MARKETING
AN INTRODUCTION

5TH
CANADIAN
EDITION

MARKETING
AN INTRODUCTION

GARY ARMSTRONG
University of North Carolina

PHILIP KOTLER
Northwestern University

VALERIE TRIFTS
Dalhousie University

LILLY ANNE BUCHWITZ
Wilfrid Laurier University

CONTRIBUTING AUTHOR: DAVID GAUDET
SAIT Polytechnic

PEARSON

Toronto

Editor-in-Chief: Claudine O'Donnell
Director of Marketing: Leigh-Anne Graham
Program Manager: Karen Townsend
Project Manager: Andrea Falkenberg
Developmental Editor: Patti Sayle
Media Editor: Nicole Mellow
Media Producer: Daniel Szabo
Production Services: Cenveo® Publisher Services
Permissions Project Manager: Joanne Tang
Photo Permissions Research: Stephanie Imhof, Q2A/Bill Smith; Kristiina Paul
Text Permissions Research: Haydee Hidalgo, Electronic Publishing Services Inc., NYC
Art Director: Jerilyn Bockorick
Cover Designer: Anthony Leung
Interior Designer: Garrett Cimms, Cenveo® Publishers Services
Cover Image: Courtesy of WestJet

Credits and acknowledgments for material borrowed from other sources and reproduced, with permission, in this textbook appear on the appropriate page within the text.

Original edition published by Pearson Education, Inc., Upper Saddle River, New Jersey, USA. Copyright © 2013 Pearson Education, Inc. This edition is authorized for sale only in Canada.

If you purchased this book outside the United States or Canada, you should be aware that it has been imported without the approval of the publisher or the author.

10 9 8 7 6 CKV

Library and Archives Canada Cataloguing in Publication

Armstrong, Gary, author

   Marketing : an introduction / Gary Armstrong, University of North Carolina, Philip Kotler, Northwestern University, Valerie Trifts, Dalhousie University, Lilly Anne Buchwitz, Wildfrid Laurier University; contributing author, David Gaudet, Southern Alberta Institute of Technology. -- Fifth Canadian edition.
Revision of: Marketing : an introduction / Gary Armstrong ...
   [et al.]; contributing author, Paul Finlayson. -- 4th Canadian
   ed. -- Toronto : Pearson Prentice Hall, 2011.

Includes bibliographical references and index. ISBN 978-0-13-337314-1 (pbk.)

   1. Marketing--Textbooks. I. Kotler, Philip, author II. Trifts, Valerie, author III. Buchwitz, Lilly Anne, author IV. Gaudet, David (Professor), author V. Title.

HF5415.M295 2014   658.8   C2013-907319-1

ISBN: 978-0-133-37314-1

Brief Contents

Contents

About the Authors

GARY ARMSTRONG is Crist W. Blackwell Distinguished Professor Emeritus of Undergraduate Education in the Kenan-Flagler Business School at the University of North Carolina at Chapel Hill. He holds undergraduate and masters degrees in business from Wayne State University in Detroit, and he received his Ph.D. in marketing from Northwestern University. Dr. Armstrong has contributed numerous articles to leading business journals. As a consultant and researcher, he has worked with many companies on marketing research, sales management, and marketing strategy.

But Professor Armstrong's first love has always been teaching. His long-held Blackwell Distinguished Professorship is the only permanent endowed professorship for distinguished undergraduate teaching at the University of North Carolina at Chapel Hill. He has been very active in the teaching and administration of Kenan-Flagler's undergraduate program. His administrative posts have included chair of marketing, associate director of the undergraduate business program, director of the business honors program, and many others. Through the years, he has worked closely with business student groups and has received several campus-wide and Business School teaching awards. He is the only repeat recipient of the school's highly regarded Award for Excellence in Undergraduate Teaching, which he received three times. Most recently, Professor Armstrong received the UNC Board of Governors Award for Excellence in Teaching, the highest teaching honour bestowed by the sixteen-campus University of North Carolina system.

PHILIP KOTLER is S. C. Johnson & Son Distinguished Professor of International Marketing at the Kellogg School of Management, Northwestern University. He received his master's degree at the University of Chicago and his Ph.D. at M.I.T., both in economics. Dr. Kotler is author of *Marketing Management* (Pearson Prentice Hall), now in its 13th edition and the world's most widely used marketing textbook in graduate schools of business worldwide. He has authored dozens of other successful books and has written more than 100 articles in leading journals. He is the only three-time winner of the coveted Alpha Kappa Psi award for the best annual article in the *Journal of Marketing*.

Professor Kotler was named the first recipient of two major awards: the Distinguished Marketing Educator of the Year Award given by the American Marketing Association and the Philip Kotler Award for Excellence in Health Care Marketing presented by the Academy for Health Care Services Marketing. His numerous other major honours include the Sales and Marketing Executives International Marketing Educator of the Year Award; The European Association of Marketing Consultants and Trainers Marketing Excellence Award; the Charles Coolidge Parlin Marketing Research Award; and the Paul D. Converse Award, given by the American Marketing Association to honour "outstanding contributions to science in marketing." In a recent *Financial Times* poll of 1000 senior executives across the world, Professor Kotler was ranked as the fourth "most influential business writer/guru" of the 21st century.

Dr. Kotler has served as chairman of the College on Marketing of the Institute of Management Sciences, a director of the American Marketing Association, and a trustee of the Marketing Science Institute. He has consulted with many major U.S. and international companies in the areas of marketing strategy and planning, marketing organization, and international marketing. He has travelled and lectured extensively throughout Europe, Asia, and South America, advising companies and governments about global marketing practices and opportunities.

VALERIE TRIFTS is an associate professor in marketing at Dalhousie University School of Business in Halifax. She received her undergraduate business degree from the University of Prince Edward Island, her MBA from Saint Mary's University, and her Ph.D. in marketing from the University of Alberta. Her primary research interests are in the area of consumer information search and decision-making. Specifically, she is interested in how firms can benefit from strategically providing their customers with information about competitors, as well as exploring individual difference variables that influence search behaviour. She integrates her research into a variety of courses she has taught, including introduction to marketing, consumer behaviour, Internet marketing, and marketing research at both the undergraduate and graduate levels. Her research has been published in *Marketing Science* and the *Journal of Consumer Psychology*, presented at numerous academic conferences, and funded by the Social Sciences and Humanities Research Council of Canada.

LILLY ANNE BUCHWITZ is an author, teacher, and expert in the field of Internet marketing and advertising who became an academic after 15 years in the professional world of high-tech product marketing and Internet services. In the early days of the Internet, she was the marketing manager for the Open Text Index, one of the original Internet search engines developed by Canadian software company Open Text; she became somewhat notorious for developing paid search advertising in 1996. She later worked for the Internet start-up that became About.com, helped launch Internet advertising network DoubleClick in Canada, and was the Internet marketing manager for Chapters Online. Her professional activities eventually led her to teaching and research in the still-developing field of Internet advertising, and she recently completed her Ph.D. in marketing at Bristol Business School, University of the West of England. She is currently working on turning her dissertation, "Exploring the Life Cycle of Advertising on a New Mass Medium: A Comparison of the Histories of Internet and Radio Advertising," into a book. She has undergraduate degrees in English literature and education from McGill University, and an MBA from Wilfrid Laurier University. She began her university teaching career at the University of New Brunswick in their emerging e-commerce program in St. John, as well as in their business education program in Beijing, China. Later, she taught marketing communications and Internet marketing at Brock University in St. Catharines, and then spent three years in the capital of Silicon Valley, as an Assistant Professor at San Jose State University. She is currently an instructor in the School of Business and Economics at Wilfrid Laurier University in Waterloo.

DAVID GAUDET is an instructor at SAIT Polytechnic and the University of Calgary, and an active business owner/consultant, operating in a diverse number of industries. Holding an MBA with high distinction, from the University of Southern Queensland, Australia, he develops and delivers business courses in subjects ranging from accounting to marketing. His embrace of new technologies and integration of social media into his teaching have made him an early adopter and pioneer of flipped classroom methodology, and a regular speaker at the annual NISOD Conference in Austin, Texas. Gaudet's professional career began in broadcasting, after earning his diploma of Applied Arts in 1983. He went on to assist in the successful launch of various radio stations in western Canada, and ultimately hold down programming duties in some of the country's most listened to stations. His passion for media converged with his entrepreneurial DNA in the early 90's when he started his first business, a media market research company, providing listener/viewer data to clients. He has added a plethora of marketing services to his portfolio over the last 20 years, providing corporate communications, project management, business analysis, crisis communications, media training, public relations, copywriting, web design, content management and strategic planning all under his third business startup, "Triceratops Brand Logic Inc".

The Fifth Canadian Edition of *Marketing: An Introduction*: Creating More Value for You!

The fifth Canadian edition of Marketing: An Introduction makes learning and teaching marketing more effective, easier, and more enjoyable than ever. Its streamlined approach strikes a careful balance between depth of coverage and ease of learning. The fifth Canadian edition's brand new design enhances student understanding. And when combined with MyMarketingLab, our online homework and tutorial system, *Marketing: An Introduction* ensures that you will come to class well prepared and leave class with a richer understanding of basic marketing concepts, strategies, and practices.

Marketing: Creating Customer Value and Relationships

Top marketers all share a common goal: putting the consumer at the heart of marketing. Today's marketing is all about creating customer value and building profitable customer relationships. It starts with understanding consumer needs and wants, deciding which target markets the organization can serve best, and developing a compelling value proposition by which the organization can attract, keep, and grow targeted consumers. If the organization does these things well, it will reap the rewards in terms of market share, profits, and customer equity. In the fifth Canadian edition of *Marketing: An Introduction*, you'll see how *customer value*—creating it and capturing it—drives every good marketing strategy.

Five Major Value Themes

The text is built around the five major themes described below. These themes and the many related key concepts are brought to life through cases and examples that have been written just for this edition by Canadian authors. Indeed the WestJet cover image sets the tone for this pervasive and strong Canadian theme. In this fifth Canadian edition, you'll find many stories about Canadian companies, such as The Running Room and RIM, and real Canadians working in fields such as marketing research and music marketing, as well as a running chapter by chapter WestJet mini-case. Each chapter also considers international marketing, both in terms of what Canadian companies are doing abroad and what interesting marketing activities foreign companies are engaging in.

The fifth Canadian edition of *Marketing: An Introduction* builds on five major value themes:

1. *Creating value for customers in order to capture value from customers in return.* Today's outstanding marketing companies understand the marketplace and customer needs, design value-creating marketing strategies, develop integrated marketing programs that deliver value and satisfaction, and build strong customer relationships. In return, they capture value from customers in the form of sales, profits, and customer equity. This

innovative customer value framework is introduced in a five-step marketing process model, which details how marketing creates customer value and captures value in return. The framework is carefully explained and integrated throughout the text.

2. ***Building and managing strong brands to create brand equity.*** Well-positioned brands with strong brand equity provide the basis upon which to build profitable customer relationships. Today's marketers must position their brands powerfully and manage them well. The fifth Canadian edition provides a deep focus on brands with expanded coverage of brand strategy and management in Chapter 9.

3. ***Measuring and managing return on marketing.*** Marketing managers must ensure that their marketing dollars are being well spent. In the past, many marketers spent freely on big, expensive marketing programs, often without thinking carefully about the financial returns on their spending. But all that has changed—measuring and managing return on marketing investments has become an important part of strategic marketing decision-making. The fifth Canadian edition specifically addresses return on marketing investment.

4. ***Harnessing new marketing technologies.*** New digital and other high-tech marketing developments are dramatically changing consumers and marketers, and the ways in which they relate to one another. The fifth Canadian edition thoroughly explores the new technologies impacting marketing, from "Web 3.0" to new-age digital marketing and from online technologies to the exploding use of social networks and customer-generated marketing.

5. ***Marketing in a socially responsible way around the globe.*** As technological developments make the world an increasingly smaller place, marketers must be good at marketing their brands globally and in socially responsible ways. The fifth Canadian edition integrates global marketing and social responsibility topics throughout the text, specifically in Chapter 3, which is dedicated to sustainable marketing.

New in the Fifth Canadian Edition

We've thoroughly revised the fifth Canadian edition of *Marketing: An Introduction* to reflect the major trends and forces impacting marketing in this era of customer value and relationships. Here are just some of the major changes you'll find in this edition.

- There is greater diversity of Canadian firms featured throughout each chapter. From the chapter opening vignettes, to the examples and cases, these companies provide broader coverage of the industries (services, manufacturing, and social media industries,) that are integral to Canadian business.

- In the fifth Canadian edition, coverage of **sustainability** is now woven into each chapter.

- The fifth Canadian edition features new discussions about timely issues such as **neuromarketing** (Chapter 5) **crowdsourcing and customer-driven idea generation** (Chapter 8), a discussion on how to **engage consumers**, and not just reach them (Chapter 12), a section on the **international advertising decisions** with references to specific Canadian examples (Chapter 12), as well as a section on: **personal selling and managing customer relationships** (Chapter 13).

- The fifth Canadian edition continues to engage students with this title's most unique feature, **the comprehensive case**. Used to further illustrate a chapter's key learnings, this case runs throughout the book, and examines WestJet's marketing strategy as it relates to the content being discussed. There is a particular focus on their planned expansion into regional and trans-Atlantic destinations.

- The fifth Canadian edition includes new coverage of technology woven throughout the textbook. With sections on **mass mingling** (Chapter 4), **shoppable media and showrooming** (Chapter 11), an expanded section on new **marketing communications models** and the impact of advances in communication technology alongside more traditional models (Chapter 12), and **Selling and the Internet** (Chapter 13) this text examines many of the most timely developments in marketing and technology.

- The fifth Canadian edition includes new sections on **Brand Communications, Brand Stories, Branded Content, Brands and Social Media** (Chapter 9), and the use of **brand ambassadors** as with the 2009 campaign by James Ready beer, or the work of Toronto-based Campus Intercept (Chapter 6).

- The fifth Canadian edition also contains a new section on the use and role of **logos** (Chapter 9).

- (Chapter 11) has been reorganized into three major sections: **Marketing Channels, Retail, and Supply Chain/Logistics**. The section on marketing channels has been re-written to explain the concepts in real marketing terms and to use real examples that will resonate with students. The emphasis in the revised retail section explains the new technological trends in retail (online, social media, mobile). Finally, this chapter discusses some global brands, with particular focus on US firms doing business in Canada and Canadian firms branching out to do more business internationally.

Real Value Through Real Marketing

Marketing: An Introduction features in-depth, real-world examples and stories that show concepts in action and reveal the drama of modern marketing. In the fifth Canadian edition, every chapter contains an opening vignette and Marketing@Work stories that provide fresh and relevant insights into real marketing practices. Learn how:

- The Running Room's obsession with creating the very best customer experience has resulted in avidly loyal customers and astronomical growth.

- Nike's customer-focused mission and deep sense of customer brand community have the company sprinting ahead while competitors are gasping for breath.

- Bullfrog Power shows how an innovative new company can address issues related to sustainability while stretching a limited marketing budget through the use of powerful public relations techniques.

- Google innovates at the speed of light—it's part of the company's DNA.

- Amazon.com has become one of the best-known names on the Web and has been viewed as the model for business in the digital age.

Beyond these features, each chapter is packed with countless real, relevant, and timely examples that reinforce key concepts. No other text brings marketing to life like the fifth Canadian edition of *Marketing: An Introduction*.

buys from the firm that offers the highest **customer-perceived value**—the customer's evaluation of the difference between all the benefits and all the costs of a market offering relative to those of competing offers. Importantly, customers often do not judge values and costs "accurately" or "objectively." They act on *perceived* value.

To some consumers, value might mean sensible products at affordable prices. To other consumers, however, value might mean paying more to get more. For example, a top-of-the-line Weber Summit E-670 barbecue grill carries a suggested retail price of US$2,600, more than five times the price of competitor Char-Broil's best grill. According to Weber, the stainless steel Summit grill "embraces true grilling luxury with the highest quality materials, exclusive features, and stunning looks." However, Weber's marketing also suggests that the grill is a real value, even at the premium price. For the money, you get practical features such as all-stainless-steel construction, spacious cooking and work areas, lighted control knobs, a tuck-away motorized rotisserie system, and an LED tank scale that lets you know how much propane you have left in the tank. Is the Weber Summit grill worth the premium price compared to less expensive grills? To many consumers, the answer is no. But to the target segment of affluent, hard-core grillers, the answer is "yes."[11] (see Marketing@Work 1.1)

Customer-perceived value
The customer's evaluation of the difference between all the benefits and all the costs of a market offering relative to those of competing offers.

MARKETING@WORK 1.1

Canada Goose: Authenticity Is Key to Customer Value

In 1957, Sam Tick founded Metro Sportswear, which produced a modest line of jackets and woollen shirts in a small manufacturing facility in Toronto. The 1970s saw the business expand to include the production of custom-ordered down-filled coats for the Canadian Rangers, city police forces, and other government workers. In 1985, the company was renamed Snow Goose, and in the early 1990s it began selling its products in Europe under the name Canada Goose. By the late 1990s the modern era of Canada Goose had begun and the real expansion of the brand began. Over the past 10 years or so, Canada Goose parka sales have soared within Canada and in more than 40 other countries worldwide. In fact, Canada Goose placed 152nd on the 2011 Profit 200 list of fastest growing Canadian companies, with 3000% growth in revenues over the last decade.

How did Canada Goose achieve such phenomenal growth? A number of factors contribute to the company's success. First, Canada Goose very carefully chose spokespeople who were highly credible users of the brand. Lance Mackey, a four-time Iditarod and Yukon

Quest champion, grew up in Alaska and is known as one of the best dogsled mushers in the world. Ray Zahab, ultra marathon runner and adventurer, and Laurie Skreslet, the first Canadian to reach the summit of Mount Everest, also joined the list of Canada Goose spokespeople. These individuals have enormous credibility with the company's core customer segment, which consists of polar expeditioners, oil riggers, and police departments alike.

Rather than using traditional advertising campaigns to build brand awareness, Canada Goose relied on consumer-driven marketing tactics to build its brand. About 10 years ago, product was placed on people who worked outside in cold environments, such as bouncers at nightclubs or doormen at hotels, who could give the brand credibility. Today, Canada Goose still employs several nontraditional forms of promotion to build brand awareness, from supplying Fairmont Hotels' doormen and valets with Expedition parkas to running a Canada Goose coat check at Toronto Maple Leafs and Toronto Raptors games where fans are offered the chance to try on parkas while checking their own garments.

Celebrities caught on camera and actors in feature films wearing the brand have also contributed to Canada Goose's success. Hayden Christensen was photographed wearing one at the Vancouver 2010 Winter Olympics. Daniel Radcliffe is often spotted wearing his Canada Goose parka. The brand has been used in the film industry for decades behind the scenes, but now appears on screen as well in such movies as *The Day After Tomorrow*, *Eight Below*, *National Treasure*, *Good Luck Chuck*, and *Whiteout*.

While Canada Goose has long been a bestseller in Europe, it has also been successful in the highly competitive US fashion market. It currently sells its products at premium department stores such as Barneys and Saks Fifth Avenue and is expanding its product offerings via collaborations with Italian cashmere and wool manufacturer Loro Piana and Japanese designer Yuki Matsuda.

Canada Goose is a company that has always chosen its own path and stayed true to its brand. As a result, it has attracted a diverse customer base who are interested in everything from function to fashion. This is perhaps the biggest reason why Canada Goose has been able

designed for kids? It's a matter of economics—this segment of young consumers is just too small. One leading cardiologist attributed the discrepancy to a "profitability gap" between the children's market and the much more profitable adult market for treating heart disease. While not supplying this market might make good economic sense for companies, it is of little comfort to the parents of these small patients.

QUESTIONS

1. Discuss the environmental forces acting on medical devices and pharmaceuticals companies that are preventing them from meeting the needs of the infant and child market segment. Is it wrong for these companies to not address the needs of this segment?

2. Suggest some solutions to this problem.

MARKETING TECHNOLOGY

If you thought that getting 50 miles per gallon (4.7L/100 km) driving a Toyota Prius hybrid was good, how about 230 miles per gallon (1L/100 km)? Or 367 miles per gallon (0.64L/100 km)? Well, you are about to see a new breed of automobiles from big and small automakers touting this level of performance. In 2010, there was GM's Volt and Nissan's Leaf, but there will also be offerings from unknown start-ups such as V-Vehicle, a California-based electric car company backed by billionaire T. Boone Pickens. These automobiles range from hybrids—a combination of gas and electric—to all-electric vehicles. This level of performance comes at a high price, however. Although US consumers will receive an expected US$7500 tax credit for purchasing one of these cars, the Volt's expected US$40 000 price tag will still cause sticker shock. Also, the lack of public recharging stations poses a significant challenge, especially for all-electric vehicles such as the Leaf,

which needs recharging approximately every 100 miles (160 km). And some might question the efficiency claims, especially since the Environmental Protection Agency is still finalizing the methodology that factors in electricity used when making miles-per-gallon equivalency claims.

QUESTIONS

1. What factors in the marketing environment present opportunities or threats to automakers?

2. Will it be possible for a start-up automaker such as V-Vehicle to compete with big automakers such as Ford, GM, Chrysler, Toyota, Honda, Nissan, Volvo, Hyundai, BMW, and Mercedes? What factors in the marketing environment will enable or inhibit new competitors?

MARKETING BY THE NUMBERS

China and India are emerging markets that will have a significant impact on the world in coming years. With China's and India's combined population of almost 2.5 billion, they are the two most populous countries, comprising almost 40 percent of the world's population. The economies of both countries are growing at phenomenal rates as well. The term *Chindia* is used to describe the growing power of these two countries, and predictions are that these two will overtake the United States as the largest economies in the world within just a few decades.

QUESTIONS

1. Discuss a demographic and an economic trend related to Chindia's power and their impact on marketers in Canada. Support your discussion of these trends with statistics.

2. Using the chain ratio method described in Appendix 3: Marketing by the Numbers, discuss factors to consider when estimating total market demand for automobiles in China or India.

Valuable Learning Aids

A wealth of chapter-opening, within-chapter, and end-of-chapter learning devices help students to learn, link, and apply major concepts:

- **Chapter-opening Content.** The new, more active and integrative opening spread in each chapter features a brief Previewing the Concepts section that includes chapter concepts, an outline of chapter content and learning objectives, and an opening vignette—an engaging, deeply developed, illustrated, and annotated marketing story that introduces the chapter material and sparks student interest.

- **Marketing@Work highlights.** Each chapter contains two highlight features that provide an in-depth look at real marketing practices of large and small companies.

- **Reviewing the Concepts.** A summary at the end of each chapter reviews major chapter concepts and links them to chapter objectives.

- **Key Terms.** A helpful listing of chapter key terms by order of appearance with page numbers facilitates easy reference.

- **Talk About Marketing.** This section contains discussion questions that require students to think about, discuss, defend, and apply the concepts in the chapter.

- **Think Like a Marketing Manager.** A very short case gives a real-world example of one of the concepts in the chapter in action, followed by application questions.

- **Marketing Ethics.** Situation descriptions and questions at the end of each chapter highlight important issues in marketing ethics and social responsibility.

- **Marketing Technology.** Application exercises at the end of each chapter facilitate discussion of important and emerging marketing technologies in this digital age.

- **Marketing by the Numbers.** An exercise at the end of each chapter lets students apply analytical and financial thinking to relevant chapter concepts and links the chapter to Appendix 3, Marketing by the Numbers.

- **Video Case.** Short vignettes with discussion questions come at the end of most chapters. These are to be used with the set of engaging 4- to 7-minute videos that accompany the fifth Canadian edition, and can be found on the MyMarketingLab.

The fifth Canadian edition of Marketing: An Introduction provides an effective and enjoyable total package for moving you down the road to learning marketing!

Comprehensive Case: WestJet®

WestJet is as authentic an example of true Canadian entrepreneurialism as there has been in the last several decades. Three forward thinking, resourceful businessmen, five planes and an idea to super-serve "guests" with value priced airfare, has gone from nothing to approximately one-third share of the Canadian domestic air travel market. In 2013, having grown to servicing 90 destinations throughout North America, Central America and the Caribbean, WestJet launched its regional subsidiary, Encore, to begin a new chapter of delivering the same WestJet brand experience to smaller Canadian communities.

We've used WestJet as our comprehensive case in the fifth edition. This case material can be found in three key areas of the text:

1. *WestJet Mini Cases*. At the end of each chapter is a short case about the company that illustrates how they employ the topics covered in that chapter.

2. *Appendix 1 – General Company Information: WestJet*. This appendix tells the story of WestJet and illustrates how its marketing strategy has been a key element of its success.

3. *Appendix 2 – The Marketing Plan: An Introduction*. Our second appendix contains a sample marketing plan that helps you to see how marketing concepts translate into real-life marketing strategies.

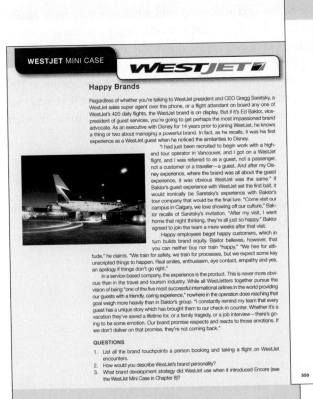

Teaching and Learning Support

A successful marketing course requires more than a well-written book. Today's classroom requires a dedicated teacher and a fully integrated teaching package. A total package of teaching and learning supplements extends this edition's emphasis on effective teaching and learning. The aids on the following page support *Marketing: An Introduction*.

Instructor's Resource Manual. This invaluable resource not only includes chapter-by-chapter teaching strategies, it also features notes about the PowerPoint slides and the video cases. This supplement is available through Pearson Education Canada's online catalogue at http://vig.pearsoned.ca, and also available through the instructor's eText.

Pearson MyTest. This computerized test bank includes multiple-choice and true/false questions, plus essay and short-answer questions. All questions include the correct answer and are linked to a learning objective from the chapter. The MyTest is available through MyMarketingLab.

PowerPoint® Presentations. Newly designed PowerPoint slides are available with this edition and include custom infographics that help bring marketing concepts to life. The PowerPoints are also available to instructors through Pearson Education Canada's online catalogue at http://vig.pearsoned.ca.

Pearson eText

Pearson eText gives students access to the text whenever and wherever they have access to the Internet. eText pages look exactly like the printed text, offering powerful new functionality for students and instructors. Users can create notes, highlight text in different colours, create bookmarks, zoom, click hyperlinked words and phrases to view definitions, and view in single-page or two-page view. Pearson eText allows for quick navigation to key parts of the eText using a table of contents and provides full-text search. The eText may also offer links to associated media files, enabling users to access videos, animations, or other activities as they read the text.

MyMarketingLab

Break through to a higher level of learning with MyMarketingLab. MyMarketingLab now allows you to assess your students at every level of learning.
Features include:

- –Chapter Quizzes

- –Video Cases

- –Marketing Mini-Cases

- –Performance Reporting

- –Pearson eText for Students and Instructors

Adaptive Learning

Dynamic Study Modules. MyMarketingLab makes studying more efficient and more effective for every student with the new Dynamic Study Modules. Leveraging research from the fields of cognitive psychology, neurobiology and game studies – the Dynamic Study Modules work by continuously assessing student performance and activity, then using data and analytics to provide personalized content in real-time to reinforce concepts that target each student's particular strengths and weaknesses. The Dynamic Study Modules in MyMarketingLab are mobile! Students can study on their phone, tablet or computer.

Writing Space. Pearson's Writing Space offers instructors powerful new tools to assign, track, and grade writing in their courses. Students can now complete and get feedback on writing assignments right within their MyLab. Writing Space assignments for this MyLab include Assisted-Graded Writing Assignments and Create Your Own Writing Assignments.

Learning Solutions Managers. Pearson's Learning Solutions Consultants work with faculty and campus course designers to ensure that Pearson technology products, assessment tools, and online course materials are tailored to meet your specific needs. This highly qualified team is dedicated to helping schools take full advantage of a wide range of educational resources, by assisting in the integration of a variety of instructional materials and media formats. Your local Pearson Education sales representative can provide you with more details on this service program.

CourseSmart goes beyond traditional expectations–providing instant, online access to the textbooks and course materials you need at a lower cost for students. And even as students save money, you can save time and hassle with a digital eTextbook that allows you to search for the most relevant content at the very moment you need it. Whether it's evaluating textbooks or creating lecture notes to help students with difficult concepts, CourseSmart can make life a little easier. See how when you visit www.coursesmart.com/instructors.

Pearson Custom Library

For enrollments of at least 25 students, you can create your own textbook by choosing the chapters that best suit your own course needs. To begin building your custom text, visit www.pearsoncustomlibrary.com. You may also work with a dedicated Pearson Custom editor to create your ideal text—publishing your own original content or mixing and matching Pearson content. Contact your local Pearson Representative to get started.

Acknowledgments

Writing a textbook, even when it is a new edition of a previous work, is a long, long process that requires a hard-working and dedicated team of people. On behalf of Gary Armstrong, Philip Kotler, and Lilly Anne Buchwitz, I would like to acknowledge the incredible team of editors, writers, and designers at Pearson without whom you would not be holding this book in your hands: Claudine O'Donnell, editor-in-chief; Deana Sigut, acquisitions editor; Patti Sayle, developmental editor; Andrea Falkenberg, project manager; Susan McNally, production editor; Leanne Rancourt, copy editor; and Leigh-Anne Graham, director of marketing.

There were many marketing instructors and professors at schools across Canada who provided valuable comments and suggestions for this edition. In particular, I would like to thank:

Lee Li, *York University*

Angelo Papadatos, *Dawson College*

Blair Lipsett, *Nova Scotia Community College – Lunenburg Campus*

Janet Bertsch, *NAIT*

Amanda Bickell, *Kwantlen Polytechnic University*

Sherry McEvoy, *Fanshawe College*

Kerry D. Couet, *Grant MacEwan University*

Don Hill, *Langara College*

Marion Hill, *SAIT*

Anne Borrowman, *Camosun College*

Wendy Tarrel, *Nova Scotia Community College*

Donna Amirault, *Nova Scotia Community College*

Lawrence Saunders, *University of Victoria*

David Moulton, *Douglas College*

We owe many thanks to our families for their constant support and encouragement. To them, we dedicate this book.

—*Valerie Trifts*

To all my past, present, and future marketing and advertising students at Wilfrid Laurier University, Brock University, San Jose State University, and Humber College. You make me a better teacher every day.

—*Lilly Buchwitz*

Jason Merritt/Staff/Getty Images Entertainment/Getty Images

AFTER STUDYING THIS CHAPTER, YOU SHOULD BE ABLE TO

1 define marketing and outline the steps in the marketing process

2 explain the importance of understanding customers and the marketplace, and identify the five core marketplace concepts

3 identify the key elements of a customer-driven marketing strategy and discuss the marketing management orientations that guide marketing strategy

4 discuss customer relationship management and identify strategies for creating value *for* customers and capturing value *from* customers in return

5 describe the major trends and forces that are changing the marketing landscape in this age of relationships

Marketing: Creating and Capturing Customer Value

PREVIEWING THE CONCEPTS

You're about to begin an exciting journey toward learning about marketing. In this chapter, we start with the question, What *is* marketing? Simply put, marketing is managing profitable customer relationships. The aim of marketing is to create value *for* customers and to capture value *from* customers in return. Next, we discuss the five steps in the marketing process—from understanding customer needs, to designing customer-driven marketing strategies and integrated marketing programs, to building customer relationships and capturing value for the firm. Finally, we discuss the major trends and forces affecting marketing in this age of customer relationships. Understanding these basic concepts and forming your own ideas about what they really mean to you will give you a solid foundation for all that follows.

Let's start with a good story about marketing in action at Loblaw, whose clothing line, Joe Fresh, has become one of Canada's most successful apparel brands. The secret to Joe Fresh's success? It's really no secret at all: Creating customer value through its "Fresh style. Fresh price." philosophy is what keeps customers coming back. You'll see this theme of creating customer value to capture value in return repeated throughout the first chapter and throughout the text.

LOBLAW'S DEVELOPMENT OF JOE FRESH: HOW "FRESH" IS CREATING VALUE FOR ITS CUSTOMERS

In the ever-changing and highly competitive fashion industry, Canadian brand Joe Fresh stands out as one of the best success stories in Canadian retail. How did they do it? By providing customers with fresh and affordable fashion in a retail setting where they shop every week—the grocery store!

As the largest food distributor and leading provider of general merchandise, drugstore, and financial products and services in Canada, Loblaw Companies operates more than 1000 stores under 22 different banners, including Superstore, Loblaw, Provigo, and Save Easy, to name a few. More than 14 million Canadians shop at a Loblaw store every week.

In an effort to compete with large US-based retailers such as Walmart and Target, Loblaw began an aggressive expansion strategy to better satisfy the needs of its customers. In 2012, Loblaw spent approximately $40 million on customer-friendly initiatives such as pricing, store execution, and customer service to set itself apart from rivals like Sobeys and Walmart. And their strategy appears to be paying off, both financially and in terms of customer satisfaction. Corporate revenues in the first quarter of 2013 topped $7.2 billion, an increase of over 3.8% from the first quarter of 2012, and marketing research polls continue to show significant gains in in-store customer satisfaction for the company. In July 2013, Loblaw also announced what may be one of the largest mergers in Canadian retail history: a $12.4 billion deal to take over Canada's largest drugstore chain, Shoppers Drug Mart.

Since the introduction of The Decadent Chocolate Chip Cookie, Loblaw has continued to provide the Canadian marketplace with a number of brands, such as PC GREEN, PC Organics, no name, and PC Blue Menu. But perhaps the company's most successful (and some would argue surprising) brand creation is Joe Fresh, which helps set the shopping experience apart from other grocery stores and has grown to become the largest apparel brand in Canada in terms of both units sold and dollars.

Joe Fresh was launched in 2006, when Loblaw hired designer Joe Mimran (the designer of the Alfred Sung and Club Monaco labels) to create an affordable brand to be sold in the Canadian grocery stores. His involvement in the project, as well as the company's decision to hold their own fashion shows twice yearly, gave instant credibility to the Joe Fresh brand and led to rapid success in a very short time frame. In its first year alone, Joe Fresh was launched in over 100 retail locations in Canada, and by its third year it grew to over 330 stores. After the hugely successful launch of the women's clothing line, Joe Fresh expanded to children's wear. "Kids and food shopping really go hand-in-hand," Mimran says, and "there is no better place for the mom to shop for kids' apparel than in the food store." The brand has further expanded to include menswear and a line of cosmetics.

In 2010, Joe Fresh launched its first stand-alone store in downtown Vancouver, targeting the younger fashionista market. Like everything else about the Joe Fresh brand, the stand-alone store concept was an instant success, and the company now operates 14 such stores in Canada. But Joe Fresh set its sights on an even more aggressive expansion strategy: entry into the highly competitive US marketplace. Five years after the initial launch in Canada, the Joe Fresh brand was poised to take the United States by storm. It opened its first US-based stand-alone store in March 2012 on Fifth Avenue in New York City. It was the brand's biggest store with the largest assortment of merchandise and made the Joe Fresh brand visible to the entire world. It even prompted a comment from New York mayor Michael Bloomberg that it was "the greatest Canadian export since Justin Bieber." Since the initial US launch, Joe Fresh has opened five other US-based stand-alone stores and, in 2013, announced a deal with JCPenney to sell the Joe Fresh brand in approximately 700 US retail locations! It appears that this brand truly resonates with consumers.

But what is it that makes Joe Fresh so successful? Although price is a key differentiator, what really makes the brand work is that it is highly accessible, and the style is constantly changing to meet the demands of consumers. In fact, new product arrives at the stores every four weeks to maintain the brand's relevancy in the fickle fashion market. The company realized quickly that customers were in the store on a weekly basis, so the assortment had to constantly change to stay "fresh."

However, the company did face an initial challenge of selling clothing in a grocery store, as customers had to adapt their buying habits. "We quickly realized we couldn't merchandise like a grocery store," said Craig Hutchinson, senior vice-president of marketing and public relations (PR). Joe Fresh's success as a major fashion brand came about largely as a result of extensive PR efforts, with over 1 billion PR hits in the brand's first five years.

Joe Fresh maintains a consistent style and image in all its promotional materials and ties its brand to its original music. The 2013 spring collection premiered at Toronto fashion week. "It's the ultimate compliment when people want to come and see what we're up to," said Joe Mimran. "It's not something you would normally expect from a brand that trades at these price points and that trades the way we do—in supermarkets." "We tend to be a brand that filters the trends and offers it to consumers," he explained. "We distill it more and are a little more realistic about our customer base." In essence, Joe Fresh has succeeded by providing customers with value—perceived customer value based on providing affordable high fashion that is accessible and constantly changing to meet customers' lifestyles.

Providing customers with affordable fashion is not the only way the Joe Fresh brand changed the global fashion industry. In the wake of the horrible Bangladesh factory collapse in 2013, which killed over 1000 garment factory workers and where many Joe Fresh items were made, Loblaw was the first corporation in the industry to promise compensation to the victims and changes to how garments are manufactured in developing countries. Rather than making the controversial decision to leave Bangladesh as some companies did, Loblaw felt a moral obligation to aid in rebuilding the country's industry and pledged that change would occur to how safety standards were met. In addition to direct financial assistance to and rehabilitation for injured workers, Loblaw committed to the proper inspection of buildings by signing the Accord on Fire and Building Safety to improve workplace safety in the Bangladesh garment industry. The company also committed to conducting their own independent inspections to ensure buildings are up to code. Certainly, their commitment to creating and capturing customer value extends well beyond the final product.[1]

TODAY'S successful companies have one thing in common: Like Loblaw, they are strongly customer focused and heavily committed to marketing. These companies share a passion for understanding and satisfying customer needs in well-defined target markets. They motivate everyone in the organization to help build lasting customer relationships based on creating value.

Customer relationships and value are especially important today. Facing dramatic technological changes and deep economic, social, and environmental challenges, today's customers are spending more carefully and reassessing their relationships with brands. In turn, it's more important than ever to build strong customer relationships based on real and enduring value.

What Is Marketing? LO1

Marketing, more than any other business function, deals with customers. Although we will soon explore more-detailed definitions of marketing, perhaps the simplest definition is this one: *Marketing is managing profitable customer relationships.* The twofold goal of marketing is to attract new customers by promising superior value and to keep and grow current customers by delivering satisfaction.

For example, McDonald's fulfills its "i'm lovin' it" motto by being "our customers' favourite place and way to eat" the world over, giving it a market share greater than that of its nearest three competitors combined. Walmart has become the world's largest retailer—and the world's largest company—by delivering on its promise, "Save Money. Live Better."[2]

Sound marketing is critical to the success of every organization. Large for-profit firms such as Procter & Gamble, Google, BlackBerry, Honda, and Marriott use marketing. But so do not-for-profit organizations such as universities, hospitals, museums, symphony orchestras, and even churches.

You already know a lot about marketing—it's all around you. Marketing comes to you in the good old traditional forms: You see it in the abundance of products at your nearby shopping mall and in the advertisements that fill your TV screen, spice up your magazines, or stuff your mailbox. But in recent years marketers have assembled a host of new marketing approaches, everything from imaginative websites and online social networks to cellphone apps. These new approaches do more than just blast out messages to the masses—they reach you directly and personally. Today's marketers want to become a part of your life and to enrich your experiences with their brands—to help you *live* their brands.

At home, at school, where you work, and where you play, you see marketing in almost everything you do. Yet there is much more to marketing than meets the consumer's casual eye. Behind it all is a massive network of people and activities competing for your attention and purchases. This book will give you a complete introduction to the basic concepts and practices of today's marketing. In this chapter, we begin by defining marketing and the marketing process.

Marketing Defined

What *is* marketing? Many people think of marketing only as selling and advertising. And no wonder—every day we are bombarded with TV commercials, direct-mail offers, sales calls, and email pitches. However, selling and advertising are only the tip of the marketing iceberg.

Today, marketing must be understood not in the old sense of making a sale—"telling and selling"—but in the new sense of *satisfying customer needs*. If the marketer understands consumer needs; develops products that provide superior customer value; and prices, distributes, and promotes them effectively, these products will sell easily. In fact, according to management guru Peter Drucker, "The aim of marketing is to make selling unnecessary."[3] Selling and advertising are only one part of a larger "marketing mix"—a set of marketing tools that work together to satisfy customer needs and build customer relationships.

Marketing

The process by which companies create value for customers and build strong customer relationships to capture value from customers in return.

Broadly defined, marketing is a social and managerial process by which individuals and organizations obtain what they need and want through creating and exchanging value with others. In a narrower business context, marketing involves building profitable, value-laden exchange relationships with customers. Hence, we define **marketing** as the process by which companies create value for customers and build strong customer relationships to capture value from customers in return.[4]

The Marketing Process

Figure 1.1 presents a simple five-step model of the marketing process. In the first four steps, companies work to understand consumers, create customer value, and build strong customer relationships. In the final step, companies reap the rewards of creating

FIGURE 1.1 A Simple Model of the Marketing Process

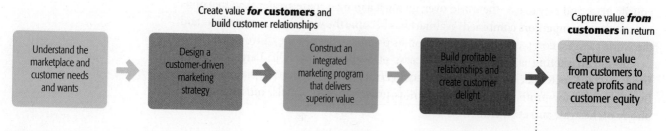

superior customer value. By creating value *for* consumers, they in turn capture value *from* consumers in the form of sales, profits, and long-term customer equity.

In this chapter and the next, we will examine the steps of this simple model of marketing. In this chapter, we will review each step but focus more on the customer relationship steps—understanding customers, building customer relationships, and capturing value from customers. In Chapter 2 we'll look more deeply into the second and third steps—designing marketing strategies and constructing marketing programs.

Understanding the Marketplace and Customer Needs L02

As a first step, marketers need to understand customer needs and wants and the marketplace within which they operate. We now examine five core customer and marketplace concepts: (1) *needs, wants, and demands*; (2) *market offerings (products, services, and experiences)*; (3) *value and satisfaction*; (4) *exchanges and relationships*; and (5) *markets*.

Customer Needs, Wants, and Demands

The most basic concept underlying marketing is that of human needs. Human **needs** are states of felt deprivation. They include basic *physical* needs for food, clothing, warmth, and safety; *social* needs for belonging and affection; and *individual* needs for knowledge and self-expression. These needs were not created by marketers; they are a basic part of the human makeup.

Wants are the form human needs take as they are shaped by culture and individual personality. A Canadian *needs* food but *wants* a breakfast sandwich and a large double-double from Tim Hortons. Wants are shaped by one's society as well as by marketing programs. They are described in terms of objects that will satisfy needs. When backed by buying power, wants become **demands**. Given their wants and resources, people demand products with benefits that add up to the most value and satisfaction.

Outstanding marketing companies go to great lengths to learn about and understand their customers' needs, wants, and demands. They conduct consumer research and analyze mountains of customer data. Their people at all levels—including top management—stay close to customers. For example, Kroger chairman and CEO David Dillon regularly dons blue jeans and roams the aisles of local Kroger supermarkets, blending in with and talking to other shoppers. He wants to see his stores through customers' eyes and understand why they make the choices they do.[5] Similarly, to stay closer to customers, Ford CEO Alan Mulally has been known to spend time selling cars at Ford dealerships.

Market Offerings—Products, Services, and Experiences

Consumers' needs and wants are fulfilled through **market offerings**—some combination of products, services, information, or experiences offered to a market to satisfy a need or want. Market offerings are not limited to physical *products*. They also include *services*—activities or benefits offered for sale that are essentially intangible and do not result in the ownership of anything. Examples include banking, airline, hotel, tax preparation, and home repair services.

More broadly, market offerings also include other entities, such as *persons, places, organizations, information,* and *ideas*. For example, the David Suzuki Foundation powerfully markets the idea that individuals and organizations can be involved in creating a healthy and sustainable environment.

Needs
States of felt deprivation.

Wants
The form human needs take as shaped by culture and individual personality.

Demands
Human wants that are backed by buying power.

Market offerings
Some combination of products, services, information, or experiences offered to a market to satisfy a need or want.

AP Photo/CP, Tom Hanson

Exhibit 1.1 **Market offerings are not limited to physical products:** The David Suzuki Foundation powerfully markets the idea that government, businesses, and individuals can be involved in creating a healthy and sustainable environment.

Many sellers make the mistake of paying more attention to the specific products they offer than to the benefits and experiences produced by these products. These sellers suffer from **marketing myopia.** They are so taken with their products that they focus only on existing wants and lose sight of underlying customer needs.[6] They forget that a product is only a tool to solve a consumer problem. A manufacturer of quarter-inch drill bits may think that the customer needs a drill bit. But what the customer *really* needs is a quarter-inch hole. These sellers will have trouble if a new product comes along that serves the customer's need better or less expensively. The customer will have the same *need* but will *want* the new product.

Marketing myopia

The mistake of paying more attention to the specific products a company offers than to the benefits and experiences produced by these products.

Smart marketers look beyond the attributes of the products and services they sell. By orchestrating several services and products, they create *brand experiences* for consumers. For example, you don't just visit Walt Disney World Resort; you immerse yourself and your family in a world of wonder, a world where dreams come true and things still work the way they should. You're "in the heart of the magic!" says Disney.

Even a seemingly functional product becomes an experience. HP recognizes that a personal computer is much more than just a cold collection of wires and electrical components. It's an intensely personal user experience. As noted in one HP ad, "There is hardly anything that you own that is *more* personal. Your personal computer is your back-up brain. It's your life . . . It's your astonishing strategy, staggering proposal, dazzling calculation." It's your connection to the world around you. HP's recent "Everybody On" marketing campaign doesn't talk much about technical specifications. Instead, it celebrates how HP's technologies help create seamless connections in today's "instant-on world."[7]

Customer Value and Satisfaction

Consumers usually face a broad array of products and services that might satisfy a given need. How do they choose among these many market offerings? Customers form expectations about the value and satisfaction that various market offerings will deliver and buy accordingly. Satisfied customers buy again and tell others about their good experiences. Dissatisfied customers often switch to competitors and disparage the product to others.

Marketers must be careful to set the right level of expectations. If they set expectations too low, they may satisfy those who buy but fail to attract enough buyers. If they raise expectations too high, buyers will be disappointed. Customer value and customer satisfaction are key building blocks for developing and managing customer relationships. We will revisit these core concepts later in the chapter.

Exchanges and Relationships

Exchange

The act of obtaining a desired object from someone by offering something in return.

Marketing occurs when people decide to satisfy needs and wants through exchange relationships. **Exchange** is the act of obtaining a desired object from someone by offering something in return. In the broadest sense, the marketer tries to bring about a response to some market offering. The response may be more than simply buying or trading products and services. A political candidate, for instance, wants votes, a church wants membership, an orchestra wants an audience, and a social action group wants idea acceptance.

Marketing consists of actions taken to build and maintain desirable exchange *relationships* with target audiences involving a product, service, idea, or other object. Beyond simply attracting new customers and creating transactions, the company wants to retain customers and grow its business. Marketers want to build strong relationships by consistently delivering superior customer value. We will expand on the important concept of managing customer relationships later in the chapter.

Markets

The concepts of exchange and relationships lead to the concept of a market. A **market** is the set of all actual and potential buyers of a product. These buyers share a particular need or want that can be satisfied through exchange relationships.

Market
The set of all actual and potential buyers of a product or a service.

Marketing means managing markets to bring about profitable customer relationships. However, creating these relationships takes work. Sellers must search for buyers, identify their needs, design good market offerings, set prices for them, promote them, and store and deliver them. Activities such as consumer research, product development, communication, distribution, pricing, and service are core marketing activities.

Although we normally think of marketing as being carried out by sellers, buyers also carry out marketing activities. Consumers do marketing when they search for products and interact with companies and obtain information and make their purchases. In fact, today's digital technologies, from websites and online social networks to smartphones, have empowered consumers and made marketing a truly interactive affair. Thus, in addition to customer relationship management, today's marketers must also deal effectively with *customer-managed relationships*. Marketers are no longer asking only "How can we reach our customers?" but also "How should our customers reach us?" and even "How can our customers reach each other?"

Figure 1.2 shows the main elements in a marketing system. Marketing involves serving a market of final consumers in the face of competitors. The company and competitors research the market and interact with consumers to understand their needs. Then they create and send their market offerings and messages to consumers, either directly or through marketing intermediaries. All the parties in the system are affected by major environmental forces (demographic, economic, physical, technological, political/legal, and social/cultural).

Each party in the system adds value for the next level. All of the arrows represent relationships that must be developed and managed. Thus, a company's success at building

FIGURE 1.2 A Modern Marketing System

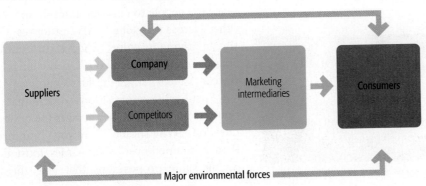

profitable relationships depends not only on its own actions but also on how well the entire system serves the needs of final consumers. Walmart cannot fulfill its promise of low prices unless its suppliers provide merchandise at low costs. And Ford cannot deliver a high-quality car ownership experience unless its dealers provide outstanding sales and service.

Designing a Customer-Driven Marketing Strategy LO3

Marketing management
The art and science of choosing target markets and building profitable relationships with them.

Once it fully understands consumers and the marketplace, marketing management can design a customer-driven marketing strategy. We define **marketing management** as the art and science of choosing target markets and building profitable relationships with them. The marketing manager's aim is to find, attract, keep, and grow target customers by creating, delivering, and communicating superior customer value.

To design a winning marketing strategy, the marketing manager must answer two important questions: *What customers will we serve (what's our target market)?* and *How can we serve these customers best (what's our value proposition)?* We will discuss these marketing strategy concepts briefly here, and then look at them in more detail in the next chapter.

Selecting Customers to Serve

The company must first decide *who* it will serve. It does this by dividing the market into segments of customers (*market segmentation*) and selecting which segments it will go after (*target marketing*). Some people think of marketing management as finding as many customers as possible and increasing demand. But marketing managers know that they cannot serve all customers in every way. By trying to serve all customers, they may not serve any customers well. Instead, the company wants to select only customers that it can serve well and profitably. For example, Holt Renfrew stores profitably target affluent professionals; Dollarama stores profitably target families with more modest means.

Ultimately, marketing managers must decide which customers they want to target based on the level, timing, and nature of their demand. Simply put, marketing management is *customer management* and *demand management*.

Choosing a Value Proposition

Exhibit 1.2 **Value propositions:** The smart car suggests that you "open your mind"—"Sorry, big guy. Efficiency is in these days."
smartUSA

The company must also decide how it will serve targeted customers—how it will *differentiate and position* itself in the marketplace. A brand's *value proposition* is the set of benefits or values it promises to deliver to consumers to satisfy their needs. Facebook helps you "connect and share with the people in your life," whereas YouTube "provides a place for people to connect, inform, and inspire others across the globe." BMW promises "the ultimate driving machine," whereas the diminutive smart car suggests that you "Open your mind to the car that challenges the status quo."

Such value propositions differentiate one brand from another. They answer the customer's question, "Why should I buy your brand rather than a competitor's?" Companies must design strong value propositions that give them the

greatest advantage in their target markets. For example, the smart car is positioned as compact yet comfortable; agile yet economical; and safe yet ecological. It offers a "guilt-free, 95% recyclable way to go from your driveway to virtually anywhere."

Marketing Management Orientations

Marketing management wants to design strategies that will build profitable relationships with target consumers. But what *philosophy* should guide these marketing strategies? What weight should be given to the interests of customers, the organization, and society? Very often, these interests conflict.

There are five alternative concepts under which organizations design and carry out their marketing strategies: the *production, product, selling, marketing,* and *societal marketing concepts.*

The Production Concept The **production concept** holds that consumers will favour products that are available and highly affordable. Therefore, management should focus on improving production and distribution efficiency. This concept is one of the oldest orientations that guides sellers.

The production concept is still a useful philosophy in some situations. For example, computer maker Lenovo dominates the highly competitive, price-sensitive Chinese PC market through low labour costs, high production efficiency, and mass distribution. However, although useful in some situations, the production concept can lead to marketing myopia. Companies adopting this orientation run a major risk of focusing too narrowly on their own operations and losing sight of the real objective—satisfying customer needs and building customer relationships.

Production concept
The idea that consumers will favour products that are available and highly affordable and that the organization should therefore focus on improving production and distribution efficiency.

The Product Concept The **product concept** holds that consumers will favour products that offer the most in quality, performance, and innovative features. Under this concept, marketing strategy focuses on making continuous product improvements.

Product quality and improvement are important parts of most marketing strategies. However, focusing *only* on the company's products can also lead to marketing myopia. For example, some manufacturers believe that if they can "build a better mousetrap, the world will beat a path to their door." But they are often rudely shocked. Buyers may be looking for a better solution to a mouse problem, but not necessarily for a better mousetrap. The better solution might be a chemical spray, an exterminating service, a housecat, or something else that works even better than a mousetrap. Furthermore, a better mousetrap will not sell unless the manufacturer designs, packages, and prices it attractively; places it in convenient distribution channels; brings it to the attention of people who need it; and convinces buyers that it is a better product.

Product concept
The idea that consumers will favour products that offer the most quality, performance, and features and that the organization should therefore devote its energy to making continuous product improvements.

The Selling Concept Many companies follow the **selling concept**, which holds that consumers will not buy enough of the firm's products unless the company undertakes a large-scale selling and promotion effort. The selling concept is typically practised with unsought goods—those that buyers do not normally think of buying, such as insurance or blood donations. These industries must be good at tracking down prospects and selling them on product benefits.

Such aggressive selling, however, carries high risks. It focuses on creating sales transactions rather than on building long-term, profitable customer relationships. The aim often is to sell what the company makes rather than making what the market wants. It assumes that customers who are coaxed into buying the product will like it. Or, if they don't like it, they will possibly forget their disappointment and buy it again later. These are usually poor assumptions.

Selling concept
The idea that consumers will not buy enough of the firm's products unless it undertakes a large-scale selling and promotion effort.

FIGURE 1.3 The Selling and Marketing Concepts Contrasted

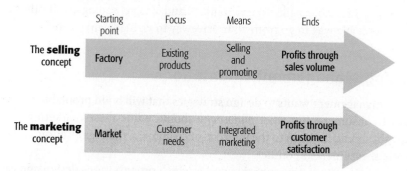

	Starting point	Focus	Means	Ends
The **selling** concept	Factory	Existing products	Selling and promoting	Profits through sales volume
The **marketing** concept	Market	Customer needs	Integrated marketing	Profits through customer satisfaction

Marketing concept
The marketing management philosophy that holds that achieving organizational goals depends on knowing the needs and wants of target markets and delivering the desired satisfactions better than competitors do.

The Marketing Concept The **marketing concept** holds that achieving organizational goals depends on knowing the needs and wants of target markets and delivering the desired satisfactions better than competitors do. Under the marketing concept, customer focus and value are the *paths* to sales and profits. Instead of a product-centred "make and sell" philosophy, the marketing concept is a customer-centred "sense and respond" philosophy. The job is not to find the right customers for your product but to find the right products for your customers.

Figure 1.3 contrasts the selling concept and the marketing concept. The selling concept takes an *inside-out* perspective. It starts with the factory, focuses on the company's existing products, and calls for heavy selling and promotion to obtain profitable sales. It focuses primarily on customer conquest—getting short-term sales with little concern about who buys or why.

In contrast, the marketing concept takes an *outside-in* perspective. As Herb Kelleher, Southwest Airlines' colourful founder, puts it, "We don't have a marketing department; we have a customer department." The marketing concept starts with a well-defined market, focuses on customer needs, and integrates all the marketing activities that affect customers. In turn, it yields profits by creating lasting relationships with the right customers based on customer value and satisfaction.

Implementing the marketing concept often means more than simply responding to customers' stated desires and obvious needs. Customer-driven companies research current customers deeply to learn about their desires, gather new product and service ideas, and test proposed product improvements. Such customer-driven marketing usually works well when a clear need exists and when customers know what they want.

In many cases, however, customers don't know what they want or even what is possible. As Henry Ford once remarked, "If I'd asked people what they wanted, they would have said faster horses."[8] For example, even 20 years ago, how many consumers would have thought to ask for now-commonplace products such as tablet computers, smartphones, digital cameras, 24-hour online buying, or GPS systems in their cars? Such situations call for customer-driving marketing—understanding customer needs even better than customers themselves do and creating products and services that meet existing and latent needs, now and in the future. As an executive at 3M puts it, "Our goal is to lead customers where they want to go before they know where they want to go."

Societal marketing concept
The idea that a company's marketing decisions should consider consumers' wants, the company's requirements, consumers' long-run interests, and society's long-run interests.

The Societal Marketing Concept The **societal marketing concept** questions whether the pure marketing concept overlooks possible conflicts between consumer *short-run wants* and consumer *long-run welfare*. Is a firm that satisfies the immediate needs and wants of target markets always doing what's best for consumers in the long run? The societal marketing concept holds that a marketing strategy should deliver value to customers in a way that maintains or improves both the consumer's *and society's* well-being.

FIGURE 1.4 The Considerations Underlying the Societal Marketing Concept

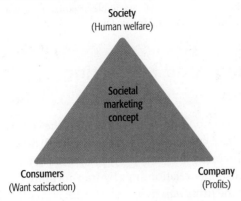

It calls for *sustainable marketing*—socially and environmentally responsible marketing that meets the present needs of consumers and businesses while also preserving or enhancing the ability of future generations to meet their needs.

Even more broadly, many leading business and marketing thinkers are now preaching the concept of *shared value,* which recognizes that societal needs, not just economic needs, define markets:

The concept of shared value focuses on creating economic value in a way that also creates value for society. A growing number of companies known for their hard-nosed approach to business—such as GE, Google, IBM, Intel, Johnson & Johnson, Nestlé, Unilever, and Walmart—have already embarked on important efforts to create shared economic and societal value by rethinking the intersection between society and corporate performance. They are concerned not just with short-term economic gains, but with the well-being of their customers, the depletion of natural resources vital to their businesses, the viability of key suppliers, and the economic well-being of the communities in which they produce and sell. One prominent marketer calls this *Marketing 3.0.* "Marketing 3.0 organizations are values-driven," he says. "I'm not talking about being value-driven. I'm talking about 'values' plural, where values amount to caring about the state of the world."[9]

As Figure 1.4 shows, companies should balance three considerations in setting their marketing strategies: company profits, consumer wants, *and* society's interests. RBC does this well:

RBC seeks more than just short-run sales and profits. Its underlying philosophy is to operate with integrity at all times and strive to have a positive impact around the globe. The firm supports many worthy causes that make real differences in people's lives. Within the community, RBC supports a variety of causes with emphasis on children and youth, sports, emerging artists, and diversity, and inclusion. RBC also created an environmental blueprint which established its environmental policy in areas of climate change, biodiversity, and fresh water. For example, the RBC Blue Water Project is a 10-year global charitable commitment of $50 million to help provide access

Exhibit 1.3 **The societal marketing concept:** RBC takes a leadership role in responsibility to the community and environmental sustainability. For example, its Blue Water Project has committed $50 million to help provide access to clean water now and for future generations.

to drinkable, swimmable, fishable water, now and for future generations. To date, the company has pledged over $38 million to more than 650 charitable organizations worldwide that protect watersheds and promote access to clean drinking water.[10]

Preparing an Integrated Marketing Plan and Program

The company's marketing strategy outlines which customers the company will serve and how it will create value for these customers. Next, the marketer develops an integrated marketing program that will actually deliver the intended value to target customers. The marketing program builds customer relationships by transforming the marketing strategy into action. It consists of the firm's *marketing mix*, the set of marketing tools the firm uses to implement its marketing strategy.

The major marketing mix tools are classified into four broad groups, called the *four Ps* of marketing: product, price, place, and promotion. To deliver on its value proposition, the firm must first create a need-satisfying market offering (product). It must decide how much it will charge for the offering (price) and how it will make the offering available to target consumers (place). Finally, it must communicate with target customers about the offering and persuade them of its merits (promotion). The firm must blend all of these marketing mix tools into a comprehensive *integrated marketing program* that communicates and delivers the intended value to chosen customers. We will explore marketing programs and the marketing mix in much more detail in later chapters.

Building Customer Relationships LO4

The first three steps in the marketing process—understanding the marketplace and customer needs, designing a customer-driven marketing strategy, and constructing marketing programs—all lead up to the fourth and most important step: building profitable customer relationships.

Customer Relationship Management

Customer relationship management is perhaps the most important concept of modern marketing. Some marketers define customer relationship management narrowly as a customer data management activity (a practice called *CRM*). By this definition, it involves managing detailed information about individual customers and carefully managing customer "touchpoints" to maximize customer loyalty. We will discuss this narrower CRM activity in Chapter 5 when dealing with marketing information.

Most marketers, however, give the concept of customer relationship management a broader meaning. In this broader sense, **customer relationship management** is the overall process of building and maintaining profitable customer relationships by delivering superior customer value and satisfaction. It deals with all aspects of acquiring, keeping, and growing customers.

Customer relationship management
The overall process of building and maintaining profitable customer relationships by delivering superior customer value and satisfaction.

Relationship Building Blocks: Customer Value and Satisfaction The key to building lasting customer relationships is to create superior customer value and satisfaction. Satisfied customers are more likely to be loyal customers and to give the company a larger share of their business.

CUSTOMER VALUE Attracting and retaining customers can be a difficult task. Customers often face a bewildering array of products and services from which to choose. A customer buys from the firm that offers the highest **customer-perceived value**—the customer's evaluation of the difference between all the benefits and all the costs of a market offering relative to those of competing offers. Importantly, customers often do not judge values and costs "accurately" or "objectively." They act on *perceived* value.

To some consumers, value might mean sensible products at affordable prices. To other consumers, however, value might mean paying more to get more. For example, a top-of-the-line Weber Summit E-670 barbecue grill carries a suggested retail price of US$2,600, more than five times the price of competitor Char-Broil's best grill. According to Weber, the stainless steel Summit grill "embraces true grilling luxury with the highest quality materials, exclusive features, and stunning looks." However, Weber's marketing also suggests that the grill is a real value, even at the premium price. For the money, you get practical features such as all-stainless-steel construction, spacious cooking and work areas, lighted control knobs, a tuck-away motorized rotisserie system, and an LED tank scale that lets you know how much propane you have left in the tank. Is the Weber Summit grill worth the premium price compared to less expensive grills? To many consumers, the answer is no. But to the target segment of affluent, hard-core grillers, the answer is "yes."[11] (see Marketing@Work 1.1)

> **Customer-perceived value**
> The customer's evaluation of the difference between all the benefits and all the costs of a market offering relative to those of competing offers.

MARKETING@WORK 1.1

Canada Goose: Authenticity Is Key to Customer Value

In 1957, Sam Tick founded Metro Sportswear, which produced a modest line of jackets and woollen shirts in a small manufacturing facility in Toronto. The 1970s saw the business expand to include the production of custom-ordered down-filled coats for the Canadian Rangers, city police forces, and other government workers. In 1985, the company was renamed Snow Goose, and in the early 1990s it began selling its products in Europe under the name Canada Goose. By the late 1990s the modern era of Canada Goose had begun and the real expansion of the brand began. Over the past 10 years or so, Canada Goose parka sales have soared within Canada and in more than 40 other countries worldwide. In fact, Canada Goose placed 152nd on the 2011 Profit 200 list of fastest growing Canadian companies, with 3000% growth in revenues over the last decade.

How did Canada Goose achieve such phenomenal growth? A number of factors contribute to the company's success. First, Canada Goose very carefully chose spokespeople who were highly credible users of the brand. Lance Mackey, a four-time Iditarod and Yukon Quest champion, grew up in Alaska and is known as one of the best dogsled mushers in the world. Ray Zahab, ultra marathon runner and adventurer, and Laurie Skreslet, the first Canadian to reach the summit of Mount Everest, also joined the list of Canada Goose spokespeople. These individuals have enormous credibility with the company's core customer segment, which consists of polar expeditioners, oil riggers, and police departments alike.

Rather than using traditional advertising campaigns to build brand awareness, Canada Goose relied on consumer-driven marketing tactics to build its brand. About 10 years ago, product was placed on people who worked outside in cold environments, such as bouncers at nightclubs or doormen at hotels, who could give the brand credibility. Today, Canada Goose still employs several nontraditional forms of promotion to build brand awareness, from supplying Fairmont Hotels' doormen and valets with Expedition parkas to running a Canada Goose coat check at Toronto Maple Leafs and Toronto Raptors games where fans are offered the chance to try on parkas while checking their own garments.

Celebrities caught on camera and actors in feature films wearing the brand have also contributed to Canada Goose's success. Hayden Christensen was photographed wearing one at the Vancouver 2010 Winter Olympics. Daniel Radcliffe is often spotted wearing his Canada Goose parka. The brand has been used in the film industry for decades behind the scenes, but now appears on screen as well in such movies as *The Day After Tomorrow*, *Eight Below*, *National Treasure*, *Good Luck Chuck*, and *Whiteout*.

While Canada Goose has long been a bestseller in Europe, it has also been successful in the highly competitive US fashion market. It currently sells its products at premium department stores such as Barneys and Saks Fifth Avenue and is expanding its product offerings via collaborations with Italian cashmere and wool manufacturer Loro Piana and Japanese designer Yuki Matsuda.

Canada Goose is a company that has always chosen its own path and stayed true to its brand. As a result, it has attracted a diverse customer base who are interested in everything from function to fashion. This is perhaps the biggest reason why Canada Goose has been able to build lasting customer relationships by creating superior customer value and satisfaction. Customers know what to expect when they buy a Canada Goose product. For example, despite the growing trend in the textile industry to ship production to overseas markets,

Kevin Van Paassen/The Globe and Mail

Exhibit 1.4 Quality, functionality, and style are central to the Canada Goose brand and are key to building customer-perceived value.

Canada Goose still manufactures approximately 250 000 parkas per year at its plant in Toronto. An in-house designer cuts the fabric, and dozens of sewers assemble the coats in much the same way as they did in the beginning. While the production of some accessories, such as gloves and mittens, has been moved to overseas plants, the company opted not to move its manufacturing of coats to Asia because it realized early on that having its clothes made in Canada was integral to the authenticity of its brand.

Canada Goose has also faced criticism from animal rights groups protesting the use of coyote fur on its hoods and down feathers in its coats. The company adheres to very strict policies on the ethical procurement of these materials, which it outlines clearly on its corporate website. Because animal products are central to the quality and warmth of Canada Goose coats, the company has opted to continue their use and do so in an ethical and sustainable manner.

Quality, functionality, and style are central to the Canada Goose brand, and maintaining these properties are key to the brand's authenticity. What does this mean for the customers' perceived value of the Canada Goose brand? It depends who you ask. While some consumers would question Canada Goose's hefty price tag and point to less expensive alternatives such as The North Face or Columbia, rarely would Canada Goose customers question the value of their chosen brand. For the extreme weather consumer, perceived value comes from the brand's functionality and protection from severe weather conditions. For the fashion-conscious consumer, the appeal is more than just about warmth. The premium pricing and limited availability (Canada Goose has deliberately undersupplied the market to protect against oversaturation) have led to Canada Goose becoming a symbol of status and wealth. So, whether you ask an adventurer trekking to the North Pole or a student trekking across the University of Alberta's campus if purchasing a Canada Goose jacket was worth it, the answer will most likely be yes!

Sources: Grant Robertson, "Year of the Goose," *Globe and Mail*, February 25, 2010, www.theglobeandmail.com/report-onbusiness/rob-magazine/year-of-the-goose/article1480120; David Kaufman, "Northern Exposure," *Financial Times*, January 13, 2012, www.ft.com/cms/s/2/b18d3dc8-36fb-11e1-b741-00144feabdc0.html#axzz1jSZ6VwAz; "Profit 200 Canada's Fastest-Growing Companies," www.profitguide.com/awards/profit200_2011; and Canada Goose's corporate website, www.canada-goose.com.

Customer satisfaction
The extent to which a product's perceived performance matches a buyer's expectations.

CUSTOMER SATISFACTION **Customer satisfaction** depends on the product's perceived performance relative to a buyer's expectations. If the product's performance falls short of expectations, the customer is dissatisfied. If performance matches expectations, the customer is satisfied. If performance exceeds expectations, the customer is highly satisfied or delighted.

Outstanding marketing companies go out of their way to keep important customers satisfied. Most studies show that higher levels of customer satisfaction lead to greater customer loyalty, which in turn results in better company performance. Smart companies aim to delight customers by promising only what they can deliver, and then delivering more than they promise. Delighted customers not only make repeat purchases, they also become willing marketing partners and "customer evangelists" who spread the word about their good experiences to others.

For companies interested in delighting customers, exceptional value and service become part of the overall company culture. For example, year after year, The Ritz-Carlton ranks at or near the top of the hospitality industry in terms of customer satisfaction. Its passion for satisfying customers is summed up in the company's credo, which promises that its luxury hotels will deliver a truly memorable experience—one that "enlivens the senses, instills well-being, and fulfills even the unexpressed wishes and needs of our guests."

Check into any Ritz-Carlton hotel around the world and you'll be amazed by the company's fervent dedication to anticipating and meeting even your slightest need. Without ever asking, they seem to know that you want a king-size bed, a nonallergenic pillow, and breakfast with decaffeinated coffee in your room. Each day, hotel staffers—from those at the front desk to those in maintenance and housekeeping—discreetly observe and record even the smallest guest preferences. Then, every morning, each hotel reviews the files of all new arrivals who have previously stayed at a Ritz-Carlton and prepares a list of suggested extra touches that might delight each guest.

Once they identify a special customer need, the Ritz-Carlton employees go to legendary extremes to meet it. For example, to serve the needs of a guest with food allergies, a Ritz-Carlton chef in Bali located special eggs and milk in a small grocery store in another country and had them delivered to the hotel. In another case, when the hotel's laundry service failed to remove a stain on a guest's suit before the guest departed, the hotel manager travelled to the guest's house and personally delivered a reimbursement cheque for the cost of the suit. As a result of such customer service heroics, an amazing 95 percent of departing guests report that their stay has been a truly memorable experience. More than 90 percent of The Ritz-Carlton's delighted customers return.[12]

However, a company doesn't have to be a luxury hotel chain with over-the-top service to create customer delight. Customer satisfaction "has a lot more to do with how well companies deliver on their basic, even plain-vanilla promises than on how dazzling the service experience might be," says one expert. "To win [customers'] loyalty, forget the bells and whistles and just solve their problems."[13]

Although a customer-centred firm seeks to deliver high customer satisfaction relative to competitors, it does not attempt to *maximize* customer satisfaction. A company can always increase customer satisfaction by lowering its price or increasing its services. But this may result in lower profits. Thus, the purpose of marketing is to generate customer value profitably. This requires a very delicate balance: The marketer must continue to generate more customer value and satisfaction but not "give away the house."

Customer Relationship Levels and Tools

Companies can build customer relationships at many levels, depending on the nature of the target market. At one extreme, a company with many low-margin customers may seek to develop *basic relationships* with them. For example, Nike does not phone or call on all of its consumers to get to know them personally. Instead, Nike creates relationships through brand-building advertising, public relations, and its numerous websites and apps. At the other extreme, in markets with few customers and high margins, sellers want to create *full partnerships* with key customers. For example, Nike sales representatives work closely with the Sport Chek, Source for Sports, Foot Locker, and other large retailers. In between these two extremes, other levels of customer relationships are appropriate.

AFP/Getty Images

Exhibit 1.5 Customer satisfaction: The Ritz-Carlton's passion for satisfying customers is summed up in its credo, which promises a truly memorable experience—one that "enlivens the senses, instills well-being, and fulfills even the unexpressed wishes and needs of our guests."

Beyond offering consistently high value and satisfaction, marketers can use specific marketing tools to develop stronger bonds with consumers. For example, many companies offer *frequency marketing programs* that reward customers who buy frequently or in large amounts. Airlines offer frequent-flyer programs, hotels give room upgrades to their frequent guests, and supermarkets give patronage discounts to "very important customers."

Other companies sponsor *club marketing programs* that offer members special benefits and create member communities. For example, buy one of those Weber grills and you can join the Weber Nation—"the site for real people who love their Weber grills." Membership gets you exclusive access to online grilling classes, an interactive recipe box, grilling tips and 24/7 telephone support, audio and video podcasts, straight-talk forums for interacting with other grilling fanatics, and even a chance to star in a Weber TV commercial. "Become a spatula-carrying member today," says Weber.[14]

The Changing Nature of Customer Relationships

Significant changes are occurring in the ways in which companies are relating to their customers. Yesterday's big companies focused on mass marketing to all customers at arm's length. Today's companies are building deeper, more direct, and lasting relationships with more carefully selected customers. Here are some important trends in the way companies and customers are relating to one another.

Relating with More Carefully Selected Customers Few firms today still practise true mass marketing—selling in a standardized way to any customer who comes along. Today, most marketers realize that they don't want relationships with every customer. Instead, they target fewer, more profitable customers. "Not all customers are worth your marketing efforts," states one analyst. "Some are more costly to serve than to lose."[15]

Many companies now use customer profitability analysis to pass up or weed out losing customers and target winning ones for pampering. One approach is to preemptively screen out potentially unprofitable customers. Progressive Insurance does this effectively. It asks prospective customers a series of screening questions to determine if they are right for the firm. If they're not, Progressive will likely tell them, "You might want to go to Allstate." A marketing consultant explains: "They'd rather send business to a competitor than take on unprofitable customers." Screening out unprofitable customers lets Progressive provide even better service to potentially more profitable ones.[16]

But what should the company do with unprofitable customers that it already has? If it can't turn them into profitable ones, the company may want to dismiss customers who are too unreasonable or that cost more to serve than they are worth. "Save your company by firing your customers," advises one marketer. "Well, not all your customers—just the ones who ask for more than they give." Adds another marketer, "Firing the customers you can't possibly please gives you the bandwidth and resources to coddle the ones that truly deserve your attention and repay you with referrals, applause, and loyalty."[17] Consider this example:

> Sprint recently sent out letters to about 1000 people to inform them that they had been summarily dismissed—but the recipients were Sprint *customers*, not employees. For about a year, the US-based wireless service provider had been tracking the number and frequency of support calls made by a group of high-maintenance users. According to a Sprint spokesperson, "in some cases, they were calling customer care hundreds of times a month . . . on the same issues, even after we felt those issues had been resolved." Ultimately, the company determined it could not meet the needs of this subset of subscribers and, therefore, waived their termination fees and cut off their service. Such "customer divestment" practices were once considered an anomaly. But new segmentation approaches and technologies have made it easier to focus on retaining the right customers and, by extension, showing problem customers the door.

Exhibit 1.6 Marketers don't want relationships with every possible customer. In fact, a company might want to "fire" customers that cost more to serve than to lose.

Memo To: **Unprofitable Customers**

You Are Fired!

Relating More Deeply and Interactively Beyond choosing customers more selectively, companies are now relating with chosen customers in deeper, more meaningful ways. Rather than relying only on one-way, mass media messages, today's marketers are incorporating new, more interactive approaches that help build targeted, two-way customer relationships.

INTERACTIVE CUSTOMER RELATIONSHIPS New technologies have profoundly changed the ways in which people relate to one another. New tools for relating include everything from email, websites, blogs, cellphones, and video sharing to online communities and social networks such as MySpace, Facebook, YouTube, and Twitter.

This changing communications environment also affects how companies and brands relate to consumers. The new communications approaches let marketers create deeper consumer involvement and a sense of community surrounding a brand—to make the brand a meaningful part of consumers' conversations and lives. "Becoming part of the conversation between consumers is infinitely more powerful than handing down information via traditional advertising," says one marketing expert. Says another, "Brands that engage in two-way conversation with their customers create stronger, more trusting relationships. People today want a voice and a role in their brand experiences. They want co-creation."[18]

However, at the same time that the new technologies create relationship-building opportunities for marketers, they also create challenges. They give consumers greater power and control. Today's consumers have more information about brands than ever before, and they have a wealth of platforms for airing and sharing their brand views with other consumers. Thus, the marketing world is now embracing not just customer relationship management, but also **customer-managed relationships**.

Greater consumer control means that, in building customer relationships, companies can no longer rely on marketing by *intrusion*. Instead, marketers must practise marketing by *attraction*—creating market offerings and messages that involve consumers rather than interrupt them. Hence, most marketers now augment their mass media marketing efforts with a rich mix of direct marketing approaches that promote brand–consumer interaction.

> **Customer-managed relationships** Marketing relationships in which customers, empowered by today's new digital technologies, interact with companies and with each other to shape their relationships with brands.

For example, many brands are creating dialogues with consumers via their own or existing *online social networks*. To supplement their marketing campaigns, companies now routinely post their latest ads and made-for-the-web videos on video-sharing sites. They join social networks. Or they launch their own blogs, online communities, or consumer-generated review systems, all with the aim of engaging customers on a more personal, interactive level.

Take Twitter, for example. Organizations ranging from Dell, West 49, lululemon, and Dalhousie University to the Edmonton Oilers and Tourism PEI have opened Twitter accounts. They use "tweets" to start conversations with Twitter's more than 500 million registered users, address customer service issues, research customer reactions, and drive traffic to relevant articles, websites, contests, videos, and other brand activities. For example, Dell monitors

Exhibit 1.7 **Online social networks:** Many organizations are creating dialogues via their own or existing networks. Tourism Prince Edward Island uses Twitter to promote events such as local golf tournaments and music festivals to visitors and Islanders alike.

PEI Tourism

Twitter-based discussions and responds quickly to individual problems or questions, and the Winnipeg Jets have almost 150 000 Twitter followers. One marketer notes that companies can "use Twitter to get the fastest, most honest research any company ever heard—the good, bad, and ugly—and it doesn't cost a cent."[19]

Similarly, almost every company has something going on Facebook these days. Starbucks has more than 20 million Facebook "fans"; Coca-Cola has more than 23 million. Social media such as Facebook, YouTube, Twitter, and even email can get consumers involved with and talking about a brand. For example, ice cream retailer Cold Stone Creamery uses all of these media to engage customers:

> On YouTube, Cold Stone posts footage from events like its annual "World's Largest Ice Cream Social," which benefits Make-A-Wish Foundation. Cold Stone's Facebook page, with more than 1.4 million friends, constitutes a modern-day online version of an ice cream social. Fans can post pictures of their favourite Cold Stone experiences, exchange views with the company and fellow ice cream lovers, learn about new flavours and happenings, or send a Cold Stone eGift—a cone, milkshake, or just a dollar amount—to a friend who needs a lift. Social media helps build both customer relationships and sales. In response to a recent 2-for-$5 coupon campaign using email and Facebook, fans printed more than 500 000 coupons in just three weeks, redeeming an amazing 14 percent of them. A new-summer–flavours contest drew 4000 entrants and 66 000 new fans in just eight weeks. According to Cold Stone, every social media campaign so far has brought a spike in store traffic and sales. More than half of the company's advertising budget is now dedicated to nontraditional activities like social media.[20]

Most marketers are still learning how to use social media effectively. The problem is to find unobtrusive ways to enter consumers' social conversations with engaging and relevant brand messages. Simply posting a humorous video, creating a social network page, or hosting a blog isn't enough. Successful social network marketing means making relevant and genuine contributions to consumer conversations. "Nobody wants to be friends with a brand," says one online marketing executive. "Your job [as a brand] is to be part of other friends' conversations."[21]

Consumer-Generated Marketing A growing part of the new customer dialogue is **consumer-generated marketing**, by which consumers themselves are playing a bigger role in shaping their own brand experiences and those of others. This might happen through uninvited consumer-to-consumer exchanges in blogs, on video-sharing sites, and other digital forums. But increasingly, companies are *inviting* consumers to play a more active role in shaping products and brand messages.

Some companies ask consumers for new product ideas. For example, Coca-Cola's vitaminwater brand recently set up a Facebook app to obtain consumer suggestions for a new flavour, promising to manufacture and sell the winner ("vitaminwater was our idea; the next one will be yours."). The new flavour—Connect (black cherry–lime with vitamins and a kick of caffeine)—was a big hit. In the process, vitaminwater doubled its Facebook fan base to more than 1 million.[22]

Other companies are inviting customers to play an active role in shaping ads. For example, PepsiCo, MasterCard, Unilever, H.J. Heinz, and many other companies have run contests for consumer-generated commercials that have been aired on national television. For the past several years, PepsiCo's Doritos brand has held a "Crash the Super Bowl" contest in which it invites 30-second ads from consumers and runs the best ones during the game. The consumer-generated ads have been a huge success. Last year, PepsiCo added the Pepsi MAX brand to the contest and consumers submitted nearly 5600 entries. The winning fan-produced ad for Doritos (called "Pug Attack") tied for number one with Bud Light's agency-produced "Dog sitter" ad in the *USA Today* Ad Meter ratings, earning the creator a $1,000,000 cash prize from PepsiCo. The ad

---

Consumer-generated marketing
Brand exchanges created by consumers themselves—both invited and uninvited—by which consumers are playing an increasing role in shaping their own brand experiences and those of other consumers.

cost only about $500 to make. In all, PepsiCo placed two consumer-made Doritos ads and two Pepsi MAX ads in the top 10 out of 61 Super Bowl ads.[23]

However, harnessing consumer-generated content can be a time-consuming and costly process, and companies may find it difficult to glean even a little gold from all the garbage. For example, when H.J. Heinz invited consumers to submit homemade ads for its ketchup brand on its YouTube page, it ended up sifting through more than 8000 entries, of which it posted nearly 4000. Some of the amateur ads were very good—entertaining and potentially effective. Most, however, were so-so at best, and others were downright dreadful. In one ad, a contestant chugs ketchup straight from the bottle. In another, the would-be film-maker brushes his teeth, washes his hair, and shaves his face with Heinz's product.[24]

Exhibit 1.8 **Harnessing consumer-generated marketing:** When H.J. Heinz invited consumers to submit homemade ads for its ketchup brand on YouTube, it received more than 8000 entries—some very good but most only so-so or even downright dreadful.

Consumer-generated marketing, whether invited by marketers or not, has become a significant marketing force. Through a profusion of consumer-generated videos, reviews, blogs, and websites, consumers are playing an increasing role in shaping their own brand experiences and those of other consumers. Beyond creating brand conversations, on their own or by invitation, customers are having an increasing say about everything from product design, usage, and packaging to pricing and distribution. Brands need to accept and embrace the emergence of consumer power. Says one analyst, "Humans, formerly known as either consumers or couch potatoes, are now creators and thought leaders, passive no more."[25]

Partner Relationship Management

When it comes to creating customer value and building strong customer relationships, today's marketers know that they can't go it alone. They must work closely with a variety of marketing partners. In addition to being good at *customer relationship management,* marketers must also be good at **partner relationship management**—working closely with others inside and outside the company to jointly bring more value to customers.

Partner relationship management
Working closely with partners in other company departments and outside the company to jointly bring greater value to customers.

Traditionally, marketers have been charged with understanding customers and representing customer needs to different company departments. However, in today's more connected world, every functional area in the organization can interact with customers. The new thinking is that—no matter what your job is in a company—you must understand marketing and be customer focused. Rather than letting each department go its own way, firms must link all departments in the cause of creating customer value.

Marketers must also partner with suppliers, channel partners, and others outside the company. Marketing channels consist of distributors, retailers, and others who connect the company to its buyers. The *supply chain* describes a longer channel, stretching from raw materials to components to final products that are carried to final buyers. Through *supply chain management,* companies today are strengthening their connections with partners all along the supply chain. They know that their fortunes rest on more than just how well they perform. Success at delivering customer value rests on how well their entire supply chain performs against competitors' supply chains.

Capturing Value from Customers

The first four steps in the marketing process outlined in Figure 1.1 involve building customer relationships by creating and delivering superior customer value. The final step involves capturing value in return in the form of current and future sales, market share, and profits. By creating superior customer value, the firm creates highly satisfied customers who stay loyal and buy more. This, in turn, means greater long-run returns for the firm. Here, we discuss the outcomes of creating customer value: customer loyalty and retention, share of market and share of customer, and customer equity.

Creating Customer Loyalty and Retention

Good customer relationship management creates customer delight. In turn, delighted customers remain loyal and talk favourably to others about the company and its products. Studies show big differences in the loyalty of customers who are less satisfied, somewhat satisfied, and completely satisfied. Even a slight drop from complete satisfaction can create an enormous drop in loyalty. Thus, the aim of customer relationship management is to create not just customer satisfaction, but customer delight.

The recent recession and the economic uncertainty that followed it put strong pressures on customer loyalty. It created a new consumer spending sensibility that will last well into the future. Recent studies show that, even in an improved economy, 55 percent of consumers say they would rather get the best price than the best brand. Some 50 percent of consumers now purchase store brands "all the time" as part of their regular shopping behaviour, up from just 12 percent in the early 1990s. Nearly two-thirds say they will now shop at a different store with lower prices even if it's less convenient. Research also shows that it's five times cheaper to keep an old customer than acquire a new one. Thus, companies today must shape their value propositions even more carefully and treat their profitable customers well to keep them loyal.[26]

Losing a customer means losing more than a single sale. It means losing the entire stream of purchases that the customer would make over a lifetime of patronage. For example, here is a classic illustration of **customer lifetime value**:

Customer lifetime value
The value of the entire stream of purchases that the customer would make over a lifetime of patronage.

> Stew Leonard, who operates a highly profitable four-store supermarket, says that he sees US$50 000 flying out of his store every time he sees a sulking customer. Why? Because his average customer spends about $100 a week, shops 50 weeks a year, and remains in the area for about 10 years. If this customer has an unhappy experience and switches to another supermarket, Stew Leonard's has lost US$50 000 in revenue. The loss can be much greater if the disappointed customer shares the bad experience with other customers and causes them to defect. To keep customers coming back, Stew Leonard's has created what the *New York Times* has dubbed the "Disneyland of Dairy Stores," complete with costumed characters, scheduled entertainment, a petting zoo, and animatronics throughout the store. From its humble beginnings as a small dairy store in 1969, Stew Leonard's has grown at an amazing pace. It has built 29 additions onto the original store, which now serves more than 300 000 customers each week. This legion of loyal shoppers is largely a result of the store's passionate approach to customer service. Rule #1: At Stew Leonard's—The customer is always right. Rule #2: If the customer is ever wrong, reread rule #1![27]

Stew Leonard is not alone in assessing customer lifetime value. Lexus, for example, estimates that a single satisfied and loyal customer is worth more than US$600 000 in lifetime sales.[28] And the estimated lifetime value of a young mobile phone consumer is US$26 000. In fact, a company can lose money on a specific transaction but still benefit greatly from a long-term relationship. This means that companies must aim high in building customer relationships. Customer delight creates an emotional relationship with a brand, not just a rational preference. And that relationship keeps customers coming back.

Growing Share of Customer

Beyond simply retaining good customers to capture customer lifetime value, good customer relationship management can help marketers to increase their **share of customer**—the share they get of the customer's purchasing in their product categories. Thus, banks want to increase "share of wallet," supermarkets and restaurants want to get more "share of stomach," car companies want to increase "share of garage," and airlines want greater "share of travel."

To increase share of customer, firms can offer greater variety to current customers. Or they can create programs to cross-sell and upsell to market more products and services to existing customers. For example, Amazon.com is highly skilled at leveraging relationships with its 90 million customers to increase its share of each customer's spending budget:

Exhibit 1.9 **Customer lifetime value:** To keep customers coming back, Stew Leonard's has created the "Disneyland of dairy stores." Rule #1—The customer is always right. Rule #2—If the customer is ever wrong, reread Rule #1.

> Originally an online bookseller, Amazon.com now offers customers a wide selection of products including music, videos, consumer electronics, toys, home improvement items, lawn and garden products, jewellery, and tools. In addition, based on each customer's purchase and search history, the company recommends related products that might be of interest. This recommendation system influences up to 30 percent of all sales. Amazon.com's ingenious Amazon Prime two-day shipping program has also helped boost the online giant's share of customers' wallets. For an annual fee of $79, Prime members receive delivery of all their purchases within two days, whether it's a single paperback book or a 60-inch HDTV. "Amazon Prime may be the most ingenious and effective customer loyalty program in all of e-commerce, if not retail in general," says one analyst. "It converts casual shoppers, who gorge on the gratification of having purchases reliably appear two days after the order, into Amazon addicts." As a result, after signing up for Prime, shoppers more than double their annual Amazon.com purchases. The shipping program is responsible for an estimated 20 percent of Amazon's sales.[29]

Share of customer
The portion of the customer's purchasing that a company gets in its product categories.

Building Customer Equity

We can now see the importance of not only acquiring customers but also keeping and growing them. The value of a company comes from the value of its current and future customers. Customer relationship management takes a long-term view. Companies want not only to create profitable customers but also "own" them for life, earn a greater share of their purchases, and capture their customer lifetime value.

What Is Customer Equity? The ultimate aim of customer relationship management is to produce high *customer equity*.[30] **Customer equity** is the total combined customer lifetime values of all of the company's current and potential customers. As such, it's a measure of the future value of the company's customer base. Clearly, the more loyal the firm's profitable customers, the higher the firm's customer equity. Customer equity may be a better measure of a firm's performance than current sales or market share. Whereas sales and market share reflect the past, customer equity suggests the future. Consider Cadillac:

Customer equity
The total combined customer lifetime values of all of the company's customers.

> In the 1970s and 1980s, Cadillac had some of the most loyal customers in the industry. To an entire generation of car buyers, the name "Cadillac" defined luxury. Cadillac's share of the luxury car market reached a whopping 51 percent in 1976. Based on market share and sales, the brand's future looked rosy. However, measures of customer equity would have

Exhibit 1.10 To increase customer lifetime value and customer equity, Cadillac is cool again. Its ad campaigns target a younger generation of consumers.

painted a bleaker picture. Cadillac customers were getting older (average age 60), and average customer lifetime value was falling. Many Cadillac buyers were on their last car. Thus, although Cadillac's market share was good, its customer equity was not.

Compare this with BMW. Its more youthful and vigorous image didn't win BMW the early market share war. However, it did win BMW younger customers (average age about 40) with higher customer lifetime values. The result: In the years that followed, BMW's market share and profits soared while Cadillac's fortunes eroded badly. In recent years, Cadillac has struggled to make the Caddy cool again by targeting a younger generation of consumers. The moral: Marketers should care not just about current sales and market share. Customer lifetime value and customer equity are the name of the game.[31]

Building the Right Relationships with the Right Customers Companies should manage customer equity carefully. They should view customers as assets that need to be managed and maximized. But not all customers, not even all loyal customers, are good investments. Surprisingly, some loyal customers can be unprofitable, and some disloyal customers can be profitable. Which customers should the company acquire and retain?

The company can classify customers according to their potential profitability and manage its relationships with them accordingly. Figure 1.5 classifies customers into one of four relationship groups, according to their profitability and projected loyalty.[32] Each group requires a different relationship management strategy.

"Strangers" show low potential profitability and little projected loyalty. There is little fit between the company's offerings and their needs. The relationship management strategy for these customers is simple: Don't invest anything in them.

"Butterflies" are potentially profitable but not loyal. There is a good fit between the company's offerings and their needs. However, like real butterflies, we can enjoy them for only a short while and then they're gone. An example is stock market investors who trade shares often and in large amounts but who enjoy hunting out the best deals without building a regular relationship with any single brokerage company. Efforts to convert butterflies into loyal customers are rarely successful. Instead, the company should enjoy

FIGURE 1.5 Customer relationship groups

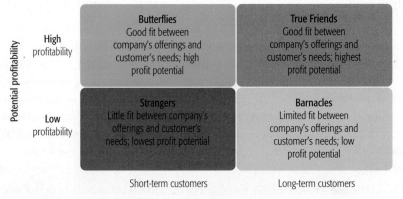

the butterflies for the moment. It should create satisfying and profitable transactions with them, capturing as much of their business as possible in the short time during which they buy from the company. Then, it should cease investing in them until the next time around.

"True friends" are both profitable and loyal. There is a strong fit between their needs and the company's offerings. The firm wants to make continuous relationship investments to delight these customers and nurture, retain, and grow them. It wants to turn true friends into "true believers," who come back regularly and tell others about their good experiences with the company.

"Barnacles" are highly loyal but not very profitable. There is a limited fit between their needs and the company's offerings. An example is smaller bank customers who bank regularly but do not generate enough returns to cover the costs of maintaining their accounts. Like barnacles on the hull of a ship, they create drag. Barnacles are perhaps the most problematic customers. The company might be able to improve their profitability by selling them more, raising their fees, or reducing service to them. However, if they cannot be made profitable, they should be "fired."

The point here is an important one: Different types of customers require different relationship management strategies. The goal is to build the *right relationships* with the *right customers.*

The Changing Marketing Landscape LO5

Every day, dramatic changes are occurring in the marketplace. Richard Love of Hewlett-Packard observes, "The pace of change is so rapid that the ability to change has now become a competitive advantage." Yogi Berra, the legendary New York Yankees catcher and manager, summed it up more simply when he said, "The future ain't what it used to be." As the marketplace changes, so must those who serve it.

In this section, we examine the major trends and forces that are changing the marketing landscape and challenging marketing strategy. We look at five major developments: the uncertain economic environment, the digital age, the growth of not-for-profit marketing, rapid globalization, and the call for more ethics and social responsibility.

The Changing Economic Environment

Beginning in 2008, world economies experienced a stunning economic meltdown, unlike anything since the Great Depression of the 1930s. The stock market plunged and trillions of dollars of market value simply evaporated. The financial crisis left shell-shocked consumers short of both money and confidence as they faced losses in income, a severe credit crunch, declining home values, and rising unemployment.

The recession caused many consumers to rethink their spending priorities and cut back on their buying. After two decades of overspending, consumers tightened their purse strings and changed their buying attitudes and habits. More than just a temporary change, the economic downturn will likely affect consumer buying attitudes and spending behaviour for many years to come. Even as the economy strengthens, consumers will continue to spend more carefully and sensibly (see Marketing@Work 1.2).

In response, companies in all industries—from discounters such as Target to luxury brands such as Lexus—have tightened their budgets and aligned their marketing strategies with the new economic realities. More than ever, marketers are emphasizing the *value* in their value propositions. They are focusing on value-for-the-money, practicality, and durability in their product offerings and marketing pitches.

MARKETING@WORK 1.2

The New Era of More Sensible Consumption

The recession of 2008–2009 and its aftermath hit consumers hard. The housing bust, credit crunch, high unemployment, and plunging stock market blew away the savings and confidence of consumers who for years operated on a buy-now, pay-later philosophy, chasing bigger homes, bigger cars, and better brands. The new economic realities forced consumers to bring their excessive consumption back in line with their incomes and rethink buying priorities. People across all income segments reined in their spending, postponed big purchases, searched for bargains, and hunkered down to weather the worst economic crisis since the Great Depression rocked the worlds of their parents or grandparents.

Today, as the world moves into the post-recession era, consumer incomes and spending are again on the rise. However, even as the economy strengthens, rather than reverting to their old free-spending ways, consumers are now showing an enthusiasm for frugality not seen in decades. Sensible consumption has made a comeback, and it might be here to stay. The behavioural shift isn't simply about spending less. The new consumption ethic emphasizes simpler living and more value for the dollar. It focuses on living with less, fixing something yourself instead of buying a new one, packing a lunch instead of eating out, spending more time in discount chains, or trading down to store brands. Despite their rebounding means, consumers are now clipping more coupons, swiping their credit cards less, and putting more in the bank.

Such new-found buying sensibilities are more than just a fad—most experts agree that the impact of the recession will last well into the future. "It is a whole reassessment of values," says a retailing consultant. "We had just been shopping until we drop, and consuming and buying it all, and replenishing before things wear out. People [have learned] again to say, 'No, not today.'"

The pain of the recession moved many consumers to reconsider their very definition of the good life, changing the way they buy, sell, and live in a post-recession society. "People are finding happiness in old-fashioned virtues—thrift, savings, do-it-yourself projects, self-improvement, hard work, faith, and community—and in activities and relationships outside the consumer realm," says John Gerzema, chief insights officer for ad agency Young & Rubicam, which maintains one of the world's largest databases of information about consumer attitudes. In what Gerzema calls the "spend shift," consumers have become uneasy with debt and excess spending and skeptical of materialistic values. "From now on, our purchases will be more considered. We are moving from mindless to mindful consumption."

Most consumers see the new frugality as a good thing. One recent survey showed that 78 percent of people believe the recession has changed their spending habits for the better. In another survey, 79 percent of consumers agreed with the statement, "I feel a lot smarter now about the way I shop versus two years ago." Some 65 percent of Americans feel that "since the recession I realize I am happier with a simpler more down-to-basic lifestyle." According to a researcher, "They look at their old spending habits and are a bit embarrassed by their behavior. So while consumption may [not] be as carefree and fun as it was before, consumers seem to like their new outlook, mindfulness, and strength."

For example, Sindi Card says her husband's job is now secure. However, because the couple has two sons in university, even in the more buoyant economy, she fixed her broken 20-year-old clothes dryer herself. It was a stark change from the past, when she would have taken the old model to the dump and had a new one delivered. With help from an appliance-repair website, she saved hundreds of dollars. "We all need to find a way to live within our means," she said.

The new, more practical spending values don't mean that people have resigned themselves to lives of deprivation. As the economy has improved, consumers

Exhibit 1.11 Even as the economy strengthens, rather than reverting to their old free-spending ways, consumers are now showing an enthusiasm for frugality not seen in decades. More sensible spending might be here to stay.

igor kisselev/Shutterstock

are indulging in luxuries and bigger-ticket purchases again, just more sensibly. "We're seeing an emergence in what we call 'conscious recklessness,' where consumers actually plan out frivolous or indulgent spending," says the researcher. It's like someone on a diet who saves up calories by eating prudently during the week and then lets loose on Friday night. But "people are more mindful now and aware of the consequences of their (and others') spending. So luxury is [again] on the 'to-do' list, but people are taking a more mindful approach to where, how, and on what they spend."

What does the new era of consumer spending mean to marketers? Whether it's for everyday products like cereal and detergents or expensive luxuries like Starbucks coffee or diamonds, marketers must clearly spell out their value propositions: what it is that makes their brands worth a customer's hard-earned money. Frugality is in; value is under scrutiny. For

companies, it's not about cutting costs and prices. Instead, they must use a different approach to reach today's more pragmatic consumers: Forego the flash and prove your products' worth. According to Starbucks CEO Howard Schultz:

> There's been a real sea change in consumer behavior. And [companies] must appeal to the consumer in a different way today than they did two or three years ago. And it's not all based on value. Cutting prices or putting things on sale is not sustainable business strategy. . . . You can't cut enough costs to save your way to prosperity. I think the question is, What is your relevancy to the new life of the consumer, who is more discriminating about what they're going to spend money on?"

Even diamond marketer De Beers has adjusted its long-standing "A diamond is forever" value proposition to these more sensible times. One ad, headlined

"Here's to Less," makes that next diamond purchase seem—what else—downright practical. "Our lives are filled with things. We're overwhelmed by possessions we own but do not treasure. Stuff we buy but never love. To be thrown away in weeks rather than passed down for generations. Perhaps we will be different now. Perhaps now is an opportunity to reassess what really matters. After all, if everything you ever bought her disappeared overnight, what would she truly miss? A diamond is forever."

Sources: Extracts, quotes, and other information from Mark Dolliver, "Will Traumatized Consumers Ever Recover?" *Adweek,* March 22, 2010, www.adweek.com; Leigh Buchanan, "Decoding the New Consumer," *Inc.,* September 2010, 159–160; Dan Sewell, "New Frugality Emerges," *Washington Times,* December 1, 2008; John Gerzema, "How U.S. Consumers Are Steering the Spend Shift," *Advertising Age,* October 11, 2010, 26; and "Howard Schultz, I'm Getting a Second Shot," *Inc.,* April 2011, 52–53.

For example, for years discount retailer Target focused on the "Expect More" side of its "Expect More. Pay Less." value proposition. It's carefully cultivated "upscale-discounter" image successfully differentiated it from Walmart's more hard-nosed "lowest price" position. But when the economy soured, many consumers worried that Target's trendier assortments and hip marketing also meant higher prices, and Target's performance slipped. So Target has shifted its balance more toward the "Pay Less" half of its slogan, making certain that its prices are in line with Walmart's and that customers know it. Although still trendy, Target's marketing now also features more practical price and savings appeals. "We let too much space drift between 'Expect More' and 'Pay Less,'" says Target's chief marketing officer. Target's latest "Life's a Moving Target" campaign seems to have found the right balance between the two sides of its positioning. "We believe we've negated the price perception issues," says the executive.[33]

At the other extreme, even luxury brands are adding value to their buying equations. For example, for years Lexus has emphasized status and performance. Its pre-Christmas ads typically feature a loving spouse giving his or her significant other a new Lexus wrapped in a big

Exhibit 1.12 In the current economic environment, companies must emphasize the value in their value propositions. Target has shifted the balance more toward the "Pay Less" half of its "Expect More. Pay Less" positioning.

Justin Sullivan/Getty Images

red bow. Lexus is still running those ads, but it's also hedging its bets by running other ads with the tagline "lowest cost of ownership," referring to Lexus' decent fuel economy, durability, and high resale value.

In adjusting to the new economy, companies might be tempted to cut marketing budgets deeply and slash prices in an effort to coax cash-strapped customers into opening their wallets. However, although cutting costs and offering selected discounts can be important marketing tactics in a down economy, smart marketers understand that making cuts in the wrong places can damage long-term brand image and customer relationships. The challenge is to balance the brand's value proposition with the current times while also enhancing its long-term equity.

"A recession creates winners and losers just like a boom," notes one economist. "When a recession ends, when the road levels off and the world seems full of promise once more, your position in the competitive pack will depend on how skillfully you managed [during the tough times]."[34] Thus, rather than slashing prices in difficult times, many marketers held the line on prices and instead explained why their brands were worth it. And rather than cutting their marketing budgets, companies such as McDonald's, Hyundai, and General Mills maintained or actually increased their marketing spending, leaving them stronger when the economy strengthened. The goal in uncertain economic times is to build market share and strengthen customer relationships at the expense of competitors who cut back.

The Digital Age

The explosive growth in digital technology has fundamentally changed the way we live—how we communicate, share information, learn, shop, and access entertainment. In turn, it has had a major impact on the ways companies bring value to their customers. For better or worse, technology has become an indispensable part of our lives:

> Carl and Maggie Frost of Regina, Saskatchewan, can remember simpler mornings not too long ago. They sat together and chatted as they ate breakfast and read the newspaper and competed only with the television for the attention of their two teenage sons. That was so last century. Today, Carl wakes around 6:00 A.M. to check his work email and his Facebook and Twitter accounts. The two boys, Cole and Brian, start each morning with text messages, video games, and Facebook. Maggie cracks open her laptop right after breakfast. The Frosts's sons sleep with their phones next to their beds, so they start the day with text messages in place of alarm clocks. Carl, an instructor at the local university, sends texts to his two sons to wake them up. "We use texting as an in-house intercom," he says. "I could just walk upstairs, but they always answer their texts." This is morning in the Internet age. After six to eight hours of network deprivation—also known as sleep—people are increasingly waking up and lunging for cellphones and laptops, sometimes even before swinging their legs to the floor and tending to more biologically current activities.[35]

The digital age has provided marketers with exciting new ways to learn about and track customers and create products and services tailored to individual customer needs. Digital technology has also brought a new wave of communication, advertising, and relationship-building tools—ranging from online advertising and video-sharing tools to online social networks and mobile phone apps. The digital shift means that marketers can no longer expect consumers to always seek them out. Nor can they always control conversations about their brands. The new digital world makes it easy for consumers to take marketing content that once lived only in advertising or on a brand website with them wherever they go and share it with friends. More than just add-ons to traditional marketing channels, the new digital media must be fully integrated into the marketer's customer-relationship-building efforts.

The most dramatic digital technology is the **Internet**. Approximately 83 percent of the Canadian population now has Internet access. On a typical day, 62 percent of adults check their email, 49 percent use Google or another search engine to find information, 43 percent get the news, 38 percent keep in touch with friends on social networking sites such as Facebook and LinkedIn, and 23 percent watch a video on a video-sharing site such as YouTube. And by 2020, many experts believe, the Internet will be accessed primarily via a mobile device operated by voice, touch, and even thought or "mind-controlled human-computer interaction."[36]

David Sacks/The Image Bank/Getty Images

Exhibit 1.13 In this digital age, for better or worse, technology has become an indispensable part of our lives. The technology boom provides exciting new opportunities for marketers.

Online marketing is now the fastest-growing form of marketing. These days, it's hard to find a company that doesn't use the web in a significant way. In addition to the click-only dot-coms, most traditional brick-and-mortar companies have now become *click-and-mortar* companies. They have ventured online to attract new customers and build stronger relationships with existing ones. Today, more than 75 percent of American online users use the Internet to shop. Last year, consumer online retail spending topped US$143 billion, up more than 11 percent over the previous year. However, Canadian consumers lag far behind Americans in terms of online shopping. The most recent Internet usage survey conducted by Statistics Canada in 2010 found that only 51 percent of Canadian online users used the Internet to shop, spending approximately $15.3 billion. Some analysts attribute this to a poor online presence by firms in Canada, which have taken a more conservative approach to e-commerce development.[37]

Thus, the technology boom is providing exciting new opportunities for marketers. We will explore the impact of digital marketing technologies in future chapters, especially Chapter 14.

Internet
A vast public web of computer networks that connects users of all types all around the world to each other and to an amazingly large information repository.

The Growth of Not-for-Profit Marketing

In recent years, marketing has also become a major part of the strategies of many not-for-profit organizations, such as universities, hospitals, museums, zoos, symphony orchestras, and even churches. The nation's not-for-profits face stiff competition for support and membership. Sound marketing can help them attract membership, funds, and support.[38] Consider the marketing efforts behind the growing success of Bust a Move for Breast Health:

> A grassroots initiative that began in Halifax in 2010, Bust a Move for Breast Health is poised to take the country by storm. The one-day fundraising event was established by the Queen Elizabeth II (QEII) Foundation and IWK Health Centre to fund an integrated, world-class Breast Health Centre in Nova Scotia. Participants enter as a team or individual and are required to raise $1000 through sponsorships. In return, they experience an unforgettable day, which includes six hours of exercise with leading fitness trainers, music and entertainment, and plenty of fun. The success of this event stems from the way QEII and IWK were able to reach out to potential participants. They quickly realized that everyone in the local community has been or knows someone who has been affected by breast cancer. Using social media sites like Facebook and Twitter and backed by TV ads, word of the event quickly spread in the local community. Celebrity hosts Richard Simmons (2010), Paula Abdul (2011), and Canadian comedian Andrea Martin (2012) brought instant publicity to the events and helped raise awareness across the country. In 2013, Haligonians raised over $515 000, bringing the four-year

Exhibit 1.14 Not-for-profit marketing: What began as a grassroots initiative in Halifax, Nova Scotia, by the QEII Foundation and the IWK Health Centre, Bust a Move for Breast Health has now raised millions of dollars for breast health in several Canadian cities and has now expanded to Australia.

total donations for the Breast Health Centre to $3.9 million. The movement has expanded to other Canadian cities, including St. John's, Ottawa, London, Saskatoon, Edmonton, Calgary, and Vancouver, and as far away as Brisbane, Australia in 2013.[39]

Government agencies have also shown an increased interest in marketing. For example, both the Canadian military and the Royal Canadian Mounted Police have marketing plans to attract recruits to their different services, and various government agencies are now designing *social marketing campaigns* to encourage energy conservation and concern for the environment or to discourage smoking, excessive drinking, and drug use. Recent reports show that the Canadian government ad expenditure has nearly tripled in recent years, peaking at $136.3 million in 2009–2010, then dropping to $78.5 million in 2011–2012.[40]

Rapid Globalization

As they are redefining their customer relationships, marketers are also taking a fresh look at the ways in which they relate with the broader world around them. In an increasingly smaller world, companies are now connected *globally* with their customers and marketing partners.

Today, almost every company, large or small, is touched in some way by global competition. A neighbourhood florist buys its flowers from Mexican nurseries, and a large US electronics manufacturer competes in its home markets with giant Korean rivals. A fledgling Internet retailer finds itself receiving orders from all over the world at the same time that a Canadian consumer goods producer introduces new products into emerging markets abroad.

North American firms have been challenged at home by the skilful marketing of European and Asian multinationals. Companies such as Honda, Nokia, Nestlé, and Samsung have often outperformed their North American counterparts. Similarly, Canadian companies in a wide range of industries have developed truly global operations, making and selling their products worldwide. Quebec-based Bombardier has become a leader in the aviation and rail transportation industries, with manufacturing, engineering, and service facilities throughout the world. British Columbia–based lululemon, a yoga-inspired athletic apparel company, manufactures its products in seven countries and operates 235 stores in Canada, the United States, Australia, China, and New Zealand. Today, companies are not only trying to sell more of their locally produced goods in international markets, they also are buying more supplies and components abroad.

Exhibit 1.15 Companies in a wide range of industries have developed truly global operations. Quebec-based Bombardier has become a leader in the aviation and rail transportation industries, with manufacturing, engineering, and service facilities throughout the world.

Thus, managers in countries around the world are increasingly taking a global, not just local, view of the company's industry, competitors, and opportunities. They are asking: What is global marketing? How does it differ from domestic marketing? How do global competitors and forces affect our business? To what extent should we "go global"? These issues will be discussed throughout this text.

Sustainable Marketing—the Call for More Social Responsibility

Marketers are re-examining their relationships with social values and responsibilities and with the very Earth that sustains us. As the worldwide consumerism and environmentalism movements mature, today's marketers are being called on to develop *sustainable marketing* practices. Corporate ethics and social responsibility have become hot topics for almost every business. And few companies can ignore the renewed and very demanding environmental movement. Every company action can affect customer relationships. Today's customers expect companies to deliver value in a socially and environmentally responsible way.

1% percent **for the planet**

Exhibit 1.16 **Sustainable marketing:** Patagonia believes in "using business to inspire solutions to the environmental crisis." It backs these words by pledging at least 1 percent of its sales or 10 percent of its profits, whichever is greater, to the protection of the natural environment.

The social responsibility and environmental movements will place even stricter demands on companies in the future. Some companies resist these movements, budging only when forced by legislation or organized consumer outcries. Forward-looking companies, however, readily accept their responsibilities to the world around them. They view sustainable marketing as an opportunity to do well by doing good. They seek ways to profit by serving both immediate needs and the best long-run interests of their customers and communities.

Some companies—such as Patagonia, Ben & Jerry's, Timberland, and others—are practising "caring capitalism," setting themselves apart by being civic-minded and responsible. They are building social responsibility and action into their company value and mission statements. For example, when it comes to environmental responsibility, outdoor gear marketer Patagonia is "committed to the core." "Those of us who work here share a strong commitment to protecting undomesticated lands and waters," says the company's website. "We believe in using business to inspire solutions to the environmental crisis." Patagonia backs these words with actions. Each year it pledges at least 1 percent of its sales or 10 percent of its profits, whichever is greater, to the protection of the natural environment.[41] We will revisit the topic of sustainable marketing in greater detail in Chapter 3.

So, What Is Marketing? Pulling it all Together

At the start of this chapter, Figure 1.1 presented a simple model of the marketing process. Now that we've discussed all of the steps in the process, Figure 1.6 presents an expanded model that will help you pull it all together. What is marketing? Simply put, marketing is the process of building profitable customer relationships by creating value for customers and capturing value in return.

FIGURE 1.6 An expanded model of the marketing process

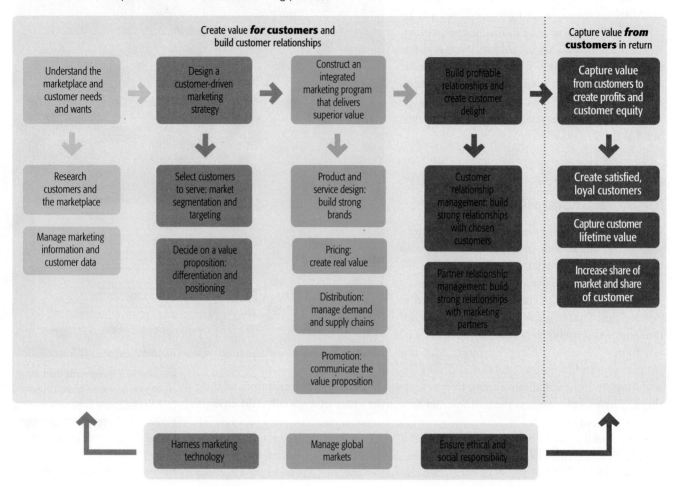

The first four steps of the marketing process focus on creating value for customers. The company first gains a full understanding of the marketplace by researching customer needs and managing marketing information. It then designs a customer-driven marketing strategy based on the answers to two simple questions. The first question is "What consumers will we serve?" (market segmentation and targeting). Good marketing companies know that they cannot serve all customers in every way. Instead, they need to focus their resources on the customers they can serve best and most profitably. The second marketing strategy question is "How can we best serve our targeted customers?" (differentiation and positioning). Here, the marketer outlines a value proposition that spells out what values the company will deliver to win target customers.

With its marketing strategy decided, the company now constructs an integrated marketing program—consisting of a blend of the four marketing mix elements, or the four *P*s—that transforms the marketing strategy into real value for customers. The company develops products and creates strong brand identities for them. It prices these offers to create real customer value and distributes the offers to make them available to target consumers. Finally, the company designs promotion programs that communicate the value proposition to target consumers and persuade them to act on the market offering.

Perhaps the most important step in the marketing process involves building value-laden, profitable relationships with target customers. Throughout the process, marketers practise customer relationship management to create customer satisfaction and delight.

In creating customer value and relationships, however, the company cannot go it alone. It must work closely with marketing partners both inside the company and throughout the marketing system. Thus, beyond practising good customer relationship management, firms must also practise good partner relationship management.

The first four steps in the marketing process create value *for* customers. In the final step, the company reaps the rewards of its strong customer relationships by capturing value *from* customers. Delivering superior customer value creates highly satisfied customers who will buy more and will buy again. This helps the company capture customer lifetime value and greater share of customer. The result is increased long-term customer equity for the firm.

Finally, in the face of today's changing marketing landscape, companies must take into account three additional factors. In building customer and partner relationships, they must harness marketing technology, take advantage of global opportunities, and ensure that they act in an ethical and socially responsible way.

Figure 1.6 provides a good road map to future chapters of the text. Chapters 1 and 2 introduce the marketing process, with a focus on building customer relationships and capturing value from customers. Chapter 3 focuses on understanding the impact marketing has on society and the ethical concerns associated with marketing practice. Chapters 4, 5, and 6 address the first step of the marketing process—understanding the marketing environment, managing marketing information, and understanding consumer and business buyer behaviour. In Chapter 7, we look more deeply into the two major marketing strategy decisions: selecting which customers to serve (segmentation and targeting) and deciding on a value proposition (differentiation and positioning). Finally, Chapters 8 through 14 discuss the marketing mix variables, one by one.

A Great Guest Experience

As the filled-to-capacity Boeing 737 taxis to the ramp at Maui's Kahului Airport, 100 weary travellers are brought back to life by the a capella stylings of the lead flight attendant's playful rendition of "Over the Rainbow." Customers, or "guests" as WestJet prefers to call them, quickly realize that they are now part of another unique WestJet moment. They chuckle as the WestJetter cleverly integrates local time, temperature, and gate information into the lyrics, but he earns genuine LOLs when he works in the verse, "flying to Hawaii is free when you're a WestJet employee."

Thus, despite being awake since 4:30 A.M., boarding a plane in Calgary in the dead of a prairie winter, and enduring a seven-hour flight with two young children who refused to sleep, these "guests" are ready to embrace the magic of Maui. The travellers may never know the reason for the improv performance, but maybe it was just another example of what the advertisements have been telling us for the better part of a decade: "Owners care," a slogan communicating how the airline's employee stock option package motivates participating WestJetters to go just a little bit further to please.

WestJet's philosophy of creating customer value is not based in its being one of the best in turnaround times, its modern fleet of planes, or even its competitively priced fares. It's more than the employee share purchase plan. It's part of their corporate culture, their DNA. Customer value stems from the core of a corporate culture, something only achievable when your people are engaged. In the words of Bob Cummings, executive vice-president of sales, marketing, and guest experience, "the big success factor in the whole corporate strategy is making sure that your employees are understanding and with you all the way." Richard Bartrem, vice-president of communications and community relations, adds "we want all of our frontline employees to leave their inhibitions at the door, knowing, one day, they'll have their WestJet moment . . . moments [that] ultimately make the WestJet flight memorable to guests."

A perennial survey chart-topper in categories such as corporate culture, best employer, and customer service, WestJet is also no stranger to industry-specific accolades, earning kudos for "Best Flight Attendants" from FlightNetwork.com. If creating customer value means exceeding as opposed to merely satisfying needs, then WestJet's "DNA" would seem to be serving both its customers and owners well.

With the song still fresh in their minds, WestJet guests join thousands from around the globe scurrying through Kahului's terminal. They're easy to identify among the throngs, though, as they're the ones talking about what made getting there half the fun.

QUESTIONS

1. What is WestJet's value proposition?
2. Explain how WestJet's "Owner's Care" ad campaign helps communicate its value proposition.
3. Which marketing management orientation does WestJet base its marketing strategies on?

REVIEWING THE CONCEPTS

1. Define marketing and outline the steps in the marketing process.

Marketing is the process by which companies create value for customers and build strong customer relationships to capture value from customers in return.

The marketing process involves five steps. The first four steps create value *for* customers. First, marketers need to understand the marketplace and customer needs and wants. Next, marketers design a customer-driven marketing strategy with the goal of getting, keeping, and growing target customers. In the third step, marketers construct a marketing program that actually delivers superior value. All of these steps form the basis for the fourth step, building profitable customer relationships and creating customer delight. In the final step, the company reaps the rewards of strong customer relationships by capturing value *from* customers.

2. Explain the importance of understanding customers and the marketplace, and identify the five core marketplace concepts.

Outstanding marketing companies go to great lengths to learn about and understand their customers' needs, wants, and demands. This understanding helps them to design want-satisfying market offerings and build value-laden customer relationships by which they can capture customer lifetime value and greater share of customer. The result is increased long-term customer equity for the firm.

The core marketplace concepts are needs, wants, and demands; market offerings (products, services, and experiences); value and satisfaction; exchange and relationships; and markets. Wants are the form taken by human needs when shaped by culture and individual personality. When backed by buying power, wants become demands. Companies address needs by putting forth a value proposition—a set of benefits that they promise to consumers to satisfy their needs. The value proposition is fulfilled through a market offering, which delivers customer value and satisfaction, resulting in long-term exchange relationships with customers.

3. Identify the key elements of a customer-driven marketing strategy and discuss the marketing management orientations that guide marketing strategy.

To design a winning marketing strategy, the company must first decide *who* it will serve. It does this by dividing the market into segments of customers (*market segmentation*)

and selecting which segments it will cultivate (*target marketing*). Next, the company must decide *how* it will serve targeted customers (how it will *differentiate and position* itself in the marketplace).

Marketing management can adopt one of five competing market orientations. The *production concept* holds that management's task is to improve production efficiency and bring down prices. The *product concept* holds that consumers favour products that offer the most in quality, performance, and innovative features; thus, little promotional effort is required. The *selling concept* holds that consumers will not buy enough of the organization's products unless it undertakes a large-scale selling and promotion effort. The *marketing concept* holds that achieving organizational goals depends on determining the needs and wants of target markets and delivering the desired satisfactions more effectively and efficiently than competitors do. The *societal marketing concept* holds that generating customer satisfaction *and* long-run societal well-being through sustainable marketing strategies are the keys to both achieving the company's goals and fulfilling its responsibilities.

4. Discuss customer relationship management and identify strategies for creating value *for* customers and capturing value *from* customers in return.

Broadly defined, *customer relationship management* is the process of building and maintaining profitable customer relationships by delivering superior customer value and satisfaction. The aim of customer relationship management is to produce high *customer equity*, the total combined customer lifetime values of all of the company's current and potential customers. The key to building lasting relationships is the creation of superior *customer value* and *satisfaction*.

Companies want not only to acquire profitable customers but also to build relationships that will keep them and grow "share of customer." Different types of customers require different customer relationship management strategies. The marketer's aim is to build the *right relationships* with the *right customers*. In return for creating value *for* targeted customers, the company captures value *from* customers in the form of profits and customer equity.

In building customer relationships, good marketers realize that they cannot go it alone. They must work closely with marketing partners inside and outside the company. In addition to being good at customer relationship management, they must also be good at *partner relationship management*.

5. Describe the major trends and forces that are changing the marketing landscape in this age of relationships.

Dramatic changes are occurring in the marketing arena. The recession left many consumers short of both money and confidence, creating a new age of consumer frugality that will last well into the future. More than ever, marketers must now emphasize the *value* in their value propositions. The challenge is to balance a brand's value proposition with the current times while also enhancing its long-term equity.

The boom in digital technology has created exciting new ways to learn about and relate to individual customers. It has also allowed new approaches by which marketers can target consumers more selectively and build closer, two-way customer relationships in the digital era.

In an increasingly smaller world, many marketers are now connected *globally* with their customers and marketing partners. Today, almost every company, large or small, is touched in some way by global competition. Today's marketers are also re-examining their ethical and societal responsibilities. Marketers are being called upon to take greater responsibility for the social and environmental impact of their actions. Finally, in recent years, marketing also has become a major part of the strategies of many not-for-profit organizations, such as universities, hospitals, museums, zoos, symphony orchestras, and even churches.

Pulling it all together, as discussed throughout the chapter, the major new developments in marketing can be summed up in a single word: *relationships*. Today, marketers of all kinds are taking advantage of new opportunities for building relationships with their customers, their marketing partners, and the world around them.

KEY TERMS

Consumer-generated marketing 20
Customer equity 23
Customer lifetime value 22
Customer-managed relationships 19
Customer-perceived value 15
Customer relationship management 14
Customer satisfaction 16
Demands 7

Exchange 8
Internet 29
Market 9
Market offerings 7
Marketing 6
Marketing concept 12
Marketing management 10
Marketing myopia 8

Needs 7
Partner relationship management 21
Product concept 11
Production concept 11
Selling concept 11
Share of customer 23
Societal marketing concept 12
Wants 7

TALK ABOUT MARKETING

1. Form a small group of three or four students. Discuss a need or want you have that is not adequately satisfied by any offerings currently in the marketplace. Think of a product or service that will satisfy that need or want. Describe how you will differentiate and position your offering in the marketplace and develop the marketing program for your offering. Present your ideas to the other groups

2. Consider a product that you use or a retailer you patronage frequently. Estimate how much you are worth to the retailer or manufacturer of the brand you prefer if you remain loyal to that marketer for the rest of your life (your customer lifetime value). What factors should you consider when deriving an estimate of your lifetime value to the company? How can the company increase your lifetime value?

3. Compare and contrast the five different marketing management orientations. For what types of products might it be most appropriate to adopt each of these

orientations? Is one orientation necessarily always the "right" one and the others "wrong"? Explain.

4. Research the following brands and try to determine the value proposition offered by each:

    a. Enterprise Rent-A-Car
    b. Lexus automobiles
    c. Gain laundry detergent
    d. iPhone

5. Browse the Canadian Marketing Association's job board at **www.marketing-jobs.ca** to learn about careers in marketing. Interview someone who works in one of the marketing jobs described here and ask him or her the following questions:

    a. What does your job entail?
    b. How did you get to this point in your career? Is this what you thought you'd be doing when you grew up? What influenced you to get into this field?

c. What education is necessary for this job?

d. What advice can you give to marketing students?

e. Add one additional question that you create.

Write a brief report of the responses to your questions, and explain why you would or would not be interested in working in this field.

THINK LIKE A MARKETING MANAGER

West 49 is a leading Canadian specialty retailer of fashion, apparel, footwear, accessories, and equipment related to the youth action sports lifestyle. The company's stores, which are primarily mall-based, carry a variety of high-performance, premium brand name and private label products that fulfill the lifestyle needs of identified target markets, primarily tweens and teens. As of January 2010, the company operated 136 stores in nine provinces under the banners West 49, Billabong, Off the Wall, Amnesia/Arsenic, and D-Tox. In addition to its private label brand, West 49 carries a wide range of products catering to skateboard, snowboard, and surfing enthusiasts, including brands such as DC, Quiksilver, Vans, Hurley, Roxy, and C1RCA.

West 49 has been successful at reaching the very loyal but often difficult to market to skateboarding segment.

The company sponsors a number of up-and-coming skateboarders and features profiles of each of them on the company website (**www.west49.com**). It also provides Canadian boarding enthusiasts with a skateboard park locator, tips and tricks for newbies, and advice on how to get sponsored. Visit the West 49 website and answer the following questions.

QUESTIONS

1. Suppose you are the marketing manager at West 49. How would you describe your value proposition?

2. What specific elements of West 49's website help create customer loyalty? What other ways could the company build relationships with its customers?

MARKETING ETHICS

Sixty years ago, about 45 percent of North Americans smoked cigarettes, but now the smoking rate is less than 20 percent. This decline is the result of increased knowledge about the potential health dangers of smoking and from marketing restrictions for this product. Although smoking rates are declining in most developed nations, more and more consumers in developing nations, such as Russia and China, are puffing away. Smoker rates in some countries run as high as 40 percent. Developing nations account for more than 70 percent of world tobacco consumption, and marketers are fuelling this growth. Most of these nations do not have the restrictions prevalent in developed nations, such as advertising bans, warning labels, and distribution restrictions. Consequently, predictions

are that 1 billion people worldwide will die this century from smoking-related ailments.

QUESTIONS

1. Given the extreme health risks, should marketers stop selling cigarettes even though they are legal and demanded by consumers? Should cigarette marketers continue to use marketing tactics that are restricted in one country in other countries where they are not restricted?

2. Research the history of cigarette marketing in North America. Are there any new restrictions with respect to marketing this product?

MARKETING TECHNOLOGY

Apple's "i" devices—iPods, iPhones, and iPads—are wildly popular. But where's the flash? Adobe Flash, that is. Adobe's Flash, the long-standing multimedia platform behind approximately 75 percent of the animated and streaming audio and video on the Internet, is not supported by Apple

devices. Many purchasers were disappointed after spending hundreds of dollars on sleek new iPads only to realize they couldn't play their favourite Internet game or watch that funny YouTube video on their device. And they still can't, even with the newer generations of the device. It seems Apple's late founder and CEO, Steve Jobs, didn't like Flash and would not support it on Apple devices. Instead, app developers must conform to Apple's operating system and existing applications on the web must convert to HTML5 to play on an Apple product. Adobe's co-founders claim Apple is "undermining the next chapter of the web" and bloggers exclaim this is not just an "Adobe/Apple problem . . . but an Apple/World problem."

QUESTIONS

1. Does Apple appear to embrace the marketing concept?

2. Research the controversy surrounding this issue and debate whether Apple did the right thing for its customers by not including the ubiquitous Adobe Flash software on its products.

MARKETING BY THE NUMBERS

Marketing is expensive! A 30-second advertising spot during the Super Bowl costs more than US$3 million, and that doesn't include the US$500 000 or more to produce the commercial. Anheuser-Busch usually purchases multiple spots each year. Similarly, sponsoring one car during a single NASCAR race costs US$500 000. But Sprint, the sponsor of the popular Sprint Cup, pays much more than that. And many marketers sponsor more than one car in more than one race. Want customers to order your product by phone? That will cost you $8 to $13 per order. Or how about a sales representative calling on customers? About $100 per sales call, and that's if the rep doesn't have to get on an airplane and stay in a hotel, which can be very costly considering some companies have thousands of sales reps calling on thousands of customers. And that $1-off coupon for Tropicana orange juice that you got in the Sunday newspaper? It costs Tropicana more than $1 when you redeem it at the store. These are all examples of just one marketing element—promotion. Marketing costs also include the costs of product research and development, the costs of distributing products to buyers, and the costs of all the employees working in marketing.

QUESTIONS

1. Select a publicly traded company and research how much was spent on marketing activities in the most recent year of available data. What percentage of sales does marketing expenditures represent for the company? Have these expenditures increased or decreased over the past five years? Write a brief report of your findings.

2. Search the Internet for salary information regarding jobs in marketing from a website such as **www .marketingsalaries.com** or a similar website. What is the national average for five different jobs in marketing? How do the averages compare in different areas of the country? Write a brief report on your findings.

VIDEO CASE

ZAPPOS

These days, online retailers are a dime a dozen, and many don't make a lasting impact. Yet in only a short time, Zappos has become a billion dollar e-tailer and an important part of the Amazon.com empire. How did Zappos hit the dot-com jackpot? By providing its customers with some of the best service available anywhere. Zappos showers its customers with such perks as free shipping both ways, surprise upgrades to overnight service, a 365-day return policy, and a call centre that is always open. Customers are also delighted by employees who are empowered to spontaneously hand out rewards based on unique needs.

With such attention to customer service, it's no surprise that Zappos has an almost cult-like following of repeat customers. However, remaining committed to the philosophy that the customer is always right can be challenging. This video highlights some of the dilemmas that can arise from a highly customer-centric strategy. Zappos also demonstrates the ultimate rewards they receive from keeping that commitment.

After viewing the video featuring Zappos, answer the following questions:

QUESTIONS

1. How would you describe Zappos' market offering?

2. What is Zappos' value proposition? How does it relate to its market offering?

3. How does Zappos build long-term customer relationships?

CONVERSE: SHAPING THE CUSTOMER EXPERIENCE

They dominated the basketball courts—both amateur and professional—for more than 40 years. The first US Olympic basketball team wore them, and Dr. J made them famous in the NBA. Punk rocker Joey Ramone made them standard issue for cult musicians; indeed, Kurt Cobain even donned a pair when he committed suicide. Today, a broad range of consumers, from the nerdiest of high school students to A-list celebrities, claim them as their own. What are they? Converse All Stars— more particularly, the famous Chuck Taylor All Stars known throughout the world as Cons, Connies, Convics, Verses, Chuckers, Chuckies, Chucks, and a host of other nicknames.

The cool quotient of the iconic Converse brand is unquestionable. However, you might wonder just how the brand has maintained its status decade after decade. The answer is this: by doing nothing. That may seem like an oversimplification, but the folks who run the Converse brand understand that to provide a meaningful customer experience, sometimes they just need to stand back and leave customers alone.

THE RISE AND FALL OF A LEGEND

Converse has been around a long time, perhaps longer than you realize. Founded in 1908 in Massachusetts, Converse introduced the canvas high-top All Star in 1917. In 1923, it renamed the shoe the Chuck Taylor, after a semiprofessional basketball player from Akron, Ohio. When his basketball career ended, Charles "Chuck" Taylor became an aggressive member of the Converse sales force. He drove throughout the Midwest, stopping at playgrounds to hawk the high tops to players. Some consider Taylor to be the original Phil Knight, Nike's CEO, who also started out by selling his shoes at track meets from the back of his van. From the 1930s to the 1960s, Chuck Taylor All Stars were *the* shoes to wear, even though they only came in basic black or white until 1969. At that time, 70 to 80 percent of all basketball players wore Converse.

There's no question that Converse invented basketball shoes. You might even say that Converse's pioneering efforts paved the way for the success of athletic shoes of all kinds. And the popularity of All Stars on the court played an instrumental role in making athletic shoes everyday footwear. But as the sneaker market began to explode in the 1970s and 1980s, shoes became more specialized, more high tech, and more expensive. As Nike, Adidas, and Reebok took over the market, Converse experienced a financial roller coaster ride. The company ultimately declared bankruptcy in 2001 as its market share bottomed out at 2 percent of the athletic shoe market, a small fraction of its prior position.

Yet even as Converse fell from market dominance, something interesting happened in the marketplace. Emerging artists, designers, and musicians began wearing Chucks because of their affordability, simplicity, and classic look. Young people caught on and adopted them as an expression of individuality. In fact, Converse's shrinking market share and ad budget made its shoes a favorite of the anti-establishment, anti-corporate crowd who were tired of trendy fashions. These people would take a cheap pair of comfy Converse All Stars and thrash them, scribble on them, and customize them as a canvas for personal expression. Perhaps the most intriguing aspect of consumers adopting Converse as a counterculture icon is that Converse itself never promoted the brand as anything but basketball shoes.

Despite its emergence as a niche counterculture brand, Converse continued to struggle. In 2003, however, Nike came to the rescue by acquiring Converse and making it part of the Nike corporate family. Many analysts speculated that this acquisition by a big-brand corporation would ruin Converse's cult caché as a "nonbrand." However, although Nike buoyed Converse with an infusion of cash and access to its product-development labs, it left Converse management pretty much alone to implement its own strategy. It kept an arms-length distance between Converse and the Nike swoosh. In fact, to this day, few consumers know that Nike owns Converse.

In the years since Nike acquired Converse, sales have improved; however, the company's market share has gone up very little. Although Converse has added different styles of shoes during the past decade (think Dwayne Wade), its primary focus has been on the original Chuck Taylor All Stars. However, Converse has branched out from that original design. For example, the Converse One Star is a low-priced line available at

Target. The company has developed thousands of higher-priced versions of All Stars created by fashion designers that are sold through upscale retailers such as Saks and Bloomingdales. And its Rock Collaborations line has featured designs created by rock legends Pink Floyd, Ozzy Osbourne, and The Who.

While some analysts worry that all these variations might detract from the authenticity of the original All Stars, so far that doesn't seem to be the case. Even the most hard-core music fans turn giddy when they see a pair of All Star high tops designed by their rock idol. These days, anti-establishment rock fans beg Converse to feature a shoe by their favorite artist.

In certain respects, the Converse brand seems to be more popular than ever. In fact, despite low market share, Converse is the most popular sneaker brand on Facebook, with more than 19 million fans—almost four times as many as market leader Nike. Converse brings in 20 000 Likes a day, versus just a few thousand for Nike. All this popularity comes from a brand that grabs less than 3 percent of the total athletic shoe market.

THE CUSTOMER IS IN CHARGE

How did Converse become the biggest little sneaker brand on Facebook? Its approach was simple: leave the brand in the hands of the customers. In fact, when Geoff Cottrill, Converse's chief marketing officer, discovered that the brand had achieved number one status on Facebook and was asked what the brand should do about it, he replied, "Nothing." By that, Cottrill explained, he meant that the brand should do nothing that would mess up Converse's valuable customer–brand relationship.

Even before Converse rose to Facebook dominance, the company had already embraced the social media. Today, Converse spends 90 percent of its marketing dollars on emerging digital media rather than traditional media. This allocation of promotional spending reflects a philosophy that customers, not companies, control brands. Although a company can influence the way its customers think, those customers ultimately decide what the brand means and how they interact with it.

As the various social media outlets emerged, Cottrill developed what he calls a "good party guest" approach to managing customer relationships. "Our philosophy in social media has been to bring our voice to the medium, which includes acting like a good party guest—we bring something to the table and we listen more than we talk." This philosophy rests on the notion of "letting go." Converse sees its role as one of making great products that its customers want to wear. Beyond that, it *participates* in consumer discussions rather than dictating them.

This is a dramatic shift from the old methods of one-way promotional brand communication. In this manner, Converse shows that it respects and trusts its customers. In turn, it fosters an emotional bond between the customer and the brand. When purchase time comes around, the strong relationship pays off. "I believe [the] brand benefits via strong advocacy—having millions of advocates can be a powerful thing," Cottrill says.

To be sure, Converse is strategic about its "stand-back" approach. The brand sponsors planned communications such as posts about products, content, and questions of the day. But it also remains flexible and ready to talk about lots of topics as they arise—just like at a dinner party. For example, when the YouTube "Yosemitebear Mountain Giant Double Rainbow" video was exploding, that inspired the Converse "Design Your Own Shoe" contest.

One of the planned elements of Converse's promotional strategy was joining forces with the (RED) Global Fund, which raises money to fight AIDS, tuberculosis, and malaria. Through the (RED) initiative, Converse has developed more than 110 artist-, designer-, and musician-designed All Stars, including limited editions by The Edge, Lupe Fiasco, Terence Koh, and Vena Kava. Up to 100 percent of the profits from the (RED) All Stars go to the Global Fund. In the five years since Converse joined forces with (RED), it has sent $160 million to the fund—no small venture. Its next five-year goal is even bigger: to deliver the first generation of babies born without HIV in nearly three decades.

In another strategic move that earned Converse a spot on *Fast Company*'s Most Innovative Companies list, the company built a music studio in Brooklyn called Converse Rubber Tracks. Although Converse is not trying to get into the music business per se, this effort keeps its brand associations with music strong. Converse offers emerging artists free recording time in exchange for agreeing to do future promotions with the brand. Converse doesn't demand anything in the way of rights or royalties to the music. Rather, the logic is that by investing in lots of unknown bands, it will have a foot in the door with those that become hits.

Converse rides a fine line: How many limited editions and upscale designs can the brand produce without losing its image as a nonmarketing marketer? How popular can the brand become without losing the core customers who love it precisely because it isn't popular? In growing the brand, Converse has been very careful in all that it does to remember one very important thing: For a brand like Converse, where authenticity is the most important trait, the customer experience should be driven by the customer.

Sources: Edmund Lee, "Major Marketers Shift More Dollars toward Social Media," *Advertising Age*, April 6, 2011, http://adage.com/article/226838; Austin Carr, "Converse: I'm with the Brand," *Fast Company*, October 7, 2010, www.fastcompany.com/1693621; Geoff Cottrill, "Our Five-Year Plan: An AIDS-Free Generation in 2015," *Advertising Age*, December 1, 2010, http://adage.com/article/147384; Todd Wasserman, "How Converse Became the Biggest Little Sneaker Brand on Facebook," *Mashable.com*, May 4, 2011, http://mashable.com/2011/05/04/converse-facebook/.

QUESTIONS FOR DISCUSSION

1. What are some examples of the needs, wants, and demands that Converse customers demonstrate? Differentiate these three concepts.

2. What are Converse and customers exchanging in the purchase transaction? Describe in detail all the facets of Converse's product and its relationship with customers.

3. Which of the five marketing management concepts best applies to Converse?

4. What are the benefits and drawbacks of Converse's "stand-back" approach?

5. How can Converse continue to grow its brand while at the same time maintaining its authentic image?

MyMarketingLab

MyMarketingLab is an online homework and tutorial system that puts you in control of your own learning with study and practice tools directly correlated to this chapter's content.

Courtesy of Christie's Digital

AFTER STUDYING THIS CHAPTER, YOU SHOULD BE ABLE TO

1 explain company-wide strategic planning and its four steps

2 discuss how to design business portfolios and develop growth strategies

3 explain marketing's role in strategic planning and how marketing works with its partners to create and deliver customer value

4 describe the elements of a customer-driven marketing strategy and mix, and the forces that influence it

5 list the marketing management functions, including the elements of a marketing plan, and discuss the importance of measuring and managing return on marketing investment

Company and Marketing Strategy: Partnering to Build Customer Relationships

PREVIEWING THE CONCEPTS

In the first chapter, we explored the marketing process by which companies create value for customers to capture value from them in return. In this chapter, we dig deeper into steps two and three of the marketing process—designing customer-driven marketing strategies and constructing marketing programs. First, we look at the organization's overall strategic planning, which guides marketing strategy and planning. Next, we discuss how, guided by the strategic plan, marketers partner closely with others inside and outside the firm to create value for customers. We then examine marketing strategy and planning—how marketers choose target markets, position their market offerings, develop a marketing mix, and manage their marketing programs. Finally, we look at the important step of measuring and managing return on marketing investment.

First, let's look at an example of a Canadian company whose careful strategic planning has helped it capitalize on a revolutionary new market—the need for ultra high tech visual display systems used in business, government, entertainment, and even advertising.

ORGANIZING AND PLANNING FOR SUCCESS AT CANADA'S CHRISTIE DIGITAL SYSTEMS

Christie Digital Systems Canada is a global visual technology company and a leader in Canada's ICT (information and communications technology) industry. The company designs and manufactures a variety of display technologies and solutions for cinema, large audience environments, control rooms, business presentations, training facilities, 3-D and virtual reality, simulation, education, media, and government. Its flagship line has been its digital cinema solutions, and Christie is the only single source provider of cinema projectors in all of North America, and one of only a handful in the world. The firm's design and engineering facility and main manufacturing facility are located in Kitchener, Ontario.

Christie Digital Systems Canada was formed in 1999, when Christie—a California-based film projector manufacturer—merged with Electrohome Visual Displays, at the time Canada's largest consumer electronics manufacturer, based in Kitchener. Over the past decade the company has experienced rapid growth. However, success didn't come overnight for Christie. When the company took its present form in late 1999, the first year's revenue for the new organization was about $100 million, and the Kitchener facility employed only 200 people. Today, annual revenues top $800 million and the employees number more than 1400 worldwide, with 700 in Kitchener.

And it was more than just the corporate letterhead that changed after the acquisition. The company had to change its business strategy, and its marketing strategy. Christie Digital Systems Canada president Gerry Remers explains: "We went from being a company that was focused on its traditional dealer channels to a company whose product strategy was focused on the entertainment and film industries—a market that changes rapidly." This flexibility and commitment to innovation has led to an evolving mission for the company, which is to help its customers create and share the world's best visual experiences. Remers says Christie has expanded beyond the entertainment industry to encompass the ". . . unlimited opportunity in the area of visual communication, so we are going to continue to develop new products and new solutions to meet the needs of the market. The fact of the matter is we're going to see pixels everywhere."

The products that Christie designs, manufactures, and markets are not sold to consumers, though most consumers are probably familiar with the results. For example, Christie's projection or image-mapping projectors and software are used by scores of amusement parks, public festivals, and advertising agencies to deliver compelling visual content to every manner of outdoor and indoor surface. And Christie's technologies are used by the post-production facilities of filmmakers such as James Cameron to produce high-resolution and immersive 3-D movie-going experiences. Christie recently signed a five-year agreement with James Cameron's Lightstorm Entertainment to exchange research, testing, development, and technical support on the industry's most exciting new technology—high frame rate (HFR) movies that end eye-strain and nausea often associated with 3-D film viewing. Cameron said he selected Christie for this "journey of discovery" because the company is fully committed to his vision and shares his dedication to continually push the boundary of digital cinema. The full potential of 3-D and high frame rate technology to fully immerse audiences in the world of the movie before them is the holy grail of cinematography. Peter Jackson's Park Road Post Production group also uses Christie technology, and Christie projectors were chosen for the world premiere of the first-ever HFR 3-D feature-length movie, *The Hobbit: An Unexpected Journey*.

Last summer, Christie's projection mapping technology turned Ottawa's Parliament Hill into a "virtual storybook," with the production of the sound and light show, "Mosaika—Canada through the Eyes of Its People" (see photo). Accompanied by lights, a 5.1 surround sound system, and audio track produced by Groupe Phaneauf, nine Christie Digital projectors painted a video canvas onto the six-story-high Parliament Building Centre Block, including the iconic Peace Tower in the middle. And those are just a few examples of where people might encounter Christie's technology. The company has installed more than 100 000 projection solutions worldwide and is recognized as one of the most innovative visual technology companies in the world, boasting 12 major patents, two Academy Awards, and countless industry awards.

In terms of top-level corporate organization, Christie Digital Systems Canada is a subsidiary of Christie Digital Systems, which in turn is a wholly owned subsidiary of Ushio Inc. of Japan. Its sister subsidiary is Christie Digital Systems USA, and both Christie Canada and Christie USA have their own presidents, reporting to the CEO and president of Christie Digital Systems, Inc. Christie has four major strategic business units (or SBUs): entertainment solutions, business products, visual environments, and managed services. Within these business units there are groups tasked with developing solutions for the following segmented markets: entertainment (both cinema and staging venues), visualization, business products, control room solutions, digital signage, managed (professional) services, medical imaging, and simulation solutions. Christie also has three subsidiary companies: Christie Medical (Memphis, Tennessee), Vista Systems (Phoenix, Arizona), and Nationwide (equipment leasing).

Christie's vice-president of global and corporate marketing, Kathryn Cress, is responsible for strategic planning and for reaching Christie's strategic marketing objectives: worldwide brand recognition and market leadership. She oversees brand equity management to ensure the delivery of tightly integrated global marketing strategies and communications. She is also responsible for outbound marketing programs, including the promotion of product launches, public relations, trade shows, events, partner marketing, advertising, web marketing, and messaging platforms. Under her supervision, Christie's marketing function is organized into six main departments: experiential marketing, digital marketing, marketing programs, communications and branding, publicity and promotions, and media and public relations.

Outside the organization, Christie's key suppliers and distributors compose part of its value delivery network—the chain of partner organizations that supply the raw materials to the manufacturing plant and the partner organizations that help to move the finished products into the hands of end-user customers. The company has a mission statement for working with supplier partners: "Our mission is to drive world class value from our supply chain to meet Christie's business goals through proactive supplier and Christie stakeholder engagement, timely responsiveness, and the relentless pursuit of continuous improvement."

As for distribution, Christie sells its products through both a direct sales force and a multichannel system including distributors who sign a contract committing them to purchase a minimum dollar amount of product, which they then resell to dealer/integrators; VIP partners, who are dealer/integrators that purchase more than six-figures annually, then sell to end-user customers. There are also rental and staging companies who purchase Christie products to run their productions, but who don't necessarily resell those products. And you might recognize the names of some of Christie's largest customers: Starbucks, Cineplex Entertainment, the London Stock Exchange, Boeing, Paramount, Cinépolis, IBM, University of Waterloo, Harrods, Industrial Light & Magic, Loews, the Montreal Police Service, Shell, and Deutsche Telekom.

In keeping with the company's leading-edge technology philosophy, Christie is fully engaged with social media. After each trade show appearance, the company's marketing managers produce an internal report on the show's effect on social media. For example, they count the number of mentions on Twitter and YouTube before and after the show. They also track the postings of industry bloggers and discover new bloggers who write about projection technology. On Facebook, they track the number of views of content related to the show, for example, the press releases and photo albums. In summarizing the social media findings after one recent trade show, the marketing managers noted that, in the future, Christie should explore using bloggers as a way of telling stories about Christie's presence at future trade shows and to develop these stories into content marketing.

As the global need for increased security and mission-critical public and private services expands, Christie is pouring more research into delivering solutions for the most complex control room environments. What sets Christie apart from—and ahead of—its global competitors? A spirit of teamwork and welcome attitude toward change are the building blocks upon which Christie has become number one in its customers' estimation, by delivering quality customer service, reliable products, and innovative solutions.[1]

LIKE CHRISTIE, outstanding marketing organizations employ strongly customer-driven marketing strategies and programs that create customer value and relationships. These marketing strategies and programs, however, are guided by broader company-wide strategic plans, which must also be customer focused. Thus, to understand the role of marketing, we must first understand the organization's overall strategic planning process.

Company-Wide Strategic Planning: Defining Marketing's Role LO1

Each company must find the game plan for long-run survival and growth that makes the most sense given its specific situation, opportunities, objectives, and resources. This is the focus of **strategic planning**—the process of developing and maintaining a strategic fit between the organization's goals and capabilities and its changing marketing opportunities.

Strategic planning sets the stage for the rest of the planning in the firm. Companies usually prepare annual plans, long-range plans, and strategic plans. The annual and long-range plans deal with the company's current businesses and how to keep them going. In contrast, the strategic plan involves adapting the firm to take advantage of opportunities in its constantly changing environment.

At the corporate level, the company starts the strategic planning process by defining its overall purpose and mission (see Figure 2.1). This mission is then turned into detailed supporting objectives that guide the whole company. Next, senior managers at the corporate level decide what portfolio of businesses and products is best for the company and how much support to give each one. In turn, each business and product develops detailed marketing and other departmental plans that support the company-wide plan. Thus, marketing planning occurs at the business-unit, product, and market levels. It supports company strategic planning with more detailed plans for specific marketing opportunities.

Defining a Market-Oriented Mission

An organization exists to accomplish something, and this purpose should be clearly stated. Forging a sound mission begins with the following questions: What is our business? Who is the customer? What do consumers value? What *should* our business be? These simple-sounding questions are among the most difficult the company will ever have to answer. Successful companies continuously raise these questions and answer them carefully and completely.

Many organizations develop formal mission statements that answer these questions. A **mission statement** is a statement of the organization's purpose—what it wants to accomplish in the larger environment. A clear mission statement acts as an "invisible hand" that guides people in the organization.

Strategic planning

The process of developing and maintaining a strategic fit between the organization's goals and capabilities and its changing marketing opportunities.

Mission statement

A statement of the organization's purpose—what it wants to accomplish in the larger environment.

FIGURE 2.1 Steps in strategic planning

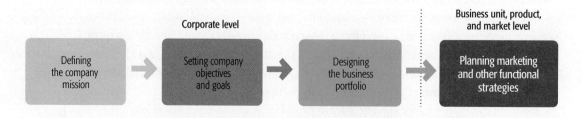

Some companies define their missions myopically in product or technology terms ("We make and sell furniture" or "We are a chemical-processing firm"). But mission statements should be *market oriented* and defined in terms of satisfying basic customer needs. Products and technologies eventually become outdated, but basic market needs may last forever. Indigo Books & Music's mission isn't simply to sell books and music. Its mission is "to provide our customers with the most inspiring retail and digital environments in the world for books and life-enriching products and experiences." Likewise, Under Armour's mission isn't just to make performance sports apparel, it's "to make all athletes better through passion, design, and the relentless pursuit of innovation." Table 2.1 provides several other examples of product-oriented versus market-oriented business definitions.[2]

Exhibit 2.1 Indigo Books & Music's mission is "to provide our customers with the most inspiring retail and digital environments in the world for books and life-enriching products and experiences."

© Helen Sessions / Alamy

Mission statements should be meaningful and specific yet motivating. They should emphasize the company's strengths in the marketplace. Too often, mission statements are written for public relations purposes and lack specific, workable guidelines. Says marketing consultant Jack Welch:[3]

> Few leaders actually get the point of forging a mission with real grit and meaning. [Mission statements] have largely devolved into fat-headed jargon. Almost no one can figure out what they mean. [So companies] sort of ignore them or gussy up a vague package deal along the lines of: "our mission is to be the best fill-in-the-blank company in our industry." [Instead, Welch advises, CEOs should] make a choice about how your company will win. Don't mince words! Remember Nike's old mission, "Crush Reebok"? That's directionally correct. And Google's mission statement isn't something namby-pamby like "To be the

TABLE 2.1 Market-Oriented Business Definitions

Company	Product-Oriented Definition	Market-Oriented Definition
Disney	We run theme parks.	We create fantasies—a place where dreams come true and America still works the way it's supposed to.
Google	We operate an online search engine.	We help you organize the world's information and make it universally accessible and useful.
Home Depot	We sell tools and home repair and improvement items.	We empower consumers to achieve the homes of their dreams.
Revlon	We make cosmetics.	We sell lifestyle and self-expression; success and status; memories, hopes, and dreams.
Ritz-Carlton Hotels & Resorts	We rent rooms.	We create the Ritz-Carlton experience—one that enlivens the senses, instills well-being, and fulfills even the unexpressed wishes and needs of our guests.

world's best search engine." It's "To organize the world's information and make it universally accessible and useful." That's simultaneously inspirational, achievable, and completely graspable.*

Finally, a company's mission should not be stated as making more sales or profits—profits are only a reward for creating value for customers. Instead, the mission should focus on customers and the customer experience the company seeks to create. Thus, McDonald's mission isn't "to be the world's best and most profitable quick-service restaurant," it's "to be our customers' favorite place and way to eat and drink." If McDonald's accomplishes this customer-focused mission, profits will follow.

Setting Company Objectives and Goals

The company needs to turn its mission into detailed supporting objectives for each level of management. Each manager should have objectives and be responsible for reaching them. For example, most consumers recognize the name Heinz for its ketchup—the

company, H.J. Heinz, sells more than 650 billion bottles of ketchup each year. But Heinz owns a breadth of other food products under a variety of brands, marketed in different countries around the world. For example, Heinz's most popular Canadian brands are Heinz Ketchup, Heinz 57, and Alpha-Getti. In New Zealand, Heinz markets food products such as condensed tomato soup under the brand Watties; and Plasmon, a Heinz-owned brand, is the leading brand of infant/nutrition products in Italy. Globally, Heinz ties this diverse product portfolio together under this mission: "As the trusted leader in nutrition and wellness, Heinz—the original Pure Food Company—is dedicated to the sustainable health of people, the planet, and our company."**

This broad mission leads to a hierarchy of objectives, including business objectives and marketing objectives. Heinz's overall objective is to build profitable customer relationships by developing foods "superior in quality, taste, nutrition, and convenience" that embrace its nutrition and wellness mission. It does this by investing heavily in research. However, research is expensive and must be funded through improved profit, so improving profits becomes another major objective for Heinz. Profits can be improved by increasing sales or reducing costs. Sales can be increased by improving the company's share of domestic and international markets. These goals then become the company's current marketing objectives.

Marketing strategies and programs must be developed to support these marketing objectives. To increase its market share, Heinz might broaden its product lines, increase product availability and promotion in existing

NO ONE GROWS KETCHUP LIKE HEINZ.

That's because every red, ripe tomato in every bottle is grown only from Heinz seeds. It's what helps us deliver the uniquely thick, rich flavor that America loves.

HEINZ. GROWN, NOT MADE.™

Learn more at www.heinzketchup.com.

Exhibit 2.2 Company objectives: Heinz's overall objective is to build profitable customer relationships by developing foods "superior in quality, taste, nutrition, and convenience" that embrace its nutrition and wellness mission.

H.J. Heinz Company, used with permission

*Jack and Suzy Welch, "State Your Business; Too Many Mission Statements Are Loaded with Fatheaded Jargon. Play It Straight," *Business Week*, January 14, 2008, p. 80.
**(c) H. J. Heinz Company, Used with permission.

markets, and expand into new markets. For example, last year Heinz added breakfast products to its Weight Watchers Smart Ones brand. And it experienced double-digit growth in emerging global markets, which now contribute 23 percent of total sales.[4]

These are Heinz's broad marketing strategies. Each broad marketing strategy must then be defined in greater detail. For example, increasing the product's promotion may require more advertising and public relations efforts; if so, both requirements will need to be spelled out. In this way, the firm's mission is translated into a set of objectives for the current period.

Designing the Business Portfolio LO2

Guided by the company's mission statement and objectives, management now must plan its **business portfolio**—the collection of businesses and products that make up the company. The best business portfolio is the one that best fits the company's strengths and weaknesses to opportunities in the environment.

Business portfolio
The collection of businesses and products that make up the company.

Most large companies have complex portfolios of businesses and brands. Strategic and marketing planning for such business portfolios can be a daunting but critical task. Consider the size and scope of Rogers Communications Inc., for example. The Rogers corporation is a large and diversified communications and media company with many business portfolios: At the top level, the corporation is organized into four major groups: Wireless, Cable, Business Solutions, and Media, each of which operates many "smaller" businesses. Rogers Wireless operates Canada's largest wireless voice and data communications network, and also operates a chain of retail stores. Rogers Cable provides consumer cable television and high-speed Internet services; Rogers Business Solutions provides business telecom, data networking and IP solutions to small, medium and large enterprise, government and carrier customers; and Rogers Media is the division that handles all media assets including television stations, radio stations, and many websites, including The Shopping Network (which is both a website and a television station). Rogers Media also oversees Rogers Publishing Ltd., which publishes dozens of magazines in English and French, including *Chatelaine, Flare, Profit, Marketing, Canadian Grocer, Canadian Business, Today's Parent,* and *Sportsnet.*

Whether the company's business portfolio consists of only one or two operations, or dozens, the strategic planning process is the same: First, the company must analyze its *current* business portfolio and determine which businesses should receive more, less, or no investment. Second, it must shape the *future* portfolio by developing strategies for growth and downsizing.

Analyzing the Current Business Portfolio

The major activity in strategic planning is business **portfolio analysis**, whereby management evaluates the products and businesses that make up the company. The company will want to put strong resources into its more profitable businesses and phase down or drop its weaker ones.

Portfolio analysis
The process by which management evaluates the products and businesses that make up the company.

Management's first step is to identify the key businesses that make up the company, called *strategic business units* (SBUs). An SBU can be a company division, a product line within a division, or sometimes a single product or brand. The company next assesses the attractiveness of its various SBUs and decides how much support each deserves. When designing a business portfolio, it's a good idea to add and support products and businesses that fit closely with the firm's core philosophy and competencies.

The purpose of strategic planning is to find ways in which the company can best use its strengths to take advantage of attractive opportunities in the environment. So most standard portfolio analysis methods evaluate SBUs on two important dimensions—the attractiveness of the SBU's market or industry, and the strength of the SBU's position in that market or industry. The best-known portfolio-planning method was developed by the Boston Consulting Group, a leading management consulting firm.[5]

The Boston Consulting Group Approach Using the now-classic Boston Consulting Group (BCG) approach, a company classifies all its SBUs according to the **growth-share matrix**, as shown in Figure 2.2. On the vertical axis, *market growth rate* provides a measure of market attractiveness. On the horizontal axis, *relative market share* serves as a measure of company strength in the market. The growth-share matrix defines four types of SBUs:

> *Stars.* Stars are high-growth, high-share businesses or products. They often need heavy investments to finance their rapid growth. Eventually their growth will slow down, and they will turn into cash cows.

> *Cash Cows.* Cash cows are low-growth, high-share businesses or products. These established and successful SBUs need less investment to hold their market share. Thus, they produce a lot of cash that the company uses to pay its bills and support other SBUs that need investment.

> *Question Marks.* Question marks are low-share business units in high-growth markets. They require a lot of cash to hold their share, let alone increase it. Management has to think hard about which question marks it should try to build into stars and which should be phased out.

> *Dogs.* Dogs are low-growth, low-share businesses and products. They may generate enough cash to maintain themselves but do not promise to be large sources of cash.

The 10 circles in the growth-share matrix represent a company's 10 current SBUs. The company has two stars, two cash cows, three question marks, and three dogs. The areas of the circles are proportional to the SBU's dollar sales. This company is in fair shape, although not in good shape. It wants to invest in the more promising question marks to make them stars and to maintain the stars so that they will become cash cows

Growth-share matrix
A portfolio-planning method that evaluates a company's strategic business units (SBUs) in terms of its market growth rate and relative market share. SBUs are classified as stars, cash cows, question marks, or dogs.

FIGURE 2.2 The BCG growth-share matrix

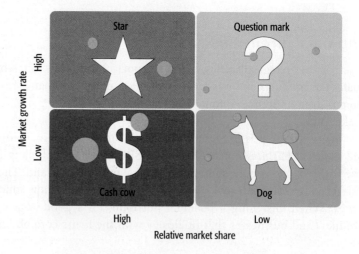

as their markets mature. Fortunately, it has two good-sized cash cows. Income from these cash cows will help finance the company's question marks, stars, and dogs. The company should take some decisive action concerning its dogs and its question marks.

Once it has classified its SBUs, the company must determine what role each will play in the future. One of four strategies can be pursued for each SBU. The company can invest more in the business unit to *build* its share. Or it can invest just enough to *hold* the SBU's share at the current level. It can *harvest* the SBU, milking its short-term cash flow regardless of the long-term effect. Finally, the company can *divest* the SBU by selling it or phasing it out and using the resources elsewhere.

As time passes, SBUs change their positions in the growth-share matrix. Many SBUs start out as question marks and move into the star category if they succeed. They later become cash cows as market growth falls, then finally die off or turn into dogs toward the end of their life cycles. The company needs to add new products and units continuously so that some of them will become stars and, eventually, cash cows that will help finance other SBUs.

Problems with Matrix Approaches The BCG and other formal methods revolutionized strategic planning. However, such centralized approaches have limitations: They can be difficult, time-consuming, and costly to implement. Management may find it difficult to define SBUs and measure market share and growth. In addition, these approaches focus on classifying *current* businesses but provide little advice for *future* planning.

Because of such problems, many companies have dropped formal matrix methods in favour of more customized approaches that better suit their specific situations. Moreover, unlike former strategic-planning efforts that rested mostly in the hands of senior managers at company headquarters, today's strategic planning has been decentralized. Increasingly, companies are placing responsibility for strategic planning in the hands of cross-functional teams of divisional managers who are close to their markets.

For example, consider The Walt Disney Company. Most people think of Disney as theme parks and wholesome family entertainment. But in the mid-1980s, Disney set up a powerful, centralized strategic planning group to guide the company's direction and growth. Over the next two decades, the strategic planning group turned The Walt Disney Company into a huge and diverse collection of media and entertainment businesses. The sprawling Walt Disney Company grew to include everything from theme resorts and film studios (Walt Disney Pictures, Touchstone Pictures, Hollywood Pictures, and others) to media networks (ABC plus Disney Channel, ESPN, A&E, History Channel, and a half-dozen others) to consumer products and a cruise line.

The newly transformed Disney proved hard to manage and performed unevenly. To improve performance, Disney disbanded the centralized strategic planning unit, decentralizing its

© Martin Beddall / Alamy

Exhibit 2.3 **Managing the business portfolio:** Most people think of Disney as theme parks and wholesome family entertainment but over the past two decades, it's become a sprawling collection of media and entertainment businesses that requires carefully planned strategic management.

functions to Disney division managers. As a result, Disney reclaimed its position at the head of the world's media conglomerates. Disney's sound strategic management of its broad mix of businesses has helped it fare better than its rival media companies through the great American recession of 2008–2010. At the end of the company's fiscal year in 2012, it reported the second year in a row of growth, with revenues topping $42.3 billion, and net income increasing 18 percent over the previous year.[6]

Developing Strategies for Growth and Downsizing Beyond evaluating current businesses, designing the business portfolio involves finding businesses and products the company should consider in the future. Companies need growth if they are to compete more effectively, satisfy their stakeholders, and attract top talent. "Growth is pure oxygen," states one executive. "It creates a vital, enthusiastic corporation where people see genuine opportunity." At the same time, a firm must be careful not to make growth itself an objective. The company's objective must be to manage "profitable growth."[7]

Marketing has the main responsibility for achieving profitable growth for the company. Marketing needs to identify, evaluate, and select market opportunities and lay down strategies for capturing them. One useful device for identifying growth opportunities is the **product/market expansion grid**, shown in Figure 2.3.[8] We apply it here to performance sports apparel maker Under Armour. Only 16 years ago, Under Armour introduced its innovative line of comfy, moisture-wicking shirts and shorts. Since then, it has grown rapidly in its performance-wear niche. Over the past five years, Under Armour's sales more than doubled and profits grew 25 percent. Looking forward, the company must look for new ways to keep it growing.[9]

First, Under Armour might consider whether the company can achieve deeper **market penetration**—making more sales without changing its original product. It can spur growth through marketing mix improvements—adjustments to its product design, advertising, pricing, and distribution efforts. For example, Under Armour offers an ever-increasing range of styles and colours in its original apparel lines. It recently boosted its promotion spending in an effort to drive home its "performance and authenticity" positioning. The company also added direct-to-consumer distribution channels, including its own retail stores, website, and toll-free call centre. Direct-to-consumer sales grew almost 60 percent last year and now account for more than 23 percent of total revenues.

Second, Under Armour might consider possibilities for **market development**—identifying and developing new markets for its current products. Under Armour could review new *demographic markets*. For instance, the company recently stepped up its emphasis on women consumers and predicts that its women's apparel business will someday be larger than its men's apparel business. The Under Armour "Athletes Run" advertising campaign includes a 30-second "women's only" spot. Under Armour could also pursue new *geographical markets*. For example, the brand has announced its intentions to expand internationally.

Product/market expansion grid
A portfolio-planning tool for identifying company growth opportunities through market penetration, market development, product development, or diversification.

Market penetration
A strategy for company growth by increasing sales of current products to current market segments without changing the product.

Market development
A strategy for company growth by identifying and developing new market segments for current company products.

FIGURE 2.3 The product/market expansion grid

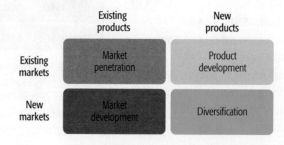

Third, Under Armour could consider **product development**—offering modified or new products to current markets. For example, after years of pitting cotton as the enemy of its sweat-absorbing synthetic materials, Under Armour recently introduced its own cotton-based line. Recognizing that many consumers simply like the feel of cotton and wear it in casual settings, the company wants a piece of the 80 percent of the active apparel market captured by cotton products. Under Armour claims that its own blend—called Charged Cotton—dries five times faster than normal cotton. "Mother nature made it," claims one ad. "We made it better."

Finally, Under Armour might consider **diversification**—starting up or buying businesses outside of its current products and markets. For example, it could move into non-performance leisurewear or begin making and marketing Under Armour fitness equipment. When diversifying, companies must be sure that any new markets they enter fit with their brands' positioning.

Companies must not only develop strategies for *growing* their business portfolios but also strategies for **downsizing** them. There are many reasons that a firm might want to abandon products or markets. The firm may have grown too fast or entered areas where it lacks experience. This can occur when a firm enters too many international markets without the proper research, or when a company introduces new products that do not offer superior customer value. The market environment might change, making some of the company's products or markets less profitable. For example, in difficult economic times, many firms prune out weaker, less-profitable products and markets to focus their more limited resources on the strongest ones. Finally, some products or business units simply age and die.

When a firm finds brands or businesses that are unprofitable or that no longer fit its overall strategy, it must carefully prune, harvest, or divest them. For example, in recent years, GM has pruned several underperforming brands from its portfolio, including the Oldsmobile, Pontiac, Saturn, and Hummer car brands and the Goodwrench parts line. Similarly, Ford recently shed its Mercury brand and sold off Jaguar, Land Rover, and Volvo. Weak businesses usually require a disproportionate amount of management attention. Managers should focus on promising growth opportunities, not fritter away energy trying to salvage fading ones.

Larry French/Getty Images for Under Armour

Exhibit 2.4 **Strategies for growth:** Under Armour is pursuing a market development strategy—identifying and developing new markets, such as women's athletic apparel.

Product development
A strategy for company growth by offering modified or new products to current market segments.

Diversification
A strategy for company growth through starting up or acquiring businesses outside the company's current products and markets.

Downsizing
Reducing the business portfolio by eliminating products or business units that are not profitable or that no longer fit the company's overall strategy.

Planning Marketing: Partnering to Build Customer Relationships LO3

The company's strategic plan establishes what kinds of businesses the company will operate and its objectives for each. Then, within each business unit, more detailed planning takes place. The major functional departments in each unit—marketing, finance, accounting, purchasing, operations, information systems, human resources, and others—must work together to accomplish strategic objectives.

Marketing plays a key role in the company's strategic planning in several ways. First, marketing provides a guiding *philosophy*—the marketing concept—that suggests that company strategy should revolve around building profitable relationships with important consumer groups. Second, marketing provides *inputs* to strategic planners by helping to identify attractive market opportunities and by assessing the firm's potential to take advantage of them. Finally, within individual business units, marketing designs *strategies* for reaching the unit's objectives. Once the unit's objectives are set, marketing's task is to help carry them out profitably.

Customer value is the key ingredient in the marketer's formula for success. However, as we noted in Chapter 1, marketers alone cannot produce superior value for customers. Although marketing plays a leading role, it can be only a partner in attracting, keeping, and growing customers. In addition to *customer relationship management*, marketers must also practise *partner relationship management*. They must work closely with partners in other company departments to form an effective internal *value chain* that serves the customer. Moreover, they must partner effectively with other companies in the marketing system to form a competitively superior external *value delivery network*. We now take a closer look at the concepts of a company value chain and a value delivery network.

Partnering with Other Company Departments

Value chain

The series of internal departments that carry out value-creating activities to design, produce, market, deliver, and support a firm's products.

Each company department can be thought of as a link in the company's internal **value chain**.[10] That is, each department carries out value-creating activities to design, produce, market, deliver, and support the firm's products. The firm's success depends not only on how well each department performs its work, but also on how well the various departments coordinate their activities.

For example, Walmart's goal is to create customer value and satisfaction by providing shoppers with the products they want at the lowest possible prices. Marketers at Walmart play an important role. They learn what customers need and stock the stores' shelves with the desired products at unbeatable low prices. They prepare advertising and merchandising programs and assist shoppers with customer service. Through these and other activities, Walmart's marketers help deliver value to customers.

However, the marketing department needs help from the company's other departments. Walmart's ability to offer the right products at low prices depends on the purchasing department's skill in developing the needed suppliers and buying from them at low cost. Walmart's information technology department must provide fast and accurate information about which products are selling in each store. And its operations people must provide effective, low-cost merchandise handling.

A company's value chain is only as strong as its weakest link. Success depends on how well each department performs its work of adding customer value and on how well the activities of various departments are coordinated. At Walmart, if purchasing can't obtain the lowest prices from suppliers, or if operations can't distribute merchandise at the lowest costs, then marketing can't deliver on its promise of unbeatable low prices.

Exhibit 2.5 **The value chain:** Walmart's ability to help you "Save money. Live Better." by offering the right products at lower prices depends on the contributions of people in all of the company's departments.

Gary Armstrong

Ideally then, a company's different functions should work in harmony to produce value for its customers. But, in practice, departmental relations are full of conflicts and misunderstandings. The marketing department strives to always understand the customer's point of view, but sometimes marketing's focus on customer satisfaction can cause other departments to do a poorer job *in their terms*. Marketing department actions can increase purchasing costs, disrupt production schedules, increase inventories, and create budget headaches. Thus, the other departments may resist the marketing department's efforts.

Yet marketers must find ways to get all departments to "think customer" and to develop a smoothly functioning value chain. Jack Welch, the highly regarded former GE CEO, emphasized that all GE people, regardless of their department, have an impact on customer satisfaction and retention. Another marketing expert puts it this way: "True market orientation does not mean becoming marketing-driven; it means that the entire company obsesses over creating value for the customer and views itself as a bundle of processes that profitably define, create, communicate, and deliver value to its target customers. . . . Everyone must do marketing regardless of function or department."[11] Thus, whether you're an accountant, operations manager, financial analyst, IT specialist, or human resources manager, you need to understand marketing and your role in creating customer value.

Partnering with Others in the Marketing System

In its quest to create customer value, the firm needs to look beyond its own internal value chain and into the value chains of its suppliers, distributors, and, ultimately, its customers. Consider McDonald's. People do not swarm to McDonald's because they love the chain's hamburgers—they flock to the McDonald's *system*, for everything it comprises and represents: a familiar restaurant; breakfast sandwiches; late night snacks; fun products and services for kids; a drive-through; and a consistent level of service and value for the money. Throughout the world, McDonald's finely tuned value delivery system delivers a high standard of QSCV—quality, service, cleanliness, and value. McDonald's is effective only to the extent that it successfully partners with its franchisees, suppliers, and others to jointly create and consistently reinforce this positioning.

More companies today are partnering with the other members of the supply chain—suppliers, distributors, and, ultimately, customers—to improve the performance of the customer **value delivery network**. For example, cosmetics maker L'Oréal knows the importance of building close relationships with its extensive network of suppliers, who supply everything from polymers and fats to spray cans and packaging to production equipment and office supplies.

Value delivery network
The network made up of the company, suppliers, distributors, and, ultimately, customers who partner with each other to improve the performance of the entire system.

> L'Oréal is the world's largest cosmetics manufacturer, with 25 brands ranging from Maybelline and Kiehl's to Lancôme and Redken. The company's supplier network is crucial to its success. As a result, L'Oréal treats suppliers as respected partners. On the one hand, it expects a lot from suppliers in terms of design innovation, quality, and socially responsible actions. The company carefully screens new suppliers and regularly assesses the performance of current suppliers. On the other hand, L'Oréal works closely with suppliers to help them meet its exacting standards. Whereas some companies make unreasonable demands of their suppliers and "squeeze" them for short-term gains, L'Oréal builds long-term supplier relationships based on mutual benefit and growth. According to the company's supplier website, it treats suppliers with "fundamental respect for their business, their culture, their growth, and the individuals who work there. Each relationship is based on . . . shared efforts aimed at promoting growth and mutual profits that make it possible for suppliers to invest, innovate, and compete." As a result, more than 75 percent of L'Oréal's supplier-partners

© imagebroker / Alamy

Exhibit 2.6 **The value delivery system:** L'Oréal builds long-term supplier relationships based on mutual benefit and growth. It "wants to make L'Oréal a top performer and one of the world's most respected companies. Being respected also means being respected by our suppliers."

Marketing strategy

The marketing logic by which the company hopes to create customer value and achieve profitable customer relationships.

have been working with the company for 10 years or more, and the majority of them for several decades. Says the company's head of purchasing, "The CEO wants to make L'Oréal a top performer and one of the world's most respected companies. Being respected also means being respected by our suppliers."[12]

Increasingly in today's marketplace, competition no longer takes place between individual competitors. Rather, it takes place between the entire value delivery networks created by these competitors. Thus, carmaker Toyota's performance against Ford depends on the quality of Toyota's overall value delivery network versus Ford's. Even if Toyota makes the best cars, it might lose in the marketplace if Ford's dealer network provides more customer-satisfying sales and service.

Marketing Strategy and the Marketing Mix LO4

The strategic plan defines the company's overall mission and objectives. Marketing's role and activities are shown in Figure 2.4, which summarizes the major activities involved in managing a customer-driven marketing strategy and the marketing mix.

Customers are at the centre of every organization's business, and the organization's goal is to create value for those customers, and to build profitable relationships with them. Next comes **marketing strategy**—the marketing logic by which the company

FIGURE 2.4 Managing marketing strategies and the marketing mix

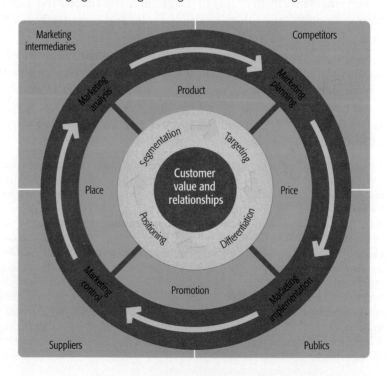

hopes to create this customer value and achieve these profitable relationships. The company decides which customers it will serve (segmentation and targeting) and how (differentiation and positioning). It identifies the total market, then divides it into smaller segments, selects the most promising segments, and focuses on serving and satisfying the customers in these segments.

Guided by marketing strategy, the company designs an integrated *marketing mix* made up of factors under its control—product, price, place, and promotion (the four *P*s). To find the best marketing strategy and mix, the company engages in marketing analysis, planning, implementation, and control. Through these activities, the company watches and adapts to the actors and forces in the marketing environment. We will now look briefly at each activity. Then, in later chapters, we will discuss each one in more depth.

Customer-Driven Marketing Strategy

As we emphasized throughout Chapter 1, to succeed in today's competitive marketplace, companies need to be customer centred. They must win customers from competitors, and then keep and grow them by delivering greater value. But before it can satisfy customers, a company must first understand their needs and wants. Effective marketing begins with careful customer analysis.

Companies know that they cannot profitably serve all customers in all markets—at least, not in the same way. There are too many different kinds of customers—both individual consumers, and business customers—with too many different kinds of needs. And most companies are in a position to serve some segments better than others. Thus, each company must divide up the total market, choose the best segments, and design strategies for profitably serving chosen segments. This process involves *market segmentation*, *market targeting*, *differentiation*, and *positioning*.

Market Segmentation The market consists of many types of customers, products, and needs. The marketer has to determine which segments offer the best opportunities. Consumers can be grouped and served in various ways based on geographic, demographic, psychographic, and behavioural factors. The process of dividing a market into distinct groups of buyers who have different needs, characteristics, or behaviours, and who might require separate products or marketing programs is called **market segmentation**.

Every market has segments, but not all ways of segmenting a market are equally useful. For example, Tylenol would gain little by distinguishing between low-income and high-income pain reliever users if both respond the same way to marketing efforts. A **market segment** consists of customers who have similar needs and requirements, and who therefore respond in a similar way to a given set of marketing efforts. In the car market, for example, consumers who want the biggest, most comfortable car regardless of price make up one market segment, while those who care mainly about price make up another segment. Plus, there are many other market segments for automobiles: corporations that purchase company cars; taxi companies; car rental companies; not to mention the different consumer segments such as families with small children, college and university students, sports car enthusiasts, and retirees. And that's just for cars—what about the different market segments for trucks? It would be impossible to make one car (or truck) model that would be favoured by customers in all these segments. That's why marketers must focus their efforts on understanding the needs of the people and organizations that make up the various market segments—and focus on meeting the needs of those market segments the company chooses to serve.

Market Targeting After a company has defined market segments, it can enter one or many of these segments. **Market targeting** involves evaluating each market segment's

Market segmentation
Dividing a market into distinct groups of buyers who have different needs, characteristics, or behaviours, and who might require separate products or marketing programs.

Market segment
A group of customers who respond in a similar way to a given set of marketing efforts.

Market targeting
The process of evaluating each market segment's attractiveness and selecting one or more segments to enter.

attractiveness and selecting one or more segments to enter. A company should target segments in which it can profitably generate the greatest customer value and sustain it over time.

A company with limited resources might decide to serve only one or a few special segments or "market niches." Such "nichers" specialize in serving customer segments that major competitors overlook or ignore. For example, Ferrari sells only 1500 of its very high-performance cars in the United States each year, but at very high prices—from an eye-opening $229 500 for its Ferrari F430 F1 Spider convertible to an astonishing more than $2 million for its FXX super sports car, which can be driven only on race tracks. Most nichers aren't quite so exotic. WhiteWave, maker of Silk Soymilk, has found its niche as North America's largest soymilk producer. And although Logitech is only a fraction the size of giant Microsoft, through skilful niching, it dominates the PC mouse market, with Microsoft as its runner-up (see Marketing@Work 2.1).

Alternatively, a company might choose to serve several related segments—perhaps those with different kinds of customers but with the same basic wants. Abercrombie & Fitch, for example, targets college students, teens, and kids with the same upscale, casual clothes and accessories in three different outlets: the original Abercrombie & Fitch, Hollister, and Abercrombie. Or a large company might decide to offer a complete range of products to serve all market segments.

Most companies enter a new market by serving a single segment, and if this proves successful, they add more segments. For example, Nike started with innovative running shoes for serious runners. Large companies eventually seek full market coverage. Nike now makes and sells a broad range of sports products for just about anyone and everyone, with the goal of "helping athletes at every level of ability reach their potential."[14] It has different products designed to meet the special needs of each segment it serves.

Market Differentiation and Positioning After a company has decided which market segments to enter, it must decide how it will differentiate its market offering for each targeted segment and what positions it wants to occupy in those segments. A product's *position* is the place the product occupies relative to competitors' products in consumers' minds. Marketers must develop a positioning strategy that makes it clear to the market what differentiates their brand from the competition.

Positioning

Arranging for a product to occupy a clear, distinctive, and desirable place relative to competing products in the minds of target consumers.

Positioning is arranging for a product to occupy a clear, distinctive, and desirable place relative to competing products in the minds of target consumers. This topic will be discussed in more detail in Chapters 7 and 8.

Marketers develop positioning strategies for their brands and products for the purpose of distinguishing them from competing brands. A positioning strategy is designed to make the consumer "think" a certain way about a brand, and, when done well, to create an emotional bond between the consumer and the brand. For example, most Canadians, when they think of Scotiabank, also think of hockey, because Scotiabank sponsors Hockey Night in Canada and many other hockey events. When they think of BMO, they think of investments; and when they think of RBC, they think of Arbie, the character with the bowler hat who is featured in most of the bank's marketing communications materials.

In positioning a product or brand, the company first identifies possible customer value differences that provide competitive advantages upon which to build the position. In other words, the company must identify what it is about their product that offers greater value, and that would motivate a customer to choose it over the competition's offering. Of course, if the company *promises* greater value, it must then *deliver* that greater value. Thus, effective positioning begins with **differentiation**—actually *differentiating* the company's market offering so that it gives consumers more value. Once the company

Differentiation

Actually differentiating the market offering to create superior customer value.

MARKETING@WORK 2.1

Nicher Logitech: The Little Mouse that Roars

Among the big tech companies, market leader Microsoft is the king of the jungle. When giant Microsoft looms, even large competitors quake. But when it comes to dominating specific market niches, overall size isn't always the most important thing. For example, in its own corner of the high-tech jungle, Logitech International is the little mouse that roars. In its niches, small but mighty Logitech is the undisputed market leader.

Logitech focuses on what it calls "personal peripherals"—interface devices for PC navigation, Internet communications, home-entertainment systems, and gaming and wireless devices. Logitech's rapidly expanding product portfolio now includes everything from cordless mice and keyboards, gaming controllers, and remote controls to webcams, PC speakers, headsets, notebook stands, and cooling pads. But it all started with computer mice.

Logitech makes every variation of mouse imaginable—including, most recently, a waterproof version. Over the years, it has flooded the world with more than 1 billion computer mice of all

varieties, mice for left- and right-handed people, wireless mice, travel mice, mini mice, 3-D mice, mice shaped like real mice for children, and even an "air mouse" that uses motion sensors to let you navigate your computer from a distance.

In the PC mouse market, Logitech competes head-on with Microsoft. At first glance it looks like an unfair contest. Microsoft's more than US$60 billion in sales is 25 times bigger than Logitech's US$2.4 billion. But when it comes to mice and other peripherals, Logitech has a depth of focus and knowledge that no other company in the world—including Microsoft—can match. Whereas mice and other interface devices are pretty much a sideline for software maker Microsoft—almost a distraction—they are the main attraction for Logitech. As a result, each new Logitech device is a true work of both art and science. Logitech's mice, for example, receive raves from designers, expert reviewers, and users alike.

A *Businessweek* analyst gives us a behind-the-scenes look at Logitech's

deep design and development prowess:

One engineer, given the moniker "Teflon Tim" by amused colleagues, spent three months scouring the Far East to find just the right nonstick coatings and sound-deadening foam. Another spent hours taking apart wind-up toys. Others poured over the contours of luxury BMW motorcycles, searching for designs to crib. They were members of a most unusual team that spent thousands of hours during the past two years on a single goal: to build a better mouse. The result: Logitech's revolutionary MX Revolution, the next-generation mouse that hit consumer electronics shelves about two years ago. It represented the company's most ambitious attempt yet to refashion the lowly computer mouse into a kind of control center for a host of PC applications. The sheer scope of the secret mission—which crammed 420 components, including a tiny motor, into a palm-sized device that usually holds about 20—brought together nearly three dozen engineers, designers, and marketers from around the globe.

Part of Logitech's product-development strategy is defensive. Once content to design mice and other peripherals for PC makers to slap their own names on, Logitech over the past half-decade has increasingly focused on selling its branded add-on equipment directly to consumers. Nearly 90 percent of Logitech's annual sales now come from retail. That forces Logitech to deliver regular improvements and new devices to entice new shoppers and purchases.

"We think of mice as pretty simple," says one industry analyst, "but there's a pretty aggressive technology battle going on to prove what the mouse can do." One of Logitech's latest feats of cutting-edge wizardry is its MX Air, which promises to change the very definition of the computer mouse as we know it. More like an airborne remote control than a traditional mouse, you

Exhibit 2.7 **Market targeting:** Logitech targets smaller market segments, sometimes referred to as "niches," with its high tech peripheral devices.

Andrew H. Walker/Staff/Getty Images Entertainment/Getty Images

can surf the web, play games, and control your home theatre PC from up to 9 metres away. There's also a cool-factor at play. Wielding the MX Air is like holding a work of art.

And at Logitech, it's not just about mice anymore. Logitech now applies its cool-factor to create sleek, stylish, and functional devices that not only enhance your PC experience, but also help you get the most out of everything from Internet navigation to all of the new gadgets in today's digital home. For example, Logitech's family of Harmony advanced universal remote controls helps even technology challenged novices tame the

complexities of their home-entertainment systems.

Logitech's business strategy is to always be aware of the ever-changing technology landscape, and to manufacture peripherals ahead of trends. Bluetooth-enabled "keyboard folios" for the iPad recently started appearing in stores. One of the new products is called the FabricSkin and, you guessed it, the keys feel like you're typing on fabric, yet the material is water resistant, so spills just wipe right off. Says one product reviewer and blogger, "If there's one accessory manufacturer that seems to be doing everything correctly at this point in time,

it's Logitech. The company apparently realizes that not only is the future pointing away from PCs and toward more portable devices like the iPad, but it's also creating many new accessories specifically for Apple products."

Sources: Steven Sande, "Three Great New iPad Keyboard Folios from Logitech," May 9, 2013, published on TUAW.com (The Unofficial Apple Weblog); Lisa Johnston and John Laposky, "Logitech Intros Accessories, Ships Billion Mouse," *TWICE*, December 15, 2008, p. 84; Cliff Edwards, "Here Comes Mighty Mouse," *Businessweek*, September 4, 2006, p. 76; Cliff Edwards, "The Mouse that Soars," *Businessweek*, August 20, 2007, p. 22; "Logitech International S.A.," *Hoover's Company Records*, March 1, 2009, p. 42459; "Haig Simonian, "Logitech Warns of Gloom Ahead," FT.com, January 21, 2009.

has chosen a desired position, it must take strong steps to deliver and communicate that position to target consumers. The company's entire marketing program should support the chosen positioning strategy.

Usually a company's differentiation and positioning strategy is a decision that is made once, then re-enforced through all its marketing and communications activities for many years. However, sometimes a brand must be re-positioned, and doing so requires just as much careful strategic planning as the original positioning required. Take Kentucky Fried Chicken, for example—or, rather, KFC, as it prefers to be known today. The name was changed in the early 1990s when the company began a carefully planned repositioning of its famous brand—an effort to change the way consumers thought about it—less emphasis on "fried" foods, more emphasis on healthier options. Though the Original Recipe fried chicken in a bucket is still available, today's KFC customers can choose grilled chicken instead of fried, and can choose from a variety of sandwiches, wraps, and chicken-related snacks. This repositioning changed the perception of KFC from "greasy fried chicken" to "healthy chicken choices."

Developing an Integrated Marketing Mix

Marketing mix
The set of controllable, tactical marketing tools—product, price, place, and promotion—that the firm blends to produce the response it wants in the target market.

After deciding on its overall marketing strategy, the company is ready to begin planning the details of the marketing mix, one of the major concepts in modern marketing. The **marketing mix** is the set of controllable, tactical marketing tools that the firm blends to produce the response it wants in the target market. The marketing mix consists of everything the firm can do to influence the demand for its product. The many possibilities can be collected into four groups of variables known as "the four Ps": *product, price, place,* and *promotion.* Figure 2.5 shows the marketing tools under each P.

- *Product* refers to the market offering—whether it is a tangible product, a service, or a combination of goods and services. For example, a Ford Escape is a product that comes in different colours and different model variations. It also has optional features that a consumer may choose to purchase. The car comes fully serviced and with a comprehensive warranty, which is also part of the product. And many Ford dealerships also include service centres to keep the Escape running smoothly.

- *Price* is the amount of money customers must pay to obtain the product. Ford calculates suggested retail prices that its dealers might *charge* for each Escape. But Ford

FIGURE 2.5 The four *P*s of the marketing mix

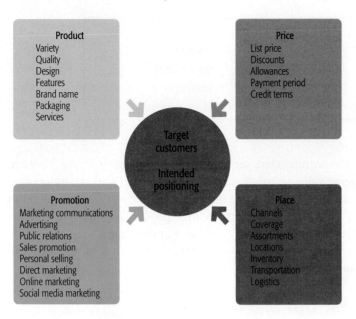

dealers rarely charge the full sticker price. Instead, they negotiate the price with each customer, offering discounts, trade-in allowances, and credit terms. These actions adjust prices for the current competitive and economic situations and bring them into line with the buyer's perception of the car's value.

- *Place* refers to the distribution of the product and the availability of the service. Ford partners with a large body of independently owned dealerships that sell the company's many different models. Ford selects its dealers carefully and supports them strongly. The dealers keep an inventory of Ford automobiles, demonstrate them to potential buyers, negotiate prices, close sales, and service the cars after the sale.

- *Promotion* means activities that communicate the merits of the product and persuade customers to buy it. Ford Motor Company spends more than US$2 billion each year on advertising to tell consumers about the company and its many products.[14] Dealership salespeople assist potential buyers and persuade them that Ford is the best car for them. Ford and its dealers offer special promotions—sales, cash rebates, low-financing rates—as added purchase incentives.

An effective marketing program blends all of the marketing mix elements into an integrated marketing program designed to achieve the company's marketing objectives by delivering value to customers. The marketing mix constitutes the company's tactical tool kit for establishing strong positioning in target markets.

The four *P*s is a conceptual model that organizes marketing activities at the top level, however, there are many other marketing functions that fall under these four headings. For example, packaging and labelling fall under Product decisions, and managing a website and a company's social media activities falls under Promotion.

The four *P*s concept takes the seller's or marketer's view of the market, and as we learned in Chapter 1, marketers must always be aware of the buyer's perspective—for, after all, the buyer *is* the market. Figure 2.6 transforms the four *P*s of the marketer into the four *C*s of the customer:

FIGURE 2.6 Transforming the Four *P*s into the Four *C*s

Four *P*s	Four *C*s
Product	Customer solution
Price	Customer cost
Place	Convenience
Promotion	Communication

Thus, whereas marketers see themselves as selling products, customers see themselves as buying value or solutions to their problems. And customers are interested in more than just the price; they are interested in the total costs of obtaining, using, and disposing of a product. Customers want the product and service to be as conveniently available as possible. Finally, they want two-way communication, especially in this age of social media. Marketers would do well to think through the four *C*s first and then build the four *P*s on that platform.

Managing the Marketing Effort `LO5`

In addition to being good at the *marketing* in marketing management, companies also need to pay attention to the *management*. Managing the marketing process requires the four marketing management functions shown in Figure 2.7—*analysis, planning, implementation*, and *control*. The company first develops company-wide strategic plans and then translates them into marketing and other plans for each division, product, and brand. Through implementation, the company turns the plans into actions. Control consists of measuring and evaluating the results of marketing activities and taking corrective action where needed. Finally, marketing analysis provides information and evaluations needed for all of the other marketing activities.

SWOT analysis
An overall evaluation of the company's strengths (S), weaknesses (W), opportunities (O), and threats (T).

Marketing Analysis

Managing the marketing function begins with a complete analysis of the company's situation. The marketer should conduct a **SWOT analysis**, by which it evaluates the

FIGURE 2.7 Managing marketing: analysis, planning, implementation, and control

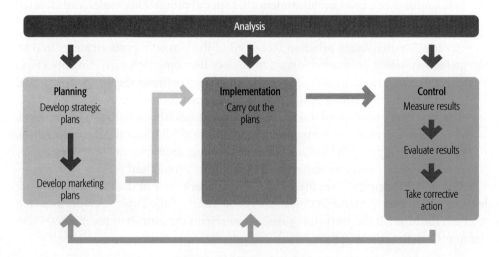

FIGURE 2.8 SWOT analysis: strengths (S), weaknesses (W), opportunities (O), and threats (T)

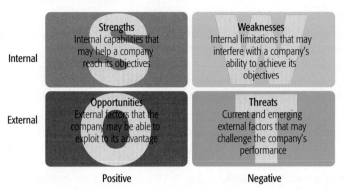

	Positive	Negative
Internal	**Strengths** Internal capabilities that may help a company reach its objectives	**Weaknesses** Internal limitations that may interfere with a company's ability to achieve its objectives
External	**Opportunities** External factors that the company may be able to exploit to its advantage	**Threats** Current and emerging external factors that may challenge the company's performance

Source: Roland T. Rust, Katherine N. Lemon, and Valerie A. Zeithaml, "Return on Marketing: Using Consumer Equity to Focus Marketing Strategy," *Journal of Marketing*, January 2004, p. 112.

company's overall strengths (S), weaknesses (W), opportunities (O), and threats (T) (see Figure 2.8). Strengths include internal capabilities, resources, and positive situational factors that may help the company to serve its customers and achieve its objectives. Weaknesses include internal limitations and negative situational factors that may interfere with the company's performance. Opportunities are favourable factors or trends in the external environment that the company may be able to exploit to its advantage. And threats are unfavourable external factors or trends that may present challenges to performance.

The company should analyze its markets and marketing environment to find attractive opportunities and identify environmental threats. It should analyze company strengths and weaknesses as well as current and possible marketing actions to determine which opportunities it can best pursue. The goal is to match the company's strengths to attractive opportunities in the environment, while eliminating or overcoming the weaknesses and minimizing the threats. Marketing analysis provides inputs to each of the other marketing management functions. We discuss marketing analysis more fully in Chapter 4.

Marketing Planning

Through strategic planning, the company decides what it wants to do with each business unit. Marketing planning involves deciding on marketing strategies that will help the company attain its overall strategic objectives. A detailed marketing plan is needed for each business, product, or brand. What does a marketing plan look like? Our discussion focuses on product or brand marketing plans.

Table 2.2 outlines the major sections of a typical product or brand marketing plan. (See Appendix 2 for a sample marketing plan.) The plan begins with an executive summary that quickly reviews major assessments, goals, and recommendations. The main section of the plan presents a detailed SWOT analysis of the current marketing situation as well as potential threats and opportunities. The plan next states major objectives for the brand and outlines the specifics of a marketing strategy for achieving them.

A *marketing strategy* consists of specific strategies for target markets, positioning, the marketing mix, and marketing expenditure levels. It outlines how the company intends to create value for target customers in order to capture value in return. In this section, the planner explains how each strategy responds to the threats, opportunities, and critical issues spelled out earlier in the plan. Additional sections of the marketing plan lay out an action program for implementing the marketing strategy, along with the details of a

TABLE 2.2 Contents of a Marketing Plan

Section	Purpose
Executive summary	Presents a brief summary of the main goals and recommendations of the plan for management review, helping top management to find the plan's major points quickly. A table of contents should follow the executive summary.
Current marketing situation	Describes the target market and company's position in it, including information about the market, product performance, competition, and distribution. This section includes: ■ A *market description* that defines the market and major segments, and then reviews customer needs and factors in the marketing environment that may affect customer purchasing. ■ A *product review* that shows sales, prices, and gross margins of the major products in the product line. ■ A review of *competition* that identifies major competitors and assesses their market positions and strategies for product quality, pricing, distribution, and promotion. ■ A review of *distribution* that evaluates recent sales trends and other developments in major distribution channels.
Threats and opportunities analysis	Assesses major threats and opportunities that the product might face, helping management to anticipate important positive or negative developments that might have an impact on the firm and its strategies.
Objectives and issues	States the marketing objectives that the company would like to attain during the plan's term and discusses key issues that will affect their attainment. For example, if the goal is to achieve 15 percent market share, this section looks at how this goal might be achieved.
Marketing strategy	Outlines the broad marketing logic by which the business unit hopes to create customer value and relationships and the specifics of target markets, positioning, and marketing expenditure levels. How will the company create value for customers in order to capture value from customers in return? This section also outlines specific strategies for each marketing mix element and explains how each responds to the threats, opportunities, and critical issues spelled out earlier in the plan.
Action programs	Spells out how marketing strategies will be turned into specific action programs that answer the following questions: *What* will be done? *When* will it be done? *Who* will do it? *How* much will it cost?
Budgets	Details a supporting marketing budget that is essentially a projected profit-and-loss statement. It shows expected revenues (forecasted number of units sold and the average net price) and expected costs of production, distribution, and marketing. The difference is the projected profit. Once approved by higher management, the budget becomes the basis for materials buying, production scheduling, personnel planning, and marketing operations.
Controls	Outlines the control that will be used to monitor progress and allow higher management to review implementation results and spot products that are not meeting their goals. It includes measures of return on marketing investment.

supporting *marketing budget*. The last section outlines the controls that will be used to monitor progress, measure return on marketing investment, and take corrective action.

Marketing Implementation

Marketing implementation
The process that turns marketing strategies and plans into marketing actions to accomplish strategic marketing objectives.

Planning good strategies is only a start toward successful marketing. A brilliant marketing strategy counts for little if the company fails to implement it properly. **Marketing implementation** is the process that turns marketing *plans* into marketing *actions* to accomplish strategic marketing objectives. Whereas marketing planning addresses the *what* and *why* of marketing activities, implementation addresses the *who*, *where*, *when*, and *how*.

Many managers think that "doing things right" (implementation) is as important as, or even more important than, "doing the right things" (strategy). The fact is that both are critical to success, and companies can gain competitive advantages through effective implementation. One firm can have essentially the same strategy as another, yet win in the marketplace through faster or better execution. Still, implementation is difficult—it is often easier to think up good marketing strategies than it is to carry them out.

In an increasingly connected world, people at all levels of the marketing system must work together to implement marketing strategies and plans. At Black & Decker, for example, marketing implementation for the company's power tools, outdoor equipment, and other products requires day-to-day decisions and actions by thousands of people both inside and outside the organization. Marketing managers make decisions about target segments, branding, packaging, pricing, promoting, and channels of distribution. They talk with engineering about product design, with manufacturing about production and inventory levels, and with finance about budgets and funding. They also work with outside organizations such as advertising agencies, sales agents, suppliers, and retailers.

Marketing Department Organization

The company must design a marketing organization that can carry out marketing strategies and plans. If the company is very small, one person might do all of the research, selling, advertising, customer service, and other marketing work. As the company expands, a marketing department emerges to plan and carry out marketing activities. In large companies, this department contains many specialists. They have product and market managers, sales managers and salespeople, market researchers, advertising experts, and many other specialists.

To head up such large marketing organizations, many companies have now created a *chief marketing officer* (or CMO) position. The CMO heads up the company's entire marketing operation and represents marketing on the company's top management team (see Marketing@Work 2.2).

Modern marketing departments can be arranged in several ways. The most common form of marketing organization is the *functional organization*. Under this organization, different marketing activities are headed by a functional specialist—a sales manager, advertising manager, marketing research manager, customer-service manager, or new-product manager. A company that sells across the country or internationally often uses a *geographic organization*. Its sales and marketing people are assigned to specific countries, regions, and districts. Geographic organization allows salespeople to settle into a territory, get to know their customers, and work with a minimum of travel time and cost. Companies with many very different products or brands often create a *product management organization*. Using this approach, a product manager develops and implements a complete strategy and marketing program for a specific product or brand.

For companies that sell one product line to many different types of markets and customers that have different needs and preferences, a *market* or *customer management organization* might be best. A market management organization is similar to the product management organization. Market managers are responsible for developing marketing strategies and plans for their specific markets or customers. This system's main advantage is that the company is organized around the needs of specific customer segments. Many companies develop special organizations to manage their relationships with large customers. For example, companies such as Procter & Gamble and Black & Decker have large teams, or even whole divisions, set up to serve large customers such as Walmart, Safeway, or Home Depot.

MARKETING@WORK   2.2

The Chief Marketing Officer

The CMO, or chief marketing officer, is the newest member of the team of senior executives at major corporations, sometimes referred to as the "C-suite." They include the chief executive officer (CEO) or chief operating officer (COO), the chief financial officer (CFO), the chief communications officer (CCO), and the chief technology officer (CTO). The chief marketing officer is responsible for all top-level marketing functions, including sales management, product development, distribution and channel management, pricing strategy, and market research; plus all marketing communications activities—advertising, sales promotions, direct marketing, online marketing; not to mention managing outside advertising and media agencies. They are even responsible for customer service in most organizations. It's no wonder that the director of McKinsey & Company says, "The job of CMO is not for the faint of heart."

The CMO position is perhaps the least secure job in top management, with the average CMO lasting just 28 months in his or her position. By comparison, the average CTO remains for 38 months, and CEOs and CFOs tend to stay in their jobs for at least four years.

Some say the reason for the high turnover among CMOs is the "Marketer's Dilemma," that is, if marketers focus on short terms results, and do the same thing that has always worked in the past, they risk getting passed by aggressive competition. But if they focus too much on the long term, and innovation, they miss today's results. Says one observer, "Try some big innovations that fail, and you lose your credibility. While effective marketing isn't rocket science, it's quite a balancing act to hit the sweet spot that delivers today's results while building the brand for the long term. And it's all played out in public." Another major challenge for CMOs is that in addition to leading everyone from the sales team through to the customer service department, CMOs invariably rely upon resources within the company that are beyond their direct control—departments such as information technology, corporate communications, legal, finance, and human resources. More than any other senior executive, the CMO must influence peers in order to achieve their own goals.

Duncan Fulton is not your typical CMO. With a background in public relations and an all-in commitment to social and digital media, he's in charge of all marketing activities at Canadian Tire Corporation. That means not only Canadian Tire stores, websites, gas stations, and service centres, but also Sport Chek, Sports Experts, Nevada Bob's Golf, Atmosphere, and Mark's stores too. Then there are the Canadian Tire private label brands, like MotoMaster, Mastercraft, and Debbie Travis. And a separate business portfolio, Canadian Tire Financial Services, which provides credit services and insurance to more than four million customers. Overall, Canadian Tire Corporation sells more

Marketing magazine

Exhibit 2.8 Not your typical CMO: Duncan Fulton, chief marketing officer at Canadian Tire Corporation, strives to rally all the company's marketing activities and personnel around the idea of inspiring consumers through sports.

products in more stores than any other Canadian retailer. That's a lot of marketing for one person to oversee.

But Fulton is up for the challenge. That's because his background is primarily in PR, consumer research, and digital—disciplines historically undervalued in the CMO role. Fulton started in communications for then-New Brunswick Premier Frank McKenna, and was appointed press secretary for Prime Minister Jean Chrétien at 25. That led to a seven-year run as GM and senior partner for PR firm Fleishman-Hillard. Recruited by Canadian Tire in 2009, Fulton immediately began making improvements: When I first got here in 2009, there were maybe two people doing PR and an annual budget of $100 000. In terms of earned media, PR was an afterthought, like "Okay, now let's get someone to put out a press release." Now we have 10 full-time people handling PR and corporate communications, which is unusual for most companies, and we've significantly increased the budget. So far this year, we have

spent about $1.7 million on earned media, but generated almost four billion media impressions and $68 million in equivalent advertising value for Canadian Tire."

The Canadian Tire CMO is an out-of-the-box thinker and creative marketing strategist. He's the brains behind some very successful and innovative marketing programs over the last few years, including Canadian Tire's Christmas in July event, for which the company rented a three-floor penthouse at the SoHo Metropolitan in downtown Toronto, decked it out with seven different Debbie Travis themes, and had staff make cookies and apple cider, so that by the time media walked in it even smelled like Christmas. The event resulted in major media coverage from 48 media organizations, including *CityLine*, *Canadian Living*, and the *Globe and Mail*. Fulton also reorganized the firm's sponsorships into a shared-services group model, so that events, sponsorships, corporate donations, and community relations are served from one group across the enterprise.

If there's one thing a career in political PR taught Duncan Fulton, it's that the public constantly judges your brand. This lesson serves him well as CMO of Canadian Tire, and especially during the recent re-branding of Sport Chek and the launch of the flagship store on Yonge Street in Toronto (see Marketing@Work 11.1). He applied the lessons learned rallying people around causes and ideas to rallying consumers around Canadian Tire and its associated retailers. Says Fulton, "We see a general inability of sporting goods retailers to inspire their customers, but when you inspire someone, you're connecting at a more emotional level than by just completing a transaction with them."

Sources: Grant Surridge, "Marketers of the Year: Duncan Fulton retells Sport Chek's story," Strategy magazine online, December 7, 2012; Alicia Androich, "Decision journeys, ROI and big data: what keeps CMOs up at night," Marketing magazine online, January 26, 2012; Canadian Tire Annual Report 2012; Chris Daniels, "The meteoric rise of Duncan Fulton," Marketing magazine online, November 24, 2011; Mike Linton, "Why Do Chief Marketing Officers Have A Short Shelf Life?" Forbes magazine online, May 15, 2009.

Large companies that produce many different products flowing into many different geographic and customer markets usually employ some *combination* of the functional, geographic, product, and market organization forms.

Marketing organization has become an increasingly important issue in recent years. More and more, companies are shifting their brand management focus toward *customer management*—moving away from managing just product or brand profitability and toward managing customer profitability and customer equity. They think of themselves not as managing portfolios of brands but as managing portfolios of customers.

Marketing Control

Because many surprises occur during the implementation of marketing plans, marketers must practise constant **marketing control**—the process of measuring and evaluating the results of marketing strategies and plans and taking corrective action to ensure that objectives are attained. Marketing control involves four steps. Management first sets specific marketing goals. It then measures its performance in the marketplace and evaluates the causes of any differences between expected and actual performance. Finally, management takes corrective action to close the gaps between its goals and its performance. This may require changing the action programs or even changing the goals.

Operating control involves checking ongoing performance against the annual plan and taking corrective action when necessary. Its purpose is to ensure that the company achieves the sales, profits, and other goals set out in its annual plan. It also involves determining the profitability of different products, territories, markets, and channels. *Strategic control* involves looking at whether the company's basic strategies are well matched to its

Marketing control
The process of measuring and evaluating the results of marketing strategies and plans and taking corrective action to ensure that objectives are achieved.

opportunities. Marketing strategies and programs can quickly become outdated, and each company should periodically reassess its overall approach to the marketplace.

Measuring and Managing Return on Marketing Investment

Return on marketing investment (or marketing ROI)
The net return from a marketing investment divided by the costs of the marketing investment.

Marketing managers must ensure that their marketing dollars are being well spent. For every planned marketing activity, whether it is creating a new product, changing the packaging, opening a new store, or developing and running an advertising campaign—there must be clearly stated objectives and a method for measuring the success of the activity after it has been completed. Marketers are increasingly being called upon to justify their activities through **return on marketing investment**, or **marketing ROI**—the net return from a marketing investment divided by the costs of the marketing investment. It measures the profits generated by investments in marketing activities. In a recent survey of CMOs in American companies, 63 percent said "ROI will be the standard for performance by 2015."[15]

A company can assess return on marketing in terms of standard marketing performance measures, such as brand awareness, sales, or market share. Marketing performance measurements are called *metrics*, and are measured and calculated using software tools, a process that has become much easier since the advent of the Internet and online advertising. Online marketing and marketing ROI expert Rex Briggs gives this example:

> P&G,* when they launched their Olay brand, had switched to Internet advertising. When they did their first set of creative, they measured consumer response, and the first set of online ads failed to connect the image of beauty with the Olay brand. What they recognized was they were using a TV model, where they would tell the story and at the end (show the) logo. That didn't work on the Internet because they needed to have their brand persistently on the screen, connected with the image of beauty, so that if (consumers) were reading content and glanced over to the ad, they'd understand the connection between Olay and the image of beauty. Within a couple of weeks they came back with newly designed creative based upon that testing, and that ad worked dramatically better. When they went through their next measure . . . there was about a 14% increase in sales lift among those who were reached by the online advertising.[16]

Some of the most frequently used marketing metrics include: measurements of customer satisfaction, customer retention, market share, marketing spending, revenue, website traffic, and profits. The challenge facing today's marketers, however, is that not everything can be reduced to numbers, and many qualitative marketing results, like enhanced brand recognition, reputation, and customer loyalty are difficult to measure. Marketing executives are under increasing pressure to show a return on investment for their programs, but many say they lack the technological resources needed to measure these programs. When asked to identify the internal barriers to implementing marketing ROI programs, nearly half of marketing managers surveyed reported problems with data availability or integrity, and more than half said that lack of technology and infrastructure was a problem. They also reported that their organizations lacked the know-how to implement marketing metrics. At the same time, 63 percent of top level executives said leadership commitment is the most important driver of marketing ROI.[17]

With the rise of social media, most companies today have a Facebook presence for their brand, and are experimenting with Twitter, Instagram, and other forms of social and mobile marketing tools. There are two major challenges facing marketers, however. The first is how to use these tools in a way that achieves marketing goals. The second is,

*Interview with Rex Briggs, published on MarketingMag.ca, December 4, 2006

how to measure the effects of social media programs. One expert suggests that marketers should look at measuring social media through engagement, retention and awareness levels, rather than in monetary terms. The key is to clearly define business, marketing and consumer objectives; however, this is often harder than it seems. "Often marketers will say, "I want to be on Facebook. I want to be on Twitter." These aren't objectives as much as they are tactics—objectives need to be measurable and achievable. For example, a marketing objective would be to improve the usability of the homepage to ultimately increase [sales] conversion."[18]

There are many tools available to assist marketers with measuring and analyzing their marketing activities. Google Analytics, for example, is a free software tool that helps marketers and website owners to understand who is coming to their website, what they are doing there, and how they can use that information to optimize their online activities. It tracks details such as which pages on the website visitors "land" on, how much time they spend on each page, and which links they click on—and collects all that data as sets of numbers, or metrics. But numbers and metrics by themselves have no meaning; they only become useable marketing information through analysis—and that's where tools such as Google Analytics come in.

Increasingly, however, beyond standard performance measures, marketers are using customer-centred measures of marketing impact, such as customer acquisition, customer retention, customer lifetime value, and customer equity. These measures capture not just current marketing performance but also future performance resulting from stronger

Google and the Google logo are registered trademarks of Google Inc., used with permission.

Exhibit 2.9 Google Analytics is used by major marketers such as Dolby, Adobe, and many other *Fortune* 500 companies. It's also used by the White House and the FBI, to analyze the activity on their websites.

FIGURE 2.9 Return on marketing investment

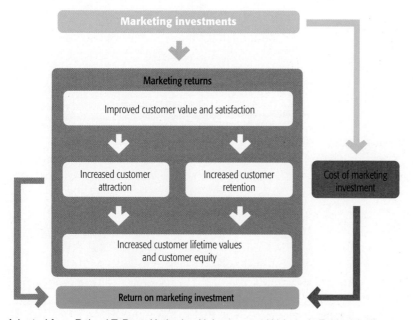

Source: Adapted from Roland T. Rust, Katherine N. Lemon, and Valerie A. Zeithaml, "Return on Marketing: Using Consumer Equity to Focus Marketing Strategy," *Journal of Marketing,* January 2004, p. 112.

customer relationships. Figure 2.9 views marketing expenditures as investments that produce returns in the form of more profitable customer relationships.[19] Marketing investments result in improved customer value and satisfaction, which in turn increase customer attraction and retention. This increases individual customer lifetime values and the firm's overall customer equity. Increased customer equity, in relation to the cost of the marketing investments, determines return on marketing investment.

Regardless of how it's defined or measured, marketing ROI is here to stay, and the modern marketing manager must learn how to use marketing metrics and analytics. In today's super-connected world, with seemingly limitless amounts of data available to marketers, the ability to measure marketing activities and analyze marketing information is the key to understanding customer behaviour, and being able to predict how target customers will react to the company's marketing offerings.

Building Momentum

The phrase was the theme of WestJet's 2012 annual report, but "building momentum" has been an unwritten part of WestJet's mission since its formation in 1996. There are few other words to explain the airline's success other than the inherent refusal to rest after conquering any single milestone. Going from zero to almost 40 per cent of Canada's domestic air travel market in a little more than 10 years is perhaps the single most impressive achievement.

The fabled beginnings of WestJet paint the picture of a typically ambitious start-up poised to change the world—with three planes, five cities, 220 employees, and blind faith. As of mid-2013, the little airline that could had 100 planes flying to 85 destinations supported by 9500 employees. As an encore, the airline launched its new regional subsidiary, called "Encore," in June 2013 to build a deeper network of destinations within Canada and serve many of Canada's smaller communities. That said, WestJet has methodically begun penetrating global markets by partnering with other airlines.

"Code-sharing and Interline agreements have allowed us to facilitate global travel for our guests, without the capital barriers of purchasing long-haul aircraft," claims WestJet vice-president of network planning, alliances, and corporate development, Chris Avery. "Each new partnership opens up more choices and flexibility for Canadian travellers who love the WestJet brand." The difference between code-sharing and interline agreements is worth noting, as it demonstrates WestJet's tactical approach to growth. The latter involves a seamless transferral of baggage for customers using WestJet and a partner airline, while the former allows WestJet passengers to book a ticket from a WestJet origin, such as Toronto, through to a non-WestJet destination, such as Seoul, South Korea. The goal is to create interline agreements and strategically evolve them into code-shares.

With these aggressive strategies to get WestJet guests to different points around the world, wouldn't it make sense to just buy bigger planes capable of trans-oceanic flights? While capital, cultural, regulatory, and competitive barriers would appear to be fairly daunting at this point, Bob Cummings, executive vice-president of sales, marketing and guest experience states with a sigh, "The intoxicating growth of China, India, and parts of South America certainly create grounds for discussion at some point."

QUESTIONS

1. WestJet's introduction of "Encore" represents an example of what form of growth strategy from the product/market expansion grid?
2. Go to www.westjet.com and create a list of airlines WestJet currently holds code-share or interline agreements with. How do these partnerships enhance WestJet's value network?
3. What specific threats would WestJet face if it were to begin flying to overseas markets in Europe, Asia, or South America?.

REVIEWING THE CONCEPTS

1. Explain company-wide strategic planning and its four steps.

Strategic planning sets the stage for the rest of the company's planning. Marketing contributes to strategic planning, and the overall plan defines marketing's role in the company.

Strategic planning involves developing a strategy for long-run survival and growth. It consists of four steps: (1) defining the company's mission, (2) setting objectives and goals, (3) designing a business portfolio, and (4) developing functional plans. The company's mission should be market oriented, realistic, specific, motivating, and consistent with the market environment. The mission is then transformed into detailed *supporting goals and objectives*, which in turn guide decisions about the *business portfolio*. Then each business and product unit must develop *detailed marketing plans* in line with the company-wide plan.

2. Discuss how to design business portfolios and develop growth strategies.

Guided by the company's mission statement and objectives, management plans its *business portfolio*, or the collection of businesses and products that make up the company. The firm wants to produce a business portfolio that best fits its strengths and weaknesses to opportunities in the environment. To do this, it must analyze and adjust its *current* business portfolio and develop growth and downsizing strategies for adjusting the *future* portfolio. The company might use a formal portfolio-planning method. But many companies are now designing more-customized portfolio-planning approaches that better suit their unique situations.

3. Explain marketing's role in strategic planning and how marketing works with its partners to create and deliver customer value.

Under the strategic plan, the major functional departments—marketing, finance, accounting, purchasing, operations, information systems, human resources, and others—must work together to accomplish strategic objectives. Marketing plays a key role in the company's strategic planning by providing a *marketing concept philosophy* and *inputs* regarding attractive market opportunities. Within individual business units, marketing designs *strategies* for reaching the unit's objectives and helps to carry them out profitably.

Marketers alone cannot produce superior value for customers. Marketers must practise *partner relationship management*, working closely with partners in other departments to form an effective *value chain* that serves the customer. And they must partner effectively with other companies in the marketing system to form a competitively superior *value delivery network*.

4. Describe the elements of a customer-driven marketing strategy and mix, and the forces that influence it.

Consumer value and relationships are at the centre of marketing strategy and programs. Through market segmentation, targeting, differentiation, and positioning, the company divides the total market into smaller segments, selects segments it can best serve, and decides how it wants to bring value to target consumers in the selected segments. It then designs an *integrated marketing* mix to produce the response it wants in the target market. The marketing mix consists of product, price, place, and promotion decisions (the four *P*s).

5. List the marketing management functions, including the elements of a marketing plan, and discuss the importance of measuring and managing return on marketing investment.

To find the best strategy and mix and put them into action, the company engages in marketing analysis, planning, implementation, and control. The main components of a *marketing plan* are the executive summary, current marketing situation, threats and opportunities, objectives and issues, marketing strategies, action programs, budgets, and controls. To plan good strategies is often easier than to carry them out. To be successful, companies must also be effective at *implementation*—turning marketing strategies into marketing actions.

Marketing departments can be organized in one or a combination of ways: *functional marketing organization, geographic organization, product management organization,* or *market management organization*. In this age of customer relationships, more and more companies are now changing their organizational focus from product or territory management to customer relationship management. Marketing organizations carry out *marketing control*, both operating control and strategic control.

Marketing managers must ensure that their marketing dollars are being well spent. In a tighter economy, today's marketers face growing pressures to show that they are adding value in line with their costs. In response, marketers are developing better measures of *return on marketing investment*. Increasingly, they are using customer-centred measures of marketing impact as a key input into their strategic decision making.

KEY TERMS

Business portfolio 49
Differentiation 58
Diversification 53
Downsizing 53
Growth-share matrix 50
Market development 52
Market penetration 52
Market segment 57
Market segmentation 57

Market targeting 57
Marketing control 67
Marketing implementation 64
Marketing mix 60
Marketing strategy 56
Mission statement 46
Portfolio analysis 49
Positioning 58
Product development 53

Product/market expansion grid 52
Return on marketing investment
  (or marketing ROI) 68
Strategic planning 46
SWOT analysis 62
Value chain 54
Value delivery network 55

TALK ABOUT MARKETING

1. Explain why it is important for all departments of an organization—marketing, accounting, finance, operations management, human resources, and so on—to "think customer." Why is it important that even people who are not in marketing understand it?

2. Imagine you are a team of marketing managers at a large consumer packaged-goods company, and you're planning the launch of a new line of shampoo. With which departments in your company will you need to work to plan the launch, and what role will each department play?

3. Discuss how TELUS might use the processes of market segmentation, market targeting, and market positioning. How is TELUS differentiated from its competitors?

4. In a small group, develop a SWOT analysis for a business in your community. From that analysis, recommend a marketing strategy and marketing mix for this business Go to **www.pg.com** to learn about the brands offered by P&G. Select one product category in which P&G offers multiple brands. What is P&G's positioning for each brand in that product category? Then, visit a store and record the prices of each brand, using a common basis such as price per millilitre. Write a brief report on what you learn. Are there meaningful positioning differences between the brands? Are any price differences you find justified?

THINK LIKE A MARKETING MANAGER

Apple markets several lines of personal electronic devices, including computers, smartphones, and tablets. Spend some time on Apple's website and learn more about its products, and then think like a marketing manager to answer the following questions.

QUESTIONS

1. Which of Apple's products are its stars, cash cows, question marks, and dogs?

2. Which of the four market growth strategies in the product/market expansion grid have you observed Apple using?

3. How does Apple employ the elements of the marketing mix—product, price, place (distribution), and promotion?

4. The iPhone was available in the United States in June 2007 but was not available in Canada until a year later. Similarly, Apple released the iPad in the United States in April 2010 but international consumers, who were only able to pre-order the product on May 10, were still faced with an "undetermined" launch date. What can you infer about Apple's international growth strategy?

MARKETING ETHICS

Ever felt like everything happens at once? Well, sometimes it does: The car breaks down, the kids are sick, the dog needs to go to the vet, and then, to top it off, the electric bill is past due again. Rather than having your kids suffer and letting the electric company cut off your lights, simply stop by and get a payday loan. Sounds easy, doesn't it? For many Canadians, payday loans have become a necessary alternative to traditional bank loans, and the trend is growing. Edmonton-based The Cash Store Financial Services Inc., with 415 stores across Canada, and Money Mart, with over 350 stores, announced record profits in 2008, with plans for future market expansion. The Canadian Payday Loan Association, which represents 20 payday loan companies, maintains that its members provide a valuable service to cash-strapped consumers, but consumer advocate groups disagree, arguing that these firms prey on those who can least afford their services—low-income families who do not qualify for low-interest bank loans. Provincial governments across the nation are now enacting legislation to protect consumers from excessive interest rates charged by many of these services.

QUESTIONS

1. What are the current and emerging external factors (i.e., opportunities and threats) contributing to the growth of payday loan companies in Canada?

2. Visit **www.apaydayloan.ca** and answer the following questions: What are they offering consumers? Do you see any problems with the service they provide? Explain. Click on the online loan application link and calculate the cost of borrowing $500 for one month. Do the cost of borrowing and the annualized interest rate surprise you? What are the implications for consumer debt in Canada? In your opinion, are payday loan companies offering a legitimate service to consumers or are they merely loan sharks in disguise?

MARKETING TECHNOLOGY

Mobile marketing is touted as the next "big thing," offering the promise of connecting with consumers on the most personal medium—their cellphones. Technological advances are letting marketers send not only text messages to cellphones but also video messages. In Japan, QR Codes (quick response codes) originally developed for manufacturing purposes are now placed on outdoor, print, and other media advertisements so that consumers can snap pictures of them and be taken directly to mobile websites. Although not yet widely practised, some marketers are now dabbling in mobile marketing. For example, Jaguar used a mobile campaign and sold over 1100 XFs in one month. Visa used mobile marketing in China to encourage consumers to pass on video commercials to their friends via mobile phones. Although there are still technical roadblocks stifling rapid expansion of this marketing method, some experts claim that marketers had better jump on this bandwagon or risk being left behind.

QUESTIONS

1. Visit the Mobile Marketing Association's website atmmaglobal.com and look for the case studies published there. Discuss one case study and describe the factors you think made that application of mobile marketing a success.

2. The rapid advance in mobile technology poses opportunities as well as threats for marketers. Discuss both the opportunities and threats for marketers.

MARKETING BY THE NUMBERS

Appendix 3, Marketing by the Numbers, discusses other marketing profitability metrics beyond the return on marketing investment (marketing ROI) measure described in this chapter. The text on the right is a profit-and-loss statement for a business. Review Appendix 3 and answer the questions below.

QUESTIONS

1. Calculate the net marketing contribution (NMC) for this company.

2. Calculate both marketing return on sales (or marketing ROS) and marketing return on investment (or marketing ROI) as described in Appendix 3. Is this company doing well?

Net Sales		$800 000 000
Cost of goods sold		(375 000 000)
Gross Margin		$425 000 000
Marketing Expenses		
Sales expenses	$70 000 000	
Promotion expenses	30 000 000	
		(100 000 000)
General and Administrative Expenses		
Marketing salaries and expenses	$10 000 000	
Indirect overhead	60 000 000	70 000 000
Net profit before income tax		$255 000 000

VIDEO CASE

LIVE NATION

Live Nation may not be a household name, but if you've been to a concert in the past few years, chances are you've purchased a Live Nation product. In fact, Live Nation has been the country's largest concert promoter for many years, promoting as many as 29 000 events annually. Through very savvy strategic planning, Live Nation is shaking up the structure of the music industry.

A recent $120 million deal with Madonna illustrates how this concert promoter is diving into other businesses as well. Under this deal, Live Nation will become Madonna's record label, concert promoter, ticket vendor, and merchandise agent. Similar deals have been reached with other performers such as Jay-Z and U2.

However, contracting with artists is only part of the picture. Live Nation is partnering with other corporations as well. A venture with Citigroup will expand its reach to potential customers through a leveraging of database technologies. Joining forces with ticket reseller powerhouses such as StubHub will give Live Nation a position in the thriving business of secondary ticket sales.

After viewing the video featuring Live Nation, answer the following questions about the role of strategic planning.

QUESTIONS

1. What is Live Nation's mission?

2. Based on the product/market expansion grid, provide support for the strategy that Live Nation is pursuing.

3. How does Live Nation's strategy provide better value for customers?

TRAP-EASE AMERICA: THE BIG CHEESE OF MOUSETRAPS

CONVENTIONAL WISDOM

One April morning, Martha House, president of Trap-Ease America, entered her office in Costa Mesa, California. She paused for a moment to contemplate the Ralph Waldo Emerson quote that she had framed and hung near her desk:

> If a man [can] . . . make a better mousetrap than his neighbor . . . the world will make a beaten path to his door.

Perhaps, she mused, Emerson knew something that she didn't. She *had* the better mousetrap—Trap-Ease—but the world didn't seem all that excited about it.

Martha had just returned from the National Hardware Show in Chicago. Standing in the trade show display booth for long hours and answering the same questions hundreds of times had been tiring. Yet, all the hard work had paid off. Each year, National Hardware Show officials held a contest to select the best new product introduced at that year's show. The Trap-Ease had won the contest this year, beating out over 300 new products.

Such notoriety was not new for the Trap-Ease mousetrap, however. *People* magazine had run a feature article on the trap, which had also been discussed on numerous talk shows. Trap-Ease was also the subject of numerous articles in various popular press and trade publications.

Despite all of this attention, however, the expected demand for the trap had not materialized. Martha hoped that this award might stimulate increased interest and sales.

BACKGROUND

A group of investors had formed Trap-Ease America in January after it had obtained worldwide rights to market the innovative mousetrap. In return for marketing rights, the group agreed to pay the inventor and patent holder, a retired rancher, a royalty fee for each trap sold. The group then hired Martha to serve as president and to develop and manage the Trap-Ease America organization.

Trap-Ease America contracted with a plastics-manufacturing firm to produce the traps. The mousetrap consisted of a square, plastic tube measuring about 6 inches long and 1-1/2 inches in diameter. The tube bent in the middle at a 30-degree angle, so that when the front part of the tube rested on a flat surface, the other end was elevated. The elevated end held a removable cap into which the user placed bait (cheese, dog food, or some other aromatic tidbit). The front end of the tube had a hinged door. When the trap was "open," this door rested on two narrow "stilts" attached to the two bottom corners of the door.

The simple trap worked very efficiently. A mouse, smelling the bait, entered the tube through the open end. As it walked up the angled bottom toward the bait, its weight made the elevated end of the trap drop downward. This action elevated the open end, allowing the hinged door to swing closed, trapping the mouse. Small teeth on the ends of the stilts caught in a groove on the bottom of the trap, locking the door closed. The user could then dispose of the mouse while it was still alive or leave it alone for a few hours to suffocate in the trap.

Martha believed the trap had many advantages for the consumer when compared with traditional spring-loaded traps or poisons. Consumers could use it safely and easily with no risk of catching their fingers while loading it. It posed no injury or poisoning threat to children or pets. Furthermore, with Trap-Ease, consumers avoided the unpleasant "mess" they often encountered with the violent spring-loaded traps. The Trap-Ease created no "clean-up" problem. Finally, the user could reuse the trap or simply throw it away.

Martha's early research suggested that women were the best target market for the Trap-Ease. Men, it seemed, were more willing to buy and use the traditional, spring-loaded trap. In contrast, the targeted women did not like the traditional trap. These women often stayed at home and took care of their children. Thus, they wanted a means of dealing with the mouse problem that avoided the unpleasantness and risks that the standard trap created in the home.

To reach this target market, Martha decided to distribute Trap-Ease through national grocery, hardware, and discount chains. She sold the trap directly to these large retailers, avoiding any wholesalers or other middlemen.

The traps sold in packages of two, with a suggested retail price of $5.99. Although this price made the Trap-Ease about five times more expensive than smaller, standard traps, consumers appeared to offer little initial price resistance. The manufacturing cost for the Trap-Ease, including freight and packaging costs, was about 59 cents per unit. The company paid an additional

19 cents per unit in royalty fees. Martha priced the traps to retailers at $2.38 per unit (two units to a package) and estimated that, after sales and volume discounts, Trap-Ease would produce net revenue from retailers of $1.50 per unit.

Martha budgeted approximately $145 000 for Trap-Ease promotion during the first year. She planned to use $100 000 of this amount for travel costs to visit trade shows and to make sales calls on retailers. The remaining $45 000 was earmarked for advertising. Since the mousetrap had generated so much publicity, Martha did not feel the need to do much advertising. Still, she had placed advertising in *Good Housekeeping* (after all, the trap had earned the *Good Housekeeping* Seal of Approval) and in other "home and shelter" magazines. Martha was the company's only salesperson, but she intended to hire more salespeople soon.

Martha had initially forecasted Trap-Ease's first-year sales at five million units. Through April, however, the company had only sold several hundred thousand units. Martha wondered if most new products got off to such a slow start, or if she was doing something wrong. She had detected some problems, although none seemed overly serious. For one, there had not been enough repeat buying. For another, she had noted that many of the retailers upon whom she called kept their sample mousetraps on their desks as conversation pieces—she wanted the traps to be used and demonstrated. Martha wondered if consumers were also buying the traps as novelties rather than as solutions to their mouse problems.

Martha knew that the investor group believed that Trap-Ease America had a "once-in-a-lifetime chance" with its innovative mousetrap, and she sensed the group's impatience with the company's progress so far. She had budgeted approximately $500 000 in administrative and fixed costs for the first year (not including marketing costs). To keep the investors happy, the company needed to sell enough traps to cover those costs and make a reasonable profit.

BACK TO THE DRAWING BOARD

In the first few months of the Trap-Ease launch, Martha learned that marketing a new product was not an easy task. Some customers were very demanding. For example, one national retailer placed a large order with instructions that Trap-Ease America was to deliver the order to the loading dock at one of the retailer's warehouses between 1:00 and 3:00 P.M. on a specified day. When the truck delivering the order arrived after 3:00 P.M., the retailer refused to accept the shipment. The retailer told Martha it would be a year before she got another chance.

As Martha sat down at her desk, she realized she needed to rethink her marketing strategy. Perhaps she had missed something or made some mistake that was causing sales to be so slow. Glancing at the quotation again, she thought that perhaps she should send the picky retailer and other customers a copy of Emerson's famous quote.

QUESTIONS FOR DISCUSSION

1. Martha and the Trap-Ease America investors believe they face a once-in-a-lifetime opportunity. What information do they need to evaluate this opportunity? How do you think the group would write its mission statement? How would *you* write it?

2. Has Martha identified the best target market for Trap-Ease? What other market segments might the firm target?

3. How has the company positioned the Trap-Ease for the chosen target market? Could it position the product in other ways?

4. How would you describe the current marketing mix for Trap-Ease? Do you see any problems with this mix?

5. Who is Trap-Ease America's competition?

6. How would you change Trap-Ease's marketing strategy? What kinds of control procedures would you establish for this strategy?

© Art Directors & TRIP / Alamy

1 define *sustainable marketing* and discuss its importance

2 identify the major social criticisms of marketing

3 define *consumer activism* and *environmentalism*, and explain how they affect marketing strategies

4 describe the principles of sustainable marketing

5 explain the role of ethics in marketing

Sustainable Marketing Social Responsibility and Ethics

PREVIEWING THE CONCEPTS

In this chapter, we'll examine the concepts of sustainable marketing, meeting the needs of consumers, businesses, and society—now and in the future—through socially and environmentally responsible marketing actions. we'll start by defining sustainable marketing and then look at some common criticisms of marketing as it impacts individual consumers and public actions that promote sustainable marketing. Finally, we'll see how companies themselves can benefit from proactively pursuing sustainable marketing practices that bring value not just to individual customers but also to society as a whole. You'll see that sustainable marketing actions are more than just the right thing to do; they're also good for business.

First, let's look at an example of sustainable marketing in action at Unilever, the world's third-largest consumer products company. For 12 years running, Unilever has been named sustainability leader in the food and beverage industry by the Dow Jones Sustainability Indexes. The company recently launched its Sustainable Living Plan, by which it intends to double its size by 2020 while at the same time reducing its impact on the planet and increasing the social benefits arising from its activities. That's an ambitious goal.

SUSTAINABILITY AT UNILEVER: CREATING A BETTER FUTURE EVERY DAY

When Paul Polman took over as CEO of Unilever in 2009, the home and personal care products company was a slumbering giant. Despite its stable of star-studded brands—including the likes of Dove, Axe, Noxema, Sunsilk, VO5, Hellmann's, Lipton, and Ben & Jerry's—Unilever had experienced a decade of stagnant sales and profits. The company needed renewed energy and purpose. "To drag the world back to sanity, we need to know why we are here," said Polman.

To answer the "why are we here" question and find a more energizing mission, Polman looked beyond the usual corporate goals of growing sales, profits, and shareholder value. Instead, he asserted, growth results from accomplishing a broader social and environmental mission. Unilever exists "for consumers, not shareholders," he said. "If we are in sync with consumer needs and the environment in which we operate, and take responsibility for our [societal impact], then the shareholder will also be rewarded."

As a result of such thinking, in 2010 Unilever launched its Sustainable Living Plan. Under this plan, the company set out to "create a better future every day for people around the world: the people who work for us, those we do business with, the billions of people who use our products, and future generations whose quality of life depends on the way we protect the environment today." According to Polman, Unilever's long-run *commercial* success depends on how well it manages the *social* and *environmental* impact of its actions.

The Sustainable Living Plan sets out three major social and environmental objectives to be accomplished by 2020: "(1) To help more than one billion people take action to improve their health and well-being; (2) to halve the environmental footprint of the making and use of our products; and (3) to source 100 percent of our agricultural raw materials sustainably."

Evaluating and working on societal and environmental impact is nothing new at Unilever. The company already had multiple programs in place to manage the impact of its products and operations. For example, over the past five years, the company's Nutrition Enhancement Program has reviewed Unilever's entire portfolio of foods—some 30 000 products—resulting in reductions in saturated and trans fat, sugar, and salt in thousands of items. And over the past decade, the company's factories have reduced CO_2 emissions by 44 percent, water use by 66 percent, and total waste disposal by 73 percent. However, the Sustainable Living Plan pulls together all of the work the company has been doing and sets ambitious new sustainability goals.

Unilever's sustainability efforts span the entire value chain, from how the company sources raw materials to how customers use and dispose of its products. "The world faces enormous environmental pressures," says the company. "Our aim is to make our activities more sustainable and also encourage our customers, suppliers, and others to do the same." On the "upstream supply side," more than two-thirds of Unilever's raw materials come from agriculture, so the company is helping suppliers develop sustainable farming practices that meet its own high expectations for environmental and social impact. Unilever assesses suppliers against two sets of standards. The first is the Unilever Supplier Code, which calls for socially responsible actions regarding human rights, labour practices, product safety, and care for the environment. The second is the Unilever Sustainable Agriculture Code, which details Unilever's expectations for sustainable agriculture practices, so that it and its suppliers "can commit to the sustainability journey together." Unilever also collaborates closely with its commercial and trade customers, such as Walmart and other large retailers, many of whom have their own ambitious goals in areas such as energy use, greenhouse gas emissions, recycling, and waste reduction.

But Unilever's Sustainable Living Plan goes far beyond simply creating more responsible supply and distribution chains. Unilever is also working with final consumers to improve the social and environmental impact of its products in use. More than 2 billion customers in 178 countries use a Unilever product on any given day. Therefore, small everyday customer actions can add up to a big difference. Unilever sums it up with this equation: "Unilever brands × small everyday events × billions of consumers = big difference."

For example, almost one-third of households worldwide use Unilever laundry products to do their washing—approximately 125 billion washes every year. Up to 70 percent of the total greenhouse gas footprint of Unilever's laundry products and 95 percent of the water footprint occur during consumer use. Therefore, under its Sustainable Living Plan, Unilever is both creating more eco-friendly laundry products and motivating consumers to improve their laundry habits.

For example, around the world, Unilever is encouraging consumers to wash clothes at lower temperatures and use the correct dosage of detergent. One Unilever product, Persil Small & Mighty laundry detergent, is a concentrated detergent that uses less packaging, making it cheaper and less polluting to transport. More importantly, it washes better at lower temperatures and uses less energy. Another Unilever product, Comfort One Rinse fabric conditioner, was created for hand-washing clothes in developing and emerging markets where water is often in short supply. The innovative product requires only one bucket of water for rinsing rather than three, saving customers time, effort, and 30 litres of water per wash. Such energy and water savings don't show up on Unilever's income statement, but they will be extremely important to the people and the planet. Similarly, small changes in product nutrition and customer eating habits can have a surprisingly big impact on human health. "In all," says the company, "we will inspire people to take small, everyday actions that can add up to a big difference for the world."

Will Unilever's Sustainable Living Plan produce results for the company? It is still too soon to tell, but so far, so good. Last year, Unilever's revenues grew 11 percent while profits grew 26 percent. The sustainability plan is not just the right thing to do for people and the environment, claims Polman, it's also right for Unilever. The quest for sustainability saves money by reducing energy use and minimizing waste. It fuels innovation, resulting in new products and new customer benefits. And it creates new market opportunities: More than half of Unilever's sales are from developing countries, the very places which face the greatest sustainability challenges.

In all, Polman predicts, the sustainability plan will help Unilever double in size by 2020, while also creating a better future for billions of people without increasing the environmental footprint. "We do not believe there is a conflict between sustainability and profitable growth," he concludes. "The daily act of making and selling consumer goods drives economic and social progress. There are billions of people around the world who deserve the better quality of life that everyday products like soap, shampoo, and tea can provide. Sustainable living is not a pipedream. It can be done, and there is very little downside."[1]*

RESPONSIBLE marketers such as Unilever discover what consumers want and respond with market offerings that create value for buyers in order to capture value in return. The *marketing concept* is a philosophy of customer value and mutual gain. Not all marketers follow the marketing concept, however. In fact, some companies use questionable marketing practices that serve their own rather than consumers' or society's interests. Responsible marketers must consider whether their actions are *sustainable* in the longer run.

Consider the sport-utility vehicles (SUVs). These large vehicles meet the immediate needs of many drivers in terms of capacity, power, and utility, however, they raise larger questions of consumer safety and environmental responsibility. For example, in accidents, SUVs are more likely to kill both their own occupants and the occupants of other vehicles. Moreover, SUVs are gas guzzlers. According to Sierra Club, a well known environmental activist group, switching from an average car to an SUV wastes more energy per year than if you left your refrigerator door open for 6 years, or left your bathroom light burning for 30 years![2]

This chapter examines *sustainable* marketing and the social and environmental effects of private marketing practices. First, we address this question: What is sustainable marketing and why is it important?

---

*Excerpts, quotes, and other information from T. L. Stanley, "Easy As Pie: How Russell Weiner Turned Sabotage Into Satisfaction," Adweek, September 13, 2010, p. 40; "Lessons from the Domino's Turnaround," Restaurant Hospitality, June 2010, p. 30; Rupal Parekh, "Marketer of the Year," Advertising Age, October 18, 2010, p. 19; Emily Bryson York, "Domino's Claims Victory with New Strategy: Pizza Wasn't Good, We Fixed It," Advertising Age, May 10, 2010, p. 4; Mark Brandau, "Domino's Do-Over,"—Nation's Restaurant News, March 8, 2010, p. 44; "Domino's Puts Customer Feedback on Times Square Billboard," Detroit News, July 26, 2011; and annual reports and other information from www.dominosbiz.com and www.pizzaturnaround.com, accessed December 2011.

Sustainable Marketing LO1

Sustainable marketing

Socially and environmentally responsible marketing that meets the present needs of consumers and businesses while also preserving or enhancing the ability of future generations to meet their needs.

Sustainable marketing calls for socially and environmentally responsible actions that meet the present needs of consumers and businesses while also preserving or enhancing the ability of future generations to meet their needs. Figure 3.1 compares the sustainable marketing concept with other marketing concepts we studied in Chapter 1 and 2.[3]

The *marketing concept* recognizes that organizations thrive from day to day by determining the current needs and wants of target group customers and fulfilling those needs and wants more effectively and efficiently than competitors do. It focuses on meeting the company's short-term sales, growth, and profit needs by giving customers what they want now. However, satisfying consumers' immediate needs and desires doesn't always serve the future best interests of either customers or the business.

Whereas the *societal marketing concept* identified in Figure 3.1 considers the future welfare of consumers and the *strategic planning concept* considers future company needs, the *sustainable marketing concept* considers both. Sustainable marketing calls for socially and environmentally responsible actions that meet both the immediate and future needs of customers and the company.

Consider McDonald's. The company's early decisions to market tasty but fat- and salt-laden fast foods created immediate satisfaction for customers and sales and profits for the company, but in the 1990s critics and activists began to blame fast food chains for contributing to the obesity problem, burdening the national health system, and causing unnecessary pollution and waste on a global scale. It was not a sustainable strategy, but in recent years, all that's changed.[4]

For the last decade McDonald's has undertaken many initiatives to change its corporate philosophy to one of sustainability, beginning by appointing a Senior Vice President, Global Corporate Social Responsibility, Sustainability and Philanthropy. The company is aware that it has a significant global "footprint"—with nearly 2 million employees and more than 5000 franchisees serving 69 million customers every day in 118 countries. McDonald's believes that because of their size, scope, and scale, they have the ability to make positive differences in the world—the very definition of sustainability. In 2007 the company created a corporate governance body called the Sustainable Supply Steering Committee (SSSC), responsible for guiding McDonald's toward their vision for sustainable supply by identifying global priorities and ensuring progress in ways that complement local priorities and efforts.

For example, McDonald's sustainable supply chain initiative means endeavouring to purchase from suppliers that follow practices that ensure the health and safety of their employees and the welfare and humane treatment of animals. In the sourcing of materials and production of packaging and other products, McDonald's works with companies that manufacture and distribute products in a way that minimizes impact on the environment. In addition, global suppliers of major products like beef and potatoes are also required to take on product-specific sustainability initiatives in their strategies.

In addition to the corporation's global initiatives, McDonald's Canada is actively engaged in national energy saving practices. For example, each year during Earth Hour, a global initiative

FIGURE 3.1 Sustainable Marketing

led by the World Wildlife Fund (WWF), McDonald's restaurants turn off their road signs and roof beams, and other lights, and in that one hour, across Canada, the company saves more than 10 000 kWh of electricity—approximately the amount required to run one Canadian household for a full year. And through energy-saving practices in the areas of ventilation, lighting, and heating, McDonald's restaurants in Canada have saved an estimated 11.7 million kWh and 770 000 cubic meters of natural gas since 2005, which equates to 4033 metric tons of carbon dioxide emissions—equal to taking approximately 739 cars off the road. In addition, two restaurants in Quebec have pioneered the use of a geothermal renewable energy system— a means of extracting heat from the earth—in the operation of quick-service restaurants.

Exhibit 3.1 **Sustainable marketing:** McDonald's sustainability strategy has created value for customers and positioned the company for a profitable future.

McDonald's Canada also engages its suppliers and encourages them to be more environmentally conscious. This led to the creation in 2007 of an annual Sustainability Award, which recognizes a supplier who has demonstrated a commitment to advancing environmental sustainability in the areas of energy conservation, solid waste mitigation and recycling, among others. McDonald's Canada also recently opened its first green restaurant in Beauport (Quebec), which is a candidate for LEED Certification. (The Leadership in Energy and Environmental Design (LEED) green building rating system encourages and accelerates global adoption of sustainable green building and development practices in Canada and the US.) As a result of its sustainability initiatives, McDonald's has been a member of the Dow Jones Sustainability Index since 2005, and was named one of the Greenest Companies in America by *Newsweek* magazine in 2010. Truly sustainable marketing requires a smooth-functioning marketing system in which consumers, companies, public policy-makers, and others work together to ensure socially and environmentally responsible marketing actions. Unfortunately, however, the marketing system doesn't always work smoothly. The following sections examine several sustainability questions: What are the most frequent social criticisms of marketing? What steps have private citizens taken to curb marketing ills? What steps have legislators and government agencies taken to promote sustainable marketing? What steps have enlightened companies taken to carry out socially responsible and ethical marketing that creates sustainable value for both individual customers and society as a whole?

Social Criticisms of Marketing L02

Marketing receives much criticism. Some of this criticism is justified; much is not. Social critics claim that certain marketing practices hurt individual consumers, society as a whole, and other business firms.

Marketing's Impact on Consumers

Consumers have many concerns about how well the marketing system serves their interests. Surveys usually show that consumers hold mixed or even slightly unfavourable attitudes toward marketing practices. Consumer advocates, government agencies, and other critics have accused marketing of harming consumers through high prices, deceptive practices, high-pressure selling, shoddy or unsafe products, planned obsolescence, and poor service to disadvantaged consumers. Such questionable marketing practices are not sustainable in terms of long-term consumer or business welfare.

High Prices Many critics charge that the marketing system causes prices to be higher than they would be under more "sensible" systems. Critics point to three factors—*high costs of distribution*, *high advertising and promotion costs*, and *excessive markups*.

HIGH COSTS OF DISTRIBUTION A long-standing charge is that channel intermediaries mark up prices beyond the value of their services. Critics charge that there are too many "middlemen," and that they are inefficient, or that they provide unnecessary or duplicate services. As a result, distribution costs too much, and consumers pay for these excessive costs in the form of higher prices.

As we'll learn in Chapter 11, marketing intermediaries provide a variety of services in the chain of distribution—the movement of products from their source of production to the hands of the final customer. The planning, organization, and ongoing management of these channels is an expensive proposition for any firm, and since all firms are concerned about their bottom line, any channel partners or intermediaries who were not adding value would quickly be cut from the process.

HIGH ADVERTISING AND PROMOTION COSTS Modern marketing is also accused of pushing up prices to finance heavy advertising and sales promotion. For example, a few dozen tablets of a heavily promoted brand of pain reliever sell for the same price as 100 tablets of less-promoted brands. Differentiated products—cosmetics, detergents, toiletries—include promotion and packaging costs that can amount to 40 percent or more of the manufacturer's price to the retailer. Critics charge that much of the packaging and promotion adds only psychological value to the product rather than functional value.

Marketers respond that although advertising is expensive, it also adds value by informing potential buyers of the availability and merits of a product. Brand name products may cost more, but branding gives buyers assurances of consistent quality. Moreover, consumers can usually buy functional versions of products at lower prices. However, they *want* and are willing to pay more for products that also provide psychological benefits—that make them feel wealthy, attractive, or special. Also, advertising and promotion are sometimes necessary, especially for marketers of products such as consumer electronics, cars, and personal care products—product categories in which there exist many brands and many competitors. Otherwise, the firm would not be able to compete.

Though it may seem logical that because advertising is expensive and therefore if firms did no advertising the price of their products would go down, this is in fact a fallacy. Without advertising, sales would decrease, therefore production would decrease. When fewer products are manufactured, the price to manufacture each product goes up—and prices would go up correspondingly. Recently in the UK, consumer activists called for more regulation in the advertising of children's toys, and argued that all toy advertising should be banned. But economics researcher and journalist Chris Snowdon argued that the prohibition of advertising would lead to monopolistic markets resulting in higher prices for consumers.[5]

Exhibit 3.2 **Criticisms of marketing:** A heavily promoted brand of Aspirin sells for much more than a virtually identical nonbranded or store-branded product. Critics charge that promotion adds only psychological value to the product rather than functional value.

© Mira / Alamy

EXCESSIVE MARKUPS Critics also charge that some companies mark up goods excessively. They point to the drug industry as an example of the worst offenders, where a pill costing five cents to make may cost the consumer $2 to buy. Marketers sometimes respond that consumers often don't understand the reasons for high markups. For example, pharmaceutical markups must cover the costs of purchasing, promoting, and distributing existing medicines plus the high research and development costs of *formulating and testing* new medicines—all of which is very expensive. The simple fact is, all companies are in business to offer something of value to the market, and producing that market offering involves much more than just the costs of the manufacturing process.

Most businesses try to deal fairly with their customers because they want to build relationships and repeat business—it's simply not in their own best interests to cheat or mislead those customers. There are, of course, exceptions to the rule, and when consumers perceive any abuse of marketing, whether it's false advertising, or unfair pricing, they should report those abuses to their local *Better Business Bureaus* or to the provincial Consumer Affairs office.

Deceptive Practices Marketers are sometimes accused of deceptive practices that lead consumers to believe they will get more value than they actually do. Deceptive practices fall into three groups: pricing, promotion, and packaging. *Deceptive pricing* includes practices such as falsely advertising "factory" or "wholesale" prices or a large price reduction from a phony high retail list price. *Deceptive promotion* includes practices such as misrepresenting the product's features or performance or luring the customers to the store for a bargain that is out of stock. *Deceptive packaging* includes exaggerating package contents through subtle design, using misleading labelling, or describing size in misleading terms.

In Canada, the Competition Bureau acts as a watchdog to prevent such practices. They are alerted to instances of deceptive marketing through consumer complaints, and they *do* take action. For example, they recently took Rogers Communications to court and charged the telecommunications giant with violating Canada's false advertising rules when they claimed their Chatr cellphone service had "fewer dropped calls" than the competition. The Bureau charged that Rogers produced "false and misleading" ads, and failed to back up its claims about dropped calls with "adequate and proper tests,"—and sought to impose a $10 million fine.[6] And just two years earlier, the federal watchdog forced Bell Canada to stop making what the Bureau had concluded were misleading representations about the prices offered for its services—and required them to pay a penalty of $10 million, the maximum amount allowed under the Competition Act.[7]

In addition to the long standing rules enforced by the Competition Bureau, new federal, provincial, and municipal guidelines and regulations are created as they become necessary. For example, as a result of claims of "greenwashing"—companies that claim to be environmentally friendly in some way, but who are not really doing what they claim to be doing—in 2008, the Competition Bureau in collaboration with the Canadian Standards Association issued guidelines to provide the business community with tools to ensure that green marketing claims are not misleading.[8]

Companies who greenwash should take note: consumers everywhere are paying attention and crying foul when they perceive they've been greenwashed. In a recent survey, four out of five residents of the UK said they suspect companies of trying to get away with false claims of green marketing. That country's watchdog organization, the Advertising Standards Authority (ASA) received

Exhibit 3.3 **Deceptive practices:** Despite plenty of regulation, some critics argue that deceptive claims are still the norm. Consider all of those "green marketing" claims.

93 complaints about 40 different ads in one month alone. Among the offenders were Lexus, who ran an ad with the headline "High Performance. Low Emissions. Zero Guilt," deemed to give the misleading impression that the car caused little or no harm to the environment. Likewise Volkswagen ran an ad that promised their car was "better for the planet,"—which was banned by the ASA because the claims were "too general."[9] And in today's always online and socially connected universe, offenders not only get caught, but information about their offences is quickly spread through social media.

The toughest problem is defining what is "deceptive." One noted marketing thinker, Theodore Levitt, once claimed that advertising puffery and alluring imagery are bound to occur—and that they may even be desirable: "There is hardly a company that would not go down in ruin if it refused to provide fluff, because nobody will buy pure functionality. . . . Worse, it denies people's honest needs and values. Without distortion, embellishment, and elaboration, life would be drab, dull, anguished, and at its existential worst."[10]

In today's world of marketing, the term puffery actually has meaning in a legal sense. The law in Canada and in the US recognizes that some statements made in advertising are not intended to be taken literally, and are therefore not illegal. A famous example that is often cited is the Barnum & Bailey Circus promoting itself as "the greatest show on earth." Puffery and hyperbole—extreme exaggeration for effect—are the staples of advertising.

Though it is sometimes debatable what constitutes deception, Ontario's Consumer Protection Act lays down some pretty clear definitions of false, misleading, and deceptive marketing practices:

1. A representation that the goods or services have sponsorship, approval, performance characteristics, accessories, uses, ingredients, benefits, or qualities they do not have.
2. A representation that the person who is to supply the goods or services has sponsorship, approval, status, affiliation, or connection the person does not have.
3. A representation that the goods or services are of a particular standard, quality, grade, style, or model, if they are not.
4. A representation that the goods are new or unused; if they are not, or are reconditioned or reclaimed, but the reasonable use of goods to enable the person to service, prepare, test, and deliver the goods does not result in the goods being deemed to be used for the purposes of this paragraph.
5. A representation that the goods have been used to an extent that is materially different from the fact.
6. A representation that the goods or services are available for a reason that does not exist.
7. A representation that the goods or services have been supplied in accordance with a previous representation, if they have not.
8. A representation that the goods or services or any part of them are available or can be delivered or performed when the person making the representation knows or ought to know they are not available or cannot be delivered or performed.
9. A representation that the goods or services or any part of them will be available or can be delivered or performed by a specified time when the person making the representation knows or ought to know they will not be available or cannot be delivered or performed by the specified time.
10. A representation that a service, part, replacement or repair is needed or advisable, if it is not.
11. A representation that a specific price advantage exists, if it does not.

12. A representation that misrepresents the authority of a salesperson, representative, employee, or agent to negotiate the final terms of the agreement.
13. A representation that the transaction involves or does not involve rights, remedies, or obligations if the representation is false, misleading, or deceptive.
14. A representation using exaggeration, innuendo or ambiguity as to a material fact or failing to state a material fact if such use or failure deceives or tends to deceive.
15. A representation that misrepresents the purpose or intent of any solicitation of or any communication with a consumer.
16. A representation that misrepresents the purpose of any charge or proposed charge.
17. A representation that misrepresents or exaggerates the benefits that are likely to flow to a consumer if the consumer helps a person obtain new or potential customers.

High-Pressure Selling Salespeople are sometimes accused of high-pressure selling that persuades people to buy goods they had no thought of buying. It is often said that insurance, real estate, and used cars are *sold*, not *bought*. Salespeople are trained to be persuasive, and their companies reward them for reaching and exceeding their sales quotas.

In Canada, there are laws that protect consumers from the dangers of being pressured into making a purchase. Ontario's Consumer Protection Act, for example, states that it is an "unconscionable representation" if "the consumer is being subjected to undue pressure to enter into a consumer transaction." In addition, the act makes several provisions for "cooling-off periods," that is, a period of time during which the consumer may change his or her mind about what they purchased, and return it or get out of the deal with no penalty. And throughout Canada there are many similar laws protecting consumers against high-pressure sales tactics.

Shoddy, Harmful, or Unsafe Products Another criticism concerns poor product quality or function. One complaint is that, too often, products are not made well and services are not performed well. A second complaint is that many products deliver little benefit, or that they might even be harmful.

In Canada, the Canada Consumer Product Safety Act (CCPSA) was updated in 2011 to introduce new requirements for the industry intended to help protect Canadians from unsafe consumer products. Manufacturers are now required to report to Health Canada any incident related to health and safety caused by a consumer product, and retailers are required to keep records that provide enough details about suppliers to be able to recall products if it becomes necessary. The CCPSA website, part of Health Canada's website, provides detailed information for both businesses and for consumers, including how to report an unsafe product, and a search engine to find information about products that have been recalled.

Product problems are not usually caused by a company's indifference or other improper behaviour—most manufacturers *want* to produce quality goods. But problems with product quality and safety do happen, and the way a company deals with them can damage or help its reputation. Companies selling poor-quality or unsafe products risk damaging their reputation, product liability suits, and large awards for damages. Also, with the ubiquity of social media, once a problem is discovered it is quickly made public, and a company's reputation becomes at stake if they don't take steps to respond. Today's marketers know that good quality results in customer value and satisfaction, which in turn creates sustainable customer relationships.

Planned Obsolescence Critics also have charged that some companies practise planned obsolescence, causing their products to become obsolete before they actually should need

Jack Hollingsworth/Corbis

Exhibit 3.4 **Planned obsolescence:**
Almost everyone, it seems, has a
"drawer filled with the detritus of
yesterday's hottest product, now
reduced to the status of fossils."

replacement. They accuse some producers of using materials and components that will break, wear, rust, or rot sooner than they should. One analyst captures the concept this way: "Planned obsolescence, a diabolical manufacturing strategy that took root with the rise of mass production in the 1920s and 1930s, has now escalated from disposable lighters to major appliances. Its evil genius is this: Make the cost of repairs close to the item's replacement price and entice us to buy new." The analyst's 12-year-old stove needed a burner repaired and 12 new screws. The price of the repair: $700, which was more than he'd paid for the stove new.[11]

Other companies are charged with continually changing consumer concepts of acceptable styles to encourage more and earlier buying. An obvious example is constantly changing clothing fashions. Still others are accused of introducing planned streams of new products that make older models obsolete. Critics claim that this occurs in the consumer electronics and computer industries. For example, consider this writer's tale about an aging cellphone:[12]

Today, most people, myself included, are all agog at the wondrous outpouring of new technology, from cellphones to iPods, iPhones, laptops, BlackBerries, and on and on. I have a drawer filled with the detritus of yesterday's hottest product, now reduced to the status of fossils. I have video cameras that use tapes no longer available, laptops with programs incompatible with anything on today's market, portable CD players I no longer use, and more. But what really upsets me is how quickly some still-useful gadgets become obsolete, at least in the eyes of their makers.

I recently embarked on an epic search for a cord to plug into my wife's cellphone to recharge it. We were travelling and the poor phone kept bleating that it was running low and the battery needed recharging. So, we began a search—from big-box technology superstores to smaller suppliers and the cellphone companies themselves—all to no avail. Finally, a salesperson told my wife, "That's an old model, so we don't stock the charger any longer." "But I only bought it last year," she sputtered. "Yeah, like I said, that's an old model," he replied without a hint of irony or sympathy. The proliferation and sheer waste of this type of practice is mind-boggling.

Marketers respond that consumers *like* style changes; they get tired of the old goods and want a new look in fashion. Or they *want* the latest high-tech innovations, even if older models still work. No one has to buy the new product, and if too few people like it, it will simply fail. Finally, most companies do not design their products to break down earlier, because they do not want to lose customers to other brands. Instead, they seek constant improvement to ensure that products will consistently meet or exceed customer expectations. Much of the so-called planned obsolescence is the working of the competitive and technological forces in a free society—forces that lead to ever-improving goods and services.

Marketing's Impact on Society as a Whole

The marketing system has been accused of adding to several "evils" in society at large. Advertising has been a special target of many of these accusations.

False Wants and Too Much Materialism Critics, such as the organization Adbusters and environmental activist Annie Leonard, have charged that the marketing system urges too much interest in material possessions, and that Americans' (and Canadians') love affair with worldly possessions is not sustainable. Too often, people are judged by what they *own* rather than by who they *are*. The critics view this "rampant consumerism" as the fault of marketing. Marketers, they claim, stimulate people's desires for goods and create false wants and materialistic models of the good life. Thus, marketers have created an endless cycle of mass consumption based on a distorted interpretation of the "American Dream."

What began in Vancouver, BC in the mid-eighties, Adbusters (www.adbusters.org) has evolved to a highly effective social-activist movement which spans the globe. The organization's magazine now reaches over 120 000 people in 40 countries around the globe, and its anti-consumption campaigns and spoof ads are getting noticed. For example, consider Buy Nothing Day, an Adbusters-sponsored campaign which began in 1992. This global event draws attention to the harmful effects of over-consumption and not only asks consumers to stop shopping for 24 hours, but also asks them to think about issues like where their products originate from, why they are making purchases, and what they do with their products after purchase. Usually held the Friday after American Thanksgiving, the day has been praised for drawing attention to issues such as how many resources consumers use in developed versus developing countries.[13]

Thus, marketing is seen as creating false wants that benefit industry more than they benefit consumers. "In the world of consumerism, marketing is there to promote consumption," says one marketing critic. It is "inevitable that marketing will promote overconsumption, and from this, a psychologically, as well as ecologically, unsustainable world."[14] This is the message that activist Annie Leonard has been promoting with the Story of Stuff project. Founded in 2008, the project's mission is to build a strong, diverse, decentralized, cross-sector movement to transform systems of production and consumption to serve ecological sustainability and social well-being. Her 20-minute web film (www.storyofstuff.com) explores the hidden consequences of North America's love affair with stuff, and her 2010 book of the same name looks deeper into the issues described in the web film.

Marketers respond that such criticisms overstate the power of business to create needs. People have strong defences against advertising and other marketing tools. Marketers are most effective when they appeal to existing wants rather than when they attempt to create new ones. Furthermore, people seek information when making important purchases and often do not rely on single sources. Even minor purchases that may be affected by advertising messages lead to repeat purchases only if the product delivers the promised customer value. Finally, the high failure rate of new products shows that companies are not able to control demand.

On a deeper level, our wants and values are influenced not only by marketers but also by family, peer groups, religion, cultural background, and education. If Americans and Canadians are highly materialistic, these values arose out of basic socialization processes that go much deeper than business and mass media could produce alone.

Moreover, consumption patterns and attitudes are also subject to larger forces, such as the economy. The 2008 recession put a damper on materialism and conspicuous spending,

Courtesy of Adbusters

Exhibit 3.5 Adbusters Media Foundation is a major critic of marketing's negative influence on our physical and cultural environments. It gets its message out through its website, *Adbusters* magazine, and worldwide campaigns such as Buy Nothing Day.

and caused consumers to re-evaluate their spending habits. Today's marketers, as a result, far from encouraging today's more frugal consumers to overspend their means, are working to help them find greater value with less. "The glib 'all your dreams will come true' approach to marketing will have to be re-evaluated," concludes another analyst.[15]

Too Few Social Goods Business has been accused of overselling private goods at the expense of public goods. As private goods increase, they require more public services that are usually not forthcoming. For example, an increase in automobile ownership (private good) requires more highways, traffic control, parking spaces, and police services (public goods). The overselling of private goods results in "social costs." For cars, some of the social costs include traffic congestion, gasoline shortages, and air pollution. Millions of litres of fuel and hours of time are wasted in traffic jams.

A way must be found to restore a balance between private and public goods. One option is to make producers bear the full social costs of their operations. For example, the government is requiring automobile manufacturers to build cars with more efficient engines and better pollution-control systems. Automakers will then raise their prices to cover the extra costs. If buyers find the price of some cars too high, however, the producers of these cars will disappear. Demand will then move to those producers that can support the sum of the private and social costs.

A second option is to make consumers pay the social costs. For example, many cities around the world are now charging "congestion tolls" in an effort to reduce traffic congestion. To unclog its streets, the city of London levies a congestion charge of £8 per day per car to drive in an eight-square-mile area downtown. The charge has not only reduced traffic congestion within the zone by 21 percent (70 000 fewer vehicles per day) and increased bicycling by 43 percent, but has also raised money to shore up London's public transportation system.[16]

Cultural Pollution Critics charge the marketing system with creating *cultural pollution*. Our senses are being constantly assaulted by marketing and advertising. Commercials interrupt television programs; pages of ads obscure magazines; billboards mar beautiful scenery; email fills our inboxes. Some feel that these interruptions continually pollute people's minds with messages of materialism, sex, power, or status.

And in the age of social media and mass electronic communications, consumer concerns about too many commercial messages have increased. For example, shortly before Facebook's IPO, the company announced it would begin showing advertisements to users on mobile devices—in an effort to increase revenue streams. The advertising product,

Exhibit 3.6 **Balancing private and public goods:** In response to lane-clogging traffic congestion, London now levies a congestion charge. The charge has reduced congestion by 21 percent and raised money to shore up the city's public transportation system.

called "featured stories," displays in the user's news feed and appears, visually, very much like "real" news about the user's friends and their activities.[17]

Marketers must proceed with caution when devising strategies for advertising and promotion campaigns, because when consumers perceive that they are being bombarded with commercial messages, they become resentful. A recent study revealed that 75 percent of respondents reported they would resent a brand after being bombarded by emails. Though consumers are used to TV commercials and billboards, they are not yet used to advertising on their personal electronic devices, which they perceive as more intimate than mass media.[18]

Marketing's Impact on Other Businesses

Critics also charge that a company's marketing practices can harm other companies and reduce competition. Three problems are involved: acquisitions of competitors, marketing practices that create barriers to entry, and unfair competitive marketing practices.

Critics claim that firms are harmed and competition reduced when companies expand by acquiring competitors rather than by developing their own new products. The large number of acquisitions and the rapid pace of industry consolidation over the past several decades have caused concern that vigorous young competitors will be absorbed and that competition will be reduced. In virtually every major industry—retailing, entertainment, financial services, utilities, transportation, automobiles, telecommunications, health care—the number of major competitors is shrinking.

Acquisition is a complex subject. Acquisitions can sometimes be good for society. The acquiring company may gain economies of scale that lead to lower costs and lower prices. A well-managed company may take over a poorly managed company and improve its efficiency. An industry that was not very competitive might become more competitive after the acquisition. But acquisitions can also be harmful and, therefore, are closely regulated by the government.

Critics have also charged that marketing practices bar new companies from entering an industry. Large marketing companies can use patents and heavy promotion spending or tie up suppliers or dealers to keep out or drive out competitors. Those concerned with antitrust regulation recognize that some barriers are the natural result of the economic advantages of doing business on a large scale. Other barriers could be challenged by existing and new laws. For example, some critics have proposed a progressive tax on advertising spending to reduce the role of selling costs as a major barrier to entry.

Finally, some firms have in fact used unfair competitive marketing practices with the intention of hurting or destroying other firms. They may set their prices below costs, threaten to cut off business with suppliers, or discourage the buying of a competitor's products. Various laws work to prevent such predatory competition. It is difficult, however, to prove that the intent or action was really predatory.

Consumer Actions to Promote Sustainable Marketing `LO3`

Sustainable marketing is a philosophy that seeks to promote the consumption of goods and services that meet basic needs and quality of life without jeopardizing the needs of future generations. It is a viewpoint that has increasingly been on the forefront of Canadian society, and while many companies are taking steps toward sustainability, there are also consumer and grassroots organizations that exist to keep businesses in line. The two major movements have been *consumer activism* and *environmentalism*.

Sustainable marketing
A philosophy that seeks to promote the consumption of goods and services that meet basic needs and quality of life without jeopardizing the needs of future generations.

Consumer Activism

The rise of *consumerism*—economic and social policies that encourage consumer spending—in Canada and the US began in the early 1900s, and though it shows no signs of slowing down, nevertheless many consumer activist organizations have risen up and attempted to do just that. The first consumer movement took place in the early 1900s. It was fuelled by rising prices, by Upton Sinclair's writings on conditions in the meat industry, and by scandals in the drug industry. The second consumer movement, in the mid-1930s, was sparked by an upturn in consumer prices during the Great Depression and another drug scandal.

The third movement began in the 1960s. Consumers had become better educated, products had become more complex and potentially hazardous, and people were unhappy with institutions. Ralph Nader appeared on the scene to force many issues, and other well-known writers accused big business of wasteful and unethical practices. President John F. Kennedy declared that consumers had the right to safety and to be informed, to choose, and to be heard. Since then, many consumer groups have been organized and in Canada, many federal and provincial laws protecting consumers have been put in place. The consumer movement has spread internationally and has become very strong in Europe.

But what is the consumer movement? **Consumer activism** is an organized movement of citizens and government agencies to improve the rights and power of buyers in relation to sellers.

Traditional *sellers' rights* include the following:

- The right to introduce any product in any size and style, provided it is not hazardous to personal health or safety; or, if it is, to include proper warnings and controls
- The right to charge any price for the product, provided no discrimination exists among similar kinds of buyers
- The right to spend any amount to promote the product, provided it is not defined as unfair competition
- The right to use any product message, provided it is not misleading or dishonest in content or execution
- The right to use any buying incentive programs, provided they are not unfair or misleading

Traditional *buyers' rights* include the following:

- The right not to buy a product that is offered for sale
- The right to expect the product to be safe
- The right to expect the product to perform as claimed

Comparing these rights, many believe that the balance of power lies on the seller's side. True, the buyer can refuse to buy. But critics feel that the buyer has too little information, education, and protection to make wise decisions when facing sophisticated sellers. Consumer advocates call for the following additional consumer rights:

- The right to be well informed about important aspects of the product
- The right to be protected against questionable products and marketing practices
- The right to influence products and marketing practices in ways that will improve the "quality of life"
- The right to consume now in a way that will preserve the world for future generations of consumers

Consumer activism
An organized movement of citizens and government agencies to improve the rights and power of buyers in relation to sellers.

Each proposed right has led to more specific proposals by activists. The right to be informed includes the right to know the true interest on a loan (truth in lending), the true cost per unit of a product (unit pricing), the ingredients in a product (ingredient labelling), the nutritional value of foods (nutritional labelling), product freshness (open dating), and the true benefits of a product (truth in advertising). Proposals related to consumer protection include strengthening consumer rights in cases of business fraud, requiring greater product safety, ensuring information privacy, and giving more power to government agencies. Proposals relating to quality of life include controlling the ingredients that go into certain products and packaging and reducing the level of advertising "noise." Proposals for preserving the world for future consumption include promoting the use of sustainable ingredients, recycling and reducing solid wastes, and managing energy consumption.

Marketing is a global societal reality, and serves an important function in promoting economic development around the world. When harnessed responsibly, marketing can encourage us as consumers to recycle, reuse, buy fair trade, eat healthily, drink sensibly, save energy, and support good causes. Sustainable marketing *is* possible, and marketing theorists believe it can be achieved through a combination of green marketing and social marketing—through the development and marketing of more sustainable products and services while introducing sustainability efforts into the core of the marketing process and business practice. A recent Boston Consulting Group study of 9000 consumers in nine countries concluded that green and ethical issues were a significant factor influencing what they chose to buy. If sustainability were to become a central component of all marketing thought and practice, consumers would undoubtedly react favourably.[19] The principle seems to be working for Canada's Bullfrog Power (see Marketing@Work 3.1).

Environmentalism

Whereas consumer activists consider whether the marketing system is efficiently serving consumer wants, environmentalists are concerned with marketing's effects on the environment and with the environmental costs of serving consumer needs and wants. **Environmentalism** is an organized movement of concerned citizens, businesses, and government agencies to protect and improve people's current and future living environment.

Environmentalists are not against marketing and consumption; they simply want people and organizations to operate with more care for the environment. The marketing system's goal, they assert, should not be to maximize consumption, consumer choice, or consumer satisfaction, but rather to maximize life quality. And "life quality" means not only the quantity and quality of consumer goods and services, but also the quality of the environment. Environmentalists want current and future environmental costs included in both producer and consumer decision making.

The first wave of modern environmentalism in North America was driven by environmental groups and concerned consumers in the 1960s and 1970s. They were concerned with damage to the ecosystem caused by strip mining, forest depletion, acid rain, global warming, toxic and solid wastes, and litter. They were also concerned with the loss of recreational areas and with the increase in health problems caused by bad air, polluted water, and chemically treated food.

The second environmentalism wave was driven by government, which passed laws and regulations during the 1970s and 1980s governing industrial practices impacting the environment. This wave hit some industries hard. Steel companies and utilities had to invest billions of dollars in pollution-control equipment and costlier fuels. The auto industry had to introduce expensive emission controls in cars. The packaging industry had

Environmentalism
An organized movement of concerned citizens, businesses, and government agencies to protect and improve people's current and future living environment.

MARKETING@WORK 3.1

Bullfrog's Green Energy

You switch on a light or leave your computer up and running without thought of the negative impact each action may have on the environment. Bullfrog Power wants to change this. With an understanding that conventional electricity generation is a leading source of carbon dioxide, the primary greenhouse gas linked to climate change, as well as other emissions that contribute to poor air quality, Bullfrog provides consumers and businesses with an easy way to green their energy and reduce their impact on the environment. It has successfully overcome a huge marketing challenge in the process: It had to convince potential customers to pay a premium for something they can't see or touch. Despite the fact that it uses relatively low-key marketing focused on building strong customer relationships, Bullfrog was named one of Marketing Magazine's top ten Marketers of the Year in 2008. It seems to have taken a page out of marketing guru Seth Godin's book: "In a field of black and white Holsteins, a purple cow gets all the attention!"

Bullfrog Power is Canada's leading green energy provider. The Toronto-based company was founded in 2005. Today it stands out as the only company providing 100 percent green energy to homes and businesses across Canada. When homes and businesses sign on for Bullfrog Power, Bullfrog's generators put renewable electricity or green natural gas onto the respective energy system to match the amount of electricity or natural gas the home or business uses; the electricity or natural gas is not injected directly into the facility. Across Canada, Bullfrog's electricity comes exclusively from wind and hydro facilities that have been certified as low impact by Environment Canada—instead of from polluting sources such as coal, oil, natural gas, and nuclear. Sourced from a unique, ground-breaking methane-capture project situated on one of Canada's thousands of landfill sites, Bullfrog's green natural gas is a climate-friendly alternative to conventional, polluting natural gas. Through this innovative technology, biogas is captured, cleaned up, and injected onto the national natural

gas pipeline, displacing fossil-fuel based gas and reducing CO_2 emissions into the atmosphere.

Bullfrog is working hard to build its customer base of both end consumers and businesses. Its business and organizational clients include such firms as Unilever Canada, Walmart Canada, BMO Financial Group, Mountain Equipment Co-op, and Staples Canada.

Bullfrog has excelled by living by strong brand values. Its mission is to provide Canadians with easy and practical 100 per cent renewable energy solutions for their homes, businesses, and transportation. The organization believes businesses can serve a vital function as community leaders in promoting and fostering responsible environmental action. It is a "double bottom line" company that maintains a dual focus on environmental responsibility and profitability. The company has pledged to donate 10 percent of profits to organizations that support sustainability. Bullfrog not only provides green energy for its customers, it empowers them to be change agents in the world. Bullfrog and its customers hope to demonstrate that change can come through collective action. The more people who sign up with Bullfrog, the more demand grows for renewable energy.

Bullfrog's brand values have resonated with many Canadians. Thus, it has been able to rely on grassroots marketing, word-of-mouth endorsements, and the Web to spread its message. "Word of mouth is an extremely powerful form of communication," says Tom Heintzman, Bullfrog's director and co-founder. "To a large measure, we divest ourselves of the brand and put it in the hands of our customers." The majority of Bullfrog's communications are done in-house to ensure that it remains true to its brand.

It's not surprising that Bullfrog is a strong believer in relationship marketing. Bullfrog works hard to add extra value for its business clients. Its website

Exhibit 3.7 **Green power:** Bullfrog Power is Canada's leading green Energy Provider. The company provides energy solutions to end consumers and businesses.

Bullfrog Power Inc. Used with permission.

features a Green Directory—an easy-to-search source of companies that support 100 percent green energy. And the company has its own YouTube channel, Facebook presence, and Twitter feed (@bullfrogpower). Bullfrog also uses more traditional tools to market its service, including national newspapers such as the *Globe and Mail*, but it has put a distinctive Bullfrog stamp on this use of traditional media by using information-rich content to explain its service and how customers can make changes.

Public relations are also a big part of Bullfrog's communication mix. Its people do a lot of public speaking to help bring home their message. The Bullfrog team can also be seen at many events linked to environmental initiatives—it is involved in hundreds of different events a year. For example, an event called the Bullfrog Bash featured supporter Gord Downie of The Tragically Hip. And in 2013, with Bruce Cockburn as its official Sustainability Ambassador, The 42nd annual JUNO Awards partnered with Bullfrog Power to provide the show with 100 per cent clean, renewable electricity. The production required 230 MWh, equivalent to the amount of electricity used by more than 1000 Canadian households for a week. The Canadian Academy of Recording Arts and Sciences (CARAS), the organization that produces the JUNO Awards, has a long tradition of being at the forefront of sustainability, and 2013 was the sixth year that Bullfrog partnered with CARAS. But for the first time, the more than 550 hotel rooms required for JUNO Week events, and all of the electricity requirements of the CARAS office and all JUNO Awards events, was "bullfrogpowered."

Sources: "Green sounds a good note: The 2013 JUNO Awards chooses 100 per cent green energy from Bullfrog Power," press release published on BullFrogPower.com, April 11, 2013; Michelle Warren, "The Best of '08 Marketers: Bullfrog Power," *Marketing*, November 24, 2008; Peter Gorrie, "Tiny Bullfrog Power Making a Mark," *The Toronto Star* online, May 26, 2008.

to find ways to improve recyclability and reduce solid wastes. These industries and others have often resented and resisted environmental regulations, especially when they have been imposed too rapidly to allow companies to make proper adjustments. Many of these companies claim they have had to absorb high costs that have made them less competitive.

The first two environmentalism waves have now merged into a third and stronger wave in which companies are accepting more responsibility for doing no harm to the environment. They are shifting from protest to prevention, and from regulation to responsibility. More and more companies are adopting policies of **environmental sustainability**. Simply put, environmental sustainability is about generating profits while helping to save the planet.

Some companies have responded to public environmental concerns by doing only what is required to avert new regulations or to keep environmentalists quiet. Enlightened companies, however, are taking action not because someone is forcing them to, or to reap short-run profits, but because it is the right thing to do—for both the company and for the planet's environmental future.

Figure 3.2 shows a grid that companies can use to gauge their progress toward environmental sustainability. It includes both internal and external "greening" activities that will pay off for the firm and environment in the short run and "beyond greening" activities

Environmental sustainability
A management approach that involves developing strategies that both sustain the environment and produce profits for the company.

FIGURE 3.2 The Environmental Sustainability Portfolio

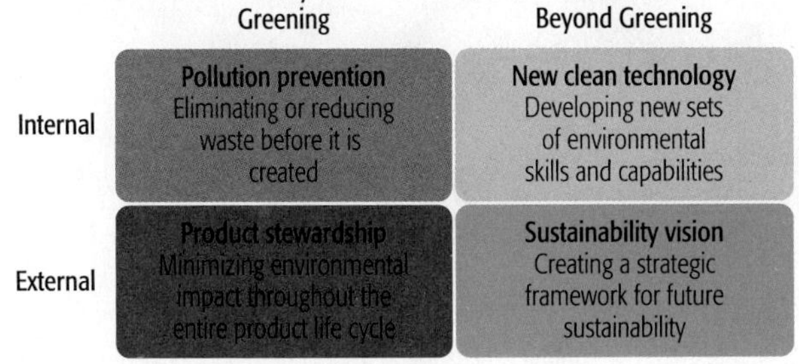

Sources: Stuart L. Hart, "Innovation, Creative Destruction, and Sustainability," *Research Technology Management,* September–October 2005, pp. 21–27.

that will pay off in the longer term. At the most basic level, a company can practice *pollution prevention*. This involves more than pollution control—cleaning up waste after it has been created. Pollution prevention means eliminating or minimizing waste before it is created. Companies emphasizing prevention have responded with internal "green marketing" programs—designing and developing ecologically safer products, recyclable and biodegradable packaging, better pollution controls, and more energy-efficient operations.

For example, Nike produces PVC-free shoes, recycles old sneakers, and educates young people about conservation, reuse, and recycling. General Mills shaved off 20 percent of the paperboard packaging for Hamburger Helper, resulting in 500 fewer distribution trucks on the road each year. UPS has been developing its "green fleet," which now boasts more than 1600 low-carbon-emissions vehicles, including electric, hybrid-electric, compressed natural gas, liquefied natural gas, and propane trucks. Sun Microsystems created its Open Work program that gives employees the option to work from home, preventing nearly 29 000 tons of CO_2 emissions, while at the same time saving US$67.8 million in real-estate costs and increasing worker productivity by 34 percent.[20]

At the next level, companies can practise *product stewardship*—minimizing not just pollution from production and product design but all environmental impacts throughout the full product life cycle, and all the while reducing costs. Many companies are adopting *design for environment (DFE)* and *cradle-to-cradle* practices. This involves thinking ahead to design products that are easier to recover, reuse, recycle, or safely return to nature after usage, becoming part of the ecological cycle. Design for environment and cradle-to-cradle practices not only help sustain the environment but can also be highly profitable for the company.

For example, more than a decade ago, IBM started a business designed to reuse and recycle parts from its mainframe computers returned from lease. Today, IBM takes in 40 000 pieces of used IBM and other equipment per week, strips them down to their chips, and recovers valuable metals. "We find uses for more than 99 percent of what we take in,

Donald Bowers/Getty Images

Exhibit 3.8 New clean technologies: Coca-Cola is investing heavily to develop new solutions to environmental issues. To reduce packaging waste problems, it's now testing new contour bottles made from corn, bioplastics, or—here—more easily recycled aluminum.

and have a return-to-landfill rate of [less than 1 percent]," says an IBM spokesperson. What started out as an environmental effort has now grown into a US$2 billion IBM business that profitably recycles electronic equipment at 22 sites worldwide.[21]

Today's "greening" activities focus on improving what companies already do to protect the environment. The "beyond greening" activities identified in Figure 3.2 look to the future. First, internally, companies can plan for *new clean technology*. Many organizations that have made good sustainability headway are still limited by existing technologies. To create fully sustainable strategies, they will need to develop innovative new technologies. For example, Coca-Cola is investing heavily in research addressing many sustainability issues:

> From a sustainability viewpoint for Coca-Cola, an aluminum can is an ideal package. Aluminum can be recycled indefinitely. Put a Coke can in a recycling bin, and the aluminum finds its way back to a store shelf in about six weeks. The trouble is, people prefer clear plastic bottles with screw-on tops. Plastic bottles account for nearly 50 percent of Coke's global volume, three times more than aluminum cans. And they are not currently sustainable. They're made from oil, a finite resource. Most wind up in landfills or, worse, as roadside trash. They can't be recycled indefinitely because the plastic discolours. To attack this waste problem, Coca-Cola will invest about US$44 million to build the world's largest state-of-the-art plastic-bottle-to-bottle recycling plant.
>
> As a more permanent solution, Coke is also investing in new clean technologies that address these and other environmental issues. For example, it's researching and testing new bottles made from aluminum, corn, or bioplastics. It's also designing more eco-friendly distribution alternatives. Currently, about ten million or so vending machines and refrigerated coolers gobble up energy and use potent greenhouse gases called HFCs to keep Cokes cold. To eliminate them, the company invested US$40 million in research and formed a refrigeration alliance with McDonald's and even competitor PepsiCo. It recently began installing a family of sleek new HFC-free coolers that use 30 to 40 percent less energy. Coca-Cola has also promised to become "water neutral" by researching ways to help its bottlers waste less water and ways to protect or replenish watersheds around the world.[22]

Finally, companies can develop a *sustainability vision*, which serves as a guide to the future. It shows how the company's products and services, processes, and policies must evolve and what new technologies must be developed to get there. This vision of sustainability provides a framework for pollution control, product stewardship, and new environmental technology for the company and others to follow.

Most companies today focus on the upper-left quadrant of the grid in Figure 3.2, investing most heavily in pollution prevention. Some forward-looking companies practise product stewardship and are developing new environmental technologies. Few companies have well-defined sustainability visions. However, emphasizing only one or a few quadrants in the environmental sustainability grid can be short-sighted. Investing only in the left half of the grid puts a company in a good position today but leaves it vulnerable in the future. In contrast, a heavy emphasis on the right half suggests that a company has good environmental vision but lacks the skills needed to implement it. Thus, companies should work at developing all four dimensions of environmental sustainability.

Alcoa, the world's leading producer of aluminum, is setting a high sustainability standard. For five years running it has been named one of the most sustainable corporations in the annual Global 100 Most Sustainable Corporations in the World ranking:

> Alcoa has distinguished itself as a leader through its sophisticated approach to identifying and managing the material sustainability risks that it faces as a company. From pollution prevention via greenhouse gas emissions reduction programs to engaging stakeholders over new environmental technology, such as controversial hydropower projects, Alcoa has the sustainability strategies in place needed to meld its profitability objectives with society's larger environmental protection goals. . . . Importantly, Alcoa's approach to sustainability is firmly rooted in the idea that sustainability programs can indeed add financial value. Perhaps the

best evidence is the company's efforts to promote the use of aluminum in transportation, where aluminum—with its excellent strength-to-weight ratio—is making inroads as a material of choice that allows automakers to build low-weight, fuel-efficient vehicles that produce fewer tailpipe emissions. This kind of forward-thinking strategy of supplying the market with the products that will help solve pressing global environmental problems shows a company that sees the future, has plotted a course, and is aligning its business accordingly. Says CEO Alain Belda, "Our values require us to think and act not only on the present challenges, but also with the legacy in mind that we leave for those who will come after us . . . as well as the commitments made by those that came before us."[23]

Environmentalism creates some special challenges for global marketers. As international trade barriers come down and global markets expand, environmental issues are having an ever-greater impact on international trade. Countries in North America, Western Europe, and other developed regions are generating strict environmental standards. A side accord to the North American Free Trade Agreement (NAFTA) set up the Commission for Environmental Cooperation for resolving environmental matters. The European Union (EU) has recently adopted a climate and energy package and legislation to reduce CO_2 emissions from new cars and transport fuels 20 percent below 1990 levels and to increase the share of renewable energy to 20 percent within one year. And the EU's Eco-Management and Audit Scheme (EMAS) provides guidelines for environmental self-regulation.[24]

However, environmental policies still vary widely from country to country. Countries such as Denmark, Germany, Japan, and the United States have fully developed environmental policies and high public expectations. But major countries such as China, India, Brazil, and Russia are in only the early stages of developing such policies. Moreover, environmental factors that motivate consumers in one country may have no impact on consumers in another. For example, PVC soft-drink bottles cannot be used in Switzerland or Germany. However, they are preferred in France, which has an extensive recycling process for them. Thus, international companies have found it difficult to develop standard environmental practices that work around the world. Instead, they are creating general policies and then translating these policies into tailored programs that meet local regulations and expectations.

Public Actions to Regulate Marketing

Citizen concerns about marketing practices will usually lead to public attention and legislative proposals. New bills will be debated—many will be defeated, others will be modified, and a few will become workable laws.

Many of the laws that affect marketing are listed in Chapter 4. The task is to translate these laws into the language that marketing executives understand as they make decisions about competitive relations, products, price, promotion, and channels of distribution.

Business Actions Toward Sustainable Marketing LO4

At first, many companies opposed the idea of social and sustainable marketing. They thought the criticisms from consumer and environmental activists were either unfair or unimportant. But by now, most companies have grown to embrace the new consumer rights, at least in principle. They might oppose certain pieces of legislation as inappropriate ways to solve specific consumer problems, but they recognize the consumer's right to information and protection. Many of these companies have responded positively to sustainable marketing as a way to create greater immediate and future customer value and to strengthen customer relationships.

Sustainable Marketing Principles

Under the sustainable marketing concept, a company's marketing should support the best long-run performance of the marketing system. It should be guided by five sustainable marketing principles: *consumer-oriented marketing, customer-value marketing, innovative marketing, sense-of-mission marketing,* and *societal marketing.*

Consumer-Oriented Marketing Consumer-oriented marketing means that the company should view and organize its marketing activities from the consumer's point of view. It should work hard to sense, serve, and satisfy the needs of a defined group of customers, both now and in the future. All of the good marketing companies that we've discussed in this text have had this in common: an all-consuming passion for delivering superior value to carefully chosen customers. Only by seeing the world through its customers' eyes can the company build lasting and profitable customer relationships.

> **Consumer-oriented marketing**
> The philosophy of sustainable marketing that holds that the company should view and organize its marketing activities from the consumer's point of view.

Customer-Value Marketing According to the principle of **customer-value marketing**, the company should put most of its resources into customer-value-building marketing investments. Many things marketers do—one-shot sales promotions, cosmetic packaging changes, direct-response advertising—may raise sales in the short run but add less *value* than would actual improvements in the product's quality, features, or convenience. Enlightened marketing calls for building long-run customer loyalty and relationships by continually improving the value customers receive from the firm's market offering. By creating value *for* customers, the company can capture value *from* customers in return.

> **Customer-value marketing**
> A principle of sustainable marketing that holds that a company should put most of its resources into customer-value-building marketing investments.

Innovative Marketing The principle of **innovative marketing** requires that the company continuously seek real product and marketing improvements. The company that overlooks new and better ways to do things will eventually lose customers to another company that has found a better way. An excellent example of an innovative marketer is Frito-Lay Canada.[25]

> **Innovative marketing**
> A principle of sustainable marketing that requires that a company seek real product and marketing improvements.

> In 2009, snack food giant Frito-Lay, maker and marketer of Sun Chips, a healthier alternative to regular potato chips, announced that it was replacing its regular plastic packaging with biodegradable chip bags that could be fully composted in 14 weeks. The change was applied to the products in both the US and Canada. It was a laudable initiative, however, it had the unfortunate effect of significantly reducing sales in the US. American consumers complained that the new bags were so loud, they didn't want to use them. The chip bag became the butt of late night comedy show jokes, and within a year the product was pulled from shelves in the US. But then, it was the American consumer that became the target of criticism. "In the grand scheme of things, this is the absolute bare-minimum level of sacrifice Americans are asked to make. . . . If the sound of a crinkly eco-chip bag is too much to handle, then the human species really is screwed," pointed out an article in *Mother Jones* magazine, itself an eco-friendly publication.
>
> In Canada, however, there was a very different reaction. Though some consumers complained about the noise, they still appreciated the eco-efforts of Frito-Lay, saying, "Yeah, the bag is noisy but given how much better it is for the environment, isn't it worth it?" This inspired the company to turn the complaints into a tongue-in-cheek advertising campaign. On the brand's Facebook page, consumers were asked to voice their opinions, and humourously told that if they didn't like the bag, Frito-Lay would send them a free pair of earplugs. The company also reached out to environmental bloggers, and produced a Web video that received widespread play on news programs.

> **Sense-of-mission marketing**
> A principle of sustainable marketing that holds that a company should define its mission in broad social terms rather than narrow product terms.

Exhibit 3.9 **Innovative (and green) marketing:** The 100 percent compostable chip bag developed by PepsiCo for its Sun Chips brand was more widely accepted by Canadians than Americans.

© Helen Sessions / Alamy

Sense-of-Mission Marketing Sense-of-mission marketing means that the company should define its mission in broad *social* terms rather than narrow *product* terms. When a company defines a social mission, employees feel better about their work and have a clearer sense of direction. Brands linked with broader missions can serve the best long-run interests of both the brand and the consumers. For example, Dove wants to do more than just sell its beauty care products. It's on a mission to discover "real beauty" and help women to be happy just the way they are:

It all started with a Unilever study that examined the impact on women of images seen in entertainment, in advertising, and on fashion runways. The startling result: Only 2 percent of 3,300 women and girls surveyed in 10 countries around the world considered themselves beautiful. Unilever's conclusion: It's time to redefine beauty. So in 2004, Unilever launched the global Dove Campaign for Real Beauty, with ads that featured candid and confident images of real women of all types (not actresses or models) and headlines that made consumers ponder their perceptions of beauty. Among others, it featured full-bodied women ("Oversized or Outstanding?"), older women ("Gray or Gorgeous?"), and a heavily freckled woman ("Flawed or Flawless?"). The following year, as the campaign's popularity skyrocketed, Dove introduced six new "real beauties" of various proportions, in sizes ranging from 6 to 14. These women appeared in ads wearing nothing but their underwear and big smiles, with headlines proclaiming, "New Dove Firming: As Tested on Real Curves." "In Dove ads," says one advertising expert, "normal is the new beautiful."

The Dove Campaign for Real Beauty quickly went digital, with a www.campaignforrealbeauty .com website and award-winning viral videos with names such as "Evolution" and "Onslaught" that attacked damaging beauty stereotypes. As the campaign took off, so did sales of Dove products. But the people behind the Dove brand and the Campaign for Real Beauty have noble motives beyond sales and profits. According to a Unilever executive, Dove's bold and compelling mission to redefine beauty and reassure women ranks well above issues of dollars and cents. "You should see the faces of the people working on this brand now," he says. "There is a real love for the brand."[26]

Such experiences taught the socially responsible business movement some hard lessons. The result is a new generation of activist entrepreneurs—not social activists with big hearts who hate capitalism, but well-trained business managers and company builders with a passion for a cause. Founded by businesspeople who are proud of it, the new mission-driven companies are just as dedicated to building a viable, profitable business as to shaping the mission. They know that to "do good," they must first "do well" in terms of successful business operations. For example, Jeff Swartz, CEO of outdoor shoe and apparel maker Timberland, refers to this as the beautiful—and profitable—nexus between "commerce and justice:"

Exhibit 3.10 **Sense-of-mission marketing:** Timberland's corporate mission is about more than just making good products; it's about "trying to make a difference in the communities where we live and work."

Frances Dean/Dean Pictures/Newscom

Timberland is no ordinary for-profit company. Its mission is to make profits while at the same time making a difference in the world. And Timberland's Jeff Swartz is no ordinary CEO. He sees Timberland's place in the world as much bigger than the products it puts into it. He believes fervently that making money should go hand in hand with making the world a better place. He's spreading the word about corporate citizenship to anyone who will listen, whether it's customers, suppliers, or employees.

For example, when Swartz met with McDonald's executives to pitch providing the fast-food giant with new uniforms, he didn't bring along any designs. In fact, he didn't even talk about clothing. Instead, he made an impassioned speech about how Timberland could help McDonald's create a more unified, motivated, purposeful workforce that would benefit both the company and the world at large. He talked about Serv-a-palooza, Timberland's annual single-day volunteer-fest, which hosts hundreds of service projects in dozens of countries and provides tens of thousands of volunteer work hours. Then, rather than trying to close the sale, Swartz left the McDonald's executives with the charge of truly helping every community in which it does business. Back at headquarters, Swartz told his team, "Find me 10 more places where I can have this conversation."

To inspire consumers to make more sustainable decisions, Timberland puts Green Index tags on its products. Modelled after the nutritional labels found on food products, the index provides a 0-to-10 rating of each product's ecological footprint in terms of climate impact, chemicals used, and resources consumed. The lower the score, the smaller the environmental footprint. The company also has a solar-powered distribution centre in California and a wind-powered factory in the Dominican Republic. And Timberland's Earthkeeper line of boots features soles made from recycled car tires. "No one believes in this more than we do, and that is our competitive advantage," says Swartz.[27]

Societal Marketing Following the principle of **societal marketing**, a company makes marketing decisions by considering consumers' wants and interests, the company's requirements, and society's long-run interests. The company is aware that neglecting consumer and societal long-run interests is a disservice to consumers and society. Alert companies view societal problems as opportunities.

Sustainable marketing calls for products that are not only pleasing but also beneficial. The difference is shown in Figure 3.3. Products can be classified according to their degree of immediate consumer satisfaction and long-run consumer benefit.

Deficient products, such as bad-tasting and ineffective medicine, have neither immediate appeal nor long-run benefits. **Pleasing products** give high immediate satisfaction but may hurt consumers in the long run. Examples include cigarettes and junk food. **Salutary products** have low immediate appeal but may benefit consumers in the long run; for instance, bicycle helmets or some insurance products. **Desirable products** give both high immediate satisfaction and high long-run benefits, such as a tasty *and* nutritious breakfast food.

Examples of desirable products abound. GE's Energy Smart compact fluorescent light bulb provides good lighting at the same time that it gives long life and energy savings. Toyota's Prius and other hybrid and electric cars are fuel efficient and less polluting than gasoline-powered vehicles. Maytag's front-loading Neptune washer provides superior cleaning along with water savings and energy efficiency.

Companies should try to turn all of their products into desirable products. The challenge posed by pleasing products is that they sell very well but may end up hurting the consumer. The product opportunity, therefore, is to add long-run benefits without reducing the product's pleasing qualities. The challenge posed by salutary products is to add some pleasing qualities so that they will become more desirable in consumers' minds.

Societal marketing
A principle of sustainable marketing that holds that a company should make marketing decisions by considering consumers' wants, the company's requirements, consumers' long-run interests, and society's long-run interests.

Deficient products
Products that have neither immediate appeal nor long-run benefits.

Pleasing products
Products that give high immediate satisfaction but may hurt consumers in the long run.

Salutary products
Products that have low appeal but may benefit consumers in the long run.

Desirable products
Products that give both high immediate satisfaction and high long-run benefits.

FIGURE 3.3 Societal Classification of Products

MARKETING@WORK 3.2

Socially Responsible Marketing: Making the World a Better Place

Chances are, when you hear the term *socially responsible business,* a handful of companies leap to mind, companies such as Mountain Equipment Co-op, Ben & Jerry's, The Body Shop, Patagonia, and TOMS Shoes, to name a few. Such companies pioneered the concept of "values-led business" or "caring capitalism." Their mission: Use business to make the world a better place.

The classic "do good" pioneer is Ben & Jerry's. Ben Cohen and Jerry Greenfield founded the company in 1978 as a firm that cared deeply about its social and environmental responsibilities. Ben & Jerry's bought only hormone-free milk and cream and used only organic fruits and nuts to make its ice cream, which it sold in environmentally friendly containers. It went to great lengths to buy from minority and disadvantaged suppliers. From its early Rainforest Crunch to its more recent Chocolate Macadamia (made with sustainably sourced macadamias and fair trade–certified cocoa and vanilla), Ben & Jerry's has championed a host of social and environmental causes over the years.

From the start, Ben & Jerry's donated a whopping 7.5 percent of pre-tax profits to support projects that exhibited "creative problem solving and hopefulness . . . relating to children and families, disadvantaged groups, and the environment." By the mid-1990s, Ben & Jerry's had become the nation's number-two super premium ice cream brand.

However, as competitors not shackled by Ben & Jerry's "principles before profits" mission invaded its markets, growth and profits flattened. After several years of lacklustre financial returns, Ben & Jerry's was acquired by consumer goods giant Unilever. What happened to the founders' lofty ideals of caring capitalism? Looking back, Ben & Jerry's may have focused too much on social issues at the expense of sound business management. Ben Cohen never really wanted to be a business person. In fact, according to one analyst, Cohen "saw businesspeople as tools of the military-industrial complex and profits as a dirty word." Cohen once commented, "There came a time [when I had to admit] 'I'm a business-

man.' And I had a hard time mouthing those words."

Having a "double bottom line" of values and profits is no easy proposition. Operating a business is tough enough. Adding social goals to the demands of serving customers and making a profit can be daunting and distracting. You can't take good intentions to the bank. In fact, many of the pioneering values-led businesses have since been acquired by bigger companies. For example, Unilever absorbed Ben & Jerry's, Clorox bought out Burt's Bees, and L'Oréal acquired The Body Shop. The experiences of pioneers like Ben & Jerry's, however, taught the socially responsible business movement some hard lessons. As a result, a new generation of mission-driven entrepreneurs emerged—not social activists with big hearts who hate capitalism, but well-trained business managers and company builders with a passion for a cause. These new double bottom-line devotees know that to "do good," they must first "do well" in terms of viable and profitable business operations.

To honour such practices, *Atlantic Business Magazine* and Dalhousie University's Faculty of Management began a CSR Awards program. Winners were selected from groups of small firms of less than 100 employees to firms that have more than 500 employees. All of the winners were well-run businesses and savvy marketers. Many were modest about their eco-friendly and responsible practices. All were high performers and innovative. Southwest Properties, a privately owned developer of residential and commercial property based in Halifax, won in the small business category and received recognition for its ongoing energy audits, energy efficiency, recycling programs, and community enhancement programs. Irving Oil won in the large firm category, largely because of its excellent human resources programs, which include its Women Leading Women program, its comprehensive

© Art Directors & TRIP / Alamy

Exhibit 3.11 Socially responsible marketing: New Brunswick's Irving Oil was one of the recent winners of the Corporate Social Responsibility (CSR) Award sponsored by *Atlantic Business Magazine* and Dalhousie University's Faculty of Management. The company won in the Human Resources category for its many leadership and development programs for female employees.[28]

safety programs, its comprehensive reviews of its social and ethical performance, and its LiveWell employee wellness program.

As the award winners demonstrate, socially responsible missions are no longer the exclusive domain of well intentioned start-ups or small firms. Social responsibility has gone mainstream, with large corporations—from TD Bank Group, to TELUS, to Walmart, to Starbucks, to PepsiCo—adopting broad-based "change the world" initiatives. For example, Walmart is fast becoming the world's leading "eco-nanny," and Starbucks created C.A.F.E. Practices, guidelines for achieving product quality, economic accountability, social responsibility, and environmental leadership.

TD Bank Group supports a broad agenda of social and environmental responsibility. It employs more than 85 000 people around the world. No matter where it operates, it is an active and responsible community member that strives to make a positive impact wherever its employees live and work. For TD this means contributing to the social and economic development of its

communities. In 2010 alone, it donated more than $57 million to support not-for-profit groups in Canada, the United States, and the UK. It works to create opportunities for young people so they can fulfill their potential, it works with diverse communities and communities in need so they can have a more prosperous and inclusive future, and it works to engage employees with communities so that positive changes can be made together.

Some brands are building their very identities around social responsibility missions. For example, Mars's PEDIGREE brand is on a "Dogs rule" mission to urge people to adopt homeless dogs and support the care of these animals in shelters. Each year, PEDIGREE has worked to raise money and has distributed $1.5 million in donations to 1000 animal shelters. PEDIGREE donates one bowl of dog food to shelters every time it gains a Facebook fan. Annually this adds up to more than 4 million bowls of dog food, enough to feed every shelter dog in the United States for one day.

Similarly, through its Pepsi Refresh Project, PepsiCo redefines its flagship

brand as not just a soft drink but as an agent for world change. In a year-long effort, the Pepsi Refresh Project awarded $20 million in grants to hundreds of individuals and organizations in local communities that propose ideas that will "make the world a better place." PepsiCo backed the effort with a big-budget traditional and social marketing campaign. This is no mere cause-related marketing effort: The Pepsi Refresh Project makes "doing good" a major element of PepsiCo's mission and positioning. Says PepsiCo's director of marketing, "We want people to be aware that every time you drink a Pepsi you are actually supporting the Pepsi Refresh Project and ideas that are going to move this country forward."

Sources: Bob Liodice, "10 Companies with Social Responsibility at the Core," *Advertising Age*, April 19, 2010, p. 88; "2011 CSR Award Winners," *Atlantic Business Magazine*, www.atlanticbusinessmagazine.ca/csr-awards-2011-winners (accessed May 2013); TD Corporate Responsibility Report 2010; Mike Hoffman, "Ben Cohen: Ben & Jerry's Homemade, Established in 1978," *Inc.*, April 30, 2001, p. 68; Sindya N. Bhanoo, "Products That Are Earth-and-Profit Friendly," *New York Times*, June 12, 2010, p. B3; Elaine Wong, "Pepsi Community Effort Finds Fans on Social Nets," *Brandweek*, June 9, 2010.

Marketing Ethics LO5

Good ethics are a cornerstone of sustainable marketing. In the long run, unethical marketing harms customers and society as a whole. Further, it eventually damages a company's reputation and effectiveness, jeopardizing the company's very survival. Thus, the sustainable marketing goals of long-term consumer and business welfare can be achieved only through ethical marketing conduct.

Conscientious marketers face many moral dilemmas. The best thing to do is often unclear. Because not all managers have fine moral sensitivity, companies need to develop *corporate marketing ethics policies*—broad guidelines that everyone in the organization must follow. These policies should cover distributor relations, advertising standards, customer service, pricing, product development, and general ethical standards.

The finest guidelines cannot resolve all the difficult ethical situations the marketer faces. In many cases, it comes down to personal choice—what kind of marketing manger do you want to be? Managers need a set of principles that will help them figure out the moral importance of each situation and decide how far they can go in good conscience. Table 3.1 lists some difficult ethical issues today's marketing managers might face during their careers.

But *what* principle should guide companies and marketing managers on issues of ethics and social responsibility? One philosophy is that such issues are decided by the

TABLE 3.1 Examples of Difficult Ethical Marketing Questions

1. Your R&D department has changed one of your products slightly. Legally speaking, if a product has changed, even it only slightly, it can be called "new and improved." But you know the product is not really new and improved. Would you use that phrase in advertising the product?

2. You are a product manager at a company that designs and manufactures televisions. The engineers have developed a component that, if used in the development of your next model, would make the TV last for ten years instead of five years (the industry standard). Would you use it? Think about how your decision would affect the pricing strategy for the new model.

3. You work for a small company that manufactures a line of cosmetics that meets all the highest standards of ethical treatment of animals yet sales are miniscule compared to similar products from larger manufacturers. You have researched the market and learned that the problem is not so much that consumers aren't aware of your product, but that they aren't aware that the big brands' products are *not* manufactured with ethical practices. You could develop a promotional campaign that, without making any untrue statements would paint the competition as unethical. Would you do it?

4. You work in the marketing department at an automobile company whose most popular product is a gas-guzzling SUV. There is independent data showing that your company's SUV has a slightly better km/100 litre gas consumption rating than some of its competitors—it ranks fifth in a field of 12. The company wants you to develop marketing materials that position the SUV as eco-friendly in the minds of consumers. What would you do?

5. You work for a pharmaceutical company that markets an over-the-counter antacid product. Advertising for this type of product typically shows someone over-indulging in spicy or fatty foods, then taking the antacid as a remedy for the resulting stomach upset. The product developers are working on a variation of the product designed to be taken *before* consuming foods. The company naturally wants to market the benefits of this product, however, you believe that to do so means communicating the message that consumers should eat whatever they want—promoting unhealthy and unsafe behaviour. How would you proceed?

Exhibit 3.12 **Marketing ethics:** Deciding whether or not to recall a product is up to the marketer. Toy-maker Mattel's open and decisive product-recall response, based on input and help from its panel of brand advisors, helped to maintain customer confidence and create even more trusting customer relationships.

free-market and legal system. Under this principle, companies and their managers are not responsible for making moral judgments. Companies can in good conscience do whatever the market and legal systems allow.

A second philosophy puts responsibility not on the system but in the hands of individual companies and managers. This more enlightened philosophy suggests that a company should have a "social conscience." Companies and managers should apply high standards of ethics and morality when making corporate decisions, regardless of "what the system allows." History provides an endless list of examples of company actions that were legal but highly irresponsible.

Each company and marketing manager must work out a philosophy of socially responsible and ethical behaviour. Under the societal marketing concept, each manager must look beyond what is legal and allowed and develop standards based on personal integrity, corporate conscience, and long-run consumer welfare.

Dealing with issues of ethics and social responsibility in an open and forthright way helps to build strong customer relationships based on honesty and trust. In fact, many companies now routinely include consumers in the social responsibility process. Consider toy maker Mattel:

> In fall 2007, the discovery of lead paint on several of its best-selling products forced Mattel to make worldwide recalls on millions of toys. Threatening as this was, rather than hesitating or hiding the incident, the company's brand advisors were up to the challenge. Their quick, decisive response helped to maintain consumer confidence in the Mattel brand, even contributing to a 6 percent sales increase over the same period in the year before. Just who were these masterful "brand advisors?" They were the 400 moms with kids aged 3 to 10 comprising The Playground Community, a private online network launched by Mattel's worldwide consumer insights department in June 2007 to "listen to and gain insight from moms' lives and needs." Throughout the crisis, The Playground Community members kept in touch with Mattel regarding the product recalls and the company's forthright response plan, even helping to shape the post-recall promotional strategy for one of the affected product lines. Even in times of crisis, "brands that engage in a two-way conversation with their customers create stronger, more trusting relationships," says a Mattel executive.[29]

As with environmentalism, the issue of ethics presents special challenges for international marketers. Business standards and practices vary a great deal from one country to the next. For example, bribes and kickbacks are illegal for Canadian firms and a variety of treaties against bribery and corruption have been signed and ratified by more than 60 countries. Yet these are still standard business practices in many countries. The World Bank estimates that more than US$1 trillion per year worth of bribes are paid out worldwide. One study showed that the most flagrant bribe-paying firms were from India, Russia, and China. Other countries where corruption is common include Iraq, Myanmar, and Haiti. The least corrupt companies were from Iceland, Finland, New Zealand, and Denmark.[30]

The question arises as to whether a company must lower its ethical standards to compete effectively in countries with lower standards. The answer is no. Companies should make a commitment to a common set of shared standards worldwide. For example, John Hancock Mutual Life Insurance Company operates successfully in Southeast Asia, an area that by Western standards has widespread questionable business and government practices. Despite warnings from locals that Hancock would have to bend its rules to succeed, the company set out strict guidelines. "We told our people that we had the same ethical standards, same procedures, and same policies in these countries that we have in the United States, and we do," said then-CEO Stephen Brown. "We just felt that things like payoffs were wrong—and if we had to do business that way, we'd rather not do business." Hancock employees feel good about the consistent levels of ethics. "There may be countries where you have to do that kind of thing," said Brown. "We haven't found that country yet, and if we do, we won't do business there."[31]

Many industrial and professional associations have suggested codes of ethics, and many companies are now adopting their own codes. For example, the Canadian Marketing Association developed the code of ethics shown in Table 3.2. Companies are also developing programs to teach managers about important ethics issues and to help them find the proper responses. They hold ethics workshops and seminars and set up ethics committees. Furthermore, most major North American companies have appointed high-level ethics officers to champion ethics issues and help resolve ethics problems and concerns facing employees.

TABLE 3.2 Excerpts from Code of Ethics and Standards of Practice of the Canadian Marketing Association (CMA)

Mission of the CMA

To create an environment which fosters the responsible growth of marketing in Canada by:
1. Representing the interests of our members on key issues;
2. Taking a leadership role in identifying, planning for, and reacting to issues affecting marketing in Canada, and
3. Influencing and shaping policy initiatives which impact marketing, through education of government, media, special interest groups, and the public;
4. Establishing and promoting ethical standards of practice for marketing and taking an active role in ensuring compliance;
5. Promoting integrity and high standards of business conduct among our members in the interests of consumers and each other;
6. Being a major source of knowledge, marketing intelligence, and professional development; and
7. Providing opportunities for members to meet, network, exchange information, and do business together.

Purpose of the CMA Code of Ethics and Standards of Practice

Marketers acknowledge that the establishment and maintenance of high standards of practice are a fundamental responsibility to the public, essential to winning and holding consumer confidence, and the foundation of a successful and independent marketing industry in Canada.

Definition of Marketing

Marketing is a set of business practices designed to plan for and present an organization's products or services in ways that build effective customer relationships.

Personal Information Practices

Marketers must promote responsible and transparent personal information management practices in a manner consistent with the provisions of the Personal Information Protection and Electronic Documents Act (Canada).

Truthfulness

Marketing communications must be clear and truthful. Marketers must not knowingly make a representation to a consumer or business that is false or misleading.

Campaign Limitations

Marketers must not participate in any campaign involving the disparagement or exploitation of any person or group on the grounds of race, colour, ethnicity, religion, national origin, gender, sexual orientation, marital status, or age.

Marketers must not knowingly exploit the credulity, lack of knowledge, or inexperience of any consumer, taking particular care when dealing with vulnerable consumers. The term "vulnerable consumer" includes, but is not limited to, children, teenagers, people with disabilities, the elderly, and those for whom English or French is not their first language.

Accuracy of Representation

Marketers must not misrepresent a product, service, or marketing program and must not mislead by statement or manner of demonstration or comparison.

Support for Claims

Test or survey data referred to in any marketing communication must be reliable, accurate, and current and must support the specific claim being made. Marketers must be able to substantiate the basis for any performance claim or comparison and must not imply a scientific, factual, or statistical basis where none exists.

Disguise

Marketers must not engage in marketing communications in the guise of one purpose when the intent is a different purpose.

Marketers must not claim to be carrying out a survey or research when their real purpose is to sell a product or service, or to raise funds.

Marketers must not mislead or deceive consumers or businesses into believing that a marketing communication is news, information, public service, or entertainment programming when its purpose is to sell products or services or to seek donations to causes or charities.

Disparagement

Marketers must not use inaccurate information to attack, degrade, discredit, or damage the reputation of competitors' products, services, advertisements, or organizations.

Protection of Personal Privacy

All consumer marketers must abide by the Personal Information Protection and Electronic Documents Act (PIPEDA), and/or applicable provincial privacy laws and the following ten Privacy Principles from the National Standard of Canada and five additional requirements as outlined in this section.

Ten Privacy Principles:

1. **Accountability:** An organization is responsible for personal information under its control and shall designate an individual or individuals who are accountable for the organization's compliance with the following principles.
2. **Identifying Purposes:** The purposes for which personal information is collected shall be identified by the organization at or before the time the information is collected.
3. **Consent:** The knowledge and consent of the individual are required for the collection, use, or disclosure of personal information, except where inappropriate.
4. **Limiting Collection:** The collection of personal information shall be limited to that which is necessary for the purposes identified by the organization. Information shall be collected by fair and lawful means.
5. **Limiting Use, Disclosure, and Retention:** Personal information shall not be used or disclosed for purposes other than those for which it was collected, except with the consent of the individual or as required by law. Personal information shall be retained only as long as necessary for the fulfillment of those purposes.
6. **Accuracy:** Personal information shall be as accurate, complete, and up-to-date as is necessary for the purposes for which it is being used.
7. **Safeguards:** Personal information shall be protected by security safeguards appropriate to the sensitivity of the information.
8. **Openness:** An organization shall make readily available to individuals specific information about its policies and practices relating to the management of personal information.
9. **Individual Access:** Upon request, an individual shall be informed of the existence, use and disclosure of his or her personal information and shall be given access to that information. An individual shall be able to challenge the accuracy and completeness of the information and have it amended as appropriate.
10. **Challenging Compliance:** An individual shall be able to address a challenge concerning compliance with the above principles to the designated individual or individuals accountable for the organization's compliance.

Source: Excerpts from Code of Ethics and Standards of Practice of the Canadian Marketing Association (CMA). Used with permission.

Do Not Contact Service and Do Not Call List In Canada, marketers have always been required by law to use the CMA's Do Not Contact Service when conducting a telemarketing or direct mail campaign. In recent years, in addition to the CMA's DNC list, the CRTC created the National Do Not Call List (in French, Liste Nationale de Numéros de Télécommunication Exclus)—and marketers are required to abide by this list as well.

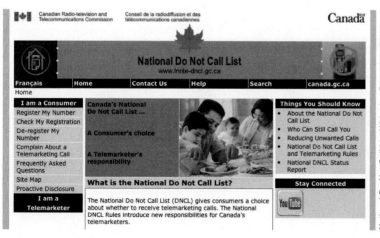

Exhibit 3.13 **Marketing ethics:** Canadian marketers are required by federal law to comply with the National Do Not Call List, maintained by the CRTC. Consumers may also use this website to complain about marketers who break the rules.

Consumers can register their telephone numbers at www.lnnte-dncl.gc.ca, and can also use the website to register complaints against offending telemarketers.

Even more recently, as part of the federal government's Task Force on Spam, a set of best practices for email marketing was developed. These and other federal guidelines and regulations governing the use of contact lists by Canadian marketers are available on Industry Canada's website (www.ic.gc.ca).

The Sustainable Company

At the foundation of marketing is the belief that companies that fulfill the needs and wants of customers will thrive. Companies that fail to meet customer needs or that intentionally or unintentionally harm customers, others in society, or future generations will decline. Sustainable companies are those that create value for customers through socially, environmentally, and ethically responsible actions.

Sustainable marketing goes beyond caring for the needs and wants of today's customers. It means having concern for tomorrow's customers in assuring the survival and success of the business, shareholders, employees, and the broader world in which they all live. Sustainable marketing provides the context in which companies can build profitable customer relationships by creating value *for* customers in order to capture value *from* customers in return, now and in the future.

Writing on the Wall

Local graffiti artists in Aquas Negra, Dominican Republic, had defaced the wall on a basketball court that had been restored through the efforts of 50 WestJetters who had travelled to the impoverished slum in 2012 to build five homes as part of the airline's community investment. They had raised funds not only to fly themselves to the country, but also to build the actual homes. Jenifer Badry, WestJet's team leader of community investment, stared at the graffiti, then said to her colleague, "That has to go. That can't be there." She was referring to the hand-painted word "WestJet." "It just felt wrong to me," she recalls. "I said to them, that is not why we do this. We do not do this to get our name on the wall."

It is a public perception dilemma faced by any for-profit organization. The spirit of corporate social responsibility is to deliver positive outcomes at the triple bottom line (profit, planet, people), and yet a firm like WestJet, who delivers at all levels, feels somewhat reluctant to communicate their acts of kindness and goodwill. "People have a cynicism today because they see that you're doing something," Badry explains, "but are you doing something because it's the right thing to do . . . or are you doing it to put a halo around your brand?"

"We have another program called 'Do the Right Thing,'" says Richard Bartrem, vice-president of communications and community relations, "where we will see something in the media which falls outside of the framework of our community investment, and yet the right thing to do is to fly someone in need, to somewhere where they can be helped. But we don't toot our horn about those."

The Dominican Republic project was the first of a new community investment program called "Hero Holiday." More significantly, it provided an opportunity for WestJetters to give back to a country that has become one of WestJet's most popular destinations. WestJet president and CEO Gregg Saretsky flew down during the final four days of the event, not just to observe but to celebrate and thank the WestJet employees who had personally raised the funds. "We will leave with memories in our hearts and minds for the love you have shown us, and gratitude for allowing us to build these homes for your beautiful families," said the emotional leader to the joyous gathering.

So did the company's name stay on the wall? According to Badry, the villagers pleaded, "Please, we want to remember you. We want to remember WestJet."

QUESTIONS

1. Do WestJet's community investment programs accurately demonstrate societal marketing? If so, how?
2. Why are companies like WestJet reluctant to communicate their acts of goodwill?
3. How do companies achieve a perception of credibility from the public if the public is inherently cynical?

REVIEWING THE CONCEPTS

1. Define *sustainable marketing* and discuss its importance.

Sustainable marketing calls for meeting the present needs of consumers and businesses while still preserving or enhancing the ability of future generations to meet their needs. Whereas the marketing concept recognizes that companies thrive by fulfilling the day-to-day needs of customers, sustainable marketing calls for socially and environmentally responsible actions that meet both the immediate and future needs of customers and the company. Truly sustainable marketing requires a smooth-functioning marketing system in which consumers, companies, public policy-makers, and others work together to ensure responsible marketing actions.

2. Identify the major social criticisms of marketing.

Marketing's *impact on individual consumer welfare* has been criticized for its high prices, deceptive practices, high-pressure selling, shoddy or unsafe products, planned obsolescence, and poor service to disadvantaged consumers. Marketing's *impact on society* has been criticized for creating false wants and too much materialism, too few social goods, and cultural pollution. Critics have also criticized marketing's *impact on other businesses* for harming competitors and reducing competition through acquisitions, practices that create barriers to entry, and unfair competitive marketing practices. Some of these concerns are justified; some are not.

3. Define *consumer activism* and *environmentalism*, and explain how they affect marketing strategies.

Concerns about the marketing system have led to *citizen action movements*. *Consumer activism* is an organized social movement intended to strengthen the rights and power of consumers relative to sellers. Alert marketers view it as an opportunity to serve consumers better by providing more consumer information, education, and protection. *Environmentalism* is an organized social movement seeking to minimize the harm done to the environment and quality of life by marketing practices. The first wave of modern environmentalism was driven by environmental groups and concerned consumers; whereas the second wave was driven by government, which passed laws and regulations governing industrial practices impacting the environment. The first two environmentalism waves are now merging into a third and stronger wave in which companies are accepting responsibility for doing no environmental harm. Companies now are adopting policies of *environmental sustainability*—developing strategies that both sustain the environment and produce profits for the company.

4. Describe the principles of sustainable marketing.

Many companies originally opposed these social movements and laws, but most of them now recognize a need for positive consumer information, education, and protection. Under the sustainable marketing concept, a company's marketing should support the best long-run performance of the marketing system. It should be guided by five sustainable marketing principles: *consumer-oriented marketing*, *customer-value marketing*, *innovative marketing*, *sense-of-mission marketing*, and *societal marketing*.

5. Explain the role of ethics in marketing.

Increasingly, companies are responding to the need to provide company policies and guidelines to help their managers deal with questions of *marketing ethics*. Of course, even the best guidelines cannot resolve all the difficult ethical decisions that individuals and firms must make. But there are some principles that marketers can choose among. One principle states that such issues should be decided by the free market and legal system. A second, and more enlightened, principle puts responsibility not on the system but in the hands of individual companies and managers. Each firm and marketing manager must work out a philosophy of socially responsible and ethical behaviour. Under the sustainable marketing concept, managers must look beyond what is legal and allowable and develop standards based on personal integrity, corporate conscience, and long-term consumer welfare.

KEY TERMS

Consumer activism 92
Consumer-oriented marketing 99
Customer-value marketing 99
Deficient products 101
Desirable products 101

Environmental sustainability 95
Environmentalism 93
Innovative marketing 99
Pleasing products 101
Salutary products 101

Sense-of-mission marketing 99
Societal marketing 101
Sustainable marketing 91

TALK ABOUT MARKETING

1. A bottle of Asacol, a drug for controlling intestinal inflammation, is more expensive than a bottle of the same drug as a generic product. Consumers accuse pharmaceutical manufacturers of unfair markups when the brand price is compared with the lower price of the generic product. As a marketer at a pharmaceutical company, how would you defend the higher prices for your company's branded products?

2. The Consumers' Association of Canada (http://consumer.ca) represents and informs consumers about issues affecting their quality of life. Visit the organization's website to learn about this association. Select one of the issues or activities listed on its home page. Discuss how the information helped you become a more informed consumer.

3. Imagine that you work for a large consumer products company that makes soaps, detergents, and other products, such as shampoos, that ultimately end up being washed down the drain. How would you go about making sure that these products are not harming the environment?

4. Choose a company that you admire, shop at, or buy from—a company that you personally believe is a responsible social marketer. Investigate its website and find out what it does that you would consider "good" social marketing. What could it improve on?

5. If Kellogg's stops advertising to children, how should it change its marketing of products such as Froot Loops and Eggo waffles?

6. Consumer activist groups are beginning to raise awareness of the horrible wastefulness of bottled water. In Canada, no cities have unsafe drinking water, and since it was recently revealed that some branded bottled waters, such as Dasani, come from public sources (i.e., they are nothing more than bottled tap water), there is, logically, no reason for anyone to buy bottled water. What can consumer groups do to discourage or ban the sale of bottled water in Canada? Or should they?

THINK LIKE A MARKETING MANAGER

A forest full of trees has been spared thanks to a new paperless wine list being used at Aureole restaurants in Las Vegas and New York. The wine selection boasts an awe-inspiring 4000 different wine labels that would be impractical to print onto paper in the form of a manageable wine list. Instead of a paper wine list, customers are presented with a lightweight, wireless computer tablet. Pages are turned and selections are made by customers using either a stylus or their fingers. Aside from the positive environmental impact, there are other marketing applications for the electronic wine list. For example, the tablet can be used to display wine reviews and narratives about the winery, customers are allowed to bookmark favourite wine selections, and the tablet has the ability to let customers request

that wine selection information and special offers be emailed to them at home.

QUESTIONS

1. What other businesses could benefit from using this sort of electronic device?

2. What sort of resistance do you think consumers may have to accessing printed material in an electronic format? How could such resistance be overcome?

3. What other typical paper documents do you commonly see when you go shopping, eat out, or purchase services that could be replaced with electronic devices?

4. List all the environmental benefits of such a system.

MARKETING ETHICS

K.G.O.Y. stands for "kids getting older younger," and marketers are getting much of the blame. Kids today see all types of messages, especially on the Internet, that they would never have seen in the past. Whereas boys may give up their G.I. Joes at an earlier age to play war games on their Xbox 360s, the greater controversy seems to surround claims of how girls have changed, or rather, how marketers have changed girls. Critics describe clothing designed for young girls aged 8 to 11 as "floozy" and sexual, with department stores selling thongs for youngsters and T-shirts that say "Naughty Girl!" Although Barbie's sexuality has never been subtle, she was originally targeted to girls 9 to 12 years old. Now, Barbie dolls target primarily 3- to 7-year-old girls.

QUESTIONS

1. Are marketers to blame for kids getting older younger? Give some examples other than those listed above.

2. Give an example of a company that is countering this trend by offering age-appropriate products for children.

MARKETING TECHNOLOGY

Does your computer have a floppy disk drive? Do you listen to music on a cassette deck or record movies on a VCR tape? Does your telephone handset have a cord? You probably answered no. All are examples of obsolete products. New products often provide greater value for customers, especially in fast-changing industries such as computers and electronics. But what happens to all the old products? This creates a growing concern over electronic waste, called *e-waste*. Although e-waste represents only 2 percent of the trash in our landfills, according to some analysts, it accounts for 70 percent of overall toxic waste. Recycling programs are increasing and are even required by law in some provinces. But the waste is often shipped for recycling or disposal to landfills in China, Kenya, India, and other developing countries, which have more lax standards concerning worker and environmental welfare.

QUESTIONS

1. Who should be responsible for properly disposing of discarded electronic products—consumers or manufacturers? Is it appropriate to ship e-waste to developing countries? Discuss alternative solutions.

2. Visit several electronics manufacturers' websites to learn whether they offer electronic recycling programs. Are manufacturers doing enough? Write a brief report on what you learned.

MARKETING BY THE NUMBERS

"High-low" pricing is popular with retailers but considered deceptive by some. Using this practice, retailers set initial prices very high for a short period and then discount the merchandise for the majority of the selling season. Critics complain that the supposed discounted price is in reality the regular price. For example, Canadian retailers such as Suzy Shier and Hudson's Bay were accused of double tagging—placing sale tags on goods right in the factory, so that the sale price was in fact the regular price.

QUESTIONS

1. Refer to Appendix 3, Marketing by the Numbers, to answer the following questions. If The Bay's cost for a piece of jewellery is $50 and it was marked up five times the cost, what is the "high" retail price? What is the "low" sales price if the price is reduced 60 percent off the "regular" price? What is Hudson's Bay's markup percentage on cost at this price? What is its markup percentage on the "low" selling price?

2. Judgments of some cases of high-low pricing have ruled that the retailer did not violate any laws and that one retailer cannot be singled out because most jewellery competitors promote sales prices in a similar way. Is it ethical for retailers to use this pricing tactic?

LAND ROVER

The automotive industry has seen better days. Many auto companies are now facing declining revenues and negative profits. Additionally, because of its primary dependence on products that consume petroleum, the auto industry has a big environmental black eye, especially companies that primarily make gas-guzzling trucks and SUVs.

During the past few years, however, Land Rover has experienced tremendous growth in revenues and profits. It is currently selling more vehicles than ever worldwide. How is this possible for a company that sells only SUVs? One of the biggest reasons is Land Rover's strategic focus on social responsibility and environmentalism. Land Rover believes that it can meet consumer needs for luxury all-terrain vehicles while at the same time providing a vehicle that is kinder to the environment. As a corporation, it is also working feverishly to reduce its carbon emissions, reduce waste, and reduce water consumption and pollution.

With actions like this, Land Rover is successfully repositioning its brand away from the standard perceptions of SUVs as environmental enemies.

After viewing the video featuring Land Rover, answer the following questions about the company's efforts toward social responsibility.

QUESTIONS

1. Make a list of social criticisms of the automotive industry. Discuss all the ways that Land Rover is combating those criticisms.

2. By the textbook's definition, does Land Rover practise sustainable marketing?

3. Do you believe that Land Rover is sincere in its efforts to be environmentally friendly? Is it even possible for a large SUV to be environmentally friendly? Present support for both sides of these arguments.

BELL CANADA'S CLEAN CAPITALISM: COMBINING PLANET AND PROFIT

When you think of the most sustainable corporations in the world, Bell Canada may not jump to mind. Nonetheless, *Corporate Knights* listed Bell as one of only eight Canadian companies to make the Global 100 list of sustainable companies for 2011. Bell Canada Enterprises (BCE) was also named by *Maclean's*/Jantzi-Sustainalytics as one of Canada's Top 50 Socially Responsible Corporations. It also made the prestigious FTSE4Good Global Index. It is not surprising that it is an active member of the United Nations Global Compact and that it adheres to the Compact's principles on human rights, labour, the environment, and anticorruption.

Bell is Canada's largest communications company, providing consumers and businesses with solutions to all of their communications needs. Bell is wholly owned by BCE Inc. It has a number of divisions including Bell Mobility and Bell Media (Canada's premier multimedia company with assets in television, radio, and digital media, including CTV, Canada's number-one television network, and the country's most-watched specialty channels).

Bell takes social responsibility and sustainability seriously. It has no doubt that acting responsibly is central to achieving the sustainable business success that is essential to achieving its corporate goal of being recognized by customers as Canada's leading communications company. "Corporate responsibility is not a program at Bell. It is a way of life," said Michael Sabia, Bell's former CEO. "Our success as a company—and as a country—will be defined by the sustainability of the communities in which we live and work."

In achieving sustainability, the company stresses that each employee has a part to play in accomplishing this agenda. George Cope, Bell's current president and CEO, adds that Bell operates "according to the highest ethical principles and remain[s] committed to the highest standards of corporate responsibility" in all of its interactions with customers, shareholders, suppliers, and team members as well as to the broader communities in which we work and live.

Bell's sustainability vision is one of contributing to the well-being of society by enabling responsible economic growth, connecting communities, and safeguarding the natural environment. As Canada's largest communications company, Bell believes that it has a responsibility to make its services accessible to all members of society, including those with disabilities or living in remote areas. The company takes pride in the fact that its founder, Alexander Graham Bell, was driven by the conviction that he could help deaf people hear and communicate better. "That same spirit—of innovation, of altruism, of service"—remains at Bell today, more than 130 years later. Not only does it still help those with disabilities to communicate easily and more efficiently, it also provides telemedicine, telepsychiatry services, and e-learning services to remote communities.

Bell has a multifaceted sustainability program. It begins with the workplace, where it strives not only to have a safe and healthy working environment, but also to have fully engaged employees. It invested almost $15 million in training and development, and was honoured in 2011 for its excellence in workplace diversity and inclusiveness. Bell conducts trend analysis and benchmark studies, monitors stakeholder feedback, and undertakes surveys to ensure that it is responding to issues relevant to Canadian consumers. Its 2010 survey revealed that privacy and data security, responsible marketing practices, protection of children in the online world, reduction of energy consumption and emissions, and the use of responsible suppliers were among the issues of greatest importance to its customers.

Bell has a wide range of responsible marketing programs. First, protecting privacy and the use of customer information is never taken lightly at Bell. In addition to having all of its team members review and sign its code of ethics on an annual basis, its representatives undergo privacy training so that customer rights are carefully protected. It has developed an easier-to-read privacy statement and has posted answers to privacy questions its customers frequently ask on its website.

Bell has been working to improve telemarketing practices and has been working with the Canadian Radiotelevision and Telecommunications Commission (CRTC) to encourage companies to respect the National Do Not Call List. It works with the CRTC to investigate complaints.

Bell knows that customers want clear price information, so it works to ensure that it provides clear descriptions of rates and charges for its products and service plans. Bell seeks out suppliers who have a commitment to sustainable development, environmental protection, health, safety, ethics, and fair labour practices. All suppliers have to conform to Bell's Supplier Code of Conduct. Rare minerals are critical inputs to many telecommunication products, but many of these come from conflict-torn countries. Many know the story of conflict diamonds, but other rare minerals also may be mined in conditions that abuse human rights or result in the support of armed conflict. Bell works with the manufacturers of its products to avoid the use of such minerals.

Life cycle issues and product disposal are growing in importance. Bell was the first company to establish a Canada-wide collection program for reusing and recycling mobile phones. Customers can drop off their old mobile devices, batteries, and accessories at Bell's authorized retailers and at participating Caisse Desjardins, or they can ship them back to Bell free of charge via Canada Post. Since 2003, Bell has recovered more than 879 000 phones. In 2010 alone, it also collected for reuse or recycling 4.7 tonnes of batteries and accessories that would have otherwise ended up in landfills.

Protecting children from exploitation in a complex communication environment is another of Bell's priorities. The company founded the Canadian Coalition Against Internet Child Exploitation. As part of this initiative, Bell developed Cleanfeed Canada, which reduces accidental access to images of child sexual abuse and discourages those trying to access or distribute child pornography. Bell is also a lead partner in www.cybertip.ca, Canada's tip line for reporting the online exploitation of children. As well, it is the founding sponsor of Media Awareness Network's Be Web Aware website, which promotes the safe use of the Internet for children and their parents.

Bell plays a leadership role in the telecommunications industry, and it takes environmental protection into account in all aspects of its operations, including the deployment and maintenance of its networks and the efficient use of energy and resources. As its 2010 Sustainability report notes, "Using energy efficiently not only helps the environment—it also saves money and supports our strategic imperative of achieving a competitive cost structure."

Bell has been working hard to reduce its carbon footprint. Since 2003, it has reduced its greenhouse gas emissions by 22 percent. It recycled 89.8 percent of its waste materials. By using more electronic billing, it saved the paper equivalent of 33 000 trees, and by using teleconferencing instead of travelling to distant meetings, it further lowered its contribution to harmful emissions. Bell has a large fleet of service vehicles. By equipping 6000 vehicles with telematics (integrated use of telecommunications and informatics), Bell was able to reduce fuel consumption in 2010 by 2.8 million litres and reduce greenhouse gas emissions by 7777 tonnes (the equivalent of taking 1900 mid-sized cars off the road for a year).

When building new facilities (called campuses at Bell), it strives to make them as environmentally friendly as possible through the use of natural light, energy recovery cooling systems, water saving devices, and landscaping that does not require irrigation. Its new Montreal campus was LEED-certified by the Canadian Green Building Council, and its Mississauga, Ontario, campus received a waste minimization award from the Recycling Council of Ontario.

Bell also supports the communities in which it operates, including northern communities. Its employees logged more than 256 000 hours as community volunteers. Bell targeted improved mental health, Canada's most pressing health concern, as its primary cause. In 2010 alone, it contributed $15.8 million to mental health and centres for addiction across the country. In a 2011 program called Bell let's Talk Day, an anti-stigma initiative, Bell contributed 5 cents for each of its customers' 66 million text messages and long distance calls, raising an additional $3.3 million for mental health programs.

Bell is also one of the chief supporters of the Kids Help Phone. The annual Walk for Kids raised $2.5 million for the cause in 2010 and drew 15 000 participants, including 2000 Bell team members.

Bell Canada is a company that certainly demonstrates that you can do well by doing good. It has been consistently profitable, and it does all of these things while sustaining the world for future generations. Indeed, Bell proves that good business and good corporate citizenship can go hand in hand.

Sources: Extracts and other case information are from Bell Canada 2010 Corporate Responsibility Report, "Let's Talk About Sustainability," (available on the Bell Canada website, BCE.ca); Bell News Release, "Bell Recognized Nationally and Internationally for Leadership in Corporate Social Responsibility," July 2007, both accessed January 2012.

QUESTIONS FOR DISCUSSION

1. Give as many examples as you can for how Bell Canada defies the common social criticisms of marketing.

2. Why is Bell successful in applying concepts of sustainability?

3. Analyze Bell according to the environmental sustainability portfolio in Figure 3.2.

4. Does Bell practise enlightened marketing? Support your answer with as many examples as possible.

5. Would Bell be more financially successful if it were not so focused on social responsibility? Explain.

MyMarketingLab

MyMarketingLab is an online homework and tutorial system that puts you in control of your own learning with study and practice tools directly correlated to this chapter's content.

© Mike Kemp/In Pictures/Corbis

AFTER STUDYING THIS CHAPTER, YOU SHOULD BE ABLE TO

1 describe the environmental forces that affect the company's ability to serve its customers

2 explain how changes in the demographic and economic environments affect marketing decisions

3 identify the major trends in the firm's natural and technological environments

4 explain the key changes in the political and cultural environments

5 discuss how companies can react to the marketing environment

Analyzing the Marketing Environment

PREVIEWING THE CONCEPTS

In Part 1, you learned about the basic concepts of marketing, the steps in the marketing process for building profitable relationships with targeted consumers, and the concepts of sustainable marketing. In Part 2, we'll look deeper into the first step of the marketing process—understanding the marketplace and customer needs and wants. In this chapter, you'll discover that marketing operates in a complex and changing environment. Other *actors* in this environment—suppliers, intermediaries, customers, competitors, publics, and others—may work with or against the company. Major environmental *forces*—demographic, economic, natural, technological, political, and cultural—shape marketing opportunities, pose threats, and affect the company's ability to build customer relationships. To develop effective marketing strategies, you must first understand the environment in which marketing operates.

To start, let's look at YouTube, the Internet video-sharing giant that burst onto the scene only a few short years ago. Today, viewers around the globe watch more than 2 billion videos a day on YouTube, giving it a 43 percent share of the online video market. To stay on top and grow profitably, however, YouTube will have to adapt nimbly to the fast-changing marketing environment.

YouTube: ADAPTING TO THE FAST-CHANGING MARKETING ENVIRONMENT

Some 2500 years ago, Greek philosopher Heraclitus observed, "Change is the only constant." That statement holds especially true today in the turbulent video entertainment industry. Today's environment is a far cry from the old days of finding video entertainment only on your TV from schedules set by the networks. Instead, consumers now face a bewildering array of choices about what they watch, as well as how, when, and where. But if the fast-changing video environment sometimes befuddles consumers, it's doubly daunting for the companies that serve them.

Perhaps no company has navigated this changeable marketing environment better than Google-owned YouTube. YouTube's mission is to provide a distribution platform through which people can discover, watch, and share video entertainment. YouTube is now so pervasive that it's hard to believe the first video was uploaded on the site in 2005. Today, viewers around the world watch more than 2 billion videos on YouTube each day and upload more than 35 hours of new video to the site every minute of every day. YouTube now captures a 43 percent share of the online video market and is the third-most visited website on the Internet, trailing only Google (its parent company) and Facebook.

Rather than simply surviving in its chaotic environment, YouTube is thriving in it, leading the way in shaping how video is produced, distributed, and monetized. For the first several years, YouTube's revenues barely covered costs. Recently, however, the video-sharing site has reached the Valhalla of dot-coms. Not only is it generating mind-numbing traffic, it's also making money; last year, income reached nearly US$1 billion.

YouTube began as a place where regular folks could upload low-quality, homemade video clips. But as the video industry has bolted forward, YouTube has adapted quickly. For example, to compete with new video-streaming competitors such as Netflix and Hulu, in 2008 YouTube created a section called "Shows," which provides access to an ever-expanding list of full-length films and television episodes accompanied by advertisements.

But more than just reacting to changes in the environment, YouTube wants to lead those changes. So rather than simply providing more access to traditional Hollywood-type content, YouTube created its Partner Program, which encourages aspiring web video producers to create original new content for YouTube. In all, more than 10 000 partners now participate in the Partner Program, producing new content and sharing the revenue that YouTube generates from ads that accompany their videos. As just one example, partner Mark Douglas produces *Key of Awesome*, a musical comedy series that spoofs celebrities and pop culture. It's now the second-most-viewed web series on YouTube. One Ke$ha parody has an incredible 75 million views, two and a half times as many views as the original Ke$ha video that it parodies.

With all the channels now available on broadcast and cable television, you'd think there would be little need for even more video content. But YouTube sees things differently. It plans to employ the power of its vast social network by creating thousands, if not hundreds, of thousands, of channels. YouTube wants to be a home for special-interest channels that have no place on network or cable TV. The aim is to provide something for everyone. "On cable, there is no kitesurfing channel, no skiing channel, no piano channel," says YouTube CEO Salar Kamangar, an avid kitesurfer, skier, and pianist. "So . . . we're helping define a new way for content creators to reach an audience, and all the topics [an individual might] care about suddenly have a home."

Creating innovative content in the topsy-turvy video environment presents a big challenge. But finding new and better ways to *distribute* that content might be an even bigger one. YouTube's favourite distribution playground has been the Internet on PCs. It has also expanded into mobile distribution with a popular app that gives people on the go full access to YouTube. But with technology exploding, that model doesn't go far enough anymore. One YouTube executive sums up the company's broader distribution ambitions this way: "YouTube is emerging as the first global TV station, the living room for the world," taking video to people wherever they are, whenever they want it.

To become the living room for the world, however, YouTube needs to be on every available screen—especially the big one in people's living rooms. Ultimately, in addition to having people access YouTube via their PCs, tablets, and phones, YouTube wants people to watch YouTube the same way they watch TV. The stakes are huge. The average YouTube session lasts only 15 minutes, whereas the average television watcher spends five hours a day in front of the TV. To that end, YouTube is working feverishly to create an experience on the big screen that will attract more people and keep them watching longer. For example, it's creating Personalized Channels, dynamic streams of videos adjusted to an individual's viewing patterns, much like Internet radio creates personalized music stations.

At the same time that YouTube is changing the way it produces and distributes video content, it's also trying to figure out the best way to monetize (or make money on) that content in an era when consumers still think that everything on the Internet should be free. To that end, YouTube is developing an advertising model that's built around the way people use the site, a model that best suits the needs of users, content providers, advertisers, and its own bottom line.

For example, YouTube worked with Kraft Food's Philadelphia Cream Cheese brand to create an effective YouTube-based campaign. Recognizing that YouTube is a haven for how-to videos, the brand came up with a "Real Women of Philadelphia" (RWoP) community website, starring Food Network chef Paula Deen. The site revolves around YouTube-hosted videos, including Paula Deen videos posted by Kraft, "how-to" recipe videos, and cooking contests that invite users to submit their own cooking videos via YouTube.

On opening day of the first season, Kraft placed a commercial for RWoP featuring Paula Deen on YouTube's home page for $375 000. The goal was to drive traffic to the RWoP site and The Philadelphia Channel on YouTube. Although $375 000 might seem expensive, the Paula Deen commercial on YouTube was seen by 51 million people, making it much cheaper than an ad with comparable reach on prime-time television. More importantly, 10 million people viewed the ad all the way through, and 100 000 people clicked through to the RWoP website. Ultimately, RWoP helped boost the brand's revenue by 5 percent, its first real sales lift in five years. "You look at those numbers; they almost don't even make sense," says Philadelphia's brand manager. "It's bigger than TV."

Even the average person can profit from their videos by signing up for YouTube Partner Program, AdSense, and allowing static ads, banner advertising, and pop-ups to be displayed. In fact, Montréal's Centre NAD will be offering scholarships to future design students based on the ad revenue generated by the recent "fake baby-snatching eagle" video. As part of a class project, students were told they would receive full marks for any video that generated 100 000 hits on YouTube. Animation students Loïc Mireault, Antoine Seigle, Félix Marquis-Poulin, and Normand Archambault's video generated over 30 million views in the first four days, and more than 41 million YouTube views since it aired on December 18, 2012.

What does the future hold for YouTube? Stay tuned. But to remain on top, the company will have to be nimble in adapting to the ever-changing marketing environment—or better, in leading the change. To repeat the words of Heraclitus, change will be the only constant. A respected current marketing thinker puts it a little differently: "In five years, if you're still in the same business you're in now, you're going to be out of business."[1]

A COMPANY'S **marketing environment** consists of the actors and forces outside marketing that affect marketing management's ability to build and maintain successful relationships with target customers. Like YouTube, companies constantly watch and adapt to the changing environment—or, in many cases, lead those changes.

Marketing environment
The actors and forces outside marketing that affect marketing management's ability to build and maintain successful relationships with target customers.

More than any other group in a company, marketers must be the environmental trend trackers and opportunity seekers. Although every manager in an organization should watch the outside environment, marketers have two special aptitudes. They have disciplined methods—marketing research and marketing intelligence—for collecting information about the marketing environment. They also spend more time in customer and competitor environments. By carefully studying the environment, marketers can adapt their strategies to meet new marketplace challenges and opportunities.

The marketing environment is made up of a *microenvironment* and a *macroenvironment*. The **microenvironment** consists of the actors close to the company that affect its ability to serve its customers—the company, suppliers, marketing intermediaries, customer markets, competitors, and publics. The **macroenvironment** consists of the larger societal forces that affect the microenvironment—demographic, economic, natural, technological, political, and cultural forces. We look first at the company's microenvironment.

Microenvironment
The actors close to the company that affect its ability to serve its customers—the company, suppliers, marketing intermediaries, customer markets, competitors, and publics.

Macroenvironment
The larger societal forces that affect the microenvironment—demographic, economic, natural, technological, political, and cultural forces.

The Company's Microenvironment LO1

Marketing management's job is to build relationships with customers by creating customer value and satisfaction. However, marketing managers cannot do this alone. Figure 4.1 shows the major actors in the marketer's microenvironment. Marketing success will require building relationships with other company departments, suppliers, marketing intermediaries, customers, competitors, and various publics, which combine to make up the company's value delivery network.

The Company

In designing marketing plans, marketing management takes other company groups into account—groups such as top management, finance, research and development (R&D), purchasing, operations, and accounting. All of these interrelated groups form the internal environment. Top management sets the company's mission, objectives, broad strategies, and policies. Marketing managers make decisions within the strategies and plans made by top management. Then, as we discussed in Chapter 2, marketing managers must work closely with other company departments. With marketing taking the lead, all departments—from manufacturing and finance to legal and human resources—share the responsibility for understanding customer needs and creating customer value.

FIGURE 4.1 Actors in the Microenvironment

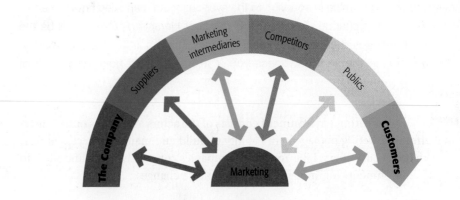

Suppliers

Suppliers form an important link in the company's overall customer value delivery network. They provide the resources needed by the company to produce its goods and services. Supplier problems can seriously affect marketing. Marketing managers must watch supply availability and costs. Supply shortages or delays, labour strikes, natural disasters, and other events can cost sales in the short-run and damage customer satisfaction in the long-run. Rising supply costs may force price increases that can harm the company's sales volume.

Most marketers today treat their suppliers as partners in creating and delivering customer value. For example, cosmetics maker L'Oréal knows the importance of building close relationships with its extensive network of suppliers, who supply everything from polymers and fats to spray cans and packaging to production equipment and office supplies:

> L'Oréal is the world's largest cosmetics manufacturer, with 23 brands in 130 countries ranging from Maybelline and Kiehl's to Lancôme and Redken. The company's supplier network is crucial to its success. As a result, L'Oréal treats suppliers as respected partners. On the one hand, the company expects a lot from suppliers in terms of design innovation, quality, and sustainability. On the other hand, L'Oréal works closely with suppliers to help them meet its exacting standards. According to the company's supplier website, it treats suppliers with "fundamental respect for their business, their culture, their growth, and the individuals who work there. Each relationship is based on . . . shared efforts aimed at promoting growth and mutual profits that make it possible for suppliers to invest, innovate, and compete." As a result, more than 75 percent of L'Oréal's supplier-partners have been working with the company for 10 years or more and the majority of them for several decades. Says the company's head of purchasing, "The CEO wants to make L'Oréal a top performer and one of the world's most respected companies. Being respected also means being respected by our suppliers."[2]

TEH ENG KOON/Getty Images

Exhibit 4.1 L'Oréal builds long-term supplier relationships based on mutual benefit and growth. It "wants to make L'Oréal a top performer and one of the world's most respected companies. Being respected also means being respected by our suppliers."

Marketing Intermediaries

Marketing intermediaries help the company to promote, sell, and distribute its products to final buyers. They include resellers, physical distribution firms, marketing services agencies, and financial intermediaries. *Resellers* are distribution channel firms that help the company find customers or make sales to them. These include wholesalers and retailers who buy and resell merchandise. Selecting and partnering with resellers is not easy. No longer do manufacturers have many small, independent resellers from which to choose. They now face large and growing reseller organizations such as Walmart, Winners, Home Depot, Costco, and Future Shop. These organizations frequently have enough power to dictate terms or even shut smaller manufacturers out of large markets.

Physical distribution firms help the company to stock and move goods from their points of origin to their destinations. *Marketing services agencies* are the marketing research firms, advertising agencies, media firms, and marketing consulting firms that help the company target and promote its products to the right markets. *Financial intermediaries* include banks, credit companies, insurance companies, and other businesses that help finance transactions or insure against the risks associated with the buying and selling of goods.

Marketing intermediaries
Firms that help the company to promote, sell, and distribute its goods to final buyers.

Like suppliers, marketing intermediaries form an important component of the company's overall value delivery system. In its quest to create satisfying customer relationships, the company must do more than just optimize its own performance. It must partner effectively with marketing intermediaries to optimize the performance of the entire system.

Thus, today's marketers recognize the importance of working with their intermediaries as partners rather than simply as channels through which they sell their products. For example, when Coca-Cola signs on as the exclusive beverage provider for a fast-food chain, such as McDonald's, Wendy's, or Subway, it provides much more than just soft drinks. It also pledges powerful marketing support.

> Coke assigns cross-functional teams dedicated to understanding the finer points of each retail partner's business. It conducts a staggering amount of research on beverage consumers and shares these insights with its partners. It analyzes the demographics of US zip code areas and helps partners to determine which Coke brands are preferred in their areas. Coca-Cola has even studied the design of drive-through menu boards to better understand which layouts, fonts, letter sizes, colours, and visuals induce consumers to order more food and drink. Based on such insights, the Coca-Cola Food Service group develops marketing programs and merchandising tools that help its retail partners to improve their beverage sales and profits. Coca-Cola Food Service's website, www.CokeSolutions.com, provides retailers with a wealth of information, business solutions, and merchandising tips. Such intense partnering efforts have made Coca-Cola a runaway leader in the US fountain soft-drink market.[3]

Competitors

The marketing concept states that to be successful, a company must provide greater customer value and satisfaction than its competitors do. Thus, marketers must do more than simply adapt to the needs of target consumers. They also must gain strategic advantage by positioning their offerings strongly against competitors' offerings in the minds of consumers.

No single competitive marketing strategy is best for all companies. Each firm should consider its own size and industry position compared with those of its competitors. Large firms with dominant positions in an industry can use certain strategies that smaller firms cannot afford. But being large is not enough. There are winning strategies for large firms, but there are also losing ones. And small firms can develop strategies that give them better rates of return than large firms enjoy.

Publics

Public

Any group that has an actual or potential interest in or impact on an organization's ability to achieve its objectives.

The company's marketing environment also includes various publics. A **public** is any group that has an actual or potential interest in or impact on an organization's ability to achieve its objectives. We can identify seven types of publics:

- *Financial publics:* This group influences the company's ability to obtain funds. Banks, investment houses, and stockholders are the major financial publics.
- *Media publics:* This group carries news, features, and editorial opinion. It includes newspapers, magazines, television stations, and blogs and other Internet media.
- *Government publics:* Management must take government developments into account. Marketers must often consult the company's lawyers on issues of product safety, truth in advertising, and other matters.
- *Citizen-action publics:* A company's marketing decisions may be questioned by consumer organizations, environmental groups, minority groups, and others. Its public relations department can help it stay in touch with consumer and citizen groups.

- *Local publics:* This group includes neighbourhood residents and community organizations. Large companies usually create departments and programs that deal with local community issues and provide community support. For example, Ronald McDonald House Charities recognize the importance of community publics.
- *General public:* A company needs to be concerned about the general public's attitude toward its products and activities. The public's image of the company affects its buying.
- *Internal publics:* This group includes workers, managers, volunteers, and the board of directors. Large companies use newsletters and other means to inform and motivate their internal publics. When employees feel good about their company, this positive attitude spills over to external publics.

Exhibit 4.2 Ronald McDonald House Charities® (RMHC®) Canada recognizes the importance of community publics. At the cornerstone of RMHC is Ronald McDonald House®. The 14 Ronald McDonald Houses play a vital role in communities across Canada, providing a home-away-from-home for out-of-town families of children with serious illnesses being treated at a nearby children's hospital.

Hand-out/OEUVRE DES MANOIRS RONALD MCDONALD/Newscom

A company can prepare marketing plans for these major publics as well as for its customer markets. Suppose the company wants a specific response from a particular public, such as goodwill, favourable word of mouth, or donations of time or money. The company would have to design an offer to this public that is attractive enough to produce the desired response.

Customers

As we've emphasized throughout, customers are the most important actors in the company's microenvironment. The aim of the entire value delivery system is to serve target customers and create strong relationships with them. The company might target any or all of five types of customer markets. *Consumer markets* consist of individuals and households that buy goods and services for personal consumption. *Business markets* buy goods and services for further processing or for use in their production process, whereas *reseller markets* buy goods and services to resell at a profit. *Government markets* are made up of government agencies that buy goods and services to produce public services or transfer the goods and services to others who need them. Finally, *international markets* consist of these buyers in other countries, including consumers, producers, resellers, and governments. Each market type has special characteristics that call for careful study by the seller.

The Company's Macroenvironment

The company and all of the other actors operate in a larger macroenvironment of forces that shape opportunities and pose threats to the company. Figure 4.2 shows the six major forces in the company's macroenvironment. In the remaining sections of this chapter, we examine these forces and show how they affect marketing plans.

Demographic Environment

Demography is the study of human populations in terms of size, density, location, age, gender, race, occupation, and other statistics. The demographic environment is of major

Demography
The study of human populations in terms of size, density, location, age, gender, race, occupation, and other statistics.

FIGURE 4.2 Major Forces in the Company's Macroenvironment

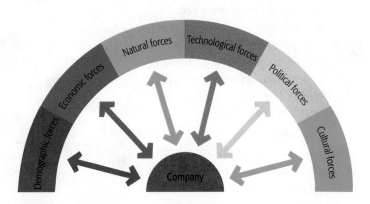

interest to marketers because it involves people, and people make up markets. The world population is growing at an explosive rate. It now exceeds 6.9 billion people and will grow to more than 8 billion by the year 2030.[4] The world's large and highly diverse population poses both opportunities and challenges.

Changes in the world demographic environment have major implications for business. Therefore, marketers keep a close eye on demographic trends and developments in their markets. They analyze changing age and family structures, geographic population shifts, educational characteristics, and population diversity. Here, we discuss the most important demographic trends in Canada.

Changing Age Structure of the Population The Canadian population exceeded 33.4 million in 2011 and is expected to reach between 40.1 and 47.7 million by 2036.[5] The single most important demographic trend in Canada is the changing age structure of the population. The Canadian population contains several generational groups. Here, we discuss the three largest groups—the Baby Boomers, Generation X, and the Millennials—and their impact on today's marketing strategies.

THE BABY BOOMERS The post–World War II baby boom, which began in 1947 and ran through 1966, produced 9.8 million **Baby Boomers** in Canada. Although there was a baby boom in both Canada and the United States, Canadian marketers have to recognize that our baby boom was unique. It started later than the American version (1947 versus 1946) and lasted longer (the American boom ended in 1964; the Canadian boom continued until 1966). While the American baby boom resulted in 3.5 children per family, the Canadian boom produced an average of 4 children. Furthermore, the baby boom was not a worldwide phenomenon. Among the other developed countries, only Australia and New Zealand experienced the same expansion in the birth rate. In Europe, there was no baby boom, and in Japan, the birth rate declined during our baby boom years, which explains why these countries have a higher proportion of older people in their societies.[6]

After years of prosperity, free spending, and saving little, the recent recession hit many Baby Boomers hard, especially the pre-retirement boomers. A sharp decline in stock prices and home values has eaten into their nest eggs and retirement prospects. As a result, many Boomers are now spending more carefully and planning to work longer.

However, although they might now be feeling the pinch of the weakened economy, the Baby Boomers are still the wealthiest generation in Canadian history. Today's Baby Boomers account for about one-third of Canada's population and control over 50 percent of the country's wealth. As they reach their peak earning and spending years, the Boomers will continue to constitute a lucrative market for financial services, new housing and

Baby Boomers
The 9.8 million Canadians born during the baby boom following World War II and lasting until the mid-1960s.

home remodelling, travel and entertainment, eating out, health and fitness products, and just about everything else.

It would be a mistake to think of the older boomers as phasing out or slowing down. Today's boomers think young no matter how old they are. One study showed that boomers, on average, see themselves 12 years younger than they actually are. And rather than viewing themselves as phasing out, they see themselves as entering new life phases. The more active boomers—sometimes called zoomers, or baby boomers with zip—have no intention of abandoning their youthful lifestyles as they age. "It is time to throw out the notion that the only things marketable to [the older boomers] are chiropractic mattresses, arthritis drugs, and [staid] cruises," says one marketer. "Boomers have sought the fountain of youth through all stages of life and have incorporated aspects of play and fun into everything from careers to cars."[7]

GENERATION X The baby boom was followed by a "birth dearth," creating another generation of 7 million Canadians born between 1967 and 1976. Author Douglas Coupland calls them **Generation X** because they lie in the shadow of the Boomers and lack obvious distinguishing characteristics.

Generation X
The 7 million Canadians born between 1967 and 1976 in the "birth dearth" following the baby boom.

Considerably smaller that the boomer generation that precedes them and the Millennials who follow, the Generation Xers are a sometimes overlooked consumer group. Although they seek success, they are less materialistic; they prize experience, not acquisition. For many of the Gen-Xers who are parents, family comes first—both children and their aging parents— and career second. From a marketing standpoint, the Gen-Xers are a more skeptical bunch. They tend to research products before they consider a purchase, preferring quality over quantity, and they tend to be less receptive to overt marketing pitches.

The Gen-Xers have grown up and are now taking over. They are increasingly displacing the lifestyles, culture, and values of the Baby Boomers. They are moving up in their careers, and many are proud homeowners with young, growing families. They are the most educated generation to date, and they possess hefty annual purchasing power. They spend 62 percent more on housing, 50 percent more on apparel, and 27 percent more on entertainment than the average. However, like the Baby Boomers, the Gen-Xers now face growing economic pressures. Like almost everyone else these days, they are spending more carefully.[8]

Still, with so much potential, many companies are focusing on Gen-Xers as an important target segment. For example, Mountain Equipment Co-op (MEC), the largest retail co-operative in Canada, appeals to the Gen X consumers—those who value family, life experience, and environmental sustainability. Celebrating its fortieth year in operation in 2011, MEC has grown to service nearly 3.3 million members worldwide. With stores in 15 Canadian cities and worldwide catalogue sales, the company has become Canada's leading supplier of quality outdoor gear, clothing, and camping equipment, surpassing $261 million in annual sales. It promotes itself

Courtesy of Mountain Equipment Co-op

Exhibit 4.3 Targeting Gen-Xers: MEC has been highly successful in serving a segment of Gen-Xers who value family, life experiences, and environmental sustainability.

as an ethical company through its commitment to green building, community grants, ethical purchasing, product sustainability, and promotion of Canada-wide parks and protected areas.[9]

Millennials (or Generation Y)
The 10.4 million children of the Canadian Baby Boomers, born between 1977 and 2000.

MILLENNIALS   Both the Baby Boomers and Gen-Xers will one day be passing the reins to the **Millennials** (also called **Generation Y** or the echo boomers). Born between 1977 and 2000, these children of the Baby Boomers number 10.4 million, dwarfing the Gen-Xers and larger even than the Baby Boomer segment. This group includes several age cohorts: *tweens* (aged 9–12), *teens* (13–18), and *young adults* (19–32). The Millennials make up a huge and attractive market.[10]

One thing that all of the Millennials have in common is their utter fluency and comfort with digital technology. They don't just embrace technology; it's a way of life. The Millennials were the first generation to grow up in a world filled with computers, cell-phones, satellite TV, iPods and iPads, and online social networks. As a result, they engage with brands in an entirely new way, such as with mobile or social media. "They tend to expect one-to-one communication with brands," says one analyst, "and embrace the ability to share the good and bad about products and services with friends and strangers."[11]

Rather than having mass marketing messages pushed at them, the Millennials prefer to seek out information and engage in two-way brand conversations. Thus, reaching them effectively requires creative marketing approaches. Consider how the New Democratic Party of Canada (NDP) succeeded in reaching this group:

In 2011, led by Jack Layton, the NDP soared to Official Opposition status for the first time in history. How was this accomplished? A big part of this success was the personality of Layton himself, but it also had a lot to do with how the party reached Canada's younger voters. While the NDP did not make a concerted effort to appeal to the youth vote during the campaign, its message of social equality, environmentalism, and health care spoke directly to the concerns of youth. And that message reached young voters in several ways. For example, all print ads contained QR codes that linked to online information. The party used Twitter, Facebook, and events streamed live on NDP.ca. By texting "NDP" to a designated number, voters could hear a message from Jack Layton detailing his campaign promises. And an iPhone app allowed voters to use their smartphones to get more information on the campaign.

Shortly after the federal election, the NDP were forced to choose a new leader after Jack Layton passed away. This time around, the party intentionally reached out to Canada's youth to make their voice heard. The social media surge surrounding the leadership campaign recognized that "today's youth don't hurl their political messages from the foot of Parliament Hill." They do it online. The NDP built on its ability to attract young voters to its campaigns, and so the leadership convention reflected its young demographic and the way in which youth communicate political messages. The hashtag that the party promoted, #ndpldr, was flooded with messages from supporters in all camps, making it one of the top trending topics on Twitter in Canada for most of the day. The names of the candidates were also trending during their time on stage during the convention, as were #Layton and the words "Jack Layton" ahead of the tribute to the party's former leader. But the real power of social media was evident during 29-year-old candidate Niki Ashton's speech to delegates. The online discussion made "Niki Ashton" a trending topic worldwide. When Toronto's CP24.com broke the news to Ashton, her response was "Holy sh**! Really? That's awesome!" When asked what she would do next she said, "I'm going to tweet about it, of course!" Ashton said it's not only about using social media, but also about the language that youth use. "We are a progressive party that wants to engage young people and we need to take on this new way of doing politics."[12]

Exhibit 4.4 The NDP's policies and presence on social media resonated with Canadian youth, whose vote helped the party win Official Opposition status in 2011, and elected Tom Mulcair as its new leader in 2012.

Sean Kilpatrick, Associated Press

GENERATIONAL MARKETING   Do marketers need to create separate products and marketing programs for each generation? Some experts warn that marketers need to be careful about turning off one generation each time they craft a product or message that appeals effectively to another. Others caution that each generation spans decades of time and many socio-economic levels. For example, marketers often split the Baby Boomers into three smaller groups—leading-edge boomers, core boomers, and trailing-edge boomers—each with its own beliefs and behaviours. Similarly, as mentioned above, they split the Millennials into tweens, teens, and young adults.

Thus, marketers need to form more precise age-specific segments within each group. More important, defining people by their birth date may be less effective than segmenting them by their lifestyle, life stage, or the common values they seek in the products they buy. We will discuss many other ways to segment markets in Chapter 7.

The Changing Canadian Household   When one uses the term *household*, a stereotype of the typical family living in the suburbs with its two children may leap to mind. However, this stereotype is far from accurate. The 2011 census reveals some interesting trends. For example, there is a growing "crowded nest" syndrome. About 42 percent of young Canadians aged 20 to 29 now live with their parents. There are almost 9.4 million families in Canada, but fewer are having children. In fact, the 2006 census marked the first time there were more census families without children than with children during the past 20 years, and this trend continued in 2011. The 2011 Census counted more one-person households than couple households with children for the first time, and the average size of the Canadian family now stands at 2.9 persons. Canada also experienced growth in diverse family structures including common-law marriages, same-sex couples, and blended families.[13] Given these trends, marketers must increasingly consider the distinctive needs and buying habits of these non-traditional households, because they are now growing more rapidly than traditional ones.

Responsibility for household tasks and the care of children is also changing. There are now more dual-income families as more and more women enter the workforce. Today women account for more than 50 percent of the Canadian workforce. The employment rate of women with children has grown particularly sharply in the past two decades, especially for those with preschool-aged children. In 2009, 72.9 percent of women with children under the age of 16 living at home were employed, more than double the figure of 1976.[14]

The significant number of women in the workforce has spawned the child day-care business and increased the consumption of career-oriented women's clothing, convenience foods, financial services, and time-saving services. Royal Caribbean targets time-crunched working moms with budget-friendly family vacations that are easy to plan and certain to wow the family. Royal Caribbean estimates that, although vacations are a joint decision, 80 percent of all trips are planned and booked by women—moms who are pressed for time, whether they work or not. "We want to make sure that you're the hero, that when your family comes on our ship, it's going to be a great experience for all of them," says a senior marketer at Royal Caribbean, "and that you, Mom, who has done all the planning and scheduling, get to enjoy that vacation."[15]

Geographic Shifts in Population   The population of Canada grew by approximately 4.7 percent between 2008 and 2012. As Table 4.1 shows, however, growth rates across all provinces and territories are not uniform. Western Canada and two of our three territories experienced the highest growth rates. Growth was also near the national average for PEI, Ontario, and Quebec, and lowest in New Brunswick, Nova Scotia, and Newfoundland and Labrador. However all provinces and territories, with the exception of the North West Territories, saw an increase in population from 2008 and 2012, which may be an indication of less interprovincial movement of Canadians over the past four years.

TABLE 4.1 Canada's Population

	2008 (thousands)	2012 (thousands)	Change (%)
Canada	33 317.7	34 880.5	4.7
Newfoundland and Labrador	506.4	512.7	1.2
Prince Edward Island	139.5	146.1	4.7
Nova Scotia	937.5	948.7	1.2
New Brunswick	746.9	756.0	1.2
Quebec	7750.5	8054.8	3.9
Ontario	12 932.5	13 505.9	4.4
Manitoba	1205.7	1267.0	5.1
Saskatchewan	1013.8	1080.0	6.5
Alberta	3592.2	3873.7	7.8
British Columbia	4384.3	4622.6	5.4
Yukon	33.1	36.1	9.1
Northwest Territories	43.7	43.3	−1.0
Nunavut	31.6	33.7	6.7

Source: "Population by Year, by Province and Territory," www.statcan.gc.ca /tables-tableaux/sum-som/l01/cst01/demo02a-eng.htm. Statistics Canada, 2013. Reproduced with the permission of the Minister of Public Works and Government Services Canada, 2010.

In fact, a recent article in the *Globe and Mail* suggests that this may be exactly what is happening in Canada. Interprovincial migration is driven by differences in unemployment rates and wages, and the oil boom in Alberta has lured many Canadians westward. However, while Alberta has seen a bump in interprovincial migration in recent years, flows between provinces remain lower than they were in the 1970s and 1980s. A recent study by Ipsos Reid found that only 20 percent of Canadians were willing to relocate to another city for a few years, even with a pay hike of at least 10 percent and all moving expenses covered. Moving costs are often cited as the single biggest reason preventing Canadians from moving, but also some professional qualifications are not transferrable between provinces, meaning that people would have to get recertified when they move. As well, many Canadians are now caring for aging parents or younger children, making moving to another province more difficult.[16]

Canada's cities are changing as well. Canadian cities are often surrounded by large suburban areas. Statistics Canada calls these combinations of urban and suburban populations Census Metropolitan Areas (CMAs). Census data for 2011 showed that 23 123 441 people, or 69.1 percent of the total population, lived in one of Canada's 33 CMAs. The three largest CMAs—Toronto, Montreal, and Vancouver—accounted for 35.0 percent of the total Canadian population. The two fastest growing CMAs were both in Alberta: Calgary, where the population rose 12.6 percent, and Edmonton, where it increased 12.1 percent.[17] The shift in where people live has also caused a shift in where they work. For example, the migration toward metropolitan and suburban areas has resulted in a rapid increase in the number of people who telecommute—that is, work at home or in a remote office, and conduct their business by phone, fax, modem, or the Internet. This trend, in turn, has created a booming SOHO (small office/home office) market. An increasing number of people are working from home with the help of electronic conveniences such as PCs, smartphones, and broadband Internet access. Statistics Canada reported that roughly 19 percent of Canada's workforce worked from home in 2008. This represents more than 1.75 million employees and 1.84 million self-employed individuals.[18]

Many marketers are actively courting the lucrative telecommuting market. For example, WebEx, the web-conferencing division of Cisco, helps overcome the isolation that often accompanies telecommuting. With WebEx, people can meet and collaborate online via computer or smartphone, no matter what their work location. Additionally, companies such as Regus or Grind rent out fully equipped shared office space by the day or month for telecommuters and others who work away from the main office.[19]

A Better-Educated, More Professional Population The Canadian population is becoming better educated. Statistics Canada reported that in 2011, 89 percent of Canadians had completed high school and 64 percent of Canadians aged 25 to 64 had completed postsecondary education (university, college, or trade school).[20] The rising number of educated people will increase the demand for quality products, books, travel, computers, and Internet services.

Courtesy of Grind

Exhibit 4.5 **Serving the telecommuter market:** Companies such as Grind rent out shared office space by the day or month to telecommuters and others who work away from the main office.

Higher education is a must to maintain a skilled labour force in Canada. It is estimated that roughly two-thirds of all job openings between 2007 and 2017 will be in occupations requiring postsecondary education (university, college, or apprenticeship training) or in management occupations. These jobs will cover a wide range of diverse options, from nursing to construction. In fact, the Canadian Chamber of Commerce predicts that over the next decade there will be labour shortfalls of 163 000 in construction, 130 000 in oil and gas, 60 000 in nursing, 37 000 in trucking, 22 000 in the hotel industry, and 10 000 in the steel trades. The Chamber also lists the skilled labour shortage as the number one barrier to increasing the country's international competitiveness.[21]

Increasing Diversity Countries vary in their ethnic and racial makeup. At one extreme is Japan, where almost everyone is Japanese. At the other extreme are countries such as Canada and the United States, with people from virtually all nations who have mixed together, but have maintained their diversity by retaining and valuing important ethnic and cultural differences. Anyone who has walked the streets of Vancouver, Montreal, Calgary, or Toronto will immediately understand that visible minorities in Canada are a force to be reckoned with. More than 5 million Canadians (16 percent) identified themselves as visible minorities in the 2006 census and more than 200 ethnic origins were reported. Between 2001 and 2006, the visible minority population increased five times faster than the population as a whole, mainly due to immigration. According to Statistics Canada's population projections, members of visible minority groups could account for over 30 percent of the total population by 2031.[22]

Most large companies—from Procter & Gamble (P&G), Walmart, Air Canada, and TD Bank to Levi Strauss and TELUS—now target specially designed products, ads, and promotions to one or more of these groups. For example, TELUS has been successfully marketing their service to Chinese Canadians since 2000 and operates two websites dedicated to Chinese and south Asian communities: chinese.telus.com and desi.telus.com.

Diversity goes beyond ethnic heritage. For example, many major companies explicitly target gay and lesbian consumers. While the exact percentage of Canadians who

Courtesy of TELUS

Exhibit 4.6 Firms such as TELUS know the importance of cultural sensitivity and building meaningful connections with people of different ethnic backgrounds.

identify themselves as lesbian, gay, bisexual, and transgender (LGBT) is unknown, Statistics Canada now identifies same-sex couples in the census. The 2011 census enumerated 64 575 same-sex couples in Canada, up 42.4 percent from 45 300 in 2006.[23] A US-based study by Simmons Research of readers of the National Gay Newspaper Guild's 12 publications found that, compared to the average American, LGBT respondents are 12 times more likely to be in professional jobs, almost twice as likely to own a vacation home, eight times more likely to own a notebook computer, and twice as likely to own individual stocks. More than two-thirds have graduated from college or university, and 21 percent hold a master's degree.[24]

As a result of TV shows such as *Modern Family, Ugly Betty* and *The Ellen DeGeneres Show,* and Oscar-winning movies such as *Brokeback Mountain*, the LGBT (lesbian, gay, bisexual, and transgender) community has increasingly emerged into the public eye. A number of media now provide companies with access to this market. For example, Planet Out Inc. offers several successful magazines (*Out,* the *Advocate, Out Traveler*) and websites (Gay.com and PlanetOut.com). Canada's only digital television channel specifically targeted at the gay and lesbian community, OUTtv, was launched nationally in 2001. By 2011, it became Canada's fastest-growing digital cable channel and had 1 million subscribers.

Companies in a wide range of industries are now targeting the LGBT community with gay-specific marketing efforts. For example, American Airlines has a dedicated LGBT sales team, sponsors gay community events, and offers a special gay-oriented website (www.aa.com/rainbow) that features travel deals, an e-newsletter, podcasts, and a gay events calendar. The airline's focus on gay consumers has earned it double-digit revenue growth from the LGBT community each year for more than a decade. And Blue Flame Ventures Inc. offers seminars and marketing consulting services to Canadian tourism businesses to better service the estimated $7 billion LGBT tourism market in Canada.[25]

Another attractive diversity segment is the 14.3 percent of the Canadian population (4.4 million) who have some form of disability. This group has considerable spending power, as well as great need for tailored products and services. Not only do they value services that make daily life easier, but they are also a growing market for travel, sports, and other leisure-oriented products. The Canadian Abilities Foundation provides a wealth of information ranging from products and services to housing and travel advice on its website (www.abilities.ca).

How are companies trying to reach consumers with disabilities? Many marketers now recognize that the worlds of people with disabilities and those without disabilities are one and the same. Marketers such as McDonald's, Verizon Wireless, Sears, Nike, and Honda have featured people with disabilities in their mainstream advertising. For instance, Samsung and Nike sign endorsement deals with Paralympic athletes and feature them in advertising.

BONNY MAKAREWICZ/EPA/Newscom

Exhibit 4.7 Targeting consumers with disabilities: Samsung features people with disabilities in its mainstream advertising and signs endorsement deals with Paralympic athletes.

Other companies use specially targeted media to reach this attractive segment. The UK website DisabledGo.com reaches people with disabilities through its website and social networking sites, including Facebook and Twitter. The site offers relevant information on everything from healthcare to education, jobs, and travel tips. Several large marketers, including Marks and Spencer, Mazda, Kia, and Ford, advertise on the site.

As the population in Canada grows more diverse, successful marketers will continue to diversify their marketing programs to take advantage of opportunities in fast-growing segments.

Economic Environment

Markets require buying power as well as people. The **economic environment** consists of factors that affect consumer purchasing power and spending patterns. Marketers must pay close attention to major trends and consumer spending patterns both across and within their world markets.

Nations vary greatly in their levels and distribution of income. Some countries have *industrial economies*, which constitute rich markets for many different kinds of goods. At the other extreme are *subsistence economies*—they consume most of their own agricultural and industrial output and offer few market opportunities. In between are *developing economies*—which can offer outstanding marketing opportunities for the right kinds of products.

Economic environment
Factors that affect consumer buying power and spending patterns.

Consider India with its population of more than 1.1 billion people. In the past, only India's elite could afford to buy a car. In fact, only one in seven Indians now owns one. But recent dramatic changes in India's economy have produced a growing middle class and rapidly rising incomes. Now, to meet the new demand, European, North American, and Asian automakers are introducing smaller, more-affordable vehicles into India. But they'll have to find a way to compete with India's Tata Motors, which has unveiled the least expensive car ever in this market, the Tata Nano. Dubbed "the people's car," the Nano sells for only 100 000 rupees (about US$2500). It can seat four passengers, gets 50 miles per gallon (4.7L/100 km), and travels at a top speed of 60 miles (96 km) per hour. The ultra-low-cost car is designed to be India's Model T—the car that puts the developing nation on wheels. "Can you imagine a car within the reach of all?" asks a Nano advertisement. "Now you can," comes the answer. Tata hopes to sell 1 million of these vehicles a year.[26]

Following are some of the major economic trends in Canada.

Exhibit 4.8 **Economic environment:** To capture India's growing middle class, Tata Motors introduced the small, affordable Tata Nano. "Can you imagine a car within the reach of all?" asks this advertisement. "Now you can."

Changes in Income and Spending Economic factors can have a dramatic effect on consumer spending and buying behaviour. For example, until fairly recently, Canadian consumers spent freely, fuelled by income growth, a boom in the stock market, rapid increases in housing values, and other economic good fortune. They bought and bought, seemingly without caution, amassing record levels of debt. However, the free spending and high expectations of those days were dashed by the worldwide recession. Says one economist, "For a generation that has substituted rising home equity and stock prices for personal savings, the . . . economic meltdown has been psychologically wrenching after a quarter century of unquestioned prosperity."[27]

As a result, consumers have now adopted a back-to-basics sensibility in their lifestyles and spending patterns that will likely persist for years to come. They are buying less, and they are looking for greater value in the things that they do buy. In turn, *value marketing* has become the watchword for many marketers. Marketers in all industries are looking for ways to offer today's more financially cautious buyers greater value—just the right combination of product quality and good service at a fair price.

You'd expect value pitches from the sellers of everyday products. For example, as Target has shifted emphasis toward the "Pay Less" side of its "Expect More. Pay Less." slogan, the once-chic headlines at the Target.com website have been replaced by more practical appeals such as "Our lowest prices of the season," "Fun, sun, save," and "Free shipping, every day." However, these days, even luxury-brand marketers are emphasizing good value. For instance, upscale car brand Infiniti now promises to "make luxury affordable."

INCOME DISTRIBUTION Marketers should pay attention to income distribution as well as income levels. Canadians in the top 5 percent of wage earners account for approximately 25 percent of the total income earned. According to the 2006 census, the median earnings among the top 20 percent of full-time workers increased over 16 percent, while the median earnings among those in the bottom one-fifth of the distribution fell by over 20 percent. In Canada, the rich are getting richer, the poor are getting poorer, and the earnings of the middle class are stagnating. Canadians are definitely feeling the effects of the recent recession. From 2009 to 2010, only 52.8 percent of Canadians saw an increase in their after-tax household income, compared to 62.4 percent from 2006 to 2007, despite the fact that the cost of living continues to rise. Furthermore, roughly 3 million Canadians (including 546 000 children) lived below the poverty line in 2010.[28]

This distribution of income has created a tiered market. Many companies—such as Holt Renfrew and La Maison Simons department stores—aggressively target the affluent. Others—such as Giant Tiger and Dollarama stores—target those with more modest means. Still other companies tailor their marketing offers across a range of markets, from the affluent to the less affluent. For example, Ford offers cars ranging from the low-priced Ford Fiesta, starting at $13 999, to the luxury Lincoln Navigator SUV, starting at $74 300.

Changes in major economic variables such as income, cost of living, interest rates, and savings and borrowing patterns have a large impact on the marketplace. Companies watch these variables by using economic forecasting. Businesses do not have to be wiped out by an economic downturn or caught short in a boom. With adequate warning, they can take advantage of changes in the economic environment.

Natural Environment

Natural environment
Natural resources that are needed as inputs by marketers or that are affected by marketing activities.

The **natural environment** involves the natural resources that are needed as inputs by marketers or that are affected by marketing activities. Environmental concerns have grown steadily during the past three decades. In many cities around the world, air and water pollution have reached dangerous levels. World concern continues to mount about the possibilities of global warming, and many environmentalists fear that we soon will be buried in our own trash.

Marketers should be aware of several trends in the natural environment. The first involves growing *shortages of raw materials*. Air and water may seem to be infinite resources, but some groups see long-run dangers. Air pollution chokes many of the world's large cities; Great Lakes water levels are low, causing problems in many Canadian interior port cities; and water shortages are already a big problem in some parts of the world. By 2030, more than one in three of the world's population will not have enough water to drink.[29] Renewable resources, such as forests and food, also have to be used wisely. Nonrenewable resources, such as oil, coal, and various minerals, pose a serious problem. Firms making products that require these scarce resources face large cost increases, even if the materials remain available.

A second environmental trend is *increased pollution*. Industry will almost always damage the quality of the natural environment. Consider the disposal of chemical and nuclear wastes; the dangerous mercury levels in the ocean; the quantity of chemical pollutants in the soil and food supply; and the littering of the environment with nonbiodegradable bottles, plastics, and other packaging materials.

A third trend is *increased government intervention* in natural resource management. The governments of different countries vary in their concern and efforts to promote a clean environment. Some, such as the German government, vigorously pursue environmental quality. Others, especially many poorer nations, do little about pollution, largely because they lack the needed funds or political will. Even the richer nations lack the vast funds and political accord needed to mount a worldwide environmental effort. The general hope is that companies around the world will accept more social responsibility, and that less expensive devices can be found to control and reduce pollution.

The Canadian government passed the Environmental Protection Act in 1989. This act established stringent pollution-control measures as well as the means for their enforcement, including fines as high as $1 million if regulations are violated. In the United States, the Environmental Protection Agency (EPA) was created in 1970 to set and enforce pollution standards and to conduct pollution research. In the future, companies doing business in Canada and the United States can expect continued strong controls from government and pressure groups. Instead of opposing regulation, marketers should help develop solutions to the material and energy problems facing the world.

Concern for the natural environment has spawned the so-called green movement. In 2008, the Canadian Standards Association published guidelines for the business community to ensure that their environmental advertising and labelling was not false and misleading.[30] Today, enlightened companies go beyond what government regulations dictate. They are developing strategies and practices that support **environmental sustainability**—an effort to create a world economy that the planet can support indefinitely.

Many companies are responding to consumer demands with more environmentally responsible products. Other companies are developing recyclable or biodegradable packaging, recycled materials and components, better pollution controls, and more energy-efficient operations. For example, PepsiCo—which owns businesses ranging from Frito Lay and Pepsi-Cola to Quaker, Gatorade, and Tropicana—is working to dramatically reduce its environmental footprint.

Environmental sustainability Developing strategies and practices that create a world economy that the planet can support indefinitely.

> PepsiCo markets hundreds of products that are grown, produced, and consumed worldwide. Making and distributing these products requires water, electricity, and fuel. In 2007, the company set as its goal to reduce water consumption by 20 percent, electricity consumption by 20 percent, and fuel consumption by 25 percent per unit of production by 2015. It's already well on its way to meeting these goals. For example, a solar-panel field now generates power for three-quarters of the heat used in Frito-Lay's Modesto, California, SunChips plant. A wind turbine now supplies more than two-thirds of the power at PepsiCo's beverage plant in Mamandur, India. On the packaging front, PepsiCo recently introduced new half-litre bottles of its Lipton iced tea, Tropicana juice, Aquafina FlavorSplash, and Aquafina Alive beverages that

AP Images/Mary Altaffer

Exhibit 4.9 **Environmental sustainability:** PepsiCo is working to reduce its environmental footprint. For example, a solar-panel field now generates three-quarters of the heat used in Frito-Lay's Modesto, California, SunChips plant, and SunChips themselves come in the world's first 100 percent compostable package.

Technological environment
Forces that create new technologies, creating new product and market opportunities.

contain 20 percent less plastic than the original packaging. Aquafina has trimmed the amount of plastic used in its bottles by 35 percent since 2002, saving 50 million pounds of plastic annually.[31]

Companies today are looking to do more than just good deeds. More and more, they are recognizing the link between a healthy ecology and a healthy economy. They are learning that environmentally responsible actions can also be good business.

Technological Environment

The **technological environment** is perhaps the most dramatic force now shaping our destiny. Technology has released such wonders as antibiotics, robotic surgery, miniaturized electronics, laptop computers, and the Internet. It also has released such horrors as nuclear missiles, chemical weapons, and assault rifles. It has released such mixed blessings as the automobile, television, and credit cards. Our attitude toward technology depends on whether we are more impressed with its wonders or its blunders.

New technologies can offer exciting opportunities for marketers. For example, what would you think about having tiny little transmitters implanted in all of the products you buy that would allow tracking products from their point of production through use and disposal? On the one hand, it would provide many advantages to both buyers and sellers. On the other hand, it could be a bit scary. Either way, it's already happening:

> Envision a world in which every product contains a tiny transmitter, loaded with information. As you stroll through supermarket aisles, shelf sensors detect your selections and beam ads to your shopping cart screen, offering special deals on related products. As your cart fills, scanners detect that you might be buying for a dinner party; the screen suggests a wine to go with the meal you've planned. When you leave the store, exit scanners total up your purchases and automatically charge them to your credit card. At home, readers track what goes into and out of your pantry, updating your shopping list when stocks run low. For Sunday dinner, you pop a Butterball turkey into your "smart oven," which follows instructions from an embedded chip and cooks the bird to perfection. Seem far-fetched? Not really. In fact, it might soon become a reality, thanks to radio-frequency identification (RFID) transmitters that can be embedded in the products you buy.

Many firms are already using RFID technology to track products through various points in the distribution channel. For example, Walmart has strongly encouraged suppliers shipping products to its distribution centers to apply RFID tags to their pallets. So far, more than 600 Walmart suppliers are doing so. And clothing retailer American Apparel uses RFID to manage inventory in many of its retail stores. Every stocked item carries an RFID tag, which is scanned at the receiving docks as the item goes into inventory. American Apparel puts only one of each item on the store floor at a time. When the item is sold, a point-of-sale RFID reader alerts the inventory system and prompts employees to bring a replacement onto the floor. Another RFID reader located between the stockroom and the store floor checks to see that this was done. In all, the system creates inventory efficiencies and ensures that the right items are always on the sales floor. As a result, American Apparel stores with RFID systems average 14 percent higher sales but 15 percent lower stockroom inventories than other stores. And the chain's RFID stores require

20 to 30 percent fewer staff because employees don't have to spend five or more hours a day doing manual inventory checks.[32]

The technological environment changes rapidly. Think of all of today's common products that were not available 100 years ago, or even 30 years ago. John A. Macdonald did not know about automobiles, airplanes, radios, or the electric light. William Lyon Mackenzie King did not know about xerography, synthetic detergents, tape recorders, birth control pills, jet engines, or Earth satellites. John Diefenbaker did not know about personal computers, cellphones, the Internet, or Google.

Exhibit 4.10 **Technological environment:** Envision a world in which every product contains a transmitter loaded with information. In fact, it's already happening on the back of RFID product labels like this one at Walmart.

New technologies create new markets and opportunities. However, every new technology replaces an older technology. Transistors hurt the vacuum-tube industry, xerography hurt the carbon-paper business, CDs hurt phonograph records, digital photography hurt the film business, and MP3 players and digital downloads are hurting the CD business. When old industries fought or ignored new technologies, their businesses declined. Thus, marketers should watch the technological environment closely. Companies that do not keep up will soon find their products outdated. And they will miss new product and market opportunities.

As products and technology become more complex, the public needs to know that these are safe. Canada has a complex web of departments and regulations devoted to issues associated with product safety. For example, Agriculture and Agri-Food Canada and the Canadian Food Inspection Agency monitor the safety of food products. The Department of Justice Canada oversees the Consumer Packaging and Labelling Act, the Food and Drug Act, and the Hazardous Products Act. Health Canada also has a food safety and product safety division. Transport Canada governs vehicle recalls. Such regulations have resulted in much higher research costs and in longer times between new-product ideas and their introduction. Marketers should be aware of these regulations when applying new technologies and developing new products.

Political and Social Environment LO4

Marketing decisions are strongly affected by developments in the political environment. The **political environment** consists of laws, government agencies, and pressure groups that influence or limit various organizations and individuals in a given society.

Legislation Regulating Business Even the most liberal advocates of free-market economies agree that the system works best with at least some regulation. Well-conceived regulation can encourage competition and ensure fair markets for goods and services. Thus, governments develop *public policy* to guide commerce—sets of laws and regulations that limit business for the good of society as a whole. Almost every marketing activity is subject to a wide range of laws and regulations.

INCREASING LEGISLATION Legislation affecting business around the world has increased steadily over the years. Canada has many laws covering issues such as competition, fair trade practices, environmental protection, product safety, truth in advertising, consumer privacy, packaging and labelling, pricing, and other important areas (see Table 4.2). The

Political environment
Laws, government agencies, and pressure groups that influence and limit various organizations and individuals in a given society.

Marc F. Henning/Alamy

TABLE 4.2 Major Federal Legislation Affecting Marketing

The Competition Act is a major legislative act affecting the marketing activities of companies in Canada. Specific sections and the relevant areas are as follows:

- Section 34: Pricing—Forbids suppliers from charging different prices to competitors purchasing like quantities of goods (price discrimination). Forbids price-cutting that lessens competition (predatory pricing).
- Section 36: Pricing and Advertising—Forbids advertising prices that misrepresent the "usual" selling price (misleading price advertising).
- Section 38: Pricing—Forbids suppliers from requiring subsequent resellers to offer products at a stipulated price (resale price maintenance).
- Section 33: Mergers—Forbids mergers by which competition is, or is likely to be, lessened to the detriment of the interests of the public.

Other selected acts that have an impact on marketing activities are the following:

- National Trade Mark and True Labelling Act—Established the term *Canada Standard,* or *CS,* as a national trademark; requires certain commodities to be properly labelled or described in advertising for the purpose of indicating material content or quality.
- Consumer Packaging and Labelling Act—Provides a set of rules to ensure that full information is disclosed by the manufacturer, packer, or distributor. Requires that all prepackaged products bear the quantity in French and English in metric as well as traditional Canadian standard units of weight, volume, or measure.
- Motor Vehicle Safety Act—Establishes mandatory safety standards for motor vehicles.
- Food and Drug Act—Prohibits the advertisement and sale of adulterated or misbranded foods, cosmetics, and drugs.
- Personal Information Protection and Electronic Documents Act—Establishes rules to govern the collection, use, and disclosure of personal information that recognize the right of privacy of individuals. The law recognizes the needs of organizations to collect, use, or disclose personal information for appropriate purposes. (For full details of the act, see http://laws.justice.gc.ca/en/P-8.6.)

European Commission has been active in establishing a new framework of laws covering competitive behaviour, product standards, product liability, and commercial transactions for the nations of the European Union.

Understanding the public policy implications of a particular marketing activity is not a simple matter. For example, in Canada, many laws are created at the federal, provincial/territorial, and municipal levels, and these regulations often overlap. Moreover, regulations are constantly changing—what was allowed last year may now be prohibited, and what was prohibited may now be allowed. Marketers must work hard to keep up with changes in regulations and their interpretations.

Business legislation has been enacted for a number of reasons. The first is to *protect companies* from each other. Although business executives may praise competition, they sometimes try to neutralize it when it threatens them. So laws are passed to define and prevent unfair competition.

The second purpose of government regulation is to *protect consumers* from unfair business practices. Some firms, if left alone, would make shoddy products, invade consumer privacy, tell lies in their advertising, and deceive consumers through their packaging and pricing. Unfair business practices have been defined and are enforced by various agencies.

The third purpose of government regulation is to *protect the interests of society* against unrestrained business behaviour. Profitable business activity does not always create a better quality of life. Regulation arises to ensure that firms take responsibility for the social costs of their production or products.

CHANGING GOVERNMENT AGENCY ENFORCEMENT   International marketers will encounter dozens, or even hundreds, of agencies set up to enforce trade policies and regulations. In Canada, several federal agencies, such as Health Canada, the Canadian Food Inspection Agency, Industry Canada, and the Canadian Environmental Assessment Agency, have been established. Because such government agencies have some discretion in enforcing the laws, they can have a major impact on a company's marketing performance.

New laws and their enforcement will continue to increase. Business executives must watch these developments when planning their products and marketing programs. Marketers need to know about the major laws protecting competition, consumers, and society. They need to understand these laws at the local, provincial/territorial, national, and international levels.

Increased Emphasis on Ethics and Socially Responsible Actions

Written regulations cannot possibly cover all potential marketing abuses, and existing laws are often difficult to enforce. However, beyond written laws and regulations, business is also governed by social codes and rules of professional ethics.

SOCIALLY RESPONSIBLE BEHAVIOUR   Enlightened companies encourage their managers to look beyond what the regulatory system allows and simply "do the right thing." These socially responsible firms actively seek out ways to protect the long-run interests of their consumers and the environment.

The recent rash of business scandals and increased concerns about the environment have created fresh interest in the issues of ethics and social responsibility. Almost every aspect of marketing involves such issues. Unfortunately, because these issues usually involve conflicting interests, well-meaning people can honestly disagree about the right course of action in a given situation. Thus, many industrial and professional trade associations have suggested codes of ethics. And more companies are now developing policies, guidelines, and other responses to complex social responsibility issues.

The boom in Internet marketing has created a new set of social and ethical issues. Critics worry most about online privacy issues. The amount of personal digital data available has exploded. Users, themselves, supply some of it. They voluntarily place highly private information on social networking sites such as Facebook or on genealogy sites, which are easily searched by anyone with a computer or smartphone.

However, much of the information is systematically developed by businesses seeking to learn more about their customers, often without consumers realizing that they are under the microscope. Legitimate businesses track consumers' Internet browsing and buying behaviour and collect, analyze, and share digital data from every move consumers make at their websites. Critics worry that companies may now know *too* much, and that some companies might use digital data to take unfair advantage of consumers. Although most companies fully disclose their Internet privacy policies, and most work to use data to benefit their customers, abuses do occur. As a result, consumer advocates and policymakers are taking action to protect consumer privacy.

CAUSE-RELATED MARKETING   To exercise their social responsibility and build more positive images, many companies are now linking themselves to worthwhile causes. These days, every product seems to be tied to some cause. Buy a pink mixer from KitchenAid and support breast cancer research. Purchase a special edition bottle of Dawn dishwashing detergent, and P&G will donate a dollar to help rescue and rehabilitate wildlife affected by oil spills. Go to Staples' DoSomething101 website or Facebook page and fill a virtual backpack with essential school supplies needed by school children living in poverty. Pay for these purchases with the right charge card and you can support a local cultural arts group or help fight heart disease.

In fact, some companies are founded entirely on cause-related missions. Under the concept of "value-led business" or "caring capitalism," their mission is to use business to make the world a better place. For example, TOMS Shoes was founded as a for-profit company—it wants to make money selling shoes. But the company has an equally important not-for-profit mission—putting shoes on the feet of needy children around the world. For every pair of shoes you buy from TOMS, the company will give another pair to a child in need on your behalf.

Cause-related marketing has become a primary form of corporate giving. It lets companies "do well by doing good" by linking purchases of the company's products or services with benefiting worthwhile causes or charitable organizations. At TOMS Shoes, the "do well" and "do good" missions go hand in hand. Beyond being socially admirable, the buy-one-give-one-away concept is also a good business proposition. "Giving not only makes you feel good, but it actually is a very good business strategy," says TOMS founder Blake Mycoskie. "Business and charity or public service don't have to be mutually exclusive. In fact, when they come together, they can be very powerful."[33]

Companies now sponsor hundreds of cause-related marketing campaigns each year. Many are backed by large budgets and a full complement of marketing activities. For example, PepsiCo's Pepsi Refresh Project awards tens of millions of dollars in grants to fund "refreshing ideas that will change the world." PepsiCo promotes the program with a full-blown multimedia campaign. More than a mere add-on cause-related marketing campaign, Pepsi Refresh puts social responsibility at the heart of Pepsi's positioning (see Marketing@Work 4.1).

Cause-related marketing has stirred some controversy. Critics worry that cause-related marketing is more a strategy for selling than a strategy for giving—that "cause-related" marketing is really "cause-exploitative" marketing. Thus, companies using cause-related marketing might find themselves walking a fine line between increased sales and an improved image, and facing charges of exploitation. For example, following the 2011 Japanese tsunami disaster, Microsoft's Bing search engine created a backlash when it posted a message on Twitter offering to donate $1 to Japan's relief efforts each time someone forwarded its message. The tweet set off a firestorm of complaints from Twitter users, who accused Bing of using the tragedy as a marketing opportunity. Microsoft quickly apologized.[34]

However, if handled well, cause-related marketing can greatly benefit both the company and the cause. The company gains an effective marketing tool while building a more positive public image. The charitable organization or cause gains greater visibility and important new sources of funding and support. Spending on cause-related marketing in the United States skyrocketed from only US$120 million in 1990 to more than US$1.7 billion by 2011.[35]

Cultural environment
Institutions and other forces that affect society's basic values, perceptions, preferences, and behaviours.

PR NEWSWIRE

Exhibit 4.11 **Cause-related marketing:** TOMS Shoes pledges: "No complicated formulas, it's simple . . . you buy a pair of TOMS and we give a pair to a child on your behalf." Here, TOMS founder and CEO Blake Mycoskie gives out shoes in Argentina.

Cultural Environment

The **cultural environment** is made up of institutions and other forces that affect a society's basic values, perceptions, preferences, and behaviours.

MARKETING@WORK 4.1

The Pepsi Refresh Project: What Does Your Brand Care About?

It seems that almost every brand is supporting some worthy cause these days, from promoting healthful living to curing cancer to ending poverty or world hunger. But the Pepsi Refresh Project is no mere cause-related marketing effort, added on to pay token homage to a borrowed cause. Instead, the Pepsi Refresh Project makes "doing good" a major element of the Pepsi brand's mission and positioning. Supported by a large budget and full complement of marketing activities, Pepsi Refresh promotes the concept of social responsibility as much as it promotes the Pepsi brand itself.

Through the Pepsi Refresh campaign, PepsiCo redefines its flagship brand not just as a soft drink but as an agent for world change. The project awards millions of dollars in grants to fund hundreds of worthwhile ideas by individuals and communities that will "refresh the world." "What do you care about?" asks one Pepsi Refresh ad. "Maybe it's green spaces. Or educational comic books. Maybe it's teaching kids to rock out. The Pepsi Refresh Project: Thousands of ideas. Millions in grants."

To obtain a Pepsi Refresh grant ranging from US$5000 to US$250 000, individuals and organizations go to the campaign's refresheverything.com website and propose ideas for how to make the world a better place. Then, consumers vote at the site for their favourite projects and Pepsi funds the winners. Last year, Pepsi accepted 1000 proposals each month in six different areas: health, arts and culture, food and shelter, the planet, neighborhoods, and education. In all, it awarded US$20 million to fund nearly 1000 projects.

The Pepsi Refresh Project not only delivers a new kind of social responsibility brand message, it delivers that message in a whole new, more social way. To engage people with the project, Pepsi is spreading the "do good" message though an integrated campaign that makes heavy use of big social networks like Facebook, Twitter,

and YouTube. It has also collaborated with Hulu to sponsor its first original series, the reality show "If I Can Dream." The Pepsi Refresh Project has even partnered with *Spin* magazine, music festival South by Southwest, and two indie bands in a web-based contest where music lovers vote between the two for their favourite band. Rock band Metric beat out Broken Social Scene for a US$100 000 grant that it gave to the Women's Funding Network.

Unlike many other cause-related marketing campaigns, Pepsi Refresh is not just an add-on that links a brand to a cause that is only peripherally relevant to the brand message. Rather, Pepsi Refresh is a fully integrated marketing campaign wrapped around Pepsi's unified "refresh your world" brand message. Beyond social media, the Pepsi Refresh Project utilizes spot ads on the major TV networks and cable channels, print ads, and a major PR effort. The campaign also employs a host of celebrity endorsers. Among others, Pepsi has recruited Demi Moore; NFL players Mark Sanchez, DeMarcus Ware, and Drew Brees; and

NASCAR veterans Jeff Gordon, Dale Earnhardt, Jr., and Jimmie Johnson to apply for grants and act as spokespeople in broadcast ads.

The projects funded by the Pepsi Refresh Project so far are almost too numerous to list. Many of the grant awards have been given to everyday people just trying to improve their own little corners of the world. In 2010, fifty-eight Canadian projects totalling nearly $1.2 million were funded, including $100 000 to Scouts Canada to send more children to summer camp, $25 000 to True North Aid to build a playground for children in Attawapiskat, $10 000 to the Alzheimer Society of York Region to provide music therapy to people with Alzheimer's disease, and $5000 to Colleen Caza of Windsor, Ontario, to distribute backpacks of food to needy children. "I'm proud of every idea we're supporting," says PepsiCo CEO Indra Nooyi, "but it's the simplicity of [these ideas that's] so innovative. You would never have thought that one simple thing could bring about [such] a big change in a community."

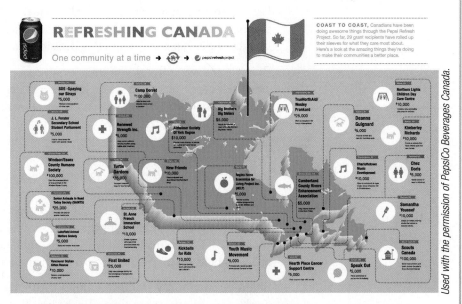

Exhibit 4.12 **Cause-related marketing:** The Pepsi Refresh Project isn't just an add-on that pays token homage to a borrowed cause. It makes "doing good" a major element of Pepsi's mission and positioning.

All of this "doing good" is admirable, but does it help sell Pepsi? After all, at the end of the day, Pepsi is in the soft drink business. In that regard, the Pepsi Refresh Project has had its share of doubters. As one social marketer states, "This is big, new, getting a lot of attention. It's impactful; it's innovative. [But] what the industry is talking about now is, is this a gamble that was worth taking in terms of a lift in sales? That's the holy grail."

After the first year of the Pepsi Refresh Project, the "sales lift" question was very much open to debate. During 2010, Pepsi and Diet Pepsi sales volumes dropped 4.8 percent and 5.2 percent, respectively, compared with a more modest industry-wide decline of 0.5 percent. Perhaps more important, Pepsi-Cola, the perennial number two soft drink brand behind Coca-Cola, dropped to number three behind Diet Coke. Even as its numbers dip, however, PepsiCo is not retreating from the good-works Pepsi Refresh Project. In fact, the company steadfastly insists that the project has surpassed its expectations. "It's a long-term play," says a Pepsi spokesperson. As a result, PepsiCo not only continued the campaign for a second year but also expanded it to other countries.

As evidence of the campaign's success, Pepsi points to impressive results in social media. Last year, consumers cast 75 million votes in awarding the US$20 million in grant funds. The number of Pepsi Facebook fans quadrupled to more than 1 million in just eight months. And whereas Pepsi used to get a Twitter tweet every five minutes or so, it now receives more tweets per minute than a person can read. PepsiCo has also developed a return-on-investment scorecard that ties different elements of the Pepsi Refresh campaign back to the health of the brand. Based on that harder analysis, the company is holding steady on its large Pepsi Refresh Project budget at the same time that it is boosting other mass-media spending for the brand.

Beyond the more tangible returns, the Pepsi Refresh Project has drawn wide attention and praise. For example, PepsiCo was named by ad industry publication *Advertising Age* as last year's runner-up "Marketer of the Year." PepsiCo CEO Nooyi received the Ad Council's Public Service Award for her commitment to social responsibility. And Pepsi bottlers assert that Refresh is a clear winner in terms of clout gained with local communities.

Regardless of where the Pepsi Refresh Project goes from here, PepsiCo and other observers will learn much from this sweeping, first-of-its-kind social responsibility campaign. Ana Maria Irazabal, director of marketing for Pepsi, wants the campaign to become the model of the future. "We want people to be aware that every time you drink a Pepsi you are actually supporting the Pepsi Refresh Project and ideas that are going to move this country forward. We may be the first to do something like this, but hopefully, we're not the last."[36]

Sources: Mike Esterl, "Pepsi Thirsty for a Comeback," *Wall Street Journal,* March 18, 2011, p. B5; Natalie Zmuda, "Pass or Fail, Pepsi's Refresh Will Be Case for Marketing Textbooks," *Advertising Age,* February 8, 2010, p. 1; Natalie Zmuda, "Who Are the Big Pepsi Refresh Winners? Local Bottlers and Community Groups," *Advertising Age,* November 1, 2010, p. 2; Natalie Zmuda, "Pepsi Expands Refresh Project: Social-Media Experiment Becomes Full-Blown Global Marketing Strategy," *Advertising Age,* September 7, 2010, accessed at www.adage.com; Stuart Elliott, "Pepsi Invites the Public to Do Good," *New York Times,* January 31, 2010, p. B6; Natalie Zmuda, "How Pepsi Blinked, Fell Behind Diet Coke," *Advertising Age,* March 21, 2011, pp. 1, 6; and www.refresheverything.com (accessed June 2011).

People grow up in a particular society that shapes their basic beliefs and values. They absorb a world view that defines their relationships with others. The following cultural characteristics can affect marketing decision making.

Persistence of Cultural Values   People in a given society hold many beliefs and values. Their core beliefs and values have a high degree of persistence. For example, many Canadians believe in cultural diversity (versus assimilation), democracy, gender equality, sustainable development, universal health care, a love of nature, hard work, and being honest. These beliefs shape more specific attitudes and behaviours found in everyday life. *Core* beliefs and values are passed on from parents to children and are reinforced by schools, churches, business, and government.

Secondary beliefs and values are more open to change. Believing in marriage is a core belief; believing that people should get married early in life is a secondary belief. Marketers have some chance of changing secondary values but little chance of changing core values. For example, family-planning marketers could argue more effectively that people should get married later than not get married at all.

Shifts in Secondary Cultural Values   Although core values are fairly persistent, cultural swings do take place. Consider the impact of popular music groups, movie personalities, and other celebrities on young people's hairstyling and clothing norms. Marketers want to predict cultural shifts to spot new opportunities or threats. The major cultural values of a society are expressed in people's views of themselves and others, as well as in their views of organizations, society, nature, and the universe.

PEOPLE'S VIEWS OF THEMSELVES   People vary in their emphasis on serving themselves versus serving others. Some people seek personal pleasure, wanting fun, change, and escape. Others seek self-realization through religion, recreation, or the avid pursuit of careers or other life goals. Some people see themselves as sharers and joiners; others see themselves as individualists. People use products, brands, and services as a means of self-expression, and they buy products and services that match their views of themselves.

Marketers can target their products and services based on such self-views. For example, TOMS Shoes appeals to people who see themselves as part of the broader world community. In contrast, Kenneth Cole shoes appeal to fashion individualists. In its ads, the company declares, "We all walk in different shoes," asserting that Kenneth Cole represents "25 years of non-uniform thinking."

PEOPLE'S VIEWS OF OTHERS   People's attitudes toward and interactions with others shift over time. In recent years, some analysts have voiced concerns that the Internet age would result in diminished human interaction, as people buried their heads in their computers or emailed and texted rather than interacting personally. Instead, today's digital technologies seem to have launched an era of what one trend watcher calls *mass mingling*. Rather than interacting less, people are using online social media and mobile communications to connect more than ever. And, often, more online and mobile interactions result in more offline mingling:

> More people than ever [are] living large parts of their lives online. Yet, those same people also mingle, meet up, and congregate more often with other "warm bodies" in the offline world. In fact, social media and mobile communications are fueling a *mass mingling* that defies virtually every cliché about diminished human interaction in our "online era." Ironically, the same technology that was once condemned for turning entire generations into mobile gaming zombies and avatars is now deployed to get people *out* of their homes.
>
> Basically, the more [people] date and network and twitter and socialize online, the more likely they are to eventually meet up with friends and followers in the real world. Thanks to social networking services such as Facebook (whose more than 500 million fans spend more than 700 *billion* minutes a month on the site), people are developing more diverse social networks, defying the notion that technology pulls people away from social engagement. Rather than being more isolated, people today are increasingly tapping into their networks of friends.[36]

This new way of interacting strongly affects how companies market their brands and communicate with customers. "Consumers are increasingly tapping into their networks of friends, fans, and followers to discover, discuss, and purchase goods and services in ever-more sophisticated ways," says one analyst. "As a result, it's never been more important for brands to make sure they [tap into these networks] too."[37]

PEOPLE'S VIEWS OF ORGANIZATIONS   People vary in their attitudes toward corporations, government agencies, trade unions, universities, and other organizations. By and large, people are willing to work for major organizations and expect them, in turn, to carry out society's work.

Donald Miralle/Getty Images

Exhibit 4.13 **Mass mingling:** Rather than diminishing human interaction, today's social media and mobile communications are causing people to increasingly tap into their networks of friends.

The past two decades have seen a sharp decrease in confidence in and loyalty toward business and political organizations and institutions. In the workplace, there has been an overall decline in organizational loyalty. Waves of company downsizings bred cynicism and distrust. In just the last decade, rounds of layoffs resulting from the recent recession; corporate scandals at Enron, WorldCom, and Tyco; the financial meltdown triggered by Wall Street bankers' greed and incompetence; and other unsettling activities have resulted in a further loss of confidence in big business. Many people today see work not as a source of satisfaction but as a required chore to earn money to enjoy their non-work hours. This trend suggests that organizations need to find new ways to win consumer and employee confidence.

PEOPLE'S VIEWS OF SOCIETY   People vary in their attitudes toward their society—nationalists defend it, reformers want to change it, and malcontents want to leave it. People's orientation to their society influences their consumption patterns and attitudes toward the marketplace. National pride in Canada has been increasing gradually for the past two decades and many Canadian companies are responding to this trend with Canadian themes and promotions. From the now infamous Molson "I am Canadian" rant to the more recent Tide commercial that claims "no self-respecting Canadian says let's wait for a warmer day!" companies are jumping on the patriotic bandwagon. In fact, since the Vancouver Olympics in 2010, national pride has soared. According to a survey conducted by Ipsos Reid, 80 percent of Canadians agree that they are Canadian nationalists, up from 72 percent polled one year before the Olympics.[38]

Marketers respond with patriotic products and promotions, offering everything from floral bouquets to clothing with patriotic themes. Although most of these marketing efforts are tasteful and well received, waving the flag can prove tricky. Except in cases where companies tie product sales to charitable contributions, such flag-waving promotions can be viewed as attempts to cash in on triumph or tragedy. Marketers must take care when responding to such strong national emotions.

PEOPLE'S VIEWS OF NATURE   People vary in their attitudes toward the natural world—some feel ruled by it, others feel in harmony with it, and still others seek to master it. A long-term trend has been people's growing mastery over nature through technology and the belief that nature is bountiful. More recently, however, people have recognized that nature is finite and fragile, that it can be destroyed or spoiled by human activities.

This renewed love of things natural has created a 63-million-person "lifestyles of health and sustainability" (LOHAS) market, consumers who seek out everything from natural, organic, and nutritional products to fuel-efficient cars and alternative medicine. This segment spends nearly US$300 billion annually on such products.[39]

Food producers have also found fast-growing markets for natural and organic products. In total, the North American organic food market generated nearly US$29 billion in sales in 2012, more than doubling over the past five years. Niche marketers, such as Planet Organic, have sprung up to serve this market, and traditional food chains, such as Loblaws and Safeway, have added separate natural and organic food sections. Even pet owners are joining the movement as they become more aware of what goes into Fido's food. Almost every major pet food brand now offers several types of natural foods.[40]

Exhibit 4.14 Riding the trend toward all things natural, Earthbound Farm has grown to become the world's largest producer of organic salads, fruits, and vegetables, with products in 75 percent of North America's supermarkets.

Scott Olson/Getty Images

PEOPLE'S VIEWS OF THE UNIVERSE Finally, people vary in their beliefs about the origin of the universe and their place in it. Although many Canadians practise religion, religious conviction and practice have been dropping off gradually through the years. Statistics Canada surveys show Canadians' continuing slide out the doors of the country's churches, temples, and synagogues. In 1946, 67 percent of adult Canadians regularly attended religious services, but by 2001 the figure had dropped to 20 percent. In fact, 19 percent of adult Canadians were reported to have no religious affiliation in 2004.[41]

However, the fact that people are dropping out of organized religion doesn't mean that they are abandoning their faith. Some futurists have noted a renewed interest in spirituality, perhaps as part of a broader search for a new inner purpose. People have been moving away from materialism and dog-eat-dog ambition to seek more permanent values—family, community, Earth, faith—and a more certain grasp of right and wrong. "We are becoming a nation of spiritually anchored people who are not traditionally religious," says one expert.[42] This changing spiritualism affects consumers in everything from the television shows they watch and the books they read to the products and services they buy.

Responding to the Marketing Environment LO5

Someone once observed, "There are three kinds of companies: those who make things happen, those who watch things happen, and those who wonder what's happened."[43] Many companies view the marketing environment as an uncontrollable element to which they must react and adapt. They passively accept the marketing environment and do not try to change it. They analyze the environmental forces and design strategies that will help the company avoid the threats and take advantage of the opportunities the environment provides.

Other companies take a *proactive* stance toward the marketing environment. "Instead of letting the environment define their strategy," advises one marketing expert, "craft a strategy that defines your environment."[44] Rather than assuming that strategic options are bounded by the current environment, these firms develop strategies to change the environment. "Business history . . . reveals plenty of cases in which firms' strategies shape industry structure," says the expert, "from Ford's Model T to Nintendo's Wii."

Even more, rather than simply watching and reacting to environmental events, these firms take aggressive actions to affect the publics and forces in their marketing environment. Such companies hire lobbyists to influence legislation affecting their industries and stage media events to gain favourable press coverage. They run *advertorials* (ads expressing editorial points of view) to shape public opinion. They press lawsuits and file complaints with regulators to keep competitors in line, and they form contractual agreements to better control their distribution channels.

By taking action, companies can often overcome seemingly uncontrollable environmental events. For example, whereas some companies try to hush up negative talk about their products, others proactively counter false information. Taco Bell did this when its brand fell victim to potentially damaging claims about the quality of the beef filling in its tacos.

When a California woman's class-action suit questioned whether Taco Bell's meat filling could accurately be labelled "beef," the company's reaction was swift and decisive. The suit claimed that Taco Bell's beef filling is 65 percent binders, extenders, preservatives, additives, and other agents. It wanted Taco Bell to stop calling it "beef." But Taco Bell fought back quickly with a major counterattack campaign, in print and on YouTube and Facebook. Full page ads in the *Wall Street Journal*, the *New York Times*, and *USAToday* boldly proclaimed: "Thank you for suing us. Here's the truth about our seasoned beef." In the ad, Taco Bell revealed its not-so-secret recipe. "Start with USDA-inspected quality beef (88%). Then add water to keep it juicy and moist (3%). Mix in Mexican spices and flavors, including salt, chili pepper, onion powder, tomato powder, sugar, garlic powder, and cocoa powder (4%). Combine a little oats, caramelized sugar, yeast, citric acid, and other ingredients that contribute to the flavor, moisture, consistency, and quality of our seasoned beef (5%). The only reason we add anything to our beef is to give the meat flavor and quality." Taco Bell further announced that it would take legal action against those making the false statements. The company's proactive counter campaign quickly squelched the false information in the law suit, which was voluntarily withdrawn only a few months later.[45]

Marketing management cannot always control environmental forces. In many cases, it must settle for simply watching and reacting to the environment. For example, a company would have little success trying to influence geographic population shifts, the economic environment, or major cultural values. But whenever possible, smart marketing managers will take a *proactive* rather than *reactive* approach to the marketing environment (see Marketing@Work 4.2).

MARKETING@WORK 4.2

When the Dialog Gets Nasty: Turning Negatives into Positives

Marketers have hailed the Internet as the great new relational medium. Companies use the web to engage customers, gain insights into their needs, and create customer community. In turn, web-empowered consumers share their brand experiences with companies and with each other. All of this back-and-forth helps both the company and its customers. But sometimes, the dialog can get nasty. Consider the following examples:

■ MSN Money columnist Scott Burns accuses Home Depot of being a "consistent abuser" of customers' time. Within hours, MSN's servers are caving under the weight of 14 000 blistering emails and posts from angry Home Depot customers who storm the MSN comment room, taking Home Depot to task for pretty much everything. It is the biggest response in MSN Money's history.

■ Blogger Jeff Jarvis posts a series of irate messages to his BuzzMachine blog about the many failings of his Dell computer and his struggles with Dell's customer support. The post quickly draws national attention, and an open letter posted by Jarvis to Dell founder Michael Dell becomes the third most linked-to post on the blogosphere the day

after it appears. Jarvis's headline—Dell Hell—becomes shorthand for the ability of a lone blogger to deliver a body blow to an unsuspecting business.

■ When eight-year-old Harry Winsor sends a crayon drawing of an airplane he's designed to Boeing with a suggestion that they might want to manufacture it, the company

responds with a stern, legal-form letter. "We do not accept unsolicited ideas," the letter states. "We regret to inform you that we have disposed of your message and retain no copies." The embarrassing blunder would probably go unnoticed were it not for the fact that Harry's father—John Winsor, a prominent ad exec—blogs and tweets about

Exhibit 4.15 **Today's empowered consumers:** Boeing's embarrassing blunder over young Harry Winsor's airplane design made instant national news. However, Boeing quickly took responsibility and turned the potential PR disaster into a positive.

© Eye Risk / Alamy

the incident, making it instant national news.

■ When United Airlines rejects musician Dave Carroll's damage claim after its baggage handlers break his guitar, he produces a catchy music video, "United Breaks Guitars," and posts it on YouTube. "I should've flown with someone else or gone by car," he despairs in the video, "'cause United breaks guitars." The video becomes one of YouTube's greatest hits—more than 10 million people have now viewed it—and causes an instant media frenzy across major global networks.

Extreme events? Not anymore. The Internet has turned the traditional power relationship between businesses and consumers upside down. In the good old days, disgruntled consumers could do little more than bellow at a company service rep or shout out their complaints from a street corner. Now, armed with only a PC or a smartphone and a broadband connection, they can take it public, airing their gripes to millions on blogs, chats, online social networks, or even hate sites devoted exclusively to their least favourite corporations.

"I hate" and "sucks" sites are almost commonplace. These sites target some highly respected companies with some highly *dis*respectful labels: PayPalSucks.com (aka NoPayPal); Walmart-blows.com; IHateStarbucks .com; DeltaREALLYsucks.com; and UnitedPackageSmashers.com (UPS), to name only a few. "Sucks" videos on YouTube and other video sites also abound. For example, a search of "Apple sucks" on YouTube turns up 5300 videos; a similar search for Microsoft finds 5360 videos. An "Apple sucks" search on Facebook links to 540 groups.

Some of these sites, videos, and other web attacks air legitimate complaints that should be addressed. Others, however, are little more than anonymous, vindictive slurs that unfairly ransack brands and cor-

porate reputations. Some of the attacks are only a passing nuisance; others can draw serious attention and create real headaches.

How should companies react to online attacks? The real quandary for targeted companies is figuring out how far they can go to protect their images without fueling the already raging fire. One point on which all experts seem to agree: Don't try to retaliate in kind. "It's rarely a good idea to lob bombs at the fire starters," says one analyst. "Preemption, engagement, and diplomacy are saner tools."

Some companies have tried to silence the critics through lawsuits, but few have succeeded. The courts have tended to regard such criticism as opinion and, therefore, protected speech. In general, attempts to block, counterattack, or shut down consumer attacks may be shortsighted. Such criticisms are often based on real consumer concerns and unresolved anger. Hence, the best strategy might be to proactively monitor these sites and respond to the concerns they express. "The most obvious thing to do is talk to the customer and try to deal with the problem, instead of putting your fingers in your ears," advises one consultant.

For example, Home Depot CEO Francis Blake drew praise when he heeded the criticisms expressed in the MSN Money onslaught and responded positively. Blake posted a heartfelt letter in which he thanked critic Scott Burns, apologized to angry customers, and promised to make things better. And Boeing quickly took responsibility for mishandling aspiring designer Harry Winsor's drawing, turning a potential PR disaster into a positive. It called and invited young Harry to visit Boeing's facilities. On its corporate Twitter site, it confessed "We're expert at airplanes but novices in social media. We're learning as we go."

United Airlines, however, hasn't fared so well. After Dave Carroll's YouTube

video went platinum, United belatedly offered to pay for his ruined guitar. Carroll politely declined but thanked the company for boosting his career—which now boasts two new United videos that air complaints on behalf of other disgruntled customers and call for United to "change in a big way."

Many companies have now created teams of specialists that monitor web conversations and engage unhappy consumers. In the years since the Dell Hell incident, Dell has set up a 40-member "communities and conversation team," which does outreach on Twitter and Facebook and communicates with bloggers. The social media team at Southwest Airlines includes a chief Twitter officer who tracks Twitter comments and monitors Facebook groups, an online representative who checks facts and interacts with bloggers, and another person who takes charge of the company's presence on sites such as YouTube, Flickr, and LinkedIn. So if someone posts an online complaint, the company can respond in a personal way.

Thus, by listening and proactively responding to seemingly uncontrollable events in the environment, companies can prevent the negatives from spiraling out of control or even turn them into positives. Who knows? With the right responses, Walmart-blows.com might even become Walmart-rules.com. Then again, probably not.

Source: Quotes, excerpts, and other information from Rupal Parekh and Edmund Lee, "How to Succeed When It's Time to Make Your Social-Media Mea Culpa," *Advertising Age*, May 10, 2010, pp. 5, 25; Michelle Conlin, "Web Attack," *Businessweek*, April 16, 2007, pp. 54–56; Christopher L. Marting and Nathan Bennett, "Corporate Reputation; What to Do About Online Attacks," *Wall Street Journal*, March 10, 2008, p. R6; "Boeing's Social Media Lesson," May 3, 2010, http://mediadecoder.blogs.nytimes.com/2010/05/03/boeings-social-medialesson/;www.youtube.com/watch?v55YGc4zOqozo (accessed June 2011); and "Corporate Hate Sites," New Media Institute, www.newmedia.org/articles/corporate-hate-sites—nmi-white-paper.html (accessed October 2011).

Blue Sky and Storm Clouds

"I remember once advising a group of students, at a business case competition, that Apple would never enter the cellphone business," admits Bob Cummings, WestJet executive vice-president of sales, marketing, and guest experience, with palpable humility. "Having spent over eight years in the mobile industry myself, I did not conceive that an outsider could revolutionize the space by bringing touch screen and a simpler navigation. I do view Apple and Virgin as unique companies that have unique perspectives and competencies that have taken them in different directions, and I say, wow—never say never."

Cummings and other senior business leaders like him can be forgiven for underestimating the broad range of certain companies when it comes to exploiting possibilities. That, however, is the driving rationale for deep examination of the marketing environment. An obsession with gathering intelligence on macroenvironmental forces has assisted WestJet leadership in key business decisions. "We look at the market in Canada, where we've penetrated, and where the other guys have penetrated the market," states Cummings. "As we analyze the markets we have not touched, we realize that we need to make some product, network and channel investments to continue growth."

Knowledge of a volatile economic landscape, and building an airline business model designed to endure that volatility, allowed WestJet to navigate through the 2008–2009 recession without layoffs. Awareness of technological trends available to the commercial airline space prompted the airline to begin using required navigation performance (RNP) technology, which allows more direct approaches in and out of airports. Keeping up with regulatory patterns with regards to flight attendant/passenger ratios earned WestJet permission from Transport Canada to effectively cut operational costs without compromising safety or the guest experience. "And that," adds Cummings, "was done only after we explained the rationale to our flight attendant group."

Aside from the launch of its regional carrier, Encore, and the inevitable discussion about someday considering new global destinations, Cummings and WestJet's leadership team would appear to have a fairly wide angle lens when it comes to growth opportunities. "You do have to know where you are coming from. Do you have a broader DNA or perspective that can be leveraged more horizontally or in different directions? But unless you are in R&D, for most of us, mixing in more incremental type innovation and executing well is the more prudent approach to business."

QUESTIONS

1. Identify the macroenvironmental forces which helped WestJet and those which threatened to hurt the airline.
2. What macroenvironmental forces prompted WestJet to introduce Encore?
3. Besides the technological opportunity in implementing RNP, why else would WestJet implement this system?

REVIEWING THE CONCEPTS

1. Describe the environmental forces that affect the company's ability to serve its customers.

The company's *microenvironment* consists of other actors close to the company that combine to form the company's value delivery network or that affect its ability to serve its customers. It includes the company's *internal environment*—its several departments and management levels—as it influences marketing decision making. *Marketing channel firms*—suppliers and marketing intermediaries, including resellers, physical distribution firms, marketing services agencies, and financial intermediaries—co-operate to create customer value. *Competitors* vie with the company in an effort to serve customers better. Various *publics* have an actual or potential interest in or impact on the company's ability to meet its objectives. Finally, five types of customer *markets* exist: consumer, business, reseller, government, and international markets.

The *macroenvironment* consists of larger societal forces that affect the entire microenvironment. The six forces making up the company's macroenvironment include demographic, economic, natural, technological, political, and cultural forces. These forces shape opportunities and pose threats to the company.

2. Explain how changes in the demographic and economic environments affect marketing decisions.

Demography is the study of the characteristics of human populations. Today's *demographic environment* shows a changing age structure, shifting family profiles, geographic population shifts, a better-educated population, and increasing diversity. The *economic environment* consists of factors that affect buying power and patterns. The economic environment is characterized by more frugal consumers who are seeking greater value—the right combination of good quality and service at a fair price. The distribution of income also is shifting. The rich have grown richer, the middle class has shrunk, and the poor have remained poor, leading to a two-tiered market.

3. Identify the major trends in the firm's natural and technological environments.

The *natural environment* shows three major trends: shortages of certain raw materials, higher pollution levels, and more government intervention in natural resource management. Environmental concerns create marketing opportunities for alert companies. The *technological environment* creates both opportunities and challenges. Companies that fail to keep up with technological change will miss out on new product and marketing opportunities.

4. Explain the key changes in the political and cultural environments.

The *political environment* consists of laws, agencies, and groups that influence or limit marketing actions. The political environment has undergone three changes that affect marketing worldwide: increasing legislation regulating business, strong government agency enforcement, and greater emphasis on ethics and socially responsible actions. The *cultural environment* is made up of institutions and forces that affect a society's values, perceptions, preferences, and behaviours. The environment shows trends toward *mass mingling*, a lessening trust of institutions, increasing patriotism, greater appreciation for nature, a changing spiritualism, and the search for more meaningful and enduring values.

5. Discuss how companies can react to the marketing environment.

Companies can passively accept the marketing environment as an uncontrollable element to which they must react as events arise. Or they can take a *proactive* stance, working to change the environment rather than simply reacting to it. Whenever possible, companies should try to be proactive rather than reactive.

KEY TERMS

Baby Boomers 124
Cultural environment 138
Demography 123
Economic environment 131
Environmental sustainability 133

Generation X 125
Macroenvironment 120
Marketing environment 119
Marketing intermediaries 121
Microenvironment 120

Millennials (or Generation Y) 126
Natural environment 132
Political environment 135
Public 122
Technological environment 134

TALK ABOUT MARKETING

1. An important macroenvironmental force on companies is the social/cultural environment, particularly in international markets. In a small group, select a country and discuss at least three elements of the cultural environment that differ from that in Canada and how they impact companies doing business in that culture.

2. The current economic crisis has been difficult for both consumers and companies. However, Tim Hortons has managed to pose record profits and sustainable growth over the past few years. Visit the company website at www.timhortons.com and review its latest annual report. What strategies have enabled Tim Hortons to continue to be successful?

3. What marketing strategies should the makers of luxury products use during tough economic times? Provide an example of one luxury brand that you think has handled the economic crisis well.

4. Are age cohorts (Millennials, Gen X, Baby Boomers) a good demographic variable to use when segmenting the marketplace? Why or why not? For what product categories might age be an important segmentation variable? For what product categories might age be less important?

5. In April 2009, the Canadian government introduced anti-spam legislation, the Electronic Commerce Protection Act (ECPA). Visit www.ic.gc.ca/eic/site/ic1 .nsf/eng/04595.html and read about this new act. Discuss the implications for electronic commerce in Canada.

6. Cause-related marketing has grown considerably over the past 10 years. Visit www.causemarketingforum.com to learn about companies that have won Halo Awards for outstanding cause-related marketing programs. Present an award-winning case study to your class.

THINK LIKE A MARKETING MANAGER

Customer loyalty for online travel companies is low because the average consumer checks three different travel websites for the best prices on air travel, hotels, and rental cars before booking. With consumers highly motivated to make their selections based on price, online travel companies are trying to figure out other ways to differentiate themselves from the competition.

QUESTIONS

1. What current macroenvironmental forces do you think are having the greatest positive and negative impact on online travel companies?

2. How can online travel companies address the negative influences of the macroenvironment?

3. How can they take advantage of the positive influences of the macroenvironment?

4. What do you think will be the most significant environmental issues facing the online travel industry in the next five years?

MARKETING ETHICS

You've probably heard of heart procedures, such as angioplasty and stents, that are routinely performed on adults. But such heart procedures, devices, and related medications are not available for infants and children, despite the fact that almost 40 000 children a year are born in the United States with heart defects that oftentimes require repair. This is a life or death situation for many young patients, yet doctors must improvise by using devices designed and tested on adults. For instance, doctors use an adult kidney balloon on an infant's heart because it is the appropriate size for a newborn's aortic valve. However, this device is not approved for the procedure. Why are specific devices and medicines developed for the multibillion-dollar cardiovascular market not also designed for kids? It's a matter of economics—this segment of young consumers is just too small. One leading cardiologist attributed the discrepancy to a "profitability gap" between the children's market and the much more profitable adult market for treating heart disease. While not supplying this market might make good economic sense for companies, it is of little comfort to the parents of these small patients.

QUESTIONS

1. Discuss the environmental forces acting on medical devices and pharmaceuticals companies that are preventing them from meeting the needs of the infant and child market segment. Is it wrong for these companies to not address the needs of this segment?

2. Suggest some solutions to this problem.

MARKETING TECHNOLOGY

If you thought that getting 50 miles per gallon (4.7L/100 km) driving a Toyota Prius hybrid was good, how about 230 miles per gallon (1L/100 km)? Or 367 miles per gallon (0.64L/100 km)? Well, you are about to see a new breed of automobiles from big and small automakers touting this level of performance. In 2010, there was GM's Volt and Nissan's Leaf, but there will also be offerings from unknown start-ups such as V-Vehicle, a California-based electric car company backed by billionaire T. Boone Pickens. These automobiles range from hybrids—a combination of gas and electric—to all-electric vehicles. This level of performance comes at a high price, however. Although US consumers will receive an expected US$7500 tax credit for purchasing one of these cars, the Volt's expected US$40 000 price tag will still cause sticker shock. Also, the lack of public recharging stations poses a significant challenge, especially for all-electric vehicles such as the Leaf, which needs recharging approximately every 100 miles (160 km). And some might question the efficiency claims, especially since the Environmental Protection Agency is still finalizing the methodology that factors in electricity used when making miles-per-gallon equivalency claims.

QUESTIONS

1. What factors in the marketing environment present opportunities or threats to automakers?

2. Will it be possible for a start-up automaker such as V-Vehicle to compete with big automakers such as Ford, GM, Chrysler, Toyota, Honda, Nissan, Volvo, Hyundai, BMW, and Mercedes? What factors in the marketing environment will enable or inhibit new competitors?

MARKETING BY THE NUMBERS

China and India are emerging markets that will have a significant impact on the world in coming years. With China's and India's combined population of almost 2.5 billion, they are the two most populous countries, comprising almost 40 percent of the world's population. The economies of both countries are growing at phenomenal rates as well. The term *Chindia* is used to describe the growing power of these two countries, and predictions are that these two will overtake the United States as the largest economies in the world within just a few decades.

QUESTIONS

1. Discuss a demographic and an economic trend related to Chindia's power and their impact on marketers in Canada. Support your discussion of these trends with statistics.

2. Using the chain ratio method described in Appendix 3: Marketing by the Numbers, discuss factors to consider when estimating total market demand for automobiles in China or India.

ECOIST

At least one company has taken the old phrase "One man's trash is another man's treasure" and turned it into a business model. Ecoist uses discarded packaging materials from multinational brands such as Coca-Cola, Frito-Lay, Disney, and Mars to craft high-end handbags that would thrill even the most discriminating fashionistas.

When the company first started in 2004, consumer perceptions of goods made from recycled materials weren't very positive. This video describes how Ecoist found its opportunity in a growing wave of environmentalism. Not only does Ecoist capitalize on low-cost materials and the brand images of some of the world's major brands,

it comes out smelling like a rose as it saves tons of trash from landfills.

After viewing the video featuring Ecoist, answer the following questions:

QUESTIONS

1. How engaged was Ecoist in analyzing the marketing environment before it launched its first company?

2. What trends in the marketing environment have contributed to the success of Ecoist?

3. Is Ecoist's strategy more about recycling or about creating value for customers? Explain.

TARGET: FROM "EXPECT MORE" TO "PAY LESS"

When you hear the term *discount retail*, two names usually come to mind: Walmart and Target. The two competitors have been compared so much that the press rarely covers one without at least mentioning the other. The reasons for the comparisons are fairly obvious. These corporations are two of the largest discount retailers in the United States. Category-for-category, they offer very similar merchandise. And they tend to build their stores in close proximity to one another, often even facing each other across major streets.

But even with such strong similarities, ask any consumer if there's a difference between the two and they won't even hesitate in offering a reply. Walmart is all about low prices; Target is about style and fashion. The "upscale discounter" label applied by consumers and the media over the years perfectly captures Target's long-standing positioning: "Expect More. Pay Less." With its numerous designer product lines, Target has been so successful with its brand positioning that for many years it has slowly chipped away at Walmart's massive market share lead. Granted, the difference in the scale of the two companies has always been huge. Walmart's most recent annual revenues of US$419 billion are more than six times Target's US$67 billion. But for many years, Target grew at a much faster pace than Walmart.

In fact, as Walmart's same-store sales began to lag in the mid-2000s, the world's largest retailer unabashedly attempted to become more like Target. It spruced up its store environment, added more fashionable clothing and housewares, and stocked organic and gourmet foods in its grocery aisles. Walmart even experimented with luxury brands. After 19 years of promoting the slogan, "Always Low Prices. Always." Walmart replaced it with the very Target-esque tagline, "Save Money. Live Better." However, none of those efforts seemed to speed up Walmart's revenue growth or slow down Target's.

But as the global recession began to tighten its grip on the world's retailers in 2008, the dynamics between the two retail giants reversed almost overnight. As unemployment rose and consumers began pinching their pennies, Walmart's familiar price "rollbacks" resonated with consumers, whereas Target's image of slightly better stuff for slightly higher prices did not. Target's well-cultivated upscale discount image was turning away customers who believed that its fashionable products and trendy advertising meant steeper prices. By mid-2008, Target had experienced three straight quarters of flat same-store sales growth and a slight dip in store traffic. At the same time, Walmart was defying the economic slowdown, posting quarterly increases in same-store sales of close to 5 percent along with substantial jumps in profits.

SAME SLOGAN, DIFFERENT EMPHASIS

In the fall of 2008, Target acknowledged the slide and announced its intentions to do something about it. CEO Gregg Steinhafel succinctly summarized the company's new strategy: "The customer is very cash strapped right now. And in some ways, our greatest strength has become somewhat of a challenge. So, we're still trying to define and find the right balance between 'Expect More. Pay Less.' The current environment means that the focus is squarely on the 'Pay Less' side of it."

In the few years since Steinhafel unveiled the new strategic plan, Target has gone through some drastic changes. The executives at Target challenged every assumption about the brand and the business model that had formerly brought Target so much success. While this adjustment certainly meant cutting costs and prices, Walmart's decades-long lead in that department meant that Target would have to do more.

According to Michael Francis, Target's chief marketing officer, doing more is exactly what happened. "There was more innovation happening within Target during the recession than in any time in my 25 years with the corporation." For starters, Target began a massive effort to redesign its stores. This included redesigning departments and making updates to store signage and lighting. But the biggest change to store design came from the PFresh concept, an expansion of the grocery section in regular Target stores to include fresh produce, meat, and dairy products. This new "mini-grocery store" was designed to provide a narrow selection of 90 percent of the food categories found in full-size grocery stores while occupying only a corner of an existing Target store.

Target's intention was to create mini-grocery stores to provide customers with a one-stop shopping experience.

One shopper's reaction was just what Target was hoping for. A Wisconsin housewife and mother of two stopped by her local Target to buy deodorant and laundry detergent before heading to the local grocery store. But as she worked her way through the fresh-food aisles, she found everything on her list. "I'm done," she said, as she grabbed for a 99-cent green pepper. "I just saved myself a trip."

While the PFresh concept demonstrated promise for increasing store traffic, groceries are a low-margin category. That's why Target's second major operational change focused on stronger sales of higher margin goods. Target surprised many analysts by unveiling a new package for its main store brand . . . one without the familiar Target bulls-eye! Instead, the new Target store brand, "up & up," featured big, colourful, upward-pointing arrows on a white background. The total number of products under the store label was expanded from 730 to 800 and promotional efforts for the store brand were increased in weekly newspaper circulars. Kathryn Tesija, Target's vice-president of merchandising, stated, "We believe that it will stand out on the shelf, and it is so distinctive that we'll get new guests that will want to try it that maybe didn't even notice the Target brand before."

The design changes to Target stores required a major shift in the company's store growth plan. In fact, Target opened only 10 new stores in 2010, the lowest number in its history. "It will be a long time before we approach the development pace of several years ago," said Doug Scovanner, Target's chief financial officer. Meanwhile, Target continues to put its money into remodeling existing stores to better accommodate the shifts in inventory.

As its product portfolio and prices began to reflect the "Pay Less" part of its slogan, Target also shifted its advertising strategy. For years, the company had featured ads that projected the "Expect More" part of its slogan. But even as it turned the stated message of its ads toward price, trendy and stylish visual-imagery continued to strike customers as "expensive." Therefore, Target put all its advertising in the hands of Wieden & Kennedy as its first-ever lead advertising agency. Wieden went to work, fine-tuning the marketing message in an effort to convince consumers that Target was just as committed to bargains as Walmart.

Target's most recent campaign, "Life's A Moving Target," is spot on. The campaign has produced in excess of 70 spots, each 15 seconds long and highlighting a specific product, ranging from flu shots to pants to cheese. The overall message that "the pace of life is complex" is much more in line with the reality that the middle class faces. In addition, each ad ultimately shows that Target is there to fill consumers' daily needs. For example, one clever shot shows a young boy at the table, sliding his Brussels sprouts under the table to the dog. But the dog won't have them and leaves, just as a bag of PEDIGREE dog food flashes on the screen, followed by the campaign's tag line. The campaign also brings in co-op dollars from vendors who are even petitioning Target to be part of the campaign.

SIGNS OF LIFE

Although Steinhafel's "Pay Less" strategy was aggressive, Target's sales and profits were slow to respond. In fact, sales initially fell, at one point dropping by 10 percent from the previous year. Target's profits suffered even more. It didn't help matters that as Target's financials suffered, Walmart bucked the recessionary retail trend by posting revenue increases.

But Target's journey over the past few years demonstrates that changing the direction of a large corporation is like trying to reverse a moving freight train. It has to slow down before going the other way. It now appears that consumers may have finally gotten the message. During 2010, Target's same-store sales rose by as much as 5 percent while profits shot up 16 percent. Both the amount spent per visit and number of store visits increased. In a sign that Target's efforts are truly paying off, Walmart's fortunes reversed as well. The retail giant saw same-store sales decline for seven straight quarters.

Steinhafel makes it clear that Target is viewing the new signs of life with cautious optimism. "Clearly the economy and consumer sentiment have improved since their weakest point in 2009," says the Target CEO. "But we believe that both are still somewhat unstable and fragile and will likely continue to experience occasional setbacks as the year progresses." Steinhafel's comments reflect an understanding that even as the recession showed signs of ending, research indicated that consumers everywhere have adopted a new-found sense of frugality and monetary responsibility. Although economic growth may have improved, inflation is on the rise and unemployment remains high.

Some Wall Street analysts have expressed concern that Target's recent value strategy may weaken the brand as customers lose sight of the distinctive features that set it apart from Walmart. But the words of one shopper are a good indication that, despite having emphasized the "Pay Less" part of its image, Target still retains the "Expect More" part: "Target is a nice place to go. Walmart may have good prices, but I would rather tell my friends that I came back from shopping at Target."

Sources: Natalie Zmuda, "Why the Bad Economy Has Been Good for Target," *Advertising Age,* October 4, 2010, accessed at www .adage.com; Rita Trichur and Marina Strauss, "Target Knows What They Are; Clean, Bright, and Well-Organized," *Globe and Mail,* January 14, 2011, p. B4; Karen Talley, "Target Profit Rises on Strong Sales, Improved Credit-Card Operations," *Wall Street Journal,* May 20, 2010, accessed at www.wsj.com; Ann Zimmerman, "Target Believes a Rebound Recipe Is in Grocery Aisle," *Wall Street Journal,* May 12, 2009, p. B1; Nicole Maestri, "Target Revamps Its Target Brand as 'Up & Up,'" *Reuters,* May 19, 2009, accessed at www .reuters.com.

QUESTIONS FOR DISCUSSION

1. What microenvironmental factors have affected Target's performance over the past few years?

2. What macroenvironmental factors have affected Target's performance during that period?

3. By focusing on the "Pay Less" part of its slogan, has Target pursued the best strategy? Why or why not?

4. What alternative strategy might Target have followed in responding to the first signs of declining revenues and profits?

5. Given Target's current situation, what recommendations would you make to CEO Steinhafel for the company's future? How might their current situation impact their entry into the Canadian market?

MyMarketingLab MyMarketingLab is an online homework and tutorial system that puts you in control of your own learning with study and practice tools directly correlated to this chapter's content.

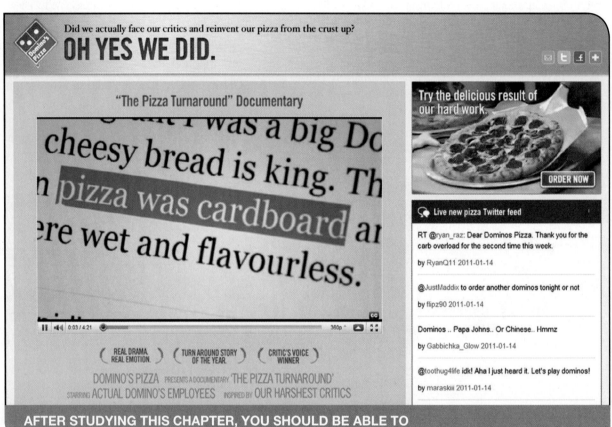

AFTER STUDYING THIS CHAPTER, YOU SHOULD BE ABLE TO

1 explain the importance of information in gaining insights about the marketplace and customers

2 define the marketing information system and discuss its parts

3 outline the steps in the marketing research process

4 explain how companies analyze and use marketing information

5 discuss the special issues some marketing researchers face, including public policy and ethics issues

Managing Marketing Information to Gain Customer Insights

PREVIEWING THE CONCEPTS

In this chapter, we continue our exploration of how marketers gain insights into consumers and the marketplace. We look at how companies develop and manage information about important marketplace elements—customers, competitors, products, and marketing programs. To succeed in today's marketplace, companies must know how to turn mountains of marketing information into fresh customer insights that will help them deliver greater value to customers.

Let's start with a story about marketing research and customer insights in action. Good marketing research can involve a rich variety of sophisticated data collection and analysis techniques. But sometimes research is as simple as just talking with customers directly, listening openly to what they have to say, and using those insights to develop better products and marketing. That's how Domino's Pizza turned a five-year revenue slide into a fresh, hot turnaround.

DOMINO'S PIZZA: LISTENING TO CONSUMERS AND LETTING THEM KNOW YOU HEARD THEM

After five years of stagnant or declining revenues, in late 2009 Domino's Pizza did something practically unheard of in the business world. "First," says an industry observer, "it asked customers for honest feedback. Second, it actually listened to the painful truth [punctuated by words like 'cardboard crust' and 'totally devoid of flavour']. Finally—and here's the most shocking part—the company reinvented its product 'from the crust up.'" What follows is the full story behind Domino's impressive "Pizza Turnaround" campaign.

The turnaround began with marketing research to understand what customers thought and wanted. Industry research showed that although Domino's was tops in service, convenience, and value for the money, it trailed far behind competitors in taste. One taste preference survey placed Domino's dead last, tied with—of all possibilities—Chuck E. Cheese, a competitor not known for culinary excellence.

To gain deeper insights into what consumers really thought about its pizzas, Domino's turned to research using social media channels and focus groups. It monitored consumer online chatter and solicited thousands of direct consumer feedback messages via Facebook, Twitter, and other social media. Then, based on insights it gained online,

Domino's launched a wave of good old-fashioned, tried-and-true focus groups to engage customers directly in face-to-face conversations.

The online feedback and focus group results were as difficult to digest as a cold Domino's pizza. The most common complaint: Domino's pizza crust "tasted like cardboard." But that was just the beginning. One after another, pizza lovers panned Domino's pies with biting comments such as "Totally devoid of flavour." "The sauce tastes like ketchup." "Worst excuse for pizza I've ever had." "Processed cheese!!" "Mass-produced, boring, bland pizza." and "Microwave pizza is far superior." One focus group participant concluded: "It doesn't feel like there's much love in Domino's pizza." "They weren't poisoning people," chuckles an analyst, "but taste was [certainly a big] glitch on the radar."

Rather than hiding from these stinging results or waving them off, Domino's executives fessed up to the problems and faced them head on. "We had a focus group webcast to our team," says a Domino's marketing executive. "When somebody's saying something terrible about your pizza, you never get used to it, but for the first time all our executives were face to face with it. They couldn't believe it. We all said: 'we can't just go to the next meeting. We have to do something.'"

Domino's began by completely reinventing its pizzas. It didn't just make improvements to the old product; it threw out the recipe and started over. According to Domino's chief marketing officer, Russell Weiner, "We weren't going to call it 'new and improved' and expect that to break through. We had to blow up the bridge."

Domino's chefs started from scratch with new crusts, sauces, cheese, and other ingredients. The result was an entirely new pizza that Domino's boasts has a "garlic seasoned crust with parsley, baked to a golden brown." The new sauce is "bright, spicy, and robust" with a "little bit of red pepper just to tingle on your tongue." And the new cheese is to die for—mozzarella, shredded not diced, flavoured with just a hint of provolone. "We changed everything," says a Domino's product-development chef. "Now it tastes better." Customers seem to agree. Two months after the new pizza was introduced, some 1800 random pizza consumers from eight US markets did a blind taste test. In head-to-head comparisons, consumers picked Domino's pizzas as tasting better than both Papa John's and Pizza Hut by a wide margin.

To announce the changes and to turn around customer opinions, Domino's launched a daring US$75 million "Pizza Turnaround" promotion campaign. In the campaign, the research itself was the message. Self-deprecating TV commercials showed real focus groups describing, in vivid detail, how dreadful the pizza was. In the ads, Domino's CEO Patrick Doyle admits that he's heard what customers had to say and has taken it to heart. "There comes a time," he acknowledges, "when you know you've got to make a change."

The startlingly honest campaign was fully integrated into the brand's Facebook and Twitter pages, where the company posted all the bad along with the good and asked for continuing feedback. The entire turnaround saga—from biting focus group footage to the shocked reactions of Domino's executives and efforts to reformulate the product—was documented for all to see in a forthright four-and-a-half minute behind-the-scenes documentary on the website www.pizzaturnaround.com. The company even posted a stream of customer comments—good, bad, or indifferent—on a 4630-square-foot billboard in New York City's Times Square area.

The campaign was risky. When Domino's admitted in its ads that its pizza was gross, some analysts predicted that the approach would be brand suicide. CEO Doyle admits that he had knots in his stomach when the chain launched the campaign. But Domino's wanted to shout out loud and clear: We've heard you! Our pizza was lousy but we fixed the recipe. "We had to be open, honest, and transparent," says CMO Weiner.

As it turns out, the upfront approach worked. In the three months following the start of the Pizza Turnaround campaign, Domino's sales soared 14.3 percent and in-store profits reached new highs. The transparent ads and message grabbed consumer attention and changed opinions. "The advertising itself scored off the charts," says Weiner. And while the ads drew people in, Domino's new pizza kept them coming back. Revenues and profits continued to climb throughout 2010, even as overall revenues for the pizza-delivery industry were declining. The Pizza Turnaround campaign even earned Domino's "marketer of the year" honours from two major marketing publications, *Advertising Age* and *Brandweek*.

The lesson for marketers is that talking to customers, hearing what they have to say, and acting on the insights gained can pay big dividends. Marketing research and really listening to customers, says Doyle, "dramatically changed our momentum, and we can build on this going forward. We feel very good now about our understanding of the brand. We're a new Domino's."[1]

AS THE Domino's story highlights, good products and marketing programs begin with good customer information. Companies also need an abundance of information on competitors, resellers, and other actors and marketplace forces. But more than just gathering information, marketers must *use* the information to gain powerful *customer and market insights*.

Marketing Information and Customer Insights LO1

To create value for customers and build meaningful relationships with them, marketers must first gain fresh, deep insights into what customers need and want. Such customer insights come from good marketing information. Companies use these customer insights to develop a competitive advantage.

For example, Apple wasn't the first company to develop a digital music player. However, Apple's research uncovered two key insights: people wanted personal music players that let them take all of their music with them, and they wanted to be able to listen to it unobtrusively. Based on these insights, Apple applied its design and usability magic to create the phenomenally successful iPod. The expanded iPod and iPod Touch lines now capture a 76 percent share of the MP3 player market. The iPod insights also spawned other Apple blockbusters such as the iPhone and iPad.[2]

Although customer and market insights are important for building customer value and relationships, these insights can be very difficult to obtain. Customer needs and buying motives are often anything but obvious—consumers themselves usually can't tell you exactly what they need and why they buy. To gain good customer insights, marketers must effectively manage marketing information from a wide range of sources.

Today's marketers have ready access to plenty of marketing information. With the recent explosion of information technologies, companies can now generate

© Caro / Alamy

Exhibit 5.1 Key customer insights, plus a dash of Apple's design and usability magic, have made the iPod a blockbuster. It now captures 76 percent of the market and has spawned other Apple blockbusters such as the iPhone and iPad.

Customer insights
Fresh understandings of customers and the marketplace derived from marketing information that becomes the basis for creating customer value and relationships.

LO2

Marketing information system (MIS)
People and procedures for assessing information needs, developing the needed information, and helping decision makers to use the information to generate and validate actionable customer and market insights.

information in great quantities. Moreover, consumers themselves are now generating tons of marketing information. Through email, text messaging, blogging, Facebook, Twitter, and other grassroots digital channels, consumers are now volunteering a tidal wave of bottom-up information to companies and to each other. Companies that tap into such information can gain rich, timely customer insights at lower cost.

Far from lacking information, most marketing managers are overloaded with data and often overwhelmed by it. For example, when a company such as Pepsi monitors online discussions about its brands by searching key words in tweets, blogs, posts, and other sources, its servers take in a stunning six million public conversations a day, more than 2 billion a year.[3] That's far more information than any manager can digest. Thus, marketers don't need *more* information; they need *better* information. And they need to make better *use* of the information they already have.

The real value of marketing research and marketing information lies in how it is used—in the **customer insights** that it provides. Based on such thinking, many companies are now restructuring their marketing research and information functions. They are creating *customer insights teams*, headed by a vice-president of customer insights and composed of representatives from all of the firm's functional areas. For example, Coca-Cola's marketing research group is headed by a vice-president of marketing strategy and insights. And at Unilever, marketing research is done by the Consumer and Market Insight division, which helps brand teams harness information and turn it into customer insights.

Customer insights groups collect customer and market information from a wide variety of sources, ranging from traditional marketing research studies, to mingling with and observing consumers, to monitoring consumer online conversations about the company and its products. Then, they *use* the marketing information to develop important customer insights from which the company can create more value for its customers.

Thus, companies must design effective marketing information systems that give managers the right information, in the right form, at the right time and help them to use this information to create customer value and stronger customer relationships. A **marketing information system (MIS)** consists of people and procedures for assessing information needs, developing the needed information, and helping decision makers to use the information to generate and validate actionable customer and market insights.

Figure 5.1 shows that the MIS begins and ends with information users—marketing managers, internal and external partners, and others who need marketing information. First, it interacts with these information users to *assess information needs*. Next, it interacts with the marketing environment to *develop needed information* through internal company databases, marketing intelligence activities, and marketing research. Finally, the MIS helps users to *analyze and use* the information to develop customer insights, make marketing decisions, and manage customer relationships.

FIGURE 5.1 The Marketing Information System

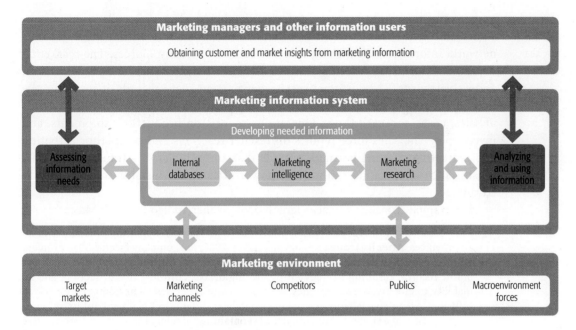

Assessing Marketing Information Needs

The marketing information system primarily serves the company's marketing and other managers. However, it may also provide information to external partners, such as suppliers, resellers, or marketing services agencies. For example, Walmart's Retail Link system gives key suppliers access to information on everything from customers' buying patterns and store inventory levels to how many items they've sold in which stores in the past 24 hours.[4]

A good MIS balances the information users would *like* to have against what they really *need* and what is *feasible* to offer. Some managers will ask for whatever information they can get without thinking carefully about what they really need. Too much information can be as harmful as too little. Other managers may omit things they ought to know, or they may not know to ask for some types of information they should have. For example, managers might need to know about surges in favourable or unfavourable consumer discussions about their brands on blogs or online social networks. Because they do not know about these discussions, they do not think to ask about them. The MIS must monitor the marketing environment to provide decision makers with information they should have to better understand customers and make key marketing decisions.

Finally, the costs of obtaining, analyzing, storing, and delivering information can mount quickly. The company must decide whether the value of insights gained from additional information is worth the costs of providing it, and both value and cost are often hard to assess.

Developing Marketing Information

Marketers can obtain the needed information from *internal data*, *marketing intelligence*, and *marketing research*.

Internal Data

Internal databases
Electronic collections of consumer and market information obtained from data sources within the company network.

Many companies build extensive **internal databases**, electronic collections of consumer and market information obtained from data sources within the company's network. Information in the database can come from many sources. The marketing department furnishes information on customer characteristics, sales transactions, and website visits. The customer service department keeps records of customer satisfaction or service problems. The accounting department provides detailed records of sales, costs, and cash flows. Operations reports on production, shipments, and inventories. The sales force reports on reseller reactions and competitor activities, and marketing channel partners provide data on point-of-sale transactions. Harnessing such information can provide powerful customer insights and competitive advantage.

For example, consider Canada's largest book retailer, Indigo Books & Music:[5]

Indigo Books & Music is the largest book retailer in Canada, operating bookstores in all 10 provinces. After its acquisition of Chapters in 2001, the company faced a huge problem with its customer databases. Customers had to be tracked through multiple retail and online records, resulting in frequent processing delays, customer dissatisfaction, and an inability to effectively analyze sales, marketing, and retail data. The company turned to Infusion, a firm specializing in customer database design, to help overhaul its systems. Infusion created a single customer database containing all retail, Internet, and prospective customer information, which was also able to track data relating to Indigo's "irewards" loyalty program.

The results for Indigo included an increase from 40 to 80 percent of new signups who provided a working email address and the re-engagement via email with more than 100 000 existing Indigo customers. Says Sumit Oberai, Chief Information Officer at Indigo, "We've stopped talking about online customers and retail store customers and loyalty customers and just talk about customers." In 2011, Indigo launched the Plum Rewards program, after getting feedback from customers that they wanted a free loyalty program that would enable them to earn and redeem points on both book and nonbook purchases. "Customization is critical" with rewards programs, says Heather Reisman, founder and CEO of Indigo Books & Music. "It's essential to make a loyalty program meaningful to customers." A large part of the success of the Indigo rewards program is a function of how personalized customer communications are; relevant messages help increase member engagement.

Competitive marketing intelligence
The systematic collection and analysis of publicly available information about consumers, competitors, and developments in the marketing environment.

Internal databases usually can be accessed more quickly and cheaply than other information sources, but they also present some problems. Because internal information is often collected for other purposes, it may be incomplete or in the wrong form for making marketing decisions. Data also ages quickly; keeping the database current requires a major effort. Finally, managing the mountains of information that a large company produces requires highly sophisticated equipment and techniques.

Competitive Marketing Intelligence

Competitive marketing intelligence is the systematic collection and analysis of publicly available information about consumers, competitors,

© Helen Sessions / Alamy

Exhibit 5.2 Internal data: Indigo Books & Music has found a wealth of actionable customer insights by analyzing internal databases.

and developments in the marketplace. The goal of competitive marketing intelligence is to improve strategic decision making by understanding the consumer environment, assessing and tracking competitors' actions, and providing early warnings of opportunities and threats. Marketing intelligence techniques range from observing consumers first-hand to quizzing the company's own employees, benchmarking competitors' products, researching the Internet, and monitoring Internet buzz.

Good marketing intelligence can help marketers to gain insights into how consumers talk about and connect with their brands. Many companies send out teams of trained observers to mix and mingle with customers as they use and talk about the company's products. Other companies routinely monitor consumers' online chatter. For example, PepsiCo's Gatorade brand has created an extensive control centre to monitor brand-related social media activity.[6]

> The Gatorade Mission Control Centre, deep within the company's Chicago headquarters, serves as a nerve centre in which Gatorade's four-member Mission Control team monitors the brand in real-time across social media. Whenever someone mentions anything related to Gatorade (including competitors, Gatorade athletes, and sports nutrition-related topics) on Twitter, Facebook, a blog, or in other social media, it pops up in various visualizations and dashboards on one of six big screens in Mission Control. Staffers also monitor online-ad and website traffic, producing a consolidated picture of the brand's Internet image.
>
> Gatorade uses what it sees and learns at Mission Control to improve its products, marketing, and interactions with customers. For example, while monitoring its "Gatorade Has Evolved" campaign, the team quickly saw that a commercial featuring a song by rap artist David Banner was being heavily discussed in social media. Within 24 hours, they had worked with Banner to put out a full-length version of the song and distribute it to Gatorade followers and fans on Twitter and Facebook. In another case, the brand knew to bulk up on production of its recovery drinks because of complaints they were selling out. Beyond just monitoring social media conversations, the Mission Control team sometimes joins them, as when staffers recently jumped into a Facebook conversation to answer a poster's questions about where to buy products.

Many companies have even appointed *chief listening officers*, who are charged with sifting through online customer conversations and passing along key insights to marketing decision makers. Dell created a position called *Listening Czar* two years ago. "Our chief listener is critical to making sure that the right people in the organization are aware of what the conversations on the web are saying about us, so the relevant people in the business can connect with customers," says a Dell marketing executive.[7]

Companies also need to actively monitor competitors' activities. Firms use competitive marketing intelligence to gain early warnings of competitor moves and strategies, new-product launches, new or changing markets, and potential competitive strengths and weaknesses. Much competitor intelligence can be collected from people inside the company—executives, engineers and scientists, purchasing agents, and the sales force. The company can also obtain important intelligence information from suppliers, resellers, and key customers. It can monitor competitors' websites and use the Internet to search specific competitor names, events, or

Exhibit 5.3 **Mission control:** PepsiCo's Gatorade brand has created an extensive control centre to monitor real-time brand-related social media activity.

© NetPhotos / Alamy

trends and see what turns up. And tracking consumer conversations about competing brands is often as revealing as tracking conversations about the company's own brands.

Intelligence seekers can also pore through any of thousands of online databases. Some are free. For example, you can search the System for Electronic Document Analysis and Retrieval (SEDAR) database for the documents and information filed by public companies and for investment funds with the Canadian Securities Administrators. The Howard Ross Library of Management at McGill University lists many resources for learning more about Canadian businesses, and www.hoovers.com has a searchable website containing financial information on publicly traded Canadian and US companies. And for a fee, companies can subscribe to any of more than 3000 online databases and information search services, such as Dialog, LCC; DataStar; LexisNexis; Dow Jones News/Retrieval; UMI ProQuest; and Dun & Bradstreet online access. Today's marketers have an almost overwhelming amount of competitor information only a few keystrokes away.

The intelligence game goes both ways. Facing determined competitive marketing intelligence efforts by competitors, most companies are now taking steps to protect their own information. The growing use of marketing intelligence also raises ethical issues. Although the preceding techniques are legal, others may involve questionable ethics. Clearly, companies should take advantage of publicly available information. However, they should not stoop to snoop. With all the legitimate intelligence sources now available, a company does not need to break the law or accepted codes of ethics to get good intelligence.

Marketing Research LO3

In addition to marketing intelligence information about general consumer, competitor, and marketplace happenings, marketers often need formal studies that provide customer and market insights for specific marketing situations and decisions. For example, Budweiser wants to know what appeals will be most effective in its Super Bowl advertising. Google wants to know how web searchers will react to a proposed redesign of its site. Or Samsung wants to know how many and what kinds of people will buy its next-generation ultrathin televisions. In such situations, managers will need marketing research.

Marketing research is the systematic design, collection, analysis, and reporting of data relevant to a specific marketing situation facing an organization. Companies use marketing research in a wide variety of situations. For example, marketing research gives marketers insights into customer motivations, purchase behaviour, and satisfaction. It can help them to assess market potential and market share, or to measure the effectiveness of pricing, product, distribution, and promotion activities.

Marketing research
The systematic design, collection, analysis, and reporting of data relevant to a specific marketing situation facing an organization.

Some large companies have their own research departments that work with marketing managers on marketing research projects. In addition, these companies—like their smaller counterparts—frequently hire outside research specialists to consult with management on specific marketing problems and conduct marketing research studies. Sometimes firms simply purchase data collected by outside firms to aid in their decision making.

The marketing research process has four steps (see Figure 5.2): defining the problem and research objectives, developing the research plan, implementing the research plan, and interpreting and reporting the findings.

Defining the Problem and Research Objectives

Marketing managers and researchers must work closely together to define the problem and agree on research objectives. The manager best understands the decision for which

FIGURE 5.2 The Marketing Research Process

| Defining the problem and research objectives | → | Developing the research plan for collecting information | → | Implementing the research plan—collecting and analyzing the data | → | Interpreting and reporting the findings |

information is needed; the researcher best understands marketing research and how to obtain the information. Defining the problem and research objectives is often the hardest step in the research process. The manager may know that something is wrong, without knowing the specific causes.

After the problem has been defined carefully, the manager and researcher must set the research objectives. A marketing research project might have one of three types of objectives. The objective of **exploratory research** is to gather preliminary information that will help define the problem and suggest hypotheses. The objective of **descriptive research** is to describe things, such as the market potential for a product or the demographics and attitudes of consumers who buy the product. The objective of **causal research** is to test hypotheses about cause-and-effect relationships. For example, would a 10 percent decrease in tuition at a university result in an enrolment increase sufficient to offset the reduced tuition? Managers often start with exploratory research and later follow with descriptive or causal research.

The statement of the problem and research objectives guides the entire research process. The manager and researcher should put the statement in writing to be certain that they agree on the purpose and expected results of the research.

Developing the Research Plan

Once the research problems and objectives have been defined, researchers must determine the exact information needed, develop a plan for gathering it efficiently, and present the plan to management. The research plan outlines sources of existing data and spells out the specific research approaches, contact methods, sampling plans, and instruments that researchers will use to gather new data.

Research objectives must be translated into specific information needs. For example, suppose that Red Bull wants to conduct research on how consumers would react to a proposed new vitamin-enhanced water drink that would be available in several flavours and sold under the Red Bull name. Red Bull currently dominates the worldwide energy drink market with a more than 40 percent market share worldwide.[8] A new line of enhanced waters—akin to Coca Cola's vitaminwater—might help Red Bull leverage its strong brand position even further. The proposed research might call for the following specific information:

■ The demographic, economic, and lifestyle characteristics of current Red Bull customers. (Do current customers also consume enhanced-water products? Are such products consistent with their lifestyles? Or would Red Bull need to target a new segment of consumers?)

■ The characteristics and usage patterns of the broader population of enhanced-water users: What do they need and expect

Exploratory research
Marketing research to gather preliminary information that will help define the problem and suggest hypotheses.

Descriptive research
Marketing research to better describe marketing problems, situations, or markets.

Causal research
Marketing research to test hypotheses about cause-and-effect relationships.

Exhibit 5.4 A decision by Red Bull to add a line of enhanced waters to its already successful mix of energy and cola drinks would call for marketing research that provides lots of specific information.

Red Bull North America

from such products, where do they buy them, when and how do they use them, and what existing brands and price points are most popular? (The new Red Bull product would need strong, relevant positioning in the crowded enhanced-water market.)

■ Retailer reactions to the proposed new product line: Would they stock and support it? Where would they display it? (Failure to get retailer support would hurt sales of the new drink.)

■ Forecasts of sales of both the new and current Red Bull products. (Will the new enhanced-waters create new sales or simply take sales away from current Red Bull products? Will the new product increase Red Bull's overall profits?)

Red Bull's marketers will need these and many other types of information to decide whether or not to introduce the new product and, if so, the best way to do it.

The research plan should be presented in a *written proposal.* A written proposal is especially important when the research project is large and complex or when an outside firm carries it out. The proposal should cover the management problems addressed and the research objectives, the information to be obtained, and how the results will help management decision making. The proposal also should include research costs.

To meet the manager's information needs, the research plan can call for gathering secondary data, primary data, or both. **Secondary data** consist of information that already exists somewhere, having been collected for another purpose. **Primary data** consist of information collected for the specific purpose at hand.

Gathering Secondary Data

Researchers usually start by gathering secondary data. The company's internal database provides a good starting point. However, the company can also tap into a wide assortment of external information sources, including commercial data services and government sources.

Companies can buy secondary data reports from outside suppliers. For example, Nielsen sells shopper insight data from a consumer panel of more than 250 000 households in 25 countries worldwide, with measures of trial and repeat purchasing, brand loyalty, and buyer demographics. Experian Consumer Research (Simmons) sells information on more than 8000 brands in 450 product categories, including detailed consumer profiles that assess everything from the products consumers buy and the brands they prefer to their lifestyles, attitudes, and media preferences. The MONITOR service by Yankelovich sells information on important social and lifestyle trends. These and other firms supply high-quality data to suit a wide variety of marketing information needs.[9]

By using **commercial online databases**, marketing researchers can conduct their own searches of secondary data sources. General database services such as ProQuest, LexisNexis, and Dialog, LCC, put an incredible wealth of information at the keyboards of marketing decision makers. Beyond commercial websites offering information for a fee, almost every industry association, government agency, business publication, and news medium offers free information to those tenacious enough to find their websites.

Internet search engines can also be a big help in locating relevant secondary information sources. However, they can also be very frustrating and inefficient. For example, a Red Bull marketer googling "enhanced water products" would come up with more than 750 000 hits! Still, well-structured, well-designed web searches can be a good starting point to any marketing research project.

Secondary data
Information that already exists somewhere, having been collected for another purpose.

Primary data
Information collected for the specific purpose at hand.

Commercial online databases
Computerized collections of information available from online commercial sources or via the Internet.

Secondary data can usually be obtained more quickly and at a lower cost than primary data. Also, secondary sources can sometimes provide data an individual company cannot collect on its own—information that either is not directly available or would be too expensive to collect. For example, it would be too expensive for Red Bull's marketers to conduct a continuing retail store audit to find out about the market shares, prices, and displays of competitors' brands. But it can buy the InfoScan service from SymphonyIRI Group, which provides this information based on scanner and other data from thousands of retail stores.[10]

Secondary data can also present problems. Researchers can rarely obtain all the data they need from secondary sources. For example, Red Bull will not find existing information about consumer reactions to a new enhanced-water line that it has not yet placed on the market. Even when data can be found, the information might not be very useable. The researcher must evaluate secondary information carefully to make certain it is *relevant* (fits research project needs), *accurate* (reliably collected and reported), *current* (up-to-date enough for current decisions), and *impartial* (objectively collected and reported).

Primary Data Collection

Secondary data provide a good starting point for research and often help define research problems and objectives. In most cases, however, the company must also collect primary data. Table 5.1 shows that designing a plan for primary data collection calls for a number of decisions on *research approaches*, *contact methods*, *sampling plan*, and *research instruments*.

Research Approaches Research approaches for gathering primary data include observation, surveys, and experiments. Here, we discuss each one in turn.

OBSERVATIONAL RESEARCH **Observational research** involves gathering primary data by observing relevant people, actions, and situations. For example, a bank might evaluate possible new branch locations by checking traffic patterns, neighbourhood conditions, and the location of competing branches.

Observational research
Gathering primary data by observing relevant people, actions, and situations.

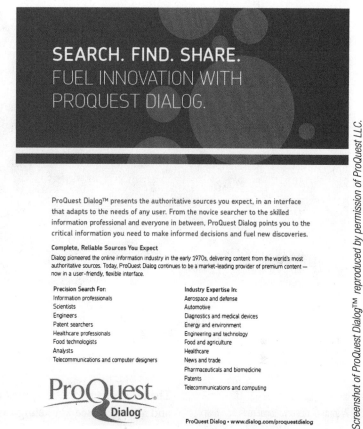

Exhibit 5.5 Online database services, such as Dialog, LCC, put an incredible wealth of information at the keyboards of marketing decision makers. Dialog provides "authoritative answers enriched by ProQuest."

TABLE 5.1 Planning Primary Data Collection			
Research Approaches	Contact Methods	Sampling Plan	Research Instruments
Observation	Mail	Sampling unit	Questionnaire
Survey	Telephone	Sample size	Mechanical instruments
Experiment	Personal Online	Sampling procedure	

(Michael Stuparyk/GetStock.com)

Exhibit 5.6 Ethnographic research: Kraft Canada sent out its president (above centre) and other high-level executives to observe actual family life in diverse Canadian homes. Videos of their experiences helped marketers and others across the company to understand the role Kraft's brands play in people's lives.

Ethnographic research

A form of observational research that involves sending trained observers to watch and interact with consumers in their "natural habitat."

Researchers often observe consumer behaviour to glean customer insights they can't obtain by simply asking customers questions. For instance, Fisher-Price has set up an observation lab in which it can observe the reactions of little tots to new toys. The Fisher-Price PlayLab is a sunny, toy-strewn space where lucky kids get to test Fisher-Price prototypes, under the watchful eyes of designers who hope to learn what will get kids worked up into a new-toy frenzy.

Marketers not only observe what consumers do, they also observe what consumers are saying. As discussed earlier, marketers now routinely listen in on consumer conversations on blogs, social networks, and websites. Observing such naturally occurring feedback can provide inputs that simply can't be gained through more structured and formal research approaches.

A wide range of companies now use **ethnographic research**. Ethnographic research involves sending trained observers to watch and interact with consumers in their "natural habitat." The observers might be trained anthropologists and psychologists, or company researchers and managers (see Marketing@Work 5.1). Also, consider this example:[11]

> Kraft Canada recently sent its president and other high-level Kraft executives to observe actual family life in a dozen diverse Canadian homes. "We went out with the purpose of understanding the Canadian family, what's going on in their homes, particularly the kitchen," says Kraft Canada's vice-president of consumer insights and strategy. After viewing hours of video of all 12 families visited, the consumer insights group found some unifying themes across Kraft's diverse markets. It learned that almost all families faced the same "mad rush to have something ready to feed the family, a hectic-ness, last-minute decisions, the need to balance the child's needs and different food needs." Kraft shared a compilation of the videos with marketing and sales teams, who used it as a basis for brainstorming sessions, and even put the video on an internal website for Kraft's 4,500 employees across Canada to view. The experience of "living with customers" helped Kraft's marketers and others understand how the company's brands help customers by providing more convenient products that reduce the stress of getting meals on the table.

Beyond conducting ethnographic research in physical consumer environments, many companies now routinely conduct *Netnography* research—observing consumers in a natural context on the Internet. Observing people as they interact on and move about the Internet can provide useful insights into both online and offline buying motives and behaviour.

Observational and ethnographic research often yields the kinds of details that just don't emerge from traditional research questionnaires or focus groups. Whereas traditional quantitative research approaches seek to test known hypotheses and obtain answers to well-defined product or strategy questions, observational research can generate fresh customer and market insights that people are unwilling or unable to provide. It provides a window into customers' unconscious actions and unexpressed needs and feelings.

In contrast, however, some things simply cannot be observed, such as feelings, attitudes, motives, or private behaviour. Long-term or infrequent behaviour is also difficult to observe. Finally, observations can be very difficult to interpret. Because of

Ethnographic Research: Watching What Consumers *Really* Do

A girl walks into a bar and says to the bartender, "Give me a Diet Coke and a clear sight line to those guys drinking Miller Lite in the corner." If you're waiting for a punch line, this is no joke. The "girl" in this situation is Emma Gilding, corporate ethnographer at ad agency Ogilvy & Mather. In this case, her job is to hang out in bars around the country and watch groups of guys knocking back beers with their friends. No kidding. This is honest-to-goodness, cutting-edge marketing research—ethnography style.

As a videographer filmed the action, Gilding kept tabs on how close the guys stood to one another. She eavesdropped on stories and observed how the mantle was passed from one speaker to another, as in a tribe around a campfire. Back at the office, a team of trained anthropologists and psychologists pored over more than 70 hours of footage from five similar nights in bars from San Diego to Philadelphia. One key insight: Miller is favoured by groups of drinkers, while its main competitor, Bud Lite, is a beer that sells to individuals. The result was a hilarious series of ads that cut from a Miller Lite drinker's weird experiences in the world—getting caught in the subway taking money from a blind musician's guitar case or hitching a ride in the desert with a deranged trucker—to shots of him regaling friends with tales over a brew. The Miller Lite ads got high marks from audiences for their entertainment value and emotional resonance.

Today's marketers face many difficult questions: What do customers *really* think about a product and what do they say about it to their friends? How do they *really* use it? Will they tell you? *Can* they tell you? All too often, traditional research simply can't provide accurate answers. To get deeper insights, many companies use ethnographic research by watching and interacting with consumers in their "natural environments."

Ethnographers are looking for "consumer truth." In surveys and interviews, customers may state (and fully believe) certain preferences and behaviours, when the reality is actually quite different. Ethnography provides an insider's tour of the customer's world, helping marketers get at what consumers *really* do rather than what they *say* they do. "That might mean catching a heart-disease patient scarfing down a meatball sub and a cream soup while extolling the virtues of healthy eating," observes one ethnographer, "or a diabetic vigorously salting his sausage and eggs after explaining how he refuses jelly for his toast."

By entering the customer's world, ethnographers can scrutinize how customers think and feel as it relates to their products. Here's another example:

Kelly Peña, also known as "the kid whisperer," was digging through a 12-year-old boy's dresser drawer one recent afternoon. Her undercover mission: to unearth what makes him tick and help the Walt Disney Company reassert itself as a cultural force among boys. Peña, a Disney researcher, heads a team zeroed in on a ratty rock 'n' roll T-shirt. Black Sabbath? "Wearing it makes me feel like I'm going to an R-rated movie," said Dean, the shy redheaded boy under scrutiny. Jackpot! Peña and her team of anthropologists have spent 18 months peering inside the heads of incommunicative boys in search of just that kind of psychological nugget.

Disney is relying on Peña's insights to create new entertainment for boys ages 6 to 14, who account for US$50 billion a year in spending worldwide. With the exception of *Cars*, Disney—home to more girl-focused fare such as the "Princesses" merchandising line, "Hannah Montana," and "Pixie Hollow"—has been notably weak on hit entertainment for boys. Peña's research is sometimes conducted in groups; sometimes it involves going shopping with a teenage boy and his mother. Walking through Dean's house, Peña looked for unspoken clues about his likes and dislikes. "What's on the back shelves that he hasn't quite gotten rid of will be telling," she said beforehand. "What's on his walls? How does he interact with his siblings?" One big takeaway from the two-hour visit: Although Dean was trying to sound grown-up and nonchalant in his answers, he still had a lot of little kid in him. He had dinosaur sheets and stuffed animals at the bottom of his bed. "I think he's trying to push a lot of boundaries for the first time," Peña said later.

Children can already see the results of Peña's scrutiny on Disney XD, a new cable channel and website. It's no accident, for instance, that the central character on "Aaron Stone" is a mediocre basketball player. Peña told producers that boys identify with protagonists who try hard to grow.

Exhibit 5.7 **Ethnographic research:** To better understand the challenges faced by elderly shoppers, Kimberly-Clark executives shopped while wearing vision-impairment glasses and bulky gloves to simulate arthritis.

(Lauren Pond/The Photo Pond)

"Winning isn't nearly as important to boys as Hollywood thinks," she said.

Ethnographic research often yields the kinds of intimate details that just don't emerge from traditional focus groups and surveys. For example, focus groups told the Best Western hotel chain that it's men who decide when to stop for the night and where to stay. But videotapes of couples on cross-country journeys showed it was usually the women. And observation can often uncover problems that customers don't even know they have. By videotaping consumers in the shower, plumbing fixture maker Moen uncovered safety risks that consumers didn't recognize—such as the habit some women have of shaving their legs while holding on to one unit's temperature control. Moen would find it almost impossible to discover such design flaws simply by asking questions.

Experiencing firsthand what customers experience can also provide powerful insights. To that end, consumer products giant Kimberly-Clark even runs a program that puts executives from retail chains such as Walgreens, Rite Aid, and Family Dollar directly into their customers' shoes—literally. The executives shop in their own stores with glasses that blur their vision, unpopped popcorn in their shoes, and bulky rubber gloves on their hands. It's all part of an exercise designed to help marketers understand the physical challenges faced by elderly shoppers, who will represent 20 percent of the total North American population by 2030.

The vision-blurring glasses simulate common vision ailments such as cataracts, macular degeneration, and glaucoma. Unpopped popcorn in shoes gives a feel for what it's like to walk with aching joints. And the bulky gloves simulate the limitations to manual dexterity brought on by arthritis. Participants come back from these experiences bursting with ideas for elderly-friendly store changes, such as bigger typefaces and more eye-friendly colors on packaging and fliers, new store lighting and clearer signage, and instant call buttons near heavy merchandise such as bottled water and laundry detergent.

Thus, more and more, marketing researchers are getting up close and personal with consumers—watching them closely as they act and interact in natural settings or stepping in to feel firsthand what they feel. "Knowing the individual consumer on an intimate basis has become a necessity," says one research consultant, "and ethnography is the intimate connection to the consumer."

Sources: Adapted excerpts and other information from Brooks Barnes, "Disney Expert Uses Science to Draw Boy Viewers," *New York Times*, April 14, 2009, p. A1; Linda Tischler, "Every Move You Make," Fast Company, April 2004, pp. 73–75; Ellen Byron, "Seeing Store Shelves Through Senior Eyes," *Wall Street Journal*, September 14, 2009, p. B1; and Natasha Singer, "The Fountain of Old Age," *New York Times*, February 6, 2011, p. BU 1.

these limitations, researchers often use observation along with other data collection methods.

Survey research
Gathering primary data by asking people questions about their knowledge, attitudes, preferences, and buying behaviour.

SURVEY RESEARCH **Survey research**, the most widely used method for primary data collection, is the approach best suited for gathering *descriptive* information. A company that wants to know about people's knowledge, attitudes, preferences, or buying behaviour can often find out by asking them directly.

The major advantage of survey research is its flexibility—it can be used to obtain many different kinds of information in many different situations. Surveys addressing almost any marketing question or decision can be conducted by phone or mail, in person, or on the web.

However, survey research also presents some problems. Sometimes people are unable to answer survey questions because they cannot remember or have never thought about what they do and why. People may be unwilling to respond to unknown interviewers or about things they consider private. Respondents may answer survey questions even when they do not know the answer in order to appear smarter or more informed. Or they may try to help the interviewer by giving pleasing answers. Finally, busy people may not take the time, or they might resent the intrusion into their privacy.

Experimental research
Gathering primary data by selecting matched groups of subjects, giving them different treatments, controlling related factors, and checking for differences in group responses.

EXPERIMENTAL RESEARCH Whereas observation is best suited for exploratory research and surveys for descriptive research, **experimental research** is best suited for gathering *causal* information. Experiments involve selecting matched groups of subjects, giving them different treatments, controlling unrelated factors, and checking for differences in group responses. Thus, experimental research tries to explain cause-and-effect relationships.

TABLE 5.2	Strengths and Weaknesses of Contact Methods			
	Mail	**Telephone**	**Personal**	**Online**
Flexibility	Poor	Good	Excellent	Good
Quantity of data that can be collected	Good	Fair	Excellent	Good
Control of interviewer effects	Excellent	Fair	Poor	Fair
Control of sample	Fair	Excellent	Good	Excellent
Speed of data collection	Poor	Excellent	Good	Excellent
Response rate	Poor	Poor	Good	Good
Cost	Good	Fair	Poor	Excellent

For example, before adding a new sandwich to its menu, McDonald's might use experiments to test the effects on sales of two different prices it might charge. It could introduce the new sandwich at one price in one city and at another price in another city. If the cities are similar, and if all other marketing efforts for the sandwich are the same, then differences in sales in the two cities could be related to the price charged.

Contact Methods Information can be collected by mail, telephone, personal interview, or online. Table 5.2 shows the strengths and weaknesses of each of these contact methods.

MAIL, TELEPHONE, AND PERSONAL INTERVIEWING *Mail questionnaires* can be used to collect large amounts of information at a low cost per respondent. Respondents may give more honest answers to more personal questions on a mail questionnaire than to an unknown interviewer in person or over the phone. Also, no interviewer is involved to bias the respondent's answers.

However, mail questionnaires are not very flexible—all respondents answer the same questions in a fixed order. Mail surveys usually take longer than other types of surveys to complete, and the response rate—the number of people returning completed questionnaires—is often very low. Finally, the researcher often has little control over the mail questionnaire sample. Even with a good mailing list, it is hard to control *who* at the mailing address fills out the questionnaire. As a result of the shortcomings, more and more marketers are now shifting to faster, more flexible, and lower-cost online surveys.

Telephone interviewing is one of the best methods for gathering information quickly, and it provides greater flexibility than mail questionnaires. Interviewers can explain difficult questions and, depending on the answers they receive, skip some questions or probe on others. Response rates tend to be higher than with mail questionnaires, and interviewers can ask to speak to respondents with the desired characteristics or even by name.

However, with telephone interviewing, the cost per respondent is higher than with mail or online questionnaires. Also, people may not want to discuss personal questions with an interviewer. The method introduces interviewer bias—the way interviewers talk, how they ask questions, and other differences may affect respondents' answers. Finally, in this age of do-not-call lists and promotion-harassed consumers, potential survey respondents are increasingly hanging up on telephone interviewers rather than talking with them.

Personal interviewing takes two forms—individual and group interviewing. *Individual interviewing* involves talking with people in their homes or offices, on the street, or in shopping malls. Such interviewing is flexible. Trained interviewers can guide interviews, explain difficult questions, and explore issues as the situation requires. They can show subjects actual products, advertisements, or packages, and observe reactions and behaviour. However, individual personal interviews may cost three to four times as much as telephone interviews.

Group interviewing consists of inviting six to ten people to meet with a trained moderator to talk about a product, service, or organization. Participants normally are paid a small sum for attending. The moderator encourages free and easy discussion, hoping that group interactions will bring out actual feelings and thoughts. At the same time, the moderator "focuses" the discussion—hence the name **focus group interviewing**.

In traditional focus groups, researchers and marketers watch the focus group discussions from behind one-way glass, and record comments in writing or on video for later study. Focus group researchers often use videoconferencing and Internet technology to connect marketers in distant locations with live focus group action. By using cameras and two-way sound systems, marketing executives in a far-off boardroom can look in and listen, using remote controls to zoom in on faces and pan the focus group at will.

Along with observational research, focus group interviewing has become one of the major qualitative marketing research tools for gaining fresh insights into consumer thoughts and feelings. However, focus group studies present some challenges. They usually employ small samples to keep time and costs down, and it may be hard to generalize from the results. Moreover, consumers in focus groups are not always open and honest about their real feelings, behaviour, and intentions in front of other people.

To overcome these problems, many researchers are tinkering with the focus group design. Some companies use *immersion groups*—small groups of consumers who interact directly and informally with product designers without a focus group moderator present. Other researchers are changing the environments in which they conduct focus groups to help consumers relax and elicit more authentic responses. For example, Lexus recently hosted a series of "An Evening with Lexus" dinners with groups of customers in customers' homes:[12]

> Nothing like citrus-cured sardines with Escabeche vegetables or baked halibut with a quail egg to get the conversation flowing. Indeed, Mark Templin, Lexus group vice-president and general manager, figures the best way to get up close and personal with customers is to dine with them—in their homes and in style. At the first dinner, held in Beverly Hills, 16 owners of Lexus, Mercedes, BMW, Audi, Land Rover, and other high-end cars traded their perceptions of the Lexus brand. Through lively talk over a sumptuous meal catered by a famous chef, Templin hoped to learn why people did or didn't become Lexus owners.
>
> While feasting on the cuisine, the high-end car consumers gave Templin many actionable insights. For example, he heard that Lexus vehicles often are tagged with being unexciting. "Everyone had driven a Lexus at some point and had a great experience," Templin says. "But the Lexus they [had] wasn't as fun to drive as the car they have now. It's our challenge to show that Lexus is more fun to drive today than it was 15 years ago." Templin was also startled by the extent to which luxury car buyers allow their grown children to decide what car they should purchase. Templin says Lexus marketing in the future also will have to aim at young adults who may not be buying luxury cars but who may strongly influence their parents' decisions.

Individual and focus group interviews can add a personal touch as opposed to more numbers-oriented research. "We get lots of research, and it tells us what we need to run our business, but I get more out of talking one-on-one," says Lexus's Templin. "It really comes to life when I hear people say it."

Focus group interviewing
Personal interviewing that involves inviting six to ten people to gather for a few hours with a trained interviewer to talk about a product, service, or organization. The interviewer "focuses" the group discussion on important issues.

ONLINE MARKETING RESEARCH The growth of the Internet has had a dramatic impact on how marketing research is conducted. Increasingly, researchers are collecting primary data through **online marketing research**: Internet surveys, online panels, experiments, and online focus groups and brand communities.

Online research can take many forms. A company can use the web as a survey medium: It can include a questionnaire on its website or use email to invite people to answer questions, create online panels that provide regular feedback, or conduct live discussions, or online focus groups. Researchers can also conduct experiments on the web. They can experiment with different prices, headlines, or product features on different websites or at different times to learn the relative effectiveness of their offers. They can set up virtual shopping environments and use them to test new products and marketing programs. Or a company can learn about the behaviour of online customers by following their click streams as they visit the website and move to other sites.

The Internet is especially well suited to *quantitative* research—for example, conducting marketing surveys and collecting data. More than three-quarters of people now have access to the web, making it a fertile channel for reaching a broad cross-section of consumers.[13] As response rates for traditional survey approaches decline and costs increase, the web is quickly replacing mail and the telephone as the dominant data collection methodology.

Web-based survey research offers many advantages over traditional phone, mail, and personal interviewing approaches. The most obvious advantages are speed and low costs. By going online, researchers can quickly and easily distribute Internet surveys to thousands of respondents simultaneously via email or by posting them on selected websites. Responses can be almost instantaneous, and because respondents themselves enter the information, researchers can tabulate, review, and share research data as the information arrives.

Online research also usually costs much less than research conducted through mail, phone, or personal interviews. Using the Internet eliminates most of the postage, phone, interviewer, and data-handling costs associated with the other approaches. Moreover, sample size has little impact on costs. Once the questionnaire is set up, there's little difference in cost between 10 respondents and 10 000 respondents on the web.

Its low cost puts online research well within the reach of almost any business, large or small. In fact, with the Internet, what was once the domain of research experts is now available to almost any would-be researcher. Even smaller, less sophisticated researchers can use online survey services such as Zoomerang (www.zoomerang.com) and SurveyMonkey (www.surveymonkey.com) to create, publish, and distribute their own custom surveys in minutes. However, tighter privacy legislation in several provinces, which was implemented in response to the US Patriot Act, now require Canadian companies to store their customer data in Canada. As a result, Canadian-based survey tools, such as FluidSurveys (fluidsurveys.com), offer similar survey tools while storing consumer data on Canadian servers.

Exhibit 5.8 **New focus group environments:** Lexus general manager Mark Templin hosts "An Evening with Lexus" dinners with luxury car buyers to figure out why they did or didn't become Lexus owners.

Courtesy of Lexus

Online marketing research
Collecting primary data online through Internet surveys, online focus groups, web-based experiments, or tracking consumers' online behaviour.

Courtesy of Fluid Surveys

Exhibit 5.9 Online research: Thanks to survey services such as FluidSurveys, almost any business, large or small, can create, publish, and distribute its own custom surveys in minutes.

Online focus groups
Gathering a small group of people online with a trained moderator to chat about a product, service, or organization and to gain qualitative insights about consumer attitudes and behaviour.

Web-based surveys also tend to be more interactive and engaging, easier to complete, and less intrusive than traditional phone or mail surveys. As a result, they usually garner higher response rates. The Internet is an excellent medium for reaching the hard-to-reach consumer—for example, the often-elusive teen, single, affluent, and well-educated audiences. It's also good for reaching working mothers and other people who lead busy lives. Such people are well represented online, and they can respond in their own space and at their own convenience.

Just as marketing researchers have rushed to use the Internet for quantitative surveys and data collection, they are now also adopting *qualitative* Internet-based research approaches, such as online focus groups, blogs, and social networks. The Internet can provide a fast, low-cost way to gain qualitative customer insights.

A primary qualitative web-based research approach is **online focus groups**. Such focus groups offer many advantages over traditional focus groups. Participants can log in from anywhere—all they need is a laptop and a web connection. Thus, the Internet works well for bringing together people from different parts of the country or world. Also, researchers can conduct and monitor online focus groups from just about anywhere, eliminating travel, lodging, and facility costs. Finally, although online focus groups require some advance scheduling, results are almost immediate.

Online focus groups can take any of several formats. Most occur in real time, in the form of online chat room discussions in which participants and a moderator sit around a virtual table exchanging comments. Alternatively, researchers might set up an online message board on which respondents interact over the course of several days or a few weeks. Participants log in daily and comment on focus group topics.

Although low in cost and easy to administer, online focus groups can lack the real-world dynamics of more personal approaches. To overcome these shortcomings, some researchers are now adding real-time audio and video to their online focus groups.

For example, online research firm Channel M2 "puts the human touch back into online research" by assembling focus group participants in people-friendly "virtual interview rooms." At the appointed time, participants sign on via their webcam-equipped computer, view live video of other participants, and interact in real-time. Researchers can "sit in" on the focus group from anywhere, seeing and hearing every respondent.[14]

Although growing rapidly, both quantitative and qualitative Internet-based research have some drawbacks. One major problem is controlling who's in the online sample. Without seeing respondents, it's difficult to know who they really are. To overcome such sample and context problems, many online research firms use opt-in communities and respondent panels. For example, Zoomerang offers an online consumer and business panel profiled on more than 500 attributes.[15]

Alternatively, many companies are now developing their own custom social networks and using them to gain customer inputs and insights. For example, in addition to picking customers' brains in face-to-face events such as "An Evening with Lexus" dinners in customers' homes, Lexus has built an extensive online research community called the Lexus Advisory Board.[16]

The Lexus Advisory Board consists of 20 000 invitation-only Lexus owners representing a wide range of demographics, psychographics, and model ownership. Lexus surveys the group regularly to obtain owner input on everything from perceptions of the brand and input on new models and features to the Lexus ownership experience and customer relationships with dealers. "As a Lexus owner, your opinion is invaluable to us," says the invitation, "which is why Lexus is inviting you to join our exclusive online research panel. By becoming a member of the Lexus Advisory Board, your feedback will help shape future product development, customer service, and marketing communications." Says a Lexus marketing executive, "This is a great way of listening to customers."

Thus, in recent years, the Internet has become an important tool for conducting research and developing customer insights. But today's marketing researchers are going even further—

Exhibit 5.10 Some researchers have now added real-time audio and video to their online focus groups. For example, Channel M2 "puts the human touch back into online research" by assembling focus group participants in people-friendly "virtual interview rooms."

well beyond structured online surveys, focus groups, and web communities. Increasingly, they are listening to and watching consumers by actively mining the rich veins of unsolicited, unstructured, "bottom up" customer information already coursing around the web.

This might be as simple as scanning customer reviews and comments on the company's brand site or on shopping sites such as amazon.ca or bestbuy.ca. Or it might mean using sophisticated web-analysis tools to deeply analyze mountains of consumer comments and messages found in blogs or on social networking sites, such as Facebook or Twitter. Listening to and watching consumers online can provide valuable insights into what consumers are saying or feeling about brands. As one information expert puts it, "The web knows what you want."[17] (See Marketing@Work 5.2.)

Sampling Plan Marketing researchers usually draw conclusions about large groups of consumers by studying a small sample of the total consumer population. A **sample** is a segment of the population selected for marketing research to represent the population as a whole. Ideally, the sample should be representative so that the researcher can make accurate estimates of the thoughts and behaviours of the larger population.

Designing the sample requires three decisions. First, *who* is to be studied (what *sampling unit*)? The answer to this question is not always obvious. For example, to learn about the decision-making process for a family automobile purchase, should the subject be the husband, wife, other family members, dealership salespeople, or all of these? The researcher must determine what information is needed and who is most likely to have it.

Second, *how many* people should be included (what *sample size*)? Large samples give more reliable results than small samples. However, larger samples usually cost more, and it is not necessary to sample the entire target market or even a large portion to get reliable results. If well chosen, samples of less than 1 percent of a population can often give good reliability.

Third, *how* should the people in the sample be *chosen* (what *sampling procedure*)? Table 5.3 describes different kinds of samples. Using *probability samples*, each population member has a known chance of being included in the sample, and researchers can

Sample
A segment of the population selected for marketing research to represent the population as a whole.

MARKETING@WORK   5.2

Listening Online: The Web Knows What You Want

Thanks to the burgeoning world of blogs, social networks, and other Internet forums, marketers now have near-real-time access to a flood of online consumer information. It's all there for the digging—praise, criticism, recommendations, actions—revealed in what consumers are saying and doing as they ply the Internet. Forward-looking marketers are now mining valuable customer insights from this rich new vein of unprompted, "bottom-up" information.

Whereas traditional marketing research provides insights into the "logical, representative, structured aspect of our consumers," says Kristin Bush, senior manager of consumer and market knowledge at P&G, online listening "provides much more of the intensity, much more of the . . . context and the passion, and more of the spontaneity that consumers are truly giving you [when they offer up their opinions] unsolicited."

Listening online might involve something as simple as scanning customer reviews on the company's brand site or on popular shopping sites such as amazon.ca or bestbuy.ca. Such reviews are plentiful, address specific products, and provide unvarnished customer reactions. Amazon.ca alone features detailed customer reviews on everything it sells, and its customers rely heavily on these reviews when making purchases. If customers in the market for a company's brands are reading and reacting to such reviews, so should the company's marketers. Many companies are now adding customer review sections to their own brand sites. Both positive and negative feedback can help the company learn what it is doing well and where improvement is needed.

At a deeper level, marketers now employ sophisticated web-analysis tools to listen in on and mine nuggets from the churning mass of consumer comments and conversations in blogs, in news articles, in online forums, and on social networking sites such as Facebook or Twitter. But beyond monitoring what customers are *saying* about them online,

companies are also watching what customers are *doing* online. Marketers scrutinize consumer web-browsing behaviour in precise detail and use the resulting insights to personalize shopping experiences. Consider this example:

A shopper at the retail site www.figleaves .com takes a close look at a silky pair of women's slippers. Next, a recommendation appears for a man's bathrobe. This could seem terribly wrong—unless, of course, it turns out to be precisely what she wanted. Why the bathrobe? Analysis of figleaves .com website behaviour data—from mouse clicks to search queries—shows that certain types of female shoppers at certain times of the week are likely to be shopping for men.

What a given customer sees at the site might also depend on other behaviours. For example, shoppers who seem pressed for time (say, shopping from work and clicking rapidly from screen to screen) might see more simplified pages with a direct path to the shopping cart and checkout. Alternatively, more leisurely shoppers (say, those shopping from home or on weekends and browsing product reviews) might receive pages with more features, video clips, and comparison information. The goal of such analysis is to teach websites "something close to the savvy of a flesh-and-blood sales clerk," says a web-analytics expert. "In the first five minutes in a store, the sales guy is observing a customer's body language and tone of voice. We have to teach machines to pick up on those same insights from movements online."

More broadly, information about what consumers do while trolling the vast expanse of the Internet—what searches they make, the sites they visit, what they buy, with whom they connect—is pure gold to marketers. And today's marketers are busy mining that gold.

On the Internet today, everybody knows who

you are. In fact, legions of Internet companies know your gender, your age, the neighbourhood you live in, who your Facebook and Twitter friends are, that you like pickup trucks, and that you spent, say, three hours and 43 seconds on a website for pet lovers on a rainy day in January. All that data streams through myriad computer networks, where it's sorted, catalogued, analyzed, and then used to deliver ads aimed squarely at you, potentially anywhere you travel on the Internet. It's called *behavioural targeting*—tracking consumers' online behaviour and using it to target ads to them. So, for example, if you place a cellphone in your Amazon.ca shopping cart but don't buy it, you might expect to see some ads for that very type of phone the next time you visit your favourite TSN site to catch up on the latest sports scores.

That's amazing enough, but the newest wave of web analytics and targeting takes online eavesdropping even further—from *behavioural* targeting to *social* targeting. Whereas behavioural targeting tracks consumer movements across websites, social targeting also mines individual online social connections. Research shows that consumers shop a lot like their friends and are five times more likely to respond to ads from brands friends use. Social targeting links customer data to social interaction data

Exhibit 5.11 Marketers watch what consumers say and do online, then use the resulting insights to personalize online shopping experiences. Is it sophisticated web research or "just a little creepy?"

(Andresr/Shutterstock)

from social networking sites. So, instead of just having a sportchek.ca ad for running shoes pop up because you've recently searched for running shoes (behavioural targeting), an ad for a specific pair of running shoes pops up because a friend that you're connected to via Twitter just bought those shoes from sportchek.ca last week (social targeting).

Online listening. Behavioural targeting. Social targeting. All of these are great for marketers as they work to mine customer insights from the massive amounts of consumer information swirling around the web. The biggest question? You've probably already guessed it. As marketers get more adept at trolling blogs, social networks, and other web domains, what happens to consumer privacy? Yup, that's the downside. At what point does sophisticated web research cross the line into consumer stalking?

Proponents claim that behavioural and social targeting benefit more than abuse consumers, by feeding back ads and products that are more relevant to their interests. But to many consumers and public advocates, following consumers online and stalking them with ads feels more than just a little creepy. Behavioural targeting, for example, has already been the subject of congressional and regulatory hearings in the United States. The Federal Trade Commission has recommended the creation of a "Do Not Track" system (the Internet equivalent to the "Do Not Call" registry), which would let people opt out of having their actions monitored online.

Despite such concerns, however, online listening will continue to grow. And, with appropriate safeguards, it promises benefits for both companies and customers. Tapping into online conversations and behaviour lets companies "get the unprompted voice of the consumer, the real sentiments, the real values, and the real points of view that they have of our products and services," says P&G's Bush. "Companies that figure out how to listen and respond . . . in a meaningful, valuable way are going to win in the marketplace." After all, knowing what customers really want is an essential first step in creating customer value. And, as one online information expert puts it, "The web knows what you want."

Sources: Adapted excerpts, quotes, and other information from Stephen Baker, "The Web Knows What You Want," *Business-Week,* July 27, 2009, p. 48; Piet Levy, "The Data Dilemma," *Marketing News,* January 30, 2011, pp. 20–21; Brian Morrissey, "Connect the Thoughts," *Adweek,* June 29, 2009, pp. 10–11; Paul Sloan, "The Quest for the Perfect Online Ad," *Business 2.0,* March 2007, p. 88; David Wiesenfeld, Kristin Bush, and Ronjan Sikdar, "Listen Up: Online Yields New Research Pathway," *Nielsen Consumer Insights,* August 2009, http://en-us.nielsen.com/; Elizabeth A. Sullivan, "10 Minutes with Kristin Bush," Marketing News, September 30, 2009, pp. 26–28; Eric Picard, "Why Consumers Think Online Marketing Is Creepy," iMedia Connection, December 9, 2010, www.imediaconnection.com/content/28158.asp; and Douglas Karr, "Do Not Track: What Marketers Need to Know," Marketing Tech Blog, January 26, 2011, www.marketingtechblog.com/technology/do-not-track/.

calculate confidence limits for sampling error. But when probability sampling costs too much or takes too much time, marketing researchers often take *nonprobability samples,* even though their sampling error cannot be measured. These varied ways of drawing samples have different costs and time limitations as well as different accuracy and statistical properties. Which method is best depends on the needs of the research project.

TABLE 5.3 Types of Samples

Probability Sample	
Simple random sample	Every member of the population has a known and equal chance of selection.
Stratified random sample	The population is divided into mutually exclusive groups (such as age groups), and random samples are drawn from each group.
Cluster (area) sample	The population is divided into mutually exclusive groups (such as blocks), and the researcher draws a sample of the groups to interview.
Nonprobability Sample	
Convenience sample	The researcher selects the easiest population members from which to obtain information.
Judgment sample	The researcher uses his or her judgment to select population members who are good prospects for accurate information.
Quota sample	The researcher finds and interviews a prescribed number of people in each of several categories.

Research Instruments In collecting primary data, marketing researchers have a choice of two main research instruments—the *questionnaire* and *mechanical instruments*.

QUESTIONNAIRES The *questionnaire* is by far the most common instrument, whether administered in person, by phone, or online. Questionnaires are very flexible—there are many ways to ask questions. *Closed-end questions* include all the possible answers, and subjects make choices among them. Examples include multiple-choice questions and scale questions. *Open-end questions* allow respondents to answer in their own words. In a survey of airline users, WestJet might simply ask, "What is your opinion of WestJet Airlines?" Or it might ask people to complete a sentence: "When I choose an airline, the most important consideration is." These and other kinds of open-end questions often reveal more than closed-end questions because they do not limit respondents' answers.

Open-end questions are especially useful in exploratory research, when the researcher is trying to find out *what* people think, but not measuring *how many* people think in a certain way. Closed-end questions, on the other hand, provide answers that are easier to interpret and tabulate.

Researchers should also use care in the *wording* and *ordering* of questions. They should use simple, direct, unbiased wording. Questions should be arranged in a logical order. The first question should create interest if possible, and difficult or personal questions should be asked last so that respondents do not become defensive.

MECHANICAL INSTRUMENTS Although questionnaires are the most common research instrument, researchers also use *mechanical instruments* to monitor consumer behaviour. Nielsen Media Research attaches *people metres* to television sets, cable boxes, and satellite systems in selected homes to record who watches which programs. Retailers use *checkout scanners* to record shoppers' purchases.

Other mechanical devices measure subjects' physical responses. For example, consider Disney Media Networks' new consumer research lab in Austin, Texas:[18]

> A technician in a black lab coat gazed at the short, middle-aged man seated inside Disney's secretive new research facility, his face shrouded with eye-tracking goggles. "Read espn .go.com on that BlackBerry," she told him soothingly, like a nurse about to draw blood. "And have fun," she added, leaving the room. In reality, the man's appetite for sports news was not of interest. (The site was a fake version anyway.) Rather, the technician and her fellow researchers from Disney Media Networks—which includes ABC, ESPN, and other networks— were eager to know how the man responded to ads of varying size. How small could the banners become and still draw his attention? A squadron of Disney executives scrutinized the data as it flowed in real time onto television monitors in an adjacent room. "He's not even looking at the banner now," said one researcher. The man clicked to another page. "There we go, that one's drawing his attention." The tools are advanced: In addition to tracking eye movement, the research team uses heart-rate monitors, skin temperature readings, and facial expressions (probes are attached to facial muscles) to gauge reactions. The goal: to learn what works and what does not in the high-stakes game of new media advertising.

Still other researchers are applying *neuromarketing*—measuring brain activity to learn how consumers feel and respond. Marketing scientists using MRI scans and EEG devices have learned that tracking brain electrical activity and blood flow can provide companies with insights into what turns consumers on and off regarding their brands and marketing. "Companies have always aimed for the customer's heart, but the head may make a better target," suggests one neuromarketer. "Neuromarketing is reaching consumers where the action is: the brain."[19]

Companies ranging from PepsiCo and Disney to Google and Microsoft now hire neuromarketing research companies such as NeuroFocus and EmSense to help figure out what people are really thinking. For example, PepsiCo's Frito-Lay unit uses neuromarketing to test commercials, product designs, and packaging. Recent EEG tests showed that, compared with shiny packages showing pictures of potato chips, matte beige bags showing potatoes and other healthy ingredients trigger less activity in an area of the brain associated with feelings of guilt. Needless to say, Frito-Lay quickly switched away from the shiny packaging. And eBay's PayPal began pitching its online payment service as "fast" after brain-wave research showed that speed turns consumers on more than security and safety—earlier themes used in eBay ad campaigns.[20]

Although neuromarketing techniques can measure consumer involvement and emotional responses second by second, such brain responses can be difficult to interpret. Thus, neuromarketing is usually used in combination with other research approaches to gain a more complete picture of what goes on inside consumers' heads.

Implementing the Research Plan

The researcher next puts the marketing research plan into action. This involves collecting, processing, and analyzing the information. Data collection can be carried out by the company's marketing research staff or by outside firms. Researchers should watch closely to make sure that the plan is implemented correctly. They must guard against problems with interacting with respondents, with the quality of participants' responses, and with interviewers who make mistakes or take shortcuts.

Researchers must also process and analyze the collected data to isolate important information and insight. They need to check data for accuracy and completeness and code it for analysis. The researchers then tabulate the results and compute statistical measures.

Exhibit 5.12 **Mechanical instruments:** To find out what ads work and why, Disney researchers have developed an array of devices to track eye movement, monitor heart rates, and measure other physical responses.

Erich Schlegel/New York Times/Redux Pictures

Interpreting and Reporting the Findings

The market researcher must now interpret the findings, draw conclusions, and report them to management. The researcher should not try to overwhelm managers with numbers and fancy statistical techniques. Rather, the researcher should present important findings and insights that are useful in the major decisions faced by management.

However, interpretation should not be left only to the researchers. They are often experts in research design and statistics, but the marketing manager knows more about the problem and the decisions that must be made. The best research means little if the manager blindly accepts faulty interpretations from the researcher. Similarly, managers may be biased—they might tend to accept research results that show what they expected and reject those that they did not expect or hope for. In many cases, findings can be interpreted in different ways, and discussions between researchers and managers will help point to the best interpretations. Thus, managers and researchers must work together closely when interpreting research results, and both must share responsibility for the research process and resulting decisions.

Analyzing and Using Marketing Information `LO4`

Information gathered in internal databases and through competitive marketing intelligence and marketing research usually requires additional analysis. And managers may need help applying the information to gain customer and market insights that will improve their marketing decisions. This help may include advanced statistical analysis to learn more about the relationships within a set of data. Information analysis might also involve the application of analytical models that will help marketers make better decisions.

Once the information has been processed and analyzed, it must be made available to the right decision makers at the right time. In the following sections, we look deeper into analyzing and using marketing information.

Customer Relationship Management (CRM)

The question of how best to analyze and use individual customer data presents special problems. Most companies are awash in information about their customers. In fact, smart companies capture information at every possible customer *touchpoint*. These touch points include customer purchases, sales force contacts, service and support calls, website visits, satisfaction surveys, credit and payment interactions, market research studies—every contact between the customer and the company.

Customer relationship management (CRM)
Managing detailed information about individual customers and carefully managing customer "touch points" to maximize customer loyalty.

Unfortunately, this information is usually scattered widely across the organization. It is buried deep in the separate databases and records of different company departments. To overcome such problems, many companies are now turning to **customer relationship management (CRM)** to manage detailed information about individual customers and carefully manage customer touch points to maximize customer loyalty.

CRM consists of sophisticated software and analytical tools from companies such as Oracle, Microsoft, www.salesforce.com, and SAS that integrate customer information from all sources, analyze it in depth, and apply the results to build stronger customer relationships. CRM integrates everything that a company's sales, service, and marketing teams know about individual customers, providing a 360-degree view of the customer relationship.

CRM analysts develop *data warehouses* and use sophisticated *data mining* techniques to unearth the riches hidden in customer data. A data warehouse is a company-wide electronic database of finely detailed customer information that needs to be sifted through for gems. The purpose of a data warehouse is not just to gather information, but to pull it together into a central, accessible location. Then, once the data warehouse brings the data together, the company uses high-powered data mining techniques to sift through the mounds of data and dig out interesting findings about customers.

These findings often lead to marketing opportunities. For example, Sobeys, the second largest grocery chain in Canada, uses CRM to provide its customers with coupons relevant to their individual needs:[21]

> Sobeys, the second largest grocery chain in Canada, operates over 1500 stores in 10 provinces under different banners including IGA, Thrifty Foods, Foodland and FreshCo. The company has invested heavily in CRM by leveraging the data from its various loyalty programs, which include Air Miles in Atlantic Canada and Quebec, Club Sobeys in Ontario and the West, and Club Thrifty Foods in British Columbia. Toronto-based Exchange Solutions, the company's CRM provider, developed an offer-targeting capability for Sobeys to ensure that consumers receive coupons they'll actually want to use. By using data from their loyalty program database, Sobeys developed six segmentation models that group consumers by a number of factors such as how often they shop, how price conscious they are, and their lifestyles. When coupon offers are entered into the system, Sobeys' offer-matching engine uses additional logic (for instance, whether you've bought the product or a similar one before) to determine the best recipients. The system ensures that you won't receive a diaper coupon if you don't have a baby, and won't tempt you to buy name-brand if you're already buying the private label equivalent. The Club Sobeys quarterly statement is sent to over two million members, containing 1.4 million unique combinations of offers. CMO, Belinda Youngs says this system results in coupon redemptions that are well above the industry average.

By using CRM to understand customers better, companies can provide higher levels of customer service and develop deeper customer relationships. They can use CRM to pinpoint high-value customers, target them more effectively, cross-sell the company's products, and create offers tailored to specific customer requirements.

CRM benefits don't come without costs or risk, either in collecting the original customer data or in maintaining and mining it. The most common CRM mistake is to view CRM as a technology and software solution only. Yet technology alone cannot build profitable customer relationships. Companies can't improve customer relationships by simply installing some new software. Instead, CRM is just one part of an effective

Exhibit 5.13 Sobeys digs deeply into data obtained from its various loyalty programs, such as Club Sobeys.

overall *customer relationship management strategy*. "There's lots of talk about CRM and these days it usually has to do with a software solution," says one analyst. But marketers should start by adhering to "some basic tenets of actual customer relationship management and *then* empower them with high-tech solutions."[22] They should focus first on the R—it's the *relationship* that CRM is all about.

Distributing and Using Marketing Information

Marketing information has no value until it is used to gain customer insights and make better marketing decisions. Thus, the marketing information system must make the information readily available to the managers and others who need it. In some cases, this means providing managers with regular performance reports, intelligence updates, and reports on the results of research studies.

But marketing managers may also need non-routine information for special situations and on-the-spot decisions. For example, a sales manager having trouble with a large customer may want a summary of the account's sales and profitability over the past year. Or a retail store manager who has run out of a bestselling product may want to know the current inventory levels in the chain's other stores. These days, therefore, information distribution involves entering information into databases and making it available in a timely, user-friendly way.

Many firms use company *intranet* and internal CRM systems to facilitate this process. These systems provide ready access to research and intelligence information, customer contact information, reports, shared work documents, and more. For example, the CRM system at phone and online gift retailer 1-800-Flowers gives customer-facing employees real-time access to customer information. When a repeat customer calls, the system immediately calls up data on previous transactions and other contacts, helping reps make the customer's experience easier and more relevant. For instance, "If a customer usually buys tulips for his wife, we [talk about] our newest and best tulip selections," says the company's vice-president of customer knowledge management. "No one else in the business is able to connect customer information with real-time transaction data the way we can."[23]

In addition, companies are increasingly allowing key customers and value-network members to access account, product, and other data on demand through *extranets*. Suppliers, customers, resellers, and select other network members may access a company's

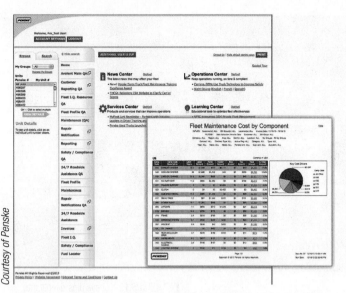

Courtesy of Penske

Exhibit 5.14 Extranets: Penske Truck Leasing's extranet site, myfleetatpenske .com, lets Penske customers access all of the data about their fleets in one spot and provides tools to help fleet managers manage their Penske accounts and maximize efficiency.

extranet to update their accounts, arrange purchases, and check orders against inventories to improve customer service. For example, Penske Truck Leasing's extranet site, www.myfleetatpenske.com, lets Penske customers access all of the data about their fleets in one spot and provides an array of tools and applications designed to help fleet managers manage their Penske accounts and maximize efficiency.[24]

Thanks to modern technology, today's marketing managers can gain direct access to the information system at any time and from virtually any location. They can tap into the system while working at a home office, from a hotel room, or from the local Starbucks through a wireless network—anyplace where they can turn on a laptop or BlackBerry. Such systems allow managers to get the information they need directly and quickly and to tailor it to their own needs. From just about anywhere, they can obtain information from company or outside databases, analyze it by using statistical software, prepare reports and presentations, and communicate directly with others in the network.

Other Marketing Information Considerations LO5

This section discusses marketing information in two special contexts: marketing research in small businesses and not-for-profit organizations, and international marketing research. Finally, we look at public policy and ethics issues in marketing research.

Marketing Research in Small Businesses and Not-for-Profit Organizations

Just like larger firms, small organizations need market information and the customer and market insights that it can provide. Managers of small businesses and not-for-profit organizations often think that marketing research can be done only by experts in large companies with big research budgets. True, large-scale research studies are beyond the budgets of most small businesses. However, many of the marketing research techniques discussed in this chapter also can be used by smaller organizations in a less formal manner and at little or no expense. Consider how one small-business owner conducted market research on a shoestring before even opening his doors:[25]

> After a string of bad experiences with his local dry cleaner, Robert Byerley decided to open his own dry-cleaning business. But before jumping in, he conducted plenty of market research. He needed a key customer insight: How would he make his business stand out from the others? To start, Byerley spent an entire week in the library and online, researching the dry-cleaning industry. To get input from potential customers, using a marketing firm, Byerley held focus groups on the store's name, look, and brochure. He also took clothes to the 15 best competing cleaners in town and had focus group members critique their work. Based on his research, he made a list of features for his new business. First on his list: quality. His business would stand behind everything it did. Not on the list: cheap prices. Creating the perfect dry-cleaning establishment simply didn't fit with a discount operation.
>
> With his research complete, Byerley opened Bibbentuckers, a high-end dry cleaner positioned on high-quality service and convenience. It featured a bank-like drive-through area with curbside delivery. A computerized bar code system read customer cleaning preferences and tracked clothes all the way through the cleaning process. Byerley added other differentiators,

such as decorative awnings, TV screens, and refreshments (even "candy for the kids and a doggy treat for your best friend"). "I wanted a place . . . that paired five-star service and quality with an establishment that didn't look like a dry cleaner," he says. The market research yielded results. Today, Bibbentuckers is a thriving six-store operation.

"Too [few] small-business owners have a . . . marketing mind-set," says a small-business consultant. "You have to think like Procter & Gamble. What would they do before launching a new product? They would find out who their customer is and who their competition is."[26]

Thus, small businesses and not-for-profit organizations can obtain good marketing insights through observation or informal surveys by using small convenience samples. Also, many associations, local media, and government agencies provide special help to small organizations. For example, the Conference Board of Canada and the Canadian Council for Small Business and Entrepreneurship offer dozens of free publications that give advice on topics ranging from preparing a business plan to ordering business signs. Other excellent web resources for small businesses include Statistics Canada (statscan.gc.ca) and Industry Canada (www.ic.gc.ca). Finally, small businesses can collect a considerable amount of information at very little cost online. They can scour competitor and customer websites and use Internet search engines to research specific companies and issues.

In summary, secondary data collection, observation, surveys, and experiments can all be used effectively by small organizations with small budgets. However, although these informal research methods are less complex and less costly, they still must be conducted with care. Managers must think carefully about the objectives of the research, formulate questions in advance, recognize the biases introduced by smaller samples and less skilled researchers, and conduct the research systematically.[27]

Exhibit 5.15 Before opening Bibbentuckers dry cleaner, owner Robert Byerly conducted research to gain insights into what customers wanted. First on the list: quality.

Courtesy of Bibbentuckers

International Marketing Research

International marketing research has grown tremendously over the past decade. International researchers follow the same steps as domestic researchers, from defining the research problem and developing a research plan to interpreting and reporting the results. However, these researchers often face more and different problems. Whereas domestic researchers deal with fairly homogeneous markets within a single country, international researchers deal with diverse markets in many different countries. These markets often vary greatly in their levels of economic development, cultures and customs, and buying patterns.

In many foreign markets, the international researcher may have a difficult time finding good secondary data. Whereas Canadian and American marketing researchers can obtain reliable secondary data from dozens of domestic research services, many countries have almost no research services at all. Some of the largest international research services operate in many countries. For example, The Nielsen Company (the world's largest marketing research company) has offices in more than 100 countries, from Schaumburg, Illinois, to Hong Kong to Nicosia, Cyprus. However, most research firms operate in only a relative handful of countries.[28] Thus, even when secondary information is available, it usually must be obtained from many different sources on a country-by-country basis, making the information difficult to combine or compare.

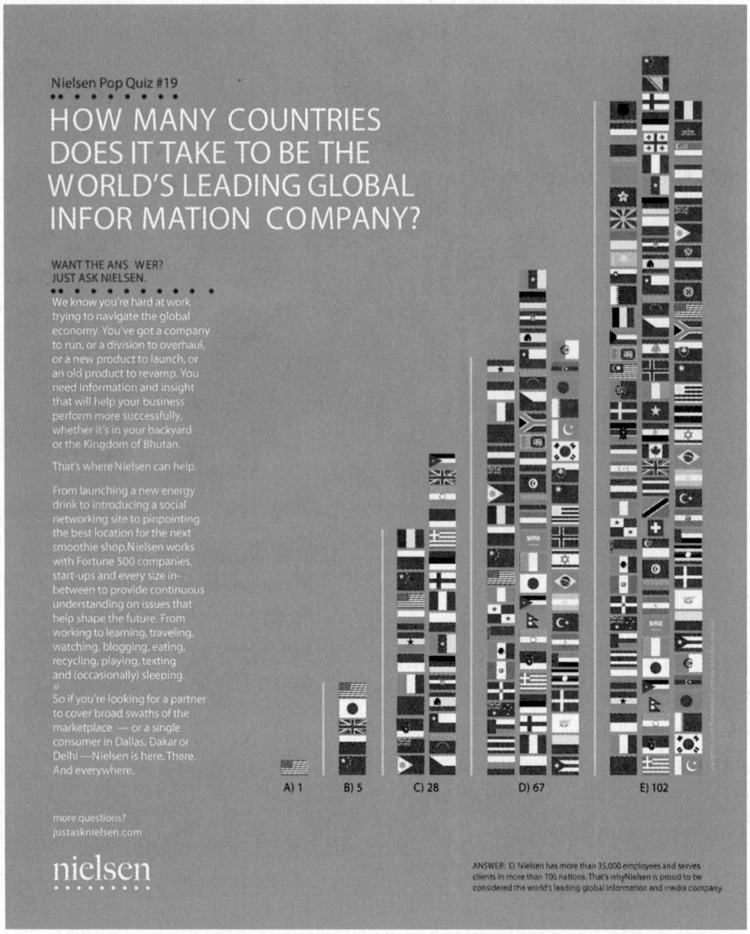

Exhibit 5.16 Some of the largest research services firms have large international organizations. ACNielsen, for example, has offices in more than 100 countries.

Because of the scarcity of good secondary data, international researchers often must collect their own primary data. However, obtaining primary data may be no easy task. For example, it can be difficult simply to develop good samples. Canadian researchers can use current telephone directories, email lists, census tract data, and any of several sources of socioeconomic data to construct samples. However, such information is largely lacking in many countries.

Once the sample is drawn, the US and Canadian researcher usually can reach most respondents easily by telephone, by mail, on the Internet, or in person. Reaching respondents is often not so easy in other parts of the world. Researchers in Mexico cannot rely on telephone, Internet, and mail data collection—most data collection is door to door and concentrated in three or four of the largest cities. In some countries, few people have phones or personal computers. For example, whereas there are 83 Internet users per 100 people in Canada, there are only 36 Internet users per 100 people in Mexico. In Rwanda, the numbers drop to 7 Internet users per 100 people. In some countries, the postal system is notoriously unreliable. In many developing countries, poor roads and transportation systems make certain areas hard to reach, making personal interviews difficult and expensive.[29]

Cultural differences from country to country cause additional problems for international researchers. Language is the most obvious obstacle. For example, questionnaires must be prepared in one language and then translated into the languages of each country researched. Responses then must be translated back into the original language for analysis and interpretation. This adds to research costs and increases the risks of error.

Translating a questionnaire from one language to another is anything but easy. Many idioms, phrases, and statements mean different things in different cultures. For example, a Danish executive noted, "Check this out by having a different translator put back into English what you've translated from English. You'll get the shock of your life. I remember [an example in which] 'out of sight, out of mind' had become 'invisible things are insane.'"[30]

Consumers in different countries also vary in their attitudes toward marketing research. People in one country may be very willing to respond; in other countries, nonresponse can be a major problem. Customs in some countries may prohibit people from talking with strangers. In certain cultures, research questions often are considered too personal. For example, in many Muslim countries, mixed-gender focus groups are taboo, as is videotaping female-only focus groups. Even when respondents are *willing* to respond, they may not be *able* to because of high functional illiteracy rates.

Despite these problems, as global marketing grows, global companies have little choice but to conduct such international marketing research. Although the costs and problems associated with international research may be high, the costs of not doing it—in terms of missed opportunities and mistakes—might be even higher. Once recognized, many of the problems associated with international marketing research can be overcome or avoided.

Public Policy and Ethics in Marketing Research

Most marketing research benefits both the sponsoring company and its consumers. Through marketing research, companies learn more about consumers' needs, resulting in more satisfying products and services, and stronger customer relationships. However, the misuse of marketing research can also harm or annoy consumers. Two major public policy and ethics issues in marketing research are intrusions on consumer privacy and the misuse of research findings.

Intrusions on Consumer Privacy Many consumers feel positive about marketing research and believe that it serves a useful purpose. Some actually enjoy being interviewed and giving their opinions. However, others strongly resent or even mistrust marketing research. They don't like being interrupted by researchers. They worry that marketers are building huge databases full of personal information about customers. Or they fear that researchers might use sophisticated techniques to probe our deepest feelings, peek over our shoulders as we shop, or eavesdrop on our conversations and then use this knowledge to manipulate our buying.

There are no easy answers when it comes to marketing research and privacy. For example, is it a good or bad thing that marketers track and analyze consumers' web clicks and target ads to individuals based on their browsing and social networking behaviour? Similarly, should we applaud or resent companies that monitor consumer discussions on YouTube, Facebook, Twitter, or other public social networks in an effort to be more responsive? For example, Dell uses web-monitoring service Radian6 to routinely track social media conversations and often responds quickly. Someone commenting about Dell on a popular blog might be surprised by receiving a response from a Dell representative within only a few hours. Dell views such monitoring as an opportunity to engage consumers in helpful two-way conversations. However, some disconcerted consumers might see it as an intrusion on their privacy.

Increasing consumer privacy concerns have become a major problem for the marketing research industry. Companies face the challenge of unearthing valuable but potentially sensitive consumer data while also maintaining consumer trust. At the same time, consumers wrestle with the trade-offs between personalization and privacy. "The debate over online [privacy] stems from a marketing paradox," says a privacy expert. "Internet shoppers want to receive personalized, timely offers based on their wants and needs. but they resent that companies track their online purchase and browsing histories." The key question: "Where is the line between questionable and acceptable customer data gathering activities?"[31] Failure to address such privacy issues could result in angry, less-cooperative consumers and increased government intervention.

The marketing research industry is considering several options for responding to intrusion and privacy issues. One example is the Marketing Research Association's "Your Opinion Counts" and "Respondent Bill of Rights" initiatives to educate consumers about the benefits of marketing research and distinguish it from telephone selling and database building. The industry also has considered adopting broad standards, perhaps based on the International Chamber of Commerce's International Code of Marketing and Social Research Practice. This code outlines researchers' responsibilities to respondents and the general public. For example, it urges that researchers make their names and addresses

Exhibit 5.17 **Misuse of research findings:** The Federal Trade Commission recently challenged research-based advertising and packaging claims stating that Kellogg's Frosted Mini-Wheats were "clinically shown to improve kids' attentiveness by nearly 20 percent."

available to participants and be open about the data they are collecting.[32]

Most major companies—including IBM, Microsoft, Facebook, and American Express—have now appointed a chief privacy officer (CPO), whose job is to safeguard the privacy of consumers who do business with the company. In the end, if researchers provide value in exchange for information, customers will gladly provide it. For example, Amazon.com's customers do not mind if the firm builds a database of products they buy as a way to provide future product recommendations. This saves time and provides value. The best approach is for researchers to ask only for the information they need, use it responsibly to provide customer value, and avoid sharing information without the customer's permission.

Misuse of Research Findings   Research studies can be powerful persuasion tools; companies often use study results as claims in their advertising and promotion. Today, however, many research studies appear to be little more than vehicles for pitching the sponsor's products. In fact, in some cases, research surveys appear to have been designed just to produce the intended effect. Few advertisers openly rig their research designs or blatantly misrepresent the findings—most abuses tend to be more subtle "stretches." Consider the following example:[33]

Based on a scientific study, the Kellogg Company proclaimed in ads and on packaging for Frosted Mini-Wheats that the cereal was "clinically shown to improve kids' attentiveness by nearly 20 percent." When challenged by the US Federal Trade Commission, however, the claims turned out to be a substantial stretch of the study results. Fine print at the bottom of the box revealed the following: "Based upon independent clinical research, kids who ate Kellogg's Frosted Mini-Wheats cereal for breakfast had up to 18 percent better attentiveness three hours after breakfast than kids who ate no breakfast." That is, as one critic noted, "Frosted Mini-Wheats are (up to) 18 percent better than starving." Moreover, according to the FTC complaint, the clinical study referred to by Kellogg actually showed that children who ate the cereal for breakfast *averaged* just under 11 percent better in attentiveness than children who ate no breakfast, and that only about one in nine improved by 20 percent or more. Kellogg settled with the FTC, agreeing to refrain from making unsubstantiated health claims about Frosted Mini-Wheats or other products, and from misrepresenting the results of scientific tests.

Recognizing that surveys can be abused, several associations—including the Marketing Research and Intelligence Association, the Canadian Marketing Association, and the American Marketing Association—have developed codes of research ethics and standards of conduct. In the end, however, unethical or inappropriate actions cannot simply be regulated away. Each company must accept responsibility for policing the conduct and reporting of its own marketing research to protect consumers' best interests and its own.

Old-School Data Mining Goes Social

So much of what you read about WestJet, in this or any other source, will tell the story of Western entrepreneurialism turned wildly successful based on two key competencies: low-cost structure and high-quality customer service. But, while always easier said than done, this is the value equation that will lead any business toward success. Those strengths began as a series of puzzles, which ultimately required solutions. Finding those solutions, as Merridy Mitchell, WestJet manager of market research, can attest, begins with asking questions—lots of questions, many times, to countless guests and WestJetters.

"We've actually been doing post-flight surveys with customers since 2005 so we have a lot of historical data to assist us with key questions around satisfaction and loyalty drivers," explains Mitchell. Data mining through this ongoing research and analysis sets off a chain reaction through the company. "Not surprisingly, customer interaction tops the list of needs guests have with WestJetters . . . more than seat comfort, TV not working, even on-time departures. So, knowing how important that is to our guests, it permeates into our training programs, our internal materials, and our creative as well."

Conventional forms of market research such as surveys and focus groups prevail as battle-tested forms of intelligence gathering; however, digital and social media communication has been a game changer in this field. So infinite is this knowledge resource that it is often overwhelming as to how to use it. "Social media and even email are different forms of intelligence than that which comes from traditional research tools. If you think about it, the feedback tends to be reactionary." The challenge, then, would be developing methods to not only mine the data, but also to make sense of it in a way that can truly benefit the company and, ultimately, its customers.

WestJet has been using what Mitchell refers to as a "voice of the guest" tool, which combines a survey system with text analytics. "Its original intention was to be used across the social digital space, but we began first using it only on email to provide us with quantitative and qualitative analysis." The result is a sophisticated tool that not only counts tweets about WestJet, for instance, but also classifies them as positive or negative and even begins to answer "why." Because, as suggested, whether it's a pen and paper survey or a Facebook post, there's a question being asked or answered, and that process, as Mitchell puts it, is what motivates her team of "research geeks."

QUESTIONS

1. What research approach has WestJet been using since 2005, and how has data been gathered?
2. How does WestJet's market research affect other areas of the organization?
3. Why should a market research analyst be particularly cautious about information gathered through social media?

REVIEWING THE CONCEPTS

1. Explain the importance of information in gaining insights about the marketplace and customers.

The marketing process starts with a complete understanding of the marketplace and consumer needs and wants. Thus, the company needs sound information to produce superior value and satisfaction for customers. The company also requires information on competitors, resellers, and other actors and forces in the marketplace. Increasingly, marketers are viewing information not only as an input for making better decisions but also as an important strategic asset and marketing tool.

2. Define the marketing information system and discuss its parts.

The *marketing information system (MIS)* consists of people and procedures for assessing information needs, developing the needed information, and helping decision makers to use the information to generate and validate actionable customer and market insights. A well-designed information system begins and ends with users.

The MIS first assesses information needs. The MIS primarily serves the company's marketing and other managers, but it may also provide information to external partners. Then, the MIS develops information from internal databases, marketing intelligence activities, and marketing research. Internal databases provide information on the company's own operations and departments. Such data can be obtained quickly and cheaply, but often needs to be adapted for marketing decisions. Marketing intelligence activities supply everyday information about developments in the external marketing environment. Market research consists of collecting information relevant to a specific marketing problem faced by the company. Lastly, the MIS helps users to analyze and use the information to develop customer insights, make marketing decisions, and manage customer relationships.

3. Outline the steps in the marketing research process.

The first step in the marketing research process involves *defining the problem and setting the research objectives*, which may be exploratory, descriptive, or causal research. The second step consists of *developing a research plan* for collecting data from primary and secondary sources. The third step calls for *implementing the marketing research plan* by gathering, processing, and analyzing the information. The fourth step consists of *interpreting and reporting the findings*. Additional information analysis helps marketing managers to apply the information and provides them with sophisticated statistical procedures and models from which to develop more rigorous findings.

Both *internal* and *external* secondary data sources often provide information more quickly and at a lower cost than primary data sources, and they can sometimes yield information that a company cannot collect by itself. However, needed information might not exist in secondary sources. Researchers must also evaluate secondary information to ensure that it is *relevant, accurate, current*, and *impartial*.

Primary research must also be evaluated for these features. Each primary data collection method—*observational, survey*, and *experimental*—has its own advantages and disadvantages. Similarly, each of the various research contact methods—mail, telephone, personal interview, and online—also has its own advantages and drawbacks.

4. Explain how companies analyze and use marketing information.

Information gathered in internal databases and through marketing intelligence and marketing research usually requires more analysis. This may include advanced statistical analysis or the application of analytical models that will help marketers to make better decisions. To analyze individual customer data, many companies have now acquired or developed special software and analysis techniques—called *customer relationship management (CRM)*—that integrate, analyze, and apply the mountains of individual customer data contained in their databases.

Marketing information has no value until it is used to make better marketing decisions. Thus, the MIS must make the information available to the managers and others who make marketing decisions or deal with customers. In some cases, this means providing regular reports and updates; in other cases it means making non-routine information available for special situations and on-the-spot decisions. Many firms use company intranets and extranets to facilitate this process. Thanks to modern technology, today's marketing managers can gain direct access to the MIS at any time and from virtually any location.

5. **Discuss the special issues some marketing researchers face, including public policy and ethics issues.**

Some marketers face special marketing research situations, such as those conducting research in small business, not-for-profit, or international situations. Marketing research can be conducted effectively by small businesses and non-profit organizations with limited budgets. International marketing researchers follow the same steps as domestic researchers, but often face more and different problems. All organizations need to act responsibly to major public policy and ethical issues surrounding marketing research, including issues of intrusions on consumer privacy and misuse of research findings.

KEY TERMS

Causal research 163
Commercial online databases 164
Competitive marketing intelligence 160
Customer insights 158
Customer relationship
  management (CRM) 178
Descriptive research 163

Ethnographic research 166
Experimental research 168
Exploratory research 163
Focus group interviewing 170
Internal databases 160
Marketing information system (MIS) 158
Marketing research 162

Observational research 165
Online focus groups 172
Online marketing research 171
Primary data 164
Sample 173
Secondary data 164
Survey research 168

TALK ABOUT MARKETING

1. In a small group, identify a problem faced by a local business or charitable organization and propose a research project addressing that problem. Develop a research proposal that implements each step of the marketing research process. Discuss how the research results will help the business or organization.

2. Want to earn a little extra cash? Businesses use focus groups and surveys to make better marketing decisions, and they might pay for your participation. Visit findfocusgroups.com and review the opportunities available for research participation. Find two more websites that recruit research participants. Write a brief report of what you found and discuss the pros and cons to companies of recruiting research participants this way.

3. Focus groups are commonly used during exploratory research. A focus group interview entails gathering a group of people to discuss a specific topic. In a small group, research how to conduct a focus group interview and then conduct one with six to ten other students to learn what services your university could offer to better meet student needs. Assign one person in your group to be the moderator while the others observe and interpret the responses from the focus group participants. Present a report of what you learned from this research.

4. Go to Strategic Business Insights (SBI) website (www.strategicbusinessinsights.com), click on the VALS survey on the left side of the webpage, and complete the survey. What type of research is being conducted—exploratory, descriptive, or causal? How can marketers use this information?

THINK LIKE A MARKETING MANAGER

Outback Steakhouse currently operates restaurants in only two provinces, Ontario and Alberta. Outback's marketing department is working on a strategic plan to open five new restaurants in Canada in the next two years. They have come to you, the head of the marketing research department, to ask for your help in providing information that will assist them in deciding where to open these five restaurants.

QUESTIONS

1. Make a list of three questions you can find the answers to in secondary sources. Which secondary sources will

you use to find the answers to these questions? Can you find the answers to all three questions just by using free Internet sources and your university's library databases?

2. You're going to have to prepare a research plan to conduct some primary research. Which type or types of research will you use: observational, experimental, or causal? Think this through and make notes. What would you observe, and for what purpose? What kind of experiment might you conduct? What cause-and-effect relationships would you want to understand?

3. What type of research would you conduct to determine which markets in Canada are likely to respond most favourably to Outback's menu?

4. Assume that the marketing department has now made the decision about which five cities to enter. How can market research help make the next decision: Where exactly, in each city, should the restaurant be opened?

MARKETING ETHICS

Marketers are hungry for customer information, and the electronic tracking industry is answering the call by gathering consumer Internet behaviour data. A recent investigation by the *Wall Street Journal* found that the 50 most popular US websites installed more than 3000 tracking files on the computer used in the study. The total was even higher for the top 50 sites popular with children and teens (4123 tracking files). Many sites installed more than 100 tracking tools each during the tests. Tracking tools include files placed on users' computers and on websites. You probably know about cookies, small files placed on your computer that contain information. Newer technology, such as web beacons (also known as web bugs, tracking bugs, pixel tags, and clear GIFs), are invisible graphic files placed on websites and in emails that, when combined with cookies, can tell a lot about the user. For example, beacons can tell a marketer if a page was viewed and for how long and can even tell if you read the email sent to you. Such tracking has become aggressive to the point where keystrokes can be analyzed for clues about a person and "flash cookies" can re-spawn after a user deletes them. Although the data do not identify users by name, data-gathering companies can construct consumer profiles that include demographic, geographic, and lifestyle information. Marketers use this information to target online advertisements.

QUESTIONS

1. Critics claim that Internet tracking infringes on consumer privacy rights. Should marketers have access to such information? Discuss the advantages and disadvantages of this activity for both marketers and consumers.

2. Visit the Network Advertising Initiative's website at www.networkadvertising.org to learn more about behavioural targeting and the advertising industry's efforts to give consumers power to protect their online privacy. Click on "Consumer Opt-out." How many active cookies have been placed on the computer you are using? After learning more from this website, discuss whether you are more or less likely to allow companies to gather your Internet behaviour data.

MARKETING TECHNOLOGY

In 1996, Marks & Spencer (M&S), the venerable British retailer, launched "lunchtogo"—an online corporate catering service (see www.lunchtogo-e.com). But M&S found it difficult to develop long-term relationships with corporate customers due to high personnel turnover within customer organizations. Therefore, it turned to EWA Bespoke Communications, a company that uses data mining to "tell you more about your customers." EWA used *propensity modelling* to develop the Critical Lag formula, which identified customers whose last order fell outside of their expected behaviour. EWA then developed an automated system to send communications to customers who have not reordered within the maximum allowed order lag determined by the formula. Whereas most customers received emails, the system flagged M&S' best corporate catering customers that should receive more personalized phone calls because of their value and importance. EWA also implemented information systems to improve the company's service. Knowing more about its customers paid off—within a short period of time, the EWA system generated more than €1 million, tripling the operation's revenues, and delivered an almost perfect order accuracy rate.

QUESTIONS

1. Visit EWA Bespoke Communications at www.ewa.ltd.uk/ to learn more about its Customer Insight services and the types of analyses performed by this company. What is propensity modelling? Review other case studies from this website and write a brief report of how data mining technology was used to gain customer insights.

2. Describe how other organizations can benefit from these types of data mining analyses. Find examples of other companies that can offer such analysis to businesses.

MARKETING BY THE NUMBERS

"Company X has 34 percent market share," "Brand A is preferred by over 60 percent of consumers," "Prices are increasing at a rate of 44 percent," and "The average customer satisfaction rating is 4, satisfied, on a 1–5 scale." These are all conclusions based on statistics. Statistics lend credibility to conclusions and can be very persuasive. But are the conclusions legitimate? Many are survey-based claims, meaning that survey research is used to substantiate them. Claiming that 60 percent of consumers prefer a brand is powerful but can be misleading if only five consumers were sampled and three preferred that brand (that is, 60 percent). Interpretation of data can vary by who's interpreting it. For example, saying that your average customer is satisfied may not be accurate, as an average rating of 4 could result from half of respondents indicating 5 (extremely satisfied) and the other half rating 3 (neither satisfied nor dissatisfied), which paints a different picture. Market share is the ratio of the company's sales to total market sales, and a 34 percent market share is nice. But how is "market" defined? As you can see, numbers can say almost anything you want them to say. For more discussion of the financial and quantitative implications of marketing decisions, see Appendix 3, Marketing by the Numbers.

QUESTIONS

1. By using Statistics Canada data on education, training, and learning (available at http://www5.statcan.gc.ca/subject-sujet/theme-theme.action?pid=1821&lang=eng&more=0), develop statistics, such as percentages, to support the argument for tuition freezes for undergraduate education in Canada. Use any portion of the data you deem important to support your argument.

2. By using the same data on that website, develop different statistics to support the counter-argument to the one above. That is, interpret the data and present it in a way that supports the universities' position for the need to increase tuition fees. Again, use any portion of the data you deem important to support your argument.

VIDEO CASE

DOMINO'S

As a delivery company, no one outdoes Domino's. Its reputation for delivering hot pizza in 30 minutes or less is ingrained in customers' minds. But not long ago, Domino's began hearing negative comments from its customers about its pizza; basically, they felt it was horrible. As a company that has long focused on solid marketing intelligence to make decisions, Domino's went to work on changing consumers' perceptions about its pizza.

Based on its marketing research, Domino's soon realized that it had to take a very risky step and completely recreate the pizza that it had been selling for more than 40 years. This video illustrates how research not only enabled Domino's to come up with a winning recipe, but laid the foundation for a successful promotional campaign that has made fans appreciate Domino's pizza as much as its delivery service.

After viewing the video featuring Domino's, answer the following questions:

QUESTIONS

1. What role did marketing research play in the creation and launch of Domino's new pizza?

2. Could Domino's have gone about its research process in a more effective way? Explain.

3. Why did it take so long for Domino's to realize that customers didn't like its pizza? Did the company come to this realization accidentally?

MEREDITH: THANKS TO GOOD MARKETING INFORMATION, MEREDITH *KNOWS* WOMEN

You may not recognize the name Meredith Corporation but you have certainly heard of the magazines it publishes. *Better Homes and Gardens, Ladies' Home Journal,* and *Family Circle* are some of its oldest and best-known titles. Meredith has been publishing magazines for more than 100 years and maintains many top-ten titles, both by category and overall. With a total of 21 subscription magazines, Meredith is also the creator of *American Baby, Parents, Fitness, Midwest Living,* and more. Meredith's magazines have a combined circulation of 30 million—*Better Homes and Gardens* alone reaches nearly 8 million paid readers each month.

If Meredith's magazines sound like something your mom would read, that's intentional. Meredith caters to women. In fact, Meredith has become the undisputed leading media and marketing company focused on women, a reputation earned by developing an expertise in managing deep relationships with female customers. With core categories of home, health, family, and personal development, Meredith's goal is to touch every life stage of women, from young adults and new parents to established families and empty nesters.

Print media is hardly a growth industry—it's been declining in recent years. In fact, Meredith no longer describes itself as a magazine publisher. It claims to be a creator of "content," delivered to women "whenever, wherever, and however [they want] it." Long before print media began its decline, Meredith expanded into television stations, cable programming, and websites. Today, Meredith has a strong foundation on the web, with more than 50 websites that reach an average of 20 million unique visitors each month. Its web empire includes bhg.com, parents.com, divinecaroline.com, and fitnessmagazine.com, to name just a few. This network allows Meredith to do more than just distribute content; the company has also become proficient in social networking.

How has Meredith been able to achieve success as the leading expert on women? In short, Meredith *knows* women. The company knows women through a continual strategic effort to manage marketing information about them. In fact, Meredith's marketing information system is its core competency. That system produces customer insights that allow the company to understand women's needs and desires, and maintain strong relationships with them.

IT STARTS WITH DATA

Meredith's core strength lies in its massive database. Meredith's database is the largest collection of customer information of any US media company. With more than 85 million unduplicated names, it contains information on 80 percent of US home-owning households, as well as a good portion of non-home-owning households. Beyond its breadth, Meredith's database also has unsurpassed depth. On average, each name in the database has more than 700 data points attached to it. Those 700 data points allow Meredith to truly know each person on an intimate level.

The basic information in Meredith's database comes from typical internal company sources. Information gathered through sales transactions alone is huge. This includes not only descriptive and demographic information, but also information on which magazines customers buy, to which magazines they subscribe, what kinds of incentive offers they like, and how they have responded to particular creative executions. Although most companies have no idea how to process and handle all that information, Meredith effectively puts it all into one place so that managers throughout the company can access it.

Beyond gathering information from internal sources, Meredith also conducts marketing research. Online and traditional surveys allow Meredith to dig deeper into attitudinal information. One of the focal points is questions about customers' life events. "Are you having a baby, are your kids about to go to school, are your oldest kids about to graduate, are you thinking about retiring?" explains Cheryl Dahlquist, director of database marketing services at Meredith. "As much as we can, we'd like to know that information because we feel like those are the things that influence really what's happening with someone." Knowing a single life event can tell a lot about a person's needs and wants. However, possessing updated information on dozens of life events for a given person becomes very powerful.

Yet, all the information in the world means little unless you can make sense of it. Fortunately, Meredith is as skilled at analyzing and using database information as it is collecting it. Through a concept Meredith calls "passion points," the company computes scores for numerous different interest areas, such as cooking, fitness, and gardening. It then segments each interest area into specifics, such that fitness becomes running, yoga, and hiking, to name just a few. Multiple data points feed into each score.

In this manner, Meredith not only knows what your primary interests are, it also knows how your interest levels compare to those of everyone else in the database. "We've developed through our statistical group the ability to say when somebody reaches a certain score, that's when they're really hot to trot in [say] cooking, and they're ready to respond to just about all the offers that come their way around the cooking category." Meredith employs 20 predictive analytical models, each designed to rank the order of a person's interests. All 20 models are scored and ranked each week. That's how Meredith gets to know women.

PUTTING CUSTOMER INSIGHTS TO USE

Based on the valuable insights that it extracts from its database, Meredith manages relationships with its customers through various means. For starters, customer insights not only drive the content of its media products, they drive the development of new products. For example, over the years, *Better Homes and Gardens* has spawned spin-offs such as *Country Home* and *Traditional Home*, not to mention bhg.com and the cable program *Better*.

But the insights that come from Meredith's marketing information system also tell the company which products are the most relevant to a given individual. And with its large and holistic portfolio of products, there is something for almost everyone. David Ball, vice-president of consumer marketing for Meredith, explains how this works: "We had *American Baby* at the very early stages of a woman going into the home-owning and child-rearing years. We filled in with *Parents* and *Family Circle*. *American Baby* is prenatal, *Parents* is postnatal, *Family Circle* is teens and tweens. And so now we're able to take someone who subscribes to *American Baby* and really graduate them into our other products."

Rich customer insights allow Meredith to meet customer needs when it comes to promotion and pricing as well. Because Meredith has so many media products, almost all of its promotional efforts are either through direct mail and email, or cross-promoting across titles. Based on what it knows about specific customers, Meredith customizes the types of offers and messages con-

tained in its promotions, often in real time. If you think about it, this is marketing at its finest. When customers and potential customers aren't bothered by irrelevant messages and products, but are approached only with offers that actually interest them, everyone wins.

Given its vast database and its skill at managing information, Meredith can sell marketing research to other companies that need insights on women. Its strength in managing marketing information has also resulted in numerous partnerships with leading companies such as Home Depot, DirecTV, Chrysler, and Carnival Cruise Lines. In addition, Meredith's database and research efforts have resulted in something else that may be a first: The Meredith Engagement Dividend, a program that guarantees Meredith advertisers an increase in sales. Meredith can make such a guarantee because, based on information in its database, advertisers are able to increase their product sales by an average of 10 percent over a one-year period.

Meredith's flat revenues over the past five years suggest that, as a company, it is still heavily tied to print media for distributing its content. But with a consistent profit margin of 8 to 10 percent of sales, Meredith is holding its own. More importantly, Meredith's core competency of managing customer information is not exclusive to print. It is something that will fuel the company's expansion into other, faster-growing media. As Meredith maintains its marketing information system strategy, it will continue to develop the right products, price, distribution methods, and promotions for each and every woman in its database.

QUESTIONS FOR DISCUSSION

1. Analyze Meredith's marketing information system. What are its strengths and weaknesses?

2. Can impersonal data points really result in meaningful relationships? Explain.

3. Does Meredith's marketing information expertise transfer into other media and products?

4. As a company still heavily rooted in print, what does Meredith's future hold?

5. What recommendations would you make to Meredith's executives?

Sources: Officials at Meredith Corporation contributed to and supported the development of this case. Additional information comes from www.meredith.com, August 2011.

Courtesy of Running Room

AFTER STUDYING THIS CHAPTER, YOU SHOULD BE ABLE TO

1 understand the consumer market and the major factors that influence consumer buyer behaviour

2 identify and discuss the stages in the buyer decision process

3 describe the adoption and diffusion process for new products

4 define the business market and identify the major factors that influence business buyer behaviour

5 list and define the steps in the business buying decision process

Understanding Consumer and Business Buyer Behaviour

PREVIEWING THE CONCEPTS

You've studied how marketers obtain, analyze, and use information to develop customer insights and assess marketing programs. In this chapter, we continue with a closer look at the most important element of the marketplace—customers. The aim of marketing is to affect how customers think and act. To affect the *whats*, *whens*, and *hows* of buyer behaviour, marketers must first understand the *whys*. We look first at *final consumer* buying influences and processes and then at the buying behaviour of *business customers*. You'll see that understanding buying behaviour is an essential but very difficult task.

To get a better sense of the importance of understanding consumer behaviour, let's look first at Running Room. What makes Running Room customers so fanatically loyal? Just what is it that makes them visit retail stores, participate in clinics, or make Running Room a part of their active lifestyle? At the core, customers buy from Running Room because the brand itself is a part of their own self-expression and lifestyle. It's a part of what the loyal Running Room customer is.

RUNNING ROOM: A PASSION FOR CREATING CUSTOMER VALUE AND RELATIONSHIPS

Perhaps no Canadian retailer has experienced growth quite as remarkable as that of the Running Room. Founded in Edmonton in 1984 by John Stanton, who was looking to purchase quality running shoes from someone knowledgeable about the sport, the Running Room has grown to over 100 locations across Canada and a handful in the United States. While exact sales numbers are not available for this family-owned business, some analysts estimate sales of over $100 million annually.

Expansion to the US market was one growth strategy of the company, but not its primary one. In 2004, Stanton announced the opening of the Walking Room, which allowed the company to grow into smaller Canadian markets, such as Sudbury, Ontario, and Fredericton, New Brunswick, which would not have been financially feasible for the Running Room alone. While expecting its new stores to cater to seniors and older boomers no longer able to handle the physical stress of running, the company soon found out that the new combined Running Room/Walking Room stores were attracting younger customers in their 20s and 30s who wanted to become more active. "A lot of younger people today work harder and longer, and they do that work in front of computers. As a result, they're more sedentary. They're looking at doing something active, but running can be intimidating," says Stanton. "Dealing with walkers of all ages was a huge learning curve for us. We discovered we weren't talking to walkers who would eventually become runners. Walkers made it clear to us that walking was their sport and that they had no intention of ever becoming runners."

In an interview with the *Calgary Herald*, John Stanton was asked about the major reason his business was expanding:

> I think everybody is concerned about childhood obesity and the aging baby boomer, and the burden that our health-care system is under. People know they have to get fit and be active. The primary thing we try to do is to show people through our Learn To Run programs and training clinics that when you engage in exercise there's a natural transition to healthy eating, and pretty soon you start to take control of your own life just by the simple thing of going for a run. If someone's overweight, walking is sometimes a great option for them to get started. It's less daunting. The number one thing I've found that keeps people from exercising is fear of embarrassment. . . . By putting people in a group environment, it's like kids joining a soccer team, a ball team, or a hockey team. All of a sudden you start having fun and enjoying it and it continues. That's what we've been able to do.*

So, what factors led to the company's success? The Running Room's reputation has been built upon product innovation, quality, and the knowledge of the sport of running. Its private label products have been developed to provide customers with the best in style, functionality, fabric innovations, and reasonable price, and have been developed with the input of customers and staff alike. The company even created a new clothing line for walkers, who require heavier, looser clothing in contrast to the close-fitting spandex garments favoured by runners. Even packs had to be specially designed for walkers. Runners may carry a nutrient bar, but walkers want room for more substantial snacks. While quality merchandise is one factor contributing to the company's success (judging by the rate at which runners and walkers alike purchase the products), it is not the main reason behind the explosive growth. In fact, the Running Room's success can be summed up in one word: *relationships*. The deep connections cultivated among the owner/company, its customers, and the broader community are the driving force behind the Running Room's success.

The Running Room has managed to create customer value and relationships in a number of ways. Service has always been an essential component of the company philosophy and is what keeps it competitive. All employees are considered Team Members, and all are runners. Who else but a runner is knowledgeable about the needs of runners, as well as the products that cater to those needs? The Running Room philosophy is that if you're out there running on the same roads as the customers, you can relate to their exact needs. The Running Room is truly a store for runners by runners. Yet, when the company opened the combined Running Room/Walking Room outlets, it had to overcome its own brand image to deal with the potential intimidation walkers may feel on entering a running store. The solution was to give equal prominence to the Walking Room brand on the exterior signs of the new combined stores. In-store signage also clearly differentiates walking and running gear.

In addition to its in-store service, the Running Room offers an incredible number of clinics such as Walking, Learn to Run, Marathon, Half Marathon, 10K Training, Personal Best, and For Women Only Running Clinics. The tremendous success of these clinics

*Yana Doyle, "Writer Makes Tracks at Marathon," Calgary Herald, June 10, 2010, at www .calgaryherald.com/Writer+makes+tracks+marathon/3135672/story.html, accessed June 2010.

is evident from the over 600 000 clinic graduates to date. The Running Room clinic program is committed to a lifestyle of fitness. The various programs meet the needs of those just getting into a fitness routine and of those contemplating a marathon. In addition, there is the Running Room Running Club, which has no membership fee and allows all levels of runners to run in a group setting twice weekly. The Running Room Running Club really adds a social component to running since you get an opportunity to run with a variety of people and receive some great coaching on running techniques and training methods.

Finally, the Running Room and its owner, John Stanton, are actively involved in building strong relationships in the community. The Running Room sponsors and helps organize and promote more than 400 walks, runs, and events that annually raise millions of dollars for local charities and non-profit organizations. For example, the Running Room hosts clinics all across Canada for runners wishing to compete in the Scotiabank Toronto Waterfront Marathon, which raised a record-breaking $4.3 million in 2012 for 181 Canadian charities. It partnered with Weight Watchers Canada to promote the country's first Walk-It Challenge, which saw over 7000 Canadians from coast-to-coast take their first steps toward physical activity. Stanton himself takes part in several of these events, from participating as the "pace bunny" in Halifax's Scotiabank Blue Nose Marathon to holding Q&A online forums on the *Globe and Mail* website.

The company's hands-on approach and deep customer focus has led to some wonderful personal success stories, including the following:

■ The Calgary writer, whose long-time dream to finish a marathon alongside her husband finally came through—she first completed 16 weeks of marathon training offered by the Running Room.

■ Sudbury, Ontario, native Kandis Stoughton, who completed the Boston Marathon, known to be one of the most challenging marathons to even qualify for—her passion for running began with a 5K clinic offered by the Running Room.

■ Darrel Wilkins of New Brunswick, who quit smoking after 33 years and has become an accomplished marathoner with over 10 races behind him, including the Boston Marathon—the path to his success began with a 5K clinic offered by the Running Room.

Personal achievements such as these have come as a result of the company's deep commitment to building lasting relationships not only with customers and community but also between customers. "We believe that the Running Room philosophy and our in-store environment are unlike any other retail business in North America. While we offer clothing, shoes, products and accessories for walkers and runners, we also help people to change their lives through fitness activities," said Stanton. "Through the Running Room and Walking Room, people can gain a tremendous sense of belonging that comes from walking or running alongside people who share similar goals: improving wellness, while having fun and adventure exploring our cities on foot. The Running Room becomes very important to our customers, because their well-being is very important to us."[1]

THE RUNNING ROOM example shows that factors at many levels affect consumer buying behaviour. Buying behaviour is never simple, yet understanding it is the essential task of marketing management. First we explore the dynamics of the consumer market and consumer buyer behaviour. We then examine business markets and the business buyer process.

Consumer Markets and Consumer Buyer Behaviour LO1

Consumer buyer behaviour
The buying behaviour of final consumers—individuals and households that buy goods and services for personal consumption.

Consumer market
All the individuals and households that buy or acquire goods and services for personal consumption.

Consumer buyer behaviour refers to the buying behaviour of final consumers—individuals and households that buy goods and services for personal consumption. All of these final consumers combine to make up the **consumer market**. The North American consumer market includes almost 342 million people in Canada and the United States who consume more than US$10 trillion worth of goods and services each year, making it one of the most attractive consumer markets in the world.[2]

Consumers around the world vary tremendously in age, income, education level, and tastes. The ways these diverse consumers relate with each other and with other elements of the world around them impact their choices among various products, services, and companies. Here we examine the fascinating array of factors that affect consumer behaviour.

What Is Consumer Behaviour?

Consumers make many purchase decisions and some are more complex than others. For example, a consumer buying a cup of coffee would go through a very different decision-making process than one buying his or her first house. Most large companies research consumer buying decisions in great detail to answer questions about what consumers buy, where they buy, how and how much they buy, when they buy, and why they buy. Marketers can study actual consumer purchases to find out what they buy, where, and how much. But learning about the *whys* of consumer buying behaviour is not so easy—the answers are often locked deep within the consumer's mind.

The central question for marketers, then, is this: Given all the characteristics (cultural, social, personal, and psychological) affecting consumer behaviour, how do we best design our marketing efforts to reach our consumers most effectively? Thus, the study of consumer behaviour begins and ends with the individual. In the past, the field was often referred to as *buyer behaviour*, reflecting an emphasis on the actual exchange of goods for money. Marketers now recognize the study of consumer behaviour is an ongoing process that starts long before the consumer purchases a product or service, and continues long after he or she consumes it. This extended definition of consumer behaviour means that marketers must be aware of a number of issues before, during, and after purchase to build brand loyalty and lasting relationships with their customers. Figure 6.1 illustrates some issues that arise during each stage of the consumption process, but there are many more.

Consumers' responses, which can range from actual purchase to merely engaging in word-of-mouth communications about the product, is the ultimate test of whether or not a marketing strategy is successful. In the next section, we will examine each of the characteristics affecting consumer behaviour in more detail.

Characteristics Affecting Consumer Behaviour

Consumer purchases are influenced strongly by cultural, social, personal, and psychological characteristics, shown in Figure 6.2. For the most part, marketers cannot control such factors, but they must take them into account.

Cultural Factors   Cultural factors exert a broad and deep influence on consumer behaviour. The marketer needs to understand the role played by the buyer's *culture*, *subculture*, and *social class*.

FIGURE 6.1 Some Issues that Arise during Stages in the Consumption Process

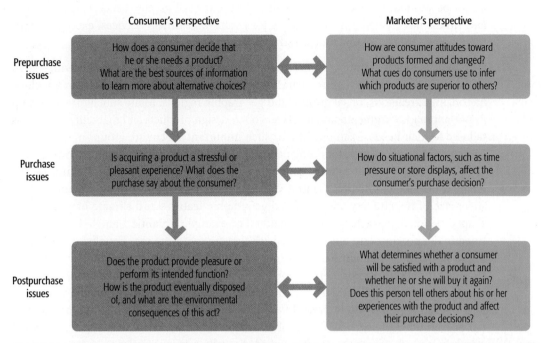

Source: Michael R. Solomon, Judith L. Zaichkowsky, and Rosemary Polegato (2011), *Consumer Behaviour: Buying, Having, and Being*, 5th Canadian Edition (Toronto, ON: Pearson Education Canada).

Culture **Culture** is the most basic cause of a person's wants and behaviour. Human behaviour is largely learned. Growing up in a society, a child learns basic values, perceptions, wants, and behaviours from the family and other important institutions. A child in the United States normally learns or is exposed to the following values: achievement and success, individualism, freedom, hard work, activity and involvement, efficiency and practicality, material comfort, youthfulness, and fitness and health. In contrast, Canadians value freedom; the beauty of our natural landscape; our belief in respect, equality, and fair treatment; family life; and being Canadian. In fact, one public opinion poll found that 86 percent of Canadians agreed with the statement that their country was "the greatest in the world."[3] Despite our differences, both the United States and Canada are consumer cultures, and marketing practices reinforce this as a way of life.

Culture
The set of basic values, perceptions, wants, and behaviours learned by a member of society from family and other important institutions.

FIGURE 6.2 Factors Influencing Consumer Behaviour

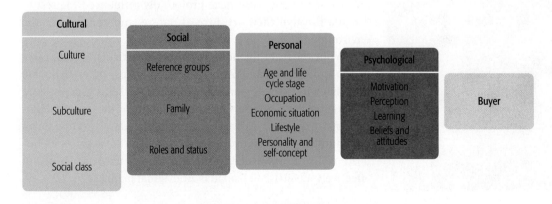

Marketers are always trying to spot *cultural shifts* to discover new products that might be wanted. For example, the cultural shift toward greater concern about health and fitness has created a huge industry for health-and-fitness services, exercise equipment and clothing, organic foods, and a variety of diets.

Subculture Each culture contains smaller **subcultures**, or groups of people with shared value systems based on common life experiences and situations. Subcultures include nationalities, religions, racial groups, and geographic regions. Many subcultures make up important market segments, and marketers often design products and marketing programs tailored to their needs. Examples of four such important subculture groups in Canada include regional subcultures, founding nations, ethnic subcultures, and mature consumers.

Canada is a regional country, so marketers may develop distinctive programs for the Atlantic provinces, Quebec, Central Canada, the Prairies, and British Columbia. The sheer size of the country and its varied geographic features and climate have certainly shaped regional character and personality. For example, Atlantic Canada is largely defined by its proximity to and historical relationship with the sea. Equally, the isolation imposed by the mountain barrier, along with the abundance and grandeur of British Columbia's natural environment, shaped the outlook of that region's residents. Immigration has also had a differential effect on the different regions within Canada. The economy of each region furthers these differences. The fate of regions linked to the rise and fall of commodities, such as fish, timber, wheat, minerals, or oil, has affected regional mindsets as well as economies. Perceived disparities in political power have also increased regionalism, especially in Quebec, Newfoundland and Labrador, and Alberta.[4]

Canada had three founding nations: the English, French, and Aboriginal peoples. The unique history and language of each of these nations has driven many of the cultural differences that result in different buying behaviours across Canada. The most recent census results (2011) reported that people noting their English-language roots (anglophones) accounted for approximately 58 percent of the population, and people whose mother tongue is French (francophones) made up approximately 22 percent of the population. In total, approximately 213 500 Canadians reported an Aboriginal language as their mother tongue.

Aboriginal Canadians are making their voices heard both in the political arena and in the marketplace. There are more than 1.17 million Aboriginal Canadians, including Métis and Inuit, and this number is expected to double by 2031.[5] Among Canada's Aboriginal population, Cree is reported as the most common mother tongue. Not only do Aboriginal Canadians have distinct cultures that influence their values and purchasing behaviour, but they also have profoundly influenced the rest of Canada through their art, love of nature, and concern for the environment.

While the banking industry has been particularly responsive to the unique needs of Aboriginal Canadians, other firms are now following suit. For example, Quality Market, a grocery store in Thunder Bay, Ontario, launched an online ordering and delivery service that will allow residents of isolated northern Ontario communities to access groceries at more affordable prices.[6] Publications like *Windspeaker* magazine are also used as vehicles to effectively advertise to Canada's Aboriginal peoples.

Subculture
A group of people with shared value systems based on common life experiences and situations.

Exhibit 6.1 *Windspeaker* magazine is one tool promoted by the Aboriginal Multi-Media Society (AMMSA) to assist marketers who want to communicate with Canada's Aboriginal peoples effectively and efficiently.

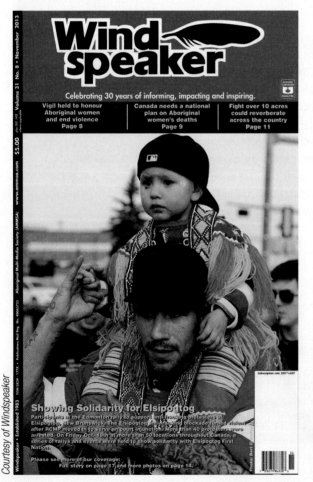

Courtesy of Windspeaker

According to Statistics Canada, roughly one out of every five people in Canada could be a member of a visible minority by 2017, when Canada celebrates its 150th anniversary. Approximately, 250 000 new immigrants come to Canada each year.[7] Thus, being sensitive to their cultural values is important, because 70 percent of the visible minority population were born outside Canada.

People with a Chinese background are still the largest group among visible minorities in Canada. Almost 4 percent of Canada's population is Chinese, with 40 percent of this group residing in Toronto and 31 percent living in Vancouver. Canadian companies are realizing the importance of culturally relevant advertising that includes a multimedia approach to reach the Chinese-Canadian market. A 2008 poll conducted by Solutions Research Group revealed that Internet use among Chinese Canadians exceeds time spent listening to radio and watching TV combined. Media outlets such as 51.ca and singtao.ca, which serve as free markets for information for Canada's Chinese community, have captured the attention of many Canadian advertisers. Chinese Canadians appreciate advertising delivered in their native tongue. "There's a certain emotional connection a person makes when somebody speaks their own language," said Solutions Research Group president Kaan Yigit. "It speaks to the issue of showing respect or feeling like you're being acknowledged."[8]

Exhibit 6.2 Since its launch in 1978, *Sing Tao Daily* (singtao.ca) has developed into one of the most influential media for Chinese Canadians, and now publishes in Toronto, Vancouver, and Calgary.

People who identified themselves as "black" in the 2006 census are Canada's third largest visible minority.[9] While some members of this group trace their ancestry back to Africa, many others have more recently emigrated from the Caribbean. In recent years, many companies have developed special products, appeals, and marketing programs for this subculture. For example, Procter & Gamble has long been the leader in black advertising, spending nearly twice as much as the second-place spender. P&G also tailors products to the specific needs of black consumers. For example, its CoverGirl Queen Latifah line is specially formulated "to celebrate the beauty of women of colour."[10]

Though age is a demographic variable, some researchers also contend that different age cohorts have distinct cultures. As of July 2012, the median age in Canada was 40.0 years and higher than ever before (*median age* is defined as the point where exactly half of the population is older, and the other half is younger). According to the 2001 census, the median age was 37.6. To see how rapidly the Canadian population has aged, it is interesting to note that the median age in Canada in 1966 (the year when the last of the Baby Boomers was born) was 25.4 years. Thus, today, Canada's working-age population is dominated by older individuals, but there are regional variations. Newfoundland and Labrador has the oldest population with a median age of 44.2. Alberta is the youngest, with a median age of 36.1. Because of high immigration rates, however, Canada's population is not aging as fast as the population of the United States.

As the Canadian population ages, mature consumers are becoming a very attractive market. By 2015, when all of the baby boomers will be 50-plus, people aged 50 to 75 will account for 40 percent of adult consumers. By 2030, adults aged 65 and older will represent nearly 20 percent of the population. And these mature consumer segments boast the most expendable cash. The 50-plus consumer segment now accounts for nearly 50 percent of all consumer spending, more than any current or previous generation. They have 2.5 times the discretionary buying power of those aged 18 to 34. As one marketing executive puts it, they have "assets, not allowances." Despite some financial setbacks resulting from the recent economic crisis, mature consumers remain an attractive market for companies in all industries, from pharmaceuticals, furniture, groceries, beauty products, and clothing, to consumer electronics, travel and entertainment, and financial services.

For decades, many marketers stereotyped mature consumers as doddering, impoverished shut-ins who are less willing to change brands. As a group, however, mature consumers are anything but "stuck in their ways." To the contrary, a recent AARP study showed that older consumers for products such as stereos, computers, and mobile phones are more willing to shop around and switch brands than their younger counterparts. Companies such as Fairmont Hotels and The McLennan Group Insurance now promote directly to mature consumers on www.carp.ca, a website designed to promote the health and well-being of Canada's aging population.

Social class
Relatively permanent and ordered divisions in a society whose members share similar values, interests, and behaviours.

SOCIAL CLASS   Almost every society has some form of social class structure. **Social classes** are society's relatively permanent and ordered divisions whose members share similar values, interests, and behaviours. Social class is not determined by a single factor, such as income, but is measured as a combination of occupation, income, education, wealth, and other variables. In some social systems, members of different classes are reared for certain roles and cannot change their social positions. In North America, however, the lines between social classes are not fixed and rigid; people can move to a higher social class or drop into a lower one.

Most Canadians see themselves as middle class, and we are less likely or willing to think of ourselves in terms of social class than our neighbours south of the border. It is for this reason that the New Democratic Party no longer tries to appeal to "the working class" but to "ordinary Canadians." Marketers are interested in social class because people within a given social class tend to exhibit similar buying behaviour. Social classes show distinct product and brand preferences in areas such as clothing, home furnishings, leisure activity, and automobiles.

Social Factors   A consumer's behaviour also is influenced by social factors, such as the consumer's *small groups*, *family*, and *social roles* and *status*.

Group
Two or more people who interact to accomplish individual or mutual goals.

GROUPS AND SOCIAL NETWORKS   Many small **groups** influence a person's behaviour. Groups that have a direct influence and to which a person belongs are called membership groups. In contrast, reference groups serve as direct (face-to-face) or indirect points of comparison or reference in forming a person's attitudes or behaviour. People often are influenced by reference groups to which they do not belong. For example, an aspirational group is one to which the individual wishes to belong, as when a young hockey player hopes to someday emulate Sidney Crosby and play in the NHL.

Marketers try to identify the reference groups of their target markets. Reference groups expose a person to new behaviours and lifestyles, influence the person's attitudes and self-concept, and create pressures to conform that may affect the person's product and brand choices. The importance of group influence varies across products and brands. It tends to be strongest when the product is visible to others whom the buyer respects.

Word-of-mouth influence can have a powerful impact on consumer buying behaviour. The personal words and recommendations of trusted friends, associates, and other consumers tend to be more credible than those coming from commercial sources, such as advertisements or salespeople. Most word-of-mouth influence happens naturally: Consumers start chatting about a brand they use or feel strongly about one way or the other. Often, however, rather than leaving it to chance, marketers can help to create positive conversations about their brands.

Marketers of brands subjected to strong group influence must figure out how to reach **opinion leaders**—people within a reference group who, because of special skills, knowledge, personality, or other characteristics, exert social influence on others. Some experts call this 10 percent of consumers the *influentials* or *leading adopters*. When influential friends talk, consumers listen. Marketers try to identify opinion leaders for their products and direct marketing efforts toward them.

Buzz marketing involves enlisting or even creating opinion leaders to serve as "brand ambassadors" who spread the word about a company's products. Many companies now create brand ambassador programs in an attempt to turn influential but everyday customers into brand evangelists. A recent study found that such programs can increase the effectiveness of word-of-mouth marketing efforts by as much as 50 percent.[11] For example, read what Campus Intercept's brand ambassadors accomplished for James Ready beer:[12]

Exhibit 6.3 Several companies now promote directly to mature consumers on CARP.ca, a website designed to promote the health and well-being of Canada's aging population.

© BSIP SA / Alamy

In 2009, James Ready beer, with the help of Toronto-based Campus Intercept, launched a unique campaign targeting its main market: students. Brand ambassadors were hired to run events at student-friendly pubs across Ontario, where participants were invited to play games, such as ring toss or beer pong, to win James Ready beer caps. They could then trade their winnings for products necessary for campus life, such as laundry detergent and deodorant.

In addition to hosting the events, brand ambassadors were responsible for marketing the campaign locally with posters, Facebook postings, and door-hangers in student housing. The unique campaign yielded a sales increase of 8.5 percent and market share growth of 31 percent for the beer company, and numerous awards for Leo Burnett, the ad agency involved in its creation. After five years of steady growth, primarily due to the male university market, the brand is poised to take its success to Western Canada and expand its primary market to include both students and blue-collar discount beer drinkers.

Over the past few years, a new type of social interaction has exploded onto the scene—online social networking. **Online social networks** are online communities where people socialize or exchange information and opinions. Social networking media range from blogs (Gizmodo, Zenhabits) and message boards (Craigslist) to social networking websites (Facebook and Twitter) and virtual worlds (Second Life). This new form of consumer-to-consumer and business-to-consumer dialogue has big implications for marketers.

Word-of-mouth influence
The impact of the personal words and recommendations of trusted friends, associates, and other consumers on buying behaviour.

Opinion leader
Person within a reference group who, because of special skills, knowledge, personality, or other characteristics, exerts social influence on others.

Online social networks
Online social communities—blogs, social networking websites, or even virtual worlds—where people socialize or exchange information and opinions.

Exhibit 6.4 Brand ambassadors: Campus Intercept hires hundreds of students on campuses across Canada to be brand ambassadors for companies such as RBC, SaskTel, and James Ready beer.

Marketers are working to harness the power of these new social networks and other "word-of-web" opportunities to promote their products and build closer customer relationships. Instead of throwing more one-way commercial messages at consumers, they hope to use the Internet and social networks to *interact* with consumers and become a part of their conversations and lives (see Marketing@Work 6.1).

For example, Red Bull has an astounding 8.4 million friends on Facebook; Twitter and Facebook are the primary ways it communicates with university students. Lululemon has over 470 000 followers on Twitter and often responds to customers' tweets. P&G's Old Spice brand put entertaining spokesman Isaiah Mustafa on the web and invited fans to use Twitter, Facebook, and other social media to pose questions that he would answer. The questions poured in and Mustafa responded quickly in more than 180 web videos, creating a real-time connection with the brand's community.[13]

Most brands have built a comprehensive social media presence. Eco-conscious outdoor shoe and gear maker Timberland has created an online community (http://community.timberland.com) that connects like-minded "Earthkeepers" with each other and the brand through a network that includes several websites, a Facebook page, a YouTube channel, a Bootmakers Blog, an email newsletter, and several Twitter feeds.

Even small brands can leverage the power of the Internet and online social networks. For example, Blendtec has developed a kind of cult following for its flood of "Will It Blend?" online videos, in which the seemingly indestructible Blendtec Total Blender grinds everything from a hockey puck and a golf club to an iPhone and iPad into dust. The low-cost, simple idea led to a fivefold increase in Blendtec's sales.

But marketers must be careful when tapping into online social networks. Results are difficult to measure and control. Ultimately, the users control the content, so social network marketing attempts can easily backfire. For example, when Skittles designed its website to include a live Twitter feed for Skittles-related tweets, pranksters laced Skittles tweets with profanities so they would end up on the candy's website. Skittles was forced to abandon the campaign. We will dig deeper into online social networks as a marketing tool in Chapter 14.

Family Family members can strongly influence buyer behaviour. The family is the most important consumer buying organization in society, and it has been researched extensively. Marketers are interested in the roles and influence of the husband, wife, and children on the purchase of different products and services.

Husband–wife involvement varies widely by product category and by stage in the buying process. Buying roles change with evolving consumer lifestyles. For example, in Canada and the United States, the wife traditionally has been considered

Word-of-Web: Harnessing the Power of Online Social Influence

People love talking with others about things that make them happy—including their favourite products and brands. Say you really like WestJet—they fly with flair and get you there at an affordable price. Or you just plain love your new Sony GPS camera—it's too cool to keep to yourself. In the old days, you'd have chatted up these brands with a few friends and family members. But these days, thanks to online technology, anyone can share brand experiences with thousands, even millions, of other consumers via the web.

In response, marketers are now feverishly working to harness today's newfound technologies and get people interacting with their brands online. Whether it's creating online brand ambassadors, tapping into existing online influentials and social networks, or developing conversation-provoking events and videos, the Internet is awash with marketer attempts to create brand conversations and involvement online.

A company can start by creating its own online brand evangelists. That's what Ford did when it launched its Fiesta subcompact model, targeted heavily toward Millennials.

Generating buzz for the Fiesta among the incredibly web-savvy Millennials generation—which includes 70 million drivers—was a must. One study found that 77 percent of Millennials use a social networking site like Facebook or Twitter daily and 28 percent of them have a personal blog. So Ford created the Fiesta Movement campaign, in which it handed Fiestas to 100 influential 20-something Millennials selected from 4000 applicants. The Fiesta ambassadors lived with the cars for six months, completed monthly "missions" with different themes, and shared their experiences via blogs, tweets, Facebook updates, YouTube, and Flickr posts. Ford didn't tell the ambassadors what to say, nor did it edit their content. "We told them to be completely honest," says Ford's social media manager. The successful Fiesta Movement ambassadors campaign generated 58 percent pre-launch awareness among Fiesta's under-30 target consumers and a 14 percent

reservation-to-purchase rate, compared to the company's usual 1 to 2 percent rate.

Beyond creating their own brand ambassadors, companies looking to harness the web's social power can work with the army of self-made influencers already plying today's Internet—independent bloggers. The blogosphere has exploded onto the scene in recent years. Two-thirds of all North American Internet users now read blogs regularly and nearly one-third write one. Believe it or not, there are almost as many people making a living as bloggers as there are lawyers. No matter what the interest area, there are probably hundreds of bloggers covering it. Moreover, research shows that 90 percent of bloggers post about their favourite and least favourite brands.

As a result, most companies try to form relationships with influential bloggers and online personalities. For example, to help build awareness for its six-year, US$3 billion Healthymagination health care innovation initiative, GE tapped well-known social network influentials, such as Justine Ezarik. Known online as iJustine, she has built a passionate,

committed, and trusting audience—more than 1 million subscribers to her YouTube channels and 1.2 million Twitter followers. At GE's request, iJustine posted a video on YouTube last year asking viewers how she can live a healthier life. More than 11 000 responded. She produced five videos about those ideas that were viewed more than 2.1 million times. GE's Healthymagination effort received a shout-out in each video. "Justine has tremendous credibility in the space," says GE global advertising chief Judy Hu. "I could not believe the numbers. The views kept going up. It has a life of its own."

The key is to find bloggers who have strong networks of relevant readers, a credible voice, and a good fit with the brand. For example, companies ranging from P&G and Johnson & Johnson to Walmart work closely with influential "mommy bloggers." And you'll no doubt cross paths with the likes of climbers blogging for North Face, bikers blogging for Harley-Davidson, and shoppers blogging for Whole Foods Market or Trader Joe's.

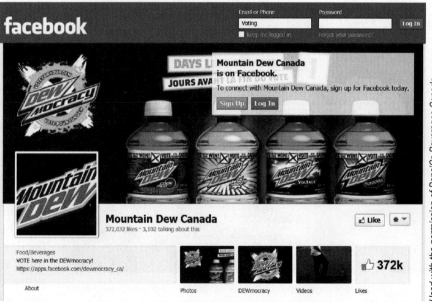

Exhibit 6.5 **Harnessing online influence:** Mountain Dew runs "DEWmocracy" campaigns that invite avid Mountain Dew customers to participate at all levels in launching a new Mountain Dew flavour.

Perhaps the best way to generate brand conversations and social involvement on the web is simply to do something conversation worthy—to actually involve people with the brand online. Pepsi's Mountain Dew brand runs "DEWmocracy" campaigns that invite avid Mountain Dew customers to participate at all levels in launching a new Mountain Dew flavour, from choosing and naming the flavour to designing the can to submitting and selecting TV commercials and even picking an ad agency and media. Presented through a dedicated website, as well as Facebook, Twitter, Flickr, and other public network pages, DEWmocracy has been a perfect forum for getting youthful, socially-savvy Dew drinkers talking with each other and the company about the brand. For example, Mountain Dew's Facebook fan page grew fivefold at the launch of the latest DEWmocracy campaign. The Canadian campaign, which allowed consumers to vote for one of four new flavours in June 2013, generated over 370 000 likes on Facebook.

Ironically, one of the simplest means of capturing social influence through the web is one of the oldest—produce a good ad that gets people talking. But in this day and age, both the ads and the media have changed. Almost every brand, large and small, is now creating innovative brand-sponsored videos, posting them online, and hoping they'll go viral. The videos range from traditional 60-second ads to intricate 10- or 12-minute film shorts. Top innovative viral video ads from the past few years, as rated by social media guide mashable.com, have included everything from a very creative three-minute ad for a small Charlotte, North Carolina, ad agency to a heart-tugging British public service announcement urging people to "Embrace Life" and always wear seatbelts. Such videos can create lots of attention and talk. For example, the Embrace Life video drew more than 13 million YouTube views. One five-minute action video for Inspired Bicycles garnered 15 million rapt views, while a 12-minute love story for Schweppes drew nearly four million views and critical acclaim.

So, whether through online ambassadors, bloggers, social networks, or talked-about videos and events, companies are finding innovative ways to tap social influence online. Called word-of-web, it's growing fast as *the* place to be—for both consumers and marketers. Last year, the time consumers spent on social networking sites nearly tripled; marketer spending at those sites nearly kept pace. "Social [media] is one of the key trends driving business," says a social marketing executive. "It's more than pure marketing. It's about fast connections with customers and building an ongoing relationship."

Sources: Elisabeth A. Sullivan, "Blog Savvy," *Marketing News*, November 15, 2009, p. 8; Keith Barry, "Ford Bets the Fiesta on Social Networking," *Wired*, April 17, 2009, accessed at www.wired.com/autopia/2009/04/how-the-fiesta; Ellen McGirt, "Mr. Social: Ashton Kutcher Plans to Be the Next New-Media Mogul," *Fast Company*, December 1, 2009, accessed at www.fastcompany.com; Josh Warner, "The Ten Most Viral Videos of 2009," December 7, 2009, accessed at www.mashable.com; Mark Borden, "The New Influentials," *Fast Company*, November 2010, p. 124; and information from www.dewmocracy.com, accessed August 2011.

the main purchasing agent for the family in the areas of food, household products, and clothing. But with more women working outside the home and the willingness of husbands to do more of the family's purchasing, all this is changing. A recent survey of men ages 18 to 74 found that more than half now identify themselves as primary grocery shoppers in their households. At the same time, today women account for 50 percent of all technology purchases and influence two-thirds of all new car purchases.[14] Such shifting roles signal a new marketing reality. Marketers in industries that have traditionally sold their products to only women or only men—from groceries and personal care products to cars and consumer electronics—are now courting the opposite sex.

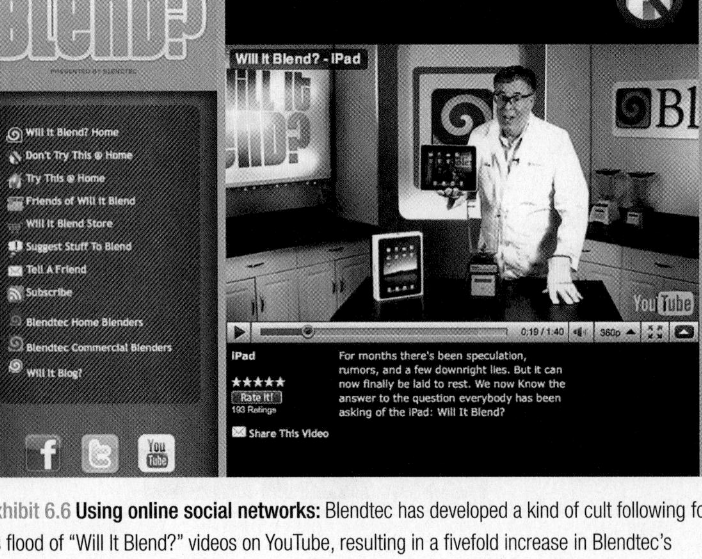

Children may also have a strong influence on family buying decisions. Canadian kids influence some $20 million in household spending each year and have memorized between 300 and 400 brand names by the age of 10. They also influence how much their families spend on them in areas

Exhibit 6.6 **Using online social networks:** Blendtec has developed a kind of cult following for its flood of "Will It Blend?" videos on YouTube, resulting in a fivefold increase in Blendtec's sales.

such as food, clothing, entertainment, and personal care items. One study found that kids significantly influence family decisions about everything from what cars they buy to where they eat out and take vacations.[15]

For example, to encourage families to take their children out to eat, several restaurants in Calgary reach out to children with everything from sophisticated children's menus and special deals, to a wealth of kid-focused activities. At Applebee's, children eat free on Mondays with the purchase of an adult entree. The Boston Pizza on Bow Trail has a magician who entertains kids with magic tricks and makes balloon animals. And Montana's paper-covered tables with crayons are always a hit with kids (and some adults).

ROLES AND STATUS   A person belongs to many groups—family, clubs, organizations. The person's position in each group can be defined in terms of both role and status. A role consists of the activities people are expected to perform according to the persons around them. Each role carries a status reflecting the general esteem given to it by society.

People usually choose products appropriate to their roles and status. Consider the various roles a working mother plays. In her company, she plays the role of a brand manager; in her family, she plays the role of wife and mother; at her favourite sporting events, she plays the role of avid fan. As a brand manager, she will buy the kind of clothing that reflects her role and status in her company.

Personal Factors   A buyer's decisions also are influenced by personal characteristics such as the buyer's *age and life-cycle stage, occupation, economic situation, lifestyle,* and *personality, and self-concept.*

AGE AND LIFE-CYCLE STAGE   People change the goods and services they buy over their lifetimes. Tastes in food, clothes, furniture, and recreation are often age-related. Buying is also shaped by the stage of the family life cycle—the stages through which families might pass as they mature over time. Life-stage changes usually result from demographics and life-changing events—marriage, having children, purchasing a home, divorce, children going to college, changes in personal income, moving out of the house, and retirement. Marketers often define their target markets in terms of life-cycle stage and develop appropriate products and marketing plans for each stage.

Consumer information giant Acxiom's PersonicX life-stage segmentation system places households into one of 70 consumer segments and 21 life-stage groups, based on specific consumer behaviour and demographic characteristics. PersonicX includes life-stage groups with names such as *Beginnings, Taking Hold, Cash & Careers, Jumbo Families, Transition Blues, Our Turn, Golden Years,* and *Active Elders.* For example, the *Taking Hold* group consists of young, energetic, well-funded couples and young families who are busy with their careers, social lives, and interests, especially fitness and active recreation. *Transition Blues* are blue-collar, less-educated, mid-income consumers who are transitioning to stable lives and talking about marriage and children.

"Consumers experience many life-stage changes during their lifetimes," says Acxiom. "As their life stages change, so do their behaviour and purchasing preferences." Armed with data about the timing and makeup of life-stage changes, marketers can create targeted, personalized campaigns.[16]

In line with today's tougher economic times, Acxiom has also developed a set of economic life-stage segments, including groups such as Squeaking By, Eye on Essentials, Tight with a Purpose, It's My Life, Full Speed Ahead, and Potential Rebounders.

PERSONICX
HOUSEHOLD SEGMENTATION
REACHES A NEW LEVEL OF ACCURACY

People aren't just a parent or only a doctor or simply a scuba diver. They can be all of these things – and more. Acxiom's 70 segments and 21 Life Stage groupings will let you know your customers and target them with unmatched precision. And PersonicX™ is the only household-level segmentation product that uses our industry-leading InfoBase-X™ data. You'll now see your prospects as they really are.

ACXIOM®

Spin our Life Stage wheel at **personicx.com** and order a free wheel for yourself.

www.personicx.com · 888-3ACXIOM

GLOBAL INTERACTIVE MARKETING SERVICES

Exhibit 6.7 **Life-stage segmentation:** PersonicX 21 life-stage groupings let marketers see customers as they really are and target them precisely. "People aren't just a parent or only a doctor or simply a scuba diver. They are all of these things."

Lifestyle
A person's pattern of living as expressed in his or her activities, interests, and opinions.

The Potential Rebounders are those more likely to loosen up on spending sooner. This group appears more likely than other segments to use online research before purchasing electronics, appliances, home decor, and jewellery. Thus, home improvement retailers appealing to this segment should have a strong online presence, providing pricing, features and benefits, and product availability.

OCCUPATION A person's occupation affects the goods and services bought. Blue-collar workers tend to buy more rugged work clothes, whereas executives buy more business suits. Marketers try to identify the occupational groups that have an above-average interest in their products and services. A company can even specialize in making products needed by a given occupational group. For example, Moores Clothing for Men has grown to become Canada's leading national retailer of men's business attire. In 30 years, the company has grown to more than 100 stores across Canada, including stores in virtually every major city. The company's founders attribute their success to their commitment to offer Canada's largest selection of quality menswear at the lowest possible everyday prices, and to customer satisfaction. The company guarantees its customers that "if for any reason you are not satisfied with any Moores purchase, simply bring it back for a full refund or exchange." The company strives "to provide customers with everything they want: high quality, outstanding selection, superior customer service, and everyday low prices."[17]

ECONOMIC SITUATION A person's economic situation will affect his or her store and product choices. Marketers watch trends in personal income, savings, and interest rates. Following the recent recession, most companies are taking steps to redesign, reposition, and reprice their products. For example, to counter the lingering long-term effects of the recession, upscale discounter Target has replaced some of its "chic" with "cheap." It has even introduced periodic "Great Save" events featuring exceptional deals on everyday essentials—a kind of treasure-hunt experience to challenge warehouse retailers such as Costco. "Our [tagline] is 'Expect more. Pay less.'" says one Target marketer. These days, "we're putting more emphasis on the pay less promise."[18] As discussed in the opening story in Chapter 1, Canadian brand Joe Fresh recently signed a deal with major US retailer JCPenney to bring "stylish, fresh and affordable fashion" to nearly 700 locations in the US market.

LIFESTYLE People coming from the same subculture, social class, and occupation may have quite different lifestyles. **Lifestyle** is a person's pattern of living as expressed in his or her psychographics. It involves measuring consumers' major AIO dimensions—activities (work, hobbies, shopping, sports, social events), interests (food, fashion, family, recreation), and opinions (about themselves, social issues, business, products). Lifestyle captures something more than the person's social class or personality. It profiles a person's whole pattern of acting and interacting in the world.

When used carefully, the lifestyle concept can help marketers understand changing consumer values and how they affect buying behaviour. Consumers don't just buy products; they buy the values and lifestyles those products represent. For example,

Triumph doesn't just sell motorcycles; it sells an independent, "Go your own way" lifestyle. Similarly, Harley-Davidson tells customers to "grab life by the bars." And Tilley Endurables doesn't just sell high quality hats and accessories. It positions itself as the hat that "goes with anywhere," targeting active Canadians travelling the world.

PERSONALITY AND SELF-CONCEPT Each person's distinct personality influences his or her buying behaviour. **Personality** refers to the unique psychological characteristics that distinguish a person or group. Personality is usually described in terms of traits such as self-confidence, dominance, sociability, autonomy, defensiveness, adaptability, and aggressiveness. Personality can be useful in analyzing consumer behaviour for certain product or brand choices.

Exhibit 6.8 Moores Clothing for Men has grown to become Canada's leading national retailer of men's business attire.

© Helen Sessions / Alamy

The idea is that brands also have personalities, and consumers are likely to choose brands with personalities that match their own. A *brand personality* is the specific mix of human traits that may be attributed to a particular brand. One researcher identified five brand personality traits: *sincerity* (down-to-earth, honest, wholesome, and cheerful); *excitement* (daring, spirited, imaginative, and up-to-date); *competence* (reliable, intelligent, and successful); *sophistication* (upper class and charming); and *ruggedness* (outdoorsy and tough). "Your personality determines what you consume, what TV shows you watch, what products you buy, and [most] other decisions you make," says one consumer behaviour expert.[19]

Personality

The unique psychological characteristics that distinguish a person or group.

Most well-known brands are strongly associated with one particular trait: Jeep with "ruggedness," Apple with "excitement," CNN with "competence," and Dove with "sincerity." Hence, these brands will attract persons who are high on the same personality traits.

Many marketers use a concept related to personality—a person's *self-concept* (also called *self-image*). The idea is that people's possessions contribute to and reflect their identities—that is, "we are what we have." Thus, to understand consumer behaviour, the marketer must first understand the relationship between consumer self-concept and possessions.

Exhibit 6.9 Tilley Endurables doesn't just sell hats and accessories, it sells "an adventurous, travel the world" lifestyle.

For example, Unilever's Axe men's personal care products brand projects a young, confident, manly, and mischievous personality. Dubbed the Axe Effect, Axe ads around the world show how men who use the brand get the woman (or women). One ad from the United Arab Emirates shows a man in a bathtub with women's feet sticking out the other side. An alternative media ad placed next to local emergency exits in Belgium shows stick figures of a man fleeing to the exit pursued by avid female admirers. An Axe ad from Brazil features a wedding cake with a bride and groom on top with other brides scaling the tiers of cake to get to the groom.[20]

Toronto Star via Getty Images

THE-AXE-EFFECT

Exhibit 6.10 **Brand personality:** Unilever's Axe brand projects a young, confident, manly, and mischievous personality.

Motive (drive)
A need that is sufficiently pressing to direct the person to seek satisfaction of the need.

Psychological Factors A person's buying choices are further influenced by four major psychological factors: *motivation*, *perception*, *learning*, and *beliefs and attitudes*.

MOTIVATION A person has many needs at any given time. Some are biological, arising from states of tension such as hunger, thirst, or discomfort. Others are psychological, arising from the need for recognition, esteem, or belonging. A need becomes a motive when it is aroused to a sufficient level of intensity. A **motive (or drive)** is a need that is sufficiently pressing to direct the person to seek satisfaction. Psychologists have developed theories of human motivation. Two of the most popular—the theories of Sigmund Freud and Abraham Maslow—have quite different meanings for consumer analysis and marketing.

Sigmund Freud assumed that people are largely unconscious about the real psychological forces shaping their behaviour. He saw the person as growing up and repressing many urges. These urges are never eliminated or under perfect control; they emerge in dreams, in slips of the tongue, in neurotic and obsessive behaviour, or ultimately in psychoses.

Freud's theory suggests that a person's buying decisions are affected by subconscious motives that even the buyer may not fully understand. Thus, an aging Baby Boomer who buys a sporty BMW 330Ci convertible might explain that he simply likes the feel of the wind in his thinning hair. At a deeper level, he may be trying to impress others with his success. At a still deeper level, he may be buying the car to feel young and independent again.

The term *motivation research* refers to qualitative research designed to probe consumers' hidden, subconscious motivations. Consumers often don't know or can't describe just why they act as they do. Thus, motivation researchers use a variety of probing techniques to uncover underlying emotions and attitudes toward brands and buying situations.

Many companies employ teams of psychologists, anthropologists, and other social scientists to carry out motivation research. One ad agency routinely conducts one-on-one, therapy-like interviews to delve into the inner workings of consumers. Another company asks consumers to describe their favourite brands as animals or cars (say, Mercedes versus Chevrolets) in order to assess the prestige associated with various brands. Still others rely on hypnosis, dream therapy, or soft lights and mood music to plumb the murky depths of consumer psyches.

Such projective techniques seem pretty goofy, and some marketers dismiss such motivation research as mumbo-jumbo. But many marketers use such touchy-feely approaches, now sometimes called *interpretive consumer research*, to dig deeper into consumer psyches and develop better marketing strategies.

Abraham Maslow sought to explain why people are driven by particular needs at particular times. Why does one person spend much time and energy on personal safety and another on gaining the esteem of others? Maslow's answer is that human needs are arranged in a hierarchy, as shown in Figure 6.3, from the most pressing at the bottom to

FIGURE 6.3 Maslow's Hierarchy of Needs

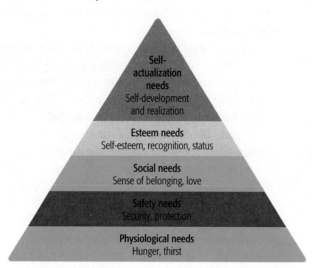

the least pressing at the top.[21] They include *physiological* needs, *safety* needs, *social* needs, *esteem* needs, and *self-actualization* needs.

A person tries to satisfy the most important need first. When that need is satisfied, it will stop being a motivator and the person will then try to satisfy the next most important need. For example, starving people (physiological need) will not take an interest in the latest happenings in the art world (self-actualization needs), nor in how they are seen or esteemed by others (social or esteem needs), nor even whether they are breathing clean air (safety needs). But as each important need is satisfied, the next most important need will come into play. Critics of Maslow's Hierarchy argue that human motivation does not always follow this hierarchical structure. For example, consumers may often seek to satisfy esteem needs by purchasing a $400 pair of designer jeans, while ignoring lower-order safety needs by not paying the rent!

PERCEPTION A motivated person is ready to act. How the person acts is influenced by his or her perception of the situation. All of us learn by the flow of information through our five senses: sight, hearing, smell, touch, and taste. However, each of us receives, organizes, and interprets this sensory information in an individual way. **Perception** is the process by which people select, organize, and interpret information to form a meaningful picture of the world.

Perception
The process by which people select, organize, and interpret information to form a meaningful picture of the world.

People can form different perceptions of the same stimulus because of three perceptual processes: selective attention, selective distortion, and selective retention. People are exposed to a great amount of stimuli every day. For example, people are exposed to an estimated 3000 to 5000 ad messages every day. It is impossible for a person to pay attention to all these stimuli. *Selective attention*—the tendency for people to screen out most of the information to which they are exposed—means that marketers must work especially hard to attract the consumer's attention.[22]

Even noticed stimuli do not always come across in the intended way. Each person fits incoming information into an existing mindset. *Selective distortion* describes the tendency of people to interpret information in a way that will support what they already believe. People also will forget much of what they learn. They tend to retain information that supports their attitudes and beliefs. *Selective retention* means that consumers are likely to remember good points made about a brand they favour and to forget good

PEOPLE HAVE BEEN TRYING TO FIND THE BREASTS IN THESE ICE CUBES SINCE 1957.

The advertising industry is sometimes charged with sneaking seductive little pictures into ads. Supposedly, these pictures can get you to buy a product without your even seeing them.

Consider the photograph above. According to some people, there's a pair of female breasts hidden in the patterns of light refracted by the ice cubes.

Well, if you really searched you probably *could see* the breasts. For that matter, you could also see Millard Fillmore, a stuffed pork chop and a 1946 Dodge.

The point is that so-called "subliminal advertising" simply doesn't exist. Overactive imaginations, however, most certainly do.

So if anyone claims to see breasts in that drink up there, they aren't in the ice cubes. They're in the eye of the beholder.

ADVERTISING
ANOTHER WORD FOR FREEDOM OF CHOICE.
American Association of Advertising Agencies

Exhibit 6.11 This classic ad from the American Association of Advertising Agencies pokes fun at subliminal advertising. "So-called 'subliminal advertising' simply doesn't exist," says the ad. "Overactive imaginations, however, most certainly do."

Learning
Changes in an individual's behaviour arising from experience.

Belief
A descriptive thought that a person holds about something.

points made about competing brands. Because of selective attention, distortion, and retention, marketers must work hard to get their messages through.

Interestingly, although most marketers worry about whether their offers will be perceived at all, some consumers worry that they will be affected by marketing messages without even knowing it—through *subliminal advertising*. More than 50 years ago, a researcher announced that he had flashed the phrases "Eat popcorn" and "Drink Coca-Cola" on a screen in a New Jersey movie theatre every five seconds for one three-hundredths of a second. He reported that although viewers did not consciously recognize these messages, they absorbed them subconsciously and bought 58 percent more popcorn and 18 percent more Coke. Suddenly advertisers and consumer-protection groups became intensely interested in subliminal perception. Although the researcher later admitted to making up the data, the issue has not died. Some consumers still fear that they are being manipulated by subliminal messages.

Numerous studies by psychologists and consumer researchers have found little or no link between subliminal messages and consumer behaviour. Recent brainwave studies have found that in certain circumstances, our brains may register subliminal messages. However, it appears that subliminal advertising simply doesn't have the power attributed to it by its critics. Scoffs one industry insider, "Just between us, most [advertisers] have difficulty getting a 2 percent increase in sales with the help of $50 million in media and extremely *liminal* images of sex, money, power, and other [motivators] of human emotion. The very idea of [us] as puppeteers, cruelly pulling the strings of consumer marionettes, is almost too much to bear."[23]

LEARNING When people act, they learn. **Learning** describes changes in an individual's behaviour arising from experience. Learning theorists say that most human behaviour is learned. Learning occurs through the interplay of drives, stimuli, cues, responses, and reinforcement.

A *drive* is a strong internal stimulus that calls for action. A drive becomes a motive when it is directed toward a particular *stimulus object*. For example, a person's drive for self-actualization might motivate him or her to look into buying a camera. The consumer's response to the idea of buying a camera is conditioned by the surrounding cues. *Cues* are minor stimuli that determine when, where, and how the person responds. For example, the person might spot several camera brands in a shop window, hear of a special sale price, or discuss cameras with a friend. These are all cues that might influence a consumer's *response* to his or her interest in buying the product.

Suppose the consumer buys a Nikon camera. If the experience is rewarding, the consumer will probably use the camera more and more, and his or her response will be *reinforced*. Then, the next time the consumer shops for a camera, or for binoculars, or some similar product, the probability is greater that he or she will buy a Nikon product. The practical significance of learning theory for marketers is that they can build up demand for a product by associating it with strong drives, by using motivating cues, and by providing positive reinforcement.

BELIEFS AND ATTITUDES Through doing and learning, people acquire beliefs and attitudes. These, in turn, influence their buying behaviour. A **belief** is a descriptive thought that a person has about something. Beliefs may be based on real knowledge, opinion, or faith and may or may not carry an emotional charge. Marketers are interested in the beliefs that people formulate about specific products and services, because these beliefs make up product and brand images that affect buying behaviour. If some of the beliefs are wrong and prevent purchase, the marketer will want to launch a campaign to correct them.

People have attitudes regarding religion, politics, clothes, music, food, and almost everything else. **Attitude** describes a person's relatively consistent evaluations, feelings, and tendencies toward an object or an idea. Attitudes put people into a frame of mind of liking or disliking things, of moving toward or away from them. Our camera buyer may hold attitudes such as "Buy the best," "The Japanese make the best electronics products in the world," and "Creativity and self-expression are among the most important things in life." If so, the Nikon camera would fit well into the consumer's existing attitudes.

Attitudes are difficult to change. A person's attitudes fit into a pattern; changing one attitude may require difficult adjustments in many others. Thus, a company should usually try to fit its products into existing attitudes rather than attempt to change attitudes. For example, today's beverage marketers now cater to people's new attitudes about health and well-being with drinks that do a lot more than just taste good or quench your thirst. Pepsi's SoBe brand, for example, offers "Lifewater," "elixirs" (juices), and teas—all packed with vitamins, minerals, herbal ingredients, and antioxidants but without artificial preservatives, sweeteners, or colours. SoBe promises drinks that are good tasting (with flavours like YumBerry Pomegranate Purify, Energize Mango Melon, and Orange Cream Tsunami) but are also good for you. By matching today's attitudes about life and healthful living, the SoBe brand has become a leader in the New Age beverage category.

We can now appreciate the many forces acting on consumer behaviour. The consumer's choice results from the complex interplay of cultural, social, personal, and psychological factors.

The Buyer Decision Process LO2

Now that we have looked at the influences that affect buyers, we are ready to look at how consumers make buying decisions. Figure 6.4 shows that the buyer decision process consists of five stages: *need recognition, information search, evaluation of alternatives, purchase decision*, and *postpurchase behaviour*. Clearly, the buying process starts long before the actual purchase and continues long after. Marketers need to focus on the entire buying process rather than on just the purchase decision.

The figure suggests that consumers pass through all five stages with every purchase. But in more routine purchases, consumers often skip or reverse some of these stages. A woman buying her regular brand of toothpaste would recognize the need and go right to the purchase decision, skipping information search and evaluation. However, we use the model in Figure 6.4 because it shows all the considerations that arise when a consumer faces a new and complex purchase situation.

Attitude
A person's consistently favourable or unfavourable evaluations, feelings, and tendencies toward an object or an idea.

Exhibit 6.12 **Beliefs and attitudes:** By matching today's attitudes about life and healthful living, the SoBe brand has become a leader in the New Age beverage category.

Ruaridh Stewart/ZUMA Press/Newscom

FIGURE 6.4 Buyer Decision Process

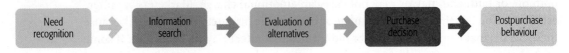

Need Recognition The buying process starts with *need recognition*—the buyer recognizes a problem or need. The need can be triggered by *internal stimuli* when one of the person's normal needs—hunger, thirst, sex—rises to a level high enough to become a drive. A need can also be triggered by *external stimuli*. For example, an advertisement or a discussion with a friend might get you thinking about buying a new car. At this stage, the marketer should research consumers to find out what kinds of needs or problems arise, what brought them about, and how they led the consumer to this particular product.

Information Search An interested consumer may or may not search for more information. If the consumer's drive is strong and a satisfying product is near at hand, the consumer is likely to buy it then. If not, the consumer may store the need in memory or undertake an *information search* related to the need. For example, once you've decided you need a new car, at the least, you will probably pay more attention to car ads, cars owned by friends, and car conversations. Or you may actively search the web, talk with friends, and gather information in other ways.

Consumers can obtain information from any of several sources. These include *personal sources* (family, friends, neighbours, acquaintances), *commercial sources* (advertising, salespeople, dealer websites, packaging, displays), *public sources* (mass media, consumer rating organizations, Internet searches), and *experiential sources* (handling, examining, using the product). The relative influence of these information sources varies with the product and the buyer.

Generally, the consumer receives the most information about a product from commercial sources—those controlled by the marketer. The most effective sources, however, tend to be personal. Commercial sources normally *inform* the buyer, but personal sources *legitimize* or *evaluate* products for the buyer. As one marketer states, "It's rare that an advertising campaign can be as effective as a neighbour leaning over the fence and saying, 'This is a wonderful product.'" Increasingly, that "fence" is a digital one. A recent study revealed that consumers find sources of user-generated content—discussion forums, blogs, online review sites, and social networking sites—three times more influential when making a purchase decision than conventional marketing methods such as TV advertising.[24]

As more information is obtained, the consumer's awareness and knowledge of the available brands and features increase. In your car information search, you may learn about the several brands available. The information might also help you to drop certain brands from consideration. A company must design its marketing mix to make prospects aware of and knowledgeable about its brand. It should carefully identify consumers' sources of information and the importance of each source.

Evaluation of Alternatives We have seen how the consumer uses information to arrive at a set of final brand choices. How does the consumer choose among the alternative brands? The marketer needs to know about *alternative evaluation*—that is, how the consumer processes information to arrive at brand choices. Unfortunately, consumers do not use a simple and single evaluation process in all buying situations. Instead, several evaluation processes are at work.

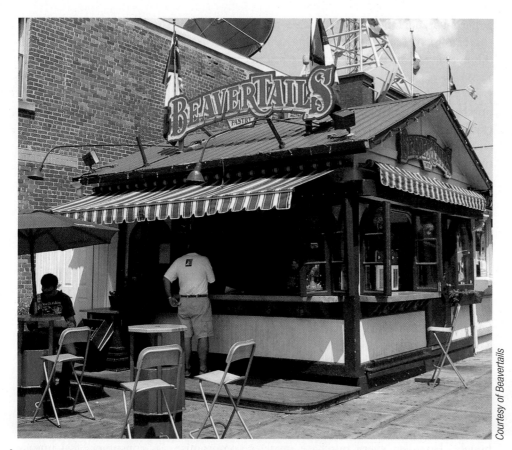

Courtesy of Beavertails

Exhibit 6.13 **Need recognition can be triggered by external stimuli:** Time for a snack?

The consumer arrives at attitudes toward different brands through some evaluation procedure. How consumers go about evaluating purchase alternatives depends on the individual consumer and the specific buying situation. In some cases, consumers use careful calculations and logical thinking. At other times, the same consumers do little or no evaluating; instead they buy on impulse and rely on intuition. Sometimes consumers make buying decisions on their own; sometimes they turn to friends, online reviews, or salespeople for buying advice.

Suppose you've narrowed your car choices to three brands. And suppose that you are primarily interested in four attributes—styling, operating economy, warranty, and price. By this time, you've probably formed beliefs about how each brand rates on each attribute. Clearly, if one car rated best on all the attributes, we could predict that you would choose it. However, the brands will no doubt vary in appeal. You might base your buying decision on only one attribute, and your choice would be easy to predict. If you wanted styling above everything else, you would buy the car that you think has the best styling. But most buyers consider several attributes, each with different importance. If we knew the importance that you assigned to each of the four attributes, we could predict your car choice more reliably.

Marketers should study buyers to find out how they actually evaluate brand alternatives. If they know what evaluative processes go on, marketers can take steps to influence the buyer's decision.

Purchase Decision In the evaluation stage, the consumer ranks brands and forms purchase intentions. Generally, the consumer's *purchase decision* will be to buy the most preferred brand, but two factors can come between the purchase *intention* and the purchase *decision*. The first factor is the *attitudes of others*. If someone important to you thinks that you should buy the lowest-priced car, then the chances of you buying a more expensive car are reduced.

The second factor is *unexpected situational factors*. The consumer may form a purchase intention based on factors such as expected income, expected price, and expected product benefits. However, unexpected events may change the purchase intention. For example, the economy might take a turn for the worse, a close competitor might drop its price, or a friend might report being disappointed in your preferred car. Thus, preferences and even purchase intentions do not always result in actual purchase choice.

Postpurchase Behaviour   The marketer's job does not end when the product is bought. After purchasing the product, the consumer will be satisfied or dissatisfied and will engage in *postpurchase behaviour* of interest to the marketer. What determines whether the buyer is satisfied or dissatisfied with a purchase? The answer lies in the relationship between the *consumer's expectations* and the product's *perceived performance*. If the product falls short of expectations, the consumer is disappointed; if it meets expectations, the consumer is satisfied; if it exceeds expectations, the consumer is delighted. The larger the gap between expectations and performance, the greater the consumer's dissatisfaction. This suggests that sellers should promise only what their brands can deliver so that buyers are satisfied.

Cognitive dissonance
Buyer discomfort caused by postpurchase conflict.

Almost all major purchases, however, result in **cognitive dissonance**, or discomfort caused by postpurchase conflict. After the purchase, consumers are satisfied with the benefits of the chosen brand and are glad to avoid the drawbacks of the brands not bought. However, every purchase involves compromise. So consumers feel uneasy about acquiring the drawbacks of the chosen brand and about losing the benefits of the brands not purchased. Thus, consumers feel at least some postpurchase dissonance for every purchase.[25]

Why is it so important to satisfy the customer? Customer satisfaction is a key to building profitable relationships with consumers—to keeping and growing consumers and reaping their customer lifetime value. Satisfied customers buy a product again, talk favourably to others about the product, pay less attention to competing brands and advertising, and buy other products from the company. Many marketers go beyond merely *meeting* the expectations of customers—they aim to *delight* the customer.

A dissatisfied consumer responds differently. Bad word-of-mouth often travels farther and faster than good word-of-mouth. It can quickly damage consumer attitudes about a company and its products. But companies cannot simply rely on dissatisfied customers to volunteer their complaints when they are dissatisfied. Most unhappy customers never tell the company about their problem. Therefore, a company should measure customer satisfaction regularly. It should set up systems that *encourage* customers to complain. In this way, the company can learn how well it is doing and how it can improve.

By studying the overall buyer decision, marketers may be able to find ways to help consumers move through it. For example, if consumers are not buying a new product because they do not perceive a need for it, marketing might launch advertising messages that trigger the need and show how the product solves customers' problems. If customers know about the product but are not buying because they

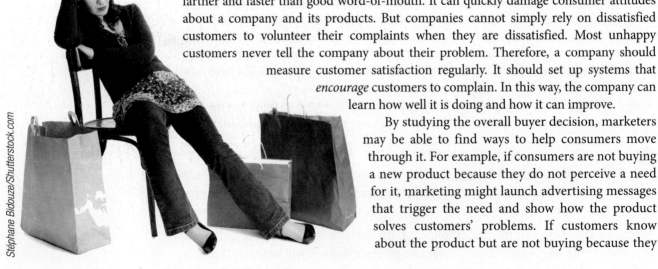

Exhibit 6.14 **Postpurchase cognitive dissonance:** No matter what choice they make, consumers feel at least some postpurchase dissonance for every decision.

Stéphane Bidouze/Shutterstock.com

hold unfavourable attitudes toward it, the marketer must find ways to change either the product or consumer perceptions.

The Buyer Decision Process for New Products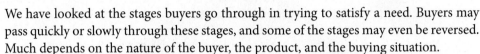

We have looked at the stages buyers go through in trying to satisfy a need. Buyers may pass quickly or slowly through these stages, and some of the stages may even be reversed. Much depends on the nature of the buyer, the product, and the buying situation.

We now look at how buyers approach the purchase of new products. A **new product** is a good, service, or idea that is perceived by some potential customers as new. It may have been around for a while, but our interest is in how consumers learn about products for the first time and make decisions on whether to adopt them. We define the **adoption process** as "the mental process through which an individual passes from first learning about an innovation to final adoption," and *adoption* as the decision by an individual to become a regular user of the product.[26]

New product
A good, service, or idea that is perceived by some potential customers as new.

Adoption process
The mental process through which an individual passes from first hearing about an innovation to final adoption.

Stages in the Adoption Process   Consumers go through five stages in the process of adopting a new product:

- *Awareness:* The consumer becomes aware of the new product, but lacks information about it.
- *Interest:* The consumer seeks information about the new product.
- *Evaluation:* The consumer considers whether trying the new product makes sense.
- *Trial:* The consumer tries the new product on a small scale to improve his or her estimate of its value.
- *Adoption:* The consumer decides to make full and regular use of the new product.

This model suggests that new-product marketers should think about how to help consumers move through these stages. For example, Best Buy recently developed a unique way to help concerned customers get past a hurdle in the buying process and make a positive buying decision for new televisions.[27]

> Prior to the recent holiday shopping season, to convince buyers to upgrade to new models, television manufacturers offered a flurry of new technologies and loaded their marketing pitches with techie jargon such as 3D, ultrathin, Wi-Fi-capable, widget-equipped, and Internet-ready. However, rather than spurring new purchases, the pitches created a barrier to buying—fear among buyers that whatever they bought might soon be obsolete. In one study, 40 percent of consumers said that concerns about technology becoming outdated were preventing them from buying electronic products such as TVs, mobile phones, and computers. That left electronics retailers like Best Buy with aisles stacked high with unsold electronics.
>
> To help customers past this buying hurdle, Best Buy began offering a Future-Proof Buy Back Program. For an up-front fee of 7 to 20 percent of the price, Best Buy promises customers that, when they're ready for something new, it will redeem purchases in good working order for up to 50 percent of the purchase price, depending on how many months pass before they upgrade. "There is a fair number of consumers on the bubble, not quite willing to make a purchase because they fear some other new thing will come down very quickly," says a Best Buy executive. "We want them to go ahead and make that purchase with confidence."

Individual Differences in Innovativeness   People differ greatly in their readiness to try new products. In each product area, there are "consumption pioneers" and early adopters. Other individuals adopt new products much later. People can be classified into the adopter categories shown in Figure 6.5. After a slow start, an increasing number of

FIGURE 6.5 Adopter Categorization on the Basis of Relative Time of Adoption of Innovations

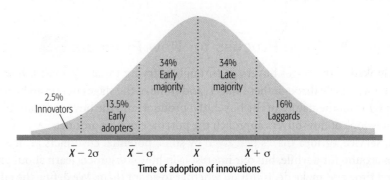

Source: From *Diffusion of Innovations*, 5th ed., by Everett M. Rogers. Copyright © 2003 by the Free Press., Simon & Schuster, Inc.

people adopt the new product. The number of adopters reaches a peak and then drops off as fewer non-adopters remain. Innovators are defined as the first 2.5 percent of the buyers to adopt a new idea (those beyond two standard deviations from mean adoption time); the early adopters are the next 13.5 percent (between one and two standard deviations); and so forth.

The five adopter groups have differing values. *Innovators* are venturesome—they try new ideas at some risk. *Early adopters* are guided by respect—they are opinion leaders in their communities and adopt new ideas early but carefully. The *early majority* are deliberate—although they rarely are leaders, they adopt new ideas before the average person. The *late majority* are skeptical—they adopt an innovation only after a majority of people have tried it. Finally, *laggards* are tradition bound—they are suspicious of changes and adopt the innovation only when it has become something of a tradition itself.

This adopter classification suggests that an innovating firm should research the characteristics of innovators and early adopters in their product categories and should direct marketing efforts toward them.

Influence of Product Characteristics on Rate of Adoption   The characteristics of the new product affect its rate of adoption. Some products catch on almost overnight—for example, the iPod and iPhone, both of which flew off retailers' shelves at an astounding rate from the day they were introduced. Others take a longer time to gain acceptance. For example, the first HDTVs were introduced in North America in the 1990s, but the percentage of households owning a high definition set stood at only 12 percent by 2007 and 61 percent by 2010.[28]

Five characteristics are especially important in influencing an innovation's rate of adoption. For example, consider the characteristics of HDTV in relation to the rate of adoption:

■ *Relative advantage:* the degree to which the innovation appears superior to existing products. HDTV offers substantially improved picture quality. This speeded up its rate of adoption.

■ *Compatibility:* the degree to which the innovation fits the values and experiences of potential consumers. HDTV, for example, is highly compatible with the lifestyles of the TV-watching public. However, in the early years, HDTV was not yet compatible with programming and broadcasting systems, slowing adoption. Now, as high definition programs and channels have become the norm, the rate of HDTV adoption has increased rapidly.

- *Complexity:* the degree to which the innovation is difficult to understand or use. HDTVs are not very complex. Therefore, as more programming has become available and prices have fallen, the rate of HDTV adoption is increasing faster than that of more complex innovations.

- *Divisibility:* the degree to which the innovation may be tried on a limited basis. Early HDTVs and HD cable and satellite systems were very expensive, slowing the rate of adoption. As prices fall, adoption rates are increasing.

- *Communicability:* the degree to which the results of using the innovation can be observed or described to others. Because HDTV lends itself to demonstration and description, its use will spread faster among consumers.

Other characteristics influence the rate of adoption, such as initial and ongoing costs, risk and uncertainty, and social approval. The new-product marketer must research all these factors when developing the new product and its marketing program.

Business Markets and Business Buyer Behaviour LO4

In one way or another, most large companies sell to other organizations. Companies such as DuPont, Bombardier, IBM, Caterpillar, and countless other firms sell *most* of their products to other businesses. Even large consumer-products companies, which make products used by final consumers, must first sell their products to other businesses. For example, General Mills makes many familiar consumer brands—Big G cereals (Cheerios, Wheaties, Trix, Chex), baking products (Pillsbury, Betty Crocker, Gold Medal flour), snacks (Nature Valley, Pop Secret, Chex Mix), Yoplait yogurt, Häagen-Dazs ice cream, and others. But to sell these products to consumers, General Mills must first sell them to its wholesaler and retailer customers, who in turn serve the consumer market.

Business buyer behaviour refers to the buying behaviour of the organizations that buy goods and services for use in the production of other products and services that are sold, rented, or supplied to others. It also includes the behaviour of retailing and wholesaling firms that acquire goods to resell or rent them to others at a profit. In the *business buying process*, business buyers determine which products and services their organizations need to purchase and then find, evaluate, and choose among alternative suppliers and brands. *Business-to-business (B-to-B) marketers* must do their best to understand business markets and business buyer behaviour. Then, like businesses that sell to final buyers, they must build profitable relationships with business customers by creating superior customer value.

Business buyer behaviour
The buying behaviour of the organizations that buy goods and services for use in the production of other products and services or to resell or rent them to others at a profit.

Business Markets

The business market is *huge*. In fact, business markets involve far more dollars and items than do consumer markets. For example, think about the large number of business transactions involved in the production and sale of a single set of Goodyear tires. Various suppliers sell Goodyear the rubber, steel, equipment, and other goods that it needs to produce tires. Goodyear then sells the finished tires to retailers, who in turn sell them to consumers. Thus, many sets of *business* purchases were made for only one set of *consumer*

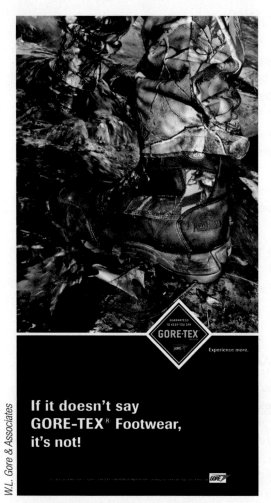

Exhibit 6.15 **Derived demand:** You can't buy anything directly from Gore, but to increase demand for Gore-Tex fabrics, the company markets directly to the buyers of outdoor apparel and other brands made from them. Both Gore and its partner brands win.
W. L. Gore & Associates, Inc. GORE-TEX is a trademark of W. L. Gore & Associates, Inc.

Derived demand
Business demand that ultimately comes from (derives from) the demand for consumer goods.

purchases. In addition, Goodyear sells tires as original equipment to manufacturers who install them on new vehicles, and as replacement tires to companies that maintain their own fleets of company cars, trucks, buses, or other vehicles.

In some ways, business markets are similar to consumer markets. Both involve people who assume buying roles and make purchase decisions to satisfy needs. However, business markets differ in many ways from consumer markets. The main differences are in *market structure and demand*, the *nature of the buying unit*, and the *types of decisions and the decision process* involved.

Market Structure and Demand The business marketer normally deals with *far fewer but far larger buyers* than the consumer marketer does. Even in large business markets, a few buyers often account for most of the purchasing. For example, when Goodyear sells replacement tires to final consumers, its potential market includes the owners of the millions of cars currently in use around the world. But Goodyear's fate in the business market depends on getting orders from one of only a handful of large automakers.

Further, business demand is **derived demand**—it ultimately derives from the demand for consumer goods. For example, W. L. Gore & Associates sells its Gore-Tex brand to manufacturers who make and sell outdoor apparel brands made from Gore-Tex fabrics. If demand for these brands increases, so does demand for Gore-Tex fabrics. So to boost demand for Gore-Tex, Gore advertises to final consumers to educate them on the benefits of Gore-Tex fabrics in the brands they buy. It also directly markets brands containing Gore-Tex—from Arc'teryx, Marmot, and The North Face to Burton and L.L. Bean—on its own website (www.gore-tex.com).

To deepen its direct relationship with outdoor enthusiasts further, Gore even sponsors an "Experience More" online community in which members can share experiences and videos, connect with outdoor experts, and catch exclusive gear offers from partner brands. As a result, consumers around the world have learned to look for the familiar Gore-Tex brand label, and both Gore and its partner brands win. No matter what brand of apparel or footwear you buy, says the label, if it's made with Gore-Tex fabric, it's "guaranteed to keep you dry."

Finally, many business markets have *inelastic and more fluctuating demand*. The total demand for many business products is not much affected by price changes, especially in the short run. A drop in the price of leather will not cause shoe manufacturers to buy much more leather unless it results in lower shoe prices that, in turn, increase consumer demand for shoes. And the demand for many business goods and services tends to change more—and more quickly—than does the demand for consumer goods and services. A small percentage increase in consumer demand can cause large increases in business demand.

Nature of the Buying Unit Compared with consumer purchases, a business purchase usually involves *more decision participants* and a *more professional purchasing effort*. Often, business buying is done by trained purchasing agents who spend their working lives learning how to buy better. The more complex the purchase, the more likely it is that several people will participate in the decision-making process. Buying committees made up of technical experts and top management are common in the buying of major goods. Beyond this, B-to-B marketers now face a new breed of higher-level, better-trained supply managers. Therefore, companies must have well-trained marketers and salespeople to deal with these well-trained buyers.

Types of Decisions and the Decision Process Business buyers usually face *more complex* buying decisions than do consumer buyers. Business purchases often involve large sums of money, complex technical and economic considerations, and interactions among many people at many levels of the buyer's organization. Because the purchases are more complex, business buyers may take longer to make their decisions. The business buying process also tends to be *more formalized* than the consumer buying process. Large business purchases usually call for detailed product specifications, written purchase orders, careful supplier searches, and formal approval.

Finally, in the business buying process, the buyer and seller are often much *more dependent* on each other. B-to-B marketers may roll up their sleeves and work closely with their customers during all stages of the buying process—from helping customers define problems, to finding solutions, to supporting after-sale operation. They often customize their offerings to individual customer needs. In the short run, sales go to suppliers who meet buyers' immediate product and service needs. In the long run, however, business-to-business marketers keep a customer's sales and create customer value by meeting current needs *and* by partnering with customers to help them solve their problems. For example, Dow Performance Plastics doesn't just sell commodity plastics *to* its industrial customers—it works *with* these customers to help them succeed in their own markets. (See Marketing @ Work 6.2.)

In recent years, relationships between customers and suppliers have been changing from downright adversarial to close and chummy. In fact, many customer companies are now practicing **supplier development**, systematically developing networks of supplier-partners to ensure a dependable supply of products and materials that they use in making their own products or reselling to others. For example, Walmart doesn't have a "Purchasing Department"; it has a "Supplier Development Department." The giant retailer knows that it can't just rely on spot suppliers who might be available when needed. Instead, Walmart manages a robust network of supplier-partners that help provide the hundreds of billions of dollars of goods that it sells to its customers each year.

Supplier development
Systematic development of networks of supplier-partners to ensure an appropriate and dependable supply of products and materials for use in making products or reselling them to others.

Business Buyer Behaviour

At the most basic level, marketers want to know how business buyers will respond to various marketing stimuli. Figure 6.6 shows a model of business buyer behaviour. In this model, marketing and other stimuli affect the buying organization and produce certain buyer responses. These stimuli enter the organization and are turned into buyer responses. To design good marketing strategies, the marketer must understand what happens within the organization to turn stimuli into purchase responses.

Within the organization, buying activity consists of two major parts: the buying centre, made up of all the people involved in the buying decision, and the buying decision process. The model shows that the buying centre and the buying decision process are influenced by internal organizational, interpersonal, and individual factors as well as by external environmental factors.

The model in Figure 6.6 suggests four questions about business buyer behaviour: What buying decisions do business buyers make? Who participates in the buying process? What are the major influences on buyers? How do business buyers make their buying decisions?

MARKETING@WORK   6.2

Dow Performance Plastics: "If You Win, We Win"

When you pick up your cellphone to text a friend or hop into your car to head for the mall, you probably don't think much about the plastics that make those state-of-the-art products possible. But at Dow Performance Plastics, thinking about how plastics can make our lives better is at the very core of its business strategy. What makes that noteworthy is that Dow doesn't sell its products to you and me. Instead, it sells mountains of raw materials to its business customers, who in turn sell parts to companies—such as Nokia and BMW—who sell their products to final users. But Dow Performance Plastics understands that its own success depends heavily on how successfully its business customers use Dow plastic polymers and resins in satisfying final consumer needs. It's not just selling commodity plastics; it's helping the businesses that buy its plastics materials to be heroes with their own customers.

To get a better perspective on this strategy, let's go back a few years. In the late 1980s, The Dow Chemical Company realigned its dozen or so widely varied plastics businesses into a single subsidiary, called Dow Plastics (now Dow Performance Plastics). One of the first things Dow had to do was to decide how to position its new division competitively. Initial research showed that Dow Plastics rated a distant third in customer preference behind industry leaders DuPont and GE Plastics. The research also revealed, however, that customers were unhappy with the service—or lack thereof—that they received from all three suppliers. "Vendors peddled resins as a commodity," said the then head of Dow Plastics' advertising agency. "They competed on price and delivered on time but gave no service."

These findings led to a positioning strategy that went far beyond simply selling good products and delivering them on time. Dow Plastics set out to build deeper relationships with business customers. The organization wasn't just selling products and value-added services; it was partnering with customers to help them win with their own final consumers. Said the agency executive, "Whether they're using Dow's plastics to make bags for Safeway or for complex [automotive] applications, we had to help them succeed in their markets." This new thinking was summed up in the positioning statement, "We don't succeed unless you do."

This new philosophy got Dow out of selling just plastics and into selling customer success. The problems of Dow's organizational customers became more than just engineering challenges. Dow's business customers sell to somebody else, so the company now faced new challenges of marketing to and helping satisfy customers' customers.

Over the past two decades, the customer success philosophy has come to permeate everything Dow does. Dow doesn't just sell plastics *to* its business customers; it works *with* them to grow and succeed together. Now, whenever Dow people encounter a new plastics product or market, the first question they always ask is, "How does this help our customers succeed?"

For example, carmaker BMW sells to some of the world's most demanding customers. BMW owners want high performance, but they also want reasonable prices and fuel economy. Thus, to help deliver more value to its customers, BMW looks for two important attributes in every vehicle component: cost savings and weight reduction. Lower costs mean more palatable prices for car buyers, and weight reduction yields customer benefits such as improved fuel economy, increased acceleration, and better handling and braking.

So when BMW and its electronic parts supplier Tyco needed an advanced electronics box for the engine compartment of BMW's latest 7 Series models, they looked for something that would not only meet complex performance specifications but also be cost efficient and lightweight. Enter Dow. Working together, the Dow-Tyco team developed a lightweight plastic box that yields "exceptional dimensional stability, low warpage, low weight, and improved hydrolysis resistance," all at a surprisingly economical cost.

That might sound like gibberish to you, but it's sweet music to companies like Tyco and BMW. In the final analysis, of course, the folks at Dow care most about how such parts will help BMW succeed with car buyers. The more cars BMW

Associated Press

Exhibit 6.16 Dow Performance Plastics isn't just selling commodity plastics—it's helping the businesses that buy its plastics to be heroes with their own customers.

sells to final buyers, the more plastics Dow sells to Tyco. Through such innovations, Dow has helped BMW give customers a full-sized 5100-pound sedan that hits 60 miles per hour from a standstill in 4.4 seconds, blasts through corners like a go-cart, and still gets decent gas mileage.

Selling customer success has turned Dow into a world-leading supplier of plastic resins and material science innovations. Plastics now account for more than 20 percent of Dow Chemical's US$54

billion in annual revenues. Dow Performance Plastics doesn't come up with winning solutions for customers by simply dipping into its current product portfolio. It works closely with customers in every stage of product development and production, from material selection through final part testing. Dow Plastics considers itself a partner, not just a supplier. As the company summarized on its website:

Think of Dow as the team behind your team. Dow Performance Plastics' greatest

asset, and the one that can make the biggest difference to your business, is our people. Knowledgeable, flexible, and committed to your success, our team puts all our resources together to provide you with a competitive edge. We believe in a simple concept . . . if you win, we win.

Sources: For historical background, see Nancy Arnott, "Getting the Picture: The Grand Design—We Don't Succeed Unless You Do," *Sales & Marketing Management,* June 1994, pp. 74–76. Current quotes and other information from www.omnexus.com/sf/dow/?id=plastics, accessed March 2010, and http://plastics.dow.com, accessed September 2011.

Major Types of Buying Situations   There are three major types of buying situations.[29] In a **straight rebuy**, the buyer reorders something without any modifications. It is usually handled on a routine basis by the purchasing department. To keep the business, "in" suppliers try to maintain product and service quality. "Out" suppliers try to find new ways to add value or exploit dissatisfaction so that the buyer will consider them.

In a **modified rebuy**, the buyer wants to modify product specifications, prices, terms, or suppliers. The "in" suppliers may become nervous and feel pressured to put their best foot forward to protect an account. "Out" suppliers may see the modified rebuy situation as an opportunity to make a better offer and gain new business.

A company buying a product or service for the first time faces a **new-task** situation. In such cases, the greater the cost or risk, the larger the number of decision participants and the greater their efforts to collect information. The new-task situation is the marketer's greatest opportunity and challenge. The marketer not only tries to reach as many key buying influences as possible but also provides help and information. The buyer makes the fewest decisions in the straight rebuy and the most in the new-task decision.

Many business buyers prefer to buy a complete solution to a problem from a single seller instead of buying separate products and services from several suppliers and putting them together. The sale often goes to the firm that provides the most complete *system* for

Straight rebuy

A business buying situation in which the buyer routinely reorders something without any modifications.

Modified rebuy

A business buying situation in which the buyer wants to modify product specifications, prices, terms, or suppliers.

New task

A business buying situation in which the buyer purchases a product or service for the first time.

FIGURE 6.6 The Model of Business Buyer Behaviour

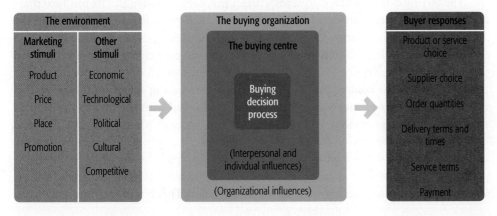

Oberhaeuser/Caro/Alamy

Exhibit 6.17 Systems selling: UPS bundles a complete system of services that support Nikon's consumer products supply chain—including logistics, transportation, freight, and customs brokerage services.

Systems selling (or solutions selling)
Buying a packaged solution to a problem from a single seller, thus avoiding all the separate decisions involved in a complex buying situation.

meeting the customer's needs and solving its problems. Such **systems selling (or solutions selling)** is often a key business marketing strategy for winning and holding accounts.

UPS does more than just ship packages for its business customers. It develops entire solutions to customers' transportation and logistics problems. For example, UPS bundles a complete system of services that support Nikon's consumer-products supply chain—including logistics, transportation, freight, and customs brokerage services—into one smooth-running system.[30]

When Nikon entered the digital camera market, it decided that it needed an entirely new distribution strategy as well. So it asked transportation and logistics giant UPS to design a complete system for moving its entire electronics product line from its Asian factories to retail stores throughout the United States, Canada, Latin America, and the Caribbean. Now, products leave Nikon's Asian manufacturing centres and arrive on retailers' shelves in as few as two days, with UPS handling everything in between. UPS first manages air and ocean freight and related customs brokerage to bring Nikon products from Korea, Japan, and Indonesia to its Louisville, Kentucky, operations centre. There, UPS can either "kit" the Nikon merchandise with accessories such as batteries and chargers or repackage it for in-store display. Finally, UPS distributes the products to thousands of retailers across the United States or exports them to Canadian, Latin American or Caribbean retail outlets and distributors. Along the way, UPS tracks the goods and provides Nikon with a "snapshot" of the entire supply chain, letting Nikon keep retailers informed of delivery times and adjust them as needed.

Participants in the Business Buying Process Who does the buying of the trillions of dollars' worth of goods and services needed by business organizations? The decision-making unit of a buying organization is called its **buying centre**—all the individuals and units that play a role in the business purchase decision-making process. This group includes the actual users of the product or service, those who make the buying decision, those who influence the buying decision, those who do the actual buying, and those who control buying information.

Buying centre
All the individuals and units that play a role in the purchase decision-making process.

The buying centre is not a fixed and formally identified unit within the buying organization. It is a set of buying roles assumed by different people for different purchases. Within the organization, the size and makeup of the buying centre will vary for different products and different buying situations. For some routine purchases, one person—say, a purchasing agent—may assume all the buying centre roles and serve as the only person involved in the buying decision. For more complex purchases, the buying centre may include 20 or 30 people from different levels and departments in the organization.

The buying centre concept presents a major marketing challenge. The business marketer must learn who participates in the decision, each participant's relative influence, and what evaluation criteria each decision participant uses. This can be difficult.

The buying centre usually includes some obvious participants who are involved formally in the buying decision. For example, the decision to buy a corporate jet will probably involve the company's CEO, chief pilot, a purchasing agent, some legal staff, a member of top management, and others formally charged with the buying decision. It may also involve less obvious, informal participants, some of whom may actually make or strongly affect the buying decision. Sometimes, even the people in the buying centre are not aware of all the buying participants. For example, the decision about which corporate jet to buy may actually be made by a corporate board member who has an interest in flying and who knows a lot about airplanes. This board member may work behind the scenes to sway the decision. Many business buying decisions result from the complex interactions of ever-changing buying centre participants.

Major Influences on Business Buyers Business buyers are subject to many influences when they make their buying decisions. Some marketers assume that the major influences are economic. They think buyers will favour the supplier who offers the lowest price or the best product or the most service. They concentrate on offering strong economic benefits to buyers. However, business buyers actually respond to both economic and personal factors. Far from being cold, calculating, and impersonal, business buyers are human and social as well. They react to both reason and emotion.

Today, most B-to-B marketers recognize that emotion plays an important role in business buying decisions. For example, you might expect that a company selling corrugated boxes, protective packaging, and point-of-purchase displays would stress objective factors such as price, quality, and delivery. However, Great Little Box Company of British Columbia has built a reputation on the strength of its people. Its tagline "Great people to deal with" sums up the company's philosophy. Owner Robert Meggy attributes the company's success to his employees, who are committed to providing the company's customers with good service, quick turnaround, and on-time delivery. "If you keep your staff happy, they will keep your customers happy," says James Palmer, vice-president of sales and marketing. The company's focus on people resulted in it being selected as one of Canada's top 100 employers, one of Financial Post's 10 best companies to work for, and one of BC's top employers in 2012.[31]

Figure 6.7 lists various groups of influences on business buyers—environmental, organizational, interpersonal, and individual. *Environmental factors* have the broadest impact. Business buyers are heavily influenced by factors in the current and expected economic environment, such as levels of primary demand and the economic outlook. Business buyers also are affected by supply, technological, political, and competitive developments in the environment. Finally, culture and customs can strongly influence business buyer reactions to the marketer's behaviour and strategies, especially in the international marketing environment. The business buyer must watch these factors, determine how they will affect the buyer, and try to turn environmental challenges into opportunities.

Organizational factors are also important. Each buying organization has its own objectives, policies, procedures, structure, and systems, and the business marketer must understand these factors well. Questions such as these arise: How many people are

Great Little Box Company

Exhibit 6.18 Emotions play an important role in business buying: Great Little Box Company has succeeded by becoming known to its customers as "great people to deal with."

FIGURE 6.7 Major Influences on Business Buyer Behaviour

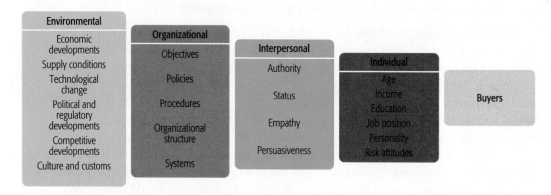

involved in the buying decision? Who are they? What are their evaluative criteria? What are the company's policies and limits on its buyers?

The buying centre usually includes many participants who influence each other, so *interpersonal factors* also influence the business buying process. However, it is often difficult to assess such interpersonal factors and group dynamics. Buying centre participants do not wear tags that label them as *key decision maker* or *not influential*. Nor do buying centre participants with the highest rank always have the most influence. Participants may influence the buying decision because they control rewards and punishments, are well liked, have special expertise, or have a special relationship with other important participants. Interpersonal factors are often very subtle. Whenever possible, business marketers must try to understand these factors and design strategies that take them into account. Finally, each participant in the business buying decision process brings in personal motives, perceptions, and preferences. These *individual factors* are affected by personal characteristics such as age, income, education, professional identification, personality, and attitudes toward risk. Also, buyers have different buying styles. Some may be technical types who make in-depth analyses of competitive proposals before choosing a supplier. Other buyers may be intuitive negotiators who are adept at pitting the sellers against one another for the best deal.

LO5 **The Business Buying Process** Figure 6.8 lists the eight stages of the business buying process.[32] Buyers who face a new-task buying situation usually go through all stages of the buying process. Buyers making modified or straight rebuys may skip some of the stages. We will examine these steps for the typical new-task buying situation.

The buying process begins with *problem recognition*—when someone in the company recognizes a problem or need that can be met by acquiring a specific product or service. Problem recognition can result from internal or external factors. Business

FIGURE 6.8 Stages of the Business Buying Process

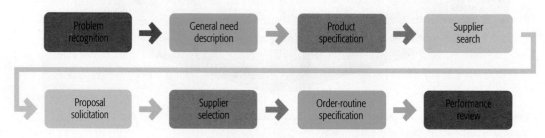

marketers use their sales forces or advertising to alert customers to potential problems and then show how their products provide solutions. For example, an award-winning ad from Quill.com, an online office products supplier that strives for strong customer service, highlights an important customer problem: what to do when your printer runs out of toner. The visual in the ad—which shows the headline fading then reappearing—effectively suggests both the problem and the solution. "If you run out of toner," says the ad, "we will replace it this quickly. At Quill.com, we are here whenever you need us."

Having recognized a need, the buyer next prepares a *general need description* that describes the characteristics and quantity of the needed items or solutions. For standard purchases, this process presents few problems. For complex items, however, the buyer may need to work with others—engineers, users, consultants—to define what's needed.

Once the buying organization has defined the need, it develops the item's technical *product specifications*, often with the help of a value analysis engineering team. **Value analysis** is an approach to cost reduction in which the company carefully analyzes a product's or service's components to determine whether they can be redesigned and made more effectively and efficiently to provide greater value. The team decides on the best product or service characteristics and specifies them accordingly. Sellers, too, can use value analysis as a tool to help secure new accounts and keep old ones. Especially in a down economy, improving customer value and helping customers find more cost-effective solutions gives the business marketer an important edge in keeping current customers loyal and winning new business.

Value analysis
Carefully analyzing a product's or service's components to determine whether they can be redesigned and made more effectively and efficiently to provide greater value.

In the next buying process step, the buyer conducts a *supplier search* to find the best vendors. The buyer can locate qualified suppliers through trade directories, computer searches, or recommendations from others. Today, more and more companies are turning to the Internet to find suppliers. For marketers, this has levelled the playing field—the Internet gives smaller suppliers many of the same advantages as larger competitors. The supplier's task is to understand the search process and make certain that their firm is considered.

In the *proposal solicitation* stage of the business buying process, the buyer invites qualified suppliers to submit proposals. When the purchase is complex or expensive, the buyer will usually require detailed written proposals or formal presentations from each potential supplier. In response, business marketers must be skilled in researching, writing, and presenting proposals. The proposals should be marketing documents, not just technical documents. They should spell out how the seller's solution creates greater value for the customer than competing solutions.

The buyer next reviews the proposals and selects a supplier or suppliers. During *supplier selection*, the buyer will consider many supplier attributes and their relative importance. Such attributes include product and service quality, reputation, on-time delivery, ethical corporate behaviour, honest communication, and competitive prices. In the end, they may select a single supplier or a few suppliers. Today's supplier development managers often want to develop a full network of supplier-partners that can help the company bring more value to its customers.

The buyer now prepares an *order-routine specification*. It includes the final order with the chosen supplier or suppliers and lists items such as technical specifications, quantity needed, expected time of delivery, return policies, and warranties. Many large buyers now practise *vendor-managed inventory*, in which they turn over ordering and inventory responsibilities to their suppliers. Under such systems, buyers share sales and inventory information directly with key suppliers. The suppliers then monitor inventories and replenish stock automatically as needed. For example, most major suppliers to large retailers such as Walmart, Home Depot, and Lowe's assume vendor-managed inventory responsibilities.

The final stage of the business buying process is the supplier *performance review*, in which the buyer assesses the supplier's performance and provides feedback. For example, Home Depot has issued a set of supplier guidelines and policies and regularly evaluates each supplier in terms of quality, delivery, and other performance variables. It gives suppliers online performance scorecards that provide ongoing feedback that helps them to improve their performance.[33] The supplier performance review may lead the buyer to continue, modify, or drop the arrangement. The seller's job is to monitor the same factors used by the buyer to make sure that the seller is giving the expected satisfaction.

The eight-stage buying-process model provides a simple view of the business buying as it might occur in a new-task buying situation. The actual process is usually much more complex. In the modified rebuy or straight rebuy situation, some of these stages would be compressed or bypassed. Each organization buys in its own way, and each buying situation has unique requirements.

Different buying centre participants may be involved at different stages of the process. Although certain buying-process steps usually do occur, buyers do not always follow them in the same order, and they may add other steps. Often, buyers will repeat certain stages of the process. Finally, a customer relationship might involve many different types of purchases ongoing at a given time, all in different stages of the buying process. The seller must manage the total customer relationship, not just individual purchases.

E-Procurement: Buying on the Internet   Advances in information technology have changed the face of the B-to-B marketing process. Electronic purchasing, often called **e-procurement**, has grown rapidly in recent years. Virtually unknown less than a decade ago, online purchasing is standard procedure for most companies today. E-procurement gives buyers access to new suppliers, lowers purchasing costs, and hastens order processing and delivery. In turn, business marketers can connect with customers online to share marketing information, sell products and services, provide customer support services, and maintain ongoing customer relationships.

Companies can do e-procurement in any of several ways. They can conduct *reverse auctions,* in which they put their purchasing requests online and invite suppliers to bid for the business. Or they can engage in online *trading exchanges*, through which companies work collectively to facilitate the trading process. Companies also can conduct e-procurement by setting up their own *company buying sites*. For example, GE operates a company trading site on which it posts its buying needs and invites bids, negotiates terms, and places orders. Or companies can create *extranet links* with key suppliers. For instance, they can create direct procurement accounts with suppliers such as Dell or Office Depot, through which company buyers can purchase equipment, materials, and supplies directly.

B-to-B marketers can help customers online and build stronger customer relationships by creating well-designed, easy-to-use websites. For example, *BtoB* magazine recently rated the site of Shaw Floors—a market leader in flooring products—as one of its "10 great B-to-B websites." The site helps Shaw build strong links with its business and trade customers.[34]

> At one time, flooring manufacturer Shaw Floors' website was nothing more than "brochure-ware." Today, however, the site is a true interactive experience. At the site, design and construction professionals as well as customers can "see"—virtually—the company's many

E-procurement

Purchasing through electronic connections between buyers and sellers—usually online.

product lines. At the popular "Try on a Floor" area, designers or retailers can even work with final buyers to upload digital images of an actual floor and put any of the company's many carpets on it to see how they look. They can select various lines and colours immediately without digging through samples. And the extremely detailed images can be rotated and manipulated so a designer, for example, can show a client what the pile of the carpet looks like and how deep it is.

For retailers, Shaw has created a website, www.shawadvantage.com. This site provides retailers the resources they need to create their own advertising materials and order point-of-sale materials for their businesses. Retailers can also check their co-op advertising accounts with the company, letting them subsidize or add to their advertising budgets. Retailer-partners can connect to their accounts and search the company's products, make inventory checks, order or reserve products, and track order status for their stores. The Shaw Web Studio lets retailers—many of which are mom-and-pop stores—create their own websites in minutes or download photography, catalogue engines, and other content to add to their existing websites. "So many retailers don't have the time or money to build their own online presence," says Shaw's interactive marketing manager, "so this really helps them."

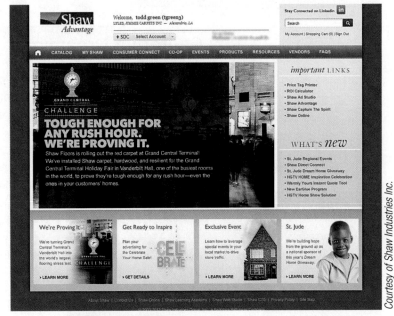

Exhibit 6.19 B-to-B websites: This Shaw Floors site builds strong links with Shaw's retailers. It provides marketing ideas and tools that make retailers more effective in selling Shaw's products to final customers.

Courtesy of Shaw Industries Inc.

Business-to-business e-procurement yields many benefits. First, it shaves transaction costs and results in more efficient purchasing for both buyers and suppliers. E-procurement reduces the time between order and delivery. And a web-powered purchasing program eliminates the paperwork associated with traditional requisition and ordering procedures and helps an organization keep better track of all purchases. Finally, beyond the cost and time savings, e-procurement frees purchasing people from a lot of drudgery and paperwork. In turn, it frees them to focus on more-strategic issues, such as finding better supply sources and working with suppliers to reduce costs and develop new products.

The rapidly expanding use of e-procurement, however, also presents some problems. For example, at the same time that the web makes it possible for suppliers and customers to share business data and even collaborate on product design, it can also erode decades-old customer–supplier relationships. Many buyers now use the power of the web to pit suppliers against one another and to search out better deals, products, and turnaround times on a purchase-by-purchase basis.

E-procurement can also create potential security concerns. Although email and home banking transactions can be protected through basic encryption, the secure environment that businesses need to carry out confidential interactions is sometimes still lacking. Companies are spending millions for research on defensive strategies to keep hackers at bay. Cisco Systems, for example, specifies the types of routers, firewalls, and security procedures that its partners must use to safeguard extranet connections. In fact, the company goes even further; it sends its own security engineers to examine a partner's defences and holds the partner liable for any security breach that originates from its computers.

California Dreaming

As Tim Croyle, vice-president of WestJet Vacations, begins to draw a sketch of how his service anticipates the needs of vacation travellers, the parallels between his sketch and the typical "consumer decision process" (noted in this textbook) become immediately obvious, but with one key difference: "The first phase is dreaming—hmm, like 'wouldn't it be nice to go to San Diego?'" and that begins the cycle. Traditional marketing theory calls this the "need recognition" phase; in true WestJet form, it becomes the "dreaming" phase.

It makes sense when analyzing the vacation consumer that a different lens is used—it is a very different form of product. First, it is a service as opposed to a concrete good. But more significantly, as Croyle puts it, "When choosing a vacation, there's a lot of money and a lot of time spent, and so it's got to be fantastic, because those memories have to last a lifetime." So what is the single biggest influencer when travellers choose their vacation provider? "With those great expectations, there has to be trust. Whoever you're giving your credit card to, you have to be confident that they're going to deliver on those expectations."

While equity in the WestJet brand helped launch the vacation business in 2006, it is product differentiation that has earned it the highest guest satisfaction rating of any Canadian tour operator in 2012. At first glance, the WestJet Vacations website might not appear to be very different from Expedia or Travelocity. However, it's what WestJet does on the ground that helps meet travellers' expectations. "In our key destinations we have WestJetters who live and work, and they will contact all WestJet guests who arrive in those destinations. They will meet the guests at their hotel and their sole focus is resolving any issues those guests have during their vacation," claims Croyle.

The final phase of the consumer decision process, according to WestJet, is "share." At this stage, where consumers will evaluate their purchase, WestJet Vacations builds in a platform for guests to rate their experience. Croyle admits, "It's like TripAdvisor, but because it's WestJet Vacations travellers, sharing their WestJet Vacations experience, we feel, again, there's a higher level of trust." And as for the inevitable bad reviews, "it gets posted—we need to get that information to our guests . . . it's a big part of building and maintaining trust."

QUESTIONS

1. How does WestJet's final phase of the buyer decision process differ from that presented in this textbook?
2. Knowledge of the buyer decision process empowers companies to help secure business from customers and to better serve them during the purchase experience. What unique way does WestJet provide for its guests once they have decided on a WestJet vacation?

REVIEWING THE CONCEPTS

1. Understand the consumer market and the major factors that influence consumer buyer behaviour.

The *consumer market* consists of all the individuals and households who buy or acquire goods and services for personal consumption. Consumer behaviour should be viewed as an ongoing process that starts long before the consumer purchases a product or service and continues long after he or she consumes it. This extended definition of consumer behaviour means that marketers must be aware of a number of issues before, during, and after purchase to build brand loyalty and lasting relationships with their customers.

Consumer buyer behaviour is influenced by four key sets of buyer characteristics: cultural, social, personal, and psychological. Understanding these factors can help marketers to identify interested buyers, and to shape products and appeals to serve consumer needs better. Each factor provides a different perspective for understanding the consumers' decision-making process.

2. Identify and discuss the stages in the buyer decision process.

When making a purchase, the buyer goes through a decision process consisting of need recognition, information search, evaluation of alternatives, purchase decision, and postpurchase behaviour. During *need recognition*, the consumer recognizes a problem or need that could be satisfied by a product or service. Once the need is recognized, the consumer moves into the *information search* stage. With information in hand, the consumer proceeds to *alternative evaluation* and assesses brands in the choice set. From there, the consumer makes a *purchase decision* and actually buys the product. In the final stage of the buyer decision process, *postpurchase behaviour*, the consumer takes action based on satisfaction or dissatisfaction. The marketer's job is to understand the buyer's behaviour at each stage and the influences that are operating.

3. Describe the adoption and diffusion process for new products.

The product *adoption process* is made up of five stages: awareness, interest, evaluation, trial, and adoption. New-product marketers must think about how to help consumers move through these stages. With regard to the *diffusion process* for new products, consumers respond at different rates, depending on consumer and product characteristics. Consumers may be innovators, early adopters, early majority, late majority, or laggards. Each group may require different marketing approaches. Marketers often try to bring their new products to the attention of potential early adopters, especially those who are opinion leaders.

4. Define the business market and identify the major factors that influence business buyer behaviour.

The *business market* comprises all organizations that buy goods and services for use in the production of other products and services, or for the purpose of reselling or renting them to others at a profit. As compared to consumer markets, business markets usually have fewer, larger buyers. Business demand is derived demand, and the business buying decision usually involves more, and more professional, buyers.

Business buyers make decisions that vary with the three types of *buying situations*: straight rebuys, modified rebuys, and new tasks. The decision-making unit of a buying organization—the *buying centre*—can consist of many different persons playing many different roles. The business marketer needs to know the following: Who are the major buying centre participants? In what decisions do they exercise influence and to what degree? What evaluation criteria does each decision participant use? The business marketer also needs to understand the major environmental, organizational, interpersonal, and individual influences on the buying process.

5. List and define the steps in the business buying decision process.

The *business buying decision process* itself can be quite involved, with eight basic stages: problem recognition, general need description, product specification, supplier search, proposal solicitation, supplier selection, order-routine specification, and performance review. Buyers who face a new-task buying situation usually go through all stages of the buying process. Buyers making modified or straight rebuys may skip some of the stages. Companies must manage the overall customer relationship, which often includes many different buying decisions in various stages of the buying decision process. Recent advances in information technology have given birth to "e-procurement," by which business buyers are purchasing all kinds of products and services online. Business marketers are increasingly connecting with customers online to share marketing information, sell products and services, provide customer support services, and maintain ongoing customer relationships.

KEY TERMS

TALK ABOUT MARKETING

1. In designing the advertising for a soft drink, which would you find more helpful, information about consumer demographics or information about consumer lifestyles? Select a new soft drink on the market and give examples of how you would use each type of information.

2. Think of a product you've purchased recently that was not a routine purchase. Describe how you progressed through each of the five stages of the consumer buyer decision process. Did you experience any cognitive dissonance during your postpurchase behaviour?

3. Now, think about the product you discussed in #2 from the perspective of a marketer. What forms of marketing communications or programs could you use to influence a prospective buyer of the product you selected, at each of the five stages?

4. Marketers often target consumers before, during, or after a trigger event—an event in one's life that triggers change. For example, after having a child, new parents have an increased need for baby furniture, clothes, diapers, car seats, and lots of other baby-related goods.

Consumers who never paid attention to marketing efforts for certain products may now be focused on those related to their life change. Discuss other trigger events that may provide opportunities to target the right buyer at the right time.

5. Business buying occurs worldwide, so marketers need to be aware of cultural factors influencing business customers. In a small group, select a country and develop a multimedia presentation on proper business etiquette and manners, including appropriate appearance, behaviour, and communication. Include a map showing the location of the country as well as a description of the country in terms of its demographics, culture, and economic history.

6. Imagine you work in the purchasing department at Canadian Tire. You are responsible for making all the purchase decisions about paint and related home decor items such as blinds and curtain rods. Which of the influences on business buyer behaviour would be your most important criteria? Are there any influences on consumer buyer behaviour that you would take into consideration when making your decisions?

THINK LIKE A MARKETING MANAGER

How would you like to sell to a customer that spends millions of dollars per year on contractors? If so, you need to learn how to crack the federal government market. The federal government purchases goods ranging from toilet paper to aircraft carriers and services from janitorial supplies to high-tech information technology (IT). This is a lucrative market—especially during economic downturns. Many companies focus their marketing solely on this market. How do businesses—big and small—find out about opportunities in this market? One way is to search the government's website for opportunities. A great deal of the government's buying is now done online.

QUESTIONS

1. Go to the Public Works and Government Services Canada website (www.tpsgc-pwgsc.gc.ca/comm/index-eng.html) and review the information for businesses. Search MERX, the government's electronic tendering services. Are there many opportunities in your province?

2. What types of products and services are most frequently listed?

3. Write a brief report describing the usefulness of this website for businesses desiring to sell to the government market.

MARKETING ETHICS

What does an "eight" mean to you? Well, if you are a female, then it means a lot, especially if you really are a "12"—size, that is. Marketers know that, too, and the trend is for larger sizes to be labelled with smaller numbers. Sizing was standardized in the 1940s and 1950s when women started purchasing mass-produced clothing. But sizes fluctuated in the following decades and the US Department of Commerce abandoned sizing standardization in 1983. Now, the size number can mean anything the marketer wants it to mean. Marketers know that a size-12 woman who finds out she can fit into an eight will get a self-esteem boost and likely purchase more. This practice, known as *vanity sizing,* has the potential to pay off big for clothing manufacturers. With 34 percent of adults in the United States overweight and another 40 percent obese, that adds up to a sizable market potential. Plus-sized

clothing designer Torrid caters to the full-sized woman with sizes ranging from zero–five, where a size four is actually a size 26. If a large number on the size label really bothers you, stick to the more expensive brands—they tend to be the ones using vanity sizing most.

QUESTIONS

1. Which factors are clothing marketers using to influence consumers? Ask five female and five male friends how much the size labelled on clothing influences their behaviour. Write a brief report of your findings.

2. Should manufacturers be allowed to pick whatever measurements they want and attach any size number they want to them? Should the government or business set standardized sizes?

MARKETING TECHNOLOGY

Have you noticed that some of your Facebook friends like certain advertisements? Marketers know what Facebook users like and are using that knowledge to influence users' friends. *Social-context ads* are based on data collected on the likes and friends of Facebook users. When you click on an ad indicating you like it, you also give Facebook permission to share that "like" with all of your friends. Marketers like this feature because it appears as though you are endorsing the brand to your friends. The more you click on the "Like" button in ads, the greater the chance they will migrate onto your wall and become part

of your conversations rather than stay on the perimeter of the page.

QUESTIONS

1. Which factors are marketers advertising on Facebook using to influence consumers? Would you be influenced by an ad if you saw that your friends liked it?

2. How would you feel about Facebook using your name in these types of ads, or advertising integrating itself in conversations with your friends?

MARKETING BY THE NUMBERS

The North American Industry Classification System (NAICS) code is very useful for marketers. It is a relatively new coding system that replaces the old product-based Standard Industrial Classification (SIC) system introduced in the 1930s. The NAICS system classifies businesses by production processes, better reflecting changes in the global economy, especially in the service and technology industries. It was developed jointly by the United States, Canada, and Mexico in 1997 in concert with the North American Free Trade Agreement (NAFTA), providing a common classification system for the three countries and better compatibility with the International Standard

Industrial Classification (ISIC) system. This six-digit number (in some cases, seven or ten digits) is very useful for understanding business markets.

QUESTIONS

1. What do the six digits of the NAICS code represent? What industry is represented by the NAICS code 721110? What information can a marketer obtain using this code?

2. Using the 721110 NAICS code, research and create a report highlighting the trends in this industry. Suggest markets that have the greatest potential.

GOODWILL INDUSTRIES

Since 1902, Goodwill Industries has funded job training and placement programs through its chain of thrift stores. Even though selling used clothing, furniture, and other items may not seem like big business, it amounts to more than US$3 billion in annual sales for Goodwill. The company is changing people's perceptions of thrift stores as musty, low-class operations by focusing on concepts of consumer behaviour. Like any good marketing company, Goodwill recognizes that not all customers are the same. This video demonstrates how Goodwill caters to different types of customers by recognizing the cultural, social, personal, and psychological factors that affect how customers make buying decisions. In this manner, Goodwill is maximizing customer value by offering the right mix of goods at unbeatable bargain prices.

After viewing the video featuring Goodwill, answer the following questions:

QUESTIONS

1. How would you describe the different types of Goodwill customers?

2. Which of the four sets of factors affecting consumer behaviour do you believe most strongly affects consumers' purchase decisions from Goodwill?

3. How does Goodwill's recognition of consumer behaviour principles affect its marketing mix?

PORSCHE: GUARDING THE OLD WHILE BRINGING IN THE NEW

Porsche (pronounced *Porsh*-uh) is a unique company. It has always been a niche brand that makes cars for a small and distinctive segment of automobile buyers. Porsche recently had annual sales of only 27 717 cars among the five models it sells in the United States. By comparison, Honda sold about 10 times that many Accords alone. But Porsche owners are as rare as their vehicles. For that reason, top managers at Porsche spend a great deal of time thinking about customers. They want to know who their customers are, what they think, and how they feel. They want to know why they buy a Porsche rather than a Jaguar, or a Ferrari, or a big Mercedes Coupe. These are challenging questions to answer—even Porsche owners themselves don't know exactly what motivates their buying. But given Porsche's low volume and the increasingly fragmented auto market, it is imperative that management understand its customers and what gets their motors running.

PROFILE OF A PORSCHE OWNER

Porsche was founded in 1931 by Ferdinand Porsche, the man credited for designing the original Volkswagen Beetle, known as Adolf Hitler's "people's car" and one of the most successful car designs of all time. For most of its first two decades, the company built Volkswagen Beetles for German citizens while making tanks and Beetles for the military. As Porsche AG began to sell cars under its own nameplate in the 1950s and 1960s, a few constants developed. The company sold very few models, creating an image of exclusivity. Those models had a rounded, bubble shape that had its roots in the original Beetle but evolved into something more Porsche-like with the world famous 356 and 911 models. Finally, Porsche's automobiles featured air-cooled four- and six-cylinder "boxer" motors (cylinders in an opposed configuration) in the rear of the car. This gave the cars a unique and often dangerous characteristic—a tendency for the rear end to swing out when cornering hard. That's one of the reasons that Porsche owners were drawn to them: since they were challenging to drive, most people stayed away.

Since its early days, Porsche has appealed to a very narrow segment of financially successful people. These are achievers who see themselves as entrepreneurial, even if they work for a corporation. They set very high goals for themselves and then work doggedly to meet them. These people expect no less from the clothes they wear, the restaurants they go to, or the cars they drive. They see themselves not as a part of the regular world, but as exceptions to it. They buy Porsches because the car mirrors their self-image—it stands for the things owners like to see in themselves and in their lives.

Most of us buy what Porsche executives call utility vehicles. That is, we buy cars to go to work, to deliver the kids, and to run errands. Because we have to use our cars to accomplish these daily tasks, we base buying decisions on features such as price, size, fuel economy, and other practical considerations. But Porsche is more than a utility car. Its owners see it as a car to be enjoyed, not just used. Most Porsche buyers are not moved by information, but by feelings. A Porsche is like a piece of clothing, something the owner "wears" and is seen in. Owners develop a personal relationship with their cars, one that has more to do with the way the car sounds, vibrates, and feels than how many cup holders it has or how much cargo it can hold in the trunk. They admire their Porsche because it is a competent performance machine without being flashy or phony.

People buy Porsches because they enjoy driving. If all they needed was something to get them from point A to point B, they could find something much less expensive. And while many Porsche owners are car enthusiasts, some of them are not. One successful businesswoman and owner of a high-end Porsche said, "When I drive this car to the high school to pickup my daughter, I end up with five youngsters in the car. If I drive any other car, I can't even find her; she doesn't want to come home."

FROM NICHE TO NUMEROUS

For the first few decades, Porsche AG lived by the philosophy of Ferry Porsche, Ferdinand's son. Ferry created the Porsche 356 because no one else made a car like the one he wanted. "We did no market research, we had no sales forecasts, no return-on-investment calculations. None of that. I very simply built my dream car and figured that there would be other people who share that dream." So really, Porsche AG from the beginning was very much like its customers: an achiever that set out to make the very best.

But as the years rolled on, Porsche management became concerned with a significant issue: Were there enough Porsche buyers to keep the company afloat? Granted, the company never had illusions of churning out the number of cars produced by Chevrolet or Toyota.

But to fund innovation, even a niche manufacturer has to grow a little. And Porsche began to worry that the quirky nature of the people who buy Porsches might just run out on them.

This led Porsche to extend its brand outside the box. In the early 1970s, Porsche introduced the 914, a square-ish, mid-engine, two-seater that was much cheaper than the 911. This meant that a different class of people could afford a Porsche. It was no surprise that the 914 became Porsche's top selling model. By the late 1970s, Porsche replaced the 914 with a hatchback coupe that had something no other regular Porsche model had ever had: an engine in the front. At less than US$20 000, more than US$10 000 less than the 911, the 924 and later 944 models were once again Porsche's pitch to affordability. At one point, Porsche increased its sales goal by nearly 50 percent to 60 000 cars a year.

Although these cars were in many respects sales successes, the Porsche faithful cried foul. They considered these entry-level models to be cheap and underperforming. Most loyalists never really accepted these models as "real" Porsches. In fact, they were not at all happy that they had to share their brand with a customer who didn't fit the Porsche owner profile. They were turned off by what they saw as a corporate strategy that had focused on *mass* over *class* marketing. This tarnished image was compounded by the fact that Nissan, Toyota, BMW, and other car makers had ramped up high-end sports car offerings, creating some fierce competition. In fact, both the Datsun 280-ZX and the Toyota Supra were not only cheaper than Porsche's 944, they were faster. A struggling economy threw more sand in Porsche's tank. By 1990, Porsche sales had plummeted and the company flirted with bankruptcy.

RETURN TO ITS ROOTS?

But Porsche wasn't going down without a fight. It quickly recognized the error of its ways and halted production of the entry-level models. It rebuilt its damaged image by revamping its higher-end model lines with more race-bred technology. In an effort to regain rapport with customers, Porsche once again targeted the high end of the market in both price and performance. It set modest sales goals and decided that moderate growth with higher margins would be more profitable in the long term. The company set out to make one less Porsche than the public demanded. According to one executive, "We're not looking for volume, we're searching for exclusivity."

Porsche's efforts had the desired effect. By the late 1990s, the brand was once again favoured by the same type of achiever who had so deeply loved the car for

decades. The cars were once again exclusive, and the company was once again profitable. But by the early 2000s, Porsche management was asking itself a familiar question: To have a sustainable future, could Porsche rely on only the Porsche faithful? According to then CEO Wendelin Wiedeking, "For Porsche to remain independent, it can't be dependent on the most fickle segment in the market. We don't want to become just a marketing department of some giant. We have to make sure we're profitable enough to pay for future development ourselves."

So in 2002, Porsche did the unthinkable. It became one of the last car companies to jump into the insatiable SUV market. At roughly 5000 pounds, the new Porsche Cayenne was heavier than anything that Porsche had ever made with the exception of some prototype tanks it made during World War II. Once again, the new model featured an engine up front. And it was the first Porsche to ever be equipped with seatbelts for five. As news spread about the car's development, howls could be heard from Porsche's customer base.

This time, however, Porsche did not seem too concerned that the loyalists would be put off. Could it be that the company had already forgotten what happened the last time it deviated from the mould? After driving one of the first Cayenne's off the assembly line, one journalist stated, "A day at the wheel of the 444 horsepower Cayenne Turbo leaves two overwhelming impressions. First, the Cayenne doesn't behave or feel like an SUV, and second, it drives like a Porsche." This was no entry-level car. Porsche had created a two-and-a-half ton beast that could accelerate to 60 miles per hour in just over five seconds, corner like it was on rails, and hit 165 miles per hour, all while coddling five adults in sumptuous leather seats with almost no wind noise from the outside world. On top of that, it could keep up with a Land Rover when the pavement ended. Indeed, Porsche had created the Porsche of SUVs.

Last year, Porsche upped the ante one more time by unveiling another large vehicle. But this time, it was a low-slung, five-door luxury sedan. The Porsche faithful and the automotive press again gasped in disbelief. But by the time the Panamera hit the pavement, Porsche had proven once again that Porsche customers could have their cake and eat it, too. The Panamera is almost as big as the Cayenne but can move four adults down the road at speeds of up to 188 miles per hour and accelerate from a standstill to 60 miles per hour in four seconds flat.

Although some Porsche traditionalists would never be caught dead driving a front engine Porsche that has more than two doors, Porsche insists that two trends will sustain these new models. First, a category of Porsche buyers has moved into life stages that have them facing inescapable needs—they need to haul more people and stuff. This not only applies to certain regular Porsche buyers, but also to new buyers entering its dealerships who otherwise wouldn't have considered a Porsche. This time, the price points of the new vehicles are drawing only the well-healed, allowing Porsche to maintain its exclusivity. These buyers also seem to fit the achiever profile of regular Porsche buyers.

The second trend is the growth of emerging economies. Whereas the United States has long been the world's biggest consumer of Porsches, the company expects China to become its biggest customer before too long. Twenty years ago, the United States accounted for about 50 percent of Porsche's worldwide sales. Now, it only buys about 26 percent. In China, many people who can afford to buy a car as expensive as a Porsche also hire a chauffer. The Cayenne and the Panamera are perfect for those who want to be driven around in style but who may also want to make a quick getaway if necessary.

The most recent economic downturn has brought down the sales of just about every maker of premium automobiles. When times are tough, buying a car like a Porsche is the ultimate deferrable purchase. But as this downturn turns back up, Porsche is better poised than it has ever been to meet the needs of its customer base. It is also in better shape than ever to maintain its brand image with the Porsche faithful, and with others as well. Sure, understanding Porsche buyers is still a difficult task. But one former chief executive of Porsche summed it up this way: "If you really want to understand our customers, you have to understand the phrase, 'If I were going to be a car, I'd be a Porsche.'"

Sources: Christoph Rauwald, "Porsche Raises Outlook," *Wall Street Journal*, June 18, 2010, accessed at www.wsj.com; Jonathan Welsh, "Porsche Relies Increasingly on Sales in China," *Wall Street Journal*, April 2, 2010, accessed at www.wsj.com; David Gumpert, "Porsche on Nichemanship," *Harvard Business Review*, March/April 1986, pp. 98–106; Peter Robinson, "Porsche Cayenne—Driving Impression," *Car and Driver*, January 2003, accessed at www.caranddriver.com; Jens Meiners, "2010 Porsche Panamera S/4S/Turbo—First Drive Review," *Car and Driver*, June 2009, accessed at www.caranddriver.com.

QUESTIONS FOR DISCUSSION

1. Analyze the buyer decision process of a traditional Porsche customer. What conclusions can you draw?

2. How does the traditional Porsche customer decision process contrast with the decision process for a Cayenne or Panamera customer?

3. Which concepts from the chapter explain why Porsche sold so many lower-priced models in the 1970s and 1980s?

4. Explain how both positive and negative attitudes toward a brand like Porsche develop. How might Porsche change consumer attitudes toward the brand?

5. What role does the Porsche brand play in the self-concept of its buyers?

MyMarketingLab

MyMarketingLab is an online homework and tutorial system that puts you in control of your own learning with study and practice tools directly correlated to this chapter's content.

Courtesy of Boston Pizza

AFTER STUDYING THIS CHAPTER, YOU SHOULD BE ABLE TO

1 define the major steps in designing a customer-driven marketing strategy: market segmentation, targeting, differentiation, and positioning

2 list and discuss the major bases for segmenting consumer and business markets

3 explain how companies identify attractive market segments and choose a market-targeting strategy

4 discuss how companies differentiate and position their products for maximum competitive advantage

Segmentation, Targeting, and Positioning

PREVIEWING THE CONCEPTS

So far, you've learned what marketing is, and about the importance of understanding consumers and the marketplace environment. With that as background, you're now ready to delve deeper into marketing strategy and tactics. This chapter looks further into key customer-driven marketing strategy decisions—how to divide up markets into meaningful customer groups (*segmentation*), choose which customer groups to serve (*targeting*), create market offerings that best serve targeted customers (*differentiation*), and position the offerings in the minds of consumers (*positioning*). Then, the chapters that follow explore the tactical marketing tools—the four *P*s—by which marketers bring these strategies to life.

At their most basic, target markets are simply groups of people with similar characteristics, and while those characteristics may have always been around for the targeting, it sometimes takes a new kind of thinking to decide to serve a particular group with a line of products that's new to them—in other words, to define a new market segment.

BOSTON PIZZA: TARGETING THE FOODIES

When it comes to their market segmentation and targeting strategy, Boston Pizza has a very specific group in mind: dads and dudes. "Going back to 2011, we carefully defined our brand as 'Dad's happy place' and established that our core guest was a male between the ages of 25–54," explains Steve Silverstone, executive vice-president of marketing at Boston Pizza International. "We focus on providing a happy place for dads and dudes, but without alienating moms." Boston Pizza is positioned as a sports bar, but the chain's key differentiator in the Canadian marketplace is that they successfully offer two experiences under one roof—a welcoming family dining room and a lively sports bar.

So what makes a successful sports bar and restaurant decide to develop an advertising campaign to appeal to foodies? Well, if you watch Boston Pizza's TV commercial, "Be Careful You Don't Become a Foodie," you'll realize the appeal is tongue-in-cheek.

The word *foodie* was coined by Paul Levy and Ann Barr, who used it in the title of their 1984 book *The Official Foodie Handbook*. It describes a group of people—a market segment—who are aficionados of food and drink. A foodie is a person who invests a keen amount of attention and energy on knowing the ingredients of food and the proper preparation of food. But a foodie is not necessarily a food snob. In fact, most foodies enthusiastically apply the term to themselves and view it as a hobby similar to being a wine aficionado, but without the snobbish overtones. On the other hand, real gourmets—or real food snobs, depending on your perspective—hate being called foodies. And while sophisticated food critics view the term *foodie* with disdain and consider it an annoying fad, real foodies revel in the humour of the situation.

It was this insight into the nature of the foodie that led Boston Pizza and its advertising agency, TAXI, to realize that their dads and dudes would enjoy a little foodie humour—and that real foodies might be persuaded to take a closer look at Boston Pizza's new menu. Silverstone explains how the idea for the campaign came about:

> The campaign was based on the insight that our signature pasta dishes are so good, our guests feel like 'foodies' when they order and eat them. Based on the ingredients and flavours, guests feel like they are experiencing a premium dining experience; however, our typical guest, the dad/dude, wouldn't necessarily label himself a foodie. We took the opportunity to play on this insight and poke a little fun at the growing trend on social media to share dining and foodie experiences by bringing it to life in our advertising in a humorous way.

The Boston Pizza Foodie campaign was a limited six-week promotion, however some of the menu items developed for the promotion will remain on the menu. "We have a two-year planning process for our menu items," says Silverstone. "A cross-functional brand planning team works with our executive chef and culinary director to identify trends or opportunities for national menu promotions. Given the time of year and climate (winter in Canada), we decided to run a pasta promotion in the first quarter of 2013 to give our guests a taste of comfort food during the coldest months of the year." The result was a feature menu of seven delicious pasta creations such as Pulled Pork Penne, Pasta Nachos, Butter Chicken Fettuccine, and Massive Meatball Spaghetti, which promised to impress taste buds across the country.

To introduce its new pasta dishes, BP called upon TAXI to develop a marketing communications campaign. The agency began by drafting a creative brief, a short document that outlines what the campaign is intended to accomplish. The goal of the BP Foodie campaign was to make BP just as famous for the quality of its pasta as its pizza. The creative brief also explains *how* the campaign will accomplish the goal: by getting people to reappraise the idea of pasta at Boston Pizza. For past guests who may have tried the pasta before, the idea was to get them to try the new dishes. For new guests, the idea was to get them to realize that Boston Pizza does pasta. And in both cases, to show that the new pasta dishes look really delicious. The message strategy was to highlight the fact that BP has pasta dishes like you've never seen before, and to inspire curiosity in the customer. With all that information firmly in mind, the agency began to develop a creative strategy.

The result was an integrated national advertising campaign that included a 30-second TV spot along with online banners, page takeovers, social media, and public relations. The tongue-in-cheek campaign warned guests that the new pasta dishes from Boston Pizza run the risk of converting them from a casual food lover into a pretentious foodie. The humorous approach was designed to highlight how the superior quality of ingredients might make an everyday guy—BP's target market, the dad/dude—suddenly feel like a food connoisseur.

In the TV spot, three friends enjoy a meal so delicious that one sprouts tiny glasses and a bow tie and calls his spaghetti "divine." The tagline cautions, "Careful you don't become a foodie!" "The foodie segment is a culture you can really rip into," says Darren

Clarke, creative director of TAXI, the Toronto-based advertising firm behind the campaign. "We play on the tension that the food is good enough for a 'foodie,' but that the restaurant is for a guy who wants to watch the hockey game and have wings with his buddies," Clarke says.

Foodies know that they're not a difficult group to tease, but the word can instantly produce an unflattering mental image. To address this, a reclamation project has emerged on such dining websites as Epicurious and Chowhound. Suddenly, a movement is under-foot to take back the term. "There's been a backlash to the backlash, because the growing tendency among foodies runs against the idea of being pretentious about food," says Shyon Baumann, professor of sociology at the University of Toronto and co-author of *Foodies: Democracy and Distinction in the Gourmet Foodscape*. According to Baumann, who has spent nearly a decade studying this subculture—or market segment, depending upon how you look at it—the majority of foodies aren't dining out on social status and care deeply about such issues as animal rights, locally sourced products, and the experience of authentic or exotic cuisine. "It's not like the stereotype's based on nothing, but the real foodie is someone who can enjoy Boston Pizza and has their favourite doughnut at Tims," Baumann says. "I think the people who use the term foodie to describe themselves are very careful about not being a snob."

The Boston Pizza Foodie campaign was about much more than just advertising. "Whenever we run a national menu-based marketing campaign, there is a lot of work that goes on across all lanes at Boston Pizza," explains Silverstone. "We provide our stores with POS materials (posters and table materials), menu inserts, and the option of purchasing additional materials like outdoor banners, server T-shirts, and other promotional items. National promotions are also supported with digital and online marketing tactics, which result in our website, bostonpizza.com, and our Facebook pages receiving complementary marketing images and support messaging throughout the campaigns." In addition to the external marketing, Boston Pizza focuses on internal marketing. Extensive kitchen and server training is conducted to ensure that every restaurant employee knows the entire new menu and how to prepare and serve the items properly. The company creates online training modules, videos, and how-to guides and posts them on their internal website. And before the new menu items are offered to guests, employees participate in live kitchen demos and server tastings across the country.

With 350 restaurants across Canada operating in every province and territory, Boston Pizza has the ability to do things that smaller, regional brands simply can't do. "Our size allows us to be on TV with advertising 52 weeks per year, keeping the Boston Pizza brand top-of-mind for our guests. Our size also presents us with a purchasing advantage as well as the ability to form national partnerships with brands and sports properties like the UFC, Toronto Blue Jays, and local NHL teams across the country," explains Silverstone. This competitive advantage, along with a clearly defined segmentation, targeting, and position-ing strategy, has made BP the number one choice for dads and dudes across Canada.[1]

COMPANIES today recognize that they cannot appeal to all buyers in the marketplace, or at least not to all buyers in the same way. Buyers are too numerous, too widely scat-tered, and too varied in their needs and buying practices. Moreover, the companies themselves vary widely in their abilities to serve different segments of the market. Instead, a company must identify the parts of the market that it can serve best and most profitably. It must design customer-driven marketing strategies that build the *right* rela-tionships with the *right* customers.

FIGURE 7.1 Designing a Customer-driven Marketing Strategy

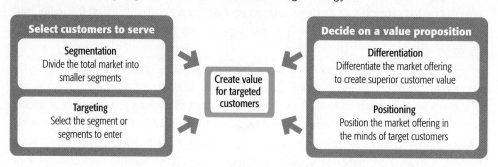

Companies are being choosier about the customers with whom they connect. Most have moved away from mass marketing and toward market segmentation and targeting—identifying market segments, selecting one or more of them as the most appropriate to serve, and developing products and marketing programs tailored to each.

Figure 7.1 shows the four major steps of designing a customer-driven marketing strategy. In the first two steps, the company selects the customers that it will serve. Market **segmentation** involves dividing a market into smaller groups of buyers with distinct needs, characteristics, or behaviours that might require separate marketing strategies or mixes. The company identifies different ways to segment the market and develops profiles of the resulting market segments. Market **targeting** consists of evaluating each market segment's attractiveness and selecting one or more market segments to enter. Next, the company decides on a value proposition—on how it will create value for target customers, and how it can stand out from its competition, or **differentiate** itself. When all these decisions have been made, the company positions its brand, or product, in the market. **Positioning** consists of arranging for a market offering to occupy a clear, distinctive, and desirable place relative to competing products in the minds of consumers. In this chapter, we'll look in detail at each of these four concepts.

Market Segmentation LO2

Buyers in any market differ in their wants, resources, locations, buying attitudes, and buying practices. Through market segmentation, companies divide large, heterogeneous markets into smaller segments that can be reached more efficiently and effectively with products and services that match their unique needs. In this section, we discuss four important segmentation topics: segmenting consumer markets, segmenting business markets, segmenting international markets, and requirements for effective segmentation.

Segmenting Consumer Markets

There is no single way to segment a market. A marketer has to try different segmentation variables, alone and in combination, to find the best way to view the market structure. Table 7.1 outlines the major variables that might be used in segmenting consumer markets. Here we look at the major *geographic*, *demographic*, *psychographic*, and *behavioural* variables.

Geographic Segmentation **Geographic segmentation** calls for dividing a market into different geographical units, such as global regions, countries, regions within a country, provinces, cities, or even neighbourhoods. A company may decide to operate in

Segmentation
Dividing a market into distinct groups with distinct needs, characteristics, or behaviours that might require separate marketing strategies or mixes.

Targeting
The process of evaluating each market segment's attractiveness and selecting one or more segments to enter.

Differentiation
Actually differentiating the market offering to create superior customer value.

Positioning
Arranging for a market offering to occupy a clear, distinctive, and desirable place relative to competing products in the minds of target consumers.

Geographic segmentation
Dividing a market into different geographical units, such as global regions, countries, regions within a country, provinces, cities, or even neighbourhoods.

TABLE 7.1 Major Segmentation Variables for Consumer Markets

Geographic Segmentation

World region	North America, South America, Western Europe, Eastern Europe, the British Isles, the Middle East, the Pacific Rim, Asia, Southeast Asia, Africa, Australia
Country	Canada, the United States, Brazil, England, China, and so on
Region of the country	The Maritimes, the prairie provinces, southern Ontario, Victoria and the Gulf Islands, Quebec
Population size	Under 5000; 5000–250 000; 250 000–500 000; 500 000–1 000 000; over 1 000 000, and so on
Type of region	Urban, suburban, rural, mountainous, far north, ocean/beaches, and so on

Demographic Segmentation

Age	Under 6, 6–12, 13–19, 20–34, 35–49, 50–64, 65+; or children, teens, young adults, middle-aged, seniors
Gender	Male, female
Family size	2, 3, 4, 5, more than 5
Life cycle	Young couple, young couple with children, single-parent family, older couple with grown children, divorced, and so on
Household income (HHI)	Under $20 000; $20 000–$50 000; $50 000–$100 000; over $100 000, and so on
Occupation	Professional, union worker, academic, small business owner, sales, farming/fishing, student, retired, homemaker, unemployed
Education	High school, college or trade school, university undergraduate, post-graduate
Ethnic or cultural group	African, Canadian, American, Chinese, Japanese, Korean, Caribbean/West Indies, East Indian, Filipino, Greek, Italian, German, Portuguese, Muslim, Jewish, Inuit, Métis, North American Indian
Generation	Baby Boomer, Generation X, Millennial

Psychographic Segmentation

Social class	Lower lowers, upper lowers, working class, middle class, upper middles, lower uppers, upper uppers
Lifestyle	Athletic/outdoors type, active suburban family, student, single urban professional, and so on
Personality	Highly organized and detail oriented; outgoing and adventurous; creative or artistic; quiet and solitary; ambitious, and so on

Behavioural Segmentation

Occasions	Regular occasion, special occasion, holiday, seasonal
Benefits	Quality, service, economy, convenience, speed
User status	Non-user, ex-user, potential user, first-time user, regular user
User rates	Light user, medium user, heavy user
Loyalty status	None, medium, strong, absolute
Readiness stage	Unaware, aware, informed, interested, desirous, intending to buy
Attitude toward product	Enthusiastic, positive, indifferent, negative, hostile

one or a few geographical areas or to operate in all areas but pay attention to geographical differences in needs and wants.

Many companies today are localizing their products, advertising, promotion, and sales efforts to fit the needs of individual regions, cities, and even neighbourhoods. For example,

Yukon Brewing Company

Exhibit 7.1 **Geographic segmentation:**
Yukon Brewing produces products like
Ice Fog beer, made especially for
Yukoners who prefer to drink their beer
from a can.

Yukon Brewing produces products made especially for residents of the Yukon Territory:[2]

> When Alan Hansen and Bob Baxter opened their craft brewery in Whitehorse their mission was to service the north with quality beer while keeping jobs and money in the territory. It didn't hurt that Yukoners consume 132 litres of beer per capita each year, more than anyone else in the country. It wasn't easy being the first craft brewery in the region, however. After years of drinking Canadian and Blue, Yukoners didn't trust the new brand, and, it seemed, they didn't like the flavourful, full-bodied brews.
>
> Success came after the company discovered the reason their beer wasn't selling wasn't because of the taste, it was because Yukoners were used to drinking beer from a can, and Yukon Brewing was only available in bottles. So in 2000 they changed their packaging to cans, and the product took off. Today, Yukon Brewing sells more draught in the territory than giants Molson-Coors and Labatt combined, and in stores, Yukon Brewing enjoys a market share most microbreweries only dream of. In addition to their colourfully named brews (Chilkoot Lager, Deadman Creek Cranberry Wheat, Ice Fog India Pale Ale, Midnight Sun Espresso Stout, and Lead Dog Olde English Ale Now), the company now markets a line of whisky, and is aiming to build a national brand.

Other companies are seeking to cultivate as-yet untapped geographic territory. For example, Four Points by Sheraton hotels has opened a chain of smaller-format hotels in places such as Kingston, Ontario, and Canmore, Alberta, that are too small for its standard-size, more upscale hotels. Small businesses such as hair salons and dentists' offices typically focus their marketing efforts on a local region within a few kilometres of their location, while destination-type businesses, such as restaurants and sporting facilities, might market to a larger region.

Demographic segmentation
Dividing the market into segments based on variables such as age, gender, family size, life cycle, household income (HHI), occupation, education, ethnic or cultural group, and generation.

Demographic Segmentation **Demographic segmentation** divides the market into segments based on variables such as age, gender, family size, life cycle, household income (HHI), occupation, education, ethnic or cultural group, and generation. Demographic factors are the most popular bases for segmenting customer groups. One reason is that consumer needs, wants, and usage rates often vary closely with demographic variables. Another is that demographic variables are easier to measure than most other types of variables. Even when marketers first define segments by using other bases, such as benefits sought or behaviour, they must know segment demographic characteristics to assess the size of the target market and to reach it efficiently.

AGE AND LIFE-CYCLE SEGMENTATION Consumer needs and wants change with age. Some companies segment the market based on age or, more specifically, family status, offering different products or using different marketing approaches for different groups. For example, for kids, Oscar Mayer offers Lunchables, full-of-fun, kid-appealing finger food. For older generations, it markets Deli Creations, everything these consumers need to create a microwaveable sandwich.

Age and life-cycle segmentation
Dividing a market into different age and life-cycle groups.

Other companies focus on marketing to groups that are in the same life-cycle stage. Some people get married and have children in their early 20s, some wait until they are 40; some people retire at age 50, some at 75, but retirement is a life-cycle stage. Companies that divide their markets by either age or life-cycle stage are using **age and life-cycle segmentation**. Disney Cruise Lines targets families with children, so most of its destinations and shipboard activities are designed with this life-cycle stage in mind. On board,

Disney provides trained counsellors who help younger kids join in hands-on activities, teen-only spaces for older children, and family-time or individual-time options for parents and other adults. It's difficult to find a Disney Cruise Line advertisement or webpage that doesn't feature a family full of smiling faces. In contrast, Viking River Cruises, the deluxe smaller-boat cruise line that offers tours along the world's great rivers, primarily targets older adults, couples and singles. You won't find a single child in a Viking ad or webpage.

GENDER **Gender segmentation** has long been used in clothing, cosmetics, toiletries, and magazines. For example, P&G was among the first with Secret antiperspirant, a brand specially formulated for a woman's chemistry, packaged and advertised to reinforce the female image. Since women make 70 percent of shopping decisions, big-box stores such as home-improvement chain RONA are courting women consumers with trendy "paint cafés" and luxurious display kitchens. Owens Corning aimed a major advertising campaign for home insulation at women, after a study showed that two-thirds of all women were involved in materials installation, with 13 percent doing it themselves.

On the other side of the gender coin, male grooming is a booming market, and developing and marketing new products that cater to this new segment has been a top trend for the last several years. There has been a huge increase not only in the level of acceptance of men's skin-care products but also in usage rates. As a result, Holt Renfrew stores in Montreal, Toronto, and Vancouver now have a large men's cosmetics area, designed with manly details such as dark hardwood floors. And many companies that traditionally marketed only to women, such as Dove, Clinique, Nivea, Lancôme, and L'Oréal, have launched complete lines of skin-care products for men.

A neglected gender segment can offer new opportunities in markets ranging from consumer electronics to motorcycles. For example, Harley-Davidson has traditionally targeted its product design and marketing to a bread-and-butter market of 35- to 55-year-old males. Women were more often just along for the ride—but no longer:[3]

> Women are now among the fastest-growing customer segments in the motorcycle business. The number of female Harley-Davidson owners has tripled in the past 20 years, and female buyers now account for over 13 percent of new Harley-Davidson purchases. So the company is boosting its efforts to move more women from the back of the bike onto the driver's seat. It started by making its product more accessible to females, modifying motorcycles to fit women's smaller frames, and offering an instructional manual and courses to teach women how to handle their bikes. Ads and other marketing materials aimed at women play to the brand's established strengths but with a softer side.
>
> Rather than indulging in female stereotypes, Harley-Davidson is appealing to "strong, independent women who enjoy taking on a challenge and a feeling of adventure," says the company's women's outreach manager. A recent ad sports the headline: "Not pictured: the weaker sex." A women's web microsite encourages women to share inspirational riding stories with one another. And to kick off Women Riders Month, Harley-Davidson recently hosted special riding events designed to "celebrate the millions of women who have already grabbed life by the handlebars."

Gender segmentation
Dividing a market into different segments based on gender.

Robert Duyos/MCT/Newscom

Exhibit 7.2 **Gender segmentation:** Rhonnie Robins, 51, of Boca Raton, Florida, with her Harley-Davidson. Women represent a significant market segment for Harley-Davidson, so the company invests in advertising campaigns that specifically target them.

© Design Pics Inc. / Alamy

Exhibit 7.3 **Income segmentation:** Luxury hotels provide amenities to attract affluent travellers. The Benjamin Hotel in New York City offers a "Dream Dog" program that pampers not just guests, but also their dogs.

Household Income (HHI) segmentation
Dividing a market into different income segments.

In marketing to women, Harley-Davidson is staying true to its tough, road tested image. "I don't think we're going to see any pink [Harley-Davidson motorcycles] on the road," says an analyst. And "they don't have to add bigger mirrors so women can do their cosmetics. . . . They want to sell Harleys to women, and they want to sell them to women who want to ride a *Harley*."

HOUSEHOLD INCOME (HHI) The marketers of products and services such as automobiles, clothing, cosmetics, financial services, and travel have long used **household income (HHI) segmentation**. Household income refers to the total income for the family, whether only one parent works or both parents work. Many companies target affluent consumers with luxury goods and convenience services. For example, for a price, luxury hotels provide amenities to attract specific groups of affluent travellers, such as families, expectant moms, and even pet owners.[4]

At the Four Seasons Hotel Chicago, guests can buy the Kids in the City package for $520 a night and, among other things, enjoy a visit in their room from the Ice Cream Man, who arrives with all the fixings to make any concoction they desire. At one spa in Scottsdale, Arizona, expectant parents can purchase the "Bundle of Joy" Babymoon package, which includes a 24-hour Cravings Chef service, a couples massage, and breakfast in bed. The Benjamin Hotel in New York City has the "Dream Dog" program, which provides dog beds in a variety of styles along with doggie bathrobes, canine room service, and DVDs for dogs, as well as access to pet spa treatments and a pet psychic. And if that isn't over the top enough, the Four Seasons Miami offers a Five Diamond package that includes a Graff diamond eternity band (or another diamond piece designed to your specifications) for $45 000, or a stay in the presidential suite with a bottle of 1990 Dom Pérignon Oenothéque champagne, caviar for two, and an 80-minute in-suite couples massage using a lotion infused with real ground diamonds, for a price tag: "From $50 000."

However, not all companies that use income segmentation target the affluent. For example, many retailers—such as No Frills, Giant Tiger, and the dollar-store chains—successfully target low- and middle-income groups. The core market for such stores is families with household incomes under $30 000.

Segmenting the market according to household income is one of the main ways car marketers divide the market, as each brand offers an economy car for the first-time buyer—the Toyota Yaris, for example—and a luxury model—like the much more expensive Lexus sedans and SUVs, which can reach nearly $100 000. A family that has a household income of $40 000 a year is not likely to purchase a car that costs twice as much as their income. Consumers at all income levels, including affluent consumers, primarily seek value from their purchases—however they personally define value.

ETHNIC OR CULTURAL GROUP Because of the multicultural makeup of Canada, and our two national languages (not to mention all the other languages spoken in our country), marketers often segment markets based on easy-to-define criteria such as race, ethnicity, and language. Statistics Canada, as we learned in Chapter 4, compiles census data about Canadians, and makes it available to marketers. It's not difficult, for example, to identify markets in Canada with high numbers of Chinese-speaking consumers, and place your advertising accordingly. Coast Capital Savings identifies a market segment of Cantonese- and Mandarin-speaking customers who have recently arrived in Canada. To promote its free chequing account to this segment, it created ads featuring Jan Walls, a well-known retired Asian studies professor from Simon Fraser University.[5]

Quebec is a large market segment of its own, defined by geography, but more importantly by ethnicity and language. Hyundai created a French-only advertising campaign featuring Quebec actor Guillaume Lemay-Thivierge, who was chosen because the marketers felt his personality was similar to the brand personality of Hyundai—dynamic and exciting. The spots show Lemay-Thivierge bungee jumping and engaging in other thrilling pastimes, after which he yawns because those activities are boring compared with his Hyundai.[6]

Psychographic Segmentation **Psychographic segmentation** divides buyers into different segments based on social class, lifestyle, or personality characteristics. People in the same demographic group can have very different psychographic makeups.

The "new luxury" market in Canada is a fast-growing market segment, comprising approximately 250 000 individuals of high net worth. As a market segment, it is defined entirely by psychographics—in this case, lifestyle and social class. Denise Pickett, president of Amex Bank of Canada, says a company that wants to reach the "new luxury" market "has to include before they purchase, during the purchase, while they use the product, and even when they decide not to use your product—making sure that the whole experience is truly luxurious for the customer."[7]

Marketers also use *personality* variables to segment markets. For example, cruise line Royal Caribbean targets adventure seekers—high-energy couples and families—with hundreds of activities such as rock wall climbing and ice skating. By contrast, Regent Seven Seas Cruises targets more serene and cerebral adventurers, mature couples seeking a more elegant ambiance and exotic destinations, such as the Orient.

One method marketers use to target consumers by personality is through the TV shows they watch. "Your personality determines what you consume, what TV shows you watch, what products you buy, and all the other decisions you make," says the CEO of Mindset Media, a company that specializes in helping advertisers target audiences through psychographics. People who watch *Mad Men* are creative and liberal, while people who enjoy cooking shows like Rachael Ray tend to be altruistic. Fans of *Family Guy* are rebels and rule breakers. And people who watch *Glee* are in touch with their own feelings, and feel happiness and sadness more intensely than others.[8]

Behavioural Segmentation **Behavioural segmentation** divides buyers into segments based on their knowledge, attitudes, uses, or responses to a product. Many marketers believe that behaviour variables are the best starting point for building market segments.

OCCASIONS Buyers can be grouped according to occasions when they get the idea to buy, actually make their purchase, or use the purchased item. **Occasion segmentation** can help firms to build up product usage. For example, most consumers drink orange juice in the morning, but orange growers have promoted drinking orange juice as a cool, healthful refresher at other times of the day. Occasion segmentation also applies to Christmas, Halloween, and other holiday decorations; food products associated with certain occasions; greeting cards; red and white products, and products adorned with maple leaves, around Canada Day; flowers for Mother's Day; and tools and ties for Father's Day.

BENEFITS SOUGHT A powerful form of segmentation is to group buyers according to the different *benefits* that they seek from the product. **Benefit segmentation** requires finding

Psychographic segmentation
Dividing a market into different segments based on social class, lifestyle, or personality characteristics.

Behavioural segmentation
Dividing a market into segments based on consumer knowledge, attitudes, uses, or responses to a product.

Occasion segmentation
Dividing the market into segments according to occasions when buyers get the idea to buy, actually make their purchase, or use the purchased item.

Benefit segmentation
Dividing the market into segments according to the different benefits that consumers seek from the product.

the major benefits people look for in the product class, the kinds of people who look for each benefit, and the major brands that deliver each benefit.

For example, when Netflix first opened its virtual doors it offered unlimited DVDs by mail for a monthly subscription rate. A few years later it added streaming video to its offering without changing the monthly subscription price. Then, in 2011 the company announced that subscribers who want unlimited access both to DVDs and streaming video would have to pay 60 percent more per month—$15.98 rather than $9.99. The strategy was to offer different price points to market segments that exhibit different behaviours, so the lower price was for those who wanted only streaming video, the higher price for those who wanted both. What the company failed to consider was that some customers still wanted a DVD-only plan. Once they understood that behaviour was still popular, they offered a $7.99/month plan for DVD-only consumers.[9] Today, in light of new viewing behaviours, Netflix no longer offers DVDs by mail, and instead offers only streaming video for $7.99/month.

USER STATUS Markets can be segmented into non-users, ex-users, potential users, first-time users, and regular users of a product. Marketers want to reinforce and retain regular users, attract non-users, and reinvigorate relationships with ex-users.

Included in the potential user group are consumers facing life-stage changes—such as newlyweds and new parents—who can be turned into heavy users. For example, up-scale kitchen and cookware retailer Williams-Sonoma actively targets newly engaged couples.[10]

> Eight-page Williams-Sonoma ad inserts in bridal magazines show a young couple strolling through a park or talking intimately in the kitchen over a glass of wine. The bride-to-be asks, "Now that I've found love, what else do I need?" Pictures of Williams-Sonoma knife sets, toasters, glassware, and pots and pans provide some strong clues. The retailer also offers a bridal registry, of course, but it takes its registry a step further. Through a program called "The Store Is Yours," it opens its stores after hours, by appointment, exclusively for individual couples to visit and make their wish lists. This segment is very important to Williams-Sonoma. About half the people who register are new to the brand—and they'll be buying a lot of kitchen and cookware in the future.

USAGE RATE Markets can also be segmented into light, medium, and heavy product users. Heavy users are often a small percentage of the market but account for a high percentage of total consumption. For example, Burger King targets what it calls "Super Fans," young (age 18 to 34), Whopper-wolfing males and females who make up 18 percent of the chain's customers but account for almost half of all customer visits, and who eat at Burger King an average of 16 times a month. And a recent study showed that, in the US, less than 5 percent of all shoppers account for 64 percent of unbreaded seafood sales, while only 2.6 percent of shoppers—mostly mothers buying breaded fish sticks and filets for their families—account for more than 54 percent of breaded seafood sales.[11] Information like this helps marketers target the heaviest users of their products more effectively.

LOYALTY STATUS A market can also be segmented by consumer loyalty. Consumers can be loyal to brands, such as Apple or Adidas; retailers, such as Forever 21 or H&M; and companies, such as Honda or Tim Hortons. Buyers can be divided into groups according to their degree of loyalty.

Some consumers are completely loyal—they buy one brand all the time. For example, Apple has an almost cult-like following of loyal users. Other consumers are somewhat loyal—they are loyal to two or three brands of a given product or favour one brand while sometimes buying others. Still other buyers show no loyalty to any brand. They either want something different each time they buy or they buy whatever's on sale.

A company can learn a lot by analyzing loyalty patterns in its market. It should start by studying its own loyal customers. For example, by studying Mac fanatics, Apple can better pinpoint its target market and develop marketing appeals. By studying its less-loyal buyers, the company can detect which brands are most competitive with its own. By looking at customers who are shifting away from its brand, the company can learn about its marketing weaknesses.

Using Multiple Segmentation Bases Marketers rarely limit their segmentation analysis to only one or a few variables. Rather, they often use multiple segmentation bases in an effort to identify smaller, better-defined target groups. For example, Rockport Canada targets 18- to 34-year-old men, in different life-cycle stages—high school graduates, new careerists, and young marrieds. Jeff Roach, managing director at market research firm Youthography, explains, "The reason for that is what we call the prolonged pre-adult life stage. Young people have been getting more adult responsibilities younger, but they're not entering full adulthood until much later in life. We see very similar values across this group right up to age 34." What are those shared characteristics? They place a high value on personal relationships, media, and technology. They are relatively affluent. And they tend to delay marriage and having children until after age 35—which means they have more discretionary income to spend on lifestyle products.[12]

There are several business information services that provide multi-variable segmentation systems that merge geographic, demographic, lifestyle, and behavioural data to help companies segment their markets down to neighbourhoods, and even households. One of the leading segmentation systems is the PRIZM system by The Nielsen Company. PRIZM classifies households based on a host of demographic factors—such as age, educational level, income, occupation, family composition, ethnicity, and housing—and behavioural and lifestyle factors—such as purchases, free-time activities, and media preferences. It then classifies and names each segment. For example, the market segment called Hunters & Collectors is described as "older homeowners, without kids . . . who care little about stocks, bonds, and other investments . . . take out personal and home improvement loans mostly to upgrade their older homes . . . have above-average rates for buying auto and residential insurance. For leisure, Hunters & Collectors households rank at the top for hunting and a number of other popular country pursuits: boating, camping, and reading Country Living and Town & Country." Other segments are given names such as "Savvy Savers," "Domestic Bliss," "School Daze," and "Corporate Climbers." The colourful names and brief descriptions help bring these market segments to life for marketers.[13]

Another example of how geographic, demographic, and psychographic characteristics can all be brought to bear in describing a market segment is the LGBT (lesbian, gay, bisexual, and transgender) market.[14]

When gay marriage was pronounced legal in Canada it created a new market segment— which was exciting news to marketers of products such as formal wear, jewellery, hotels, and vacation packages. The new type of engaged couple includes both men and women, and is spawning segmentation of other areas, as well. Toronto magazine *Wedding Essentials* now publishes *Wedding Essentials for Same-Sex Couples*. Wedding trade shows and expos catering to the needs and tastes of same-sex couples are springing up all over the place, and so are specialized wedding planners. "For the gay community, weddings are as new to us as they are to the marketers," says Shane Wagg, owner of Wilde Marketing in Toronto, a gay consulting agency. For this new market segment, there is no such thing as a traditional wedding.

The new group is also an extremely desirable segment for marketers to target. Gay consumers earn on average 20 percent more than straight consumers, and spend approximately 10 percent more on their weddings. "With a projected $641 billion in purchasing power and higher discretionary-spending patterns than mainstream consumers," states Harris Interactive,

Connect in Ontario, Canada.

It's hard to imagine a more gay and lesbian-friendly place than Ontario, Canada. Home to the third largest gay and lesbian population in the world, Toronto is a mature, laid-back big city of flair and sophistication, generosity and warmth. Film. Theater. Art. Music. Food. Wine. We've got them all here. And more. Plus a fabulous gay village, alive with bars and discos, cafes and clubs.

Just over an hour away is the Niagara Region, the location of Niagara Falls and center of one of the world's most exciting emerging wine regions. Drive the Wine Route, lunch in a vineyard, then head back to Toronto for an evening of theater, a late supper in a downtown bistro and a nightcap in a friendly, cosmopolitan bar.

For more information, visit **www.ontariotravel.net/GLBT** or call 1-800-ONTARIO.

ONTARIO CANADA

Exhibit 7.4 **Multiple segmentation bases:** The market segment comprising gay and lesbian couples is defined partly by gender and marital status (demographic segmentation), mainly by lifestyle (psychographic segmentation), but also by country, province, and city (geographic segmentation). The Ontario Tourism Marketing Partnership is just one organization that targets this segment through its advertising.

a market research company, "the gay, lesbian, bisexual and transgender (GLBT) market segment has become an important target for some of the biggest brands." Not only that, but the new market segment is attracting American consumers—gays and lesbians who are increasingly choosing Canada as a travel destination and a place to get married—and American marketers, such as jeweller Cartier, which ran an ad in *Vanity Fair* that featured Melissa Etheridge and her partner wearing Cartier's handcuff bracelets.

Such segmentation provides a powerful tool for marketers of all kinds. It can help companies to identify and better understand key customer segments, target them more efficiently, and tailor market offerings and messages to their specific needs.

Segmenting Business Markets

Consumer and business marketers use many of the same variables to segment their markets. Business buyers can be segmented geographically, demographically (industry, company size), or by benefits sought, user status, usage rate, and loyalty status. Yet, business marketers also use some additional variables, such as customer *operating characteristics*, *purchasing approaches*, *situational factors*, and *personal characteristics*.

Almost every company serves at least some business markets. For example, American Express targets businesses in three segments—merchants, corporations, and small businesses. It has developed distinct marketing programs for each segment. In the merchants segment, American Express focuses on convincing new merchants to accept the card and on managing relationships with those that already do. For larger corporate customers, the company offers a corporate card program, which includes extensive employee expense and travel management services. It also offers this segment a wide range of asset management, retirement planning, and financial education services. For small business customers, American Express created OPEN: The Small Business Network, a system of small business cards and financial services. It includes credit cards and lines of credit, special usage rewards, financial monitoring and spending report features, and 24/7 customized financial support services. "OPEN is how we serve small business," says American Express.[15]

Many companies set up separate systems for dealing with larger or multiple-location customers. For example, Steelcase, a major producer of office furniture, first segments customers into seven industries, including banking, biosciences, health care, and higher education. Next, company salespeople work with independent Steelcase dealers to handle smaller, local, or regional Steelcase customers in each segment. But many national, multiple-location customers, such as ExxonMobil or IBM, have special needs that may reach beyond the scope of individual dealers. So Steelcase uses national account managers to help its dealer networks handle its national accounts.

Finally, a company need not choose between business and consumer market segments. Many companies, such as Blackberry and Dell successfully target both, and sometimes a company known for its business products decides to enter the consumer market. Cisco, for example, has long been known to large- and medium-sized businesses around the globe as a marketer of networking and teleconferencing hardware, but Cisco also competes in the consumer market with its Linksys home networking products and more recently with products for the home entertainment segment, and Cisco's Flip-branded products bring high-quality videoconferencing technology to the home user.

Within a given target industry and customer size, the company can segment by purchase approaches and criteria. As in consumer segmentation, many marketers believe that *buying behaviour* and *benefits* provide the best basis for segmenting business markets.

Segmenting International Markets

Few companies have either the resources or the will to operate in all, or even most, of the countries that dot the globe. Although some large companies, such as Coca-Cola and Sony, sell products in more than 200 countries, most international firms focus on a smaller set. Operating in many countries presents new challenges. Different countries, even those that are close together, can vary greatly in their economic, cultural, and political makeup. Thus, just as they do within their domestic markets, international firms need to group their world markets into segments with distinct buying needs and behaviours.

Companies can segment international markets by using one or a combination of several variables. They can segment by *geographic location*, grouping countries by regions such as Western Europe, the Pacific Rim, the Middle East, or Africa. Geographic segmentation assumes that nations close to one another will have many common traits and behaviours. Although this is often the case, there are many exceptions. For example, some US marketers lump all Central and South American countries together, and assume they all speak Spanish, even though Brazilians speak Portuguese, and millions in other countries speak a variety of Indian dialects. And North America consists of three countries, though Mexico is usually ignored when marketers consider the North American market. Even Canada and the United States, though they have much in common, differ culturally, socially, and economically, and cannot be assumed to respond the same way to marketing offers.

World markets can also be segmented on the basis of *economic factors*. Countries might be grouped by population income levels or their overall level of economic development. A country's economic structure shapes its population's product and service needs and, therefore, the marketing opportunities it offers. For example, many companies are now targeting the BRIC countries—Brazil, Russia, India, and China—fast-growing developing economies with rapidly increasing buying power.

Countries can also be segmented by *political and legal factors* such as the type and stability of government, receptivity to foreign firms, monetary regulations, and amount of bureaucracy. *Cultural factors* can also be used, grouping markets according to common languages, religions, values and attitudes, customs, and behavioural patterns.

Exhibit 7.5 **Intermarket segmentation:** Swedish furniture giant IKEA targets the aspiring global middle class—it sells good-quality furniture that ordinary people worldwide can afford.

Intermarket segmentation
Forming segments of consumers who have similar needs and buying behaviour even though they are located in different countries.

Segmenting international markets based on geographic, economic, political, cultural, and other factors assumes that segments should consist of clusters of countries. However, as new communications technologies, such as satellite TV and the Internet, connect consumers around the world, marketers can define and reach segments of like-minded consumers no matter where in the world they are. Using **intermarket segmentation** (also called *cross-market segmentation*), they form segments of consumers who have similar needs and buying behaviours even though they are located in different countries. For example, Lexus targets the world's well-to-do—the "global elite" segment—regardless of their country. Coca-Cola creates special programs to target teens, core consumers of its soft drinks the world over. And Swedish furniture giant IKEA targets the aspiring global middle class—it sells good-quality furniture that ordinary people worldwide can afford.

Requirements for Effective Segmentation

Clearly, there are many ways to segment a market, but not all segmentation methods are effective. For example, buyers of table salt could be divided into blond and brunette customers, but hair colour obviously is not a relevant criterion because it doesn't influence a consumer's choice of salt brand. Furthermore, if all salt buyers bought the same amount of salt each month, believed that all salt is the same, and wanted to pay the same price, the company would not benefit from segmenting this market.

To be useful, market segments must be the following:

- *Measurable:* The size, purchasing power, and profiles of the segments can be measured. Certain segmentation variables are difficult to measure. For example, although approximately 7 to 10 percent of adults are left-handed, there is no way to identify and target them. Perhaps this is why so few products are targeted toward this market segment.

- *Accessible:* The market segments can be effectively reached and served. Suppose a fragrance company finds that heavy users of its brand are single men and women who stay out late and socialize a lot. Unless this group lives or shops at certain places and is exposed to certain media, its members will be difficult to reach.

- *Substantial:* The market segments are large or profitable enough to serve. A segment should be the largest possible homogeneous group worth pursuing with a tailored marketing program. It would not pay, for example, for an automobile manufacturer to develop cars especially for people whose height is greater than seven feet (2.13 metres).

- *Differentiable:* The segments are conceptually distinguishable and respond differently to different marketing-mix elements and programs. If married and unmarried women respond similarly to a sale on perfume, they do not constitute separate segments.

■ *Actionable:* Effective programs can be designed for attracting and serving the segments. For example, although one small airline identified seven market segments, its staff was too small to develop separate marketing programs for each segment.

Market Targeting LO3

Market segmentation reveals the firm's market segment opportunities. The firm now has to evaluate the various segments and decide how many and which segments it can serve best. We now look at how companies evaluate and select target segments.

Evaluating Market Segments

In evaluating different market segments, a firm must look at three factors: segment size and growth, segment structural attractiveness, and company objectives and resources. The company must first collect and analyze data on current segment sales, growth rates, and expected profitability for various segments. It will be interested in segments that have the right size and growth characteristics.

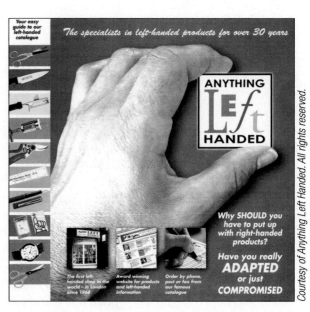

Exhibit 7.6 **Measurable market segments:** The "leftie" segment can be hard to identify and measure. As a result, few companies tailor their offers to left-handers. However, some nichers such as Anything Left-Handed in the United Kingdom target this segment.

But "right size and growth" is a relative matter. The largest, fastest-growing segments are not always the most attractive ones for every company. Smaller companies may lack the skills and resources needed to serve the larger segments. Or they may find these segments too competitive. Such companies may target segments that are smaller and less attractive, in an absolute sense, but that are potentially more profitable for them. And if a company identifies a segment as being unprofitable, they might take steps to encourage that group to shop at the competition instead. Best Buy in the United States, for example, identified its "demon" or unprofitable customers, and implemented a segmentation strategy to discourage them from shopping at Best Buy.

The company also needs to examine major structural factors that affect long-run segment attractiveness, such as the number and aggressiveness of *competitors*.[16] The existence of many actual or potential *substitute products* may limit prices and the profits that can be earned in a segment. The relative *power of buyers* also affects segment attractiveness. Buyers with strong bargaining power relative to sellers will try to force prices down, demand more services, and set competitors against one another—all at the expense of seller profitability. Finally, a segment may be less attractive if it contains *powerful suppliers* who can control prices or reduce the quality or quantity of ordered goods and services.

Even if a segment has the right size and growth and is structurally attractive, the company must consider its own objectives and resources. Some attractive segments can be dismissed quickly because they do not mesh with the company's long-run objectives. Or the company may lack the skills and resources needed to succeed in an attractive segment. For example, given current economic conditions, the economy segment of the automobile market is large and growing. But given its objectives and resources, it would make little sense for luxury-performance carmaker BMW to enter this segment. A company should enter only segments in which it can create superior customer value and gain advantages over competitors.

Selecting Target Market Segments

After evaluating different segments, the company must decide which and how many segments it will target. A **target market** consists of a set of buyers who share common needs

Target market
A set of buyers sharing common needs or characteristics that the company decides to serve.

FIGURE 7.2 Market Targeting Strategies

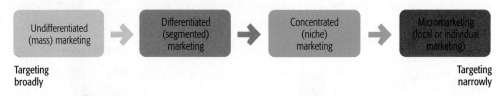

or characteristics that the company decides to serve. Market targeting can be carried out at several different levels. Figure 7.2 shows that companies can target very broadly (undifferentiated marketing), very narrowly (micromarketing), or somewhere in between (differentiated or concentrated marketing).

By using an **undifferentiated marketing (or mass marketing)** strategy, a firm might decide to ignore market segment differences and target the whole market with one offer. This mass-marketing strategy focuses on what is *common* in the needs of consumers rather than on what is *different*. The company designs a product and a marketing program that will appeal to the largest number of buyers.

As noted earlier in the chapter, most modern marketers have strong doubts about this strategy. Difficulties arise in developing a product or brand that will satisfy all consumers. Moreover, mass marketers often have trouble competing with more-focused firms that do a better job of satisfying the needs of specific segments and niches.

Differentiated Marketing By using a **differentiated marketing (or segmented marketing)** strategy, a firm decides to target several market segments and designs separate offers for each. Toyota, for example, produces many different brands of cars, from Yaris to Lexus, each targeting a different group of car buyers—a different market segment. Procter & Gamble markets six different laundry detergent brands, which compete with each other on supermarket shelves. And VF Corporation offers a closet-full of more than 30 clothing brands, including Lee, Wrangler, and The North Face, each of which "taps into consumer aspirations to fashion, status, and well-being" in a well-defined segment.[17]

By offering product and marketing variations to segments, companies hope for higher sales and a stronger position within each market segment. Developing a stronger position within several segments creates more total sales than undifferentiated marketing across all segments. VF Corporation's combined brands give it a much greater, more stable market share than any single brand could. The company's jeans brands alone account for a quarter of all jeans sold in the United States. Similarly, P&G's multiple detergent brands capture four times the market share of nearest rival Unilever.

But differentiated marketing also increases the costs of doing business. A firm usually finds it more expensive to develop and produce, say, 10 units of 10 different products than 100 units of one product. Developing separate marketing plans for the separate segments requires extra marketing research, forecasting, sales analysis, promotion planning, and channel management. And trying to reach different market segments with different advertising campaigns increases promotion costs. Thus, the company must weigh increased sales against increased costs when deciding on a differentiated marketing strategy.

Concentrated Marketing

By using a **concentrated marketing (or niche marketing)** strategy, instead of going after a small share of a large market, the firm goes after a large share of one or a few smaller

Undifferentiated (mass) marketing
A market-coverage strategy in which a firm decides to ignore market segment differences and go after the whole market with one offer.

Differentiated (segmented) marketing
A market-coverage strategy in which a firm decides to target several market segments and designs separate offers for each.

segments or niches. Through concentrated marketing, the firm achieves a strong market position because of its greater knowledge of consumer needs in the niches it serves and the special reputation it acquires. It can market more *effectively* by fine-tuning its products, prices, and programs to the needs of carefully defined segments. It can also market more *efficiently*, targeting its products or services, channels, and communications programs toward only consumers that it can serve best and most profitably. Consider Sabian, the second largest cymbal manufacturer in the world:[18]

Concentrated (niche) marketing
A market-coverage strategy in which a firm goes after a large share of one or a few segments or niches.

> The village of Meductic, New Brunswick, has a population of only a few hundred people, and you've likely never heard of it—unless you're a musician. More specifically, a drummer. Neil Peart and Phil Collins, two of the most respected drummers in the world, have visited Meductic, because it's home to Sabian, a world-renowned cymbal maker. Sabian employs 130 people, sells its cymbals in 120 countries, and holds about half the market share.
>
> How big is the worldwide market for cymbals? In dollar terms, it's less than $100 million per year, which definitely qualifies it as a niche market. Sabian's only competitor to speak of is the company that holds the other half of this small market segment, the Avedis Zildjian Company of Boston. Sabian differentiates itself from Zildjian by projecting the idea that it is a creative, innovative company, whereas Zildjian is more traditional. Sabian invites the world's best drummers to New Brunswick to invent new cymbal sounds, which the company then markets as a signature line. One of these lines, called Paragon, was designed in collaboration with legendary Rush drummer Neil Peart, and featured an advertisement showing Canada's most famous drummer playing in a forest.

Whereas most market segments are fairly large and normally attract several competitors, niche markets are smaller and may attract only one or two competitors. Niche marketing lets smaller companies focus their limited resources on serving very small groups of customers that may be unimportant to or overlooked by larger competitors. Many companies start as niche marketers to get a foothold against larger, more-resourceful competitors and then grow into broader competitors. For example, Enterprise Rent-A-Car began by building a network of neighbourhood offices that served the niche market of city dwellers who don't own a car, rather than competing with Hertz and Avis in airport locations, but is now one of the largest car rental companies.

Today, the low cost of setting up shop on the Internet plus the instant access to global markets makes it even more profitable to serve seemingly miniscule niches. Fancy Feather (FancyFeather .com), for example, sells items such as feather boas, fans, and masks to consumers around the world, and Edmonton's Kinnikinnick Foods reaches a worldwide market of consumers with its gluten-free baked goods.

Micromarketing Differentiated and concentrated marketers tailor their offers and marketing programs to meet the needs of market segments consisting of groups of people, however, they do not go so far as to customize their offers to each

Sabian Ltd

Exhibit 7.7 **Niche marketing:** Though the market for cymbals is small, New Brunswick cymbal manufacturer Sabian holds approximately half the market share. Their marketing strategy includes designing custom lines in collaboration with world-renowned drummers, such as Nickelback's Daniel Adair.

Micromarketing

The practice of tailoring products and marketing programs to the needs and wants of specific individuals and local customer segments—includes *local marketing and individual marketing.*

Local marketing

A small group of people who live in the same city, or neighbourhood, or who shop at the same store.

individual customer. **Micromarketing** is the practice of tailoring products and marketing programs to suit the tastes of specific individuals and locations. Micromarketing is an extreme form of market segmentation, where the market segment is so small it is contained within a small geographic area—*local marketing*—or so small that it consists of only one person—*individual marketing*.

LOCAL MARKETING **Local marketing** involves tailoring brands and promotions to the needs and wants of a small group of people who live in the same city, or neighbourhood, or who shop at the same store. Most convenience stores practise local marketing, stocking their shelves with the items they know the people in their neighbourhood are likely to want.

Advances in communications technology have given rise to a new high-tech version of location-based marketing. Using location-based social networks such as Foursquare, and local marketing deal-of-the-day services such as Groupon, local retailers can target consumers directly (see Marketing@Work 7.1).

Local marketing has some drawbacks. It can drive up manufacturing and marketing costs by reducing economies of scale. It can also create logistics problems as companies try to meet the varied requirements of different regional and local markets. Further, a brand's overall image might be diluted if the product and message vary too much in different localities.

Still, as companies face increasingly fragmented markets, and as new supporting technologies develop, the advantages of local marketing often outweigh the drawbacks. Local marketing helps a company to market more effectively in the face of pronounced regional and local differences in demographics and lifestyles. It also meets the needs of the company's first-line customers—retailers—who prefer more finely tuned product assortments for their neighbourhoods.

Individual marketing (mass customization)

Tailoring products and marketing programs to the needs and preferences of individual customers.

INDIVIDUAL MARKETING In the extreme, micromarketing becomes **individual marketing**—tailoring products and marketing programs to the needs and preferences of individual customers. Individual marketing is also known as **mass customization**.

The modern custom of mass marketing has obscured the fact that for centuries consumers *were* served as individuals: The tailor custom made a suit, the cobbler designed shoes for an individual, the cabinetmaker made furniture to order. So, in a sense we are returning to a time-honoured tradition, but employing contemporary technology to improve upon it. Computer databases, robotic production, flexible manufacturing, and interactive communication media have combined to foster mass customization. Today's marketers have the tools to interact on a one-to-one basis with masses of customers to produce products that are in some way customized to the individual. For example, Dell creates custom-configured computers, and hockey-stick maker Branches Hockey lets customers choose from more than two dozen options—including stick length, blade patterns, and blade curve—and turns out a customized stick in five days. Visitors to Nike's Nike ID website can personalize their sneakers by choosing from hundreds of colours and putting an embroidered word or phrase on the tongue. At www .myMMs.com, you can upload your photo and order a batch of M&Ms with your face and a personal message printed on each little candy. Toyota even lets Scion owners design their own personal "coat of arms" online, "a piece of owner-generated art that is meant to reflect their own job, hobbies, and—um, okay—Karma." Customers can download their designs and have them made into window decals or professionally airbrushed onto their cars.[19]

Marketers are also finding new ways to personalize promotional messages. For example, large screens placed in shopping malls around the country can now analyze

MARKETING@WORK   7.1

Location-Based Micromarketing Equals Macro Opportunities

Marketers have always used a variety of characteristics to target customers, and today's marketers are adding an important new targeting variable: location—*where you are right now*. Thanks to smartphones with GPS capabilities and location-based social networks and their associated mobile apps, companies can now track your whereabouts closely and customize their offers accordingly.

Location-based apps such as Foursquare, CheckPoints, and Shopkick are all check-in services that offer users some kind of rewards, whether real or virtual. Shoppers using Shopkick collect points called "kicks" just by walking into stores, and CheckPoints users collect points by checking into locations or checking out (i.e., looking at) certain products within a store. Similarly, Foursquare encourages users to check in at each location they visit and collect points toward earning virtual badges and becoming the "mayor" of a particular location—all the while being alerted to special offers from nearby retailers.

There's also Scvngr, a mobile app that is basically a game. By going places and doing challenges, players can earn points, unlock badges, and redeem real-world rewards such as discounts or free items. And Facebook Places—the new giant in location-based marketing services—suggests that you "share where you are, connect with friends nearby, *and* find local deals." The check-in networks provide attractive targeting opportunities to retailers, letting them market to people on the go, when they're nearby and ready to eat, shop, and spend.

These location-based check-in services bridge the gap between the digital world and the real bricks-and-mortar world. But more than just passing out e-coupons and other rewards, Foursquare and the other check-in services are becoming full-fledged, location-based lifestyle networks. The aim is to enrich people's lives by helping them to learn the whereabouts of friends, share location-related experiences, and discover new places—all while linking

them to sponsoring locations that match their interests.

Recently, Foursquare announced plans to create a new ad product that will generate revenue outside its app—selling advertising space that would use Foursquare's location and behavioural data to contextualize ads on other platforms. Advertisers will use Foursquare data to target ads purchased through ad exchanges or networks. That data includes the 3.5 billion check-ins made on its platform and the data it receives from the more than 40 000 developers that have integrated Foursquare's location database in their apps, including the popular apps Instagram, Uber, and Evernote.

Another form of location-based marketing is "deal-of-the-day" websites such as Groupon, which partner with local businesses to offer local shopping deals to subscribers based on where they live and what they like. Groupon offers subscribers at least one deal each day in their city—such as paying $40 for an $80 voucher at a local restaurant. But the coupon deals kick in only if enough people sign up, encouraging subscribers to spread word of the deal to friends and neighbours and via social media such as Twitter and Facebook. Hence, the name *Groupon*—group plus coupon. Its customers are typically small businesses, who use the marketer as a way to promote their goods and services to their local market. But global giants such as Starbucks, Best Buy, and PepsiCo have also gotten into the Groupon act.

Living Social has been operating in Canada since 2010, but it is not nearly as popular here as it is in the United States, where it is Groupon's biggest rival. Instead, homegrown deal sites like WagJag, TeamBuy, and Tuango dominate the Canadian market. Recently, Starbucks Canada worked with Living Social on a daily deal promotion that was redeemed by 150 000 consumers and generated $750 000 in sales. Dan Stuart, Living Social's Canadian general manager, said

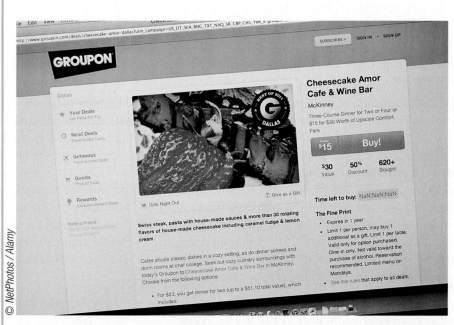

Exhibit 7.8 Location-based marketing: Groupon provides local marketers with a way to advertise deals to consumers in their city.

the deal sold out at the 150 000 person cap set by Starbucks about 48 hours after it went live. "It was huge for us," he said. "It took off very quickly. No one had done anything of this scale in Canada. It was treading new ground." According to the Canadian Deals Association, which tracks the group buying market, the deal represented the highest number of vouchers ever redeemed for a daily deal in Canada.

TikTok, a Vancouver-based company, came out in 2012 with a new daily deal model that it claimed is was the antithesis of Groupon and its many clones. TikTok was a mobile app that worked on your smartphone and sent out 500 offers per day. Users would get some but not all of the offers, and the offers always expired, usually the same day. TikTok's creators encouraged users to share with their friends via Facebook and Twitter to earn "Karma Points," which, if you collected enough, might win you an iPad or a prepaid Visa card. The advantage for

businesses (the ones giving out the coupons) was that they could set up the application for free and push out offers to as many as a thousand people at a time. TikTok's creators believed they had an app that could beat Groupon, and they may have had a point—Groupon's business model is flawed because it attracts only the shopper looking for deep discounts. Sadly, being right doesn't always equal success. TikTok closed its doors in late 2013.

But the landscape of location-based marketers changes drastically from year to year. Gowalla, Whrr, TikTok, and many others have come and gone. Though Facebook attempted to launch a competitor, Facebook Deals, they gave up the attempt after only four months. Groupon simply dominates the market with more than 70 million subscribers in 500 cities worldwide—but there may be trouble on the horizon there, too. Groupon's stock plummeted a staggering 77 percent last year.

"When any business operates by putting more focus on getting new customers than on retaining existing customers, it's going to pay the price of constant churn," says one strategic marketing expert. "They need to put as much focus on helping businesses retain their existing customers as they do in attracting those new customers."

Recently, Google launched Google Offers, a competitor to Groupon, but only time will tell which of these business models will survive in the long run.

Sources: John McDermott, "Foursquare Planning to Offer Check-in Data to Target Ads on Other Platforms," AdAge.com, April 12, 1013; Russ Martin, "Living Social Makes Canadian Inroads with Big Starbucks Program," *Marketing Magazine* online, January 24, 2013; Steve Olenski, "Is Location Based Advertising the Future of Mobile Marketing and Mobile Advertising?" Forbes.com, January 17, 2013; Noah Fleming, "How Groupon Can Save Itself," *Fast Company* online, October 1, 2012; Eve Lazarus, "Daily Deal Offering TikTok Turns Groupon Model on Its Head," *Marketing Magazine* online, June 19, 2012; and information from Groupon.com, TikTok.com, Scvngr.com, and Facebook.com.

shoppers' faces and place ads based on an individual shopper's gender, age, or ethnicity:[20]

> Watch an advertisement on a video screen in a mall, health club, or grocery store and there's a growing chance that the ad is watching you too. Small cameras can now be embedded in or around the screen, tracking who looks at the screen and for how long. With surprising accuracy, the system can determine the viewer's gender, approximate age range and, in some cases, ethnicity—and change the ads accordingly. That could mean razor ads for men, cosmetics ads for women, and videogame ads for teens. Or a video screen might show a motorcycle ad for a group of men, but switch to a minivan ad when women and children join them. "This is proactive merchandising," says a media executive. "You're targeting people with smart ads."

Business-to-business marketers are also finding new ways to customize their offerings. For example, John Deere manufactures seeding equipment that can be configured in more than 2 million versions to individual customer specifications. The seeders are produced one at a time, in any sequence, on a single production line. Mass customization provides a way to stand out against competitors.

Unlike mass production, which eliminates the need for human interaction, mass customization has made relationships with customers more important than ever. Just as mass production was the marketing principle of the past century, mass customization is becoming a marketing principle for the twenty-first century. The world appears to be coming full circle—from the good old days when customers were treated as individuals, to mass marketing when nobody knew your name, and back again.

Choosing a Targeting Strategy Companies need to consider many factors when choosing a market-targeting strategy. Which strategy is best depends on *company resources*. When the firm's resources are limited, concentrated marketing makes the most sense. The best strategy also depends on the degree of *product variability*. Undifferentiated marketing is more suited for uniform products such as grapefruit or steel. Products that can vary in design, such as cameras and cars, are more suited to differentiation or concentration. The *product's life-cycle stage* also must be considered. When a firm introduces a new product, it may be practical to launch only one version, and undifferentiated marketing or concentrated marketing may make the most sense. In the mature stage of the product life cycle, however, differentiated marketing often makes more sense.

Another factor is *market variability*. If most buyers have the same tastes, buy the same amounts, and react the same way to marketing efforts, undifferentiated marketing is appropriate. Finally, *competitors' marketing strategies* are important. When competitors use differentiated or concentrated marketing, undifferentiated marketing can be suicidal. Conversely, when competitors use undifferentiated marketing, a firm can gain an advantage by using differentiated or concentrated marketing, focusing on the needs of buyers in specific segments.

© PhotoAlto sas / Alamy

Exhibit 7.9 **Individual marketing:** Video screens in malls and stores can now determine who's watching them and change ads accordingly.

Socially Responsible Target Marketing

Smart targeting helps companies become more efficient and effective by focusing on the segments that they can satisfy best and most profitably. Targeting also benefits consumers—companies serve specific groups of consumers with offers carefully tailored to their needs. However, target marketing sometimes generates controversy and concern. The biggest issues usually involve the targeting of vulnerable or disadvantaged consumers with controversial or potentially harmful products.

For example, over the years marketers in a wide range of industries—from cereal, soft drinks, and fast food to toys and fashion—have been heavily criticized for their marketing efforts directed toward children. Critics worry that premium offers and high-powered advertising appeals presented through the mouths of lovable animated characters will overwhelm children's defences.

Other problems arise when the marketing of adult products spills over into the children's segment—intentionally or unintentionally. For example, Victoria's Secret targets its highly successful Pink line of young, hip, and sexy clothing to young women from 18 to 30 years old. However, critics charge that Pink is now all the rage among girls as young as 11 years old. Responding to Victoria's Secret's designs and marketing messages, tweens are flocking into stores and buying Pink, with or without their mothers. More broadly, critics worry that marketers of everything from lingerie and cosmetics to Barbie dolls are, directly or indirectly, targeting young girls with provocative products, promoting a premature focus on sex and appearance.[21]

Ten-year-old girls can slide their low-cut jeans over "eye-candy" panties. French maid costumes, garter belt included, are available in preteen sizes. Barbie now comes in a "bling-bling" style, replete with halter top and go-go boots. Abercrombie & Fitch markets a padded "push-up" bikini top for girls as young as eight. Walmart is marketing a make-up line to tweens. And it's not unusual for girls under 12 years old to sing, "Don't cha wish your girlfriend was hot like me?" American girls, say experts, are increasingly being fed a cultural catnip of products and images that promote looking and acting sexy. "The message we're telling our girls is a simple one," laments one reporter about the Victoria's

Jarrod Weaton/Weaton Digital, Inc.

Exhibit 7.10 Socially responsible marketing: Critics worry that marketers of everything from lingerie and cosmetics to Barbie dolls are targeting young girls with provocative products.

Secret Pink line. "You'll have a great life if people find you sexually attractive. Grown women struggle enough with this ridiculous standard. Do we really need to start worrying about it at 11?" Adds another parenting expert, "The sexualization of teens is bad enough, and now this trend is trickling down to our babies."

In Canada, advertising to children is strictly controlled by several organizations, including Advertising Standards Canada, which publishes the Canadian Code of Advertising Standards; the Canadian Association of Broadcasters, which has its own code for television advertising aimed at children; and Concerned Children's Advertisers, an advocacy group dedicated to promoting media literacy, ethics, and responsibility in advertising to children. Still, many consumers feel that more should be done to protect vulnerable groups from being targeted.

Most market targeting, however, draws no criticism because it benefits consumers. For example, all shampoo marketers target multiple market segments defined by various demographic characteristics, by offering products for different colours of hair; for hair that is colour treated; for grey hair; and special products for men's hair. Samsung markets the Jitterbug, an easy-to-use phone, directly to seniors who need a simpler cellphone with bigger buttons, large screen text, and a louder speaker. And Colgate makes a large selection of toothbrush shapes and toothpaste flavours for children—from Colgate SpongeBob SquarePants Mild Bubble Fruit toothpaste to Colgate Dora the Explorer character toothbrushes. Such products help make tooth brushing more fun and get children to brush longer and more often.

Therefore, in target marketing, the issue is not really who is targeted but rather how and for what. Controversies arise only when unscrupulous marketers attempt to profit by unfairly targeting vulnerable segments with questionable products or tactics. Socially responsible marketing calls for segmentation and targeting that serve not just the interests of the company but also the interests of those targeted.

Differentiation and Positioning LO4

Beyond deciding which segments of the market it will target, the company must decide on a *value proposition*—on how it will create differentiated value for targeted segments, and what positions it wants to occupy in those segments. A **product position** is the way the product is *defined by consumers* on important attributes—the place the product occupies in consumers' minds relative to competing products. More often, positioning is based not just on the product, but on the product's brand name. "Products are created in the factory, but brands are created in the mind," says a positioning expert.[22]

For example, most smartphones have similar features, so marketers attempt to position their smartphone's brand in the mind of the consumer by using emotional appeals. BlackBerry is positioned as a personal and business productivity aid, while iPhone is positioned as high tech with high style. Meanwhile Samsung, a brand previously known for its cheap microwave ovens, broke through in 2012 with its Galaxy line of smartphones, positioning them as the technology of the future—and became the top selling smartphone, overtaking Apple's long standing top position.

Tide is positioned through its advertising as a powerful, all-purpose family detergent, while Ivory Snow is positioned as the detergent for baby clothes. In the growing

Product position

The way the product is defined by consumers on important attributes—the place the product occupies in consumers' minds relative to competing products.

market for men's personal care products, Old Spice is positioned as being the choice for "manly men," Axe is the brand for young men who want to score with the opposite sex, and Dove is for the regular, everyday family man. Subway restaurants positioned themselves with spectacular success as the healthy fast food. Beer is a relatively undifferentiated product, so beer brands position themselves on the basis of lifestyle: Corona is for when you're on vacation (or want to feel like you are); Molson Canadian is the hockey fan's beer, and Kokanee is for the outdoorsy type.

Consumers are overloaded with information about products and services. They cannot re-evaluate products every time they make a buying decision. To simplify the buying process, consumers organize products, services, and companies into categories and "position" them in their minds. A product's position is the complex set of perceptions, impressions, and feelings that consumers have for the product compared with competing products.

Consumers position products with or without the help of marketers. But marketers do not want to leave their products' positions to chance. They must *plan* positions that will give their products the greatest advantage in selected target markets, and they must design marketing mixes to create these planned positions.

Positioning Maps

In planning their differentiation and positioning strategies, marketers often prepare *perceptual positioning maps*, which show consumer perceptions of their brands versus competing products on important buying dimensions. Figure 7.3 shows a positioning map for the US large luxury sport-utility-vehicle market. The position of each circle on the map indicates the brand's perceived positioning on two dimensions—price and orientation (luxury versus performance). The size of each circle indicates the brand's relative market share.

Customers view the market-leading Cadillac Escalade as a moderately priced, large, luxury SUV with a balance of luxury and performance. The Escalade is positioned on urban luxury, and, in its case, performance probably means power and safety performance. You'll find no mention of off-road adventuring in an Escalade ad.

FIGURE 7.3 Positioning Map: Large Luxury SUVs

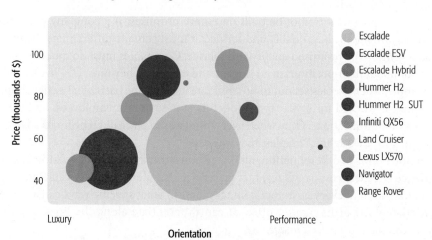

Sources: SUV sales data provided by WardsAuto.com, March 2011; price data from Edmunds.com, March 2011.

Exhibit 7.11 Positioning: Advertising for Toyota's Land Cruiser shows the vehicle performing in rough terrain, reinforcing its positioning as a rugged off-road vehicle.

By contrast, Range Rover and Land Cruiser are positioned on luxury with nuances of off-road performance. For example, the Toyota Land Cruiser began in 1951 as a four-wheel drive, Jeep-like vehicle designed to conquer the world's most gruelling terrains and climates. In recent years, Land Cruiser has retained this adventure and performance positioning but with luxury added. The Toyota website describes the Land Cruiser as "off-road prowess meets on-road refinement." Despite its ruggedness, this SUV is not lacking in comfort and technology—it's equipped with a leather trimmed, heated steering wheel, Bluetooth, rear seat entertainment, and 14 JBL speakers.

Choosing a Differentiation and Positioning Strategy

Some marketers find it easy to choose a differentiation and positioning strategy for their products and brands. For example, a brand well known for its high quality and style in its existing market segments will continue to position its new products in a similar manner. But when two or more brands go after the same position, each will have to find other ways to set itself apart. Marketers must differentiate their product offerings by building a unique bundle of benefits that appeals to a substantial group within the segment. Above all else, a brand's positioning must serve the needs and preferences of well-defined target markets.

The differentiation and positioning task consists of three steps: identifying a set of differentiating competitive advantages upon which to build a position, choosing the right competitive advantages, and selecting an overall positioning strategy. The company must then effectively communicate and deliver the chosen position to the market.

Identifying Possible Value Differences and Competitive Advantages To build profitable relationships with target customers, marketers must understand customer needs better than competitors do and deliver more customer value. To the extent that a company can differentiate and position itself as providing superior customer value, it gains **competitive advantage**.

But solid positions cannot be built on empty promises. If a company positions its product as *offering* the best quality and service, it must actually differentiate the product so that it *delivers* the promised quality and service. Companies must do much more than simply shout out their positions in ad slogans and taglines. They must first *live* the slogan. For example, when Staples set out to differentiate itself on the basis of an easier shopping experience, it worked for a year to remodel its stores, retrain employees, and simplify customer communications. Only when everything was in place did it begin its advertising campaign with the tagline, "Staples: that was easy."[23]

To find points of differentiation, marketers must think through the customer's entire experience with the company's product or service. An alert company can find ways to differentiate itself at every customer contact point. In what specific ways can a company differentiate itself or its market offer? It can differentiate along the lines of *product*, *services*, *channels*, *people*, or *image*.

Through *product differentiation* brands can be differentiated on features, performance, or style and design. For example, Maple Leaf Foods claims that its Maple Leaf

Competitive advantage

An advantage over competitors gained by offering greater customer value, either through lower prices, or by providing more benefits that justify higher prices.

Prime Naturally–branded chicken is fresher and more tender—and gets a price premium based on this differentiation. Whirlpool promotes its dishwashers on performance—they run more quietly—and Bose positions its speakers on their striking design characteristics. Similarly, companies can differentiate their products on attributes such as consistency, durability, reliability, or repairability.

Beyond differentiating its physical product, a firm can also differentiate the services that accompany the product. Some companies gain *services differentiation* through speedy, convenient, or careful delivery. For example, TD Canada Trust positions itself as the bank that makes banking "comfortable," and differentiates itself by offering services other banks don't, such as branches that are open on Sundays. Others differentiate their service based on high-quality customer care. Lexus makes fine cars but is perhaps even better known for the quality service that creates outstanding ownership experiences for Lexus owners.

Firms that practise *channel differentiation* gain competitive advantage through the way they design their channel's coverage, expertise, and performance. Caterpillar's success in the heavy equipment industry is based on its superior marketing channels starring local Caterpillar dealers. Online marketers such as Amazon and Dell similarly distinguish themselves by their high-quality direct channels.

Companies can also gain a strong competitive advantage through *people differentiation*—hiring and training better people than their competitors do. Singapore Airlines enjoys an excellent reputation, largely because of the beauty and grace of its flight attendants, and WestJet staffers are known for their sense of humour. People differentiation requires that a company select its customer-contact people carefully and train them well.

Even when competing offers look the same, buyers may perceive a difference based on company or brand *image differentiation*. For example, Dippity-do hair gel was for many years positioned as the "value brand," but in 2008, on the advice of research and strategic branding company White-Space, it repositioned itself as an "image brand" and redesigned its packaging to look more modern.[24] Similarly, Alberto-Culver successfully transitioned its TRESemmé brand from unremarkable to "professional affordable."[25] We will look more closely at developing and managing a brand image in Chapter 9.

Choosing the Right Competitive Advantages   Suppose a company is fortunate enough to discover several potential differentiations that provide competitive advantages. It now must choose the ones on which it will build its positioning strategy. It must decide *how many* differences to promote and *which ones*.

HOW MANY DIFFERENCES TO PROMOTE   Some marketers believe that the best approach is to aggressively promote only one benefit to the target market, in other words, to focus on the product or brand's *unique selling proposition (USP)*. If a product has a clear USP, all marketing communications in support of it then focus on saying, "Buy this product, and you will receive this benefit." For example, Head & Shoulders shampoo's USP is that it gets rid of dandruff, and FedEx's USP is overnight delivery.

Other marketers choose to position their brands on more than one differentiator. This may be necessary if two or more companies or products are claiming to be best on the same attribute, especially today, when what was once a mass market is fragmenting into many small market segments.

For example, SC Johnson introduced Pledge multi-surface cleaner, an extension of its well-known furniture polish brand. The new Pledge product was positioned as a cleaner that works on wood, electronics, glass, marble, stainless steel, and other surfaces. The benefit it provides is the ability to use only one product to clean everything in a room. Almost certainly, consumers want these multiple benefits, however, it can be a challenge to convince them that one product can do it all. As companies increase the number of claims for their brands, they risk disbelief and a loss of clear positioning.

WHICH DIFFERENCES TO PROMOTE Not all brand differences are meaningful or worthwhile; not every difference makes a good differentiator. Each difference has the potential to create company costs as well as customer benefits. A difference is worth establishing to the extent that it satisfies the following criteria:

- *Important:* The difference delivers a highly-valued benefit to target buyers.
- *Distinctive:* Competitors do not offer the difference, or the company can offer it in a more distinctive way.
- *Superior:* The difference is superior to other ways that customers might obtain the same benefit.
- *Communicable:* The difference is communicable and visible to buyers.
- *Preemptive:* Competitors cannot easily copy the difference.
- *Affordable:* Buyers can afford to pay for the difference.
- *Profitable:* The company can introduce the difference profitably.

Many companies have introduced differentiations that failed one or more of these tests. When the Westin Stamford Hotel in Singapore once advertised that it is the world's tallest hotel, it was a distinction that was not important to most tourists—in fact, it turned many off. Polaroid's Polarvision, a unique product (for its time) that produced instantly developed home movies, turned out to offer a benefit no one wanted.

Choosing competitive advantages upon which to position a product or service can be difficult, yet such choices may be crucial to success. Choosing the right differentiators can help a brand to stand out from the pack of competitors. For example, when carmaker Nissan introduced its funky little Cube, it didn't position the car only on attributes shared with competing models, such as affordability and customization. Instead, it turned the Cube into something more—a "mobile device" (see Marketing@ Work 7.2).

Value proposition

The full positioning of a brand—the full mix of benefits upon which it is positioned.

Selecting an Overall Positioning Strategy The full positioning of a brand is called the brand's **value proposition**—the full mix of benefits upon which the brand is differentiated and positioned. It is the answer to the customer's question "Why should I buy your brand?" Volvo's value proposition hinges on safety but also includes reliability, roominess, and styling, all for a price that is higher than average but seems fair for this mix of benefits.

Figure 7.4 (see p. 264) shows possible value propositions upon which a company might position its products. In the figure, the five green cells represent winning value propositions—differentiation and positioning that gives the company competitive advantage. The red cells, however, represent losing value propositions. The centre cell represents at best a marginal proposition. In the following sections, we discuss the five winning value propositions upon which companies can position their products: more for more, more for the same, the same for less, less for much less, and more for less.

MORE FOR MORE "More-for-more" positioning involves providing the most upscale product or service and charging a higher price to cover the higher costs. Four Seasons hotels, Montblanc writing instruments, Mercedes automobiles, LG electronics and appliances—each claims superior quality, craftsmanship, durability, performance, or style and charges a price to match. Not only is the market offering high in quality, it also gives prestige to the buyer. It symbolizes status and a loftier lifestyle. Often, the price difference exceeds the actual increment in quality.

MARKETING@WORK 7.2

Nissan's Cube is Not Just a Car, It's a Mobile Device

When Nissan introduced its new model, the Cube—a smallish, city car with a funky look—the carmaker knew that, to be successful, it would have to align all of the Cube's intricate marketing facets into a winning pattern that would differentiate the car from competing models.

Introducing a new car to the market is difficult enough in normal times, but Nissan introduced the Cube in mid-2009, in the midst of a recession and plummeting auto sales. And although the Cube had been a huge hit in Japan for several years, Nissan was late to enter the American market with a small vehicle aimed at the 20-something first-car buyer. Honda and Toyota had already made their mark six years earlier with the boxy Honda Element (positioned as "a dorm room on wheels") and eccentric-looking Toyota Scion (also known as "the toaster"). By the time Nissan launched the Cube, the Canadian market was already crammed full of competing small cars such as the Toyota Yaris, Ford Focus, Kia Rio, and the startling, unique Smart Car marketed by Mercedes. Before introducing the Cube, Nissan needed to figure out

how to make its car distinctive. How could Nissan differentiate the Cube to make it stand out from the pack?

The Cube and its competitors primarily target Millennials, 18-to-25-year-old drivers for whom it would be their first car, or at least their first new car. Many of these buyers are in college or university, or are just starting their careers, so they often don't have much money. Millennials are an expressive, hypercreative bunch who are setting out to establish their independence. They value things built just for them, with lots of room for personalization. These younger buyers grew up with the web, blogs, cellphones, text messaging, and social networks. They're a uniquely social group, with both the need and the technical savvy to stay in touch—anywhere, anytime. They communicate constantly.

The Cube's young target buyers are looking for an affordable car, and for a car that lets them express their individuality. Cube has plenty of both qualities. The base model was originally priced at $17 400, and Nissan helped with the financing. Buyers could select from more

than 40 accessories to customize the car. One writer described the Cube as "an inspiring canvas for personalization." But many Cube competitors also offer these attributes. Many have base prices even lower than the Cube's, and others feature personalization as their main value proposition. For example, Toyota initially positioned its Scion with the slogan, "Personalization begins here—what moves you?"

So, to stand out from this crowded field, Nissan needed something more, something truly unique. The answer: Position the Cube not just as another small *car* but as a personal *mobile device*—as something that enhances young customers' individual, mobile, connected lifestyles. Nissan decided to present the Cube "as a part of a fun, busy life that can be customized and personalized as easily as a cellphone ring tone or a webpage," notes an analyst. "We decided we wouldn't think about it as a car," says the creative director at Nissan's advertising agency. Instead, Nissan designed the Cube "to bring young people together—like every mobile device they have."

The Cube, then, becomes a mobile space where young people can connect with friends. It's also a space that's their own, just like a Facebook page, where they can hang out and create. Nissan Canada created a blog (at CubeCommunity.ca) for Cube owners to post pictures and stories about their experiences with their Cubes, and launched it by giving away several Cubes.

With this novel positioning in mind, Nissan put together a marketing mix that delivers the desired value proposition. Advertising for the Cube reinforces the positioning, with messages such as "Say hello to a Cube that's extremely well-rounded. Personalize it. Share it. Connect with it." Promotion for the Cube supported and extended its targeting and innovative positioning. To reach the Millennials and draw them into Nissan's showrooms, the company peppered its communications and product

Trigger Happy Photography

Exhibit 7.12 The Nissan Cube targets Millennials looking for an affordable car that lets them express their personality, but the car is positioned as a personal mobile device.

descriptions with terms such as *search engine*, *browse*, *storage capacity*, *add friends*, and *set preferences;* and avoided the usual ho-hum car advertising in favour of non-traditional media, such as iPhone games, computer wallpaper, text messaging, a Facebook page, and MP3 downloads. Even ads in traditional media were designed as "all-screen videos," ready for viewing on everything from TVs and computers to cellphone and movie-theatre screens.

Then there's the car itself. As the name suggests, the Cube looks sort of like—you guessed it—a cube, but not an ordinary one. Its wrap-around rear window helps it to stand out visually. With its peppy 4-cylinder, 122-horsepower engine, the fun-to-drive Cube gets a combined 8.1litres per 100 km. Although small, the Cube feels roomy inside, with

comfortable seats and a high ceiling that gives passengers, especially those in the back seat, the sense that they are in a living room, not a car. In all, with its eye-catching but sensible design, the Cube is "more studio loft rather than economy car," says an analyst.

You don't just drive a Cube—it becomes a part of the mobile, connected you. The top-of-the-line Cube Krom (pronounced *chrome*), one of four Cube models, offers a Bluetooth hands-free phone system, an upgraded audio system with six speakers and Rockford Fosgate subwoofer, an interface for an iPod, titanium trim accents, automatic temperature control, an interior illumination system with 20 lights, and 16-inch aluminum-alloy wheels. Add in the abundance of customizing accessories and Nissan hopes you've got everything a

young Millennial could want—a personalized, connected mobile device at an affordable price.

The Cube represents an innovative differentiation and positioning strategy in an otherwise me-too segment. Nissan thinks it has a winner, and many agree; in fact, *Automobile* magazine named the Cube its 2010 Design of the Year, calling the car "charming" and "funny-looking, but in an especially agreeable way."

Sources: Stuart Elliott, "With the Car Industry in Trouble, Nissan Rolls Out the Mobile Device," *New York Times*, April 6, 2009; Jeff Sabatini, "The Driver's Seat: Nissan's Compact: It's Fun Cubed," *Wall Street Journal*, March 28, 2009, p. W7; Jennifer Wells, "An Out-of-Box Campaign for a Square-Boned Newcomer," *Globe and Mail*, March 20, 2009, p. B5; Dan Neil, "Nissan's Cube is Coolness in a Box," *Los Angeles Times*, March 6, 2009, p. 1; "Nissan North America, Inc.," *Science Letter*, February 24, 2009, p. 3836; Robert Cumberford, "2010 Design of the Year: 2010 Nissan Cube," *Automobile* magazine, November 2009; www.nissan.ca and www.cubecommunity.ca, accessed May 2010.

Sellers offering "only the best" can be found in every product and service category, from hotels, restaurants, food, and fashion to cars and household appliances. Consumers are sometimes surprised, even delighted, when a new competitor enters a category with an unusually high-priced brand. Starbucks coffee entered as a very expensive brand in a largely commodity category. When Apple premiered its iPhone, it offered higher-quality features than a traditional cellphone with a hefty price tag to match, and Häagen-Dazs entered the market as a premium ice cream brand at a price never before charged.

In general, companies should be on the lookout for opportunities to introduce a more-for-more brand in any underdeveloped product or service category. Yet more-for-more brands can be vulnerable. They often invite imitators who claim the same quality

FIGURE 7.4 Possible Value Propositions

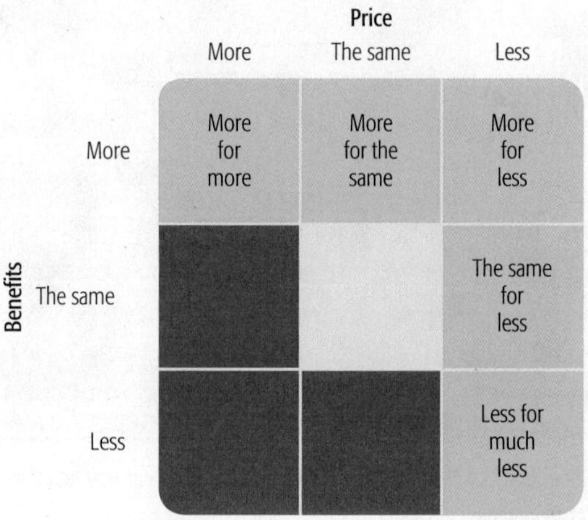

but at a lower price. For example, Starbucks now faces "gourmet" coffee competition from McDonald's McCafé. Also, luxury goods that sell well during good times may be at risk during economic downturns when buyers become more cautious in their spending.

MORE FOR THE SAME Companies can attack a competitor's more-for-more positioning by introducing a brand offering comparable quality but at a lower price. For example, Toyota introduced its Lexus line with a "more-for-the-same" value proposition versus Mercedes and BMW. Its first ad headline read "Perhaps the first time in history that trading a $72 000 car for a $36 000 car could be considered trading up." It communicated the high quality of its new Lexus through rave reviews in car magazines and through a widely distributed videotape showing side-by-side comparisons of Lexus and Mercedes automobiles. It published surveys showing that Lexus dealers were providing customers with better sales and service experiences than were Mercedes dealerships. Many Mercedes owners switched to Lexus, and the Lexus repurchase rate has been 60 percent, twice the industry average.

THE SAME FOR LESS Offering "the same for less" can be a powerful value proposition—everyone likes a good deal. Discount stores such as Walmart and "category killers" such as Best Buy, PetSmart, and Payless Shoes use this positioning. They don't claim to offer different or better products. Instead, they offer many of the same brands as department stores and specialty stores but at deep discounts based on superior purchasing power and lower-cost operations. Other companies develop imitative but lower-priced brands in an effort to lure customers away from the market leader. For example, drug stores offer lower priced versions of the "fancy" soaps and creams sold at high end specialty bath shops.

LESS FOR MUCH LESS A market almost always exists for products that offer less and therefore cost less. Few people need, want, or can afford "the very best" in everything they buy. In many cases, consumers will gladly settle for less than optimal performance or give up some of the bells and whistles in exchange for a lower price. For example, many travellers seeking lodgings prefer not to pay for what they consider unnecessary extras, such as a pool, attached restaurant, or mints on the pillow. Hotel chains such as Ramada Limited suspend some of these amenities and charge less accordingly.

"Less-for-much-less" positioning involves meeting consumers' lower performance or quality requirements at a much lower price. For example, Giant Tiger, Winners, and the many "dollar stores" offer more affordable goods at very low prices.

MORE FOR LESS Of course, the winning value proposition would be to offer "more for less." Many companies claim to do this. And, in the short run, some companies can actually achieve such lofty positions. For example, when it first opened for business, Home Depot had arguably the best product selection, the best service, *and* the lowest prices compared with local hardware stores and other home improvement chains, but today Home Depot is positioned more on selection than on price.

Yet in the long run, companies will find it very difficult to sustain such best-of-both positioning. Offering more usually costs more, making it difficult to deliver on the "for-less" promise. Companies that try to deliver both may lose out to more focused competitors. For example, facing determined competition from Canadian Tire and RONA stores, Home Depot must now decide whether it wants to compete primarily on superior service or on lower prices.

HÄAGEN-DAZS® is a registered trademark of General Mills, Inc. and is used with permission.

Before we knew it we were having Häagen-Dazs.

Fall deeply in Häagen-Dazs.

Exhibit 7.13 **More-for-more positioning:** Everything about Häagen-Dazs ice cream, from its price and packaging to its advertising, suggests luxury. Some marketers refer to this positioning as "*much* more for much more."

All said, each brand must adopt a positioning strategy designed to serve the needs and wants of its target markets. "More for more" will draw one target market, "less for much less" will draw another, and so on. Thus, in any market, there is usually room for many different companies, each successfully occupying different positions. The important thing is that each company must develop its own winning positioning strategy, one that makes it special to its target market.

Developing a Positioning Statement   Company and brand positioning should be summed up in a **positioning statement**. The statement should follow the form: To (target segment and need) our (brand) is (concept) that (point of difference).[26] For example, "To busy, mobile professionals who need to always be in the loop, BlackBerry is a wireless connectivity solution that gives you an easier, more reliable way to stay connected to data, people, and resources while on the go."

Note that the positioning first states the product's membership in a category (wireless connectivity solution) and then shows its point of difference from other members of the category (easier, more reliable connections to data, people, and resources). Placing a brand in a specific category suggests similarities that it might share with other products in the category. But the case for the brand's superiority is made on its points of difference.

Positioning statement
A statement that summarizes company or brand positioning—it takes this form: To (target segment and need) our (brand) is (concept) that (point of difference).

Sometimes marketers put a brand in a surprisingly different category before indicating the points of difference. For example, Delissio frozen pizza is positioned in the delivered pizza category. Advertising for Delissio features the tagline "It's not delivery. It's Delissio!" and television commercials feature characters trying to trick each other into believing that they ordered takeout pizza when they really made Delissio at home.

Communicating and Delivering the Chosen Position

Once it has chosen a position, the company must take strong steps to deliver and communicate the desired position to target consumers. All the company's marketing-mix efforts must support the positioning strategy.

Positioning the company calls for concrete action, not just talk. If the company decides to build a position on better quality and service, it must first *deliver* that position. Designing the marketing mix—product, price, place, and promotion—involves working out the tactical details of the positioning strategy. Thus, a firm that seizes on a more-for-more position knows that it must produce high-quality products, charge a high price, distribute through high-quality dealers, and advertise in high-quality media. It must hire and train more service people, find retailers who have a good reputation for service, and develop sales and advertising

Courtesy of Nestle

Pizza this delicious definitely calls for a replay.

DELISSIO   DELISSIO   DELISSIO   DELISSIO
RISING CRUST   Harvest Wheat   Express

It's not delivery. It's Delissio.

Exhibit 7.14 Positioning by points of difference: Delissio positions its frozen pizza brand by suggesting it belongs in a different category altogether—home-delivered pizza.

messages that broadcast its superior service. This is the only way to build a consistent and believable more-for-more position.

Companies often find it easier to come up with a good positioning strategy than to implement it. Establishing a position or changing one usually takes a long time. In contrast, positions that have taken years to build can quickly be lost. Once a company has built the desired position, it must take care to maintain the position through consistent performance and communication. It must closely monitor and adapt the position over time to match changes in consumer needs and competitors' strategies. However, the company should avoid abrupt changes that might confuse consumers. Instead, a product's position should evolve gradually as it adapts to the ever-changing marketing environment.

Road Warriors

It has always been one of WestJet's most visible inflight distinctions from the beginning: the absence of a curtain separating business class from economy. When employed by most other successful commercial airlines, the curtain draws a physical line between those who paid a premium and those who did not—a metaphor for the division of social classes. In WestJet's world, the curtain was just never on-brand, and the profit margins associated with having an actual business class was in conflict with WestJet's cost-saving business model. So why, in 2013, would Canada's preferred airline, where WestJetters care and everybody loves everybody, decide to introduce a "class" system of seating?

It is important to first distinguish between the perception of business class in other airlines, and WestJet's "Plus" seating, which is merely a new product targeted at a specific segment. As Marshall Wilmot, vice-president of product and distribution, explains, "We're not going after the super-elite business traveller, principally because we want to focus on a market that fits well with our network and stays true to the WestJet brand—this is not about anyone on the plane getting special treatment."

Since its inception in 1996, WestJet has been a value airline serving a wide variety of travellers, with a focus largely on the leisure market. That emphasis evolved as the airline began serving vacation destinations in the United States before ultimately launching WestJet Vacations in 2006. Price-sensitive business travellers were always more than happy to climb aboard and take advantage of WestJet's value proposition, but the airline saw an opportunity to develop that market further.

"We took a look at the key drivers to that segment," explains Wilmot. The introduction of WestJet Rewards, a loyalty program, along with the WestJet RBC MasterCard, were key steps in attracting the business segment. "Convenience, flexibility, and comfort were other important drivers." To provide additional comfort, WestJet reconfigured its entire fleet of 737s to create extra legroom for 18 seats. "These are road warriors," Wilmot says. "They're on the road all the time, and a little bit of extra legroom added value."

The cost of the legroom makeover made for an interesting business decision for West-Jet. "It had to make sense from an ROI perspective." In order to recover some of the associated costs while adding value, the extra legroom seats were branded as WestJet's "Plus" seating, available to any guest, road warrior or not.

QUESTIONS

1. Describe the psychographic and behavioural traits of the WestJet "road warrior" segment.
2. What segment was WestJet targeting almost exclusively prior to going after business travellers?
3. Is WestJet attempting to reposition itself in light of this deliberate pursuit of a different segment?

REVIEWING THE CONCEPTS

1. Define the major steps in designing a customer-driven marketing strategy: market segmentation, targeting, differentiation, and positioning.

Customer-driven marketing strategy begins with selecting which customers to serve and with deciding on a value proposition that best serves the targeted customers. It consists of four steps. *Market segmentation* is the act of dividing a market into distinct segments of buyers with different needs, characteristics, or behaviours who might require separate products or marketing mixes. Once the groups have been identified, *market targeting* evaluates each market segment's attractiveness and selects one or more segments to serve. Market targeting consists of designing strategies to build the *right relationships* with the *right customers*. *Differentiation* involves actually differentiating the market offering to create superior customer value. *Positioning* consists of positioning the market offering in the minds of target customers.

2. List and discuss the major bases for segmenting consumer and business markets.

There is no single way to segment a market. Therefore, the marketer tries different variables to see which give the best segmentation opportunities. For consumer marketing, the major segmentation variables are geographic, demographic, psychographic, and behavioural. In *geographic segmentation*, the market is divided into different geographical units, such as nations, regions, states, counties, cities, or neighbourhoods. In *demographic segmentation*, the market is divided into groups based on demographic variables, including age, gender, family size, family life cycle, income, occupation, education, religion, race, generation, and nationality. In *psychographic* segmentation, the market is divided into different groups based on social class, lifestyle, or personality characteristics. In *behavioural segmentation*, the market is divided into groups based on consumers' knowledge, attitudes, uses, or responses to a product. Business marketers use many of the same variables to segment their markets. But business markets also can be segmented by business consumer *demographics* (industry, company size), *operating characteristics*, *purchasing approaches*, *situational factors*, and *personal characteristics*. The effectiveness of segmentation analysis depends on finding segments that are *measurable*, *accessible*, *substantial*, *differentiable*, and *actionable*.

3. Explain how companies identify attractive market segments and choose a market-targeting strategy.

To target the best market segments, the company first evaluates each segment's size and growth characteristics, structural attractiveness, and compatibility with company objectives and resources. It then chooses one of four market-targeting strategies—ranging from very broad to very narrow targeting. The seller can ignore segment differences and target broadly by using *undifferentiated (or mass) marketing*. This method involves mass producing, mass distributing, and mass promoting about the same product in about the same way to all consumers. Or the seller can adopt *differentiated marketing*—developing different market offers for several segments. *Concentrated marketing (or niche marketing)* involves focusing on only one or a few market segments. Finally, *micromarketing* is the practice of tailoring products and marketing programs to suit the tastes of specific individuals and locations. *Local marketing* refers to customizing marketing offers to a small group of people living in the same city, or neighbourhood, or who shop at the same store, and *individual marketing*, better known as *mass customization*, is the practice of customizing a marketing offer to an individual.

4. Discuss how companies differentiate and position their products for maximum competitive advantage.

Once a company has decided which segments to enter, it must decide on its *differentiation and positioning strategy*. The differentiation and positioning task consists of three steps: identifying a set of possible differentiations that create competitive advantage, choosing advantages upon which to build a position, and selecting an overall positioning strategy. The brand's full positioning is called its *value proposition*—the full mix of benefits upon which the brand is positioned. In general, companies can choose from one of five winning value propositions upon which to position their products: more for more, more for the same, the same for less, less for much less, or more for less. Company and brand positioning are summarized in positioning statements that state the target segment and need, positioning concept, and specific points of difference. The company must then effectively communicate and deliver the chosen position to the market.

KEY TERMS

Age and life-cycle segmentation 242
Behavioural segmentation 245
Benefit segmentation 245
Competitive advantage 260
Concentrated (niche) marketing 253
Demographic segmentation 242
Differentiated (segmented) marketing 252
Differentiation 240
Gender segmentation 243

Geographic segmentation 240
Household income (HHI) segmentation 244
Individual marketing (mass customization) 254
Intermarket segmentation 250
Local marketing 254
Micromarketing 253
Occasion segmentation 245
Positioning 240

Positioning statement 266
Product position 258
Psychographic segmentation 245
Segmentation 240
Target market 251
Targeting 240
Undifferentiated (mass) marketing 252
Value proposition 262

TALK ABOUT MARKETING

1. Think of a product or a brand that you're familiar with that caters to a niche market. Describe the shared characteristics of consumers in that market, in terms of the four main bases of segmentation: geography, demographics, psychographics, and behaviour.

2. Geography, in terms of a basis of market segmentation, can refer to a country, region of a country, or region that is defined by its climate or its terrain, such as coastal areas, the far north, the prairies, or the Rockies. Describe three distinct geographic market segments in Canada. Then think of a product that could be successfully marketed to each of those segments but might not be as successful in another geographic market segment.

3. The George Foreman Grill is a compact cooking appliance with a double-sided cooking surface that is angled to allow fat to drip off the food and out of the grill. Describe a likely target market for this product in terms of its geographic, demographic, psychographic,

and behavioural characteristics. How does this target market rate with respect to size, growth, and structural attractiveness?

4. Find out what is the bestselling beer in Quebec and one other province. Describe each province as a market segment. Why do you think those particular beers have the most appeal in those provinces?

5. Think of an example of a hotel chain that falls into each of the five general value propositions. What does each hotel you selected do on the benefits dimension to offer more, the same, or less than competitors?

6. When A&W celebrated its fiftieth anniversary, it invited customers to write in about their favourite memories. Many customers, most of them Baby Boomers, reminisced about carhop service. Do you think that A&W should target Baby Boomers by reinstating carhops?

THINK LIKE A MARKETING MANAGER

A new trend in the market is men's group vacations, or, as they call them in Hollywood (in movies such as *Sideways*), "mancations." This is an example of creating a new market segment by virtue of behaviour with the product, something marketers refer to as behavioural segmentation. The size of this market indicates that it is worthwhile for marketers to target: According to one online survey, 34 percent of American male respondents said they had taken at least one trip with guy friends in the past year.

QUESTIONS

1. Imagine you are the marketing director at a hotel in Banff. What services could you offer that would appeal to this market segment? What forms of marketing communications would you use to reach this target market?

2. What tourist destinations in Canada, specifically, would appeal to this market? (For example, could Canada's Wonderland appeal to this group effectively?)

3. There are cruises that cater to families, cruises that cater to singles, and cruises that cater to gays and lesbians. Do you think it would be worthwhile for a cruise line to create a special cruise to cater to the mancationer market segment? How would you go about evaluating the potential value? Do you consider this a niche market? What ports of call would such a cruise visit, and what sorts of activities could the cruise company offer?

4. Choose a city or town in Canada that is near one of the tourist destinations you listed in #2 above. What local marketing could be done to attract mancationers?

MARKETING ETHICS

A few years ago Anheuser-Busch (A-B) launched the Bud Light "Fan Can," a promotion that included 27 different colour combinations of its cans in college team colours. For example, students at Louisiana State University could purchase purple-and-gold cans of Bud Light. Anheuser-Busch timed the campaign, called "Team Pride," to coincide with students returning to campus and with the kick-off of the football season. Several schools, such as Wisconsin, Michigan, Iowa State, University of Colorado, and others, objected strenuously. As a result, A-B halted the program in those markets. The promotion also caught the attention of the Federal Trade Commission (FTC). Both the FTC and college officials are concerned about the high rate of underage and binge drinking on college campuses. Some school officials also were concerned about trademark infringements, and about the appearance that they support Budweiser's activities. As criticism brewed around the country, A-B released a statement claiming that

it did not mean to encourage underage drinking—it just wanted to create more fun for sports fans. Although the company halted the promotion in areas where college officials objected, controversy surrounding the promotion appeared in American news media.

QUESTIONS

1. What type of market-targeting strategy was Anheuser-Busch using with the Team Pride promotion?

2. In the United States, students typically attend college from the ages of 18–22, and the legal drinking age is 21 in all states. That means most students reach legal drinking age only during their last year at school. With that in mind, do you think the Team Pride promotion—or any other campus-based promotion by a beer marketer—is ethical? Would a similar promotion be ethical in Canada, in your opinion?

MARKETING TECHNOLOGY

Today's micromarketing technology enables marketers to mass customize products ranging from clothing, skin-care products, and vitamin supplements to furniture, automobiles, and even postage stamps. And through behavioural targeting technologies, marketing communications also can be customized, based on web surfing behaviour and television viewership, often without consumers being aware that their behaviour is being tracked.

QUESTIONS

1. At NikeID.com, consumers can design their own shoe. Go through the process on the website—design your

own shoe and then price it. Do you feel the price is appropriate for the value you received from being able to customize your shoe? Find two other websites that allow consumers to similarly customize a product.

2. Online advertising technology has the ability to allow marketers to deliver Internet ads to individuals based on their Internet behaviour, for example, search terms they typed into a search engine, or how frequently they visit a particular website. As a marketer, how might you use this information to target a particular market?

MARKETING BY THE NUMBERS

Tesla Motors is a publicly traded company based in California that produces fully electric sports cars. To date, Tesla has delivered almost 10 000 electric vehicles to customers in 31 countries. The Tesla Roadster entered production in 2008 and released the Tesla Model S in 2012. In April, 2013 the company announced that sales of its Model S vehicle exceeded the target of 4500 as sales to that date had exceeded 4750 units. The next model, the Tesla Model X, is scheduled to begin deliveries in 2014.The company needs to estimate the market potential for the Tesla Model X before doing a full scale market launch in Canada.

QUESTIONS

1. Discuss variables Tesla should consider when estimating the potential number of buyers for the Tesla X.

2. Using the chain ratio method described in Appendix 3, Marketing by the Numbers, estimate the market potential for the Tesla X. Search the Internet for reasonable numbers to represent the factors you identified in the previous question. Assume each buyer will purchase only one automobile and that the average purchase price is $100 000.

SCOUTS CANADA: REPOSITIONING THE BRAND

Scouts Canada, a venerable volunteer-led organization known for its legendary merit badges, was born in Canada in 1907. A few years ago, it began to think that its image was a little worn since it was experiencing a precipitous decline in membership and volunteer support. More recently, it has been plagued by scandal, as a number of former Scout leaders were charged with sexual abuse. Not surprisingly, Scouts Canada needed to think about how to grow its membership and reposition itself in the minds of its key stakeholders: parents, volunteers, children, and donors. The organization had to come up with a way to reposition itself as modern, ethical, and relevant. Embarking on a repositioning program is always risky, because the organization doesn't want to make changes so drastic as to alienate its current membership—that is, its core customers.

Membership in Scouts Canada had been declining for many years, ever since its peak in the 1960s, at around 320 000. It went down by 18 percent between 1996 and 2000 alone. Then, in late 2008, it bottomed out at about 97 000 members. Numbers started to grow in 2009 and have grown steadily since then. Most members join when they are very young, but many lose interest after a few years. More and more, however, Scouts are becoming more committed and are staying involved with the organization into adulthood. Programs have been updated, and Scouts Canada has made it easier to volunteer. The organization has also worked hard to get more young people involved in leadership positions. To help modernize the Scouts, Joe Fresh was hired to redesign their uniforms. But repositioning doesn't mean everything needs to change—Scouts Canada also focused on reiterating its original environmentally oriented values. Steve Kent, chief commissioner of Scouts Canada, notes, "We were the original environmentalist . . . long before it was cool or trendy to go green, Scouts were planting trees and engaged in other environmental projects."

For some members, the most valuable benefit is the friends they make through Scouts. For others, it is the self-esteem they gain. "I was one of those kids who was shy and wouldn't go up to another kid and start a conversation, but now I'm comfortable talking to people I don't know," says one Calgary member.

To build its membership and reposition its image, Scouts Canada took a strategic marketing approach. As a recent annual report noted, "It began with a vision. It was nurtured with passion. It will succeed through action."

Scouts Canada was very focused in its efforts, developing a new strategic plan around a new positioning strategy that mixed its traditional values with new insights to take it forward during the period 2010 to 2016. Its goals are to remain relevant to Canadian society and ensure that its programs are affordable and attractive to both youth and adult volunteers. It began by clearly defining what the organization was all about—the key values at the heart of the new positioning: leadership, healthy active living, and a clean environment. The values provided a foundation for the new promise of "adventures to come," of scouting being a "healthier way to live," and the positive impact that youth can have on society in general and Canada in particular.

Scouts Canada knew that the new values had to be lived, so it undertook an internal marketing campaign. This included writing a new manual designed to ensure that the new brand positioning would be used consistently by all of its management team. The manual not only outlines Scouts Canada's new standards for the brand, but it also stresses that a brand is more than a name and a logo—it's all the attributes that give meaning to that name. The new brand positioning focuses on communicating scouting as a positive experience and on the fact that Scouts Canada is "an organization committed to providing children with new adventures and experiences—all of which help them develop into capable and confident individuals, better prepared for success in the world."

As a result of its efforts, Scouts Canada has a new logo and motto in both French and English. The English version proclaims, "It starts with Scouts!" The French translation is "Tout commence avec les Scouts." It launched a new print advertising campaign to reinforce the new brand positioning externally. Scouts Canada wants to convey the idea that scouting is all about great adventures and first-time discoveries. In an age when many children are obese and unfit, it also wants to stress the benefits children receive from exploring the outdoors. The campaign also took a shot at more passive indoor activities: one poster shows a tent in the middle of a field at night, with mountains in the background, along with copy that reads, "Try finding this on a search engine." Another poster depicts a sunlit forest accompanied by orders to parents to "Show them where Discovery Channel got its name."

Initial results from the new positioning strategy have been encouraging. By 2010, membership had increased in every province, and almost 600 scouting groups had increased their membership by more than 15 percent.

Sources: Scouts Canada, "Strategic Directions 2006–2016—Creating the Environment for Growth," www.scouts.ca/media/documents/p15FEB06.pdf, accessed September 2010; Matt Semansky, "Scouts Canada Begins 'Outdoors' Campaign," *Marketing Magazine*, September 3, 2010; Scouts Canada Style Guide, August 19, 2010, www.scouts.ca/dnn/LinkClick.asp x?fileticket=TC1MvHv0MJs%3d&tabid=133&mid=480; Scouts Canada, 2009–10%20 Annual%20 report%20Eng.pdf, accessed January 2011; "Recruitment and Retention Rates Rising at Scouts Canada," *CTV News*, March 25, 2011, www.ctv.ca/CTVNews/Canada/20111008/scouts-canada-membershipnumbers-retention-111008/, accessed April 2012.

QUESTIONS FOR DISCUSSION

1. Using the full spectrum of segmentation variables, describe how Scouts Canada could segment its marketplace.

2. What changed first: the potential Scouts member or the Scouts experience? Explain your response by discussing the principles of market targeting.

3. Now that you've learned what steps Scouts Canada took to reposition its brand, what steps would you take to reinforce that positioning on an ongoing basis?

4. Do you think Scouts Canada will ever reach the membership levels of the 1960s? Why or why not?

 MyMarketingLab is an online homework and tutorial system that puts you in control of your own learning with study and practice tools directly correlated to this chapter's content.

Courtesy of Nissan

AFTER STUDYING THIS CHAPTER, YOU SHOULD BE ABLE TO

1 define *product* and describe and classify different types of product offerings

2 list and define the steps in the new-product development process and the major considerations in managing this process, and explain why new products fail

3 describe the stages of the product life cycle and how marketing strategies change during the product's life cycle

4 describe the decisions companies make regarding their individual products and services, product lines, and product mixes

5 identify the four characteristics that affect the marketing of services and the additional marketing considerations that services require

Developing and Managing Products and Services

Now that you've had a good look at customer-driven marketing strategy, we'll take a deeper look at the marketing mix—the tactical tools that marketers use to implement their strategies and deliver superior customer value. In this chapter, we'll study how a product is defined, how companies develop new products, and how marketers manage products over time. You'll see that every product passes through several life-cycle stages and that each stage poses new challenges requiring different marketing strategies and tactics. We'll also consider the special challenges of marketing services—which are actually a type of product. But first let's look at the story of a how a revolutionary new product was recently brought to market.

BRINGING A NEW PRODUCT TO MARKET: THE STORY OF THE NISSAN LEAF

In August 2009, the Nissan Motor Company unveiled the Nissan LEAF, the world's first affordable, zero-emission car powered by a lithium-ion battery. Three years later the Nissan LEAF became the best-selling electric vehicle of all time. How did this revolutionary new car become so successful so quickly? The secret lies in the years of careful planning that went into bringing this new product to market. "There are many challenges when launching a ground-breaking product like the Nissan LEAF and from a marketing perspective, the top priority is to ensure that consumers understand what the product offers," said Judy Wheeler, director of marketing at Nissan Canada. "There are lots of misperceptions about electric vehicles, so one of our top priorities was to educate consumers that the Nissan LEAF is a real car. It seats five people, has lots of space, meets every safety standard, and is really fun to drive!"

Production of the Nissan LEAF began in October 2010 in Oppama, Japan, and that same year Nissan built a battery manufacturing plant in Smyrna, Tennessee, capable of producing 200 000 advanced-technology batteries annually. The plant is located adjacent to Nissan's existing vehicle assembly plant in Tennessee, which was retooled to accommodate production of the LEAF.

The name LEAF makes a significant statement about the car itself. Just as leaves purify the air in nature, so the Nissan LEAF purifies mobility by taking emissions out of the driving experience. And because there's no traditional engine, the LEAF is completely quiet. It's also ultra-high tech and includes an IT system complete with an on-board remote-controlled timer that can be programmed to recharge batteries. The instrument panel provides the driver with regular updates on range and driving efficiency, and using a system called CARWINGS the driver can communicate with the car via a smartphone and the Nissan LEAF app, which allows users to check the state of the battery charge, begin charging, check when the battery charge is complete, see estimated driving range, and turn the climate control system on or off. Nissan views the IT system as a partner for the driver and an enhancement for the passengers. It's also an important aspect of the new product's positioning.

The LEAF is positioned in the Canadian market as the first mass-market, affordable fully electric car that provides environmentally conscious drivers with a zero-emission option for real environmental impact; that provides 90 percent of Canadians with the range needed for daily commutes; and at the same time has plenty of room, comfort, and style and an uncompromising driving experience. The environmentally friendly theme is communicated through the car's name, the "Blue Ocean" body colour of the introductory model, and the interior blue dashboard highlights and instrument illumination.

While the product developers in Japan worked on producing the Nissan LEAF, the marketing team at Nissan Canada focused on preparing the Canadian market for its first fully electric car. The first step was to establish relationships with energy producers like Hydro-Québec and governments such as the City of Toronto and the Government of Manitoba so that all could work together to plan for the necessary charging infrastructure and pave the way for the arrival of electric vehicles on Canada's streets.

Then there was the task of getting Nissan dealers ready to sell and service the LEAF. The project began with the certification of 27 selected retailers located in regions where Nissan had established partnerships with local governments. In order to be certified these dealers had to pass a rigorous training process and complete modifications to their sales and service departments. Special lifts and pallets to handle the battery along with EV-skilled technicians are required to service the car.

One of the most important marketing programs for the LEAF in Canada is the online reservation system. Electric cars are not for everyone, they're just for most people, but until charging systems are as common as gas stations, consumers who want a Nissan LEAF must live in the vicinity of a certified dealer, and in a municipality whose government and utilities are making preparations for electric vehicles. Interested prospective customers must register online at Nissan.ca/leaf, and answer a few basic questions to make sure they are eligible to own a LEAF. Once qualified, these customers are given a "reservation" to purchase the car. Through model year 2012, Nissan prepared to release around 600 Nissan LEAFs on the Canadian market through several waves of reservations.

All these market preparations were done months, even years, before the first LEAF rolled into Canada for a brief visit in December 2009. The first market-ready LEAF was viewed at the Montreal Auto Show in January 2011. That April, at the Green Living Show in Toronto, Canadians were allowed to test drive the car for the first time. Throughout the fall of 2011 Nissan Canada orchestrated a cross-Canada tour, allowing Canadians to test drive and learn more about the LEAF at certified dealer locations. The Drive Electric Tour began in Montreal and ended in Vancouver in late October, stopping at all 27 LEAF certified dealers across the country for one or two days each.

The first Canadian sales happened in the summer of 2011, when PowerStream, an electricity distribution company in Ontario, purchased two of the vehicles for its fleet. Nissan Canada and PowerStream demonstrated the Nissan "LEAF to Home" charging system for the first time in Canada at the Georgian College Auto Show in Barrie (see photo). Two months later the first Canadian consumer took possession of a LEAF. Ricardo Borba of Ottawa, a 44-year-old electric engineer and software developer with IBM, was the first person in Canada to place a Nissan LEAF order, and said his LEAF would be the family's primary car. "My family and I were starting to look for a new car last year when the Deepwater Horizon oil spill occurred and prompted us to think about alternatives to gas-powered vehicles," said Borba.

The promotions didn't end with the first sales, however. Nissan Canada launched the Nissan LEAF consumer website in April 2010 and promoted it with a 60-second commercial that aired in movie theatres across Canada. A year later the Canadian LEAF Facebook page opened with a promotion that saw 40 lucky fans invited to a ride and drive event held at Nissan Canada's head office in Mississauga, Ontario. Around the same time, the Nissan LEAF Twitter account (@NissanLEAF_CAN) began to share up-to-date news and information on all things related to the Nissan LEAF's arrival in Canada. A dedicated moderator from Nissan was assigned to manage the Facebook and Twitter accounts and to engage in conversation with and answer questions from fans across Canada.

In 2012 Nissan Canada sponsored the second annual National Tree Day and awarded a 2012 Nissan LEAF SL as the grand prize in a contest that asked Canadians to "Get Treemotional" by submitting an image of their favourite tree and explaining what makes that tree special. The company participated in National Tree Day events in Ottawa as well as in tree planting events across the country by offering Nissan LEAF test drives. And that fall at the Toronto International Film Festival (TIFF) attendees were offered free taxi rides in two Nissan LEAF taxis based in the Entertainment District. The Nissan LEAF taxis were driven by professional drivers, and winners of free rides were chosen at random from tweets sent with the hashtag #LEAFTAXI.

Perhaps the largest social media promotion was 2012's "The Big Turn On," Nissan's ambitious online campaign designed to get 1 million people worldwide "turned on" to electric vehicles. The initial plan was to reach the 1 million mark in 100 days, but the campaign so captured the imagination of the public that the milestone was reached 15 days ahead of schedule. Many promotional events were held in Europe in conjunction with "The Big Turn On," including setting a new Guinness World Record with the Nissan LEAF for the fastest time over a distance of one mile in reverse.

Not only do consumers worldwide seem to be loving their LEAFs, but the car has won numerous awards and accolades. It was named 2011 European Car of the Year and World Car of the Year. Also in 2011, the European New Car Assessment Programme (Euro NCAP) awarded the LEAF the highest level of car safety following its performance in the independent organization's stringent crash tests. Similarly in the United States, the LEAF earned a five-star overall vehicle rating for safety as part of the National Highway Traffic Safety Administration's New Car Assessment Program (NCAP)—the first electric vehicle to earn this distinction from the program. It was also awarded a "Top Safety Pick" rating from the Insurance Institute for Highway Safety in the United States. In Canada, the LEAF was recognized as the most fuel-efficient vehicle in the mid-size class for 2012 by the Government of Canada's ecoENERGY for Vehicles Awards. All of this allows marketers to add a new element to the car's positioning: Not only is the LEAF the most innovative car on the planet, it is also one of the safest.[1]*

*All information provided by Nissan Canada, and available at media.nissan.ca/leaf

AS THE NISSAN LEAF story suggests, companies that excel at developing and managing new products reap big rewards. Product is the first "*P*" of marketing, and is usually the first and most basic marketing consideration. It's also the subject of this chapter. We'll start with a seemingly simple question: What is a product? As it turns out, however, the answer is not so simple.

What Is a Product? LO1

Product

Anything that can be offered to a market for attention, acquisition, use, or consumption that might satisfy a want or need.

We define a **product** as anything that can be offered to a market for attention, acquisition, use, or consumption that might satisfy a want or need. Products include more than just tangible objects, such as cars, computers, or cellphones. Broadly defined, "products" also include services, events, persons, places, organizations, ideas, or mixes of these. Throughout this text, we use the term *product* broadly to include any or all of these entities—so an Apple iPad, a Toyota Camry, and a box of Timbits are products; but so are Air Canada flights and BMO investments.

Because of their importance in the world economy, we give special attention to services. **Services** are a form of product that consists of activities, benefits, or satisfactions offered for sale that are essentially intangible and do not result in the ownership of anything, for example, a day at an amusement park or a night in a hotel. We will look at services more closely later in this chapter.

Service

An activity, benefit, or satisfaction offered for sale that is essentially intangible and does not result in the ownership of anything.

Products, Services, and Experiences

Product is a key element in the overall *market offering*. Marketing-mix planning begins with building an offering that brings value to target customers. This offering becomes the basis upon which the company builds profitable customer relationships.

A company's market offering often includes both tangible goods and services. At one extreme, the offer may consist of a *pure tangible good*, such as soap, toothpaste, or salt—no services accompany the product. At the other extreme are *pure services*, for which the offer consists primarily of a service. Examples include a checkup at your dentist or an Air Canada flight. Between these two extremes, however, many goods-and-services combinations are possible.

Today, as products and services become more commoditized, many companies are moving to a new level in creating value for their customers. To differentiate their offers, beyond simply making products and delivering services, they are creating and managing customer *experiences* with their brands or their company.

Experiences have always been an important part of marketing for some companies. Disney has long manufactured dreams and memories through its movies and theme parks. Today, however, all kinds of firms are recasting their traditional goods and services to create experiences.

Organizations, Persons, Places, and Ideas

In addition to tangible products and services, marketers have broadened the concept of a product to include other market offerings—organizations, persons, places, and ideas. Organization marketing consists of activities undertaken to create, maintain, or change the attitudes and behaviour of customers and the general public toward an organization. Both profit and not-for-profit organizations practise organization marketing.

People can also be thought of as products. Person marketing consists of activities undertaken to create, maintain, or change attitudes or behaviour toward particular people.

People ranging from politicians, entertainers, and sports figures to professionals such as real-estate agents, lawyers, and architects use person marketing to build their reputations.

Place marketing involves activities undertaken to create, maintain, or change attitudes or behaviour toward particular places. Cities and countries compete to attract tourists, new residents, conventions, and company offices and factories. For example, Canada is marketed around the world by the Canadian Tourism Commission (CTC), a federal Crown corporation. And many foreign countries are marketed to Canadians as travel destinations, for example the government of China operates the China National Tourist Office (CNTO), with 15 overseas offices, including one in Toronto, for the purpose of promoting travel to China, which has been booming since the Beijing Olympics.

Ideas can also be marketed. For example, Molson regularly runs ads warning of the dangers of drunk driving, and various Canadian health services promote the idea of getting a flu shot when flu season rolls around. In one sense, all marketing is the marketing of an idea, whether it is the general idea of brushing your teeth, or the specific idea that Crest toothpastes create "healthy, beautiful smiles for life." So we see that the line between hard products and pure services is not clear cut, but rather is a continuum, and today's marketing managers think about products and services in terms of levels.

Exhibit 8.1 **Marketing a place as a product:** The Canadian Tourism Commission develops and pays for advertising campaigns in Europe and the U.S. that promote Canada as a tourism destination.

Levels of Products and Services

Product marketers need to think about the product they manage as consisting of three levels (see Figure 8.1). Each level adds more customer value. The most basic level is the *core customer value*, which addresses the question *"What is the buyer really buying?"* When designing products, marketers must first define the core problem-solving benefits or services that consumers seek. For example, the core product of all beauty products is the feeling of being beautiful, and the core product of all smartphones is constant connectivity.

At the second level, product marketers must turn the core benefit into an *actual product*—the physical device with all its features and associated brand name and packaging. Finally, marketers must consider the augmented product—the additional services and benefits that go with it. So, for example, if the core product of a smartphone is constant connectivity, and the actual product is an iPhone 5, then the augmented product is the iPhone 5 plus a calling plan and data plan.

Consumers see products as complex bundles of benefits that satisfy their needs. When developing products, marketers first must identify the *core customer value* that consumers seek from the product. They must then design the *actual* product and find ways to *augment* it to create this customer value and the most satisfying customer experience.

Product and Service Classifications

Products and services fall into two broad classes: consumer products and industrial products. **Consumer products** are purchased by consumers for their personal (i.e. non

FIGURE 8.1 Three Levels of Product: Core, Actual, and Augmented

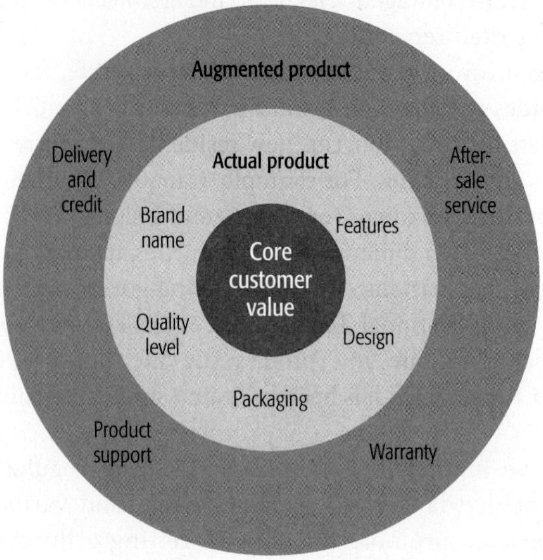

business) use. Marketers usually classify these products and services further based on how consumers go about buying them. Consumer products include *convenience products*, *shopping products*, *specialty products*, and *unsought products*. These products differ in the ways consumers buy them and, therefore, in how they are marketed (see Table 8.1).

Convenience products are consumer products and services that customers usually buy frequently, immediately, and with a minimum of comparison and buying effort. Convenience products are distributed through drug stores, grocery stores, and, of course, convenience stores, and include such things as laundry detergent, candy, magazines, and

Consumer products

Products purchased by consumers for their personal (i.e. non business) use.

TABLE 8.1 Marketing Considerations for Consumer Products

Marketing Considerations	Type of Consumer Product			
	Convenience	**Shopping**	**Specialty**	**Unsought**
Customer buying behaviour	Frequent purchase, little planning, little comparison or shopping effort, low customer involvement	Less frequent purchase, much planning and shopping effort, comparison of brands on price, quality, style	Strong brand preference and loyalty, special purchase effort, little comparison of brands, low price sensitivity	Little product awareness, knowledge (or, if aware, little or even negative interest)
Price	Low price	Higher price	High price	Varies
Distribution	Widespread distribution, convenient locations	Selective distribution in fewer outlets	Exclusive distribution in only one or a few outlets per market area	Varies
Promotion	Mass promotion by the producer	Advertising and personal selling by both producer and resellers	More carefully targeted promotion by both producer and resellers	Aggressive advertising and personal selling by producer and resellers
Examples	Toothpaste, magazines, laundry detergent	Major appliances, televisions, furniture, clothing	Luxury goods, such as Rolex watches or fine crystal	Life insurance, donations to Canadian Blood Services

fast food. Convenience products are usually low priced, and marketers place them in many locations to make them readily available when customers need them.

Shopping products are less frequently purchased consumer products and services that shoppers compare carefully on suitability, quality, price, and style. When buying shopping products and services, consumers spend much time and effort in gathering information and making comparisons. Examples include furniture, clothing, used cars, major appliances, and hotel and airline services. Shopping-products marketers usually distribute their products through fewer outlets but provide deeper sales support to help customers in their comparison efforts.

Specialty products are consumer products and services with unique characteristics or brand identification for which a significant group of buyers is willing to make a special purchase effort. Examples include specific brands of cars, high-priced photographic equipment, designer clothes, and the services of medical or legal specialists. A Lamborghini automobile, for example, is a specialty product because buyers are usually willing to travel great distances to buy one. Buyers normally do not compare specialty products. They invest only the time needed to reach dealers carrying the wanted products.

Unsought products are consumer products that the consumer either does not know about or knows about but does not normally think of buying. Most major new innovations are unsought until the consumer becomes aware of them through advertising. Classic examples of known but unsought products and services are life insurance, pre-planned funeral services, and blood donations. By their very nature, unsought products require a lot of advertising, personal selling, and other marketing efforts.

Marketing unsought products requires a different approach from typical product marketing. For example, consider the challenges of marketing funeral services and cemetery plots. Montreal's Mount Royal Commemorative Services has one of the nicer products to offer in that category: the cemetery is located on the mountain in the middle of the city, and designated a national historic site by the federal government. It has a certain celebrity cachet by virtue of the former prime ministers, hockey stars, and Titanic victims who rest there. But it's still not easy to promote this product to customers who would rather not think about it. When market research revealed the single biggest thing consumers want from the funeral industry is information, Mount Royal decided to focus their market efforts on educating Montrealers. They purchased easy-to-remember toll free phone numbers, then launched a radio advertising campaign with a "Did you know . . . ?" theme. At the end of each spot consumers were encouraged to call to request a no obligation information kit.[2]

Industrial Products **Industrial products** are those purchased for further processing or for use in conducting a business. The distinction between a consumer product and an industrial product is based on the *purpose* for which the product is bought. If a consumer buys a lawn mower for use around home, the lawn mower is a consumer product. If the same consumer buys the same lawn mower for use in a landscaping business, the lawn mower is an industrial product.

Convenience product
A consumer product that customers usually buy frequently, immediately, and with a minimum of comparison and buying effort.

Shopping product
Less frequently purchased consumer products and services that shoppers compare carefully on suitability, quality, price, and style

Specialty product
A consumer product with unique characteristics or brand identification for which a significant group of buyers is willing to make a special purchase effort.

Unsought product
A consumer product that the consumer either does not know about or knows about but does not normally think of buying.

Industrial product
A product bought by individuals and organizations for further processing or for use in conducting a business.

© Rubens Abboud / Alamy

Exhibit 8.2 **Unsought products:** Even with a beautiful product, like the Mount Royal Cemetery in Montreal, marketers have a difficult time promoting services people would rather not think about.

The three groups of industrial products and services include materials and parts, capital items, and supplies and services. *Materials and parts* include raw materials and manufactured materials and parts. Raw materials consist of farm products (wheat, cotton, livestock, fruits, vegetables) and natural products (fish, lumber, crude petroleum, iron ore). Manufactured materials and parts consist of component materials (iron, yarn, cement, wires) and component parts (small motors, tires, castings). Most manufactured materials and parts are sold directly to industrial users. Price and service are the major marketing factors; branding and advertising tend to be less important.

Capital items are industrial products that aid in the buyer's production or operations, including installations and accessory equipment. Installations consist of major purchases such as buildings (factories, offices) and fixed equipment (generators, drill presses, large computer systems, elevators). Accessory equipment includes portable factory equipment and tools (hand tools, lift trucks) and office equipment (computers, scanners, desks). They have a shorter life than installations and simply aid in the production process.

The final group of industrial products is *supplies and services*. Supplies include operating supplies (lubricants, coal, paper, pencils) and repair and maintenance items (paint, nails, brooms). Supplies are the convenience products of the industrial field because they are usually purchased with a minimum of effort or comparison. Business services include maintenance and repair services (window cleaning, computer repair) and business advisory services (legal, management consulting, advertising). Such services are usually supplied under contract.

New Product Development LO2

Now that we've learned that there's more to the first *P* of marketing, the product, than just hard goods, let's look at how new products are developed and managed.

Whether it's a new type of credit card from the Bank of Montreal or a new snowmobile from Bombardier, Canadians have a long history as inventors of new products. McIntosh apples, Pablum, frozen fish, and instant mashed potatoes are food products that all originated in Canada. Canadians are responsible for developing such sports and leisure activities as basketball, five-pin bowling, table hockey, and Trivial Pursuit. Many Canadian inventions spawned entire industries. Reginald Fessenden, born near Sherbrooke, Quebec, was known as the father of radio after he invented amplitude modulation (AM) radio and transmitted his first broadcast in 1900. In 1844, Nova Scotia's Charles Fenerty developed the product we now call newsprint, which is made from wood pulp. Modern air travel was made possible by another Canadian, Wallace Rupert Turnbull, who developed the variable-pitch propeller. Canadian marketers are leaders in technology, e-commerce, and especially telecommunications: from Bell Canada to Nortel to BlackBerry.

Let's look at the formal process for developing, managing, and marketing new products.

New Product Development Strategy

New-product development
The development of original products, product improvements, product modifications, and new brands through the firm's own product-development efforts.

A firm can obtain new products in two ways. One is through *acquisition*—by buying a whole company, a patent, or a license to produce someone else's product. The other is through the firm's own **new-product development** efforts. By *new products*, we mean original products, product improvements, product modifications, and new brands that the firm develops through its own research-and-development (R&D) efforts.

New products may also be improvements to existing products, like the new waterproof and washable keyboard recently developed by Logitech. It resists spills and can actually be immersed in water, washed, and set on its edge to dry. Water runs out of small drainage holes, and the letters are laser printed and UV coated to ensure they won't fade in the wash.

New products are important to both customers and the marketers who serve them. For customers, they bring new solutions and variety to their lives. For companies, new products are a key source of growth. Yet innovation can be very expensive and very risky, because a surprisingly high percentage—some say as high as 80 percent—of new products fail.

Why New Products Fail

No one knows exactly how many new products fail each year, but all marketing managers are aware that the number is very high, and it's a frightening thought. Still, companies are in the business of continually offering new products to the market, and so, every year, consumers see a parade of new products on the shelves.

Many new beers are launched on the market every year, most of which fail, and for reasons that have nothing to do with taste. Molson's A Marca Bavaria, a premium lager imported from Brazil, didn't sell because consumers were confused by the brand—a German name on a Brazilian beer.

Exhibit 8.3 **New products:** Sometimes new products are completely new inventions, but more frequently they are improvements to existing products, like the Logitech K310 Washable Keyboard.

Raina + Wilson, Raina + Wilson Photography

The major soft drink companies also launch many new products every year, most of which are destined for failure for various reasons. Pepsi Blue, a too-sweet blue drink, lasted less than six months on store shelves because people didn't want to drink something that looked like window cleaner. Lifesavers soda bombed because consumers thought it would taste like liquid candy. And when Coke and Nestle partnered to produce Enviga, a drink that claimed to have "negative calories," production ceased after several lawsuits challenged claims made by the beverage makers.

Not every electronic device is a hit, either. Just ask Apple about its Newton, or Microsoft about Zune, the music player that was supposed to rival the iPod. Even marketers of well established brands can fail with product line extensions that somehow hit a wrong note with consumers: Ben-Gay Aspirin, Smith and Wesson Mountain Bikes, Cosmopolitan (the magazine) Yogurt, and Colgate Kitchen Entrees.

One study of 128 senior marketers from some of the world's leading consumer packaged-goods companies suggests that the biggest problem with most new products is that they lack differentiation. In fact, of the marketing managers surveyed, only 12 percent felt that their own recently launched products were differentiated. At the same time, these marketers reported operating in highly competitive categories which suggests an explanation for the problem: If everyone is exploiting similar technology within a given

Exhibit 8.4 **Failed products:** Enviga, a beverage created by Coca-Cola and Nestlé, claimed to have "negative calories." It failed when those claims couldn't stand up to challenges from scientists, consumers, and other beverage companies.

Diffusion of innovations theory
A social sciences theory that divides members of a social group into segments according to how likely they are to adopt a new idea.

Technology Adoption Life Cycle
A marketing theory that proposes that when marketing a technology product, marketers must cross a chasm, or significant gap, between members of the early adopters segment and members of the early majority segment, before a new product will become successful.

category, the market is sure to be flooded with products too similar in design, features and benefits.[3]

Another reason why new products fail can be explained by the **diffusion of innovations theory**, a social sciences theory that divides members of a social group into segments according to how likely they are to adopt a new idea. The theory suggests that the new idea must be diffused through the group via various forms of communications, and that because each group has very different motivations and beliefs, that diffusion is much more difficult than it might seem. Marketers have adopted this theory to explain why it is difficult to get a new product adopted, even when it has obvious advantages. While there are always a few early adopters of any new idea, product, or technology, most people tend to wait until the idea is proven before they are willing to try it.

In the marketing of high tech products, marketers believe there is a "chasm" that must be crossed before mainstream consumers will accept the product—that is, before the product can become a success. Figure 8.2 illustrates where the chasm occurs in the **Technology Adoption Life Cycle**, a model created by Geoffrey Moore, the author of *Crossing the Chasm*, which is based on the diffusions of innovations theory. The theory proposes that when marketing a technology product, marketers must cross a chasm, or significant gap, between members of the early adopters segment and members of the early majority segment, before a new product will become successful.

Each of the groups in Moore's model can be viewed as a different market segment, each with its own characteristics. Moore suggests that *innovators* pursue new technology for its own sake—they are the kind of people who line up overnight to be among the first to purchase the new iPhone or iPad. *Early adopters* will purchase new technology soon after it is released, but only if they have a use or purpose for it. The *early majority* are the more practical market segment. While they might want the new gadget, they wait until they have a real need for it, or

FIGURE 8.2 Developed by Geoffrey Moore, the Technology Adoption Life Cycle shows five different market segments, each separated by a gap. The "chasm," or most significant gap, occurs between members of the early adopters and members of the early majority segments.

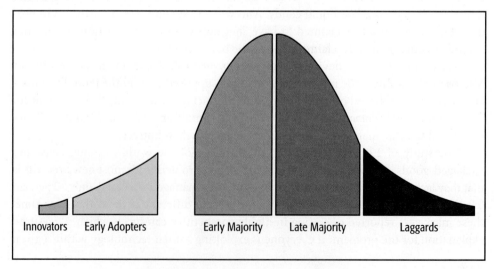

until the price becomes more affordable. Members of the *late majority* are those who wait until the new technology has been proven and has more or less become a standard. Once "everyone" is using it, so will they. And finally, *laggards* are people who are not comfortable with technology or have no interest in it, and so are not a valuable market to pursue.

High-tech marketing requires marketers to understand the psychographics of the target market, that is, the lifestyle and behaviours that will make it more likely for a consumer to fall into the innovator or early adopter category—the first market segments that must be targeted. Notice that in Figure 8.2 there are gaps between each of the groups. These gaps symbolize the dissociation between the two groups—that is, the difficulty any group will have in accepting a new product if it is presented in the same way as it was to the group to its immediate left. For example, a message designed to persuade an innovator to try a new product will not be effective with a member of the early or late majority. Marketers, therefore, must choose a different approach in their positioning strategy and marketing communications if they decide to target more than one of these market segments.

Finally, consumers in the two groups on each side of the chasm make their purchase decision about the new technology largely on the basis of benefits sought. Early adopters are seeking in the new technology a change agent—they want something radically different, which they believe will be better, and will therefore give them some sort of advantage over the competition. By contrast, the early majority are seeking a productivity improvement in the new technology. They want evolution, not revolution.[4]

The New-Product Development Process

Companies face a problem—they must develop new products, but the odds weigh heavily against success. In all, to create successful new products, a company must understand its consumers, markets, and competitors and develop products that deliver superior value to customers. It must carry out strong new-product planning and set up a systematic, customer-driven *new-product development process* for finding and growing new products. This process consists of eight major stages (see Figure 8.3).

Idea Generation   New-product development starts with **idea generation**—the systematic search for new-product ideas. A company typically generates hundreds of ideas, even thousands, in order to find a few good ones. Major sources of new-product ideas include internal sources and external sources such as customers, competitors, distributors and suppliers, and others.

Companies can also obtain good new-product ideas from any of a number of external sources. For example, *distributors and suppliers* can contribute ideas. Distributors are

Idea generation
The systematic search for new-product ideas.

FIGURE 8.3 Major Stages in New-Product Development

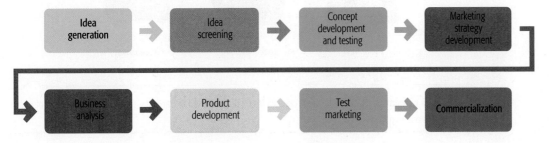

close to the market and can pass along information about consumer problems and new-product possibilities. Suppliers can tell the company about new concepts, techniques, and materials that can be used to develop new products. *Competitors* are another important source. Companies watch competitors' ads to get clues about their new products. They buy competing new products, take them apart to see how they work, analyze their sales, and decide whether they should bring out a new product of their own. Other idea sources include trade magazines, shows, and seminars; government agencies; advertising agencies; marketing research firms; university and commercial laboratories; and inventors.

Perhaps the most important source of new-product ideas is *customers* themselves. The company can analyze customer questions and complaints to find new products that better solve consumer problems. Their questions, complaints, and comments on social media provide insights into what new products the market wants. For example, Canada Goose's customers said they wanted a jacket they could wear when a parka was too warm; something that was more than a non-insulated coat but less than a full parka. This generated an idea for a new line of lightweight down outerwear products. Canada Goose developed the new line, incorporating a new technology called Thermal Mapping (which takes into consideration unique male and female heat conservation needs), while still retaining the traditional Canada Goose soft shell lightness and flexibility.

Customers have always found new uses for products beyond what the company originally envisioned, and sometimes those new uses can lead to the development of new products. For example, the makers of Arm & Hammer baking soda learned that customers used baking soda as a deodorant for their cat litter boxes, and for other purposes such as brushing their teeth. This led to the development of many new products including Arm & Hammer cat litter, Arm & Hammer laundry detergent, Arm & Hammer deodorant, and Arm & Hammer toothpaste. Some companies, such as LEGO Group, actively involve their customers in the new-product development process—see Marketing@ Work 8.1.

Several companies, including Eli Lilly, SAP, Fujitsu, and the World Bank, have implemented an "idea market" within the company, where any employee can submit

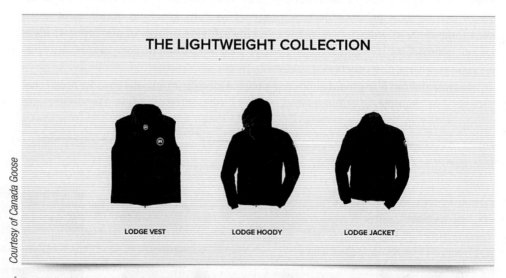

Courtesy of Canada Goose

THE LIGHTWEIGHT COLLECTION

LODGE VEST   LODGE HOODY   LODGE JACKET

Exhibit 8.5 **Idea generation:** Suggestions and requests from customers led to Canada Goose's new product line of lightweight down outerwear.

MARKETING@WORK 8.1

LEGO Group: Including Customers in the New-Product Development Process

Classic LEGO plastic bricks have been fixtures in homes around the world for more than 60 years. Today, Denmark-based LEGO Group (TLG) markets their products in 130 countries and sells seven LEGO sets every second. But only seven years ago, the company was near bankruptcy. The problem? The classic toy company had fallen out of touch with its customers, and its products were not in keeping with the times. In the age of the Internet, videogames, iPods, and high-tech playthings, traditional toys like LEGO bricks had been pushed to the back of the closet. So in 2004, the company set out to rebuild its aging product line—brick by brick.

The LEGO product makeover didn't start with engineers working in design labs—it started by listening to customers, understanding them, and including them in the new-product development process. Then it used the insights it gained to develop new generations of more relevant products. Rather than simply pushing the same old construction sets out to customers, TLG worked *with* customers to create new products and concepts.

To get to know its customers better, LEGO conducted up-close-and-personal ethnographic studies—hanging out with and observing children ages seven to nine on their home turf. "We thought we understood our consumers, the children of the world," says a LEGO Group marketer, but it turns out that "we didn't know them as well as we thought." The ethnographic research produced a lot of "Aha! moments" that shattered many of the brand's long-held traditions.

For example, the company had long held fast to a "keep it simple" mantra. From the beginning, it offered only basic play sets—bricks, building bases, beams, doors, windows, wheels, and slanting roof tiles—with few or no instructions. The philosophy was that giving children unstructured building sets would stimulate their imaginations and foster creativity. But that concept just wasn't cutting it in today's fast-moving

environment where children are exposed to so many characters and themes. So LEGO shifted toward more specialized, more structured products. It now churns out some 7000 unique building pieces each year, which support a seemingly endless assortment of themed product lines and specific building projects. So instead of just buying a set of basic square LEGO bricks and building a house or a car, children can now buy specialized kits to construct anything from a realistic fire engine to a city police helicopter to a working robot. And the LEGO brick lineup is refreshed regularly; 60 percent of the core LEGO product assortment changes every year.

In addition, LEGO now builds plays sets around popular movie and TV themes and characters. It offers an ever-changing assortment of licensed lines based on everything from *Indiana Jones* and *Star Wars* to *Toy Story*. Marketing these thematic and structured new products has given a big boost to sales, but not everyone is thrilled. One industry observer notes, "What LEGO loses is what makes it so special. When you have a less-structured, less-themed set, kids [can] start from scratch. When you have kids playing out Indiana Jones, they're playing out Hollywood's imagination, not their own." But LEGO doesn't see this shift as a compromise of values, and most customers agree. For example, one father of two recognizes that LEGO toys have changed since he was a boy, but he thinks

that they have retained their innocence. "The most exotic thing I could build when I was a kid was an ambulance," he says. "Now [my kids] can build the Death Star." The fact that "the pieces and the sets are a lot cooler than they were 30 years ago" means that they lure kids away from less imaginative pastimes. "Instead of watching TV or playing computer games, the kids are building something, and [we] build stuff together."

Surprisingly, kids aren't the only ones playing with LEGO bricks. The classic brick sets have a huge fan base of adults—as many as 250 000 active AFOLs (adult fans of LEGO) around the globe who spend large sums on LEGO products. These adults maintain thousands of LEGO fan sites and blogs, flock to conventions with names such as

Exhibit 8.6 LEGO Japan's Mindstorm NXT robot carries a ball at the Robot Awards 2007 in Tokyo, Japan. LEGO robots are built using standard LEGO Technic parts and a special microcomputer.

FRANCK ROBICHON/EPA/Newscom

BrickFest, and compete with each other to construct "the Biggest LEGO Train Layout Ever (3343 feet; it ran through an entire LEGO cityscape) or beat the Fastest Time to Build the LEGO Imperial Star Destroyer (3104 pieces; five builders maximum and no presorting allowed; record: 1 hour, 42 minutes, 43 seconds)."

In developing new products, TLG actively taps into the AFOL community. It has created a roster of customer ambassadors who provide regular input, and it even invites customers to participate directly in the product development process. For example, it invited 250 LEGO train-set enthusiasts to visit its New York office to assess new designs. The result was the LEGO Santa Fe Super Chief set, which sold out the first 10 000 units in less than two weeks with virtually no additional marketing. Listening to adult customers also led to the development of the LEGO Design by Me site, which lets customers download 3-D design software, create a LEGO toy, and then order the kit to build it. And LEGO

Universe, an MMOG (massively multiplayer online game), lets both adults and children act out roles from LEGO sets and build toys from virtual blocks. Working with customers led to the development of the company's most popular product ever, LEGO MINDSTORMS, a build-it-yourself robot created in partnership with MIT. Within three weeks of its introduction more than 1000 intrigued customers formed their own web community to outdo each other in making it better. LEGO Group quickly embraced the co-creation idea. The next generation of LEGO MINDSTORMS featured user-defined parts. Then, LEGO made customer co-creation official by creating the MINDSTORMS Development Program (MDP), through which it selected the most avid MINDSTORMS fans—100 pioneers, inventors, and innovators from across the globe—to play with LEGO MINDSTORMS and create innovative new features and applications. The MDP fans share their ideas with other customers and invite feedback.

Thanks to customer-centred new-product development, LEGO Group is now thriving. In the past five years, even as the overall toy market declined and competitors such as Mattel and Hasbro struggled, LEGO's sales soared 66 percent, and its profits have jumped tenfold. "Kids [including the adult variety] are ruthless," says a senior LEGO executive. "If they don't like the product, then at the end of the day . . . all the rest of it won't make any difference. What counts, all that counts, is that you're at the top of kids' wish lists." Thanks to all that listening and customer involvement, that's where the LEGO Group is again.

Sources: "LEGO Grows by Listening to Customers," *Advertising Age,* November 9, 2009, p. 15; Nelson D. Schwartz, "Beyond the Blocks," *New York Times,* September 6, 2009, p. BU1; Jon Henley, "Toy Story," *Guardian,* March 26, 2009, p. F4; Kevin O'Donnell, "Where Do the Best Ideas Come From? The Unlikeliest Sources," *Advertising Age,* July 14, 2008, p. 15; Lewis Borg Cardona, "LEGO Learns a Lesson," *Change Agent,* June 2008; "Toy Company Lego Reports 69 Percent Rise in Net Profit," *McClatchy-Tribune Business News,* March 3, 2011; and LEGO's websites lego.com and mindstorms.lego.com, accessed February 2013.

---

suggestions for solving a problem, or for a new product, in return for a reward. Fusenet, a software developer based in Oakville, Ontario, reports that they have in at least five instances offered equity participation to employees who have come up with ideas for a new product. With today's technology, a secure internal network can serve as a suggestion box for the digital age.[5]

A new approach to idea generation that some companies are employing today is **crowdsourcing**—inviting broad communities of people such as customers, employees, independent scientists and researchers, and even the public at large, into the new product innovation process. "The first rule of innovation these days is that the most powerful ideas often come from the most unexpected places—the quiet genius of employees inside your company, the hidden genius of customers," says one expert. "Tapping into this hidden genius doesn't require fancy technology or deep pockets—it just requires a leadership mindset that invites outside brainpower into the organization."[6]

Crowdsourcing
Inviting broad communities of people such as customers, employees, independent scientists and researchers, and even the public at large, into the new product innovation process.

For example, Frito Lay recently organized an initiative to crowdsource new flavours for Lay's potato chips from anyone in the consumer public. Consumers submitted their ideas through the company's Facebook page, and the company eventually chose three finalists (Cheesy Garlic Bread, Chicken & Waffles, and Sriracha). Consumers were then asked to vote on Facebook or via text message for the flavour that would then be produced as a new product.[7] A senior executive at Facebook believes that brand fans like these could be the new marketers, and that companies should take advantage of these passionate and interested consumers to generate new ideas: "A marketer's goal is for their product to rise above being a commodity to something that triggers an emotional response and that the consumer feels a personal connection with. Crowdsourcing . . . lets people express that emotional connection they have with the brand."[8]

Rather than creating and managing their own crowdsourcing platforms, companies can use third-party crowdsourcing networks, such as InnoCentive, TopCoder, Hypios, and jovoto. For example, organizations ranging from Facebook and PayPal to ESPN, NASA, and the Salk Institute tap into TopCoder's network of nearly 300 000 mathematicians, engineers, software developers, and designers for ideas and solutions, offering prizes of $100 to $100 000. PayPal recently posted a challenge to the TopCoder community seeking the development of an innovative Android or iPhone app that would successfully and securely run its checkout process, awarding the winners $5000 each. After only four weeks of competition and two weeks of review, PayPal had its solutions. The Android app came from a programmer in the United States; the iPhone app from a programmer in Colombia.[9]

Idea Screening The purpose of idea generation is to create a large number of ideas. The purpose of the succeeding stages is to *reduce* that number. The first idea-reducing stage is **idea screening**, which helps spot good ideas and drop poor ones as soon as possible. Product development costs rise greatly in later stages, so the company wants to go ahead only with the product ideas that will turn into profitable products.

Idea screening
Screening new-product ideas to spot good ideas and drop poor ones as soon as possible.

This more detailed consideration of the new product idea may be reviewed by a committee, who will consider such things as the proposed customer value proposition, the target market, and the competition. They will make rough estimates of market size, product price, development time and costs, manufacturing costs, and rate of return, then recommend which ideas should go forward into the concept development and testing stage.

One marketing expert proposes an R-W-W ("real, win, worth it") new-product screening framework that asks three questions. First, *Is it real?* Is there a real need and desire for the product and will customers buy it? Is there a clear product concept and will the product satisfy the market? Second, *Can we win?* Does the product offer a sustainable competitive advantage? Does the company have the resources to make the product a success? Finally, *Is it worth doing?* Does the product fit the company's overall growth strategy? Does it offer sufficient profit potential? The company should be able to answer yes to all three R-W-W questions before developing the new-product idea further.[10]

Product concept
A detailed version of the new-product idea stated in meaningful consumer terms.

Concept Development and Testing Once the company has generated, and then screened, new-product ideas, the next step is to develop those ideas into a product concept. Whereas a product idea is an idea for a possible product that the company can potentially offer to the market, a **product concept** is a detailed description, drawing, or prototype of that idea that can be shown to potential customers. That product concept must then be developed and tested, that is, the new product idea is developed in various alternative forms, and tested with a group of potential customers.

Every year automobile marketers promote their latest "concept cars" at auto shows. Concept cars are real cars that can be driven; however, they are not yet in production, which means they are not yet available to the public. Concept cars are displayed at auto shows so that the automobile marketers can gauge the market's response to their product concept. Automobile marketers may also let journalists from magazines like

Imago stock&people/Newscom

Exhibit 8.7 **Concept development and testing:** BMW's i8 electric concept car is displayed at the Canadian International Car Show in Toronto.

Motor Trend and *Car And Driver* drive and review their concept cars in hopes that a good review will result in enough market interest to justify a full-scale development and release of the new car.

Marketing Strategy Development After the product concept has been tested with members of the target market, and their opinions about the concept have been collected, the next step in the product development process is to design the marketing strategy. **Marketing strategy development** involves designing an initial marketing strategy for a new product based on the product concept. The strategy must answer questions about how, when, where, and to whom the product will be introduced.

The marketing strategy begins with a detailed description of the target market for the new product. It outlines the value proposition of the new product, and describes its positioning with respect to existing product. The strategy and plan must describe where and how the product will be made available to customers. It also proposes a target launch date, and the details of advertising and other promotional activities that must accompany the release of the new product. Finally, the marketing strategy must state sales goals, market share goals, and profit goals. Typically this initial marketing strategy encompasses plans for the first year of the product.

Business Analysis Once management has decided on its product concept and marketing strategy, it can evaluate the business attractiveness of the proposal. **Business analysis** involves a review of the sales, costs, and profit projections for a new product to find out whether they satisfy the company's objectives. If they do, the product can move to the product development stage.

To estimate sales, the company might look at the sales history of similar products and conduct market surveys. It can then estimate minimum and maximum sales to assess the range of risk. After preparing the sales forecast, management can estimate the expected costs and profits for the product, including marketing, R&D, operations, accounting, and finance costs. The company then uses the sales and costs figures to analyze the new product's financial attractiveness.

Product Development So far, for many new-product concepts, the product may have existed only as a word description, a drawing, or perhaps a crude mock-up. If the product concept passes the business test, it moves into **product development**. Here, R&D or engineering develops the product concept into a physical product. The product development step, however, now calls for a large jump in investment. It will show whether the product idea can be turned into a workable product.

Developing the new product, that is, turning the new product idea into a workable, mass-produced market offering, takes months, even years. During the development process the new product will undergo rigorous testing to make sure that it works the way it is supposed to work, and that customers will be able to use it safely and effectively.

Marketers often involve actual customers in product testing. For example, New Balance's Wear Test Program engages consumers throughout the product development process to field test new shoe designs under real life conditions. Consumer testers attend The New Balance Tester School to learn how to analyze the fit, function, and durability of their assigned test shoes. As they test shoes over an eight-week period, they log on to their Wear Test account and complete online surveys and feedback forms documenting

Marketing strategy development
Designing an initial marketing strategy for a new product based on the product concept.

Business analysis
A review of the sales, costs, and profit projections for a new product to find out whether these factors satisfy the company's objectives.

Product development
Developing the product concept into a physical product to ensure that the product idea can be turned into a workable market offering.

Exhibit 8.8 **Product development and testing:** Throughout the product development stage, New Balance uses customers to field test its new shoe designs under real life conditions.

New Balance

their experiences with the test product. Says New Balance, "We believe that subjecting our product line to rigorous field testing ensures that all of our products perform at their peak—so you can too."[11]

Test Marketing   If the product passes concept and product tests, the next step is **test marketing**, the stage at which the product and marketing program are introduced into realistic market settings. Test marketing gives the marketer experience with marketing the product before going to the great expense of full introduction. It lets the company test the product and its entire marketing program—targeting and positioning strategy, advertising, distribution, pricing, branding and packaging, and budget levels.

Companies typically invest in a test marketing program when the new product required a major investment in development, or when the risks of taking it to market are particularly high. For example, Starbucks' VIA instant coffee was one of the company's biggest, most risky product rollouts ever and had been in development for 20 years. Before releasing the product nationally in Canada and the US, Starbucks first test marketed VIA in Chicago and Seattle. The test marketing program lasted approximately six months, during which time Starbucks customers in the test cities were offered coupons and free samples of VIA to take home with them. In addition, Taste Challenges were held to help drum up interest and induce trial. Performance of VIA exceeded expectations and the promotional efforts were applied to the national rollout as well.[12]

Commercialization   The final step in the new-product development process is **commercialization**, or the full-scale introduction of the product into the market. If the company goes ahead with this stage, it will invest heavily in advertising and promotion.

The Product Life Cycle LO3

The new-product development process gets the new product to market, and marks the beginning of the product's life. Every company wants its new products to enjoy a long, happy, and profitable life, but realistically, they realize that the new product won't sell forever. Marketing managers must understand that each product launched in the market will have a life cycle. The **product life cycle**, or PLC, is the course that a product's sales and profits take over its lifetime. Figure 8.4 shows a typical progression of a new product over the course of its life.

The typical product life cycle sees the product move through five stages: *product development*, *introduction*, *growth*, *maturity*, and *decline*. In theory, all products follow the PLC—eventually—though some well-established and mature products such as Coca-Cola and Tide laundry detergent may stay in the mature stage indefinitely, and never decline. The many products that are introduced to the market and then fail can be viewed as having skipped their growth and maturity stages, and gone directly to decline. And some products that enter the decline stage are saved by revitalizing them or somehow making them "new and improved,"—which sends them back to the introduction stage.

Stages of the Product Life Cycle

We looked at the product-development stage of the product life cycle earlier in this chapter. We now look at strategies for each of the other life-cycle stages.

© studiomode / Alamy

Exhibit 8.9 Test marketing: Starbucks test marketed its new product, VIA instant coffee, for six months in Chicago and Seattle before rolling it out to all Starbucks locations.

Test marketing
The stage of new-product development in which the product and marketing program are tested in realistic market settings.

Commercialization
The full-scale introduction of the new product into the market.

FIGURE 8.4 Representation of Sales and Profits over a Typical New Product's Life Cycle

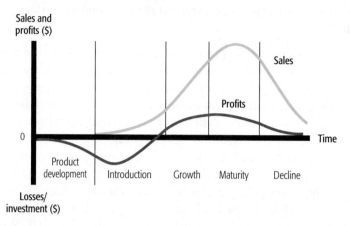

Product life cycle

The course of a product's sales and profits over its lifetime. It involves five stages: product development, introduction, growth, maturity, and decline.

Introduction stage

The product life-cycle stage in which the new product is first distributed and made available for purchase.

Introduction Stage   The **introduction stage** starts when the new product is first launched. Introduction takes time, and sales growth is apt to be slow. Well-known products such as instant coffee, frozen foods, and HDTVs lingered for many years before they entered a stage of more rapid growth.

In this stage, as compared to other stages, profits are negative or low because of the low sales and high distribution and promotion expenses. Much money is needed to attract distributors and build their inventories. Promotion spending is relatively high to inform consumers of the new product and get them to try it. Because the market is not generally ready for product refinements at this stage, the company and its few competitors produce basic versions of the product. These firms focus their selling on those buyers who are the most ready to buy.

Only successful new products will make it past the introduction stage, and begin to see growth. At the end of each calendar year, the best new products in Canada, as voted by consumers, are awarded "Product of the Year" status. Some recent winners were Smirnoff Premium Vodka Mixed Drinks (alcoholic beverages category), BlueWater Seafoods Simply Bake (frozen foods category), Cascades Enviro Ultra (personal care category), Cadbury Pieces (confectionary category), and Essilor Optifog lenses and activator (personal comfort category).

Growth stage

The product life-cycle stage in which a product's sales start climbing quickly.

Exhibit 8.10 **Introduction stage:** Tide Pods are a new product that combines detergents, stain fighters, and brighteners in a single pod with multiple chambers.

Growth Stage   If the new product satisfies the market, it will enter a **growth stage**, in which sales will start climbing quickly. The early adopters will continue to buy, and later buyers will start following their lead, especially if they hear favourable word of mouth. Competitors will release their versions of the new product, and the first marketer will need to make improvements or lower prices in order to compete. Profits increase during the growth stage as promotion costs are spread over a larger volume and unit manufacturing costs fall. During this stage, the marketing strategy is to sustain the growth for as long as possible, perhaps by adding new features or new models, or by targeting new market segments, or

© Richard Levine / Alamy

adding new distribution channels. Some examples of products that are currently in the growth stage are computer tablets, and smartphones.

Maturity Stage   At some point, a product's sales growth will slow down, and the product will enter a **maturity stage**. This maturity stage normally lasts longer than the previous stages, and it poses strong challenges to marketing management. Most products are in the maturity stage of the life cycle, and therefore most of marketing management deals with the mature product.

The main marketing goal when a product is in the mature stage is to prevent it from declining. Marketers who handle mature products must constantly be developing strategies and managing marketing programs to keep their product consistently profitable. One way to do this is by *modifying the market*, or trying to increase consumption by finding new market segments. The company might also try *modifying the product*— changing characteristics such as quality, features, style, or packaging to attract new users and inspire more usage. It can improve the product's styling and attractiveness. It might improve the product's quality and performance—its durability, reliability, speed, and taste. Marketers of consumer food and household products introduce new flavours, colours, scents, ingredients, or packages to enhance performance and revitalize consumer buying.

Finally, the company can try *modifying the marketing mix*—improving sales by changing one or more marketing mix elements. The company can offer new or improved services to buyers. It can cut prices to attract new users and competitors' customers. It can launch a better advertising campaign or use aggressive sales promotions—trade deals, cents-off, premiums, and contests. In addition to pricing and promotion, the company can also move into new marketing channels to help serve new users.

Decline Stage   Many mature products that continue to be useful, such as brands of laundry detergent and shampoo, can stay in the maturity stage indefinitely, but other products such as computers, televisions, and telephones will eventually decline, die, and be replaced by different new products. Some products that are currently in the **decline stage** are small digital cameras, which have become unnecessary due to the growth of smartphones. Home or "landline" telephones are also on the decline, as many consumers use only a cellphone.

Marketing product managers need not despair because their product is in decline, however. Some marketers decide to maintain their declining products without change in the hope that competitors will leave the industry. For example, P&G made good profits by remaining in the declining liquid soap business as others withdrew. Another strategy for managing products as they decline is to reposition them and try to appeal to a new market segment. For example TAB, the original diet soda, had practically disappeared from the market before being repositioned as an energy drink for women; and Old Spice, known for years as your father's aftershave, repositioned itself to appeal to a younger generation of men.

If decline is unpreventable, marketers may decide to *harvest* the product, which means reducing various costs (plant and equipment, maintenance, R&D, advertising, sales force) and hoping that sales hold up. If successful, harvesting will increase the company's profits in the short run. Sometimes declining products can be sold to another firm or simply liquidated at salvage value. In recent years, P&G has sold off a number of lesser or declining brands such as Crisco oil, Comet cleanser, Sure deodorant, and Duncan Hines cake mixes.

Table 8.2 summarizes the key characteristics of each stage of the product life cycle. The table also lists the marketing objectives and strategies for each stage.[13]

Maturity stage
The product life-cycle stage in which sales growth slows or levels off.

Decline stage
The product life-cycle stage in which a product's sales decline.

TABLE 8.2   Summary of Product Life-Cycle Characteristics, Objectives, and Strategies

	Introduction	Growth	Maturity	Decline
Characteristics				
Sales	Low sales	Rapidly rising sales	Peak sales	Declining sales
Costs	High cost per customer	Average cost per customer	Low cost per customer	Low cost per customer
Profits	Negative	Rising profits	High profits	Declining profits
Customers	Innovators	Early adopters	Middle majority	Laggards
Competitors	Few	Growing number	Stable number beginning to decline	Declining number
Marketing Objectives				
	Create product awareness and trial	Maximize market share	Maximize profit while defending market share	Reduce expenditure and milk the brand
Strategies				
Product	Offer a basic product	Offer product extensions, service, warranty	Diversify brand and models	Phase out weak items
Price	Use cost-plus	Price to penetrate market	Price to match or beat competitors	Cut price
Distribution	Build selective distribution	Build intensive distribution	Build more intensive distribution	Go selective: phase out unprofitable outlets
Advertising	Build product awareness among early adopters and dealers	Build awareness and interest in the mass market	Stress brand differences and benefits	Reduce to level needed to retain hard-core loyalists
Sales Promotion	Use heavy sales promotion to entice trial	Reduce to take advantage of heavy consumer demand	Increase to encourage brand switching	Reduce to minimal level

Source: Kotler, Philip R; and Keller, Kevin Lane, *Marketing Management,* 13th ed., © 2009, p. 288. Reprinted and Electronically reproduced by Pearson Education, One Lake Street, Upper Saddle River, NJ 07458

Styles, Fashions, and Fads

Style

A basic and distinctive mode of expression.

Fashion

A currently accepted or popular style of design, colour, or theme.

Fad

A temporary period of unusually high sales driven by consumer enthusiasm and immediate product or brand popularity.

The PLC concept also can be applied to *styles*, *fashions* and *fads* (see Figure 8.5). A **style** is a basic and distinctive mode of expression. For example, styles appear in homes (colonial, ranch, transitional), clothing (formal, casual), and art (realist, surrealist, abstract). Once a style is invented, it may last for generations, passing in and out of vogue. A style has a cycle showing several periods of renewed interest. A **fashion** is a currently accepted or popular style of design, colour, or theme. There are fashions in clothing, of course, but also in cars, furniture, music, and even sports. Punk was a fashion in music, clothing, and hairstyles in the 1970s. Playing handball was fashionable in the 1980s, golf was a fashion in the 1990s but is now declining, and snowboarding is a new fashion, still on the rise. Fashions tend to grow slowly, remain popular for a while, and then decline slowly.

Fads are new products that are extremely popular for a very short period of time, then disappear almost completely. Every decade has its memorable fads, but they are not usually identified as fads until years later. In the last ten years, new products such as razor scooters, Crocs, and the Big Mouth Billy Bass were viewed in retrospect as fads. The upside-down Christmas tree was a fad in 2005. Luxury gadget catalogue marketer

FIGURE 8.5 Styles, Fashions, and Fads

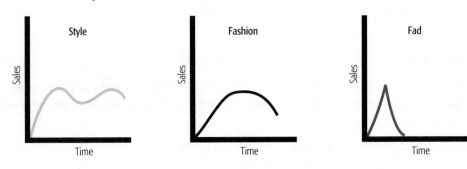

Hammacher Schlemmer sold one that came pre-strung with 800 clear commercial-grade lights, and sold for $599.95.

Some say the plastic wrist bands and energy drinks that are so popular today will be viewed as fads 10 years from now. But just because something is a fashion or a fad doesn't mean it wasn't successful as a new product. Take Guitar Hero, for example.[14]

> Guitar Hero, the hugely popular video game with the guitar-shaped controller, was in production for only six years, from 2005-2011. The first version of Guitar Hero sold 1.5 million copies and generated US$45 million in revenue, prompting Activison Blizzard Inc., the makers of World of Warcraft, to purchase the company. They launched Guitar Hero II which improved the product by doubling the song selection and adding stage effects, and made US$200 million in profit.
>
> Competitors such as Rock Band soon appeared on the market, and Guitar Hero released a stream of new products such as Guitar Hero: Aerosmith, Guitar Hero: Metallica, and Guitar Hero World Tour. At the height of its popularity an entire episode of South Park was dedicated to Guitar Hero. Rick Mercer played Guitar Hero with Rush guitarist Alex Lifeson on an episode of *The Rick Mercer Report,* musicians like Dave Navarro and Matt Sorum helped promote the latest edition of the game in live events, and endless Hollywood celebrities were photographed enthusiastically playing the game.
>
> Sadly, the game's stratospheric growth didn't last long. By 2009 sales had declined, and in 2010 only one new title was released (Guitar Hero: Warrior of Rock). Finally, in 2011, Activision shut down Guitar Hero operations for good.

How long does a new product's life cycle have to last? As the example of Guitar Hero shows, there are no hard and fast rules. Some might say Guitar Hero was a wildly successful new product that simply followed the PLC: it grew quickly, generated millions in sales, matured three years after it was introduced, and declined three years later. But one day, marketing historians may look back on Guitar Hero as "just a fad."

Product and Service Decisions LO4

Marketers make product and service decisions at three levels. At the first level, they make individual product decisions, which include decisions about product attributes such as *quality, features,* and *style and design,* as well as decisions about packaging, labelling, and product support services for each product. At the next level are decisions

Exhibit 8.11 Was it a fad, or a wildly successful new product? Hollywood celebrities Adam Gregory, Brandon Michael Vayda, and Matt Prokop play Guitar Hero during the Guitar Hero World Tour VIP Launch Event in 2008 at Best Buy in Los Angeles.

Tony D iPhoto Inc./Newscom

about product lines, or groups of products. Finally, marketers make decisions about the company's overall product portfolio, or product *mix*.

Individual Product and Service Decisions

The important decisions in the development and marketing of individual products and services include decisions about *product attributes*, *packaging*, *labelling*, and *product support* services.

Product and Service Attributes   Developing a product or service involves defining the benefits that it will offer. These benefits are communicated and delivered by product attributes such as *quality*, *features*, and *style and design*.

Product quality

The characteristics of a product or a service that bear on its ability to satisfy stated or implied customer needs.

PRODUCT QUALITY   **Product quality** is one of the marketer's major positioning tools. Quality has a direct impact on product or service performance; thus, it is closely linked to customer value and satisfaction. In the narrowest sense, quality can be defined as "freedom from defects." But most customer-centred companies go beyond this narrow definition. Instead, they define quality in terms of creating customer value and satisfaction. Product quality is a serious matter for marketers, many of whom belong to the Society of Quality Assurance (SQA), an international professional membership organization that provides a forum for organizations to exchange information about research and regulations that govern quality assurance practices.

The level of quality a product has determines the type of marketing programs that will be created to promote it, for example, Rolex watches are the highest quality watch available on the market, and all point-of-sale materials and advertising tend to mention the craftsmanship and length of time that goes into building one. Similarly, marketers of high end sports cars focus on promoting the quality of their vehicles, while smaller, less expensive cars focus on price promotions.

Exhibit 8.12 **Marketing that focuses on features:** The new Samsung T9000 LCD refrigerator is the latest in high tech for appliances, with features such as commercial grade humidity control and a built-in computer screen.

David Becker/Getty Image

PRODUCT FEATURES   A product can be offered with varying features. A stripped-down model, one without any extras, is the starting point. The company can create higher-level models by adding more features. Features are a competitive tool for differentiating the company's product from competitors' products. Being the first producer to introduce a valued new feature is one of the most effective ways to compete. When the new product is a new version in a well-established product category such as home appliances, the marketing strategy should focus on what makes this new product different from all the others. One way to do that is to promote new features, especially if they are unique or the latest in technology. For example, Samsung recently launched the T9000 LCD refrigerator at the Consumer Electronics Show, where visitors were impressed with its innovative and modern features.[15]

The four-door Samsung T9000 represents the next evolution in refrigerators. It is both beautiful and high performance: Samsung's Triple Cooling system, with two compressors, three evaporators, and an array of sensors, keeps produce fresher longer by ensuring optimal temperature and commercial grade humidity control. The Samsung T9000 features a large capacity French door refrigerator compartment on top, and two smaller compartments below. The lower left side is a freezer, and the lower right side can be used as either a refrigerator or a freezer—making the T9000 both unique and versatile.

The most innovative new feature, however, is the LCD display that lets families stay organized and connected. It includes apps such as calendars, weather, and Evernote, which allows members of the family to share photos, videos, and even recipes. Samsung says the T9000 LCD refrigerator redefines the kitchen appliance experience as "the home entertainer's ultimate refrigerator."

STYLE AND DESIGN Another way to add customer value is through distinctive *style and design*. Design is a larger concept than style. *Style* simply describes the appearance of a product. Styles can be eye-catching or yawn producing. A sensational style may grab attention and produce pleasing aesthetics, but it does not necessarily make the product *perform* better. Unlike style, *design* is more than skin deep—it goes to the very heart of a product. Good design contributes to a product's usefulness as well as to its looks.

To understand the importance of style and design on products, one only need look at any product made by Apple. From their first computers to their latest iPads and iPhones, Apple products have a design that is instantly recognizable and uniquely Apple. The way a product is *designed*—what features it has, where they are located, and how they are used—and the way a product looks—*its style*—are important factors that influence consumers to choose one company's product over another. Good design begins with observing customers and developing a deep understanding of their needs. More than simply creating product or service attributes, it involves shaping the customer's product-use experience.

The design of a product involves both aesthetics and functionality, so there can be a fine line between what is strictly design, and what are features. Take the case of Denmark-based Bodum, for example. The company, famous for its French press coffee maker, attempted to register the design of a new product—a double wall glass intended to insulate hot and cold beverages. But while registering a design protects visual features such as a logo or the shape of a bottle, it is not the same as registering a patent, which protects useful features and new inventions. A few years later Bodum's competitor, Quebec-based Trudeau Corp., began marketing a line of double wall glassware, and Bodum sued. The Federal Court of Canada has ruled in favor of Trudeau by rejecting the claim of industrial design infringement made by Bodum USA and PI Design, a case filed in February of 2007. The Court also invalidated both of Bodum's industrial design registrations Nos. 107,736 and 114,070 covering the configuration of double-walled glasses and found that Trudeau branded products were dissimilar and did not infringe Bodum's industrial designs. Today Trudeau markets a full line of double wall glassware, and Trudeau's in-house design team continues to produce new products at the rate of about 100 per year.[16]

Packaging and Labelling

Packaging is much more than just the container to hold the product—it's an important marketing tool as well. The main functions of packaging are as follows:[17]

- **Protection**—from breakage, spoilage, contamination, tampering, and theft
- **Promotion**—packaging describes the product, lists ingredients, identifies the brand, and draws attention to features and benefits
- **Information**—packaging identifies the product, describes its preparation and usage, gives opening instructions, storage details, safety warnings, and contact information
- **Convenience**—especially in food products, packaging contains prepared servings and portioning

Packaging
The activities of designing and producing the container or wrapper for a product.

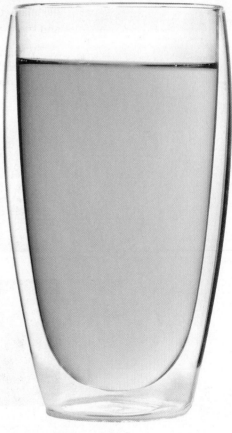

© Robert Mora / Alamy

Exhibit 8.13 **Design:** The shape, colour, or "look" of a product is part of its design, not a feature—as a judge ruled in the case of Trudeau and Bodum's double wall glassware.

- **Unitization**—packaging allows for the provision of consumer units, retail units, and transport units
- **Handling**—packaging offers ease of transportation from producer to retailer, and point of sale display

Innovative packaging can give a company an advantage over competitors and boost sales. For example, Heinz revolutionized the condiments industry by inverting the good old ketchup bottle, letting customers quickly squeeze out even the last bit of ketchup. Marketers of other squeezable products such as mustard, shampoo, and toothpaste quickly followed suit. And Amazon.com has developed Certified Frustration-Free Packaging that is recyclable and comes without excess materials such as hard plastic clamshell casings and wire ties. It's designed to be opened without the use of a box cutter or knife, yet it protects products as well as traditional packaging. Many products can even be shipped in their own boxes, without an additional shipping box.[18]

How much does the package influence shopping decisions? A recent study by OgilvyAction of 14 000 shoppers in 24 countries found that 28 percent of shoppers wait until they are in the store to decide which brand they will buy. One in 10 shoppers change their mind in the store, and buy a different brand from what they originally intended, and 20 percent of shoppers will buy products they had no intention of buying before entering the store—all based on the packaging they see while shopping.[19]

Sometimes, the package is the most important marketing tool of all. "The fundamental truth about packaging is that it's the only marketing vehicle that 100 percent of the shoppers who buy your product actually see," points out Jason Dubroy, VP of shopper marketing at DDB Canada. Pet food marketer Petcurean took this advice to heart and spent a year redesigning its packaging.[20]

When Vancouver's Subplot Design was hired by Petcurean to redesign the packaging for their Go and Now Fresh lines of premium dog and cat food, the first thing creative director Matthew Clark thought of was packaging in Europe—it's more minimalist, more frugal, and

Courtesy of Petcurean

Exhibit 8.14 **Packaging:** Petcurean spent a year redesigning the packaging for its Go and Now Fresh lines of pet food because the company's marketing manager believes there is nothing more vital to the brand than its package.

usually has some level of higher engagement through fun, wit, or whimsy. His package design philosophy is to be simpler and quieter, to free up space, and to say one thing clearly, not 12 things in a cluttered way.

The redesigned packaging for the Go product line brings to life the tagline, "created to put more life into your pet." It features black and white action shots of dogs and cats on a hi-gloss metallic foil. The formerly small and hard to read type was replaced with large type that communicates the product flavour and nutritional benefits clearly and simply.

For the Now Fresh product line, Subplot designed the package with a "Fresh Market" sign that reinforces the brand's "100% fresh" positioning, and used burlap textures and a warmer, softer design.

The project took a full year, which explains why some marketers shy away from major redesigns of their packaging, but Petcurean's marketing manager, Jaimie Turkington, had a different vision: "There is nothing more vital to this brand than packaging, because in the absence of everything else, it's the entire consumer experience. So why wouldn't we put all our money, effort, and time into it?"

Sustainable Packaging   In today's marketing environment, consumers are increasingly aware of which products are environmentally responsible and sustainable, and which are not. Whether or not a particular product's packaging is excessive or recyclable can make the difference between whether a consumer purchases that product or not. Today, many marketers are exploring options for **sustainable packaging**—packaging that meets the requirements of the product while minimizing the environmental, economic, and social impacts of the product and its package.

The Sustainable Packaging Coalition, an organization of retailers, manufacturers, designers, educational institutions, and government agencies, promotes the idea of using sustainable packaging. Sustainable packaging made from materials that are sourced, manufactured, transported, and recycled using renewable energy. It optimizes the use of renewable or recycled source materials, and is manufactured using clean production technologies. Sustainable packaging should also be recyclable, thus creating a closed loop system for all packaging materials.

Green options help consumers feel better about purchasing, and one marketing strategist believes sustainability in packaging is a growing trend influencing consumer behaviour: "It has been embraced by consumers. I only have to look at how quickly consumers have adopted 'no plastic bags' at grocery stores. Consumers are certainly willing to do their part, and manufacturers know they have to put forward greener options."[21] Not only are consumers willing to do their part, they are demanding marketers do theirs. In response, Coca-Cola and Pepsi introduced beverage bottles made from sugar cane and plant waste.

Sustainable packaging
Packaging that meets the requirements of the product while minimizing the environmental, economic, and social impacts of the product and its package.

Labelling   Labels range from simple tags attached to products to complex graphics that are part of the package. They perform several functions. At the very least, the label *identifies* the product or brand, such as the name Sunkist stamped on oranges. The label might also *describe* several things about the product—who made it, where it was made, when it was made, its contents, how it is to be used, and how to use it safely. For many companies, labels have become an important element in broader marketing campaigns. In Canada, labelling decisions play a very important role in product marketing, because what must be, and what can be, included on a label is strictly regulated. Health Canada, a federal department responsible for helping Canadians maintain and improve their health, regulates labelling for all food products. To that end, nutrition labelling of all prepackaged foods became mandatory in Canada in 2007. Regulations governing the packaging of non-food items is defined in the Consumer Packaging and Labelling Act. Some forward-thinking packaged-food marketers benefited from these regulations by promoting the nutritious features of their products long before it became trendy to do so.

Product Support Services Customer service is another element of product strategy. A company's offer usually includes some support services, which augment actual products.

Many companies use the Internet to provide support services that were not possible before. For example, HP offers a complete set of sales and after-sale services. It promises "HP Total Care—expert help for every stage of your computer's life. From choosing it, to configuring it, to protecting it, to tuning it up—all the way to recycling it." Customers can click onto the HP Total Care service portal that offers online resources for HP products and 24/7 tech support, which can be accessed via email, instant online chat, and telephone.[22]

Product Line Decisions

Product line
A group of products that are closely related because they function in a similar manner, are sold to the same customer groups, are marketed through the same types of outlets, or fall within given price ranges.

Beyond decisions about individual products and services, product strategy also calls for building a product line. A **product line** is a group of products that are closely related because they function in a similar manner, are sold to the same customer groups, are marketed through the same types of outlets, or fall within given price ranges. For example, Nike produces several lines of athletic shoes and apparel, and Marriott offers several lines of hotels.

The major product line decision involves *product line length*—the number of items in the product line. The line is too short if the manager can increase profits by adding items; the line is too long if the manager can increase profits by dropping items.

Product line length is influenced by company objectives and resources. For example, one objective might be to allow for upselling. Thus, BMW wants to move customers up from its 3-series models to 5- and 7-series models. Another objective might be to allow cross-selling: Hewlett-Packard sells printers as well as cartridges. Still another objective might be to protect against economic swings: Gap runs several clothing-store chains (Gap, Old Navy, and Banana Republic), covering different price points.

A company can expand its product line in two ways: by *line filling* or *line stretching*. *Product line filling* involves adding more items within the present range of the line. There are several reasons for product line filling: reaching for extra profits, satisfying dealers, using excess capacity, being the leading full-line company, and plugging holes to keep out competitors. However, line filling is overdone if it results in cannibalization and customer confusion. The company should ensure that new items are noticeably different from existing ones.

Product line stretching occurs when a company lengthens its product line beyond its current range. The company can stretch its line downward, upward, or both ways. Companies located at the upper end of the market can stretch their lines *downward*. A company may stretch downward to plug a market hole that otherwise would attract a new competitor or to respond to a competitor's attack on the upper end. Or it may add low-end products because it finds faster growth taking place in the low-end segments.

Companies can also stretch their product lines *upward*. Sometimes, companies stretch upward to add prestige to their current products. Or they may be attracted by a faster growth rate or higher margins at the higher end. For example, some years ago, each of the leading Japanese auto companies introduced an upmarket automobile: Honda launched Acura; Toyota launched Lexus; and Nissan launched Infiniti. They used entirely new names rather than their own names.

Companies in the middle range of the market may decide to stretch their lines in *both directions*. Marriott did this with its hotel product line. Along with regular Marriott hotels, it added eight new branded hotel lines to serve both the upper and lower ends of the market.

For example, Renaissance Hotels & Resorts aims to attract and please top executives; Fairfield Inn by Marriott, vacationers and business travellers on a tight travel budget; and Courtyard by Marriott, salespeople and other "road warriors."[23] The major risk with this strategy is that some travellers will trade down after finding that the lower-price hotels in the Marriott chain give them pretty much everything they want. However, Marriott would rather capture its customers who move downward than lose them to competitors.

Product Mix Decisions

An organization with several product lines has a product mix. A **product mix (or product portfolio)** consists of all the product lines and items that a company markets. Some companies manage very complex product portfolios. For example, the Campbell Soup Company's product mix consists of three product lines: healthy beverages, baked snacks, and simple meals. Each product line consists of several sub-lines. For example, the simple meals line consists of soups, sauces, and pastas, and each of these has many individual items. Altogether, Campbell's product mix includes hundreds of items.

> **Product mix (or product portfolio)** The set of all product lines and items that a company markets.

A company's product mix has four important dimensions: width, length, depth, and consistency.

Product mix *depth* refers to the number of versions offered of each product in the line. Campbell's has a very deep product mix. For example, it makes and markets many kinds of soups, sauces, and other food products. Finally, the *consistency* of the product mix refers to how closely related the various product lines are in end use, production requirements, distribution channels, or some other way. Within each of their three major product lines, Campbell's products are fairly consistent in that they perform similar functions for buyers and go through the same distribution channels.

Finally, product managers must not only make strategic decisions about marketing their products at home, but in international markets, where some adaptation of product strategy may be required. KFC and Kraft Foods are two marketers that have successfully adapted their product and marketing strategies for the large Chinese market—see Marketing@Work 8.2.

MARKETING@WORK 8.2

Adapting Products for the Biggest Market on Earth

Kraft Foods had a problem—the Chinese weren't buying Oreos. Introduced to the world's most populous nation in 1996, the company's most popular cookie saw only modest sales growth in the ensuing decade. By 2005, it controlled a mere 3 percent of the Chinese cookie market.

For anyone raised in North America, this was a shocking fall for the King of All Cookies. "When I worked in the US, it was the biggest mega-brand we had," says Shawn Warren, a native of Kitchener, Ont., who arrived in 2005 as the company's newly assigned vice-president of

snacks for Asia-Pacific. "Then, when I came over here, Oreo was just this really small brand."

What could possibly be the problem in China? It's a question faced by many western brands that over the past 15 years have flocked east, eager for the potential profits presented by a nation of 1.5 billion people with a ballooning middle class. But brands have often relied too heavily on the same approach that made them popular in the West. Same product, same marketing, just a different language. And it rarely works. As Oreo learned,

scoring success in China requires both exploiting the appeal that big brands have to Chinese consumers and adapting products for local tastes. This small insight led the cookie to go from a piddling three percent to 15 percent in a few short years.

The best example of this approach is KFC—Chinese sales account for nearly 40 percent of worldwide operating profits for its parent company Yum Brands, which also owns Pizza Hut and Taco Bell. The Colonel has dominated China's fast-food landscape since it first landed in

Exhibit 8.15 KFC has been successful in China because it adapts its products for the market. Here, boys dressed as Colonel Sanders promote egg tarts in a KFC restaurant in Shanghai.

1987, thanks, in part, to adding items like breakfast congee and rice dishes to the menu. Last year there were more than 3700 KFC outlets in China, compared to 1464 McDonald's restaurants. For many years they were alone in realizing you need to adapt to succeed in China, but recently other major western brands have begun focusing on the needs of Chinese consumers. For example, Estee Lauder launched an entirely new beauty brand specifically for the Chinese market called Osiao, which the company says was formulated for various types of Asian skin and includes traditional Chinese herbal ingredients like ginseng. Colgate introduced its Flax Fresh tea mouthwash flavour, catering to China's love of all things tea-related. BMW created a longer version of its 5 Series sedan exclusively for the Chinese car market, where the wealthy have personal drivers and want more room in the back seat. And Nestlé altered its Nescafé instant coffee recipe after its research showed Chinese consumers preferred a smoother, milkier "cup of joe" than their European or North American counterparts.

When it comes to adapting product-marketing strategies for China, one of the biggest success stories is Oreo. The billion-dollar Chinese biscuit market can be roughly split into seven categories: sandwich biscuits, plain sweet biscuits,

wafers, plain savory cookies, soda crackers, and egg-roll biscuits. In 2005, Kraft Foods China simply copied each Oreo product manufactured for the United States, and competed solely in the sandwich biscuit category. Its 19 percent share in that segment translated into just 3.5 percent of the overall biscuit market. Since then, the brand has increased its sandwich biscuit take to 46 percent and launched an Oreo wafer cookie that's nabbed 30 percent of the wafer market, to boost its overall share to almost 15 percent. That's the highest market share for Oreo anywhere in the world, including the United States or Canada.

In addition to product form, product flavour must be adapted to local tastes. While we like the classic Oreo, in India for example, consumers think it's not sweet enough. Conversely, Oreo discovered back in 2005 Chinese consumers thought our North American version of the Oreo was too sweet. According to Kraft, there are 135 components to an Oreo cookie, including roastedness, burntness, bitterness, and 132 other "nesses." To create an "original" Oreo for China, Kraft tested more than 20 unique Oreo formulations.

As the company delved deeper into its China market research, they found sales of cookies and other chocolate products tend to slow down in the summer. The

Chinese have what they call "heaty" foods and cooling foods, the former for colder months and the latter for warmer times of the year. Cookies were traditionally a "heaty" food. To boost summer sales, in 2009 Oreo developed a crème that had a cooling sensation when licked to create both a vanilla and green-tea ice-cream-flavoured cookie. It's now the second-most-popular flavour after original Oreo. Fruits are also cooling foods, so the success of the ice-cream-flavoured cookies led them to try more cooling variations. In 2011, after researching what fruit flavours Chinese consumers would like best, they launched Oreo double fruits that put combinations like orange-mango and blueberry-raspberry between the familiar biscuits. "It's about taking a local cultural consumer insight and finding ways to innovate with it," says Warren.

It wasn't just the cookies that needed to change. Kraft also found that its traditional package size was too big and expensive for the average Chinese consumer, so they introduced smaller sizes so they could get into smaller grocery stores and mom-and-pop stores. For advertising, the company ditched the subtitled American ads in favour of a focus on kids, who are at the centre of the Chinese family, and home-grown spokespeople like former NBA star Yao Ming.

All of these strategies helped Oreo grow its market share by 10 times over the past five years. Warren says the Oreo model in China has become the company's model for all its other products. That means get ready for Ritz cracker flavours like "fantastic beef stew" and "very spicy chicken." "There's now a different formulation for Chips Ahoy cookies here than in North America," says Warren. "We've also got the packaging and advertising localized, and as a result over the last few years we've tripled the Chips Ahoy business."

Despite the different shapes, colours and flavours that have catapulted Oreo to the top of the cookie heap in China, some things remain universal. "We do it in different ways around the world," says Warren. "But it's still the ritual of twist, lick and dunk."

Source: "Oreos's Chinese Twist", Jeff Beer, originally published in *Canadian Business*, December 10, 2012, pp. 66–67.

Services Marketing `LO5`

Services are considered a type of product because they are a marketing offer, but marketing offers that are not tangible hard goods, have special considerations when it comes to marketing.

The "service sector," as it is called, is bigger, in terms of dollar value, than the retail sector. Services constitute the single most important industry in Canada's economy, with 68 percent of total gross domestic product, 75 percent of employment, and 53 percent of consumer spending. Service industries in Canada have grown faster than both goods-producing industries and the economy as a whole. The services sector is also a much larger employer than the goods-producing sector. Almost 12 million Canadians were employed in the service sector compared with the 4 million people working in the goods-producing sector. And the biggest service is the retail industry, with 132 000 workers.[24]

The service sector includes all government services, hospitals, the military, police and fire departments, Canada Post, schools, colleges, and universities. It also includes not-for-profit organizations such as museums, charities, and churches. The largest part of the service industry is the business services segment, that is, for-profit companies that market and sell services to either consumers or businesses, and develop and maintain profitable customer relationships. Business services include airlines, banks, hotels, insurance companies, consulting firms, law and accounting firms, entertainment companies, real-estate firms, and advertising agencies.

Nature and Characteristics of a Service

A company must consider four special service characteristics when designing marketing programs: *intangibility*, *inseparability*, *variability*, and *perishability* (see Figure 8.6).

Service intangibility means that services cannot be seen, tasted, felt, heard, or smelled before they are bought. For example, people undergoing cosmetic surgery cannot see the result before the purchase. Airline passengers have nothing but a ticket and the promise that they and their luggage will arrive safely at the intended destination, ideally at the same time. To reduce uncertainty, buyers look for "signals" of service quality. They draw conclusions about quality from the place, people, price, equipment, and communications that they can see.

Therefore, the service provider's task is to make the service tangible in one or more ways and to send the right signals about quality. One analyst calls this *evidence management*, in which the service organization presents its customers with organized, honest evidence of its capabilities.

Service intangibility
A major characteristic of services—they cannot be seen, tasted, felt, heard, or smelled before they are bought.

FIGURE 8.6 Special Characteristics of Services

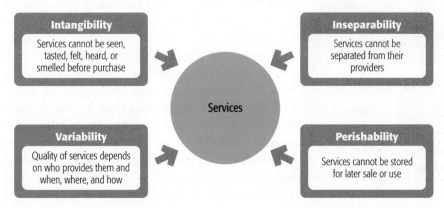

Intangibility
Services cannot be seen, tasted, felt, heard, or smelled before purchase

Inseparability
Services cannot be separated from their providers

Services

Variability
Quality of services depends on who provides them and when, where, and how

Perishability
Services cannot be stored for later sale or use

Courtesy of Scotiabank

Service inseparability

A major characteristic of services—they are produced and consumed at the same time and cannot be separated from their providers.

Service variability

A major characteristic of services—their quality may vary greatly, depending on who provides them and when, where, and how.

Service perishability

A major characteristic of services—they cannot be stored for later sale or use.

Physical goods are produced, then stored, later sold, and still later consumed. In contrast, services are first sold, then produced and consumed at the same time. In services marketing, the service provider is the product. **Service inseparability** means that services cannot be separated from their providers, whether the providers are people or machines. If a service employee provides the service, then the employee becomes a part of the service. Because the customer is also present as the service is produced, *provider–customer interaction* is a special feature of services marketing. Both the provider and the customer affect the service outcome.

Service variability means that the quality of services depends on who provides them as well as when, where, and how they are provided. For example, some hotels—say, Marriott—have reputations for providing better service than others. Still, within a given Marriott hotel, one registration-counter employee may be cheerful and efficient, whereas another standing just a metre away may be unpleasant and slow. Even the quality of a single Marriott employee's service varies according to his or her energy and frame of mind at the time of each customer encounter.

Service perishability means that services cannot be stored for later sale or use. Some salons charge customers for missed appointments because the service value existed only at that point and disappeared when the customer did not show up. The perishability of services is not a problem when demand is steady. However, when demand fluctuates, service firms often have difficult problems. For example, because of rush-hour demand, public transportation companies have to own much more equipment than they would if demand were even throughout the day. Service firms must therefore design strategies for producing a better match between demand and supply. Hotels and resorts charge lower prices in the off-season to attract more guests. And restaurants hire part-time employees to serve during peak periods.

Marketing Strategies for Service Firms

As we have seen, differentiation is very important for new products. It is perhaps even more important for services because they are intangible. To the extent that customers view the services of different providers as similar, they care less about the provider than the price. The solution to price competition is to develop a differentiated offer, delivery, and image—in other words, to establish a clear *positioning*.

Without a physical product, positioning is based on associations and advertising messages. Take banks, for example. RBC uses a brand icon named Arbie—a cartoon gentleman in a blue suit and a top hat, in all their advertising and signage. Arbie is seen interacting with bank offerings, and projects an affable personality. RBC associates itself with TIFF, the Toronto International Film Festival, and positions itself as being dedicated to culture. Scotiabank, on the other hand, uses "real people" in authentic situations to demonstrate that there is more to life than money, and their association with hockey, through numerous sponsorships, is a further extension and support of their value proposition "enabling richer lives" through community support.

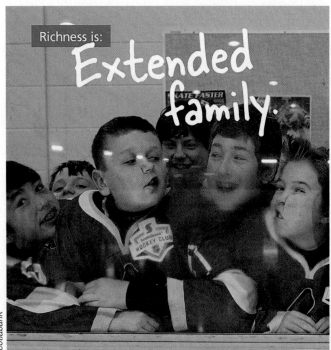

Richness is:
Extended family.

Proudly supporting 3,700 community teams.

f /scotiahockeyclub   @scotiahockey   You're richer than you think: **Scotiabank**®

Exhibit 8.16 Positioning of service firms: Scotiabank's positioning as the bank that helps real people do more with their money is reinforced with its slogan, "You're richer than you think," which appears on all the bank's marketing materials.

Because services differ from tangible products, they often require additional marketing approaches. These include understanding and managing the *service-profit chain*, and *internal marketing*.

The Service-Profit Chain   In a service business, the customer and front-line service employee *interact* to create the service. Effective interaction, in turn, depends on the skills of front-line service employees and on the support processes backing these employees. Because of this, successful service companies must focus their attention on *both* their customers and their employees. They understand the **service-profit chain**, which links service firm profits with employee and customer satisfaction. This chain consists of five links (see Figure 8.7):[25]

Service-profit chain
The chain that links service firm profits with employee and customer satisfaction.

- *Internal service quality:* superior employee selection and training, a quality work environment, and strong support for those dealing with customers, which results in . . .

- *Satisfied and productive service employees:* more satisfied, loyal, and hard-working employees, which results in . . .

- *Greater service value:* more effective and efficient customer value creation and service delivery, which results in . . .

- *Satisfied and loyal customers:* satisfied customers who remain loyal, repeat purchase, and refer other customers, which results in . . .

- *Healthy service profits and growth:* superior service firm performance.

An important aspect of the service-profit chain is **internal marketing**, or orienting and motivating customer-contact employees and supporting service people to work as a team to provide customer satisfaction. Part of the job for marketing managers in a service firm is to get everyone in the organization to be customer centred. In fact, internal marketing should precede external marketing. For example, Four Seasons Hotels and Resorts starts by hiring the right people and carefully orienting and inspiring them to give unparalleled customer service.[26]

Internal marketing
Orienting and motivating customer-contact employees and supporting service people to work as a team to provide customer satisfaction.

> Four Seasons has perfected the art of high-touch, carefully crafted service that pampers its guests with elegant surroundings and highly personalized 24-hour service. "What you see from the public point of view is a reflection of our people—they are the heart and soul of what makes this company succeed," says Four Seasons founder and CEO Isadore Sharp.

FIGURE 8.7 The Service-Profit Chain

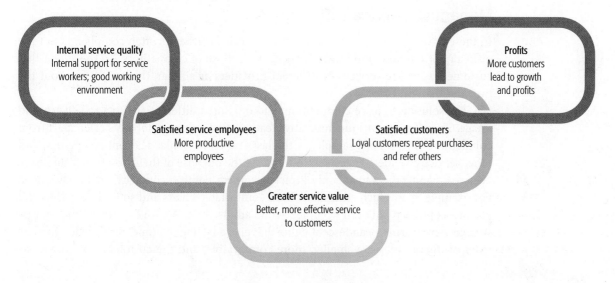

Robyn Twomey

Exhibit 8.17 **The service-profit chain:** Happy employees make for happy customers. At Four Seasons, employees feel as important and pampered as the guests.

"When we say people are our most important asset—it's not just talk." Just as it does for customers, Four Seasons respects and pampers its employees. It knows that happy, satisfied employees make for happy, satisfied customers.

"Personal service is not something you can dictate as a policy," he adds. "How you treat your employees is a reflection of how you expect them to treat customers." Four Seasons brings this culture to life by hiring the best people, orienting them carefully, instilling in them a sense of pride, and motivating them by recognizing and rewarding outstanding service deeds. "Every job applicant, whether hoping to fold laundry or teach yoga, goes through at least four interviews," notes one reporter. "We look for employees who share that Golden Rule—people who, by nature, believe in treating others as they would have them treat us," says Sharp.

Four Seasons employees earn higher than industry-average salaries, have generous retirement and profit sharing plans, and enjoy perks such as free meals and free rooms. As a result, the Four Seasons staff loves the hotel just as much as customers do. Although guests can check out anytime they like, employees never want to leave. The annual turnover for full-time employees is only 18 percent, half the industry average. Four Seasons has been included on *Fortune* magazine's list of 100 Best Companies to Work For every year since the list began in 1998. And that's the biggest secret to Four Seasons' success. Just as the service-profit chain suggests, taking good care of customers begins with taking good care of those who take care of customers.

Today, as competition and costs increase, and as productivity and quality decrease, more service marketing sophistication is needed. Service companies face three major marketing tasks: They want to increase their *service differentiation*, *service quality*, and *service productivity*.

Managing Service Differentiation

In these days of intense price competition, service marketers often complain about the difficulty of differentiating their services from those of competitors. To the extent that customers view the services of different providers as similar, they care less about the provider than the price.

The solution to price competition is to develop a differentiated offer, delivery, and image. The offer can include innovative features that set one company's offer apart from competitors' offers. For example, in the last few years, banks, telecom companies, and other service providers have been re-thinking the purpose of their storefronts, and have been redesigning them to not only attract customers, but to encourage them to stay longer. For example, many such stores now have comfortable chairs and sofas, free coffee, and play areas to keep children occupied while adults shop. At Rogers stores, one-on-one stations have warm, incandescent lights that give a feeling of home. BMO redesigned its teller counters—they are smaller, more comfortable, and the customer now has a bar stool to sit on—to reduce the confrontational nature of sales and the psychological distance between seller and customer. And some banks have hired greeters to welcome customers and answer basic questions.[27]

Managing Service Quality

A service firm can differentiate itself by delivering consistently higher quality than its competitors provide. Like manufacturers before them, most service industries have now joined the customer-driven quality movement. And like product marketers, service providers need to identify what target customers expect in regards to service quality.

Unfortunately, service quality is harder to define and judge than product quality. For instance, it is harder to agree on the quality of a haircut than on the quality of a hair dryer. Customer retention is perhaps the best measure of quality—a service firm's ability to hang onto its customers depends on how consistently it delivers value to them.

Top service companies set high service-quality standards. They watch service performance closely, both their own and that of competitors. They do not settle for merely good service; they strive for 100 percent defect-free service. A 98 percent performance standard may sound good, but using this standard, 64 000 FedEx packages would be lost each day, 10 words would be misspelled on each printed page, 400 000 prescriptions would be misfiled daily, and drinking water would be unsafe eight days a year.[28]

Managing Service Productivity

With their costs rising rapidly, service firms are under great pressure to increase service productivity. They can do so in several ways. They can train current employees better or hire new ones who will work harder or more skilfully. Or they can increase the quantity of their service by giving up some quality. The provider can "industrialize the service" by adding equipment and standardizing production, as in McDonald's assembly-line approach to fast-food retailing. Finally, the service provider can harness the power of technology. Although we often think of technology's power to save time and costs in manufacturing companies, it also has great—and often untapped—potential to make service workers more productive.

However, companies must avoid pushing productivity so hard that doing so reduces quality. Attempts to industrialize a service or cut costs can make a service company more efficient in the short run. But they can also reduce its longer-run ability to innovate, maintain service quality, or respond to consumer needs and desires. For example, some airlines have learned this lesson the hard way as they attempt to economize in the face of rising costs. They stopped offering even the little things for free—such as inflight snacks—and began charging extra for everything from curbside luggage check-in to aisle seats. The result is a plane full of resentful customers who avoid the airline whenever they can. In their attempts to improve productivity, these airlines mangled customer service.

Thus, in attempting to improve service productivity, companies must be mindful of how they create and deliver customer value. In short, they should be careful not to take the "service" out of service.

A Baby Airline Is Born

It was, in many ways, like anticipating the arrival of a child. After two years of research, discussion, analysis, more discussion, and then commitment, "Encore," WestJet's new regional subsidiary, was due in mere weeks and the excitement could be felt throughout the company in the spring of 2013. "47 days!" shouted WestJet's vice-president of communications and community relations, Richard Bartrem, to a colleague as the two WestJetters scurried past one another in front of the "History Wall," where every significant WestJet milestone is enshrined. Something like, "June 24, 2013—WestJet Encore takes flight" will also have its place on the wall.

"Encore was a natural evolution for us," recalls Chris Avery, vice-president of network planning, alliances, and corporate development. "We wanted to solidify our foundation here in Canada with regional coverage, as a complementing piece to our growing North American network and international partnerships." Based upon research and industry trends, Encore would serve two segments: those who wanted to fly to WestJet's established Canadian network from currently unserved destinations, and those who wanted to fly to a hub which, through WestJet's interline and code-sharing partnerships, could connect them with the rest of the world.

WestJet Encore would not have received permission for take-off without first having the buy-in from WestJetters themselves. As president and CEO Gregg Saretsky commented during the early stages of analysis, "one of the cornerstones of our success is engaging with employees early on in key decisions." WestJet employees, of course, were doubly invested, both as employees and shareholders. "Going to them and telling the story was key," recalls Bob Cummings, executive vice-president of sales, marketing and guest experience. "Once they saw the strategic value, they were on board."

When that key stakeholder group gave the green light, the product development was set to begin. Given the generally shorter haul nature of the anticipated flights, WestJet, for the first time in its 16-year existence, had to examine alternative aircraft. Within months of meeting with WestJetters, a deal was inked with Montreal-based Bombardier to purchase 20 Q400 NextGen planes. Next came the extremely complex task of building a new network of destinations where the airline would fly.

Naming the new airline was a fun but important final step. Once again it was put to a WestJetter vote and christened "Encore." The name spoke for all WestJetters, according to Cummings. "Encore reinforced that WestJetters were ready to repeat the success of WestJet."

QUESTIONS

1. How did WestJet use internal marketing to gain support for Encore among its employees?
2. In what stage of new-product development were WestJet executives when they presented the idea of Encore to employees?
3. In what way did WestJet's introduction of Encore represent a product line expansion?

REVIEWING THE CONCEPTS

1. Define *product* and describe and classify different types of product offerings.

Broadly defined, a *product* is anything that can be offered to a market for attention, acquisition, use, or consumption that might satisfy a want or need. Products include physical objects but also services, events, persons, places, organizations, ideas, or mixes of these entities. *Services* are products that consist of activities, benefits, or satisfactions offered for sale that are essentially intangible, such as banking, hotel, tax preparation, and home-repair services.

A product is more than a simple set of tangible features. Each product or service offered to customers can be viewed on three levels. The *core customer value* consists of the core problem-solving benefits that consumers seek when they buy a product. The *actual product* exists around the core and includes the quality level, features, design, brand name, and packaging. The *augmented product* is the actual product plus the various services and benefits offered with it, such as a warranty, free delivery, installation, and maintenance.

Products and services fall into two broad classes based on the types of consumers that use them. *Consumer products*—those bought by final consumers—are usually classified according to consumer shopping habits (convenience products, shopping products, specialty products, and unsought products). *Industrial products*—purchased for further processing or for use in conducting a business—include materials and parts, capital items, and supplies and services. Other marketable entities—such as organizations, persons, places, and ideas—can also be thought of as products.

2. List and define the steps in the new-product development process and the major considerations in managing this process, and explain why new products fail.

The new-product development process consists of eight stages, starting with *idea generation*. A new approach to idea generation that some companies are employing today is *crowdsourcing*—inviting broad communities of people such as customers, employees, independent scientists and researchers, and even the public at large, into the new product innovation process. Next comes *idea screening*, which reduces the number of ideas based on the company's own criteria. Ideas that pass the screening stage continue through *product concept development*, in which a detailed version of the new-product idea is stated in meaningful consumer terms. In the next stage, *concept testing*, new-product concepts are tested with a group of target consumers to determine whether the concepts have strong consumer appeal. Strong concepts proceed to *marketing strategy development*, in which an initial marketing strategy for the new product is developed from the product concept. In the *business-analysis* stage, a review of the sales, costs, and profit projections for a new product is conducted to determine whether the new product is likely to satisfy the company's objectives. With positive results here, the ideas become more concrete through *product development* and *test marketing* and finally are launched during *commercialization*.

Despite this careful process, many new products fail, sometimes because they lack differentiation, and sometimes because they were not positioned properly, or the wrong market segment was targeted. The diffusion of innovations theory suggests that new products sometimes fail because they are unable to cross the gaps between the different market segments of innovators, early adopters, early majority, and late majority. The Technology Adoption Life Cycle suggests that in the marketing of high-tech products a chasm exists between the early adopters and the early majority, and that only new technology products that are able to cross that gap will be successful.

3. Describe the stages of the product life cycle and how marketing strategies change during the product's life cycle.

Each product has a *life cycle* marked by a changing set of problems and opportunities. The sales of the typical product follow an S-shaped curve made up of five stages. The cycle begins with the *product development stage* in which the company finds and develops a new-product idea. The *introduction stage* is marked by slow growth and low profits as the product is distributed to the market. If successful, the product enters a *growth stage*, which offers rapid sales growth and increasing profits. Next comes a *maturity stage* in which sales growth slows down and profits stabilize. Finally, the product enters a *decline stage* in which sales and profits dwindle. The company's task during this stage is to recognize the decline and to decide whether it should maintain, harvest, or drop the product.

In the *introduction stage*, the company must choose a launch strategy consistent with its intended product positioning. Much money is needed to attract distributors, build inventories, and inform consumers of the new product to achieve the trial phase. In the *growth stage*, companies continue to educate potential consumers and distributors.

In addition, the company works to stay ahead of the competition and sustain rapid market growth by improving product quality, adding new product features and models, entering new market segments and distribution channels, shifting advertising from building product awareness to building product conviction and purchase, and lowering prices at the right time to attract new buyers.

In the *maturity stage*, companies continue to invest in maturing products and consider modifying the market, the product, and the marketing mix. When *modifying the market*, the company attempts to increase the consumption of the current product. When *modifying the product*, the company changes some of the product's characteristics—such as quality, features, or style—to attract new users or inspire more usage. When *modifying the marketing mix*, the company works to improve sales by changing one or more of the marketing-mix elements. Once the company recognizes that a product has entered the *decline stage*, management must decide whether to *maintain* the brand without change, hoping that competitors will drop out of the market; *harvest* the product, reducing costs and trying to maintain sales; or *drop* the product, selling it to another firm or liquidating it at salvage value.

4. Describe the decisions companies make regarding their individual products and services, product lines, and product mixes.

Individual product decisions involve product attributes, packaging, labelling, and product support services. *Product attribute* decisions involve product quality, features, and style and design. *Packaging* provides many key benefits, such as protection, economy, convenience, and promotion. Today, many marketers are exploring options for *sustainable packaging*—packaging that meets the requirements of the product while minimizing the environmental, economic, and social impacts of the product and its package. Package decisions often include designing *labels*, which identify, describe, and possibly promote the product. Companies also develop *product support services* that enhance customer service and satisfaction and safeguard against competitors.

Most companies produce a product line rather than a single product. A *product line* is a group of products that are related in function, customer-purchase needs, or distribution channels. *Line stretching* involves extending a line downward, upward, or in both directions to occupy a gap that might otherwise be filled by a competitor. In contrast, *line filling* involves adding items within the present range of the line. All product lines and items offered to customers by a particular seller make up the *product mix*. The mix can be described by four dimensions: width, length, depth, and consistency. These dimensions are the tools for developing the company's product strategy.

5. Identify the four characteristics that affect the marketing of services and the additional marketing considerations that services require.

Services are characterized by four key characteristics: they are *intangible*, *inseparable*, *variable*, and *perishable*. Each characteristic poses problems and marketing requirements. Marketers work to find ways to make the service more tangible, to increase the productivity of providers who are inseparable from their products, to standardize the quality in the face of variability, and to improve demand movements and supply capacities in the face of service perishability.

Good service companies focus attention on *both* customers and employees. They understand the *service-profit chain*, which links service firm profits with employee and customer satisfaction. Services marketing strategy calls not only for external marketing but also for *internal marketing* to motivate employees. To succeed, service marketers must create *competitive differentiation*, offer high *service quality*, and find ways to increase *service productivity*.

KEY TERMS

TALK ABOUT MARKETING

1. Choose a company whose products you are familiar with. If you were a marketing manager at that company, what specific sources might you turn to for new-product ideas? Assuming the company has a website, how might it be used to interact with the market to generate new-product ideas? Brainstorm your own new product ideas for this company.

2. Choose three of the products mentioned in this chapter. Which stage of the product life cycle is each of these products in? Explain how you were able to identify the stage. How long do you think it will be before each product enters the next stage of the life cycle?

3. Yoplait markets a product called Yoplait Tubes that is targeted to children. Visit the Yoplait website and learn about this product. Now, assume the role of the product manager responsible for Yoplait Tubes. You have been asked to modify the market for this product. Do you think this product can be adapted for the adult market?

Devise a plan for testing the product concept with 25- to 45-year-olds. What factors would be critical to your test? What questions would you ask the testers?

4. Visit a large department store, drug store, or grocery store and find a product you believe is an example of a fad. What evidence can you find—through online research or by asking people you know who have experience with the product—that supports your theory? Explain why you believe the product won't last in the market.

5. If you were a marketing manager at Tim Hortons' head office, what sort of internal and interactive marketing programs would you develop?

6. Discuss how the four characteristics of services—intangibility, inseparability, variability, and perishability—affect Air Canada. What marketing initiatives could Air Canada employ to try to mitigate the negative effects of these characteristics as much as possible?

THINK LIKE A MARKETING MANAGER

Dell revolutionized the personal computer industry in the 1990s by giving consumers what they wanted at the time: commodity components they needed without having to buy the ones they didn't need. The focus was on functionality, not on style. Now that all personal computers are functional, and prices have come down, computer makers compete on the basis of features and design. Dell's latest line of new personal computer products is the Ultrabook, a slim design laptop that converts to a tablet.

QUESTIONS

1. As a consumer, what do you value most in your personal computer? Talk to your friends and find out whether they value the same thing, or whether they name other

features or benefits as most important. How could the marketers at Dell use this information to develop its next new personal computer?

2. Dell also marketed a line of its popular Inspiron laptops in colours, from pink to "spring green." Find out whether they are still available. If not, were they just a fad?

3. Dell has trademarked the name Ultrabook, but other computer manufacturers may offer similar products. Find out what similar products are available. What is the Ultrabook's point of differentiation?

4. What else could Dell do to make its computers more stylish?

MARKETING ETHICS

You may be using a book you purchased or borrowed from another student. People sell or share books all the time, but not e-books! With the growth of electronic readers,

such as Amazon.com's Kindle, buying electronic books is easy and growing in popularity. But purchasers of e-books don't have the same rights as those purchasing physical books. Some consumers found out that it is just as easy for sellers to take them back as it is for buyers to get them. For instance, Amazon.com realized it did not have the proper rights to sell certain books—such as George Orwell's *1984*—and used its wireless technology to delete them from its customers' Kindle e-readers. While purchases were refunded, some called the company an Orwellian "Big Brother" because the deletion was done without their knowledge. Imagine if you purchased *1984* and tried to read it right before the test only to learn it had disappeared from your Kindle. Owning an e-book is much like licensing software with digital rights management software embedded to prevent sharing and selling. Such digital rights management software also confuses consumers and limits the number of devices that can play a single e-book.

QUESTIONS

1. How would you classify e-books—a tangible good, an experience, or a service? Explain your choice.

2. Amazon.com had the legal right to delete e-books from the Kindle, but did the company do it the right way? Also, should consumers be able to do whatever they want with an e-book once they purchase it, just as they can with a tangible book?

MARKETING TECHNOLOGY

An exciting new technology that has begun to be employed by marketers is 3-D projection mapping. The technique allows marketers to use the facade of a building as a screen onto which images are projected, with the projection programmed to utilize the façade's features (doors, windows, etc.) in a mixture of real 3-D objects and images which are huge, bright, and can be seen from miles away. The technology was used during the closing ceremonies of the London Olympics to create jaw-dropping images on the face of Buckingham Palace. Tech product marketers like LG, Nokia, and Samsung have used the technology to create larger than life advertising displays, but so have companies like Ralph Lauren and Red Bull. The company behind most of the 3-D projection technology in use today is Christie Digital.

QUESTIONS

1. Christie Digital is a large Japanese company with offices around the world, including Canadian headquarters in Kitchener, Ontario. Their name is not well known, however. How might Christie Digital use its own technology to increase awareness of its brand?

2. Most marketing applications of 3-D mapping technology so far have been to advertise brands or products in an entertaining way. How could this technology be used in a more engaging manner to promote a service business?

MARKETING BY THE NUMBERS

When introducing new products, it's usually not easy to determine at what price it should be offered. At the very least, however, a marketer must understand the costs associated with producing the product and set the price at some level above those costs. For example, suppose that a manufacturer of lawn mowers incurs a cost of $75 for each mower it produces and that it produces a total of 1 million mowers each year. Fixed costs for this company are $5 million.

QUESTIONS

1. What is the unit cost for each mower this company produces?

2. If the manufacturer desires a markup of 60 percent on sales, at what price should this product be sold to a reseller such as a wholesaler or a distributor?

SUBARU

When a company has a winning product, everything else falls into place. Or does it? Subaru is a winning company (one of the few automotive companies to sustain growth and profits in hard economic times) with various winning products, including the Impreza, Legacy, Forester, and Outback. But what happens when any one product starts to decline in popularity?

This video demonstrates how Subaru constantly engages in new-product development as part of its efforts to manage the product life cycle for each of its models. Subaru is focused on both developing the next version of each existing model and developing possible new models to boost its product portfolio.

After viewing the video, answer the following questions:

QUESTIONS

1. Choose one of Subaru's current models and describe its life cycle so far. Which stage do you think it is currently in?

2. What consumer trends were mentioned in the video, and how do they affect Subaru's product development?

3. What does Subaru do, specifically, to remain customer-focused as it develops new products?

GRAF CANADA–FOCUSED ON FIT AND PERFORMANCE

Case prepared by David Rose, Wilfrid Laurier University

The people at Graf Canada are crazy about the foot and what it can do, so it is not surprising that the company's mission is all about fit and producing a better pair of skates. The company sells skates at price and performance levels ranging from entry level to performance to pro level. A customer's skill level and budget will influence their choice of model, but no matter which level they choose they get Graf's True 3-D fit, based on their heel width, backstay shape, and heel instep depth. Graf skates are only available through authorized dealers because the company is convinced that it takes an experienced professional to determine the right skate to match a customer's foot type. They devote considerable time to educating and training their dealers in the science of fit and continually work to better understand the foot and how the fit can be improved.

Graf Canada chairman of the board and four-time Stanley Cup winner Claude Lemieux knows all too well the importance of high-performance equipment. "As a hockey player, what you need is a great pair of skates. If you can't skate, you can't play." After 21 years in the NHL, Lemieux has seen what happens when skates don't fit properly and he's warning people of the alarming increase in foot injuries caused by modern skates. He describes an "epidemic of bone spurs and lace bite" resulting from ill-fitting skates.

Lace bite is an inflammation of the foot's exterior tendons, which in hockey is caused by the boot or skate laces continually rubbing on the tendons on the top of the foot or ankle bones. These can sometimes get so painful that players have trouble tying their skates. Bone spurs are tiny bone outgrowths from joints that form in response to pressure, rubbing, or stress that continues over a period of time, and can limit joint movement and cause sharp pain.

Lemieux has seen players having to take two or three days off the ice because of these injuries and wearing ice packs on their feet after practices because they are in so much pain. He also sees players trying to avoid this pain by adding gel pads inside their skates. The problem with this solution? The pads can affect the fit of the skate in ways that actually affect the player's skating ability. Lemieux himself never suffered foot problems, but many former teammates did. "I've been around many locker rooms at the NHL level and just looking at players' feet,

I can tell who is having problems. They are the ones wearing the really, really stiff skates."

Lemieux attributes his ability to avoid foot problems to always wearing a traditional, soft leather skate, which provides extra flexibility. "I was very happy with the way my skates felt and I was very happy with the boots we had way back in the 1990s and early 2000s." Over the years, most skate manufacturers have made their skates stiffer and lighter, assuming that would make hockey players faster, but Lemieux is not convinced. "I don't know how it developed. All I can tell you, as a player when I saw it, I didn't like it. Everyone has been sold on the 'lighter is better, faster', but we're working on a study that's going to prove that's not the case."

Lemieux and Graf Canada have teamed up with Kelly Lockwood, an associate professor in the kinesiology department at Brock University in St. Catharines, Ontario, to examine the link between foot injuries and skate design, hopefully to find ways to build a better skate that can prevent bone spurs and lace bite. Lockwood has been working in Brock's state-of-the-art skating lab for more than a decade, with athletes, sporting bodies, and equipment companies. She is enthusiastic about working with Lemieux: "He's passionate and it's nice to see a skate company chaired by someone who has worn skates. He's walked the walk and it's nice he can talk the talk as well."

The ultimate goal of Lockwood's research is to design a boot that permits the forward flexing required in a powerful skating stride. She feels the lighter, stiffer boots that are so common today don't allow athletes to bend or get down to their knees, a position of power as a skater. "It's the ability of the boot to complement the biomechanics of the skater. If you need to flex, that boot has to flex. The way athletes today permit forward flexion is by not tying up the boot all the way. Some kids can get away with it, but other kids end up with a lot of lateral movement. That's a real floppy or inefficient translation. You have a loss of force that could have been translated to the ice."

The first phase of Lockwood's study, funded by a provincial grant, is to provide proof that forward flexion in skate boots enhances skating ability. Her study will involve controlled lab-based data as well as on-ice testing that consists of skill drills to assess skaters under three different conditions: wearing the boot of their choice, wearing a custom-fit boot provided by Graf, and wearing a custom-fit boot with a device that permits more forward flexion. Her 60 test subjects include minor hockey players, Brock varsity players, OHL players, professionals, retired NHL players, recreational players, coaches, and referees. If her study proves that a more flexible boot makes hockey players faster, Graf would be the benefactor since they have been one of the few skate manufacturers not to buy the lighter and stiffer argument.

Graf's position in the skate industry is based on the *science* of skating and producing skates with superior fit. They are now taking that scientific approach to other areas of hockey, expanding their product line beyond skates into hockey sticks, hockey gloves, and protective equipment. Sticks are the number one product line in the hockey market and players purchase sticks more frequently than other equipment, so it is an attractive area to enter. However, Lemieux sees opportunities to enhance the performance of their sticks and give players the level of technology they expect from a Graf product. For example, they are the only ones to offer a junior stick with whip flex technology. "It's like a golf club—you can feel it in the stick," he says.

With gloves, it's also a story about fit. Most gloves have straight thumbs, but that is not the way the hand works, so Graf has introduced the first glove that fits the anatomical structure of the hand with a natural gap between the thumb and hand.

Graf's focus on fit and performance and their ongoing research into new product designs has given them a loyal following of over 100 professional hockey players and many NHL referees who have chosen Graf skates without being paid to do so. They feel their greatest endorsement is the person who chooses their product because it provides the fit and quality they are looking for.

Sources: Bernie Puchalski, "Building a Better Skate," *St. Catharines Standard*, October 18, 2011; "Research Story: Professor Kelly Lockwood–Graf Canada," Brock University website, accessed March 2013; "Kelly L. Lockwood Research," Brock University website, accessed March 2013; "Bone Spur," Cigna health services website, accessed March 2013; Graf Canada website, grafcanada.com; John Matisz, "Claude Lemieux; Hockey Connoisseur," *The Good Point*, September 12, 2011; Matt Horner, "Hockey Skate Trend Increases Injury, Study Suggests," *The Good Point*, October 20, 2011; "Discovering a Better Boot Design," Brock University website, accessed March 2013; "Researcher Works with NHL Veterans to Improve the Hockey Skate," *The Brock News*, December 21, 2011.

QUESTIONS FOR DISCUSSION

1. What type of consumer product is Graf selling? Has Graf considered the marketing mix recommendations in this chapter? In what ways, if any, could the marketing mix be changed to better reflect this type of product?

2. Which stage of the product life cycle do you think hockey skates are in? How does Graf's focus on improving the design of the skate fit with suggested marketing strategies for products at this stage?

3. Is Graf following the new-product development process described in this chapter? What stage are they at? What's next?

MyMarketingLab

 *Courtesy of Flying Monkeys Craft Brewery*

AFTER STUDYING THIS CHAPTER, YOU SHOULD BE ABLE TO

1 define and describe the concept of a brand

2 explain the roles of brand personality, brand status, and brand equity in building brands

3 list and describe the major strategic and ongoing management decisions marketers must make about brands

4 summarize the ways marketers can engage consumers through brand communications

5 describe the roles of storytelling, branded content, branded entertainment, and social media in brand communications

Brand Strategy and Management

PREVIEWING THE CONCEPTS

In this chapter, we'll study how companies create, develop, and manage brands—but what, exactly, is a brand? Many people think that a brand is just a logo, but it is so much more than that. A strong brand gives meaning to a name; it stands for something in the mind of the consumer. Some marketers say a brand is the sum total of what the company stands for.

The first step in creating a brand is giving it a name. Once the brand is named, marketers can begin positioning the brand, developing the brand's personality, and telling the brand story. We'll learn more about the importance of brand stories later in this chapter, but first, let's look at a how one beer marketer created a unique and colourful brand—twice.

FLYING MONKEYS: BUILDING A BRAND FROM THE GROUND UP—TWICE

Marketing is all about building brands that connect deeply with customers, and when it comes to branding beer, a product that is not highly differentiated, creating that connection may be the most important part of the company's marketing strategy. At Flying Monkeys Craft Brewery in Barrie, Ontario, the creator and manager of the Flying Monkeys brand is Andrea Chiodo. What started out small and local is now a brewery that does $3.5 million in annual sales. Flying Monkeys is available in more than 1000 retailers and bars in Ontario, is distributed across Canada, and even ships to Scandinavia. Andrea says, "If you had told me twenty years ago, when I was an English professor at the University of Mississippi, that I would be creating a company called Flying Monkeys Craft Brewery, I would have said it sounds like something spit out by a random word generator."

Flying Monkeys is more than just the name of the company, it's a *brand*—Flying Monkeys means craft beer that is not afraid to be different. And in the craft beer business, being successful requires more than just brewing a good product. It requires building a strong, memorable brand that is able to establish a clear position in the mind of the beer drinking consumer. The Flying Monkeys brand is rich, colourful, and quirky. It is brought to life in their crazy packaging, their slogan, "Normal is weird," and their pun (and fun)-filled product names: Antigravity Light Ale, Hoptical Illusion Almost Pale Ale, Netherworld Cascadian Dark Ale, and Smashbomb Atomic IPA. Their website (see photo) is reminiscent of Monty Python artist Terry Gilliam's surrealist style: Monkeys parachuting from bottle caps, giant green fingers crushing hops, and pails of lard on the ingredients page are not meant to be taken literally: "We could reference the Beer Purity Law of 1516 (Reinheitsgebot), but it just comes off sounding pretentious. We don't put junk in our beer because it's just not right." Every illustration, every communication, and every product that comes out of Flying Monkeys headquarters represents this brand personality, right down to the bottle caps with their offbeat, fortune cookie-esque sayings. It's a brand personality that grew and developed from the personalities of Andrea and Peter Chiodo.

The story of the Flying Monkeys brand is inextricably wound up in the story of Andrea and her husband, Peter, and the brand's personality is, in many ways, an extension of their personalities. Says Andrea, "When Peter told me he wanted to quit his job and start a craft brewery in Barrie I figured he would work on the plan for a while, discover holes in his theories and declare the idea dead." But what seemed at the time to be a crazy idea eventually turned into the couple following their passions—Peter's for brewing beer, and Andrea's for creativity.

Peter had grown up in the suburbs of Toronto and used to help his grandfather brew beer in his basement. What was for the grandfather an exercise in thrift became for his grandson an introduction to a passion he'd continue for life. In grad school Peter and his friends started brewing concoctions in a spare closet of his student house, and on weekends Peter and Andrea would explore the region and sample all the interesting, flavourful, craft beer they could find. Hooked on the beer bug, they bought some recipe books, better home-brewing supplies, sought out advice, and with time their beer got better.

In 2002 the couple, now married and with three small children, moved to Barrie and began to make serious plans to open a microbrewery. At that time there were small breweries like Sleeman and Creemore in Ontario, but the term "craft beer" didn't yet exist. The market didn't seem to have a palate for bolder flavoured beers, but Andrea and Peter did. "We loved to take little day trips to small breweries and we always asked for local brews when we visited places," continues Andrea. "In the States, I loved the funky names of beers: Turbo Dog, Pete's Wicked Ale, Grant's Perfect Porter, Purple Haze—and the folksy, edgy art that adorned their labels. Little did I know our hobby was actually market research!"

While Peter worked on beer recipes, Andrea thought about the brand. What should they call their brewery? What names should they give to their beers? What would their story be? At the time, the city of Barrie was gearing up for its sesquicentennial and Andrea, being a history buff, loved the story of Robert Simpson, the first reeve and mayor of Barrie, and renowned brewmaster—so she named their brewery the Simcoe Steam Brewing Company. It was a brand that fit right in with the trend, as most Ontario breweries were named after historically significant people and geographical regions—Great Lakes, Wellington County, Mill Street, Muskoka. But that was the problem. "We had our brand, and it fit right in with all the other beer brands," says Andrea. "We were in the middle of the pack. We took our place in the tradition. Our brand was nationalistic yet local, catchy, yet still classy. We thought of ourselves as the Creemore of Barrie."

Then one fateful night the phone rang and the Chiodos were told that the San Francisco Bay Brewing Company, brewers of Anchor Steam, had a trademark on the word steam as it applies to steam beer and brewing. Anyone using the word "steam" in the name of a brewery or a beer was subject to a trademark infringement lawsuit. Says Andrea, "After the shock subsided we started thinking, maybe this was our chance to change our brand. Maybe we should forget about Ontario history and create a brand with a name like

Dogfish Head—something that was truly our own." They wanted to do it, and in retrospect they wish they had, but it was just too difficult. "We chickened out," admits Andrea.

Instead of re-creating the brand, they simply changed the name to Robert Simpson Brewing Company, and continued what they had been doing. Says Andrea, "Here's the thing—we owned a microbrewery, yet we looked forward to trips to the States where we would stock up on the beers we *wanted* to drink; beers that were unlike anything we could find in Ontario!"

In 2007 the couple attended a symposium put on by the recently formed Ontario Craft Brewers Association. Microbrewers were on the fringe of the market, always struggling to find a place to sell their beers. The American consultants who had been invited to talk about the future of the micro beer market politely pointed out that Ontario craft beers, although clean and palatable, were, well, stuffy. Says Andrea, "It raised the hackles of a few brewers in the room, but, you know what? We agreed."

And so, for the second time, the Chiodos took a good hard look at their brand and no longer liked what they saw. There they were, bland, stuffy, and brewing their "inoffensive" beer, which they sold to consumers but preferred not to drink themselves. "We asked ourselves, 'What had happened to the revolutionary spirit of the independent brewer that had lured us to this place? What had happened to our passion? Why weren't we brewing the kinds of beers we want to drink?'"

They realized that their serious brand image, while successfully keeping them in the middle of a respectable pack, was boring—and that was the last straw. They decided to get funky, be true to their off-centred nature, and craft the kind of brews they wanted to drink themselves. They realized it was "weird to be normal." So they threw out what Andrea later referred to as the "dead white guy" branding, and went back to the drawing board. They brainstormed crazy new brand names that just got weirder and weirder: BioEngibeer, Hopzilla, Hopnotic Suggestion, Moon Radio, Genius of Suburbia, Dark Succubus, Braincube, Time Warp, Polar Bomb, Borealis Lamp . . . and all of a sudden they realized that anything could be a beer or brewery name!

So they became the Flying Monkeys Craft Brewery. The flying monkeys are, of course, characters from the Wizard of Oz, but that's not why Andrea chose the name. The brand has a more personal meaning to the Chiodos: "There's a sign in the mudroom of our house that reads, 'Don't make me get my Flying Monkeys!' It's a joke and a threat telling our kids to put their crap away, or else. It also brings to mind the words of Walt Whitman, 'all goes onward and outward,' and our mission to keep the craft beer revolution in Ontario going. To brew bigger beers, with higher alcohol contents, with strange new ingredients—onward and outward."

The market for beer in Canada and the United States is currently in the midst of a structural shift, marked by changing tastes and increasing competition. What was once a market dominated by two large breweries with a few smaller brands in each province is now a highly fragmented market with hundreds of craft breweries. Beer consumers who once favoured the premium lagers bearing the big brand names are becoming increasingly educated and selective, and their taste for hoppier, fuller flavoured beers is increasing. And that's good news for Flying Monkeys. No longer an inoffensive brand surrounded by similar brews, it is now the leader of the pack—well ahead of the trend that has recently seen major breweries scrambling to create their own "craft-like" beers. For example, Labatt's recently introduced Alexander Keith's Hallertauer Hop Ale, and Moosehead launched a new brand called Barking Squirrel, designed to look and feel like a craft brew.

Each beer has a story, a personality, an ethos. "We name our beers to reflect flavour and the spirit of the brew," says Andrea. "What we discovered in both the brewing of Hoptical Illusion and the package design was that our competitive advantage was our creativity." Our packaging has become synonymous with our name, and, really, all we have is our brand to convey our brewery's mission, and explain our mantra *Normal is weird*."[1]

IN CHAPTER 8 we learned that when developing a new product, marketers must make many important decisions about features, style, and design; level of quality; packaging; and labelling. In addition to these important decisions about how the product looks, feels, and works, marketers must make decisions about branding—which has more to do with how customers *perceive* the product. Brands have personality, brands have value, brands position the product in the mind of the consumer, and perform many other important functions in product marketing, yet a brand is not the same as a product. In this chapter, we'll look more closely at the abstract concepts of brands and branding, and how they are applied in marketing.

What Is a Brand? LO1

Brand

A name, symbol, icon, design, or a combination of these, that identifies the maker or marketer of a product.

Perhaps the most distinctive skill of professional marketers is their ability to build and manage brands. The basic definition of a **brand** is a name, symbol, icon, design, or a combination of these, that identifies the maker or marketer of a product. But truly understanding what a brand is, and the important role it plays in marketing, is far from simple. Says one advertising expert, "What's a brand? You realize that no two people, let alone two marketers, agree on the answer. It's a word, a metaphor, an analogy, a concept or some sort of thing with an existence and personality."[2]

A brand is not a logo, not a corporate identity system, and not a product. Branding expert Marty Neumeier, author of two books on the subject, says, "Marketing people often talk about managing their brands, but what they usually mean is managing their products. To manage a brand is to manage something much less tangible—an aura, an invisible layer of meaning that surrounds the product."[3] That said, a brand name may identify a company, one of their products, or a product line. If used for the firm as a whole, the preferred term is *trade name*—but a brand is much more than just a trade name. Brands are powerful. Brands have status and value. Brands have personality, and so they involve our emotions as consumers, and as human beings. But for all that, a brand is not real. It can't be touched, or even pointed at. A brand is nothing more than an idea—and for the biggest brands in the world, it is precisely that idea that generates most of the company's revenue.

Even though the idea of a brand has been around for thousands of years, in today's information-rich modern society, where each purchase requirement offers a multitude of choices, we no longer have time to make comparisons based on features and benefits. We base our choices on more symbolic attributes, like what kind of people buy it, and what other people are saying about it. In other words, we make our purchase decisions based on what we know, feel, or believe, about the brand.[4]

Courtesy of BC Tree Fruits Cooperative

Exhibit 9.1 **Anything can be branded:** Apples are a fruit, Royal Gala is a name, but "BC Brand" is a trade name that differentiates this brand of Royal Gala apples from any other.

Branding has become so strong that, today, hardly anything goes unbranded. Salt is packaged in branded containers, common nuts and bolts are packaged with a distributor's label, and automobile parts—spark plugs, tires, filters—bear brand names that differ from those of the automakers. Even fruits, vegetables, dairy products, and poultry are branded—Sunkist oranges, BC–brand apples, Neilson Dairy Oh! milk, and Maple Leaf Prime chickens.

Branding helps buyers in many ways. Brand names help consumers to identify products that might benefit them. Brands also say something about product quality and consistency—buyers who always buy the same brand know that they will get the same level of quality each time they buy. Branding also gives the marketer several advantages. The brand name becomes the basis on which a whole story can be built about a product's special qualities. The brand name and trademark provide legal protection for unique product features that otherwise might be copied by competitors. And branding helps the marketer to segment markets. For example, Toyota Motor Corporation can offer the major Lexus, Toyota, and Scion brands, each with numerous sub-brands—such as Camry, Corolla, Prius, Matrix, Yaris, Tundra, Land Cruiser, and others—not just one general product for all consumers.

Brand Meaning

In the beginning, products were just products, and they stayed that way for a long time. Then, someone came up with the idea of trademarks. Consumers came to trust trademarks, because they reassured them that the product they were getting had the attributes they wanted and expected from that maker. One of the first makers of products to learn the value of trademarking was Louis Vuitton. The company designed and patented its signature quatrefoil and flowers pattern, and the LV monogram in 1896, to protect itself from counterfeit luggage makers. Today the Louis Vuitton brand is one of the most valuable luxury brands in the world.

Trademarks can be names, symbols, characters (like the Pillsbury Doughboy), even shapes, such as the Coca-Cola bottle, whose design was registered as a trademark in 1960. Trademark names have monetary value, and therefore must be protected, and distinguished from regular or generic words with a similar meaning. Trademarked names are indicated with a superscript TM, and after the company has gone through a lengthy legal process of registering their trademark, they indicate it with this symbol: ®. The name Kleenex, for example, is a registered trademark belonging to Kimberly-Clark Worldwide, which means it should always be spelled with a capital and used to refer to the name brand tissue. This is an important issue, important enough for Kimberly-Clark to take out ads

You may not realize it, but by using the name **Kleenex®** as a generic term for tissue, you risk erasing our coveted brand name that we've worked so hard for all these years. **Kleenex®** is a registered trademark and should *always* be followed by a ® and the words 'Brand Tissue'. Just pretend it's in permanent marker.

Kimberly-Clark Worldwide, Inc.

Exhibit 9.2 **Trademarks:** The name Kleenex® is a registered trademark, which means it should always be spelled with a capital and used to refer to the name brand tissue.

to explain it (see Exhibit 9.2). Companies can lose their trademarks if their name becomes a generic word, for example, Aspirin was originally a trademarked name for acetylsalicylic acid, owned by Bayer. It is still a trademark in Canada and in many countries in Europe, but it has become a generic term in the US. Other trademarks that have been lost for this reason are lanolin, kerosene, thermos, zipper, and escalator.

Trademarks and logos often represent brands, yet the meaning of a brand encompasses much more than just a name and a logo. Customers attach meanings to brands and develop brand relationships that go well beyond a product's physical attributes. For example, consider what this experiment illustrates about the meaning of Coca-Cola:[5]

> In one interesting taste test of Coca-Cola versus Pepsi, 67 subjects were hooked up to brain-wave-monitoring machines while they consumed both products. When the soft drinks were unmarked, consumer preferences were split down the middle. But when the brands were identified, subjects chose Coke over Pepsi by a margin of 75 percent to 25 percent. When drinking the identified Coke brand, the brain areas that lit up most were those associated with cognitive control and memory—a place where culture concepts are stored. That didn't happen as much when drinking Pepsi. Why? According to one brand strategist, it's because of Coca-Cola's long-established brand imagery—the almost 100-year-old contour bottle and cursive font, and its association with iconic images ranging from Mean Joe Greene and the Polar Bears to Santa Claus. Pepsi's imagery isn't quite as deeply rooted. Although people might associate Pepsi with a hot celebrity or the "Pepsi generation" appeal, they probably don't link it to the strong and emotional American icons associated with Coke. The conclusion? Plain and simple: consumer preference isn't based on taste alone. Coke's iconic brand appears to make a difference.

Branding expert Al Reis says the key to communicating brand meaning is to get consumers to associate your brand with just one word, so that your brand "owns" that word in terms of brand positioning. For example Volvo owns the word "safety," and Coors Light owns the word "cold." Another example is Red Bull, which owns the word "extreme." The energy drink brand has built its reputation by associating itself with, and sponsoring, extreme sports and activities around the world. Red Bull Racing is a Formula One racing team that drives cars built by Infiniti and competes in Formula One races around the world; the Red Bull Storm Chase is a windsurfing competition that takes place in cold water and storm-force winds. The brand is associated with every extreme cycling, aerial, and water sport, some of which they create themselves, like Red Bull Crashed Ice, the annual tournament where skaters race down and around a half kilometre long ice track in the middle of a city. Perhaps the most extreme activity this extreme brand has ever sponsored was daredevil Felix Baumgartner's jump to Earth from the stratosphere in 2012, during which he became the first human to break the sound barrier without vehicular power.

Exhibit 9.3 **Brand meaning:** Red Bull is synonymous with the word "extreme" due to its sponsorship of extreme activities, such as daredevil Felix Baumgartner's jump from Red Bull Stratos, nearly 40 km high in the stratosphere.

Red Bull Stratos/EPA/Newscom

Brand Relationships

Brands are more than just names and symbols. They are a key element in the company's relationships with consumers. Brands represent consumers' perceptions and feelings about a product and its performance—everything that the product or service means to consumers. In the final analysis, brands exist in the heads of consumers. As one well-respected marketer once said, "Products are created in the factory, but brands are created in the mind."[6]

Successful brands are created by marketers who view them, and treat them, much the way we think about people: Brands have good, memorable names, personalities, and stories to tell. And when a brand has all that going for it, it is able to enter into a relationship with consumers—or, rather, consumers form relationships with their favourite brands. Branding expert Kevin Roberts points out that human beings are powered by emotion, not by reason, and that brand marketers must strive to inspire among consumers a loyalty beyond reason for their brands.[7]

"Lovemarks" is Roberts' term for brands that inspires the kind of loyalty we exhibit toward those we love. And consumers *do* love their brands! One Michigan couple had such a passion for Black & Decker's DeWalt power tool brand that they designed their entire wedding around it. They wore trademark DeWalt black-and-yellow T-shirts, made their way to a wooden chapel that they'd built with their DeWalt gear, exchanged vows and power tools, and even cut cake with a power saw. Joked the wife about her husband, who is a carpenter by trade, "He loves DeWalt nearly as much as he loves me."[8]

Exhibit 9.4 **People as brands:** Justin Bieber's first branded fragrance was called "Someday by Justin Bieber." It was followed two years later by a second fragrance called "Girlfriend by Justin Bieber."

Mayer RCF / Splash News/Newscom

People As Brands

People become brands when, just as with products, their name takes on meanings that transcend the person. The true mark of any brand is the ability to apply it to products in other categories and have the same meaning and positioning transfer with it—the way Red Bull has done with extreme sports and events. A true brand has life beyond its original product, and in the case of people as brands, the brand must have life and meaning outside the person. For example, Gianni Versace, Coco Chanel, Louis Vuitton, and Levi Strauss are all people who became brands that live on today, even though the people themselves are all dead. Today we have Trump, Rachael Ray, Beyoncé, and Oprah brands, not to mention the Kardashians and Justin Bieber.

Some of these names may still be living as brands ten or even a hundred years from now; others may not. Developing, growing, and managing a person as a brand requires the same amount of dedication to marketing as marketers apply to products. Today's athletes who aspire to become brands begin their marketing efforts before their playing days are over. For example, Canadian basketball star Steve Nash promotes his brand in a variety of ways. He doesn't just appear in Nike commercials, he helps make them. He wrote the script for a viral video called Training Day, which showed the basketball star practising on the court. Included in the spot was a new product Nash developed with Nike, a sneaker called Trash Talk that's made entirely from recycled materials.[9]

Brand Characteristics `LO2`

Most established brands are represented by a powerful name, a logo, or an icon, however, these symbols are only part of what makes up the brand. Brands ultimately exist in the minds and hearts of consumers, but it is the job of brand managers to create representations of the brand, such as *logos*. Brands also have *personality*, *status*, and value (*brand equity*).

Logos

Logos are designs that represent the brand, and that may or may not incorporate the brand name. The Nike swoosh, for example, originally appeared in conjunction with the word Nike, but once the market had been "trained" to recognize the swoosh as a representation of the Nike brand, the name was removed from the logo.

Sometimes brand managers feel their logo needs an update. The Royal Bank, for example, updates its lion every ten years or so, to make it more modern looking. Pepsi updated its red, white and blue swirl logo a few years ago to make it look more like a smile. And recently the Hudson's Bay Company rebranded its stores from "The Bay" to "Hudson's Bay," unveiling a redesigned logo to communicate the change.

Not all logo updates are met with a favourable response from consumers, however. When Gap tried to introduce a contemporary redesign of its familiar old logo, the well-known white text on a blue square, customers went ballistic and imposed intense online pressure: industry commentators called it a disaster, and mock Facebook pages and Twitter feeds quickly sprang up to make fun of it. Gap is one of the most valuable brands in the world, and consumers felt strongly that the logo was a brand icon that shouldn't be messed with. Gap reinstated the old logo after only one week.

Brand Personality

Brand personality
The sum total of all the attributes of a brand, and the emotions it inspires in the minds of consumers.

Many of the most successful brands are those that have a distinctive *personality*. A **brand personality** is the sum total of all the attributes of a brand, and the emotions it inspires in the minds of consumers. Brand managers describe their brands by using the same kinds of adjectives we might use to describe people, and they use those attributes to establish the brand's positioning. For example, Coca-Cola is "traditional," while Pepsi is "youthful," Apple is "stylish," and Mac is "hip." Starbucks is "sophisticated," and Ford is "reliable," IBM is "conservative" and "practical," while Google is "quirky" and "fun-loving." In fact, Google is a brand that just oozes brand personality.

Every April 1, Google's home page announces a new product, such as Google Custom Time or Google Surface Mail—which are not real products at all, but spoofs to celebrate April Fool's Day. And Google Doodles, the playful versions of Google's logo, are so well known as part of the Google personality, that today there are Google Doodle contests and fan-created logos. Says the company, "Having a little bit of fun with the corporate logo by redesigning it from time to time is unheard of at many companies but at Google, it is a part of the brand. While the doodle is primarily a fun way for the company to recognize events and notable people, it also illustrates the creative and innovative personality of the company itself."[10]

Another aspect of a brand's personality is its *status*. Brands occupy a level of social regard with respect to one another. Rolls-Royce and Bentley are higher-status car brands than Ford and Toyota; and Hyundai and Kia are lower-status brands. Within just about every product category there are high-status and low-status brands, however, status should not be confused with value or popularity. Many high-status brands, such as Chanel and Rolex, tend to be exclusive rather than popular, while lower-status brands, such as Canadian Tire and Keds, can still be highly popular.

A brand's personality is an important part of what establishes the positioning of that brand. Just as we learned about the positioning of products and services, so too must brands be positioned, and the task is difficult for beer brands, which compete in a market where the products are not highly differentiated. One Canadian beer marketer has done an exceptional job creating a personality for its brand—Sleeman's "owns" the word notorious (see Marketing@Work 9.1).

Exhibit 9.5 **Brand personality:** Google Doodles are both a representation of the Google brand and an illustration of the brand's personality. Hundreds of Doodles have been designed to mark special occasions.

© sjscreens / Alamy

Brand Equity

A powerful brand has monetary value and equity. **Brand equity** is the dollar amount attributed to the value of the brand, based on all the intangible qualities that create that value. Brand equity is difficult to calculate, but one indicator is the extent to which people are willing to pay more for the brand.

John Stewart, co-founder of Quaker Oats, once said, "If this business were split up, I would give you the land and bricks and mortar, and I would keep the brands and trademarks, and I would fare better than you." The CEO of McDonald's agrees: "A McDonald's board member who worked at Coca-Cola once talked to us about the value of our brand. He said if every asset we own, every building, and every piece of equipment were destroyed in a terrible natural disaster, we would be able to borrow all the money to replace it very quickly because of the value of our brand. And he's right. The brand is more valuable than the totality of all these assets."[11]

Advertising agency Young & Rubicam developed a methodology called the **brand asset valuator,** or BAV, which measures the value of a brand along four consumer perception dimensions: *differentiation* (what makes the brand stand out), *relevance* (how consumers feel it meets their needs), *knowledge* (how much consumers know about the brand), and *esteem* (how highly consumers regard and respect the brand). Brands with strong brand equity rate high on all of these dimensions. A brand must be distinct, or consumers will have no reason to choose it over other brands. But the fact that a brand is highly differentiated doesn't necessarily mean that consumers *will* buy it. The brand must stand out in ways that are relevant to consumers' needs, and even a differentiated, relevant brand is far from a shoo-in. Before consumers will respond to the brand, they must first know about and understand it. And that familiarity must lead to a strong, positive consumer-brand connection.[12]

Every two years, consulting firm Interbrand evaluates and ranks the top 100 global brands and the top 25 Canadian brands in terms of their value, or brand equity (see Table 9.1). To qualify for the global list, a brand must derive one-third of its earnings from outside its home country, be recognizable to people who are not customers, and have publicly available marketing and financial data. The ranking is then done through a complex

Brand equity
The dollar amount attributed to the value of the brand, based on all the intangible qualities that create that value.

Brand asset valuator (BAV)
An international research project that has been taking place for the past 16 years, in which 38 000+ brands are tested.

TABLE 9.1   Top 10 Global and Canadian Brands

Global rank	Brand	Value (US$ million)	Canadian rank	Brand	Value (CA$ million)
1	Coca-Cola	77 839	1	TD	9 693
2	Apple	76 568	2	Thomson Reuters	9 548
3	IBM	75 532	3	RBC	7 929
4	Google	69 726	4	BlackBerry	6 466
5	Microsoft	57 853	5	Scotiabank	3 965
6	GE	43 682	6	Tim Hortons	3 441
7	McDonald's	40 062	7	Lululemon	3 245
8	Intel	39 385	8	Shoppers Drug Mart	3 179
9	Samsung	32 893	9	Bell	3 059
10	Toyota	30 280	10	Rogers	2 998

Source: Interbrand, "Best Canadian Brands 2012" and "Best Global Brands 2012," available at www.interbrand.com.

MARKETING@WORK   9.1

Sleeman's Notorious Brand

The word notorious is not usually considered a good personality trait—it has connotations of being dangerous. But John Sleeman doesn't mind if you call his brand notorious, because he is some-what notorious himself. In the 1970s, he opened a pub in Oakville, Ontario, and started a company to import and distribute beers from abroad in Canada. In 1984, his aunt thought it was time he found out about his family heritage, since he was in the beer business anyway, and she encouraged him to restart the family brewery, which had closed in 1933. "They were told no one with the name Sleeman would get a liquor licence for 50 years," said Sleeman's aunt. "Now it's 51. Here you go." Then she handed him an old bottle and a leather-bound book filled with his grandfather's beer recipes, and the rest is history.

Sleeman traced the ownership of the dormant company to Nabisco, purchased the rights for just a few dollars, and opened the new brewery in Guelph, Ontario. Like any good notorious character, he's had his ups and downs. "There are few things that motivate me as much as somebody telling me I'm wrong or I'm going to fail," he said. But fail he did. When the bank called in a loan a year after the brewery relaunched, John Sleeman lost his family home. He didn't stay down for long, though. He sought refinancing from a US bank and

5 GENERATIONS OF INFAMOUS FAMILY BREWING HERITAGE.

SLEEMAN
NOTORIOUSLY GOOD
SINCE 1834

Sleeman's Brewery, Ltd.

Exhibit 9.6 The cast of characters from the original Notorious campaign, including John Sleeman and his aunt (far left), who is holding the original bottle and the black book.

rose from the ashes to build Canada's largest microbrewery and create a brand based on the family's history. His grandfather's brewery had been called The Sleeman Brewing and Malting Company, but it went out of business after suffering the consequences of selling contraband liquor to the United States during Prohibition. "We haven't hidden the fact that my grandfather's brothers got caught smuggling," says Sleeman, though he adds that the family is not particularly proud of it.

Sleeman's beer bottles are notorious, too. The first product developed by the newly reopened brewery was a cream ale, painstakingly recreated from his grandfather's recipe and bottled in a re-creation of the original clear glass bottle, a move unique among beer brands in the 1980s. Unfortunately, it doubled packaging costs and increased quality control expenses, because clear bottles make the beer more susceptible to light. "We felt we needed to stay as close to the original as possible, and went over budget to get everything right," says Sleeman. In the days before the company could afford to advertise, the bottles got the beer noticed. Consumers liked the bottles so much that they kept them instead of returning them to the beer store. There was even a time in the 1990s when the company put out a call to consumers to please return them, as they were running out.

In 2006, Sapporo Breweries purchased Sleeman, a match that seems to be built in brand heaven. Sapporo is one of Japan's oldest beers, dating back to 1876. It has a firmly established brand image, and its own unique packaging, the asymmetric top-heavy silver can. Sapporo recognized the unique talent of John Sleeman, who had managed to build the largest craft brewery in Canada in a market dominated by two very large players, and invited him to stay on and run the company's operations in Canada. Sleeman agreed. "I explained to [Sapporo] that as consumers, Canadians are very proud of our beer and our heritage. . . . We still talk about the things that got us here: heritage, quality, caring about our customers, and putting money back into the community."

With this new financial support, Sleeman hired advertising agency Dentsu Canada for a brand positioning project, and after two years of working on it, the "Notorious" strategy was born. The creative genius behind the campaign was Glen Hunt, who is notorious himself in advertising circles as the writer behind the famous Molson Canadian "I Am Canadian" commercial, featuring a plaid-shirted "Joe" proclaiming his pride in being Canadian. About the new campaign, Hunt jokes, "Notoriously good targets individuals 25 and older who are looking for a 'notoriously good evening.'"

The Notorious campaign was launched in 2010 with a 60-second spot that introduced viewers to a cast of real-life characters who inspired the brewery's beginnings, while the shorter ads focused on individual characters. All five original spots were done in the style of a vaudeville-era theatre. The first ad began with a red velvet curtain under the title "Our History." The curtain opened to reveal a Sleeman beer case on the stage floor. The top opened, and the colourful, historical characters (shown in Exhibit 9.6) climbed out: a pirate, a beer wench holding frosty mugs, dancing girls, a smuggler, and a philanderer. They gathered on the stage in the manner of a cast assembling for their curtain call at the end of a play. Finally, a tuxedo-clad John Sleeman emerged from the box, holding the signature Sleeman clear bottle in one hand, and the famous black leather book in the other, as the announcer proclaimed, "Five generations of infamous family brewing heritage. Sleeman: Notoriously good since 1834."

Subsequent executions on the Notorious theme elaborated on the brand story. "Some of John Sleeman's early ancestors were pirates, philanderers, bootleggers, and smugglers," said one ad; another showed a pirate climbing slyly out of the Sleeman beer case on the stage as the announcer tells us, "Our ancestors were pirates. The name was Slyman. On land they opened taverns. The name became Sleeman. Born of pirates. Brewed in Guelph." In another, we learn, "Prohibitionists wanted to run George Sleeman out of town. But George Sleeman ran for mayor, and ran *them* out of town." And finally, we are told of a particularly famous notorious character: "Sleeman beer was enjoyed by Al Capone. A man who did what he did, and took what he wanted."

Today, Sleeman's continues to use their Notorious theme in their TV commercials, and all the original Notorious spots can still be viewed on Sleeman's YouTube channel. Says John Sleeman, "I restarted a 100-and-something-year-old business thinking I was going to be this generation's custodian, and that someone in my family might be interested in taking over when I ended up in my pine box." With nearly two centuries of notorious history behind it, there seems to be no end to the potential for telling stories about this brand, even long after its founder is no longer part of the story.

Sources: Kristin Laird, "Dentsu Launches Sapporo's First National Canadian Campaign," *Marketing Magazine*, June 7, 2010, accessed at marketingmag.ca; Kristin Laird, "Sleeman Puts Its Notorious History on TV," *Marketing Magazine*, May 7, 2010, accessed at marketingmag.ca; "Sleeman Brews Up a Crafty Takeover of Established Quebec-based Beermaker," *Canadian Packaging*, May 2004, *57*(5), p. 7; Andy Holloway, "John Sleeman," *Canadian Business*, Summer 2004, *77*(10), pp. 204–205; Interview with John Sleeman in "Ask the Legends," *Profit*, November 2008, pp. 112–113; Colin Campbell, "Our Beer Sure Goes Down Smooth," *Maclean's*, September 4, 2006, pp. 38–39; Alicia Clegg, "Old Brands in New Bottles," *Financial Times*, June 1, 2006, p. 12.

procedure of calculating what percentage of the company's revenues can be credited to the brand. Interbrand then projects five years of earnings and sales for the brand, deducts operating costs and taxes, and strips out intangibles such as patents and management. Interbrand believes this figure comes closest to representing a brand's true economic worth.

Thomson Reuters is the only Canadian brand that ranked on the global list (at number 44). The corporation is the world's leading source of information for businesses and professionals, and employs 60 000 people in over 100 countries. Not bad for an organization that began in the 1930s with a single Canadian newspaper, *The Timmins Daily Press*.

A powerful brand forms the basis for building strong and profitable customer relationships. The fundamental asset underlying brand equity is *customer equity*—the value of the customer relationships that the brand creates. A powerful brand is important, but what it really represents is a profitable set of loyal customers. The proper focus of marketing is building customer equity, with brand management serving as a major marketing tool.

Branding Strategy & Management `LO3`

Marketing managers responsible for brands must make high-level strategic decisions that govern the management of the brand and that guide the public and market perceptions about the brand. The main branding strategy decisions are *brand name selection*, *brand positioning*, and *brand sponsorship*. In addition, because brands are valuable corporate assets, they must be carefully developed, either by creating *line extensions* or *brand extensions*; pursuing a *multibrand* strategy, or creating entirely *new brands*. Finally, it is the job of the brand manager to manage and protect the brand on an ongoing basis.

Brand Name Selection

A good name can add greatly to a product's success. However, finding the best brand name is a difficult task. It begins with a careful review of the product and its benefits, the target market, and proposed marketing strategies. After that, naming a brand becomes part science, part art, and a measure of instinct. Here are what brand experts say are the things to consider when coming up with a new brand name:

- It should suggest something about the type of products it will brand, such as Beautyrest, Craftsman, Snuggle.
- It should be easy to pronounce, recognize, and remember, such as Tide, Crest, Ziploc.
- It should be distinctive, such as Google, Lexus, BlackBerry.
- It should be extendable, that is, not tied too closely to one product. Good names that illustrate this example are Oracle, Amazon.com, and Nike.
- It should be pronounceable in many languages, such as Kodak.
- It should be capable of registration and protection as a trademark. A brand name cannot be registered if it infringes on existing brand names. Unique, "made up" names work best for this: Yahoo!, Novartis, Ugg.

A great brand absolutely requires a good, strong, memorable name. When Google burst onto the scene in 1998, no one had to say the name twice. It was instantly memorable, and, only a few short years later, it had become synonymous with "Internet search." Sometimes companies resurrect brand names from the past and give them a new life. Ford sold more than seven million cars branded with the name Taurus, then changed the car's name to Ford Five Hundred. Even though it was essentially the same car, the Five Hundred flopped, because the name had no meaning to consumers. Consumer research conducted by Ford revealed that only 25 percent of people were aware of the Ford Five Hundred, but 80 percent of people recognized the name Taurus—in fact, it was the third strongest of all Ford's brand names (after F-150 and Mustang). So the company decided to switch the car's name back to Taurus.[13]

When Canadian Pacific Hotels & Resorts bought Fairmont Hotels in 1999, they picked up some of the most legendary hotel properties in the world, including the famous Fairmont San Francisco. But they also faced a challenge: what to call the hotels under the newly merged CP-Fairmont brand?

CP purchased the hotel chain because they felt it was a good fit with their existing grand railroad hotels, like Quebec City's Chateau Frontenac and Toronto's Royal York, all of which were already associated with the Canadian Pacific brand. With the acquisition of American hotels and the aspirations to take the hotel brand global, CP felt their corporate brand wasn't the right choice. For people outside Canada, the name conjured up images of railways, if anything at all—not luxury hotels.

The decision was made to combine the Fairmont brand name with the local hotel names, so today we have The Fairmont Banff Springs and The Fairmont Jasper Park Lodge. It was a brilliant strategy, because it protects the attachment local consumers already had for their hotels, while at the same time making the connection with the well-established Fairmont brand in the minds of foreign travellers. Not only that, but it allows for infinite growth, in any market in the world.[14]

Krzysztof Dydynski/Getty Images

Exhibit 9.7 **Brand names:** When two businesses join forces, choosing a new brand name can be a challenge. Canadian Pacific opted to add the Fairmont brand to the well-known local names of its hotels.

Brand Positioning

In Chapter 7 we learned about the importance of segmenting the market and positioning a product in the marketplace, and positioning is even more important for brands, because they are intangible. Canadian branding expert Ted Matthews says, "To stand out in our over-communicated world, brands must establish and own a unique, honest, meaningful and clear position."[15]

Brands can be positioned based on *product attributes*. For example, P&G invented the disposable diaper category with its Pampers brand. Early Pampers marketing focused on attributes such as fluid absorption, fit, and disposability. In general, however, attributes are the least desirable quality for brand positioning, because competitors can easily copy them.

Consumers are more interested in what the products will do for them, so a better positioning strategy is to associate the brand with a particular *benefit*. Pampers' later marketing communications focused on the benefits of dry baby bottoms. Other successful brands positioned on benefits are Volvo (safety), FedEx (guaranteed on-time delivery), Nike (performance), and Staples (that was easy).

The strongest brands go beyond attribute or benefit positioning. They are positioned on strong *beliefs and values*, and as such they engage consumers on a deep, emotional level. Brands such as Godiva, Starbucks, Apple, and Victoria's Secret rely less on a product's tangible attributes and more on creating surprise, passion, and excitement.

Brand Sponsorship

Brand sponsorship is an important branding strategy decision, and begins with the question, "To brand or not to brand?" Not all products are branded, but those that are may be *national brands* or *private brands*. Marketers may choose *licensing* as a method of branding a new product, or they may partner with another firm to *co-brand* a product.

National brand (or manufacturer's brand)

A brand created and owned by the manufacturer of the product.

National Brands A new product may be launched as a **national brand (or manufacturer's brand)**, as when Sony and Kellogg sell their output under their own brand names (Sony Bravia or Kellogg's Frosted Flakes). National brands are so called because they are well known and well established throughout the country, or even internationally.

Private brand (store brand, private label)

Brand names applied by the marketer to products manufactured for them under contract.

Private Brands **Private brands**, also called **store brands** and **private label**, are brand names applied by the marketer to products manufactured for them under contract. Shoppers Drug Mart's Life Brand is a private label; so is Walmart's Great Value brand. Perhaps the most well known private brand of all is President's Choice, which has reached the status of a national brand and has spawned many brand extensions.

In Canada, private-label products account for approximately 25 percent of Canadian grocery stores' and drug stores' revenues. Private label products are often manufactured by companies that also manufacture national brands, for example Sears Canada recently partnered with Aldo Group to design and manufacture footwear lines for their Nevada, Attitude, and Jessica brands; and with Buffalo International to produce their line of Nevada denim apparel for women and men.[16] Sometimes, though, a company can be *only* a manufacturer of private label products. Toronto's Cott Corp is the world's largest producer of store-branded private label soft drinks. It has operations in Canada, the United States, the United Kingdom, and Mexico, and manufactures soda, energy drinks, flavoured water, sports drinks, and juices for major retailers, including Walmart.[17]

President's Choice is a private label that has become so popular in Canada it now enjoys a status on par with national brands. So strong is the President's Choice brand, it has many brand extensions: President's Choice Financial, PC Blue Menu, PC Organics—and now, President's Choice Black Label collection.[18]

Loblaw's is attempting to position the new brand to compete with the likes of Pusateri's, a high end grocery store for discriminating upper middle class "foodies." This positioning is reinforced by extremely polished online videos created by Toronto ad agency Bensimon Byrne that consciously imitate the high tone of videos on gourmet websites such as that of *Saveur* magazine. Other marketing materials boast of the line's "rich artisanal provenance," and the ads use the tagline, "satisfy your inner foodie." Positioning the brand this way is the beginning of a long-term marketing effort.

Carlos Osorio/ZUMA Press/Newscom

Exhibit 9.8 Private brands: Loblaws launched its new black label brand at an event called "The Dinner Party," held in an *avant garde* art gallery with a who's who list of gourmets and foodies in attendance.

The brand was launched at an event held in the *avant garde* art gallery, Neubacher Shor Contemporary, in Toronto's Parkdale neighbourhood. Everything about it was upscale, from the valet parking to the black carpet leading from the street to the gallery door. Inside, celebrity photographers stood at the ready to snap pictures of guests while high-profile Toronto chefs cooked with black label products in one of the galleries. Petite Thuet's Marc Thuet created soy and ginger marinated salmon, while Canoe's Anthony Walsh offered a Montmorency Cherry Lacquered Squab. Sarah Bell and Allyson Meredith from Bobbette & Belle brought things to a sweet end with Dark Venezuelan Chocolate Cake served on edible candy plates. Twelve product images taken around the world by Toronto photographer Michael Mahovlich for the product labels were transferred to canvas and hung in the gallery.

Loblaw isn't using the words "Black Label" on its packaging, claiming that they prefer to let the packaging speak for itself—all products in the black label collection feature labels with a plain black background, high end photos and a few simple descriptive words. When the products are described in writing, it's important to note which words are capitalized, and which aren't: PC® black label Cherry Shiraz Wine Jelly, PC® black label Pomegranate Lemonade Sparkling Soda, PC® black label Salted Caramel Ice Cream, PC® black label Fiorelli Pasta, and PC® black label Vodka Pasta Sauce. Though President's Choice and its abbreviation, PC, are both registered trademarks, the new brand cannot be trademarked as Black Label—because that name is owned by Diageo, makers of Johnnie Walker.

In the so-called battle of the brands between national and private brands, retailers have many advantages. They control what products they stock, where they go on the shelf, what prices they charge, and which ones they will feature in local circulars. Retailers often price their store brands lower than comparable national brands, thereby appealing to the budget-conscious shopper in all of us. Although store brands can be hard to establish and costly to stock and promote, they also yield higher profit margins for the reseller. And they give resellers exclusive products that cannot be bought from competitors, resulting in greater store traffic and loyalty.

Licensing   While some manufacturers take years and spend millions to create their own brand names, others *license* the right to use a brand name, then focus on marketing and selling their products under that name. **Licensing** is the buying and selling of the rights to use a brand name, logo, character, icon, or image.

Many makers of clothing and other soft goods license the rights to use the names of well-known celebrities, or characters from popular movies and books. If you've ever bought an NHL team jersey or any other item bearing the logo of a professional sports team, you own an item made by a company that licensed the right to make that item. The value of a brand can be determined, in part, by the willingness of other companies to purchase the rights to use it.

Name brand soft drinks are bottled and distributed by licensed bottlers who have purchased the right to do so. Many beer brands, too, are brewed under license by local brewers though their bottles may bear a foreign brand. For example, for many years Molson Coors Canada had a licensing agreement with the Miller Brewing Company, a subsidiary of UK corporation SABMiller PLC, which saw Molson Coors producing beer under the brands Miller Genuine Draft, Miller Lite, and Miller High Life, for distribution in Canada. But after seeing the success of its brands in the Canadian market, Miller Brewing decided to revoke its license—which any marketer has the right to do, so long as they follow whatever procedure was outlined in the license agreement—and produce Miller beer brands in Canada itself.[19]

Co-branding   One branding strategy that's growing in popularity is to partner with another company, take the strongest elements of your each of your products, and combine them to produce a *co-branded* offering. **Co-branding** occurs when two established brand names of different companies are used on the same product. For example, financial services firms often partner with other companies to create co-branded credit cards,

Licensing
The buying and selling of the rights to use a brand name, logo, character, icon, or image.

Co-branding
The practice of using the established brand names of two different companies on the same product.

such as when CIBC and Air Canada joined forces to create the Aeroplan Visa card. Similarly, Costco teamed up with mattress maker Stearns & Foster to market a line of Kirkland Signature by Stearns & Foster mattress sets.

In order for co-branding to work, the two brands must be complementary, for example Cold Stone Creamery, an American quick service ice cream parlour, partnered with Oreo and Jell-O Pudding to create co-branded ice cream products, and with Tim Hortons and Rocky Mountain Chocolate Factory to create co-branded stores. Says Dan Beem, president of Cold Stone Creamery, "The combination of these premium brands and iconic flavors are a draw for our customers and a natural fit in quality and reputation. . . . In other words, the potential worth of the whole may be greater than the sum of the individual brands."[20]

Co-branding offers many advantages. Because each brand dominates in a different category, the combined brands create broader consumer appeal and greater brand equity. Co-branding also allows a company to expand its existing brand into a category it might otherwise have difficulty entering alone.

Brand Development

Brands are powerful, valuable assets that must be carefully developed. In general, a company has four options when it comes to developing brands (see Figure 9.1). It can create *line extensions* or *brand extensions*; pursue a *multibrand* strategy, or create entirely *new brands*.

Line extensions

Extending an existing brand name to new forms, colours, sizes, ingredients, or flavours of an existing product category.

Line Extensions **Line extensions** occur when a company extends existing brand names to new forms, colours, sizes, ingredients, or flavours of an existing product category, for example, Honey Nut Cheerios and MultiGrain Cheerios are extensions of the Cheerios product line.

A company might use line extensions as a low-cost, low-risk way to introduce new products. Or it might want to meet consumer desires for variety, to use excess capacity, or simply to command more shelf space from resellers. However, line extensions involve some risks. An overextended brand name might lose its specific meaning. Another risk is that sales of an extension may come at the expense of other items in the line. For example, the original Doritos Tortilla Chips have now morphed into a full line of 20 different types and flavours of chips, including such high-decibel flavours as Jalapeno & Cheddar, Sweet Chili Heat, Spicy Nacho, and Scream Cheese. Although the line seems to be doing well, the original Doritos chips seem like just another flavour. A line extension works

FIGURE 9.1 Brand Development Strategies

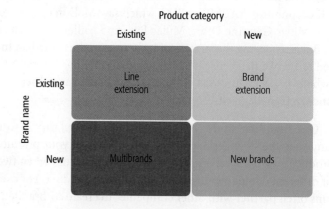

best when it takes sales away from competing brands, not when it "cannibalizes" the company's other items.

Brand Extensions   **Brand extensions** extend a current brand name to new or modified products in a new category. For example, Campbell Soup extended its V8 juice brand to a line of soups, and Ritz co-branded with Kraft to create mini Ritz Bits Sandwiches (with Real Kraft Cheese). Procter & Gamble leveraged the strength of its Mr. Clean brand to launch several new lines: cleaning pads (Mr. Clean Magic Eraser), bathroom cleaning tools (Mr. Clean Magic Reach), and at-home auto cleaning kits (Mr. Clean AutoDry). And KitKat, one of Canada's most popular chocolate bars, introduced many brand extensions including KitKat Chunky, KitKat Chunky Peanut Butter, and KitKat Chunky Caramel.

A brand extension gives a new product instant recognition and faster acceptance. It also saves the high advertising costs usually required to build a new brand name. At the same time, a brand extension strategy involves some risk. Brand extensions such as Cheetos lip balm, Heinz pet food, and Life Savers gum met early deaths. The extension may confuse the image of the main brand. And if a brand extension fails, it may harm consumer attitudes toward the other products carrying the same brand name.

Exhibit 9.9 Brand extensions: One of Canada's most popular chocolate bars, KitKat introduced brand extensions including KitKat Chunky, KitKat Chunky Peanut Butter, and KitKat Chunky Caramel.

Multibrands   **Multibranding** is a brand development strategy in which the same manufacturer produces many different brands in a given product category. For example, in the United States, P&G sells six brands of laundry detergent (Tide, Cheer, Gain, Era, Dreft, and Ivory), five brands of shampoo (Pantene, Head & Shoulders, Aussie, Herbal Essences, and Infusium 23); and four brands of dishwashing detergent (Dawn, Ivory, Joy, and Cascade). *Multibrands* are a way to establish different features that appeal to different customer segments, lock up more reseller shelf space, and capture a larger market share. Together, those six brands capture a whopping 62 percent of the US laundry detergent market.

> **Brand extensions**
> Extending an existing brand name to new product categories.

A major drawback of multibranding is that each brand might obtain only a small market share, and none may be very profitable. The company may end up spreading its resources over many brands instead of building a few brands to a highly profitable level. This happened to General Motors, which was forced to cut several unprofitable brands from its portfolio, including Saturn, Oldsmobile, Pontiac, Hummer, and Saab.

> **Multibranding**
> A brand development strategy in which the same manufacturer produces many different brands in the same product category.

New Brands   Sometimes a company with a long-established name, that has been in business for many years decides to adopt a new strategy—to brand itself and its products. This is what Montreal's Gildan did recently.[21]

> Gildan Activewear Inc., with its headquarters in Montreal, has been in business since 1984; is publically traded on the TSX and the NYSE; has 30 000 employees worldwide, and has registered the trademark of its name: Gildan®. The company sells T-shirts, sport shirts and fleece as undecorated "blanks," which are subsequently decorated by screenprinters with designs and logos (which they license).
>
> Gildan is also one of the world's largest suppliers of athletic, casual and dress socks, which in the US are sold under a diversified portfolio of company-owned brands, including Gold Toe®, PowerSox®, SilverToe®, Auro®, All Pro®, GT®, and the Gildan® brand. In addition, the company supplies selective national retailer brands. Gildan is also the exclusive US sock licensee for the Under Armour® and New Balance® brands. Last year, Gildan sold more than

Gildan Branded Retail, division of Gildan Activewear Inc.

Exhibit 9.10 New brands: Gildan is an established Montreal company that recently adopted a strategy of branding its T-shirts.

650 million T-shirts and 600 million pairs of socks, largely through wholesale and screen-printers. "The average American consumer has about 10 of our products in their closet," says CEO Glenn Chamandy. Problem is, most of them have no idea any of those products are a Gildan.

Today that's changing. Gildan is pursuing a strategy to grow its sales of branded underwear and activewear products in the US retail market. The maker of T-shirts, underwear, and socks is trying to make inroads into the competitive apparel business by selling its own Gildan-branded products. The company bought a 30-second ad during the 2013 Super Bowl to launch its $25 million branding campaign. In the spot, a young man wakes up on the floor of a rumpled bedroom. He gathers his things to leave, but at the door he realizes he doesn't have his T-shirt, and returns to the bedroom where we see that a sleeping girl is wearing it. The young man hesitates, wondering whether he should wake her, then decides that his favourite T-shirt is worth it. As the girl's cat watches, the man gently tugs at his shirt, and the caption reads, "It's about time you had a favourite T-shirt." Then it fades to the brand identification: Gildan.

A second spot that aired during the game and was posted online showed a roller coaster rider taking extreme measures to protect his Gildan underwear. "As we are building our brand in the retail channel, we want to start making a connection between the brand name and the shirts people already have and which might already be their favourite," explained company spokesperson Genevieve Gosselin.

More frequently, an established company creates a new brand when it develops a new product or product line. For example, Toyota created the Scion brand to appeal to Millennials, and Grocery chain Sobeys redesigned some of its suburban stores under the banner of a new brand name, FreshCo. The new stores are positioned as high-quality products at low prices, with a focus on multicultural and ethnic foods, and were developed as a result of market research that described the changing consumer landscape, especially in the Greater Toronto Area. "In Brampton, the South Asian population has grown 250 percent in about 12 or 13 years, and there are varieties of produce that are important and relevant and required to satisfy that marketplace," said Sobeys president and CEO Bill McEwan.[22]

Ongoing Brand Management

One of the most important marketing management roles is that of the brand manager. The brand manager's job, day in and day out, is to be responsible for, and to manage, a brand. Brand managers need to continually audit their brands' strengths and weaknesses, and ask (and answer) questions such as the following: Does our brand excel at delivering benefits that consumers truly value? Is the brand properly positioned? Do all of our consumer touchpoints support the brand's positioning? Do the brand's managers understand what the brand means to consumers? Does the brand receive proper, sustained support? The brand manager makes decisions about which brands need more support, which brands need to be dropped, and which brands should be rebranded or repositioned because of changing customer preferences or new competitors.

Another of the brand manager's ongoing tasks is to carefully manage the marketing communications and advertising that communicates the brand's attributes and positioning to the market. Brands must be maintained, not just by advertising but by the overall brand experience, points of purchase, word of mouth, websites, and, increasingly, social media.

Why is it so important to manage brands? Does it really matter whether Rachael Ray says "olive oil" or "EVOO," or whether Mickey Mouse has two buttons or five on his pants? To brand managers, it's everything. Brand images and logos must be consistent and exact to be recognizable, so the way Mickey Mouse looks—his white gloves, the two buttons on his pants, and the proportional size of his ears—must be carefully controlled and managed. In fact, it is illegal for a manufacturer to print Mickey Mouse T-shirts without Disney's permission. Disney actually polices the use of its brand images and goes after offenders with all its legal guns. If that seems harsh, consider what would happen if a company didn't carefully manage its brands. It wouldn't be long before Mickey would start to look different, and we wouldn't recognize him anymore.

Brand Communications LO4

Brand communications is a specialized form of marketing communications and advertising that focuses on communicating brand positioning, or image, rather than on product features. In addition to advertising, brand messages are communicated through *brand experiences*, *touchpoints*, brand *icons* and *characters*, *brand ambassadors*, *brand stories*, *branded content*, and *branded entertainment*. Furthermore, with the increasing use and popularity of *social media*, consumers become a part of the brand communications, and can serve as *brand advocates*.

Brand Experiences and Touchpoints

Advertising campaigns can help to create name recognition, brand knowledge, and maybe even some brand preference. However, the fact is that brands are not maintained by advertising but by people's brand experiences. Today, customers come to know a brand through a wide range of contacts and **touchpoints**. These include advertising and other forms of marketing communications, but also personal experience with the brand, word of mouth, social media, company and brand websites, store displays, and many others. The company must put as much care into managing these touchpoints as it does into producing its ads. "Managing each customer's experience is perhaps the most important ingredient in building [brand] loyalty," states one branding expert. "Every memorable interaction . . . must be completed with excellence and . . . must reinforce your brand essence." A former Disney executive agrees: "A brand is a living entity, and it is enriched or undermined cumulatively over time, the product of a thousand small gestures."[23]

Touchpoints
Advertising, marketing communications, personal experience with the brand, word of mouth, social media, company and brand websites, store displays, and anything else that brings a consumer into contact with a brand.

Brand experience is composed of four dimensions: sensory, affective, behavioural, and intellectual. These responses are evoked in consumers when they come into contact with brand-related stimuli (i.e., touchpoints) like brand design, communications, and environments. Researchers have found that affective brand experiences affect brand trust and brand commitment positively, and that a behavioural brand experience positively affects brand commitment. All in all, brand experiences are crucial for building a brand relationship and brand loyalty.[24]

For example, when people are considering buying a new car, their consideration set—the brands they will consider—is created almost entirely based on their experiences with various car brands. According to a recent study by Starcom MediaVest Group, people in the US talk about their auto purchases 30 000 times a day on social media, and that if a brand is not part of the social conversation during consideration phase, it rarely gets purchased. Social media has dramatically altered the purchase decision "journey" for automobiles. The journey now includes an expanded "purchase" phase that reflects the rise of social check-ins and status updates via mobile devices, and a new "post purchase satisfaction and dissatisfaction" stage. For automobile marketers, that means brand experiences need to be created, and brand ambassadors assigned to watch and respond to post purchase dissatisfaction in social media.[25]

Brand Icons and Characters

Brand icons
Objects with distinct shapes, colours, or patterns that are associated with the brand.

Brand characters
Lifelike brand icons, or mascots, that can move speak, and interact, and that have personality traits.

Brands with well established histories and personalities often develop **brand icons** or characters (sometimes called *brand mascots*), to aid with brand communications. Brand icons are objects associated with the brand, such as the unique shape of the Volkswagen Beetle and a Corvette Stingray, Coca-Cola's red and white swoosh, NBC's peacock, and Disney's castle. **Brand characters**, also called mascots, are also icons but they move, speak, interact, and have personality traits.

The Pillsbury Doughboy, Tony the Tiger, and the Michelin Man are all examples of brand characters which have been used by brand managers for decades to help establish and communicate the meaning of the brand. In fact the Michelin Man, whose name is actually Bibendum, has been demonstrating the safety features of Michelin tires for more than 120 years! Brand characters can also be human, like Betty Crocker, who was created by Gold Medal Flour in 1921. Her name was the signature on letters responding to customer questions, her voice was on the radio in the 1920s as host of The Betty Crocker School of the Air, the first radio cooking show in the US. According to *Fortune Magazine*, Betty Crocker was the second most famous American woman, after Eleanor Roosevelt. In 1936 the company created the visual representation of Betty Crocker, and her look has been updated approximately every ten years, so that she always appears modern. And she has always embodied the brand's attributes: she's resourceful, committed to family, community-minded, and likes to bake.[26]

Brand engagement
The interaction between consumers and brands, based on the emotional connection consumers feel toward the brand.

Brand icons and characters help to establish the brand personality, and because they can move, speak, and interact, they are also an important tool for **brand engagement**. Brand engagement is the interaction between consumers and brands, based on the emotional connection consumers feel toward the brand. Marketers and brand managers work to develop marketing programs, especially through the use of social media, that serve to engage consumers with their brand.

For example, Mars Canada's "Find Red" campaign for M&M's was a digital treasure hunt that engaged consumers with the M&M's brand through its animated candy-coated characters, one of whom is named Red.[27]

Red is not simply an M&M's candy with legs, he's a fully developed character with a distinct personality and attitude. His "resume" appears on the M&M's website and describes his physical attributes (Age: He says 30-something but we're checking on it; Weight: perfect for his shell size) and personality (Hidden Talent: Can turn simple chores into complicated tasks; Turn-ons: when people blindly follow his wise advice). Red also has a Twitter feed (@mmsred) and his own Facebook page, where he is listed as a public figure. His profile says: "Well what can I say about me that hasn't already been said? I'm smart, savvy and if I was any sharper it'd be illegal to carry me in a concealed place." Clearly, Red has attitude!

In 2011 Mars Canada was honoured as one of *Marketing Magazine*'s top marketers of the year, and won three Bronze Lions at the Cannes International Festival of Creativity for its "Find Red" campaign, a comprehensive sales promotion with a grand prize of a red Smart

Courtesy of Mars, Incorporated and its affiliates. The M Logo, M&M'S® and the M&M'S® Characters are trademarks of Mars, Incorporated and its affiliates.

Exhibit 9.11 Brand characters: Red M&M is a brand character with a fully developed personality and his own Facebook page.

Car. The company had placed Red M&M images in various places across Toronto, and three of those images had been captured by Google's cameras and posted to Google Street View. When the contest began, consumers searched for Red using Street View and a contest microsite at findred.ca. Clues were posted on YouTube, the website, Twitter, and Facebook. Mobile marketing was also used: Clues were placed on real-world posters with QR codes, and appeared in Foursquare check-ins.

The results? According to a follow-up video posted on YouTube by Mars Canada, the campaign generated 225 000 Twitter impressions, seven million QR code poster views, and participants spent an average of 19 minutes at findred.ca. Now that's brand engagement!

Brand Ambassadors **Brand ambassadors** are real people who, under contract with the brand's marketing organization, act as spokespersons for the brand. Popular Quebec actress Sonia Vachon served as the first brand ambassador for plus-size clothing brand Pennington's. She was introduced on the Pennington's Facebook page and only a few days later the post was liked by 2543 fans, shared 177 times and got 406 positive comments out of the first 410 posted. "Finally a beautiful and real woman who feels good about herself, very inspiring," wrote one fan. In her role as ambassador, Ms. Vachon will appear in television ads, online videos, at live events, and be featured in "fashion file" TV segments broadcast on TVA.[28]

Unlike political ambassadors or traditional marketing spokespeople, brand ambassadors are typically selected for their looks, and may be used for a limited time. For example, alternative clothing brand Benetton, known for its provocative print ads, recently ran an advertising campaign that featured a cast of brand ambassadors selected for their unusual characteristics, none of which are obvious in the photos: Mario Galla, a disabled model from Germany; transsexual Brazillian model Lea T, Kiera Chaplin, granddaughter of Charlie Chaplin, who is an active supporter of UNESCO; Dudley O'Shaughnessy, British former national welterweight boxing champion; Uruguayan chef Matias Perdomo; and Californian Charlotte Free, who is known for her pink hair. Benetton describes the campaign as "an effort to confront prejudice."[29]

> **Brand ambassador**
> A real person who, under contract with the brand's marketing organization, acts as a spokesperson for the brand.

Brand Stories LO5

Every brand has a history, and smart brand managers use some history, as well as elements of fiction, to create stories for their brands. Branding expert Kevin Roberts says that stories are what bring brands to life and keep them interesting. Stories are how we explain the world to ourselves, and give value to the things we love, and businesses that have a good story that involves the listeners—that is, consumers—will succeed in capturing their attention and cultivating favourable feelings toward the brand. A great story can never be told too often; that's why the really good ones become classics, even legends. This is the kind of storytelling brand managers should aspire to. "Ask your friends if they can tell you a story about your brand. If they haven't got one, you have work to do," he says.[30]

Today's brand managers think of their brands as a form of storytelling. When brand managers tell stories about brands, the rich details of character, place, and action embellish the basic "information maps" we all keep in our heads. Psychologists refer to these information maps as *schemas*, basically the structures of information about products and objects, upon which we "hang" new information that we learn. While new products provide us with new information—this is what it's called, this is what it looks like, and this is what it does—brands enrich this information with details that give the new information *meaning*.

A good story has characters we care about interacting in a world or a situation in which something happens or changes. We all love stories *because* we care about the characters, and as we watch or hear about what happens to them, we experience strong emotions.

In brand storytelling, the goal is to elicit those feelings, and transfer them to the brand. For example, think about the Budweiser Clydesdales, the horses that have been featured in the brand's Super Bowl ads for years. The "episode" of the Clydesdale story that aired during the 2013 Super Bowl was called "Brotherhood," and told the story of the man who raised one of the horses, then gave it to Budweiser. Three years later the man goes to see the Clydesdales in a parade, and the horse recognizes him. It is a beautifully told, emotional story that displays the Budweiser product only briefly—this ad isn't about beer, it's about the brand. It was also the first time social media was used to engage viewers with the Clydesdales—at the end viewers were invited to help name the baby horse shown in the commercial by tweeting #Clydesdales.

Brand stories are an excellent strategy for inspiring loyalty among consumers for a brand that might otherwise go unnoticed. Take potatoes, for example. They are ubiquitous, inexpensive, and popular, but rarely inspire emotion. Cavendish Farms changed all that by creating a rich story for its From the Farm brand of frozen potato products—see Marketing@Work 9.2.

MARKETING@WORK 9.2

What's the Story—of Your Brand?

What's your story? It's common slang for "What are you doing?" or "What's happening?" but when branding experts like Mark Thomson ask that question, they mean something very different. They mean, what is the story of your brand? Stories are "one of the primary ways we make sense of our world and our place in it," says Thomson. And the same is true of brands: "Brands are the stories that unite us all in a common purpose within an enterprise, and connect us with the people we serve on the outside . . . brand stories give meaning to who we are and what we do . . . they're strategic."

At Cavendish Farms, marketers are telling the story of their From The Farm brand using the voices of their key suppliers—PEI potato farmers—in an advertising campaign. These farmers love what they do, and they don't just *talk* about their passion for potatoes in the commercials, they literally sing their praises. The commercial shows the farmers in their fields, on their trucks (with their potatoes), and at a large picnic table, enjoying Cavendish Farms From the Farm potatoes with their families. Oh, and singing. It's a catchy jingle, one that gets stuck in your head and delivers a clear, believable message about the From the Farm brand:

There's nothing like a PEI potato,
From the farm we harvest them with pride.
In our hearts we know wherever they go,
The taste of PEI is there inside.

Halfway through the commercial, titles appear on the screen: "Actual PEI farmers." Pause, then, "Actually singing." It's hard not to feel a wide range of favourable emotions towards these lovable characters, and to admire their bravery in singing, slightly off key, on national television. It just goes to prove how much they really love and believe in their product. Cavendish Farms senior brand manager Suzanne Milner explains: "We wanted to make a connection between the pride our farmers take in growing the potatoes and the product that's delivered to consumers' homes."

J.D. Irving, Limited

Actual PEI potato farmers. Actually singing.

Exhibit 9.12 **Brand stories:** Cavendish Farms tells the story of its From the Farm brand by having real PEI potato farmers literally singing its praises in a television commercial.

The spot actually has two different endings which aired in rotation. In one, a farmer jokingly tells another, "You have a great voice," and in the other he says, "You're off-key." The spot aired on national network television in Central and Eastern Canada, as well as on the Food Network.

Cavendish Farms is a member of the J.D. Irving, Limited group of companies, a family-owned organization whose commitment to quality products and services dates back over 130 years. The Cavendish Farms brand story began in 1980, when Irving purchased a PEI-based producer of frozen vegetables and French fries, and renamed the company. Right away, they dropped the focus on frozen products and began acting on a vision to become "The Potato Specialists." The From The Farm brand was introduced by Cavendish Farms in 2007, and positioned as a "natural" food brand. And the story of the potatoes, which, really, is the story of the From The Farm brand—is told on the Cavendish Farms website: "Harvested exclusively from the rich red soil of PEI, we carefully select only the most delicious, premium potatoes. We leave the skin on and prepare them with 100 percent canola oil and lightly season them with sea salt. Your family will love the unforgettable real potato taste and homestyle appearance. You'll love the fact that they're also low in saturated fat. We put a lot of pride into our From the Farm frozen potatoes to ensure you are serving your family the very best!"

Toronto-based Yield Branding is the creative talent behind the TV commercial, and the agency's philosophy is in perfect keeping with the brave singing farmers. They believe that "To break through today's fragmented media environment, marketers and agencies need to take risks—not foolish risks, not uninformed risks, but risks calculated to make the most of what we know in order to push through to the next level. Without fearlessness, we're doomed to sameness." Adds Milner, "We felt they really understood our business issues. Having not worked with frozen food previously, they invested the time to really understand the category and our current status within it."

The brand's suppliers "are all PEI. potato farmers and that's such a great Canadian story to tell," said Chris Torbay, creative director at Yield. He said that throughout the day of the shoot, the farmers "loosened up … and by the end of the day, we started to have some fun. We tried a bunch of [friendly jabs] that fit in with their personalities after their personalities started to come out. That really plays to the honesty of the spot, that these aren't actors, they're real guys."

Sources: Rebecca Harris, "Farmers Sing Potato Praises for Cavendish Farms," *Marketing Magazine,* January 15, 2013; Chris Powell, "Cavendish Farms Chooses Yield and Cairns O'Neil," *Marketing Magazine,* May 29, 2012; Mark Thomson, "The Power of a Good Brand Story," BrandChannel.com, October 25, 2004; and information from CavendishFarms.com, YieldBranding.com, ThomsonBrands.com.

Branded Content   In addition to advertising and other traditional marketing communications channels, brand stories can also be communicated through *branded content* or *content marketing*. **Branded content** is any form of information or story written and produced by a brand marketer, with the brand clearly and prominently featured. Branded content is also referred to as content marketing, and defined by some Canadian marketers as "telling real stories that help and entertain," and "using the power of storytelling to move consumers into action."[31]

> **Branded content (content marketing)**
> Any form of information or story written and produced by a brand marketer, with the brand clearly and prominently featured.

The word content traditionally applied to the editorial content of a newspaper or magazine; the stories written by journalists, managed by editors, and for the purpose of engaging readers. In today's brand-driven world, some content is now being written about and for the purpose of promoting brands—and it's created a new opportunity for traditional content providers. The *Globe and Mail* now operates a Custom Content Group that writes and produces content for marketers like Toronto's Sunnybrook Health Sciences Centre. The *Globe's* Custom Content Group works for and with the Sunnybrook Foundation, the fundraising arm of the Centre, to produce a twice-yearly magazine called *Sunnybrook*, a 52-page glossy publication distributed to donors, patients and visitors to the hospital, and 50 000 *Globe* subscribers.[32]

Branded Entertainment   Another vehicle through which brands can tell stories is to partner with filmmakers, musicians, and other artists to create *branded entertainment*. **Branded entertainment** is a form of entertainment, usually video, that is created with the cooperation or financial support of a marketer.

> **Branded entertainment**
> A form of entertainment, usually video, that is created with the cooperation or financial support of a marketer.

The first brand to create branded entertainment was BMW, with its series of short films called BMW Films. Each was written, acted, directed, and produced with the flair of a Hollywood movie, but the star of each film was a BMW car. The success of BMW Films led many marketers to produce their own films and music videos. Since then, Martin Scorsese produced an award-winning short film called "The Key to Reserva" for Frexinet champagne, and Lady Gaga and Beyoncé produced a short film

Exhibit 9.13 Branded content:
Content providers such as the *Globe and Mail* are now working with marketers to produce branded or custom content, like *Sunnybrook* magazine.

in the form of a music video called "Telephone," which clearly shows the main characters using a Virgin Mobile cellphone and a Polaroid camera; eating a Subway sandwich; logging into the dating site PlentyOfFish (www.pof.com); and whipping up a poison-laced lunch with Wonder Bread and Miracle Whip.

Kokanee went so far as to create a feature-length motion picture titled *The Movie Out Here*, starring the brand's colourful cast of spokescharacters—Glacier and Fresh, the Glacier Girls and Sasquatch. The film was produced by Alliance Films and Grip, Labatt's advertising agency, with help from professional screenwriters and Canadian beer fans. It's the story is a comedy/adventure that follows a group of friends who reunite in a ski town in Western Canada—and will only be available in theatres in that part of the country. The idea behind the branded movie is to take engagement to the next level and make it more than just a 90-second commercial. Says Grip's creative director, "People are more than willing to watch branded entertainment as long as it entertains them."[33]

Branded entertainment is on the rise and could soon prove to be the single most effective way for advertisers to engage audiences online with video. Canada is the number one per capita consumer of online video according to comScore, and so it is only a matter of time before this opportunity is more fully exploited by Canadian brands.

Brands and Social Media

Social media and other emerging technologies are radically changing how consumers think, act, and relate to others, which in turn is forcing brand managers to re-think their marketing strategies and tactics. "Your brand is more than what you say it is; it's also what you produce and the experiences you create," advises a senior brand analyst.[34] Today's brand managers must create social groups and fan pages; host dialogues with consumers and solicit feedback from them. In other words, they must *engage* them.

"In the era of the social web, we are all brand advocates and managers," says Brian Solis, author of the book *Engage!*[35] He advises brand managers to use social media to define the face, voice, and personality of the brand. Good advice, but not so easy to accomplish because of the challenges posed by how, exactly, to display and present a long established brand across the social web. This challenge is further complicated by the addition of consumer voices and personalities into the mix. But for brand marketers willing to develop well planned social media campaigns, there are rewards to be had.

For example, Hudson's Bay, Dockers, and Old Navy have all developed social media campaigns using the popular music matching app, Shazam. Hudson's Bay ran a national radio advertising campaign promoting its Bay Day sales and used Shazam to drive listeners to its mobile site. The app recognizes codes embedded into the commercials and listeners who have Shazam active when the spots air are taken to that item on the site where it can be viewed or purchased. Dockers embedded Shazam codes in a TV commercial called "Men Without Pants" that drove viewers to a branded content page. And Old Navy integrated Shazam's content discovery app throughout a music-based marketing campaign that included TV, online, in-store, and mobile.[36]

Brand Advocates Today consumers are telling stories about brands and spreading them through social media. Though it is not possible for brand managers to control what consumers say about their brands, it *is* possible to encourage feedback and storytelling from those consumers who love the brand, and to create **brand advocates**—customers, employees, and others who willingly and voluntarily promote their favourite brands.

Brand advocates
Customers, employees, and others who willingly and voluntarily promote their favourite brands.

Brand advocacy is a powerful marketing tool, but how can it be created and used effectively? Inter-brand offers the following suggestions:[37]

- *Advocacy begins with trust:* Word of mouth, good or bad, has always influenced perceptions of brands. Online consumer opinions have also gained importance as new communications channels have emerged. Build trust with potential advocates by nurturing their recommendations and opinions.

- *Advocacy starts close to home:* Oprah telling the world she used her BlackBerry to write an article about First Lady Michelle Obama is a great brand story. But it is unlikely that a brand can capture Oprah's attention without first building a strong base of brand supporters. Brands must start by creating advocates in the world around them. If you gain the passionate support of customers and employees, their enthusiasm for the brand will spill over into words and actions.

Exhibit 9.14 **Branded entertainment:** New forms of entertainment such as Lady Gaga's "Telephone" blend elements of music videos, short film, drama (or comedy), and advertising.

PR NEWSWIRE

- *Make customers and employees part of the brand story:* Transforming customers and employees into advocates puts them at the heart of the brand. Zappos, the online clothing and shoe retailer, has employees who are valued and empowered partners in creating and delivering the customer experience. Real customer-service calls were featured in television commercials; "I hear Zappos" stories are posted online; and CEO Tony Hsieh tells brand stories on his numerous speaking tours.

- *Deliver an experience that gets them talking:* Creating brand advocates requires persistence and effort. Loyalty is not enough, because loyalists can be quiet and passive, for example, Microsoft's customers. On the other hand, Apple's advocates go beyond loyalty to actively promote the brand.

- *Outperform where they care the most:* The secret to creating advocates is to outperform for brand participants when they most need it. Understanding and solving problems is universally one of the most effective ways to create brand advocates.

Social media campaigns engage consumers, and now there's proof that engagement works. According to a study of over 100 social gaming campaigns commissioned by MediaBrix, a company that develops and produces in-app and in-game social and mobile advertising solutions for Fortune 500 brands, social and mobile gaming ads give advertisers 20 percent engagement rates. The study also showed that gaming ads outperformed mobile banner ads, Facebook ads, and standard banner ads in average click-through rates. "It comes as no surprise that social and mobile gaming advertising sees results 30 to 100 times better than standard online advertising campaigns," says Ari Brandt, CEO and co-founder, MediaBrix. "This is largely due to the fact that people are driven by a deep well of positive emotions—such as joy, excitement, and brand affinity—when playing social and mobile games."[38]

To sum up, brand management and brand marketing are all about building brands that connect deeply with customers. In the era of social media, marketers must rethink their processes, broaden the channels of communication available to consumers who seek information about their products and services, and engage consumers in conversations about brands.

Happy Brands

Regardless of whether you're talking to WestJet president and CEO Gregg Saretsky, a WestJet sales super agent over the phone, or a flight attendant on board any one of WestJet's 500 daily flights, the WestJet brand is on display. But if it's Ed Baklor, vice-president of guest services, you're going to get perhaps the most impassioned brand advocate. As an executive with Disney for 14 years prior to joining WestJet, he knows a thing or two about managing a powerful brand. In fact, as he recalls, it was his first experience as a WestJet guest when he noticed the similarities to Disney.

"I had just been recruited to begin work with a high-end tour operator in Vancouver, and I got on a WestJet flight, and I was referred to as a guest, not a passenger, not a customer or a traveller—a guest. And after my Disney experience, where the brand was all about the guest experience, it was obvious WestJet was the same." If Baklor's guest experience with WestJet set the first bait, it would ironically be Saretsky's experience with Baklor's tour company that would be the final lure. "Come visit our campus in Calgary, we love showing off our culture," Baklor recalls of Saretsky's invitation. "After my visit, I went home that night thinking, they're all just so happy." Baklor agreed to join the team a mere weeks after that visit.

Happy employees beget happy customers, which in turn builds brand equity. Baklor believes, however, that you can neither buy nor train "happy." "We hire for attitude," he claims. "We train for safety, we train for processes, but we expect some key unscripted things to happen. Real smiles, enthusiasm, eye contact, empathy and yes, an apology if things don't go right."

In a service-based company, the experience is the product. This is never more obvious than in the travel and tourism industry. While all WestJetters together pursue the vision of being "one of the five most successful international airlines in the world providing our guests with a friendly, caring experience," nowhere in the operation does reaching that goal weigh more heavily than in Baklor's group. "I constantly remind my team that every guest has a unique story which has brought them to our check-in counter. Whether it's a vacation they've saved a lifetime for, or a family tragedy, or a job interview—there's going to be some emotion. Our brand promise respects and reacts to those emotions. If we don't deliver on that promise, they're not coming back."

QUESTIONS

1. List all the brand touchpoints a person booking and taking a flight on WestJet encounters.
2. How would you describe WestJet's brand personality?
3. What brand development strategy did WestJet use when it introduced Encore (see the WestJet Mini Case in Chapter 8)?

REVIEWING THE CONCEPTS

1. Define and describe the concept of a brand. Differentiate between brands and the symbols, logos, and trade names that represent them.

The basic definition of a *brand* is a name, symbol, icon, design, or a combination of these, that identifies the maker or marketer of a product. A brand may identify a company, one of their products, or a product line, but a brand is much more than just a *trade name*. Brands are powerful, and appeal to our emotions. They have status, personality, and monetary value. However, brands are intangible. A brand is an abstract concept or an idea—and for the biggest brands in the world, it is precisely that idea that generates most of the company's revenue.

Today, hardly anything goes unbranded. Branding helps consumers to identify products that might benefit them. For marketers, the brand name becomes the basis on which a whole story can be built about a product's special qualities. The brand name and *trademark* provide legal protection for unique product features that otherwise might be copied by competitors. Trademarked names are indicated with a superscript TM, and registered trademarks are indicated with the symbol®.

Consumers attach meanings to brands and develop *brand relationships* that go well beyond a product's physical attributes. The most powerful brands are those that consumers associate with just one word. Finally, people can become brands when, just as with products, their name takes on meanings that transcend the person.

2. Explain the role of a logo in branding. Define brand personality, brand status, and brand equity, and explain why each is important to brand marketers.

While brands ultimately exist only as an abstract concept in the minds and hearts of consumers, it is the job of brand managers to create representations of the brand, such as *logos*. Logos are designs that represent the brand, and that may or may not incorporate the brand name. Logos may be redesigned from time to time, but these updates must be done without changing the meaning of the brand.

The most successful brands are those that have a distinctive personality. A *brand personality* is the sum total of all the attributes of a brand, and the emotions it inspires in the minds of consumers. Brand personalities are described in the same manner as human personalities, using words such as fun-loving, conservative, colourful, shy, and friendly. Another aspect of a brand's personality is its *status*, or level of social regard. Within every product

category there are high-status and low-status brands, however, status should not be confused with value or popularity. Many high-status brands tend to be exclusive rather than popular, while lower-status brands can still be highly popular. A brand's personality and status are key to establishing the positioning of that brand.

A powerful brand has monetary value and equity. *Brand equity* is the dollar amount attributed to the value of the brand, based on all the intangible qualities that create that value. Brand equity is difficult to calculate, but one indicator is the extent to which people are willing to pay more for the brand.

3. List and describe the major strategic and ongoing management decisions marketers must make about brands.

Marketing managers responsible for brands must make high-level strategic decisions that govern the management of the brand, and that guide the public and market perceptions about the brand. The first is *brand name selection*. A great brand requires a good, strong, memorable name. Brand experts advise that a new brand name should suggest something about the type of products it will brand; be easy to pronounce, recognize, and remember; be distinctive, extendable, pronounceable in many languages, and capable of registration and protection as a trademark.

To stand out in our over-communicated world, brands must establish and own a unique, honest, meaningful and clear position. Brand *positioning* based on product attributes, benefits, or beliefs and values. The strongest brands are those that engage consumers on a deep, emotional level.

Brand sponsorship is an important branding strategy decision, and begins with the question, "To brand or not to brand?" Not all products are branded, but those that are may be *national brands* or *private brands* (also called *store brands* and *private label*). Private brands are brand names applied by the marketer to products manufactured for them under contract. While some manufacturers take years and spend millions to create their own brand names, others *license* the right to use a brand name, then focus on marketing and selling their products under that name. Finally, marketers may partner with another company, take the strongest elements of each company's products, and combine them to produce a *co-branded* offering.

In addition, because brands are valuable corporate assets, they must be carefully developed, either by creating *line extensions* or *brand extensions*; pursuing a *multibrand* strategy, or creating entirely *new brands*. Finally, it is the job of the brand manager to manage and protect the brand on an ongoing basis, by carefully managing the marketing communications and advertising that communicates the brand's attributes and positioning to the market. Brands must be maintained, not just by advertising, but by the overall brand experience, points of purchase, word of mouth, websites, and, increasingly, social media.

4. **Differentiate between brand communications and traditional product-focused advertising. Explain the need for brand engagement, and summarize the ways marketers can engage consumers through brand communications.**

Brand communications is a specialized form of marketing communications and advertising that focuses on communicating brand positioning, or image, rather than on product features. Advertising campaigns can help to create name recognition and product knowledge, but consumers "get to know" a brand through their own *brand experiences* and through a wide range of *touchpoints* such as other forms of marketing communications, word of mouth, social media, company and brand websites, store displays, and many others. Brand experiences are evoked in consumers when they come into contact with brand touchpoints.

Brand communications efforts may employ *brand icons* or *characters* (sometimes called *brand mascots*). Brand icons are objects associated with the brand, while *brand characters*, also called *mascots*, are icons that move, speak, interact, and have personality traits. Brand icons and characters are also an important tool for *brand engagement*, the interaction between consumers and brands, based on the emotional connection consumers feel toward the brand. Marketers and brand managers work to develop marketing programs, especially through the use of social media, that serve to engage consumers with their brand. Brand communications tactics may also include *brand ambassadors*, real people who, under contract with the brand's marketing organization, act as spokespersons for the brand.

5. **Describe the role of storytelling in brand management. Explain how branded content, branded entertainment, social media, and brand advocates can be used to tell brand stories.**

Today's brand managers use elements of a company's history, as well as elements of fiction, to create stories for their brands. In fact, brands themselves can be thought of as a form of storytelling. While new products provide us with new information, brand stories enrich this information with details that give the facts *meaning*.

In addition to advertising and other traditional marketing communications channels, brand stories can also be communicated through *branded content* or *content marketing*, the production of any form of information or story by a brand marketer, in which the brand is clearly and prominently featured. A similar form of storytelling is *branded entertainment*, which is any form of entertainment, usually video, that is created with the co-operation or financial support of a marketer.

Brand managers can use social media to tell brand stories. In addition, they can cultivate consumers who are telling stories about their brands, and turn them into *brand advocates*. Brand advocates are people who care about, or are interested in, the brand, and who willingly and voluntarily promote it. In the era of social media, marketers must engage consumers in conversations about brands.

KEY TERMS

TALK ABOUT MARKETING

1. Visit a TELUS retail store, and spend some time browsing the TELUS website. How would you describe TELUS' brand personality? What role does packaging play in TELUS' brand communications strategy?

2. Think of a specialty product you purchased in the past. How important was brand to your purchase decision? What other aspects of the product played important roles in your decision to purchase that brand of that particular product?

3. Choose a car manufacturer and brand that you are familiar with. How would you describe the brand's attributes, personality, and positioning? How do you feel about the brand? In other words, describe your emotions and beliefs about it.

4. Find or describe three TV commercials you remember seeing recently. Are these examples of brand communications? Explain why or why not.

5. Find an example of a brand extension and a line extension. Why do you think the marketers made these brand decisions for the products you've chosen? In other words, why do you think they decided on a brand extension instead of a line extension, and vice versa?

6. NextPhase Strategy is a branding and marketing agency in Vancouver. Visit its website, and examine some of the work it has done for clients. How does it help clients to manage brands?

THINK LIKE A MARKETING MANAGER

General Mills owns, markets, and manages over 300 brands. On the company's website (www.generalmills.com), these brands are organized by food category: baking, breads, cereals, pasta, and so on. Visit the company's website, and choose one of the food categories to examine, and then answer the following questions about the brands in that category.

QUESTIONS

1. How many brands are in your food category? Are they line extensions, brand extensions, or new brand names? Briefly describe the positioning and brand personality for each.

2. Let's say General Mills wants to launch a new brand in your category. Would you recommend a line extension, brand extension, or new brand name? Briefly describe how the new brand should be positioned, for example, should it be a new flavour, or colour, and if so, what? Come up with a new brand name for your product.

MARKETING ETHICS

There are hundreds of different beer brands available to Canadian consumers, most of which are marketed to different segments based on lifestyle, and with advertising campaigns based on communicating brand personality. Yet alcohol is a controlled substance and cannot legally be promoted to underage drinkers. Visit the "Our Brands" section of Labatt Breweries of Canada website, and consider the following ethical questions.

QUESTIONS

1. Labatt has a Facebook page, and there is also a Facebook page for each of their beer brands. For marketers, the main reason for having a Facebook page is to get as many people as possible to "like" it—yet there are no controls for keeping underage children from liking a beer page on Facebook. Visit the Facebook pages of three of Labatt's beer brands and compare the fans on both. How many are there? Do most of them seem to be of legal drinking age? If you were a marketing manager at Labatt, what additional steps would you recommend to attempt to prevent children from becoming fans of the beers on Facebook?

2. Look closely at the website of your favourite Labatt beer brand. Does it offer any communications that associate their brand with responsible drinking? Do you think the marketers are making any attempt to position the brand as "responsible?"

MARKETING TECHNOLOGY

BlackBerry, Apple, and Samsung are all well known and well respected technology brands whose smartphone brands (BlackBerry, iPhone, and Galaxy respectively) are in direct competition with one another. The smartphone brands are not highly differentiated in terms of features, functionality, or pricing.

QUESTIONS

1. Research the latest smartphone from each company. If you were the brand manager for BlackBerry, what technical details would you highlight in your brand communications to position your brand against the iPhone and the Galaxy?

2. Describe the brand personality for all three smartphone brands. Are technical qualities or attributes part of the personality for either of the brands? Which brand do you think does a better job of communicating its brand personality to the market?

MARKETING BY THE NUMBERS

Special K is the number one brand in the diet food category, and the Kellogg Company is planning to turn it into a megabrand. Brand extensions must be consistent with the brand's positioning as a weight-management food, and so the company will roll out Special K–branded protein waters and protein bars. Sales of Special K–branded cereals were $500 million worldwide last year, an increase of 16 percent from the previous year. The budget for advertising was $45 million. The worldwide market for bottled water is worth approximately $75 billion. Retail sales in the snack food category in Canada were approximately $500 million last year. The snack food category includes candy, gum, snacks, and bars. The natural snacks and bars segment of the market is approximately 10 percent of the larger snack category.

QUESTIONS

1. Kellogg hopes to capture 3 percent of the market with its new Special K protein water products by the end of next year. How much should the company spend on advertising in Canada to support this new product line?

2. How much should the company spend to advertise the new Special K protein bars in Canada? What percentage of the snack food market do you think they will be able to capture in the first year, and what is the value of that market?

VIDEO CASE

Life Is Good

Life Is Good is a clothing brand created in Boston in the late 1970s, and represented by a quirky smiley-face logo that is printed on all the items the company sells. The company's slogan is "Spread optimism," and optimistic sayings appear on many of their T-shirts. While the company has enjoyed considerable success, still the founders think that consumers aren't getting the complete image that the Life Is Good brand stands for. This video illustrates the challenges a company faces in balancing the customer's role with that of the company in determining and communicating brand meaning. After viewing the video, answer the following questions:

QUESTIONS

1. What are people really buying when they purchase a Life Is Good product?

2. Other than the logo and the company slogan, what other representations or factors contribute to the Life Is Good brand image?

3. What recommendations would you make to Life Is Good regarding future brand development?

CAFFEINE AND CHOCOLATE: A WINNING COMBINATION FOR AWAKE CHOCOLATE

Case prepared by David Rose, Wilfrid Laurier University

Targeting a perennially sleep-deprived population with chocolate can be a hard sell in an already crowded market, but a bolt of caffeine and delightfully quirky packaging has given Awake Chocolate a sweet start.

The idea to create a caffeine-infused bar of milk chocolate came from Awake founders Matt Schnarr, Adam Deremo, and Dan Tzotzis, a Toronto-based trio with a consumer packaged-goods pedigree at companies such as Kraft Foods and PepsiCo. Over lunch one day in 2010, they decided to go into business together. "We didn't know what the idea was, nor did we have any clue as to where we'd end up," Tzotzis said.

In the ensuing months, the trio, who collectively have 35 years of packaged goods experience, brainstormed and soon realized that products with functional benefits have been the single biggest driver of growth in consumer packaged goods in the past decade. "Whether it's probiotics or Greek yogurt, which is fortified with protein, or fibre and omega in granola bars . . . and what vitamin water and energy drinks have done within the carbonated drinks space, they've delivered solid growth," Tzotzis said.

Between 2003 and 2010, global functional food sales growth outpaced that of standard food and beverages, growing at about 14 percent a year compared with 4 percent, according to Leatherhead Food Research, a British market analysis firm. It predicts sales in the category will hit US$29.8 billion by 2014, and noted the number of new products making functional claims has also grown at the rate of 28 percent a year. There is an added benefit of price stability in the budding category, Schnarr said: the herbs, tinctures, supplements, and vitamins added to juices and other products allow those products to enjoy a premium regular soft drinks and candy bars no longer command—a perceived value people are willing to pay for.

"With functional products like probiotic yogurt, energy drinks, and vitamin water, you can get away a bit from the price game," he said. "With water and pop like Pepsi and Coke, for a long time [competitors focused on] how low can you go. With Vitamin Water and Aquafina Plus, however, you get back into re-establishing the

[pricing] base." And compared to Coke, energy drinks command an average price of $3.49.

While standard milk chocolate bars have some naturally occurring caffeine in their cocoa base—about 10 mg to 20 mg—Awake, at 101 mg, packs a punch. That's more than the caffeine found in a can of the Red Bull energy drink, but below the jitters one might experience after ingesting a 12 oz "tall" bold-drip coffee at Starbucks, which contains a whopping 260 mg.

Some products with functional benefits had entered the chocolate space, but all had committed a significant sin: They compromised taste. To deliver a product that satisfied on both fronts, the three men and a friend with expertise in building chocolate manufacturing facilities gathered in Tzotzis's Stoney Creek, Ontario, kitchen to cook up the right mix. The result was Awake, a chocolate bar that delivers 101 mg of caffeine. "Not only did we have something that tasted great but it provided the added pick-me-up caffeine typically adds," Tzotzis said.

Although multinational food firms are getting into the functional foods business in a big way by starting smaller sub-brands or doing line extensions—PepsiCo's Frito-Lay division recently introduced Cracker Jack'd, which includes caffeinated varieties of its classic Cracker Jack snack—Schnarr said he and his partners chose to go out on their own so they could be completely in charge of their brand.

"There is also obviously a chance to have a greater stake in the company [as entrepreneurs], but positive or negative, as an owner you are fully accountable for the results," he said. "At a big company, sometimes it doesn't matter how many hours you work personally, you are sometimes subject to what the other 20 000 people in the company are doing."

By early 2011, with the product formula down, they set about formulating a business plan, reaching out to investors, and building a brand. The trio's extensive network helped them secure funding. They raised about $1 million through friends, family, and seasoned investors such as Andrew Black, former president of Virgin Mobile Canada, and Tony Chapman, chief executive of ad agency Capital C and judge on the Food Network reality TV series *Recipe to Riches*. Investor Stanley Hainsworth, former vice-president of global creative at Starbucks and head of the design firm Tether Inc., created Awake's distinctive packaging and look, with an owl design on its packaging and etched into the chocolate bars.

"Beyond taste, we knew design and packaging was the top thing you can do," Schnarr said. "Most decisions in chocolate happen at the shelf. Packaging is going to be the most visible element of the marketing mix, period." The number of consumer impressions that a package design has is higher than everything, he said, because merchandise displays itself at stores everywhere. He feels the packaging has the right elements to capture people looking for a pick-me-up that tastes great. The wrapper colour looks like chocolate, giving high taste appeal. The irreverent personality of Nevil, the owl mascot, creates brand character, while the clear, unambiguous labelling of caffeine and nutritional content is straight to the point. The packaging and the Awake name tested well with Awake's target consumers—socially connected 18- to 30-year-olds who live an active lifestyle and like to discover new things.

To raise awareness with these target consumers, more than 180 000 samples were given out during a coast-to-coast sampling program at Canadian colleges and universities. The program paid off, with on-campus retail locations among the top retail locations. On a number of campuses, Awake has become the number one selling chocolate bar. Social media and Awake brand ambassadors are being used to generate buzz. Overwhelmingly positive feedback from credible food and media sites is also generating consumer awareness and interest. An *Elle Canada* magazine article provided "Five Reasons Why We Love AWAKE Chocolate Bars," while *Tasting Toronto* asked "Why didn't anyone come up with this before?"

Armed with national and regional retailer commitments, including Shell, Shoppers Drug Mart, and Gateway News, and promising sales growth the partners decided it was time to enter the CBC's *Dragons' Den*, where aspiring entrepreneurs pitch their business concepts and products to a panel of Canadian business moguls who have the cash and the know-how to make it happen. The entrepreneurs asked for $200 000 in exchange for a 20 percent stake in their business. A deal was struck with two of the dragons, David Chilton and Kevin O'Leary. In due diligence, O'Leary opted out and within weeks the Awake founders came to terms with Chilton. "We knew we wanted a strategic partner with public relations expertise and Dave Chilton was top of our list," Tzotzis said.

Chilton felt the upside was outstanding based on how well energy beverages have done. "When you look at drinks that have been caffeinated, they have resonated with a significant size demographic. The taste of the chocolate brought me in. I expected it to have a caffeine aftertaste and be an inferior chocolate and neither was the case."

"I also thought they were very credible, they answered all the questions well, the math was right, they had the right backgrounds. It was an unusual pitch in that I liked everything about it," Chilton said. From an investor's point of view, he is pleased with Awake's progress. "They are in good shape. There is no debt at this point. But it's still a highly competitive business and they are up against major players that dominate shelf space and that hurts. The big focus is Canada and the US for now. Getting on shelves is incredibly difficult and these guys have done that better than anyone we've seen on *Dragons' Den*."

The next step, he said, is to create demand: "That's the piece they are working on. They are using old-fashioned sampling and new techniques like social media to create a buzz; they are doing it all. That includes guerrilla marketing, testing, and in-store promotion to see what gives them the best ROI. At any one time they are trying between five and 20 initiatives to see what grabs hold. The consumer feedback has been really good," Chilton said.

He also likes that the entrepreneurs love to learn: "They call up, tell me what they are working on, and ask me to recommend some books that will help with the initiative and they will read them within two or three days."

Sources: Mary Teresa Bitti, "Dragons Eat up Awake Chocolate's Pitch," *Financial Post*, February 11, 2013; Hollie Shaw, "Caffeine Fuels Awake Chocolate's Success," *Financial Post*, January 28, 2013; Awake Chocolate website, AwakeChocolate.com; Dragons' Den website, CBC.ca/dragonsden; company documents.

QUESTIONS FOR DISCUSSION

1. Do you think Awake is a good brand name? Explain why or why not.

2. Do you think Nevil, the irreverent owl, is a good brand mascot?

3. Briefly describe the brand personality of Awake Chocolate. What attributes or elements of the company and the product contribute to this personality?

4. What suggestions do you have for managing the Awake brand in the future?

MyMarketingLab is an online homework and tutorial system that puts you in control of your own learning with study and practice tools directly correlated to this chapter's content.

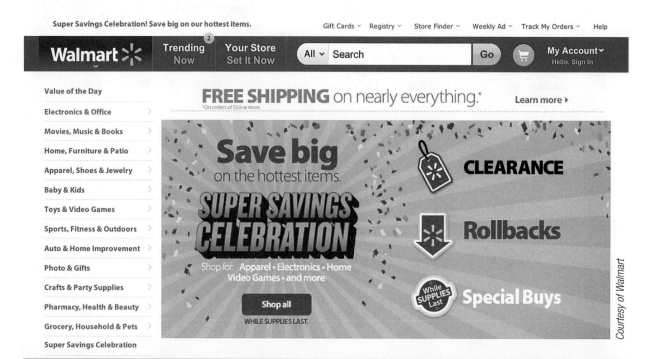

Courtesy of Walmart

AFTER STUDYING THIS CHAPTER, YOU SHOULD BE ABLE TO

1 identify the three major pricing strategies and discuss the importance of understanding customer-value perceptions, company costs, and competitor strategies when setting prices

2 identify and define the other important external and internal factors affecting a firm's pricing decisions

3 describe the major strategies for pricing new products

4 explain how companies find a set of prices that maximizes the profits from the total product mix

5 discuss how companies adjust their prices to take into account different types of customers and situations

6 discuss the key issues related to initiating and responding to price changes

7 list and briefly describe the major legislation in Canada that affect marketers' pricing decisions

Pricing: Understanding and Capturing Customer Value

PREVIEWING THE CONCEPTS

We continue your marketing journey with a look at another major marketing mix tool—pricing. If effective product development, promotion, and distribution sow the seeds of business success, effective pricing is the harvest. Firms successful at creating customer value with the other marketing mix activities must still capture some of this value in the prices they earn. Yet, despite its importance, many firms do not handle pricing well. In this chapter, we begin with the following question: What is a price? Next, we look at three major pricing strategies—customer value-based, cost-based, and competition-based pricing—and at other factors that affect pricing decisions. Finally, we examine strategies for new-product pricing, product-mix pricing, price adjustments, and dealing with price changes.

For openers, let's examine an interesting online pricing story. In case you haven't noticed, there's a war going on—between Walmart, by far the world's largest retailer, and Amazon.com, the world's largest online merchant. The weapon of choice? Prices. Only time will tell who will win on the web. But for now, the two retailers, especially Walmart, seem determined to fight it out on price.

AMAZON VS. WALMART: FIGHTING IT OUT ONLINE ON PRICE

Walmart to Amazon: "Let's Rumble" read the headline. Just like Coke has Pepsi, Walmart, the mightiest retail giant in history, has met its own worthy adversary: Amazon.com. In the United States, the two heavyweight retailers are waging a war online. The weapon of choice? Prices—not surprising, given the two combatants' long-held low-cost positions.

The price war between Walmart and Amazon.com began in 2009, with skirmishes over online prices for new books and DVDs. It then escalated quickly to video game consoles, mobile phones, and even toys. At stake was not only the fortunes of the two companies, but also those of whole industries whose products they sell, both online and in retail stores. Price can be a potent strategic weapon, but it can also be a double-edged sword.

Amazon.com, it seems, wants to be the "Walmart of the web"—our digital general store—and it's well on its way to achieving that goal. Although Amazon's $60-plus billion in annual sales is small compared to Walmart's, which in 2013 was an incredible $466 billion ($135 billion of which comes from international markets, including Canada), on the other hand Amazon's online sales are nearly seven times greater than Walmart's online sales. Moreover, Amazon attracts more than 100 million unique visitors to its US website monthly, almost triple Walmart's number. One analyst estimates that more than one-half of all US consumers who look online for retail items start their search at Amazon.com.

Why does this worry Walmart? After all, online sales account for only 5 percent of its overall US retail sales. Walmart captures most of its business by offering affordable prices to average consumers in its more than 4000 brick-and-mortar stores. By comparison, according to one analyst, Amazon.com sells mostly to "affluent urbanites who would rather click with their mouse than push around a cart."

But this battle isn't about now, it's about the future. Although still a small market by Walmart's standards, online sales will soar within the next decade to an estimated 15 percent of total US retail sales. And, increasingly, Amazon.com owns the online space. In 2012, Amazon's net sales increased 27 percent from the previous year to $61.09 billion. Furthermore, Amazon is continually adding new product lines, such as its recent launch of Kindle Stores in Brazil, Canada, China, and Japan. And for eight years in a row, Amazon has ranked number one in customer satisfaction during the holiday shopping season according to the ForeSee annual Holiday E-Retail Satisfaction Index. Perhaps of greatest concern to Walmart, however, is the fact that Amazon is continually lowering its prices— there were 10 price reductions in 2012 alone.

Amazon has shown a relentless ambition to offer more of almost everything on the web. It started by selling only books online, but now it sells everything from books, movies, and musicals to consumer electronics, home and garden products, clothing, jewellery, toys, tools, and even groceries in some markets. Its selection expanded further after it purchased online shoe retailer Zappos and baby products retailer Diapers.com. It's even beefing up its private label selection, adding new lines of Amazon-branded goods. If Amazon.com's expansion continues and online sales grow as predicted, the giant web retailer will eat further and further into Walmart's bread-and-butter store sales.

But Walmart isn't about to let that happen. Instead, it's taking the battle to Amazon. com's home territory—the web. Through aggressive pricing, it is now fighting for every dollar consumers spend online. Walmart fired the first shot before the 2009 holiday shopping season. It announced that it would take online preorders for 10 soon-to-be-released hardback books—all projected best sellers by authors such as John Grisham, Stephen King, Barbara Kingsolver, and James Patterson—at an unprecedented low price of just $10 each. (Actually, the new hardcover prices matched the $9.99 price that Amazon was already charging for e-book versions of bestsellers that are downloaded to its Kindle or other readers; Walmart, however, doesn't sell e-books.) To take it a step further, Walmart also cut prices by 50 percent on 200 other best sellers, undercutting Amazon's prices. When Amazon quickly announced that it would match Walmart's $10 price on the 10 best sellers, the price war was on. Walmart dropped its price to $9.00, Amazon.com did likewise, and Walmart lowered its prices yet again, to $8.98.

These low book prices represented a 59 to 74 percent reduction off the list price, much more than the 30 to 40 percent reduction you might expect in traditional retail bookstores like Barnes & Noble. In fact, Walmart and Amazon discounted these best sellers below costs—as so-called loss leaders—to lure shoppers to their online stores in hopes that they would buy other, more profitable items.

Today, the book price war continues. And it's having an impact beyond the two primary combatants, causing collateral damage across the entire book industry. "When your product is treated as a loss leader, it lowers its perceived value," says one publishing executive. In the long run, that's not great for either the companies that publish the books or the retailers who sell them. Price carries messages about customer value, notes another publisher. Companies want to be careful about the messages they send. Moreover, the price war is not just taking place over books. If you compare prices at Walmart.com and Amazon.com, you'll find the price battle raging across a broad range of product categories.

Who will win the online battle for the hearts and dollars of online buyers? Certainly, low prices will be an important factor. And when it comes to low prices, Walmart appears to have the upper hand. With its huge size, it can negotiate better terms with its suppliers. And by combining its online and offline operations, it can provide some unique services, such as free and convenient delivery and returns of online orders to stores (Walmart's site gives you three buying options: online, in-store, and site-to-store). Walmart is even experimenting with drive-through windows where shoppers can pick up their Internet orders. But Amazon.com also has advantages, including a highly recognizable online brand, a sophisticated distribution network built specifically for online shopping, a much larger assortment, an unparalleled online customer shopping experience, and fast and free shipping with Amazon Prime. And, of course, Amazon is no stranger to low prices.

In the long run, however, reckless price cutting will likely do more damage than good to both Walmart and Amazon. Price wars can turn whole product categories into unattractive, low-margin commodities (think DVDs, for example). And buying online is about much more than just getting the best prices, even in today's economy. In the end, winning online consumers will require offering not only the lowest prices but also the best customer value in terms of price and product selection, speed, convenience, and overall shopping experience.

For now, the two retailers seem determined to fight it out on price. Amazon's CEO, Jeff Bezos, has long maintained that there's plenty of room for all competitors in the big world of retailing. However, Paul Vazquez, president and CEO of Walmart.com, says that it's "only a matter of time" before Walmart dominates web shopping. Pricing, he thinks, will be key. "Our company is based on low prices," says Vazquez, laying down the challenge. "Even in books, we kept going until we were the low-priced leader. And we will do that in every category we need to. Our company is based on low prices." Offering the low price "is in our DNA."[1*]

Exhibit 10.1 **Pricing:** No matter what the state of the economy, companies should sell value, not price.

Little Whale / Shutterstock.com

COMPANIES TODAY face a fierce and fast-changing pricing environment. As a result of increased information and online price comparison tools, plus the increasing number of low price and discount retailers, today's value-seeking shoppers have put increased pricing pressure on many companies. It would seem that all companies should respond by tightening their belts and reducing their prices, yet cutting prices is often not the best answer. Reducing prices unnecessarily can lead to lost profits and damaging price wars. It can cheapen a brand by signalling to customers that the price is more important than the value the brand delivers. Instead, companies should sell value, not price. In some cases, that means selling lesser products at rock-bottom prices. But in most cases, it means persuading customers that paying a higher price for the company's brand is justified by the greater value they gain.

*"Q4 2013 WalMart Stores, Inc. Prerecorded Earnings Conference Call—Final," Fair Disclosure Wire [Waltham], February 21, 2013; "Amazon.com Announces Fourth Quarter Sales up 22% to $21.27 Billion," press release published on Business Wire, January 29, 2013; Brad Stone and Stephanie Rosenbloom, "The Gloves Come Off at Amazon and Walmart," New York Times, November 24, 2009, p. 1; Gayle Feldman, "Behind the US Price War," Bookseller, November 13, 2009, p. 16; Jeffrey A. Trachtenberg and Miguel Bustillo, "Amazon, Walmart Cut Deeper in Book Duel," Wall Street Journal, October 19, 2009, p. B1; Josh Smith, "2010 Marks Return of Price Wars Between Amazon, Best Buy, and Walmart," published on DailyFinance.com, January 19, 2010; Brad Stone, "Can Amazon Be Walmart of the Web," New York Times, September 20, 2009, p. 1; Jonathan Birchall, "Walmart Tweaks Price in Amazon Battle," Financial Times, October 17, 2009; Curt Woodward, "Amazon: Feds OK Diapers.com Deal," published on XConomy.com, March 24, 2011; Matthew Boyle and Douglas MacMillan, "Walmart's Rocky Path from Bricks to Clicks," Bloomberg Businessweek, July 25-July 31, 1022, pp. 31-33; and information from Walmart.com and Amazon.com websites.

FIGURE 10.1 Considerations in Setting Price

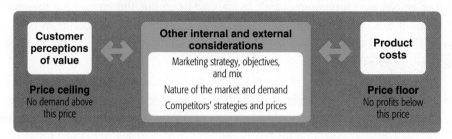

What Is a Price?

Price
The amount of money charged for a product or a service, or the sum of the values that customers exchange for the benefits of having or using the product or service.

In the narrowest sense, **price** is the amount of money charged for a product or a service. More broadly, price is the sum of all the values that customers give up to gain the benefits of having or using a product or service. Historically, price has been the major factor affecting buyer choice. In recent decades, non-price factors have gained increasing importance. However, price still remains one of the most important elements determining a firm's market share and profitability.

Price is the only element in the marketing mix that produces revenue; all other elements represent costs. Price is also one of the most flexible marketing mix elements. Unlike product features and channel commitments, prices can be changed quickly. At the same time, pricing is the number one problem facing many marketing executives, and many companies do not handle pricing well. Some managers view pricing as a big headache, preferring instead to focus on the other marketing mix elements. However, smart managers treat pricing as a key strategic tool for creating and capturing customer value. Prices have a direct impact on a firm's bottom line. A small percentage improvement in price can generate a large percentage in profitability. More importantly, as a part of a company's overall value proposition, price plays a key role in creating customer value and building customer relationships. "Instead of running away from pricing," says the expert, "savvy marketers are embracing it."[2]

Major Pricing Strategies LO1

The price the company charges will fall somewhere between one that is too high to produce any demand and one that is too low to produce a profit. Figure 10.1 summarizes the major considerations in setting price. Customer perceptions of the product's value set the ceiling for prices. If customers perceive that the price is greater than the product's value, they will not buy the product. Product costs set the floor for prices. If the company prices the product below its costs, company profits will suffer. In setting its price between

FIGURE 10.2 Value-based Pricing versus Cost-based Pricing

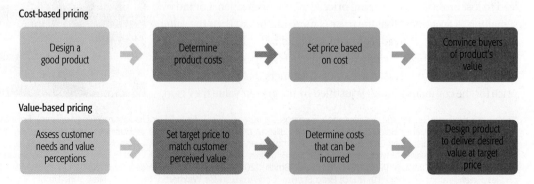

these two extremes, the company must consider a number of other internal and external factors, including competitors' strategies and prices, the company's overall marketing strategy and mix, and the nature of the market and the demand.

The figure suggests three major pricing strategies: customer value-based pricing, cost-based pricing, and competition-based pricing.

Customer value-based pricing
Setting price based on buyers' perceptions of value rather than on the seller's cost.

Customer Value-Based Pricing

In the end, the customer will decide whether a product's price is right. Pricing decisions, like other marketing mix decisions, must start with customer value. When customers buy a product, they exchange something of value (the price) to get something of value (the benefits of having or using the product). Effective, customer-oriented pricing involves understanding how much value consumers place on the benefits they receive from the product and setting a price that captures this value.

Customer value-based pricing uses buyers' perceptions of value, not the seller's cost, as the key to pricing. Value-based pricing means that the marketer cannot design a product and marketing program and then set the price. Price is considered along with the other marketing mix variables *before* the marketing program is set.

Figure 10.2 compares value-based pricing with cost-based pricing. Although costs are an important consideration in setting prices, cost-based pricing is often product driven. The company designs what it considers to be a good product, adds up the costs of making the product, and sets a price that covers costs plus a target profit. Marketing must then convince buyers that the product's value at that price justifies its purchase. If the price turns out to be too high, the company must settle for lower markups or lower sales, both resulting in disappointing profits.

Value-based pricing reverses this process. The company first assesses customer needs and value perceptions. It then sets its target price based on customer perceptions of value. The targeted value and price drive decisions about what costs can be incurred and the resulting product design. As a result, pricing begins with analyzing consumer needs and value perceptions, and price is set to match consumers' perceived value.

It's important to remember that "good value" is not the same as "low price." For example, a Steinway piano—any Steinway piano—costs a lot. But to those who own one, a Steinway is a great value:[3]

At the Steinway Piano Gallery Toronto you can purchase a custom-made Crown Jewel Edition Steinway piano, encased in your choice of magnificent woods, with the grain meticulously matched from one end of the piano to the other. It's not just a piano, it's an original, handmade work of art, unique in the world—but it will cost you about $800 000. For the less extravagant buyer, a Steinway piano can be had for $26 000. But ask anyone who owns one and they'll tell you that, when it comes to Steinway, price is nothing, the Steinway experience is everything. Steinway makes very high quality pianos—handcrafting each Steinway requires up to one full year. But more important, owners get the Steinway mystique. The Steinway name evokes images of classical concert stages and the celebrities and performers who've owned and played Steinway pianos across more than 155 years.

World renowned Canadian classical pianist Glenn Gould owned one—in fact his favourite

Exhibit 10.2 **Perceived value:** A Steinway piano—any Steinway piano—costs a lot. But to those who own one, price is nothing; the Steinway experience is everything.

Robert Caplin/NY Times/Redux Pictures

Steinway is on permanent display at The National Arts Centre in Ottawa. But Steinways aren't just for world-class pianists and the wealthy. Ninety-nine percent of all Steinway buyers are amateurs who perform only in their dens. To such customers, whatever a Steinway costs, it's a small price to pay for the value of owning one. As one Steinway owner puts it, "My friendship with the Steinway piano is one of the most important and beautiful things in my life." Who can put a price on such feelings?

Companies often find it hard to measure the value customers will attach to its product. For example, calculating the cost of ingredients in a meal at a fancy restaurant is relatively easy. But assigning a value to other satisfactions such as taste, environment, relaxation, conversation, and status is very hard. These values are subjective—they vary both for different consumers and different situations.

Still, consumers will use these perceived values to evaluate a product's price, so the company must work to measure them. Sometimes, companies ask consumers how much they would pay for a basic product and for each benefit added to the offer. Or a company might conduct experiments to test the perceived value of different product offers. According to an old Russian proverb, there are two fools in every market—one who asks too much and one who asks too little. If the seller charges more than the buyers' perceived value, the company's sales will suffer. If the seller charges less, its products sell very well but they produce less revenue than they would if they were priced at the level of perceived value.

We now examine two types of value-based pricing: *good-value pricing* and *value-added pricing*.

Good-Value Pricing   Recent economic events have caused a fundamental shift in consumer attitudes toward price and quality. In response, many companies have changed their pricing approaches to bring them into line with changing economic conditions and consumer price perceptions. More and more, marketers have adopted **good-value pricing** strategies—offering just the right combination of quality and good service at a fair price.

Good-value pricing
Offering just the right combination of quality and good service at a fair price.

In many cases, this has involved introducing less expensive versions of established, brand-name products. For example, fast-food restaurants such as Taco Bell and McDonald's offer value meals and dollar menu items. Armani offers the less-expensive, more-casual Armani Exchange fashion line. Alberto-Culver's TRESemmé hair care line promises "A salon look and feel at a fraction of the price." And every car company now offers small, inexpensive models better suited to the first time car buyer's budget.

In other cases, good-value pricing has involved redesigning existing brands to offer more quality for a given price or the same quality for less. Some companies even succeed by offering less value but at rock-bottom prices. For example, passengers flying low-cost European airline Ryanair won't get much in the way of free amenities, but they'll like the airline's unbelievably low prices.[4]

Ireland's Ryanair bills itself as "Europe's only ultra–low cost carrier," and it seems no other EU airline can match Ryanair's fares—because they are nearly free! What's their secret? Ryanair sells seats on a one-way basis, regardless of fare. Prices are set based on the demand for a particular flight and the period remaining until the departure date, with higher fares charged on flights with higher demand, and with bookings made nearer to the date of departure. For its most popular route, Dublin to London, prices range from an incredible low of €0.99 to €199.99.

FERNANDO ALVARADO/EPA/Newscom

Exhibit 10.3 **Good-value pricing:** Passengers on budget-minded Ryanair don't get much by way of amenities, but they love the unbelievably low prices. Ryanair's sometimes outrageous CEO, Michael O'Leary, hopes one day to make flying free.

There is a catch, however. The airline charges for virtually everything except the seat itself, from baggage check-in to seat-back advertising space. Once in the air, flight attendants hawk everything from scratch-card games to perfume and digital cameras to their captive audience. Upon arrival at some out-of-the-way airport, Ryanair will sell you a bus or train ticket into town. The airline even gets commissions from sales of Hertz rental cars, hotel rooms, ski packages, and travel insurance. Despite Ryanair's sometimes pushy efforts to extract more revenue from each traveller, customers aren't complaining. In a recent survey of 10 000 passengers, 87 percent were satisfied or very satisfied with their Ryanair flight, 93 percent said they would fly Ryanair again, and a whopping 95 percent said Ryanair provides excellent value for the money.

Ryanair's seemingly outrageous pricing strategy seems to be working, because the airline continues to grow at a rapid rate, adding new routes and acquiring new aircraft every year. And despite the global recession, in 2011 Ryanair paid a special dividend of €483m to shareholders.

An important type of good-value pricing at the retail level is *everyday low pricing (EDLP)*. EDLP involves charging a constant, everyday low price with few or no temporary price discounts. Retailers such as Costco and furniture seller Leon's, with its Integrity Pricing guarantee, practise EDLP. The king of EDLP is Walmart, which practically defined the concept. Except for a few sale items every month, Walmart promises everyday low prices on everything it sells. In contrast, *high-low pricing* involves charging higher prices on an everyday basis but running frequent promotions to lower prices temporarily on selected items. Department stores such as Sears and Hudson's Bay practise high-low pricing by having frequent sales days, early-bird savings, and bonus earnings for store credit-card holders.

Value-Added Pricing   Value-based pricing doesn't mean simply charging what customers want to pay or setting low prices to meet the competition. Instead, many companies adopt **value-added pricing** strategies. Rather than cutting prices to match competitors, they attach value-added features and services to differentiate their offers and justify higher prices. Similarly, some movie theatre chains are *adding* amenities and charging *more* rather than cutting services to maintain lower admission prices.[5]

> **Value-added pricing**
> Attaching value-added features and services to differentiate a company's offers and charging higher prices.

Some theatre chains are turning their multiplexes into smaller, roomier viewing rooms with luxurious features such as high-backed leather seats, food service, and even alcohol. Cineplex Entertainment, for example, recently announced a new premium theatre experience called VIP Cinemas. When purchasing tickets, guests choose exactly where they would like to sit in the auditorium, and all seats are reserved. Each VIP Cinema auditorium features stadium seating with extra leg room and luxurious high-back leather seats fitted with movable tray tables. When a guest takes their seat they are presented with a menu, and their order is taken and delivered in the same manner as in a restaurant. There's also a licensed lounge for the exclusive use of VIP Cinema guests. The strategy is designed to appeal to adults, and only those of legal drinking age will be allowed in. One observer describes VIP Cinema as a movie experience that is "heavy on the amenities, and short on some of the irritants that keep [adults] at home." The move is part of an industry-wide trend to offer services that increase the bottom line. In the United States, movie theatre chain AMC is experimenting with a "dinner and a movie" concept, and a Mexico-based chain that expanded

Exhibit 10.4 **Value-added pricing:** Some Cineplex theatres are adding value to movie tickets by providing luxurious seating and tray tables.

© david pearson / Alamy

into Southern California offers an extensive gourmet menu and equips theatre seats with call buttons that summon servers (who are referred to as "cast members."

The Cineplex example illustrates that people are motivated not by price, but by what they get for what they pay. "If consumers thought the best deal was simply a question of money saved, we'd all be shopping in one big discount store," says one pricing expert. "Customers want value and are willing to pay for it. Savvy marketers price their products accordingly."[6]

Cost-Based Pricing

Cost-based pricing
Setting prices based on the costs for producing, distributing, and selling the product plus a fair rate of return for effort and risk.

Whereas customer-value perceptions set the price ceiling, costs set the floor for the price that the company can charge. **Cost-based pricing** involves setting prices based on the costs for producing, distributing, and selling the product plus a fair rate of return for its effort and risk. A company's costs may be an important element in its pricing strategy.

Some companies, such as Ryanair, Walmart, and Dell, work to become the "low-cost producers" in their industries. Companies with lower costs can set lower prices that result in smaller margins but greater sales and profits. Other companies, however, intentionally pay higher costs so that they can claim higher prices and margins. For example, it costs more to make a handcrafted Steinway piano than a Yamaha production model, but the higher costs result in higher quality, justifying the much higher price. The key is to manage the spread between costs and prices—how much the company makes for the customer value it delivers.

Fixed costs (overhead)
Costs that do not vary with production or sales level.

Variable costs
Costs that vary directly with the level of production.

Types of Costs   A company's costs take two forms, fixed and variable. **Fixed costs** (also known as **overhead**) are costs that do not vary with production or sales level. For example, a company must pay each month's bills for rent, heat, interest, and executive salaries, whatever the company's output. **Variable costs** vary directly with the level of production. For example, each computer produced by HP involves a cost of computer chips, wires, plastic, packaging, and other inputs. These costs tend to be the same for each unit produced. They are called variable because their total varies with the number of units produced. **Total costs** are the sum of the fixed and variable costs for any given level of production. Management wants to charge a price that will at least cover the total production costs at a given level of production.

Total costs
The sum of the fixed and variable costs for any given level of production.

The company must watch its costs carefully. If it costs the company more than competitors to produce and sell a similar product, the company will need to charge a higher price or make less profit, putting it at a competitive disadvantage.

Cost-plus pricing (or markup pricing)
Adding a standard markup to the cost of the product.

Cost-Plus Pricing   The simplest pricing method is **cost-plus pricing (or markup pricing)**—adding a standard markup to the cost of the product. For example, an electronics retailer might pay a manufacturer $20 for an HDMI cable and mark it up to sell at $30, a 50 percent markup on cost. The retailer's gross margin is $10. If the store's operating costs amount to $8 per HDMI cable sold, the retailer's profit margin will be $2. The manufacturer that made the HDMI cable probably used cost-plus pricing, too. If the manufacturer's standard cost of producing the HDMI cable was $16, it might have added a 25 percent markup, setting the price to the retailers at $20.

Does using standard markups to set prices make sense? Generally, no. Any pricing method that ignores consumer demand and competitor prices is not likely to lead to the best price. Still, markup pricing remains popular for many reasons. First, sellers are more certain about costs than about demand. By tying the price to cost, sellers simplify pricing. Second, when all firms in the industry use this pricing method, prices tend to be similar, minimizing price competition.

FIGURE 10.3 Break-even Chart for Determining Target Return Price and Break-even Volume

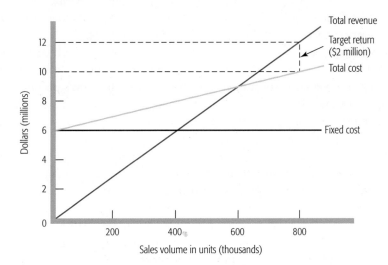

Another cost-oriented pricing approach is **break-even pricing**, or a variation called **target return pricing**. The firm tries to determine the price at which it will break even or make the target return it is seeking. Target return pricing uses the concept of a *break-even chart*, which shows the total cost and total revenue expected at different sales volume levels. Figure 10.3 shows a break-even chart for the HDMI cable manufacturer discussed previously. Fixed costs are $6 million regardless of sales volume, and variable costs are $5 per unit. Variable costs are added to fixed costs to form total costs, which rise with volume. The slope of the total revenue curve reflects the price. Here, the price is $15 (for example, the company's revenue is $12 million on 800 000 units, or $15 per unit).

At the $15 price, the manufacturer must sell at least 600 000 units to *break even* (break-even volume = fixed costs ÷ (price − variable costs) = $6 000 000 ÷ ($15 − $5) = 600 000). That is, at this level, total revenues will equal total costs of $9 million, producing no profit. If the manufacturer wants a target return of $2 million, it must sell at least 800 000 units to obtain the $12 million of total revenue needed to cover the costs of $10 million plus the $2 million of target profits. In contrast, if the company charges a higher price, say $20, it will not need to sell as many units to break even or to achieve its target profit. In fact, the higher the price, the lower the manufacturer's break-even point will be.

The major problem with this analysis, however, is that it fails to consider customer value and the relationship between price and demand. As the *price* increases, *demand* decreases, and the market may not buy even the lower volume needed to break even at the higher price. For example, suppose the HDMI cable manufacturer calculates that, given its current fixed and variable costs, it must charge a price of $30 for the product in order to earn its desired target profit. But marketing research shows that few consumers will pay more than $25. In this case, the company must trim its costs to lower the break-even point so that it can charge the lower price consumers expect.

Thus, although break-even analysis and target return pricing can help the company to determine minimum prices needed to cover expected costs and profits, they do not take the price–demand relationship into account. When using this method, the company must also consider the impact of price on sales volume needed to realize target profits and the likelihood that the needed volume will be achieved at each possible price.

Break-even pricing (or target return pricing)
Setting price to break even on the costs of making and marketing a product, or setting price to make a target return.

Competition-Based Pricing

Competition-based pricing
Setting prices based on competitors'
strategies, prices, costs, and market
offerings.

Competition-based pricing involves setting prices based on competitors' strategies, costs, prices, and market offerings. Consumers will base their judgments of a product's value on the prices that competitors charge for similar products.

In assessing competitors' pricing strategies, the company should ask several questions. First, how does the company's market offering compare with competitors' offerings in terms of customer value? If consumers perceive that the company's product or service provides greater value, the company can charge a higher price. If consumers perceive less value relative to competing products, the company must either charge a lower price or change customer perceptions to justify a higher price.

Next, how strong are current competitors and what are their current pricing strategies? If the company faces a host of smaller competitors charging high prices relative to the value they deliver, it might charge lower prices to drive weaker competitors out of the market. If the market is dominated by larger, low-price competitors, the company may decide to target unserved market niches with value-added products at higher prices.

For example, Pete's, an independent grocer with three locations in Nova Scotia, isn't likely to win a price war against Sobeys or Superstore—it doesn't even try. Instead, the store relies on its personal approach, high-quality produce, cozy atmosphere, and friendly and knowledgeable staff to turn local food lovers into loyal patrons, even if they have to pay a little more.

> Emily F. wrote this review of Pete's on Yelp: "I am always amazed each time I visit at actually how much fresh produce is here, beautifully displayed, and really affordable. They always mark clearly which comes from our farms right here in NS and which are from Canada, and recently they've been putting special stickers in the dry goods aisles marking which products are local. Pete's has everything you need, plus imported goods, and the staff are just excellent. It's always busy and for good reason. The sushi is a steal of a deal and this is not grocery store sushi but the real stuff with a chef preparing it in front of you—but fast. If you haven't had one of the salads you are truly missing out—you never thought one could pack THAT MUCH STUFF into such a small box. Fills you up every time. Feels like such a deal. This year they opened a gluten free eatery with the BEST chocolate cake I have ever put in my mouth. We love Pete's. All the mature ladies swoon over Pete when he's on location and I hear he has a

© Ron Buskirk / Alamy

Exhibit 10.5 Pricing against larger, low-price competitors: Independent grocer Pete's isn't likely to win a price war against Sobeys or Superstore. Instead, it relies on outstanding customer service, a premium selection, relationships with local suppliers, and a traditional market atmosphere to turn food lovers into loyal customers.

great sign-up for his cruises too." Another Yelp reviewer, Travelin G., summed up Pete's this way: "A+ to this place! Montreal bagels! HOOORAY! Imported Parisian brie? Don't mind if I do! I could spend a million dollars here EASILY!"[7]

What principle should guide decisions about what price to charge relative to those of competitors? The answer is simple in concept but often difficult in practice: no matter what price you charge—high, low, or in between—be certain to give customers superior value for that price.

Other Internal and External Considerations Affecting Pricing Decisions LO2

Beyond customer value perceptions, costs, and competitor strategies, the company must consider several additional internal and external factors. Internal factors affecting pricing include the company's overall marketing strategy, objectives, and marketing mix, as well as other organizational considerations. External factors include the nature of the market and the demand and other environmental factors.

Overall Marketing Strategy, Objectives, and Mix

Price is only one element of the company's broader marketing strategy. Before setting price, the company must decide on its overall marketing strategy for the product or the service. If the company has selected its target market and positioning carefully, then its marketing mix strategy, including price, will be fairly straightforward. For example, when Honda developed its Acura brand to compete with European luxury-performance cars, it needed to set prices in line with luxury performance cars. In contrast, when it introduced the Honda Fit subcompact, it needed to set a price in line with subcompacts. Thus, pricing strategy is largely determined by decisions on brand positioning. Burt's Bees positioned their brand right from the beginning as natural and eco-friendly, and set a correspondingly high price for their products. (See Marketing@ Work 10.1.)

Pricing may play an important role in helping to accomplish company objectives at many levels. A firm can set prices to attract new customers or to profitably retain existing ones. It can set prices low to prevent competition from entering the market, or set prices at competitors' levels to stabilize the market. It can price to keep the loyalty and support of resellers or to avoid government intervention. Prices can be reduced temporarily to create excitement for a brand. Or one product may be priced to help the sales of other products in the company's line.

Price is only one of the marketing mix tools that a company uses to achieve its marketing objectives. Pricing decisions must be coordinated with product design, distribution, and promotion decisions to form a consistent and effective integrated marketing program. Decisions made for other marketing mix variables may affect pricing decisions. For example, a decision to position the product on high-performance quality will mean that the seller must charge a higher price to cover higher costs. And producers whose resellers are expected to support and promote their products may have to build larger reseller margins into their prices.

Companies often position their products on price and then tailor other marketing mix decisions to the prices they want to charge. Here, price is a crucial product-positioning factor that defines the product's market, competition, and design. Many firms support such price-positioning strategies with a technique called **target costing**. Target

Target costing
Pricing that starts with an ideal selling price, and then targets costs that will ensure that the price is met.

MARKETING@WORK 10.1

Burt's Bees: Wilfully Overpriced

How much are you willing to pay for a standard-sized tube of lip balm? The market leader charges just a bit more than $1. But would you pay $2 for a comparable product? How about $3? When it comes to price, your first thought might be, "The lower the better." Many companies follow this reasoning and try to out-do each other by providing the cheapest option, but such a strategy can lead to razor thin margins and even losses. Although low price might seem to be the most attractive way to lure customers into purchasing goods and services, when it comes to actually creating value for customers, that's not always the case.

Burt's Bees understands that sometimes it pays to charge more. Just

10 years ago, the popular maker of natural personal care products was a niche brand, distributed only in boutiques and natural foods stores. But Burt's Bees' sales exploded when major supermarket and discount retail chains started carrying the small company's line. Although Walmart and other national chains are known for pressuring manufacturers to cut costs and lower prices, Burt's Bees achieved its distribution victory through a strategy that has been called "wilful overpricing." In Burt's Bees' case, that means charging price premiums of 80 percent or more over comparable non-natural brands. Burt's Bees lip balm, the brand's best-selling product, sells for $4.89 a tube in Canada, while market-leading ChapStick can be had for about a third of that price. A 300 ml bottle of Burt's Bees shampoo costs $10, and a bar of soap (or, in Burt's Bees terms, an energizing or replenishing body bar) costs $8. A pricing strategy like this can only succeed if there's something about the brand that makes it special.

Burt's Bees started like many entrepreneurial ventures, with founders that had a good idea but not a penny to their names. In the late 1980s, Burt Shavitz was a beekeeper in northern Maine selling honey out of his pickup truck and living in a modified turkey coop. Roxanne Quimby, a wife and mother looking for a way to supplement the family income, had the idea to buy Burt's surplus beeswax to make and sell candles. Later, Roxanne happened upon a nineteenth-century book

of homemade personal care recipes and acquired a second-hand industrial mixer from a university cafeteria. That's when the Burt's Bees brand began to take shape. The main product line of natural beeswax candles was slowly replaced by personal care products, including the brand's famous lip balm made with beeswax, coconut and sunflower oils, and other ingredients that you could just as easily eat as put on your lips.

As Burt's Bees grew, it automated its manufacturing processes, yet the products that rolled off those automated lines maintained the quality and feel of natural homemade goods. Right from the start, the Burt's Bees brand stood for natural ingredients, and today that continues to be the brand's main point of differentiation, as is clear from its "about us" statement on its website: "Your well-being is affected every single day by the personal care products you use. Our goal is to create and educate people on truly natural products that have a positive effect on both you and the world you live in for the good of your well-being, for the good of the environment and for The Greater Good. Simply put, we strive to make people's lives better every day—naturally."

It seems that part of the reason for Burt's Bees success is its prestige pricing strategy. Higher prices serve as an indicator of quality level and, in the case of Burt's Bees, higher prices also served to peak customer curiosity. When people compare brands, a moderately higher-priced option causes them to take notice and look a little deeper to understand why a certain brand is more expensive. They may learn that the product contains features that justify the higher price—features they may not have even considered before. Customers then ask themselves, "Do I need this benefit or not?" Some studies show that in such situations, customers recall nearly twice as much product information and can cite more arguments in favour of buying the products. If the price premium charged is

Exhibit 10.6 Burt's Bees prides itself on its products made from natural ingredients, its eco-friendly and socially responsible attitude, and its pricing strategy.

Bloomberg via Getty Images

too high or too low, however, shoppers ignore the option.

Fortunately for Burt's Bees, its strategy of wilful overpricing coincided with a trend of growing consumer preference toward natural products and environmentally friendly goods. Burt's Bees' natural ingredients and company values were enough to justify the brand's higher prices for many. But can a pricing strategy that relies on trends in consumer preferences work forever?

In 2007 Clorox purchased Burt's Bees for a whopping $925 million as part of its comprehensive strategy to become more environmentally friendly. They immediately ran magazine ads comparing natural ingredients in Burt's Bees to chemical ingredients found in other products. For all intents and purposes, Clorox allows Burt's Bees

to operate as an independent division, remaining true to its original mission and values. Four years after the Burt's Bees acquisition, Clorox announced that it was writing off almost $250 million— about 25 percent—of the price it paid for the brand due to overvaluation at the time of the deal. You might take this as a sign that Burt's Bees isn't doing so well these days, but that's not the case. The Burt's Bees brand remains a very solid contributor to Clorox's results, with sales growth and profit margins above the company average, and it's the fastest growing business unit in the company.

If Burt's Bees' Facebook fan base is any indication, that growth is continuing. In little more than a year's time, Burt's Bees went from about 100 000 fans to more than 650 000, and today the US

Facebook page has more than one million "likers," while the Canadian Burt's Bees page boasts close to 100 000. The corporate buyout and economic trends appear to have had little impact on the brand. In the end, it just may be that Burt's Bees' pricing strategy is proof that, by leveraging a brand's strengths, customers will continue to buy on value, not just on price.

Sources: Tess Stynes and Paul Ziobro, "Clorox Forecasts Profit, Sales Below Expectations," *Wall Street Journal*, January 3, 2011; Tim Donnelly, "How to Sell on Value Rather Than Price," *Inc.*, July 20, 2011; Marco Bertini and Luc Wathieu, "How to Stop Customers from Fixating on Price," *Harvard Business Review*, May 2010, pp. 85–91; Mitch Maranowski, "The Triple Value Proposition: Why Inauthentic Green Brands Are Doomed to Fail," *Fast Company*, May 18, 2011; and information from BurtsBees.ca, accessed April 2013.

costing reverses the usual process of first designing a new product, determining its cost, and then asking, "Can we sell it for that?" Instead, it starts with an ideal selling price based on customer-value considerations, and then targets costs that will ensure that the price is met. For example, when Honda set out to design the Fit, it began with a US$13 950 starting price point and 33-miles-per-gallon operating efficiency firmly in mind. It then designed a stylish, peppy little car with costs that allowed it to give target customers those values.

Other companies de-emphasize price and use other marketing mix tools to create *non-price* positions. Often, the best strategy is not to charge the lowest price but rather to differentiate the marketing offer to make it worth a higher price. For example, Bang & Olufsen—known for its cutting-edge consumer electronics—builds more value into its products and charges sky-high prices. There are only five B&O retailers in Canada, all of which are located in extremely high end shopping districts—like Bang & Olufsen Custom Home in Calgary, which specializes in working with the customer's designer to create a custom built-in home entertainment system. If you have to ask how much it costs, you probably can't afford it, but for those customers who can, Bang & Olufsen's very high quality is worth the price.

Some marketers even position their products on *high* prices, featuring high prices as part of their product's allure. For example, Grand Marnier offers a US$225 bottle of Cuvée du Cent Cinquantenaire that's marketed with the tagline "Hard to find, impossible to pronounce, and

INTS KALNINS/Reuters /Landov

Exhibit 10.7 Positioning on high price: Some brands, like Bang & Olufsen, deliberately charge prices that are significantly higher than competitors' products. If you have to ask how much it is, you probably can't afford it.

prohibitively expensive." And Titus Cycles, a premium bicycle manufacturer, features its high prices in its advertising. Ads humorously show people working unusual second jobs to earn the money to afford a Titus. Suggested retail price for a Titus Solera: US$7750. But "It's worth a second job," the ads confirm.

Marketers must consider the total marketing strategy and mix when setting prices, but even when featuring price, marketers need to remember that customers rarely buy on price alone. Instead, they seek products that give them the best value in terms of benefits received for the prices paid.

Organizational Considerations

Management must decide who within the organization should set prices. Companies handle pricing in a variety of ways. In small companies, prices are often set by top management rather than by the marketing or sales departments. In large companies, pricing is typically handled by divisional or product line managers. In industrial markets, salespeople may be allowed to negotiate with customers within certain price ranges. Even so, top management sets the pricing objectives and policies, and it often approves the prices proposed by lower-level management or salespeople.

In industries in which pricing is a key factor (airlines, aerospace, steel, railroads, oil companies), companies often have pricing departments to set the best prices or help others in setting them. These departments report to the marketing department or top management. Others who have an influence on pricing include sales managers, production managers, finance managers, and accountants.

The Market and Demand

As noted earlier, good pricing starts with an understanding of how customers' perceptions of value affect the prices they are willing to pay. Both consumer and industrial buyers balance the price of a product or a service against the benefits of owning it. Thus, before setting prices, the marketer must understand the relationship between price and demand for the company's product. In this section, we take a deeper look at the price–demand relationship and how it varies for different types of markets. We then discuss methods for analyzing the price–demand relationship.

Pricing in Different Types of Markets The seller's pricing freedom varies with different types of markets. Economists recognize four types of markets, each presenting a different pricing challenge.

Under *pure competition*, the market consists of many buyers and sellers trading in a uniform commodity such as wheat, copper, or financial securities. No single buyer or seller has much effect on the going market price. In a purely competitive market, marketing research, product development, pricing, advertising, and sales promotion play little or no role. Thus, sellers in these markets do not spend much time on marketing strategy.

Under *monopolistic competition*, the market consists of many buyers and sellers who trade over a range of prices rather than a single market price. A range of prices occurs because sellers can differentiate their offers to buyers. Sellers try to develop differentiated offers for different customer segments and, in addition to price, freely use branding, advertising, and personal selling to set their offers apart. For example, the Nissan LEAF is positioned as the first mass-market fully-electric car. It is not the first electric car, nor is it the only electric car currently available on the market, however, it is the first mass-market electric car, positioned against the Tesla, which, though electric, is a much more expensive sports car. Because there are many competitors in such markets, each firm is less affected by competitors' pricing strategies than in oligopolistic markets.

FIGURE 10.4 Demand Curve

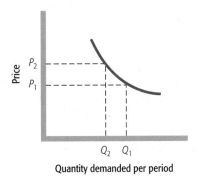

Quantity demanded per period

Under *oligopolistic competition*, the market consists of a few sellers who are highly sensitive to each other's pricing and marketing strategies. Because there are few sellers, each seller is alert and responsive to competitors' pricing strategies and moves.

In a *pure monopoly*, the market consists of one seller. The seller may be a government monopoly (Canada Post), a private regulated monopoly (a power company), or a private non-regulated monopoly (DuPont when it introduced nylon). Pricing is handled differently in each case.

Analyzing the Price–Demand Relationship Each price the company might charge will lead to a different level of demand. The relationship between the price charged and the resulting demand level is shown in the **demand curve** in Figure 10.4. The demand curve shows the number of units the market will buy in a given time period at different prices that might be charged. In the normal case, demand and price are inversely related; that is, the higher the price, the lower the demand. Thus, the company would sell less if it raised its price from $P1$ to $P2$. In short, consumers with limited budgets probably will buy less of something if its price is too high.

Understanding a brand's price–demand curve is crucial to good pricing decisions. ConAgra Foods learned this lesson when pricing its Banquet frozen dinners.[8]

> ConAgra Foods, the company behind popular food brands such as Hunt's, Reddi Wip, PAM, and Orville Redenbacher, found out the hard way about the perils of pushing up the price of a Banquet frozen dinner. When it tried to recoup high commodity costs by hiking the wholesale price, many retailers began charging up to $1.25 a meal. The response from shoppers used to paying $1? The cold shoulder. The resulting sales drop forced ConAgra to peddle excess dinners to discounters and contributed to a 40 percent drop in the company's stock price for the year. It turns out that "the key component for Banquet dinners—the key attribute—is you've got to be at $1," says ConAgra's CEO, Gary Rodkin. "Everything else pales in comparison to that." The price is now back to a buck a dinner. To make money at that price, ConAgra is doing a better job of managing costs. It tossed out pricey items such as barbecued chicken and country-fried pork in favour of grilled meat patties and rice and beans. It also shrank portion sizes while swapping in cheaper ingredients, such as mashed potatoes for brownies. Consumers are responding well to the brand's efforts to keep prices down. Where else can you find dinner for $1?

Most companies try to measure their demand curves by estimating demand at different

Demand curve
A curve that shows the number of units the market will buy in a given time period, at different prices that might be charged.

Exhibit 10.8 **The price–demand curve:** When ConAgra raised prices on its Banquet frozen dinners, sales fell sharply. "You've got to be at $1," says CEO Gary Rodkin. "Everything else pales in comparison to that."

Associated Press

prices. The type of market makes a difference. In a monopoly, the demand curve shows the total market demand resulting from different prices. If the company faces competition, its demand at different prices will depend on whether competitors' prices stay constant or change with the company's own prices.

Price elasticity

A measure of the sensitivity of demand to changes in price.

Price Elasticity of Demand   Marketers also need to know **price elasticity**—how responsive demand will be to a change in price. If demand hardly changes with a small change in price, we say demand is *inelastic*. If demand changes greatly, we say the demand is *elastic*.

If demand is elastic rather than inelastic, sellers will consider lowering their prices. A lower price will produce more total revenue. This practice makes sense as long as the extra costs of producing and selling more do not exceed the extra revenue. At the same time, most firms want to avoid pricing that turns their products into commodities. The ease of finding pricing information on the Internet has increased consumer price sensitivity, turning products ranging from cellphones and televisions to new automobiles into commodities in some consumers' eyes.

The Economy

Economic conditions can have a strong impact on the firm's pricing strategies. Economic factors such as a boom or a recession, inflation, and interest rates affect pricing decisions because they affect consumer spending, consumer perceptions of the product's price and value, and the company's costs of producing and selling a product.

In the aftermath of the 2008 recession in the United States and the corresponding economic downturn in Canada, consumers began to rethink the price–value equation. Many consumers tightened their belts and became more value conscious. As a result, many marketers increased their emphasis on value-for-the-money pricing strategies. "Value is the magic word," says a P&G marketer. "In these economic times, people are doing the math in their heads, and they're being much more thoughtful before making purchases. . . . Now, we're going to be even more focused on helping consumers see value."[9]

The most obvious response to a slow economy is to cut prices and offer deep discounts. And thousands of companies did just that. Lower prices make products more affordable and help spur short-term sales. However, such price cuts can have undesirable long-term consequences. "Tempted to cut prices?" asks one pricing consultant. "You're not alone. With slumping sales, many businesses have been quick to offer discounts. But price cuts raise some tough questions: Will deep discounts cheapen your brand? Once you cut prices, can you raise them again? How do you deal with narrower margins?"[10] Consider upscale brands such as Starbucks, Tiffany's or Whole Foods Market, which position themselves on providing premium products at premium prices—the "more for more" strategy. When consumer spending rates decrease, companies like these face the difficult task of realigning their value propositions with their positioning.

Rather than cut prices, marketers can instead shift their focus to more affordable items in their product mixes. For example, whereas its previous promotions emphasized high-end products, and pricey concepts such as creating dream kitchens, Home Depot's post-recession advertising pushed items such as potting soil and hand tools. Another approach is to hold steady on price but redefine the "value" in value propositions. For instance, Unilever repositioned its higher-end Bertolli frozen meals as an eat-at-home brand that's more affordable than eating out, and Kraft's advertising for Velveeta cheese communicates the value of a package of Velveeta being twice the size of a package of cheddar.

Remember, no matter what state the national economy is in, people continue to make purchases, and their purchase decisions are not based on prices alone. They balance the price they pay against the value they receive. For example, despite selling its shoes for as much as $150 a pair, Nike continues to command a high degree of customer loyalty, because consumers perceive the value of Nike's products and the Nike ownership experience to be well worth the price. And Whole Foods Markets, a grocery retailer known for its high quality and high prices, adjusted marketing strategies without lowering prices (see Marketing@Work 10.2). The marketing lesson? No matter what price they charge—low or high—companies need to offer great *value for the money*.

MARKETING@WORK 10.2

Whole Foods Market: Modifying Price and Value Strategies for Changing Economic Times

In the early years of the 2000s, consumers were flush with cash, and Whole Foods Market was thriving. The upscale grocery retailer was a model "more for more" marketer, offering premium value at premium prices. Under its motto, "Whole Foods, Whole People, Whole Planet," it served up a gourmet assortment of high-quality grocery items, including a strong mix of natural and organic foods and health products. Stores were strategically located in upper middle class neighbourhoods such as Oakville, Yorkville, and West Vancouver, where upscale, health-conscious customers were willing and able to pay higher prices for the extra value they got. In the two decades before the recession, Whole Foods Market's sales had soared, and its stock price had grown at a compounded annual rate of 25 percent.

Then came the Great Recession of 2008. People in all walks of life began rethinking the price-value equation and looking for ways to save. They asked tough questions, such as: "I love the wonderful foods and smells in my Whole Foods Market, but is it worth the extra 30 percent versus shopping at Walmart?" All of a sudden, Whole Foods Market's seemingly perfect premium marketing strategy looked less like a plum and more like a bruised organic banana. Even affluent customers were cutting back and spending less. For the first time in its history, the company faced declines in same-store sales, and its stock price plunged to a shocking low

of close to $8. "The company had long touted its premium food offerings in its marketing, and that branding [was] now actually hurting them," observed a retail analyst. Some joked that the company's motto should be changed to "Whole Foods, Whole Paycheck."

Hit hard by the economic downturn, Whole Foods Market faced difficult questions. Should it hold the line on the premium positioning that had won it so much success in the past? Or should it cut prices and reposition itself to fit the leaner times? On the one hand, it could simply batten down the hatches and wait for the economic storm to pass. But a wait-and-see strategy made little sense—the newfound consumer frugality probably will last for years to come. At the other extreme, Whole Foods could reshuffle its product assortment, cut prices, and reposition downward to fit the new times. But that strategy would sacrifice most of what had made the upscale grocer unique over the years.

Faced with these alternatives, Whole Foods Market decided to stick with its core up-market positioning but subtly realign its value proposition to better meet the needs of recession-rattled customers. It set out to downplay the gourmet element of its positioning while playing up the real value of the healthy but exciting food it offers. First, rather than dropping its everyday prices across the board, Whole Foods lowered prices on many basic items that customers demand most and bolstered these savings by offering

significant sales on selected other items. It also started emphasizing its private-label brand, 365 Everyday Value.

Next, Whole Foods Market launched a new marketing program aimed at tempering the chain's high-price reputation, reconnecting with customers, and convincing them that Whole Foods Market was, in fact, an affordable place to shop. To help consumers see the value, it beefed up its communications about private-label and sale items using newsletters, coupons, and its website. It assigned workers to serve as "value tour guides" to escort shoppers around stores and point out value items. New ads featured headlines such as "No wallets were harmed in the buying of our 365 Everyday Value products," and "Sticker shock, but in a good way."

The new marketing efforts actually did more than simply promote more affordable merchandise. They worked to convince shoppers that Whole Foods Market's regular products and prices offer good value as well—that when it comes to quality food, price isn't everything. As one tour guide notes, wherever you go, you'll have to pay a premium for organic food. "Value means getting a good exchange for your money." Such conversations helped to shift customers' eyes off the price and back to value.

To strengthen customer relationships further in tighter times, Whole Foods Market also boosted its social media presence. It set up a Facebook page and dozens of Twitter accounts to address specific value and other topics related to every product category and every store. Videos on its Whole Tube YouTube channel advised customers to "waste not, want not." At the official Whole Foods Market blog—The Whole Story—customers learned about and exchanged views on organic and natural food, recipes, and other topics. Interestingly, customer conversations on this blog tended to focus more heavily on the "what you get" from Whole Foods Market than the "what you pay."

Customers more interested in the value side of the price-value equation could log onto The Whole Deal, an official blog that offers coupons, deals, budget-friendly recipes, and other things that help you make "wiser

choices for your budget, the Earth, and your fellow Earthlings." Whole Foods also offered iPhone and iPod apps, providing more than 2000 recipes using Whole Foods Market natural and organic products, and highlighting meals that feed a family of four for less than $15.

How has the Whole Foods Market value realignment worked out? So far, so good. By 2010, sales and earnings were again growing at a healthy clip, and a year later stock prices had climbed back up to $65. And by 2013, operations were returning to normal—that is, successful. Annual sales were in excess of $12 billion; more than 30 new stores per year are being planned for the United States, Canada, and the UK; and Whole Foods Market ranked #19 in *Fortune* magazine's

World's Most Admired Companies list, and #16 on the magazine's Best Companies to Work for list.

Regarding the move to value offerings, says Whole Foods Market's COO, "We did it early, we did it strong, and we've done it consistently." Customers now "give us credit for being more competitive and for meeting their needs in these times, and now they can see the better deals, the better pricing, the better choices."

Most important, however, Whole Foods Market has managed to realign its value proposition in a way that preserves all the things that have made it special to its customers through the years. In all, things aren't really much different inside a local Whole Foods Market these days. There are more sale items, and the private-label 365 Everyday Value brand is more prominently presented, but customers can still find the same alluring assortment of high-quality, flavourful, and natural foods wrapped in Whole Foods, Whole People, Whole Planet values. Thanks to the subtle shifts in its value strategy, however, customers might just appreciate the value side of the Whole Foods Market formula a little bit more.

Librado Romero/The New York Times/Redux Pictures

Exhibit 10.9 When the economy dipped, rather than cutting prices, Whole Foods set out to convince shoppers that it was, in fact, an affordable place to shop. It even assigned workers to serve as "value tour guides," like the one above, to escort shoppers around stores pointing out value items.

Sources: Mike Duff, "Whole Foods Dropping Prices to Raise Its Prospects," *R&FF Retailer*, November 2009, p. 14; David Kesmodel, "Whole Foods Net Falls 31% in Slow Economy," *Wall Street Journal*, August 6, 2008, p. B1; Stuart Elliott, "With Shoppers Pinching Pennies, Some Big Retailers Get the Message," *New York Times*, April 13, 2009, p. B6; "Whole Web," *Progressive Grocer*, June 19, 2009; Annie Gasparro and Matt Jarzemsky, "Earnings: Whole Foods Boosts View as Net Rises 61%," *Wall Street Journal*, February 10, 2011, p. B4; "What Is It that Only I Can Do?" *Harvard Business Review*, January–February 2011, pp. 119–123; and information from Blog.WholeFoodsMarket.com, and WholeFoodsMarket.com, accessed March 2013.

Other External Factors

When setting prices, beyond the market and the economy, the company must consider a number of other factors in its external environment. It must know what impact its prices will have on other parties in its environment. How will *resellers* react to various prices? The company should set prices that give resellers a fair profit, encourage their support, and help them to sell the product effectively. The *government* is another important external influence on pricing decisions. Finally, *social concerns* may need to be taken into account.

In setting prices, a company's short-term sales, market share, and profit goals may need to be tempered by broader societal considerations. We will examine public policy issues in pricing later in the chapter.

We've now seen that pricing decisions are subject to a complex array of customer, company, competitive, and environmental forces. To make things even more complex, a company sets not a single price but rather a *pricing structure* that covers different items in its line. This pricing structure changes over time as products move through their life cycles. The company adjusts its prices to reflect changes in costs and demand, and to account for variations in buyers and situations. As the competitive environment changes, the company considers when to initiate price changes and when to respond to them.

We now examine additional pricing approaches used in special pricing situations, or to adjust prices to meet changing situations. We look in turn at *new-product pricing* for products in the introductory stage of the product life cycle, *product mix pricing* for related products in the product mix, *price adjustment tactics* that account for customer differences and changing situations, and strategies for initiating and responding to *price changes*.[11]

New-Product Pricing `LO3`

Pricing strategies usually change as the product passes through its life cycle. The introductory stage is especially challenging. Companies bringing out a new product face the challenge of setting prices for the first time. They can choose between two broad strategies: *market-skimming pricing* and *market-penetration pricing*.

Market-Skimming Pricing

Many companies that invent new products set high initial prices to "skim" revenues layer by layer from the market. Sony frequently uses this strategy, called **market-skimming pricing (or price skimming)**. For example, every time Apple introduces a new iPhone or iPad model, the initial price is very high, because for the type of customer who anxiously awaits the newest gadget, price is no object. After about six months the prices come down slightly; after a year they are lowered even more; and after two years, when rumours of the next version appear, the prices drop again. Finally, when the latest model is released, the prices of the last generation model are drastically discounted. During that period, carriers such as Bell and Rogers typically offer the older models as free upgrades in exchange for a renewed three year contract. There is a segment of the market that waits for that to happen, and then buys the older model for the lowest possible price.

Market skimming makes sense only under certain conditions. First, the product's quality and image must support its higher price and enough buyers must want the product at that price. Second, the costs of producing a smaller volume cannot be so high that they cancel the advantage of charging more. Finally, competitors should not be able to enter the market easily and undercut the high price.

Market-skimming pricing (or price skimming) Setting a high price for a new product to skim maximum revenues layer by layer from the segments willing to pay the high price; the company makes fewer but more profitable sales.

Market-Penetration Pricing

Rather than setting a high initial price to skim off small but profitable market segments, some companies use **market-penetration pricing**. They set a low initial price in order to *penetrate* the market quickly and deeply—to attract a large number of buyers quickly and win a large market share. The high sales volume results in falling costs, allowing the

Market-penetration pricing Setting a low initial price for a new product in order to attract a large number of buyers and a large market share.

Exhibit 10.10 **Penetration pricing:** To lure famously frugal Chinese customers, IKEA slashed its prices. The strategy worked. Weekend crowds at its cavernous Beijing store are so big that employees need to use megaphones to keep them in control.

companies to cut their prices even further. For example, giant Swedish retailer IKEA used penetration pricing to boost its success in the Chinese market:[12]

> When IKEA first opened stores in China in 2002, people crowded in, but not to buy home furnishings. Instead, they came to take advantage of the freebies—air conditioning, clean toilets, and even decorating ideas. Chinese consumers are famously frugal. When it came time to actually buy, they shopped instead at local stores just down the street that offered knockoffs of IKEA's designs at a fraction of the price. So to lure the finicky Chinese customers, IKEA slashed its prices in China to the lowest in the world, the opposite approach of many Western retailers there. By increasingly stocking its Chinese stores with China-made products, the retailer pushed prices on some items as low as 70 percent below prices in IKEA's outlets outside China. The penetration pricing strategy worked. IKEA now captures a 43 percent market share of China's fast-growing homewares market alone, and the sales of its six mammoth Chinese stores surged 25 percent last year. The cavernous Beijing store draws nearly 6 million visitors annually. Weekend crowds are so big that employees need to use megaphones to keep them in control.

Several conditions must be met for this low-price strategy to work. First, the market must be highly price sensitive so that a low price produces more market growth. Second, production and distribution costs must fall as sales volume increases. Finally, the low price must help keep out the competition, and the penetration price must maintain its low-price position—otherwise, the price advantage may be only temporary.

Product Mix Pricing LO4

The strategy for setting a product's price often has to be changed when the product is part of a product mix. In this case, the firm looks for a set of prices that maximizes the profits on the total product mix. Pricing is difficult because the various products have related demand and costs, and face different degrees of competition. We now take a closer look at the five product mix pricing situations summarized in Table 10.1: *product line pricing, optional-product pricing, captive-product pricing, by-product pricing,* and *product bundle pricing.*

Product Line Pricing

Companies usually develop product lines rather than single products. For example, Samsonite offers some 20 different collections of bags, from its Aramon NXT line of laptop bags, ranging in price from $20 to $35; to its high end Cosmolite luggage line, where a small suitcase retails for more than $500. In **product line pricing**, management must decide on the price steps to set between the various products in a line.

The price steps should take into account cost differences between the products in the line. More importantly, they should account for differences in customer perceptions of the value of different features. For example, TurboTax, the best-selling tax software in Canada, offers multiple versions of its personal tax software, including Standard,

Product line pricing
Setting the price steps between various products in a product line based on cost differences between the products, customer evaluations of different features, and competitors' prices.

TABLE 10.1 Product Mix Pricing

Pricing Situation	Description
Product line pricing	Setting prices across an entire product line
Optional-product pricing	Pricing optional or accessory products sold with the main product
Captive-product pricing	Pricing products that must be used with the main product
By-product pricing	Pricing low-value by-products to get rid of them
Product bundle pricing	Pricing bundles of products sold together

Premier, and Home & Business, priced at $17.99, $32.99, and $44.99 respectively. Although it costs Intuit, the software company that markets TurboTax, no more to produce the CD and packaging containing the Home & Business version than the CD containing the Standard version, many buyers happily pay more to obtain additional features. Intuit's task is to establish perceived value differences that support the price differences.

Optional-Product Pricing

Many companies use **optional-product pricing**—offering to sell optional or accessory products along with their main product. For example, a car buyer may choose to order a GPS navigation system and Bluetooth wireless communication. Refrigerators come with optional ice makers. And when you purchase a new computer or tablet, you can select from a bewildering array of hard drives, docking systems, software options, service plans, and carrying cases. Pricing these options is a sticky problem. Companies must decide which items to include in the base price and which to offer as options.

Optional-product pricing
The pricing of optional or accessory products along with a main product.

Captive-product pricing
Setting a price for products that must be used along with a main product, such as blades for a razor and games for a video-game console.

Captive-Product Pricing

Companies that make products that must be used along with a main product are using **captive-product pricing**. Examples of captive products are razor blade cartridges, video games, and ink cartridges for printers. Producers of the main products (razors, video-game consoles, and printers) often price them low and set high markups on the supplies.

However, companies that use captive-product pricing must be careful. Finding the right balance between the main product and captive-product prices can be tricky. For example, Kodak introduced its line of EasyShare printers in 2007, and promoted them as a new concept in pricing—the printers sold for $150–$300 (about $50 higher than competitors' models), but the ink cartridges sold for $10–$15.[13] It was a bold strategy, but it failed. Five years later, Kodak filed for

Exhibit 10.11 **Product line pricing:** Intuit offers an entire line of tax preparation software under its TurboTax brand, at various prices.

Courtesy Intuit Canada

Exhibit 10.12 **Captive-product pricing:** At Canada's Wonderland, you pay a daily-ticket or season-pass charge plus additional fees for food and other in-park features.

bankruptcy. What's more, consumers trapped into buying expensive captive products may come to resent the brand that ensnared them—this has happened to some extent in the printer and cartridges industry.

In the case of services, this captive-product pricing is called *two-part pricing*. The price of the service is broken into a *fixed fee* plus a *variable usage rate*. For example, at Canada's Wonderland and other amusement parks, you pay a daily-ticket or season-pass charge plus additional fees for food and other in-park features.

By-Product Pricing

By-product pricing

Setting a price for by-products to make the main product's price more competitive.

Producing products and services often generates by-products. If the by-products have no value and if getting rid of them is costly, this will affect the pricing of the main product. Using **by-product pricing**, the company seeks a market for these by-products to help offset the costs of disposing of them and to help make the price of the main product more competitive. The by-products themselves can even turn out to be profitable—turning trash into cash. For example, MacTara Limited, Nova Scotia's largest sawmill, is the only one in Canada that uses all of the wood by-products. Wood chips are turned into paper, shavings are used to heat the company's kilns, and bark is turned into wood pellets used in old coal furnaces.[14]

And at the Toronto Zoo, one of its major by-products, animal feces, has turned out to be an excellent source of revenue:[15]

> What happens to all that poo at the Toronto Zoo? Each year, 3000 tonnes of animal waste is dumped into an open-air compost pit. With all that methane gas going straight up in the air, it was bad for the environment. Now ZooShare, a nonprofit renewable energy cooperative, is building a community-owned biogas plant on the grounds of the Toronto Zoo that will turn animal waste, as well as food and other organic waste from neighbouring farms and major retailers into methane gas that can be used to produce power.
>
> ZooShare is investing $5.4 million to design, develop and build the plant which, when completed, will provide power to 750 homes as well as generating $50 000 in annual revenue for the zoo. The plant will also produce compost and farm fertilizers, and the co-op plans to build a greenhouse to use up the nominal amount of heat that will be produced. "We want to be a leader in environmental practices. Solar, thermal, and geothermal energy is already used on zoo premises," Mr. Tracogna, chief operating officer at the zoo says. For its efforts, ZooShare was recognized as a 2012 winner of the Toronto Community Foundation's Green Innovation Award.

Product Bundle Pricing

Product bundle pricing

Combining several products and offering the bundle at a reduced price.

By using **product bundle pricing**, sellers often combine several of their products and offer the bundle at a reduced price. For example, fast-food restaurants bundle a burger, fries, and a soft drink at a "combo" price. Bath & Body Works offers "three-fer" deals on its soaps and lotions (such as three antibacterial soaps for $10). And EastLink, Rogers Communications, and other telecommunications companies bundle TV service, phone service, and high-speed Internet connections at a low combined price. Price bundling

TABLE 10.2 Price Adjustments

Strategy	Description
Discount and allowance pricing	Reducing prices to reward customer responses such as paying early or promoting the product
Segmented pricing	Adjusting prices to allow for differences in customers, products, or locations
Psychological pricing	Adjusting prices for psychological effect
Promotional pricing	Temporarily reducing prices to increase short-run sales
Geographical pricing	Adjusting prices to account for the geographic location of customers
Dynamic pricing	Adjusting prices continually to meet the characteristics and needs of individual customers and situations
International pricing	Adjusting prices for international markets

can promote the sales of products consumers might not otherwise buy, but the combined price must be low enough to get them to buy the bundle.[16]

Price Adjustment Strategies LO5

Companies usually adjust their basic prices to account for various customer differences and changing situations. Here we examine the seven price adjustment strategies summarized in Table 10.2: *discount and allowance pricing, segmented pricing, psychological pricing, promotional pricing, geographical pricing, dynamic pricing,* and *international pricing.*

Discount and Allowance Pricing

Most companies adjust their basic price to reward customers for certain responses, such as early payment of bills, volume purchases, and off-season buying. These price adjustments—called *discounts* and *allowances*—can take many forms.

The many forms of **discounts** include a *cash discount*, a price reduction to buyers who pay their bills promptly. A typical example is "2/10, net 30," which means that although payment is due within 30 days, the buyer can deduct 2 percent if the bill is paid within 10 days. A *quantity discount* is a price reduction to buyers who buy large volumes. Under the provisions of the Competition Act, quantity discounts must be offered equally to all customers and must not exceed the seller's cost savings associated with selling large quantities. A *seasonal discount* is a price reduction to buyers who buy merchandise or services out of season.

Allowances are another type of reduction from the list price. For example, *trade-in allowances* are price reductions given for turning in an old item when buying a new one. Trade-in allowances are most common in the automobile industry but are also given for other durable goods. *Promotional allowances* are payments or price reductions to reward dealers for participating in advertising and sales support programs.

Segmented Pricing

Companies will often adjust their basic prices to allow for differences in customers, products, and locations. In **segmented pricing**, the company sells a product or service at

Discount

A straight reduction in price on purchases during a stated period of time or on larger quantities.

Allowance

Promotional money paid by manufacturers to retailers in return for an agreement to feature the manufacturer's products in some way.

Segmented pricing

Selling a product or service at two or more prices, where the difference in prices is not based on differences in costs.

two or more prices, even though the difference in prices is not based on differences in costs.

Segmented pricing takes several forms. Under *customer-segment pricing*, different customers pay different prices for the same product or service. Museums, for example, may charge a lower admission for students and senior citizens. Under *product-form pricing*, different versions of the product are priced differently but not according to differences in their costs. For example, a round trip economy seat on a flight from Toronto to London might cost $1200, whereas a business class seat on the same flight might cost $5000 or more. Although business class customers receive roomier, more comfortable seats and higher quality food and service, the differences in costs to the airlines are much less than the additional prices to passengers. However, to passengers who can afford it, the additional comfort and services are worth the extra charge.

By using *location-based pricing*, a company charges different prices for different locations, even though the cost of offering each location is the same. For instance, sports arenas and theatres vary their seat prices because of audience preferences for certain locations. Finally, by using *time-based pricing*, a firm varies its price by the season, the month, the day, and even the hour. Movie theatres charge matinee pricing during the daytime. Resorts give weekend and seasonal discounts.

For segmented pricing to be an effective strategy, certain conditions must exist. The market must be segmentable, and the segments must show different degrees of demand. The costs of segmenting and watching the market cannot exceed the extra revenue obtained from the price difference. Of course, the segmented pricing must also be legal.

Most importantly, segmented prices should reflect real differences in customers' perceived value. Consumers in higher price tiers must feel that they're getting their extra money's worth for the higher prices paid. By the same token, companies must be careful not to treat customers in lower price tiers as second-class citizens. Otherwise, in the long run, the practice will lead to customer resentment and ill will. For example, in recent years, the airlines have incurred the wrath of frustrated customers at both ends of the airplane. Passengers paying full fare for business or executive seats often feel that they are being gouged. At the same time, passengers in lower-priced economy seats feel that they're being ignored or treated poorly.

Psychological Pricing

Psychological pricing
Pricing that considers the psychology of prices and not simply the economics; the price is used to say something about the product.

Price says something about the product. For example, many consumers use price to judge quality. A $100 bottle of perfume may contain only $3 worth of materials, but some people are willing to pay the $100 because this price indicates something special.

In using **psychological pricing**, sellers consider the psychology of prices and not simply the economics. For example, consumers usually perceive higher-priced products as having higher quality. When they can judge the quality of a product by examining it or calling on past experience with it, they use price less to judge quality. But when they cannot judge quality because they lack the information or skill, price becomes an important quality signal. For example, who's the better lawyer, one who charges $50 per hour or one that charges $500 per hour? You'd have to do a lot of digging into the respective lawyers' credentials to answer this question objectively, and even then, you might not be able to judge accurately. Most of us would simply assume that the higher-priced lawyer is better.

Reference prices
Prices that buyers carry in their minds and refer to when they look at a given product.

Another aspect of psychological pricing is **reference prices**—prices that buyers carry in their minds and refer to when looking at a given product. The reference price might be formed by noting current prices, remembering past prices, or assessing the buying situation. Sellers can influence or use these consumers' reference prices when setting price. For example, a company could display its product next to more expensive ones to imply that it belongs in the same class, as when a grocery retailer shelves its store brand of bran flakes-and-raisins cereal priced at $3.99 next to Kellogg's Raisin Bran priced at $5.29.

For most purchases, consumers don't have all the skill or information they need to figure out whether they are paying a good price. They don't have the time, ability, or inclination to research different brands or stores, compare prices, and get the best deals. Instead, they may rely on certain cues that signal whether a price is high or low. Interestingly, such pricing cues are often provided by sellers, in the form of sales signs, price-matching guarantees, loss-leader pricing, and other helpful hints.[17]

Even small differences in price can signal product differences. Consider a flat screen TV priced at $500 compared to one priced at $499.99. The actual price difference is only one cent, but the psychological difference can be much greater. For example, some consumers will see the $499.99 as a price in the $400 range rather than the $500 range. The $499.99 will more likely be seen as a bargain price, whereas the $500 price suggests more quality. Some psychologists argue that each digit has symbolic and visual qualities that should be considered in pricing. Thus, eight is round and even and creates a soothing effect, whereas seven is angular and creates a jarring effect.

Promotional Pricing

With **promotional pricing**, companies will temporarily price their products below list price and sometimes even below cost to create buying excitement and urgency. Promotional pricing takes several forms. A seller may simply offer *discounts* from normal prices to increase sales and reduce inventories. Sellers also use *special-event pricing* in certain seasons to draw more customers. For example, electronics retailers such as Best Buy typically offer promotional pricing (i.e., discounts) in November and December to attract Christmas shoppers into stores.

Manufacturers sometimes offer *cash rebates* to consumers who buy the product from dealers within a specified time; the manufacturer sends the rebate directly to the customer. Rebates have been popular with automakers and producers of cellphones and small appliances, but they are also used with consumer packaged-goods. Some manufacturers offer *low-interest financing*, *longer warranties*, or *free maintenance* to reduce the consumer's "price." This practice has become another favourite of the auto industry.

Promotional pricing, however, can have adverse effects. Used too frequently and copied by competitors, price promotions can create "deal-prone" customers who wait until brands go on sale before buying them. Or, constantly reduced prices can erode a brand's value in the eyes of customers. Marketers sometimes become addicted to promotional pricing, especially in difficult economic times. They use price promotions as a quick fix instead of sweating through the difficult process of developing effective longer-term strategies for building their brands. But companies

Promotional pricing
Temporarily pricing products below the list price and sometimes even below cost to increase short-run sales.

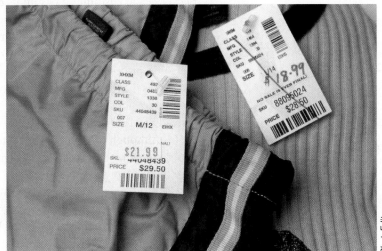

Exhibit 10.13 Psychological pricing: What do the prices marked on this tag suggest about the product and buying situation?

PhotoEdit

must be careful to balance short-term sales incentives against long-term brand building. One analyst advises:[18]

> When times are tough, there's a tendency to panic. One of the first and most prevalent tactics that many companies try is an aggressive price cut. Price trumps all. At least, that's how it feels these days. 20% off. 30% off. 50% off. Buy one, get one free. Whatever it is you're selling, you're offering it at a discount just to get customers in the door. But aggressive pricing strategies can be risky business. Companies should be very wary of risking their brands' perceived quality by resorting to deep and frequent price cuts. Some discounting is unavoidable in a tough economy, and consumers have come to expect it. But marketers have to find ways to shore up their brand identity and brand equity during times of discount mayhem.

The point is that promotional pricing can be an effective means of generating sales for some companies in certain circumstances. But it can be damaging for other companies if taken as a steady diet.

Geographical Pricing

A company also must decide how to price its products for customers located in different parts of the country or the world. Should the company risk losing the business of more-distant customers by charging them higher prices to cover the higher shipping costs? Or should the company charge all customers the same prices regardless of location? We will look at three **geographical pricing** strategies for the following hypothetical situation:

Geographical pricing
Setting prices for customers located in different parts of the country or the world.

> The Peerless Paper Company is located in Vancouver and sells paper products to customers all over Canada. The cost of freight is high and affects the companies from whom customers buy their paper. Peerless wants to establish a geographical pricing policy. It is trying to determine how to price a $10 000 order to three specific customers: Customer A (Vancouver), Customer B (Winnipeg), and Customer C (Halifax).

One option is for Peerless to ask each customer to pay the shipping cost from the Vancouver factory to the customer's location. All three customers would pay the same factory price of $10 000, with Customer A paying, say, $100 for shipping; Customer B, $150; and Customer C, $250. Called *FOB-origin pricing*, this practice means that the goods are placed *free on board* (hence, *FOB*) a carrier. At that point the title and responsibility pass to the customer, who pays the freight from the factory to the destination. Because each customer picks up its own cost, supporters of FOB pricing feel that this is the fairest way to assess freight charges. The disadvantage, however, is that Peerless will be a high-cost firm to distant customers.

Uniform-delivered pricing is the opposite of FOB pricing. Here, the company charges the same price plus freight to all customers, regardless of their location. The freight charge is set at the average freight cost. Suppose this is $150. Uniform-delivered pricing therefore results in a higher charge to the Vancouver customer (who pays $150 freight instead of $100) and a lower charge to the Halifax customer (who pays $150 instead of $250). Although the Vancouver customer would prefer to buy paper from another local paper company that uses FOB-origin pricing, Peerless has a better chance of winning over the Halifax customer.

Zone pricing falls between FOB-origin pricing and uniform-delivered pricing. The company sets up two or more zones. All customers within a given zone pay a single total price; the more distant the zone, the higher the price. For example, Peerless might set up a West Zone and charge $100 freight to all customers in this zone, a Central Zone in which it charges $150, and an East Zone in which it charges $250. In this way, the customers within a given price zone receive no price advantage from the company. For example, customers in Vancouver and Calgary pay the same total price to Peerless. The complaint, however, is that the Vancouver customer is paying part of the Calgary customer's freight cost.

Dynamic Pricing

Throughout most of history, prices were set by negotiation between buyers and sellers. *Fixed price* policies—setting one price for all buyers—is a relatively modern idea that arose with the development of large-scale retailing at the end of the nineteenth century. Today, most prices are set this way. However, some companies are now reversing the fixed pricing trend. They are using **dynamic pricing**—adjusting prices continually to meet the characteristics and needs of individual customers and situations.

For example, think about how the Internet has affected pricing. From the mostly fixed pricing practices of the past century, the web seems now to be taking us back—into a new age of fluid pricing. The flexibility of the Internet allows web sellers to instantly and constantly adjust prices on a wide range of goods based on demand dynamics (sometimes called *real-time* pricing). In other cases, customers control pricing by bidding on auction sites such as eBay, or negotiating on sites such as Priceline. Still other companies customize their offers based on the characteristics and behaviours of specific customers.

Dynamic pricing
Adjusting prices continually to meet the characteristics and needs of individual customers and situations.

Dynamic pricing offers many advantages for marketers. For example, online retailers such as Amazon can mine their databases to gauge a specific shopper's desires, measure his or her means, instantaneously tailor products to fit that shopper's behaviour, and price products accordingly. Catalogue retailers such as L.L.Bean or Tilley Endurables can change prices on the fly according to changes in demand or costs, changing prices for specific items on a day-by-day or even hour-by-hour basis. And many direct marketers monitor inventories, costs, and demand at any given moment and adjust prices instantly.

Consumers also benefit from the web and dynamic pricing. Price comparison sites—such as Shopbot.ca, RedFlagDeals.com, and PriceGrabber.ca—offer instant product and price comparisons from thousands of vendors. Shopbot.ca, for instance, lets shoppers browse by category or search for specific products and brands in either English or French. It lists only products available from reliable Canadian retailers, allows users to compare prices from various sellers, and enables shoppers to order them right on the site.

In addition, consumers can negotiate prices at online auction sites and exchanges. Suddenly the centuries-old art of haggling is back in vogue. Want to sell that antique pickle jar that's been collecting dust for generations? Post it on eBay or Kijiji. Want to name your own price for a hotel room or a rental car? Visit Priceline.com or another reverse auction site. Want to bid on a ticket to a Coldplay show? Check out Ticketmaster.com, which now offers an online auction service for concert tickets.

Dynamic pricing makes sense in many contexts—it adjusts prices according to market forces, and it often works to the benefit of the customer. But marketers need to be careful not to use dynamic pricing to take advantage of certain customer groups, damaging important customer relationships.

International Pricing

Companies that market their products internationally must decide what prices to charge in the different countries in which they operate. In some cases, a company can set a uniform worldwide price. For example, Bombardier sells its jetliners at about the same price everywhere, whether Canada, Europe, or a developing country. However, most companies adjust their prices to reflect local market conditions and cost considerations.

The price that a company should charge in a specific country depends on many factors, including economic conditions, competitive situations, laws and regulations, and development of the wholesaling and retailing system. Consumer perceptions and preferences also may vary from country to country, calling for different prices. Or the company may have different marketing objectives in various world markets, which require changes in pricing strategy. For example, Samsung might introduce a new product into mature markets in highly developed countries with the goal of quickly gaining mass-market share—this would call for a penetration-pricing strategy. In contrast, it might enter a less-developed market by targeting smaller, less price-sensitive segments; in this case, market-skimming pricing makes sense.

Costs play an important role in setting international prices. Travellers abroad are often surprised to find that goods that are relatively inexpensive at home may carry outrageously higher price tags in other countries. A pair of Levi's selling for $50 in Canada might go for $150 in Tokyo and $100 in Paris. A McDonald's Big Mac selling for a modest $3.50 here might cost $7.50 in Reykjavik, Iceland, and an Oral-B toothbrush selling for $2.49 at home may cost $10 in China. Conversely, a Gucci handbag going for only $140 in Milan, Italy, might fetch $240 in Canada. In some cases, such *price escalation* may result from differences in selling strategies or market conditions. In most instances, however, it is simply a result of the higher costs of selling in another country—the additional costs of product modifications, shipping and insurance, import tariffs and taxes, exchange-rate fluctuations, and physical distribution.

Price has become a key element in the international marketing strategies of companies attempting to enter emerging markets, such as China, India, and Brazil. Consider Unilever's pricing strategy for developing countries:

> There used to be one way to sell a product in developing markets, if you bothered to sell there at all: Slap on a local label and market at premium prices to the elite. Unilever—maker of such brands as Dove, Lipton, and Vaseline—changed that. Instead, it built a following among the world's poorest consumers by shrinking packages to set a price even consumers living on $2 a day could afford. The strategy was forged about 25 years ago when Unilever's Indian subsidiary found its products out of reach for millions of Indians. To lower the price while making a profit, Unilever developed single-use packets for everything from shampoo to laundry detergent, costing just pennies a pack. The small, affordable packages put the company's premier brands within reach of the world's poor. Today, Unilever continues to woo cash-strapped customers with great success. For example, its approachable pricing helps explain why Unilever now captures 70 percent of the Brazil detergent market.[19]

Price Changes LO6

After developing their pricing structures and strategies, companies often face situations in which they must initiate price changes or respond to price changes by competitors.

Initiating Price Changes

In some cases, the company may find it desirable to initiate either a price cut or a price increase. In both cases, it must anticipate possible buyer and competitor reactions.

Initiating Price Cuts   Several situations may lead a firm to consider cutting its price. One such circumstance is excess capacity. Another is falling demand in the face of strong price competition or a weakened economy. In such cases, the firm may aggressively cut prices to boost sales and share. But as the airline, fast-food, automobile, and other industries have learned in recent years, cutting prices in an industry loaded with excess capacity may lead to price wars as competitors try to hold on to market share.

A company may also cut prices in a drive to dominate the market through lower costs. Either the company starts with lower costs than its competitors, or it cuts prices in the hope of gaining market share that will further cut costs through larger volume. Bausch & Lomb used an aggressive low-cost, low-price strategy to become an early leader in the competitive soft contact lens market. Costco used this strategy to become the world's largest warehouse retailer.

Initiating Price Increases A successful price increase can greatly improve profits. For example, if the company's profit margin is 3 percent of sales, a 1 percent price increase will boost profits by 33 percent if sales volume is unaffected. A major factor in price increases is cost inflation. Rising costs squeeze profit margins and lead companies to pass cost increases along to customers. Another factor leading to price increases is overdemand: When a company cannot supply all that its customers need, it may raise its prices, ration products to customers, or both. Consider today's worldwide oil and gas industry.

When raising prices, the company must avoid being perceived as a *price gouger*. For example, when gasoline prices rise rapidly, angry customers often accuse the major oil companies of enriching themselves at the expense of consumers. Customers have long memories, and they will eventually turn away from companies or even whole industries that they perceive as charging excessive prices. In the extreme, claims of price gouging may even bring about increased government regulation.

There are some techniques for avoiding these problems. One is to maintain a sense of fairness surrounding any price increase. Price increases should be supported by company communications that tell customers why prices are being raised.

Wherever possible, the company should consider ways to meet higher costs or demand without raising prices. For example, it can consider more cost-effective ways to produce or distribute its products. It can shrink the product or substitute less-expensive ingredients instead of raising the price, as ConAgra did in an effort to hold its Banquet frozen dinner prices at $1. Or it can "unbundle" its market offering, removing features, packaging, or services and separately pricing elements that were formerly part of the offer.

Buyer Reactions to Price Changes Customers do not always interpret price changes in a straightforward way. A price *increase*, which would normally lower sales, may have some positive meanings for buyers. For example, what would you think if Rolex *raised* the price of its latest watch model? On the one hand, you might think that the watch is even more exclusive or better made. On the other hand, you might think that Rolex is simply being greedy by charging what the market will bear.

Similarly, consumers may view a price *cut* in several ways. For example, what would you think if Rolex were to suddenly cut its prices? You might think that you are getting a better deal on an exclusive product. More likely, however, you'd think that quality had been reduced, and the brand's luxury image might be tarnished.

A brand's price and image are often closely linked. A price change, especially a drop in price, can adversely affect how consumers view the brand. Tiffany found this out when it attempted to broaden its appeal by offering a line of more affordable jewellery:[20]

> Tiffany is all about luxury and the cachet of its blue boxes. However, in the late 1990s, the high-end jeweller responded to the "affordable luxuries" craze with a new "Return to Tiffany" line of less expensive silver jewellery. The "Return to Tiffany" silver charm bracelet quickly

Time & Life Pictures/Getty Images

Exhibit 10.14 **Price changes:** A brand's price and image are often closely linked. Tiffany found this out when it attempted to broaden its appeal by offering a line of more affordable jewellery.

became a must-have item, as teens jammed Tiffany's hushed stores clamouring for the $110 silver bauble. Sales skyrocketed. But despite this early success, the bracelet fad appeared to alienate the firm's older, wealthier, and more conservative clientele, damaging Tiffany's reputation for luxury. So, in 2002, the firm began re-emphasizing its pricier jewellery collections. Although high-end jewellery has once again replaced silver as Tiffany's fastest growing business, the company has yet to fully regain its exclusivity. Says one well-heeled customer: "You used to aspire to be able to buy something at Tiffany, but now it's not that special anymore."

Competitor Reactions to Price Changes A firm considering a price change must worry about the reactions of its competitors as well as those of its customers. Competitors are most likely to react when the number of firms involved is small, when the product is uniform, and when the buyers are well informed about products and prices.

How can the firm anticipate the likely reactions of its competitors? The problem is complex because, like the customer, the competitor can interpret a company price cut in many ways. It might think the company is trying to grab a larger market share, or that it's doing poorly and trying to boost its sales. Or it might think that the company wants the whole industry to cut prices to increase total demand.

The company must guess each competitor's likely reaction. If all competitors behave alike, this amounts to analyzing only a typical competitor. In contrast, if the competitors do not behave alike—perhaps because of differences in size, market shares, or policies—then separate analyses are necessary. However, if some competitors will match the price change, there is good reason to expect that the rest will also match it.

Responding to Price Changes

Here we reverse the question and ask how a firm should respond to a price change by a competitor. The firm needs to consider several issues: Why did the competitor change the price? Is the price change temporary or permanent? What will happen to the company's market share and profits if it does not respond? Are other competitors going to respond? Besides these issues, the company must also consider its own situation and strategy and possible customer reactions to price changes.

Figure 10.5 shows the ways a company might assess and respond to a competitor's price cut. Suppose the company learns that a competitor has cut its price and decides that this price cut is likely to harm company sales and profits. It might simply decide to hold its current price and profit margin. The company might believe that it will not lose too much market share, or that it would lose too much profit if it reduced its own price. Or it might decide that it should wait and respond when it has more information on the effects of the competitor's price change. However, waiting too long to act might let the competitor get stronger and more confident as its sales increase.

If the company decides that effective action can and should be taken, it might make any of four responses. First, it could *reduce its price* to match the competitor's price.

FIGURE 10.5 Assessing and Responding to Competitor Price Changes

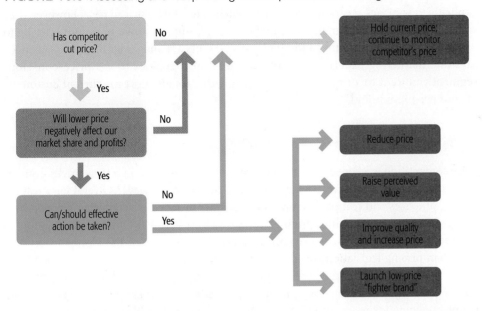

It may decide that the market is price sensitive and that it would lose too much market share to the lower-priced competitor. Cutting the price will reduce the company's profits in the short run. Some companies might also reduce their product quality, services, and marketing communications to retain profit margins, but this will ultimately hurt long-run market share. The company should try to maintain its quality as it cuts prices.

Alternatively, the company might maintain its price but *raise the perceived value* of its offer. It could improve its communications, stressing the relative value of its product over that of the lower-price competitor. The firm may find it cheaper to maintain price and spend money to improve its perceived value than to cut price and operate at a lower margin. Or, the company might *improve quality and increase price*, moving its brand into a higher price–value position. The higher quality creates greater customer value, which justifies the higher price. In turn, the higher price preserves the company's higher margins.

Finally, the company might *launch a low-price "fighter brand"*—adding a lower-price item to the line or creating a separate lower-price brand. This is necessary if the particular market segment being lost is price sensitive and will not respond to arguments of higher quality. For example, Telus created Koodo, a telecommunications brand with a very different pricing structure than its Telus-branded services, to fight against

Exhibit 10.15 **Fighter brands:** Telus markets its lower priced mobile phone services under the brand Koodo, represented by the character El Tabador.

market share being lost to Mobilicity and Wind Mobile. Fighter brands are created explicitly to win back customers that have switched to a lower priced rival, however, they sometimes result in customers switching from the company's own premium offering to its fighter brand. "Positioning a fighter brand presents a manager with a dual challenge," says one marketing expert. "You must ensure that it appeals to the price-conscious segment you want to attract while guaranteeing that it falls short for current customers of your premium brand."[21]

Public Policy and Pricing LO7

Price competition is a core element of our free-market economy. In setting prices, companies usually are free to charge whatever prices they wish, however, several laws restrict pricing practices and companies must also consider broader societal pricing concerns.

Legal issues surrounding pricing are outlined in Part VI: Offences in Relation to Competition and Part VII.1: Deceptive Marketing Practices of the Competition Act. Canadian pricing legislation was designed with two goals in mind: to foster a competitive environment and to protect consumers.[22] Although pricing decisions made by firms do not generally require regulatory approval, Canadian marketers should be aware of the major public policy issues in pricing outlined in Figure 10.6. These include potentially damaging pricing practices within a given level of the channel (price-fixing and predatory pricing) and across levels of the channel (retail price maintenance, discriminatory pricing, and deceptive pricing).[23]

Pricing Within Channel Levels

Federal legislation on *price-fixing* states that sellers must set prices without talking to competitors. Otherwise, price collusion is suspected. Price-fixing is illegal per se—that is, the government does not accept any excuses for price-fixing. Under the Competition Act, the legal charge for offences of this nature is *conspiracy*. Companies found guilty of such practices can receive heavy fines. In fact, 2009 changes to the Competition Act increased potential fines by as much as $25 million and increased jail sentences for breaching new conspiracy provisions to 14 years.[24]

Section 47 of the act also identifies bid rigging, where one party agrees not to submit a bid or tender in response to a call, or agrees to withdraw a bid or tender submitted at the request of another party, as another indictable offense pertaining to price-fixing. Under Section 78 (abuse of dominant position) of the Competition Act, sellers are

FIGURE 10.6 Public Policy Issues in Pricing

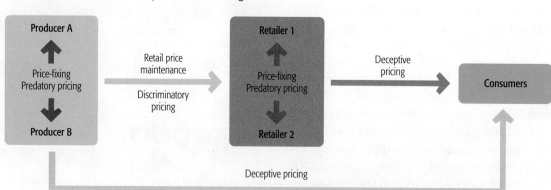

prohibited from using *predatory pricing*—selling below cost with the intention of punishing a competitor, or gaining higher long-run profits by putting competitors out of business. This protects small sellers from larger ones who might sell items below cost temporarily or in a specific locale to drive them out of business. The biggest problem is determining just what constitutes predatory pricing behaviour. Selling below cost to unload excess inventory is not considered predatory; selling below cost to drive out competitors is. For example, in 2001 the short-lived Roots Air accused Air Canada of predatory pricing designed to drive it out of business. The competition bureau ordered Air Canada to stop offering deeply discounted fares on some of its routes, however, that didn't save Roots Air from going out of business. Thus, the same action may or may not be predatory depending on intent, and intent can be very difficult to determine or prove.

Pricing Across Channel Levels

The Competition Act seeks to prevent unfair *price discrimination* by ensuring that sellers offer the same price terms to customers at a given level of trade. For example, every retailer is entitled to the same price terms from a given manufacturer, whether the retailer is Sears or your local bicycle shop. However, price discrimination is allowed if the seller can prove that its costs are different when selling to different retailers—for example, that it costs less per unit to sell a large volume of bicycles to Sears than to sell a few bicycles to the local dealer. In other words, quantity or volume discounts are not prohibited. However, discriminatory promotional allowances (those not offered on proportional terms to all other competing customers) are illegal. Thus, large competitors cannot negotiate special discounts, rebates, and price concessions that are not made proportionally available to smaller competitors. For example, a small customer purchasing one-third as much as a larger competitor must receive a promotional allowance equal to one-third of what the large competitor was offered.

Although functional discounts (offering a larger discount to wholesalers than to retailers) are legal in the United States, they are illegal in Canada. In Canada, retailers and wholesalers are considered competing customers who must receive proportionally equal promotional allowances. Often, Canadian marketers who work for multinational firms must explain the differences in the law to their US counterparts. Canadian marketers must also keep in mind that it is illegal for a buyer to knowingly benefit from any form of price discrimination. Price differentials may be used to "match competition" in "good faith," provided the firm is trying to meet competitors at its own level of competition, and the price discrimination is temporary, localized, and defensive, rather than offensive.

Canadian marketers are allowed to offer price breaks for one-shot deals, such as store-opening specials, anniversary specials, and stock clearance sales. However, regional price differentials that limit competition are illegal. Canadian firms cannot price products unreasonably low in one part of the country with the intent of driving out the competition.

Laws also prohibit *retail (or resale) price maintenance*—a manufacturer cannot require dealers to charge a specified retail price for its product. Although the seller can propose a manufacturer's *suggested* retail price to dealers, it cannot refuse to sell to a dealer who takes independent pricing action, nor can it punish the dealer by shipping late or denying advertising allowances.

Deceptive pricing practices are outlined in Section 74 of the Competition Act. For example, firms cannot advertise a product at a low price, carry very limited stock, and then tell consumers they are out of the product so that they can entice them to switch to a higher-priced item. This "bait and switch" advertising is illegal in Canada. Firms must offer their customers "rain checks" to avoid legal sanctions if advertised items are not stocked in sufficient quantities to cover expected demand.

Deceptive pricing occurs when a seller states prices or price savings that are not actually available to consumers. Some deceptions are difficult for consumers to discern, such as when an airline advertises a low one-way fare that is available only with the purchase of a round-trip ticket, or when a retailer sets artificially high "regular" prices, and then announces "sale" prices close to its previous everyday prices.

Other deceptive pricing issues include *scanner fraud* and price confusion. The widespread use of scanner-based computer checkouts has led to increasing complaints of retailers overcharging their customers. Most of these overcharges result from poor management—from a failure to enter current or sale prices into the system. Other cases, however, involve intentional overcharges. Price confusion results when firms employ pricing methods that make it difficult for consumers to understand just what price they are really paying. Canadian law requires firms to charge consumers the lesser price in cases where more than one price is supplied by the seller either through its advertising, packaging, or in-store display.

Building Value in a Bundle

Sell the product. This is the essential objective of any for-profit organization. So why would WestJet be concerned because its load factor (percentage of seats sold) increased steadily from its inception in 1996 to the present? "High load factors are good things," explains WestJet vice-president of revenue management Paul Harvalias. "But when your value proposition is partially based on low price, it becomes harder and harder to grow revenue the more you fill a plane." A classic catch-22: WestJet could charge more per fare, but not without compromising its brand. In the meantime, it needs to generate more revenue to continue pursuing growth objectives.

"It's great when all of your performance indicators are pointed in the right direction, but at some point, when you can't fill any more seats because you're full, the only way to grow revenue profitably is to get more revenue per available seat." Harvalias and his team are thus charged with an intriguing business case: Make more money per seat without raising the price. "That's my predicament every day— sell sufficient numbers of seats to meet total revenue objectives while still being perceived as a value airline."

Enter bundle pricing, a resourceful way of achieving WestJet's conflicting goals. In early 2013 WestJet broke the tradition of a one-price strategy to move to a tiered pricing system. As discussed in Chapter 7, this decision was made concurrent with, or perhaps because of, its decision to target the business segment. "We really hadn't developed a product for the business traveller, so this allowed us to add some utilities desired by that market at an incremental price increase per seat." Three price bundles were offered: Econo, Flex, and Plus. These, as you might expect, provided varying degrees of value-added amenities. "Econo seating was for those that just want to get the plane to go from A to B," explains Harvalias, whereas "Flex gave you select additional features, while Plus provided all of the extras—more legroom, no-fee cancellation, pre-boarding, some extra onboard amenities, extra luggage, etc."

For someone who wonders why marketing students would care about "boring revenue management stuff," Harvalias teaches an important lesson on how the price "*P*" can be as important as any other part of the marketing mix. Fare bundling has allowed WestJet to "generate higher revenue from business passengers as a means of subsidizing the lower priced seats which appeal to the larger of our segments." Presto, the brand image of WestJet stays intact, but revenues grow thanks to the magic of the bundle.

QUESTIONS

1. Does WestJet risk compromising its brand by offering tiered pricing for seats?
2. WestJet calls this practice "bundle pricing," but when analyzing the definition of this term, does what WestJet is doing still qualify, or is it more consistent with segmented pricing?
3. Which WestJet segment (leisure or business) is more price sensitive?

REVIEWING THE CONCEPTS

1. **Identify the three major pricing strategies and discuss the importance of understanding customer-value perceptions, company costs, and competitor strategies when setting prices.**

A price is the sum of all the values that customers give up to gain the benefits of having or using a product or service. The three major pricing strategies include customer value-based pricing, cost-based pricing, and competition-based pricing. Good pricing begins with a complete understanding of the value that a product or service creates for customers and setting a price that captures that value. The price the company charges will fall somewhere between one that is too high to produce any demand, and one that is too low to produce a profit.

Customer perceptions of the product's value set the ceiling for prices. If customers perceive that the price is greater than the product's value, they will not buy the product. At the other extreme, company and product costs set the floor for prices. If the company prices the product below its costs, its profits will suffer. Between these two extremes, consumers will base their judgments of a product's value on the prices that competitors charge for similar products. Thus, in setting prices, companies need to consider all three factors: customer-perceived value, costs, and competitor's pricing strategies.

2. **Identify and define the other important external and internal factors affecting a firm's pricing decisions.**

Other *internal* factors that influence pricing decisions include the company's overall marketing strategy, objectives, and marketing mix, as well as organizational considerations. Price is only one element of the company's broader marketing strategy. If the company has selected its target market and positioning carefully, then its marketing mix strategy, including price, will be fairly straightforward. Some companies position their products on price and then tailor other marketing mix decisions to the prices they want to charge. Other companies de-emphasize price and use other marketing mix tools to create *non-price* positions.

Other *external* pricing considerations include the nature of the market and the demand and environmental factors such as the economy, reseller needs, and government actions. The seller's pricing freedom varies with different types of markets. Ultimately, the customer decides whether the company has set the right price. The customer weighs the price against the perceived values of using the product—if the price exceeds the sum of the values, consumers will not buy. So the company must understand concepts such as demand curves (the price–demand relationship) and price elasticity (consumer sensitivity to prices).

Economic conditions can also have a major impact on pricing decisions. The recent recession caused consumers to rethink the price–value equation. Marketers have responded by increasing their emphasis on value-for-the-money pricing strategies. Even in tough economic times, however, consumers do not buy based on prices alone. Thus, no matter what price they charge—low or high—companies need to offer superior value for the money.

3. **Describe the major strategies for pricing new products.**

Pricing is a dynamic process. Companies design a *pricing structure* that covers all their products. They change this structure over time and adjust it to account for different customers and situations. Pricing strategies usually change as a product passes through its life cycle. The company can decide on one of several price–quality strategies for introducing an imitative product, including premium pricing, economy pricing, good value, or overcharging. In pricing innovative new products, it can use *market-skimming pricing* by initially setting high prices to "skim" the maximum amount of revenue from various segments of the market. Or it can use *market-penetrating pricing* by setting a low initial price to penetrate the market deeply and win a large market share.

4. **Explain how companies find a set of prices that maximizes the profits from the total product mix.**

When the product is part of a product mix, the firm searches for a set of prices that will maximize the profits from the total mix. In *product line pricing*, the company decides on price steps for the entire set of products it offers. In addition, the company must set prices for *optional products* (optional or accessory products included with the main product), *captive products* (products that are required for use of the main product), *by-products* (waste or residual products produced when making the main product), and *product bundles* (combinations of products at a reduced price).

5. Discuss how companies adjust their prices to take into account different types of customers and situations.

Companies apply a variety of *price adjustment strategies* to account for differences in consumer segments and situations. One is *discount and allowance pricing*, whereby the company establishes cash, quantity, functional, or seasonal discounts, or varying types of allowances. A second strategy is *segmented pricing*, where the company sells a product at two or more prices to accommodate different customers, product forms, locations, or times. Sometimes companies consider more than economics in their pricing decisions, using *psychological pricing* to better communicate a product's intended position. In *promotional* pricing, a company offers discounts or temporarily sells a product below list price as a special event, sometimes even selling below cost as a loss leader. Another approach is *geographical pricing*, whereby the company decides how to price to distant customers, choosing from such alternatives as FOB-origin pricing, uniform-delivered pricing, and zone pricing. Finally, *international pricing* means that the company adjusts its price to meet different conditions and expectations in different world markets.

6. Discuss the key issues related to initiating and responding to price changes.

When a firm considers initiating a *price change*, it must consider customers' and competitors' reactions. There are different implications to *initiating price cuts* and *initiating price increases*. Buyer reactions to price changes are influenced by the meaning customers see in the price change. Competitors' reactions flow from a set reaction policy or a fresh analysis of each situation.

There are also many factors to consider in responding to a competitor's price changes. The company that faces a price change initiated by a competitor must try to understand the competitor's intent as well as the likely duration and impact of the change. If a swift reaction is desirable, the firm should preplan its reactions to different possible price actions by competitors. When facing a competitor's price change, the company might sit tight, reduce its own price, raise perceived quality, improve quality and raise price, or launch a fighting brand.

KEY TERMS

Allowance 373
Break-even pricing
  (or target return pricing) 359
By-product pricing 372
Captive-product pricing 371
Competition-based pricing 360
Cost-based pricing 358
Cost-plus pricing
  (or markup pricing) 358
Customer value-based pricing 355
Demand curve 365

Discount 373
Dynamic pricing 377
Fixed costs (overhead) 358
Geographical pricing 376
Good-value pricing 356
Market-penetration pricing 369
Market-skimming pricing
  (or price skimming) 369
Optional-product pricing 371
Price 254
Price elasticity 366

Product bundle pricing 372
Product line pricing 370
Promotional pricing 375
Psychological pricing 374
Reference prices 374
Segmented pricing 373
Target costing 361
Total costs 358
Value-added pricing 357
Variable costs 358

TALK ABOUT MARKETING

1. Identify three price-comparison shopping websites, and shop for a tablet of your choice. Compare the price ranges given at these three websites.

2. You are an owner of a small independent chain of coffeehouses competing head-to-head with Starbucks. The retail price your customers pay for coffee is exactly the same as at Starbucks. The wholesale price you pay for roasted coffee beans has increased by 25 percent. You know that you cannot absorb this increase and that you must pass it on to your customers. However, you are concerned about the consequences of an open price increase. Discuss three alternative price-increase strategies that address these concerns.

3. Why do marketers charge customers different prices for the same product or service? Explain how this type of pricing is implemented and the conditions under which it is effective.

4. Explain market-skimming and market-penetration pricing strategies. Why would a marketer of innovative high-tech products choose market-skimming pricing rather than market-penetration pricing when launching a new product?

5. What does the following positioning statement suggest about the firm's marketing objectives, marketing-mix strategy, and costs? "No one beats our prices. We crush the competition."

6. Retailers often use psychological pricing as a price-adjustment strategy. Explain this pricing strategy. How do reference prices affect psychological pricing decisions?

THINK LIKE A MARKETING MANAGER

The printer industry is intensively competitive with respect to pricing. The first home printers, marketed by companies such as Epson and Hewlett-Packard, were almost as expensive as computers themselves. But like most technology products, as technology improves and features are added, the price is forced down. Today, consumers can choose from a wide range of desktop printers for home use. Printers come with a variety of features and can be purchased from many different vendors.

QUESTIONS

1. What role does price play in a consumer's selection of a home printer? What about a business buyer making a purchase decision about an office printer? What about a business person selecting a portable printer to take on business trips?

2. List all the different features a printer can have. Which of these do you think are most important to consumers, and how much extra are they willing to pay for them? Which do you think are most important to business buyers?

3. Do some online research and find three different marketers that sell printers that are suitable for home use. Are the prices of the three brands the same or very different? If they are different, what accounts for the difference? What pricing strategy do you think each marketer is using?

4. Today, many printers designed for home use are "all in one" devices that print, scan, and fax. Explain the pricing strategy used by marketers of all-in-one printers.

MARKETING ETHICS

Businesses often charge different prices to different customers. For example, movie theatres charge less to students and senior citizens, and prices vary across times of the day. Women are charged more for dry cleaning and haircuts. Business flyers pay more than leisure travellers. And that person sitting next to you on the airplane may have paid more or less than you did—the same goes for hotel rooms. Consumers with arthritis pay more per milligram of pain relief when they buy the Tylenol Arthritis product than when they buy regular Tylenol, even though the active ingredient, acetaminophen, and dosage over an eight-hour period are identical. Technology offers marketers the ability to price-discriminate in various ways. For example, Coca-Cola once experimented with vending machines that raised prices as outdoor temperatures went higher. Electronic shelf labels allow retailers to change prices based on supply and demand. Moreover, the Internet provides the capability for businesses to charge different prices on their websites to different customers of the same product.

QUESTIONS

1. Is it fair for businesses to charge different prices to different customers?

2. Go to Wikipedia and research the "three degrees of price discrimination." Does this discussion impact your opinion stated in #1 regarding the fairness of this practice? Explain.

MARKETING TECHNOLOGY

You know what an auction is, but what about a *reverse auction*? In a typical auction, a seller offers a good or service for sale and buyers bid on it, with the highest bidder winning the auction. In a reverse auction, however, buyer and seller roles are reversed. A buyer wants to purchase a good or service and solicits sellers to make an offer, with the lowest bidder winning the sale. Like traditional auctions that take place on websites such as eBay, the Internet is facilitating reverse auctions that drive down a company's procurement costs as much as 25 percent to 50 percent. The key to reverse auctions is that they take place quickly and sellers see the lowest bid, which drives down price for the host buyer. Basically, sellers are bidding for how low they are willing to sell a product or service to the buyer. Reverse auctions became popular in the 1990s, and one researcher estimates that almost half of all corporate expenditures will soon be done through reverse auctions. Reverse auctions aren't just for business-to-business purchases anymore, either. They are now used in the business-to-consumer and consumer-to-consumer marketspace as well. Because of technology, businesses and consumers are now able to set the price they are willing to pay and have sellers compete for their business from anywhere in the world.

QUESTIONS

1. Search the Internet for reverse auction sites. Learn how these sites operate, and explain how they work and the costs associated with conducting a reverse auction.

2. Search for articles about reverse auctions. What are the advantages and disadvantages of using reverse auctions to purchase products and services for businesses? For consumers?

MARKETING BY THE NUMBERS

When introducing new products, some manufacturers use a price-skimming strategy by setting a high initial price and then reducing the price later. However, reducing the price also reduces contribution margins, which in turn impacts profitability. To be profitable, the reduced price must sufficiently increase sales. For example, a company with a contribution margin of 30 percent on sales of $60 million realizes a total contribution to fixed costs and profits of $18 million ($60 million 0.30 = $18 million). If this company decreases price, the contribution margin will also decrease. So to maintain or increase profitability, the price reduction must increase sales considerably.

QUESTIONS

1. Refer to Appendix 3, Marketing by the Numbers, and calculate the new contribution margin for the company discussed above if it reduces price by 10 percent. Assume that unit variable costs are $70 and the original price was $100.

2. What total sales must the company capture at the new price to maintain the same level of total contribution (that is, total contribution = $18 million)?

VIDEO CASE

Hammerpress

Printing paper goods may not sound like the best business to get into these days, but Hammerpress is nonetheless carving out a niche in this old industry. And they're doing it by returning to old technology. Most of today's printing firms use computer-driven graphic design techniques and printing processes. But Hammerpress creates greeting cards, calendars, and business cards that are hand-crafted by professional artists and printed using traditional letterpress technology.

When it comes to competing, this old-fashioned process presents both opportunities and challenges. While Hammerpress's products certainly stand out as works of art, the cost for producing such goods is considerably higher than the industry average. This video illustrates how Hammerpress employs dynamic pricing techniques to meet the needs of various customer segments and thrive in a competitive environment.

After viewing the video featuring Hammerpress, answer the following questions:

QUESTIONS

1. How does Hammerpress employ the concept of dynamic pricing?

2. Discuss Hammerpress in relation to the three major pricing strategies. Which of these three strategies is the company's core strategy?

3. Does it make sense for Hammerpress to compete in product categories where the market dictates a price that is not profitable for the company? Explain.

FUZION WINES CATCHES THE ATTENTION OF ONTARIO WINE DRINKERS

Case prepared by David Rose, Wilfrid Laurier University

The Liquor Control Board of Ontario (LCBO) is one of the world's largest buyers and retailers of beverage alcohol with more than 630 retail stores throughout the province of Ontario, offering nearly 19 000 products directly to consumers and also to licensed establishments. LCBO sales are over $4 billion per year, with spirit sales making up about 43 percent, wine 36 percent, and beer 21 percent of the total. As an Ontario government enterprise, LCBO pays dividends to the province that helps pay for healthcare, education, and other important services. Since 1990, LCBO has won more than 200 awards in customer service, innovative retailing, social responsibility, staff training, store design, marketing, and corporate communications.

In setting retail prices for the products it sells, the LCBO strives to balance several key elements of its mandate, including promoting social responsibility in the sale and consumption of beverage alcohol, providing excellent customer service, including offering customers a broad product selection and value at all price points, and generating maximum profit to fund government programs and priorities. The LCBO also ensures that it meets the legislated requirements under the Liquor Control Act concerning minimum price and uniform price. (Minimum prices are the lowest prices that products can be sold for, and uniform price requires the price for a particular product to be the same throughout the province.)

To achieve this necessary balance among the key elements of its mandate, and to meet public sector standards of openness, fairness, and transparency when it buys products for resale, the LCBO uses a standard mark-up pricing structure. Mark-ups vary by product category (among beer, wine, fortified wine, spirits, and liqueurs, for example) and there is an additional charge on imports to cover supplementary costs associated with those products, but otherwise the mark-up is consistent for all products. This standard mark-up pricing structure, established by the LCBO in consultation with the Ministry of Finance many years ago, allows suppliers to be confident that the LCBO provides fair and equitable treatment to its business partners.

As a result of the LCBO's fixed mark-up structure, when LCBO buyers and suppliers discuss possible purchases they focus on the product's final retail price. The payment to the supplier for the products follows automatically from the application of the fixed mark-ups and other elements of the pricing structure (for example, freight costs and currency exchange rates if the purchase is in a foreign currency). As part of the agreement to purchase, the supplier must provide the final quote or cost to the LCBO, usually per case.

LCBO buyers make every effort to get the best products in each price band, whether for sub-$8 wines, or super-premium spirits. They review more than 50 000 submissions annually and negotiate with suppliers to make the best of these products available at good prices. The LCBO is an attractive customer for manufacturers, and there is fierce competition for listings. As a result, suppliers frequently submit products to the LCBO at prices lower than those charged to other jurisdictions.

Some of the newer products included in the LCBO's lineup carry the Fuzion brand name, a line of affordable wines from Argentina's Familia Zuccardi, one of that country's largest and most famous wineries. Making wine in the South American country of Argentina is not new—they've been doing it for 400 years—but sometimes a tiny push in the right direction is all a region needs to put it on the map, and that push came in the form of Fuzion. When the shiraz-malbec blend was first launched in Ontario in 2008, it caused near riots in the aisles of LCBO stores, as the fruity, soft sensation—at the time $7.45 per bottle (now $7.95)—was snapped up at an alarming rate after receiving favourable reviews and being compared to wines at twice and three times the cost. Such was the frenzy over the new wine that LCBO instituted a waiting list and reported jammed phone lines as customers called to add their names to the list. Customers spent so much time searching for Fuzion that they bought it by the case when they did find a supply, prompting the LCBO to stack cases near checkout counters rather than trying to keep up with restocking of shelves.

Fuzion did for Argentina what Yellow Tail did for Australia—sending exports soaring and other wineries scrambling to catch the wave of excitement. At one time, Fuzion was not only the hottest selling wine in Ontario, it was also the fourth best selling product at the LCBO behind only Heineken, Smirnoff, and Corona. While sales have since cooled, the company has added to the portfolio with a wide range of new wines including a Blanc de Blancs Chardonnay that lists for $24.95, an Organic Malbec Cabernet at $12.95, Fuzion Alta Reserve Malbec at $9.95, and a couple of easy-drinking white wines in the under $10 category.

While the Fuzion hysteria has subsided, there is no denying that consumers have come to love the bold fruity flavours and soft tannins of malbec, the main ingredient in the red wines of Argentina. The country's profile has been elevated and the door opened to so many other interesting wines, many of them attractive for their low price, but also because the wines are so consumer friendly. Perfect growing conditions in the regions near the Andes and Colorado River have allowed varieties such as cabernet sauvignon, malbec, pinot noir, semillon, merlot, and chardonnay to grow successfully. Today, over 230 000 hectares of vineyards are planted in Argentina—almost half of those to red varieties and a quarter each to "pink" and white varieties. The most popular grapes are malbec, chardonnay, cabernet sauvignon, and various indigenous grapes.

While Argentina is currently the world's fifth largest wine producer by volume—after France, Italy, Spain, and the United States—it is only in recent years that it has emerged as a major player in the wine world. The most important aspect of Argentina's wine boom is what people usually call the price–quality ratio. Argentina's grape-growing regions are warm and dry, which means there are few problems with pests and moulds, so little need to buy pesticides, fungal treatments, and so on. Argentina's other production costs (labour, grapes) are also generally low by international standards. Together, these low costs mean that Argentinian wineries can offer the same quality product for less money than other producers.

However, Argentine wines are not the only value-priced wines available in Ontario. The LCBO lists more than 500 wines for under $10, with products from all of the world's major wine-producing regions. How was the launch of one wine—Fuzion's original shiraz-malbec—able to create such a sensation in this very crowded market? The situation was different in 2008 and the timing was perfect for Fuzion's entry. At the time, the LCBO was being challenged for moving away from wines selling below $10 and not searching out suppliers in the low-price category. In response to this criticism, the LCBO began

looking for added-value brands for its product lineup and picked Fuzion, thinking it would be perfect to address consumer demands for better, cheaper wines. They were right; Fuzion found the magical boundary between the affordable and the highly enjoyable, and the rest is history.

Meanwhile, value-seeking wine lovers in the United States are lamenting the end of the "Two-Buck Chuck" era. For more than a decade, shoppers at Trader Joe's stores in California have paid just $1.99 for a bottle of Charles Shaw shiraz or cabernet sauvignon, making it Trader Joe's best selling wine, with 5 million cases sold in 2012. While the price has been higher in other parts of the United States for years, the increase to $2.49 in California is creating quite a stir. According to Bronco Wine, the company that produces the Charles Shaw brand, they were able to maintain such low prices for so long in part because they own 45 000 acres of vineyard land, which helps the company ride out wild fluctuations in grape prices like those the industry has seen in recent years. However, bad crops in 2010 and 2011 spelled the end of "Two-Buck Chuck."

Sources: LCBO website www.lcbo.com; Gord Stimmell, "Fuzion Frenzy Uncorked", *Toronto Star*, January 24, 2009, www.thestar.com/life/2009/01/24/fuzion_frenzy_uncorked.html; "Plonk for the Priviledged: Fuzion Malbec," *Choosy-Beggars*, June 10, 2009, www.choosy-beggars.com/index.php/2009/06/10/plonk-for-the-priviledged-fuzion-malbec; Rick VanSickle, "Argentina Wines," *Traveling Golfer*, February 1, 2011, www.travelinggolfer.net/2011/02/01/argentina-wines; "Canada Signs up for the Cult of Fuzion," *Ontario Wine Review*, October 8, 2008, http://ontariowinereview.com/print/Canada_FuZion.pdf; Cathy Bussewitz, "Price Hiked for 'Two-Buck Chuck," *The Press Democrat*, January 23, 2013, www.pressdemocrat.com/article/20130122/BUSINESS/130129860.

QUESTIONS FOR DISCUSSION

1. Which of the major pricing strategies does the LCBO employ when introducing new products?

2. What other factors does the LCBO consider when setting prices for its products?

3. By pricing the first shiraz-malbec blend below the value perceived by most of the wine drinkers who tried it, Fuzion created a sensation in the Ontario wine market. Are there any risks involved when selling a product for less than other products of similar quality?

MyMarketingLab MyMarketingLab is an online homework and tutorial system that puts you in control of your own learning with study and practice tools directly correlated to this chapter's content.

Target/TARGET/Newscom

AFTER STUDYING THIS CHAPTER, YOU SHOULD BE ABLE TO

1 list and describe the major types of marketing channel partners. Explain why companies need channel partners, and describe the roles and responsibilities channel partners may perform

2 describe the major methods of organizing channel members, and the problems that can arise in managing channels

3 describe the importance of retail in Canada, and list and briefly describe the major types of retailers

4 name and describe the current trends in retail marketing (including online retail) and describe the new technologies retail marketers are employing

5 describe the role of supply chain management and logistics management in a company's distribution system

Marketing Channels

PREVIEWING THE CONCEPTS

Marketing channels, or channels of distribution, collectively comprise the "third P" or third marketing mix tool—place. Marketers in every organization must design, develop, and manage the channels through which their products and services move from their point of production to the hands of the final customer. Some products, like software, move electronically while others, like clothing, furniture, and cars, move physically. Sometimes a firm's overall success can depend on how well it designs its channels or how well it manages them compared to its competitors. The first part of this chapter describes marketing channels and channel partners (also known as intermediaries), and explores some of the issues in designing and managing effective marketing channels. Because retail is such an important (and visible) marketing channel, we take a closer look at the business of retail in Canada, and new trends and technology that are driving retail marketing. Finally, we'll take a look at the supply chain—the back end of the distribution channel—and consider the challenges of inventory movement and logistics management. But first let's take a closer look at one of the newest entrants into the Canadian retail landscape: the hugely popular American discount chic retailer, Target.

TARGET LOVES CANADA!

When popular American discount retailer Target announced plans to expand into Canada, the cover of *Marketing Magazine* proclaimed, "Canadian retail will never be the same again," and months before the first store even opened that prediction was already coming true. On a cold winter day in downtown Toronto, people lined up for hours just for a chance to squeeze into a small "pop-up" store Target had built in a vacant lot (see photo) and for the opportunity to buy a limited edition Jason Wu design—from Jason Wu himself. The Jason Wu for Target collection sold out in less than five hours, and Target donated 100 percent of the sales from the event to United Way Toronto. How can a new entrant into the market become so successful so quickly?

Target stores appeal to price-conscious but fashion-forward shoppers, as do many other retailers—but Target has a way of making them feel like they're part of an exclusive club. Everyone who works at Target is a brand ambassador, and they all know and live the brand's promise: Expect more. Pay less. The brand is positioned firmly against Walmart:

Whereas Walmart has consistently promised to be the store that offers low prices on everything and appeals to the extremely price-conscious shopper (the kind of person who gladly sacrifices fashion and even quality for price), Target promises low prices *and* fashion chic. Target stores are carefully designed to appeal to the fashion-conscious at every touchpoint, with wide aisles, bright lights, carefully and attractively presented merchandise, and graphic signs reminiscent of modern art. The brand imagery is tastefully reinforced at every turn. They contrast sharply with Walmart's obstacle course of bargain bins and cardboard displays flagged by discount "rollback" signs.

And Target didn't wait until the first Canadian stores opened to begin its marketing plan. The marketing began nearly two years before the first store opened with a cross-country tour. "The Target Road Trip was about getting to know our Canadian guests and sharing something special with them along the way," said Livia Zufferli, director of marketing at Target Canada.

At every stop the Target team and Bullseye, the brand's loveable mascot, staged events to interact with Canadians. In Quebec City, folk musician Yves Lambert and singer Nadja invited guests of the event to join them on stage. A surprise free concert in Toronto's Yonge-Dundas square by The Tenors thrilled passers-by during the lunch hour, and Target's 30-vehicle fleet provided complimentary car service for travellers in the downtown core. The Target Road Trip took over the Pete Palangio Arena in North Bay for a hockey game, and the retailer's canine mascot, Bullseye, dropped the puck. Later in Sudbury, they set up a pop-up Christmas tree farm and gave away Christmas trees. The final stop on the Target Road Trip was Mission, British Columbia, home of Canadian singer Carly Rae Jepsen, where Target organized a free concert at the Clarke Foundation Theatre.

While the road trip was in full swing, marketers at Target Canada headquarters were busy making other preparations. To make shopping easier for consumers, Target partnered with the Royal Bank of Canada to offer a Target Debit Card (which can be used only at Target stores) and Target MasterCard, which offers REDcard Rewards (Target's loyalty program). Even though the stores were months from opening, there were Halloween and Christmas promotions, a Meet Us at the Beach promotion in August with events at beaches in Ottawa, Toronto, Vernon, British Columbia, and Sylvan Lake, Alberta. Target was also an active participant at Fashion Week in Montreal.

All marketing communications in advance of the stores' opening directed attention to recruiting and to Target's focus on design and corporate responsibility. No traditional mass media advertising was used during this period; rather, Target actively worked its social-media channels to engage Canadian consumers.

In August 2012, almost a year before a single store opened, Target Canada created its Facebook page featuring a big red box that said simply, "hello." The information section on its Facebook site included a store locator that indicated when each location would be opening, and an Ask Target section, where Target representatives answered questions (in both official languages) like "What brands will be carried in Canadian Target stores?

Two new Twitter accounts were created, @target_ca for English Canadians and @target_fr for French Canadians, and they quickly grew to more than 20 000 followers. The accounts were actively monitored by Target's marketing team, who engaged with consumers and encouraged them to create their own hashtags. Just a few of the hashtags created by followers were #targetisawesome and #fashionthatrocks.

One of the keys to Target's success in Canada was this early and constant engagement with consumers via social media. When the NHL lockout ended in January 2013, Target Canada's Facebook page showed a picture of a hockey puck with the red Target swirls and the caption, "Welcome back, hockey. We missed you." Tweets and Facebook posts were constantly being re-tweeted by Target's tweeters. And Target Canada also has its own YouTube channel.

Meanwhile, Canadian consumers and competing retailers were anxious to learn what products and brands Target would be featuring. Grocery retailers, especially, wondered how much food Target would be selling, and what kind of threat it would pose. Then Target announced that it had inked a supply deal with Canada's second largest grocery chain, Sobeys, and that its stores would feature food brands Up and Up, Market Pantry, and Archer Farms. Up and Up, with its minimalist packaging and pops of colour, poses the most direct challenge to existing Canadian private label lines, including the Loblaw behemoth President's Choice. Archer Farms is a premier grocery line, similar to Compliments (Sobeys), President's Choice (Loblaw's) and Irresistibles (Metro); while Market Pantry is the low-cost grocery brand, similar to Signal (Sobeys), No Name (Loblaw's), and Selection (Metro).

Aside from food, Target's design and brand partners for Canada include the Nate Berkus home collection, Sonia Kashuk make-up line, Giada De Laurentiis cookware and cookbook line, and Shaun White for Target. And the biggest news of all, Roots! The launch of Target Canada coincided with the fortieth anniversary of Roots, and so the beloved Canadian brand produced a new, limited-time-only collection for the retailer. The new line is called Roots Outfitters Collection for Target and will include sweat pants, sweatshirts, and graphic tees at prices ranging from $7.99 to $34.99—in typical Roots style, athletic heritage, cozy, and comfortable. At an event announcing Target's Canadian brand partners, product lines from Merona, Mossimo, and Pixi were on display surrounding an ice track where skaters modelled items from the apparel collections.

The company also worked at becoming a good Canadian citizen: As part of Target's long-term commitment to sustainable business practices, the company sought Leadership in Energy & Environmental Design (LEED) certification from the US Green Building Council for all its Canadian stores. The sites for Target's stores were renovated at a cost of more than $10 million per location. Design plans include conserving energy and water, reducing greenhouse gas emissions, and limiting waste sent to landfill, among other features. Target's approach to environmental sustainability is integrated throughout the business, from how stores are built to the products on the shelves. "We take our role as good corporate citizen very seriously, and we're proud that Target is making a firm commitment to sustainability in Canada," said Tony Fisher, president of Target Canada. "Striving for LEED certification at our 124 stores opening in 2013 is important as we seek to use our resources responsibly and maintain the health of our communities."

While some established Canadian retailers are worried about their newest competition, consumers are clearly overjoyed, and Target could have other positive effects. Retail marketing experts are keenly observing the effect Target will have on Canada's retail landscape, and while they disagree about what exactly that effect might be, no one doubts that Target's entry into Canada will have lasting effects. One marketing observer suggests that Target will reinvigorate the suburban strip malls currently anchored by fading Zellers stores—good news for surrounding retailers. Another peripheral effect may be to keep Canadian shoppers from crossing the border. Says one Canadian retail expert, "Consumers will come to expect a higher quality product at a more reasonable price point, which will affect all players in the retail landscape." And that's good news for both consumers and retailers.[1]*

*Sources: Target Canada press releases published on Canada Newswire in 2012-2013; Kristin Laird, "Target finds Canadian Roots With New Partnership," Marketing magazine online, January 25, 2013; Kristin Laird, "Everybody Loves Target," Marketing, May 7, 2012, 44-49; Duncan Hood, "Target Won't Kill Canadian Retail. It Will Save It," Canadian Business, October 15, 2012, 4; Richard Warnica, "Target's Friendly Invasion," Canadian Business, October 15, 2012, 32-36; "WSL/Strategic Retail: Canada Represents Opportunities for U.S. Retailers," Entertainment Close - Up, September 21, 2012; Beth Mattson-Teig, "Walmart Blazes a Trail for Other Value Retailers in Expanding Internationally," Retail Traffic, May 22, 2012; Ron Margulis, "Here Comes TARGET," Canadian Grocer 126, no. 9 (2012): 38-42,44; Megan Haynes, "Target to Bring Archer Farms, Market Pantry and Up And Up to Canada," Strategy magazine online (StrategyOnline.ca), January 24, 2013.

AS THE TARGET STORY SHOWS, marketing channel decisions such as when and how to enter a new market take careful planning, but if done well can result in superior customer value and competitive advantage—both for the firm and for its channel partners. Retailers such as Target cannot bring value to customers by themselves, but must work closely with other firms in a larger value delivery network. In this chapter, we consider marketing channels, or channels of distribution; why they are important, and the major marketing decisions companies make in managing their channels. We then look at the task of supply chain management, or the "back end" of the distribution channel. Finally, we examine closely the business of retail, the most visible marketing channel of them all.

Marketing and Distribution Channels `LO1`

Producing a product or service and making it available to buyers requires building relationships not just with customers, but also with key suppliers "upstream" in the company's *supply chain,* and distributers and resellers who act as intermediaries to help move the product "downstream." Upstream from the company is the set of firms that supply the raw materials, components, parts, information, finances, and expertise needed to create a product or service. Marketers, however, have traditionally focused on the "downstream" side—the *marketing channels* (or *distribution channels*) that look toward the customer. Downstream marketing channel partners, such as wholesalers and retailers, form a vital connection between the firm and its customers.

Consider the many suppliers and distributors involved in the process of building and selling a car: from the makers of the tires, the engines, the windows, and every other part; to the movement of the finished vehicles on trucks and trains; to the neighbourhood car dealership that displays, markets, and sells the vehicle to a consumer. Viewed from beginning to end these chains and channels comprise a continually evolving *value delivery network.* A firm's **value delivery network** is made up of the company, suppliers, distributors, and ultimately customers who "partner" with each other to improve the performance of the entire system.

Value delivery network
The network made up of the company, suppliers, distributors, and ultimately customers who "partner" with each other to improve the performance of the entire system in delivering customer value.

What Is a Channel?

Few producers, whether they are tire manufacturers or farmers, sell their goods directly to the final users of their products. Instead, most use intermediaries to bring their products to market. They forge a **marketing channel (or distribution channel)**—a set of interdependent organizations that help make a product or service available for use or consumption by the consumer or business customer.

A company's channel decisions directly affect every other marketing decision. Pricing depends on whether the company works with national discount chains, uses high-quality specialty stores, or sells directly to consumers online. The firm's sales force and communications decisions depend on how much persuasion, training, motivation, and support its channel partners need. Whether a company develops or acquires certain new products may depend on how well those products fit the capabilities of its channel members.

Marketing channel (or distribution channel)
A set of interdependent organizations that help make a product or service available for use or consumption by the consumer or business customer.

Designing channels and choosing channel partners are strategic marketing decisions, made only after carefully studying the market and considering its opportunities. Enterprise Rent-A-Car, for example, looked at the saturated market of car rental companies servicing airports and decided to take a different approach:[2]

> With annual revenues of more than $14 billion and more than 65 000 employees (2800 in Canada), Enterprise Rent-a-Car is the largest car rental company in North America and, by

all estimates, the most profitable. How did Enterprise become such a dominating industry leader? The company might argue that it was through better prices or better marketing, but what contributed most to Enterprise taking the lead was an industry-changing, customer-driven distribution strategy. While competitors such as Hertz focused on serving travellers at airports, Enterprise developed a new distribution doorway to a large and untapped segment. It opened off-airport, neighbourhood locations that provided short-term car-replacement rentals for people whose cars were wrecked, stolen, or being serviced, or for people who simply wanted a different car for a short trip or a special occasion.

In many cases Enterprise's rental offices are located in residential neighbourhoods, close to target customers, which gives Enterprise a cost advantage—property rents are typically lower than airport neighbourhoods, and there are no airport taxes and fees. Enterprise branch managers develop relationships with local auto insurance adjusters, dealership sales and service personnel, and body shops and service garages, making Enterprise their preferred neighbourhood rental-car provider. Today, Enterprise has a virtual lock on the "home-city" market, but they're not resting on their laurels. The company is continually striving to improve customer convenience in all its locations. Many Enterprise locations in Canada now offer hybrid cars, and new self-serve touch-screen kiosks enable customers to skip the rental counter and initiate both reserved and walk-up transactions with just a valid driver's license and major credit card.

Exhibit 11.1 **Marketing channel decisions:** Enterprise's distribution strategy is to serve the home city market, rather than to focus on the crowded airport market.

Enterprise Holdings Inc.

Sometimes developing a marketing channel, especially in a new country, requires changing the brand name. For example, the Coastal Forest and Lumber Association, marketers of BC hemlock, a hardwood grown in abundance in that province, renamed their product Canada Tsunga for the Japanese market, and created a multi-million dollar marketing campaign to support the channel partners in that country. Marketers designed a new logo and created an advertising campaign to communicate the fact that Canada Tsunga was stronger than other hardwoods. The ads featured a well-known but comparatively light-weight Sumo wrestler named Mai-no-umi, and compared his qualities to that of the lumber.[3]

How Channel Partners Add Value

Producers use intermediaries because they reduce the amount of work that must be done to reach customers. For example, Figure 11.1A shows three manufacturers, which each use direct channels to reach three customers. This system requires nine different contacts. Figure 11.1B shows the three manufacturers working through one channel partner, which contacts the three customers. This system requires only six contacts.

From the economic system's point of view, the role of marketing intermediaries is to transform the assortments of products made by producers into the assortments wanted by consumers. Producers make narrow assortments of products in large quantities, but consumers want broad assortments of products in small quantities. Marketing channel members buy large quantities from many producers and break them down into the smaller quantities and broader assortments wanted by consumers.

FIGURE 11.1 How Adding a Distributor Reduces the Number of Channel Transactions

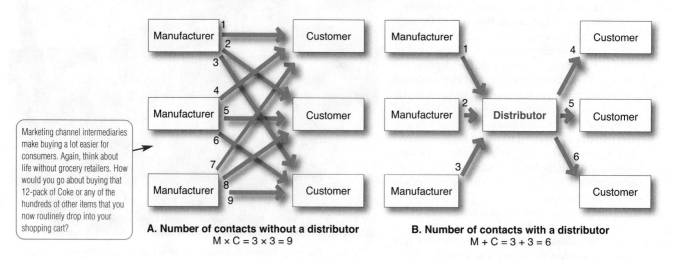

A. Number of contacts without a distributor
M × C = 3 × 3 = 9

B. Number of contacts with a distributor
M + C = 3 + 3 = 6

Marketing channel intermediaries make buying a lot easier for consumers. Again, think about life without grocery retailers. How would you go about buying that 12-pack of Coke or any of the hundreds of other items that you now routinely drop into your shopping cart?

In general, channel members add value by bridging the major time, place, and possession gaps that separate goods and services from those who would use them. These are some of the specific functions channel partners can perform:

- *Information gathering and distribution:* Channel partners such as retailers who are closer to the final customer have access to information the manufacturer might not have. Channel partners can collect market intelligence and communicate it back to the original producer.

- *Promotion at point of purchase:* National brand advertising is typically handled by the manufacturer, but promotions at point of purchase, such as locally-advertised sales, are handled by distributers and retailers.

- *Contact:* Channel members such as sales agents operating in the field and in local markets can find new customers.

- *Matching and arranging:* Channel partners often play a role in adapting the product to fit the buyer's needs, such as customizing the installation of kitchen cabinets. Channel members such as specialty retailers also display and arrange products to offer customers a choice.

- *Negotiation:* Channel partners such as brokers and agents negotiate price and terms of delivery so that the product can move from one channel member to another.

- *Physical distribution:* Trucking and other transportation companies act as channel members by transporting and storing products as they move through the channel.

- *Financing:* Companies such as Canadian Tire that offer store credit cards, and companies that sell large products such as cars, may have finance organizations as channel partners.

- *Risk taking:* Depending upon the partner arrangement, channel members may assume the risk of handling, transporting, and storing the product as it moves through the channel.

- *After-sales support:* Some products, such as electronics and automobiles, require after-sales support and servicing. These functions are typically performed by channel partners.

Associated Press

Exhibit 11.2 **Functions served by channel members:** Caterpillar's local dealers are the main point of contact with the customer and perform many other channel functions including matching the customer with the right product, negotiating terms, communicating information about Caterpillar to the customer (and collecting intelligence from the customers to report back to Caterpillar). They also handle the last leg of the physical distribution of the product, and they take care of all the after sales support.

The question is not *whether* these functions need to be performed—they must be—but rather *who* will perform them. Consider the many valuable functions served by the channel partners of heavy-equipment manufacturer Caterpillar, for example:

> Caterpillar produces innovative, high-quality products, yet the most important reason for Caterpillar's dominance is its value delivery network of outstanding independent dealers worldwide. Caterpillar and its dealers work as partners. According to a former Caterpillar CEO: "After the product leaves our door, the dealers take over. They are the ones on the front line. They're the ones who live with the product for its lifetime. They're the ones customers see." When a big piece of Caterpillar equipment breaks down, customers know that they can count on Caterpillar and its outstanding dealer network for support. Dealers play a vital role in almost every aspect of Caterpillar's operations, from product design and delivery to product service and support.
>
> Caterpillar equipment is currently being used on major construction sites around the world, including the construction of the world's third largest hydroelectric dam in Brazil, an iron ore mine in Sierra Leone, and almost a million kilometres of new roads in China. There's just no way the company could cover that kind of territory alone! As a result of its channel partnerships, Caterpillar dominates the world's markets for heavy construction, mining, and logging equipment.[4]

We've learned about one type of channel partner, the independent dealer, now let's look at what other types of businesses and organizations can act as channel partners in a company's supply chain and distribution channels.

Types of Channel Partners

Channel partners are businesses that are owned and operated independently from the manufacturer, and who are contracted by the manufacturer to perform a specific function in the movement of the product. The major types of channel partners are *retailers*, *wholesalers*, *drop shippers*, *rack jobbers*, *brokers*, and *agents*.

Retailers **Retailing** is the business of selling products and services directly to consumers for their personal use. It includes all the activities involved in running the business, such

Retailing
The business of selling goods or services to consumers for their personal use.

Retailer
A business that primarily sells products and services to consumers.

as operating and managing a bricks-and-mortar location and/or a website; selecting, purchasing, and displaying merchandise; and marketing and sales. Though some wholesalers and manufacturers engage in some retailing, either by having a storefront at their location, or by opening their doors to the public on occasion, **retailers** are businesses whose sales come primarily from retailing.

Retail is one of the most important, and certainly the most visible, of marketing channels. Every store that is open to the public, from your corner convenience store to that big box store in the suburbs, is a retailer, but so is your local bank branch, your regular gas station, and your favourite restaurant or bar. Because retail is such an important and complex marketing channel, we will look at it in more detail at the end of this section on marketing channels.

Wholesaling
All activities involved in selling goods and services to those buying for resale or business use.

Wholesalers
Companies whose primary business is wholesaling.

Wholesalers   **Wholesaling** includes all activities involved in selling goods and services to those buying for resale or business use. **Wholesalers** are companies that buy from producers and sell to retailers, business customers, and other wholesalers. In Canada, wholesaling contributes nearly $60 billion to the economy every year.[5] Because wholesalers do not sell directly to consumers, you may never have heard of some of the largest and most important wholesalers like Grainger, a company with more than 1.8 million business and institutional customers around the world.[6]

> Grainger may be the biggest market leader you've never heard of. It's a $7.2 billion business with 18 500 employees that wholesales and distributes maintenance, repair, and operating (MRO) products such as pumps, motors, hand tools, and janitorial supplies. These products are purchased by Grainger from its "upstream" supply chain network of more than 3000 vendors, then resold "downstream" to its more than two million customers in 157 countries. Most of Grainger's customers are in the healthcare, manufacturing, government, and hospitality industries, and some of their more noteworthy customers include General Motors, Honeywell, the Campbell Soup company, and the US Postal Service.
>
> Grainger's Canadian subsidiary, Acklands-Grainger, manages distribution centres in Vancouver, Dartmouth, Edmonton, Winnipeg, Richmond Hill, and Saskatoon. In addition, National Technical Service Centres provide customers with expert product knowledge and keep up with the new and expanding product lines. This very large wholesaler manages a highly integrated value-delivery network which includes its 3000 vendors; local branches with showrooms that serve customers directly; regional warehouses that ship customer orders and are typically smaller than 20 000 square feet; much larger distribution centres that receive inventory from suppliers, replenish the branch network and ship orders to customers; and a central logistics system that keeps it all running smoothly.

Wholesalers like Grainger are also referred to as *merchant wholesalers* and *distributors* because they purchase and take possession of the products, then physically distribute them to their customer. A wholesaler who takes possession of inventory also assumes the risk (of theft, damage, spoilage) that goes with it.

Drop Shippers and Rack Jobbers   There are other types of intermediaries who do not take possession of merchandise and who instead perform very specific functions in the distribution channel.

Drop shipping refers to a process in which the intermediary takes the order from the

© Randy Duchaine / Alamy

Exhibit 11.3 Wholesaling: Wholesalers such as Grainger and Acklands-Grainger distribute maintenance, repairs, and operating (MRO) products such as pumps, motors, hand tools, and janitorial supplies to thousands of business and industrial customers around the world.

customer, passes the order to a manufacturer or wholesaler, who then ships the item directly to the customer. Some retailers engage in drop shipping at times, especially for large items that are not kept in stock at each store location. For example, if a consumer orders a mattress set from Sears (whether online, over the phone, or in the store), the Sears employee takes the payment and delivery information, then passes it to the Sears distribution centre. From there it is drop shipped to the customer. Smaller retailers might also engage in drop shipping if they receive a large order from a customer that exceeds the stock they have on hand.

There are also businesses that never keep inventory or handle the product, and so are full time **drop shippers**. Examples of this type of business are companies that sell customized clothing and other small items like key chains and mouse pads to groups such as minor-league sports teams and small businesses. Many of these vendors do not have physical storefronts but operate only online; they do not manufacture the goods they sell, but rather they choose from a network of suppliers to produce the customer's order. When Amazon.com began operations, they only drop shipped books from the publisher to the consumer. Today, they still drop ship certain titles, but maintain warehouses to handle more popular and frequently ordered books. Because drop shippers take payment from the customer (i.e., sell) and later pay the supplier for the order (i.e., buy), they are considered wholesalers.

Another type of wholesaler is the **rack jobber**. Rack jobbers buy merchandise and then set up "rack" displays inside retail stores, where the merchandise is sold to customers. Rack jobbers typically serve grocery and drug retailers, mostly in non-food items. They set up point-of-purchase displays, keep inventory records, and retain ownership of the goods until they are sold. The consumer who purchases an item from the display pays at the retailer's checkout, and later, the rack jobber bills the retailer for the items that were sold.

Brokers Brokers differ from merchant wholesalers in two ways: They do not take title to goods, and they perform only a few functions. Like merchant wholesalers, they generally specialize by product line or customer type. A **broker** brings buyers and sellers together and assists in negotiation, but does not carry inventory, get involved in financing, or assume risk. Think of a stock broker, who buys stocks on behalf of a client and earns a commission.

Agents Agents are similar to brokers in that they perform only a few functions and do not take title to goods, but while a broker makes deals with many different buyers and sellers, an **agent** typically has a more permanent relationship representing either one or the other. A real estate agent, for example, typically represents the seller of a home, and performs functions such as taking pictures, listing it on the MLS, producing marketing support materials, and advising the seller about how best to attract a buyer.

Manufacturers' agents are a common type of agent, typically contracted by smaller manufacturers who do not have their own sales staff. The agent sells the manufacturer's goods to buyers and receives a commission from the manufacturer.

Advertising agencies are another type of agent, and valuable members of the marketing channel. They provide marketing communications services such as designing and producing advertisements, and buying the media (television, radio, magazines, Internet) in which to run them.

Traditionally, advertising agencies refer to their upstream channel partners as clients, but that may be changing. The CEO of 72andSunny, *Advertising Age* magazine's 2013 Agency of the Year, recently directed his employees to stop using the word client and to instead refer to them by name, or as partners. He said, "By removing the label, we have found it easier to empathize with our partners and their situations."[7] Having an

Drop shipper
An intermediary who takes orders and payment from the customer, then arranges to have the merchandise shipped to the customer directly from the supplier.

Rack jobber
A wholesaler who buys merchandise and re-sells it on "racks" inside a retail store, in partnership with the retailer.

Broker
A wholesaler who does not take title to goods and whose function is to bring buyers and sellers together and assist in negotiation.

Agent
A representative, either of a buyer or a seller, who performs only a few functions and does not take title to goods.

© Athol Pictures / Alamy

Exhibit 11.4 **Advertising agencies as channel partners:** Sun Life is a household name in Canada, but when they moved into the United States they needed a marketing-communications partner who understood the American market. Today, the company's name is on the Miami stadium that is home to the Dolphins.

advertising agency as marketing channel partner can help to open doors when entering a new market, as Sun Life Financial learned:[8]

> Sun Life Financial is a household name in Canada, but when they expanded into the United States they knew they'd need a strong marketing-communications partner to help them gain recognition and respect in that fiercely competitive market. The company had already established a channel of distribution in the United States, but had been hearing that the job of those sales representatives was very difficult. "It's one thing," they said, "to explain very complex financial products and services to consumers. It's quite another to have to explain who Sun Life is." So Sun Life went shopping for an agency partner and ultimately chose The Martin Agency.
>
> Martin is responsible for creating the Geico gecko, and for the great advertising slogan, "Virginia is for Lovers." They are based in Richmond, Virginia, and that's part of the reason why Sun Life chose them. Many large agencies are located in New York or Chicago, which gives them something of a skewed view of what the average American consumer is really like. As Martin's senior vice-president of marketing communications explains, "I remember when we were in a review for Saab, we were the only agency whose employees drove to work every day. When we were in the review for Walmart, we were the only agency with Walmarts in our town. There are no Walmarts in Manhattan." Martin won the accounts.
>
> Martin was able to create a successful advertising campaign that "taught" Americans who Sun Life was by using Canadian images that Americans recognize. In one television commercial, for example, representatives of Sun Life try to persuade Cirque de Soleil to change its name to Cirque de Sun Life.

We've seen how some of the major types of channel members provide valuable services in the movement of goods and associated services from producers to final customers, but there are many other companies and organizations that can play a role in a well designed channel. We'll look at the "back end" or "upstream" members, the channel partners in the supply chain, later in this chapter.

Organization and Management of Channels LO2

Marketing channels don't happen by themselves, rather, they must be built and designed to meet strategic business goals. Many decisions about the organization of the channel, and the number and types of channel members, must be made.

Direct vs. Indirect Channels   The number of levels of the channel, or number of channel members who function as intermediaries between the producer and the consumer, constitutes the *length* of a channel. The shortest possible channel is a channel with no intermediaries—this is referred to as a *direct marketing channel*, where the producer of the goods sells directly to the final customer. Most channels, however, have one or more intermediaries and therefore are *indirect marketing channels*.

While it may seem at first glance that companies like Mary Kay, Avon, and The Pampered Chef are direct marketing channels, they are, in fact, more complex than that. Mary Kay and The Pampered Chef sell their products through home parties, which are organized by independent representatives acting as an agent. Avon and other marketers sell products in a similar manner, or door-to-door, but also offer online sales which truly are a direct channel—unless, of course, the products are drop shipped. Insurance companies and other service providers often sell their services via the telephone, and that means either an inside sales staff or, more likely, a third-party telephone-marketing company—another channel partner.

In reality, there are very few companies that sell directly to customers without the assistance of any intermediaries or channel partners.

Channel Conflict   Each channel member plays an important role in the marketing channel, but sometimes disagreements over goals, roles, and rewards among channel members can create what is known as **channel conflict**. Take the distribution and marketing of cellphones, for example. A mobile phone manufacturer like BlackBerry wants their product distributed as widely as possible, so as to end up in the hands of as many consumers as possible. However, their distributors, telecommunications companies such as Rogers, Bell, and TELUS, see things a little differently: they want to distribute as many new devices as possible to their customers, but they don't favour one manufacturer over another, which can lead to channel conflict among those manufacturers.

Companies that market and sell their products through bricks-and-mortar and online channels are especially susceptible to channel conflict. Toy marketer Mattel, for example, sells through thousands of retailers and also online at Shop.Mattel.com, Fisher-Price.com, MattyCollector.com, BarbieCollector.com and HotWheelsCollectors. com. The sites target different segments of the toy-buying population, and cater to serious aficionados of those brands, many of whom subscribe to receive certain new Mattel toys the day they become available. But according to Mike Young, director of ecommerce for Mattel, the main goal of the sites isn't necessarily to generate revenue. Mattel avoids channel conflict with retailers by not competing online on the basis of price.[9]

In extreme situations, channel conflict can result in *disintermediation*.

Disintermediation   *Disintermediation* is an economics term that became popular with the advent of the Internet and the new types of online businesses that came with it. As the Internet developed as a channel of distribution, some traditional businesses which had once held an important role in the channel became, unfortunately, unnecessary. The classic example of **disintermediation** is online travel sites such as Travelocity that allowed consumers to book their own travel arrangements, thus rendering the neighbourhood travel agent redundant. Traditional travel agencies were said to have been disintermediated, or cut out of the channel.

The latest example of an online-only business that successfully changed a traditional distribution model is Netflix, which created a subscription business that distributed movies and TV series on DVD to consumers via the mail, then later evolved into online-only distribution via streaming video. Netflix disintermediated bricks-and-mortar movie rental retailers such as Blockbuster, which once could be found in every neighbourhood and have now virtually disappeared.

The taxi business is also facing threats from new technology, and traditional local taxi cab companies might very well one day be disintermediated. Several startups in recent years have created smartphone apps that make it easy for customers to order a taxi to their location, bypassing the need to call the taxi company's dispatcher. One such app, Uber, found itself going up against a taxi industry that is willing to fight to maintain its control. Uber ceased its taxi operations in New York following

Channel conflict
Disagreement among marketing channel members over goals, roles, and rewards.

Disintermediation
The cutting out of marketing channel intermediaries by product or service producers, or the displacement of traditional resellers by radical new types of intermediaries.

BROWN ADRIAN/SIPA/Newscom

Exhibit 11.5 **Channel conflict:** BlackBerry distributes its devices not just through Rogers, but through all the major telecommunications companies. They must carefully manage their pricing and promotion so as not to cause conflict among channel members.

Exhibit 11.6 **Disintermediation?** Not if Beck Taxi has its way. The company offers its own smartphone app.

Vertical marketing system (VMS)

A distribution channel structure in which producers, wholesalers, and retailers act as a unified system. One channel member owns the others, has contracts with them, or has so much power that they all co-operate.

Corporate VMS

A vertical marketing system that combines successive stages of production and distribution under single ownership—channel leadership is established through common ownership.

opposition from the city's Taxi & Limousine commission, and in Toronto the company discovered it must become a licensed taxi brokerage in order to operate there. Uber feels they shouldn't be regulated in this manner because they're not the ones driving the cars or running the taxi company, but the City of Toronto says Uber is refusing to follow the bylaws. Meanwhile Beck Taxi, the largest taxi operator in Toronto, doesn't seem to be too concerned about the potential threat—it offers its own smartphone app.[10]

Vertical Marketing Systems In traditional, or conventional, distribution systems one producer distributes products through one wholesaler or distributer, and from there to several or many retailers. Each of the businesses in the process is independently owned and is seeking to maximize its own profits, perhaps even at the expense of the others. No channel member has much control over the other members, and no formal means exists for assigning roles and resolving channel conflict.

In contrast, a **vertical marketing system (VMS)** consists of producers, wholesalers, and retailers acting as a unified system. One channel member owns the others, has contracts with them, or wields so much power that they must all co-operate. The VMS can be dominated by the producer, wholesaler, or retailer. Three types of VMSs are *corporate*, *administered*, and *contractual*.

A **corporate VMS** integrates successive stages of production and distribution under single ownership. Coordination and conflict management are attained through regular organizational channels. For example, George Weston Limited is a corporation that owns and operates Weston Foods and Loblaw Companies Limited. Weston Foods produces and distributes baked goods under the brands Weston, Wonder, Colonial Cookies, and ACE Bakery. Their largest retail customer is Loblaws, which owns more than 1000 retail grocery stores operating under 22 different banners including Real Canadian Superstore, No Frills, Fortinos, Zehrs, Provigo, Dominion, and Wholesale Club. It also owns many well-known food brands which it produces under contract and distributes through its retail stores: President's Choice, Joe Fresh, Blue Menu, and The Decadent.

Another example of a vertical marketing system is popular fashion brand Zara, a prototype "fast fashion" house that owes its success to the fact that it controls every member of its marketing and distribution channel:[11]

> Fashion retailer Zara is known for cheap chic—designs that resemble those of big-name fashion houses but at moderate prices. It's a new breed of retailer that responds to the latest fashion trends quickly and nimbly, thanks to its cutting-edge distribution system and its vertical marketing strategy. Zara controls all phases of its supply chain, marketing channel, and distribution channel, and that allows the company to take a new fashion concept through design, manufacturing, and store-shelf placement in as little as two weeks.
>
> How can they move so quickly? One reason is the value of timely information provided by Zara's store managers, who use handheld computers to report in real time what's selling and what's not. They talk with customers to learn what they're looking for but not yet finding. At the same time, Zara trend-seekers roam fashion shows in Paris and concerts

in Tokyo, looking for young people who might be wearing something new or different. When they find something, they notify company headquarters in tiny La Coruña, Spain, and the company's team of 300 designers conjures up a version of the new item.

Once the designers have done their work, production begins. But rather than relying on a hodgepodge of slow-moving suppliers in Asia, as most competitors do, Zara makes 40 percent of its own fabrics and produces more than half of its own clothes. Even farmed-out manufacturing goes primarily to local contractors. Almost all clothes sold in Zara's stores worldwide are made quickly and efficiently at or near company headquarters in the remote northwest corner of Spain. Finished goods then feed into Zara's modern, highly automated distribution centres, which can sort, pack, label, and allocate up to 80 000 items an hour, readying them for direct shipment to Zara stores around the world. Now that's fast!

Exhibit 11.7 **Corporate vertical marketing system:** Zara either owns or controls most of its distribution system, from manufacturing through to retailing.

© Caro / Alamy

There are many such corporate VMSs, though the names of the overseeing corporations may not be ones we recognize. You've probably never heard of an Italian company called Luxottica, for example, but you're likely familiar with its well-known sunglasses brands, Ray-Ban and Oakley. Luxottica also produces eyewear under license for brands such as Polo Ralph Lauren, Dolce & Gabbana, Prada, Versace, and Bulgari. It then sells these brands through two of the world's largest optical chains, LensCrafters and Sunglass Hut, which it also owns.

In an **administered VMS**, leadership is assumed not through common ownership or contractual ties, but through the size and power of one or a few dominant channel members. Manufacturers of a top brand can obtain strong trade co-operation and support from resellers. For example, General Electric, Procter & Gamble, and Kraft can command unusual co-operation from retailers regarding displays, shelf space, promotions, and price policies. In turn, large retailers can exert strong influence on the many manufacturers that supply the products they sell.

The third type of vertical marketing system is the **contractual VMS**, which consists of independent firms at different levels of production and distribution who work together under contract. The companies that band together in such a system do so to achieve economies of scale and other efficiencies that are greater than if each business were to operate on its own. The most common type of contractual vertical marketing system is the franchise organization.

Administered VMS
A vertical marketing system that coordinates successive stages of production and distribution, not through common ownership or contractual ties, but through the size and power of one of the parties.

Contractual VMS
A vertical marketing system in which independent firms at different levels of production and distribution work together under contract.

Franchise Organizations A franchise organization is a special type of contractual vertical marketing system, and perhaps the one most familiar to us as consumers. A *franchise* is a retailer or service provider that operates under licence using another firm's proven, successful business model. McDonald's, for example, began as one restaurant in 1940, but was the first restaurant to serve what we now call fast food. It was a new business model, and it became successful, and therefore franchisable. In terms of marketing and distribution, the *franchisor* is the corporation that owns the rights to the brand and the business model, and who allows independent business owners called *franchisees* to use their trademark. The franchisor dictates and controls the look and feel of the franchisee's operation, and also typically supplies the franchisee with the necessary ingredients

Franchise organization
A marketing system that links several stages in the production and distribution process, and controls operations from a central head office.

to run the franchise. Together the franchisor and franchisees comprise the **franchise organization**, a marketing system that links several stages in the production and distribution process, and controls operations from a central head office.

There are three types of franchises. The first type is the *manufacturer-sponsored retailer franchise system*—for example, Ford and its network of independent franchised dealers. The second type is the *manufacturer-sponsored wholesaler franchise system*—Coca-Cola licenses bottlers (wholesalers) in various markets who buy Coca-Cola syrup concentrate and then bottle and sell the finished product to retailers in local markets.

The third type is the *service-firm sponsored retailer franchise system*—for example, Edmonton-based Boston Pizza, a Canadian owned and operated restaurant and sports bar chain with over 340 locations from coast to coast and annual sales in excess of $853 million. Boston Pizza franchisees run their own local restaurant and pay a royalty of seven percent on gross food sales to the corporation. Once a franchisee's application is approved, decisions must be made, and agreements entered into, between the parties, for example, the specific location of the new franchise must be selected, and the land or building lease secured. There are also contractual agreements governing the design of the interior, the use of the Boston Pizza logo, and a co-op fund to pay for national advertising.[12]

Franchising is a common way for people who want to run their own businesses to do so, and in Canada, franchise owners have formed a trade association called the Canadian Franchise Association (CFA) to assist franchisees. They offer events, programs, and publications to help educate Canadians about how to get into franchising, how to choose a franchise, and what franchise opportunities are available. The CFA publishes *Franchise-Canada* magazine, a bi-monthly consumer publication for entrepreneurs interested in acquiring a franchise.

Horizontal Marketing Systems   Another type of co-operative marketing system is the **horizontal marketing system**, in which two or more companies that operate at the same channel level join together to follow a new marketing opportunity. By working together, companies can combine their financial, production, or marketing resources to accomplish more than any one company could alone.

Horizontal marketing system
An arrangement in which two or more companies that operate at the same channel level join together to follow a new marketing opportunity.

Companies in a horizontal marketing system might join forces with competitors or non-competitors. They might work with each other on a temporary or permanent basis, or they may create a separate company. For example, Tim Hortons set up express versions of their stores at Esso gas stations so commuters can fill up and get a coffee on the way to work without making two stops. Similarly, many Home Depot stores in Canada have a self-contained Subway restaurant. Each business is run by its own corporate management, but the companies join forces to reach the same market—hungry shoppers.

Exhibit 11.8 **Franchise:** Boston Pizza is one of Canada's largest and most successful franchise operations.

The Star Alliance is an example of companies that compete in the same industry, air travel, and co-operate in a marketing system that allows frequent fliers of one of the member airlines to book travel on another member's planes. More than 25 airlines, including Air Canada, Lufthansa, and United, are members of the Star Alliance.

Multichannel (Hybrid) Distribution Systems   We have seen that there are many different types of distribution systems a company can use to move its products from their point of origin to the hands of the consumer or business customer, but companies are not restricted to choosing one or the other.

© Helen Sessions / Alamy

With so many channel opportunities available, both online and offline, many companies opt for a **multichannel or hybrid distribution system**. This form of multichannel marketing occurs when a single firm sets up two or more marketing channels to reach one or more market segments.

Some of the examples we've already looked at are, in fact, multichannel distribution systems. Many fashion brands and retailers such as Zara sell their merchandise online as well as through their traditional retail distribution channel. A business-to-business marketer may operate a channel that includes wholesalers and distributors, but may also sell directly through its own sales force.

These days, almost every large company and many small ones distribute through multiple channels. For example, John Deere sells its familiar green and yellow lawn and garden tractors, mowers, and outdoor power products to consumers and commercial users through several channels, including John Deere retailers, Lowe's home improvement stores, independent equipment retailers in its smaller markets (such as Green Diamond Equipment Ltd. in Nova Scotia), and online. It sells and services its tractors, combines, planters, and other agricultural equipment through its premium John Deere dealer network. And it sells large construction and forestry equipment through selected large, full-service John Deer dealers and their sales forces.

Multichannel distribution systems offer many advantages to companies facing large and complex markets. With each new channel, the company expands its sales and market coverage and gains opportunities to tailor its products and services to the specific needs of diverse customer segments. But such multichannel systems are harder to control, and they generate conflict as more channels compete for customers and sales.

Distribution Strategy

As we have seen, there are many marketing management decisions involved in creating channels of distribution, and in the ongoing organization and management of them. We now consider the decisions a marketer must make not just about *where* and *how* to distribute its products, but *in how many places*. At first glance it may seem like all marketers would wish to distribute their products in as many locations as possible—*intensive* distribution—but that's not always the best strategy. Sometimes it's better to choose *selective* or even *exclusive* distribution.

Intensive Distribution   Marketers of everyday convenience products such as soft drinks and snack foods typically choose **intensive distribution**, a strategy in which they stock their products in as many outlets as possible. The types of products found in convenience stores are often impulse purchases, and so the marketing strategy is to make them available where and when consumers want them. Other necessities such as toothpaste and toilet paper are often purchased hastily when the consumer has just run out of them, and so marketers like

Multichannel (hybrid) distribution system

A distribution system in which a single firm sets up two or more marketing channels to reach one or more market segments.

Intensive distribution

A marketing strategy in which the product is stocked in as many outlets as possible.

Courtesy of Lowes

Exhibit 11.9 Multichannel (or hybrid) distribution system: John Deere doesn't just use one channel to distribute its tractors and mowers; it uses many different channels, including retail, independent dealers, and a sales force.

Kimberly-Clark choose intensive distribution to make their products available at just about every store the consumer might run to in a shopping emergency.

Selective Distribution   Selective distribution is a marketing strategy typically chosen by makers of brand name appliances, furniture, and electronics. In **selective distribution** the marketer selects a set of retailers that specialize in their product category. For example, Whirlpool and General Electric sell their major appliances at Sears and other large department stores, and Le Creuset sells its cookware through specialty stores such as Williams-Sonoma, William Ashley, and independent retailers of fine cookware.

Often, the selection of which retailers to use as channel partners is made so as to reflect the status of the brand. For example, midmarket mattress brands such as Sealy and Serta are distributed through Leon's (a furniture retailer) and Sleep Country (a mattress specialty store), but more upscale mattress brands such as Hypnos (found in the homes of royalty and celebrities) are only available in very high-end specialty stores such as The Bedroom Shoppe in Calgary. Similarly, high quality brands such as the Sony Bravia are distributed at high-end electronics retailers but would not be found at discount retailers, and designer clothing labels such as Stella McCartney and Burberry are available at retailers such as Holt Renfrew but would never be found in a store like Giant Tiger.

Exclusive Distribution   Exclusive distribution is a deliberate marketing strategy chosen by brands that wish to associate themselves with an air of, well, exclusivity. It is usually associated with luxury brands such as Rolex and Tiffany, which give exclusive rights to carry their products in a particular region to one retailer, but it is also the distribution strategy employed by IKEA. In **exclusive distribution** the marketer gives the rights to distribute its products to only one retailer, or to only one retailer in a particular geographic territory. Sleep Number beds, for example, are available exclusively at Radisson Hotels and Resorts; Breville designer toasters are available exclusively at The Bay; and the Cindy Crawford line of home furnishings is available exclusively at The Brick.

Another form of exclusive distribution is when the manufacturer of a line of products makes those products available only though its own retail channels, whether they be in stores, online, or through catalogues. (It's also a vertical marketing system.) For example Veritas Tools of Ottawa is a world leader in woodworking tool design and is the manufacturing arm of retailer Lee Valley Tools. The company distributes its 250 products exclusively through its own outlets:[13]

Selective distribution
A distribution strategy in which the marketer selects a set of retailers that specialize in their product category.

Exclusive distribution
A distribution strategy in which the marketer gives the rights to distribute its products to only one retailer, or to only one retailer in a particular geographic territory.

Exhibit 11.10 **Exclusive distribution:** Lee Valley is the exclusive distributor of Veritas Tools of Ottawa.

Lee Valley Tools is a family business founded in Ottawa in 1978 by Leonard Lee. It manufactures many of its high quality woodworking and gardening tools through its own manufacturing arm, Veritas. It prides itself on its high level of customer satisfaction, and customers can return any product for a full refund within three months of purchase. To ensure that its customers are served by people with a high level of knowledge about its products, and given good advice about products and their uses, the company sells through its 13 retail stores located across Canada and through its catalogues and website. Such exclusive distribution enables it to promise to "treat every customer like a friend." Close customer relationships have helped the company better understand customer needs and get ideas about how to improve its tools or design new tools. In fact, in 1998, it developed a line of tools for surgeons after it discovered that one plastic surgeon, Michael Bell, was using Lee Valley tools in his practice.

Now that we've learned about channels of distribution, channel partners, and channel strategy, let's look more closely at the most visible channel of distribution for consumer products: retail.

Retailing LO3

As we have already learned, retailing is the business of selling products and services directly to consumers for their personal use. Retailers are important channel partners for manufacturers of every consumer product from breath mints to automobiles, and, of course, we as consumers deal with them every day. The business of retail is a major contributor to our economy, and one of the most visible aspects of marketing. For that reason, it's worth examining in more detail.

Retail in Canada

In Canada, jobs in retail trade account for the largest labour force segment in the country and in most of the provinces. Retailing provides more than 2.1 million jobs Canadawide, which is 11.5 percent of the total labour force.

All together Canadian retailers generate more than $450 billion in sales each year. The largest sector is food and beverages retailers, contributing more than $104 billion to our economy. The automotive sector, which includes new car dealerships, used car dealerships, and retailers that sell parts, supplies, and tires, is almost as large ($100 billion). Next is supermarkets and other grocery (except convenience) stores ($74 billion), followed by gasoline stations ($58 billion), general merchandise stores ($56 billion), health and personal care ($33 billion), and building and gardening supplies ($27 billion).[14] Each year the Retail Council of Canada compiles monthly retail sales across all sectors, and produces a pie chart that shows at a glance the breakdown of retail in Canada (see Figure 11.2).

FIGURE 11.2 Annual Summary of Retail Sales in Canada, 2012

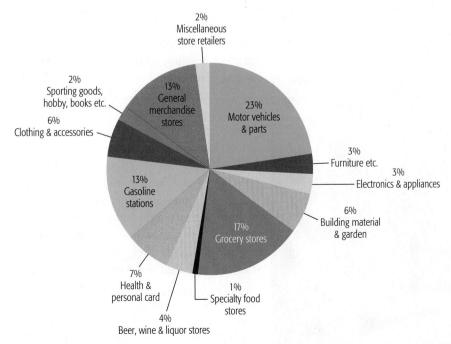

Source: Pie chart published in Retail Council of Canada's Retail Fast Facts Report - December 2012.

Because it is such a large industry, employs so many people, and is therefore so important to our economy, Statistics Canada publishes detailed monthly reports on the state of retail in Canada. Each report includes the total retail sales for that month, whether sales rose or declined, and by how much. It then goes into great detail about each sector. This is just a sample: "Sales at motor vehicle and parts dealers rose 1.8 percent in November. New car dealers (+1.6 percent) led the increase, rising for a sixth straight month. Gains were also reported in the 'other motor vehicle dealers' industry (+3.9 percent) and used car dealers (+3.9 percent). Automotive parts, accessories, and tire stores declined 0.6 percent, partially offsetting the gain in October."[15]

Differences between the United States and Canada   Walmart is one of the most popular retailers in Canada, and every mall includes retail brands we know originate in the United States. But the Canadian consumer is very different from the typical American, and so retailers must learn to adapt. Canadians tend to take a more balanced approach when choosing where to shop, and we don't make lists as often as Americans do. We focus less on price, more on convenience, assortment, and rewards programs. We pay closer attention to in-store displays and are more likely to be influenced by them. "There are vast differences between Canadian and US ethnographic and retailer landscapes. What works in the United States doesn't necessarily work in Canada. The research shows that we Canadians need to be engaged both by brands and by channel in our own unique ways," says Molly Spinak, president of Quadrant Marketing.[16]

One of those differences is our attitude toward layaway, a rather old-fashioned retail practice that was popular before the days of credit cards. Consumers who couldn't afford to pay the full price of an item they wanted could "lay it away" or put it on hold, and pay for it in instalments. After the recent American credit crunch, layaway was reinstituted by retailers like Sears, to make it possible for consumers to get that new refrigerator if they needed it. The practice was briefly attempted in Canadian Sears stores during the Christmas shopping season, but there were no takers. Instead, Sears offered an interest-free, equal-billing plan to customers with a Sears card.[17]

Canadian consumers' grocery shopping habits have also changed radically in the last ten years, in part because of their increased knowledge. Food-related television programs are so popular there's a channel devoted to airing them 24 hours a day, and of course anyone thinking about what to prepare for tonight's dinner has an endless source of ideas available to them on the Internet. Gone are the days when big box grocery retailers controlled our shopping baskets with items at their convenience. Consumers want more, and today they are finding it at specialty "foodie" stores and ethnic retailers.

Which brings us to perhaps the biggest difference between Canadian and American shoppers: our ethnic makeup. The largest visible ethnic group in Canada today, and the one that's growing the fastest, is Canadians of South Asian descent. Walmart Canada took notice, and launched a fashion line called Bollywood Signature:[18]

Retailers across Canada are pursuing multicultural markets directly with products designed to appeal to their tastes. Walmart Canada introduced its Bollywood Signature line of traditional women's wear by hosting a fashion show at a Brampton, Ontario, store.

Exhibit 11.11 Walmart held a fashion show in Brampton to announce its new Bollywood Signature line of clothing for men and women.

© Visage / Alamy

Women in large Canadian cities can now shop at Walmart for a Salwar Kameez, a traditional Indian three-piece suit that consists of pyjama-like trousers, a long shirt or tunic and a matching scarf. The retailer offers nine different styles, all priced to sell for less than $80. The clothing line is made by Ranka, a family-run company owned by Canadians of Indian descent, and based in Markham, Ontario.

Clearly, Walmart is reaching out to its multicultural customers, and so far the response has been favourable. One customer in Surrey, British Columbia, said, "I think it's wonderful. It's about time. Vancouver is a multicultural city and we're all from different backgrounds. What better place than Walmart to bring it to."

In another retail area, food service, the United States has been in decline for the past decade while in Canada it has grown 2 percent during that same period. Our more stable economy has American chain restaurants eyeing us greedily. One of the first to cross our border was Panera Bread, known for its fresh ingredients and bakery goods, which grew from 242 locations and $200 million in revenue in 2000 to more than 1500 locations and revenues of $1.82 billion in 2013. Other entrants into the Canadian market in the last few years have been Chipotle Mexican Grill, Smashburger, Buffalo Wild Wings, P.F. Chang's, Carl's Jr., and Five Guys. Though most of these offer burgers and fast foods, retail experts believe the next invasion will be from the "fast casual" chains, the ones that offer a slightly fancier décor, better food, and higher prices.[19]

And while American retailers are entering the Canadian market, Canadian retailers are going global. Lululemon is less than 20 years old but is already thriving in the United States, New Zealand, Australia, China, and the UK. Loblaw's Joe Fresh apparel brand recently opened four stores in the United States, and Tim Hortons has plans to be a global brand by 2015. The iconic coffee brand already has 290 self-serve kiosks in convenience stores in England and Ireland, and a number of locations in the United States including on military bases and at Fort Knox.

Financial analysts believe this is the right move. Says one, "I think it's that Canada has a finite size and if you have a company that's growing and doing well, eventually you have to decide whether you're going to leap over the border." Though it may be comfortable for Canadian and American retailers to test the new market waters in their neighbouring countries, their ultimate goal is the young, emerging, high-growth markets in Asia and South America.[20]

Types of Retailers

Retailers can be classified by industry. For example Statistics Canada uses the following classifications: motor vehicles and parts dealers; furniture and home furnishings stores; electronics and appliance stores; building material and garden equipment and supplies dealers; food and beverage stores; health and personal care stores; gasoline stations; clothing and clothing accessories stores; sporting goods, hobby, book and music stores; and general merchandise stores (including department stores).

Retailers can also be classified by the level of service they offer. Convenience stores and discount stores are typically *self-serve retailers*, which allow customers to perform their own locate-compare-select process to save time or money. Today most gas stations are self-serve, though some still offer limited service. *Limited-service retailers*, such as Home Depot, Canadian Tire, and Best Buy provide some sales assistance because they carry products that often require the customer to seek expert advice and information. In *full-service retailers*, salespeople assist customers in every phase of the shopping process. Full-service retailers are typically those that serve a higher end market (Holt Renfrew), or that sell luxury goods (jewellery stores), or that sell specialty items such as expensive cookware or wedding dresses.

Exhibit 11.12 **Retailer classification by price:** Warehouse clubs such as Costco are a type of retailer defined by their relative prices.

Another way to define retailers is by the breadth and depth of their product lines. *Specialty stores*, for example, carry narrow product lines with deep assortments within those lines. Shoe stores, women's clothing stores, toy stores, and electronics stores are all specialty stores. In contrast, *department stores* carry a wide variety of product lines, organized into shoe, clothing, toy, and electronics departments. *Supermarkets* carry a wide assortment of food and grocery products. *General merchandise* stores such as Walmart and Target, and even some drug stores, also sell food, but offer a much narrower selection. *Convenience stores* carry a small selection of high-turnover convenience goods, while *superstores* are much larger than regular supermarkets and offer a large assortment of routinely purchased food products, non-food items, and services. Very large specialty stores that carry thousands of products in a particular category, such as Home Depot and Best Buy, are sometimes referred to as *category killers* or *big box stores*. For some retailers the product line they offer is actually a service. Hotels, banks, airlines, movie theatres, and restaurants are *service retailers*.

Retailers can also be classified according to the prices they charge. *Discount stores* such as Giant Tiger and Dollarama sell standard merchandise at lower prices by accepting lower margins and selling higher volume. *Off-price retailers* such as Winners and Marshall's buy end-of-season or overstock goods at less than regular wholesale prices and charge lower prices for brand name merchandise, although they offer a very limited selection. *Factory outlets* are manufacturer-owned and operated stores by firms such as J. Crew, Gap, and Levi Strauss, and are usually grouped together in malls. And *warehouse clubs* such as Costco operate in huge, warehouse-like facilities and offer few frills. Customers themselves must wrestle furniture, heavy appliances, and other large items to the checkout line. Warehouse clubs make no home deliveries and often accept no credit cards; however, they do offer ultralow prices and surprise deals on selected branded merchandise.

It's important to recognize that all these types of retailers are just the ones we're most familiar with today. But the retail landscape is constantly changing, and all retailers must be aware of the latest trends and technology in retailing.

Trends and Technology in Retailing

Retailers operate in a harsh and fast-changing environment, which offers threats as well as opportunities. New retail forms continue to emerge to meet new situations and consumer needs, but the life cycle of new retail forms is getting shorter. Department stores took about 100 years to reach the mature stage of the life cycle; more recent forms, such as warehouse stores, reached maturity in about 10 years. To remain successful, retailers must continually monitor the new trends and new technology available to them, and keep evolving.

Experiential Retail One marketer who is adapting well is BMW—it is not just renovating, but entirely rethinking what its dealerships look like. The first BMW "concept store" opened in Paris and it looks nothing like a traditional Canadian or American dealership. For one thing, there are no giant signs, which makes it difficult to find, but also gives it an air of exclusivity. Once found, the dealer showroom looks and feels like entering a really posh department store. The sleek, high-ceilinged space is mostly white and equipped with giant flat-screens and other digital technology. BMW is referring to its new store as "future retail" and says it offers a whole range of initiatives and tools designed to enhance the customer experience and to set new standards for retail in the automotive industry and beyond.[21]

BMW's new concept store, like Target's pop-up store, are variations of what marketers have come to call experiential retailing—the idea that the retail environment should not be simply a display of products for sale, but rather an experience that engages the customer. The concept was pioneered by Rainforest Café and the Hard Rock Café, but today retailers like IKEA and even Home Depot are running with experiential retail. And no one has done it quite like Sport Chek (see Marketing@Work 11.1).

In-Store Technology   Sport Chek has gone all-out with digital in its new store, but it's not the only retailer to be embracing in-store technology. Walmart is testing Scan and Go, a checkout system that would allow shoppers to skip checkout lines by using their mobile phone to scan items and pay at self-serve kiosks. Chapters and Indigo stores have kiosks that allow customers to order books not available in the store. And New Balance and L.L.Bean are using RFID tags to launch product-related video when a consumer picks up a shoe from a display.

The latest buzzword in retail marketing is "shoppable media," meaning video or print vehicles that encourage customers to immediately purchase products using various technologies, especially their personal mobile devices. For example, Target produced a video called "Falling for You," a three-part romantic comedy featuring Kristen Bell and 110 Target products. Consumers, while viewing the video, could click on a product and order it from Target right then and there.[22]

There's even new technology that brings the consumer's sense of smell into play. Retailers have long understood that scents can lead to more lingering and ultimately more spending, and now they can create digital interactive installations that include scent. Intel, HP, and 5thScreen Digital Services worked together to create five interactive scent-based games at The McCormick World of Flavors, in the McCormick spice company's flagship store in Baltimore. Games include "Guess That Spice" and "FlavorPrint," which allows consumers to find spices to match their taste preferences.[23]

Increasing Use of Gift Cards   Gift cards are a billion dollar industry in Canada and one of the fastest growing areas of retail, and it's not just the big retailers who are offering them. Today, many restaurants, salons, and even gas stations have their own gift cards, and retailers are developing new ways to incorporate them into their marketing efforts. The attraction for retailers goes beyond generating sales. Gift cards attract new customers and build brand awareness. "It's like having a billboard in your wallet," said one retailer.

One of the reasons gift cards are so popular with retailers is because they are profitable, because many cards go unused—by some estimates one in four gift cards remains unused a year after it was received. To help solve that problem for consumers, two Canadian entrepreneurs founded a business called CardSwap.ca, which allows consumers to buy, sell, and swap unwanted gift cards for cash. If you buy a gift card you pay the face value of the card, and if you sell a card you receive between 75 and 90 percent of its value. You can also sell a gift card to CardSwap and it will turn it into a donation to a charitable organization, and the charity will provide the donor with a tax receipt.[24]

Shopper Marketing   Many retail marketers are now embracing the concept of **shopper marketing**, using point-of-purchase promotions and advertising to extend brand equity to "the last mile" and encouraging favourable point-of-purchase decisions. Shopper marketing involves focusing the entire marketing process—from product and brand development

Shopper marketing
Using point-of-sale promotions and advertising to extend brand equity to "the last mile" and encourage favourable in-store purchase decisions.

MARKETING@WORK   11.1

Experiential Retail Goes Digital at Sport Chek Concept Store

Canadian retailer Sport Chek has combined the latest trends in concept stores and experiential retailing into a new "retail lab" store in downtown Toronto. The 12 000 square foot location, designed by the architectural division of advertising agency Sid Lee, was created to test and demonstrate the latest in retail technology.

Sport Chek is owned by FGL Sports Ltd., Canada's largest national retailer of sporting goods, which operates more than 500 stores from coast to coast under the banners Sport Chek, Sports Experts, Atmosphere, Sport Mart, Athletes World, National Sports, Intersport, Econosports, Nevada Bob's Golf, Hockey Experts, Fitness Source, and S3. The corporation also owns Canadian Tire and Marks and is said to be testing the new retail model for possible rollout in those stores in the future.

The Sport Chek retail lab incorporates the latest digital technology to enable interaction between customers and the brand in every corner of the store. Samsung installed 140 digital screens with ultra-thin borders, touch technology, and near-field communication (NFC) capabilities, which allow customers to interact with the merchandise. There are smaller format screens such as digital tiles built into display tables, tablets that have been incorporated into the top of clothing racks, and loads of digital displays to showcase videos and still images. The Yonge Street exterior of the store features a five-foot by 32-foot digital projection screen that displays high-definition video, still images, and may eventually show live feeds of sporting events. Next to the store's escalator is a wall of 19 screens. When consumers approach, an Xbox Kinect activates and displays promotions or a simulated chairlift on the screens. An electronic community board on the second floor provides customers with schedules of fitness classes, and updates and statistics for local sports teams, and visitors to the store can log onto the Sport Chek Facebook page to submit photos for

the board. And customers will soon be able to access offers and discounts through a Sport Chek app while in the store.

All of the digital content is controlled from a facility in Calgary, which can produce and send material to specific screens within 12 minutes. The store is believed to be the most advanced digital retail space of any category in North America.

Sport Chek's product strategy is to sell sporting equipment and apparel by the top brands in the world, and in this new store it has partnered more closely than usual with those brands to market and advertise them to customers in mid-experience. For example, each sales associate is equipped with a tablet that allows them to take over the larger screens when they feel it's appropriate to showcase brands for the customers. In addition, the sports brands themselves have created their own in-store experiences for customers.

Reebok, for instance, installed a build-your-own sneaker kiosk, where the finished product will be shipped to the consumer approximately four-to-six weeks later. Meanwhile, Adidas set up a permanent digital shoe wall to showcase

each of its shoe models with content such as product features, live Twitter feeds, videos, images, and facts about athletes' accomplishments while wearing that shoe. Not to be outdone, Nike offers the Nike Shoe VJ Experience, where customers can use Nike shoes fitted with a game controller to design art and sound—with the palettes by artists James Jean and David Choe, and sound courtesy of world-renowned DJ Cut Chemist—and display their creations on a 12-foot digital wall.

It's not all digital and video, though. The new store is chock full of high tech devices for customers to interact with: There's a dynamic gait analysis machine that helps you find the perfect shoe for your sport or activity, an automated ski and snowboard tuning machine, and a Sidas custom ski and snowboard boot insert system that creates a 3-D map of the customer's foot, which is then reflected in a boot insert that provides maximum support, shock absorption and comfort within 30 minutes. If tennis is your sport, there's a Wilson Baiardo racquet stringer that precisely tunes your racquet to within one decimal point of poundage

Courtesy of FGL Sports Ltd.

Exhibit 11.13 Sport Chek's new "retail lab" store in Toronto demonstrates the latest in retail technology combined with the high energy environment of a sports stadium.

in just 12 minutes. And sunglass brand Oakley has installed an interactive design kiosk where customers can create the perfect customized pair of Oakley sunglasses, which are then built in-store by specially trained staff in minutes.

Sales associates and employees of Sport Chek act as brand ambassadors, defined by their passion for sports and living active lifestyles—as well as providing excellent customer service. They are assigned to sections of the store that match their own personal expertise so that they may share in-depth product

knowledge and insights from their experiences using the gear. Multimedia stories detailing the sporting lives of store employees are also featured content on the many digital screens throughout the store, inspiring consumers and addressing product questions and expert recommendations.

The Sport Chek brand promise seeks to inspire its customers to be a "better you," whether that means looking better, feeling better, or performing better in sport. This message is captured in the brand's tagline, "Your Better Starts Here." Ultimately,

though, the retail environment is the primary execution of the Sport Chek brand, and the retailer's marketing management team believes that a fundamentally better and more inspiring retail environment can be achieved through the combination of world-class products, an all-star staff, and digital innovations that keep customers engaged.

Sources: Kristin Laird, "Sport Chek Turns Digital Focus In-Store with New Retail Concept," *Marketing Magazine* online, January 29, 2013; "Sport Chek Changes the Game with Retail Lab in Toronto," press release issued by FGL Sports on Canada Newswire, January 28, 2013.

---

to logistics, promotion, and merchandising—toward turning shoppers into buyers at the point of sale.

Retail marketing used to be about guiding the consumer along the last few steps on the path to purchase, but the shopping experience and consumer behaviour is no longer that clear cut. The typical path to purchase began with awareness, then moved through investigation and selection, and finally to purchase—a straight line, or linear process. Today that process is anything but linear, and retailers are looking beyond traditional in-store marketing tactics to digital, mobile, and social media to create ongoing bonds with consumers—hence, shopper marketing. It's more of a circular process.

Consumers today are exposed to a constant flow of information through various media, which means they are always on a potential purchase path. Today, brand experiences can begin on Facebook, when a consumer is notified that a friend has enjoyed a particular restaurant, or purchased a new brand of jeans. "The path to purchase has gone mobile, multimedia, and social all at once," says Kelly McCarten, vice-president of Marketing Core, a Toronto-based full-service agency with shopper marketing expertise. Retailers today are increasingly hiring shopper marketing consultants, like ChaseDesign, a 50-year old shopper design consultancy, that works with major advertising agencies like McCann to develop product innovation, package design, and in-store experiences for retail clients.

In order to be competitive, retailers are paying closer attention to the three elements of shopper marketing: pre-shopping, shopping, and post-shopping, and are using methods such as social media and search engine marketing to reach consumers at every stage in the process. For example, because 80 percent of consumers research their purchases online before going into a store, retailers can reach consumers in this pre-shopping stage by purchasing relevant keywords on Google. "Consumers are researching what's relevant to them in their terms," says McCarten. "They don't generally type in a brand name, but instead perhaps a phrase like 'healthy heart solutions.' The key is to have your brand be optimized first by offering a relevant recipe or product."

During stage two, the actual shopping process, retailers use digital technologies to provide a more personalized shopping experience. For example,

Exhibit 11.14 Shopper marketing: The dramatic growth of digital shopping has added a new dimension to "point of purchase." Influencing consumers' buying decisions as they shop now involves efforts aimed at in-store, online, and mobile shopping.

Wu Kaixiang/ZUMAPRESS/Newscom

Indigo suggests specific books to members of its Plum Rewards loyalty program through direct email, online, and at its in-store kiosks. These personalized recommendations are driven in part by members' previous purchases and the preferences they've selected in their account profile. While browsing at a Chapters or Indigo store, members can insert their rewards membership card into a kiosk to access their recommendations.

In the post-shopping stage, retailers continue to engage with customers through social media. For example, Best Buy makes sure that any questions they receive through their social channels are always followed by a response by an appropriate employee. Technical questions are answered by a "Geek Agent," and in Best Buy's online community forum, "Plug In," customers can converse with one another and get answers to questions from Best Buy experts. In shopper marketing, this type of consumer plus expert forum exemplifies shopper marketing, which is all about sharing and conversing.[25]

Online Retail

Canadians have always been leaders in communications technologies, Internet usage, and e-commerce, and today regular home use of the Internet is commonplace. Statistics Canada reports that 80 percent of Canadian households have access to the Internet, and half of those use more than one device to go online. The rates of access are highest in British Columbia (84 percent), followed closely by Alberta (83 percent) and Ontario (81 percent). As for online shopping, 65 percent of Canadians say they use the Internet for "window shopping"—browsing for goods or services but not placing an order—and 50 percent use it to order personal goods or services, spending a total of more than $13 billion.[26]

Online retail in Canada continues to grow at astonishing rates—in the double digits every year for the last four years. The most popular online retailers for Canadians, according to Mastercard, are The Source, Sephora, The Gap, Dell, Chapters-Indigo, and Old Navy.[27] Bricks-and-mortar retailers aren't going to disappear any time soon, but online retail offers an additional channel for retailers to increase their reach, and therefore their sales. When Canadian consumers shop both online and in-store, the majority (53 percent) spend more at their favourite retailer than they would through a single-channel. Furthermore, almost a third (30 percent) increase their spending by at least 10 percent.[28]

A report from the NPD Group, a leading market research firm, revealed that consumers between the ages of 25 and 44 are the "sweet spot" for online retailers, because they are the generation that feels most at home online. Says Rick Brown, director of analytic solutions at NPD Group, "The online super buyers that exist in this age bracket are drawn to how easy it is to research and compare the products they're interested in buying, but their dexterity in hunting for discounts means that they expect to find better deals on the web."

The report also shows a surprising fact that men tend to spend more online than women. Men shopped for an average of $371 last year in comparison to women who spend $266 shopping online. Men seem to prefer online shopping over manual shopping as they actually find better shopping deals online, and are able to compare popular products in real-time. On the other hand, women seem to shop online for products that are not easily available in retail stores across Canada. Further, they seem to enjoy the convenience of online shopping, which is more hassle-free than manual shopping.[29]

Retailers' websites also influence a large amount of in-store buying. In the United States, 80 percent of shoppers said they research products online before going to a store to make a purchase, and 62 percent say that they spend at least 30 minutes online every week to help them decide whether and what to buy. A whopping 92 percent said they had more confidence in information they seek out online than anything coming from a sales clerk or other source. So shoppers are devoting time and energy to ferreting out detailed info before they buy. Whether it's cars, homes, or electronics, nearly four in five shoppers say they gather information online before buying. Customers appear at the car dealership with the wholesale price and the model already picked out. Now this trend is spreading down the product chain. In the survey, 24 percent of shoppers said they are doing online research before buying shampoo. And they have questions: How does this shampoo work on different hair types, thicknesses, and colours? Are the bottles recyclable? Has the product been tested on animals?[30]

It's the influence of retailer's websites on traditional retailing that has led to a new phenomenon called *showrooming*—and it has many retailers, including Future Shop, worried. Showrooming refers to the fact that consumers are increasingly treating bricks-and-mortar retailers as showrooms, where they view and test products before leaving to buy them elsewhere or online for a lower price. Showroomers tend to be young female shoppers who frequently purchase online, have a lower household income, and are therefore motivated almost exclusively by price. One study found that finding a mere 2.5 percent discount on an in-store item online is enough to entice 5 percent of customers to leave a store; 60 percent would leave for a 5 percent discount, and 87 percent would leave if they found the same product online for 20 percent less. To combat showrooming, Best Buy and Future Shop created a new marketing program called the "Price Beat Promise," which states that if a competitor—either online or in-store—has an item selling for less, they will beat it by 10 percent of the difference for up to 30 days.[31]

Some online retailers welcome the idea of showrooming—so long as the customer does their viewing and testing elsewhere, and comes back to their website to make the purchase. And other formerly online-only retailers such as eBay and Etsy are testing the idea of creating temporary physical stores. Though retailers like Target have bemoaned the impact of showrooming, it's an opportunity for e-commerce players to showcase their products while carrying less inventory, hiring fewer salespeople and investing less in real estate. As much as consumers crave the convenience of online shopping, there are still times when they'd like to step into a physical location to try on a pair of shoes or pants; and despite the fact that online retail is booming, the majority of sales still happen in bricks-and-mortar retail locations.[32]

Social Media and Mobile

The use of social media and mobile devices by shoppers is on the increase, and retailers who know how to use them will develop a competitive advantage. Smartphones and other handheld electronic devices are becoming like "butlers" to shoppers. They assist consumers with everything from finding a particular retailer's nearest location, to checking on product availability and price. A recent study found that in a one month period, 8 million Canadians used a mobile device to help them shop, and those numbers are likely to increase as more consumers adopt mobile devices with Internet access.[33]

While many retailers have rushed to create Facebook pages and Twitter accounts, fewer have figured out how to use them effectively. While 90 percent of the top 50 retailers (in the United States) have a presence on Twitter, a mere 29 percent use it to actively engage with consumers. One expert says the number one mistake retailers make is to create a Twitter account and then ignore it: "More often than not they [the retailer] assign either an already over-worked marketer or young, inexperienced, entry-level person to man the Twitter account. This person will do the obligatory Tweets during the course of a day without any thought to content or more importantly, engagement." The solution, suggests a public relations expert, is that brands should view Twitter just as they do customer call centres—as a customer service communication tool that everyone sees.[34]

So while social media is easy and fun for consumers to use, retail marketers must carefully plan their use of it. For an example of how an Indian ice cream retailer, Hokey Pokey, created a social media campaign that actually showed a return on investment, see Marketing@Work 11.2.

MARKETING@WORK 11.2

Hokey Pokey uses Social Media Marketing

Now that so many people worldwide participate in online social networks—over 1 billion on Facebook alone—influencing consumer preferences and purchase decisions through these networks and word of mouth (WOM) is an increasingly important part of every marketer's job. In fact, 78% of consumers claim that social media posts from companies influence their purchases.[1] As a result, many enterprises are investing in social channels to rapidly create or propagate their brand through viral content, social media contests, and other consumer engagement efforts. Companies such as Geico, Dell, and eBay are augmenting the traditional "one-way" broadcast format by using it as a stepping-stone to establish a two-way conversation with consumers via social media.

Researchers worked with an ice cream retailer in India, Hokey Pokey, whose stores allow customers to custom-mix flavours, a retail concept that appeals mostly to the Millennial demographic. Hokey Pokey executives wanted to connect better with this target market, acquire and retain profitable customers, and develop a social media strategy that would create a buzz about Hokey Pokey while ensuring a high ROI—all within a limited marketing budget. Together, Hokey Pokey's marketing managers and the researchers developed a seven-step framework[2] for successfully using social media in retailing:

Step 1: Study the flow of information across social networks. By monitoring brand-related conversations in social media, businesses can gain intelligence on prevalent brand/category perceptions and the purchase decision making process in the category.

Step 2: Analyse the spread of influence in a social network. Retailers can use the information from social media to identify a pool of "influencers," and measure the degree of each influencer's influence.

Step 3: Develop target "influencer" profiles for future activation. Retailers should find commonalities among the candidates and create profiles of typical influencers to find similar such influencers for activation/ seeding.

Step 4: Shortlist relevant potential influencers. It's not enough to identify social media users with influence; instead, a company needs to identify those influential users who show special interest in the company's category of goods and services, and can be considered "subject matter experts" on the category in a social network.

Step 5: Recruit those influencers to talk about the company's product or service. Enlist those influencers in the company's social media campaign by developing interactive online content and inducing them to act as positive WOM "agents" of the company.

Step 6: Incentivize those influencers to spread positive WOM about the product or service. Offer incentives such as discounts or freebies, or intangible incentives such as recognition, to influencers to encourage them to promote your brand.

Step 7: Track the performance of the campaign. At the firm level, metrics such as overall brand sentiment, buzz, and engagement, along with actual conversions/sales and the resultant campaign ROI need to be tracked judiciously. At the customer level, the value of a customer needs to be measured in terms of his/her social influence as well as the quality of his/her referrals. As a backend measure for the accurate attribution of offline sales to online activity and for streamlining campaign related conversations, customized tracking and analytics need to be implemented consistently.

Hokey Pokey developed a social media campaign[3] that was executed in two stages. The first was called "Creations on the Wall," which encouraged the recruited influencers to make custom ice cream creations at any Hokey Pokey location, identify themselves with their creations, and post pictures on their Facebook wall and other social media networks. They could also post their creations and their recipes on the real wall in the Hokey Pokey store to help walk-in customers place orders. In the second phase, "Share Your Brownies," the influencers who had collected "Brownie Points" for each social media post about Hokey Pokey, tweeted about their creations and competed for incentives such as T-shirts.

Courtesy Hokey Pokey

Exhibit 11.15 Hokey Pokey, an ice cream retailer in India where customers can custom-mix flavours, developed a seven-step framework for successfully using social media in retailing.

Throughout the campaign, the researchers tracked its social media success as well as actual business impact. This campaign yielded Hokey Pokey an increase of 49% in brand awareness, 83% in ROI, 40% in sales growth, and also a 33.5 times increase in positive WOM. Thus, while most companies are still grappling with social media accountability, Hokey Pokey gained an important competitive edge by being able to measure and leverage the value of its social media investments.

Source: Adapted from V. Jumar & Rohan Mirchandani, "Increasing the ROI of Social Media Marketing," *MIT Sloan Management Review* 54 (Fall 2012). http://sloanreview.mit.edu/article/increasing-the-roi-of-social-media-marketing (accessed September 20, 2013).

Supply Chain Management and Logistics LO5

At the beginning of this chapter, we learned that the supply chain is the "upstream" part of any channel of distribution. The supply chain supplies the manufacturer with the parts and supplies it needs to be able to create products that it then sells "downstream" through its marketing channels to, eventually, its customers. The task of coordinating and controlling the physical flow of all those supplies and products—the logistics—is called *logistics management* or *supply chain management.*

Modern logistics is much more than just trucks and warehouses. **Logistics management** requires planning, implementing, and controlling the physical flow of goods, services, and related information from points of origin to points of consumption to meet customer requirements at a profit. In short, it involves getting the right product to the right customer in the right place at the right time.

In the days before technology, distribution managers (as they were called then) typically started with products at the plant and then tried to find the least expensive method to get them to their customers. Today, logistics managers use sophisticated computer systems which allow them to see the bigger picture, and to plan the movement of supplies by starting with the customer and the marketplace, and working backward to the factory, or even to sources of supply. Logistics involves not only *outbound distribution* (moving products from the factory to resellers and ultimately to customers) but also *inbound distribution* (moving products and materials from suppliers to the factory) and *reverse distribution* (moving broken, unwanted, or excess products returned by consumers or resellers). That is, it involves management of the entire supply chain—upstream and downstream value-added flows of materials, final goods, and related information among suppliers, the company, resellers, and customers.

Logistics management is also concerned with the management of inventory—the delicate balance between carrying too little inventory and carrying too much (which is very expensive). Many companies have greatly reduced their inventories and related costs through **just-in-time logistics systems.** With such systems, producers and retailers carry only small inventories of parts or merchandise, often only enough for a few days of operations. New stock arrives exactly when needed, rather than being stored in inventory until being used. Just-in-time systems require accurate forecasting and can result in substantial savings in inventory-carrying and handling costs.

Companies today are placing greater emphasis on logistics for several reasons. First, companies can gain a powerful competitive advantage by using improved logistics to give customers better service or lower prices. Second, improved logistics can yield tremendous cost savings to both the company and its customers. As much as 20 percent of an average product's price is accounted for by shipping and transport alone. This far exceeds the cost of advertising and many other marketing costs.

Logistics management
Planning, implementing, and controlling the physical flow of materials, final goods, and related information from points of origin to points of consumption to meet customer requirements at a profit.

Just-in-time logistics systems
A type of inventory management system in which only small inventories of parts or merchandise are held, and new stock arrives "just in time" when it is needed.

Warehousing and Distribution Centres

Production and consumption cycles rarely match, so most companies must store their goods while they wait to be sold. For example, Snapper, Toro, and other lawn mower

photo courtesy of Staples

Exhibit 11.16 **High-tech distribution centres:** Staples employs a team of super-retrievers—robots—to move inventory through its distribution centres as efficiently as possible.

manufacturers run their factories all year long and store up products for the heavy spring and summer buying seasons. The storage function overcomes differences in needed quantities and timing, ensuring that products are available when customers are ready to buy them.

Warehouses may or may not also function as distribution centres. Distribution centres are designed to move goods in and out, and to store them for as little time as possible. Today's warehouses and distribution centres could not function without technology such as computers, scanners, and robots. Staples, for example, uses electronic "super-retrievers" to move inventory through its distribution centres as efficiently as possible:[35]

Imagine a team of employees that works 16 hours a day, seven days a week. They never call in sick or show up late, because they never leave the building. They demand no benefits, require no health insurance, and receive no pay cheques. And they never complain. Sounds like a bunch of robots, huh? They are, in fact, robots—and they're dramatically changing the way Staples delivers notepads, pens, and paper clips to its customers. Every day, Staples' huge Chambersburg, Pennsylvania, distribution centre receives thousands of customer orders, each containing a wide range of office supply items. Having people run around a warehouse looking for those items is expensive, especially when the company has promised to delight customers by delivering orders the next day.

Enter the robots. On the distribution centre floor, the 150 robots most resemble a well-trained breed of working dogs, say, golden retrievers. When orders come in, a centralized computer tells the robots where to find racks with the appropriate items. The robots retrieve the racks and carry them to picking stations, then wait patiently as humans pull the correct products and place them in boxes. When orders are filled, the robots neatly park the racks back among the rest. The robots pretty much take care of themselves. When they run low on power, they head to battery-charging terminals, or, as warehouse personnel say, "They get themselves a drink of water." The robots now run 50 percent of the Chambersburg facility, where average daily output is up 60 percent since they arrived on the scene.

Logistics Technology

Improvements in information technology have created opportunities for major gains in distribution efficiency. Today's companies are using sophisticated supply-chain management software, online real-time logistics systems, point-of-sale scanners, satellite tracking, and electronic transfer of order and payment data. Such technology lets them quickly and efficiently manage the flow of goods, information, and finances through the supply chain.

Another important technology for logistics management is RFID or radio frequency ID tags, tiny computer chips embedded in products or product containers that allow scanners to track their movement without touching them. The use of RFID tags by manufacturers is increasing, and the latest technology allows an RFID software system to be used at every stage of the supply chain, from producing the tags, to tagging the goods, to recording the movement of items from the warehouse to the sales floor, tracking in-store inventory, and recording items that have left the system at the retailer's checkout process. The information provided to the logistics system by the RFID tags is then stored and can be analyzed later to improve the efficiency of the distribution channel.

Collecting information about the movement of goods is important, and that information must be shared between the parties involved in the transactions. Most information sharing takes place through electronic data interchange or EDI, computer systems that allow members of the supply chain to communicate and share information. A retailer the size of Target, for example, has thousands of suppliers, so keeping track of all that inventory, and knowing where it is and where it's headed, requires a great deal of data to be shared in real time or near real time.

Some retailers and suppliers even set up vendor-managed inventory systems, sometimes called *continuous inventory replenishment systems*. These systems allow the supplier to keep track of what the retailer needs, and to generate orders and arrange deliveries.

Third Party Logistics

Logistics management is a complex activity, and one that is critically important to many businesses. It is not, however, usually a business's "core competency." As such, some companies choose to outsource their logistics management to firms that specialize in just that. These companies are called **third-party logistics (3PL) providers**. For example, Whirlpool uses third-party logistics supplier Ryder to provide order fulfillment and worldwide distribution of Whirlpool's service parts across six continents to hundreds of customers that include (in addition to consumers) the Sears service network, authorized repair centres, and independent parts distributors that in turn ship parts out to a network of service companies and technicians. The are many other 3PLs, including UPS Supply Chain Solutions, Penske Logistics, BAX Global, DHL Logistics, and FedEx Logistics.

Third-party logistics (3PL) provider An independent logistics provider that performs any or all of the functions required to get its client's product to market.

Environmental Impact of Logistics

More than almost any other business activity, logistics affects the environment and a firm's environmental sustainability efforts. Transportation, warehousing, and packaging are typically the biggest supply chain contributors to the company's environmental footprint. At the same time, they also provide one of the most fertile areas for cost savings. So developing a green supply chain is not only environmentally responsible, it can also be profitable.

One way logistics managers can reduce the environmental impact of their activities is by adopting slow shipping, the simple practice of slowing the speed at which ships travel so as to save fuel and reduce pollution. International shipping contributes nearly 3 percent to global greenhouse gas emissions, compare to the 1.5 percent generated by airplanes. An environmental group called Seas at Risk commissioned a study and found that companies can reduce emissions by as much as 30 percent, just by slowing the ships.[36]

Managing the supply chain—the "chain" of businesses that supply a manufacturer or producer—and managing the downstream distribution of products from the producer to the consumer, is a complex task. Logistics managers plan and coordinate the movement of all these goods and supplies, and sometimes use third parties to do the job. Companies use 3PL providers because getting the product to market is their main focus, and these providers can often do it more efficiently and at lower cost. Finally, whether logistics management is handled in-house or by a third party, managers must constantly strive to find lower cost and more environmentally friendly solutions.

The Digital Storefront

Up until the advent of e-commerce, the intermediary of the commercial travel sector was the brick-and-mortar travel agency. Today, of course, that space is reliant on e-tailers led by Expedia, Travelocity, and more recently unique blind auction sites such as Hotwire. "These services are partners for WestJet," states Manoj Jasra, WestJet's digital director, "but my mandate is to gain as much channel share as possible, which means making the guest online experience as positive as possible."

In 2013, WestJet invested $40 million into a system upgrade to assist Jasra and his team. "We replaced our Internet booking engine with a system that allowed us

greater merchandising capabilities . . . things like cross-selling flights with cars, having a shopping cart, and a better booking management system for customers who may want or need to change their flights." These and other features allowed WestJet to compete with substitutes like Expedia and rivals like Air Canada.

That said, an online guest experience is predicated first upon guests visiting a site. Jasra explains the two key components toward driving that traffic. "Analytics measures everything about the number and nature of visits to our website: where they came from, how long they stayed, where did they drop off, and so on. Optimization attempts to maximize traffic to our website by knowing where people search and what they search with."

If technology built the perfect beast known as the Internet, then it is also responsible for the tools used to slay the dragon. "We know that 25% of our customers begin their search on Google, so it is easy to ensure that we show up number one in Google searches using the word 'WestJet.' It becomes more challenging, although not impossible, to earn a high ranking on searches like 'cheap flights to Vegas.'"

The user's online expectation continues to change, however, and every company relying on online shopping has found themselves painted into a corner where everything that was once done on a 21-inch screen must now be doable on a smartphone device. Admitting that WestJet was late in launching an app, Jasra says overcoming that issue is made more challenging by today's customer expectations. "If you're late to the party, you better come up with something really strong. What is that set of functionality features which will really resonate with our guests? My vision is one which encompasses the different parts of a guest's journey. So what if you can book a flight—our app needs to do more."

QUESTIONS

1. What does Manoj Jasra mean by "channel share?"
2. Why is it important to increase channel share?
3. Are intermediaries like Expedia a necessary evil for airlines, hotels, and car rental companies? Explain your answer.

REVIEWING THE CONCEPTS

1. List and describe the major types of marketing channel partners. Explain why companies need channel partners, and describe the roles and responsibilities channel partners may perform.

Making products available to buyers requires building relationships with key suppliers "upstream" in the company's *supply chain*, and distributers and resellers who act as intermediaries to help move the product "downstream" through *marketing channels* or *channels of distribution*. Viewed from beginning to end this channel is a continually evolving *value delivery network* connecting the company, suppliers, distributors, and ultimately customers.

Designing channels and choosing channel partners are strategic marketing decisions. Companies need channel partners to reduce the amount of work that must be done to reach customers, and to transform the assortments of products made by producers into the assortments wanted by consumers. Channel members add value by bridging the major time, place, and possession gaps that separate goods and services from those who would use them, specifically by performing functions such as gathering and distributing information, promoting products at point of purchase, contacting new customers, customizing installations, negotiating price and delivery, moving and distributing the products (and assuming the risk that goes with it), financing purchases, and supporting customers after the sale.

The major types of channel partners are: *retailers*, or businesses whose primary activity is selling products and services directly to consumers for their personal use; *wholesalers*, or companies that buy from producers and sell to retailers, business customers, and other wholesalers; *drop shippers*, or intermediaries who take orders and payment from the customer, then arrange to have the merchandise shipped to the customer directly from the supplier; *rack jobbers*, or wholesalers who buy merchandise and re-sell it on "racks" inside a retail store, in partnership with the retailer; *brokers*, who do not take title to goods and whose function is to bring buyers and sellers together and assist in negotiation; and *agents*, who are representatives, either of a buyer or a seller, who perform only a few functions and do not take title to goods.

2. Describe the major methods of organizing channel members, and the problems that can arise in managing channels.

Marketing channels must be built and designed to meet strategic business goals. The shortest possible channel is a *direct marketing channel*, where the producer of the goods sells directly to the final customer. Most channels, however, have one or more intermediaries, and therefore are *indirect marketing channels*.

A *vertical marketing system* or *VMS* is a distribution channel structure in which producers, wholesalers, and retailers act as a unified system. One channel member owns the others, has contracts with them, or has so much power that they all co-operate. A *franchise organization* is a type of contractual VMS, in which several stages in the production and distribution process are linked among *franchisees* and operations are controlled from a central head office run by the *franchisor*. Another method of organization is the *horizontal marketing system*, in which two or more companies that operate at the same channel level join together to follow a new marketing opportunity. A distribution system in which a single firm sets up two or more marketing channels to reach one or more market segments is a *multichannel* or *hybrid distribution system*.

In designing a retail marketing channel, the marketer must also consider a strategy for how many locations in which to make the product available. *Intensive distribution* is a strategy in which the product is stocked in as many outlets as possible; *selective distribution* is a distribution strategy in which the marketer selects a set of retailers that specialize in their product category; and *exclusive distribution* is a strategy in which the marketer gives the rights to distribute its products to only one retailer, or to only one retailer in a particular geographic territory.

Each channel member plays an important role in the marketing channel, but sometimes disagreements over goals, roles, and rewards among channel members can create *channel conflict*. In extreme situations, channel conflict can result in *disintermediation*, where a channel member is rendered redundant and cut out of the channel.

3. Explain the differences between Canadian and American shoppers, and why retail marketers need to understand them. List and briefly describe the major types of retailers common to both countries.

Retailing is one of the largest contributors to the Canadian economy, therefore it is important for Canadian retailers to understand the characteristics of Canadian shoppers in order to be successful. It is especially important for retailers carrying American products such as automobiles and clothing; and retailers such as Target, which originate in the United States but operate in Canada, to understand the differences between Canadian and American shoppers in order to be successful.

Canadians don't make shopping lists as often as Americans do, which means we pay closer attention to in-store displays and are more likely to be influenced by them. We focus less on price, more on convenience, assortment, and rewards programs. Our economy wasn't affected by the credit card "crunch" the way the American economy was, which means we are better able to handle store credit. Our grocery shopping habits have changed radically in the last ten years, and we are more interested in local markets and ethnic foods than Americans tend to be. The biggest difference in our culture is our ethnic makeup as a country. Not only are our largest ethnic groups different from those in the United States, but our attitude towards them is different. Canadians celebrate their ethnic heritage, and so retailers need to pay attention to the ethnic makeup of their target markets to be able to serve them appropriately.

In Canada, like in the United States, the major types of in-store retailers are: *specialty stores*, which carry narrow product lines with deep assortments within those lines; *department stores,* which carry a wide variety of product lines organized in departments within the store; *supermarkets* and *general merchandise* stores such as Walmart and Target; and *convenience stores, superstores,* and very large specialty stores called *category killers* or *big box stores.* Retailers that compete on price are *discount stores* such as Giant Tiger and Dollarama, *off-price retailers* such as Winners and Marshall's, *factory outlets,* and *warehouse clubs.*

4. Name and describe the current trends in retail marketing (including online retail), and describe the new technologies retail marketers are employing.

Retailers operate in a harsh and fast-changing environment, which offers threats as well as opportunities. To remain successful, retailers must continually monitor the new trends and new technology available to them, and keep evolving. *Experiential retailing* refers to a retail environment that offers a fuller customer experience (more than just shopping). Some of these new experienced-based retail outlets are also referred to as *concept stores.* *Pop-up retail*, or stores that "pop up" temporarily in a location such as an empty lot, are being used more frequently by both large and small retailers. *Gift cards* are also a rising trend among large and small retailers.

A new area of interest to retailers is *shopper marketing*, the focus on marketing to customers just before and during their shopping excursions. Shopper marketing attempts to communicate with consumers during the entire shopping process, from product and brand development to logistics, promotion, and merchandising, in an attempt to convert shoppers into buyers at the point of sale. Online retail is growing in Canada as more and more men and women shop online, in addition to shopping in stores, and because most consumers research their purchases online before they go to a store, retailers are also increasingly using search advertising and social media to communicate with consumers, provide them with information, and drive them to their websites. The use of social media and mobile devices by shoppers is on the increase, and retailers who know how to use them will develop a competitive advantage. Many retailers are concerned about *showrooming*, or having customers treat their retail stores like a showroom, then leave to purchase products online at a lower price.

In terms of in-store technology retailers employ large and small digital screens, often in many locations within the store; self-scanning checkout systems; systems that allow customers to interact in-store with their mobile devices; interactive maps; RFID tags; kiosks that engage customers and can even emit scents; and shoppable media, or electronic devices or media that encourage customers to use their mobile devices to purchase.

5. Describe the role of supply chain management and logistics management in a company's distribution system.

While marketing channels, or channels of distribution, move manufacturers' products "downstream" into the hands of customers, the supply chain is the "upstream" section of the channel that supplies the manufacturer with the parts and supplies it needs to be able to create those products. The task of coordinating and controlling the physical flow of all the products in the supply chain is called *supply chain management*, while the task of coordinating and controlling the physical movements of *all* supplies and products, both upstream and downstream, is called *logistics management.*

Logistics management requires planning, implementing, and controlling the physical flow of goods, services, and related information from points of origin to points of consumption, to meet customer requirements at a profit. In short, it involves getting the right product to the right customer in the right place at the right time. Logistics managers use sophisticated computer systems which allow them to plan the movement of supplies from one end of the *value delivery network* to the other. That is, it involves management of the entire supply chain—upstream and downstream value-added flows of materials, final goods, and related information among suppliers, the company, resellers, and customers.

Logistics management is also concerned with the management of inventory in warehouses and distribution centres. Many companies have greatly reduced their inventories and related costs through *just-in-time logistics systems*, in which they carry only small inventories and arrange for new stock to arrive exactly when it is needed. Finally, because logistics management is a complex activity, and one that is not usually a business's "core competency," some companies choose to outsource their logistics management to *third-party logistics providers*, or *3PL* providers.

KEY TERMS

Administered VMS 405
Agent 401
Broker 401
Channel conflict 403
Contractual VMS 405
Corporate VMS 404
Disintermediation 403
Drop shipper 401
Exclusive distribution 408
Franchise organization 406

Horizontal marketing system 406
Intensive distribution 407
Just-in-time logistics systems 419
Logistics management (or supply
    chain management) 419
Marketing channel (distribution
    channel) 396
Multichannel (hybrid) distribution
    system 407
Rack jobber 401

Retailer 400
Retailing 399
Selective distribution 408
Shopper marketing 413
Third-party logistics (3PL)
    provider 421
Value delivery network 396
Vertical marketing system (VMS) 404
Wholesaler 400
Wholesaling 400

TALK ABOUT MARKETING

1. Describe the marketing channel, and all the intermediaries, that would be involved in moving apples produced in British Columbia's Okanagan Valley to a grocery store in Kingston, Ontario, and for moving T-shirts manufactured in Montreal, Quebec, to an independent clothing retailer in Saskatoon, Saskatchewan.

2. What is *disintermediation*? Think of an example (other than those given in the chapter) of a company that has been disintermediated and one that has disintermediated another type of company. Do you think that bricks-and-mortar retailers will ever be completely disintermediated?

3. Which distribution strategy—intensive, selective, or exclusive—is used for the following products and why? (a) Piaget watches, (b) Acura automobiles, and (c) Snickers chocolate bars.

4. Why do you think a company would choose to use an intermediary to distribute its products rather than handling the distribution itself? What are the benefits and risks of using a channel partner for this function?

5. Coca-Cola markets an astonishing 2800 different beverages. Not all these beverages are available for sale in all areas, and certainly there is no retailer that offers all 2800. What marketing decisions does the retailer need to make when deciding which of those 2800 to stock on its shelves? How can the distributor (the bottler) help the retailer with this decision?

6. List all the services you can think of that can be delivered from the producer to the customer via the Internet (that is, with no physical distribution required). Can you think of any other levels of the marketing channel that could be conducted online or electronically, rather than physically?

THINK LIKE A MARKETING MANAGER

A group of 50 Coca-Cola bottlers in the United States sued the Coca-Cola Company when it announced a plan to ship its Powerade sports drink directly to Walmart warehouses, thus upsetting the established chain of distribution. Coca-Cola uses a distribution system called "direct-to-store delivery" that relies on the licensed bottlers to package and deliver Coca-Cola products to retailers. Bottlers also set up retail displays and stock the shelves. Rival Pepsi-Cola, which markets Gatorade, the competitor to Powerade, ships its products directly to retailers' warehouses. Coca-Cola says forcing them to distribute their products through bottlers will make them less competitive. From Walmart's perspective, cutting the bottlers out of the channel of distribution could reduce their operating costs and therefore increase their profits. Walmart's margin on Gatorade is 30 percent, but on Powerade it is only 20 percent.

QUESTIONS

1. Not all retailers have warehouses. Convenience stores and smaller independent grocery stores don't have

them. Assuming that the Coca-Cola bottlers deliver to these stores as well as Walmart, why were they so upset about the possibility of losing just one customer?

2. Walmart makes more profit on each bottle of Gatorade that it sells than on a bottle of Powerade. List all the things a Walmart store manager could do to encourage consumers to choose Gatorade over Powerade.

3. If it wants to be more competitive with Pepsi, why doesn't Coca-Cola simply increase Walmart's margin on Powerade?

4. If Pepsi has been shipping direct to Walmart's warehouse all along, why aren't its bottlers upset?

MARKETING ETHICS

Tension is escalating between apparel retailers and suppliers during the economic recovery. Retailers previously placed orders almost a year in advance, and suppliers produced high volumes cheaply. Now many retailers are placing small initial orders, and if styles take off with consumers, they quickly reorder—a tactic known as "chasing." Teen retailer Aéropostale has been buying conservatively and chasing for items that are hot with buyers. Appropriate inventory levels in the apparel industry have always

been difficult to predict, but it appears that retailers are pushing this worry back to suppliers.

QUESTIONS

1. Discuss the concerns of suppliers and retailers in the apparel channel of distribution. Is it fair that retailers should expect suppliers to respond so quickly? Is it fair that suppliers should demand long lead times?

2. Is this an example of channel conflict?

MARKETING TECHNOLOGY

Brewing craft beer is both an art and a science, and Sonia Collin, a Belgian researcher, is trying to devise a way for this highly perishable beer to have a longer shelf life. If successful, brewers can ship more for longer distances. Hoping to boost exports of homegrown products, the Belgian government is investing $7 million for research, with $1.7 million of that allocated to Collin's research. The $250 000 tasting machine in her laboratory identifies the chemical compounds in a sample of beer, which allowed researchers to recommend using organic ingredients, adjusting the oxygen and yeast levels, and reducing the time the beer spends at high temperatures in the brewing process. While pasteurization and bottling methods allow giants such as Heineken and Molson to export their brews,

aficionados prefer the more delicate flavour of craft beers. But craft brews don't travel well—sunlight is their worst enemy, and most craft beers lose flavour in less than three months.

QUESTIONS

1. Describe the channel of distribution for a craft beer from Belgium to your city or town. How many channel levels will be involved?

2. Is there a small brewer in your area whose distribution is limited to the local market? List all the marketing decisions that brewer would have to make if brewing technology improves to the point where it would be possible to increase its distribution.

MARKETING BY THE NUMBERS

One external factor manufacturers must consider when setting prices is reseller margins. Manufacturers do not have the final say concerning the price to consumers—

retailers do. So, manufacturers must start with their suggested retail prices and work back, subtracting out the markups required by resellers that sell the product to consumers. Once that is considered, manufacturers know at what price to sell their products to resellers, and they can determine what volume they must sell to break even at that price and cost combination. To answer the following questions, refer to Appendix 3, Marketing by the Numbers.

QUESTIONS

1. A consumer purchases a flat iron to straighten her hair for $150 from a salon at which she gets her hair cut. If the salon's markup is 40 percent and the wholesaler's markup is 15 percent, both based on their selling prices, for what price does the manufacturer sell the product to the wholesaler?

2. If the unit variable costs for each flat iron are $40 and the manufacturer has fixed costs totalling $200 000, how many flat irons must this manufacturer sell to break even? How many must it sell to realize a profit of $800 000?

VIDEO CASE

GAVIÑA GOURMET COFFEE

These days, there seems to be plenty of coffee to go around. So how does a small time coffee roaster like Gaviña succeed in an industry dominated by big players? By carefully crafting a distribution strategy that moves its products into the hands of consumers. Without a big advertising budget, Gaviña has creatively pursued channel partners in the grocery, restaurant, and hospitality industries. Now, major chains such as McDonald's carry Gaviña's coffees. This video illustrates the company's distribution strategy and its impact on supply chain and product development issues. After watching the video, answer the following questions:

QUESTIONS

1. Describe, using a diagram, Gaviña's supply chain.

2. List and describe each channel of distribution, and explain how each channel meets a particular customer need.

3. How has Gaviña's distribution strategy affected its product strategy?

MABEL'S LABELS: MOVING FROM ONLINE TO WALMART

Case prepared by David Rose, Wilfrid Laurier University

While many brick-and-mortar retailers are developing multichannel marketing systems by adding online options to their distribution strategies, one Canadian online retailer is moving in the other direction. Mabel's Labels, a Hamilton, Ontario, company that manufactures and markets personalized labels for children's clothing, lunch boxes, and other items, has started selling its products through Walmart Canada.

Mabel's Labels began when four moms—Julie Cole, Julie Ellis, Tricia Mumby, and Cynthia Esp—grew tired of their kids coming home from daycare, school, or camp without all of their belongings and decided to come up with a solution to the problem. They created a line of personalized labels that can be affixed to clothes, lunch boxes, backpacks, water bottles, and anything else kids tote around and often leave behind. Ten years later, the business has sold more than 50 million labels in 97 countries through its website, and they have registered the trademark for the slogan, "Labels for the stuff kids lose!" They have mastered social media, hired public relations companies to generate attention in mom-oriented media, won plenty of business awards, and built an incredibly loyal customer base. Many celebrity moms have used Mabel's Labels, including Jennifer Garner, Rachel Weisz, Reese Witherspoon, Gwyneth Paltrow, and Victoria Beckham.

Despite the devoted online following, the move to sell products through retailers was in response to the needs of the market, particularly the calls from customers needing labels quickly. As Julie Cole explains, "We all know that feeling—you've procrastinated ordering and your child leaves for camp TOMORROW. Now when you're having a last-minute panic, you'll have the convenience of being able to pick something up in a nearby retail location."

The move to Walmart also provides a convenient way for parents to experience and access the products. The labels are now more widely available to busy moms on the go, who can grab the labels along with other essentials ahead of sending kids off to camp or back to school. People who don't feel comfortable shopping online can now get their hands on Mabel's Labels, too. The partners worried about cannibalizing their own online business by going the retail route, but after conducting market research and focus groups they determined that the two channels served different markets.

A NEW PRODUCT FOR A NEW CHANNEL

Mabel's Labels come in a variety of styles, including sticky labels, clothing labels, shoe tags, and bag tags. All labels can be personalized by choosing the label style and a colourful design and adding the child's name. This highly individualized approach works well in an online environment but created a major challenge when the partners decided to make their labels available in a retail setting. One approach they considered was to stock the most popular names in spinning racks at the stores, the way some other personalized products are displayed, but they were concerned about the potential challenges of managing that system. Cole says, "How do you keep track? Oh, the Jennifers are sold out there and the Alexes are all gone there. It was too overwhelming."

Mabel's Labels's solution was to create a new line of products for the retail channel. After two years of development, they created Write Away!, a new line of peel-and-stick labels that are written on with marker and a clear overlay that is pressed over top as a lamination, making the labels dishwasher and microwave proof. They sell at Walmart for $10.47 for a package of 30.

WORKING WITH WALMART

The partners were intimidated at the thought of approaching such a big retailer, but they had an incredible experience. From the outset, Walmart Canada was extremely open to learning about an offering from a small Canadian manufacturer, especially one with a strong online presence but no retail presence. They discovered it is important to Walmart buyers that they stay in touch with what Canadian moms are buying online and what brands they care about. Businesses owned by women are also a big focus for Walmart. Cole describes their reception by Walmart: "Here's little Mabel and big, old Walmart. But they responded really warmly to us. They recognized the value of the product and knew their customers would love it."

DEVELOPING NEW CAPABILITIES

Retail was a whole new territory for the partners and it was hard for them to even know where to start. Walmart could move vast quantities of their Write Away! Labels, but what they didn't realize at first was how thoroughly a Walmart listing would transform their business—and how quickly. From establishing a new supply chain from China to decoding the world of third-party logistics, Mabel's Labels had just four months to reinvent the way it did business to meet Walmart's deadline for the 2012 back-to-school season. "It was as if we were starting a second company," says Cole.

The firm approached this task systematically, doing intensive preparations under the guidance of a key adviser with experience dealing with Walmart and carefully executing the sweeping changes needed to become a Walmart supplier. The Mabel's Labels team's copious preparations helped it overcome the "be careful what you wish for" moment many Walmart suppliers experience when they realize how much they'll have to do to meet the retailer's exacting standards. They first needed to develop realistic sales projections. From there, they determined the production volumes and capital they'd need and they mapped out how they'd pick an overseas manufacturer to produce enough labels for 275 Walmart Canada stores. A month after the pitch meeting with Walmart, the two parties struck a deal that met Walmart's two key requests. One was that Mabel's Labels would charge 15 percent more for the labels on its website, $12 a pack, than the $10.47 that Walmart would sell them for. "They need their everyday low prices," says Cole. The other was that Walmart would have exclusivity on the Write Away! line among big-box stores for one year.

With the deal done, two of the Mabel's Labels partners flew to China to tour three factories recommended by manufacturers they respected. The partners had each plant manufacture a limited run of the labels and then went through a round of quality testing before making a selection. Next, they hired a China-based company recommended by the Canadian consulate in Hong Kong to conduct continuous quality control. As well, they hired a third-party firm in Canada to handle electronic data interchange, the paperless system that Walmart uses to issue purchase orders, receive invoices, process credit memos, and handle other administrative tasks. Finally, they hired a third-party logistics firm to manage shipping the labels from China, taking them through customs, unloading the container, packing smaller shipments, and trucking them to Walmart warehouses across Canada.

They also had to come up with the financing to make all of this happen months before the products hit Walmart's shelves, long before the label maker saw a cent. Cole says the upfront preparatory work that they had done for the Walmart pitch prepared the partners for how much credit their firm would need. They were careful to have this financing in place before even pitching to Walmart.

Cole says the Walmart deal is a huge step for the company and will mean some hiring. "I can hardly believe it. The labels are on the shelves as of last week. I have never been to Walmart so many times in my life," she jokes. "It was a huge investment, but the outlay of time and money is already paying off."

The strong performance of the Write Away! line in the first few months of sales in Canada helped persuade Walmart to carry the labels in some of its US stores for the 2013 back-to-school season. Plans are also underway for Mabel's Labels products to soon be available in Target.

Sources: Company website, www.mabelslabels.com; Mabel's Labels press releases published on Market Wire, December 8, 2009, and June 25, 2012; Eleanor Beaton, "Wowing Wal-Mart (W100 profile)," *PROFITGuide.com*, October 1, 2012; Francine Kopun, "Mabel's Labels at Wal-Mart Canada," *Moneyville.ca*, June 25, 2012; Julie Cole, "Big News for Mabel's Labels and Other Local Mompreneurs," *YummyMummyClub.ca*, June 20, 2012; Meredith MacLeod, "Mabel Sticking to Walmart," *HamiltonBusiness.com*, June 26, 2012; Julie Cole, "The Mabel's Labels Story," *RaiseTheHammer.org*, June 6, 2012.

QUESTIONS FOR DISCUSSION

1. Why has Mabel's Labels been so successful selling exclusively online?

2. Can Mabel's Labels maintain their competitive advantage when selling through retail stores? How can they reduce the threat of other competitors entering the write-on label market?

3. Should Mabel's Labels be concerned about Write Away! labels cannibalizing their online products? Should they continue to sell a different product in stores than online?

4. Channel conflict does not appear to be an issue yet, provided Walmart is able to sell at a retail price lower than Mabel's online prices. What steps does Mabel's Labels need to take to prevent channel conflict once they start to sell through other retail chains?

5. Mabel's Labels's website was very focused on their target market of moms. Now that products are available in retail stores, should they consider targeting other segments that might have different uses for write-on labels?

 MyMarketingLab is an online homework and tutorial system that puts you in control of your own learning with study and practice tools directly correlated to this chapter's content.

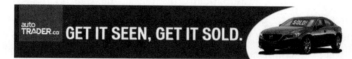

AFTER STUDYING THIS CHAPTER, YOU SHOULD BE ABLE TO

1. define the five promotion mix tools for communicating customer value

2. discuss the changing communications landscape and the need for integrated marketing communications

3. describe how advertising objectives are set and how advertising strategy is developed

4. explain how advertising effectiveness is evaluated and the role of the advertising agency

5. explain how companies use public relations to communicate with their publics

Communicating Customer Value: Advertising and Public Relations

PREVIEWING THE CONCEPTS

We'll forge ahead now into the last of the marketing mix tools—promotion. Companies must do more than just create customer value. They must also use promotion to clearly and persuasively communicate that value. You'll find that promotion is not a single tool but rather a mix of several tools. Ideally, under the concept of *integrated marketing communications,* the company will carefully coordinate these promotion elements to deliver a clear, consistent, and compelling message about the organization and its products. We'll begin by introducing you to the various promotion mix tools. Next, we'll examine the rapidly changing communications environment and the need for integrated marketing communications. Finally, we'll look more closely at two of the promotion tools—advertising and public relations. In the next chapter, we'll visit two other promotion mix tools—sales promotion and personal selling. Then, in Chapter 14, we'll explore direct and online marketing.

Let's start by looking at a good integrated marketing communications campaign—autoTRADER.ca's "The Most Cars In One Place" campaign. From TV and radio to engaging websites and a unique Facebook app, the campaign employed a rich mix of promotional elements, and was recently named top Canadian ad campaign of 2012.

autoTRADER.CA: THE MOST CARS IN ONE PLACE

Looking to buy or sell a car? A couple of years ago, your first inclination may have been to check out listings on Craigslist or Kijiji. But before the world went digital, autoTRADER magazine was the go-to-source for Canadians in the market to buy or sell vehicles for over 25 years. The magazine dominated the marketplace—that is, it did until the Internet came along. Then things changed rapidly for the company. More and more consumers were finding information online, and new websites such as Craigslist and Kijiji provided consumers with thousands of vehicles for them to view. Gradually, autoTRADER's dominance eroded as consumers chose digital information over print. So the company made the tough decision to go 100 percent digital to capture a larger slice of the dealer market, boost customer traffic, and work toward recapturing the number one position as the resource for consumers looking to buy and sell automobiles.

However, autoTRADER.ca began their move to digital with a shaky start. In 2011, autoTRADER.ca's traffic performance was in a downward spiral, declining on average

4 percent per month. In just seven months, the site experienced a decline of over 1.7 million visitors, which represented a 31 percent decrease in traffic. The company desperately needed to reinvigorate the brand and breathe life into a struggling digital endeavour.

In order to deal with stiff competition from Craigslist and Kijiji, the company enlisted the help of advertising agency DDB Canada, which identified a number of core business objectives. First, the ad agency wanted to attract at least 500 000 visitors per month in 2012. They also wanted to increase private seller listings to the site by 25 percent and dealer listings by 10 percent during the new ad campaign. Finally, the new ad campaign was intended to drive traffic growth by at least 5 percent, especially in Western Canada where site traffic levels were the lowest.

The overall communication objective of this new campaign was to make autoTRADER .ca relevant in the minds of Canadian car buyers and sellers, and to become the number one digital automotive destination in the country. When examining autoTRADER.ca's strengths, DDB Canada quickly realized that it had the largest car inventory of any digital site in the country. This factor became a major selling feature in the new ad campaign. To ensure this was a valuable feature to consumers, the advertising agency conducted a qualitative research study that concluded that a large inventory was a very strong motivator for consumers because it made them feel as if they had "left no stone unturned" in their quest to find the perfect car.

The new tagline, "The Most Cars in One Place," quickly became the driving force behind the new ad campaign. No matter where or how the brand was going to be communicated, it would always be clear: autoTRADER.ca was the online destination with "The Most Cars in One Place." The new campaign incorporated a number of different mediums including TV, radio, online, social media, public relations, and business-to-business communications. The campaign launched across the country in both French and English and used humour to get the message across to consumers. For example, the TV ad depicted in this chapter opening photo shows a young couple enjoying a dinner date. All is going well, and then the conversation turns to "children" and "the future." The man realizes he has a potential future with an attractive woman and quickly agrees that children are part of his future. As he glances outside at his obviously impractical-for-a-family Hummer, he quickly lists it on autoTRADER.ca. The next shot shows a huge bodybuilder looking at his perfect new automobile, the Hummer, on a laptop. The goal: to convince consumers that no matter what the reason for selling or buying, autoTRADER.ca is the place online to shop for or sell a vehicle.

Other forms of media soon followed the TV campaign. The firm used radio ads specific to Calgary and Edmonton where the online adoption of autoTRADER.ca lagged behind the rest of the country. Standard online banner ads reinforced the "most cars" message and reminded consumers that autoTRADER.ca specialized in vehicles only, not the wide variety of listings found on Craigslist or Kijiji. The campaign also used geotargeted homepage takeovers on YouTube and MSN.ca to show potential consumers the breadth of vehicle selection on autoTRADER.ca. As a consumer scrolled over the vehicles, they were provided with a real-time count of how many of a certain vehicle type were available within a 100 kilometre radius of their current location.

autoTRADER.ca also created a unique Facebook application labelled "the autoLYZER." This app was designed to help Canadians discover three automobiles for sale on autoTRADER.ca that best suited their personality and social life. The app was designed to analyze real-time Facebook data by looking at an individual's lifestyle, interests, social activities, and Facebook friends' opinions via existing posts. This information was then compiled and used to recommend cars currently for sale that would best match the customer's personality.

autoTRADER.ca's promotional activities were equally aggressive toward auto dealers. The landing page on autoTRADER.ca was developed to introduce dealers to the new message and strategy and to convince them that autoTRADER.ca was investing in their current and future business success.

This new marketing campaign rolled out in February 2012 with a national TV campaign coupled with the B2B initiative targeting dealers. autoTRADER.ca simultaneously engaged in heavy public relations to bring media attention to the new campaign. The company followed up a month later with the online banner ads, followed by the social media push and the introduction of the autoLYZER app in May.

The results of this campaign were astounding. Since the launch of this integrated marketing campaign (IMC), website traffic increased over 18 percent, with a 27 percent increase in growth in monthly unique visitors. Not only were consumers visiting the site, but the results proved they were interested in what the company had to offer, as page views were up over 76 percent from the previous year.

Unaided awareness of the autoTRADER.ca brand also increased post-campaign. The launch of the autoLYZER app and the publicity it generated resulted in substantial interest in the brand. The company now has over 14 000 likes on Facebook and over 3200 followers on Twitter. Dealer listings on the site increased over 18 percent and private listings skyrocketed, up 169 percent since the launch of the campaign. Even in Edmonton and Calgary, where web traffic was the lowest, autoTRADER.ca saw an immediate spike in web traffic of close to 15 percent.

The national campaign for autoTRADER.ca was an overwhelming success for the company and the ad agency responsible for it. In fact, DDB Canada was the Grand Prix winner at the 2013 CASSIES awards, which recognize the best business-building communication campaigns in Canada. This unique and highly creative campaign certainly repositioned autoTRADER.ca as the number one destination for car buyers and sellers and also generated triple-digit growth in consumer traffic for the website.[1]

BUILDING good customer relationships calls for more than just developing a good product, pricing it attractively, and making it available to target customers. Companies must also *communicate* their value propositions to customers, and what they communicate should not be left to chance. All of their communications must be planned and blended into carefully integrated marketing communications programs. Just as good communication is important in building and maintaining any kind of relationship, it is a crucial element in a company's efforts to build profitable customer relationships.

The Promotion Mix LO1

A company's total **promotion mix**—also called its **marketing communications mix**—consists of the specific blend of advertising, public relations, personal selling, sales promotion, and direct-marketing tools that the company uses to persuasively communicate customer value and build customer relationships. Definitions of the five major promotion tools follow:[2]

- **Advertising:** any paid form of non-personal presentation and promotion of ideas, goods, or services by an identified sponsor

Promotion mix (or marketing communications mix)
The specific blend of promotion tools that the company uses to persuasively communicate customer value and build customer relationships.

Advertising
Any paid form of non-personal presentation and promotion of ideas, goods, or services by an identified sponsor.

Sales promotion
Short-term incentives to encourage the purchase or sale of a product or a service.

Personal selling
Personal presentation by the firm's sales force for the purpose of making sales and building customer relationships.

Public relations (PR)
Building good relations with the company's various publics by obtaining favourable publicity, building up a good corporate image, and handling or heading off unfavourable rumours, stories, and events.

Direct marketing
Direct connections with carefully targeted individual consumers to both obtain an immediate response and cultivate lasting customer relationships.

■ **Sales promotion**: short-term incentives to encourage the purchase or sale of a product or a service

■ **Personal selling**: personal presentation by the firm's sales force for the purpose of making sales and building customer relationships

■ **Public relations (PR)**: building good relations with the company's various publics by obtaining favourable publicity, building up a good corporate image, and handling or heading off unfavourable rumours, stories, and events

■ **Direct marketing**: direct connections with carefully targeted individual consumers to both obtain an immediate response and cultivate lasting customer relationships

Each category involves specific promotional tools used to communicate with consumers. For example, advertising includes broadcast, print, Internet, mobile, outdoor, and other forms. Sales promotion includes discounts, coupons, displays, and demonstrations. Personal selling includes sales presentations, trade shows, and incentive programs. Public relations (PR) includes press releases, sponsorships, events, and web pages. And direct marketing includes catalogues, direct-response TV, kiosks, the Internet, mobile marketing, and more.

At the same time, marketing communication goes beyond these specific promotion tools. The product's design, its price, the shape and colour of its package, and the stores that sell it *all* communicate something to buyers. Thus, although the promotion mix is the company's primary communication activity, the entire marketing mix—promotion *and* product, price, and place—must be coordinated for greatest communication impact.

Integrated Marketing Communications

In past decades, marketers perfected the art of mass marketing—selling highly standardized products to masses of customers. In the process, they developed effective mass-media communications techniques to support these strategies. Large companies now routinely invest millions or even billions of dollars in television, magazine, and other mass-media advertising, reaching tens of millions of consumers with a single ad. Today, however, marketing managers face some new marketing communications realities. Perhaps no other area of marketing is changing so profoundly as marketing communications, creating both exciting and scary times for marketing communicators.

The New Marketing Communications Model

Several major factors are changing the face of today's marketing communications. First, *consumers* are changing. In this digital, wireless age, they are better informed and more communications empowered. Rather than relying on marketer-supplied information, they can use the Internet and other technologies to seek out information on their own. They can connect more easily with other consumers to exchange brand-related information or even to create their own marketing messages.

Second, *marketing strategies* are changing. As mass markets have fragmented, marketers are shifting away from mass marketing. More and more, they are developing focused marketing programs designed to build closer relationships with customers in more narrowly defined micromarkets.

Finally, sweeping advances in *communications technology* are causing remarkable changes in the ways in which companies and customers communicate with each other. The digital age has spawned a host of new information and communication tools—from smartphones and iPads to satellite and cable television systems to the many faces of the Internet (email, brand websites, online social networks, blogs, and so much more). These explosive developments have had a dramatic impact on marketing communications. Just as mass marketing once gave rise to a new generation of mass-media communications, the new digital media have given birth to a new marketing communications model.

Although network television, magazines, newspapers, and other traditional mass media remain very important, their dominance is declining. In their place, advertisers are now adding a broad selection of more-specialized and highly-targeted media to reach smaller customer segments with more-personalized, interactive messages. The new media range from specialty cable television channels and made-for-the-web videos to Internet catalogues, email, blogs, mobile phone content, and online social networks. In all, companies are doing less *broadcasting* and more *narrowcasting*.

Exhibit 12.1 **The new marketing communications model:** Rethink Breast Cancer, a Canadian not-for-profit focused on young women concerned about and affected by breast cancer uses an innovative approach to promote early detection and risk reductions with their Your Man Reminder Campaign.

Courtesy of Rethink

Some advertising industry experts even predict that the old mass-media communications model will eventually become obsolete. Mass media costs are rising, audiences are shrinking, ad clutter is increasing, and viewers are gaining control of message exposure through technologies such as video streaming or DVRs that let them skip disruptive television commercials. As a result, they suggest, marketers are shifting ever-larger portions of their marketing budgets away from old-media mainstays and moving them to digital and other new-age media. In recent years, although TV still dominates as an advertising medium, ad spending on the major TV networks has stagnated as ad spending on the Internet and other digital media has surged. Ad spending in magazines, newspapers, and radio, in contrast, has lost considerable ground.[3]

When Rethink Breast Cancer, a Canadian not-for-profit that promotes awareness of the disease to the under-40 crowd, hired John St. advertising agency, they exceeded all expectations with their award-winning campaign, "Your Man Reminder." The public service announcement (PSA), designed to encourage young women to conduct regular breast self-exams, went viral with more than 2.3 million views on YouTube (www.youtube .com/watch?v=VsyE2rCW71o), and the smartphone app has been downloaded more 70 000 times, becoming the number two app in Canada in the health and wellness category. The campaign also earned John St. a Webby award, which recognizes the best interactive content on the web. Similarly, commercials from Heineken's recent "Open your world" campaign debuted first on the brand's YouTube channel and Facebook page before making their way onto TV in 30 countries three months later. The first humorous spot, called "The Entrance," had been watched more than 3.6 million times on YouTube by the time it hit TV. Heineken later brought out 11 video clips, featuring characters from "The Entrance," that ran *only* online.[4]

In the new marketing communications world, rather than using old approaches that interrupt customers and force-feed them mass messages, new media formats let marketers reach smaller groups of consumers in more interactive, engaging ways. For example, think about television viewing these days. Consumers can now watch their favourite programs on just about anything with a screen—on televisions but also laptops, mobile phones, or iPads. And they can choose to watch programs whenever and wherever they wish, often with or without commercials. Increasingly, some programs, ads, and videos are being produced only for Internet viewing.

Despite the shift toward new digital media, however, traditional mass media still capture a lion's share of the promotion budgets of most major marketing firms, a fact that probably won't change quickly. For example, P&G, a leading proponent of digital media, still spends the majority of its huge advertising budget on mass media. Although P&G's digital outlay more than doubled last year to US$169 million, digital still accounts for less than 5 percent of the company's annual global advertising budget.[5]

At a broader level, although some may question the future role of TV advertising, it's still very much in use today. Last year, more than 41 percent of US advertising dollars was spent on television advertising versus 16 percent on Internet advertising. Says one media expert, "Traditional TV [is] still king."[6] It's a similar story in Canada where TV ad spending accounts for roughly 38 percent of total advertising expenditure. And while Internet and mobile media spending in Canada have experienced the largest increases, Tom Keane, president of Strategic Marketing Counsel, states "Advertisers believe in TV's ability to deliver what it's supposed to deliver." As such, it is expected to remain the dominant form of advertising in the near future.[7]

Thus, rather than the old media model rapidly collapsing, most industry insiders see a more gradual blending of new and traditional media. The new marketing communications model will consist of a shifting mix of both traditional mass media and a wide array of exciting, new, more-targeted, and more-personalized media. The challenge is to bridge the "media divide" that too often separates traditional creative and media approaches from new interactive and digital ones. Many advertisers and ad agencies are now grappling with this transition (see Marketing@Work 12.1). In the end, however, regardless of whether it's traditional or digital, the key is to find the mix of media that best communicates the brand message and enhances the customer's brand experience.

The Need for *Integrated* Marketing Communications

The shift toward a richer mix of media and communication approaches poses a problem for marketers. Consumers today are bombarded by commercial messages from a broad range of sources. But consumers don't distinguish between message sources the way marketers do. In the consumer's mind, messages from different media and promotional approaches all become part of a single message about the company. Conflicting messages from these different sources can result in confused company images, brand positions, and customer relationships.

All too often, companies fail to integrate their various communications channels. The result is a hodgepodge of communications to consumers. Mass-media advertisements say one thing, whereas an in-store promotion sends a different signal, and company sales literature creates still another message. Furthermore, the company's website, emails, Facebook page, or videos posted on YouTube say something altogether different.

The problem is that these communications often come from different parts of the company. Advertising messages are planned and implemented by the advertising department or an advertising agency. Personal-selling communications are developed by sales management. Other company specialists are responsible for public relations, sales

The Shifting Advertising Universe: SoBe It!

SoBe made a big splash during the 2008 Super Bowl with a big-budget, 60-second commercial produced by the Arnell Group, an old-line Madison Avenue creative ad agency. The ad extravaganza featured supermodel Naomi Campbell and a full troupe of SoBe lizards, energized by colourful droplets of the brand's then-new enhanced water, LifeWater. The computer-generated graphics were stunning, the colours alluring, and Naomi Campbell was, well, Naomi Campbell. However, although the ad drew attention, it was not a viewer favourite. It just didn't connect with consumers.

Not to be denied, for the 2009 Super Bowl, SoBe and its parent company, PepsiCo, assigned the Arnell Group to create an even more elaborate (and even more expensive) commercial, a 3D spectacular featuring pro football players in white tutus performing a ballet, directed by a SoBe lizard. Once the athletes and lizards got a taste of SoBe LifeWater, a DJ cranked up the music, and the dance switched to hip-hop. Once again, although the ad generated a ton of awareness, it simply didn't deliver much in the way of consumer-brand engagement. As one journalist stated bluntly: "The SoBe spots [were] among the biggest wastes of money in Super Bowl history."

Finally the wiser, SoBe stopped running Super Bowl ads. In fact, in a move that sent shivers down the spines of many old-line Madison Avenue agencies, SoBe abandoned its traditional big-media, "TV-first," advertising approach altogether and adopted a more bottom-up, digital, new-media approach. It fired the Arnell Group, replacing the big creative agency with a team of smaller digital, PR, creative, and promotion shops.

SoBe's new advertising model turns the old approach upside down. Instead of starting with mass-market TV and print advertising, SoBe now aims first to hook its 18- to 29-year-old target audience with more focused and involving interactive media. Rather than developing a TV plan and then creating content to fill it, SoBe starts with engaging brand message content and then figures out where to put it to reach customers in the most effective way. In a reverse of past thinking, SoBe now favours a collaborative approach that integrates digital, traditional, and event media. In fact, content often appears online first and then moves to traditional TV. That kind of thinking causes concern for many traditional Madison Avenue creative agencies, which cut their teeth on developing creative ads for big-budget, mostly television and print campaigns.

SoBe's new advertising approach reflects a broader industry trend. In today's splintering advertising universe, in which there are more new places than ever to stick ads—online, on mobile phones, in all places digital and interactive—advertisers and traditional ad agencies alike are scrambling to stay relevant. For decades, the big traditional creative agencies ruled the roost. They were about coming up with strategic Big Ideas that would connect brands emotionally with millions of consumers through large-scale mass-media campaigns. But today, the Small Idea is on the rise. Increasingly, like SoBe, marketers are adding a host of new digital and interactive media—websites, viral video, blogs, social networks, street events—that let them target individuals or small communities of consumers rather than the masses.

In this shifting advertising universe, traditional creative agencies, such as the Arnell Group, often find themselves outmaneuvered by smaller, more nimble, and specialized digital, interactive, media, and creative agencies. However, these smaller digital shops sometimes lack experience in leading accounts and driving brand strategy. The competition is fierce, with traditional agencies struggling to become more digital and digital agencies struggling to become more traditional. "We in the ad business are faced with the question of who is going to lead this new world," says an industry analyst. "Will it be digitized traditional agencies or the new breed of digital agencies with big ambitions? The outcome . . . is far from clear."

At SoBe, however, things seem clear enough. Its latest marketing campaign—called "Try Everything"—is a true 360-degree effort developed by a diverse team of agencies including Firstborn (a digital shop), Weber Shandwick (a PR agency), Motive (in-market sampling and events), and Anomaly (advertising). Under the old approach, the SoBe brand team would have developed a "creative brief" that outlined the brand and advertising strategy and then let the Arnell Group take the lead in creating the advertising (usually a traditional television-plus-print campaign). Under the new approach, the SoBe brand team and the team of agencies workshop jointly in an ongoing process to create and distribute engaging message content using an integrated mix of new and old media.

SoBe's "Try Everything" campaign blends TV ads with the brand's website, Facebook page, YouTube channel, iPhone app, and other digital elements designed to drive home the brand message that "Life is more exciting—and more fun—when you try new things." TV ads draw viewers to the SoBe website and other digital elements, which offer a range of virtual experiences inspired by one of SoBe's 31 flavours, from "tickling Kiwis" (inspired by Strawberry Kiwi LifeWater) to "kissing the office hottie" (fuelled by SoBe Citrus Energy). The TV and digital efforts are supported by hands-on PR in the form of "Try Everything" street events in New York, Chicago, Los Angeles, Denver, Seattle, and other cities, which encourage locals to experience everything from milking (fake) Orange Cream cows or bowling with melons (Mango Melon) to building sandcastles (SoBe Pina Colada Elixir) or joining in on a rooftop dance party (SoBe Lean Honey Green Tea).

The immersive "Try Everything" effort isn't your traditional "advertising-led" campaign—it's a true team effort.

© studiomode / Alamy

Exhibit 12.2 Rather than starting with traditional mass-market TV and print ads, SoBe's new bottom-up approach blends interactive digital content with traditional media and hands-on PR to engage customers in the most effective way.

The team's diverse agencies are "all working together to come back with the most compelling approach," says Andrew Katz, SoBe's marketing director. Even the agency that's creating the "Try Everything" ads—Anomaly—prides itself on being anything *but* traditional. Instead, Anomaly is "ideas-led, media-neutral, integrated, and multidisciplinary . . . at its core."

Consumer relevance and interaction seem to be the key to the new approach. For example, go to the SoBe website and you'll see customer testimonials from real on-the-street tastings of SoBe flavours or even a "Join the Debate" feature inviting consumers to vote for the next SoBe flavour.

Interestingly, SoBe's shifting communication strategy came at a time when the brand was already doing extremely well. SoBe LifeWater's share of the enhanced and flavoured water market grew from 5.9 percent in 2008 to 13.9 percent in

2010. It seems the new advertising approach evolved not to meet a crisis but as a forward-thinking effort to adjust to the new advertising environment.

Thus, for advertisers and their agencies, as oft-misspoken baseball legend Yogi Berra once said, "The future ain't what it used to be." In the fast-changing advertising universe, SoBe and other brands are moving to master the new digital and interactive technologies and merge them effectively with traditional approaches. For advertisers and agencies alike, the message is clear. Says one agency CEO, "We've got to reinvent and transform the way we work."

Sources: Quotes and other information from Ken Wheaton, "Is Pepsi's Pass on Super Bowl an Offensive or Defensive Move?" *Advertising Age,* January 4, 2010, p. 12; Tony Quin, "Race to Relevance: Why the Winners Will Come from Both Sides," *Brandweek,* March 15, 2010, p. 14; Natalie Zmuda, "SoBe Ditches Creative Agency in New Marketing Approach," *Advertising Age,* April 14, 2010, http://adage.com/agencynews/article?article_id=143303; "Jered Weaver, Kate Upton to Star in New SoBe Ad Campaign," *Advertising Age,* May 17, 2011, http://adage.com/print/227607; "SoBe Celebrates 'Try Everything,'" PRNewswire, May 25, 2011; "PepsiCo; SoBe Rallies Millennials to 'Try Everything,'" *Entertainment Newsweekly,* June 3, 2011, p. 139; and www.sobe.com/#/tryeverything, accessed November 2011.

---

promotion events, Internet marketing, and other forms of marketing communications. However, whereas these companies have separated their communications tools, customers won't. Mixed communications from these sources will result in blurred brand perceptions by consumers. "This new world of [the Internet, social networks,] tablet computers, smartphones, and apps presents both opportunities and challenges," says one marketing executive. "The biggest issue is complexity and fragmentation . . . the amount of choice out there," he says. The challenge is to "make it come together in an organized way."[8]

Integrated marketing communications (IMC)

Carefully integrating and coordinating the company's many communications channels to deliver a clear, consistent, and compelling message about the organization and its products.

Today, more companies are adopting the concept of **integrated marketing communications (IMC)**. Under this concept, as illustrated in Figure 12.1, the company carefully integrates its many communications channels to deliver a clear, consistent, and compelling message about the organization and its brands.

Integrated marketing communications calls for recognizing all touchpoints where the public may encounter the company and its brands. Each *brand contact* will deliver a message, whether good, bad, or indifferent. The company's goal should be to deliver a consistent and positive message to each contact. IMC leads to a total marketing communications strategy aimed at building strong customer relationships by showing how the company and its products can help customers solve their problems.

Integrated marketing communications tie together all of the company's messages and images. Its television and print ads have the same message, look, and feel as its email

FIGURE 12.1 Integrated Marketing Communications

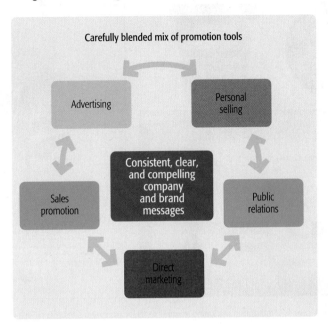

and personal selling communications. And its PR materials project the same image as its website, online social networks, or mobile marketing efforts. Often, different media play unique roles in attracting, informing, and persuading consumers; these roles must be carefully coordinated under the overall marketing communications plan.

A great example of a well-integrated marketing communications effort comes from premium ice cream maker Häagen-Dazs. To strengthen its emotional connection with consumers, Häagen-Dazs launched the "Häagen-Dazs loves honey bees" campaign, centred on an issue that's important to both the brand and its customers—a mysterious colony-collapse disorder threatening the honey bee population. Honey bees pollinate one-third of all the natural products we eat and up to 40 percent of the natural flavours used in Häagen-Dazs ice cream, making the "HD loves HB" message a natural for the brand. But perhaps even more important than the "help the honey bees" message itself is the way that Häagen-Dazs communicates that message:[9]

> More than just running a few ads, Häagen-Dazs has created a full-fledged, beautifully integrated marketing communications campaign, using a wide range of media that work harmoniously for the cause. It starts with broadcast and print ads that drive traffic to the campaign's helpthehoneybees.com website, a kind of honey bee central where customers can learn about the problem and how to help. At the site, visitors can tap into a news feed called *The Buzz*, turn on "Bee TV," purchase Bee-Ts with phrases like "Long live the queen" and "Bee a hero," send "Bee-mail" messages to friends, or make donations to support honey bee research. To create even more bee buzz, Häagen-Dazs hands out samples of Vanilla Honey Bee ice cream and wildflower seeds at local farmers markets across the country and sponsors fund-raisers by local community and school groups. The campaign also incorporates social networks such as Twitter and Facebook. In all, the rich, well-coordinated blend of communications elements successfully delivers Häagen-Dazs' unique message and positioning. It is now "a brand with a heart and a soul," says the brand's director. "We're not only raising brand awareness," she says, "but making a difference in the world."

In the past, no one person or department was responsible for thinking through the communication roles of the various promotion tools and coordinating the promotion mix. To help implement integrated marketing communications, some companies appoint

HDIP, Inc.

Exhibit 12.3 The "HD loves HB" integrated marketing communications campaign uses a rich, well-coordinated blend of promotion elements to successfully deliver Häagen-Dazs' unique message.

a marketing communications director who has overall responsibility for the company's communications efforts. This helps to produce better communications consistency and greater sales impact. It places the responsibility in someone's hands—where none existed before—to unify the company's image as it is shaped by thousands of company activities.

Shaping the Overall Promotion Mix

The concept of integrated marketing communications suggests that the company must blend the promotion tools carefully into a coordinated *promotion mix*. But how does the company determine what mix of promotion tools to use? Companies within the same industry differ greatly in the design of their promotion mixes. For example, Mary Kay spends most of its promotion funds on personal selling and direct marketing, whereas competitor CoverGirl spends heavily on mass media advertising. We now look at factors that influence the marketer's choice of promotion tools.

The Nature of Each Promotion Tool

Each promotion tool has unique characteristics and costs. Marketers must understand these characteristics in shaping the promotion mix.

Advertising Advertising can reach masses of geographically dispersed buyers at a low cost per exposure, and it enables the seller to repeat a message many times. For example, an estimated 108 million people tuned in to watch Super Bowl XLVII and about 40 million people watched at least part of the eighty-fifth Academy Awards broadcast. For companies that want to reach a mass audience, TV is the place to be.[10]

Beyond its reach, large-scale advertising says something positive about the seller's size, popularity, and success. Because of advertising's public nature, consumers tend to view advertised products as more legitimate. Advertising is also very expressive—it allows the company to dramatize its products through the artful use of visuals, print, sound, and colour. On the one hand, advertising can be used to build up a long-term image for a product (such as Coca-Cola ads).On the other hand, advertising can trigger quick sales (as when Home Hardware advertises weekend specials).

Advertising also has some shortcomings. Although it reaches many people quickly, advertising is impersonal and cannot be as directly persuasive as can company sales-people. For the most part, advertising can carry on only a one-way communication with the audience, and the audience does not feel that it has to pay attention or respond. In addition, advertising can be very costly. Although some advertising forms, such as news-paper and radio advertising, can be done on smaller budgets, other forms, such as net-work TV advertising, require very large budgets.

Personal Selling   Personal selling is the most effective tool at certain stages of the buy-ing process, particularly in building up buyers' preferences, convictions, and actions. It involves personal interaction between two or more people, so each person can observe the other's needs and characteristics and make quick adjustments. Personal selling also allows all kinds of customer relationships to spring up, ranging from matter-of-fact sell-ing relationships to personal friendships. An effective salesperson keeps the customer's interests at heart to build a long-term relationship by solving a customer's problems. Fi-nally, with personal selling, the buyer usually feels a greater need to listen and respond, even if the response is a polite "No thank-you."

These unique qualities come at a cost, however. A sales force requires a longer-term commitment than does advertising—advertising can be turned up or down, but sales force size is harder to change. Personal selling is also the company's most expensive pro-motion tool, costing companies on average $350 or more per sales call, depending on the indus-try.[11] Most firms spend up to three times as much on personal selling as they do on advertising.

Sales Promotion   Sales promotion includes a wide assortment of tools—coupons, rebates, contests, discounts or "sales," "buy one get one free" offers, and other limited time offers. Sales promotions are designed to achieve one or more of the following goals: attract consumer atten-tion, offer strong incentives to purchase, drama-tize product offers, encourage trial, or boost sag-ging sales. For example, furniture retailer Leon's offers regular but different sales promotions, each typically lasting one month. Sometimes sales promotions may be combined, such as the "Honey! They Shrunk the Prices!" sale com-bined with a special financing offer, "Don't pay for 16 months!"

Sales promotions invite and reward quick response—whereas advertising says, "Buy our product," sales promotion says, "Buy it now." Sales promotion effects are often short-lived, however, and often are not as effective as adver-tising or personal selling in building long-run brand preference and customer relationships.

Courtesy of Leon's Furniture Ltd.

Exhibit 12.4 **Sales promotion:** Leon's "Ho! Ho! Hold the Payment" sales promotion offers strong incentives to purchase, but always for a limited time, to encourage consumers to purchase now rather than wait until later.

Public Relations Public relations (PR) is very believable—news stories, features, sponsorships, and events seem more real and believable to readers than ads do. Public relations can also reach many prospects who avoid salespeople and advertisements—the message gets to the buyers as "news" rather than as a sales-directed communication. And, as with advertising, PR can dramatize a company or product. Marketers tend to underuse PR or to use it as an afterthought. Yet a well-thought-out PR campaign used with other promotion mix elements can be very effective and economical.

Direct Marketing Although there are many forms of direct marketing—direct mail and catalogues, online marketing, telephone marketing, and others—they all share four distinctive characteristics. Direct marketing is *less public*: The message is normally directed to specific persons. Direct marketing is *immediate* and *customized*: Messages can be prepared very quickly and can be tailored to appeal to specific consumers. Finally, direct marketing is *interactive*: It allows a dialogue between the marketing team and the consumer, and messages can be altered depending on the consumer's response. Thus, direct marketing is well suited to highly-targeted marketing efforts and to building one-to-one customer relationships.

Promotion Mix Strategies

Marketers can choose from two basic promotion mix strategies—*push* promotion or *pull* promotion. Figure 12.2 contrasts the two strategies. The relative emphasis given to the specific promotion tools differs for push and pull strategies. A **push strategy** involves "pushing" the product through marketing channels to final consumers. The producer directs its marketing activities (primarily personal selling and trade promotion) toward channel members to induce them to carry the product and promote it to final consumers. For example, John Deere does very little promoting of its lawn mowers, garden tractors, and other residential consumer products to final consumers. Instead, John Deere's sales force works with RONA, Home Depot, independent dealers, and other channel members, who in turn push John Deere products to final consumers.

Using a **pull strategy**, the producer directs its marketing activities (primarily advertising and consumer promotion) toward final consumers to induce them to buy the product. For example, Unilever promotes its Axe grooming products directly to its young male target market by using TV and print ads, a brand website, its YouTube channel, and other marketing channels. If the pull strategy is effective, consumers will then demand the brand from

Push strategy
A promotion strategy that calls for using the sales force and trade promotion to push the product through channels. The producer promotes the product to channel members who in turn promote it to final consumers.

Pull strategy
A promotion strategy that calls for spending a lot on advertising and consumer promotion to induce final consumers to buy the product, creating a demand vacuum that "pulls" the product through the channel.

FIGURE 12.2 Push versus Pull Promotion Strategy

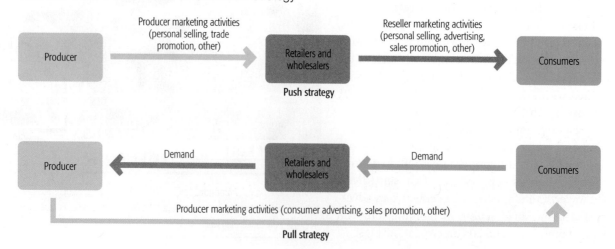

retailers, such as Shoppers Drug Mart or Walmart, who will in turn demand it from Unilever. Thus, under a pull strategy, consumer demand "pulls" the product through the channels.

Some business-to-business marketers use only push strategies; some consumer-products companies use only pull. However, most large companies use some combination of both. For example, Unilever spends more than US$6 billion worldwide each year on media advertising and consumer sales promotions to create brand preference and pull customers into stores that carry its products. At the same time, it uses its own and distributors' sales forces and trade promotions to push its brands through the channels, so that they'll be available on store shelves when consumers come calling. Companies consider many factors when designing their promotion mix strategies, including the type of product and market. For example, the importance of different promotion tools varies between consumer and business markets. Business-to-consumer companies usually pull more, putting more of their funds into advertising, followed by sales promotion, personal selling, and then PR. In contrast, business-to-business marketers tend to push more, putting more of their funds into personal selling, followed by sales promotion, advertising, and PR.

Now that we've examined the concept of integrated marketing communications and the factors that firms consider when shaping their promotion mixes, let's look more closely at the specific marketing communications tools.

Advertising LO3

Advertising can be traced back to the very beginnings of recorded history. Archaeologists working in the countries around the Mediterranean Sea have dug up signs announcing various events and offers. The Romans painted walls to announce gladiator fights, and the Phoenicians painted pictures promoting their wares on large rocks along parade routes. During the golden age in Greece, town criers announced the sale of cattle, crafted items, and even cosmetics. An early "singing commercial" went as follows: "For eyes that are shining, for cheeks like the dawn / For beauty that lasts after girlhood is gone / For prices in reason, the woman who knows / Will buy her cosmetics from Aesclyptos."

Modern advertising, however, is a far cry from these early efforts. Canadian advertisers now run up an estimated annual bill of over CDN$14 billion on measured advertising media; worldwide ad spending exceeds an estimated US$500 billion. P&G, the world's largest advertiser, last year spent US$8.7 billion worldwide.[12]

Although advertising is used mostly by business firms, a wide range of not-for-profit organizations, professionals, and social agencies also use advertising to promote their causes to various target publics. For example, the Canadian government boosted ad spending to more than $136 million in 2009–2010, up from only $41 million just four years earlier.[13] Advertising is a good way to inform and persuade, whether the purpose is to sell Coca-Cola worldwide or to encourage people in a developing nation to use birth control.

Marketing management must make four important decisions when developing an advertising program (see Figure 12.3): *setting advertising objectives, setting the advertising budget, developing advertising strategy (message decisions and media decisions), and evaluating advertising campaigns.*

Setting Advertising Objectives

The first step is to set *advertising objectives*. These objectives should be based on past decisions about the target market, positioning, and the marketing mix, which define the job that advertising must do in the total marketing program. The overall advertising objective is to help build customer relationships by communicating customer value. Here, we discuss specific advertising objectives.

FIGURE 12.3 Major Advertising Decisions

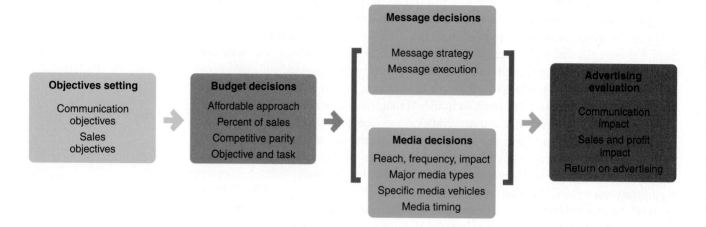

Advertising objective

A specific communication *task* to be accomplished with a specific *target* audience during a specific period of *time*.

An **advertising objective** is a specific communication *task* to be accomplished with a specific *target* audience during a specific period of *time*. Advertising objectives can be classified by primary purpose—whether the aim is to *inform*, *persuade*, or *remind*. Table 12.1 lists examples of each of these specific objectives.

Informative advertising is used heavily when introducing a new-product category. In this case, the objective is to build primary demand. Thus, early producers of HDTVs first had to inform consumers of the image quality and size benefits of the new product. *Persuasive advertising* becomes more important as competition increases. Here, the company's objective is to build selective demand. For example, once HDTVs became established, Samsung began trying to persuade consumers that *its* brand offered the best quality for their money.

Some persuasive advertising has become *comparative advertising* (or *attack advertising*), in which a company directly or indirectly compares its brand with one or more other brands. You see examples of comparative advertising in almost every product category,

TABLE 12.1 Possible Advertising Objectives

Informative Advertising

Communicating customer value	Suggesting new uses for a product
Building a brand and company image	Informing the market of a price change
Telling the market about a new product	Describing available services and support
Explaining how a product works	Correcting false impressions

Persuasive Advertising

Building brand preference	Persuading customers to purchase now
Encouraging switching to a brand	Persuading customers to receive a sales call
Changing customer's perception of product value	Convincing customers to tell others about the brand

Reminder Advertising

Maintaining customer relationships	Reminding consumers that the product may be needed in the near future
Reminding consumers where to buy the product	Keeping the brand in the consumer's mind during off-seasons

ranging from sports drinks, coffee, and soup to computers, car rentals, and credit cards. For example, Pepsi revived its once famous taste challenge in 2012. The company's TV and Facebook campaign kicked off early in 2012, and the company targeted millions of Canadians in blind-taste tests across the nation during the summer. Using touchscreen tablets, consumer were able to instantly see their results, have them emailed to them, and were able to share their results with friends on Facebook.

Advertisers should use comparative advertising with caution. All too often, such ads invite competitor responses, resulting in an advertising war that neither competitor can win. Upset competitors might also take more drastic action, such as filing complaints with the Competition Bureau or even filing false-advertising lawsuits. For example, in the past few years multiple lawsuits have been filed in the Canadian telecommunications industry in several provinces by Bell, Rogers, and TELUS.[14]

Exhibit 12.5 **Comparative advertising:** Pepsi ran its taste challenge across Canada in the summer of 2012 and used TV and social media to spread the word.

Reminder advertising is important for mature products; it helps to maintain customer relationships and keep consumers thinking about the product. Expensive Coca-Cola television ads primarily build and maintain the Coca-Cola brand relationship rather than inform consumers or persuade them to buy it in the short run.

Advertising's goal is to help move consumers through the buying process. Some advertising is designed to move people to immediate action. For example, a direct-response television ad by Weight Watchers urges consumers to pick up the phone and sign up right away, and a Best Buy newspaper insert for a weekend sale encourages immediate store visits. However, many ads focus on building or strengthening long-term customer relationships. For example, a Nike television ad in which well-known athletes work through extreme challenges in their Nike gear never directly asks for a sale. Instead, the goal is to somehow change the way the people think or feel about the brand.

Setting the Advertising Budget

After determining its advertising objectives, the company next sets its **advertising budget** for each product. Here, we look at four common methods used to set the total budget for advertising: the *affordable method*, the *percentage-of-sales method*, the *competitive-parity method*, and the *objective-and-task method*.[15]

Affordable Method   Some companies use the **affordable method:** They set the advertising budget at the level they think the company can afford. Small businesses often use this method, reasoning that the company cannot spend more on advertising than it has. They start with total revenues, deduct operating expenses and capital outlays, and then devote some portion of the remaining funds to advertising.

Unfortunately, this method of setting budgets completely ignores the effects of advertising on sales. It tends to place promotion last among spending priorities, even in situations in which advertising is critical to the firm's success. It leads to an uncertain annual promotion budget, which makes long-range market planning difficult. Although the affordable method can result in overspending on advertising, it more often results in underspending.

Advertising budget
The dollars and other resources allocated to a product or company advertising program.

Affordable method
Setting the advertising budget at the level management thinks the company can afford.

Percentage-of-sales method
Setting the promotion budget at a certain percentage of current or forecasted sales, or as a percentage of the unit sales price.

Percentage-of-Sales Method Other companies use the **percentage-of-sales method**, setting the promotion budget at a certain percentage of current or forecasted sales. Or they budget a percentage of the unit sales price. The percentage-of-sales method has advantages. It is simple to use and helps management to think about the relationships among promotion spending, selling price, and profit per unit.

Despite these claimed advantages, however, the percentage-of-sales method has little to justify it. It wrongly views sales as the *cause* of promotion rather than as the *result*. Although studies have found a positive correlation between promotional spending and brand strength, this relationship often turns out to be effect and cause, not cause and effect. Stronger brands with higher sales can afford the biggest ad budgets.

Thus, the percentage-of-sales budget is based on availability of funds rather than on opportunities. It may prevent the increased spending sometimes needed to turn around falling sales. Because the budget varies with year-to-year sales, long-range planning is difficult. Finally, the method does not provide any basis for choosing a *specific* percentage, except what has been done in the past or what competitors are doing.

Competitive-parity method
Setting the promotion budget to match competitors' outlays.

Competitive-Parity Method Still other companies use the **competitive-parity method**, setting their promotion budgets to match competitors' outlays. They monitor competitors' advertising or get industry promotion spending estimates from publications or trade associations, and then set their budgets based on the industry average.

Two arguments support this method. First, competitors' budgets represent the collective wisdom of the industry. Second, spending what competitors spend helps prevent promotion wars. Unfortunately, neither argument is valid. There are no grounds for believing that the competition has a better idea of what a company should be spending on promotion than does the company itself. Companies differ greatly, and each has its own special promotion needs. Finally, there is no evidence that budgets based on competitive parity prevent promotion wars.

Objective-and-task method
Developing the advertising budget by (1) defining specific objectives, (2) determining the tasks that must be performed to achieve these objectives, and (3) estimating the costs of performing these tasks. The sum of these costs is the proposed advertising budget.

Objective-and-Task Method The most logical budget-setting method is the **objective-and-task method**, whereby the company sets its advertising budget based on what it wants to accomplish with promotion. This budgeting method entails (1) defining specific promotion objectives, (2) determining the tasks needed to achieve these objectives, and (3) estimating the costs of performing these tasks. The sum of these costs is the proposed advertising budget.

The advantage of the objective-and-task method is that it forces management to spell out its assumptions about the relationship between dollars spent and promotion results. But it is also the most difficult method to use. Often, it is hard to figure out which specific tasks will achieve stated objectives. For example, suppose Sony wants 95 percent awareness for its latest Blu-ray player during the six-month introductory period. What specific advertising messages and media schedules should Sony use to attain this objective? How much would these messages and media schedules cost? Sony management must consider such questions, even though they are hard to answer.

No matter what method is used, setting the advertising budget is no easy task. John Wanamaker, the department store magnate, once said, "I know that half of my advertising is wasted, but I don't know which half. I spent $2 million for advertising, and I don't know if that is half enough or twice too much."

As a result of such thinking, advertising is one of the easiest budget items to cut when economic times get tough. Cuts in brand-building advertising appear to do little short-term harm to sales. For example, in the wake of the 2008 recession, US advertising expenditures plummeted 12 percent over the previous year. In the long run, however, slashing ad spending risks long-term damage to a brand's image and market share. In fact, companies that can maintain or even increase their advertising spending while competitors are decreasing theirs can gain competitive advantage. For example, during the recent recession, while competitors were cutting back, car maker Audi actually increased its marketing and advertising spending. Audi "kept its foot on the pedal while everyone else is pulling back," said an Audi ad executive at the time. "Why would we go backwards now when the industry is generally locking the brakes and cutting spending?" As a result, Audi's brand awareness and buyer consideration reached record levels during the recession, outstripping those of BMW, Mercedes, and Lexus, and positioning Audi strongly for the post-recession era. Audi is now one of the hottest auto brands on the market.[16]

Developing Advertising Strategy

Advertising strategy consists of two major elements: creating advertising *messages* and selecting advertising *media*. In the past, companies often viewed media planning as secondary to the message-creation process. The creative department first created good advertisements, and then the media department selected and purchased the best media for carrying these advertisements to desired target audiences. This often caused friction between creatives and media planners.

Today, however, soaring media costs, more-focused target marketing strategies, and the blizzard of new media have promoted the importance of the media-planning function. The decision about which media to use for an ad campaign—television, newspapers, magazines, a website or online social network, mobile phones, or email—is now sometimes more critical than the creative elements of the campaign. As a result, more and more, advertisers are orchestrating a closer harmony between their messages and the media that deliver them. In fact, in a really good ad campaign, you often have to ask, "Is that a media idea or a creative idea?"

Creating the Advertising Message No matter how big the budget, advertising can succeed only if advertisements gain attention and communicate well. Good advertising messages are especially important in today's costly and cluttered advertising environment. In 1950, the average household received only three network television channels and a handful of major national magazines. Today, the average household receives about 119 channels, and consumers have more than 20 000 magazines from which to choose.[17] Add in the countless radio stations and a continuous barrage of catalogues, direct mail, email and online ads, and out-of-home media, and consumers are being bombarded with ads at home, work, and all points in between. As a result, consumers are exposed to as many as 3000 to 5000 commercial messages every day.[18]

BREAKING THROUGH THE CLUTTER If all this advertising clutter bothers some consumers, it also causes huge headaches for advertisers. Take the situation facing network television advertisers. They pay an average of US$302 000 to make a single 30-second commercial. Then, each time they show it, they pay an average of US$122 000 for 30 seconds of advertising time during a popular prime-time program. They pay even more if it's an especially popular program, such as *American Idol* (US$468 000), *Sunday Night Football* (US$415 000), *Glee* (US$273 000), *Family Guy* (US$259 000), or a mega-event such as the Super Bowl (US$3 million per 30 seconds!).[19] In comparison, Canadian advertising is a bargain, but the reach is smaller. For example, the number of TV households in Canada is only 13.7 million, compared to 114.7 million in the United States. In Canadian dollars, advertisers in Canada spent

Advertising strategy
The strategy by which the company accomplishes its advertising objectives. It consists of two major elements: creating advertising messages and selecting advertising media.

Exhibit 12.6 **Advertising clutter:** Today's consumers, armed with an arsenal of weapons, can choose what they watch and don't watch. Increasingly, they are choosing not to watch ads.

© Andrew Rubtsov / Alamy

approximately $3.4 billion versus $59.1 billion in the United States on TV advertising in 2010.[20]

Then, their ads are sandwiched in with a clutter of other commercials, announcements, and network promotions, totalling nearly 20 minutes of non-program material per prime-time hour with commercial breaks coming every six minutes on average. Such clutter in television and other ad media has created an increasingly hostile advertising environment. According to one study, more than 70 percent of viewers think there are too many ads on TV, and 62 percent of national advertisers believe that TV ads have become less effective, citing clutter as the main culprit.[21]

Until recently, television viewers were pretty much a captive audience for advertisers. But today's digital wizardry has given consumers a rich new set of information and entertainment choices. With the growth in cable and satellite TV, the Internet, video streaming, and smartphones, today's viewers have many more options.

Digital technology has also armed consumers with an arsenal of weapons for choosing what they watch or don't watch. Increasingly, thanks to the growth of DVR systems, consumers are choosing *not* to watch ads. Approximately 30 percent of Canadian TV households now have DVRs, and that number is likely to increase. One ad agency executive calls these DVR systems "electronic weedwhackers" when it comes to viewing commercials. DVR owners view only about 45 percent of the commercials during DVR playback. At the same time, VOD and video downloads are exploding, letting viewers watch entertainment on their own time—with or without commercials.[22]

Thus, advertisers can no longer force-feed the same old cookie-cutter ad messages to captive consumers through traditional media. Just to gain and hold attention, today's advertising messages must be better planned, more imaginative, more entertaining, and more emotionally engaging. Simply interrupting or disrupting consumers no longer works. Unless ads provide information that is interesting, useful, or entertaining, many consumers will simply skip by them.

MERGING ADVERTISING AND ENTERTAINMENT To break through the clutter, many marketers have subscribed to a new merging of advertising and entertainment, dubbed "Madison & Vine." You've probably heard of Madison Avenue, the New York City street that houses the headquarters of many of the largest advertising agencies in the United States. You may also have heard of Hollywood & Vine, the intersection of Hollywood Avenue and Vine Street in Hollywood, California, long the symbolic heart of the US entertainment industry. Now, Madison Avenue and Hollywood & Vine have come together to form a new intersection—Madison & Vine—that represents the merging of advertising and entertainment in an effort to create new avenues for reaching consumers with more engaging messages.

This merging of advertising and entertainment takes one of two forms: advertainment or branded entertainment. The aim of *advertainment* is to make ads themselves so entertaining, or so useful, that people *want* to watch them. There's no chance that you'd watch ads on purpose, you say? Think again. For example, the Super Bowl has become an annual advertainment showcase. Tens of millions of people tune in to the Super Bowl each year, as much to watch the entertaining ads as to see the game.

In fact, DVR systems can actually *improve* viewership of a really *good* ad. For example, most Super Bowl ads last year were viewed more in DVR households than non-DVR households. Rather than zipping past the ads, many people were skipping back to rewatch them during halftime and following the game.[23]

Beyond making their regular ads more entertaining, advertisers are also creating new advertising forms that look less like ads and more like short films or shows. For example, Dove's "Evolution" video wasn't technically an ad, but it drew more—and more meaningful—views than many TV ads do, and the views were initiated by consumers.

A range of new brand messaging platforms—from webisodes and blogs to viral videos and apps—are now blurring the line between ads and entertainment. These days, it's not unusual to see an entertaining ad or other brand message on YouTube before you see it on TV. And you might well seek it out at a friend's suggestion rather than having it forced on you by the advertiser.

Branded entertainment (or *brand integrations*) involves making the brand an inseparable part of some other form of entertainment. The most common form of branded entertainment is product placements—embedding brands as props within other programming. It might be a brief glimpse of the latest LG phone on *Grey's Anatomy,* or the product placement might be scripted into an episode. For example, one entire episode of *Modern Family* centred around the Dunphy family trying to find the recently released, hard-to-find Apple iPad their father, Phil, coveted as his special birthday present. Finally, the placement could be worked into the show's overall storyline. For example, NBC's *The Biggest Loser* and health-club chain 24 Hour Fitness have created a product placement partnership that fully and thematically integrates the brand with the show.[24]

Exhibit 12.7 **Madison & Vine:** NBC's *The Biggest Loser* and health-club chain 24 Hour Fitness have created a product placement partnership that fully and thematically integrates the brand with the show.

> 24 Hour Fitness built and furnished the state-of-the-art gym on the *Loser* set and has been a key integrated brand in the show for nine seasons. On the show, workouts in 24 Hour Fitness are common. Simultaneously, out-of-show marketing has been nearly as extensive. The chain has used the show's contestants in its promotions and the brand outfits every contestant with its branded Bodybugg, so she can calculate her calories in and out. "The fact is, you can tell a great story *and* meet the advertisers' needs," says the show's director.

Originally created with TV in mind, branded entertainment has spread quickly into other sectors of the entertainment industry. For example, it is widely used in movies. Last year's 33 top films contained 592 identifiable brand placements—*Iron Man 2* alone had 64 placements. Morgan Spurlock even created a movie documentary—*POM Wonderful Presents: The Greatest Movie Ever Sold*—which examines the art of the branded entertainment deal and was itself paid for by product placements.[25] If you look carefully, you'll also see product placements in video games, comic books, Broadway musicals, and even pop music. For example, there's a sandwich-making scene featuring Wonder Bread and Miracle Whip in the middle of Lady Gaga's 10-minute "Telephone" video (which captured more than 50 million YouTube views in less than a month).

So, Madison & Vine is now the meeting place for the advertising and entertainment industries. The goal is for brand messages to become a part of the entertainment rather than interrupting it. As advertising agency JWT puts it, "We believe advertising needs to stop *interrupting* what people are interested in and *be* what people are interested in." However, advertisers must be careful that the new intersection itself doesn't become too congested. With all the new ad formats and product placements, Madison & Vine threatens to create even more of the very clutter that it was designed to break through. At that point, consumers might decide to take yet a different route.

MESSAGE STRATEGY The first step in creating effective advertising messages is to plan a *message strategy*—to decide what general message will be communicated to the audience. The purpose of advertising is to get consumers to think about or react to the product or the company in a certain way. People will react only if they believe that they will benefit from doing so. Thus, developing an effective message strategy begins with identifying customer *benefits* that can be used as advertising appeals.

Ideally, advertising-message strategy will follow directly from the company's broader positioning and customer value strategies. Message-strategy statements tend to be plain, straightforward outlines of benefits and positioning points that the advertiser wants to stress. The advertiser must next develop a compelling **creative concept**—or *"big idea"*—that will bring the message strategy to life in a distinctive and memorable way. At this stage, simple message ideas become great ad campaigns. Usually, a copywriter and art director will team up to generate many creative concepts, hoping that one of these concepts will turn out to be the big idea. The creative concept may emerge as a visualization, a phrase, or a combination of the two.

The creative concept will guide the choice of specific appeals to be used in an advertising campaign. *Advertising appeals* should have three characteristics. First, they should be *meaningful*, pointing out benefits that make the product more desirable or interesting to consumers. Second, appeals must be *believable*—consumers must believe that the product or service will deliver the promised benefits.

However, the most meaningful and believable benefits may not be the best ones to feature. Appeals should also be *distinctive*—they should tell how the product is better than the competing brands. For example, the most meaningful benefit of owning a wristwatch is that it keeps accurate time, yet few watch ads feature this benefit. Instead, based on the distinctive benefits they offer, watch advertisers might select any of a number of advertising themes. For years, Timex has been the affordable watch. Last Father's Day, for example, Timex ads suggested, "Tell Dad more than time this Father's Day. Tell him that you've learned the value of a dollar." Similarly, Rolex ads never talk at all about keeping time. Instead, they talk about the brand's "obsession with perfection" and the fact that "Rolex has been the preeminent symbol of performance and prestige for more than a century."

MESSAGE EXECUTION The advertiser now has to turn the big idea into an actual ad execution that will capture the target market's attention and interest. The creative team must find the best approach, style, tone, words, and format for executing the message. Any message can be presented in different **execution styles**, such as the following:

- *Slice of life:* This style shows one or more "typical" people using the product in a normal setting. For example, a Silk Soymilk "Rise and Shine" ad shows a young professional starting the day with a healthier breakfast and high hopes.

- *Lifestyle:* This style shows how a product fits in with a particular lifestyle. For example, an ad for Athleta activewear shows a woman in a complex yoga pose and states, "If your body is your temple, build it one piece at a time."

- *Fantasy:* This style creates a fantasy around the product or its use. For example, recent IKEA ads show consumers creating fanciful room designs with IKEA furniture, such as "a bedroom for a queen made by Bree and her sister, designed by IKEA."

- *Mood or image:* This style builds a mood or image around the product or service, such as beauty, love, intrigue, or serenity. Few claims are made about the product except through suggestion. For example, a Nestlé Toll House ad shows a daughter hugging her mother after surprising her with an unexpected weekend home from college. The mother responds, "So I baked her the cookies she's loved since she was little."

- *Musical:* This style shows people or cartoon characters singing about the product. For example, Chevrolet recently ran a two-minute-long TV commercial featuring

Creative concept
The compelling "big idea" that will bring the advertising-message strategy to life in a distinctive and memorable way.

Execution style
The approach, style, tone, words, and format used for executing an advertising message.

most of the cast of the TV show Glee in an elaborate production number set to the 1950s brand jingle, "See the U.S.A. in Your Chevrolet."

■ *Personality symbol:* This style creates a character that represents the product. The character might be animated (Mr. Clean, the GEICO Gecko, or the Zappos Zappets) or real (perky Progressive Insurance spokeswoman Flo, the E*TRADE babies, Ronald McDonald).

■ *Technical expertise:* This style shows the company's expertise in making the product. Thus, natural-foods maker Kashi shows its buyers carefully selecting ingredients for its products, and Jim Koch of the Boston Beer Company tells about his many years of experience in brewing Samuel Adams beer.

■ *Scientific evidence:* This style presents survey or scientific evidence that the brand is better, or better liked than one or more other brands. For years, Crest toothpaste has used scientific evidence to convince buyers that Crest is better than other brands at fighting cavities.

■ *Testimonial evidence or endorsement:* This style features a highly believable or likable source endorsing the product. It could be ordinary people saying how much they like a given product. For example, Subway uses spokesman Jared, a customer who lost 245 pounds on a diet of Subway heroes. Or it might be a celebrity presenting the product, such as Sidney Crosby speaking for Reebok.

The advertiser also must choose a *tone* for the ad. Procter & Gamble always uses a positive tone: Its ads say something very positive about its products. Other advertisers now use edgy humour to break through the commercial clutter. Bud Light commercials are famous for this.

The advertiser must use memorable and attention-getting *words* in the ad. For example, rather than claiming simply that its laundry detergent is "superconcentrated," Method asks customers, "Are you jug addicted?" The solution: "Our patent-pending formula that's so fricken' concentrated, 50 loads fits in a teeny bottle. . . . With our help, you can get off the jugs and get clean."

Finally, *format* elements make a difference in an ad's impact as well as in its cost. A small change in ad design can make a big difference in its effect. In a print ad, the *illustration* is the first thing the reader notices—it must be strong enough to draw attention. Next, the *headline* must effectively entice the right people to read the copy. Finally, the *copy*—the main block of text in the ad—must be simple but strong and convincing. Moreover, these three elements must effectively work *together* to persuasively present customer value.

CONSUMER-GENERATED MESSAGES Taking advantage of today's interactive technologies, many companies are now tapping consumers for message ideas or actual ads. They are searching existing video sites, setting up their own sites, and sponsoring ad-creation contests and other promotions. Sometimes the results are outstanding; sometimes they are forgettable. If done well, however, user-generated content can incorporate the voice of the customer into brand messages and generate greater consumer brand involvement (see Marketing@Work 12.2).

Exhibit 12.8 **Message execution:** Advertisers often use fantasy and humour as a way of encouraging consumers to engage in their products.

© volke/Fotolia

MARKETING@WORK 12.2

Consumer-Generated Advertising: When Done Well, It Can Be Really Good

Fuelled by the user-generated content craze made popular by the likes of YouTube, Facebook, and other online content-sharing communities, the move toward consumer-generated advertising has spread like wildfire in recent years. Companies large and small—including the likes of PepsiCo, Unilever, P&G, CareerBuilder, and other blue-chip marketers—have fast recognized the benefits (and the drawbacks) of inviting customers to co-create brand messages.

Perhaps no brand has been more successful with user-generated advertising than PepsiCo's Doritos brand. For seven years running, the Doritos "Crash the Super Bowl" contest has invited consumers to create their own 30-second video ads featuring the market-leading tortilla chip. A jury of ad pros and Doritos brand managers whittle down the thousands of entries submitted and post the finalists online. Consumers vote for the winners, who receive cash prizes and have their ads run during the Super Bowl.

For the Super Bowl in 2009, PepsiCo threw prize money around like a rich uncle home for the holidays. Six finalists each claimed US$25 000, and PepsiCo aired the ads during the game. To put more icing on the cake, Doritos promised to pay a whopping US$1 million to any entrant whose ad placed first in the *USA Today* Ad Meter ratings. Second place was good for US$600 000, and third place would take home US$400 000. If the winners swept the top three Ad Meter spots, each would receive an additional US$1 million. Not surprisingly, the contest attracted nearly 5600 entries.

In 2012, one of the consumer-made Doritos ads—"Pug goes for the chips"—tied with a Bud Light commercial, the first tie ever in the *USA Today* ratings. Tie or not, the person behind the winning Doritos ad, 31-year-old J.R. Burningham of Utah, took home the US$1 million prize—not a bad return for an ad that cost only US$500 to produce. In all, three "Crash the Super Bowl" ads finished in *USA Today's* top five. Moreover, the ads

finished strongly in virtually every consumer survey. One rating firm judged four of the six consumer-generated ads (two Doritos ads and two Pepsi Max ads) as the top four most effective Super Bowl ads overall. In fact, the ads were a hit before the Super Bowl even began. Prior to the game, PepsiCo aired the ads on YouTube and Facebook and tweeted feverishly about them. By game day, the videos already had 3 million-plus views each. The 2013 entrants may not have won the extra prize money, but "Fashionista Dad" placed fourth and "Goat 4 Sale" ranked seventh in the *USA Today* Ad Meter ratings.

It seems that many other companies are also getting into the consumer-generated content act. According to one global report that ranks the world's top creative work, nine of last year's top 10 campaigns involved some kind of consumer input. "This is a big seismic shift in our business," says the former ad agency executive who assembled the report. "We've had 100 years of business-to-consumer advertising, but now the web has enabled us to get people actively involved in talking to each other. If the idea is interesting enough, consumers will do the work for you." Even more, they'll work for little or no pay.

That kind of talk makes some ad agencies nervous. However, the idea isn't that companies should fire their ad agencies and have consumers create their ads instead. In fact, most consumer-generated ad campaigns are coordinated by ad agencies. For example, Unilever is expanding its crowdsourcing efforts with a video ad contest that involves 13 of its brands, including Ben & Jerry's, Dove, Lipton, and Vaseline. However, the company is quick to clarify the role of its user-generated content strategy.

> This in no way is a replacement for our ad agencies. The real reason for it is to offer more participation for our consumers, to get closer to consumers, and allow them to be more involved with our brands. It will help them become advocates, help them have more of a connection with the brands if they've been a part of helping to create it. It's not one of our objectives to save money. I mean it's a nice benefit, if we can get great stuff. But it's not really the objective. We believe that marketing will be much more participatory in the next few years and we want to be at the leading edge of that.

Although most consumer-generated content efforts are limited to ad and video messages, PepsiCo's award-winning Mountain Dew crowdsourcing campaign—called "Dewmocracy"—has

Exhibit 12.9 **Consumer-generated messages:** Three Doritos "Crash the Super Bowl" ads finished in *USA Today's* top five. This "Pug goes for the chips" ad tied for first place.

Frito-Lay, Inc.

involved consumers in decisions across the entire range of marketing for the brand. Dewmocracy seeks inputs from ardent brand fans on everything from product development to ad messages and ad agency selection.

At the start of the most recent Dewmocracy campaign, Mountain Dew asked loyal fans to submit ideas for three new flavours. It sent 50 finalists home-tasting kits and Flip video cameras and encouraged them to upload videos about their experience to YouTube. With three finalists selected, Mountain Dew asked consumers to pick names (Typhoon, Distortion, and White Out rose to the top), colours, and package designs for the new flavours on the Dewmocracy website, Facebook, Twitter, and other social media sites. The three flavours were rolled out over the summer, and fans were asked to try them and vote for a favourite, which became a permanent addition to the Mountain Dew lineup.

As for advertising, rather than having consumers submit their own video ads, Mountain Dew invited fans to help choose the ad agencies that would do the job. Consumers "built these products and had a clear idea of the products," said Mountain Dew's director of marketing. They "challenged us to say, who is going to do our advertising, and how do we get

some new thinking?" Ad agencies and individuals submitted more than 200 12-second videos outlining their ideas for promoting the three new flavours. Consumers cast 15 000 votes. In the end, three small ad shops landed the jobs.

The Dewmocracy consumer-generated marketing campaigns have produced successful new, customer-approved Mountain Dew flavours at very little cost (the brand didn't spend a dollar on media throughout the process). But they met an even bigger objective. They have "allowed us to have as rich a dialogue as we could with consumers," says the brand's marketing director. The average loyal Mountain Dew drinker is male, between the ages of 18 and 39, with 92 percent on Facebook, and 50 percent using YouTube. The digital Dewmocracy campaigns have been incredibly success-ful at engaging this group and giving them an ownership stake in the brand.

There are downsides to consumer-generated ads, of course. Although it might seem "free," the process of wading through hundreds—or even thousands—of entries can be difficult, costly, and time consuming. In dealing with user-created content, copyright issues, poor produc-tion quality, offensive themes, and even attacks on the brand are all par for the

course. And in the end, you never know what you're going to get. For every hit Doritos ad, there are hundreds that are uninspired or just plain dreadful. Many Madison Avenue advertising pros write off consumer-generated efforts as mostly amateurish, crudely produced, and ineffective.

But when it's done well, it can be very good. Despite "a lot of advertising people" playing it down as "a seventh-grader in his backyard with a video camera," says one advertising expert, "it complements efforts by marketers to engage and involve consumers. Consumer-generated content really can work."

Sources: Extracts, quotes, and other information from Stuart Elliott, "Do-It Yourself Super Ads," *New York Times*, February 9, 2010, p. B3; Andrew McMains, "Unilever Embraces UGC," *Adweek*, April 20, 2010, accessed at www.adweek.com; Emma Hall, "Most Winning Creative Work Involves Consumer Participation," *Advertising Age*, January 6, 2010, http://adage.com/print/141329; Natalie Zmuda, "Why Mountain Dew Let Skater Dudes Take Control of Its Marketing," *Advertising Age*, February 22, 2010, p. 30; "Doritos and Pepsi Max's '*Crash the Super Bowl* Contest' Delivered Top 4 Most Effective Super Bowl Ads," *BusinessWire*, February 8, 2011; Bruce Horovitz, "Admeter First: A Doggone Tie," *USA Today*, February 7, 2011, p. 6B; Bruce Horovitz, "Super Bowl Ads Win with Social-Media Play," *USA Today*, February 8, 2011, p. 3B; and "Mtn Dew Thanks Fans by Name in New Campaign," *Advertising Age*, June 14, 2011, http://adage.com/print/228189; Christopher Heine, "Frito-Lay Likes the Data from Doritos' "Crash the Superbowl"," *Adweek*, February 7, 2013, www.adweek.com/news/technology/frito-lay-likes-data-doritos-crash-super-bowl-147127.

Many brands hold contests that invite consumers to submit ad message ideas and videos. For example, for the past several years, PepsiCo's Doritos brand has held its annual "Crash the Super Bowl Challenge" contest that invites consumers to create their own video ads about the tasty triangular corn chips. The consumer-generated Doritos ads have been a smashing success. At the other end of the size spectrum, the Canadian Tourism Commission used user-generated videos from visitors to bolster Canada's share of the competitive international tourism market.[26]

Facing tough international competition, Canada saw its share of the international tourism industry decline by 22 percent in the seven years leading up to 2009, despite tourism being one of fastest-growing sectors in the global economy. After the 2010 Olympics, the Canadian Tourism Commission came up with a strategy to turn awareness of Canada into visits. The organization launched the "Keep Exploring" campaign in May 2010, using a combination of traditional and online media that allowed visitors to tell their own stories. For example, TV ads sourced user-generated videos from YouTube. Print ads emulated Flickr and Facebook, while major newspapers used "spadea" wraps that looked like an online blog. The campaign propelled Canada to the number-one country brand in the world. It also delivered a government-approved return on investment (ROI) of 101:1—for every dollar invested, $101 was generated in tourism revenues.

Hand-out/CANADIAN TOURISM COMMISSION/Newscom

Exhibit 12.10 **Consumer-generated advertising:** The Canadian Tourism Commission created its "Keep Exploring" campaign using user-generated videos visitors uploaded to YouTube.

Advertising media

The types of media and media vehicles through which advertising messages are delivered to their intended audiences.

Not all consumer-generated advertising efforts, however, are so successful. As many big companies have learned, ads made by amateurs can be . . . well, pretty amateurish. If done well, however, consumer-generated advertising efforts can produce new creative ideas and fresh perspectives on the brand from consumers who actually experience it. Such campaigns can boost consumer involvement and get consumers talking and thinking about a brand and its value to them.[27]

Selecting Advertising Media   The major steps in **advertising media** selection are (1) deciding on *reach*, *frequency*, and *impact*; (2) choosing among major *media types*; (3) selecting specific *media vehicles*; and (4) deciding on *media timing*.

DECIDING ON REACH, FREQUENCY, AND IMPACT To select media, the advertiser must decide on the reach and frequency needed to achieve advertising objectives. *Reach* is a measure of the *percentage* of people in the target market who are exposed to the ad campaign during a given period of time. For example, the advertiser might try to reach 70 percent of the target market during the first three months of the campaign. *Frequency* is a measure of how many *times* the average person in the target market is exposed to the message. For example, the advertiser might want an average exposure frequency of three.

But advertisers want to do more than just reach a given number of consumers a specific number of times. The advertiser also must decide on the desired *media impact*—the *qualitative value* of a message exposure through a given medium. For example, the same message in one magazine (say, *Newsweek*) may be more believable than in another (say, the *National Enquirer*). For products that need to be demonstrated, messages on television may have more impact than messages on radio because television uses sight *and* sound. Products for which consumers provide input on design or features might be better promoted at an interactive website than in a direct mailing.

More generally, the advertiser wants to choose media that will *engage* consumers rather than simply reach them. In any medium, how relevant an ad is for its audience is often much more important than how many people it reaches. For example, in an effort to make every advertising dollar count, Ford has recently been selecting TV programs based on viewer engagement ratings:[28]

> Ford had little apparent reason to advertise on the Discovery Channel's *Dirty Jobs* series, which stars Mike Rowe. The show delivers puny Nielsen ratings. But when engagement metrics were applied to the program, the viewers most deeply absorbed in the show turned out to be truck-buying men between the ages of 18 and 49—a ripe demographic for Ford. That prompted Ford to advertise heavily and hire Rowe to appear in highly successful web videos demonstrating the durability of the F-Series pickup.

Although Nielsen is beginning to measure the levels of television *media engagement*, such measures are hard

Fordimages.com and Mike Rowe/MikeRoweWorks.com

Exhibit 12.11 **Viewer engagement:** Viewers most deeply engaged in the Discovery Channel's *Dirty Jobs* series turned out to be truck-buying men, a ripe demographic for Ford's F-Series pickups.

to come by for most media. Current media measures are things such as ratings, readership, listenership, and click-through rates. However, engagement happens inside the consumer. Notes one expert, "Just measuring the number of eyeballs in front of a television set is hard enough without trying to measure the intensity of those eyeballs doing the viewing."[29] Still, marketers need to know how customers connect with an ad and brand idea as a part of the broader brand relationship.

Engaged consumers are more likely to act upon brand messages and even share them with others. Thus, rather than simply tracking *consumer impressions* for a media placement—how many people see, hear, or read an ad—Coca-Cola now also tracks the *consumer expressions* that result, such as a comment, a "like," uploading a photo or video, or passing content onto their networks. Today's empowered consumers often generate more messages about a brand than a company can. Through engagement, "instead of having to always pay for their message to run somewhere, [marketers] can 'earn' media for free, via consumer spreading YouTube clips, Groupons, and tweets," says an advertising consultant.[30]

For example, Coca-Cola estimates that on YouTube there are about 146 million views of content related to Coca-Cola. However, only about 26 million of those are of content that Coca-Cola created. The other 120 million are of content created by engaged consumers. "We can't match the volume of our consumers' output," says Coca-Cola's chief marketing officer, "but we can spark it with the right type [and placement] of content."[31]

CHOOSING AMONG MEDIA TYPES As summarized in Table 12.2, the major media types are television, newspapers, the Internet, direct mail, magazines, radio, and outdoor. Advertisers can also choose from a wide array of new digital media, such as mobile phones and other digital devices, which reach consumers directly. Each medium has its advantages and its limitations.

Media planners want to choose media that will effectively and efficiently present the advertising message to target customers. Thus, they must consider each medium's impact,

TABLE 12.2 Profiles of Major Media Types

Medium	Advantages	Limitations
Television	Good mass-marketing coverage; low cost per exposure; combines sight, sound, and motion; appealing to the senses	High absolute costs; high clutter; fleeting exposure; less audience selectivity
Newspapers	Flexibility; timeliness; good local market coverage; broad acceptability; high believability	Short life; poor reproduction quality; small pass-along audience
The Internet	High selectivity; low cost; immediacy; interactive capabilities	Potentially low impact; the audience controls exposure
Direct mail	High audience selectivity; flexibility; no ad competition within the same medium; allows personalization	Relatively high cost per exposure; "junk mail" image
Magazines	High geographic and demographic selectivity; credibility and prestige; high-quality reproduction; long life and good pass-along readership	Long ad purchase lead time; high cost; no guarantee of position
Radio	Good local acceptance; high geographic and demographic selectivity; low cost	Audio only; fleeting exposure; low attention ("the half-heard" medium); fragmented audiences
Outdoor	Flexibility; high repeat exposure; low cost; low message competition; good positional selectivity	Little audience selectivity; creative limitations

message effectiveness, and cost. Typically, it's not a question of which one medium to use. Rather, the advertiser selects a mix of media and blends them into a fully integrated marketing communications campaign.

The mix of media must be re-examined regularly. For a long time, television and magazines dominated the media mixes of national advertisers, with other media often neglected. However, as discussed previously, the media mix appears to be shifting. As mass-media costs rise, audiences shrink, and exciting new digital and interactive media emerge, many advertisers are finding new ways to reach consumers. They are supplementing the traditional mass media with more-specialized and highly targeted media that cost less, target more effectively, and engage consumers more fully.

In addition to the explosion of online media, cable and satellite television systems are thriving. Such systems allow narrow programming formats, such as all sports, all news, nutrition, arts, home improvement and gardening, cooking, travel, history, finance, and others that target select groups. Cable operators are even testing systems that will let them target specific types of ads to TVs in specific neighbourhoods, or individually to specific types of customers. For example, ads for a French-language channel would run in only Francophone neighbourhoods, or only pet owners would see ads from pet food companies. Advertisers can take advantage of such *narrowcasting* to "rifle in" on special market segments rather than use the "shotgun" approach offered by network broadcasting.

Finally, in their efforts to find less-costly and more-highly targeted ways to reach consumers, advertisers have discovered a dazzling collection of *alternative media*. These days, no matter where you go or what you do, you will probably run into some new form of advertising.

Tiny billboards attached to shopping carts urge you to buy JELL-O Pudding Pops or Pampers, while ads roll by on the store's checkout conveyor touting your local Chevy dealer. Step outside and there goes a city trash truck sporting an ad for Glad trash bags or a school bus displaying a Little Caesar's pizza ad. A nearby fire hydrant is emblazoned with advertising for KFC's "fiery" chicken wings. You escape to the ballpark, only to find billboard-size video screens running Budweiser ads while a blimp with an electronic message board circles lazily overhead. In mid-winter, you wait in a city bus shelter that looks like an oven—with heat coming from the coils—introducing Caribou Coffee's line-up of hot breakfast sandwiches. How about a quiet trip in the country? Sorry—you find an enterprising farmer using his milk cows as four-legged billboards mounted with ads for Ben & Jerry's ice cream.

These days, you're likely to find ads—well—anywhere. Taxi cabs sport electronic messaging signs tied to GPS location sensors that can pitch local stores and restaurants wherever they roam. Ad space is being sold on DVD cases, parking-lot tickets, airline boarding passes, subway turnstiles, golf scorecards, ATMs, municipal garbage cans, and even police cars, doctors' examining tables, and church bulletins. One agency even leases space on the shaved heads of college students for temporary advertising tattoos ("cranial advertising").

Such alternative media seem a bit far-fetched, and they sometimes irritate consumers who resent it all as "ad nauseam." But for many marketers, these media can save money and provide a way to hit selected consumers where they live, shop, work, and play. Of course, all this may leave you wondering if there are any commercial-free havens remaining for ad-weary consumers. Public

Exhibit 12.12 Marketers have discovered a dazzling array of alternative media, like this heated Caribou Coffee bus shelter.

elevators, perhaps, or stalls in a public restroom? Forget it! Each has already been invaded by innovative marketers.

Another important trend affecting media selection is the rapid growth in the number of *media multitaskers*, people who absorb more than one medium at a time. For example, it's not uncommon to find someone watching TV with a smartphone in hand, posting on Facebook, texting friends, and chasing down product information on Google. One recent survey found that a whopping 86 percent of mobile Internet users watch TV with their devices in hand. Another study found that 60 percent of TV viewers go online via their smartphones, tablets, or PCs during their TV viewing time. Still another study found that a majority of these multitaskers "are 'primarily focused' on the Internet rather than TV, and their online viewing is overwhelmingly unrelated to the TV programs or commercials they are watching." Marketers need to take such media interactions into account when selecting the types of media they will use.[32]

SELECTING MEDIA VEHICLES The media planner now must choose the best **media vehicles**—specific media within each general media type. Television is a media type, but CTV and *Hockey Night in Canada* are media vehicles. Similarly magazines are a media type, but *Maclean's* and *Chatelaine* are media vehicles.

Media planners must compute the cost per 1000 persons reached by a vehicle. For example, if a full-page, four-colour advertisement in *Newsweek* costs $168 300 and *Newsweek's* readership is 1.5 million people, the cost of reaching each group of 1000 persons is about $112. The same advertisement in *Bloomberg BusinessWeek* may cost only $139 500 but reach only 900 000 people—at a cost per 1000 of about $155. The media planner ranks each magazine by cost per 1000 and favours those magazines with the lower cost per 1000 for reaching target consumers.[33]

Media planners must also consider the costs of producing ads for different media. Whereas newspaper ads may cost very little to produce, flashy television ads can be very costly. Many online ads cost little to produce, but costs can climb when producing made-for-the-web videos and ad series.

In selecting specific media vehicles, media planners must balance media costs against several media effectiveness factors. First, the planner should evaluate the media vehicle's audience quality. For a Huggies disposable diapers advertisement, for example, *Parents* magazine would have a high exposure value; *Maxim* would have a low exposure value. Second, the media planner should consider audience engagement. Readers of *Vogue*, for example, typically pay more attention to ads than do *Newsweek* readers. Third, the planner should assess the vehicle's editorial quality. *Time* and the *Wall Street Journal* are more believable and prestigious than *Star* or the *National Enquirer*.

DECIDING ON MEDIA TIMING The advertiser must also decide how to schedule the advertising over the course of a year. Suppose sales of a product peak in December and drop in March (for winter sports gear, for instance). The firm can vary its advertising to follow the seasonal pattern, oppose the seasonal pattern, or be the same all year. Most firms do some seasonal advertising. For example, Mars currently runs M&M's special ads for almost every holiday and "season," from Easter and Halloween to the Super Bowl season and the Oscar season. Some marketers do *only* seasonal advertising: For instance, P&G advertises its Vicks NyQuil only during the cold and flu season.

Finally, the advertiser has to choose the pattern of the advertising schedule. *Continuity* means scheduling ads evenly within a given period. *Pulsing* means scheduling ads unevenly over a given time period. Thus, 52 ads could either be scheduled at one per week during the year or pulsed in several bursts. The idea behind pulsing is to advertise heavily for a short period to build awareness that carries over to the next advertising

Media vehicle
The specific media (publication or program) within a general media type (magazine, radio, television).

Exhibit 12.13 Media timing: Vicks NyQuil runs ads like this only during the cold and flu season.

Procter and Gamble

Return on advertising investment
The net return on advertising investment divided by the costs of the advertising investment.

period. Those who favour pulsing feel that it can be used to achieve the same impact as a steady schedule but at a much lower cost. However, some media planners believe that although pulsing achieves minimal awareness, it sacrifices depth of advertising communications.

Evaluating Advertising Effectiveness and Return on Advertising Investment LO4

Measuring advertising effectiveness and the **return on advertising investment** has become a hot issue for most companies, especially in a tighter economic environment. A less friendly economy "has obligated us all to pinch pennies all the more tightly and squeeze blood from a rock," says one advertising executive.[34] That leaves top management at many companies asking their marketing managers, "How do we know that we're spending the right amount on advertising?" and "What return are we getting on our advertising investment?"

Advertisers should regularly evaluate two types of advertising results: the communication effects and the sales and profit effects. Measuring the *communication effects* of an ad or ad campaign tells whether the ads and media are communicating the ad message well. Individual ads can be tested before or after they are run. Before an ad is placed, the advertiser can show it to consumers, ask how they like it, and measure message recall or attitude changes resulting from it. After an ad is run, the advertiser can measure how the ad affected consumer recall or product awareness, knowledge, and preference. Pre- and post-evaluations of communication effects can be made for entire advertising campaigns as well.

Advertisers have gotten pretty good at measuring the communication effects of their ads and ad campaigns. However, *sales and profit* effects of advertising are often much harder to measure. For example, what sales and profits are produced by an ad campaign that increases brand awareness by 20 percent and brand preference by 10 percent? Sales and profits are affected by many factors other than advertising—such as product features, price, and availability.

One way to measure the sales and profit effects of advertising is to compare past sales and profits with past advertising expenditures. Another way is through experiments. For example, to test the effects of different advertising spending levels, Coca-Cola could vary the amount it spends on advertising in different market areas and measure the differences in the resulting sales and profit levels. More complex experiments could be designed to include other variables, such as differences in the ads or media used.

However, because so many factors affect advertising effectiveness, some controllable and others not, measuring the results of advertising spending remains an inexact science. Managers often must rely on large doses of judgment along with quantitative analysis when assessing advertising performance.

Other Advertising Considerations

In developing advertising strategies and programs, the company must address two additional questions. First, how will the company organize its advertising function—who will perform which advertising tasks? Second, how will the company adapt its advertising strategies and programs to the complexities of international markets?

Organizing for Advertising Different companies organize in a variety of ways to handle advertising. In small companies, advertising might be handled by someone in the sales department. Large companies set up advertising departments whose job it is to set the advertising budget, work with the advertising agency, and handle other advertising not done by the agency. Most large companies use outside advertising agencies because they offer several advantages.

How does an **advertising agency** work? Advertising agencies originated in the mid- to-late-1800s by salespeople and brokers who worked for the media and received a commission for selling advertising space to companies. As time passed, the salespeople began to help customers prepare their ads. Eventually, they formed agencies and grew closer to the advertisers than to the media.

Today's agencies employ specialists who can often perform advertising tasks better than the company's own staff can. Agencies also bring an outside point of view to solving the company's problems, along with lots of experience from working with different clients and situations. So, today, even companies with strong advertising departments of their own use advertising agencies.

Some ad agencies are huge; the largest US agency, McCann Erickson Worldwide, has annual gross US revenues of more than US$457 million. In recent years, many agencies have grown by gobbling up other agencies, thus creating huge agency holding companies. The largest of these megagroups, WPP, includes several large advertising, PR, and promotion agencies with combined worldwide revenues of US$14.4 billion.[35] Most large advertising agencies have the staff and resources to handle all phases of an advertising campaign for their clients, from creating a marketing plan to developing ad campaigns and preparing, placing, and evaluating ads.

Advertising agency
A marketing services firm that assists companies in planning, preparing, implementing, and evaluating all or portions of their advertising programs.

International Advertising Decisions International advertisers face many complexities not encountered by domestic advertisers. The most basic issue concerns the degree to which global advertising should be adapted to the unique characteristics of various country markets.

Some advertisers have attempted to support their global brands with highly standardized worldwide advertising, with campaigns that work as well in Bangkok as they do in Baltimore. For example, McDonald's unifies its creative elements and brand presentation under the familiar "i'm lovin' it" theme in all its 100-plus markets worldwide. Visa coordinates worldwide advertising for its debit and credit cards under the "more people go with Visa" creative platform, which works as well in Korea as it does in Canada or Brazil. And ads from Brazilian flip-flops maker Havaianas make the same outrageously colourful splash worldwide, no matter what the country.

In recent years, the increased popularity of online social networks and video sharing has boosted the need for advertising standardization for global brands. Most big marketing and advertising campaigns include a large online presence. Connected consumers can now zip easily across borders via the Internet, making it difficult for advertisers to roll out adapted campaigns in a controlled, orderly fashion. As a result, at the very least, most global consumer brands coordinate their websites internationally. For example, check out the McDonald's websites from Germany to Jordan to China. You'll find the golden arches logo, the "i'm lovin' it" logo and jingle, a Big Mac equivalent, and maybe even Ronald McDonald himself.

Standardization produces many benefits—lower advertising costs, greater global advertising coordination, and a more consistent worldwide image. But it also has drawbacks. Most importantly, it ignores the fact that country markets differ greatly in their cultures, demographics, and economic conditions. Thus, most international advertisers "think globally but act locally." They develop global advertising *strategies* that make their

Exhibit 12.14 Ads from colourful Brazilian flip-flops maker Havaianas make the same outrageously colourful splash worldwide, no matter what the country.

worldwide efforts more efficient and consistent. Then they adapt their advertising *programs* to make them more responsive to consumer needs and expectations within local markets. For example, although Visa employs its "more people go with Visa" theme globally, ads in specific locales employ local language and inspiring local imagery that make the theme relevant to the local markets in which they appear.

Global advertisers face several special problems. For instance, advertising media costs and availability differ vastly from country to country. Countries also differ in the extent to which they regulate advertising practices. Many countries have extensive systems of laws restricting how much a company can spend on advertising, the media used, the nature of advertising claims, and other aspects of the advertising program. Such restrictions often require advertisers to adapt their campaigns from country to country.

For example, alcohol products cannot be advertised in India or in Muslim countries. In many countries, such as Sweden and Canada, junk food ads are banned from children's television programming. To play it safe, McDonald's advertises itself as a family restaurant in Sweden. Comparative ads, although acceptable and even common in the United States and Canada, are less commonly used in the United Kingdom and are illegal in India and Brazil. China bans sending email for advertising purposes to people without their permission, and all advertising email that is sent must be titled "advertisement."

China also has restrictive censorship rules for TV and radio advertising; for example, the words *the best* are banned, as are ads that "violate social customs" or present women in "improper ways." McDonald's once avoided government sanctions in China by publicly apologizing for an ad that crossed cultural norms by showing a customer begging for a discount. Similarly, Coca-Cola's Indian subsidiary was forced to end a promotion that offered prizes, such as a trip to Hollywood, because it violated India's established trade practices by encouraging customers to "gamble."

Thus, although advertisers may develop global strategies to guide their overall advertising efforts, specific advertising programs must usually be adapted to meet local cultures and customs, media characteristics, and regulations.

Public Relations LO5

Another major mass-promotion tool is public relations (PR)—building good relations with the company's various publics. Public relations departments may perform any or all of the following functions:[36]

■ *Press relations or press agency:* creating and placing newsworthy information in the news media to attract attention to a person, a product, or a service

■ *Product publicity:* publicizing specific products

■ *Public affairs:* building and maintaining national or local community relations

■ *Lobbying:* building and maintaining relations with legislators and government officials to influence legislation and regulation

- *Investor relations:* maintaining relationships with shareholders and others in the financial community
- *Development:* working with donors or members of not-for-profit organizations to gain financial or volunteer support

Public relations is used to promote products, people, places, ideas, activities, organizations, and even nations. Companies use PR to build good relations with consumers, investors, the media, and their communities. Trade associations have used PR to rebuild interest in commodities, such as eggs, apples, potatoes, milk, and even onions. For example, the Vidalia Onion Committee built a PR campaign around the DreamWorks character Shrek—complete with Shrek images on packaging and in-store displays with giant inflatable Shreks—that successfully promoted onions to children. Even government organizations use PR to build awareness. For example, the National Heart, Lung, and Blood Institute (NHLBI) of the National Institutes of Health in the United States and the Heart and Stroke Foundation in Canada sponsor a long-running PR campaign that builds awareness of heart disease in women:[37]

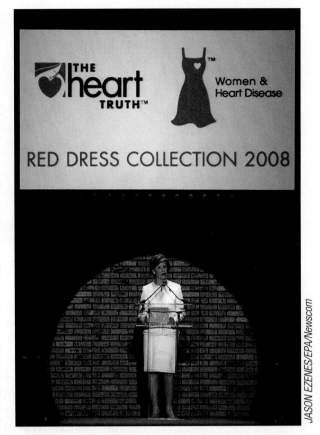

Exhibit 12.15 **Public relations campaigns:** NHLBI's "The Heart Truth" campaign has produced impressive results in raising awareness of the risks of heart disease in women.
(Courtesy of the National Heart, Lung, and Blood Institute)

> Heart disease is the number one killer of women; it kills more women each year than all forms of cancer combined. But a 2000 survey by the NHLBI showed that only 34 percent of women knew this, and that most people thought of heart disease as a problem mostly affecting men. So with the help of Ogilvy Public Relations Worldwide, the NHLBI set out to "create a personal and urgent wakeup call to American women." In 2002, it launched a national PR campaign—"The Heart Truth"—to raise awareness of heart disease among women and get women to discuss the issue with their doctors.
>
> The centerpiece of the campaign is the Red Dress, now the national symbol for women and heart disease awareness. The campaign creates awareness through an interactive website, mass media placements, and campaign materials—everything from brochures, DVDs, and posters to speaker's kits and airport dioramas. It also sponsors several major national events, such as the National Wear Red Day, an annual Red Dress Collection Fashion Show, and The Heart Truth Road Show, featuring heart disease risk factor screenings in major cities. Finally, the campaign works with more than three-dozen corporate sponsors, such as Diet Coke, St. Joseph aspirin, Tylenol, Cheerios, CVS Pharmacy, Swarovski, and Bobbi Brown Cosmetics. So far, some 2.65 billion product packages have carried the Red Dress symbol.
>
> The results are impressive: Awareness among women of heart disease as the number one killer of women has increased to 57 percent, and the number of heart disease deaths in women has declined steadily from one in three women to one in four. The American Heart Association has also adopted the Red Dress symbol and introduced its own complementary campaign.

The Role and Impact of Public Relations

Public relations can have a strong impact on public awareness at a much lower cost than advertising can. The company does not pay for the space or time in the media. Rather, it pays for a staff to develop and circulate information and to manage events. If the company develops an interesting story or event, it could be picked up by several different media, having the same effect as advertising that would cost millions of dollars. And it would have more credibility than advertising.

PR results can sometimes be spectacular. Consider the launches of Apple's iPad and iPad 2:[38]

Associated Press

Exhibit 12.16 **The power of PR:** Apple's iPad and iPad 2 launches created unbounded consumer excitement, a media frenzy, and long lines outside retail stores—all with no advertising, just PR.

Apple's iPad was one of the most successful new-product launches in history. The funny thing: Whereas most big product launches are accompanied by huge pre-launch advertising campaigns, Apple pulled this one off with no advertising. None at all. Instead, it simply fed the PR fire. It built buzz months in advance by distributing iPads for early reviews, feeding the offline and online press with tempting tidbits, and offering fans an early online peek at thousands of new iPad apps that would be available. At launch time, it fanned the flames with a cameo on the TV sitcom *Modern Family*, a flurry of launch-day appearances on TV talk shows, and other launch-day events. In the process, through PR alone, the iPad launch generated unbounded consumer excitement, a media frenzy, and long lines outside retail stores on launch day. Apple sold more than 300 000 of the sleek gadgets on the first day alone and more than two million in the first two months—even as demand outstripped supply. Apple repeated the feat a year later with the equally successful launch of iPad 2, which sold close to one million devices the weekend of its launch.

Despite its potential strengths, public relations is occasionally described as a marketing stepchild because of its sometimes limited and scattered use. The PR department is often located at corporate headquarters or handled by a third-party agency. Its staff is so busy dealing with various publics—shareholders, employees, legislators, and the press—that PR programs to support product marketing objectives may be ignored. Moreover, marketing managers and PR practitioners do not always speak the same language. Whereas many PR practitioners see their jobs as simply communicating, marketing managers tend to be much more interested in how advertising and PR affect brand building, sales and profits, and customer involvement and relationships.

This situation is changing, however. Although public relations still captures only a small portion of the overall marketing budgets of most firms, PR can be a powerful brand-building tool. And in this digital age, the lines between advertising and PR are becoming more and more blurred. For example, are brand websites, blogs, online social networks, and viral brand videos advertising efforts or PR efforts? All are both. The point is that PR should work hand in hand with advertising within an integrated marketing communications program to help build brands and customer relationships.

"This is PR's time to shine," says P&G's global marketing and brand building officer. "PR is going to grow its impact on the future [of] marketing because it is a great amplifier, builds relationships, and invites consumer participation," he says. "PR [gives] our big ideas a megaphone that we used to spur participation [leading] to spontaneous combustion."[39]

Major Public Relations Tools

Public relations uses several tools. One of the major tools is *news*. Public relations professionals find or create favourable news about the company and its products or people. Sometimes news stories occur naturally, and sometimes the PR person can suggest events or activities that would create news. Another common PR tool is *special events*, ranging from news conferences and speeches, press tours, grand openings, and fireworks displays to laser shows, hot air balloon releases, multi-media presentations, or educational programs designed to reach and interest target publics.

Public relations people also prepare *written materials* to reach and influence their target markets. These materials include annual reports, brochures, articles, and company newsletters and magazines. *Audiovisual materials*, such as DVDs and online videos are being used increasingly as communication tools. *Corporate identity materials* can also help create a corporate identity that the public immediately recognizes. Logos, stationery, brochures, signs, business forms, business cards, buildings, uniforms, and company cars and trucks—all become marketing tools when they are attractive, distinctive, and memorable. Finally, companies can improve public goodwill by contributing money and time to *public service activities.*

As previously discussed, the web is also an important PR channel. Websites, blogs, and social networks such as YouTube, Facebook, and Twitter are providing new ways to reach more people. "The core strengths of public relations—the ability to tell a story and spark conversation—play well into the nature of such social media," says a PR expert. Consider the recent "Harlequin Office for the Preservation of the Kiss" PR campaign.[40]

> In 2010, NATIONAL, Canada's largest PR firm, recommended that its client Harlequin take its promotional campaign digital. The result was a truly innovative and award-winning PR campaign. The goal of the "Harlequin Office for the Preservation of the Kiss" campaign was to enhance consumer engagement with the brand and prove that "Harlequin owns romance." The first step in the campaign was literally to patent the "Essential Romantic Kiss" with the United States Patent and Trademark Office (patent pending). It also launched www.patentyourkiss.com, which became an instant online hit. The site received more than 50 000 visitors from more than 164 countries, and celebrities such as Kim Kardashian were tweeting about "patenting a kiss" and engaging with the online kiss-creation tool. According to NATIONAL, the site achieved its goal of brand engagement, with users spending an average of more than six minutes on the campaign in the first week it launched. The website and patent story were discussed in top-tier media outlets, including *InTouch*, *Life & Style*, AOL, *The New Yorker*, the *Today* show, *ET Canada*, the *Globe and Mail*, and *Canada AM*, among many others.

By itself, a company's website is an important PR vehicle. Consumers and other publics often visit websites for information or entertainment. Websites can also be ideal for handling crisis situations. For example, when several bottles of Odwalla apple juice sold on the West Coast of the United States were found to contain *E. coli* bacteria, Odwalla initiated a massive product recall. Within only three hours, it set up a website laden with information about the crisis and Odwalla's response. Company staffers also combed the Internet looking for newsgroups discussing Odwalla and posted links to the site. In this age where "it's easier to disseminate information through email marketing, blogs, and online chat," notes an analyst, "public relations is becoming a valuable part of doing business in a digital world."[41]

As with the other promotion tools, in considering when and how to use product public relations, management should set PR objectives, choose the PR messages and vehicles, implement the PR plan, and evaluate the results. The firm's PR should be blended smoothly with other promotion activities within the company's overall integrated marketing communications effort.

Exhibit 12.17 The Harlequin Office for the Preservation of the Kiss PR campaign used social media to prove that "Harlequin owns romance."

Telling Stories

At first viewing, the mock-u-mercial depicting two children riding the "travel toboggan" (a plastic bin) down the WestJet check-in baggage conveyor belt en route to the "Kargo Kids" compartment in the lower fuselage of a WestJet aircraft is almost believable. Richard Bartrem, WestJet's vice-president of communications, skilfully sells the story, reading a script suitable for a *Saturday Night Live* skit: "On board each flight, we have a Kargo Kids counsellor . . . with plenty of toys and a state-of-the-art food trough . . . your kids will be able to eat, play and scream all they want."

The annual WestJet April Fool's gag has grown to become a much anticipated production from year to year, and its 2013 theme, "Furry Family" (promoting the airline's new pet policy), generated over half a million YouTube views within days of its launch. That year, WestJet decided to leverage the viral reach of the gag to offer viewers special April Fool's fares (real ones), a promotion that Bartrem reveals produced double-digit percent increases in sales compared to similar time frames the previous year.

Bob Cummings, WestJet executive vice-president of sales, marketing, and guest experience, cites one of his company's five secrets, "Celebration and Kudos" (Secret #4 if you're keeping track), as a driving force behind WestJet's success. "Despite now having over 9000 employees, the underdog label still fits, and part of that is having fun and not taking ourselves too seriously." The annual April Fool's spoof is something Bartrem transformed from a tongue-in-cheek news release, which sometimes got picked up depending on how slow the news day was, to its current status as "an institutionalized and strategically planned event."

Of course, Bartrem's role stretches infinitely beyond planning, producing, and disseminating the annual joke. "I take my responsibility as WestJet's story-teller very seriously," he says. "When I think that there are WestJetters across the country at any given moment, scrubbing planes, resolving issues, and of course creating a great guest experience, I know it's on me to tell their story and communicate that passion and that level of care."

Though it has become an anxiously anticipated event externally, the April Fool's video is among a handful of projects that WestJet's creative services department will produce every year as internal communications strategies. "Sometimes there will be a business message in terms of what we want them to understand," says Bartrem, "but mostly they're intended to have fun and celebrate what we do."

QUESTIONS

1. What are the promotional tools being integrated into WestJet's April Fool's campaign?
2. What role does communications play in creating and sustaining brand equity for WestJet?
3. View WestJet's archives of April Fool's day spoofs at www.youtube.com/user/WestJet and comment on the evolution of the mock-u-mercials over time.

REVIEWING THE CONCEPTS

1. Define the five promotion mix tools for communicating customer value.

A company's total *promotion mix*—also called its *marketing communications mix*—consists of the specific blend of *advertising, personal selling, sales promotion, public relations (PR),* and *direct-marketing* tools that the company uses to persuasively communicate customer value and build customer relationships. Advertising includes any paid form of non-personal presentation and promotion of ideas, goods, or services by an identified sponsor. In contrast, public relations focuses on building good relations with the company's various publics. Personal selling is any form of personal presentation by the firm's sales force for the purpose of making sales and building customer relationships. Firms use sales promotion to provide short-term incentives to encourage the purchase or sale of a product or a service. Finally, firms seeking immediate response from targeted individual customers use direct-marketing tools to communicate with customers and cultivate relationships with them.

2. Discuss the changing communications landscape and the need for integrated marketing communication.

The explosive developments in communications technology and changes in marketer and customer communication strategies have had a dramatic impact on marketing communications. Advertisers are now adding a broad selection of more-specialized and highly-targeted media—including digital media—to reach smaller customer segments with more-personalized, interactive messages. As they adopt richer but more fragmented media and promotion mixes to reach their diverse markets, they risk creating a communications hodgepodge for consumers. To prevent this, more companies are adopting the concept of *integrated marketing communications (IMC)*. Guided by an overall IMC strategy, the company works out the roles that the various promotional tools will play and the extent to which each will be used. It carefully coordinates the promotional activities and the timing of when major campaigns take place.

3. Describe how advertising objectives are set and how advertising strategy is developed.

Advertising—the use of paid media by a seller to inform, persuade, and remind about its products or organization—is a strong promotion tool that takes many forms and has many uses. *Advertising decision making* involves decisions about the objectives, the budget, the message, and the media. Advertisers begin by setting a clear *objective* as to whether the advertising is supposed to inform, persuade,

or remind buyers. The advertising *budget* can be based on what is affordable, on sales, on competitors' spending, or on the objectives and tasks. Developing the *advertising strategy* begins by determining what *message* the advertising must send to the target audience, and then developing a compelling *creative concept* to communicate the message. Message *execution* refers to the style, tone, words, and format of the ad. Finally, the *media decision* involves defining reach, frequency, and impact goals; choosing major media types; selecting media vehicles; and deciding on media timing. Message and media decisions must be closely coordinated for maximum campaign effectiveness.

4. Explain how advertising effectiveness is evaluated and the role of the advertising agency.

Evaluating advertising calls for evaluating the communication and sales effects of advertising before, during, and after the advertising is placed, and measuring advertising return on investment. Companies must measure the effectiveness of their advertising, and specifically try to measure the *return on advertising investment*. Advertising must be measured in terms of its *communication effects*, as well as its sales and profit effects. Measuring return on advertising is difficult; however, most companies today recognize its importance and are constantly looking for new methods. Advertising *agencies* work with the company (i.e., the advertiser) to develop, produce, plan, and execute advertising campaigns. Most large companies use agencies, which employ specialists in design, production, and media planning.

5. Explain how companies use public relations to communicate with their publics.

Public relations (PR) involves building good relations with the company's various publics. Its functions include *press agentry, product publicity, public affairs, lobbying, investor relations,* and *development*. Public relations can have a strong impact on public awareness at a much lower cost than advertising can, and PR results can sometimes be spectacular. Despite its potential strengths, however, PR sometimes sees only limited and scattered use. Public relations tools include *news, speeches, special events, buzz marketing, written materials, audiovisual materials, corporate identity materials,* and *public service activities*. A company's website can be a good PR vehicle. In considering when and how to use product PR, management should set PR objectives, choose the PR messages and vehicles, implement the PR plan, and evaluate the results. PR should be blended smoothly with other promotion activities within the company's overall IMC effort.

KEY TERMS

Advertising 433
Advertising agency 459
Advertising budget 445
Advertising media 454
Advertising objective 444
Advertising strategy 447
Affordable method 445
Competitive-parity method 446

Creative concept 450
Direct marketing 434
Execution style 450
Integrated marketing
   communications (IMC) 438
Media vehicle 457
Objective-and-task method 446
Percentage-of-sales method 446

Personal selling 434
Promotion mix (or marketing
   communications mix) 433
Public relations (PR) 434
Pull strategy 442
Push strategy 442
Return on advertising investment 458
Sales promotion 434

TALK ABOUT MARKETING

1. The shift from mass marketing to targeted marketing and the corresponding use of a richer mix of marketing communications tools pose challenges for many marketers. If you were responsible for promoting your college or university, which of the five major forms of marketing communications would you use? How would you make sure they were integrated? Who are your publics and target audience, and how can you best reach them with your communications?

2. Imagine that you are the marketing communications manager for a small local brewery (pick one that you know about). Make a list of your top five competitors. Which method of setting the advertising budget do you think each of your competitors uses? Which method will you use?

3. Any message can be presented using different execution styles. Select a brand and target audience and design two advertisements, each using a different execution style to deliver the same message to the target audience but in a different way. Identify the types of execution styles you are using and present your advertisements.

4. Marketers are developing branded web series to get consumers involved with their brands. One successful series is "The Real Women of Philadelphia" from Kraft (www.realwomenofphiladelphia.com). Fans can watch videos of professionals making delicious, simple recipes with one common ingredient—Philadelphia Cream Cheese, of course! The site features a recipe contest, and entrants even get training on how to photograph their entries to make them look as yummy as possible. Visit this website and find two other branded web series. Critique the sites and describe how viewers interact with the websites.

5. In a small group, discuss the major public relations tools and develop three public relations items for each of the following: (a) a charity, (b) a bank, (c) a brand of beer, (d) a health club.

6. Press releases are one of the tools of the public relations manager. Go to the website of *Canada Newswire*, and read some of today's press releases. If you were a business journalist, which of the press releases would you choose to write a story about? Explain why you picked that one over all the others.

THINK LIKE A MARKETING MANAGER

In Germany, it's "*Ich liebe es*"; in France, "*C'est tout ce que j'aime*." In China, it translates into "I like it," because one doesn't say "love" lightly in that culture. The McDonald's "i'm lovin' it" campaign was launched simultaneously in more than 100 countries. It was unprecedented in McDonald's history because it was the first time an international campaign was consistent in flavour and brand message in every country McDonald's serves. "It's much

more than just a new tagline or commercials—it's a new way of thinking about and expressing our worldwide brand appeal to the consumer," said Larry Light, McDonald's executive vice-president and global chief marketing officer, and the man behind the campaign. The McDonald's website at McDonalds.com features an international welcome page with a drop-down selection for each country's site. Here the online marketing is localized, the campaign adapted, the words translated, but even while capturing the spirit, music, and flavour of each country, the brand message remains consistent.

QUESTIONS

1. List all the publics and audiences that McDonald's' main corporate website communicates with.

2. Go to the McDonald's site, choose a country, and explore that country's site. How is the "i'm lovin' it" message translated and adapted? What are the signs that local culture, language, and customs have been incorporated into the campaign?

3. Find out what the most recent new menu item available at your local McDonald's is. Is it being promoted through advertising? What other forms of marketing communications are being used to promote it, and how are they integrated?

4. In response to public pressure and claims that fast food makes children obese, McDonald's geared up a major public relations campaign on the theme "It's what I eat and what I do . . . i'm lovin' it." Describe how this new public relations initiative could be integrated with each of the other four major elements of marketing communications for McDonald's.

MARKETING ETHICS

The US Food and Drug Administration (FDA) is enlisting doctors in its battle against misleading and deceptive prescription drug advertisements targeted toward consumers (called direct-to-consumer or DTC ads) and other promotional activities directed at medical professionals. You've probably seen the TV commercials for Viagra, Lipitor, Chantix, and other prescription drugs. Since the FDA relaxed the rules regarding broadcast prescription drug advertising in the late 1990s, DTC advertising has increased more than 300 percent, with US$4.5 billion spent in 2009. That's actually down from the peak of $US5.5 billion in 2006 because of the recession. It's difficult for the FDA to monitor DTC ads and other promotional activity aimed at medical professionals, so it created the "Bad Ad Program" and spent most of 2010 educating doctors about why it exists.

QUESTIONS

1. Visit www.fda.gov and search for "Bad Ad Program" to learn more about it. What is the FDA asking medical professionals to look for in DTC ads and other promotional activities directed toward them? How might this program be abused by the pharmaceutical industry?

2. Many consumers are not aware of the FDA's regulations regarding DTC advertising. The agency has a parallel program—called EthicAd—to educate consumers and to encourage them to report violations. Search the FDA's website for this program, look at the examples of correct and incorrect ads, and evaluate two prescription drug advertisements using these guidelines.

3. In Canada, the Food and Drug Act regulations are supposed to prevent pharmaceutical companies from advertising directly to consumers, but enforcement has been difficult, especially online. Search for information about Canada's regulations. Are Canadians still exposed to pharmaceutical ads? If so, how are the drug companies reaching Canadian audiences?

MARKETING TECHNOLOGY

Marketers today are constantly experimenting with new technologies, most of them online, to help them promote their products—but the technologies come and go so quickly, what's a marketer to do? MySpace was the first social networking site and was once highly desired by advertisers, but within a few short years it was overshadowed by Facebook to the point where MySpace is now struggling to survive. When virtual world Second Life launched in 2003, it quickly grew to more than 9 million inhabitants, who created online digital alter egos called *avatars*, to speak to each other. Marketers such as IBM, Sony, Adidas, Pontiac, Kraft, Coca-Cola, and even Canada Post, set up virtual presences in Second Life—much like product placement in other forms of media. Yet by 2010 Second Life was declared lifeless. Today, Twitter is going strong, marketing-wise. It's extremely popular with celebrities such as Ashton Kutcher and his millions of followers—consumers—but advertisers are still trying to figure out how to make money by using it.

QUESTIONS

1. If you haven't already done so, sign up on Twitter and search for your favourite brand or company. Are they represented? Follow them on Twitter and observe how they are using this social media tool for promotion.

2. How much does it cost to advertise on Facebook, and what different forms of advertising does it offer? If you were the marketing communications manager for Axe or Mac, would you recommend they purchase advertising on Facebook? Why or why not?

3. Besides Facebook, Twitter, and YouTube, what other social media sites is your favourite brand using to promote their business? How is this brand integrating social media into its overall IMC strategy?

MARKETING BY THE NUMBERS

Nielsen ratings are very important to both advertisers and television programmers because the cost of television advertising time is based on this rating. A show's *rating* is the number of households in Nielsen's sample tuned to that program divided by the number of television-owning households. A show's *share* of the viewing audience is the number of households watching that show divided by the number of households using TV at that time. That is, ratings consider all TV-owning households whereas share considers only households that actually have the television turned on at the time. Ratings and share are usually given together. For example, suppose that one hour on Sunday evening showed the following ratings/shares for the major broadcast networks:

Network	Program	Rating/Share
NBC	*Sunday Night Football* (played on Thursday)	13.6/22
CBS	*Big Brother 14*	4.6/8
ABC	*Wipeout*	3.1/5
FOX	*Bones*	2.9/5
The CW	*The Vampire Diaries*	2.0/3

QUESTIONS

1. If one rating point represents 1 percent of TV households, how many households were watching football that evening? How many households were tuned into *The Vampire Diaries*?

2. What total share of the viewing audience was captured by all five networks? Explain why share is higher than the rating for a given program.

VIDEO CASE

OXO

For over 20 years, OXO has put its well-known kitchen gadgets into almost every home in North America through word-of-mouth, product placement, and other forms of non-traditional promotional techniques. While OXO is a leading national brand, it competes in product categories that are small in size. With its tight advertising budgets, mass-media promotions are not feasible.

This video demonstrates how OXO is moving forward with its promotional mix through online and social media campaigns. For its Good Grips, Steel, Candela, Tot, and Staples/OXO brands, OXO is making extensive use of the major social networks, expanding into the blogosphere, developing online ad campaigns, and more.

After viewing the video featuring OXO, answer the following questions:

1. How would you describe OXO's overall advertising strategy?

2. Why has OXO chosen to change its promotional strategy at this time?

3. Is OXO abandoning its old promotional methods? How is OXO blending a new advertising strategy with the promotional techniques that have made it a success?

OgilvyOne: IT'S NOT CREATIVE UNLESS IT SELLS

These days, there are some extremely creative ads fighting for our attention. Television spots are often on par with feature films in terms of artistic quality. Print ads and billboards rival works of art. Such ads can move our emotions powerfully. They can make us laugh, cry, or sing; they can produce feelings of guilt, fear, or joy. Ads themselves are often as entertaining as the programming in which they appear. However, although highly creative ads might dazzle us and even win awards from advertising critics, they sometimes overlook a very important fundamental truth: Truly creative advertising is advertising that creates sales.

Not all ads have forgotten this truth. But too often, advertisers become so enamored with the artistry of advertising that they forget about the selling part. After all, the ultimate objective of advertising is not to win awards or even to make people like an ad. It's to get people to think, feel, or *act* in some way after being exposed to an ad. Ultimately, no matter how entertaining or artistic an ad, it's not creative unless it sells.

This thinking prompted one of the world's premiere advertising agencies—OgilvyOne Worldwide—to run a unique contest. Part of Ogilvy & Mather Worldwide, OgilvyOne launched a contest to search for the World's Greatest Salesperson. According to Rory Sutherland, vice chairman for the British operations of Ogilvy & Mather, the goal of the contest was "recreating the noble art of ka-ching. There's an interesting case to be made that advertising has strayed too far from the business of salesmanship."

"Salesmanship has been lost in the pursuit of art or the dazzle of technology," said Brian Fetherstonhaugh, chairman and CEO at OgilvyOne. "It needs to be rekindled in this post-recession environment, as consumers are making more informed and deliberate choices." But as Fetherstonhaugh also points out, the return to selling through advertising is more challenging today than ever. Technologies such as TiVo, SPAM filters, and viewing-on-demand through the Internet have put consumers in control of the media more than ever. For this reason, advertisers not only need to become great salespeople, they need to be salespeople that get invited into the consumer's environment. According to Fetherstonhaugh, advertising needs to be "less about intrusion and repetition and more about engagement and evangelizing."

THE CONTEST

OgilvyOne chose a popular format for its "World's Greatest Salesperson" contest. Entrants prepared one- to two-minute video clips selling the assigned product and submitted them via YouTube. Viewers voted for their favourite videos and a panel of judges winnowed the field down to a set of finalists.

However, the product that contestants were assigned to sell was anything but the usual. They weren't asked to sell a glitzy new smartphone or super-thin large-screen TV. Instead, they had to make a pitch for a brick. That's right, a common, every day red brick. Why a brick? "If you can sell a red brick, maybe you can sell anything," said Mat Zucker, executive creative director for OgilvyOne and the creator of the contest. Some people at Ogilvy pushed for a more exciting product. But Mish Fletcher, worldwide marketing director at OgilvyOne, pointed out that perhaps those exciting products don't need "the World's Greatest Salesperson" as much.

A HERITAGE IN SALES

The "World's Greatest Salesperson" contest was a nod to advertising legend David Ogilvy, who founded Ogilvy & Mather more than 60 years ago. Prior to entering the advertising world, Ogilvy sold stoves door-to-door in Scotland. He sold so many stoves, the company asked him to write a manual for other salesmen. That manual was dubbed "the finest sales instruction manual ever written" by the editors of *Fortune* magazine, who still used it as a resource guide 30 years after Ogilvy wrote it. Ogilvy once revealed the secret to his success as a stove salesman: "No sale, no commission. No commission, no eat. That made an impression on me." That notion forms the basis for Ogilvy's credo, "We sell, or else."

David Ogilvy left sales, but sales never left him. He founded Ogilvy & Mather in 1949 based on the principles that the function of advertising is to sell, and that successful advertising for any product is based on customer information. Ogilvy's principles worked for major corporation after major corporation. In 1962, *Time* magazine called Ogilvy "the most sought-after wizard in today's advertising industry." He was so successful at expanding the bounds of creativity in advertising that he has often been called "The Father of Advertising." The list of iconic advertising campaigns that he developed is as long as anyone's in the business.

Based on this heritage, Zucker came up with the idea for the "World's Greatest Salesperson" contest. "If we believe in selling, and our founder was a salesman, we have a special responsibility to reassert the importance of sales," Zucker said.

CREATIVE PITCHES

More than 230 videos from entrants in 12 countries were uploaded to Ogilvy's YouTube contest site. Ogilvy eventually narrowed the entrants down to three finalists. The first finalist was Todd Herman, an international performance coaching and training expert from Edmonton, Canada. Herman pitched a single brick as a symbol of something that can be used as the first step in building something great. He started his video with a brick in hand, saying "The story of a simple, red brick is one filled with power, struggle, and romance. And now you have the chance to capture some of its magic." From there, Herman summarized various ways that bricks have been used throughout history to build and connect civilizations. His pitch was based on the idea that a red brick is not just a common object but a symbol of a dream that was acted upon.

Eric Polins, managing partner of a marketing consulting firm in Tampa, Florida, was the second finalist. Polins, who left broadcast news because of extreme stage fright every time he stepped in front of a camera, sold his brick as an intangible asset—a good luck charm. In a clever way, he pointed out that the classic good luck charms all have problems. A rabbit's foot is too morbid. A four-leaf clover is too hard to come by in a paved-over world. The "knock on wood" gesture is outdated as hardly anything is made out of wood anymore. And a horseshoe . . . who can afford a horse?

The third finalist was Lee Abbas, a former Panasonic marketing executive from Japan. She organized her approach around a reinvention of the classic old brick—a must-have purse with chrome steel handles. She demonstrated this new product from a brick factory and maker of high-strength, lightweight bricks. She then related how a friend of hers was mugged. Rather than reaching into her purse for a can of pepper spray, she simply whacked her assailant over the head with a brick, knocking him out cold.

All three finalists were winners in one respect. Each received an all-expense-paid trip to Cannes, France, for the fifty-seventh annual Cannes Lions International Advertising Festival. There, each had to make a live presentation for a second product in front of a studio audience and panel of judges. This time, the finalists had to sell a Motorola Droid phone. They made their presentations, the audience voted, and Todd Herman emerged as the "World's Greatest Salesperson."

"I honestly can't believe I'm standing here with the World's Greatest Salesperson award," Herman stated. "[I]t's such an honour to be working with a company whose founder has been such a huge influence on my business philosophy." Perhaps the biggest part of the prize was a job with OgilvyOne. Herman was given the opportunity to fulfill a three-month fellowship with the agency with the express purpose of crafting a sales guide to the twenty-first century. The principles in the guide will be presented at the Direct Marketing Association's annual conference.

As would be expected of the World's Greatest Salesperson, Fetherstonhaugh pointed out, Herman "is a true student of persuasion and motivation. It shone through at every stage of the World's Greatest Salesperson competition." Herman's own words seem to reflect the principles of David Ogilvy and the true nature of advertising. "People always think of sales as the in-your-face-used-car salesman. But selling happens all the time. Really great selling is never noticed. You should feel like you just bought something, not like you just got sold."

Sources: Stuart Elliott, "In a Test of Sales Savvy, Selling a Red Brick on YouTube," *New York Times*, March 29, 2010, p. B3; "Todd Herman Voted World's Greatest Salesperson," PRNewswire.com, July 2010; Robert Trigaux, "To Be 'Greatest Salesperson,' Just Sell a Measly Red Brick," *St. Petersburg Times*, June 15, 2010, p. 1B; Florence Loyie, "Patter to Sell Brick Wins Trip to Cannes," *Edmonton Journal*, June 10, 2010, p. A3.

QUESTIONS FOR DISCUSSION

1. Do you agree with David Ogilvy that the primary function of advertising is selling? How does that fit with the three advertising objectives of informing, persuading, and reminding?

2. If the primary purpose of advertising is to sell, are there any message execution techniques that seem best predisposed to this purpose?

3. As a creator of advertising, what kind of return on investment did OgilvyOne get out of this promotional contest?

4. Do you agree or disagree with the premise that the primary function of advertising is to sell? Give examples of ad campaigns to support your position.

MyMarketingLab

MyMarketingLab is an online homework and tutorial system puts you in control of your own learning with study and practice tools directly correlated to this chapter's content.

Bloomberg/Getty Images

1 discuss the role of a company's salespeople in creating value for customers and building customer relationships

2 identify and explain the six major sales force management steps

3 discuss the personal selling process, distinguishing between transaction-oriented marketing and relationship marketing

4 explain how sales promotion campaigns are developed and implemented

Personal Selling and Sales Promotion

PREVIEWING THE CONCEPTS

In the previous chapter, you learned about communicating customer value through integrated marketing communications (IMC) and about two elements of the promotion mix—advertising and public relations. In this chapter, we'll look at two more IMC elements—personal selling and sales promotion. Personal selling is the interpersonal arm of marketing communications, in which the sales force interacts with customers and prospects to build relationships and make sales. Sales promotion consists of short-term incentives to encourage purchase or sale of a product or a service. As you read on, remember that although this chapter examines personal selling and sales promotion as separate tools, they must be carefully integrated with other elements of the promotion mix.

When you think of salespeople, perhaps you think of pushy retail sales clerks, "yell and sell" TV pitchmen, or the stereotypical "used-car salesman." But such stereotypes simply don't fit the reality of most of today's salespeople—well-trained, well-educated, dedicated sales professionals who succeed not by taking advantage of customers but by listening to their needs and forging solutions to their problems. For most companies, personal selling plays an important role in building profitable customer relationships. Consider Procter & Gamble, whose customer-focused sales force as long been considered one of the best.

P&G: IT'S NOT SALES, IT'S CUSTOMER BUSINESS DEVELOPMENT

For decades, Procter & Gamble has been at the top of almost every expert's A-list of outstanding marketing companies. The experts point to P&G's stable of top-selling consumer brands or that, year in and year out, P&G is the world's largest advertiser. Consumers seem to agree. You'll find at least one of P&G's blockbuster brands in 99 percent of all households; in many homes, you'll find a dozen or more familiar P&G products. But P&G is also highly respected for something else—its top-notch customer-focused sales force.

P&G's sales force has long been an icon for selling at its very best. When it comes to selecting, training, and managing salespeople, P&G sets the gold standard. The company employs a massive sales force of more than 5000 salespeople worldwide. At P&G, however, they rarely call it *sales*. Instead, it's *customer business development (CBD)*. And P&G sales reps aren't *salespeople*—they're *CBD managers* or *CBD account executives*. All this might seem like just so much "corp-speak," but at P&G the distinction goes to the very core of how selling works.

P&G understands that if its customers don't do well, neither will the company. To grow its own business, therefore, P&G must first grow the business of the retailers that sell its brands to final consumers. And at P&G, the primary responsibility for helping customers grow falls to the sales force. Rather than just selling *to* its retail and wholesale customers, CBD managers partner strategically *with* customers to help develop their business in P&G's product categories. "We depend on them as much as they depend on us," says one CBD manager. By partnering with each other, P&G and its customers create "win–win" relationships that help both companies prosper.

Most P&G customers are huge and complex businesses—such as Shoppers Drug Mart, Walmart, or Dollar General—with thousands of stores and billions of dollars in revenues. Working with and selling to such customers can be a very complex undertaking, more than any single salesperson or sales team could accomplish. Instead, P&G assigns a full CBD team to every large customer account. Each CBD team contains not only salespeople, but also a full complement of specialists in every aspect of selling P&G's consumer brands at the retail level.

CBD teams vary in size depending on the customer. For example, P&G's largest customer, Walmart—which accounts for an amazing 20 percent of the company's sales—commands a 350-person CBD team. By contrast, the P&G Dollar General team consists of about 30 people. Regardless of size, every CBD team constitutes a complete, multifunctional customer service unit. Each team includes a CBD manager and several CBD account executives (each responsible for a specific P&G product category), supported by specialists in marketing strategy, product development, operations, information systems, logistics, finance, and human resources.

To deal effectively with large accounts, P&G salespeople must be smart, well trained, and strategically grounded. They deal daily with high-level retail category buyers who may purchase hundreds of millions of dollars' worth of P&G and competing brands annually. It takes a lot more than a friendly smile and a firm handshake to interact with such buyers. Yet individual P&G salespeople can't know everything, and thanks to the CBD sales structure they don't have to. Instead, as members of a full CBD team, P&G salespeople have at hand all the resources they need to resolve even the most challenging customer problems. "I have everything I need right here," says a household care account executive. "If my customer needs help from us with in-store promotions, I can go right down the hall and talk with someone on my team in marketing about doing some kind of promotional deal. It's that simple."

Customer business development involves partnering with customers to jointly identify strategies that create shopper value and satisfaction and drive profitable sales at the store level. When it comes to profitably moving Tide, Pampers, Gillette, or other P&G brands off store shelves and into consumers' shopping carts, P&G reps and their teams often know more than the retail buyers they advise. In fact, P&G's retail partners often rely on CBD teams to help them manage not only the P&G brands on their shelves but also entire product categories, including competing brands.

Wait a minute. Does it make sense to let P&G advise on the stocking and placement of competitors' brands as well as its own? Would a P&G CBD rep ever tell a retail buyer to stock fewer P&G products and more of a competing brand? Believe it or not, it happens all the time. The CBD team's primary goal is to help the customer win in each product category. Sometimes analysis shows that the best solution for the customer is "more of the other guy's product." For P&G, that's okay. It knows that creating the best situation for the retailer ultimately pulls in more customer traffic, which in turn will likely lead to increased sales for other P&G products in the same category. Because most of P&G's brands are market share leaders, it stands to benefit more from the increased traffic than competitors do. Again, what's good for the customer is good for P&G—it's a win–win situation.

Honest and open dealings also help to build long-term customer relationships. P&G salespeople become trusted advisers to their retailer partners, a status they work hard to maintain. "It took me four years to build the trust I now have with my buyer," says a veteran CBD account executive. "If I talk her into buying P&G products that she can't sell, or talk her out of stocking competing brands that she should be selling, I could lose that trust in a heartbeat."

Finally, collaboration is usually a two-way street—P&G gives and customers give back in return. "We'll help customers run a set of commercials or do some merchandising events, but there's usually a return-on-investment," explains another CBD manager. "Maybe it's helping us with distribution of a new product or increasing space for fabric care. We're very willing if the effort creates value for us as well as for the customer and the final consumer."

According to P&G, "Customer business development is selling and a whole lot more. It's a P&G-specific approach [that lets us] grow business by working as a 'strategic partner' with our accounts, focusing on mutually beneficial business building opportunities. All customers want to improve their business; it's [our] role to help them identify the biggest opportunities."

Thus, P&G salespeople aren't the stereotypical glad-handers that some people have come to expect when they think of selling. In fact, they aren't even called *salespeople*. They are *customer business development managers*—talented, well-educated, well-trained sales professionals who do all they can to help customers succeed. They know that good selling involves working with customers to solve their problems for mutual gain. They know that if customers succeed, they succeed.[1]

IN THIS CHAPTER, we examine two more promotion mix tools: *personal selling* and *sales promotion*. Personal selling consists of interpersonal interactions with customers and prospects to make sales and maintain customer relationships. Sales promotion involves using short-term incentives to encourage customer purchasing, reseller support, and sales force efforts.

Personal Selling `LO1`

Robert Louis Stevenson once noted, "Everyone lives by selling something." Companies around the world use sales forces to sell products and services to business customers and final consumers, but sales forces are also found in many other kinds of organizations. For example, colleges and universities use recruiters to attract new students, and museums use fundraisers to contact donors and raise money. In the first part of this chapter, we examine personal selling's role in the organization, sales force management decisions, and the personal selling process.

The Nature of Personal Selling

Personal selling is one of the oldest professions in the world. The people who do the selling go by many names, including salespeople, sales representatives, agents, district managers, account executives, sales consultants, and sales engineers.

Personal selling
Personal presentation by the firm's sales force for the purpose of making sales and building customer relationships.

Exhibit 13.1 **Professional selling:** It takes more than fast talk and a warm smile to sell high-tech diesel locomotives. GE's real challenge is to win buyers' business by building day-in, day-out, year-in, year-out partnerships with customers.

© Rick Pisio\RWP Photography / Alamy

People hold many stereotypes of salespeople—including some unfavourable ones. "Salesman" may bring to mind the image of Dwight Schrute, the opinionated Dunder Mifflin paper salesman from the TV show *The Office*, who lacks both common sense and social skills. Or they may think of the real-life "yell-and-sell" TV pitchmen, who hawk everything from ShamWow to the Swivel Sweeper and Point 'n Paint in infomercials. However, the majority of salespeople are a far cry from these unfortunate stereotypes.

As the opening P&G story shows, most salespeople are well-educated and well-trained professionals who add value for customers and maintain long-term customer relationships. They listen to their customers, assess customer needs, and organize the company's efforts to solve customer problems. The best salespeople are the ones who work closely with customers for mutual gain.

Consider GE's diesel locomotive business. It takes more than fast talk and a warm smile to sell a batch of US$2 million high-tech locomotives. A single big sale can easily run into the hundreds of millions of dollars. GE salespeople head up an extensive team of company specialists—all dedicated to finding ways to satisfy the needs of large customers. The selling process can take years from the first sales presentation to the day the sale is announced. The real challenge is to win buyers' business by building day-in, day-out, year-in, year-out partnerships with them based on superior products and close collaboration.

The term **salesperson** covers a wide range of positions. At one extreme, a salesperson might be largely an *order taker*, such as the department store salesperson standing behind the counter. At the other extreme are *order getters*, whose positions demand *creative selling* and *relationship building* for products and services ranging from appliances, industrial equipment, and airplanes to insurance and information technology services. In this chapter, we focus on the more creative types of selling and the process of building and managing an effective sales force.

Salesperson

An individual representing a company to customers by performing one or more of the following activities: prospecting, communicating, selling, servicing, information gathering, and relationship building.

The Role of the Sales Force

Personal selling is the interpersonal arm of the promotion mix. Advertising consists largely of nonpersonal communication with mass audiences. In contrast, personal selling involves interpersonal interactions between salespeople and individual customers—whether face to face, by telephone, via email, through video or web conferences, or by other means. Personal selling can be more effective than advertising in more complex selling situations. Salespeople can probe customers to learn more about their problems and then adjust the marketing offer and presentation to fit each customer's special needs.

The role of personal selling varies from company to company. Some firms have no salespeople at all—for example, companies that sell only online or through catalogues, or companies that sell through manufacturer's reps, sales agents, or brokers. In most firms, however, the sales force plays a major role. In companies that sell business products and services, such as IBM, DuPont, or Boeing, the company's salespeople work directly with customers. In consumer-products companies such as Nestlé and Nike, the sales force plays an important behind-the-scenes role. It works with wholesalers and retailers to gain their support and help them be more effective in selling the company's products.

Linking the Company with Its Customers
The sales force serves as a critical link between a company and its customers. In many cases, salespeople serve two masters—the seller and the buyer. First, they *represent the company to customers*. They find and develop new customers and communicate information about the company's products and services. They sell products by approaching customers, presenting their offerings, answering objections, negotiating prices and terms, closing sales, and servicing accounts.

At the same time, salespeople *represent customers to the company*, acting inside the firm as "champions" of customers' interests and managing the buyer–seller relationship. Salespeople relay customer concerns about company products and actions back inside to those who can handle them. They learn about customer needs

Exhibit 13.2 Salespeople link the company with its customers. To many customers, the salesperson is the company.

yellowdog/cultura/Corbis

and work with other marketing and nonmarketing people in the company to develop greater customer value.

In fact, to many customers, the salesperson *is* the company—the only tangible manifestation of the company that they see. Hence, customers may become loyal to salespeople as well as to the companies and products they represent. This concept of "salesperson-owned loyalty" lends even more importance to the salesperson's customer-relationship-building abilities. Strong relationships with the salesperson will result in strong relationships with the company and its products. Conversely, poor salesperson relationships will probably result in poor company and product relationships.

Given its role in linking the company with its customers, the sales force must be strongly customer-solutions focused. In fact, such a customer-solutions focus is a must not just for the sales force, but also for the entire organization. Says Anne Mulcahy, successful former CEO and chairman of Xerox, who started her career in sales, a strong customer service focus "has to be the centre of your universe, the heartland of how you run your company."[2]

Coordinating Marketing and Sales Ideally, the sales force and other marketing functions (marketing planners, brand managers, and researchers) should work together closely to jointly create value for customers. Unfortunately, however, some companies still treat marketing and sales as separate functions. When this happens, the separated marketing and sales functions often don't get along well. When things go wrong, marketers blame the sales force for its poor execution of an otherwise splendid strategy. In turn, the sales team blames the marketers for being out of touch with what's really going on with customers. Neither group fully values the other's contributions. If not repaired, such disconnects between marketing and sales can damage customer relationships and company performance.

A company can take several actions to help bring its marketing and sales functions closer together. At the most basic level, it can increase communications between the two groups by arranging joint meetings and spelling out communication channels. It can create opportunities for salespeople and marketers to work together. Brand managers and researchers can tag along on sales calls or sit in on sales planning sessions. In turn, salespeople can sit in on marketing planning sessions and share their firsthand customer knowledge.

A company can also create joint objectives and reward systems for sales and marketing teams or appoint marketing-sales liaisons—people from marketing who "live with the sales force" and help coordinate marketing and sales force programs and efforts. Finally, it can appoint a high-level marketing executive to oversee both marketing and sales. Such a person can help infuse marketing and sales with the common goal of creating value for customers to capture value in return.[3]

Managing the Sales Force LO2

Sales force management

Analyzing, planning, implementing, and controlling sales force activities.

We define **sales force management** as analyzing, planning, implementing, and controlling sales force activities. It includes designing sales force strategy and structure, as well as recruiting, selecting, training, compensating, supervising, and evaluating the firm's salespeople. These major sales force management decisions are shown in Figure 13.1 and discussed in the following sections.

Designing Sales Force Strategy and Structure

Marketing managers face several sales force strategy and design questions. How should salespeople and their tasks be structured? How big should the sales force be? Should salespeople sell alone or work in teams with other people in the company? Should they sell in the field or by telephone or on the web? We address these issues next.

The Sales Force Structure   A company can divide sales responsibilities along any of several lines. The structure decision is simple if the company sells only one product line to one industry with customers in many locations. In that case the company would use a *territorial sales force structure*. However, if the company sells many products to many types of customers, it might need either a *product sales force structure* or a *customer sales force structure*, or a combination of the two.

Territorial sales force structure

A sales force organization that assigns each salesperson to an exclusive geographic territory in which that salesperson sells the company's full line.

In the **territorial sales force structure**, each salesperson is assigned to an exclusive geographic area and sells the company's full line of products or services to all customers in that territory. This organization clearly defines each salesperson's job and fixes accountability. It also increases the salesperson's desire to build local customer relationships that, in turn, improve selling effectiveness. Finally, because each salesperson travels within a limited geographic area, travel expenses are relatively small. A territorial sales organization is often supported by many levels of sales management positions. For example, individual territory sales reps may report to area managers, who in turn report to regional managers who report to a director of sales.

Product sales force structure

A sales force organization under which salespeople specialize in selling only a portion of the company's products or lines.

If a company has numerous and complex products, it can adopt a **product sales force structure**, in which the sales force specializes along product lines. For example, GE employs different sales forces within different product and service divisions of its major businesses. Within GE Infrastructure, for instance, the company has separate sales forces for aviation, energy, transportation, and water processing products and technologies. No single salesperson can become expert in all of these product categories, so product

FIGURE 13.1 Major Steps in Sales Force Management

specialization is required. Within GE Healthcare, it employs different sales forces for diagnostic imaging, life sciences, and integrated IT solutions products and services. In all, a company as large and complex as GE might have dozens of separate sales forces serving its diverse product and service portfolio.

Using a **customer (or market) sales force structure**, a company organizes its sales force along customer or industry lines. Separate sales forces may be set up for different industries, for serving current customers versus finding new ones, and for major accounts versus regular accounts.[4] Many companies even have special sales forces set up to handle the needs of individual large customers. For example, appliance maker Whirlpool assigns individual teams of salespeople to big retail customers such as Sears, Best Buy, and Home Depot. Each Whirlpool sales team aligns with the large customer's buying team.

Exhibit 13.3 **Sales force structure:** Whirlpool specializes its sales force by customer and by territory for each key customer group.

Paul SANCYA, Associated Press

When a company sells a wide variety of products to many types of customers over a broad geographic area, it often employs a *complex sales force structure,* which combines several types of organization. Salespeople can be specialized by customer and territory; product and territory; product and customer; or territory, product, and customer. For example, Whirlpool specializes its sales force by customer (with different sales teams for Sears, Lowe's, Best Buy, Home Depot, and smaller independent retailers) *and* by territory for each key customer group (territory representatives, territory managers, regional managers, and so on). No single structure is best for all companies and situations. Each company should select a sales force structure that best serves the needs of its customers and fits its overall marketing strategy.

Customer (or market) sales force structure
A sales force organization under which salespeople specialize in selling only to certain customers or industries.

Sales Force Size   Once the company has set its structure, it is ready to consider *sales force size.* Sales forces may range in size from only a few salespeople to tens of thousands. Some sales forces are huge—for example, PepsiCo employs 36 000 salespeople; American Express, 23 400; GE, 16 400; and Xerox, 15 000.[5] Salespeople constitute one of the company's most productive—and most expensive—assets. Therefore, increasing their number will increase both sales and costs.

Many companies use some form of *workload approach* to set sales force size. When using this approach, a company first groups accounts into different classes according to size, account status, or other factors related to the amount of effort required to maintain them. It then determines the number of salespeople needed to call on each class of accounts the desired number of times.

The company might think as follows: Suppose we have 1000 Type-A accounts and 2000 Type-B accounts. Type-A accounts require 36 calls a year and Type-B accounts require 12 calls a year. In this case, the sales force's *workload*—the number of calls it must make per year—is 60 000 calls [(1000 × 36) + (2000 × 12) = 36 000 + 24 000 = 60 000]. Suppose our average salesperson can make 1000 calls a year. Thus, we need 60 salespeople (60 000 ÷ 1000).

Other Sales Force Strategy and Structure Issues   Sales management must also decide who will be involved in the selling effort and how various sales and sales support people will work together.

Outside sales force (or field sales force)
Salespeople who travel to call on customers in the field.

Inside sales force
Salespeople who conduct business from their offices via telephone, the Internet, or visits from prospective buyers.

OUTSIDE AND INSIDE SALES FORCES   The company may have an **outside sales force (or field sales force)**, an **inside sales force**, or both. Outside salespeople travel to call on customers in the field. Inside salespeople conduct business from their offices via telephone, the Internet, or visits from buyers.

Some inside salespeople provide support for the outside sales force, freeing them to spend more time selling to major accounts and finding new prospects. For example, *technical sales support people* provide technical information and answers to customers' questions. *Sales assistants* provide administrative backup for outside salespeople. They call ahead and confirm appointments, follow up on deliveries, and answer customers' questions when outside salespeople cannot be reached. Using such combinations of inside and outside salespeople can help to serve important customers better. The inside rep provides daily access and support; the outside rep provides face-to-face collaboration and relationship building.

Other inside salespeople do more than just provide support. *Telemarketers* and *Internet sellers* use the phone and Internet to find new leads and qualify prospects or to sell and service accounts directly. Telemarketing and Internet selling can be very effective, less costly ways to sell to smaller, harder-to-reach customers. Depending on the complexity of the product and the customer, for example, a telemarketer can make from 20 to 33 decision maker contacts a day, compared with the average of four that an outside salesperson can make. And whereas an average business-to-business field sales call costs $350 or more, a routine industrial telemarketing call costs only about $5 and a complex call about $20.[6]

Although the federal government's Do Not Call Registry put a dent in telephone sales to consumers, telemarketing remains a vital tool for many business-to-business marketers. For some smaller companies, telephone and web selling may be the primary sales approaches. However, larger companies also use these tactics, either to sell directly to small and mid-size customers or to help out with larger ones. Especially in the leaner times following the recent recession, many companies are cutting back on in-person customer visits in favour of more telephone, email, and Internet selling.

For many types of products and selling situations, phone or web selling can be as effective as a personal sales call:[7]

Exhibit 13.4 For many types of selling situations, phone or web selling can be as effective as a personal sales call. At Climax Portable Machine Tools, phone reps build surprisingly strong and personal customer relationships.

Helen King / Corbis

Climax Portable Machine Tools, which manufactures portable maintenance tools for the metal cutting industry, has proven that telemarketing can save money and still lavish attention on buyers. Under the old system, Climax sales engineers spent one-third of their time on the road, training distributor salespeople and accompanying them on calls. They could make about four contacts a day. Now, each of five sales engineers on Climax's inside sales team calls about 30 prospects a day, following up on leads generated by ads and emails. Because it takes about five calls to close a sale, the sales engineers update a prospect's profile after each contact, noting the degree of commitment, requirements, next call date, and personal comments. "If anyone mentions he's going on a fishing trip, our sales engineer enters that in the sales information system and uses it to personalize the next phone call," says Climax's president, noting that this is one way to build good relations.

Another is that the first contact with a prospect includes the sales engineer's business card with his or her picture on it. Climax's customer information system also gives inside reps instant access to customer information entered by the outside sales force and service people. Armed with all the information, inside reps can build surprisingly strong and personal customer relationships. Of course, it takes more than friendliness to sell US$15 000 machine tools over the phone (special orders may run US$200 000), but the telemarketing approach works well. When Climax customers were asked, "Do you see the sales engineer often enough?" the response was overwhelmingly positive. Obviously, many people didn't realize that the only contact they had with Climax had been on the phone.

TEAM SELLING As products become more complex, and as customers grow larger and more demanding, a single salesperson simply can't handle all of a large customer's needs. Instead, most companies now use **team selling** to service large, complex accounts. Sales teams can unearth problems, solutions, and sales opportunities that no individual salesperson could. Such teams might include experts from any area or level of the selling firm—sales, marketing, technical and support services, R&D, engineering, operations, finance, and others.

> **Team selling**
> Using teams of people from sales, marketing, engineering, finance, technical support, and even upper management to service large, complex accounts.

In many cases, the move to team selling mirrors similar changes in customers' buying organizations. Many large customer companies have implemented team-based purchasing, requiring marketers to employ equivalent team-based selling. When dealing with large, complex accounts, one salesperson can't be an expert in everything the customer needs. Instead, selling is done by strategic account teams, quarterbacked by senior account managers or customer business managers.

Some companies, such as IBM, Xerox, and P&G, have used teams for a long time. P&G sales reps are organized into "customer business development (CBD) teams." Each CBD team is assigned to a major P&G customer, such as Walmart, Safeway, or Shoppers Drug Mart. Teams consist of a customer business development manager, several account executives (each responsible for a specific category of P&G products), and specialists in marketing strategy, operations, information systems, logistics, and finance. This organization places the focus on serving the complete needs of each important customer. It lets P&G "grow business by working as a 'strategic partner' with our accounts, not just as a supplier."[8]

Team selling does have some pitfalls. For example, salespeople are by nature competitive and have often been trained and rewarded for outstanding individual performance. Salespeople who are used to having customers all to themselves may have trouble learning to work with and trust others on a team. In addition, selling teams can confuse or overwhelm customers who are used to working with only one salesperson. Finally, difficulties in evaluating individual contributions to the team selling effort can create some sticky compensation issues.

Recruiting and Selecting Salespeople

At the heart of any successful sales force operation is the recruitment and selection of good salespeople. Once selected, the new members of the sales team must be trained—they must learn about the company and its products, and how those products can benefit customers. The performance difference between an average salesperson and a top salesperson can be substantial. In a typical sales force, the top 30 percent of the salespeople might bring in 60 percent of the sales. Beyond the differences in sales performance, poor selection results in costly turnover. When a salesperson quits, the costs of finding and training a new salesperson—plus the costs of lost sales—can be very high. Also, a sales force with many new people is less productive, and turnover disrupts important customer relationships.

What sets great salespeople apart from all the rest? In an effort to profile top sales performers, Gallup Management Consulting Group, a division of the well-known Gallup

Adam Gregor/Shutterstock

Exhibit 13.5 Great salespeople: The best salespeople possess intrinsic motivation, a disciplined work style, the ability to close a sale, and, perhaps most important, the ability to build relationships with customers.

polling organization, has interviewed hundreds of thousands of salespeople. Its research suggests that the best salespeople possess four key talents: intrinsic motivation, disciplined work style, the ability to close a sale, and, perhaps most important, the ability to build relationships with customers.[9]

Super salespeople are motivated from within—they have an unrelenting drive to excel. Some salespeople are driven by money, a desire for recognition, or the satisfaction of competing and winning. Others are driven by the desire to provide service and build relationships. The best salespeople possess some of each of these motivations. They also have a disciplined work style. They lay out detailed, organized plans and then follow through in a timely way.

But motivation and discipline mean little unless they result in closing more sales and building better customer relationships. Super salespeople build the skills and knowledge they need to get the job done. Perhaps most important, top salespeople are excellent customer problem solvers and relationship builders. They understand their customers' needs. Talk to sales executives and they'll describe top performers in these terms: empathetic, patient, caring, responsive, good listeners. Top performers can put themselves on the buyer's side of the desk and see the world through their customers' eyes. They don't want just to be liked, they want to add value for their customers.

That said, there is no one right way to sell. Each successful salesperson uses a different approach, one that best applies his or her unique strengths and talents. For example, some salespeople enjoy the thrill of a harder sell in confronting challenges and winning people over. Others might apply "softer" talents to reach the same goal. "The key is for sales reps to understand and nurture their innate talents so they can develop their own personal approach and win business *their* way," says a selling expert.[10]

When recruiting, a company should analyze the sales job itself, and the characteristics of its most successful salespeople to identify the traits needed by a successful salesperson in their industry. Then it must recruit the right salespeople. The human resources department looks for applicants by getting names from current salespeople, using employment agencies, searching the Internet, placing classified ads, and working through college placement services. Another source is to attract top salespeople from other companies. Proven salespeople need less training and can be productive immediately.

Recruiting will attract many applicants from which the company must select the best. The selection procedure can vary from a single informal interview to lengthy testing and interviewing. Many companies give formal tests to sales applicants. Tests typically measure sales aptitude, analytical and organizational skills, personality traits, and other characteristics. But test scores provide only one piece of information in a set that includes personal characteristics, references, past employment history, and interviewer reactions.

Training Salespeople

New salespeople may spend anywhere from a few weeks or months to a year or more in training. After the initial training ends, most companies provide continuing sales training via seminars, sales meetings, and Internet e-learning throughout the salesperson's career. In all, companies spend billions of dollars annually on training salespeople, and sales training typically captures the largest share of the training budget. Although training can be expensive, it can also yield dramatic returns. For instance, one recent study showed that sales training conducted by ADP, an administrative services firm, resulted in an ROI of nearly 338 percent in only 90 days.[11] In Canada, the Canadian Professional Sales Association (CPSA), in conjunction with Human Resources Skills Development Canada, offers sales training and certification to sales professionals in a wide range of industries, and have trained over 12 000 salespeople.[12]

Training programs have several goals. First, salespeople need to know about customers and how to build relationships with them. So the training program must teach them about different types of customers and their needs, buying motives, and buying habits. And it must teach them how to sell effectively and train them in the basics of the selling process. Salespeople also need to know and identify with the company, its products, and its competitors. So an effective training program teaches them about the company's objectives, organization, chief products and markets, and about the strategies of major competitors.

Today, many companies are adding e-learning to their sales training programs. Online training may range from simple text-based product training and Internet-based sales exercises that build sales skills to sophisticated simulations that re-create the dynamics of real-life sales calls. Training online instead of on-site can cut travel and other training costs, and it takes up less of a salesperson's selling time. It also makes on-demand training available to salespeople, letting them train as little or as much as needed, whenever and wherever needed. Although most e-learning is web-based, many companies now offer on-demand training from anywhere via almost any digital device.

Many companies are now using imaginative and sophisticated e-learning techniques to make sales training more efficient—and sometimes even more fun. For example, Bayer HealthCare Pharmaceuticals worked with Concentric Pharma Advertising, a health care marketing agency, to create a role-playing simulation video game to train its sales force on a new drug marketing program:[13]

Most people don't usually associate fast-paced rock music and flashy graphics with online sales training tools. But Concentric Pharma Advertising's innovative role-playing video game—Rep Race: The Battle for Office Supremacy—has all that and a lot more. Rep Race gives Bayer sales reps far more entertainment than the staid old multiple-choice skills tests it replaces. The game was created to help breathe new life into a mature Bayer product—Betaseron, an 18-year-old multiple sclerosis (MS) therapy treatment. The aim was to find a fresh, more active way to help Bayer sales reps apply the in-depth information they learned about Betaseron to actual selling and objections-handling situations. Bayer also wanted to increase rep engagement through interactive learning and feedback through real-time results. Bayer reps liked Rep Race from the start. According to Bayer, when the game was first launched, reps played it as many as 30 times. In addition to its educational and motivational value, Rep Race allowed Bayer to measure sales reps' individual and collective performance. In the end, Bayer calculated that the Rep Race simulation helped improve the Betaseron sales team's effectiveness by 20 percent.

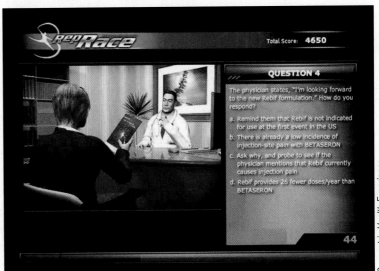

Concentric Health Experience

Exhibit 13.6 E-training can make sales training more efficient—and more fun. Bayer HealthCare Pharmaceuticals' role-playing video game—Rep Race—helped improve sales rep effectiveness by 20 percent.

Compensating Salespeople

To attract good salespeople, a company must have an appealing compensation plan. Compensation is made up of four elements—a fixed amount, a variable amount, expenses, and fringe benefits. The fixed amount, usually a salary, gives the salesperson some stable income. The variable amount, which might be commissions or bonuses based on sales performance, rewards the salesperson for greater effort and success.

Management must determine what *mix* of these compensation elements makes the most sense for each sales job. Different combinations of fixed and variable compensation give rise to four basic types of compensation plans: straight salary, straight commission, salary plus bonus, and salary plus commission. According to one study of sales force compensation, 18 percent of companies pay straight salary, 19 percent pay straight commission, and 63 percent pay a combination of salary plus incentives. A study showed that the average salesperson's pay consists of about 67 percent salary and 33 percent incentive pay.[14]

The sales force compensation plan can both motivate salespeople and direct their activities. Compensation should direct salespeople toward activities that are consistent with overall sales force and marketing objectives. For example, if the strategy is to acquire new business, grow rapidly, and gain market share, the compensation plan might include a larger commission component, coupled with a new-account bonus to encourage high sales performance and new-account development. In contrast, if the goal is to maximize current account profitability, the compensation plan might contain a larger base-salary component with additional incentives for current account sales or customer satisfaction.

In fact, more and more companies are moving away from high commission plans that may drive salespeople to make short-term grabs for business. They worry that a salesperson who is pushing too hard to close a deal may ruin the customer relationship. Instead, companies are designing compensation plans that reward salespeople for building customer relationships and growing the long-run value of each customer.

When times get tough economically, some companies are tempted to cut costs by reducing sales compensation. However, although some cost-cutting measures make sense when business is sluggish, cutting sales force compensation across the board is usually a "don't-go-there, last-of-the-last-resorts" action, says one sales compensation expert. "Keep in mind that if you burn the salesperson, you might burn the customer relationship." If the company must reduce its compensation expenses, says the expert, a better strategy than across-the-board cuts is to "keep the pay up for top performers and turn the [low performers] loose."[15]

Supervising and Motivating Salespeople

New salespeople need more than a territory, compensation, and training—they need supervision and motivation. The goal of *supervision* is to help salespeople "work smart" by doing the right things in the right ways. The goal of *motivation* is to encourage salespeople to "work hard" and energetically toward sales force goals. If salespeople work smart and work hard, they will realize their full potential, to their own and the company's benefit.

Supervising Salespeople   Companies vary in how closely they supervise their salespeople. Many help salespeople to identify target customers and set call norms. Some may also specify how much time the sales force should spend prospecting for new accounts and set other time management priorities. One tool is the weekly, monthly, or annual *call plan* that shows which customers and prospects to call on and which activities to carry out. Another tool is *time-and-duty analysis*. In addition to time spent selling, the salesperson spends time travelling, waiting, taking breaks, and doing administrative chores.

Figure 13.2 shows how salespeople spend their time. On average, active selling time accounts for only 11 percent of total working time! If selling time could be raised from

FIGURE 13.2 How Salespeople Spend Their Time

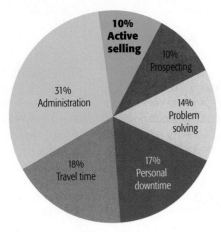

Source: Proudfoot Consulting. Data used with permission.

11 percent to 33 percent, this would triple the time spent selling.[16] Companies always are looking for ways to save time—simplifying administrative duties, developing better sales-call and routing plans, supplying more and better customer information, and using phones, email, or video conferencing instead of travelling.

Many firms have adopted *sales force automation systems*: computerized, digitized sales force operations that let salespeople work more effectively anytime, anywhere. Companies now routinely equip their salespeople with technologies such as laptops or tablets, smartphones, wireless connections, videoconferencing technologies, and customer-contact and relationship management software. Armed with these technologies, salespeople can more effectively and efficiently profile customers and prospects, analyze and forecast sales, schedule sales calls, make presentations, prepare sales and expense reports, and manage account relationships. The result is better time management, improved customer service, lower sales costs, and higher sales performance. In all, technology has reshaped the ways in which salespeople carry out their duties and engage customers.

Selling And The Internet

Perhaps the fastest-growing sales technology tool is the Internet. The Internet offers explosive potential for conducting sales operations and interacting with and serving customers. Some analysts even predict that the Internet will mean the death of person-to-person selling, as salespeople are ultimately replaced by websites, online social networking, mobile apps, and other tools that allow direct customer contact. "Don't believe it," says one sales expert (see Marketing@Work 13.1). Sales organizations are now both enhancing their effectiveness and saving time and money by using a host of innovative Internet approaches to

Exhibit 13.7 **Sales force automation:** Technology has reshaped the ways in which salespeople carry out their duties and engage customers.

© Blend Images / Alamy

MARKETING@WORK 13.1

B-to-B Salespeople: Who Needs Them Anymore?

It's hard to imagine a world without salespeople. But according to some analysts, there will be a lot fewer of them a decade from now. With the explosion of the Internet, mobile devices, and other technologies that link customers directly with companies, they reason, who needs face-to-face selling anymore? According to the doubters, salespeople are rapidly being replaced by websites, email, blogs, mobile apps, video sharing, virtual trade shows, social networks like Facebook and LinkedIn, and a host of other new-age interaction tools.

Research firm Gartner predicts that by 2020, 85 percent of all interactions between businesses will be executed without human intervention, requiring fewer salespeople. Of the 18 million salespeople now employed in the United States, the firm says, there will be only about 4 million left. "The world no longer needs salespeople," one doomsayer boldly proclaims. "Sales is a dying profession and soon will be as outmoded as oil lamps and the rotary phone." Says another, "If we don't find and fill a need faster than a computer, we won't be needed."

So, is business-to-business selling really dying? Will the Internet, mobile technologies, and online networks replace the age-old art of selling face to face? To answer these questions, *SellingPower* magazine called together a panel of five sales experts and asked them to weigh in on the future of B-to-B sales. The panel members agreed that technology is radically transforming the selling profession. Today's revolutionary changes in how people communicate are affecting every aspect of business, and selling is no exception.

But is B-to-B selling dead in this Internet age? Don't believe it, says the *SellingPower* panel. "The assumption that technology, especially the Internet, will replace person-to-person buying and selling is ... ridiculous," declares one panelist. "Has selling changed? Of course. But when it comes to B-to-B sales, the profession is only going to

become more valuable ... in the future." Other panelists agreed: "The Internet can take orders and disseminate content, but what it can't do is discover customer needs," says one. "It can't build relationships, and it can't prospect on its own." Adds another panelist, "Someone must define the company's value proposition and unique message and communicate it to the market, and that person is the sales rep."

What is dying, however, is what one panelist calls the account-maintenance role—the order taker who stops by the customer's office on Friday and says, "Hey, got anything for me?" Such salespeople are not creating value and can easily be replaced by automation. However, salespeople who excel at new-customer acquisition, relationship management, and account growth with existing customers will always be in high demand.

There's no doubt about it—technology is transforming the profession of selling. Instead of relying on salespeople for basic

information and education, customers can now do much of their own pre-purchase research via websites, Internet searches, online-community contacts, and other venues. "The conversation with the customer starts online," says a panelist. "Customers often come to the initial meeting already having done their homework about you, your products, and your competitors. They're ready to go deeper. [So] instead of focusing on educating, the salesperson needs to move into the discovery and relationship-building phase, uncovering pain points and focusing on the prospect's business."

Rather than replacing salespeople, however, technology is augmenting them. "We're really not doing anything fundamentally different than what we and our predecessors have been doing for decades," observes a sales executive. Selling has always involved buyers and sellers doing research and social networking. Only now, we're "doing it on steroids" with a wider range of tools and applications.

UWE ANSPACH/EPA/Newscom

Exhibit 13.8 German-based software giant SAP created a community-driven marketplace called EcoHub, an online environment where SAP customers can easily discover, evaluate, and purchase software solutions. Rather than replacing salespeople, EcoHub is a B-to-B selling tool that extends their reach and effectiveness.

For example, many companies are moving rapidly into online community-based selling. Case in point: enterprise-software company SAP, which has set up EcoHub, its own online, community-powered marketplace consisting of customers, partners, and almost anyone else who wants to join. The EcoHub community (ecohub.sap.com) has two million users in 200 countries and extends across a broad Internet spectrum—a dedicated website, Twitter channels, LinkedIn groups, Facebook fan pages, YouTube channels, Flickr groups, mobile apps, and more. It includes 600 "solution storefronts" where visitors can "easily discover, evaluate, and initiate the purchase of software solutions and services from SAP and its partners." EcoHub also lets users rate the solutions and advice they get from other community members.

SAP was surprised to learn that what it had originally seen as a place for customers to discuss issues, problems, and solutions has turned into a significant point of sale. The information, give-and-take discussions, and conversations at the site draw in customers, even for big-ticket sales. "Some customers are spending US$20 to US$30 million due to EcoHub," says the SAP vice-president who heads up the community.

However, although EcoHub draws in new potential customers and takes them through many of the initial stages of product discovery and evaluation, it doesn't replace SAP's or its partners' salespeople. Instead, it extends their reach and effectiveness. The real value of EcoHub is the flood of sales leads it creates for the SAP and partner sales forces. Once prospective customers have discovered, discussed, and evaluated SAP solutions on EcoHub, SAP invites them to "initiate contact, request a proposal, or start the negotiation process." That's where the person-to-person selling begins.

All this suggests that B-to-B selling isn't dying, it's just changing. "It may take on a different appearance, employ different tools and techniques, and adapt to the changes in the marketplace," concludes one of the *SellingPower* panelists, "but I don't think you can ever replace the value of a strong sales team, particularly in a B-to-B environment." Salespeople who can discover customer needs, solve customer problems, and build relationships will be needed and successful, regardless of what else changes. Especially for those big-ticket B-to-B sales, "all the new technology may make it easier to sell by building strong ties to customers even before the first sit-down, but when the signature hits the dotted line, there will be a sales rep there."

Sources: Quotes and other information from Robert McGarvey, "All About Us," *SellingPower*, March 7, 2011, p. 48; Lain Chroust Ehmann, "Sales Up!" *SellingPower*, January/February, 2011, p. 40; James Ledbetter, "Death of a Salesman. Of Lots of Them, Actually," *Slate*, September 21, 2010, www.slate.com/id/2268122; Sean Callahan, "Is B-to-B Marketing Really Obsolete?" *BtoB*, January 17, 2011, p. 1; Gerhard Gschwandtner, "How Many Salespeople Will Be Left by 2020?" *Selling Power*, May/June 2011, p. 7; and "Getting Started with SAP EcoHub," http://ecohub.sap.com/getting-started, accessed November 2011.

train sales reps, hold sales meetings, service accounts, and conduct sales meetings with customers:[17]

> With the Internet as a new business platform, all stakeholders—prospects, customers, salespeople, and marketers—can now connect, learn, plan, analyze, engage, collaborate, and conduct business together in ways that were not even imaginable a few years ago. The Internet supports customer-focused methodologies and productivity-enhancing technologies that transform selling from an art to an interactive science. It has forever changed the process by which people buy and companies sell. Will all this new sales technology reduce the role of face-to-face selling? The good news is that the Internet will not make salespeople obsolete. It will make them a lot more productive and effective.

Internet-based technologies can produce big organizational benefits for sales forces. They help conserve salespeople's valuable time, save travel dollars, and give salespeople a new vehicle for selling and servicing accounts. Over the past decade, customer buying patterns have changed. In today's digital world, customers often know almost as much about a company's products as their salespeople do. This gives customers more control over the sales process than they had in the days when brochures and pricing were only available from a sales rep. New sales force technologies recognize and take advantage of these buying process changes, creating new avenues for connecting with customers in the Internet age.

For example, sales organizations now generate lists of prospective customers from online databases and networking sites, such as Hoovers and LinkedIn. They create dialogues when prospective customers visit their websites through live chats with the sales team. They use web conferencing tools such as WebEx, GoToMeeting, or TelePresence to talk live with customers about products and services. Other digital tools allow salespeople to monitor Internet interactions between customers about how they would like to buy, how they feel about a vendor, and what it would take to make a sale.

Courtesy of Makino, Inc.

Exhibit 13.9 **Selling on the Internet:** Machinery manufacturer Makino makes extensive use of online social networking—everything from proprietary online communities and webinars to Twitter, Facebook, and YouTube.

Today's sales forces are also ramping up their use of social networking media, from proprietary online customer communities to webinars and even Twitter, Facebook, and YouTube applications. A recent survey of business-to-business marketers found that, although they have recently cut back on traditional media and event spending, 68 percent are investing more in social media. Consider Makino, a leading manufacturer of metal cutting and machining technology:[18]

> Makino complements its sales force efforts through a wide variety of social media initiatives that inform customers and enhance customer relationships. For example, it hosts an ongoing series of industry-specific webinars that position the company as an industry-thought leader. Makino produces about three webinars each month and has archived more than 100 on topics ranging from how to get the most out of your machine tools to how metal-cutting processes are done. Webinar content is tailored to specific industries, such as aerospace or medical, and is promoted through carefully targeted banner ads and email invitations. The webinars help to build Makino's customer database, generate leads, build customer relationships, and prepare the way for salespeople by serving up relevant information and educating customers online. Makino even uses Twitter, Facebook, and YouTube to inform customers and prospects about the latest Makino innovations and events, and dramatically demonstrate the company's machines in action. "We've shifted dramatically into the electronic marketing area," says Makino's marketing manager. "It speeds up the sales cycle and makes it more efficient—for both the company and the customer. The results have been 'outstanding.'"

Ultimately, digital technologies are "delivering instant information that builds relationships and enables sales to be more efficient and cost-effective and more productive," says one sales technology analyst. "Think of it as . . . doing what the best reps always did but doing it better, faster, and cheaper," says another.[19]

However, the technologies also have some drawbacks. For starters, they're not cheap. In addition, such systems can intimidate low-tech salespeople or clients. Even more, there are some things you just can't present or teach via the Internet—things that require personal interactions. For these reasons, some high-tech experts recommend that sales executives use Internet technologies to supplement training, sales meetings, and preliminary client sales presentations, but resort to old-fashioned, face-to-face meetings when the time draws near to close the deal.

Motivating Salespeople

Beyond directing salespeople, sales managers must also motivate them. Some salespeople will do their best without any special urging from management. To them, selling may be the most fascinating job in the world. But selling can also be frustrating. Salespeople often work alone and they must sometimes travel away from home. They may face aggressive competing salespeople and difficult customers. Therefore, salespeople often need special encouragement to do their best.

Management can boost sales force morale and performance through its organizational climate, sales quotas, and positive incentives. *Organizational climate* describes the feeling that salespeople have about their opportunities, value, and rewards for a good performance. Some companies treat salespeople as if they are not very important, so performance suffers accordingly. Other companies treat their salespeople as valued contributors and allow virtually unlimited opportunity for income and promotion. Not surprisingly, these companies enjoy higher sales force performance and less turnover.

Many companies motivate their salespeople by setting **sales quotas**—standards stating the amount they should sell and how sales should be divided among the company's products. Compensation is often related to how well salespeople meet their quotas. Companies also use various *positive incentives* to increase sales force effort. *Sales meetings* provide social occasions, breaks from routine, chances to meet and talk with "company brass," and opportunities to air feelings and identify with a larger group. Companies also sponsor *sales contests* to spur the sales force to make a selling effort above what would normally be expected. Other incentives include honours, merchandise and cash awards, trips, and profit-sharing plans.

Sales quota
A standard that states the amount a salesperson should sell and how sales should be divided among the company's products.

Evaluating Salespeople and Sales Force Performance

We have thus far described how management communicates what salespeople should be doing and how it motivates them to do it. This process requires good feedback, which means getting regular information about salespeople to evaluate their performance.

Management gets information about its salespeople in several ways. The most important source is *sales reports*, including weekly or monthly work plans and longer-term marketing plans. Salespeople also write up their completed activities on *call reports* and turn in *expense reports* for which they are partly or wholly reimbursed. The company can also monitor the sales and profit performance data in the salesperson's territory. Additional information comes from personal observation, customer surveys, and talks with other salespeople.

Using various sales force reports and other information, sales management evaluates the members of the sales force. It evaluates salespeople on their ability to "plan their work and work their plan." Formal evaluation forces management to develop and communicate clear standards for judging performance. It also provides salespeople with constructive feedback and motivates them to perform well.

On a broader level, management should evaluate the performance of the sales force as a whole. Is the sales force accomplishing its customer relationship, sales, and profit objectives? Is it working well with other areas of the marketing and company organization? Are sales force costs in line with outcomes? As with other marketing activities, the company wants to measure its *return on sales investment*.

The Personal Selling Process LO3

We now turn from designing and managing a sales force to the actual personal selling process. The **selling process** consists of several steps that salespeople must master. These steps focus on the goal of getting new customers and obtaining orders from them. However, most salespeople spend much of their time maintaining existing accounts and building long-term customer *relationships*. We discuss the relationship aspect of the personal selling process in a later section.

Selling process
The steps that salespeople follow when selling, which include prospecting and qualifying, preapproach, approach, presentation and demonstration, handling objections, closing, and follow-up.

Steps in the Selling Process

As shown in Figure 13.3, the selling process consists of seven steps: prospecting and qualifying, preapproach, approach, presentation and demonstration, handling objections, closing, and follow-up.

FIGURE 13.3 Steps in the Selling Process

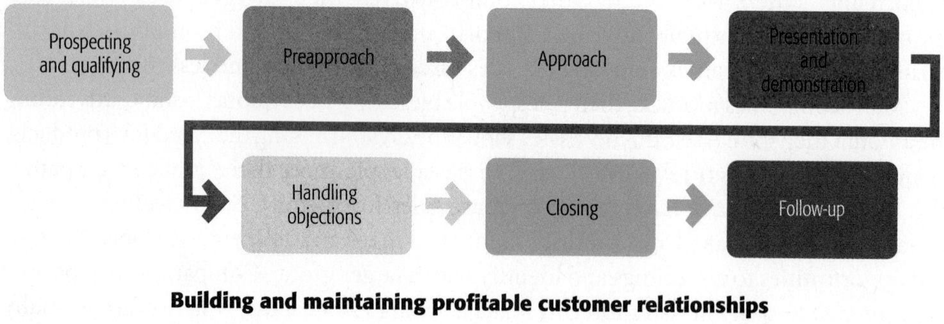

Building and maintaining profitable customer relationships

Prospecting

The step in the selling process in which the salesperson or company identifies qualified potential customers.

Prospecting and Qualifying The first step in the selling process is **prospecting**—identifying qualified potential customers. Approaching the right potential customers is crucial to selling success. Salespeople don't want to call on just any potential customers. They want to call on those who are most likely to appreciate and respond to the company's value proposition—those the company can serve well and profitably.

The salesperson must often approach many prospects to get just a few sales. Although the company supplies some leads, salespeople need skill in finding their own. The best source is referrals. Salespeople can ask current customers for referrals and cultivate other referral sources, such as suppliers, dealers, non-competing salespeople, and web or other social networks. They can also search for prospects in directories or on the web and track down leads by using the telephone and email. Or they can drop in unannounced on various offices—a practice known as *cold calling*.

Salespeople also need to know how to *qualify* leads—that is, how to identify the good ones and screen out the poor ones. Prospects can be qualified by looking at their financial ability, volume of business, special needs, location, and possibilities for growth.

Preapproach

The step in the selling process in which the salesperson learns as much as possible about a prospective customer before making a sales call.

Preapproach Before calling on a prospect, the salesperson should learn as much as possible about the organization (what it needs, who is involved in the buying) and its buyers (their characteristics and buying styles). This step is known as the **preapproach**. A successful sale begins long before the salesperson sets foot into a prospect's office. Preapproach begins with good research and preparation. The salesperson can consult standard industry and online sources, acquaintances, and others to learn about the company. Then the salesperson must apply the research gathered to develop a customer strategy.

The salesperson should set *call objectives*, which may be to qualify the prospect, gather information, or make an immediate sale. Another task is to decide on the best approach, which might be a personal visit, a phone call, or a letter or email. The best timing should be considered carefully because many prospects are busiest at certain times. Finally, the salesperson should give thought to an overall sales strategy for the account.

Approach

The step in the selling process in which the salesperson meets the customer for the first time.

Approach During the **approach** step, the salesperson should know how to meet and greet the buyer and get the relationship off to a good start. This step involves the salesperson's appearance, opening lines, and the follow-up remarks. The opening lines should be positive to build goodwill from the beginning of the relationship. This opening might be followed by some key questions to learn more about the customer's needs or by showing a display or sample to attract the buyer's attention and curiosity. As in all stages of the selling process, listening to the customer is crucial.

Presentation

The step in the selling process in which the salesperson tells the "value story" to the buyer, showing how the company's offer solves the customer's problems.

Presentation and Demonstration During the **presentation** step of the selling process, the salesperson tells the "value story" to the buyer, showing how the company's offer solves the customer's problems. The *customer-solution approach* fits better with today's relationship marketing focus than does a hard-sell or glad-handing approach. Buyers today want answers, not smiles; results, not razzle-dazzle. Moreover, they don't want just products, they want to know how those products will add value to their businesses. They want salespeople who listen to their concerns, understand their needs, and respond with the right products and services.

But before salespeople can *present* customer solutions, they must *develop* solutions to present. The solutions approach calls for good listening and problem-solving skills. The qualities that buyers *dislike most* in salespeople include being pushy, late, deceitful, unprepared, disorganized, or overly talkative. The qualities they *value most* include good listening, empathy, honesty, dependability, thoroughness, and follow-through. Great salespeople know how to sell, but more importantly they know how to listen and build strong customer relationships. According to an old sales adage, "You have two ears and one mouth. Use them proportionally." A classic ad from office products maker Boise Cascade makes the listening point. It shows a Boise salesperson with huge ears drawn on. "With Boise, you'll notice a difference right away, especially with our sales force," says the ad. "At Boise . . . our account representatives have the unique ability to listen to your needs."

Courtesy of OfficeMax Incorporated. BOISE CASCADE, BC CALC, and BCI are trademarks of Boise Cascade Company, or its affiliates.

Exhibit 13.10 This classic ad from Boise makes the point that good selling starts with listening. "Our account representatives have the unique ability to listen to your needs."

Finally, salespeople must also plan their presentation methods. Good interpersonal communication skills count when it comes to making effective sales presentations. However, today's media-rich and cluttered communications environment presents many new challenges for sales presenters. Today's information-overloaded customers demand richer presentation experiences. For their part, presenters now face multiple distractions during presentations from cellphones, text messages, and mobile Internet devices. As a result, salespeople must deliver their messages in more engaging and compelling ways.

Thus, today's salespeople are employing advanced presentation technologies that allow for full multimedia presentations to only one or a few people. The venerable old flip chart has been replaced with sophisticated presentation software, online presentation technologies, interactive whiteboards, tablet computers, and digital projectors.

Handling Objections   Customers almost always have objections during the presentation or when asked to place an order. The problem can be either logical or psychological, and objections are often unspoken. In **handling objections**, the salesperson should use a positive approach, seek out hidden objections, ask the buyer to clarify any objections, take objections as opportunities to provide more information, and turn the objections into reasons for buying. Every salesperson needs training in the skills of handling objections.

Handling objections
The step in the selling process in which the salesperson seeks out, clarifies, and overcomes customer objections to buying.

Closing   After handling the prospect's objections, the salesperson now tries to close the sale. Some salespeople do not get around to **closing** or do not handle it well. They may lack confidence, feel guilty about asking for the order, or fail to recognize the right moment to close the sale. Salespeople should know how to recognize closing signals from the buyer, including physical actions, comments, and questions. For example, the customer might sit forward and nod approvingly or ask about prices and credit terms.

Closing
The step in the selling process in which the salesperson asks the customer for an order.

Salespeople can use one of several closing techniques. They can ask for the order, review points of agreement, offer to help write up the order, ask whether the buyer wants this model or that one, or note that the buyer will lose out if the order is not placed now. The salesperson may offer the buyer special reasons to close, such as a lower price or an extra quantity at no charge.

Follow-Up The last step in the selling process—**follow-up**—is necessary if the salesperson wants to ensure customer satisfaction and repeat business. Right after closing, the salesperson should complete any details on delivery time, purchase terms, and other matters. The salesperson then should schedule a follow-up call when the initial order is received to make sure there is proper installation, instruction, and servicing. This visit would reveal any problems, assure the buyer of the salesperson's interest, and reduce any buyer concerns that might have arisen since the sale.

Follow-up
The last step in the selling process in which the salesperson follows up after the sale to ensure customer satisfaction and repeat business.

Personal Selling and Managing Customer Relationships

The steps in the just-described selling process are *transaction oriented*—their aim is to help salespeople close a specific sale with a customer. But in most cases, the company is not simply seeking a sale. Rather, it wants to serve the customer over the long haul in a mutually profitable *relationship*. The sales force usually plays an important role in customer relationship-building. Thus, as shown in Figure 13.3, the selling process must be understood in the context of building and maintaining profitable customer relationships.

Successful sales organizations recognize that winning and keeping accounts requires more than making good products and directing the sales force to close lots of sales. If the company wishes only to close sales and capture short-term business, it can do this by simply slashing its prices to meet or beat those of competitors. Instead, most companies want their salespeople to practice *value selling*—demonstrating and delivering superior customer value and capturing a return on that value that is fair for both the customer and the company.

Unfortunately, in the heat of closing sales—especially in a tight economy—salespeople too often take the easy way out by cutting prices rather than selling value. Sales management's challenge is to transform salespeople from customer advocates for price cuts into company advocates for value. Here's how Rockwell Automation sells value and relationships rather than price:[20]

Facing pressure from Walmart to lower its prices, a condiment producer hastily summoned several competing supplier representatives—including Rockwell Automation sales rep Jeff Policicchio—who were given full access to the plant for one day and asked to find ways to dramatically reduce the customer's operating costs. Policicchio quickly learned that a major problem stemmed from lost production and down time due to poorly performing pumps on 32 huge condiment tanks. Policicchio gathered relevant cost and usage data and then used a Rockwell Automation laptop value-assessment tool to construct the best pump solution for the customer.

The next day, Policicchio and the competing reps presented their solutions to plant management. Policicchio's value proposition: "With this Rockwell Automation pump solution, through less downtime, reduced administrative costs in procurement, and lower spending on repair parts, your company will save at least $16 268 per pump—on up to 32 pumps—relative to our best competitor's solution." It turns out that Policicchio was the only rep to demonstrate tangible cost savings for his proposed solution. Everyone else made fuzzy promises about possible benefits or offered to save the customer money by simply shaving their prices.

The plant managers were so impressed with Policicchio's value proposition that—despite its higher initial price—they immediately purchased one Rockwell Automation pump solution for a trial. When the actual savings were even better than predicted, they placed orders for the remaining pumps. Thus, Policicchio's value-selling approach rather than price-cutting approach not only landed the initial sale but also provided the basis for a profitable long-term relationship with the customer.

Value selling requires listening to customers, understanding their needs, and carefully coordinating the whole company's efforts to create lasting relationships based on customer value.

Sales Promotion LO4

Personal selling and advertising often work closely with another promotion tool, sales promotion. **Sales promotion** consists of short-term incentives to encourage purchase or sales of a product or a service. Whereas advertising offers reasons to buy a product or service, sales promotion offers reasons to buy *now*.

Examples of sales promotions are found everywhere. A freestanding insert in the *Globe and Mail* contains a coupon offering $1 off PEDIGREE GoodBites treats for your dog. A Bed Bath & Beyond ad in your favourite magazine offers 20 percent off on any single item. The end-of-the-aisle display in the local supermarket tempts impulse buyers with a wall of Coca-Cola cases—four 12-packs for $12. Buy a new HP laptop and get a free memory upgrade. A hardware store chain receives a 10 percent discount on selected Stihl power lawn and garden tools if it agrees to advertise them in local newspapers. Sales promotion includes a wide variety of promotion tools designed to stimulate earlier or stronger market response.

Sales promotion
Short-term incentives to encourage the purchase or sale of a product or a service.

Rapid Growth of Sales Promotion

Sales promotion tools are used by most organizations, including manufacturers, distributors, retailers, and not-for-profit institutions. They are targeted toward consumers (*consumer promotions*), retailers and wholesalers (*trade promotions*), business customers (*business promotions*), and members of the sales force (*sales force promotions*). Today, in the average consumer packaged-goods company, sales promotion accounts for 74 percent of all marketing expenditures.[21]

Several factors have contributed to the rapid growth of sales promotion, particularly in consumer markets. First, inside the company, product managers face greater pressures to increase their current sales, and promotion is viewed as an effective short-run sales tool. Second, externally, the company faces more competition and competing brands are less differentiated. Increasingly, competitors are using sales promotion to help differentiate their offers. Third, advertising efficiency has declined because of rising costs, media clutter, and legal restraints. Finally, consumers have become more deal oriented, demanding lower prices and better deals. Sales promotions can help attract today's more thrift-oriented consumers.

The growing use of sales promotion has resulted in *promotion clutter*, similar to advertising clutter. According to one recent study, for example, in 70 percent of packaged-goods categories last year, 30 percent of all merchandise was sold with some sort of promotional support.[22] A given promotion runs the risk of being lost in a sea of other promotions, weakening its ability to trigger immediate purchase. Manufacturers are now

Exhibit 13.11 **Sales promotion:** Bed Bath & Beyond often uses a common form of sales promotion, the "limited time" offer, to encourage consumers to visit their stores.

© Jeff Greenberg / Alamy

searching for ways to rise above the clutter, such as offering larger coupon values, creating more dramatic point-of-purchase displays, or delivering promotions through new interactive media, such as the Internet or mobile phones.

In developing a sales promotion program, a company must first set sales promotion objectives and then select the best tools for accomplishing these objectives.

Sales Promotion Objectives

Sales promotion objectives vary widely. Marketers may use *consumer promotions* to urge short-term customer buying or enhance customer brand involvement. Objectives for *trade promotions* include getting retailers to carry new items and more inventory, buy ahead, or promote the company's products and give them more shelf space. For the *sales force*, objectives include getting more sales force support for current or new products or getting salespeople to sign up new accounts.

Sales promotions are usually used together with advertising, personal selling, direct marketing, or other promotion mix tools as part of an integrated marketing campaign. Consumer promotions must be advertised and can add excitement and pulling power to ads. Trade and sales force promotions support the firm's personal selling process.

When the economy tightens and sales lag, it's tempting to offer deep promotional discounts to spur consumer spending. In general, however, rather than creating only short-term sales or temporary brand switching, sales promotions should help to reinforce the product's position and build long-term *customer relationships*. If properly designed, every sales promotion tool has the potential to build both short-term excitement and long-term consumer relationships. Marketers should avoid "quick fix," price-only promotions in favour of promotions that are designed to build brand equity. Examples include the various *frequency marketing programs* and loyalty cards that have mushroomed in popularity in recent years. Most hotels, supermarkets, and airlines offer frequent-guest/buyer/flyer programs that give rewards to regular customers to keep them coming back. All kinds of companies now offer rewards programs. Such promotional programs can build loyalty through added value rather than discounted prices. It's estimated that over 94 percent of Canadians belong to some type of loyalty program, which is the highest usage rate in the world.[23]

Consumer promotions

Sales promotion tools used to boost short-term customer buying and involvement or to enhance long-term customer relationships.

For example, Shoppers Drug Mart, Canada's largest drug store chain, has the most successful loyalty program offered by any Canadian retailer. Members of the Optimum program spend 60 percent more on their purchases than non-members, and overall, Shoppers generates two-thirds of its non-prescription sales from Optimum cardholders.[24]

Major Sales Promotion Tools

Many tools can be used to accomplish sales promotion objectives, however, the decision about which form of sales promotion should be employed depends on whether it is a consumer, trade, or business promotion.

The Canadian Press

Exhibit 13.12 Customer loyalty programs: Canadians are among the highest users of loyalty programs in the world.

Consumer Promotions **Consumer promotions** include a wide range of tools—from samples, coupons, rebates, premiums, and point-of-purchase displays to contests, sweepstakes, and event sponsorships.

SAMPLES Samples are offers of a trial amount of a product. Sampling is the most effective—but most expensive—way to introduce a new product or create new excitement for an existing one. Some samples are free; for others, the company charges a small amount to offset its cost. The sample might be delivered door-to-door, sent by mail, handed out in a store or a kiosk, attached to another product, or featured in an ad. Sometimes, samples are combined into sample packs, which can then be used to promote other products and services. Sampling can be a powerful promotional tool.

COUPONS Coupons are certificates that give buyers a saving when they purchase specified products. Most consumers love coupons. Major packaged-goods companies distributed more than 305 billion coupons in 2012 with an average face value of $1.53, and consumers redeemed more than 2.9 billion of them for a total savings of about US$3.8 billion.[25] Coupons can promote early trial of a new brand or stimulate sales of a mature brand. However, as a result of coupon clutter, redemption rates have been declining in recent years. Thus, most major consumer-goods companies are issuing fewer coupons and targeting them more carefully.

Marketers are also cultivating new outlets for distributing coupons, such as supermarket shelf dispensers, electronic point-of-sale coupon printers, and online and mobile coupon programs. According to a recent study, digital coupons now outpace printed newspaper coupons by 10 to 1. Almost one-third of all coupon users are digital coupon users who only get coupons online or by phone, via sites such as smartcanucks.ca, Groupon.ca, RedFlagDeals.ca, and Cellfire.ca (see Marketing@Work 13.2).

REBATES Rebates, or cash refunds, are like coupons except that the price reduction occurs after the purchase rather than at the retail outlet. The consumer sends a "proof of purchase" to the manufacturer, who then refunds part of the purchase price by mail. For example, Toro ran a clever pre-season promotion on some of its snow blower models, offering a rebate if the snowfall in the buyer's market area turned out to be below average. Competitors were not able to match this offer on such short notice, and the promotion was very successful.

PRICE PACKS Price packs (also called *cents-off deals*) offer consumers savings off the regular price of a product. The producer marks the reduced prices directly on the label or the package. Price packs can be single packages sold at a reduced price (such as two for the price of one) or two related products banded together (such as a toothbrush and toothpaste). Price packs are very effective—even more so than coupons—in stimulating short-term sales.

PREMIUMS Premiums are goods offered either free or at low cost as an incentive to buy a product, ranging from toys included with kids' products to phone cards and DVDs. A premium may come inside the package (in-pack), outside the package (on-pack), or through the mail. For example, over the years, McDonald's has offered a variety of premiums in its Happy Meals—from *Kung Fu Panda* characters to *My Little Pony* and *Pokémon* toy figures. Customers can visit www.happymeal.com to play games and watch commercials associated with the current Happy Meal sponsor.[26]

ADVERTISING SPECALTIES Advertising specialties, also called promotional products, are useful articles imprinted with an advertiser's name, logo, or message that are given as gifts to consumers. Typical items include T-shirts and other apparel, pens, coffee mugs, calendars, key rings, mouse pads, matches, tote bags, coolers, golf balls, and caps. US marketers spent nearly US$17 billion on advertising specialties last year. Such items can be very effective. The "best of them stick around for months, subtly burning a brand name into a user's brain," notes a promotional products expert.[27]

MARKETING@WORK 13.2

Mobile Coupons: Reaching Customers Where They Are—Now

As mobile phones become appendages that many people can't live without, businesses are increasingly eyeing them as prime real estate for marketing messages. Whether it's to build a brand, boost business, or reward loyalty, more merchants are using mobile marketing to tap into the mobile phone's power of immediacy.

"It's cool," said Kristen Palestis recently at her local Jamba Juice after she opted in to receive a 20 percent-off coupon on her mobile phone. "I'm spending less money and it was real easy," she said after she used the coupon to buy a smoothie. Palestis received the coupon within seconds of texting a special five-digit code from her mobile phone.

Retailers' mobile marketing messages can include text messages with numeric "short codes" that customers dial to receive a promotion, bar-coded digital coupons, website links, and display advertisements. "We know the most effective way to reach the customer is to be where they are," says a marketer at Jamba Juice, a chain that sells smoothies and other "better-for-you" beverages and foods. "For our customers this means both on the Internet and on their mobiles."

Jamba Juice and a growing host of other retailers want to get special offers quickly into the hands of the consumers who are most apt to use them. These mobile social users—as they're called—represent 11 percent of online adults, but their ranks are growing. They're more likely to respond to ads on their mobile phones, buy mobile content and services, and access the mobile web.

Estimates of adoption rates for smartphones in Canada vary substantially, but one thing is clear—mobile usage is growing. One study suggests that the number of mobile phones or wireless devices in Canada surpassed 26 million in 2012, and over 50 percent of these are smartphones. In the 18–34 age group, smartphones account for nearly 70 percent of all mobile devices used.

So what does this mean for electronic coupons? Enormous potential. In fact, the number of mobile coupon users worldwide is forecast to triple by 2014 to more than 300 million people.

While Canadian firms have been slower to adopt mobile couponing than their American counterparts, that is about to change. Two Canadian companies, MyMobileMarketing (mymobilemarketing.ca) and Retail Common (retailcommon.com) offer software platforms to retailers and malls wishing to create and distribute online coupons directly to customers via text messages and social media. With a simple click of a mouse, businesses can create and send mobile coupons, as well as track their effectiveness in the

marketplace. For example, when Quiznos Canada used Clip Mobile to distribute mobile coupons, the redemption rate was 35 percent and the resulting return on marketing investment was 300 percent.

Still, mobile coupons aren't for everyone. Some consumers just don't want marketing messages delivered to their phones. So many digital coupon marketers include print and email delivery options as well. Challenges aside, companies ranging from Mark's Work Wearhouse and Sport Chek to Wendy's and Best Buy are testing the digital couponing waters. And while mobile apps are currently limited to major cities in Canada, national coverage is bound to grow as it has done in the United States.

Associated Press

Exhibit 13.13 **Mobile coupons:** While relatively new to Canada, mobile coupons are poised to take off.

Over the past few years, a growing list of online coupon sites—such as smartcanucks.ca, RedFlagDeals.ca, Groupon.ca, and Cellfire.com—have sprung up. These sites allow consumers to find coupons online and download them to mobile devices, print them out at home, or transfer them to store loyalty cards for later redemption at stores.

Mobile coupons offer distinct advantages to both consumers and marketers. Consumers don't have to find and clip paper coupons or print out web coupons and bring them along when they shop. They always have their cellphone coupons with them. To use the coupons, users simply call up stored digital coupons on their phones and present them at a retail location for scanning. For marketers, mobile coupons allow more careful targeting and eliminate the costs of printing and distributing paper coupons. The redemption rates can be dazzling—as high as 20 percent—whereas the industry average paper-coupon response is less than 1 percent.

Thus, when properly used, mobile coupons can both cost less and be more immediate and effective. When it comes to digital couponing, marketers are increasingly echoing the sentiments of Jamba Juice customer Kristen Palestis. "It's cool."

Sources: Portions adapted from Arlene Satchel, "More Merchants Embrace Mobile Coupons," *McClatchy-Tribune News Service*, February 10, 2010; with information from Erik Sass, "Is Digital Coupons' Rise Print Inserts' Demise?" *MediaDailyNews*, February 17, 2010, http://tinyurl.com/25vh966; "Digital Coupons Overtaking Print Coupons," *BusinessWire*, February 8, 2011, www.businesswire.com/news/home/20110208007022/en/Digital-Coupons-Represent-Fastest-Growing-Coupon-Segment; Canadian data obtained from "Canadian Mobile Coupon Shop Retail Common Raises Another $250,000 for Rollout Plans," Canada Newswire, www.newswire.ca/en/story/907887/canadian-mobile-coupon-shop-retailcommon-raises-another-250-000-for-rollout-plans, June 2012; Susan Kuchinskas "Mobile Coupon Service Takes on Daily Deals in Canada," www.clickz.com/clickz/news/2111483/mobile-coupon-service-daily-deals-canada, June 2012; Rita Trichur, "Canada on Track to Pass 100 Per Cent Wireless Penetration Rate." *Globe and Mail*, June 2012, www.theglobeandmail.com/report-on-business/canada-on-track-to-pass-100-per-cent-wireless-penetration-rate/article4230795/?cmpid=rss1; and information from retailcommon.com, mymobilemarketing.ca, getclip.ca, and pushadeal.com.

POINT-OF-PURCHASE (POP) Point-of-purchase (POP) promotions include displays and demonstrations that take place at the point of sale. Think of your last visit to your local convenience store, grocery store, liquor store, or drug store. Chances are good that you were tripping over aisle displays, promotional signs, "shelf talkers," or demonstrators offering free tastes of featured food products. Unfortunately, many retailers do not like to handle the hundreds of displays, signs, and posters they receive from manufacturers each year, and some end up unused or discarded. Manufacturers have responded by offering better POP materials, offering to set them up, and tying them in with television, print, or online messages.

CONTESTS AND SWEEPSTAKES Contests, sweepstakes, and games give consumers the chance to win something, such as cash, trips, or goods, by luck or through extra effort. A contest calls for consumers to submit an entry—a jingle, guess, suggestion—to be judged by a panel that will select the best entries. A sweepstakes calls for consumers to submit their names for a draw. A game presents consumers with something—bingo numbers, missing letters—every time they buy, which may or may not help them win a prize. Such promotions can create considerable brand attention and consumer involvement.

For example, Tim Hortons has been running one of the most successful consumer promotions in Canada to reward and thank their loyal guests for over twenty-five years. The annual "Roll up the Rim to Win" ® campaign has been a hit with coffee drinkers from coast to coast. With the purchase of any size hot coffee, or any hot beverage or cold coffee, Tim Hortons guests have a chance to win prizes ranging from a free cup of coffee to a brand new car. The company awarded nearly 25 000 prizes valued over $100, including 36 cars—and that's in addition to the millions of free coffee and doughnuts won![28]

Tim Hortons, RRRoll up the Rim to Win and Dérrroulez le rebord pour gagner are registered trademarks of the TDL Marks Corporation. Used with permission.

Exhibit 13.14 Games can create considerable consumer involvement: The 2014 version of Tim Hortons popular "Roll up the Rim to Win" promotion marked its twenty-eighth year in Canada.

Event marketing

Creating a brand-marketing event or serving as a sole or participating sponsor of events created by others.

EVENT MARKETING Marketers can promote their brands through **event marketing** (or *event sponsorships*), either by creating their own brand marketing events or by serving as a sponsor of events created by others. The events might include anything from mobile brand tours to festivals, reunions, marathons, concerts, or other sponsored gatherings. Event marketing is huge, and it may be the fastest-growing area of promotion.

Effective event marketing links events and sponsorships to a brand's value proposition. For example, to help build awareness of its new LEAF electric vehicle, Nissan signed on to a two-year sponsorship as the official vehicle of the Amgen Tour of California, an 800-mile, eight-day cycling road race. Last year, Nissan supplied 40 LEAFs to serve as lead, support, medical, and VIP vehicles for the event. The Amgen event links well with the brand's positioning; sponsoring an event for people living healthy lifestyles is a no-brainer for a car that promises "100% electric. Zero gas. Zero tailpipe." According to a senior Nissan marketer, "This event offers a unique opportunity to not only participate in America's largest cycling event but to also reaffirm the company's commitment to supporting healthy lifestyles." In addition to such sponsorships, Nissan fields its own national event, the Nissan LEAF Drive Electric Tour. The tour takes the LEAF to the streets in major cities, giving prospective buyers an opportunity to learn about the innovative car, kick the tires, and sign up for test drives.[29]

Event marketing can also take place online. For example, Dove Canada hosted its first ever live-streamed event, "Women Who Should be Famous", in June 2012 at www.facebook.com/dove. Building on the company's successful "Campaign for Real Beauty," Dove hoped to inspire women and girls to reach their full potential by showing stories of four inspirational women in the fields of science, leadership, environmentalism and the arts. Any Canadian with a Facebook account and access to a computer could register on Dove's page and was encouraged to participate in this free event with a girl in their life.[30]

Trade promotions

Sales promotion tools used to persuade resellers to carry a brand, give it shelf space, promote it in advertising, and push it to consumers.

Trade Promotions Manufacturers direct more sales promotion dollars toward retailers and wholesalers (81 percent) than to final consumers (16 percent).[31] **Trade promotions** can persuade resellers to carry a brand, give it shelf space, promote it in advertising, and push it to consumers. Shelf space is so scarce these days that manufacturers often have to offer price-offs, allowances, buy-back guarantees, or free goods to retailers and wholesalers to get products on the shelf and, once there, to keep them on it.

Manufacturers use several trade promotion tools. Many of the tools used for consumer promotions—contests, premiums, displays—can also be used as trade promotions. Or the manufacturer may offer a straight *discount* off the list price on each case purchased during a stated period of time (also called a *price-off, off-invoice,* or *off-list*). Manufacturers also may offer an *allowance* (usually so much off per case) in return for the retailer's agreement to feature the manufacturer's products in some way. For example, an advertising allowance compensates retailers for advertising the product, whereas a display allowance compensates them for using special displays.

Manufacturers may offer *free goods*, which are extra cases of merchandise, to resellers who buy a certain quantity or who feature a certain flavour or size. They may also offer *push money*—cash or gifts to dealers for their sales forces to "push" the manufacturer's goods. Manufacturers may give retailers free *specialty advertising items* that carry the company's name, such as pens, calendars, memo pads, flashlights, and tote bags.

Business promotions

Sales promotion tools used to generate business leads, stimulate purchases, reward customers, and motivate salespeople.

Business Promotions Companies spend billions of dollars each year on promotion to industrial customers. **Business promotions** are used to generate business leads, stimulate purchases, reward customers, and motivate salespeople. Business promotions include many of the same tools used for consumer or trade promotions. Here, we focus on two additional major business promotion tools—conventions and trade shows, and sales contests.

Many companies and trade associations organize *conventions and trade shows* to promote their products. Firms selling to the industry show their products at the trade show.

Vendors receive many benefits, such as opportunities to find new sales leads, contact customers, introduce new products, meet new customers, sell more to present customers, and educate customers with publications and audiovisual materials. Trade shows also help companies to reach many prospects not reached through their sales forces.

Some trade shows are huge. For example, at the 2013 International Consumer Electronics Show in Las Vegas, 3250 exhibitors, displaying over 20 000 products, attracted more than 150 000 professional visitors. Even more impressive, at the Bauma mining and construction equipment trade show in Munich, Germany, more than 3200 exhibitors from 53 countries presented their latest product innovations to more than 420 000 attendees from more than 200 countries.[32]

Exhibit 13.15 Some trade shows are huge. At the 2013 International Consumer Electronics Show 3250 exhibitors attracted more than 150 000 professional visitors.

A *sales contest* is a contest for salespeople or dealers to motivate them to increase their sales performance over a given period. Sales contests motivate and recognize good company performers, who may receive trips, cash prizes, or other gifts. Some companies award points for performance, which the receiver can turn in for any of a variety of prizes. Sales contests work best when they are tied to measurable and achievable sales objectives (such as finding new accounts, reviving old accounts, or increasing account profitability).

Developing the Sales Promotion Program

Beyond selecting the types of promotions to use, marketers must make several other decisions in designing the full sales promotion program. First, they must decide on the *size of the incentive*. A certain minimum incentive is necessary if the promotion is to succeed; a larger incentive will produce more sales response. The marketer also must set *conditions for participation*. Incentives might be offered to everyone or only to select groups.

Marketers must decide how to *promote and distribute the promotion* program itself. A $2-off coupon could be given out in a package, at the store, via the Internet, or in an advertisement. Each distribution method involves a different level of reach and cost. Increasingly, marketers are blending several media into a total campaign concept. The *length of the promotion* is also important. If the sales promotion period is too short, many prospects (who may not be buying during that time) will miss it. If the promotion runs too long, the deal will lose some of its "act now" force.

Evaluation is also very important. Many companies fail to evaluate their sales promotion programs, and others evaluate them only superficially. Yet marketers should work to measure the returns on their sales promotion investments, just as they should seek to assess the returns on other marketing activities. The most common evaluation method is to compare sales before, during, and after a promotion. Marketers should ask: Did the promotion attract new customers or more purchasing from current customers? Can we hold onto these new customers and purchases? Will the long-run customer relationship and sales gains from the promotion justify its costs?

Clearly, sales promotion plays an important role in the total promotion mix. To use it well, the marketer must define the sales promotion objectives, select the best tools, design the sales promotion program, implement the program, and evaluate the results. Moreover, sales promotion must be coordinated carefully with other promotion mix elements within the overall integrated marketing communications program.

The Profit of Loyalty

Once upon a time there were frequent-flyer programs, designed by airlines to build loyalty. The problem was they didn't really build loyalty as much as they did confusion and resentment. The fractional rewards subscribers received in exchange for their patronage was such that these promotions soon became widely criticized as an ineffective means of short-term inducement of sales—the main objective of sales promotions. Recently, more successful loyalty programs have occurred through partnerships between airlines and financial services companies, namely banks and credit cards.

"We actually launched a guest rewards program and a credit card program separately in 2010," recalls Brenda Wallace-Ionescu, WestJet's senior manager of program marketing, who guided the implementation of the WestJet Rewards program. "We saw the guest rewards program as a way of really adding value to very frequent guests, and the MasterCard as a means of building mass awareness." The sales promotion strategy eventually brought the two programs together along with RBC. "We discovered along the way that they are both really one and the same. In fact, in 2012 we re-branded the two programs together under WestJet Rewards, acknowledging the need for them both to be marketed as one in order to build a very powerful value proposition." And powerful it was, as the WestJet Rewards program saw a year-over-year growth of 265 percent between 2012 and 2013.

"What is crucial to the success of our program is that our guests understand our currency. In keeping with WestJet's brand, it is simple to use and transparent." The WestJet Rewards program, like others linked with a credit card, rewards travellers on a dollar-for-dollar exchange. Unlike other loyalty programs, the dollar-spent, dollar-used model is not capped at a seasonal fare. "In those programs if the value of the fare goes up, it changes the value of your points," explains Wallace-Ionescu. "With WestJet Rewards, if you want to book a flight to Vegas, you simply go to WestJet.com and use all or part of what's in your WestJet Rewards account to pay for your flight. Book it. Done."

The sky would appear to be the limit as far as growth opportunities are concerned for WestJet Rewards. "When you think of our code-sharing agreements with a growing number of international airlines, and our ancillary partners in car and hotels, there really is nothing but growth ahead."

QUESTIONS

1. In addition to the WestJet Rewards MasterCard, RBC also carries the Visa Avion card, another air travel loyalty program. Research to identify what the key differences are between the two.
2. What does Wallace-Ionescu claim to be the two key benefits of the WestJet rewards program?
3. How does the WestJet Rewards program qualify as a sales promotion based on the definition in this textbook?

REVIEWING THE CONCEPTS

1. Discuss the role of a company's salespeople in creating value for customers and building customer relationships.

Most companies use salespeople, and many companies assign them an important role in the marketing mix. For companies selling business products, the firm's salespeople work directly with customers. Often, the sales force is the customer's only direct contact with the company and therefore may be viewed by customers as representing the company itself. In contrast, for consumer-product companies that sell through intermediaries, consumers usually do not meet salespeople or even know about them. The sales force works behind the scenes, dealing with wholesalers and retailers to obtain their support and helping them become effective in selling the firm's products.

As an element of the promotion mix, the sales force is very effective in achieving certain marketing objectives and carrying out such activities as prospecting, communicating, selling and servicing, and information gathering. But with companies becoming more market oriented, a customer-focused sales force also works to produce both *customer satisfaction* and *company profit*. The sales force plays a key role in developing and managing profitable *customer relationships*.

2. Identify and explain the six major sales force management steps and the role of sales force automation.

High sales force costs necessitate an effective sales management process consisting of six steps: designing sales force strategy and structure, recruiting and selecting, training, compensating, supervising, and evaluating salespeople and sales force performance. In designing a sales force, sales management must address strategy issues such as what type of sales force structure will work best (*territorial*, *product*, *customer*, or *complex* structure), how large the sales force should be, who will be involved in the selling effort, and how its various salespeople and sales-support people will work together (inside or outside sales forces and team selling).

Salespeople must be recruited and selected carefully. In recruiting salespeople, a company may look to the job duties and the characteristics of its most successful salespeople to suggest the traits it wants in new salespeople. It must then look for applicants through recommendations of current salespeople, ads, and the Internet and other social networks, as well as college recruitment/placement centers. In the selection process, the procedure may vary from a single informal interview to lengthy testing and interviewing. After the selection process is complete, training programs familiarize new salespeople not only with the art of selling, but also with the company's history, its products and policies, and the characteristics of its customers and competitors.

The sales force compensation system helps to reward, motivate, and direct salespeople. In addition to compensation, all salespeople need supervision, and many need continuous encouragement because they must make many decisions and face many frustrations. Periodically, the company must evaluate their performance to help them do a better job. In evaluating salespeople, the company relies on information gathered from sales reports, personal observations, customer surveys, and conversations with other salespeople.

3. Discuss the personal selling process, distinguishing between transaction-oriented marketing and relationship marketing.

The art of selling involves a seven-step selling process: *prospecting* and *qualifying*, *preapproach*, *approach*, *presentation* and *demonstration*, *handling objections*, *closing*, and *follow-up*. These steps help marketers to close a specific sale and as such are transaction oriented. However, a seller's dealings with customers should be guided by the larger concept of relationship marketing. The company's sales force should help to orchestrate a whole-company effort to develop profitable long-term relationships with key customers based on superior customer value and satisfaction.

4. Explain how sales promotion campaigns are developed and implemented.

Sales promotion campaigns call for setting sales promotions objectives (in general, sales promotions should be *consumer relationship building*); selecting tools; and developing and implementing the sales promotion program by using *consumer promotion tools* (from coupons, refunds, premiums, and point-of-purchase promotions to contests, sweepstakes, and events), *trade promotion tools* (from discounts and allowances to free goods and push money), and *business promotion tools* (conventions, trade shows, and sales contests), as well as determining such things as the size of the incentive, the conditions for participation, how to promote and distribute the promotion package, and the length of the promotion. After this process is completed, the company must evaluate its sales promotion results.

KEY TERMS

Approach 490
Business promotions 498
Closing 491
Consumer promotions 494
Customer (or market)
   sales force structure 479
Event marketing 498
Follow-up 492
Handling objections 491

Inside sales force 480
Outside sales force
   (or field sales force) 480
Personal selling 475
Preapproach 490
Presentation 490
Product sales force
   structure 478
Prospecting 490

Sales force management 478
Sales promotion 493
Sales quota 489
Salesperson 476
Selling process 489
Team selling 481
Territorial sales force
   structure 478
Trade promotions 498

TALK ABOUT MARKETING

1. For what kinds of products and services, and what kind of situations, is personal selling a more effective marketing communications tool than advertising?

2. Cellphone companies such as Rogers, Bell, and TELUS have both inside and outside sales forces. List all the tasks that each performs. Where might you encounter these sales forces as a consumer?

3. If you've ever worked in retail, you know something about personal selling. Which of the seven steps in the personal selling process do you think is the most difficult? Which step is the most critical to successful selling?

4. Sales promotions are sometimes used to encourage use of seasonal facilities (sports arenas, ski hills, amusement parks, and so on) during the off-season. Choose a seasonal facility near you that is currently in the off-season. Visit the facility's website. Are there any offers designed to encourage immediate purchase during the off-season?

5. Which of the sales promotion tools described in the chapter would be best for stimulating sales of the following products or services? (a) a dry cleaner wanting to emphasize low prices on washed and pressed dress shirts, (b) Gummy Bears new black cherry flavour, (c) Procter & Gamble's efforts to bundle laundry detergent and fabric softener together in a combined marketing effort, and (d) a company that wants its customers to aid in developing a new jingle.

6. Sales promotions frequently include an online and an offline component. If you were designing a sales promotion for your favourite car brand, how would you use Facebook, Twitter, or other social media tools to engage your target market and provide them with an incentive to purchase your cars?

THINK LIKE A MARKETING MANAGER

After riding high for so many years, Starbucks's steamy-hot growth has gone cold. The coffee house's sales, profits, and stock price have plummeted, resulting in layoffs and store closures. Much of the blame goes to increased consumer frugality brought on by tough economic times. Newly intensified competition hasn't helped Starbucks either, especially from companies now selling premium brews at much lower prices. Starbucks has tried various tactics to convince customers that its products offer high value for the price. It has also tenaciously avoided reducing prices, doing everything possible to maintain its premium image. Instead, Starbucks is putting efforts into things like its Starbucks Card Rewards, a major sales promotion initiative designed to generate customer loyalty.

The rewards program offers incentives such as free add-ins to coffee drinks, free in-store refills on drip coffee, complimentary in-store Wi-Fi, and free coffee with the purchase of a pound of coffee beans. The company hopes that such incentives will entice customers to visit more often and to spend more when they visit. Starbucks asserts that, as it gains experience in using the program to gather customer information and track customer purchases, Starbucks Card Rewards will become more effective in achieving its goals.

QUESTIONS

1. Find out what other forms of marketing communications Starbucks uses in Canada and the United States.

Does it advertise? Use public relations? What about social media? Is the Starbucks loyalty card program well integrated with these other forms of marketing communications?

2. Starbucks's baristas are sales representatives. What other forms of personal selling does—or could—Starbucks use?

3. Does the Starbucks Card Rewards program go far enough in providing incentives to increase customer spending in the wake of the economic downturn? What else could Starbucks do with the program?

4. What other forms of sales promotion could Starbucks use that might provide a sufficient incentive to increase sales, yet stay true to its premium brand image?

MARKETING ETHICS

Hank is a sales representative for a customer relationship management (CRM) software company and makes several cold calls each day prospecting for customers. He usually starts his call to a technology professional in a company by introducing himself and asking the person if he or she would take a few moments to participate in a survey on technology needs in companies. After a few questions, however, it becomes obvious that Hank is trying to sell software solutions to the potential customer.

QUESTIONS

1. Is Hank being ethical? Discuss other sales tactics that might be unethical.

2. What traits and behaviours characterize an ethical salesperson? What role does the sales manager play in ethical selling behaviour?

MARKETING TECHNOLOGY

The humble coupon has gotten a boost from social media. Groupon, the group deal-of-the-day coupon service that started in late 2008 and is exceeding even Google's and Facebook's phenomenal early growth rates, now offers about 1000 deals every day to more than 70 million subscribers in almost 50 countries. The business model is simple. A business sets up a deal through Groupon, such as offering $50 worth of merchandise for $25, but the deal is only honoured if enough people sign up for it. Groupon typically takes a 50 percent cut of all the revenue generated on the deal (that is, $12.50 of the $25 the consumer pays for the Groupon deal). In return, the business gets a lot of store traffic from the deal. Because the business model is so simple and the entry barriers so small, there are now more than 600 of these digital daily-deal websites.

QUESTIONS

1. Debate the pros and cons of offering coupons through digital deal-of-the-day websites such as Groupon from the perspective of the businesses offering the deal.

2. Create an idea for a local group-buying promotional service based on Groupon's model as a class project or as a fund-raiser for a student organization at your school. Students will be the target market of this digital deal website. Develop a sales plan to recruit local businesses to offer deals as well as the promotion plan to attract students to the website. Present your plans to the class.

MARKETING BY THE NUMBERS

FireSpot, Inc. is a manufacturer of drop-in household fireplaces sold primarily in the eastern United States. The company has its own sales force that does more than just sell products and services—it manages relationships with retail customers to enable them to better meet consumers' needs. FireSpot's sales reps visit customers several times per year—often for hours at a time. Thus, sales managers must ensure that they have enough salespeople to adequately deliver value to customers. Refer to Appendix 3, Marketing by the Numbers, to answer the following questions.

QUESTIONS

1. Determine the number of salespeople FireSpot needs if it has 1000 retail customer accounts that need to be called on five times per year. Each sales call lasts approximately 2.5 hours, and each sales rep has approximately 1250 hours per year to devote to customers.

2. FireSpot wants to expand to the Midwest and Western United States and intends to hire ten new sales representatives to secure distribution for its products. Each sales rep earns a salary of $50 000 plus commission. Each retailer generates an average $50 000 in revenue for FireSpot. If FireSpot's contribution margin is 40 percent, what increase in sales will it need to break even on the increase in fixed costs to hire the new sales reps? How many new retail accounts must the company acquire to break even on this tactic? What average number of accounts must each new rep acquire?

VIDEO CASE

MedTronic

Many companies sell products that most customers can live without. But MedTronic's devices are literally a matter of life and death. Patient well-being depends upon the insulin delivery devices, implantable defibrillators, and cardiac pacemakers designed and manufactured by MedTronic. In some markets, seven out of eight medical devices in use are MedTronic devices.

But what happens when MedTronic has a product that it knows will help a given business or institutional customer in terms of cost, time, and end-user well-being, but it can't get a foot in the door to communicate that information? This video demonstrates how MedTronic sales representatives maintain a customer-centred approach to the personal selling process as a means for effectively communicating their product benefits.

After viewing the video featuring MedTronic, answer the following questions:

QUESTIONS

1. How is the sales force at MedTronic structured?

2. Can you identify the selling process for MedTronic? Give an example of each step.

3. Is MedTronic effective at building long-term customer relationships through its sales force? How?

HEWLETT-PACKARD: OVERHAULING A VAST CORPORATE SALES FORCE

Imagine this scenario: You need a new digital camera. You're not sure which one to buy or even what features you need, so you visit your nearest electronics superstore to talk with a salesperson. You walk through the camera section but can't find anyone to help you. When you finally find a salesperson, he yawns and tells you that he's responsible for selling all the products in the store, so he doesn't really know all that much about cameras. Then, he reads some information from the box of one of the models that you ask about, as if he is telling you something that you can't figure out for yourself. He then suggests that you should talk to someone else. You finally find a camera-savvy salesperson. However, after answering a few questions, she disappears to handle some other task, handing you off to someone new. And the new salesperson seems to contradict what the first salesperson said, even quoting different prices on a couple of models you like.

That imaginary situation may actually have happened to you. If so, then you can understand what many business buyers face when attempting to buy from a large corporate supplier. This was the case with business customers of technology giant Hewlett-Packard before Mark Hurd took over as HP's CEO in 2005. Prior to Hurd assuming command, HP's revenues and profits had flattened and its stock price had plummeted. To find out why, Hurd first talked directly with 400 corporate customers. Mostly what he heard were gripes about HP's corporate sales force.

Customers complained that they had to deal with too many salespeople, and that HP's confusing management layers made it hard to figure out whom to call. They had trouble tracking down HP sales representatives. And once found, the reps often came across as apathetic, leaving the customer to take the initiative. HP reps were responsible for a broad range of complex products, so they sometimes lacked the needed depth of knowledge on any subset of them. Customers grumbled that they received varying price quotes from different sales reps and that it often took weeks for reps to respond to seemingly simple requests. In all, HP's corporate customers were frustrated, not a happy circumstance for a company that gets more than 70 percent of its revenues from businesses.

But customers weren't the only ones frustrated by HP's unwieldy and unresponsive sales force structure. HP was organized into three main product divisions:

the Personal Systems Group (PSG), the Technology Solutions Group (TSG), and the Image and Printing Group (IPG). However, HP's corporate sales force was housed in a fourth division, the Customer Sales Group (CSG). All salespeople reported directly to the CSG and were responsible for selling products from all three product divisions. To make matters worse, the CSG was bloated and underperforming. According to one reporter, "Of the 17 000 people working in HP's corporate sales, only around 10 000 sold directly to customers. The rest were support staff or in management." HP division executives were frustrated by the CSG structure. They complained that they had little or no direct control over the salespeople who sold their products. Furthermore, the multiple layers of management slowed sales force decision making and customer responsiveness.

Finally, salespeople themselves were frustrated by the structure. They weren't being given the time and support they needed to serve their customers well. Burdened with administrative tasks and bureaucratic red tape, they were spending less than a third of their time with customers. In addition, they had to work through multiple layers of bureaucracy to get price quotes and sample products for customers. "The customer focus was lacking," says an HP sales vice-president. "Trying to navigate inside HP was difficult. It was unacceptable."

As then-CEO Mark Hurd (he left the company in 2010) peeled back the layers, it became apparent that HP's organizational problems went deeper than the sales force. The entire company had become so centralized, with so many layers of management, that it was unresponsive and out of touch with customers. Hurd had come to HP with a reputation for cost-cutting and ruthless efficiency. Prior to his position at HP, he spent 25 years at NCR where he ultimately headed the company. Although it was a considerably smaller company than HP, Hurd had it running like a well-oiled machine. Nothing bothered him more than the discoveries he made about HP's inefficient structure.

Thus began what one observer called "one of Hurd's biggest management challenges: overhauling HP's vast corporate sales force." For starters, Hurd eliminated the CSG division, instead assigning salespeople directly to the three product divisions. He also did away with three layers of management and cut hundreds of unproductive sales workers. This move gave divisional marketing and sales executives direct control over a leaner, more efficient sales process, resulting in speedier sales decisions and quicker market response.

Hurd also took steps to reduce salesperson and customer frustrations. Eliminating the CSG meant that each salesperson was responsible for selling a smaller number of products and was able to develop expertise in a specific product area. Hurd urged sales managers to cut back on salesperson administrative requirements and to improve sales support so that salespeople could spend more quality time with customers. As a result, salespeople now spend more than 40 percent of their time with customers, up from just 30 percent before. And HP salespeople are noticing big changes in the sales support they receive:

> Salesman Richard Ditucci began noticing some of the changes late last year. At the time, Ditucci was trying to sell computer servers to Staples. As part of the process, Staples had asked him to provide a sample server for the company to evaluate. In the past, such requests typically took two to three weeks to fulfill because of HP's bureaucracy. This time, Ditucci got the server he needed within three days. The quick turnaround helped him win the contract, valued at several million dollars.

To ensure that important customers are carefully tended, HP assigned each salesperson three or fewer accounts. The top 2000 accounts were assigned just one salesperson—"so they'll always know whom to contact." Because of this change, customers are noticing differences in the attention that they get from HP salespeople:

> James Farris, a senior technology executive at Staples, says HP has freed up his salesman to drop by Staples at least twice a month instead of about once a month before. The extra face time enabled the HP salesman to create more valuable interactions, such as arranging a workshop recently for Staples to explain HP's technology to the retailer's executives. As a result, Farris says he is planning to send more business HP's way. Similarly, Keith Morrow, chief information officer of convenience-store chain 7-Eleven, says his HP sales representative is now "here all the time" and has been more knowledgeable in pitching products tailored to his business. As a result, last October, 7-Eleven began deploying in its US stores 10 000 HP pen pads—a mobile device that helps 7-Eleven workers on the sales floor.

A SALESMAN AT HEART

Once the new sales force started to take shape, Hurd began to focus on the client's role in the sales process. The fact that HP refers to its business buyers as "partners" says a lot about its philosophy. "We heavily rely on [our partners]. We look at them as an extension of the HP sales force," Hurd said. To strengthen the relationship between HP and its partners, HP has partners participating in account planning and strategy development, an activity that teams the partners with HP sales reps and its top executive team.

Because Hurd wanted the sales force to have strong relationships with its partners, he practiced what he preached. He spent up to 60 percent of the year on the road with various channel partners and *their* customers. Part of his time was funnelled through HP's Executive Connections program, roundtable meetings that take place all over the world. But many of Hurd's interactions with HP partners took place outside that program as well. This demonstration of customer commitment at the highest level created some fierce customer loyalty toward HP.

"I've probably met Mark Hurd more times in the last three or four years than all the CEOs of our other vendors combined," said Simon Palmer, president of California-based STA, one of HP's fastest growing solution provider partners. "There's no other CEO of any company that size that's even close. He's such a down-to-earth guy. He presents the HP story in very simple-to-understand terms." Mark Sarazin, executive vice-president of AdvizeX Technologies, an HP partner for 25 years, sings similar praises. "He spent two-and-a-half hours with our customers. He talked in terms they could relate with, about his own relationship with HP IT. He knocked the ball out of the park with our 25-plus CIOs who were in the room. One said it was the best event he'd been to in his career."

In the five years that Hurd was CEO, HP's revenues, profits, and stock price increased by 44 percent, 123 percent, and 50 percent, respectively. Still, with HP's markets as volatile as they've been, Hurd took HP into new equipment markets as well as gaining a substantial presence in service solutions. Each time the company enters a new market and faces new competitors, the HP sales force is at the centre of the activity. In an effort to capture market share from Dell, Cisco, and Lexmark in the server market, HP opened a new sales operation in New Mexico called the SMB Exchange. It combines a call centre, inside sales, and channel sales teams. Observers have noted that, whereas HP's sales force was known for being more passive in the past, it is now much more aggressive—like Cisco's.

Hurd knew that because of HP's enormous size, it walks a fine line. In fact, he referred to the company's size as a "strange friend." On the one hand, it allows the company to offer a tremendous portfolio of products and services with support from a massive sales force.

On the other hand, multiple organizational layers can make it more difficult to create solutions for partners and customers. Hurd is doing everything he can to make HP leaner and meaner so that it can operate with the nimbleness and energy of a much smaller company.

The changes that have taken place at HP have made most everyone more satisfied. And happier salespeople are more productive, resulting in happier customers. That should mean a bright future for HP. With a continued focus on the sales force and the sales process, HP is developing a structure that creates better value for its business customers. Now, if your local electronics superstore could only do the same for you.

Sources: Quotes and adapted examples from Pui-Wing Tam, "System Reboot: Hurd's Big Challenge at HP: Overhauling Corporate Sales," *Wall Street Journal*, April 3, 2006, p. A1; Damon Poeter, "Never Enough," *Computer Reseller News*, April 1, 2010, p. 24; and Steven Burke, "HP Vs. Cisco: It's Personal," *Computer Reseller News*, November 1, 2009, p. 8.

QUESTIONS FOR DISCUSSION

1. Which of the sales force structures described in the text best describes HP's structure?

2. What are the positive and negative aspects of HP's new sales force structure?

3. How would you describe some of the differences in the selling process steps that an HP sales rep might face in selling to a long-term established customer versus a prospective customer?

4. Given that Hurd has an effective sales force, does he really need to meet with HP partners as much as he does?

5. Is it possible for HP to function like a smaller company? Why or why not?

MyMarketingLab MyMarketingLab is an online homework and tutorial system that puts you in control of your own learning with study and practice tools directly correlated to this chapter's content.

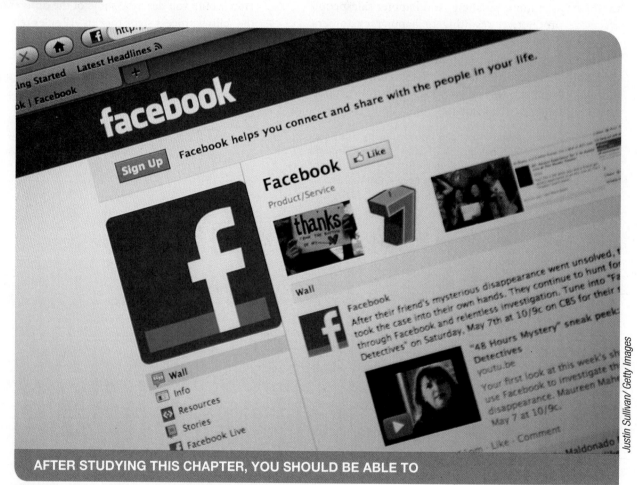

Justin Sullivan/ Getty Images

AFTER STUDYING THIS CHAPTER, YOU SHOULD BE ABLE TO

1 define direct marketing and discuss its benefits to customers and companies

2 identify and discuss the major forms of direct marketing

3 discuss how companies go about conducting online marketing to profitably deliver more value to customers

4 discuss the public policy and ethical issues presented by direct marketing

Direct and Online Marketing

PREVIEWING THE CONCEPTS

In the previous two chapters, you learned about communicating customer value through integrated marketing communication (IMC) and about four specific elements of the marketing communications mix—advertising, publicity, personal selling, and sales promotion. In this chapter, we'll look at the final IMC element, direct marketing, and at its fastest-growing form, online marketing. Actually, direct marketing can be viewed as more than just a communications tool. In many ways it constitutes an overall marketing approach—a blend of communication and distribution channels all rolled into one. As you read on, remember that although this chapter examines direct marketing as a separate tool, it must be carefully integrated with other elements of the promotion mix.

Let's start by looking at Facebook, a company that exists only online. The giant online social network promises to become one of the world's most powerful and profitable online marketers. Yet, as a marketing company, Facebook is just getting started.

FACEBOOK: WE ARE ONE PERCENT DONE WITH OUR MISSION

The world is rapidly going social and online, and no company is more social or more online than Facebook. The huge online social network has a deep and daily impact on the lives of hundreds of millions of members around the world. Yet Facebook is now grappling with a crucial question: How can it profitably tap the marketing potential of its massive community to make money without driving off its legions of loyal users?

Facebook is humongous. In only eight years, it surpassed 1.06 billion monthly active members by the end of 2012. It recently passed Google to become the most visited site on the Internet. Every 60 seconds, Facebook users send 230 000 messages, update 95 000 statuses, write 80 000 wall posts, tag 65 000 photos, share 50 000 links, and write a half-million comments affirming or disparaging all that activity.

With that many eyeballs glued to one virtual space, Facebook has tremendous impact and influence, not just as a sharing community but also as an Internet gateway. It is the default home page for many users, and some users have it on their screens 24/7. But Facebook's power comes not just from its size and omnipresence. Rather, it lies in the deep social connections between users. Facebook's mission is "Giving people the power to share." It's a place where friends and family meet, share their stories, display their photos, and chronicle their lives. Hordes of people have made Facebook their digital home.

By wielding all of that influence, Facebook has the potential to become one of the world's most powerful and profitable online marketers. Yet the burgeoning social network is only now beginning to realize that potential. Although Facebook's membership exploded from the very start, CEO Mark Zuckerberg and the network's other idealistic young co-founders gave little thought to making money. They actually opposed running ads or other forms of marketing, worried that marketing might damage Facebook's free (and commercial-free) sharing culture. So instead they focused on simply trying to manage the online revolution they'd begun.

In fact, without any help from Facebook, companies themselves were the first to discover the network's commercial value. Most brands—small and large—have now built their own Facebook pages, gaining free and relatively easy access to the gigantic community's word-of-web promise. Today, people "like" a Facebook brand page 50 million times every day. At one extreme, little Café Bica in Vancouver, British Columbia, has 123 Facebook fans. At the other extreme, the Montréal Canadiens have almost 997 000 fans (the Toronto Maple Leafs have almost 647 000 fans).

As the company has matured, however, Zuckerberg has come to realize that Facebook must make its own marketing and money-making moves. If Facebook doesn't make money, it can't continue to serve its members. As a first step, Facebook changed its philosophy on advertising. Today, for a fee, companies can place display or video ads on users' home, profile, or photo pages. The ads are carefully targeted based on user profile data. Or brands can pay Facebook to promote "sponsored stories," by which one member's interactions with a brand (check-ins, recommendations, likes) appear in the news feeds on their friends' Facebook pages. For example, if you see an item that says "Harry Gold: Second time today at Starbucks with Jenny Novak," followed by a Starbucks logo and link, Starbucks paid a fee for the placement. The organic feel of these sponsored stories increases user involvement by making the ads feel like just another part of the Facebook experience.

Advertising is proving to be a real moneymaker for Facebook. The company generated an estimated $1.33 billion in advertising revenues in the fourth quarter of 2012, with mobile advertising representing 23 percent of Facebook's ad revenue. But advertising revenues are only the tip of the marketing iceberg for Facebook. As a global gathering place where people spend time with friends, Facebook is also a natural for selling entertainment. For example, recognizing that members often exit the Facebook environment to listen to music or watch movies, the company is now moving to provide these services. For instance, Facebook has partnered with music-streaming service Spotify to integrate a Pandora-like listening function into the site. Similarly, Facebook is now entering the movie rental business. With 42 million viewers, Facebook is already the sixth most-popular video site in the United States. Until recently, however, that included only user-generated and music videos. Now, Facebook is partnering with content providers like Warner Bros. Entertainment to make streamed movies available within the Facebook community.

Beyond entertainment, Facebook is also entering the location-based and deal-of-the-day online markets. Its Facebook Places feature takes on Foursquare and other check-in services. Although Foursquare had a two-year head start and became the undisputed market leader with 9.5 million users, Facebook passed it with a flip of the switch. Almost immediately after its 2011 release, Facebook Places was registering more check-ins than

Foursquare. Facebook next fired a shot over the bow of deal-of-the-day merchants such as Groupon and LivingSocial by launching Facebook Deals. True to Facebook form, Deals not only lets users buy deals, it also employs its vast referral power in letting users share deals and see what deals friends have grabbed for themselves.

If Facebook can market digital entertainment and coupons, can it do the same with tangible goods? Many companies think so. Procter & Gamble sells Pampers via Facebook, and 1-800-Flowers has made a selection of floral bouquets available there as well. But more telling, JCPenney recently put its entire catalogue on Facebook—not just for browsing, but also for buying. The veteran catalogue retailer hopes that as users see any of its 250 000 items in their friends' news feeds, referral power will kick in to boost sales. In all, e-commerce offers huge revenue potential: Facebook takes as much as a 30 percent cut for every song, movie download, diaper, or flower bouquet sold.

In line with its goal to keep everything within the community, Facebook has even entered the banking business. That's right, banking. Facebook users can now exchange any of 15 world currencies for Facebook Credits, then use those credits to purchase anything sold within the Facebook universe. Facebook will soon require that all transactions within Facebook use its Facebook Credits currency. With Facebook's massive membership and growing e-commerce presence, it could soon pass PayPal as the online payments leader. Perhaps more impressive, Facebook Credits could become a powerful global currency all by itself.

Will increased marketing on Facebook alienate loyal Facebook fans? Not if it's done right. Research shows that online users readily accept—even welcome—well-targeted online advertising and marketing. Tasteful and appropriately targeted offers can enhance rather than detract from the Facebook user experience. "We've found, frankly, that users are getting more value [because of our marketing efforts]," says a Facebook marketing executive, so that companies are "getting value putting more [marketing] in."

It's too soon to say whether Facebook will eventually challenge the likes of Google in online advertising or Amazon.com in selling all things online. But its immense, closely knit social network gives Facebook staggering potential. As a marketing company, Facebook is just getting started. Carolyn Everson, Facebook's vice-president of global sales, sums up Facebook's growth potential this way: "I'm not sure the marketing community understands our story yet. We evolve so quickly. We have a saying here: 'We are one percent done with our mission.'"[1]

MANY of the marketing and promotion tools that we've examined in previous chapters were developed in the context of *mass marketing*: targeting broad markets with standardized messages and offers distributed through intermediaries. Today, however, with the trend toward more narrowly targeted marketing, many companies are adopting *direct marketing*, either as a primary marketing approach or as a supplement to other approaches. In this section, we explore the exploding world of direct marketing.

Direct marketing consists of connecting directly with carefully targeted consumers, often on a one-to-one, interactive basis. Using detailed databases, companies tailor their marketing offers and communications to the needs of narrowly defined segments or individual buyers.

Beyond brand and relationship building, direct marketers usually seek a direct, immediate, and measurable consumer response. For example, Amazon.ca interacts directly with customers on its website or mobile app to help them to discover and buy almost anything and everything on the Internet. Similarly, TD Canada Trust interacts directly

LO1

Direct marketing
Connecting directly with carefully targeted individual consumers to both obtain an immediate response and cultivate lasting customer relationships.

with customers—by telephone, through its website, or even on its Facebook, Twitter, and YouTube pages, as well as iPhone and Android apps—to build individual brand relationships, provide financial advice, or service customer accounts.

The New Direct Marketing Model

Early direct marketers—catalogue companies, direct mailers, and telemarketers—gathered customer names and sold goods mainly by mail and telephone. Today, however, spurred by rapid advances in database technologies and new interactive media—especially the Internet—direct marketing has undergone a dramatic transformation.

In previous chapters, we've discussed direct marketing as direct distribution—as marketing channels that contain no intermediaries. We also include direct marketing as one element of the promotion mix—as an approach for communicating directly with consumers. In actuality, direct marketing is both of these things and more.

Most companies still use direct marketing as a supplementary channel or medium. Thus, Lexus markets mostly through mass-media advertising and its high-quality dealer network. However, it also supplements these channels with direct marketing, such as promotional DVDs and other materials mailed directly to prospective buyers, and a website that provides consumers with information about various models, competitive comparisons, financing, and dealer locations. Similarly, most retail stores, such as Sears or Canadian Tire, sell the majority of their merchandise off their store shelves, but they also sell through direct mail and online catalogues.

However, for many companies today, direct marketing is more than just a supplementary channel or advertising medium—it constitutes a complete model for doing business. Firms employing this *direct model* use it as the *only* approach. Companies such as Amazon, eBay, Priceline, Netflix, and eLUXE have built their entire approach to the marketplace around direct marketing. Many, like Amazon.com, have employed this model with tremendous success (see Marketing@Work 14.1).

Exhibit 14.1 **The new direct marketing model:** Companies such as Toronto-based eLUXE have built their entire approach to the marketplace around direct marketing—just visit eluxe.ca.

Courtesy of eLuxe

Growth and Benefits of Direct Marketing

Direct marketing has become the fastest-growing form of marketing. According to Direct Marketing (www.dmn.ca), Canada's leading publication in the field, Canadian companies spend in excess of $8 billion annually on direct marketing, resulting in approximately $51 billion in sales. While direct mail is still the primary channel of direct marketing (Canadians receive about 1.5 billion pieces of targeted mail each year), response rates have dropped almost 25 percent in the last nine years to under 4 percent. Despite this, direct mail campaigns still draw better overall response rates than digital channels (email response rates in 2012 were reported at 0.12 percent), but other forms of direct marketing are definitely on the rise.[2]

Direct marketing continues to become more web-oriented, and Internet marketing is claiming a fast-growing share of direct-marketing spending and sales. Canadian online advertising revenues topped $2.59 billion in 2011, up 23 percent from 2010. Of this, approximately 19 percent

Amazon.com: *The* Model for Direct Marketing in the Digital Age

When you think of shopping online, chances are good that you think first of Amazon. The online pioneer first opened its virtual doors in 1995, selling books out of founder Jeff Bezos's garage in suburban Seattle. Amazon still sells books—*lots and lots* of books. But it now sells just about everything else as well, from music, videos, electronics, tools, housewares, apparel, mobile phones, and groceries to loose diamonds and even lobsters. Many analysts view Amazon.com as *the* model for direct marketing in the digital age.

From the start, Amazon has grown explosively. Its annual sales have rocketed from a modest US$150 million in 1997 to more than US$34 billion today. In the past five years, despite the shaky economy, its sales have more than quadrupled. Although it took the company eight years to turn its first full-year profit in 2003, Amazon's profits have since surged more than 30-fold. Last year alone, sales grew 40 percent; profits popped nearly 28 percent. This past holiday season, at one point, the online store's more than 120 million active customers worldwide were purchasing 110 items per second.

What has made Amazon one of the world's premier direct marketers? To its core, the company is relentlessly customer driven. "The thing that drives everything is creating genuine value for customers," says Bezos. The company starts with the customer and works backward. "Rather than ask what are we good at and what else can we do with that skill," says Bezos, "we ask, who are our customers? What do they need? And then [we] learn those skills."

For example, when Amazon saw an opportunity to serve its book-buying customers better through access to e-books and other e-content, it developed its own product for the first time ever—the innovative Kindle, a wireless reading device for downloading books, blogs, magazines, newspapers, and other matter. The Kindle took more than four years and a whole new set of skills to develop. But Amazon's start-with-the-customer thinking paid off handsomely.

The Kindle is now the company's number one selling product, and Amazon.com currently sells more e-books than hardcovers and paperbacks combined. The Kindle Store now offers more than 550 000 e-books, including new releases and bestsellers, at $11.99 or less. And various Kindle apps let customers enjoy e-books on devices ranging from BlackBerrys and Droids to iPhones and iPads.

Perhaps more important than *what* Amazon sells is *how* it sells. The company wants to do much more than just sell books, DVDs, or digital cameras. It wants to deliver a special *experience* to every customer. "The customer experience really matters," says Bezos. "We've focused on just having a better store, where it's easier to shop, where you can learn more about the products, where you have a bigger selection, and where you have the lowest prices."

Most Amazon.com regulars feel a surprisingly strong relationship with the company, especially given the almost complete lack of actual human interaction. Amazon obsesses over making each customer's experience uniquely personal. For example, the website greets customers with their very own personalized home pages, and its "Recommendations for You" feature offers personalized product recommendations. Amazon was the first company to use "collaborative filtering"

Associated Press

Exhibit 14.2 Online pioneer Amazon.com does much more than just sell goods on the web. It creates direct, personalized online customer experiences. "The thing that drives everything is creating genuine value for customers," says founder and CEO Jeff Bezos, pictured above.

technology, which sifts through each customer's past purchases and the purchasing patterns of customers with similar profiles to come up with personalized site content. "We want Amazon.com to be the right store for you as an individual," says Bezos. "If we have 120 million customers, we should have 120 million stores."

Visitors to Amazon.com receive a unique blend of benefits: huge selection, good value, and convenience. But it's the "discovery" factor that makes the buying experience really special. Once on the Amazon.com site, you're compelled to stay for a while—looking, learning, and discovering. Amazon.com has become a kind of online community in which customers can browse for products, research purchase alternatives, share opinions and reviews with other visitors, and chat online with authors and experts. In this way, Amazon does much more than just sell goods online. It creates direct, personalized customer relationships and satisfying online experiences. Year after year, Amazon comes in number one or number two on the American

Customer Satisfaction Index, regardless of industry.

To create even greater selection and discovery for customers, Amazon.com allows competing retailers—from mom-and-pop operations to Marks & Spencer department stores—to offer their products on Amazon.com, creating a virtual shopping mall of incredible proportions. It even encourages customers to sell used items on the site. The broader selection attracts more customers, and everyone benefits. "We are becoming increasingly important in the lives of our customers," says an Amazon marketing executive.

Based on its powerful growth, many have speculated that Amazon.com will become the Walmart of the web. In fact, some argue, it already is. Although Walmart's total sales of more than US$419 billion dwarf Amazon's US$34 billion in sales, Amazon's Internet sales are 12 times greater than Walmart's. So it's Walmart that's chasing Amazon on the web. Put another way, Walmart wants to become the Amazon.com of the web, not

the other way around. However, despite its mammoth proportions, to catch Amazon online, Walmart will have to match the superb Amazon customer experience, and that won't be easy.

Whatever the eventual outcome, Amazon has forever changed the face of direct marketing. Most importantly, the innovative direct retailer has set a very high bar for the online customer experience. "The reason I'm so obsessed with ... the customer experience is that I believe [our success] has been driven exclusively by that experience," says Bezos. "We are not great advertisers. So we start with customers, figure out what they want, and figure out how to get it to them."

Sources: See Daniel Lyons, "The Customer Is Always Right," *Newsweek,* January 4, 2010, p. 85; Brad Stone, "Can Amazon Be the Walmart of the Web?" *New York Times,* September 20, 2009, p. BU1; Joe Nocera, "Putting Buyers First? What a Concept," *New York Times,* January 5, 2008, www.nytimes.com; Scott Cendrowski, "How Amazon Keeps Cranking," *Fortune,* February 28, 2011, p. 18; Andrew Edgecliffe-Johnson, "Amazon's Electronic Book Sales Beat Print," *Financial Times,* May 20, 2011, p. 22; and annual reports and other information found at www.amazon.com and http://local.amazon.com/businesses, accessed October 2011.

were French language ads. In 2011, Canadian online ad revenue grew 16 percent, and now accounts for 21.7 percent of the total advertising revenue in Canada, second only to television advertising. According to a 2010 survey conducted by the Interactive Advertising Bureau of Canada (IAB), the Internet now stands third in Canada (just behind TV and radio) in terms of total weekly time spent by all adults with all media, and it reaches more adults each week than either magazines or newspapers. The Internet's share of media time has grown from 8 percent in 2001 to 16 percent in 2009 and is the number one form of media in the 18–24 age group. The IAB predicts that by 2016, the Internet will be the number one medium for most consumers, thus, it is imperative that advertisers shift significant portions of their budgets from TV to the Internet.[3]

Benefits to Buyers

For buyers, direct marketing is convenient, easy, and private. Direct marketers never close their doors, and customers don't have to trek to and through stores to find products. From their homes, offices, or almost anywhere else, customers can shop the Internet at any time of the day or night. Likewise, business buyers can learn about products and services without tying up time with salespeople.

Direct marketing gives buyers ready access to a virtually unlimited assortment of products that would be physically impossible to contain in a brick-and-mortar store. For instance, log onto Bulbs.com, "the web's number one light bulb superstore," and you'll have instant access to every imaginable kind of light bulb or lamp—incandescent bulbs, fluorescent bulbs, projection bulbs, surgical bulbs, automotive bulbs—you name it.

Similarly, Shop.ca provides Canadians with access to millions of products and services across 25 different categories from a community of retailers and manufacturers, all from the convenience of a single online shopping site. Launched in 2012, Shop.ca has become the fastest growing retail site in Canada, and was a top 10 most-visited Canadian-owned e-commerce site by the fourth quarter of 2012.

Direct marketing channels also give buyers access to a wealth of comparative information about companies, products, and competitors. Good catalogues or websites often provide more information in more useful forms than even the most helpful retail salesperson can provide. For example, Amazon.com offers more information than most of us can digest, ranging from top-ten product lists, extensive product descriptions, and expert and user product reviews to recommendations based on customers' previous purchases. Catalogues from Sears offer a treasure trove of information about the store's merchandise and services. In fact, you probably wouldn't think it strange to see a Sears' salesperson referring to a catalogue in the store for more detailed product information while trying to advise a customer.

Finally, direct marketing is immediate and interactive: Buyers can interact with sellers by phone or on the seller's website to create exactly the configuration of information, products, or services they desire and then order them on the spot. Moreover, direct marketing gives consumers a greater measure of control. Consumers decide which catalogues they will browse and which websites they will visit.

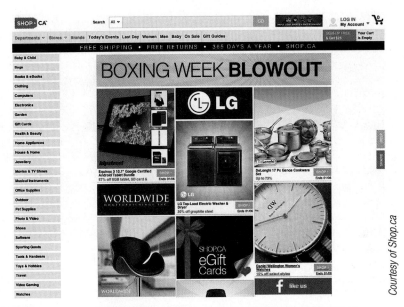

Exhibit 14.3 **Benefits of direct marketing:** Competing with giant US retailers, Shop.ca allows Canadian consumers access to millions of products and services from Canadian manufacturers and retailers from the convenience of a single shopping site.

Courtesy of Shop.ca

Benefits to Sellers

For sellers, direct marketing is a powerful tool for building customer relationships. By using database marketing, today's marketers can target small groups or individual consumers and promote their offers through personalized communications. Because of the one-to-one nature of direct marketing, companies can interact with customers by phone or online, learn more about their needs, and tailor products and services to specific customer tastes. In turn, customers can ask questions and volunteer feedback.

Direct marketing also offers sellers a low-cost, efficient, speedy alternative for reaching their markets. Direct marketing has grown rapidly in business-to-business marketing, partly in response to the ever-increasing costs of marketing through the sales force. When personal sales calls cost an average of $350 or more per contact, they should be made only when necessary and only to high-potential customers and prospects.[4] Lower-cost-per-contact media—such as business-to-business telemarketing, direct mail, and company websites—often prove more cost effective.

Similarly, online direct marketing results in lower costs, improved efficiencies, and speedier handling of channel and logistics functions, such as order processing, inventory handling, and delivery. Direct marketers such as Amazon.com or Netflix also avoid the expense of maintaining a store and the related costs of rent, insurance, and utilities, passing the savings along to customers.

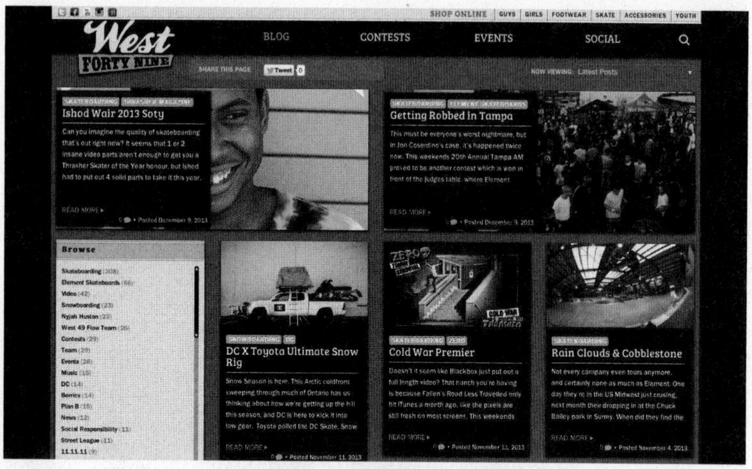

Courtesy of West 49

Exhibit 14.4 West 49 uses a variety of tools—including email, text messages, and blogs—to personalize messages and better connect with their customers.

Direct marketing can also offer greater flexibility. It allows marketers to make ongoing adjustments to its prices and programs, or to make immediate, timely, and personal announcements and offers. For example, Canadian clothing company West49 has used direct marketing to personalize its offerings in a variety of ways:[5]

Canadian clothing retailer West49 has experienced great success in reaching customers with various direct marketing campaigns. The company's All Access Pass loyalty program has led to growth by providing personalized communications to the teenage customer base. Through various incentives, West49 collects information about their customers, which is then used to create targeted email promotions. For example, the company uses knowledge about customers' gender, location, and even membership levels to segment their customer base and provide more targeted communications. West49 also uses SMS contests allowing customers to cast ballots with text messages, and provides an interactive website including blogs that consumers can post to. In some cases, West49's segmented campaigns have resulted in a doubling of in-store visits and spending habits of loyalty program members, leading to an incredible 100 percent increase in ROI.

Finally, direct marketing gives sellers access to buyers that they could not reach through other channels. Smaller firms can mail catalogues to customers outside their local markets and offer toll-free telephone numbers to handle orders and inquiries. Internet marketing is a truly global medium that allows buyers and sellers to click from one country to another in seconds. A web user from Paris or Istanbul can access an online L.L.Bean catalogue as easily as someone living in Freeport, Maine, the direct retailer's hometown. Even small marketers find that they have ready access to global markets.

Customer Databases and Direct Marketing

Customer database

An organized collection of comprehensive data about individual customers or prospects, including geographic, demographic, psychographic, and behavioural data.

Effective direct marketing begins with a good customer database. A **customer database** is an organized collection of comprehensive data about individual customers or prospects. A good customer database can be a potent relationship-building tool. The database gives companies a 360-degree view of their customers and how they behave. A company is no better than what it knows about its customers.

In consumer marketing, the customer database might contain a customer's geographic data (address, region), demographic data (age, income, family members, birthdays), psychographic data (activities, interests, and opinions), and buying behaviour (buying preferences and the recency, frequency, and monetary value [RFM] of past purchases). In B-to-B marketing, the customer profile might contain the products and services the customer has bought, past volumes and prices, key contacts, competing suppliers, the status of current contracts, estimated future spending, and competitive strengths and weaknesses in selling and servicing the account. Some of these databases are huge. For example, casino operator Harrah's Entertainment has built a customer database containing 700 terabytes worth of customer information. It uses this data to create special customer experiences. Similarly, Walmart captures data on every item, for every customer, for every store, every day. Its database contains more than 2.5 petabytes of data—that's equivalent to two billion copies of Moby Dick.[6]

Companies use their databases in many ways. They use databases to locate good potential customers and generate sales leads. They can mine their databases to learn about customers in detail, and then fine-tune their market offerings and communications to the special preferences and behaviours of target segments or individuals. In all, a company's database can be an important tool for building stronger long-term customer relationships.

For example, retailer Best Buy mines its huge customer database to glean actionable insights, which it uses to personalize promotional messages and offers:[7]

> Best Buy's 15-plus terabyte customer database contains seven years of data on more than 75 million customer households. The retail chain captures every scrap of store and online interaction data—from purchase transactions to phone calls and mouse clicks to delivery and rebate cheque addresses—and merges it with third-party and publicly available data to create multidimensional customer profiles. Then, sophisticated match-and-merge algorithms score individual customers in terms of their interests, lifestyles, and passions, and use this information to identify their likely next purchases.

Exhibit 14.5 **Customer databases:** Best Buy mines its huge database to glean actionable insights on customer interests, lifestyles, passions, and likely next purchases. It uses this information to develop personalized, customer-triggered promotional messages and offers.

Richard Sennott/ZUMAPRESS/Newscom

> Through such analysis, Best Buy categorizes three-quarters of its customers—more than 100 million individuals—into segments with names like Buzz (the young tech enthusiast), Jill (the suburban soccer mom), Larry (the wealthy professional guy), Ray (the family man), and Charlie and Helen (empty nesters with money to spend). Based on these profiles and individual transaction information, Best Buy then develops personalized, customer-triggered promotional messages and offers. So if your previous interactions suggest that you are a young Buzz assembling a home entertainment system, and you recently used Best Buy's smartphone app to look up product details and customer ratings on a specific component, you might soon receive a spot-on mobile coupon offering discounts on that and related products.

Like many other marketing tools, database marketing requires a special investment. Companies must invest in computer hardware, database software, analytical programs, communication links, and skilled personnel. The database system must be user-friendly and available to various marketing groups, including those in product and brand management, new-product development, advertising and promotion, direct mail, telemarketing, web marketing, field sales, order fulfillment, and customer service. However, a well-managed database should lead to sales and customer-relationship gains that will more than cover its costs.

Forms of Direct Marketing `LO2`

The major forms of direct marketing—as shown in Figure 14.1—include personal selling, direct-mail marketing, catalogue marketing, telephone marketing, direct-response television marketing, kiosk marketing, new digital direct-marketing technologies, and online marketing. We examined personal selling in depth in Chapter 13. Here, we examine the other direct-marketing forms.

Direct-Mail Marketing

Direct-mail marketing involves sending an offer, announcement, reminder, or other item to a person at a particular physical or virtual address. Using highly selective mailing

Direct-mail marketing
Direct marketing by sending an offer, announcement, reminder, or other item to a person at a particular physical or virtual address.

FIGURE 14.1 Forms of Direct Marketing

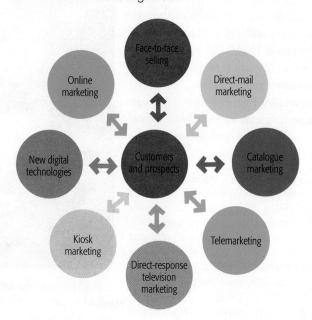

lists, direct marketers send out millions of mail pieces each year—letters, catalogues, ads, brochures, samples, DVDs, and other "salespeople with wings." Direct mail is by far the largest direct marketing medium. The Direct Marketing Association reports that US marketers spent US$45 billion on direct mail in 2010 (including both catalogue and non-catalogue mail), which accounted for 29 percent of all US direct marketing spending and generated nearly a third of direct marketing sales. In Canada, direct mail expenditures were estimated to exceed $1.24 billion of the approximately $14.4 billion spent on advertising in 2011.[8]

Direct mail is well suited to direct, one-to-one communication. It permits high target-market selectivity, can be personalized, is flexible, and allows easy measurement of results. Although direct mail costs more per thousand people reached than mass media such as television or magazines, the people it reaches are much better prospects. For example, a study conducted by Canada Post in 2011 suggested that only 18 percent of consumers who receive addressed print advertising discard it without even reading it, compared to approximately 32 percent of those who discard unaddressed print ads; and direct mail is even more effective when the company sending the mail is located within 20 minutes of the consumer.[9] Direct mail has proved successful in promoting all kinds of products, from books, music, DVDs, and magazine subscriptions to insurance, gift items, clothing, gourmet foods, and industrial products. Charities also use direct mail heavily to raise billions of dollars each year.

Some analysts predict a decline in the use of traditional forms of direct mail in coming years, as marketers switch to newer digital forms, such as email and mobile marketing. Email, mobile, and other newer forms of direct marketing deliver messages at incredible speeds and lower costs compared to the post office's "snail mail" pace. We will discuss email and mobile marketing in more detail later in the chapter.

However, even though the new digital forms of direct mail are gaining popularity, the traditional form is still by far the most widely used. Mail marketing offers some distinct advantages over digital forms. It provides something tangible for people to hold and keep and it can be used to send samples. "Mail makes it real," says one analyst. It "creates an emotional connection with customers that digital cannot. They hold it, view it, and engage with it in a manner entirely different from their online experiences." In contrast, email is easily screened or trashed. "[With] spam filters and spam folders to keep our messaging away from consumers' inboxes," says a direct marketer, "sometimes you have to lick a few stamps."[10]

Traditional direct mail can be an effective component of a broader integrated marketing campaign. For example, most large companies rely heavily on TV advertising to establish broad customer awareness and positioning. However, companies also use direct mail to break through the clutter of TV advertising. Consider 1-800-GOT-JUNK:[11]

> In 1989, Vancouver student Brian Scudamore started a small junk removal service to pay for his college education. In less than 15 years, this small business grew into one of Canada's most successful franchises, now with over 200 locations in three countries. When 1-800-GOT-JUNK decided to test a new direct marketing program to support its North American franchises, it turned to Vancouver-based Kirk Marketing for help. The direct mail creative included a personalized URL (PURL), a die-cut truck, and a scratch card. Created for both the French and English market, the campaign had to work with both Canada Post and the US Postal Service. Franchise owners benefited greatly from the centrally managed data collection done by corporate head office. In fact, one franchise in Austin, Texas saw an incredible return on investment of over 1000 percent. For every card sent to customers at a cost of $0.50 per card, the franchise made $11.00 in revenue.

Direct mail may be resented as junk mail or spam if sent to people who have no interest in it. For this reason, smart marketers are targeting their direct mail carefully so as not to waste their money and recipients' time. They are designing permission-based programs that send email and mobile ads only to those who want to receive them.

Catalogue Marketing

Advances in technology, along with the move toward personalized, one-to-one marketing have resulted in exciting changes in **catalogue marketing**. *Catalog Age* magazine used to define a *catalogue* as "a printed, bound piece of at least eight pages, selling multiple products, and offering a direct ordering mechanism." Today, this definition is sadly out of date.

In the age of the Internet, more and more catalogues are going digital. A variety of web-only cataloguers have emerged, and most print cataloguers have added web-based catalogues and smartphone catalogue shopping apps to their marketing mixes. For example, IKEA created a mobile shopping app in 2012, and Canada was one of three countries to pilot it, before it was implemented worldwide in 2013. And customers can browse and purchase any of the thousands of products available on Sears Canada's website (www.sears.ca), download the mobile app, or request a print copy by mail.

Digital catalogues eliminate production, printing, and mailing costs, and whereas print-catalogue space is limited, online catalogues can offer an almost unlimited amount of merchandise. They also offer a broader assortment of presentation formats, including search and video. Finally, online catalogues allow real-time merchandising—products and features can be added or removed as needed and prices can be adjusted instantly to match demand.

Catalogue marketing
Direct marketing through print, video, or digital catalogues that are mailed to select customers, made available in stores, or presented online.

Exhibit 14.6 Creative direct mail campaigns can be a cost effective way to grow any business.

CIRO CESAR La Opinion Photos/Newscom

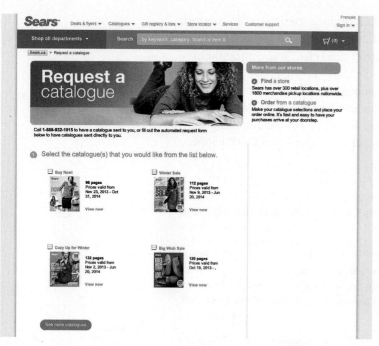

Used with the permission of Sears Canada Inc.

Exhibit 14.7 Printed catalogues are one of the best ways to drive online sales. Thus, even when Sears Canada moved their catalogue online, the company still gave consumers the option of requesting a print copy by mail.

However, despite the advantages of web-based catalogues, as your overstuffed mailbox may suggest, printed catalogues are still thriving. US direct marketers mail out some 20 billion catalogues each year—about 64 per person. Why aren't companies ditching their old-fashioned paper catalogues in this new digital era? For one thing, paper catalogues create emotional connections with customers that web-based sales spaces simply can't. "Glossy catalogue pages still entice buyers in a way that computer images don't," says an analyst. "Among retailers who rely mainly on direct sales, 62 percent say their biggest revenue generator is a paper catalogue."[12]

In addition, printed catalogues are one of the best ways to drive online sales, making them more important than ever in the digital era. According to a recent study, 70 percent of web purchases are driven by catalogues. Another study found that consumers who received catalogues from the retailer spent 28 percent more on that retailer's website than those who didn't get a catalogue. Thus, even dedicated online-only retailers, such as Zappos.com, have started producing catalogues with the hopes of driving online sales.[13]

Telephone Marketing

Telephone marketing, or telemarketing, involves using the telephone to sell directly to consumers and business customers. Telephone marketing now accounts for more than 19 percent of all direct marketing-driven sales. We're all familiar with telephone marketing directed toward consumers, but business-to-business marketers also use telephone marketing extensively, accounting for more than 55 percent of all telephone marketing sales. Marketers use *outbound* telemarketing to sell directly to consumers and businesses. They use *inbound* toll-free numbers to receive orders from television and print ads, direct mail, or catalogues.

Properly designed and targeted telemarketing provides many benefits, including purchasing convenience and increased product and service information. However, the explosion in unsolicited outbound telephone marketing over the years annoyed many consumers, who objected to the almost daily "junk phone calls."

In Canada, telephone marketing is controlled by a National Do Not Call List. Canadian consumers can reduce the number of telemarketing calls they receive by registering their residential, wireless, fax, or VoIP telephone number through the website at DNCL.gc.ca. The website is maintained by the CRTC, the Canadian Radio-television and Telecommunications Commission, and it also provides online forms for consumers to register complaints against telemarketers. Canadian marketers must register with the National DNCL, and are required by law to periodically verify that any consumer on the DNCL list is removed from their telemarketing database. Marketers who violate the rules are investigated by the CRTC and can face fines of up to $15 000 per violation. And even when marketers abide by the DNCL rules, they must follow certain procedures when making legal telemarketing calls. For example, at the beginning of a call telemarketers must tell you why they're calling, they must identify on whose behalf the call is being made, and calls may be made only within certain calling hours.

Do-not-call legislation has hurt the consumer telemarketing industry. However, two major forms of telemarketing—inbound consumer telemarketing and outbound B-to-B telemarketing—remain strong and growing. Telemarketing also remains a major fund-raising tool for not-for-profit and political groups. Interestingly, do-not-call regulations appear to be helping many direct marketers more than it's hurting them. Rather than making unwanted calls, many of these marketers are developing "opt-in" calling systems, in which they provide useful information and offers to customers who have invited the company to contact them by phone or email. The opt-in model provides better returns for marketers than the formerly invasive one.

Meanwhile, marketers who violate do-not-call regulations have themselves increasingly become the targets of crusading consumer activist groups, who return the favour by flooding the violating company's phone system with return calls and messages.[14]

Direct-Response Television Marketing

Direct-response television marketing takes one of two major forms. The first is *direct-response television advertising* (DRTV). Direct marketers air television spots, often 60 or 120 seconds long, which persuasively describe a product and give customers a toll-free number or website for ordering. Television viewers also often encounter full 30-minute or longer advertising programs, or *infomercials*, for a single product.

Successful direct-response advertising campaigns can ring up big sales. For example, little-known infomercial maker Guthy-Renker has helped propel its Proactiv Solution acne treatment and other "transformational" products into power brands that pull in $1.5 billion in sales annually to five million active customers (compare that to only about $150 million in annual drugstore sales of acne products in the United States).[15]

DRTV ads are often associated with somewhat loud or questionable pitches for cleaners, stain removers, kitchen gadgets, and nifty ways to stay in shape without working very hard at it. For example, over the past few years yell-and-sell TV pitchmen like Anthony Sullivan (Swivel Sweeper, Awesome Auger) and Vince Offer (ShamWow, SlapChop) have racked up billions of dollars in sales of "As Seen on TV" products. Brands like OxiClean, ShamWow, and the Snuggie (a blanket with sleeves) have become DRTV cult classics. And infomercial viral sensation Shake Weight created buzz on everything from YouTube to *Late Night with Jimmy Fallon*, selling more than 2 million units for $40 million in revenues in less than a year.[16]

In recent years, however, a number of large companies—from P&G, Disney, Revlon, Apple, and Kodak to Coca-Cola, Anheuser-Busch, and even the US Navy—have begun using infomercials to sell their wares, refer customers to retailers, recruit members, or attract buyers to their websites.

A more recent form of direct-response television marketing is *interactive TV (iTV)* marketing. It lets viewers interact with television programming and advertising using their remote controls. Interactive TV gives marketers an opportunity to reach targeted audiences in an interactive, more involved way.

In the past, iTV has been slow to catch on. However, the technology now appears poised to take off as a direct marketing medium. Research shows that the level of viewer engagement with iTV is much higher than with regular 30-second spots. A recent poll indicated that 66 percent of viewers would be "very interested" in interacting with commercials that piqued their interest. And broadcasting systems such as DIRECTV, EchoStar, and Time Warner are now offering iTV capabilities.[17]

Direct-response television marketing
Direct marketing via television, including direct-response television advertising (or infomercials) and home shopping channels.

New York area cable provider Cablevision offers an iTV service by which advertisers can run interactive 30-second spots.[18]

During the ads, a bar at the bottom of the screen lets viewers use their remotes to choose additional content and offers, such as on-demand free product samples, brand channels, video showcases, or emailed brochures or coupons. For example, a Gillette ad offered to send free samples of its body wash product, Benjamin Moore offered coupons for paint colour samples, and Century 21 offered $10 gift cards. Advertisers such as Mattel Barbie and the US Navy invited viewers to select their branded Cablevision channels for optional information and entertainment. So far, response rates for the interactive content have been impressive. For example, in an early test last year, the Disney Travel Channel allowed subscribers to browse information about Disney theme parks and then request a call from an agent. The booking rate for people requesting a call was an amazing 25 percent.

 appears in left margin as vertical text: *The Canadian Press/David Friend*

Exhibit 14.8 **Kiosk marketing:** Redbox recently entered the Canadian market, signing a deal with Walmart Canada and national convenience store operator Alimentation Couche-Tard Inc. to place kiosks in stores across the country.

Kiosk Marketing

As consumers become more and more comfortable with digital and touch-screen technologies, many companies are placing information and ordering machines—called *kiosks* (good old-fashioned vending machines but so much more)—in stores, airports, hotels, university campuses, and other locations. Kiosks are everywhere these days, from self-service hotel and airline check-in devices to in-store ordering devices that let you order merchandise not carried in the store. "Flashy and futuristic, souped-up machines are popping up everywhere," says one analyst. "They have touch screens instead of buttons, facades that glow and pulse ... [they] bridge the gap between old-fashioned stores and online shopping."[19]

In-store Kodak, Fuji, and HP kiosks let customers transfer pictures from memory sticks, mobile phones, and other digital storage devices; edit them; and make high-quality colour prints. Kiosks in Hilton hotel lobbies let guests view their reservations, get room keys, view pre-arrival messages, check in and out, and even change seat assignments and print boarding passes for flights on any of 18 airlines. At Toronto's Pearson International Airport, you can purchase headphones, MP3 players, iPods, and other electronics at Best Buy Canada kiosks. And Redbox operates DVD rental kiosks in hundreds of Canadian Safeway and Walmart stores from Ontario to British Columbia. Customers make their selections on a touch screen, then swipe a credit or debit card to rent DVDs. Customers can even pre-reserve DVDs online to ensure that their trip to the kiosk will not be a wasted one. In the United States, more than 27 000 Redbox Kiosks operate at various retail outlets. The market share for standalone kiosk movie rentals surpassed that of traditional retail store rentals in the United States last year and continues to grow here in Canada.[20]

Online Marketing LO3

Online marketing
Efforts to market products and services and build customer relationships over the Internet.

As noted earlier, **online marketing** is the fastest-growing form of direct marketing. Widespread use of the Internet is having a dramatic impact on both buyers and the marketers who serve them. In this section, we examine how marketing strategy and practice are changing to take advantage of today's Internet technologies.

Marketing and the Internet

Much of the world's business today is carried out over digital networks that connect people and companies. The **Internet**, a vast public web of computer networks, connects users of all types all around the world to each other and an amazingly large information repository. These days, people connect with the Internet at almost any time and from almost anywhere using their computers, smartphones, tablets, or even TVs. The Internet has fundamentally changed customers' notions of convenience, speed, price, product information, and service. As a result, it has given marketers a whole new way to create value for customers and build relationships with them.

Internet usage and impact continues to grow steadily. In 2012, 83 percent of the Canadian population or 28.5 million people, had access to the Internet, compared to 77 percent of the US population. The average Canadian spends 43.5 hours a month on the web, compared to the worldwide average of 23.1 hours. In a recent survey, Canada ranked first in the number of website visits per user per month, and ranked second only to South Korea in the number of pages viewed. Virtually all Internet users in Canada have access to broadband services either through land-line or satellite facilities. Social networking is also a major trend in this country. For example, more than 18 million Canadians have a Facebook account. Canada is also one of the leading countries in mobile Internet access, with over 26 million wireless phone subscribers. Worldwide mobile Internet access topped 6 billion in 2012.[21]

To reach this burgeoning market, all kinds of companies now market online. **Click-only companies** operate on the Internet only. They include a wide array of firms, from *e-tailers* such as Amazon.ca and Expedia.ca that sell products and services directly to final buyers via the Internet to *search engines and portals* (such as Bing, Google, and MSN), *transaction sites* (eBay, Craigslist), *content sites* (the *Globe and Mail* on the web, TSN.com, and *Encyclopedia Britannica*), and *online social networks* (Facebook, YouTube, Twitter, and Flickr).

The success of the dot-coms has caused existing *brick-and-mortar* manufacturers and retailers to re-examine how they serve their markets. Now, almost all of these traditional companies have created their own online sales and communications channels, becoming **click-and-mortar companies**. It's hard to find a company today that doesn't have a substantial online presence.

In fact, many click-and-mortar companies are now having more online success than their click-only competitors. A recent ranking of the world's ten largest online retail sites contained only one click-only retailer (Amazon.com, which was ranked number one). All the others were multichannel retailers.[22] For example, number two on the list was Staples, the US$24.5 billion office supply retailer. Staples operates more than 2280 superstores worldwide. But you might be surprised to learn that more than half of Staples' North American sales and profits come from its online and direct marketing operations.[23]

> Selling on the web lets Staples build deeper, more personalized relationships with customers large and small. A large customer, such as GE or P&G, can create lists of approved office products at discount prices and then let company departments or even individuals do their own online purchasing. This reduces ordering costs, cuts through the red tape, and speeds up the ordering process for customers. At the same time, it encourages companies to use Staples as a sole source for office supplies. Even the smallest companies and individual consumers find 24-hour-a-day online ordering via Staples mobile phone app easier and more efficient.

Internet
A vast public web of computer networks that connects users of all types around the world to each other and an amazingly large information repository.

Click-only companies
The so-called dot-coms, which operate online only and have no brick-and-mortar market presence.

Click-and-mortar companies
Traditional brick-and-mortar companies that have added online marketing to their operations.

Courtesy of Staples the Office Superstore, LLC & Staples, Inc.

Exhibit 14.9 **Click-and-mortar marketing:** Staples backs its "that was easy" positioning by offering a full range of contact points and delivery modes.

In addition, Staples' web operations complement store sales. The Staples.com and Staples.ca sites and smartphone apps build store traffic by offering hot deals and by helping customers find a local store and check stock and prices. In return, the local store promotes the website through in-store kiosks. If customers don't find what they need on the shelves, they can quickly order it via the kiosk. Thus, Staples backs its "that was easy" positioning by offering a full range of contact points and delivery modes—online, catalogues, phone, and in the store. No click-only or brick-only seller can match that kind of call, click, or visit convenience and support.

Online Marketing Domains

The four major online marketing domains are shown in Figure 14.2. They include B2C (business-to-consumer), B2B (business-to-business), C2C (consumer-to-consumer), and C2B (consumer-to-business).

Business-to-Consumer (B2C)   The popular press has paid the most attention to **business-to-consumer (B2C) online marketing**—businesses selling goods and services online to individual consumers for their personal needs. Today's consumers can buy almost anything online—from clothing, kitchen gadgets, and airline tickets to computers and cars. In 2012, online sales of retail and travel products topped $21 billion in Canada and over $340 billion in the United States. Growth in Canadian B2C e-commerce is estimated at between 10 and 15 percent per year up to 2016.[24]

Perhaps even more important, by one estimate, the Internet influences a staggering 50 percent of retail sales—including sales transacted online plus those made in stores but encouraged by online research. Some 97 percent of web-goers now use the Internet to research products before making purchases.[25] And a growing number of consumers armed with smartphones use them while shopping to find better deals and score price-matching offers. Thus, smart marketers are employing integrated multichannel strategies that use the Internet to drive sales to other marketing channels.

Online buyers differ from traditional offline consumers in their approaches to buying and their responses to marketing. In the online exchange process, customers initiate and control the contact. Traditional marketing targets a somewhat passive audience. In contrast, online marketing targets people who actively select which websites and shopping apps they will use and what marketing information they will receive about which products. Thus, online marketing requires new marketing approaches.

Business-to-Business (B2B)   Although the popular press has given the most attention to B2C websites, **business-to-business (B2B) online marketing** is also flourishing. Business-to-business marketers use B2B websites, email, online product catalogues, online trading networks, mobile apps, and other online resources to reach new business customers, sell to current customers, and serve customers more efficiently and effectively. Beyond simply selling their products and services online, companies can use the Internet to build stronger relationships with important business customers.

Business-to-consumer (B2C) online marketing
Businesses selling goods and services online to final consumers.

Business-to-business (B2B) online marketing
Businesses using online marketing to reach new business customers, serve current customers more effectively, and obtain buying efficiencies and better prices.

FIGURE 14.2 Online Marketing Domains

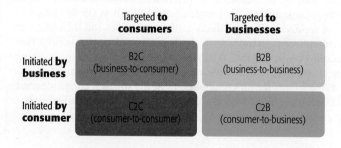

Most major B2B marketers now offer product information, customer purchasing, and customer-support services online. For example, corporate buyers can visit networking equipment and software maker Cisco Systems website (www.cisco.com), select detailed descriptions of Cisco's products and service solutions, request sales and service information, attend events and training seminars, view videos on a wide range of topics, have live chats with Cisco staff, and place orders. Some major companies conduct almost all of their business on the web. For example, Cisco Systems takes more than 80 percent of its orders over the Internet.

Consumer-to-Consumer (C2C)   Much **consumer-to-consumer (C2C) online marketing** and communication occurs on the web between interested parties over a wide range of products and subjects. In some cases, the Internet provides an excellent means by which consumers can buy or exchange goods or information directly with one another. For example, eBay and craigslist offer popular market spaces for displaying and selling almost anything, from art and antiques, computers and consumer electronics to cars. eBay's C2C online trading community of more than 100 million active users worldwide (that's more than the total populations of Great Britain, Egypt, or Turkey) transacted over US$62 billion in trades in 2010—more than $2000 every second.[26]

In other cases, C2C involves interchanges of information through Internet forums that appeal to specific special-interest groups. Such activities may be organized for commercial or noncommercial purposes. Web logs, or **blogs**, are online journals where people post their thoughts, usually on a narrow topic. Blogs can be about anything, from politics or baseball to haiku, car repair, or the latest television series. According to Nielsen, there are now more than 163 million blogs. Many bloggers use social networks such as Twitter and Facebook to promote their blogs, giving them huge reach. Such numbers give blogs—especially those with large and devoted followings—substantial influence.[27]

Many marketers are now tapping into the blogosphere as a medium for reaching carefully targeted consumers. For example, many companies have set up their own blogs. Sony has a PlayStation Blog, where fans can exchange views and submit and vote on ideas for improving PlayStation products. The Disney Parks Blog is a place to learn about and discuss all things Disney, including a Behind the Scenes area with posts about dance rehearsals, sneak peeks at new construction sites, interviews with employees, and more.[28]

Dell has a dozen or more blogs that facilitate "a direct exchange with Dell customers about the technology that connects us all." The blogs include Direct2Dell (the official Dell corporate blog), Dell TechCenter (IT brought into focus), DellShares (insights for investor relations), Health Care (about health care technology that connects us all), and Education (insights on using technology to enhance teaching, learning, and educational administration). Dell also has a very active and successful YouTube presence which it calls Dell Vlog, with 750 videos and more than 5 million video views. Dell bloggers often embed these YouTube videos into blog posts.

Companies can also advertise on existing blogs or influence content there. Alternatively, they might encourage "sponsored conversations" by influential bloggers. For example, IZEA's SocialSpark is an online marketplace that helps marketers and bloggers get together to create sponsored posts relevant to both the brand's customers and the blog's fans.[29]

Brands ranging from Bloomingdale's, British Airways, Coldwell Banker, and HP to Kraft Foods and Purex have used SocialSpark to place sponsored messages about their brands and promotions on blogs that reach targeted consumers. For instance, Purex used SocialSpark to help introduce its Purex Complete 3-in-1 Laundry Sheets via blogs such as Bargain Briana, Freaky Frugalite, 3 Kids and Us, and others that reach homemakers. The blog posts, written by the bloggers with IZEA's help, were clearly identified as being sponsored by Purex. They described the new Complete 3-in-1 Laundry Sheets product and analyzed in detail its convenience versus

Consumer-to-consumer (C2C) online marketing
Online exchanges of goods and information between final consumers.

Blog
Online journals where people post their thoughts, usually on a narrowly defined topic.

cost benefits—complete with photos and links to free sample offers from Purex. "I'm a mom with four kids and five pets and a husband who works with mail and newspapers all day," wrote enthusiastic Freaky Frugalite blogger Rebecca Mecomber. "I am basically doomed to a life of laundry. The amazing dudes at Purex recognized my plight; and when they offered to make my life EASIER, ... I grabbed at the chance."

As a marketing tool, blogs offer some advantages. They can offer a fresh, original, personal, and cheap way to enter into consumers' online conversations. However, the "blogosphere" is cluttered and difficult for marketers to control. Although companies can sometimes leverage blogs to engage in meaningful customer relationships, consumers remain largely in control.

Whether or not they actively participate in the blogosphere or other C2C conversations, companies should monitor and listen to them. C2C means that online buyers don't just consume product information—increasingly, they create it. As a result, *word of web* is joining *word of mouth* as an important buying influence. Marketers should use insights from consumer online conversations to improve their marketing programs.

Consumer-to-business (C2B)
online marketing
Online exchanges in which consumers search out sellers, learn about their offers, initiate purchases, and sometimes even drive transaction terms.

Consumer to Business (C2B) The final online marketing domain is **consumer-to-business (C2B) online marketing**. Thanks to the Internet, today's consumers are finding it easier to communicate with companies. Most companies now invite prospects and customers to send in suggestions and questions via company websites. Beyond this, rather than waiting for an invitation, consumers can search out sellers on the web, learn about their offers, initiate purchases, and give feedback. By using the web, consumers can even drive transactions with businesses, rather than the other way around. For example, by using Priceline.com, would-be buyers can bid for airline tickets, hotel rooms, rental cars, cruises, and vacation packages, leaving the sellers to decide whether to accept their offers.

Consumers can also use websites such as Gripevine.com, GetSatisfaction.com, and Complaints.com, to ask questions, offer suggestions, lodge complaints, or deliver compliments to companies. Co-founded in 2012 by Canadian musician Dave Carroll (creator of the viral video "United Breaks Guitars"), Gripevine.com provides an online forum for consumers to post complaints. Companies are then given the opportunity to resolve these complaints directly, before the consumer posting goes live to other users. If the company doesn't respond right away, consumers can go public with their complaint by inviting their social network friends and followers to provide support. The more times the gripe is viewed and the more people share it, the more the company will be motivated to work to resolve the issue. Companies such as Canada Post, Rogers, Coca-Cola, and Mazda Canada have used the site to handle customer complaints.[30]

Setting Up an Online Marketing Presence

In one way or another, most companies have now moved online. Companies conduct online marketing in any or all of the five ways shown in Figure 14.3: creating websites, placing ads and promotions online, setting up or participating in online social networks, sending email, or using mobile marketing.

Courtesy Gripevine

Exhibit 14.10 **C-to-B marketing:** Gripevine.com encourages consumers to "Be heard. Get results." by posting their complaints to the website that connects them directly with company decision makers.

FIGURE 14.3 Setting up for Online Marketing

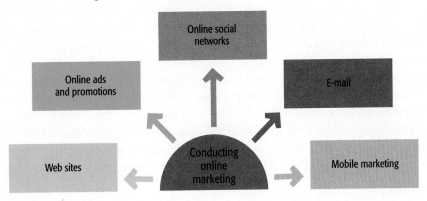

Creating a Website For most companies, the first step in conducting online marketing is to create a website. However, beyond simply creating a website, marketers must design an attractive site and find ways to get consumers to visit the site, stay around, and come back often.

Websites vary greatly in purpose and content. The most basic type is a **corporate (or brand) website**. These sites are designed to build customer goodwill, collect customer feedback, and supplement other sales channels, rather than to sell the company's products directly. They typically offer a rich variety of information and other features in an effort to answer customer questions, build closer customer relationships, and generate excitement about the company or the brand.

For example, you can't buy anything at Nestlé's colourful Wonka.com site, but you can learn about different Nestlé candy products, enter the latest contest, or hang around a while and doodle with Nerds, "paint your dreams" with the Wonka imaginator, or post Wonka-inspired digital art. Similarly, you can't buy anything at GE's corporate website. Instead, the site serves as a global public face for the huge company. It presents a massive amount of product, service, and company information to a diverse audience of customers, investors, journalists, and employees. It's both a B2B site and a portal for consumers, whether it's a Canadian consumer researching a microwave, an Indonesian business buyer checking into eco-friendly locomotives, or a German investor looking for shareholder information.

Other companies create a **marketing website**. These sites interact with consumers to move them closer to a direct purchase or other marketing outcome. For example, MINI USA operates a marketing website at www.miniusa.com. Once a potential customer clicks in, the carmaker wastes no time trying to turn the inquiry into a sale and then into a long-term relationship. The site offers a garage full of useful information and interactive selling features, including detailed and fun descriptions of current MINI models, tools for designing your very own MINI, information on dealer locations and services, and even tools for tracking your new MINI from factory to delivery.

Corporate (or brand) website
A website designed to build customer goodwill, collect customer feedback, and supplement other sales channels, rather than to sell the company's products directly.

Marketing website
A website that engages consumers in interactions that will move them closer to a direct purchase or other marketing outcome.

Exhibit 14.11 **Corporate websites:** You can't buy anything at Nestlé's colourful Wonka.com site, but you can learn about different Nestlé candy products or just hang around for a while and "feed your imagination."

© Mim Friday / Alamy

Creating a website is one thing; getting people to *visit* the site is another. To attract visitors, companies aggressively promote their websites in offline print and broadcast advertising and through ads and links on other sites. But today's web users are quick to abandon any website that doesn't measure up. The key is to create enough value and excitement to get consumers who come to the site to stick around and come back again. At the very least, a website should be easy to use, professional looking, and physically attractive. Ultimately, however, websites must also be *useful*. When it comes to web browsing and shopping, most people prefer substance over style, and function over flash. Thus, effective websites contain deep and useful information, interactive tools that help buyers find and evaluate products of interest, links to other related sites, changing promotional offers, and entertaining features that lend relevant excitement.

Placing Ads and Promotions Online   As consumers spend more and more time on the Internet, companies are shifting more of their marketing dollars to **online advertising** to build their brands or to attract visitors to their sites. The web has become a major advertising medium. According to the Interactive Advertising Bureau (IAB) of Canada, online advertising revenue exceeded $2.5 billion in 2011, and has continued to grow at a rate of about 10 percent per year. The IAB survey also revealed that mobile advertising revenues in Canada exceeded $52 million in 2010 and were projected to reach $82 million in 2011.[31] Of all forms of major mass-media advertising (TV, newspapers, Internet, radio, magazines, and out-of-home), online now ranks third in terms of spending by advertisers. Here, we discuss forms of online advertising and promotion and their future.

The major forms of online advertising are search-related ads, display ads, and online classifieds. Online display ads might appear anywhere on an Internet user's screen and are often related to the information being viewed. For instance, while browsing vacation packages on Travelocity.com, you might encounter a display ad offering a free upgrade on a rental car from Enterprise Rent-A-Car. Or while visiting the Yahoo! Finance site, a flashing E*TRADE ad might promise a free BlackBerry smartphone when you open a new account. Internet display ads have come a long way in recent years in terms of attracting and holding consumer attention. New *rich media* ads now incorporate animation, video, sound, and interactivity.

The largest form of online advertising is *search-related ads* (or *contextual advertising*), which accounted for 46 percent of all online advertising spending last year. In search advertising, text-based ads and links appear alongside search engine results on sites such as Yahoo! and Google. For example, search Google for "LCD TVs." At the top and side of the resulting search list, you'll see inconspicuous ads for ten or more advertisers, ranging from Samsung and Dell to Best Buy, Sears, Amazon.com, Walmart.com, and Nextag.com. Nearly all of Google's US$29 billion in revenues last year came from ad sales. Search is an always-on kind of medium. And in today's tight economy, the results are easily measured.[32]

A search advertiser buys search terms from the search site and pays only if consumers click through to its site. For instance, type "Coke" or "Coca-Cola" or even just "soft drinks" or "rewards" into your Google or Yahoo! search engine and almost without fail "My Coke Rewards" comes up as one of the top options. This is no coincidence. Coca-Cola supports its popular online loyalty program largely through search buys. The soft drink giant started first with traditional TV and print advertising but quickly learned that search was the most effective way to bring consumers to its www.mycokerewards.com website to register. Now, any of dozens of purchased search terms will return MyCokeRewards.com at or near the top of the search list.

Other forms of online promotions include content sponsorships and viral advertising. Using content sponsorships, companies gain name exposure on the Internet by sponsoring special content on various websites, such as news or financial information or

---

Online advertising

Advertising that appears while consumers are browsing the web, including display ads, search-related ads, online classifieds, and other forms.

special interest topics. For example, Alamo sponsors the "Vacation and Travel Planner and Guides" on Weather.com. And Marriott sponsors a "Summer to the Rescue!" microsite at Travelocity.com. Sponsorships are best placed in carefully targeted sites where they can offer relevant information or service to the audience.

Finally, online marketers use **viral marketing**, the Internet version of word-of-mouth marketing. Viral marketing involves creating a website, video, email, mobile message, advertisement, or other marketing event that is so infectious that customers will seek it out or pass it along to their friends. Because customers find and pass along the message or promotion, viral marketing can be very inexpensive. And when the information comes from a friend, the recipient is much more likely to view or read it.

For example, P&G's Old Spice brand created a viral sensation with its "Smell like a man, man" campaign featuring Isaiah Mustafa. The campaign consisted of TV ads and made-for-the-web videos designed to go viral on YouTube, Facebook, and other social media. The initial campaign garnered tens of millions of viral views. A second campaign, which consisted of nearly 200 videos in which Mustafa responded personally to digital inquiries from users including Ellen DeGeneres and Alyssa Milano, scored 21 million views in only its first week. It increased the brand's Facebook interaction by 800 percent and OldSpice.com traffic by 300 percent. After the introduction of these videos, Old Spice's YouTube page became the all-time-most-viewed channel on the site.[33]

Sometimes a well-made regular ad can go viral with the help of targeted "seeding." For example, Volkswagen's clever "The Force" Super Bowl ad, featuring a pint-sized Darth Vader using The Force to start a VW Passat, turned viral after a team at VW's ad agency seeded it to selected auto, pop culture, and Star Wars sites the week before the sporting event. By the time the ad aired during the Super Bowl, it had received more than 18 million hits online.

However, marketers usually have little control over where their viral messages end up. They can seed messages online, but that does little good unless the message itself strikes a chord with consumers. For example, why did the seeded VW Darth Vader ad explode virally? Because the sentimental ad appeals to parents—the car's target demographic—who want a responsible suburban family ride. And it appeals to the child inside the parent, who may have once been wowed by *Star Wars* and now wants a car with a little bit of magic. Says one creative director, "You hope that the creative is at a high enough mark where the seeds grow into mighty oaks. If they don't like it, it ain't gonna move. If they like it, it'll move a little bit; and if they love it, it's gonna move like a fast-burning fire through the Hollywood hills."[34]

Creating or Participating in Online Social Networks

As we discussed in Chapters 1 and 6, the popularity of the Internet has resulted in a rash of **online social networks** or *web communities*. Countless independent and commercial websites have arisen that give consumers online places to congregate, socialize, and exchange views and information. These days, it seems, almost everyone is buddying up on Facebook, checking in with Twitter, tuning into the day's hottest videos at YouTube, or checking out photos on Flickr. And, of course, wherever consumers congregate, marketers will surely follow. Most marketers are now riding the huge social networking wave.

> **Viral marketing**
> The Internet version of word-of-mouth marketing: a website, video, email message, or other marketing event that is so infectious that customers will seek it out or pass it along to friends.

> **Online social networks**
> Online communities where people congregate, socialize, and exchange views and information.

LUCASFILM/MCT/Newscom

Exhibit 14.12 Viral marketing: Sometimes a well-made regular ad can go viral. For example, Volkswagen's clever "The Force" Super Bowl ad, featuring a pint-sized Darth Vader, received more than 18 million online hits the week before it aired on TV during the Super Bowl.

Marketers can engage in online communities in two ways: They can participate in existing web communities or they can set up their own. Joining existing networks seems the easiest. Thus, most major brands—from Tim Hortons and Harley-Davidson to Nissan and Victoria's Secret—have created YouTube channels. GM and other companies have posted visual content on Flickr. Coca-Cola's Facebook page has 61 million likes.

Some of the major social networks are huge. The largest social network—Facebook—by itself commands 70 percent of all social network traffic. Forty-seven percent of the online population visits Facebook every day. That rivals the 55 percent who watch any TV channel and trounces the percentage listening to radio (37 percent) and reading newspapers (22 percent) daily. Early in 2013, Facebook announced it had reached its goal of over 1 billion active members.[35]

Although large online social networks such as Facebook, YouTube, and Twitter have grabbed most of the headlines, a new breed of more focused niche networks has emerged. These networks cater to the needs of smaller communities of like-minded people, making them ideal vehicles for marketers who want to target special interest groups. There's at least one social network for just about every interest or hobby.[36]

> Yub.com and kaboodle.com are for shopaholics, moms advise and commiserate at CafeMom.com, and PassportStamp.com is one of several sites for avid travellers. GoFISHn, a community of 4000 anglers, features maps that pinpoint where fish are biting and a photo gallery where members can show off their catches. At Dogster, 700 000 members set up profiles of their four-legged friends, read doggy diaries, or just give a dog a bone. On Ravelry.com, 1.4 million registered knitters, crocheters, designers, spinners, and dyers share information about yarn, patterns, methods, and tools.
>
> Some niche sites cater to the obscure. Passions Network is an "online dating niche social network" with 600 000 members and 145 groups for specific interests, including Star Trek fans, truckers, atheists, and people who are shy. Others reach more technical communities: More than a million scientists use ResearchGATE to coordinate research in areas such as artificial intelligence and cancer biology. And at myTransponder.com, pilots find work, students locate flight instructors, and trade-specific advertisers—such as aviation software maker ForeFlight—hone in on a hard-to-reach audience of more than 2000 people who love aviation. The myTransponder community aims to "make aviation more social."

But participating successfully in existing online social networks presents challenges. First, most companies are still experimenting with how to use them effectively, and results are hard to measure. Second, such online networks are largely user controlled. The company's goal is to make the brand a part of consumers' conversations and their lives. However, marketers can't simply muscle their way into consumers' online interactions—they need to earn the right to be there. A brand has no right to be there unless the conversation is already about that brand. Rather than intruding, marketers must learn to become a valued part of the online experience.

To avoid the mysteries and challenges of building a presence on existing online social networks, many companies have created their own targeted web communities. For example, on Nike's Nike+ website, more than 4 million runners with more than 375 million miles logged in 243 countries join together online to upload, track, and compare their performances. Nike

Dogster/Catster/Saymedia

Exhibit 14.13 Thousands of social networking sites have popped up to cater to specific interests, backgrounds, professions, and age groups. At Dogster, 700 000 members set up profiles of their four-legged friends, read doggy diaries, or just give a dog a bone.

plans eventually to have 15 percent or more of the world's 100 million runners actively participating in the Nike+ online community.[37]

Similarly, *Men's Health* magazine created a web community in conjunction with its Belly Off! program (http://my.menshealth.com/bellyoff). The magazine's long-running program helps readers develop a solid plan for exercise and diet over a set schedule. The community website incorporates user-generated content and offers workout and eating plans, reports on progress, how-to videos, and success stories. In all, the Belly Off! site serves a community of nearly 125 000 members who share similar weight-loss and fitness goals. Since 2001, the program has helped 400 000 people lose nearly 2 million pounds.[38]

Sending Email   **Email marketing** is an important and growing online marketing tool. Email is a much-used communication tool; by one estimate, the number of worldwide email accounts will grow from the current 2.9 billion to more than 3.8 billion over the next five years. Not surprisingly then, a recent study by the DMA found that 79 percent of all direct marketing campaigns employ email. US companies now spend more than US$660 million a year on email marketing, and this spending will grow by an estimated 13.6 percent annually through 2014.[39] However, click through rates have been trending downwards in Canada since 2010 and may be the result of subscriber fatigue. Despite this, 47 percent of Canadians voluntarily receive direct mail advertising from two to five retailers.[40]

When used properly, email can be the ultimate direct marketing medium. Most blue-chip marketers use it regularly and with great success. Email lets these marketers send highly targeted, tightly personalized, relationship-building messages. For example, the National Hockey League (NHL) sends hypertargeted e-newsletters to fans based on their team affiliations and locations. It sends 62 versions of the e-newsletter weekly—two for each of the 30 teams, tailored to fans in the United States and Canada, respectively, and two generic league e-newsletters for the two countries. Another NHL email campaign promoting the start of single-game ticket sales had 930 versions.[41]

But there's a dark side to the growing use of email marketing. The explosion of **spam**—unsolicited, unwanted commercial email messages that clog up our email boxes—has produced consumer irritation and frustration. According to one research company, spam now accounts for almost 75 percent of all email sent.[42] Email marketers walk a fine line between adding value for consumers and being intrusive.

To address these concerns, most legitimate marketers now practice *permission-based email marketing*, sending email pitches only to customers who "opt in." Many companies use configurable email systems that let customers choose what they want to get. Amazon.com targets opt-in customers with a limited number of helpful "we thought you'd like to know" messages based on their expressed preferences and previous purchases. Few customers object, and many actually welcome such promotional messages. Similarly,

Email marketing
Sending highly targeted, tightly personalized, relationship-building marketing messages via email.

Spam
Unsolicited, unwanted commercial email messages.

(left) iStockphoto International; (right) ICP/incamerastock/Alamy

Exhibit 14.14 Email can be an effective marketing tool. But there's a dark side—spam, unwanted commercial email that clogs up our inboxes and causes frustration.

StubHub redesigned its email system to make certain that its emails go only to consumers who actually *want* to receive them:[43]

> As a start-up almost a decade ago, online ticket merchant StubHub ran "batch-and-blast" email campaigns focused on building awareness. For years, sheer volume far outweighed email relevancy. But StubHub has now learned the value of carefully targeted, relevant email messages. It now lets customers opt in for email at registration, during purchases, and at sign-up modules throughout the StubHub site. Using opt-in customer data, StubHub targets designated consumer segments with ticket and event information closely aligned with their interests. Incorporating customer data produced immediate and stunning results. Email click-through rates quickly jumped 30 percent, and the company saw a 79 percent year-over-year increase in ticket sales despite having sent fewer emails. "The results speak for themselves," says a StubHub marketer. "These [new targeted campaigns] are driving 2500 percent more revenue per email than [our] average marketing campaigns."

Given its targeting effectiveness and low costs, email can be an outstanding marketing investment. According to the DMA, email marketing produces the greatest return on investment of all direct marketing media.[44]

Mobile marketing

Marketing to on-the-go consumers through mobile phones, smartphones, tablets, and other mobile communication devices.

Using Mobile Marketing   **Mobile marketing** features marketing messages and promotions delivered to on-the-go consumers through their mobile devices. Marketers use mobile marketing to reach and interact with customers anywhere, anytime during the buying and relationship-building processes. The widespread adoption of mobile devices and the surge in mobile web traffic have made mobile marketing a must for most brands.

With the recent proliferation of mobile phones, smartphone devices, and tablet PCs, more than 96 percent of North American households own some sort of mobile device. Canada's mobile subscriber base reached almost 21 million in 2012, of which approximately 55 percent used smartphones. They not only browse the mobile web but are also avid mobile application users. The mobile apps market is exploding: The Apple App Store offers 425 000 iPhone apps plus another 90 000 iPad apps. Android Market offers upwards of 150 000 apps.[45]

A recent study estimates that mobile advertising spending in the United States will grow from US$743 million in 2010 to US$2.5 billion by 2014. Marketers of all kinds—from Pepsi and Nordstrom to nonprofits such as the SPCA to the local bank or supermarket—are now integrating mobile platforms into their direct marketing. Sixty percent of mobile users currently click on a mobile ad at least once a week.[46]

A mobile marketing campaign might involve placing display ads, search ads, or videos on relevant mobile websites and online communities such as Facebook or YouTube. Today's rich media mobile ads can create substantial impact and involvement. For example, HBO ran engaging mobile ads for the season premiere of its *True Blood* series:[47]

> Imagine browsing through the Flixter app looking for a movie or browsing the Variety app, and the first touch of the screen turns into a bloody fingerprint. Touch again and get another fingerprint, then the blood pours down and takes over the screen and the activation pops up, a tap-to-watch-trailer call-to-action screen with a banner ad at the bottom. HBO's *True Blood* mobile ad campaign sent chills down consumers' spines and increased viewership 38 percent; 5.1 million viewers tuned in to view the season premiere.

A mobile marketing effort might be as simple as inviting people to text a number, such as when the Red Cross asked for Japan earthquake and tsunami relief donations (text "JAPAN" to 90999 to donate $10). It might involve texting promotions to consumers—anything from retailer announcements of discounts, brand coupons, and gift suggestions to mobile games and contests. Many marketers have also created their own mobile websites, optimized for specific phones and mobile service providers. Others have created useful or entertaining mobile apps to engage customers with their brands and help them shop (see Marketing@Work 14.2). For example, Nike gained unprecedented direct access to runners with a Nike+ GPS iPhone app for real-time tracking of runs and bike rides.

MARKETING@WORK 14.2

Mobile Marketing: Customers Come Calling

You're at the local Best Buy checking out portable GPS navigation systems. You've narrowed it down to the latest Garmin nüvi versus a less-expensive competing model, but you're not certain that Best Buy has the best prices. Also, you'd love to know how other consumers rate the two brands. No problem. Just pull out your smartphone and launch your Amazon Mobile app, which lets you browse the brands you're considering, read customer reviews, and compare prices of portable GPS systems sold by Amazon.com and its retail partners. The application even lets you snap a photo or scan a barcode from an item; Amazon.com employees will then search for a similar item available from Amazon. If Amazon.com offers a better deal, you can make the purchase directly from the application.

Welcome to the new world of mobile marketing. Today's new smartphones are changing the way we live—including the way we shop. And as they change how we shop, they also change how marketers sell to us.

A growing number of consumers—especially younger ones—are using their mobile phones as a "third screen" for texting, browsing the mobile web, watching videos and shows, and checking email. According to one expert, "the mobile phone ... is morphing into a content device, a kind of digital Swiss army knife with the capability of filling its owner's every spare minute with games, music, live and on-demand TV, web browsing, and, oh yes, advertising." Says the president of the Mobile Marketing Association, "It's only a matter of time before mobile is the 'first screen.'" According to another industry insider:

Mobile phones, iPads, and other mobile devices have quietly become the hottest new frontier for marketers, especially those targeting the coveted 18- to 34-year-old set. TV networks are prodding viewers to send text messages to vote for their favourite reality TV character. Wireless websites are lacing sports scores and news digests with banner ads for Lexus, Burger King, and Sheraton. A few companies are

even customizing 10-second video ads for short, TV-style episodes that are edging their way onto mobile phones. For advertisers, the young audience is just one selling point. Mobile gadgets are always-on, ever-present accessories. The fact that a phone or other device is tethered to an individual means that ads can be targeted. And users can respond instantly to time-sensitive offers. The mobile phone is very personal, and it's always with you.

Marketers large and small are weaving mobile marketing into their direct marketing mixes. For example, Walmart uses text message alerts to spread the news about sales; once you receive a text, you can click on links within the messages to go to the retailer's mobile website and check on details. Unilever phones out mobile coupons for Ragu pasta sauce, Dove body wash, Breyers ice cream, and its other brands: Just hold up your mobile phone at the checkout, and the cashier will scan the barcode off the screen. Tide's Stain Brain app helps customers find ways to remove stains. A

Sit or Squat app that directs people to nearby public restrooms opens with a splash page for Charmin bathroom tissue.

Beyond helping you buy, other mobile marketing applications provide helpful services, useful information, and entertainment. TD's iPhone banking app lets you check your balance, transfer funds, and even buy and sell stocks via a mobile phone. Zipcar's app lets members find and reserve a Zipcar, honk the horn (so they can find it in a crowd), and even lock and unlock the doors—all from their phones. REI's The Snow and Ski Report app gives ski slope information for locations throughout the United States and Canada, such as snow depth, snow conditions, and the number of open lifts. The app also links you to "Shop REI," for times "when you decide you can't live without a new set of K2 skis or a two-man Hoo-Doo tent."

For entertainment, carmaker Audi offers the Audi A4 Driving Challenge game for the iPhone, iPod, and iPod Touch, which features a tiny A4 that

Exhibit 14.15 **Mobile marketing:** Zipcar's iPhone app lets members find and book a Zipcar, honk the horn (so they can find it in a crowd), and even lock and unlock the doors—all from their iPhone.

Courtesy Zipcar

maneuvers its way through different driving courses—to steer, you tilt your phone right or left. Similarly, Audi's "Truth in 24" app lets you in on the action behind the notorious 24 Hours of Le Mans Audi auto race, including an iPhone game that "puts the excitement of LeMans racing right in the palm of your hand." For customers interested in reviewing Audi's cars, Audi A4 and A8 "Experience" apps let you explore these models interactively inside and out. Audi claims that such apps have been downloaded millions of times, drawing hundreds of thousands of visitors to its mobile websites.

One of the most effective mobile marketing applications is Kraft's iFood Assistant, which provides easy-to-prepare recipes for food shoppers on the go, how-to videos, a recipe box, and a built-in shopping list. iFood Assistant supplies advice on how to prepare some 7000 simple but satisfying meals—at three meals a day, that's almost 20 years worth of recipes. The iFood Assistant will even give you directions to local stores. Of course, most of the meals call for ingredients that just happen to be Kraft brands. The iFood Assistant app cost Kraft less than US$100 000 to create but has engaged millions of shoppers, providing great marketing opportunities for Kraft and its brands.

Many consumers are initially skeptical about mobile marketing. But they often change their minds if mobile marketers deliver value in the form of useful brand and shopping information, entertaining content, or discounted prices and coupons for their favourite products and services. Most mobile marketing efforts target only consumers who voluntarily opt in or who download apps. In the increasingly cluttered mobile marketing space, customers just won't do that unless they see real value in it. The challenge for marketers: Develop useful and engaging mobile marketing apps that make customers come calling.

Sources: Adapted extracts, quotes, and other information from Christine Birkner, "Mobile Marketing: This Time It's Different," *Marketing News*, January 30, 2011, pp. 17–18; Richard Westlund, "Mobile on Fast Forward," *Brandweek*, March 15, 2010, pp. M1–M5; Todd Wasserman, "I'm on the Phone!" *Adweek*, February 23, 2009, pp. 6–7; Alice Z. Cuneo, "Scramble for Content Drives Mobile," *Advertising Age*, October 24, 2005, p. S6; Jen Arnoff, "Wising Up to Smart Phones," *News & Observer* (Raleigh), April 22, 2009, p. 5B; Carol Angrisani, "Priced to Cell," *Supermarket News*, June 1, 2009, p. 28; Reena Jana, "Retailers Are Learning to Love Smartphones," *Businessweek*, October 26, 2009, p. 49; and www.usaa.com/inet/pages/usaa_mobile_main, accessed August 2011.

As with other forms of direct marketing, however, companies must use mobile marketing responsibly or risk angering already ad-weary consumers. "If you were interrupted every two minutes by advertising, not many people want that," says a mobile marketing expert. "The industry needs to work out smart and clever ways to engage people on mobiles." The key is to provide genuinely useful information and offers that will make consumers want to opt in or call in. One study found that 42 percent of cellphone users are open to mobile advertising if it's relevant.[48]

In all, online marketing continues to offer both great promise and many challenges for the future. Its most ardent apostles still envision a time when the Internet and online marketing will replace magazines, newspapers, and even stores as sources for information and buying. Most marketers, however, hold a more realistic view. To be sure, online marketing has become a successful business model for some companies—Internet firms such as Amazon.com, Facebook, and Google, as well as direct marketing companies such as GEICO and Netflix. However, for most companies, online marketing will remain just one important approach to the marketplace that works alongside other approaches in a fully integrated marketing mix.

Public Policy Issues in Direct Marketing LO4

Direct marketers and their customers usually enjoy mutually rewarding relationships. Occasionally, however, a darker side emerges. The aggressive and sometimes shady tactics of a few direct marketers can bother or harm consumers, giving the entire industry a black eye. Abuses range from simple excesses that irritate consumers to instances of unfair practices or even outright deception and fraud. The direct marketing industry has also faced growing privacy concerns, and online marketers must deal with Internet security issues.

Irritation, Unfairness, Deception, and Fraud Direct marketing excesses sometimes annoy or offend consumers. For example, most of us dislike direct-response TV commercials that are too loud, long, and insistent. Our mailboxes fill up with unwanted junk mail, our email boxes bulge with unwanted spam, and our computer screens flash with unwanted display or pop-up ads.

Beyond irritating consumers, some direct marketers have been accused of taking unfair advantage of impulsive or less-sophisticated buyers. Television shopping channels and program-long infomercials targeting television-addicted shoppers seem to be the worst culprits. They feature smooth-talking hosts, elaborately staged demonstrations, claims of drastic price reductions, "while they last" time limitations, and unequalled ease of purchase to inflame buyers who have low sales resistance. Worse yet, so-called heat merchants design mailers and write copy intended to mislead buyers.

Fraudulent schemes, such as investment scams or phony collections for charity, have also multiplied in recent years. *Internet fraud*, including identity theft and financial scams, has become a serious problem. The Canadian Anti-Fraud Centre (CAFC) collects information and criminal intelligence on mass marketing fraud (telemarketing), advanced-fee fraud letters (Nigerian letters), Internet fraud, and identity theft complaints from Canadian and American consumers and victims. It receives approximately 120 000 calls each year and 40 000 email messages each month. Some estimates put the total dollar value of fraud in Canada as high as $30 billion.[49]

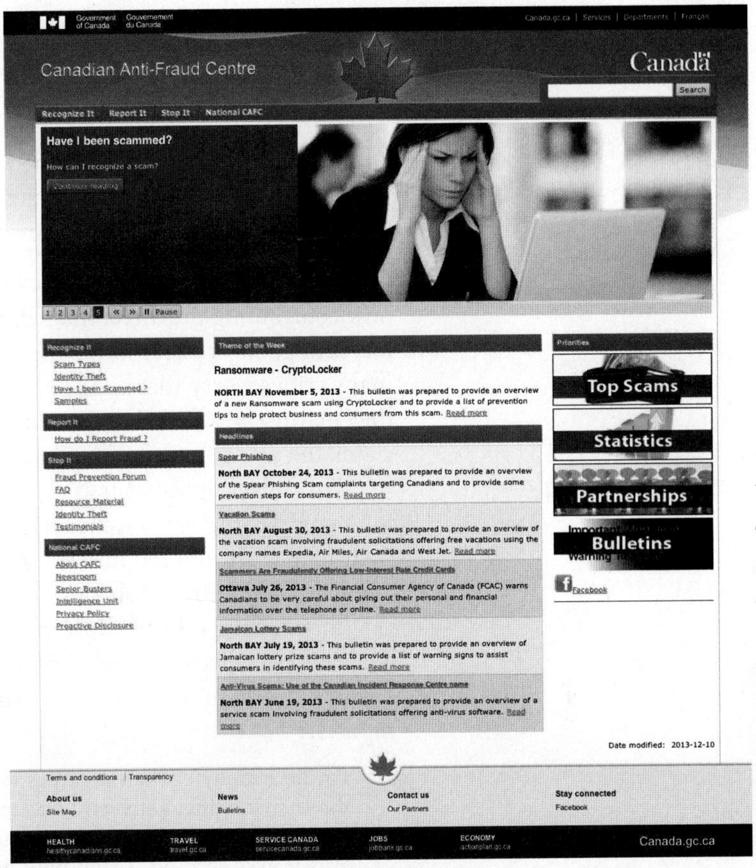

Exhibit 14.16 The Canadian Anti-Fraud Centre provides a wealth of information to help Canadians avoid online scams and telephone fraud.

Public Works and Government Services Canada

One common form of Internet fraud is *phishing*, a type of identity theft that uses deceptive emails and fraudulent websites to fool users into divulging their personal data. For example, consumers may receive an email, supposedly from their bank or credit card company, saying that their account's security has been compromised. The sender asks them to log onto a provided web address and confirm their account number, password, and perhaps even their social insurance number. If they follow the instructions, they are actually turning this sensitive information over to scam artists. Although many consumers are now aware of such schemes, phishing can be extremely costly to those caught in the net. It also damages the brand identities of legitimate online marketers who have worked to build user confidence in web and email transactions.

Many consumers also worry about *online security*. They fear that unscrupulous snoopers will eavesdrop on their online transactions, picking up personal information or intercepting credit and debit card numbers. Although online shopping has grown rapidly, 75 percent of participants in one survey said they still do not like sending personal or credit card information over the Internet.[50] Internet shoppers are also concerned about contracting annoying or harmful viruses, spyware, and other malware (malicious software).

Another Internet marketing concern is that of *access by vulnerable or unauthorized groups*. For example, marketers of adult-oriented materials and sites have found it difficult to restrict access by minors. A survey by *Consumer Reports* found 5 million US children under age 10 on Facebook, which supposedly allows no children under age 13 to have a profile. It found another 2.5 million 11- and 12-year-old Facebook subscribers. And it's not just Facebook. Young users are logging onto social networks such as Formspring, tweeting their location to the web, and making friends out of strangers on Disney and other games sites. Concerned lawmakers are currently debating legislation that would help better protect children online. Unfortunately, this requires the development of technology solutions, and as Facebook puts it, "That's not so easy."[51]

Consumer Privacy Invasion of privacy is perhaps the toughest public policy issue now confronting the direct marketing industry. Consumers often benefit from database marketing; they receive more offers that are closely matched to their interests. However, many critics worry that marketers may know *too* much about consumers' lives and that they may use this knowledge to take unfair advantage of consumers. At some point, they claim, the extensive use of databases intrudes on consumer privacy.

These days, it seems that almost every time consumers enter a sweepstakes; apply for a credit card; visit a website; or order products by mail, telephone, or the Internet, their names are entered into some company's already bulging database. Using sophisticated computer technologies, direct marketers can use these databases to "microtarget" their selling efforts. Most marketers have become highly skilled at collecting and analyzing detailed consumer information. Even the experts are sometimes surprised by how much marketers can learn. Consider this account by one *Advertising Age* reporter:[52]

> I'm no neophyte when it comes to targeting—not only do I work at *Ad Age*, but I cover direct marketing. Yet even I was taken aback when, as an experiment, we asked the database-marketing company to come up with a demographic and psychographic profile of me. Was it ever spot-on. Using only publicly available information, it concluded my date of birth, home phone number, and political-party affiliation. It gleaned that I was a college graduate, that I was married, and that one of my parents had passed away. It found that I have several bank, credit, and retail cards at "low-end" department stores. It knew not just how long I've lived at my house but how much it costs, how much it was worth, the type of mortgage that's on it, and—within a really close ballpark guess—how much is left to pay on it. It estimated my household income—again nearly perfectly—and determined that I am of British descent.
>
> But that was just the beginning. The company also nailed my psychographic profile. It correctly placed me into various groupings such as: someone who relies more on their own opinions than the recommendations of others when making a purchase; someone who is turned off by loud and aggressive advertising; someone who is family-oriented and has an interest in music, running, sports, computers, and is an avid concert-goer; someone who is never far from a web connection, generally peruses sports and general news updates; and someone who sees health as a core value. Scary? Certainly.*

Some consumers and policy makers worry that the ready availability of information may leave consumers open to abuse. For example, they ask, should web sellers be allowed to plant cookies in the browsers of consumers who visit their sites and use tracking information to target ads and other marketing efforts? Should credit card companies be allowed to make data on their millions of cardholders worldwide available to merchants who accept their cards? Or is it right for provinces to sell the names and addresses of driver's license holders, along with height, weight, and gender information, allowing apparel retailers to target tall or overweight people with special clothing offers?

---

*Adapted from information in Michael Bush, "My Life, Seen through the Eyes of Marketers," Advertising Age, April 26, 2010, http://adage.com/print/143479. Reprinted by permission from Advertising Age

A Need for Action   In response to these concerns, the Canadian government passed the Personal Information Protection and Electronic Documents Act (PIPEDA) in 2001. It came into full force in 2004. The act is based on four key principles:

- *Consumer knowledge and consent.* Consumers must know that information about them is being gathered and they must provide consent before firms can collect, use, or disclose consumers' personal information.

- *Limitations.* Firms can only collect and use information appropriate to the transaction being undertaken. For example, if a firm needs to mail you something, it can ask for your home address, but it may not request additional information unrelated to this task.

- *Accuracy.* Firms must be sure that the information they gather is recorded accurately. Firms must appoint a privacy officer to be responsible for this task.

- *Right to access.* Finally, individuals have the right to know what information is being held about them. They can also demand that errors in their personal information be corrected, and they may request that their personal information be withdrawn from a firm's database.

In 2009, the Government of Canada announced that it is delivering on its commitment to protect consumers and businesses from the most dangerous and damaging forms of spam. It proposed the Electronic Commerce Protection Act (ECPA), legislation designed to boost confidence in online commerce by protecting privacy and addressing the personal security concerns that are associated with spam, counterfeit websites, and spyware. The proposed legislation also amends PIPEDA, which covers online privacy in detail and contains many provisions relevant to email marketing.[53]

Many companies have responded to consumer privacy and security concerns with actions of their own. Still others are taking an industry-wide approach. For example, TRUSTe, a not-for-profit self-regulatory organization, works with many large corporate sponsors, including Microsoft, Yahoo!, AT&T, Facebook, Disney, and Apple, to audit privacy and security measures and help consumers navigate the web safely. According to the company's website, "TRUSTe believes that an environment of mutual trust and openness will help make and keep the Internet a free, comfortable, and richly diverse community for everyone." To reassure consumers, the company lends its TRUSTe privacy seal to websites that meet its privacy and security standards.[54]

The Canadian Marketing Association, which has 800 corporate members, also provides consumers with a wealth of information and smart shopping tips. It posts pages that help consumers know how to deal with online issues such as spam, identifying fraudulent offers, and protecting privacy. Ethical corporations are concerned with poor practices since they know that direct-marketing abuses will lead to increasingly negative consumer attitudes, lower response rates, and calls for more restrictive provincial and federal legislation. Most direct marketers want the same things that consumers want: honest and well-designed marketing offers targeted only at consumers who will appreciate and respond to them. Direct marketing is just too expensive to waste on consumers who don't want it.

Visitors, Fans, and Brand Advocates

Having an effective social media program for business purposes is a multidimensional pursuit. According to Greg Hounslow, WestJet's emerging media advisor, there are three things his team focuses on: "First, brand engagement, getting our message out on Twitter, Facebook, Instagram, YouTube—any place where our guests are hanging out. Second is customer service, providing answers to questions via our digital channels, including social media and email. Third, revenue generation: converting visits to purchases."

To accomplish these objectives, Hounslow works alongside one other teammate to plan and manage content—a tall order when you consider the size of WestJet's online community. Proactive messaging of new communications, reactive communications to guests who have used social media to reach you, and analytics that evaluate your effectiveness in using social media, according to Hounslow, together make up 90 percent of a given day. The other 10 percent is spread around supporting other areas of the organization in which there is overlap with social media.

Sophisticated web analytics assists in tracking the activity of WestJet's online community, as the really valuable information isn't how many fans, followers, hits, and visits exist, but how the life cycle of each contact point evolved. "When we first began using Twitter and Facebook, we would use those to promote seat sales. That would lead them to WestJet.com to actually perform the transaction. Our analytics have advanced to the point where we can actually see where visits originated, like Google or Facebook, and where they terminated, like at the completion of a transaction or prior."

Engaged members of an organization's digital community become brand advocates who often come to the aid of other visitors seeking information. Sometimes they'll even defend the brand where criticisms occur. WestJet vice-president of communications and community relations Richard Bartrem chuckles as he recalls some backlash to WestJet's 2012 and 2013 April Fool's videos posted to YouTube. "We did 'Kargo Kids' in 2012 and 'Furry Friends' in 2013 with tongue-in-cheek themes of how kids could be seated in our cargo bay and animals of all kinds would be admitted to general seating." While the vast majority of viewers got the joke, there were those that took offence. "So before we could even formulate a tactful response to these complaints, several members of the community jumped to our defence, using a particular tone that we, as an organization, wouldn't dream of."

QUESTIONS

1. How is WestJet using social media as a direct marketing platform?
2. Despite the availability to purchase Facebook fans and Twitter followers, WestJet has earned the members of its online community one at a time. Why would it resist taking such a shortcut toward building its membership?
3. As WestJet's online community continues to grow, what do you think are some of the challenges it faces?

REVIEWING THE CONCEPTS

1. Define direct marketing and discuss its benefits to customers and companies.

Direct marketing consists of direct connections with carefully targeted segments or individual consumers. Beyond brand and relationship building, direct marketers usually seek a direct, immediate, and measurable consumer response. Using detailed databases, direct marketers tailor their offers and communications to the needs of narrowly defined segments or even individual buyers.

For buyers, direct marketing is convenient, easy to use, and private. It gives buyers ready access to a wealth of products and information, at home and around the globe. Direct marketing is also immediate and interactive, allowing buyers to create exactly the configuration of information, products, or services they desire and then order them on the spot. For sellers, direct marketing is a powerful tool for building customer relationships. Using database marketing, today's marketers can target small groups or individual customers, tailor offers to individual needs, and promote these offers through personalized communications. It also offers them a low-cost, efficient alternative for reaching their markets. As a result of these advantages to both buyers and sellers, direct marketing has become the fastest-growing form of marketing.

2. Identify and discuss the major forms of direct marketing.

The main forms of direct marketing are *personal face-to-face selling, direct-mail marketing, catalogue marketing, telemarketing, DRTV marketing, kiosk marketing,* and *online marketing.* We discussed personal selling in the previous chapter.

Direct-mail marketing, the largest form of direct marketing, consists of the company sending an offer, announcement, reminder, or other item to a person at a specific address. Some marketers rely on catalogue marketing—selling through catalogues mailed to a select list of customers, made available in stores, or accessed on the web. Telemarketing consists of using the telephone to sell directly to consumers. DRTV marketing has two forms: direct-response advertising (or infomercials) and interactive television (iTV) marketing. Kiosks are information and ordering machines that direct marketers place in stores, airports, hotels, and other locations. Online marketing involves online channels that digitally link sellers with consumers.

3. Explain how companies have responded to the Internet and other powerful new technologies with online marketing strategies.

Online marketing is the fastest-growing form of direct marketing. The *Internet* enables consumers and companies to access and share huge amounts of information through their computers, smartphones, tablets, and other devices. In turn, the Internet has given marketers a whole new way to create value for customers and build customer relationships. It's hard to find a company today that doesn't have a substantial online marketing presence.

Online consumer buying continues to grow at a healthy rate. Most Canadian online users now use the Internet to shop. Perhaps more importantly, the Internet influences offline shopping as well. Thus, smart marketers are employing integrated multichannel strategies that use the Internet to drive sales to other marketing channels.

4. Discuss how companies go about conducting online marketing to profitably deliver more value to customers.

Companies of all types are now engaged in online marketing. The Internet gave birth to the *click-only companies* that operate online only. In addition, many traditional brick-and-mortar companies have added online marketing operations, transforming themselves into *click-and-mortar companies.* Many click-and-mortar companies are now having more online success than the click-only companies.

Companies can conduct online marketing in any or all of these five ways: creating websites, placing ads and promotions online, setting up or participating in web communities and online social networks, sending email, or using mobile marketing. The first step typically is to create a website. Beyond simply creating a site, however, companies must make their sites engaging, easy to use, and useful to attract visitors, hold them, and bring them back again.

Online marketers can use various forms of online advertising and promotion to build their Internet brands or attract visitors to their websites. Forms of online promotion include online display advertising, search-related advertising, content sponsorships, and *viral marketing,* the Internet version of word-of-mouth marketing. Online marketers can also participate in online social networks and other web communities, which take advantage of the *C2C* properties of the web. Finally, email and mobile marketing have become a fast-growing tool for both *B2C* and *B2B* marketers. Whatever direct marketing tools they use, marketers must work hard to integrate them into a cohesive marketing effort.

5. Overview the public policy and ethical issues presented by direct marketing.

Direct marketers and their customers usually enjoy mutually rewarding relationships. Sometimes, however, direct marketing presents a darker side. The aggressive and sometimes shady tactics of a few direct marketers can bother or harm consumers, giving the entire industry a black eye. Abuses range from simple excesses that irritate consumers to instances of unfair practices or even outright deception and fraud. The direct marketing industry has also faced growing concerns about invasion-of-privacy and Internet security issues. Such concerns call for strong action by marketers and public policy makers to curb direct marketing abuses. In the end, most direct marketers want the same things that consumers want: honest and well-designed marketing offers targeted only toward consumers who will appreciate and respond to them.

KEY TERMS

Blog 525
Business-to-business (B2B)
  online marketing 524
Business-to-consumer (B2C)
  online marketing 524
Catalogue marketing 519
Click-and-mortar
  companies 523
Click-only companies 523

Consumer-to-business (C2B)
  online marketing 526
Consumer-to-consumer (C2C)
  online marketing 525
Corporate (or brand) website 527
Customer database 516
Direct marketing 511
Direct-mail marketing 517
Direct-response television marketing 521

Email marketing 531
Internet 523
Marketing website 527
Mobile marketing 532
Online advertising 528
Online marketing 522
Online social networks 529
Spam 531
Viral marketing 529

TALK ABOUT MARKETING

1. Collect all the direct mail that arrives at your home during a one-week period. Look through the collection and identify the "call to action" in each piece. If the direct-mail piece was addressed to you by name, it means that you are in the sending organization's customer database. Do you remember how you got there? Some pieces of direct mail are not addressed, but are delivered by Canada Post as "unaddressed ad mail." If you have any pieces of unaddressed ad mail in your collection, why do you think the marketers chose to deliver that particular piece to your mailbox?

2. Think about the last advertising message you received on your mobile phone. Who was the advertiser, and what was the promotion? Did you take advantage of the offer? What kinds of marketing promotions or offers would you be willing to receive on your phone?

3. Choose your favourite news or information website and explore its various sections. What forms of online advertising are sold on the site?

4. In a small group, design and deliver a direct-response television ad (DRTV) for a national brand not normally associated with this type of promotion, such as an athletic shoe, automobile, or food product.

5. Describe the differences between a B2B marketer such as Cisco Systems and a B2C marketer such as La Senza. Dell is a company that markets its products both to businesses and consumers. How does its website serve these two separate markets? In which ways (if any) does Dell also incorporate C2C or C2B marketing?

6. Find articles about two data security breaches in the news. How did the breaches occur and who is potentially affected by them?

THINK LIKE A MARKETING MANAGER

Maestro S.V.P. is an upscale seafood restaurant and oyster bar on trendy St. Laurent Boulevard in Montreal. The clientele of the restaurant is mainly tourists, especially during the summer season, but there are also many regular customers who return again and again because they enjoy the food and the atmosphere, and because they have an oyster shell with their name on it installed on the oyster wall of fame. The chef is famous for his unique and flavourful seafood sauces, and customers often ask whether they can purchase these sauces to take home. Responding to market demand, the owner has recently begun packaging and retailing a line of Maestro sauces, such as Havane sauce for tuna, and Porto & Raspberry sauce, which is excellent with mussels. So far, sauces have been sold only from within the restaurant. Lately, the owner has been wondering which forms of Internet marketing might help grow her business.

QUESTIONS

1. If Maestro began the task of creating a customer database, what forms of direct marketing would you recommend it employ to promote its business?

2. Visit the restaurant's website at MaestroSVP.com. Would you recommend that the owner include e-commerce capabilities on the site? Explain why or why not.

3. Maestro is a small business and doesn't have a budget for mass-media advertising. Investigate possible opportunities for inexpensive online advertising for Maestro.

4. How is Maestro using social media to promote its business? Be specific.—Are there other social media sites that you would recommend it participate in that it is not currently using, and, if so, how should they be used? Are there any niche social network sites that would be appropriate for Maestro?

MARKETING ETHICS

The World Wide Web is often referred to as the Wild West. Unlike advertising, which openly identifies the sponsor, much product and brand information seen on the Internet does not reveal sponsorship. You may read about a product in a blog, see it in a YouTube video, or follow it on Twitter, often unaware that the person was paid or provided free merchandise or goodies to say positive things. These undercover company shills are difficult to detect. Kmart, Sony Pictures, HP, and other marketers use companies like IZEA to develop sponsored conversations using its network of bloggers. Sponsored conversations generated by IZEA disclose sponsorships, but many others do not. However, that could be changing soon. The US Federal Trade Commission (FTC) recently updated its endorsement guidelines requiring bloggers to disclose sponsorships. Violators could be slapped with a fine of US$11 000 per violation, but with almost 30 million bloggers out there—80 percent of whom occasionally or frequently post product or brand reviews—it will be difficult, if not impossible, to enforce this rule. Even with the new rules, sponsored conversations are growing rapidly.

QUESTIONS

1. Find examples of product information posted in blogs. Did the blogger indicate in the post that he or she was paid or provided with free products? Should the government enact laws to require bloggers and others on the Internet to disclose sponsorship from marketers? Explain.

2. Review the FTC's revised guidelines on endorsements and testimonials in advertising (www.ftc.gov/os/2009/10/091005revisedendorsementguides.pdf) and visit the Word of Mouth Marketing Association's website (http://womma.org/main) and the website of a social marketing company, such as http://izea.com. Write a report on how marketers can effectively use sponsored conversations within the FTC's guidelines.

MARKETING TECHNOLOGY

Your smartphone might someday be the only thing you'll need for locking your door, starting a car, paying for purchases, or even simply paying your friend the $20 you owe him. Mobile technologies allow users to do almost anything remotely and allow marketers to target services and promotions directly to consumers based on where they are. You may have noticed some Starbucks customers just wave their phones in front of a scanner—

no wallet, cash, or card required. Those customers may have gotten discount offers that lured them to Starbucks because their phone tipped the marketer off that they were nearby.

QUESTIONS

1. What mobile applications currently exist and what's on the horizon? How many of these applications do you or someone you know use?

2. What are the barriers to adoption of mobile applications?

MARKETING BY THE NUMBERS

Marketers know that Facebook is a force to be reckoned with, but until now they have not been able to measure that force and compare it to traditional media. Whereas traditional media have established metrics, such as ratings, to measure what marketers are getting for their money, an entirely new set of metrics—such as *click-through rates* and *impressions*—has evolved for online media. Unfortunately, the two metrics are not comparable. ComScore and Nielsen are two companies attempting to rectify that situation by developing a rating system based on *gross rating points* to show the power of Facebook as a marketing tool.

QUESTIONS

1. Research marketing expenditure trends in social media marketing as well as other forms of online advertising. Compare these trends with traditional advertising media expenditures. Develop a presentation illustrating those trends.

2. Visit www.comScore.com and www.Nielsen.com to learn more about the measures these companies have developed for measuring the marketing exposure of brands on Facebook. How do these metrics differ from those that have been used with regard to measuring online advertising impact?

VIDEO CASE

Home Shopping Network

Long ago, television marketing was associated with low-quality commercials broadcast in the wee hours of the morning that offered obscure merchandise. But Home Shopping Network (HSN) has played an instrumental role in making television shopping a legitimate outlet. Around the clock, top-quality programming featuring name-brand merchandise is now the norm.

But just like any retailer, HSN has had its share of challenges. This video illustrates how HSN has focused on principles of direct marketing in order to overcome these challenges and form strong customer relationships.

As market conditions continue to shift, HSN explores new ways to form and strengthen direct relationships with customers.

After viewing the video featuring HSN, answer the following questions:

1. What are the different ways that HSN engages in direct marketing?

2. What advantages does HSN specifically have over brick-and-mortar retailers?

3. What recommendations would you suggest for how HSN could make better use of its role as a direct marketer?

EBAY: FIXING AN ONLINE MARKETING PIONEER

Pop quiz: Name the high-tech company that got its start in someone's living room, grew from zero revenue to a multi-billion-dollar corporation in less than a decade, and pioneered the model for an entire industry to follow. If you're thinking that the list of companies that fit this description is a mile long, you're right. But in this case, we're talking about eBay.

eBay is one of the biggest web success stories in the history of, well, the World Wide Web. But sooner or later, every high-growth company hits a speed bump and experiences growing pains. After amazing growth for its first 15 years, eBay has hit that speed bump. Current CEO John Donahoe is faced with the difficult challenge of putting eBay back on the superhighway to prosperity.

eBay started in 1995 as an auction house. Unlike most dot-coms, eBay was based on a model that produced profits, not just revenue. Whenever a user posted an item for auction, eBay collected a fee. The more products that went up for auction, the more money eBay made. eBay has tinkered with its fee structure over the years, but the basic idea has remained the same. The online auction formula took off like wildfire and eBay dominated the industry. eBay's revenue, stock price, profits, and number of employees soared. By the year 2000, eBay was the number one e-commerce site in the world by sales revenue.

THE CHANGING FACE OF A GROWING COMPANY

With explosive growth, change is inevitable. According to many industry observers, the face of eBay slowly began to change based on two dynamics. The first was expansion. eBay's list of categories and subcategories grew into the hundreds. The e-commerce giant also added international sites for different countries. And it began to launch subsites (such as eBay Motors) and to acquire other dot-coms relevant to its business. Such acquisitions ultimately included Half.com, PayPal, StubHub, Shopping.com, and Skype.

The second dynamic driving change in eBay was the addition of fixed-price selling options. During its early years, open auction was the only option buyers and sellers had. Sellers put up an item for sale with a designated starting price for a period of one to ten days and sold to the highest bidder. In 1999, eBay augmented that core method with a fixed-price, "Buy It Now" option. Two years later, it took that concept much further with the introduction of eBay stores. With eBay stores, a seller could create an online "storefront" within eBay. The feature allowed sellers to post items more quickly, making it easier for high-volume sellers to do business. It also gave fixed-price options with no bidding whatsoever and virtually eliminated the sales period for an item.

Both of these dynamics continued to fuel eBay's steady, strong growth for years. For 2006, US$52.5 billion worth of goods were sold on eBay. Those sales were generated by 222 million users posting 610 million new listings. eBay's take was US$5.97 billion in revenue and US$1.12 billion in net income. These numbers were tremendous for a company that had only been doing business for a single decade. They also marked a zenith for the company.

In 2007, however, eBay began to show signs of slowing down. In early 2008, John Donahoe took over as CEO, replacing Meg Whitman, the mastermind behind the company's success for 10 of its 12 years. Donahoe acknowledged that eBay faced issues, including the fact that it had been resting on its laurels. "We were the biggest and the best. eBay has a storied past. But frankly, it's a past we've held onto too much." Consumer behaviour was shifting. When eBay was new, many users were thrilled by the uncertainty of bidding against other buyers for a bargain. But as online shopping went mainstream, more people opted for the tried-and-true method of finding the best price on a new piece of merchandise and buying it from a reputable retailer.

The consumer shift to buying new products at fixed prices was evident in the growth experienced by online retailers such as Amazon.com, Buy.com, and Walmart.com, companies that eBay had previously refused to recognize as competitors. Amazon had passed eBay as the largest online retailer a number of years earlier by continuing to expand its selection of fixed-price items, often with free shipping.

Shortly after taking over from Whitman, Donahoe said at a public event, "We need to redo our playbook, we need to redo it fast, and we need to take bold actions." He unveiled the details of a new strategy for eBay's turnaround, one that focused on changing the identity of the eBay marketplace. Donahoe specified that the new strategy would focus on building the site's business in the secondary market, the US$500-billion-a-year slice of retail that included out-of-season and over-stock items as well as the used and antique items for which eBay had always been known.

Core to Donahoe's strategy, eBay changed its fee structure, search-engine algorithm, and feedback rating system in ways that favoured highly rated sellers, fixed-price listings, and sellers offering free shipping. Donahoe claimed that all these tactics helped align eBay's interests with those of its best sellers. But the moves also created tension among two groups of sellers that had been growing apart for years. The traditional eBay seller sold typical flea market wares including used, vintage, antique, and homemade items. These sellers typically included mom-and-pop operations that dealt in low to moderate volumes. These merchants gave eBay its start and continued to be a sizable portion of eBay's business. Such sellers were a sharp contrast to eBay's high-volume PowerSellers. These sellers were often major operations employing dozens if not hundreds of people. They most often sold new, refurbished, or overstock items in bulk. High-volume sellers sold tens of thousands, hundreds of thousands, and even millions of items on eBay every year.

In light of the site's changes, the traditional eBay sellers cried foul, asserting that the company's new strategy made it harder for them to do business profitably while favouring the high-volume sellers. Donahoe responded that the managers at eBay knew there would be growing pains, but that the transformation was essential. "We have to create a marketplace where we're helping our sellers give our buyers what they want," he said. He added that he strongly believed that buyers wanted a fixed price, quick service, and free shipping. For eBay to not focus on market demands would ultimately be bad for everyone.

FROM BAD TO WORSE

All that may have ended well had eBay's numbers turned around. Instead, eBay's financials slid badly. In the last quarter of 2008, typically eBay's strongest period with holiday shopping, eBay experienced its first ever quarterly decline. For its core marketplace, revenue was down 16 percent from the previous year, while net income dropped a whopping 31 percent. It would have been very easy for Donahoe and his team to blame the company's woes on the economic downturn. But as eBay experienced a drop in traffic, competitors Amazon.com and Walmart.com enjoyed increases.

Still, Donahoe moved forward with even greater resolve. "The 'buyer beware' experience has run its course,"

he said. He reiterated eBay's plans to focus on the secondary market. "We're going to focus where we can win," Donahoe said, indicating that the shift away from new merchandise where its biggest competitors dominated would give eBay a strong point of differentiation. "We have begun significant change. The eBay you knew is not the eBay we are, or the eBay we will become." As these changes began to take root, eBay's financials began to stabilize. But with total e-commerce growth in the low double digits and the likes of Amazon.com growing considerably faster, it was clear that eBay would continue to lag behind for the foreseeable future.

eBay could take some solace in the strength of its non-marketplace division, PayPal. PayPal had been growing at a considerably faster rate than the core eBay site for a number of years. As the demand for secure online payment services exploded, PayPal was optimally poised as the market leader to take advantage. In fact, as eBay executives forecasted 5 to 7 percent growth for its core marketplace through 2013, it was estimated that PayPal's revenue would double to a whopping US$7 billion. Based on those growth dynamics, PayPal would shortly account for more than half of eBay's corporate revenues.

A NEW POINT OF DIFFERENTIATION

Even with the strength of PayPal, eBay is not turning its back on the eBay brand. As Donahoe's initial turnaround strategy plays out, eBay is working to stimulate stronger marketplace growth. Under Donahoe's direction, eBay's focus is, and will continue to be, on enhancing the shopping experience. To this end, the e-commerce pioneer is once again braving new frontiers, only this time it is capitalizing on the explosive growth of mobile communications.

eBay is exploring several initiatives for making shopping on mobile devices easier and more fulfilling. eBay's RedLaser bar-code scanning tool lets users scan just about any product on a shelf for immediate comparison with online sources. It even suggests nearby stores that have the product in stock. Soon, eBay will enable shoppers to tap into the same shopping tools by merely taking a photo of a product, on or off the shelf. If you like the shoes your friend is wearing, you can buy them and have them on the way to you within seconds.

The idea is to engage consumers even when they aren't thinking about buying something. To this end, eBay is also creating some big app innovations. To make its array of product categories less daunting, eBay has launched specialty apps such as eBay Fashion. This app emphasizes browsing over buying, featuring a style guide and a shared virtual closet where users can mix, match, and model different outfits with friends. But even though the focus is on browsing, eBay knows that browsers will buy. Users spend an average of 10 minutes browsing on the eBay Fashion app—40 percent longer than they spend on the main eBay app. In the Fashion app's first year, eBay mobile fashion sales tripled.

eBay hopes to carry the niche app success into other areas, including automotive, electronics, and home-and-garden sales. And although Amazon is still way ahead in terms of total sales and sales growth, eBay now has the jump in mobile commerce. Last year, eBay sold almost US$2 billion worth of goods via smartphones and tablets, more than double its total from the year before. Amazon claims just over US$1 billion in mobile sales, including Kindle e-books. Given that expert projections suggest that mobile commerce will top US$119 billion by 2015, being on top of this trend is a great place to be.

With the developments in eBay's marketplace, mobile commerce, and online payments, Donahoe's confidence is becoming more credible. "We have gone from turnaround to offensive," the CEO states. "Our purpose is to bring consumers the best experience to find what they want, how they want, and when they want it, whether

it's on eBay or otherwise." As -e-commerce continues to evolve at a blistering pace, only time will tell if Donahoe's strategy will pay off.

Sources: Dan Macsai, "eBay Dials M for Makeover," *Fast Company*, November 16, 2010; Geoffrey Fowler, "Auctions Fade in eBay's Bid for Growth," *Wall Street Journal*, May 26, 2009, p. A1; Peter Burrows, "eBay Outlines Three-Year Revival Plan," *Businessweek*, March 12, 2009; Max Colchester and Ruth Bender, "eBay CEO Continues to Seek Acquisitions," *Wall Street Journal*, May 23, 2011 accessed at www.wsj.com.

QUESTIONS FOR DISCUSSION

1. Analyze the marketing environment and the forces shaping eBay's business over the years. What conclusions can you draw?

2. How has the change in the nature of eBay sellers affected the creation of value for buyers?

3. Do you agree or disagree with CEO Donahoe that eBay's turnaround strategy is the best way to go?

4. Based on eBay's current developments with PayPal and mobile apps, what do you predict the outcome for the company will be in five years?

MyMarketingLab

MyMarketingLab is an online homework and tutorial system that puts you in control of your own learning with study and practice tools directly correlated to this chapter's content.

1

General Company Information: WestJet

Introduction

WestJet is a publicly traded company founded and headquartered in Calgary, Alberta. Embodying the western entrepreneurial spirit, the airline was the vision of Clive Beddoe and a team of partners who financed the purchase of three planes and began flying between Calgary, Edmonton, Kelowna, Abbotsford, and Winnipeg in 1996. Within two years WestJet had added Saskatoon, Regina, and Vancouver to its growing Western Canada network and quickly started munching into Canada's scheduled passenger air transport market, transforming it from the Air Canada/Canadian Airlines duopoly into a true oligopoly. By 1999 it was clear that the airline was here to stay and it went public, instantly raising $25 million through its initial public offering.

Despite the years that have passed, the accolades and awards received, the addition of a vacation package business and a regional subsidiary, yesterday's founders and today's WestJetters alike would no doubt agree that what gave them initial success is what has sustained that success throughout its history. Clear and judicious cost management processes coupled with a customer service experience rooted in the golden rule have been the cornerstones to consistent profitability.

The growth curve has been phenomenal in an industry fraught with paper-thin margins and repeated business failures. Between 1996 and 2013, WestJet has grown from a fleet of 3 to 123 planes, 5 to 87 destinations, and 225 to 9000 employees. Along the way it has been the media darling of a highly criticized industry, consistently accumulating notable awards as not only Canada's favourite airline, but also its best employer. Yet somehow the little airline that could maintains its folksy, grounded charm. And despite an extraordinarily tight-fisted approach to cost management, it is a company rich with a culture of employee engagement, where 85 percent of WestJetters are invested, literally, in the corporate stock option package.

While the "owners care" advertising campaign became a tremendously successful brand builder in the mid-2000s, it still persists as WestJet's unofficial mission, position, tag line, and value proposition all rolled into one. The logic was quite simple: Share ownership and profits with employees and they'll be motivated to create positive travel experiences for guests. Yet to suggest WestJetters are motivated solely by monetary reward would be a clear misrepresentation of their psyche. "It's in our DNA," explains Bob Cummings, executive vice-president of sales, marketing, and guest experience, referring to the fun-loving, genuinely caring type of individual WestJet strives to place with every hire.

Development of WestJet

WestJet's first major phase of growth occurred between 1998 and 2000. At this time it became clear that growth potential existed and the product created by Beddoe and his team was being embraced by an increasingly price-sensitive market. WestJet purchased more Boeing 737s and began its invasion of Eastern Canada, using the airport in Hamilton, Ontario, as its anchor in the east to avoid cost-prohibitive access to Toronto's

Pearson International Airport. It wasn't perfect, but like the decision to penetrate British Columbia's lower mainland through Abbotsford Airport (rather than Vancouver International), the cost savings could be passed on to the customer.

Air Canada's takeover of rival Canadian Airlines in 2000 could easily have doomed WestJet, but instead the company forged ahead relentlessly through the early to mid-2000s, adding Grande Prairie, Prince George, Comox, and Fort McMurray to the west side of its route map while dotting the east with Ottawa, Sudbury, Sault Ste. Marie, London, Windsor, Montreal, Moncton, Halifax, St. John's, and Gander. The route map had transformed as WestJet continued to beat the odds in its assault on the Canadian travel industry. In 2003, it even got its first taste of international exposure through an alliance with Canadian tour operator Air Transat, which used WestJet planes and crew to fly into vacation destinations in Mexico and the Caribbean.

Clearly now a threat to Air Canada, things got ugly in 2004 when the market leader filed a lawsuit against WestJet, accusing it of accessing confidential and strategically sensitive information to gain a business advantage. WestJet countersued, alleging Air Canada had used illegal measures to obtain proof that it had been spying on Air Canada. A very public PR battle ensued for two years before WestJet apologized and admitted wrongdoing, ultimately settling on paying Air Canada's $5.5 million in legal fees and making a total donation of $10 million to children's charities.

With its first major brush with adversity behind it, WestJet continued its growth pattern. It had finally seen a positive break-even point in flying into Toronto's Pearson International and summarily anointed it as its logical eastern hub. Despite an already crowded market space and competitive volatility, WestJet expanded its route map southward, adding several American cities, including New York, Los Angeles, Phoenix, Orlando, Las Vegas, and Hawaii. By 2006 it had achieved another milestone, adding the Bahamas to its network, marking its first visit outside Canada or the United States.

Additional Canadian, American, Mexican, and Caribbean markets have been added (and some deleted) since the mid-2000s, and certainly WestJet's domestic profile has increased rapidly. International growth beyond the northern half of the Western hemisphere, however, is stifled due to the cruising range of the Boeing 737 aircraft and WestJet's staunch commitment to it. While economies of scale created by the use of one type of aircraft has been a significant component to WestJet's success, it has proven to be an inevitable non-starter for any vision of expansion into lucrative overseas markets.

Strategic Direction

As emerging economies like China, India, Southeast Asia, and Brazil present irresistibly attractive destinations for an airline, which claims a vision of being "one of the five most successful international airlines in the world" by 2016, WestJet would appear to be on a methodical trajectory toward transoceanic flights at some point in the next five years. While increasing and protecting market share in Canada will always be the priority, there are three key strategies in play that support both domestic dominance as well as global penetration: rapid development of network partnerships, development of the business segment, and the launch of WestJet Encore.

Airline Partnerships

Interline agreements and code sharing allow airlines to connect their passengers with networks served by other airlines—and vice versa. For WestJet, this has not only created new revenues, but it has been a means of feeling out the international market. It has exposed the brand to the global industry, earned it competitive and market experience, and aligned it with key international partners. The initiative has provided valuable learning, global brand exposure, and new revenue streams without taking on the incredibly high capital burden of long-range aircraft.

By mid-2013, WestJet had consummated partnerships with 33 other airlines, including code shares with leading global brands such as British Airways, Cathay Pacific, and American Airlines, and interline agreements with the likes of Air China, Air India, Aeromexico, Qantas, Emirates, and Qatar Airways. The agreements aren't restricted to big brands in faraway places, however, as WestJet has also sealed deals with potential Canadian competitors like Canadian North.

Business Segment

WestJet has estimated a large market exists that is willing to embrace a value proposal that provides business-travel-related amenities, highlighted by leg space and booking flexibility, in exchange for an incremental increase in air fare. This "Plus Seating" concept, along with the creation of "Flex" and "Econo" bundles, has deepened WestJet's product line, but more importantly it has begun to reposition the company within the business segment as an alternative to Air Canada.

Going forward, the business segment is expected to help fill established domestic/transborder flights while deriving new revenue, fill the new WestJet Encore routes, and feed into WestJet's international partnerships.

While the leisure market has been the focus of WestJet's marketing efforts to date, the company has realized the opportunity of the business segment and is reacting in kind.

WestJet Encore

WestJet Encore represents various milestones for the parent company. First, the WestJet value proposition of creating a remarkable experience will be delivered to several new geographic segments. Second, for the first time since WestJet's inception in 1996 the company will depart from the one-plane business model, adding Bombardier's Q400 to its fleet of Boeing 737s. It is expected that WestJet will be able to secure similar economies of scale using the twin props for its Encore line as it has done with the 737s for the parent brand. Third, Encore is not only expected to satisfy the needs of guests needing to travel in and out of Canada's small to medium markets, it is also expected that Encore will link guests in those areas to the rest of WestJet's world.

WestJet Encore will be a mirror image of its parent company in every aspect aside from the aircraft itself. Concentration on the guest experience supported by employee engagement, cost management, and operational efficiency will be keys to transitioning the brand across to the regional airline.

Sustaining Brand Despite Growth

Perhaps the biggest challenge facing WestJet in the face of its aggressive growth pursuits is keeping its brand intact. Is it possible that "the little airline who could" can be viewed in the same manner if and when it overtakes Air Canada for market share domestically, and is no longer the underdog?

It will be vital that the culture of care at WestJet is maintained and protected at all costs, and yet doing so will become increasingly challenging as the company grows beyond 10 000 employees and stretches is network to new territories, markets, and cultures. Thus, no matter how big it gets and no matter how fast it grows, WestJet's people are the link to assuring that the powerful brand is protected.

Questions

1. What are WestJet's key strategies for growth? How would you rank them in order of importance toward reaching the company's vision?

2. Using your highest-ranking growth strategy (from the previous question), elaborate on how you would develop the strategy further.

3. How would you describe WestJet's brand? What strategies would you recommend for WestJet to ensure that this brand is sustained regardless of how large it grows?

2

The Marketing Plan

Introduction

As a marketer, you'll need a good marketing plan to provide direction and focus for your brand, product, or company. With a detailed plan, any business will be better prepared to launch a new product or build sales for existing products. Not-for-profit organizations also use marketing plans to guide their fundraising and outreach efforts. Even government agencies put together marketing plans for initiatives such as building public awareness of proper nutrition and stimulating area tourism.

The Purpose and Content of a Marketing Plan

Unlike a business plan, which offers a broad overview of the entire organization's mission, objectives, strategy, and resource allocation, a marketing plan has a more limited scope. It serves to document how the organization's strategic objectives will be achieved through specific marketing strategies and tactics, with the customer as the starting point. It is also linked to the plans of other departments within the organization. Suppose a marketing plan calls for selling 200 000 units annually. The production department must gear up to make that many units; the finance department must arrange funding to cover the expenses; the human resources department must be ready to hire and train staff; and so on. Without the appropriate level of organizational support and resources, no marketing plan can succeed.

Although the exact length and layout will vary from company to company, a marketing plan usually contains the sections described in Chapter 2. Smaller businesses may create shorter or less formal marketing plans, whereas corporations frequently require highly structured marketing plans. To guide implementation effectively, every part of the plan must be described in considerable detail. Sometimes a company will post its marketing plan on an internal website, which allows managers and employees in different locations to consult specific sections and collaborate on additions or changes.

The Role of Research

Marketing plans are not created in a vacuum. To develop successful strategies and action programs, marketers need up-to-date information about the environment, the competition, and the market segments to be served. Often, analysis of internal data is the starting point for assessing the current marketing situation, supplemented by marketing intelligence and research investigating the overall market, the competition, key issues, and threats and opportunities. As the plan is put into effect, marketers use a variety of research techniques to measure progress toward objectives and to identify areas for improvement if results fall short of projections.

Finally, marketing research helps marketers learn more about their customers' requirements, expectations, perceptions, and satisfaction levels. This deeper understanding provides a foundation for building competitive advantage through well-informed segmenting, targeting, differentiating, and positioning decisions. Thus, the marketing plan should outline what marketing research will be conducted and how the findings will be applied.

The Role of Relationships

The marketing plan shows how the company will establish and maintain profitable customer relationships. In the process, however, it also shapes a number of internal and external relationships. First, it affects how marketing personnel work with each other and with other departments to deliver value and satisfy customers. Second, it affects how the company works with suppliers, distributors, and strategic alliance partners to achieve the objectives listed in the plan. Third, it influences the company's dealings with other stakeholders, including government regulators, the media, and the community at large. All of these relationships are important to the organization's success, and so they should be considered when a marketing plan is being developed.

From Marketing Plan to Marketing Action

Companies generally create yearly marketing plans, although some plans cover a longer period. Marketers start planning well in advance of the implementation date to allow time for marketing research, thorough analysis, management review, and coordination between departments. Then, after each action program begins, marketers monitor ongoing results, compare them with projections, analyze any differences, and take corrective steps as needed. Some marketers also prepare contingency plans for implementation if certain conditions emerge. Because of inevitable and sometimes unpredictable environmental changes, marketers must be ready to update and adapt marketing plans at any time.

For effective implementation and control, the marketing plan should define how progress toward objectives will be measured. Managers typically use budgets, schedules, and performance standards for monitoring and evaluating results. With budgets, they can compare planned expenditures with actual expenditures for a given week, month, or other period. Schedules allow management to see when tasks were supposed to be completed—and when they were actually completed. Performance standards track the outcomes of marketing programs to see whether the company is moving toward its objectives. Some examples of performance standards are market share, sales volume, product profitability, and customer satisfaction.

Abbreviated Sample Marketing Plan for WestJet

What follows is an example of how a typical marketing plan is structured in terms of main sections and sequence. The example draws from primary and secondary research captured in the creation of the end-of-chapter mini cases for this text, but in no way is intended to represent WestJet's actual marketing plan nor specific strategies. What follows is a deliberately abbreviated marketing plan sample demonstrating the application of theory to a real company.

Executive Summary

WestJet is the challenger in Canada's commercial domestic air-travel market, having captured 36 percent of the market since its inception in 1996 but trailing Air Canada (which has 56 percent) in overall market share. Until recently, the company's target market has been the price-sensitive leisure traveller who is primarily interested in travelling within Canada. Bolstered by successfully tapping into the vacation market, both through the addition of southern US and Caribbean destinations and through the introduction of WestJet Vacations in 2006, WestJet has become a powerful brand within the vacation travel segment as well. In the second half of 2013, WestJet is implementing two key growth strategies.

First, through the creation of a three-tier product line for seating, WestJet is aggressively going after the business traveller segment. Second, and more ambitiously, WestJet Encore, a regional carrier aimed at providing the same WestJet value proposition to a growing number of small to medium-sized Canadian markets, launched in June 2013. While each of these initiatives requires considerable capital investment, the second one in particular, sealed by a partnership with Montreal-based Bombardier, is a milestone for WestJet because for the first time in its history an aircraft other than the Boeing 737 has become part of its fleet. Beginning with the delivery of two NextGen Q400s, WestJet will acquire roughly one new aircraft every month until its initial order of 20 planes is complete.

As the reality of WestJet's added capacity neared, the financial market began to show signs of concern that there would not be demand to fill the new supply of seats created. Despite growth in revenue and profit in the first quarter of 2013, WestJet's share price fell. With a sense of conviction that has become expected from WestJet leadership, the airline is motivated by the challenge at hand. "Encore will be a game changer in the industry, the same as WestJet has been for the last 17 years," claimed executive vice-president of sales, marketing, and guest experience, Bob Cummings.

In targeting the business segment and launching Encore, WestJet is using a market development strategy of growth with the objective of continuing to grow its share of the Canadian market. The success of both initiatives will rely on the airline leveraging its brand, which has come to stand for "great guest experience" at a great price.

This marketing plan describes the value proposition and target market of WestJet Encore and analyzes the internal and external factors (SWOT) for WestJet to consider in developing Encore through its first six months. Marketing objectives include building brand awareness of Encore while maintaining load factors between 75 and 80 percent.

The plan concludes with a *pro forma* income statement for year-end 2013, analyzing only the Calgary–Fort St. John and Calgary–Nanaimo service, where earnings before taxes are projected to be in the range of $5.5 million.

Current Marketing Situation

Current marketing situation
This section provides a brief synopsis of the competitive landscape and business environment in which the company will operate in marketing products described in the marketing plan.

Canadian passenger air transport is a $17 billion market. By definition it is an oligopoly, with 56 percent of that market owned by Air Canada, 36 percent by WestJet, and 8 percent by all other airlines, including looming new entrant Porter. The total market is expected to grow, particularly within the small-to-medium centres across the country.

Regulations within Canada's air transport industry continue to evolve under the jurisdiction of Transport Canada, with additional key stakeholders including provincial and municipal governments and the various airport authorities. A key participant, which WestJet Encore will be liaising with going forward, will be Billy Bishop Airport (a.k.a. Toronto Island Airport) as it plays directly into the strategic growth of the airline, leveraging the opportunities available when operating a smaller aircraft like Encore's new Bombardier Q400.

Economically, Canada is well positioned to provide demand for Encore with key unserved destinations in Western Canada, buoyed by the expanding energy sector in northeastern British Columbia as well as the myriad of network pieces still untapped across the prairies, southern Ontario, Quebec, and the Maritimes. The new Bombardier planes will also create workable economies of scale between markets where WestJet's 737s cannot be used without significant drops in load factor.

Sociodemographically, the Canadian landscape provides two main opportunities for WestJet Encore. In addition to linking burgeoning business communities such as Fort St. John, British Columbia, with corporate headquarter hubs like Calgary, Encore will also link leisure travellers from small-to-medium markets with WestJet's growing international vacation network.

Technologically, WestJet's newly established partnership with Bombardier, which will see the delivery of 20 NextGen Q400s within 18 months, connects the carrier with a manufacturer that invested almost $2 billion in research and development in 2012. Bombardier's core focus on "the evolution of mobility" provides WestJet with ongoing access to leading-edge aerospace technologies going forward.

Market Description

Market description
Describing the targeted segments in detail provides context for the marketing strategies and detailed action programs discussed later in the plan.

Having taken delivery of its first two Q400s, WestJet launched Encore with services connecting Fort St. John in northeastern British Columbia and Nanaimo, on Vancouver Island, with its established Canadian network. In addition to the feat of getting a new airline into the sky, the selection of these two markets is significant because Nanaimo represents WestJet's leisure/vacation segment while Fort St. John, a rapidly developing centre of British Columbia's booming energy sector, is clearly a play toward the business segment. While these two destinations were the first served by Encore, Brandon, Manitoba, came on-stream in September 2013, and according to president/CEO Gregg Saretsky, Encore will "march eastward, province by province" as new Bombardier planes are delivered.

While WestJet may have initially penetrated the market through a cost structure, which permitted profitable value pricing, it has been the airline's culture of care that has truly differentiated it from Air Canada. Thus, despite nearing 10 years in use, the "owners care" campaign shows little sign of fatigue and continues to be a brand personality that successfully resonates with the growing segment of loyal WestJet guests. Business and leisure travellers alike have at least two choices to fly with in Canada. Knowledge of its target market's needs have been as vital to WestJet's success as its cost management.

Demographically, the WestJet guest is male or female of any age, race, or ethnicity. While price sensitivity has always been a dominant psychographic trait, the desire for an experiential relationship while travelling is clearly a behavioural characteristic of WestJet's segment. Geographically, WestJet's network, served exclusively by its fleet of workhorse Boeing 737s, grew to accommodate Canada's largest metro areas from province to province as well as smaller remote (but strategically important) markets served by their own municipal airports.

WestJet Encore was so named to bring the same travel experience to travellers in those Canadian markets currently unserved or underserved by WestJet or Air Canada and its regional subsidiary Jazz. Ontario's Porter Airlines, and its customers travelling in and out of Toronto Island Airport and the growing Porter network, represent a large potentially swayable market, as do other southern Ontario markets and the eastern business travel triangle of Toronto, Montreal, and Ottawa.

An overview of WestJet Encore's target segment through 2013 is presented in the following table using geographic, demographic, psychographic, and behavioural variables.

Product Review

Product review
The product review summarizes the main features for all the company's products, organized by product line, type of customer, market, or order of product introduction.

WestJet promotes its product as a "great guest experience." While this is the desired position of the company's collective operational and marketing endeavours, technically WestJet, like its competitors, provides a passenger (and cargo) air transportation

Segment Variable	Variable Characteristics
Geographic	British Columbia, Alberta, and Manitoba
	Small to medium-sized cities (20 000–100 000)
	Municipal airport serviceable
Demographic	Male/female, all ages
	Singles, couples, families
	Business: professionals and tradespeople
	Leisure: domestic and international destinations
Psychographic	Thinkers, Believers, Experiencers, Makers (VALS descriptors)
	Sociable
	Time-starved
	Value-conscious
Behavioural	Desire value and personal experience
	Desire feeling valued
	Frequent flyers (20+ flights/year)
	Brand-conscious and loyal

service to over 80 scheduled and charter destinations across Canada, the United States, Mexico, and the Caribbean. Thus, its product is a combination of the destinations to which WestJet flies plus the total experience through the five steps of a consumer purchase decision process.

The following product/market grid categorizes WestJet's product lines by segment targeted. The first product line, WestJet Encore, is the subject of this marketing plan. Other product lines are shown to provide context of WestJet's overall product mix.

Competitive Review

In the middle of 2013, WestJet found itself in a unique competitive position. In front of WestJet was the familiar market leader, Air Canada, with its rich 80-year history and globally recognized brand. Behind WestJet, for the first time since WestJet itself assumed the position of true market challenger, was Toronto-based Porter Airlines, which is poised to take its established eastern Canada network and begin expanding westward. From a WestJet Encore perspective, both Air Canada and Porter have a strategic asset coveted by WestJet—access to Toronto's Billy Bishop (Island) Airport.

While all major US airlines, technically, qualify as competitors to WestJet in its expanding US network, they have little bearing on Encore's near-term plans. Furthermore, WestJet has code share or interline agreements established with five major US carriers, which for the moment provide some competitive cushioning in and out of the United States.

Distribution (Channel) Review

The growing reliance from travellers upon online planning was the catalyst behind the launch of WestJet Vacations in 2006. The fact that consumer online travel management is now conducted for any scale of travel, be it a global leisure excursion or a spontaneous interprovincial flight, has exposed WestJet as lagging in the arena of offering a mobile app to provide immediate, anytime, anywhere access to flight booking. At the time of writing, WestJet's emerging media team is busy in the development stages of a product to provide users with this experience. As direct channel marketing (i.e., selling through

Competitive review
The purpose of a competitive review is to identify key competitors, describe their market positions, and briefly discuss their strategies.

Distribution (channel) review
In this section, marketers list the most important channels, provide an overview of each channel arrangement, and identify developing issues in channels.

Product Line	Strategic Goal and Target Market
WestJet Encore Domestic	Market penetration and development of existing demographic/psychographic segments by entering unserved, small-to-medium geographic segments
	Small-to-medium Canadian urban centres
WestJet Domestic	Market penetration and development of existing demographic/psychographic segment by continuing to service existing medium-to-large market segments
	Small-to-large Canadian urban centres
WestJet Transborder (US)	Market development into growing list of US-based business and tourism destinations
	Unlimited demographic segments, value-conscious, sociable psychographic segment
WestJet Mexico & Caribbean	Market development into growing list of sun-seeker international tourism destinations
	Young adults or young families, value-conscious, sociable psychographic segment
WestJet Vacations	Product development combining online vacation package planning consisting of WestJet Vacations destinations and partner hotels and car rental companies
	Young adults or young families, value-conscious, sociable, psychographic segment, convenience-motivated behavioural segment
WestJet Cargo	Market development strategy to provide added value to guests and/or shippers
	Business market
Plus Seating	Product development strategy to provide a bundle of seating amenities for guests desiring additional legroom, in-flight snacks, flexible flight changes or cancellations
	Business traveller
Flex Seating	Product development strategy to provide a bundle of seating amenities for guests desiring flexible flight changes or cancellations
	Business traveller and leisure traveller desiring extra amenities and conveniences
Econo Seating	Market penetration strategy providing same product to typical WestJet guest currently satisfied with value proposition
	All segments

WestJet.com or a WestJet ticket agent) is clearly the most profitable for the airline, the prompt delivery of such an app is key to WestJet and WestJet Encore's success.

SWOT Analysis

SWOT is arguably the single most important concept toward the understanding and successful execution of marketing. It is essentially an inventory tool to compile an objective and exhaustive list of a company's internal and external forces. The resulting analysis is then used to identify objectives and determine the viability of strategies to achieve objectives. Strengths are internal controllable forces the company does well. Weaknesses are internal controllable forces the company needs to address to be successful. Opportunities are external noncontrollable forces that the company can use to its advantage. Threats are external noncontrollable forces for which the company must identify and prepare to minimize damage. Note that opportunities and threats are identified using an environmental scan, which is a sub-task of SWOT analysis. SWOTs are typically presented in matrix form for quick reference to the most vital items, followed by more in-depth explanation.

The following SWOT analysis pertains to WestJet's launch and near-term financial sustainability of Encore. As is the case with SWOT analyses in general, various internal and external factors can be interpreted as having both positive and negative influences on the company. For example, WestJet's network expansion is viewed as a strength, but some analysts suggest the airline's capacity increase is risky and thus perceive it as a weakness. Components of the SWOT are described in more detail following the matrix.

Strengths	Weaknesses
■ Brand: WestJet & Bombardier	■ Capacity increase
■ People: WestJetters & leadership	■ Limited experience & network
■ Management: Operations & financial	■ Unmet expectations
■ Network: Established & expansion	■ Absence of executive VP of operations
■ Marketing communications	■ Negative economic impact
■ Corporate social responsibility	■ Lack of mobile booking app

Opportunities		Threats	
Competitive	■ Air Canada's labour issues ■ Porter's fleet size, scope, and lack of brand awareness	Competitive	■ Air Canada & Porter access to Billy Bishop ■ Air Canada Jazz, an established regional brand network
Regulatory	■ Transport Canada's approval of WestJet's flight attendant ratio & AOC clearance	Regulatory	■ Transport Canada approval required for each airport/community entered
Economic	■ Bullish commodity-based economy in northeastern BC ■ Stability and growth of Canadian economy ■ Market outlook on WestJet stock	Economic	■ Reliance upon commodity-based economy in northeastern BC to sustain demand in that geographic segment ■ Canadian economic stability vulnerable to global economics
Social	■ Canadian market demand for travel domestically and abroad ■ Many communities vying for access to Encore's network	Social	■ Lack of confidence in financial markets ■ Low demand ■ Negative perception of airline industry
Technology	■ Advancements that enhance guest experience ■ WiFi in the sky ■ Bombardier R&D commitment	Technology	■ Advancements that are difficult to deliver

Strengths

Brand

- Industry recognition: *Canadian Business* ranks WestJet as the number two brand in Canada, behind only Tim Hortons. The same survey also found WestJet to be the top Canadian company in terms of corporate governance and workplace. In 2013, Leger Marketing ranked WestJet Canada's Most Preferred Airline, Most Trusted Airline, Best Customer Service, and Most Reputable Transportation Company. Randstad Canada named WestJet Canada as the Most Attractive Employer for a second consecutive year. All of these are to be assimilated within the Encore brand.

- Underdog Perception: Despite having displaced nearly 40 percent of the Canadian domestic airline market away from Air Canada since 1996, WestJet remains the smaller of the two airlines and will always be seen as the underdog as long as it has a lower market share. The label is advantageous as there is a natural human inclination toward supporting the underdog. Government, media, and even non-governmental organizations (NGOs) are often more supportive of upstarts than the market leader in the face of adversity.

- Everyday Low Price (EDLP) Perception: Despite being competitively priced, West-Jet still reaps the rewards of the perception created when it launched in 1996. At that time guests could clearly see the difference in price between Canada's airlines. Today the gap has narrowed, but WestJet is still widely perceived as the lower-priced of the two airlines.

- Bombardier Brand: The Montreal-based transportation manufacturer brings tremendous brand equity association to WestJet. Seen globally as an innovator and nationally as a source of pride, the partnership bodes well for both companies.

- Technology: The Q400 Turboprop aircraft would appear to be the perfect plane to create the same efficiencies to regional flying that WestJet has created in its longer haul network with Boeing 737s. The factory-to-fleet delivery also ensures WestJet gets the very latest technology to compete with older, smaller turbo props operated by Air Canada and Porter.

People

- WestJetters: WestJetters number 9000 and counting, with seemingly unanimous buy-in to WestJet's culture of care, 85 percent acceptance rate of WestJet's corporate stock option package offered to employees, and 91 percent voter support to Encore and the Encore business concept.

- Leadership: WestJet and WestJet Encore's leadership team is rich in experience in commercial aviation and across a multitude of sectors. President/CEO Gregg Saretsky brings almost 30 years of experience in the airline industry, while Encore's president Ferio Pugliese is an internal hire, having been an integral part of West-Jet's corporate culture development as former executive vice-president of people, culture, and inflight services.

- Board of Directors: WestJet's board is led by chair and co-founder, Clive Beddoe, and supported by a wide breadth of internal and external representation across many industry sectors.

Management

- Operations: The business model has always created positive economies of scale using a single aircraft model and other cost-reducing strategies. The single model aircraft will for the first time be disrupted as WestJet brings Bombardier's Q400 into its fleet, however. With an initial order of 20 planes to serve the needs of network communities, it is expected that WestJet Encore will leverage economies experience gained through 17 years of WestJet operations. The Sabresonic reservation system has enabled increased direct marketing channel growth.

- Financial: WestJet has seen 28 consecutive quarters of profitability, and year-over-year net earnings increase of 33 percent for Q1 2013 were record breaking. Capital acquisition appears to come easily to WestJet through share issues, stock splits, or more recently the sale of assets such as ten 737s to US-based Southwest Airlines.

Network

- Established: WestJet currently has more than 85 destinations in North America and the Caribbean. All of these are potential final destinations for WestJet Encore guests, who will board flights in smaller, underserved Canadian markets with the ultimate intention of flying somewhere within WestJet's network.

- Expansion: While continuously researching viable new destinations for scheduled flights within its own network, WestJet also grows its list of code share and interline agreements, which essentially give WestJet Encore guests access to the world through their Encore ticket purchase.

Marketing Communications

- Whether it is the ongoing and effective "Owners Care" ad campaign, a timely seat sale, the WestJet Rewards program, or one of the many iconic (albeit satiric) publicity grabs, WestJet continues to be visible within the market space. Its recognition, noted in strengths under "Brand," is not only the result of delivering customer value, but also communicating the WestJet story frequently and widely across all available communications channels.

Corporate Social Responsibility

- WestJet's community investment programs continue to make a difference in all communities served both domestically and abroad. The Gift of Flight, Caring for Our Communities, and Hero Holidays are examples of WestJet initiatives in this regard, while the airline has also partnered with established organizations such as Make a Wish Foundation and Boys and Girls Club of Canada to further its influence on the greater good. Environmentally, WestJet is committed to minimizing its ecological footprint through the use of fuel-efficient aircraft. This was never more visible than in its selection and acquisition of the Bombardier Q400 as Encore's aircraft—it is the industry standard in performance and energy efficiency.

Weaknesses

Capacity Increase

- While the WestJet Encore story has been one of entrepreneurial ambition that leverages a proven model and brand, the fact remains that it will add 78 new seats with each Q400 delivery (1560 new seats within the first two years). Filling them to sustainable load factors will be a challenge.

Limited Experience and Network

- Limited Experience: The entry into regional short-haul flights using a smaller, nimbler aircraft, the Q400, is new territory for WestJet, which has created effective economies of scale relying solely on Boeing 737s. There will be some hiccups in gaining a similar experiential curve with Encore planes and processes.

- Limited Initial Network: Due to Bombardier's time requirements to manufacture Q400s and WestJet's time requirements to finance each new delivery, Encore will use a phased approach to developing its network, commencing with a small network of only three new destinations within the first three months of operations. While this may satisfy demand on one level, it may create dilemmas in terms of promoting the airline on a national scale. Access to Billy Bishop Airport on Toronto Island has been publicly identified as a strategic need for WestJet.

Unmet Customer Expectations

- Despite proactive communication efforts, there will be travellers who will be disappointed with the relatively decreased personal space and services available on the Q400 aircraft.

Absence of Vice-President of Operations

- The departure of Cam Kenyon in May 2013 left WestJet vulnerable in a key senior management position and may be partially responsible for recently sagging on-time performance issues. WestJet reported year-over-year decreases in on-time performance in Q4 2012 and Q1 2013. While harsh weather was cited as the root cause, the metrics must be addressed at an operational level.

Negative Economic Impact

- While Encore commences flights in and out of Nanaimo, Fort St. John, and Brandon, smaller independent air travel businesses, such as Brandon Air Shuttle, will suffer, possibly creating a ripple effect on local economies and resulting in negative publicity.

Lack of Mobile Booking App

- In a world where everything is expected to be doable through a mobile device, WestJet has acknowledged a slow reaction to develop an app that allows guests to research, plan, book, and check-in seamlessly through their smartphone. While direct rival Air Canada has been equally slow to the table, upstart Porter has already developed such an app.

Opportunities

Competition

- Air Canada's decision to apply for a reduction in flight attendants, similar to WestJet's bid, has drawn resistance from its flight attendants' union, who have in turn drawn support from NDP transport critic Olivia Chow.

- Porter's recent announcement to begin a strategic market development growth pattern westward is limited by its own capital barriers and lack of brand awareness beyond the Eastern Business Triangle (Toronto, Montreal, and Ottawa).

Regulation

- Transport Canada's recent approval of WestJet's exemption application on flight attendant/passenger ratio will assist in its goal of significant cost cutting.

- Transport Canada granted WestJet its Air Operator Certificate to officially gain clearance for take-off of Encore on June 24, 2013. It is expected that the chief Canadian air transport regulator will be cooperative as Encore grows its network.

Economic

- The expanding economy in northeastern British Columbia, with Fort St. John in particular viewed as the centre of BC's energy "boom," will be helpful to WestJet Encore. Billions of dollars of capital investment and revenues are expected from the region, which is rich in accessible fossil fuel deposits.

- The stable (albeit slowly expanding) economy across Canada suggests at least incremental growth in discretionary spending and thus favours increased demand for business and leisure travel domestically and abroad.

- General financial market activity has led WestJet's stock to what *Forbes* calls a favourable Relative Strength Index (RSI), which suggests imminent buy mode and an increase in share value.

Social

- Demand for flights to and from newly added network destinations appears to be keeping up with capacity based on booking rates for Nanaimo, Fort St. John, and Brandon. Many communities are promoting themselves for access to the Encore network, including 32 cities that actually sent representatives to Calgary to pitch their communities as desired stops in Encore's network.

Technology

- Any technological advancement that enhances the guest experience is an opportunity for WestJet. WiFi in the sky, for instance, is now available and WestJet has indicated its intent to integrate by the end of 2014. This will be accompanied by expanded on-board digital entertainment amenities.

- The Encore partnership with Bombardier is clearly a WestJet strength because of the fact that Bombardier, regardless of its relationship with any client, is driven by innovation. Its commitment to R&D provides WestJet Encore with built-in exposure to the latest developments in aeronautical technology.

Threats

Competition

- Air Canada and Porter both have what WestJet Encore wants in its grand strategic scheme—access to Billy Bishop Airport. Together, they may do everything in their power, including collusion, to keep WestJet out.

- Air Canada's regional affiliate, Jazz, is an established brand across Canada and Porter is established throughout the east.

Regulation

- Encore's expansion into new communities across Canada over the near and long term will rely on various levels of government approval with regard to securing access to airports, all of which are regulated by Transport Canada.

Economic

- In a commodities-driven economy, especially the resources of the Western Canada Sedimentary Basin, usership of WestJet Encore will rely heavily on continued industry expansion as well as access to discretionary income amongst leisure travellers. Fort St. John in particular represents a network addition based solely upon its hub-centre status of British Columbia's natural gas and liquid natural gas sector. Slowdowns in the industry would negatively impact Encore's bottom line.

Social

- The combination of WestJet's announced decrease in load factor and increase in capacity sent the investor market into sell mode in May 2013. Despite early presales on flights between WestJet's established network and the new Encore destinations, only time will tell whether the market demand is truly there to keep the Q400's 78-seat capacity at a sustainable load factor.

- The airline industry has been subjected to harsh criticism recently, creating a public perception of decreasing overall service, comfort, and reliability in spite of WestJet's pledge to the contrary. Strategic alliances with a growing list of code shares and interline agreements expose WestJet to damage brought on by poor performance from other airlines.

- Finally, of the 32 cities who campaigned to WestJet in June 2012 to be included in Encore's new network, only three destinations have been chosen to date. Only a handful more will be selected before the end of 2013 and 2014. Excluded communities will be disappointed and could create negative publicity.

Technology

- The only threat posed by technology is the speed at which it advances and the readjusted levels of expectations from society. Keeping up with technology is a challenge for all companies in all sectors. WestJet has acknowledged its slow reaction to mobile delivery of services for its guests. At the time of writing, a mobile app was in development stages. Air Canada has also lagged behind, although upstart Porter Airlines already has a mobile app.

Objectives and Issues

The following are the financial, marketing, and brand objectives for WestJet Encore for the six-month period commencing June 24, 2013, to December 31, 2013.

Financial Objectives

- Generate $50 million in revenue on fares sold for Calgary–Fort St. John and Calgary–Nanaimo services.
- Operate at profit that is at or near WestJet's average 10 percent earnings before taxes (EBT).
- Penetrate the S1.1B domestic/regional market.

Objectives and issues
Objectives and issues should be defined in specific terms so management can measure progress and plan corrective action if needed to stay on track. This section describes any major issues that might affect the company's marketing strategy and implementation.

Marketing Objectives

- Expand from inaugural BC destinations Nanaimo and Fort St. John to Brandon, Manitoba, and further eastward. As president/CEO Gregg Saretsky says "one province at a time, we're going to continue our march east."
- Position WestJet Encore as the great guest experience for short-haul business and leisure flights within Canada.

Brand Objectives

- Create similar culture of care within Encore as with WestJet and communicate this culture accordingly.
- Build brand awareness of WestJet Encore.
- Celebrate and give back to communities in which WestJet Encore serves.

Issues

- Can WestJet Encore fill capacity to sustainable load factor metrics of 75–80 percent?
- Can WestJet gain access to additional key strategic destination communities?

Marketing Strategy

Beginning with a positioning statement, the following pages summarize recommended strategies using WestJet Encore's marketing mix of product, price, channel, and marketing communications.

Positioning and Value Proposition

Positioning and value proposition A position built on a meaningful value proposition, supported by appropriate strategy and implementation, can help the company build competitive advantage. A positioning statement provides a compass for the company, directing it to the place it wishes to occupy in the mind of its target market.

WestJet Encore will operate in the spirit of its parent airline. It will create a great guest experience while keeping prices low through judicious operations management. It will essentially do for Canadian regional air travel what WestJet has provided for longer-haul travel throughout Canada since 1996.

WestJet Encore will strive to add unserved or underserved communities across Canada to its network, eventually connecting all the dots on the WestJet and WestJet Encore network map.

WestJet Encore will leverage WestJet's award-winning and trusted brand and its engaged and enthusiastic owners to grow a new kind of regional air travel experience.

Product Strategy

At its core, WestJet Encore's product is a service—a means of flying from point A to point B. However, its differentiation will be a travel experience like no other in the regional airline market space. Combining brand new, 78-seat, state-of-the-art, fuel-efficient, nimble, and quick Bombardier Q400s with WestJet's established culture of care, the guest experience from ticket purchase to baggage collection will need to meet the high expectations established by the parent airline. This would not only include a friendly inflight crew, but also quick turnaround times, on-time departures and arrivals, efficient processes, and of course a safe and caring guest experience.

Pricing Strategy

WestJet Encore's pricing strategy will emulate the model established by WestJet: grounded in customer value, cognizant of competition, and responsible to owner equity

Airline	Fort St. John	Nanaimo
WestJet Encore	$310.00	$350.00
Air Canada	$545.00	$340.00

(Source: WestJet.com and AirCanada.com, accessed June 12, 2013. Lowest departure and return fares available the week of June 24, 2013, were selected, rounded to the nearest $5.)

and the bottom line. Price comparisons between WestJet Encore and Air Canada will be made on a regular basis by travellers and analysts alike. A small sample comparison is shown above for the Calgary–Fort St. John and Calgary–Nanaimo services. Note that the customer value in both of these flights is the nonstop travel with Encore, whereas with Air Canada one stop is required for both fares.

Channel Strategy

WestJet Encore will be the beneficiary of WestJet's Sabresonic reservations management system, providing third-party retailers and direct consumers alike with easy access to shopping, pricing, purchasing, and even changing tickets. WestJet.com will continue to be key in the company's pursuit of increasing direct channel sales, but the need for a mobile app to create a seamless and elegant smartphone purchasing experience has yet to be fulfilled. WestJet has committed to deploying a new mobile app, which will combine Sabre's sophisticated database management back end with an innovative customer interface experience. This will tilt the scales toward sales growth in the direct marketing channel.

Continued strategic alliance channels, established through code share and interline agreements will enhance indirect channel sales for Encore, as its guests can purchase a fare to any destination in the world with WestJet partners, originating with the first leg of their journey from their hometown served by Encore.

Marketing Communications Strategy

The following marketing communications strategies will be integrated into a coordinated promotional program over the course of this plan's life cycle:

Strategy	Description
Advertising	■ Continued leverage of "owners care"
	■ Encore-specific "owners care" campaign with appropriate production elements that distinguish it from WestJet (different imagery, graphics, and voiceover elements)
Sales Promotion	■ Cross-sell WestJet Rewards and WestJet Rewards card loyalty program as fully earnable and redeemable on Encore flights
	■ Yield management pricing where lost revenue, due to idle capacity, can be salvaged
Public Relations	■ Emphasis on community engagement in newly acquired network communities
	■ Stage WestJet-esque inaugural flight publicity events (i.e., bathtub race at YYC for first service to Nanaimo)
	■ Research to identify areas of need where gift of flight could apply
	■ Implement "Caring for Our Community" program
Direct Response	■ Engage guests through social networks, particularly Twitter and Facebook, setting up Encore-specific pages, handles, hashtags, and so on
	■ Leverage sophisticated SEO and analytic tools to create and maintain meaningful online guest engagement
Personal Selling	■ Internal communications program directed at educating contact-point WestJetters on new destinations
	■ Help WestJetters become brand advocates for newly added communities

Marketing Controls and Income Statement

WestJet uses the following measurement calculations to monitor and control its marketing efforts:

- Revenue: total tickets sold × average price per ticket
- Earnings before taxes (EBT): revenue less cost and expenses before taxes
- Available seat miles (ASM): total capacity from all seats in all flights
- Revenue passenger miles (RPM): total seats purchased on all flights
- Load factor: percentage of RPM relative to ASM
- Yield: revenue per revenue passenger mile
- Revenue per available seat mile (RASM)
- Cost per available seat mile (CASM)

The following simplified pro forma income statement is a high-level forecast of profit for WestJet Encore through its first six months using only estimations based on return flights from Calgary to Fort St. John and Nanaimo.

Data used reflects revenue based on a total of 16 return flights per day to Fort St. John and Nanaimo from Calgary. This is multiplied by 180 days, representing July–December 2013, then multiplied by 0.75 to represent a conservative load factor within the 78-seat capacity of the Q400. The resultant total estimation of revenue seats is then calculated by $330, representing a conservative average price of fares to both destinations from Calgary.

Cost of sales and expenses, based on prorated data from WestJet's annual report, are then subtracted, resulting in the EBT figure provided.

Revenue	$55 600 000
Cost of Sales & Expenses	$50 000 000
EBT	$5 600 000

Marketing by the Numbers

Marketing managers are facing increased accountability for the financial implications of their actions. This appendix provides a basic introduction to measuring marketing financial performance. Such financial analysis guides marketers in making sound marketing decisions and in assessing the outcomes of those decisions.

The appendix is built around a hypothetical manufacturer of consumer electronics products—ConnectPhone. In the past, ConnectPhone has concentrated on making Internet modems. However, the company is now introducing a new type of product— a *media phone* that replaces a household's telephone and provides "always-on" Internet connectivity and wireless phone access through VoIP (Voice over Internet Protocol) technology. In this appendix, we will analyze the various decisions ConnectPhone's marketing managers must make before and after the new-product launch.

The appendix is organized into *three sections*. The *first section* introduces pricing, break-even, and margin analysis assessments that will guide the introduction of ConnectPhone's new product. The *second section* discusses demand estimates, the marketing budget, and marketing performance measures. It begins with a discussion of estimating market potential and company sales. It then introduces the marketing budget, as illustrated through a *pro forma* profit-and-loss statement followed by the actual profit-and-loss statement. Next, we discuss marketing performance measures, with a focus on helping marketing managers to better defend their decisions from a financial perspective. In the *third section*, we analyze the financial implications of various marketing tactics.

Each of the three sections ends with a set of quantitative exercises that provide you with an opportunity to apply the concepts you learned to situations beyond ConnectPhone.

Pricing, Break-Even, and Margin Analysis

Pricing Considerations

Determining price is one of the most important marketing-mix decisions. The limiting factors are demand and costs. Demand factors, such as buyer-perceived value, set the price ceiling. The company's costs set the price floor. In between these two factors, marketers must consider competitors' prices and other factors such as reseller requirements, government regulations, and company objectives.

Current competing media phone products in this relatively new product category were introduced in 2009 and sell at retail prices between $500 and $1,000. ConnectPhone plans to introduce its new product at a lower price in order to expand the market and gain market share rapidly. We first consider ConnectPhone's pricing decision from a cost perspective. Then, we consider consumer value, the competitive environment, and reseller requirements.

Determining Costs

Recall from Chapter 10 that there are different types of costs. **Fixed costs** do not vary with production or sales level and include costs such as rent, interest, depreciation, and

Fixed costs
Costs that do not vary with production or sales level.

Variable costs
Costs that vary directly with the level of production.

Total costs
The sum of the fixed and variable costs for any given level of production.

clerical and management salaries. Regardless of the level of output, the company must pay these costs. Whereas total fixed costs remain constant as output increases, the fixed cost per unit (or average fixed cost) will decrease as output increases because the total fixed costs are spread across more units of output. **Variable costs** vary directly with the level of production and include costs related to the direct production of the product (such as costs of goods sold—COGS) and many of the marketing costs associated with selling it. Although these costs tend to be uniform for each unit produced, they are called *variable* because their total varies with the number of units produced. **Total costs** are the sum of the fixed and variable costs for any given level of production.

ConnectPhone has invested $10 million in refurbishing an existing facility to manufacture the new media phone product. Once production begins, the company estimates that it will incur fixed costs of $20 million per year. The variable cost to produce each device is estimated to be $250 and is expected to remain at that level for the output capacity of the facility.

Setting Price Based on Costs

Cost-plus pricing (or markup pricing)
A standard markup to the cost of the product.

ConnectPhone starts with the cost-based approach to pricing discussed in Chapter 10. Recall that the simplest method, **cost-plus pricing (or markup pricing)**, simply adds a standard markup to the cost of the product. To use this method, however, ConnectPhone must specify expected unit sales so that total unit costs can be determined. Unit variable costs will remain constant regardless of the output, but *average unit fixed costs* will decrease as output increases.

To illustrate this method, suppose ConnectPhone has fixed costs of $20 million, variable costs of $250 per unit, and expects unit sales of 1 million media phones. Thus, the cost per unit is given by

$$\text{Unit cost} = \text{variable cost} + \frac{\text{fixed costs}}{\text{unit sales}} = \$250 + \frac{\$20\ 000\ 000}{1\ 000\ 000} = \$270$$

Relevant costs
Costs that will occur in the future and that will vary across the alternatives being considered.

Note that we do *not* include the initial investment of $10 million in the total fixed cost figure. It is not considered a fixed cost because it is not a *relevant* cost. **Relevant costs** are those that will occur in the future and that will vary across the alternatives being considered. ConnectPhone's investment to refurbish the manufacturing facility was a one-time cost that will not reoccur in the future. Such past costs are *sunk costs* and should not be considered in future analyses.

Break-even price
The price at which total revenue equals total cost and profit is zero.

Also notice that if ConnectPhone sells its product for $270, the price is equal to the total cost per unit. This is the **break-even price**—the price at which unit revenue (price) equals unit cost and profit is zero.

Suppose ConnectPhone does not want to merely break even but rather wants to earn a 25 percent markup on sales. ConnectPhone's markup price is[1]

$$\text{Markup price} = \frac{\text{unit cost}}{(1 - \text{desired return on sales})} = \frac{\$270}{1 - 0.25} = \$360$$

This is the price at which ConnectPhone would sell the product to resellers such as wholesalers or retailers to earn a 25 percent profit on sales.

Return on investment (ROI) pricing (or target-return pricing)
A cost-based pricing method that determines price based on a specified rate of return on investment.

Another approach ConnectPhone could use is called **return on investment (ROI) pricing (or target-return pricing)**. In this case, the company *would* consider the initial $10 million investment, but only to determine the dollar profit goal. Suppose the company wants a 30 percent return on its investment. The price necessary to satisfy this requirement can be determined by

$$\text{ROI price} = \text{unit cost} + \frac{\text{ROI} \times \text{investment}}{\text{unit sales}} = \$270 + \frac{0.3 \times \$10\ 000\ 000}{1\ 000\ 000} = \$273$$

That is, if ConnectPhone sells its product for $273, it will realize a 30 percent return on its initial investment of $10 million.

In these pricing calculations, unit cost is a function of the expected sales, which were estimated to be 1 million units. But what if actual sales were lower? Then the unit cost would be higher because the fixed costs would be spread over fewer units, and the realized percentage markup on sales or ROI would be lower. Alternatively, if sales are higher than the estimated 1 million units, unit cost would be lower than $270, so a lower price would produce the desired markup on sales or ROI. It's important to note that these cost-based pricing methods are *internally* focused and do not consider demand, competitors' prices, or reseller requirements. Because ConnectPhone will be selling this product to consumers through wholesalers and retailers offering competing brands, the company must consider markup pricing from this perspective.

Setting Price Based on External Factors

Whereas costs determine the price floor, ConnectPhone also must consider external factors when setting price. ConnectPhone does not have the final say concerning the final price of its media phones to consumers—retailers do. So it must start with its suggested retail price and work back. In doing so, ConnectPhone must consider the markups required by resellers that sell the product to consumers.

In general, a dollar **markup** is the difference between a company's selling price for a product and its cost to manufacture or purchase it. For a retailer, then, the markup is the difference between the price it charges consumers and the cost the retailer must pay for the product. Thus, for any level of reseller,

$$\text{Dollar markup} = \text{selling price} - \text{cost}$$

Markups are usually expressed as a percentage, and there are two different ways to compute markups—on *cost* or *selling price*:

$$\text{Markup percentage on cost} = \frac{\text{dollar markup}}{\text{cost}}$$

$$\text{Markup percentage on selling price} = \frac{\text{dollar markup}}{\text{selling price}}$$

To apply reseller margin analysis, ConnectPhone must first set the suggested retail price and then work back to the price at which it must sell the product to a wholesaler. Suppose retailers expect a 30 percent margin and wholesalers want a 20 percent margin based on their respective selling prices. And suppose that ConnectPhone sets a manufacturer's suggested retail price (MSRP) of $599.99 for its product.

Recall that ConnectPhone wants to expand the market by pricing low and generating market share quickly. ConnectPhone selected the $599.99 MSRP because it is lower than most competitors' prices, which can be as high as $1000. And the company's research shows that it is below the threshold at which more consumers are willing to purchase the product. By using buyers' perceptions of value and not the seller's cost to determine the MSRP, ConnectPhone is using **value-based pricing**. For simplicity, we will use an MSRP of $600 in further analyses.

To determine the price ConnectPhone will charge wholesalers, we must first subtract the retailer's margin from the retail price to determine the retailer's cost ($600 − [$600 × 0.30] = $420). The retailer's cost is the wholesaler's price, so ConnectPhone next subtracts the wholesaler's margin ($420 − [$420 × 0.20] = $336). Thus, the **markup chain**

Markup
The difference between a company's selling price for a product and its cost to manufacture or purchase it.

Value-based pricing
Offering just the right combination of quality and good service at a fair price.

Markup chain
The sequence of markups used by firms at each level in a channel.

representing the sequence of markups used by firms at each level in a channel for ConnectPhone's new product is

Suggested retail price:	$600
minus retail margin (30%):	− $180
Retailer's cost/wholesaler's price:	$420
minus wholesaler's margin (20%):	− $ 84
Wholesaler's cost/ConnectPhone's price:	$336

By deducting the markups for each level in the markup chain, ConnectPhone arrives at a price for the product to wholesalers of $336.

Break-Even and Margin Analysis

The previous analyses derived a value-based price of $336 for ConnectPhone's product. Although this price is higher than the break-even price of $270 and covers costs, that price assumed a demand of 1 million units. But how many units and what level of dollar sales must ConnectPhone achieve to break even at the $336 price? And what level of sales must be achieved to realize various profit goals? These questions can be answered through break-even and margin analysis.

Determining Break-Even Unit Volume and Dollar Sales

Based on an understanding of costs, consumer value, the competitive environment, and reseller requirements, ConnectPhone has decided to set its price to wholesalers at $336. At that price, what sales level will be needed for ConnectPhone to break even or make a profit on its media phones? **Break-even analysis** determines the unit volume and dollar sales needed to be profitable given a particular price and cost structure. At the break-even point, total revenue equals total costs and profit is zero. Above this point, the company will make a profit; below it, the company will lose money. ConnectPhone can calculate break-even volume by using the following formula:

Break-even analysis
Analysis to determine the unit volume and dollar sales needed to be profitable given a particular price and cost structure.

$$\text{Break-even volume} = \frac{\text{fixed costs}}{\text{price} - \text{unit variable cost}}$$

The denominator (price – unit variable cost) is called **unit contribution** (sometimes called *contribution margin*). It represents the amount that each unit contributes to covering fixed costs. Break-even volume represents the level of output at which all (variable and fixed) costs are covered. In ConnectPhone's case, break-even unit volume is

Unit contribution
The amount that each unit contributes to covering fixed costs—the difference between price and variable costs.

$$\text{Break-even volume} = \frac{\text{fixed costs}}{\text{price} - \text{unit variable cost}} = \frac{\$20\,000\,000}{\$336 - \$250} = 232\,558.1 \text{ units}$$

Thus, at the given cost and pricing structure, ConnectPhone will break even at 232 559 units.

To determine the break-even dollar sales, simply multiply unit break-even volume by the selling price:

$$\text{BE}_{\text{sales}} = \text{BE}_{\text{vol}} \times \text{price} = 232\,559 \times \$336 = \$78\,139\,824$$

Another way to calculate dollar break-even sales is to use the percentage contribution margin (hereafter referred to as **contribution margin**), which is the unit contribution divided by the selling price:

Contribution margin
The unit contribution divided by the selling price.

$$\text{Contribution margin} = \frac{\text{price} - \text{unit variable cost}}{\text{price}} = \frac{\$336 - \$250}{\$336} = 0.256 \text{ or } 25.6\%$$

Then,

$$\text{Break-even sales} = \frac{\text{fixed costs}}{\text{contribution margin}} = \frac{\$20\,000\,000}{0.256} = \$78\,125\,000$$

Note that the difference between the two break-even sales calculations is due to rounding.

Such break-even analysis helps ConnectPhone by showing the unit volume needed to cover costs. If production capacity cannot attain this level of output, then the company should not launch this product. However, the unit break-even volume is well within ConnectPhone's capacity. Of course, the bigger question concerns whether ConnectPhone can sell this volume at the $336 price. We'll address that issue a little later.

Understanding contribution margin is useful in other types of analyses as well, particularly if unit prices and unit variable costs are unknown or if a company (say, a retailer) sells many products at different prices and knows the percentage of total sales variable costs represent. Whereas unit contribution is the difference between unit price and unit variable costs, total contribution is the difference between total sales and total variable costs. The overall contribution margin can be calculated by

$$\text{Contribution margin} = \frac{\text{total sales} - \text{total variable costs}}{\text{total sales}}$$

Regardless of the actual level of sales, if the company knows what percentage of sales is represented by variable costs, it can calculate contribution margin. For example, ConnectPhone's unit variable cost is $250, or 74 percent of the selling price ($250 ÷ $336 = 0.74). That means for every $1 of sales revenue for ConnectPhone, $0.74 represents variable costs, and the difference ($0.26) represents contribution to fixed costs. But even if the company doesn't know its unit price and unit variable cost, it can calculate the contribution margin from total sales and total variable costs or from knowledge of the total cost structure. It can set total sales equal to 100 percent regardless of the actual absolute amount and determine the contribution margin:

$$\text{Contribution margin} = \frac{100\% - 74\%}{100\%} = \frac{1 - 0.74}{1} = 1 - 0.74 = 0.26 \text{ or } 26\%$$

Note that this matches the percentage calculated from the unit price and unit variable cost information. This alternative calculation will be very useful later when analyzing various marketing decisions.

Determining "Breakeven" for Profit Goals

Although it is useful to know the break-even point, most companies are more interested in making a profit. Assume ConnectPhone would like to realize a $5 million profit in the first year. How many units must it sell at the $336 price to cover fixed costs and produce this profit? To determine this, ConnectPhone can simply add the profit figure to fixed costs and again divide by the unit contribution to determine unit sales:

$$\text{Unit volume} = \frac{\text{fixed cost} - \text{profit goal}}{\text{price} - \text{variable cost}} = \frac{\$20\,000\,000 + \$5\,000\,000}{\$336 - \$250} = 290\,697.7 \text{ units}$$

Thus, to earn a $5 million profit, ConnectPhone must sell 290 698 units. Multiply by price to determine dollar sales needed to achieve a $5 million profit:

$$\text{Dollar sales} = 290\,698 \text{ units} \times \$336 = \$97\,674\,528$$

Or use the contribution margin:

$$\text{Sales} = \frac{\text{fixed cost} + \text{profit goal}}{\text{contribution margin}} = \frac{\$20\,000\,000 + \$5\,000\,000}{0.256} = 97\,656\,250$$

Again, note that the difference between the two break-even sales calculations is due to rounding.

As we saw previously, a profit goal can also be stated as a return on investment goal. For example, recall that ConnectPhone wants a 30 percent return on its $10 million investment. Thus, its absolute profit goal is $3 million ($10 000 000 × 0.30). This profit goal is treated the same way as in the previous example:[2]

$$\text{Unit volume} = \frac{\text{fixed cost} + \text{profit goal}}{\text{price} - \text{variable cost}} = \frac{\$20\ 000\ 000 + \$3\ 000\ 000}{\$336 - \$250} = 267\ 442 \text{ units}$$

$$\text{Dollar sales} = 267\ 442 \text{ units} \times \$336 = \$89\ 860\ 512$$

Or

$$\text{Dollar sales} = \frac{\text{fixed cost} + \text{profit goal}}{\text{contribution margin}} = \frac{\$20\ 000\ 000 + \$3\ 000\ 000}{0.256} = \$89\ 843\ 750$$

Finally, ConnectPhone can express its profit goal as a percentage of sales, which we also saw in previous pricing analyses. Assume ConnectPhone desires a 25 percent return on sales. To determine the unit and sales volume necessary to achieve this goal, the calculation is a little different from the previous two examples. In this case, we incorporate the profit goal into the unit contribution as an additional variable cost. Look at it this way: If 25 percent of each sale must go toward profits, that leaves only 75 percent of the selling price to cover fixed costs. Thus, the equation becomes

$$\text{Unit volume} = \frac{\text{fixed cost}}{\text{price} - \text{variable cost} - (0.25 \times \text{price})} \text{ or } \frac{\text{fixed cost}}{(0.75 \times \text{price}) - \text{variable cost}}$$

So,

$$\text{Unit volume} = \frac{\$20\ 000\ 000}{(0.75 \times \$336)} = 10\ 000\ 000 \text{ units}$$

$$\text{Dollar sales necessary} = 10\ 000\ 000 \text{ units} \times \$336 = \$3\ 360\ 000\ 000$$

Thus, ConnectPhone would need more than $3 billion in sales to realize a 25 percent return on sales given its current price and cost structure! Could it possibly achieve this level of sales? The major point is this: Although break-even analysis can be useful in determining the level of sales needed to cover costs or to achieve a stated profit goal, it does not tell the company whether it is *possible* to achieve that level of sales at the specified price. To address this issue, ConnectPhone needs to estimate demand for this product.

Before moving on, however, let's stop here and practise applying the concepts covered so far. Now that you have seen pricing and break-even concepts in action as they related to ConnectPhone's new product, here are several exercises for you to apply what you have learned in other contexts.

Marketing by the Numbers Exercise Set One

Now that you've studied pricing, break-even, and margin analysis as they relate to ConnectPhone's new-product launch, use the following exercises to apply these concepts in other contexts.

1.1 Sanborn, a manufacturer of electric roof vents, realizes a cost of $55 for every unit it produces. Its total fixed costs equal $2 million. If the company manufactures 500 000 units, compute the following:
   a. unit cost
   b. markup price if the company desires a 10 percent return on sales
   c. ROI price if the company desires a 25 percent return on an investment of $1 million

1.2 An interior decorator purchases items to sell in her store. She purchases a lamp for $125 and sells it for $225. Determine the following:
   a. dollar markup
   b. markup percentage on cost
   c. markup percentage on selling price

1.3 A consumer purchases a toaster from a retailer for $60. The retailer's markup is 20 percent, and the wholesaler's markup is 15 percent, both based on selling price. For what price does the manufacturer sell the product to the wholesaler?

1.4 A vacuum manufacturer has a unit cost of $50 and wishes to achieve a margin of 30 percent based on selling price. If the manufacturer sells directly to a retailer who then adds a set margin of 40 percent based on selling price, determine the retail price charged to consumers.

1.5 Advanced Electronics manufactures DVDs and sells them directly to retailers who typically sell them for $20. Retailers take a 40 percent margin based on the retail selling price. Advanced cost information is as follows:

DVD package and disc	$2.50/DVD
Royalties	$2.25/DVD
Advertising and promotion	$500 000
Overhead	$200 000

Calculate the following:
a. contribution per unit and contribution margin
b. break-even volume in DVD units and dollars
c. volume in DVD units and dollar sales necessary if Advanced's profit goal is 20 percent profit on sales
d. net profit if 5 million DVDs are sold

Demand Estimates, the Marketing Budget, and Marketing Performance Measures

Market Potential and Sales Estimates

ConnectPhone has now calculated the sales needed to break even and to attain various profit goals on its new product. However, the company needs more information regarding demand to assess the feasibility of attaining the needed sales levels. This information is also needed for production and other decisions. For example, production schedules need to be developed and marketing tactics need to be planned.

The **total market demand** for a product or a service is the total volume that would be bought by a defined consumer group in a defined geographic area in a defined time period in a defined marketing environment under a defined level and mix of industry marketing effort. Total market demand is not a fixed number but a function of the stated conditions. For example, next year's total market demand for media phones will depend on how much other producers spend on marketing their brands. It also depends on many environmental factors, such as government regulations, economic conditions, and the level of consumer confidence in a given market. The upper limit of market demand is called **market potential**.

One general but practical method that ConnectPhone might use for estimating total market demand uses three variables: (1) the number of prospective buyers, (2) the quantity purchased by an average buyer per year, and (3) the price of an average unit. Using these numbers, ConnectPhone can estimate total market demand as follows:

$$Q = n \times q \times p$$

Where

Q = total market demand
n = number of buyers in the market
q = quantity purchased by an average buyer per year
p = price of an average unit

Total market demand
The total volume that would be bought by a defined consumer group in a defined geographic area in a defined time period in a defined marketing environment under a defined level and mix of industry marketing effort.

Market potential
The upper limit of market demand.

A variation of this approach is the **chain ratio method**. This method involves multiplying a base number by a chain of adjusting percentages. For example, ConnectPhone's product is designed to replace a household's telephone as well as provide "always on" Internet access. Thus, only households with broadband Internet access will be able to use the product. Finally, not all Internet households will be willing and able to purchase the new product. ConnectPhone can estimate US demand by using a chain of calculations like the following:

Total number of US households

$\times$ The percentage of US households with broadband Internet access

$\times$ The percentage of these households willing and able to buy this device

The US Census Bureau estimates that there are approximately 113 million households in the United States.[3] Research also indicates that 50 percent of US households have broadband Internet access.[4] Finally, ConnectPhone's own research indicates that 33.1 percent of households possess the discretionary income needed and are willing to buy a device such as this. Then, the total number of households willing and able to purchase this product is

113 million households $\times$ 0.50 $\times$ 0.331 = 18.7 million households

Households will need only one media phone. Assuming the average retail price across all brands is $750 for this product, the estimate of total market demand is as follows:

18.7 million households $\times$ 1 device per household $\times$ \$750 = \$14 billion

This simple chain of calculations gives ConnectPhone only a rough estimate of potential demand. However, more detailed chains involving additional segments and other qualifying factors would yield more accurate and refined estimates. Still, these are only *estimates* of market potential. They rely heavily on assumptions regarding adjusting percentages, average quantity, and average price. Thus, ConnectPhone must make certain that its assumptions are reasonable and defendable. As can be seen, the overall market potential in dollar sales can vary widely given the average price used. For this reason, ConnectPhone will use unit sales potential to determine its sales estimate for next year. Market potential in terms of units is 18.7 million (18.7 million households $\times$ 1 device per household).

Assuming that ConnectPhone wants to attain 2 percent market share (comparable to its share of the Internet modem market) in the first year after launching this product, then it can forecast unit sales at 18.7 million units $\times$ 0.02 = 374 000 units. At a selling price of $336 per unit, this translates into sales of $125 664 000 (374 000 units $\times$ \$336 per unit). For simplicity, further analyses will use forecasted sales of $125 million.

This unit volume estimate is well within ConnectPhone's production capacity and exceeds not only the break-even estimate (232 559 units) calculated earlier but also the volume necessary to realize a $5 million profit (290 698 units) or a 30 percent return on investment (267 442 units). However, this forecast falls well short of the volume necessary to realize a 25 percent return on sales (10 million units!) and may require that ConnectPhone revise expectations.

To assess expected profits, we must now look at the budgeted expenses for launching this product. To do this, we will construct a pro forma profit-and-loss statement.

The Profit-and-Loss Statement and Marketing Budget

All marketing managers must account for the profit impact of their marketing strategies. A major tool for projecting such profit impact is a **pro forma (or projected) profit-and-loss**

statement (also called an **income statement or operating statement**). A pro forma statement shows projected revenues less budgeted expenses and estimates the projected net profit for an organization, a product, or a brand during a specific planning period, typically a year. It includes direct product production costs, marketing expenses budgeted to attain a given sales forecast, and overhead expenses assigned to the organization or the product. A profit-and-loss statement typically consists of several major components (see Table A3.1):

- *Net sales*—gross sales revenue minus returns and allowances (e.g., trade, cash, quantity, and promotion allowances). ConnectPhone's net sales for 2010 are estimated to be $125 million, as determined in the previous analysis.

- *Cost of goods sold*—(sometimes called cost of sales)—the actual cost of the merchandise sold by a manufacturer or a reseller. It includes the cost of inventory, purchases, and other costs associated with making the goods. ConnectPhone's cost of goods sold is estimated to be 50 percent of net sales, or $62.5 million.

- *Gross margin (or gross profit)*—the difference between net sales and cost of goods sold. ConnectPhone's gross margin is estimated to be $62.5 million.

- *Operating expenses*—the expenses incurred while doing business. These include all other expenses beyond the cost of goods sold that are necessary to conduct business. Operating expenses can be presented in total or broken down in detail. Here, ConnectPhone's estimated operating expenses include marketing expenses and general and administrative expenses.

    Marketing expenses include sales expenses, promotion expenses, and distribution expenses. The new product will be sold through ConnectPhone's sales force, so the company budgets $5 million for sales salaries. However, because sales representatives earn a 10 percent commission on sales, ConnectPhone must also add a variable component to sales expenses of $12.5 million (10 percent of $125 million net sales), for a total budgeted sales expense of $17.5 million. ConnectPhone sets its advertising and promotion to launch this product at $10 million. However, the company also budgets 4 percent of sales, or $5 million, for co-operative advertising allowances to retailers who promote ConnectPhone's new product in their advertising. Thus, the total budgeted advertising and promotion expenses are $15 million ($10 million for advertising plus $5 million in co-op allowances). Finally, ConnectPhone budgets 10 percent of net sales, or $12.5 million, for freight and

TABLE A3.1 Pro Forma Profit-and-Loss Statement for the 12-Month Period Ended December 31, 2010

			% of Sales
Net Sales		$125 000 000	100%
Cost of Goods Sold		62 500 000	50%
Gross Margin		$ 62 500 000	50%
Marketing Expenses			
Sales expenses	$17 500 000		
Promotion expenses	15 000 000		
Freight	12 500 000	45 000 000	36%
General and Administrative Expenses			
Managerial salaries and expenses	$2 000 000		
Indirect overhead	3 000 000	5 000 000	4%
Net Profit Before Income Tax		$12 500 000	10%

delivery charges. In all, total marketing expenses are estimated to be $17.5 million + $15 million + $12.5 million = $45 million.

General and administrative expenses are estimated at $5 million, broken down into $2 million for managerial salaries and expenses for the marketing function, and $3 million of indirect overhead allocated to this product by the corporate accountants (such as depreciation, interest, maintenance, and insurance). Total expenses for the year, then, are estimated to be $50 million ($45 million marketing expenses + $5 million in general and administrative expenses).

- *Net profit before taxes*—profit earned after all costs are deducted. ConnectPhone's estimated net profit before taxes is $12.5 million.

In all, as Table A3.1 shows, ConnectPhone expects to earn a profit on its new product of $12.5 million in 2010. Also note that the percentage of sales that each component of the profit-and-loss statement represents is given in the right-hand column. These percentages are determined by dividing the cost figure by net sales (i.e., marketing expenses represent 36 percent of net sales determined by $45 million ÷ $125 million). As can be seen, ConnectPhone projects a net profit return on sales of 10 percent in the first year after launching this product.

Marketing Performance Measures

Now let's fast-forward a year. ConnectPhone's product has been on the market for one year and management wants to assess its sales and profit performance. One way to assess this performance is to compute performance ratios derived from ConnectPhone's **profit-and-loss statement (or income statement or operating statement)**.

Profit-and-loss statement (or income statement or operating statement)
A statement that shows actual revenues less expenses and net profit for an organization, product, or brand during a specific planning period, typically a year.

Whereas the pro forma profit-and-loss statement shows *projected* financial performance, the statement given in Table A3.2 shows ConnectPhone's *actual* financial performance based on actual sales, cost of goods sold, and expenses during the past year. By comparing the profit-and-loss statement from one period to the next, ConnectPhone can gauge performance against goals, spot favourable or unfavourable trends, and take appropriate corrective action.

The profit-and-loss statement shows that ConnectPhone lost $1 million rather than making the $12.5 million profit projected in the pro forma statement. Why? One obvious

TABLE A3.2 Profit-and-Loss Statement for the 12-Month Period Ended December 31, 2010

			% of Sales
Net Sales		$100 000 000	100%
Cost of Goods Sold		55 000 000	55%
Gross Margin		$ 45 000 000	45%
Marketing Expenses			
Sales expenses	$15 000 000		
Promotion expenses	14 000 000		
Freight	10 000 000	39 000 000	39%
General and Administrative Expenses			
Managerial salaries and expenses	$2 000 000		
Indirect overhead	5 000 000	7 000 000	7%
Net Profit Before Income Tax		($1 000 000)	(1%)

reason is that net sales fell $25 million short of estimated sales. Lower sales translated into lower variable costs associated with marketing the product. However, both fixed costs and the cost of goods sold as a percentage of sales exceeded expectations. Hence, the product's contribution margin was 21 percent rather than the estimated 26 percent. That is, variable costs represented 79 percent of sales (55 percent for cost of goods sold, 10 percent for sales commissions, 10 percent for freight, and 4 percent for co-op allowances). Recall that contribution margin can be calculated by subtracting that fraction from one (1 − 0.79 = 0.21). Total fixed costs were $22 million, $2 million more than estimated. Thus, the sales that ConnectPhone needed to break even given this cost structure can be calculated as

$$\text{Break-even sales} = \frac{\text{fixed costs}}{\text{contribution margin}} = \frac{\$22\,000\,000}{0.21} = \$104\,761\,905$$

If ConnectPhone had achieved another $5 million in sales, it would have earned a profit.

Although ConnectPhone's sales fell short of the forecasted sales, so did overall industry sales for this product. Overall industry sales were only $2.5 billion. That means that ConnectPhone's **market share** was 4 percent ($100 million ÷ $2.5 billion = 0.04 = 4%), which was higher than forecasted. Thus, ConnectPhone attained a higher-than-expected market share but the overall market sales were not as high as estimated.

Market share
Company sales divided by market sales.

Analytic Ratios

The profit-and-loss statement provides the figures needed to compute some crucial **operating ratios**—the ratios of selected operating statement items to net sales. These ratios let marketers compare the firm's performance in one year to that in previous years (or with industry standards and competitors' performance in that year). The most commonly used operating ratios are the gross margin percentage, the net profit percentage, and the operating expense percentage. The inventory turnover rate and return on investment (ROI) are often used to measure managerial effectiveness and efficiency.

Operating ratios
The ratios of selected operating statement items to net sales.

The **gross margin percentage** indicates the percentage of net sales remaining after cost of goods sold that can contribute to operating expenses and net profit before taxes. The higher this ratio, the more a firm has left to cover expenses and generate profit. ConnectPhone's gross margin ratio was 45 percent:

Gross margin percentage
The percentage of net sales remaining after cost of goods sold—calculated by dividing gross margin by net sales.

$$\text{Gross margin percentage} = \frac{\text{gross margin}}{\text{net sales}} = \frac{\$45\,000\,000}{\$100\,000\,000} = 0.45 = 45\%$$

Note that this percentage is lower than estimated, and this ratio is seen easily in the percentage of sales column in Table A3.2. Stating items in the profit-and-loss statement as a percent of sales allows managers to quickly spot abnormal changes in costs over time. If there was previous history for this product and this ratio was declining, management should examine it more closely to determine why it has decreased (i.e., because of a decrease in sales volume or price, an increase in costs, or a combination of these). In ConnectPhone's case, net sales were $25 million lower than estimated, and cost of goods sold was higher than estimated (55 percent rather than the estimated 50 percent).

The **net profit percentage** shows the percentage of each sales dollar going to profit. It is calculated by dividing net profits by net sales:

Net profit percentage
The percentage of each sales dollar going to profit—calculated by dividing net profits by net sales.

$$\text{Net profit percentage} = \frac{\text{net profit}}{\text{net sales}} = \frac{-\$1\,000\,000}{\$100\,000\,000} = -0.01 = -1.0\%$$

This ratio is easily seen in the percent of sales column. ConnectPhone's new product generated negative profits in the first year, not a good situation given that before the product launch net profits before taxes were estimated at more than $12 million. Later in this appendix, we will discuss further analyses the marketing manager should conduct to defend the product.

Operating expense percentage
The portion of net sales going to operating expenses—calculated by dividing total expenses by net sales.

The **operating expense percentage** indicates the portion of net sales going to operating expenses. Operating expenses include marketing and other expenses not directly related to marketing the product, such as indirect overhead assigned to this product. It is calculated by

$$\text{Operating expense percentage} = \frac{\text{total expenses}}{\text{net sales}} = \frac{\$46\,000\,000}{\$100\,000\,000} = 0.46 = 46\%$$

This ratio can also be quickly determined from the percent of sales column in the profit-and-loss statement by adding the percentages for marketing expenses and general and administrative expenses (39% + 7%). Thus, 46 cents of every sales dollar went for operations. Although ConnectPhone wants this ratio to be as low as possible, and 46 percent is not an alarming amount, it is of concern if it is increasing over time or if a loss is realized.

**Inventory turnover rate
(or stock-turn rate)**
The number of times an inventory turns over or is sold during a specified time period (often one year)—calculated based on costs, selling price, or units.

Another useful ratio is the **inventory turnover rate** (also called **stockturn rate** for resellers). The inventory turnover rate is the number of times an inventory turns over or is sold during a specified time period (often one year). This rate tells how quickly a business is moving inventory through the organization. Higher rates indicate that lower investments in inventory are made, thus freeing up funds for other investments. It may be computed on a cost, selling price, or unit basis. The formula based on cost is

$$\text{Inventory turnover rate} = \frac{\text{cost of goods sold}}{\text{average inventory at cost}}$$

Assuming ConnectPhone's beginning and ending inventories were $30 million and $20 million, respectively, the inventory turnover rate is

$$\text{Inventory turnover rate} = \frac{\$55\,000\,000}{(\$30\,000\,000 + \$20\,000\,000)/2} = \frac{\$55\,000\,000}{\$25\,000\,000} = 2.2$$

That is, ConnectPhone's inventory turned over 2.2 times in 2010. Normally, the higher the turnover rate, the higher the management efficiency and company profitability. However, this rate should be compared with industry averages, competitors' rates, and past performance to determine whether ConnectPhone is doing well. A competitor with similar sales but a higher inventory turnover rate will have fewer resources tied up in inventory, allowing it to invest in other areas of the business.

Return on investment (ROI)
A measure of managerial effectiveness and efficiency—net profit before taxes divided by total investment.

Companies frequently use **return on investment** (**ROI**) to measure managerial effectiveness and efficiency. For ConnectPhone, ROI is the ratio of net profits to total investment required to manufacture the new product. This investment includes capital investments in land, buildings, and equipment (here, the initial $10 million to refurbish the manufacturing facility) plus inventory costs (ConnectPhone's average inventory totalled $25 million), for a total of $35 million. Thus, ConnectPhone's ROI for this product is

$$\text{Return on investment} = \frac{\text{net profit before taxes}}{\text{investment}} = \frac{\$1\,000\,000}{\$35\,000\,000} = -0.0286 = -2.86\%$$

ROI is often used to compare alternatives, and a positive ROI is desired. The alternative with the highest ROI is preferred to other alternatives. ConnectPhone needs to be concerned with the ROI realized. One obvious way ConnectPhone can increase ROI is to increase net profit by reducing expenses. Another way is to reduce its investment, perhaps by investing less in inventory and turning it over more frequently.

Marketing Profitability Metrics

Given the above financial results, you may be thinking that ConnectPhone should drop this new product. But what arguments can marketers make for keeping or dropping this product? The obvious arguments for dropping the product are that first-year sales were well below expected levels and the product lost money, resulting in a negative return on investment.

So what would happen if ConnectPhone did drop this product? Surprisingly, if the company drops the product, the profits for the total organization will decrease by $4 million! How can that be? Marketing managers need to look closely at the numbers in the profit-and-loss statement to determine the *net marketing contribution* for this product. In ConnectPhone's case, the net marketing contribution for the product is $4 million, and if the company drops this product, that contribution will disappear as well. Let's look more closely at this concept to illustrate how marketing managers can better assess and defend their marketing strategies and programs.

Net Marketing Contribution

Net marketing contribution (NMC), along with other marketing metrics derived from it, measures *marketing* profitability. It includes only components of profitability that are controlled by marketing. Whereas the previous calculation of net profit before taxes from the profit-and-loss statement includes operating expenses not under marketing's control, NMC does not. Referring back to ConnectPhone's profit-and-loss statement given in Table A3.2, we can calculate net marketing contribution for the product as

$$\text{NMC} = \text{net sales} - \text{cost of goods sold} - \text{marketing expenses}$$
$$= \$100 \text{ million} - \$55 \text{ million} - \$41 \text{ million} = \$4 \text{ million}$$

Net marketing contribution (NMC) A measure of marketing profitability that includes only components of profitability controlled by marketing.

The marketing expenses include sales expenses ($15 million), promotion expenses ($14 million), freight expenses ($10 million), and the managerial salaries and expenses of the marketing function ($2 million), which total $41 million.

Thus, the product actually contributed $4 million to ConnectPhone's profits. It was the $5 million of indirect overhead allocated to this product that caused the negative profit. Further, the amount allocated was $2 million more than estimated in the pro forma profit-and-loss statement. Indeed, if only the estimated amount had been allocated, the product would have earned a *profit* of $1 million rather than losing $1 million. If ConnectPhone drops the product, the $5 million in fixed overhead expenses will not disappear—it will simply have to be allocated elsewhere. However, the $4 million in net marketing contribution *will* disappear.

Marketing Return on Sales and Investment

To get an even deeper understanding of the profit impact of marketing strategy, we'll now examine two measures of marketing efficiency—*marketing return on sales* (marketing ROS) and *marketing return on investment* (marketing ROI).[5]

Marketing return on sales (or marketing ROS) shows the percent of net sales attributable to the net marketing contribution. For our product, ROS is

$$\text{Marketing ROS} = \frac{\text{net marketing contribution}}{\text{net sales}} = \frac{\$4\,000\,000}{\$100\,000\,000} = 0.04 = 4\%$$

Marketing return on sales (or marketing ROS) The percent of net sales attributable to the net marketing contribution—calculated by dividing net marketing contribution by net sales.

Thus, out of every $100 of sales, the product returns $4 to ConnectPhone's bottom line. A high marketing ROS is desirable. But to assess whether this is a good level of performance, ConnectPhone must compare this figure to previous marketing ROS levels for the product, the ROSs of other products in the company's portfolio, and the ROSs of competing products.

Marketing return on investment (or marketing ROI) measures the marketing productivity of a marketing investment. In ConnectPhone's case, the marketing investment is represented by $41 million of the total expenses. Thus, marketing ROI is

$$\text{Marketing ROI} = \frac{\text{net marketing contribution}}{\text{marketing expenses}} = \frac{\$4\,000\,000}{\$41\,000\,000} = 0.0976 = 9.76\%$$

Marketing return on investment (or marketing ROI) A measure of the marketing productivity of a marketing investment—calculated by dividing net marketing contribution by marketing expenses.

As with marketing ROS, a high value is desirable, but this figure should be compared with previous levels for the given product and with the marketing ROIs of competitors' products. Note from this equation that marketing ROI could be greater than 100 percent. This can be achieved by attaining a higher net marketing contribution and/or a lower total marketing expense.

In this section, we estimated market potential and sales, developed profit-and-loss statements, and examined financial measures of performance. In the next section, we discuss methods for analyzing the impact of various marketing tactics. However, before moving on to those analyses, here's another set of quantitative exercises to help you apply what you've learned to other situations.

Marketing by the Numbers Exercise Set Two

2.1. Determine the market potential for a product that has 50 million prospective buyers who purchase an average of three per year and price averages $25. How many units must a company sell if it desires a 10 percent share of this market?

2.2. Develop a profit-and-loss statement for the Westgate division of North Industries. This division manufactures light fixtures sold to consumers through home improvement and hardware stores. Cost of goods sold represents 40 percent of net sales. Marketing expenses include selling expenses, promotion expenses, and freight. Selling expenses include sales salaries totalling $3 million per year and sales commissions (5 percent of sales). The company spent $3 million on advertising last year, and freight costs were 10 percent of sales. Other costs include $2 million for managerial salaries and expenses for the marketing function, and another $3 million for indirect overhead allocated to the division.
   a. Develop the profit-and-loss statement if net sales were $20 million last year.
   b. Develop the profit-and-loss statement if net sales were $40 million last year.
   c. Calculate Westgate's break-even sales.

2.3. Using the profit-and-loss statement you developed in question 2.2b, and assuming that Westgate's beginning inventory was $11 million, ending inventory was $7 million, and total investment was $20 million, including inventory, determine the following:
   a. gross margin percentage
   b. net profit percentage
   c. operating expense percentage
   d. inventory turnover rate
   e. return on investment (ROI)
   f. net marketing contribution
   g. marketing return on sales (marketing ROS)
   h. marketing return on investment (marketing ROI)
   i. Is the Westgate division doing well? Explain your answer.

Financial Analysis of Marketing Tactics

Although the first-year profit performance for ConnectPhone's new product was less than desired, management feels that this attractive market has excellent growth opportunities. Although the sales of ConnectPhone's product were lower than initially projected, they were not unreasonable given the size of the current market. Thus, ConnectPhone wants to explore new marketing tactics to help grow the market for this product and increase sales for the company.

For example, the company could increase advertising to promote more awareness of the new product and its category. It could add salespeople to secure greater product distribution. ConnectPhone could decrease prices so that more consumers could afford its product. Finally, to expand the market, ConnectPhone could introduce a lower-priced model in addition to the higher-priced original offering. Before pursuing any of these tactics, ConnectPhone must analyze the financial implications of each.

Increase Advertising Expenditures

Although most consumers understand the Internet and telephones, they may not be aware of media phones. Thus, ConnectPhone is considering boosting its advertising to make more people aware of the benefits of this device in general and of its own brand in particular.

What if ConnectPhone's marketers recommend increasing national advertising by 50 percent to $15 million (assume no change in the variable co-operative component of promotional expenditures)? This represents an increase in fixed costs of $5 million. What increase in sales will be needed to break even on this $5 million increase in fixed costs?

A quick way to answer this question is to divide the increase in fixed cost by the contribution margin, which we found in a previous analysis to be 21 percent:

$$\text{Increase in sales} = \frac{\text{increase in fixed cost}}{\text{contribution margin}} = \frac{\$5\ 000\ 000}{0.21} = \$23\ 809\ 524$$

Thus, a 50 percent increase in advertising expenditures must produce a sales increase of almost $24 million to just break even. That $24 million sales increase translates into an almost 1 percentage point increase in market share (1 percent of the $2.5 billion overall market equals $25 million). That is, to break even on the increased advertising expenditure, ConnectPhone would have to increase its market share from 4 percent to 4.95 percent ($123 809 524 ÷ $2.5 billion = 0.0495 or 4.95% market share). All of this assumes that the total market will not grow, which might or might not be a reasonable assumption.

Increase Distribution Coverage

ConnectPhone also wants to consider hiring more salespeople in order to call on new retailer accounts and increase distribution through more outlets. Even though ConnectPhone sells directly to wholesalers, its sales representatives call on retail accounts to perform other functions in addition to selling, such as training retail salespeople. Currently, ConnectPhone employs 60 sales reps who earn an average of $50 000 in salary plus 10 percent commission on sales. The product is currently sold to consumers through 1875 retail outlets. Suppose ConnectPhone wants to increase that number of outlets to 2500, an increase of 625 retail outlets. How many additional salespeople will ConnectPhone need, and what sales will be necessary to break even on the increased cost?

One method for determining what size sales force ConnectPhone will need is the **workload method**. The workload method uses the following formula to determine the sales force size:

Workload method
An approach to determining sales force size based on the workload required and the time available for selling.

$$NS = \frac{NC \times FC \times LC}{TA}$$

where

NS = number of salespeople
NC = number of customers
FC = average frequency of customer calls per customer
LC = average length of customer call
TA = time an average salesperson has available for selling per year

ConnectPhone's sales reps typically call on accounts an average of 20 times per year for about 2 hours per call. Although each sales rep works 2000 hours per year (50 weeks per year × 40 hours per week), they spent about 15 hours per week on nonselling activities, such as administrative duties and travel. Thus, the average annual available selling time per sales rep per year is 1250 hours (50 weeks × 25 hours per week). We can now calculate how many sales reps ConnectPhone will need to cover the anticipated 2500 retail outlets:

$$NS = \frac{2500 \times 20 \times 2}{1250} = 80 \text{ salespeople}$$

Therefore, ConnectPhone will need to hire 20 more salespeople. The cost to hire these reps will be $1 million (20 salespeople × $50 000 salary per sales person).

What increase in sales will be required to break even on this increase in fixed costs? The 10 percent commission is already accounted for in the contribution margin, so the contribution margin remains unchanged at 21 percent. Thus, the increase in sales needed to cover this increase in fixed costs can be calculated by

$$\text{Increase in sales} = \frac{\text{increase in fixed cost}}{\text{contribution margin}} = \frac{\$1\,000\,000}{0.21} = \$4\,761\,905$$

That is, ConnectPhone's sales must increase almost $5 million to break even on this tactic. So, how many new retail outlets will the company need to secure to achieve this sales increase? The average revenue generated per current outlet is $53 333 ($100 million in sales divided by 1875 outlets). To achieve the nearly $5 million sales increase needed to break even, ConnectPhone would need about 90 new outlets ($4 761 905 ÷ $53 333 = 89.3 outlets), or about 4.5 outlets per new rep. Given that current reps cover about 31 outlets apiece (1875 outlets ÷ 60 reps), this seems very reasonable.

Decrease Price

ConnectPhone is also considering lowering its price to increase sales revenue through increased volume. The company's research has shown that demand for most types of consumer electronics products is elastic—that is, the percentage increase in the quantity demanded is greater than the percentage decrease in price.

What increase in sales would be necessary to break even on a 10 percent decrease in price? That is, what increase in sales will be needed to maintain the total contribution that ConnectPhone realized at the higher price? The current total contribution can be determined by multiplying the contribution margin by total sales:[6]

$$\text{Current total contribution} = \text{contribution margin} \times \text{sales}$$
$$= 0.21 \times \$100 \text{ million} = \$21 \text{ million}$$

Price changes result in changes in unit contribution and contribution margin. Recall that the contribution margin of 21 percent was based on variable costs representing 79 percent of sales. Therefore, unit variable costs can be determined by multiplying the original price by this percentage: $336 × 0.79 = $265.44 per unit. If price is decreased by 10 percent, the new price is $302.40. However, variable costs do not change just because price decreased, so the contribution and contribution margin decrease as follows:

	Old	New (reduced 10%)
Price	$336	$302.40
– Unit variable cost	$265.44	$265.44
= Unit contribution	$70.56	$36.96
Contribution margin	$70.56/$336 = 0.21 or 21%	$36.96/$302.40 = 0.12 or 12%

So a 10 percent reduction in price results in a decrease in the contribution margin from 21 percent to 12 percent.[7] To determine the sales level needed to break even on this price reduction, we calculate the level of sales that must be attained at the new contribution margin to achieve the original total contribution of $21 million:

$$\text{New contribution margin} \times \text{new sales level} = \text{original total contribution}$$

So,

$$\text{New sales level} = \frac{\text{original contribution}}{\text{new contribution margin}} = \frac{\$21\,000\,000}{0.21} = \$175\,000\,000$$

Thus, sales must increase by $75 million ($175 million – $100 million) just to break even on a 10 percent price reduction. This means that ConnectPhone must increase market share to 7 percent ($175 million ÷ $2.5 billion) to achieve the current level of profits (assuming no increase in the total market sales). The marketing manager must assess whether or not this is a reasonable goal.

Extend the Product Line

As a final option, ConnectPhone is considering extending its product line by offering a lower-priced model. Of course, the new, lower-priced product would steal some sales from the higher-priced model. This is called **cannibalization**—the situation in which one product sold by a company takes a portion of its sales from other company products. If the new product has a lower contribution than the original product, the company's total contribution will decrease on the cannibalized sales. However, if the new product can generate enough new volume, it is worth considering.

Cannibalization
The situation in which one product sold by a company takes a portion of its sales from other company products.

To assess cannibalization, ConnectPhone must look at the incremental contribution gained by having both products available. Recall in the previous analysis we determined that unit variable costs were $265.44 and unit contribution was just over $70. Assuming costs remain the same next year, ConnectPhone can expect to realize a contribution per unit of approximately $70 for every unit of the original product sold.

Assume that the first model offered by ConnectPhone is called MP1 and the new, lower-priced model is called MP2. MP2 will retail for $400, and resellers will take the same markup percentages on price as they do with the higher-priced model. Therefore, MP2's price to wholesalers will be $224 as follows:

Retail price:	$400
minus retail margin (30%):	– $120
Retailer's cost/wholesaler's price:	$280
minus wholesaler's margin (20%):	– $ 56
Wholesaler's cost/ConnectPhone's price	$224

If MP2's variable costs are estimated to be $174, then its contribution per unit will equal $50 ($224 – $174 = $50). That means for every unit that MP2 cannibalizes from MP1, ConnectPhone will *lose* $20 in contribution toward fixed costs and profit (i.e., contributionMP2 – contributionMP1 = $50 – $70 = –$20). You might conclude that ConnectPhone should not pursue this tactic because it appears as though the company will be worse off if it introduces the lower-priced model. However, if MP2 captures enough *additional* sales, ConnectPhone will be better off even though some MP1 sales are cannibalized. The company must examine what will happen to *total* contribution, which requires estimates of unit volume for both products.

Originally, ConnectPhone estimated that next year's sales of MP1 would be 600 000 units. However, with the introduction of MP2, it now estimates that 200 000 of those sales will be cannibalized by the new model. If ConnectPhone sells only 200 000 units of the new MP2 model (all cannibalized from MP1), the company would lose $4 million in total contribution (200 000 units × –$20 per cannibalized unit = –$4 million)—not a good outcome. However, ConnectPhone estimates that MP2 will generate the 200 000 of cannibalized sales plus an *additional* 500 000 unit sales. Thus, the contribution on these additional MP2 units will be $25 million (i.e., 500 000 units × $50 per unit = $25 million). The net effect is that ConnectPhone will gain $21 million in total contribution by introducing MP2.

The following table compares ConnectPhone's total contribution with and without the introduction of MP2:

	MP1 only	MP1 and MP2
MP1 contribution	600 000 units × $70 = $42 000 000	400 000 units × $70 = $28 000 000
MP2 contribution	0	700 000 units × $50 = $35 000 000
Total contribution	$42 000 000	$63 000 000

The difference in the total contribution is a net gain of $21 million ($63 million – $42 million). Based on this analysis, ConnectPhone should introduce the MP2 model because it results in a positive incremental contribution. However, if fixed costs will increase by more than $21 million as a result of adding this model, then the net effect will be negative and ConnectPhone should not pursue this tactic.

Now that you have seen these marketing tactic analysis concepts in action as they related to ConnectPhone's new product, here are several exercises for you to apply what you have learned in this section in other contexts.

Marketing by the Numbers Exercise Set Three

3.1 Kingsford Inc. sells small plumbing components to consumers through retail outlets. Total industry sales for Kingsford's relevant market last year were $80 million, with Kingsford's sales representing 10 percent of that total. Contribution margin is 25 percent. Kingsford's sales force calls on retail outlets and each sales rep earns $45,000 per year plus 1 percent commission on all sales. Retailers receive a 40 percent margin on selling price and generate average revenue of $10,000 per outlet for Kingsford.

a. The marketing manager has suggested increasing consumer advertising by $300,000. By how much would dollar sales need to increase to break even on this expenditure? What increase in overall market share does this represent?

b. Another suggestion is to hire three more sales representatives to gain new consumer retail accounts. How many new retail outlets would be necessary to break even on the increased cost of adding three sales reps?

c. A final suggestion is to make a 20 percent across-the-board price reduction. By how much would dollar sales need to increase to maintain Kingsford's current contribution? (See endnote 7 to calculate the new contribution margin.)

d. Which suggestion do you think Kingsford should implement? Explain your recommendation.

3.2 PepsiCo sells its soft drinks in approximately 400 000 retail establishments, such as supermarkets, discount stores, and convenience stores. Sales representatives call on each retail account weekly, which means each account is called on by a sales rep 52 times per year. The average length of a sales call is 75 minutes (or 1.25 hours). An average salesperson works 2000 hours per year (50 weeks per year × 40 hours per week), but each spends 10 hours a week on non-selling activities, such as administrative tasks and travel. How many sales people does PepsiCo need?

3.3 Hair Zone manufactures a brand of hair-styling gel. It is considering adding a modified version of the product—a foam that provides stronger hold. Hair Zone's variable costs and prices to wholesalers are as follows:

	Current Hair Gel	New Foam Product
Unit selling price	2.00	2.25
Unit variable costs	0.85	1.25

Hair Zone expects to sell 1 million units of the new styling foam in the first year after introduction, but it expects that 60 percent of those sales will come from buyers who normally purchase Hair Zone's styling gel. Hair Zone estimates that it would sell 1.5 million units of the gel if it did not introduce the foam. If the fixed cost of launching the new foam will be $100 000 during the first year, should Hair Zone add the new product to its line? Why or why not?

Endnotes

CHAPTER 1

1. Kelly Gadzala, "Joe Keeps It Fresh," *Strategy,* October 5, 2011, http://strategyonline.ca/2011/10/05/joe-keeps-it-fresh; Megan Durisin, "Can Canada's Joe Fresh Save JCPenney?" *Financial Post*, March 15, 2013, http://business.financialpost .com/2013/03/16/can-canadas-joe-fresh-save-jcpenney; Jessica Allen, "Backstage with Joe Mimran: The Joe Fresh Designer—and Canadian Fashion Mogul—on What Inspired His 2013 Spring Collection," *Maclean's*, October 26, 2012, http://www2.macleans .ca/2012/10/26/backstage-with-joe-mimran; Hollie Shaw, "Brands Like Joe Fresh, President's Choice Set Loblaw Apart, Weston Tells AGM," *Financial Post*, May 3, 2012, http://business.financialpost .com/2012/05/03/brands-like-joe-fresh-presidents-choice-set-loblaw-apart-weston-tells-agm; and information from www .joefresh.com and www.loblaws.ca.

2. See "U.S. Market Leaders," *Advertising Age*, December 10, 2010, 14.

3. See Philip Kotler and Kevin Lane Keller, *Marketing Management,* 14th ed. (Upper Saddle River, NJ: Prentice Hall, 2012), 5.

4. The American Marketing Association offers the following definition: "Marketing is an organizational function and a set of processes for creating, communicating, and delivering value to customers and for managing customer relationships in ways that benefit the organization and its stakeholders." See www .marketingpower.com/_layouts/Dictionary.aspx?dLetter=M (accessed November 2011).

5. See Dan Sewell, "Kroger CEO Often Roams Aisles, Wielding Carte Blanche," *Journal Gazette* (Fort Wayne, IN), November 15, 2010, www.journalgazette.net/article/20101115/BIZ/311159958/-1/BIZ09.

6. See Theodore Levitt's classic article, "Marketing Myopia," *Harvard Business Review* (July–August 1960): 45–56. For more recent discussions, see "What Business Are You In?" *Harvard Business Review* (October 2006): 127–137; Lance A. Bettencourt, "Debunking Myths about Customer Needs," *Marketing Management*, January/February 2009, 46–51; and N. Craig Smith, Minette E. Drumright, and Mary C. Gentile, "The New Marketing Myopia," *Journal of Public Policy & Marketing* (Spring 2010): 4–11.

7. Information from HP's recent "The Computer Is Personal Again" and "Everybody On" marketing campaigns. See www.hp.com/ united-states/personal_again/index.html and www.hp.com/global/ us/en/everybody-on/ribbons/passionTVSpot.html (accessed September 2011).

8. "Henry Ford, Faster Horses and Market Research," *Research Arts,* January 25, 2011, www.researcharts.com/2011/01/henry-ford-faster-horses-and-market-research.

9. Adapted from information found in Michael E. Porter and Mark R. Kramer, "Creating Shared Value," *Harvard Business Review* (January–February 2011): 63–77; and Michael Krauss, "Evolution of an Academic: Kotler on Marketing 3.0," *Marketing News*, January 30, 2011, 12.

10. Based on information from RBC's website, "Community and Sustainability," www.rbc.com/community-sustainability/index.html (accessed June 28, 2013).

11. Based on information from Weber Grill's website, www.weber.com (accessed September 2011).

12. Based on information from Michael Bush, "Why You Should Be Putting on the Ritz," *Advertising Age*, June 21, 2010, 1; Julie Barker, "Power to the People," *Incentive*, February 2008, 34; Carmine Gallo, "Employee Motivation the Ritz-Carlton Way," *BusinessWeek*, February 29, 2008, www.businessweek.com/ smallbiz/content/feb2008/sb20080229_347490.htm; and Kotler and Keller, *Marketing Management,* 14th ed., 381. Also see http://corporate.ritzcarlton.com/en/About/Awards.htm#Hotel (accessed September 2011).

13. Matthew Dixon, Karen Freeman, and Nicholas Toman, "Stop Trying to Delight Your Customers," *Harvard Business Review* (July–August 2010), 116–122. Also see Chris Morran, "Stop Treating Customers like Liabilities, Start Treating Them like People," *Advertising Age,* February 14, 2011, 10.

14. Information about Weber Nation from www.webernation.com (accessed September 2011).

15. Elisabeth A. Sullivan, "Just Say No," *Marketing News*, April 15, 2008, 17. Also see Raymund Flandez, "It Just Isn't Working? Some File for Customer Divorce," *Wall Street Journal*, November 16, 2009, B7.

16. Sullivan, "Just Say No," 17.

17. The following example is adapted from information found in Vikas Mittal, Matthew Sarkees, and Feisal Murshed, "The Right Way to Manage Unprofitable Customers," *Harvard Business Review* (April 2008), 95–102. Quotes from Whitney Hess, "Fire Your Worst Customers," *Pleasure and Pain* Weblog, entry posted February 21, 2010, http://whitneyhess.com/blog/2010/02/21/fire-your-worst-customers; and Jeff Schmidt, "Save Your Company by Firing Your Customers," *Bloomberg Businessweek*, April 5, 2011, www.businessweek.com/managing/content/apr2011/ ca2011045_952921.htm?campaign_id=rss_topStories.

18. Quotes from Andrew Walmsley, "The Year of Consumer Empowerment," *Marketing*, December 20, 2006, p. 9; and Jeff Heilman, "Rules of Engagement: During a Recession, Marketers Need to Have Their Keenest Listening-to-Customers Strategy in Place," *The Magazine of Branded Content*, Winter 2009, p. 7. Also see Frank Striefler, "5 Marketing Principles Brands Should Embrace in 2010," *Adweek*, January 13, 2010, accessed at www.adweek.com.

19. See Brian Morrissey, "Brand Sweepstakes Get Twitterized," *Adweek*, November 22, 2009, accessed at www.adweek.com/news/ advertising-branding/brand-sweepstakes-get-twitterized-100954; Alicia Wallace, "Owing Social: Businesses Dial in to Facebook,

Twitter to Build Business," *McClatchy-Tribune Business News*, April 26, 2010; Judah Schiller, "Social Media Isn't the Problem, It's Your Culture," The Employee Engagement Group, February 22, 2011, http://employeeengagement.com/2011/02/social-media-isnt-the-problem-its-your-culture/; and Mark Milian, "The App Maker Said to Be Planning Twitter Competitor," *CNN*, April 13, 2011, http://articles.cnn.com/2011-04-13/tech/ubermedia.twitter_1_tweet-deck-twitter-blackberry-app?_s=PM:TECH.

20. Casey Hibbard, "Cold Stone Transforms the Ice Cream Social with Facebook," *Social Media Examiner*, November 22, 2010, www.socialmediaexaminer.com/cold-stone-transforms-the-ice-cream-social-with-facebook; Heba Hornsby, "Social Media Success Stories: See How Cold Stone Ice Cream Became So 'Hot' on Facebook," *Garious* Weblog, posted February 10, 2011, http://garious.com/blog/2011/02/cold-stone-creamery-success-story; and www.facebook.com/coldstonecreamery (accessed August 2011).

21. Elisabeth A. Sullivan, "We Were Right!" *Marketing News*, December 15, 2008, 17.

22. Joel Rubenstein, "Marketers, Researchers, and Your Ears," *Brandweek*, February 15, 2010, 34. For other discussion and examples, see Venkat Ramaswamy and Francis Gouillart, "Building the Co-Creative Enterprise," *Harvard Business Review* (October 2010), 100–109.

23. Tim Nudd, "Doritos 'Pug Attack' Director Wins $1 Million," *Ad Freak* Weblog, posted February 7, 2011, http://adweek.blogs.com/adfreak/2011/02/doritos-pug-attack-director-wins-1-million.html; Bruce Horowitz, "Ad Meter 1st: A Doggone Tie," *USA Today*, February 7, 2011, 68; and www.crashthesuperbowl.com (accessed April 2011).

24. Gavin O'Malley, "Entries Pour in for Heinz Ketchup Commercial Contest," *Online Media Daily*, August 13, 2007, www.mediapost.com/publications/article/65597/entries-pour-in-for-heinz-ketchup-commercial-conte.html#axzz2cfA7rxoM.

25. Steven Rosenbaum, "Teaching Brands New Tricks," *Adweek*, April 4, 2011, 12–13. Also see Steven Rosenbaum, *Curator Nation: How to Win in the World Where Consumers Are Creators* (New York: McGraw-Hill, 2011).

26. "Consumer 'New Frugality' May Be an Enduring Feature of Post-Recession Economy, Finds Booz & Company Survey," *Business Wire*, February 24, 2010; "Private Label Gets a Quality Reputation, Causing Consumers to Change Their Buying Habits," *PR Newswire*, January 20, 2011; and Ely Portillo, "In Weak Economy, Store Brands Prosper," *McClatchy-Tribune News Service*, March 18, 2011.

27. "Stew Leonard's," *Hoover's Company Records*, July 15, 2011, http://subscriber.hoovers.com/H/company360/overview.html?companyId=104426000000000; and www.stew-leonards.com/html/about.cfm (accessed November 2011).

28. Graham Brown, "MobileYouth Key Statistics," March 28, 2008, www.mobileyouth.org/?s=MobileYouth+ Key+ Statistics. For interesting discussions of customer lifetime value, see Sunil Gupta et al., "Modeling Customer Lifetime Value," *Journal of Service Research* (November 2006) 139–146; Jason Q. Zhang, Ashutosh Dixit, and Roberto Friedman, "Customer Loyalty and Lifetime

Value: An Empirical Investigation of Consumer Packaged Goods," *Journal of Marketing Theory and Practice* (Spring 2010), 127; and Norman W. Marshall, "Commitment, Loyalty, and Customer Lifetime Value: Investigating the Relationships among Key Determinants," *Journal of Business & Economics Research* (August 2010), 67–85.

29. Based on quotes and information from Heather Green, "How Amazon Aims to Keep You Clicking," *BusinessWeek*, March 2, 2009, 34–40; Geoffrey A. Fowler, "Corporate News: Amazon's Sales Soar, Lifting Profit," *Wall Street Journal*, April 23, 2010, B3; and Brad Stone, "What's in the Box? Instant Gratification," *Bloomberg Businessweek*, November 29–December 5, 2010, 39–40.

30. For more discussion on customer equity, see Roland T. Rust, Valerie A. Zeithaml, and Katherine A. Lemon, *Driving Customer Equity* (New York: Free Press, 2000); Roland T. Rust, Katherine A. Lemon, and Valerie A. Zeithaml, "Return on Marketing: Using Customer Equity to Focus Marketing Strategy," *Journal of Marketing* (January 2004), 109–127; Dominique M. Hanssens, Daniel Thorpe, and Carl Finkbeiner, "Marketing When Customer Equity Matters," *Harvard Business Review* (May 2008), 117–124; V. Kumar and Denish Shaw, "Expanding the Role of Marketing: From Customer Equity to Market Capitalization," *Journal of Marketing* (November 2009), 119; and Philip E. Pfeifer, "On Estimating Current-Customer Equity Using Company Summary Data," *Journal of Interactive Marketing* (February 2011), 1.

31. This example is adapted from information found in Roland T. Rust, Katherine A. Lemon, and Valerie A. Zeithaml, "Where Should the Next Marketing Dollar Go?" *Marketing Management* (September–October 2001), 24–28; with information from Grace Hamulic, "Audi, Cadillac, Lexus Buyer Demographics Exhibit Most Changes," *Motorway America*, May 2010, www.motorwayamerica.com/editorial/audi-cadillac-lexus-buyer-demographics-exhibit-most-changes.

32. Based on Werner Reinartz and V. Kumar, "The Mismanagement of Customer Loyalty," *Harvard Business Review* (July 2002), 86–94. Also see Stanley F. Slater, Jakki J. Mohr, and Sanjit Sengupta, "Know Your Customer," *Marketing Management* (February 2009), 37–44.

33. Natalie Zmuda, "Why the Bad Economy Has Been Good for Target," *Advertising Age*, October 4, 2010, 1; and Sharon Edelson, "Target Eying $100 Billion in Sales," *WWD*, February 25, 2011, 2.

34. Emily Thornton, "The New Rules," *Businessweek*, January 19, 2009, 30–34.

35. Adapted from information in Brad Stone, "Breakfast Can Wait. Today's First Stop Is Online," *New York Times*, August 10, 2009, A1. Also see Rich Gagnon, "2011: A Pivotal Year for Marketing," *Adweek*, January 17, 2011, www.adweek.com/news/advertising-branding/2011-pivotal-year-marketing-125424.

36. Internet usage stats from www.internetworldstats.com/stats.htm (accessed June 2011); Pew/Internet, "The Future of the Internet III," December 14, 2008, www.pewinternet.org/Reports/2008/The-Future-of-the-Internet-III.aspx; "Digital Hotlist: By the Numbers," *Adweek*, October 11, 2010, 20; and James Lewin, "Pew Internet and the American Life Project: Trend Data," www.pewinternet.org/Trend-Data.aspx (accessed June 2011).

37. "Pew Internet and the American Life Project: Trend Data," and "comScore Reports Record-Breaking $43.4 Billion in Q4 2010 U.S. Retail E-Commerce Spending, Up 11 Percent vs. Year Ago," *PR Newswire*, February 8, 2011; Statistics Canada, "Individual Internet Use and E-commerce," October 12, 2011, *The Daily*, www .statcan.gc.ca/daily-quotidien/111012/dq111012a-eng.htm; and Samantha Hornby, "How Canadian E-commerce Can Catch up to the Competition," *Techvibes*, January 8, 2013, www.techvibes.com/ blog/canadian-e-commerce-competition-2013-01-08.

38. For examples and for a good review of not-for-profit marketing, see Philip Kotler and Alan R. Andreasen, *Strategic Marketing for Nonprofit Organizations*, 7th ed. (Upper Saddle River, NJ: Prentice Hall, 2008); Philip Kotler and Karen Fox, *Strategic Marketing for Educational Institutions* (Upper Saddle River, NJ: Prentice Hall, 1995); Philip Kotler, John Bowen, and James Makens, *Marketing for Hospitality and Tourism*, 4th ed. (Upper Saddle River, NJ: Prentice Hall, 2006); and Philip Kotler and Nancy Lee, *Marketing in the Public Sector: A Roadmap for Improved Performance* (Philadelphia: Wharton School Publishing, 2007).

39. "Bust a Move for Breast Health Delivers Unforgettable Day and Important Funds for Breast Health," *Canadian Newswire*, March 24, 2012, www.newswire.ca/en/story/943491/bust-a-move-for-breast-healthtm-delivers-unforgettable-day-and-important-funds-for-breast-health; Jeremy Webb, "Martin Adds Giggles to Bust a Move," *The Chronicle Herald*, April 1, 2012, http:// thechronicleherald.ca/artslife/79808-martin-adds-giggles-bust-move; Tara Bradbury, "Bust a Move Breaks the Bank," *The Telegram*, April 2, 2012, www.thetelegram.com/News/Local/2012-04-02/ article-2944894/Bust-a-Move-breaks-thebank/1; Patricia Kozicka, "Hundreds Bust a Move for Breast Health," *Global News*, March 24, 2012, http://globalnews.ca/news/226315/hundreds-bust-a-move-for-breast-health; and information at www.bustamove.ca.

40. "Leading National Advertisers," *Advertising Age*, June 21, 2010, 10–12; Bill Curry, "Tory Government Hiked Ad Spending to Promote Stimulus Projects," *Globe and Mail*, January 4, 2012, www.theglobeandmail.com/news/politics/tory-government-hiked-ad-spending-to-promote-stimulus-projects/article1357867; and information from Public Works and Government Services Canada, www.tpsgc-pwgsc.gc.ca/pub-adv/rapports-reports/2011-2012/ deppub-advexp-eng.html. For more on social marketing, see Philip Kotler, Ned Roberto, and Nancy R. Lee, *Social Marketing: Improving the Quality of Life*, 2nd ed. (Thousand Oaks, CA: Sage Publications, 2002);

41. Quotes and information found at www.patagonia.com/web/us/ contribution/patagonia.go?assetid=2329 (accessed August 2011).

CHAPTER 2

1. See "Christie Projection Mapping Display Transforms Canada's Parliament Hill Centre Block into Virtual Storybook," press release published by Christie Digital, February 27, 2013; "Branham 300 NOW Spotlight Company: Christie Digital Systems Canada," published by Branham Group Inc., Ottawa, September 2011; and information from ChristieDigital.com, media articles about Christie, and Facebook.com/ChristieDigital.

2. Mission statements are from Indigo Books & Music at www. chapters.indigo.ca/our-company/mission (accessed August 2013),

and Under Armour at www.uabiz.com/company/mission.cfm (accessed August 2013).

3. Jack and Suzy Welch, "State Your Business: Too Many Mission Statements Are Loaded with Fatheaded Jargon. Play It Straight," *Businessweek*, January 14, 2008, p. 80. Also see Leia Fransisco, "A Good Mission Statement Can Lead a Business," *McClatchy-Tribune Business News*, November 8, 2008.

4. Based on information found at "Heinz Profit Slips; Emerging Markets Grow," *Wall Street Journal*, February 27, 2013, http:// online.wsj.com/article/SB10001424127887324503204578318622723158276.html (accessed August 2013).

5. The following discussion is based in part on information found at www.bcg.com/documents/file13904.pdf (accessed August 2013).

6. The Walt Disney Company's 2012 Annual Report; Jason Garcia, "Disney Profit Leaps 54 Percent," *Orlando Sentinel*, February 11, 2011.

7. For an interesting discussion on managing growth, see Matthew S. Olson, Derek van Bever, and Seth Verry, "When Growth Stalls," *Harvard Business Review*, March 2008, pp. 51–61.

8. H. Igor Ansoff, "Strategies for Diversification," *Harvard Business Review*, September–October 1957, pp. 113–124.

9. Matt Townsend, "Under Armour Advances After Raising Sales Forecast," *Bloomberg Businessweek*, January 27, 2011; Kyle Stack, "How Under Armour Learned to Love Cotton Fiber," *Wired*, February 9, 2011.

10. See Michael E. Porter, *Competitive Advantage: Creating and Sustaining Superior Performance* (New York, NY: Free Press, 1985); and Michel E. Porter, "What Is Strategy?" *Harvard Business Review*, November–December 1996, pp. 61–78; also see "The Value Chain" at www.quickmba.com/strategy/value-chain (accessed July 2008); and Philip Kotler and Kevin Lane Keller, *Marketing Management* (Upper Saddle River, NJ: Prentice Hall, 2009), pp. 35–36 and pp. 252–253.

11. Nirmalya Kumar, "The CEO's Marketing Manifesto," *Marketing Management*, November–December 2008, pp. 24–29.

12. Rebecca Ellinor, "Crowd Pleaser," *Supply Management*, December 13, 2007, pp. 26–29; and information from www.loreal .com/_en/_ww/html/suppliers/index.aspx (accessed August 2009).

13. See www.nikebiz.com/company_overview (accessed April 2009).

14. "100 Leading National Advertisers," special issue of *Advertising Age*, June 23, 2008, p. 10.

15. Based on information at CMOSurvey.org.

16. Interview with Rex Briggs, published on MarketingMag.ca, December 4, 2006.

17. Kristin Laird, "Marketing's Barriers to ROI," *Marketing Magazine*, December 4, 2008.

18. Kristin Laird, "Social Media Week: ROI vs. Value," *Marketing Magazine*, February 16, 2012.

19. For a full discussion of this model and details on customer-centred measures of return on marketing investment, see Roland

T. Rust, Katherine N. Lemon, and Valerie A. Zeithaml, "Return on Marketing: Using Customer Equity to Focus Marketing Strategy," *Journal of Marketing*, January 2004, pp. 109–127; Roland T. Rust, Katherine N. Lemon, and Das Narayandas, *Customer Equity Management* (Upper Saddle River, NJ: Prentice Hall, 2005); David Tiltman, "Everything You Know Is Wrong," *Marketing*, June 13, 2007, pp. 28–29; Roland T. Rust, "Seeking Higher ROI? Base Strategy on Customer Equity," *Advertising Age*, September 10, 2007, pp. 26–27; and Thorsen Wiesel, Bernd Skiera, and Julián Villanueva, "Customer Equity: An Integral Part of Financial Reporting," *Journal of Marketing*, March 2008, pp. 1–14.

CHAPTER 3

1. Excerpts, quotes, and other information from T. L. Stanley, "Easy As Pie: How Russell Weiner Turned Sabotage Into Satisfaction," *Adweek*, September 13, 2010, p. 40; "Lessons from the Domino's Turnaround," *Restaurant Hospitality*, June 2010, p. 30; Rupal Parekh, "Marketer of the Year," *Advertising Age*, October 18, 2010, p. 19; Emily Bryson York, "Domino's Claims Victory with New Strategy: Pizza Wasn't Good, We Fixed It," *Advertising Age*, May 10, 2010, p. 4; Mark Brandau, "Domino's Do-Over," *Nation's Restaurant News*, March 8, 2010, p. 44; "Domino's Puts Customer Feedback on Times Square Billboard," *Detroit News*, July 26, 2011; and annual reports and other information from www.dominosbiz.com and www.pizzaturnaround.com (accessed December 2011).

2. Information from Sierra Club website at SierraClub.org, and from non-profit organization Public Citizen's website at Citizen.org.

3. The figure and the discussion in this section are adapted from Philip Kotler, Gary Armstrong, Veronica Wong, and John Saunders, *Principles of Marketing: European Edition*, 5th ed. (London: Pearson Publishing, 2009), Chapter 2.

4. Corporate information from AboutMcDonalds.com; "McDonald's® restaurants in Canada to turn off the lights again in support of Earth Hour," press release published on Canada Newswire, March 24, 2009.

5. Chris Snowdon, "Absurd prohibition of toy advertising will lead to higher prices," April 11, 2013. BBC Radio program, published and available on the website of the Institute of Economic Affairs (iae.org.uk).

6. Jeff Gray, "Rogers violated false-advertising rules with 'fewest dropped-call' claims, court hears," *Globe and Mail*, May 13, 2013.

7. "Bell Canada to Pay $10 Million Fine for Misleading Ads," *Canadian Press*, June 29, 2011.

8. "Environmental Claims: A Guide for Industry and Advertisers," published by the Competition Bureau, and available on its website at CompetitionBureau.gc.ca.

9. Emma Hall, "Green Murder," *Marketing*, October 29, 2007, p. 11.

10. Theodore Levitt, "The Morality (?) of Advertising," *Harvard Business Review* (July–August 1970), pp. 84–92.

11. See Gerri Hirshey, "Time to Buy a New Stove. Again." *New York Times*, December 14, 2008, p. LI 4.

12. Adapted from David Suzuki, "We All Pay for Technology," *Niagara Falls Review*, March 15, 2007, p. A4. For more discussion,

see Joseph Guiltinan, "Creative Destruction and Destructive Creations: Environmental Ethics and Planned Obsolescence," *Journal of Business Ethics* (May 2009), pp. 19–28.

13. Information from AdBusters.org.

14. The quote is from Oliver James, "It's More Than Enough to Make You Sick," *Marketing*, January 23, 2008, pp. 26–28.

15. "Consumerism: New Era of Frugality Dawns," *Marketing Week*, December 18, 2008, p. 12; and "The American Dream Has Been Revised Not Reversed," *Business Wire*, March 9, 2009.

16. Transport for London website, tfl.gov.uk.

17. Tim Bradshaw, "Facebook to tap mobiles ads for revenue," *Financial Times* (FT.com), February 5, 2012.

18. Emailvision Survey: Bombarding Consumers with Marketing Creates Brand Resentment, *Wireless News*, January 24, 2013.

19. Ross Gordon, Marylyn Carrigan, and Gerard Hastings, "A Framework for Sustainable Marketing," *Marketing Theory*, 11 (2011), p. 143.

20. For these and other examples, see "Strong Growth in Green Logistics," *World Trade*, December 28, 2008, p. 13; Mark Borden et al., "50 Ways to Green Your Business," *Fast Company*, November 2007; and Jack Neff, "Green-Marketing Revolution Defies Economic Downturn," *Advertising Age*, April 20, 2009, accessed at http://adage.com/print?article_id=136091.

21. See Brown, "The Many Shades of Green," *M. E. Magazine*, accessed at http://memagazine.asme.org/Articles/2009/January/Many_Shades_Green.cfm.

22. Based on information from Marc Gunther, "Coca-Cola's Green Crusader," *Fortune*, April 28, 2008, p. 150; "Cold Test Markets Aluminum Bottles," February 20, 2008, accessed at www.bevnet.com/news/2008/02-20-2008-Coke.asp; Jessie Scanlon, "The Shape of a New Coke," *BusinessWeek*, September 2008, p. 72; and "Coca-Cola to Install 1800 CO_2 Coolers in North America," April 30, 2009, accessed at www.r744.com/articles/2009-04-30-coca-cola-toinstall-1800-co2-coolers-in-north-america.php.

23. Adapted from "The Top 3 in 2005," *Global 100*, accessed at www.global100.org, July 2005. See also "Alcoa Again Named One of the World's Most Sustainable Companies at Davos," January 29, 2009, accessed at www.alcoa.com; and information from www.global100.org, accessed August 2009. For further information on Alcoa's sustainability program, see Alcoa's Sustainability Report, found at www.alcoa.com.

24. See Geoffrey Garver and Aranka Podhora, "Transboundary Environmental Impact Assessment as Part of the North American Agreement on Environmental Cooperation," *Impact Assessment & Project Appraisal*, December 2008, pp. 253–263; http://ec.europa.eu/environment/index_en.htm, accessed May 2009; and "What is EMAS?" at http://ec.europa.eu/environment/emas/index_en.htm, accessed October 2009.

25. Jeff Beer, "Frito-Lay Canada Defends Noisy Bag With New Campaign," *Marketing* magazine online, October 29, 2010; Jeff Beer, "Breaking Down the Sun Chips Bag Story," *Marketing*, October 25, 2010, p. 6.

26. See Laurel Wentz, "'Evolution' Win Marks Dawn of New Cannes Era," *Advertising Age*, June 25, 2007, p. 1; Theresa Howard, "Ad Campaign Tells Women to Celebrate How They Are," *USA Today*, August 7, 2005, (accessed at www.usatoday.com); "Cause: Conscience Marketing. You Stand for Something. Shouldn't Your Brand?" *Strategy*, June 2007, p. 22; and information found at www.campaignforrealbeauty.com, accessed September 2009. For a thorough case study on the brand, see Jennifer Millard, "Performed Beauty: Dove's 'Real Beauty' Campaign" *Symbolic Interaction*, Spring 2009, pp. 146–168.

27. Mark Borden and Anya Kamenetz, "The Prophet CEO," *Fast Company*, September 2008, p. 126; Jennifer Reingold, "Walking the Walk," *Fast Company*, November 2005, pp. 81–85; Elaine Wong, "Timberland Kicks Off Earth Day Effort," *Adweek*, March 24, 2009, accessed at www.adweek.com; "From the Power of One to the Effort of Many," *Business Wire*, April 19, 2009; and information from Timberland.com, accessed May 2013.

28. Philip Kotler, Gary Armstrong, Peggy H. Cunningham, and Valerie Trifts, *Principles of Marketing*, 9th Canadian ed. (Toronto: Pearson, 2013), 130.

29. Based on Jeff Heilman, "Rules of Engagement," *The Magazine of Branded Engagement*, Winter 2009, pp. 7–8.

30. See The World Bank, "The Costs of Corruption," April 8, 2004, accessed at www.worldbank.org; Joseph A. McKinney and Carlos W. Moore, "International Bribery: Does a Written Code of Ethics Make a Difference in Perceptions of Business Professionals," *Journal of Business Ethics* (April 2008), 103–111; and *Global Corruption Report 2009*, Transparency International, accessed at www.transparency.org/publications/gcr/download_gcr#download.

31. John F. McGee and P. Tanganath Nayak, "Leaders' Perspectives on Business Ethics," *Prizm*, first quarter, 1994, pp. 71–72. Also see Adrian Henriques, "Good Decision—Bad Business?" *International Journal of Management & Decision Making* (2005), 273; and Marylyn Carrigan, Svetla Marinova, and Isabelle Szmigin, "Ethics and International Marketing: Research Background and Challenges," *International Marketing Review* (2005), 481–494.

CHAPTER 4

1. Danielle Sacks, "How YouTube's Global Platform Is Redefining the Entertainment Business," *Fast Company*, February 2011, p. 58; Jessica E. Vascellaro, Amir Efrati, and Ethan Smith, "YouTube Recasts for New Viewers," *Wall Street Journal*, April 7, 2011, p. B1; www.youtube.com/t/about_youtube, www.youtube.com/shows, www.youtube.com/partners, and www.realwomenofphiladelphia.com, (accessed July 2011); Nelson Wyatt, "Fake Baby-Snatching Eagle Video Helps Fund Scholarship" TheStar.com, January 2013 (accessed February 1, 2013) at www.thestar.com/news/canada/2013/01/29/fake_babysnatching_eagle_video_helps_fund_scholarship.html; Curtis Rush, "Baby-Snatching Eagle Video Goes Viral, but Montreal Animation School Admits It Was Fake," TheStar.com, December 2012 (accessed February 1, 2013) at www.thestar.com/news/canada/2012/12/19/babysnatching_eagle_video_goes_viral_but_montreal_animation_school_admits_it_was_fake.html.

2. "Asia: L'Oréal's Long-Term Commitment," *Premium Beauty News*, April 12, 2011, www.premiumbeautynews.com/ Asia-L-Oreal-s-long-term,2918; Rebecca Ellinor, "Crowd Pleaser," *Supply Management*, December 13, 2007, pp. 26–29; and information from www.loreal.com/_en/_ww/html/suppliers/index.aspx (accessed December 2011).

3. Information from Robert J. Benes, Abbie Jarman, and Ashley Williams, "2007 NRA Sets Records," at www.chefmagazine.com (accessed September 2007); and www.thecoca-colacompany.com/presscenter/presskit_fs.html and www.cokesolutions.com (accessed November 2011).

4. World POPClock, U.S. Census Bureau, at www.census.gov/main/www/popclock.html (accessed July 2011). This website provides continuously updated projections of the US and world populations.

5. Statistics Canada, "Population Projections for Canada, Provinces and Territories," at www.statcan.gc.ca/pub/91-520-x/91-520-x2010001-eng.htm (accessed June 2012).

6. Daniel Stoffman, "Completely Predictable People," *Report on Business*, November 1990, pp. 78–84; David Foot and Daniel Stoffman, *Boom, Bust and Echo*, (Toronto: Macfarlane Walter & Ross, 1996), 18–22.

7. See Simon Hudson, "Wooing Zoomers: Marketing to the Mature Traveler," *Marketing Intelligence & Planning*, 28 (2010), 444–461; and Gavin O'Malley, "Boomers Value Brands That Champion 'Youthful' Style," *MediaPostNews*, April 12, 2011, www.mediapost.com.

8. For more discussion, see R. K. Miller and Kelli Washington, *Consumer Behavior 2009* (Atlanta, GA: Richard K. Miller & Associates, 2009), Chapter 27; Bernadette Turner, "Generation X . . . Let's GO!" *New Pittsburgh Courier*, March 2–March 8, 2011, p. A11; and Piet Levy, "Segmentation by Generation," *Marketing News*, May 15, 2011, pp. 20–23.

9. Information from www.mec.ca (accessed June 2012).

10. Julie Liesse, "Getting to Know the Millennials," *Advertising Age*, July 9, 2007, pp. A1–A6; and "The Millennials," *Time*, Spring 2008, p. 55.

11. Piet Levy, "Segmentation by Generation," p. 22; and Jon Lafayette, "Marketers Targeting Generation of Millennials," *Broadcasting Cable*, April 11, 2011, p. 23.

12. Christian Cotroneo, "NDP Leadership Convention: Social Media Is Writing the Ticket To The Top," *Huffington Post Canada*, March, 2012, accessed at www.huffingtonpost.ca/2012/03/24/ndp-leadership-convention-social-media_n_1377115.html; Heather Scoffield, "NDP Is Tops with Young Voters in All Regions Except Alberta: Poll," *Canadian Press*, May 2011, accessed at www.680news.com/news/national/article/224444–ndp-is-tops-with-young-voters-in-all-regions-except-alberta-poll; Rachel Mendleson, "NDP Youth: At Convention, Next Generation Sees Hope in Candidates," *Huffington Post Canada*, March 2012, accessed at www.huffingtonpost.ca/2012/03/23/ndp-youth-convention_n_1375898.html; and Sandie Benitah, "Social Media, Youth Take Centre Stage at NDP Convention," cp24.com, March 2012, accessed at www.cp24.com/servlet/an/local/CTVNews/20120323/032312_social_media_ndp?hub=CP24Home.

13. Statistics Canada, "Study: Generational Change in Paid and Unpaid Work—2010," *The Daily,* July 12, 2011, accessed at www .statcan.gc.ca/daily-quotidien/110712/dq110712c-eng.htm; 2011 census data www12.statcan.gc.ca/census-recensement/2011/ as-sa/98-312-x/98-312-x2011003_1-eng.cfm; www12.statcan.gc.ca/ census-recensement/2011/as-sa/98-312-x/98-312-x2011003_2-eng .cfm; http://www12.statcan.gc.ca/census-recensement/2011/as-sa/ 98-312-x/98-312-x2011001-eng.cfm.

14. "Women Outnumber Men in Canadian Workforce," *Canadian Press,* September 2009, www.ctv.ca/CTVNews/Canada/20090905/ women_workforce_090905 (accessed June 2012); Statistics Canada, "Women in Canada: Paid Work—2009," *The Daily,* December 9, 2010, accessed at www.statcan.gc.ca/daily-quotidien/ 101209/dq101209a-eng.htm.

15. See Marissa Miley and Ann Mack, "The New Female Consumer: The Rise of the Real Mom," *Advertising Age,* November 16, 2009, p. A1; and Christine Birkner, "Mom's the Word," *Marketing News,* May 15, 2011, p. 8.

16. Tavia Grant, "Stuck in Place: Canada's Mobility Problem." *Globe and Mail,* June, 2012, accessed at www.theglobeandmail. com/report-on-business/economy/canada-competes/stuck-in-place-canadas-mobility-problem/article4237314.

17. Statistics Canada, "2011 Census: Population and Dwelling Counts," *The Daily,* February 8 2012, www.statcan.gc.ca/daily-quotidien/120208/dq120208a-eng.htm.

18. Martin Turcotte, "Working at Home: An Update," December 2010, www.statcan.gc.ca/pub/11-008-x/2011001/article/11366-eng .htm (accessed June 2012).

19. See "About WebEx," at www.webex.com/about-webex/index.html (accessed November 2012); and www.regus.com and http:// grindspaces.com (accessed November 2012).

20. Statistics Canada, "Educational Attainment of the Population Aged 25 to 64, Off-Reserve Aboriginal, Non-Aboriginal, and Total Population, Canada, Provinces and Territories, 2009, 2010 and 2011," www.statcan.gc.ca/pub/81-582-x/2012001/tbl/tbld6.3-eng .htm (accessed June 2012).

21. *CBC News,* "Labour Shortage 'Desperate,' Chamber Says," February 2012, accessed at www.cbc.ca/news/business/story/ 2012/02/08/canada-labourshortage.html; and Human Resources and Skills Development Canada, "Looking Ahead: A 10-Year Outlook for the Canadian Labour Market (2008–2017)," November 2008, accessed at www23.hrsdc.gc.ca/l.3bd.2t.1ilshtml@-eng.jsp ?lid=1&fid=1&lang=en#ExecutiveSummary.

22. Statistics Canada, "2006 Census: Ethnic Origin, Visible Minorities, Place of Work and Mode of Transportation," *The Daily,* April 2, 2008, www.statcan.gc.ca/daily-quotidien/080402/ dq080402a-eng.htm; www.statcan.gc.ca/pub/12-581-x/2012000/ pop-eng.htm#t03.

23. Statistics Canada, "2006 Census: Family Portrait: Continuity and Change in Canadian Families and Households in 2006: Highlights," www12.statcan.ca/census-recensement/2006/ as-sa/97-553/p1-eng.cfm, April 2009; www12.statcan.gc.ca/ census-recensement/2011/as-sa/98-312-x/98-312-x2011001-eng .cfm.

24. For these and other statistics, see Witeck-Combs Communications, "Buying Power of Gay Men and Lesbians in 2008," June 2008; accessed at www.rivendellmedia.com/ngng/executive_summary/ NGNG.PPT and www.gaymarket.com/ngng/ngng_reader.html (accessed April 2009); and Paul Morrissette, "Market to LGBT Community," *American Agent & Broker,* July 2010, p. 50.

25. See Brandon Miller, "And the Winner Is . . ." *Out Traveler,* Winter 2008, pp. 64–65; www.aa.com/rainbow (accessed August 2010); and http://blueflameventures.ca (accessed June 2012).

26. Gavin Rabinowitz, "India's Tata Motors Unveils $2,500 Car, Bringing Car Ownership within Reach of Millions," *Associated Press,* January 10, 2008; Jessica Scanlon, "What Can Tata's Nano Teach Detroit?" *Businessweek,* March 19, 2009, accessed at www .businessweek.com/innovate/content/mar2009/id20090318_012120 .htm; Mark Phelan, "Engineers Study the Magic Behind Tata Nano," *Pittsburgh Tribune Review,* April 17, 2010, www.pittsburghlive .com; and http://tatanano.inservices.tatamotors.com/tatamotors/ nano_brochure.pdf (accessed August 2011).

27. Noreen O'Leary, "Squeeze Play," *Adweek,* January 12, 2009, pp. 8–9. Also see Alessandra Stanley, "For Hard Times, Softer Sells," *New York Times,* February 6, 2009, www.nytimes.com; and Kenneth Hein, "Why Price Isn't Everything," *Brandweek,* March 2, 2009, p. 6.

28. Statistics Canada, "Income in Canada—2010," www.statcan .gc.ca/pub/75-202-x/75-202-x2010000-eng.htm (accessed June 2012); Statistics Canada, "Study: High Income Canadians," September 2007, www.statcan.gc.ca/daily-quotidien/070924/ dq070924a-eng.htm (accessed April 2009); "2006 Census: Earnings, Income, and Shelter Costs," May 2008, www.statcan .gc.ca/daily-quotidien/080501/dq080501a-eng.htm (accessed April 2009); and "Census Release Topics," www12.statcan.ca/census-recensement/2006/rt-td/index-eng.cfm (accessed April 2009).

29. The 2030 Water Resources Group, "Charting Our Water Future: Executive Summary," 2009, accessed at www.mckinsey .com/clientservice/water/charting_our_water_future.aspx.

30. Canadian Standards Association, "PLUS 14021—Environmental Claims: A Guide for Industry and Advertisers," June 2008, www .csa.ca/Default.asp?language=english (accessed April 29, 2009).

31. Facts from www.pepsico.com/Purpose/Environmental-Sustainability.html (accessed June 2011).

32. See "American Apparel RFID Case Study," accessed at www .apparel.averydennison.com/solutions/american-apparel-rfid.asp, June 2011; and Mary Catherine O'Connor, "American Apparel Adding 50 More Stores in Aggressive RFID Rollout," *RFID Journal,* April 26, 2011, www.rfidjournal.com/article/view/8374.

33. See Tamara Schweitzer, "The Way I Work," *Inc.,* June 2010, pp. 112–116; Christina Binkley, "Style—On Style: Charity Gives Shoe Brand Extra Shine," *Wall Street Journal,* April 1, 2010, p. D7; and www.toms.com (accessed June 2011).

34. Emily Steel, "Cause-Tied Marketing Requires Care," *Wall Street Journal,* March 21, 2011, p. B4.

35. See "The Growth of Cause Marketing," at www .causemarketingforum.com/page.asp?ID=188 (accessed June 2011).

36. See "10 Crucial Consumer Trends for 2010," Trendwatching .com, http://trendwatching.com/trends/pdf/trendwatching%20 2009-12%2010trends.pdf; and "The F-Factor," Trendingwatching .com, May 2011, http://trendwatching.com/trends/pdf/ trendwatching%202009-12%2010trends.pdf.

37. "The F-Factor," Trendingwatching.com, p. 1.

38. "Survey Measures the 'Olympic Effect' on National Pride," March 2010, www.historica-dominion.ca/node/1003 (accessed June 2012).

39. Sarah Mahoney, "Report: LOHAS Market Nears $300 Billion," *Marketing Daily*, April 26, 2010, www.mediapost.com/ publications/?art_aid=126836&fa=Articles.showArticle; and www.lohas.com (accessed November 2011).

40. "Organic Farming Grows to $29-Billion Industry," *Western Farm Press*, April 26, 2011.

41. Michael Valpy, "Religious Observance Continues to Decline," *Globe and Mail*, March 19, 2003; and Statistics Canada, "Who's Religious?" www.statcan.gc.ca/pub/11-008-x/2006001/9181-eng .htm (accessed June 2012).

42. Dan Harris, "America Is Becoming Less Christian, Less Religious," *ABC News*, March 9, 2009, accessed at http://abcnews.go.com.

43. See Philip Kotler, *Kotler on Marketing* (New York: Free Press, 1999), 3; and Kotler, *Marketing Insights from A to Z* (Hoboken, NJ: John Wiley & Sons, 2003), 23–24.

44. W. Chan Kim and Renée Mauborgne, "How Strategy Shaped Structure," *Harvard Business Review* (September 2009), 73–80.

45. Paula Forbes, "Taco Bell Ad: Thank You for Suing Us," January 28, 2011, *Eater*, http://eater.com/archives/2011/01/28/taco-bell-ad-thanks-firm-for-law-suit.php; Courtney Hutchinson and Katie Moisse, "Taco Bell Fights 'Where's the Beef' Lawsuit," January 28, 2011, http://abcnews.go.com/Health/Wellness/taco-bell-defends-beef-legal-action/story?id=12785818; and "Law Firm Voluntarily Withdraws Class-Action Lawsuit against Taco Bell," April 19, 2011, http://money.msn.com/business-news/article.aspx?feed=BW&date=20110419&id=13327023.

CHAPTER 5

1. Excerpts, quotes, and other information from T. L. Stanley, "Easy As Pie: How Russell Weiner Turned Sabotage into Satisfaction," *Adweek*, September 13, 2010, p. 40; "Lessons from the Domino's Turnaround," *Restaurant Hospitality*, June 2010, p. 30; Rupal Parekh, "Marketer of the Year," *Advertising Age*, October 18, 2010, p. 19; Emily Bryson York, "Domino's Claims Victory with New Strategy: Pizza Wasn't Good, We Fixed It," *Advertising Age*, May 10, 2010, p. 4; Mark Brandau, "Domino's Do-Over," *Nation's Restaurant News*, March 8, 2010, p. 44; "Domino's Puts Customer Feedback on Times Square Billboard," *Detroit News*, July 26, 2011; and annual reports and other information from www.dominosbiz .com and www.pizzaturnaround.com, accessed December 2011.

2. Dan Frommer, "Apple iPod Still Obliterating Microsoft Zune," *Business Insider*, July 12, 2010, accessed at http://read.bi/axUYCO.

3. Carey Toane, "Listening: The New Metric," *Strategy*, September 2009, p. 45.

4. Warren Thayer and Michael Sansolo, "Walmart: Our Retailer of the Year," *R&FF Retailer*, June 2009, pp. 14–20; and information from http://walmartstores.com/Suppliers/248.aspx, accessed December 2011.

5. Alicia Androich, "Indigo Launches Plum Rewards to Connect with Customers," *Marketing Magazine*, April 6, 2011, accessed at www.marketingmag.ca/news/marketer-news/indigo-launches-plum-rewards-toconnect-with-customers-25608; "Infusion Case Study: Indigo Customer Database," accessed at www.infusion.com/PDF/ Cases/Infusion-RetailandServices-IndigoCustomerDatabase.pdf.

6. Based on information from Adam Ostrow, "Inside the Gatorade's Social Media Command Center," June 6, 2010, accessed at http:// mashable.com/2010/06/15/gatorade-sical-media-mission-control; and Valery Bauerlein, "Gatorade's 'Mission': Using Social Media to Boost Sales," *Wall Street Journal Asia*, September 15, 2010, p. 8.

7. Irena Slutsky, "Chief Listeners Use Technology to Track, Sort Company Mentioned," *Advertising Age*, August 30, 2010, accessed at http://adage.com/digital/article?article_id=145618.

8. See http://biz.yahoo.com/ic/101/101316.html, accessed September 2011.

9. For more on research firms that supply marketing information, see Jack Honomichl, "2010 Honomichl Top 50," special section, *Marketing News*, June 17, 2010. Other information from www .nielsen.com/us/en/measurement/retail-measurement.html and www.yankelovich.com, accessed September 2011.

10. See http://symphonyiri.com/?TabId=159&productid=84, accessed September 2011.

11. Example adapted from Dana Flavelle, "Kraft Goes Inside the Kitchen of the Canadian Family," *Toronto Star*, January 16, 2010, accessed at www.thestar.com/business/article/751507. For other examples, see Philip Kotler and Kevin Lane Keller, *Marketing Management*, 14th ed. (Upper Saddle River, NJ: Prentice Hall, 2012), p. 101.

12. Example adapted from information found in "My Dinner with Lexus," *Automotive News*, November 29, 2010, accessed at www.autonews.com/apps/pbcs.dll/article?AID=/20101129/ RETAIL03/311299949/1292.

13. See www.internetworldstats.com/stats14.htm, accessed July 2011.

14. Based on information found at www.channelm2.com/ HowOnlineQualitativeResearch.html, accessed December 2011.

15. See "Online Panel," www.zoomerang.com/online-panel, accessed December 2011.

16. Derek Kreindler, "Lexus Soliciting Customer Feedback with Lexus Advisory Board," *Auto Guide*, August 24, 2010, accessed at www.autoguide.com/auto-news/2010/08/lexus-soliciting-customer-feedback-with-lexus-advisory-board.html; and "20,000 Customers Sign up for the Lexus Advisory Board," *4WheelsNews*, August 30, 2010, accessed at www.4wheelsnews .com/20000-customers-signed-up-for-the-lexus-advisory-board.

17. Stephen Baker, "The Web Knows What You Want," *Businessweek*, July 27, 2009, p. 48.

18. Adapted from Brooks Barnes, "Lab Watches Web Surfers to See Which Ads Work," New York Times, July 26, 2009; and "Walt Disney Company's Media Networks to Develop Emerging Media and Advertising Research Lab," accessed at http://corporate. disney.go.com/corporate/moreinfo/media_advertising_research_ lab.html, August 2011.

19. Jessica Tsai, "Are You Smarter than a Neuromarketer?" *Customer Relationship Management*, January 2010, pp. 19–20.

20. For these and other neuromarketing examples and discussion, see Laurie Burkitt, "Neuromarketing: Companies Use Neuroscience for Consumer Insights," *Forbes*, November 16, 2009, www.forbes.com; Ilan Brat, "The Emotional Quotient of Soup Shopping," *Wall Street Journal*, February 17, 2010, p. B6; Natasha Singer, "Making Ads That Will Spur the Brain," *New York Times*, November 14, 2010, p. BU4; and Deena Diggs, "Emotional Marketing," *Editor & Publisher*, January 2010, p. 7.

21. Melinda Mattos, "A Fresh Start for Sobeys," *Strategy*, December 1, 2010, accessed at http://strategyonline.ca/2010/ 12/01/moysobeys-20101201/; and information from www .sobeyscorporate.com.

22. Gillian S. Ambroz, "CRM: Getting Back to Basics," *Folio*, January 2010, p. 97.

23. "SAS Helps 1-800-Flowers.com Grow Deep Roots with Customers," accessed at www.sas.com/success/1800flowers.html, September 2011.

24. See www.pensketruckleasing.com/leasing/precision/ precision_features.html, accessed September 2011.

25. Adapted from information in Ann Zimmerman, "Small Business; Do the Research," *Wall Street Journal*, May 9, 2005, p. R3; with information from John Tozzi, "Market Research on the Cheap," *Businessweek*, January 9, 2008, accessed at www.business-week.com/smallbiz/content/jan2008/sb2008019_352779.htm; and www.bibbentuckers.com, accessed September 2011.

26. Zimmerman, "Small Business; Do the Research," *Wall Street Journal*, p. R3.

27. For some good advice on conducting market research for a small business, see "Conducting Market Research," www.sba.gov/ content/conducting-market-research, accessed August 2011; and "Researching Your Market," *Entrepreneur*, accessed at www.entrepreneur.com/article/43024-1, March 2011.

28. See "Top 25 Global Market Research Organizations," *Marketing News*, August 30, 2010, p. 16; and www.nielsen.com/us/en/about-us .html, accessed September 2011.

29. Internet stats are from www.internetworldstats.com, accessed May 14, 2013.

30. Subhash C. Jain, *International Marketing Management*, 3rd ed. (Boston: PWS-Kent, 1990), p. 338. For more discussion on international marketing research issues and solutions, see Warren J. Keegan and Mark C. Green, *Global Marketing*, 6th ed. (Upper Saddle River, NJ: Prentice Hall, 2011), pp. 170–201.

31. For these quotes and excellent discussions of online privacy, see Juan Martinez, "Marketing Marauders or Consumer Counselors?" *CRM Magazine*, January 2011, accessed at www .destinationcrm.com; and Lauren McKay, "Eye on Customers: Are Consumers Comfortable with or Creeped out by Online Data Collection Tactics?" *CRM Magazine*, January 2011, accessed at www.destinationcrm.com.

32. "ICC/ESOMAR International Code of Marketing and Social Research Practice," accessed at www.esomar.org/index.php/codes-guidelines.html, July 2011. Also see "Respondent Bill of Rights," www.mra-net.org/ga/billofrights.cfm, accessed November 2011.

33. Federal Trade Commission, "Kellogg Settles FTC Charges that Ads for Frosted Mini-Wheats Were False," April 20, 2009, accessed at www.ftc.gov/opa/2009/04/kellogg.shtm; "Kellogg's Frosted Mini-Wheats Neuroscience: The FTC Reckoning," accessed at http://rangelife.typepad.com/rangelife/2009/04/kelloggs-frosted-miniwheats-neuroscience-the-ftc-reckoning.html, April 21, 2009; Todd Wasserman, "New FTC Asserts Itself," *Brandweek*, April 27, 2009, p. 8; and "FTC Investigation of Ad Claims that Rice Krispies Benefits Children's Immunity Leads to Stronger Order against Kellogg," *US Fed News Service*, June 4, 2010.

CHAPTER 6

1. Norma Ramage, "Slowing Down," *Marketing Magazine*, May 2005, p. 9; Jason Kirby, "The Marathon Man," *Maclean's*, August 6, 2007, p. 44; "Ask a Running Expert: John Stanton Takes Your Questions," *Globe and Mail*, accessed at www.theglobeandmail.com/life/health/ running/ask-a-running-expert-johnstanton-takes-your-questions/ article1589817, June 2010; information obtained from Running Room website at www.runningroom.com, accessed June 2010; Yana Doyle, "Writer Makes Tracks at Marathon," *Calgary Herald*, June 10, 2010, accessed at www.calgaryherald.com/Writer+makes +tracks+marathon/3135672/story.html, June 2010; Laura Young, "Stoughton Takes Down Boston Marathon," *Sudbury Star*, accessed at www.thesudburystar.com/ArticleDisplay.aspx?e=2601158, June 2010; Pat O'Brien, "Butt Out, Grab Your Sneakers and Hit the Road," *Times & Transcript*, June 14, 2010, accessed at http://timestranscript .canadaeast.com/lifetimes/article/1093234, June 2010; Keith B., "Q&A with Running Room Founder John Stanton," *Calgary Herald*, May 16, 2010, accessed at http://communities.canada .com/calgaryherald/blogs/calgaryrunner/archive/2010/05/16/q-amp-a-with-running-room-founder-john-stanton.aspx, May 2010; Press release, "Canadians Coolsaet and Gillis Qualify for London Olympics at 2011 Scotiabank Toronto Waterfront Marathon," accessed at www.newswire.ca/en/story/859427/canadians-coolsaet-and-gillis-qualify-forlondon-olympics-at-2011-scotiabank-toronto-waterfrontmarathon, December 2011; Press release, "More Than 7,000 Canadians Together Log Thousands of Kilometres in National Walking Event Highlighting the Benefits of Physical Activity," accessed at www.newswire.ca/en/releases/archive/June2010/24/ c7851.html, June 2010.

2. Consumer expenditure figures from http://en.wikipedia.org/ wiki/Gross_domestic_product. Population figures from the World POPClock, U.S. Census Bureau, www.census.gov/main/ www/popclock.html, accessed May 2011. This website provides continuously updated projections of US and world populations. Information from Statistics Canada, www12.statcan.gc.ca/ census-recensement/2011/dp-pd/hlt-fst/pd-pl/Table-Tableau .cfm?LANG=Eng&T=101&S=50&O=A.

3. Nicholas Köhler, "Canadians Feel like They're on Top of the World," *Macleans.ca*, www2.macleans.ca/2011/12/19/on-top-of-the-world-2, accessed April 16, 2012.

4. The Centre for Canadian Studies, "The Political Voice of Canadian Regional Identities," 2001, accessed at http://culturescope.ca/ev_en.php?ID=9417_201&ID2=DO_TOPIC, September 2006.

5. *CBC News*, "Aboriginal People Could Number 2.2M by 2031," December 7, 2011, accessed at www.cbc.ca/news/canada/story/2011/12/07/aboriginalpopulation-forecast.html.

6. James Murray, "Quality Market Launches New Online Store That Is Easy and Fun!" April 15, 2012, accessed at http://netnewsledger.com/2012/04/15/quality-market-launches-new-onlinestore-that-is-easy-and-fun.

7. Statistics Canada, "Study: Canada's Visible Minority Population in 2017," *The Daily*, March 22, 2005; and "Canada Welcomes Highest Number of Legal Immigrants in 50 Years While Taking Action to Maintain the Integrity of Canada's Immigration System," February 13, 2011, accessed at www.cic.gc.ca/english/department/media/releases/2011/2011-02-13.asp.

8. Huixia Sun, "Chinese Websites Beat Economic Blues," *Vancouver Sun*, May 15, 2009; Chris Powell, "New Chinese Canadians Prefer Internet to TV: Diversity Study," *Marketing Magazine*, April 2008.

9. Statistics Canada, "2006 Census Data Products," accessed at www12.statcan.ca/census-recensement/2006/dp-pd/index-eng.cfm, May 15, 2009.

10. "Procter & Gamble; P&G's My Black Is Beautiful TV Series Celebrates Another Successful Season on BET Networks," *Marketing Weekly News*, January 1, 2011, p. 76; "Procter & Gamble's My Black Is Beautiful Honored with City of Cincinnati Proclamation," *PR Newswire*, May 21, 2010; and information from www.myblackisbeautiful.com, accessed October 2011.

11. "Research Reveals Word-of-Mouth Campaigns on Customer Networks Double Marketing Results," *Business Wire*, October 27, 2009.

12. Katie Bailey, "James Ready Barters with Beer Caps," *Media in Canada*, October 14, 2009, http://mediaincanada.com/2009/10/14/jamesready-20091014/; Michelle Warren, "Engagement Marketing: The Back-to-School Edition," *Marketing Magazine*, September 2011, accessed at www.interceptgroup.com/pdf/Marketing%20Mag_Sept%202011.pdf; and Megan Haynes, "James Ready Expands in 2012," January 24, 2012, accessed at http://strategyonline.ca/2012/01/24/james-readyexpands-in-2012.

13. Victoria Taylor, "The Best-Ever Social Media Campaign," *Forbes*, August 17, 2010, accessed at www.forbes.com; Bruce Horovitz, "Marketers: Inside Job on College Campuses," *USA Today*, October 4, 2010, p. B1; and "Old Spice Guy Isaiah Mustafa Says Fans Love to Smell Him," *TV Replay*, February 2, 2011, accessed at www.tvsquad.com/2011/02/02/old-spice-guy-isaiah-mustafa-says-fans-love-to-smell-him-video.

14. See Eleftheria Parpis, "She's in Charge," *Adweek*, October 6–13, 2008, p. 38; Abigail Posner, "Why Package-Goods Companies Should Market to Men," *Advertising Age*, February 9, 2009, accessed at http://adage.com/print?article_id=134473; and Marissa Miley and Ann Mark, "The New Female Consumer: The Rise of the Real Mom," *Advertising Age*, November 16, 2009, pp. A1–A27.

15. Laura A. Flurry, "Children's Influence in Family Decision Making: Examining the Impact of the Changing American Family," *Journal of Business Research*, April 2007, pp. 322–330; and "Tween Years Prove to Be Rewarding for Toymakers," *USA Today*, December 22, 2010, p. 1B. Also see Michael R. Solomon, Judith L. Zaichkowsky, and Rosemary Polegato, *Consumer Behaviour: Buying, Having, and Being*, 5th Canadian edition (Toronto, ON: Pearson Canada, 2011).

16. For information on Acxiom's PersonicX segmentation system, see "PersonicX Interactive Wheel," accessed at www.acxiom.com/products_and_services/Consumer%20Insight%20Products/segmentation/Pages/index.html, October 2011.

17. Quotes from www.mooresclothing.com/mor/index.jsp.19. See "Target Introduces the Great Save," Business Wire, January 4, 2010; and John Ewold, "How Does Target's Great Save Compare to Costco and Sam's?" Star Tribune (Minneapolis-St. Paul), January 7, 2011, accessed at www.startribune.com/lifestyle/yourmoney/blogs/113095249.html.

18. Kenneth Hein, "Target Tries Price Point Play," Adweek.com, January 15, 2009, accessed at www.adweek.com/aw/content_display/creative/news/e3i0b84325122066ed9830db4ccb41e7ecf; "Target Introduces the Great Save," *Business Wire*, January 4, 2010; and John Ewold, "How Does Target's Great Save Compare to Costco and Sam's?" *Star Tribune* (Minneapolis-St. Paul), January 7, 2011, accessed at www.startribune.com/lifestyle/yourmoney/blogs/113095249.html.

19. See Jennifer Aaker, "Dimensions of Measuring Brand Personality," *Journal of Marketing Research*, August 1997, pp. 347–356; Kevin Lane Keller, *Strategic Brand Management*, 3rd ed. (Upper Saddle River, NJ, 2008), pp. 66–67; Beth Snyder Bulik, "You Want to Watch, Market Data Suggests," *Advertising Age*, November 1, 2010, p. 12; and Michael R. Solomon, *Consumer Behavior*, 9th ed. (Upper Saddle River, NJ: Prentice Hall, 2011), pp. 221–226.

20. "Axe: Let Me Entertain You," *Brand Strategy*, October 9, 2007, p. 20; and www.unilever.com/brands/personalcarebrands/axe/index.aspx, accessed September 2011.

21. See Abraham H. Maslow, "A Theory of Human Motivation," *Psychological Review*, 50 (1943), pp. 370–396. Also see Maslow, *Motivation and Personality*, 3rd ed. (New York: HarperCollins Publishers, 1987); and Leon G. Schiffman and Leslie Lazar Kanuk, *Consumer Behavior* (Upper Saddle River, NJ: Prentice Hall, 2010), pp. 98–106.

22. See Louise Story, "Anywhere the Eye Can See, It's Likely to See an Ad," *New York Times*, January 15, 2007, accessed at www.nytimes.com/2007/01/15/business/media/15everywhere.html; Matthew Creamer, "Caught in the Clutter Crossfire: Your Brand," *Advertising Age*, April 1, 2007, p. 35; and Ruth Mortimer, "Consumer Awareness: Getting the Right Attention," *Brand Strategy*, December 10, 2008, p. 55.

23. See Bob Garfield, "'Subliminal' Seduction and Other Urban Myths," *Advertising Age*, September 18, 2000, pp. 4, 105; Cahal Milmo, "Power of the Hidden Message Is Revealed," *Independent* (London), September 28, 2009, p. 8; "50 Great Myths of Popular Psychology," *McClatchy-Tribune Business News*, May 3, 2010; and

Michael R. Solomon, *Consumer Behavior*, 9th ed. (Upper Saddle River, NJ: Prentice Hall, 2011), pp. 73–75.

24. Quotes and information from Yubo Chen and Jinhong Xie, "Online Consumer Review: Word-of-Mouth as a New Element of Marketing Communication Mix," *Management Science*, March 2008, pp. 477–491; "Leo J. Shapiro & Associates: User-Generated Content Three Times More Influential Than TV Advertising on Consumer Purchase Decisions," *Marketing Business Weekly*, December 28, 2008, p. 34; and *Customer Experience Report, North America, 2010*, RightNow Technologies, October 13, 2010, accessed at www.rightnow.com/cx-news-16097.php#.

25. See Leon Festinger, *A Theory of Cognitive Dissonance* (Stanford, CA: Stanford University Press, 1957); Cynthia Crossen, "'Cognitive Dissonance' Became a Milestone in the 1950s Psychology," *Wall Street Journal*, December 12, 2006, p. B1; and Anupam Bawa and Purva Kansal, "Cognitive Dissonance and the Marketing of Services: Some Issues," *Journal of Services Research*, October 2008–March 2009, p. 31.

26. The following discussion draws from the work of Everett M. Rogers. See his *Diffusion of Innovations*, 5th ed. (New York: Free Press, 2003).

27. Jackie Crosbie, "Best Buy Launches Gadget Buyback," *Star Tribune* (Minneapolis-St. Paul), January 10, 2011; "How Marketing Missteps Stalled TV Sales," *Bloomberg Businessweek*, January 30, 2011, pp. 24–25; and www.bestbuy.com/site/Misc/Buy-Back-Program/pcmcat230000050010.c?id=pcmcat230000050010&DCMP=rdr2161 (accessed August 2011).

28. "HDTV Households Now Dominate U.S. Viewing Landscape, According to LRG Study," *Broadcast Engineering*, December 30, 2010, accessed at http://broadcastengineering.com/hdtv/hdtv-households-dominate-viewing-landscape-according-to-lrg-study-20110104.

29. This classic categorization was first introduced in Patrick J. Robinson, Charles W. Faris, and Yoram Wind, *Industrial Buying Behavior and Creative Marketing* (Boston, MA: Allyn & Bacon, 1967). Also see James C. Anderson, James A. Narus, and Das Narayandas, *Business Market Management*, 3rd ed. (Upper Saddle River, NJ: Prentice Hall, 2009), Chapter 3; and Philip Kotler and Kevin Lane Keller, *Marketing Management*, 14th ed. (Upper Saddle River, NJ: Prentice Hall, 2012), Chapter 7.

30. Example adapted from information found in "Nikon Focuses on Supply Chain Innovation—and Makes New Product Distribution a Snap," UPS case study, www.ups-scs.com/solutions/case_studies/cs_on.pdf, accessed November 2011.

31. Information accessed at Industry Canada's Small Business Research and Statistics website, www.ic.gc.ca/eic/site/sbrp-rppe.nsf/eng/rd02456.html; and Great Little Box Company website: www.greatlittlebox.com.

32. Robinson, Faris, and Wind, *Industrial Buying Behavior*, p. 14. Also see Philip Kotler and Kevin Lane Keller, *Marketing Management*, pp. 197–203.

33. See https://suppliercenter.homedepot.com/wps/portal, accessed October 2011.

34. For this and other examples, see "10 Great Web Sites," *BtoB Online*, September 13, 2010. Other information from www.shawfloors.com/About-Shaw/Retailer-Support, accessed October 2011.

CHAPTER 7

1. Information supplied by Kate Weersink, High Road Communications; and from interviews with representatives of Boston Pizza and TAXI (Steve Silverstone, EVP marketing, Boston Pizza International; Scott Dane, account manager, PHD; Niall Kelly, creative director, TAXI Canada; Edith Rosa, group account director, TAXI Canada; Tamara Gervais, account director, TAXI Canada); Ben Kaplan, "The Other F-Word: Reclaiming 'Foodie' and the Snobby and Stigmatized Terrain of Gastronomic Culture," February 27, 2013, accessed at http://life.nationalpost.com/2013/02/27/the-other-f-word-reclaiming-foodie-and-the-snobby-terrain-of-gastronic-culture; "Careful: New Boston Pizza Dishes Could Elevate You to Foodie Status," press release published on Canada Newswire, January 28, 2013, accessed at www.newswire.ca/fr/story/1105315/careful-new-boston-pizza-dishes-could-elevate-you-to-foodie-status?relation=org; Valerie Lugonja, "Canadian Food Trends 2013," published on ACanadianFoodie.com, January 2, 2013; John Kessler, "Is There a Better Word than 'Foodie?'" Food and More [Blog], February 4, 2010, accessed at http://blogs.ajc.com/food-and-more/2010/02/04/is-there-a-better-word-than-foodie; Cole Danehower, "The New Foodie," Culinate.com, June 8, 2009, accessed at http://www.culinate.com/articles/opinion/the_new_foodie.

2. Elizabeth Hames, "The Beer Up Here," *Canadian Business*, March 18, 2013, pp. 8–9; and information from Yukon Brewing's website at YukonBeer.com (accessed March 2013).

3. Elisabeth A. Sullivan, "H.O.G.: Harley-Davidson Shows Brand Strength as It Navigates Down New Roads—and Picks Up More Female Riders Along the Way," November 1, 2008, p. 8; and "Harley-Davidson Hosts Special Rides to Kick Off Women Riders Month," *PR Newswire*, March 23, 2009.

4. Adapted from information found in Laura Koss-Feder, "At Your Service," *Time*, June 11, 2007, p. 1; and "Guide to Hotel Packages," *Travel + Leisure*, www.travelandleisure.com/articles/thesuspicious-package/sidebar/1, accessed February 2009.

5. Eve Lazarus, "Coast Capital Singing a Chinese Song," *Marketing Daily*, July 24, 2007, accessed at www.marketingmag.ca.

6. Kristin Laird, "Hyundai Harnesses Star Power in Quebec," *Marketing Daily*, March 28, 2008, accessed at www.marketingmag.ca.

7. Rebecca Harris, "Rich Rewards," *Marketing Magazine*, June 25, 2007, p. 17.

8. Beth Snyder Bulik, "You Are What You Watch, Market Data Suggest," AdAge.com, November 1, 2010.

9. Brian Steinberg, "How Netflix's New Prices Are Like Selling Coke on a Summer Day," AdAge.com, July 14, 2011.

10. See Louise Story, "Finding Love and the Right Linens," *New York Times*, December 13, 2006, accessed at www.nytimes.com; and www.williams-sonoma.com/cust/storeevents/index.cfm (accessed September 2009).

11. Carolyn Chapin, "Seafood Nets Loyal Consumers," *Refrigerated & Frozen Foods*, June 2009, p. 42.

12. Matt Semansky, "The 'ME' Years," *Marketing*, November 12, 2007, pp. 34–35.

13. Information from the Neilsen Company website, www.claritas.com.

14. "The Legalization of Gay Marriage in California Offers New Opportunity for the Jewelry Industry," a press release issued by Platinum Guild International USA, July 14, 2008; "The Impact of Extending Marriage to Same-Sex Couples on the California Budget," published by the Williams Institute, June 2008; Andrea Zoe Aster, "... and the Grooms Wore Pink," *Marketing*, May 10, 2004, pp. 11–12; Michelle Halpern, "Gay Getaways: Canada is a Popular Vacation Spot for Gay Americans," *Marketing*, May 22/29, 2006, p. 4.

15. Information from American Express's website, www201 .americanexpress.com/business-credit-cards, accessed July 2010.

16. See Michael Porter, *Competitive Advantage* (New York, NY: Free Press, 1985), pp. 4–8, 234–236. For more recent discussions, see Stanley Slater and Eric Olson, "A Fresh Look at Industry and Market Analysis," *Business Horizons*, January–February 2002, pp. 15–22; Kenneth Sawka and Bill Fiora, "The Four Analytical Techniques Every Analyst Must Know: 2. Porter's Five Forces Analysis," *Competitive Intelligence Magazine*, May–June 2003, p. 57; and Philip Kotler and Kevin Lane Keller, *Marketing Management*, 13th ed. (Upper Saddle River, NJ: Prentice Hall, 2009), pp. 342–343.

17. See Suzanne Kapner, "How Fashion's VF Supercharges Its Brands," *Fortune*, April 14, 2008, pp. 108–110; and www.vfc.com, accessed October 2009.

18. Kathleen Martin, "Global Cymbals," *Marketing*, March 22, 2004, p. 13; Sabian website at www.sabian.com.

19. For these and other examples, see Lynnley Browning, "Do-It-Yourself Logos for Proud Scion Owners," *New York Times*, March 24, 2008, accessed at www.nytimes.com; and Mike Beirne, "Mars Gives M&M's a Face," *Brandweek*, May 22, 2008, accessed at www.brandweek.com.

20. Adapted from information found in "When You Watch These Ads, the Ads Check You Out," *New York Times*, January 31, 2009, accessed at www.nytimes.com.

21. Adapted from portions of Fae Goodman, "Lingerie Is Luscious and Lovely," *Chicago Sun-Times*, February 19, 2006, p. B2; and Stacy Weiner, "Goodbye to Girlhood," *Washington Post*, February 20, 2007, p. HE01. Also see Suzanne C. Ryan, "Would Hannah Montana Wear It?" *Boston Globe*, January 10, 2008, www.boston .com; and Betsy Cummings, "Tickled Pink," *Brandweek*, September 8, 2008, pp. MO26–MO28.

22. Jack Trout, "Branding Can't Exist without Positioning," *Advertising Age*, March 14, 2005, p. 28.

23. Michael Myser, "Marketing Made Easy," *Business 2.0*, June 2006, pp. 43–44.

24. Lisa Hannam, "Spot the Difference," *Marketing*, January 26, 2009.

25. Jack Neff, "Why Tiny Tresemme Is Rising to Top of Hair-Care Heap," AdAge.com, August 30, 2010.

26. See Bobby J. Calder and Steven J. Reagan, "Brand Design," in Dawn Iacobucci, ed., *Kellogg on Marketing* (New York, NY: John Wiley & Sons, 2001), p. 61. For more discussion, see Philip Kotler and Kevin Lane Keller, *Marketing Management*, 13th ed. (Upper Saddle River, NJ: Prentice Hall, 2009), pp. 315–316.

CHAPTER 8

1. All information provided by Nissan Canada and available at media.nissan.ca/leaf.

2. Danny Kucharsky, "Friendly Funerals," *Marketing*, April 10, 2006, p. 17–18.

3. Barry Curewitz, "Want New Products That Get Noticed? Change the Process," *Advertising Age*, October 1, 2007.

4. For more about the diffusion of innovations theory and the technology adoption life cycle, see any edition of Geoffrey A. Moore, *Crossing the Chasm* (New York: HarperCollins, 1991); and Everett M. Rogers, *Diffusion of Innovations* (New York: The Free Press, originally published 1962).

5. Michael McCullough, "The Best Ideas Come from the Janitor . . ." *Canadian Business*, April 11, 2011, p. 61.

6. Bill Taylor, "John Fluevog: Ideas with Sole—In Tough Times, Tap the 'Hidden Genius' of Your Customers," *Harvard Business Review* Blog Network (blogs.hbr.org), March 5, 2009; "Entrepreneurs Seek Input from Outsiders," *Wall Street Journal*, December 22, 2010.

7. See the Frito Lay website, www.fritolay.com.

8. Russ Martin, "SXSW: Why Brand Fans Are the New Marketers," *Marketing Magazine*, March 9, 2013.

9. Andrew Abbott, "Announcing the PayPal Mobile App Challenge Winners!" TopCoder.com, February 8, 2011.

10. George S. Day, "Is It Real? Can We Win? Is It Worth Doing?" *Harvard Business Review*, December 2007, pp. 110–120.

11. For a more comprehensive discussion of marketing strategies over the course of the product life cycle, see Philip Kotler and Kevin Lane Keller, *Marketing Management*, 9th Canadian ed., Chapter 10.

12. Ibid.

13. Ibid.

14. Angelina Chapin, "Guitar Hero (2005–2011)," *Canadian Business*, March 14, 2011, p. 25.

15. Samsung Canada press release, January 7, 2013.

16. Matthew McClearn, "Through a Glass, Doubled," *Canadian Business*, Winter 2012/2013, p. 9.

17. "The Packaging Brief for Category Managers," published by the Food Marketing Institute and available on its website at fmi.org.

18. "Amazon Certified Frustration-Free Packaging," information available on amazon.com, accessed February 18, 2013.

19. Rebecca Harris, "Nice Package," *Marketing*, April 9, 2012, pp. 26–31.

20. Ibid.

21. Ibid.

22. See "HP Total Care," a section of the HP website at www.hp.com, accessed August 2010.

23. Information from the "Our Brands" section of the Marriott website, www.marriott.com, accessed August 2010.

24. Information from the Statistics Canada website, www.statcan.gc.ca, accessed March 2010.

25. See James L. Heskett, W. Earl Sasser Jr., and Leonard A. Schlesinger, *The Service Profit Chain: How Leading Companies Link Profit and Growth to Loyalty, Satisfaction, and Value* (New York: Free Press, 1997); Heskett, Sasser, and Schlesinger, *The Value Profit Chain: Treat Employees Like Customers and Customers Like Employees* (New York: Free Press, 2003); John F. Milliman, Jeffrey M. Ferguson, and Andrew J. Czaplewski, "Breaking the Cycle," *Marketing Management*, March–April 2008, pp. 14–17; and Christian Homburg, Jan Wieseke, and Wayne D. Hoyer, "Social Identity and the Service-Profit Chain," *Journal of Marketing*, March 2009, pp. 38–54.

26. Jeffrey M. O'Brien, "A Perfect Season," *Fortune*, January 22, 2008, pp. 62–66; Michael B. Baker, "Four Seasons Tops Ritz-Carlton in Deluxe Photo-Finish," *Business Travel News*, March 23, 2009, p. 10; Sean Drakes, "Keeping the Brand Sacred," *Black Enterprise*, April 2009, p. 47.

27. Sarah Barmak & Graham F. Scott, "Yes, We Sell No Bananas," *Canadian Business*, October 1, 2012.

28. See James L. Heskett, W. Earl Sasser Jr., and Christopher W.L. Hart, *Service Breakthroughs* (New York: Free Press, 1990).

CHAPTER 9

1. Website of Ontario Craft Brewers, a trade association for small breweries in Ontario, OntarioCraftBrewers.com; BMO Nesbitt Burns, "Good Time for a Beer?" August 15, 2012; Chris Powell, "Labatt's New Keith's Brew Takes Aim at Craft Crowd," *Marketing*, March 12, 2013; Ike Wilson, "Craft Beer Industry's Growth Reflected Locally," *McClatchy-Tribune Business News*, April 1, 2013; James Wilmore, "US: Craft Beer Volumes Jump in 2012—Figures," *Just Drinks Global News* [Bromsgrove], March 19, 2013. Christine Sismondo, "Canada's Coolest Job: Beer Cicerone," *Canadian Business*, March 18, 2013, p. 57; and information provided by Andrea and Peter Chiodo.

2. Jonathan Salem Baskin, "Our Measurement Problem Begins with Definitions," AdAge.com, May 17, 2010.

3. Marty Neumeier, *The Brand Gap* (Berkeley, CA: New Riders, 2006).

4. Neumeier, *The Brand Gap*.

5. Andy Goldsmith, "Coke vs. Pepsi: The Taste They Don't Want You to Know About," *The 60-Second Marketer*, at www.60secondmarketer.com/60SecondArticles/Branding/cokevs.pepsitast.html (accessed March 2013).

6. Jack Trout, "'Branding' Simplified," *Forbes*, April 19, 2007, accessed at www.forbes.com.

7. Kevin Roberts, *Lovemarks: The Future Beyond Brands* (New York, NY: powerHouse Books, 2004).

8. Al Ehrbar, "Breakaway Brands," *Fortune*, October 31, 2005, pp. 153–170; "DeWalt Named Breakaway Brand," *Snips*, January 2006, p. 66.

9. Matt Semansky, "Brand Nash," *Marketing Magazine*, September 8, 2009, p. 11.

10. "Google Doodle History," www.google.com/doodles (accessed March 2013).

11. "McAtlas Shrugged," *Foreign Policy*, May–June 2001, pp. 26–37; Philip Kotler, *Marketing Management*, 11th ed. (Upper Saddle River, NJ: Prentice Hall, 2003), p. 423.

12. See young-rubicam.de and www.brandassetvaluator.be.

13. Jean Halliday, "Ford Resurrects Taurus Name," AdAge.com, February 7, 2007.

14. Ted Matthews, *Brand: It Ain't the Logo*, Instinct Brand Equity Coaches Inc., 2012.

15. Ibid.

16. Canadian Press, "Sears Canada Taps Aldo, Buffalo for Private Label Brands," *Marketing Magazine*, January 17, 2013.

17. Canadian Press, "Cott Focuses on Private Brands," *Marketing Magazine*, June 19, 2008.

18. Susan Krashinsky, "Marketers Develop a Taste for Aspiring Foodies," *Globe and Mail*, December 27, 2012; Anne Kingston and Jennifer Bain, "Loblaws Throws Parkdale Bash for New Gourmet Products," *Toronto Star*, September 23, 2011; Fraser Abe, "President's Choice Gets in on the Bacon-Everything Trend with the New, Upscale Black Label Line," *Toronto Life*, September 13, 2011; Dana Flavelle, "Loblaws Gambles on Luxury Food Line," *Toronto Star*, September 13, 2011.

19. Canadian Press, "Miller Brewing to Terminate Canadian Licensing Agreement with Molson Coors," *Toronto Star*, February 27, 2013.

20. Dan Beem, "The Case for Co-Branding," Forbes.com, March 16, 2010.

21. Canadian Press, "Gildan Activewear Makes Super Bowl Play with TV Spot," *Marketing Magazine*, February 5, 2013; Jeff Beer, "Out of the Closet: Why Gildan Went Big on TV," *Marketing Magazine*, March 14, 2013.

22. Canadian Press, "Sobeys Inc. Launches FreshCo Brand in Ontario," *Marketing Magazine*, May 12, 2010.

23. Stephen Cole, "Value of the Brand," *CA Magazine*, May 2005, pp. 39–40; and Lawrence A. Crosby and Sheree L. Johnson, "Experience Required," *Marketing Management*, July/August 2007, pp. 21–27.

24. Lee Hee Jung and Kang Myung Soo, "The Effect of Brand Experience on Brand Relationship Quality," *Academy of Marketing Studies Journal*, 2012, 16(1), pp. 87–98.

25. "While TV Gets Auto Ad Dollars; Social Is the Critical Inflection Point in Purchase Decisions," *Business Wire*, February 21, 2013.

26. Robert Klara, "Five Famous Female Frontwomen," AdWeek.com, February 26, 2013; Old Time Radio Catalogue, OTRCat.com.

27. Matt Semansky, "Mars Canada (One of the Top Marketers of 2011)," *Marketing Magazine*, November 28, 2011, p. 37; description of Red from M&M's website, www.mms.com/us/about/characters/red, and Red's Facebook page, accessed February 2013.

28. Caroline Fortin, "Penningtons Moving in New Direction with Vachon," *Marketing Magazine*, January 23, 2013.

29. Emma Hall, "New Benetton Ads Confront Prejudice, But Don't Shock," AdAge.com, January 23, 2013.

30. Kevin Roberts, *Lovemarks*.

31. "The Power of Story," *Marketing Magazine*, September 12, 2012, p. 19.

32. Chris Powell, "Custom Takes Off," *Marketing Magazine*, June 4, 2012, pp. 23–28.

33. Kristin Laird, "Kokanee Goes to the Movies," *Marketing Magazine*, May 23, 2012.

34. Anthony Mullen, "Emerging Technologies Demand New Marketing Fundamentals," AdAge.com, March 4, 2013.

35. Brian Solis, *Engage!* John Wiley & Sons, 2010.

36. Kristin Laird, "As Seen on the Radio," *Marketing Magazine*, December 17, 2012, p. 10.

37. Interbrand, "Best Canadian Brands 2010."

38. *The MediaBrix Social and Mobile Gaming Report*, MediaBrix .com, March 2013; James Dohnert, "Social and Mobile Gaming Ads Offer 20 Percent Engagement Rates," ClickZ.com, March 4, 2013.

CHAPTER 10

1. "Q4 2013 WalMart Stores, Inc. Prerecorded Earnings Conference Call—Final," Fair Disclosure Wire [Waltham], February 21, 2013; "Amazon.com Announces Fourth Quarter Sales up 22% to $21.27 Billion," press release published on Business Wire, January 29, 2013; Brad Stone and Stephanie Rosenbloom, "The Gloves Come Off at Amazon and Walmart," *New York Times*, November 24, 2009, p. 1; Gayle Feldman, "Behind the US Price War," *Bookseller*, November 13, 2009, p. 16; Jeffrey A. Trachtenberg and Miguel Bustillo, "Amazon, Walmart Cut Deeper in Book Duel," *Wall Street Journal*, October 19, 2009, p. B1; Josh Smith, "2010 Marks Return of Price Wars Between Amazon, Best Buy, and Walmart," published on DailyFinance .com, January 19, 2010; Brad Stone, "Can Amazon Be Walmart of the Web?" *New York Times*, September 20, 2009, p. 1; Jonathan Birchall, "Walmart Tweaks Price in Amazon Battle," *Financial Times*, October 17, 2009; Curt Woodward, "Amazon: Feds OK Diapers.com Deal," published on XConomy.com, March 24, 2011; Matthew Boyle and Douglas MacMillan, "Walmart's Rocky Path from Bricks to Clicks," *Bloomberg Businessweek*, July 25–July 31, 2011, pp. 31–33; and information from Walmart.com and Amazon.com websites.

2. For more on the importance of sound pricing strategy, see Thomas T. Nagle and John Hogan, *The Strategy and Tactics of Pricing: A Guide to Growing More Profitably,* 4th ed. (Upper Saddle River, NJ: Prentice Hall, 2007), Chapter 1.

3. Anne Marie Chaker, "For a Steinway, I Did It My Way," *Wall Street Journal*, May 22, 2008; and information from the Steinway Piano Gallery Toronto, March 2013.

4. Information from Ryanair's website, Ryanair.com, accessed March 2013.

5. "Cineplex to Debut VIP Cinemas in Quebec at Cineplex Odeon Brossard Cinemas," press release published on Canada Newswire, January 23, 2012; Simon Houpt and Steve Ladurantaye, "Why Cineplex Put the Adult Back into Adult Entertainment," *Globe and Mail*, October 15, 2012.

6. Elisabeth A. Sullivan, "Value Pricing: Smart Marketers Know Cost-Plus Can Be Costly," *Marketing News*, January 15, 2008, p. 8. Also see Venkatesh Bala and Jason Green, "Charge What Your Products Are Worth," *Harvard Business Review*, September 2007, p. 22; and Peter J. Williamson and Ming Zeng, "Value-for-the-Money Strategies," *Harvard Business Review*, March 2009, pp. 66–74.

7. Emily F.'s review published on Yelp.ca March 13, 2013; Travelin G.'s review published August 6, 2012.

8. Adapted from information found in Joseph Weber, "Over a Buck for Dinner? Outrageous," *Businessweek*, March 9, 2009, p. 57.

9. Laura Petrecca, "Marketers Try to Promote Value without Cheapening Image," *USA Today*, November 21, 2008.

10. Ryan McCarthy, "Pricing: How Low Can You Go?" *Inc.*, March 2009, pp. 91–92.

11. For comprehensive discussions of pricing strategies, see Nagle and Hogan, *The Strategy and Tactics of Pricing*, 4th ed. (Upper Saddle River, NJ: Prentice Hall, 2007).

12. Adapted from information found in Mei Fong, "IKEA Hits Home in China; The Swedish Design Giant, Unlike Other Retailers, Slashes Prices for the Chinese," *Wall Street Journal*, March 3, 2006, p. B1; and "IKEA China to Boost Sales by Slashing Prices," *China Knowledge*, March 9, 2009, accessed at www.chinaknowledge.com.

13. Beth Snyder Bulik, "Kodak Develops New Model: Inexpensive Printer, Cheap Ink," *Advertising Age*, March 12, 2007, p. 4.

14. Information from "Pollution Prevention Success Stories: MacTara Limited," Environment Canada, accessed at www.atl .ec.gc.ca/epb/pollprev/mactara.html; "MacTara Jobs May Be Safe After Deal with Creditors," *CBC News*, March 11, 2008, www .cbc.ca/canada/nova-scotia/story/2008/03/11/lumber-yard.html; Monique Chiasson, "Deal in the Works for MacTara," *Truro Daily News*, March 13, 2008, www.atlanticfarmfocus.ca/index .cfm?sid=124503&sc=586, accessed July 2009.

15. May Jeong, "Powering Homes with Poo from the Zoo," *Globe and Mail*, August 17, 2011; "Green Innovation Awards for 'Zoo Poo' Energy and Urban 'Mini-Farms' Culminate ClimateSpark Social Venture Challenge," published on Canada Newswire, February 8, 2012.

16. See Nagle and Hogan, *The Strategy and Tactics of Pricing*, 4th ed. (Upper Saddle River, NJ: Prentice Hall, 2007), pp. 244–247; Bram Foubert and Els Gijsbrechts, "Shopper Response to Bundle

Promotions for Packaged Goods," *Journal of Marketing Research*, November 2007, pp. 647–662; Roger M. Heeler et al., "Bundles = Discount? Revisiting Complex Theories of Bundle Effects," *Journal of Product & Brand Management* 16(7), 2007, pp. 492–500; and Timothy J. Gilbride et al., "Framing Effects in Mixed Price Bundling," *Marketing Letters*, June 2008, pp. 125–140.

17. Based on information from Eric Anderson and Duncan Simester, "Mind Your Pricing Cues," *Harvard Business Review*, September 2003, pp. 96–103. Also see Monika Kukar-Kinney et al., "Consumer Responses to Characteristics of Price-Matching Guarantees," *Journal of Retailing*, April 2007, p. 211; and Peter J. Boyle and E. Scott Lathrop, "Are Consumers' Perceptions of Price-Quality Relationships Well Calibrated?" *International Journal of Consumer Studies*, January 2009, p. 58.

18. Adapted from information found in Elisabeth A. Sullivan, "Stay on Course," *Marketing News*, February 15, 2009, pp. 11–13. Also see Stuart Elliott, "Never Mind What It Costs. Can I Get It 70 Percent Off?" *New York Times*, April 27, 2009.

19. Based on information found in "The World's Most Influential Companies: Unilever," *Businessweek*, December 22, 2008, p. 47; and www.unilever.com/sustainability/people/consumers/affordability, accessed June 2009.

20. Example adapted from information found in Ellen Byron, "Fashion Victim: To Refurbish Its Image, Tiffany Risks Profits," *Wall Street Journal*, January 10, 2007, p. A1; and Aliza Rosenbaum and John Christy, "Financial Insight: Tiffany's Boutique Risk; By Breaking Mall Fast, High-End Exclusivity May Gain Touch of Common," *Wall Street Journal*, October 20, 2007, p. B14. Also see Bernadette Morra, "Tiffany Seeks to Break Down Some Barriers," *Toronto Star*, April 23, 2009, p. L3.

21. Mark Ritson, "Should You Launch a Fighter Brand?" *Harvard Business Review*, October 2009.

22. See the Competition Act, Sections 34–38, http://laws.justice.gc.ca/en/C-34/.

23. For discussions of these issues, see Dhruv Grewel and Larry D. Compeau, "Pricing and Public Policy: A Research Agenda and Overview of Special Issue," *Journal of Public Policy and Marketing*, Spring 1999, pp. 3–10; and Michael V. Marn, Eric V. Roegner, and Craig C. Zawada, *The Price Advantage* (Hoboken, NJ: John Wiley & Sons, 2004), Appendix 2.

24. Jim Middlemiss, "Don't Get Caught Offside in Rule Changes," *Financial Post*, March 23, 2009.

CHAPTER 11

1. Target Canada press releases published on Canada Newswire in 2012–2013; Kristin Laird, "Target Finds Canadian Roots with New Partnership," *Marketing Magazine*, January 25, 2013; Kristin Laird, "Everybody Loves Target," *Marketing Magazine*, May 7, 2012, pp. 44–49; Duncan Hood, "Target Won't Kill Canadian Retail. It Will Save It," *Canadian Business*, October 15, 2012, p. 4; Richard Warnica, "Target's Friendly Invasion," *Canadian Business*, October 15, 2012, pp. 32–36; "WSL/Strategic Retail: Canada Represents Opportunities for U.S. Retailers," *Entertainment Close Up*, September 21, 2012; Beth Mattson-Teig, "Walmart Blazes a Trail

for Other Value Retailers in Expanding Internationally," *Retail Traffic*, May 22, 2012; Ron Margulis, "Here Comes TARGET," *Canadian Grocer* 126 (9) (2012): 38–42, 44; Megan Haynes, "Target to Bring Archer Farms, Market Pantry and Up And Up to Canada," *Strategy*, January 24, 2013.

2. Enterprise Canada website, enterpriserentacar.ca, accessed January 24, 2013; Lisa Brown, "BRIEF: Enterprise Holdings Grows Fiscal 2012 Revenue," *McClatchy-Tribune Business News*, October 26, 2012; "New Self-Service Kiosks Save Time for Alamo, Enterprise and National Customers," *Leisure & Travel Business*, October 21, 2012, p. 114; "Enterprise Rent-A-Car Launches New Ads, Brings Back $9.99 Weekend Special," press release published on Canada Newswire, September 18, 2012; Stephan Stern, "Revealed: The Secret to Survival in 2009 (Pass It On)," *Financial Times*, December 23, 2008, p. 12.

3. Eve Lazarus, "Branching Out," *Marketing Magazine*, October 20, 2003, p. 29.

4. Caterpillar 2011 Annual Report; Alex Taylor III, "Caterpillar," *Fortune*, August 20, 2007, pp. 48–54; Donald V. Fites, "Make Your Dealers Your Partners," *Harvard Business Review*, March–April 1996, pp. 84–95.

5. Statistics Canada.

6. *Grainger 2011 Fact Book* and other information available from the company's website, Grainger.com, accessed January 2013.

7. John Boiler, "Five Reasons You Should Quit Using the Word 'Client,'" *Advertising Age*, January 29, 2013.

8. Christopher Loudon, "The Sun Life," *Marketing Magazine*, March 1, 2010, pp. 27–32.

9. Beth Negus Viveiros, "Mattel Uses Web to Boost Retail Sales and Bond with Collectors," *Chief Marketer*, September 23, 2012.

10. Jeff Beer, "Fight Over Taxi Apps Hits the Streets," *Canadian Business*, November 26, 2012, p. 12.

11. Cecilie Rohwedder, "Zara Grows as Retail Rivals Struggle," *Wall Street Journal*, March 26, 2009, p. B1; "Inditex Outperforms with Growth in All Its Markets," *Retail Week*, March 27, 2009, accessed at www.retail-week.com; Kerry Capell, "Fashion Conquistador," *Businessweek*, September 4, 2006, pp. 38–39; Cecilie Rohwedder, "Turbocharged Supply Chain May Speed Zara Past Gap as Top Clothing Retailer," *Globe and Mail*, March 26, 2009, p. B12.

12. Boston Pizza website, bostonpizza.com, accessed February 2013.

13. Information from Lee Valley and Veritas websites, leevalley.com and veritastools.ca, accessed February 2013.

14. "Retail Fast Facts," December 2012, published by the Retail Council of Canada.

15. *Statistics Canada Retail Trade* report, November 2012.

16. Jeff Beer, "Canada and U.S. Are Shoppers Apart: Study," *Marketing Magazine*, August 24, 2010.

17. Jaclyn Law, "Layaway . . . On Hold," *Marketing Magazine*, January 12, 2009, p. 7.

18. "Walmart Targets South Asian Market," *CBC News,* March 19, 2008; Susan Catto, "The People in Your Neighbourhood," *Marketing Magazine,* March 23, 2009, p. 44.

19. Jeff Beer, "Invasion of the Burger Joints," *Canadian Business,* November 12, 2012, pp. 36–39.

20. Dana Flavelle, "Canadian Retailers Go Global," *Toronto Star,* February 23, 2011; "Tim Hortons Charts Course for Global Expansion," *Canadian Press,* May 17, 2010.

21. Rupal Parekh, "Test Driving BMW's First Concept Store in Paris," *Advertising Age,* June 1, 2012.

22. "Shoppable Media, In-Store Technology and Physical Presences for Online Stores," AdAge.com, January 9, 2013.

23. Natalie Galiordi, "Intel's Interactive Display Spices Up the Customer Experience," accessed at RetailCustomerExperience.com, January 30, 2013.

24. Sandra Hermiston & Lynda Steele, "Swap Your Unwanted Gift Cards," *CTV British Columbia,* January 30, 2013; CardSwap.ca website, accessed February 2013; Michelle Warren, "The Amazing, Versatile Gift Card," *Marketing Magazine,* May 26, 2008, pp. 29–31.

25. Alicia Androich, "Shopper Marketing: Around and Around We Go," *Marketing Magazine,* June 7, 2012; Rupal Parekh, "McCann's Momentum Ups Shopper-Marketing Expertise with Acquisition," AdAge.com, August 8, 2012.

26. Statistics Canada, *Canadian Internet Use Survey 2010.*

27. Michael Oliveira, "Holiday Retail Sales Canada: MasterCard Says Online Shopping Shot Up 26 Per Cent," *Canadian Press,* January 17, 2013.

28. *2013 Global Multi-Channel Retail Survey* conducted by PricewaterhouseCoopers.

29. Vijay Kumar, "Canadians Prefer Online Shopping to Retail Shopping," *International Business Times* (ibtimes.com), January 24, 2013.

30. Mark Penn, "New Info Shoppers," *Wall Street Journal* online, January 8, 2009.

31. Chris Powell, "GroupM Gets Inside the 'Showrooming' Trend," *Marketing Magazine,* August 22, 2012.

32. "Shoppable Media, In-Store Technology and Physical Presences for Online Stores," AdAge.com, January 9, 2013.

33. Chris Powell, "Mobile Devices Becoming a Bigger Part of Retail: Study," *Marketing Magazine,* May 31, 2012.

34. Steve Olenski, "The Number One Mistake Retail Brands Make When It Comes to Twitter," *Forbes,* January 24, 2013.

35. Example adapted from Evan West, "These Robots Play Fetch," *Fast Company,* July/August 2007, pp. 49–50. Also see John Teresko, "Getting Lean with Armless Robots," *Industry Week,* September 2008, p. 26.

36. Laura Cameron, "The Big Money in Slow Shipping," *Canadian Business,* May 10, 2010, p. 22.

CHAPTER 12

1. Information from http://cassies.ca/entry/viewcase/7162, accessed March 22, 2013.

2. For other definitions, see www.marketingpower.com/_layouts/Dictionary.aspx, accessed November 2011.

3. See Martin Peers, "Television's Fuzzy Ad Picture," *Wall Street Journal,* May 10, 2011, p. C22; and Lisa Waananen, "How Agencies Are Spending Online Media Budgets," Mashable.com, June 9, 2011, http://mashable.com/2011/06/09/media-agency-budgets.

4. "Canadian Winners at Webbys Honoured for Interactive Ads, Community Activism," www.mediacastermagazine.com/news/canadian-winnersat-webbys-honoured-for-interactive-ads-communityactivism/1001120953; information from http://rethinkbreastcancer.com and www.johnst.com/#/work/rethink-breast-cancer; and Stuart Elliott, "Heineken Aims Ads at Young Digital Devotees," *New York Times,* May 26, 2011, p. B6.

5. Jim Edwards, "P&G's $1 Billion Problem: Is Its Ad Budget too Big?" *BNET,* August 4, 2010, www.bnet.com/blog/advertising-business/p-g-8217s-1-billion-problem-is-its-ad-budget-too-big/5368; and "Procter & Gamble Names New Top Digital Marketer," *The Ratti Report,* May 2, 2011, www.the-ratti-report.com/blog/622492-procter-gamble-names-new-top-digital-marketer.

6. Quote from Michael Schneider, "Nielsen: Traditional TV Still King," *Variety,* December 7, 2009; TV and Internet advertising stats from Lisa Waananen, "How Agencies Are Spending Online Media Budgets," Mashable.com, June 9, 2011, http://mashable.com/2011/06/09/media-agency-budgets.

7. Chris Powell, "ACA Study Shows Marketing Spend Trending Upwards," *Marketing Magazine,* October 26, 2010, www.marketingmag.ca/news/marketer-news/aca-study-shows-marketing-spendtrending-upwards-5554; and information from Association of Canadian Advertisers at www.acaweb.ca/en/mediareleases/aca-releases-report-on-marcom-expendituretrends-and-uses.

8. Jon Lafayette, "4A's Conference: Agencies Urged to Embrace New Technologies," *Broadcasting & Cable,* March 8, 2011, www.broadcastingcable.com/article/464951-4A_s_Conference_Agencies_Urged_To_Embrace_New_Technologies.php.

9. See "Integrated Campaigns: Häagen-Dazs," *Communication Arts Advertising Annual 2009,* pp. 158–159; Tiffany Meyers, "Marketing 50: Häagen-Dazs, Katty Pien," *Advertising Age,* November 17, 2008, p. S15; "Häagen-Dazs Loves Honey Bees," April 28, 2010, a summary video accessed at http://limeshot.com/2010/haagen-dazs-loves-honey-bees-titanium-silver-lion-cannes-2009; Alan Bjerga, "U.S. Queen Bees Work Overtime to Save Hives," *Bloomberg Businessweek,* April 3, 2011, pp. 27–28; and information from www.helpthehoneybees.com, accessed October 2011.

10. "Super Bowl 2013 Attracts 108 Million Viewers," www.nola.com/superbowl/index.ssf/2013/02/super_bowl_2013_attracts_108_m.html; and Scott Collins, "Oscars 2013: TV Ratings Rise with Seth MacFarlane as Host," *Los Angeles Times,* February 25, 2013, www.latimes.com/entertainment/envelope/tv/la-et-st-oscars-2013-tv-ratings-rise-with-seth-macfarlane-as-host-20130225,0,6794036.story.

11. See discussions at "What Is the Real Cost of a B2B Sales Call?" www.marketing-playbook.com/sales-marketing-strategy/what-is-the-real-cost-of-a-b2b-sales-call, accessed June 2011; and "The Costs of Personal Selling," April 13, 2011, www.seekarticle.com/business-sales/personal-selling.html.

12. Adam Smith, "GroupM Forecasts Global Ad Spending to Surpass $500 Billion in 2011," December 6, 2010, www.aaaa.org/news/agency/Pages/120610_groupm_forecast.aspx; "Top 100 Global Advertisers See World of Opportunity," *Advertising Age*, December 6, 2010, http://adage.com/print?article_id=147436; "Advertising Spending," *Advertising Age*, December 20, 2010, p. 10; "Which Marketer Has the Deepest Pockets? Ask the DataCenter," special promotional supplement, *Advertising Age,* February 14, 2011, p. 3; and "Marketing Facts 2013: Statistics and Trends for Marketing in Canada," Canadian Marketing Association, 2012.

13. Bill Curry, "Tory Government Hiked Ad Spending to Promote Stimulus Projects," *Globe and Mail*, January 4, 2012, www .theglobeandmail.com/news/politics/tory-government-hiked-ad-spending-to-promote-stimulusprojects/article2291855.

14. For these and other examples of comparative advertising, see Emily Bryson York and Natalie Zmuda, "So Sue Me: Why Big Brands Are Taking Claims to Court," *Advertising Age*, January 4, 2010, pp. 1, 23; Simon Houpt, "Rogers Suit Targets Bell Ad Claims" *Globe and Mail*, December 2009, www.theglobeandmail.com/globe-investor/rogers-suit-targets-bell-ad-claims/article1384460; Jamie Sturgeon, "BCE Dispute with Rival TV Providers Faces Final Arbitration," *Financial Post*, May 2012, www.canada.com/business/fp/dispute+with+rival+providers+faces+final+arbitration/6708846/story.html; and Isabella Soscia, Simona Girolamo, and Bruno Busacca, "The Effect of Comparison Advertising on Consumer Perceptions: Similarity or Differentiation?" *Journal of Business and Psychology*, March 2010, pp. 109–118.

15. For more on setting promotion budgets, see W. Ronald Lane, Karen Whitehill King, and J. Thomas Russell, *Kleppner's Advertising Procedure*, 18th ed. (Upper Saddle River, NJ: Prentice Hall, 2011), Chapter 6.

16. See Jean Halliday, "Thinking Big Takes Audi from Obscure to Awesome," *Advertising Age*, February 2, 2009, http://adage.com/print?article_id=134234; Chad Thomas and Andreas Cremer, "Audi Feels a Need for Speed in the U.S.," *Bloomberg Businessweek*, November 22, 2010, p. 1; and Tito F. Hermoso, "Watch Out for Audi," *BusinessWorld*, June 15, 2011, p. 1.

17. "Average U.S. Home Now Receives a Record 118.6 TV Channels, According to Nielsen," June 6, 2008, http://en-us .nielsen.com/content/nielsen/en_us/news/news_releases/2008/june/average_u_s__home.html; and "Number of Magazines Titles," www.magazine.org/ASME/EDITORIAL_TRENDS/1093.aspx, accessed July 2011.

18. Louise Story, "Anywhere the Eye Can See, It's Likely to See an Ad," *New York Times*, January 15, 2007, p. A12; and James Othmer, "Persuasion Gives Way to Engagement," *Vancouver Sun*, August 20, 2009, p. A13.

19. "Executive Summary of the 4A's Television Production Cost Survey," December 15, 2009, www.aaaa.org/news/bulletins/Documents/2008TVPCSExecSumcosts.pdf; "Prime Time

Programs & 30 Second Ad Costs: Historical Look 2000–2011," www.frankwbaker.com/prime_time_programs_30_sec_ad_costs. htm, accessed July 2011; and Aaron Smith "Super Bowl Ad: Is $3 Million Worth It?" CNNMoney.com, February 3, 2011.

20. Information from Television Bureau of Canada, "TV Basics: 2011–2012," www.tvb.ca/page_files/pdf/InfoCentre/TVBasics.pdf.

21. "Advertising in the U.S.: Synovate Global Survey Shows Internet, Innovation and Online Privacy a Must," December 3, 2009, www.synovate.com/news/article/2009/12/advertising-in-the-us-synovate-global-survey-shows-internet-innovation-and-online-privacy-a-must.html; and Katy Bachman, "Survey: Clutter Causing TV Ads to Lack Effectiveness," *MediaWeek*, February 8, 2010.

22. Wayne Freedman, "Nielsen: DVR Playback Doubles, More Ads Watch," *MediaPostNews,* August 5, 2010, www.mediapost .com/publications/?fa=Articles.showArticle&art_aid=133321; and information from Television Bureau of Canada, "TV Basics: 2011–2012," www.tvb.ca/page_files/pdf/InfoCentre/TVBasics.pdf.

23. "Rentrak Reports That Many Super Bowl Commercials Are Watched Over and Over via Viewers' DVR," February 21, 2011, www.rentrak.com/section/corporate/press_room/press_release_detail.html?release_no=1803.

24. T. L. Stanley, "A Place for Everything," *Brandweek,* March 1, 2010, p. 12.

25. Wayne Friedman, "Lights, Camera, Apple! Tech Giant Product Placement King," *MediaPostNews*, February 22, 2011, www.media-post.com/publications/?fa=Articles.showArticle&art_aid=145480; and Stuart Elliott, "Film on Branded Content Examines a Blurred Line," *New York Times*, April 22, 2011, p. B3.

26. "CASSIES Bronze: CTC Asks Visitors to Keep Exploring," *Strategy*, January 2012, http://strategyonline.ca/2012/01/23/cassies-bronze-ctc-asks-visitors-to-keepexploring; and information accessed at http://cassies.ca/entry/viewcase/4612.

27. For more on consumer-generated advertising, see Emma Hall, "Most Winning Creative Work Involves Consumer Participation," *Advertising Age*, January 6, 2010, http://adage.com/print?article_id=141329; Stuart Elliott, "Do-It-Yourself Super Ads," *New York Times*, February 8, 2010; Rich Thomaselli, "If Consumer Is Your Agency, It's Time for Review," *Advertising Age*, May 17, 2010, p. 2; and Colin Campbell et al., "Understanding Consumer Conversations around Ads in Web 2.0 World," *Journal of Advertising*, Spring 2011, p. 87.

28. See David Kiley, "Paying for Viewers Who Pay Attention," *Businessweek*, May 18, 2009, p. 56.

29. Brian Steinberg, "Viewer-Engagement Rankings Signal Change for TV Industry," *Advertising Age*, May 10, 2010, p. 12.

30. Tavis Coburn, "Mayhem on Madison Avenue," *Fast Company,* January 2011, pp. 110–115.

31. Joe Tripoti, "Coca-Cola Marketing Shifts from Impressions to Expressions," April 27, 2011, http://blogs.hbr.org/cs/2011/04/coca-colas_marketing_shift_fro.html.

32. See Jon Swartz, "Multitasking at Home: Internet and TV Viewing," *USA Today*, July 6, 2010, www.usatoday.com; Dan

Zigmond and Horst Stipp, "Vision Statement: Multitaskers May Be Advertisers' Best Audience," *Harvard Business Review*, January–February 2011, http://hbr.org/2011/01/vision-statement-multitaskers-may-be-advertisers-best-audience/ar/1; and Kunar Patel, "When's Prime Time in Mobile? Same as TV," *Advertising Age*, July 5, 2011, www.adage.com/print/228536.

33. *Newsweek* and *Businessweek* cost and circulation data online at www.bloombergmedia.com/magazine/businessweek and www.newsweekmediakit.com, accessed October 2010.

34. Kate Maddox, "Optimism, Accountability, Social Media Top Trends," *BtoB*, January 18, 2010, p. 1.

35. Information on advertising agency revenues from "Agency Report," *Advertising Age*, April 25, 2011, pp. 24–41.

36. Adapted from Scott Cutlip, Allen Center, and Glen Broom, *Effective Public Relations*, 10th ed. (Upper Saddle River, NJ: Prentice Hall, 2009), Chapter 1.

37. Information from "The Heart Truth: Making Healthy Hearts Fashionable," Ogilvy Public Relations Worldwide, www.ogilvypr.com/en/case-study/heart-truth?page=0; www.goredforwomen.org; and www.nhlbi.nih.gov/educational/hearttruth/about/index.htm, accessed October 2011.

38. See Geoffrey Fowler and Ben Worthen, "Buzz Powers iPad Launch," *Wall Street Journal*, April 2, 2010; "Apple iPad Sales Top 2 Million Since Launch," *Tribune-Review* (Pittsburgh), June 2, 2010; "PR Pros Must View Apple's iPad as a True Game-Changer," *PRweek*, May 2010, p. 23; and Yukari Iwatani Kane, "Apple's iPad 2 Chalks Up Strong Sales in Weekend Debut," *Wall Street Journal*, March 14, 2011, http://online.wsj.com/article/SB100014240527487 0402750457619883266773 2862.html.

39. Michael Bush, "P&G's Marc Pritchard Touts Value of PR," *Advertising Age*, October 27, 2010, http://adage.com/article/news/p-g-s-marc-pritchard-touts-pr/146749.

40. "National Public Relations Wins Big at the 2012 SABRE Awards in New York and 2012 CPRS Toronto ACE Awards," May 2012, www.newswire.ca/en/story/971897/national-public-relations-wins-big-atthe-2012-sabre-awards-in-new-york-and-2012-cprs-torontoace-awards; information accessed at www.national.ca/Selected-Work/Harlequin-2.aspx; and www.patentyourkiss.com.

41. Paul Holmes, "Senior Marketers Are Sharply Divided about the Role of PR in the Overall Mix," *Advertising Age*, January 24, 2005, pp. C1–C2. For another example, see Jack Neff, "How Pampers Battled Diaper Debacle," *Advertising Age*, May 10, 2010, http://adage.com/article?article_id=143777.

CHAPTER 13

1. Based on information from numerous P&G managers; with information from "500 Largest Sales Forces in America," *Selling Power*, October 2010, pp. 39–56; and www.experiencepg.com/jobs/customer-business-development-sales.aspx, accessed November 2011.

2. See Henry Canaday, "Sales Rep to CEO: Anne Mulcahy and the Xerox Revolution," *Selling Power*, November/December 2008, pp. 53–57.

3. See Philip Kotler, Neil Rackham, and Suj Krishnaswamy, "Ending the War between Sales and Marketing," *Harvard Business Review*, July–August 2006, pp. 68–78; Elisabeth A. Sullivan, "The Ties That Bind," *Marketing News*, May 15, 2010; Alan Edwards, "On the Road to Know-How," *Marketing*, March 23, 2011, p. 19; and Philip Kotler and Kevin Lane Keller, *Marketing Management,* 14th ed. (Upper Saddle River, NJ: Prentice Hall, 2012), p. 554.

4. See Henry Canaday, "Give It a Whirl," *Selling Power,* May/June 2010, pp. 22–24.

5. "Selling Power 500: The Largest Sales Force in America," *Selling Power,* September/October 2010, pp. 44–56.

6. See discussions at "What Is the Real Cost of a B2B Sales Call?" www.marketing-playbook.com/sales-marketing-strategy/what-is-the-real-cost-of-a-b2b-sales-call, accessed June 2011; and "The Costs of Personal Selling," April 13, 2011, www.seekarticle.com/business-sales/personal-selling.html.

7. See "Case Study: Climax Portable Machine Tools," www.selltis.com/productSalesCaseStudyClimax.aspx, accessed November 2011.

8. "Customer Business Development," www.experiencepg.com/jobs/customer-business-development-sales.aspx, accessed November 2011.

9. For this and more information and discussion, see www.gallup.com/consulting/1477/Sales-Force-Effectiveness.aspx, accessed October 2010; "The 10 Skills of 'Super' Salespeople," www.businesspartnerships.ca/articles/the_10_skills_of_super_salespeople.phtml, accessed May 2010; and Lynette Ryals and Iain Davies, "Do You Really Know Who Your Best Salespeople Are?" *Harvard Business Review*, December 2010, pp. 34–35.

10. Barbara Hendricks, "Strengths-Based Selling," February 8, 2011, www.gallup.com/press/146246/Strengths-Based-Selling.aspx.

11. "ADP Case Study," Corporate Visions, Inc., http://win.corporatevisions.com/caseStudy_ADP.html, accessed July 2011.

12. Website of the Canadian Professional Sales Association, www.cpsa.com.

13. Based on information found in Sara Donnelly, "Staying in the Game," *Pharmaceutical Executive*, May 2008, pp. 158–159; "Improving Sales Force Effectiveness: Bayer's Experiment with New Technology," Bayer Healthcare Pharmaceuticals, Inc., 2008, www.icmrindia.org/casestudies/catalogue/Marketing/MKTG200.htm; and Tanya Lewis, "Concentric," *Medical Marketing and Media*, July 2008, p. 59. For more on e-learning, see "Logging on for Sales School," *CustomRetailer*, November 2009, p. 30; and Sarah Boehle, "Global Sales Training's Balancing Act," *Training*, January 2010, p. 29.

14. See Joseph Kornak, "07 Compensation Survey: What's It All Worth?" *Sales & Marketing Management*, May 2007, pp. 28–39; William L. Cron and Thomas E. DeCarlo, *Dalrymple's Sales Management*, 10th ed. (New York: John Wiley & Sons Inc., 2009), p. 303; and Alexander Group, "2011 Sales Compensation Trends Survey Results," January 5, 2011, http://salescompsolutions.com/downloads/2011SCTExecSummFinal.pdf.

15. Susan Greco, "How to Reduce Your Cost of Sales," *Inc.*, March 5, 2010, www.inc.com/guide/reducing-cost-of-sales.html. Also see Robert McGarvey, "Pay for Performance," *Selling Power*, February 2011, p. 54.

16. See Charles Fifield, "Necessary Condition #3—The Right Day-to-Day Operational Focus," December 2010, www.baylor.edu/content/services/document.php/127101.pdf. For another summary, see Gerhard Gschwandtner, "How Much Time Do Your Salespeople Spend Selling?" *Selling Power*, March/April 2011, p. 8.

17. Quote above from Lain Chroust Ehmann, "Sales Up!" *Selling Power*, January/February 2011, p. 40. Extract adapted from information found in Pelin Wood Thorogood, "Sales 2.0: How Will It Improve Your Business?" *Selling Power*, November/December 2008, pp. 58–61; Gerhard Gschwandtner, "What Is Sales 2.0, and Why Should You Care?" *Selling Power*, March/April 2010, p. 9. Also see Michael Brenner, "The State of the Union in B2B Marketing," January 25, 2011, www.b2bmarketinginsider.com/strategy/the-state-of-the-union-in-b2b-marketing.

18. Adapted from information in Elisabeth A. Sullivan, "B-to-B Marketers: One-to-One Marketing," *Marketing News*, May 15, 2009, pp. 11–13. Also see "Social Media to Lead Growth in Online B2B Marketing," *Min's b2b*, February 8, 2010, www.minonline.com/b2b/13441.html; and Robert McGarvey, "All About Us: How the Social-Community Phenomenon Has Affected B2B Sales," *Selling Power*, November/December 2010, p. 48.

19. Quotes from David Thompson, "Embracing the Future: A Step by Step Overview of Sales 2.0," *Sales and Marketing Management*, July/August 2008, p. 21; and "Ahead of the Curve: How Sales 2.0 Will Affect Your Sales Process—For the Better," *Selling Power*, March/April 2010, pp. 14–17. Also see Robert McGarvey, "All About Us," *Selling Power*, March 7, 2011, p. 48; and Lain Chroust Ehmann, "Sales Up!" *Selling Power*, January/February 2011, p. 40.

20. Example based on information from James C. Anderson, Nirmalya Kumar, and James A. Narus, "Become a Value Merchant," *Sales & Marketing Management*, May 6, 2008, pp. 20–23; and "Business Market Value Merchants," *Marketing Management*, March/April 2008, pp. 31+. For another value selling example, see Heather Baldwin, "Deeper Value Delivery," *Selling Power*, September/October 2010, p. 16.

21. *Transforming Trade Promotion/Shopper-Centric Approach* (Wilton, CT: Kantar Retail, June 2010), p. 8.

22. Jack Neff, "Why Promotion May End Up a Bad Deal for Packaged Goods," *Advertising Age*, January 31, 2011, p. 11.

23. Alicia Androich and Kristin Laird, "Secrets of Canada's Top Loyalty Programs," *Marketing Magazine*, April 07, 2011, http://www.marketingmag.ca/uncategorized/secrets-of-canadas-top-loyalty-programs-2-25684.

24. "Shoppers Drug Mart Tightens up Optimum Rewards," Canadian Press, June 18, 2010.

25. See "Coupon Facts Report Indicates Marketers Continue Steady Use of Coupons," PR Newswire, January 24, 2013.

26. See www.happymeal.com/en_US, accessed July 2011.

27. See "2010 Estimate of Promotional Products Distributor Sales," www.ppai.org/inside-ppai/research/Documents/2010%20Sales%20Volume%20Sheet.pdf, accessed June 2011.

28. Based on information accessed at www.rolluptherimtowin.com/en/index.php, June 2012.

29. "Nissan Returns as Official Automotive Sponsor of the 2011 Amgen Tour of California," May 11, 2011, www.amgentourofcalifornia.com/news/press/Nissan-returns-as-official-automotive-sponsor-of-the-2011-Amgen-Tour-of-California.html; and www.nissanusa.com/leaf-electric-car/events/index#/leaf-electric-car/events/index, accessed July 2011.

30. "Dove Shines the Spotlight on 'Women Who Should Be Famous' to Create Strong Role Models for Girls," Canada Newswire, www.newswire.ca/en/story/987681/dove-shines-the-spotlight-on-women-whoshould-be-famous-to-create-strong-role-models-for-girls, accessed June 2012; and information accessed at www.facebook.com/dove/app_120750214630623.

31. *Transforming Trade Promotion/Shopper-Centric Approach*, p. 8.

32. See "CES Press Release," www.cesweb.org/News/CES-Press-Releases/CES-Press-Release.aspx?NodeID=ca38b9c2-1106-41b7-b44b-23b7b8959ad6, accessed May 7, 2013; and "Bauma 2010 Closing Report," www.bauma.de/en/Press/Closingreport, accessed October 2011.

CHAPTER 14

1. Leah Fabel, "The Business of Facebook," *Fast Company*, April 1, 2011, www.fastcompany.com; E. B. Boyd, "Facebook Deals Out-Groups Groupon," *Fast Company*, April 26, 2011; Michelle Kung and Geoffrey A. Fowler, "Warner 'Likes' Facebook Rentals," *Wall Street Journal*, March 9, 2011, p. B4; Parmy Olson, "Facebook to Launch Music Service with Spotify," *Forbes*, May 25, 2011, http://blogs.forbes.com/parmyolson/2011/05/25/facebook-to-launch-music-service-with-spotify; Venessa Miemis, "The Bank of Facebook: Currency, Identity, Reputation," *Forbes*, April 4, 2011, http://blogs.forbes.com/venessamiemis/2011/04/04/the-bank-of-facebook-currency-identity-reputation; "Facebook's Sales Chief: Madison Avenue Doesn't Understand Us Yet," *Advertising Age*, April 29, 2011, http://adage.com/print/227314/; Brian Womack, "Facebook Ad Rates Hold as Inventory Rises," *Bloomberg Businessweek*, July 6, 2011; and information from www.facebook.com, accessed October 2011; Alexei Oreskovic, "Facebook Doubles Its Mobile Advertising Revenue," *Globe and Mail*, January 30, 2013, www.theglobeandmail.com/globe-investor/facebook-doubles-its-mobile-advertising-revenue/article8015772.

2. See Direct Marketing media kit, accessed at www.dmn.ca/2012%20Media%20Kit_DM.pdf; and "Marketing Facts 2013: Statistics and Trends for Marketing in Canada," Canadian Marketing Association, 2012.

3. "IAB Canada's 2010 Canadian Media Usage Trend Study," www.iabcanada.com/insight-research, February 2013; and "IAB Canadian Online Advertising Revenue Survey—2011 Actual and 2012 Estimated," www.iabcanada.com/wp-content/uploads/2010/09/Canadian_Online_Advertising_Revenue_Survey_en.pdf.

4. See discussions at "What Is the Real Cost of a B2B Sales Call?" www.marketing-playbook.com/sales-marketing-strategy/what-is-the-real-cost-of-a-b2b-sales-call, accessed June 2011; and "The Costs of Personal Selling," April 13, 2011, www.seekarticle.com/business-sales/personal-selling.html.

5. "Customer Spotlight—Retailer West 49," http://blog.campaigner.com/2009/02/retailer-west49-keeps-teenage-customers.html; and information from www.west49.com, accessed February 22, 2013.

6. Mike Freeman, "Data Company Helps Walmart, Casinos, Air-lines Analyze Data," *Knight Ridder Business Tribune News*, February 24, 2006, p. 1; Eric Lai, "Teradata Creates Elite Club for Petabyte-Plus Data Warehouse Customers," *Computer World*, October 14, 2008, www.computerworld.com/s/article/9117159/Teradata_creates_elite_club_for_petabyte_plus_data_warehouse_customers; and "Data, Data Everywhere," *Economist*, February 27, 2010, p. 3.

7. See "Best Buy Plugs into the Power of Customer Centricity," FICO.com, 2009, www.fico.com/en/FIResourcesLibrary/Best_Buy_Success_2271CS_EN.pdf; and Philip Kotler and Kevin Lane Keller, *Marketing Management,* 14th ed. (Upper Saddle River, NJ: Prentice Hall, 2012), p. 71.

8. See DMA, *The Power of Direct Marketing, 2009–2010 Edition;* and "It's Never Been Easier to Send Direct Mail," PR Newswire, June 8, 2011; Jennifer Horn, "Mobile Ad Spend to Make Biggest Jump: Report," October 4, 2012, http://mediaincanada.com/2012/10/04/mobile-ad-spend-makes-biggest-jump-report; and "Marketing Facts 2013: Statistics and Trends for Marketing in Canada," Canadian Marketing Association, 2012.

9. "Marketing Facts 2013: Statistics and Trends for Marketing in Canada," Canadian Marketing Association, 2012.

10. Julie Liesse, "When Times Are Hard, Mail Works," *Advertising Age*, March 30, 2009, p. 14; and Paul Vogel, "Marketers Are Rediscovering the Value of Mail," *Deliver Magazine*, January 11, 2011, www.delivermagazine.com/2011/01/marketers-are-rediscovering-the-value-of-mail.

11. Information obtained from www.1800gotjunk.com/ca_en/about/press_room.aspx and www.kirkmarketing.com/case-studies/1-800-got-junk, accessed February 22, 2013.

12. Jeffrey Ball, "Power Shift: In Digital Era, Marketers Still Prefer a Paper Trail," *Wall Street Journal*, October 16, 2009, p. A3; and Jennifer Valentino-DeVries, "With Catalogs, Opt-Out Policies Vary," *Wall Street Journal,* April 13, 2011, p. B7.

13. Ball, "Power Shift: In Digital Era, Marketers Still Prefer a Paper Trail"; and "Report: Catalogs Increasingly Drive Online Sales," RetailCustomerExperience.com, March 17, 2010, www.retailcustomerexperience.com/article/21521/Report-Catalogs-increasingly-drive-online-sales.

14. See Geoffrey A. Fowler, "Peeved at Auto Warranty Calls, a Web Posse Strikes Back," *Wall Street Journal*, May 15, 2009, A1.

15. See Rachel Brown, "Perry, Fischer, Lavigne Tapped for Proactiv," *WWD*, January 13, 2010, p. 3; www.proactiv.com, accessed July 2011.

16. Darren Rovell, "The Shake Weight Hits $40 Million in Sales," August 2010, www.cnbc.com/id/38788941/The_Shake_Weight_Hits_40_Million_In_Sales; and "Sporting Activities, Baseball; Shake Weight Gets Serious," *Entertainment Newsweekly,* June 10, 2011, p. 126.

17. Shahnaz Mahmud, "Survey: Viewers Crave TV Ad Fusion," Adweek.com, January 25, 2008; Andrew Hampp, "Scorecard: Were We Wrong or Almost Right on ITV?" *Advertising Age*, April 12, 2010, http://adage.com/cabletv10/article?article_id=143163; John M. Smart, "Tomorrow's Interactive Television," *The Futurist,* November/December 2010, p. 41; and David Verklin, "Boost Sales with Interactive TV," *DM News,* February 23, 2011, p. 24.

18. Adapted from information in Zachary Rodgers, "Cablevision's Interactive TV Ads Pay Off for Gillette," *ClickZ*, October 21, 2009, www.clickz.com/3635413/print; David Goetzl, "Interactive Ads Pay Off for Cablevision," *MediaPost News*, January 12, 2010, www.mediapost.com/publications; and "Cable Television Companies; Advertisers Embrace New Feature of Optimum Select RFI to Immediately Deliver Brochures, Coupons, Offers, and Other Information to Consumers Via E-Mail," *Marketing Weekly News,* July 2, 2011, p. 158.

19. Stephanie Rosenbloom, "The New Touch-Face of Vending Machines," *New York Times*, May 25, 2010, www.nytimes.com/2010/05/26/business/26vending.html.

20. Rebecca Troyer, "Redbox DVD Rental Kiosks Now at CVS Store in Bloomington," *McClatchy-Tribune Business News,* May 14, 2011; and www.redbox.com, accessed October 2011.

21. Internet World Stats, Usage and Population Statistics, www.internetworldstats.com/am/ca.htm, accessed June 2012; Omarel Akkad, "Canadians' Internet Usage Nearly Double the Worldwide Average," *Globe and Mail*, March 2011, www.theglobeandmail.com/technology/tech-news/canadians-internet-usage-nearly-double-theworldwide-average/article569916; "Marketing Facts 2013: Statistics and Trends for Marketing in Canada," Canadian Marketing Association, 2012; and "Global Mobile Statistics 2013 Part A: Mobile Subscribers; Handset Market Share; Mobile Operators," *MobiThinking*, March, 2013, http://mobithinking.com/mobile-marketing-tools/latest-mobile-stats/a#subscribers.

22. See "Internet Retailer: Top 500 Guide," www.internetretailer.com/top500/list, accessed July 2011.

23. Staples data from annual reports and other information found at www.staples.com, accessed October 2011.

24. "Marketing Facts 2013: Statistics and Trends for Marketing in Canada," Canadian Marketing Association, 2012.

25. Anna Johnson, "Local Marketing: 97 Percent of Consumers Use Online Media for Local Shopping," *Kikabink News*, March 17, 2010, www.kikabink.com/news/local-marketing-97-percent-of-consumers-use-online-media-for-local-shopping; and "Web Influence on Retail Sales," *South Carolina Business Blog*, January 5, 2011, www.framelegal.com/blog/articletype/articleview/articleid/306/2011-web-influence-on-retail-sales.aspx.

26. See facts from eBay annual reports and other information at www.ebayinc.com, accessed March 2013.

27. Jon Sobel, "State of the Blogosphere 2010," *Technorati*, November 3, 2010, http://technorati.com/blogging/article/state-of-the-blogosphere-2010-introduction; and www.blogpulse.com, accessed July 2011.

28. For these and other examples, see Erica Swallow, "15 Excellent Corporate Blogs to Learn from," August 13, 2010, http://mashable.com/2010/08/13/great-corporate-blogs; and http://share.blog.us.playstation.com, http://disneyparks.disney.go.com/blog, and http://en.community.dell.com/dell-blogs/default.aspx, accessed October 2011.

29. See "IZEA and ImageShack Partner to Form Largest Global Social Media Sponsorship Network," *The Pak Banker*, March 27, 2011; and http://socialspark.com/advertisers/sample-campaigns, accessed October 2011.

30. Mark Evans, "Broken Guitar Leads to Startup Consumer Gripe Site," *Globe and Mail*, February 13, 2012, www.theglobeandmail.com/report-on-business/small-business/starting-out/broken-guitar-leads-to-startup-consumergripesite/article4171528; and http://gripevine.com, accessed June 2012.

31. "IAB Canadian Online Advertising Revenue Survey—2011 Actual and 2012 Estimated," www.iabcanada.com/wp-content/uploads/2010/09/Canadian_Online_Advertising_Revenue_Survey_en.pdf; and "Marketing Facts 2013: Statistics and Trends for Marketing in Canada," Canadian Marketing Association, 2012.

32. Internet Advertising Bureau, *IAB Internet Advertising Revenue Report*, May 26, 2011, www.iab.net/media/file/IAB_Full_year_2010_0413_Final.pdf; and Google annual reports, http://investor.google.com/proxy.html.

33. See "Campaigns Creativity Liked," *Advertising Age*, December 13, 2010, p. 18; Thomas Pardee, "Think the Old Spice Guy Is So 2010? Think Again," *Advertising Age*, February 16, 2011, http://adage.com/print/148911; and Dan Sewell, "Old Spice Teases Its Sexy New Ad Campaign," *USA Today*, January 26, 2011, www.usatoday.com/money/advertising/2011-01-26-old-spice-mustafa-ad_N.htm.

34. David Gelles, "The Public Image: Volkswagen's 'The Force' Campaign," *Financial Times*, February 22, 2011, p. 14; and Troy Dreier, "The Force Was Strong with This One," *Streaming Media Magazine*, April/May 2011, pp. 66–68.

35. Brian Morrissey, "Social Media Use Becomes Pervasive," *Adweek*, April 15, 2010; and www.checkfacebook.com, accessed July 2011.

36. For these and other examples, see Douglas MacMillan, "With Friends like This, Who Needs Facebook?" *Bloomberg Businessweek*, September 13–19, 2010, pp. 35–37; and www.mytransponder.com/home.php, www.gofishn.com, www.ravelry.com, www.dogster.com, www.researchgate.net, www.passionsnetwork.com, www.passportstamp.com/welcome, and www.cafemom.com, all accessed October 2011.

37. "Happy Birthday to Nike+," *Run247*, May 23, 2011, www.run247.com/articles/article-1337-happy-birthday-to-nike%2B.html.

38. See http://my.menshealth.com/bellyoff, accessed July 2011.

39. See Ken Magill, "E-mail ROI Still Stunning, Still Slipping: DMA," *Direct Magazine*, October 20, 2009, http://directmag.com/magilla/1020-e-mail-roi-still-slipping; "E-Mail," *Advertising Age's Digital Marketing Facts 2010* section, February 22, 2010; and "Think E-Mail Marketing Is Dying? Think Again," PR Newswire, May 3, 2011.

40. "Marketing Facts 2013: Statistics and Trends for Marketing in Canada," Canadian Marketing Association, 2012.

41. Elisabeth A. Sullivan, "Targeting to the Extreme," *Marketing News*, June 15, 2010, pp. 17–19.

42. Symantec, *The State of Spam and Phishing: Home of the Monthly Report—May 2011*, http://go.symantec.com/spam_report.

43. Jessica Tsai, "How Much Marketing Is Too Much?" DestinationCRM.com, October 1, 2008; "StubHub Increases Revenue Per E-Mail by Over 2,500 Percent with Responsys Interact and Omniture Recommendations," February 18, 2009, www.responsys.com/company/press/2009_02_18.php.

44. Carroll Trosclair, "Direct Marketing, Advertising and ROI: Commercial E-Mail Delivers Highest DM Return on Investment," Suite101.com, April 2, 2010, http://advertising.suite101.com/article.cfm/direct-marketing-advertising-and-roi. For examples of outstanding e-mail marketing campaigns, see "MarketingSherpa Email Awards 2011," *MarketingSherpa*, www.marketingsherpa.com/EmailAwards2011/EmailAwards2011Winners.pdf.

45. Facts in this paragraph are from *State of Mobile Advertising 2011*, *Mobile Marketer*, June 2011, www.mobilemarketer.com/cms/lib/12311.pdf; "Marketing Facts 2013: Statistics and Trends for Marketing in Canada," Canadian Marketing Association, 2012; and www.apple.com/ipad/from-the-app-store and www.apple.com/iphone/apps-for-iphone, accessed October 2011.

46. *State of Mobile Advertising 2011*, p. 4; Dan Frommer, "The Future of Mobile Advertising," *Business Insider*, June 8, 2011, www.sfgate.com/cgi-bin/article.cgi?f=/g/a/2011/06/08/businessinsider-future-of-mobile-advertising-2011-6.DTL; and Giselle Tsirulnik, "In-App Mobile Ad Spend to Reach $685M in 2011," *Mobile Marketer*, September 21, 2010, www.mobilemarketer.com/cms/news/research/7424.html.

47. Adapted from Giselle Tsirulnik, "Most Impressive Mobile Advertising Campaigns in 2010," December 29, 2010, www.mobilemarketer.com/cms/news/advertising/8617.html.

48. See Emily Burg, "Acceptance of Mobile Ads on the Rise," *MediaPost Publications*, March 16, 2007, www.mediapost.com/publications; Steve Miller and Mike Beirne, "The iPhone Effect," Adweek.com, April 28, 2008; Cyril Altmeyer, "Smart Phones, Social Networks to Boost Mobile Advertising," Reuters.com, June 29, 2009; and Richard Westlund, "Mobile on Fast Forward," *Brandweek*, March 15, 2010, pp. M1–M5.

49. See Canadian Anti-Fraud Centre, www.antifraudcentrecentre-antifraude.ca/english/home-eng.html.52; Greg Sterling, "Pew: Americans Increasingly Shop Online But Still Fear Identity Theft," SearchEngineLand.com, February 14, 2008, http://searchengine-land.com/pew-americans-increasingly-shop-online-but-still-fear-identity-theft-13366. See also www.ftc.gov/bcp/edu/microsites/idtheft and www.spendonlife.com/guide/identity-theft-statistics, accessed November 2011.

50. Ibid.

51. See Cecilia Kang, "Underage and on Facebook," *Washington Post*, June 13, 2011, www.washingtonpost.com/blogs/post-tech/post/underage-and-on-facebook/2011/06/12/AGHKHySH_blog.html.

52. Adapted from information in Michael Bush, "My Life, Seen through the Eyes of Marketers," *Advertising Age,* April 26, 2010, http://adage.com/print/143479.

53. "Anti-Spam Laws in Canada," *Email Marketing Reports,* www.email-marketing-reports.com/canspam/Canada, accessed July 2009; "Government of Canada Protects Canadians with the Electronic Commerce Protection Act," Industry Canada News Release, April 24, 2009, www.ic.gc.ca/eic/site/ic1.nsf/eng/04595.html, accessed July 2009.

54. Information on TRUSTe at www.truste.com, accessed October 2011.

Chapter 11 Box 1.2

1. Social Media Today (June 2013), "Unignorable Stats About How Social Media Influences Purchase Behaviour", http://social-mediatoday.com/rgbsocial/1532766/unignorable-stats-about-how-social-media-influences-purchase-behaviour

2. Kumar, V., & Mirchandani, Rohan (2012), "Increasing The ROI Of Social Media Marketing", MIT Sloan Management Review, 54(1), 54-61.

3. Kumar, V., et al (2013), "Creating A Measurable Social Media Marketing Strategy For Hokey Pokey: Increasing The Value And ROI Of Intangibles And Tangibles", Marketing Science, 32(2), 194-212.

APPENDIX 3

1. This is derived by rearranging the following equation and solving for price: Percentage markup = (price − cost) ÷ price.

2. Again, using the basic profit equation, we set profit equal to ROI × I: $ROI \times I = (P \times Q) - TFC - (Q \times UVC)$. Solving for Q gives $Q = (TFC + (ROI \times I)) \div (P - UVC)$.

3. U.S. Census Bureau, available at www.census.gov/prod/1/pop/p25-1129.pdf , accessed October 26, 2009.

4. See Roger J. Best, *Market-Based Management*, 4th ed. (Upper Saddle River, NJ: Prentice Hall, 2005).

5. Total contribution can also be determined from the unit contribution and unit volume: Total contribution unit contribution = unit sales. Total units sold in 2012 were 595,238 units, which can be determined by dividing total sales by price per unit ($100 million ÷ $168). Total contribution = $35.28 contribution per unit × 595,238 units = $20,999,996.64 (difference due to rounding).

6. Recall that the contribution margin of 21 percent was based on variable costs representing 79 percent of sales. Therefore, if we do not know price, we can set it equal to $1.00. If price equals $1.00, 79 cents represents variable costs and 21 cents represents unit contribution. If price is decreased by 10 percent, the new price is $0.90. However, variable costs do not change just because price decreased, so the unit contribution and contribution margin decrease as follows:

	Old	New (reduced 10 percent)
Price	$1.00	$0.90
− Unit variable cost	$0.79	$0.79
= Unit contribution	$0.21	$0.11
Contribution margin	$0.21/$1.00 = 0.21 or 21%	$0.11/$0.90 = 0.12 or 12%

Glossary

Administered VMS A vertical marketing system that coordinates successive stages of production and distribution, not through common ownership or contractual ties, but through the size and power of one of the parties.

Adoption process The mental process through which an individual passes from first hearing about an innovation to final adoption.

Advertising agency A marketing services firm that assists companies in planning, preparing, implementing, and evaluating all or portions of their advertising programs.

Advertising Any paid form of non-personal presentation and promotion of ideas, goods, or services by an identified sponsor.

Advertising budget The dollars and other resources allocated to a product or company advertising program.

Advertising media The types of media and media vehicles through which advertising messages are delivered to their intended audiences.

Advertising objective A specific communication *task* to be accomplished with a specific *target* audience during a specific period of *time*.

Advertising strategy The strategy by which the company accomplishes its advertising objectives. It consists of two major elements: creating advertising messages and selecting advertising media.

Affordable method Setting the advertising budget at the level management thinks the company can afford.

Age and life-cycle segmentation Dividing a market into different age and life-cycle groups.

Agent A representative, either of a buyer or a seller, who performs only a few functions and does not take title to goods.

Allowance Promotional money paid by manufacturers to retailers in return for an agreement to feature the manufacturer's products in some way.

Approach The step in the selling process in which the salesperson meets the customer for the first time.

Attitude A person's consistently favourable or unfavourable evaluations, feelings, and tendencies toward an object or an idea.

Baby Boomers The 9.8 million Canadians born during the baby boom following World War II and lasting until the mid-1960s.

Behavioural segmentation Dividing a market into segments based on consumer knowledge, attitudes, uses, or responses to a product.

Belief A descriptive thought that a person holds about something.

Benefit segmentation Dividing the market into segments according to the different benefits that consumers seek from the product.

Blog Online journals where people post their thoughts, usually on a narrowly defined topic.

Brand A name, symbol, icon, design, or a combination of these, that identifies the maker or marketer of a product.

Brand advocates Customers, employees, and others who willingly and voluntarily promote their favourite brands.

Brand ambassador A real person who, under contract with the brand's marketing organization, acts as a spokesperson for the brand.

Brand asset valuator (BAV) An international research project that has been taking place for the past 16 years, in which 38 000+ brands are tested.

Brand characters Lifelike brand icons, or mascots, that can move speak, and interact, and that have personality traits.

Branded content (content marketing) Any form of information or story written and produced by a brand marketer, with the brand clearly and prominently featured.

Branded entertainment A form of entertainment, usually video, that is created with the cooperation or financial support of a marketer.

Brand engagement The interaction between consumers and brands, based on the emotional connection consumers feel toward the brand.

Brand equity The dollar amount attributed to the value of the brand, based on all the intangible qualities that create that value.

Brand extensions Extending an existing brand name to new product categories.

Brand icons Objects with distinct shapes, colours, or patterns that are associated with the brand.

Brand personality The sum total of all the attributes of a brand, and the emotions it inspires in the minds of consumers.

Break-even analysis Analysis to determine the unit volume and dollar sales needed to be profitable given a particular price and cost structure.

Break-even price The price at which total revenue equals total cost and profit is zero.

Break-even pricing (or target return pricing) Setting price to break even on the costs of making and marketing a product, or setting price to make a target return.

Broker A wholesaler who does not take title to goods and whose function is to bring buyers and sellers together and assist in negotiation.

Business analysis A review of the sales, costs, and profit projections for a new product to find out whether these factors satisfy the company's objectives.

Business buyer behaviour The buying behaviour of the organizations that buy goods and services for use in the production of other products and services or to resell or rent them to others at a profit.

Business portfolio The collection of businesses and products that make up the company.

Business promotions Sales promotion tools used to generate business leads, stimulate purchases, reward customers, and motivate salespeople.

Business-to-business (B2B) online marketing Businesses using online marketing to reach new business customers, serve current customers more effectively, and obtain buying efficiencies and better prices.

Business-to-consumer (B2C) online marketing Businesses selling goods and services online to final consumers.

Buying centre All the individuals and units that play a role in the purchase decision-making process.

By-product pricing Setting a price for by-products to make the main product's price more competitive.

Cannibalization The situation in which one product sold by a company takes a portion of its sales from other company products.

Captive-product pricing Setting a price for products that must be used along with a main product, such as blades for a razor and games for a video-game console.

Catalogue marketing Direct marketing through print, video, or digital catalogues that are mailed to select customers, made available in stores, or presented online.

Causal research Marketing research to test hypotheses about cause-and-effect relationships.

Chain ratio method Estimating market demand by multiplying a base number by a chain of adjusting percentages.

Channel conflict Disagreement among marketing channel members over goals, roles, and rewards.

Click-and-mortar companies Traditional brick-and-mortar companies that have added online marketing to their operations.

Click-only companies The so-called dot-coms, which operate online only and have no brick-and-mortar market presence.

Closing The step in the selling process in which the salesperson asks the customer for an order.

Co-branding The practice of using the established brand names of two different companies on the same product.

Cognitive dissonance Buyer discomfort caused by postpurchase conflict.

Commercialization The full-scale introduction of the new product into the market.

Commercial online databases Computerized collections of information available from online commercial sources or via the Internet.

Competition-based pricing Setting prices based on competitors' strategies, prices, costs, and market offerings.

Competitive advantage An advantage over competitors gained by offering greater customer value, either through lower prices, or by providing more benefits that justify higher prices.

Competitive marketing intelligence The systematic collection and analysis of publicly available information about consumers, competitors, and developments in the marketing environment.

Competitive-parity method Setting the promotion budget to match competitors' outlays.

Competitive review The purpose of a competitive review is to identify key competitors, describe their market positions, and briefly discuss their strategies.

Concentrated (niche) marketing A market-coverage strategy in which a firm goes after a large share of one or a few segments or niches.

Consumer activism An organized movement of citizens and government agencies to improve the rights and power of buyers in relation to sellers.

Consumer buyer behaviour The buying behaviour of final consumers—individuals and households that buy goods and services for personal consumption.

Consumer-generated marketing Brand exchanges created by consumers themselves—both invited and uninvited—by which consumers are playing an increasing role in shaping their own brand experiences and those of other consumers.

Consumer market All the individuals and households that buy or acquire goods and services for personal consumption.

Consumer-oriented marketing The philosophy of sustainable marketing that holds that the company should view and organize its marketing activities from the consumer's point of view.

Consumer products Products purchased by consumers for their personal (i.e. non business) use.

Consumer promotions Sales promotion tools used to boost short-term customer buying and involvement or to enhance long-term customer relationships.

Consumer-to-business (C2B) online marketing Online exchanges in which consumers search out sellers, learn about their offers, initiate purchases, and sometimes even drive transaction terms.

Consumer-to-consumer (C2C) online marketing Online exchanges of goods and information between final consumers.

Contractual VMS A vertical marketing system in which independent firms at different levels of production and distribution work together under contract.

Contribution margin The unit contribution divided by the selling price.

Convenience product A consumer product that customers usually buy frequently, immediately, and with a minimum of comparison and buying effort.

Corporate (or brand) website A website designed to build customer goodwill, collect customer feedback, and supplement other sales channels, rather than to sell the company's products directly.

Corporate VMS A vertical marketing system that combines successive stages of production and distribution under single ownership—channel leadership is established through common ownership.

Cost-based pricing Setting prices based on the costs for producing, distributing, and selling the product plus a fair rate of return for effort and risk.

Cost-plus pricing (or markup pricing) A standard markup to the cost of the product.

Creative concept The compelling "big idea" that will bring the advertising-message strategy to life in a distinctive and memorable way.

Crowdsourcing Inviting broad communities of people such as customers, employees, independent scientists and researchers, and even the public at large, into the new product innovation process.

Cultural environment Institutions and other forces that affect society's basic values, perceptions, preferences, and behaviours.

Culture The set of basic values, perceptions, wants, and behaviours learned by a member of society from family and other important institutions.

Current marketing situation This section provides a brief synopsis of the competitive landscape and business environment in which the company will operate in marketing products described in the marketing plan.

Customer database An organized collection of comprehensive data about individual customers or prospects, including geographic, demographic, psychographic, and behavioural data.

Customer equity The total combined customer lifetime values of all of the company's customers.

Customer insights Fresh understandings of customers and the marketplace derived from marketing information that becomes the basis for creating customer value and relationships.

Customer lifetime value The value of the entire stream of purchases that the customer would make over a lifetime of patronage.

Customer-managed relationships Marketing relationships in which customers, empowered by today's new digital technologies, interact with companies and with each other to shape their relationships with brands.

Customer (or market) sales force structure A sales force organization under which salespeople specialize in selling only to certain customers or industries.

Customer-perceived value The customer's evaluation of the difference between all the benefits and all the costs of a market offering relative to those of competing offers.

Customer relationship management (CRM) The overall process of building and maintaining profitable customer relationships by delivering superior customer value and satisfaction.

Customer satisfaction The extent to which a product's perceived performance matches a buyer's expectations.

Customer value-based pricing Setting price based on buyers' perceptions of value rather than on the seller's cost.

Customer-value marketing A principle of sustainable marketing that holds that a company should put most of its resources into customer-value-building marketing investments.

Decline stage The product life-cycle stage in which a product's sales decline.

Deficient products Products that have neither immediate appeal nor long-run benefits.

Demand curve A curve that shows the number of units the market will buy in a given time period, at different prices that might be charged.

Demands Human wants that are backed by buying power.

Demographic segmentation Dividing the market into segments based on variables such as age, gender, family size, life cycle, household income (HHI), occupation, education, ethnic or cultural group, and generation.

Demography The study of human populations in terms of size, density, location, age, gender, race, occupation, and other statistics.

Derived demand Business demand that ultimately comes from (derives from) the demand for consumer goods.

Descriptive research Marketing research to better describe marketing problems, situations, or markets.

Desirable products Products that give both high immediate satisfaction and high long-run benefits.

Differentiated (segmented) marketing A market-coverage strategy in which a firm decides to target several market segments and designs separate offers for each.

Differentiation Actually differentiating the market offering to create superior customer value.

Diffusion of innovations theory A social sciences theory that divides members of a social group into segments according to how likely they are to adopt a new idea.

Direct-mail marketing Direct marketing by sending an offer, announcement, reminder, or other item to a person at a particular physical or virtual address.

Direct marketing Direct connections with carefully targeted individual consumers to both obtain an immediate response and cultivate lasting customer relationships.

Direct-response television marketing Direct marketing via television, including direct-response television advertising (or infomercials) and home shopping channels.

Discount A straight reduction in price on purchases during a stated period of time or on larger quantities.

Disintermediation The cutting out of marketing channel intermediaries by product or service producers, or the displacement of traditional resellers by radical new types of intermediaries.

Distribution (channel) review In this section, marketers list the most important channels, provide an overview of each channel arrangement, and identify developing issues in channels.

Diversification A strategy for company growth through starting up or acquiring businesses outside the company's current products and markets.

Downsizing Reducing the business portfolio by eliminating products or business units that are not profitable or that no longer fit the company's overall strategy.

Drop shipper An intermediary who takes orders and payment from the customer, then arranges to have the merchandise shipped to the customer directly from the supplier.

Dynamic pricing Adjusting prices continually to meet the characteristics and needs of individual customers and situations.

Economic environment Factors that affect consumer buying power and spending patterns.

Email marketing Sending highly targeted, tightly personalized, relationship-building marketing messages via email.

Environmentalism An organized movement of concerned citizens, businesses, and government agencies to protect and improve people's current and future living environment.

Environmental sustainability A management approach that involves developing strategies that both sustain the environment and produce profits for the company.

E-procurement Purchasing through electronic connections between buyers and sellers—usually online.

Ethnographic research A form of observational research that involves sending trained observers to watch and interact with consumers in their "natural habitat."

Event marketing Creating a brand-marketing event or serving as a sole or participating sponsor of events created by others.

Exchange The act of obtaining a desired object from someone by offering something in return.

Exclusive distribution A distribution strategy in which the marketer gives the rights to distribute its products to only one retailer, or to only one retailer in a particular geographic territory.

Execution style The approach, style, tone, words, and format used for executing an advertising message.

Experimental research Gathering primary data by selecting matched groups of subjects, giving them different treatments, controlling related factors, and checking for differences in group responses.

Exploratory research Marketing research to gather preliminary information that will help define the problem and suggest hypotheses.

Fad A temporary period of unusually high sales driven by consumer enthusiasm and immediate product or brand popularity.

Fashion A currently accepted or popular style of design, colour, or theme.

Fixed costs (overhead) Costs that do not vary with production or sales level.

Focus group interviewing Personal interviewing that involves inviting six to ten people to gather for a few hours with a trained interviewer to talk about a product, service, or organization. The interviewer "focuses" the group discussion on important issues.

Follow-up The last step in the selling process in which the salesperson follows up after the sale to ensure customer satisfaction and repeat business.

Franchise organization A marketing system that links several stages in the production and distribution process, and controls operations from a central head office.

Gender segmentation Dividing a market into different segments based on gender.

Generation X The 7 million Canadians born between 1967 and 1976 in the "birth dearth" following the baby boom.

Geographical pricing Setting prices for customers located in different parts of the country or the world.

Geographic segmentation Dividing a market into different geographical units, such as global regions, countries, regions within a country, provinces, cities, or even neighbourhoods.

Good-value pricing Offering just the right combination of quality and good service at a fair price.

Gross margin percentage The percentage of net sales remaining after cost of goods sold—calculated by dividing gross margin by net sales.

Group Two or more people who interact to accomplish individual or mutual goals.

Growth-share matrix A portfolio-planning method that evaluates a company's strategic business units (SBUs) in terms of its market growth rate and relative market share. SBUs are classified as stars, cash cows, question marks, or dogs.

Growth stage The product life-cycle stage in which a product's sales start climbing quickly.

Handling objections The step in the selling process in which the salesperson seeks out, clarifies, and overcomes customer objections to buying.

Horizontal marketing system An arrangement in which two or more companies that operate at the same channel level join together to follow a new marketing opportunity.

Household Income (HHI) segmentation Dividing a market into different income segments.

Idea generation The systematic search for new-product ideas.

Idea screening Screening new-product ideas to spot good ideas and drop poor ones as soon as possible.

Individual marketing (mass customization) Tailoring products and marketing programs to the needs and preferences of individual customers.

Industrial product A product bought by individuals and organizations for further processing or for use in conducting a business.

Innovative marketing A principle of sustainable marketing that requires that a company seek real product and marketing improvements.

Inside sales force Salespeople who conduct business from their offices via telephone, the Internet, or visits from prospective buyers.

Integrated marketing communications (IMC) Carefully integrating and coordinating the company's many communications channels to deliver a clear, consistent, and compelling message about the organization and its products.

Intensive distribution A marketing strategy in which the product is stocked in as many outlets as possible.

Intermarket segmentation Forming segments of consumers who have similar needs and buying behaviour even though they are located in different countries.

Internal databases Electronic collections of consumer and market information obtained from data sources within the company network.

Internal marketing Orienting and motivating customer-contact employees and supporting service people to work as a team to provide customer satisfaction.

Internet A vast public web of computer networks that connects users of all types all around the world to each other and to an amazingly large information repository.

Introduction stage The product life-cycle stage in which the new product is first distributed and made available for purchase.

Inventory turnover rate or stock-turn rate) The number of times an inventory turns over or is sold during a specified time period (often one year)—calculated based on costs, selling price, or units.

Just-in-time logistics systems A type of inventory management system in which only small inventories of parts or merchandise are held, and new stock arrives "just in time" when it is needed.

Learning Changes in an individual's behaviour arising from experience.

Licensing The buying and selling of the rights to use a brand name, logo, character, icon, or image.

Lifestyle A person's pattern of living as expressed in his or her activities, interests, and opinions.

Line extensions Extending an existing brand name to new forms, colours, sizes, ingredients, or flavours of an existing product category.

Local marketing A small group of people who live in the same city, or neighbourhood, or who shop at the same store.

Logistics management Planning, implementing, and controlling the physical flow of materials, final goods, and related information from points of origin to points of consumption to meet customer requirements at a profit.

Macroenvironment The larger societal forces that affect the microenvironment—demographic, economic, natural, technological, political, and cultural forces.

Market The set of all actual and potential buyers of a product or a service.

Market description Describing the targeted segments in detail provides context for the marketing strategies and detailed action programs discussed later in the plan.

Market development A strategy for company growth by identifying and developing new market segments for current company products.

Marketing channel (or distribution channel) A set of interdependent organizations that help make a product or service available for use or consumption by the consumer or business customer.

Marketing concept The marketing management philosophy that holds that achieving organizational goals depends on knowing the needs and wants of target markets and delivering the desired satisfactions better than competitors do.

Marketing controls and pro forma income statement Managers use pro forma income statements to project profitability and plan for marketing expenditures, scheduling, and operations. Marketing controls are used to monitor progress toward achieving financial goals and profitability.

Marketing control The process of measuring and evaluating the results of marketing strategies and plans and taking corrective action to ensure that objectives are achieved.

Marketing environment The actors and forces outside marketing that affect marketing management's ability to build and maintain successful relationships with target customers.

Marketing implementation The process that turns marketing strategies and plans into marketing actions to accomplish strategic marketing objectives.

Marketing information system (MIS) People and procedures for assessing information needs, developing the needed information, and helping decision makers to use the information to generate and validate actionable customer and market insights.

Marketing intermediaries Firms that help the company to promote, sell, and distribute its goods to final buyers.

Marketing management The art and science of choosing target markets and building profitable relationships with them.

Marketing mix The set of controllable, tactical marketing tools—product, price, place, and promotion—that the firm blends to produce the response it wants in the target market.

Marketing myopia The mistake of paying more attention to the specific products a company offers than to the benefits and experiences produced by these products.

Marketing research The systematic design, collection, analysis, and reporting of data relevant to a specific marketing situation facing an organization.

Marketing return on investment (or marketing ROI) A measure of the marketing productivity of a marketing investment—calculated by dividing net marketing contribution by marketing expenses.

Marketing return on sales (or marketing ROS) The percent of net sales attributable to the net marketing contribution—calculated by dividing net marketing contribution by net sales.

Marketing strategy development Designing an initial marketing strategy for a new product based on the product concept.

Marketing strategy The marketing logic by which the company hopes to create customer value and achieve profitable customer relationships.

Marketing The process by which companies create value for customers and build strong customer relationships to capture value from customers in return.

Marketing website A website that engages consumers in interactions that will move them closer to a direct purchase or other marketing outcome.

Market offerings Some combination of products, services, information, or experiences offered to a market to satisfy a need or want.

Market penetration A strategy for company growth by increasing sales of current products to current market segments without changing the product.

Market-penetration pricing Setting a low initial price for a new product in order to attract a large number of buyers and a large market share.

Market potential The upper limit of market demand.

Market segmentation Dividing a market into distinct groups of buyers who have different needs, characteristics, or behaviours, and who might require separate products or marketing programs.

Market segment A group of customers who respond in a similar way to a given set of marketing efforts.

Market share Company sales divided by market sales.

Market-skimming pricing (or price skimming) Setting a high price for a new product to skim maximum revenues layer by layer from the segments willing to pay the high price; the company makes fewer but more profitable sales.

Market targeting The process of evaluating each market segment's attractiveness and selecting one or more segments to enter.

Markup chain The sequence of markups used by firms at each level in a channel.

Markup The difference between a company's selling price for a product and its cost to manufacture or purchase it.

Maturity stage The product life-cycle stage in which sales growth slows or levels off.

Media vehicle The specific media (publication or program) within a general media type (magazine, radio, television).

Microenvironment The actors close to the company that affect its ability to serve its customers—the company, suppliers, marketing intermediaries, customer markets, competitors, and publics.

Micromarketing The practice of tailoring products and marketing programs to the needs and wants of specific individuals and local customer segments—includes *local marketing and individual marketing.*

Millennials (or Generation Y) The 10.4 million children of the Canadian Baby Boomers, born between 1977 and 2000.

Mission statement A statement of the organization's purpose—what it wants to accomplish in the larger environment.

Mobile marketing Marketing to on-the-go consumers through mobile phones, smartphones, tablets, and other mobile communication devices.

Modified rebuy A business buying situation in which the buyer wants to modify product specifications, prices, terms, or suppliers.

Motive (drive) A need that is sufficiently pressing to direct the person to seek satisfaction of the need.

Multibranding A brand development strategy in which the same manufacturer produces many different brands in the same product category.

Multichannel (hybrid) distribution system A distribution system in which a single firm sets up two or more marketing channels to reach one or more market segments.

National brand (or manufacturer's brand) A brand created and owned by the manufacturer of the product.

Natural environment Natural resources that are needed as inputs by marketers or that are affected by marketing activities.

Needs States of felt deprivation.

Net marketing contribution (NMC) A measure of marketing profitability that includes only components of profitability controlled by marketing.

Net profit percentage The percentage of each sales dollar going to profit—calculated by dividing net profits by net sales.

New product A good, service, or idea that is perceived by some potential customers as new.

New-product development The development of original products, product improvements, product modifications, and new brands through the firm's own product-development efforts.

New task A business buying situation in which the buyer purchases a product or service for the first time.

Objective-and-task method Developing the advertising budget by (1) defining specific objectives, (2) determining the tasks that must be performed to achieve these objectives, and (3) estimating the costs of performing these tasks. The sum of these costs is the proposed advertising budget.

Objectives and issues Objectives and issues should be defined in specific terms so management can measure progress and plan corrective action if needed to stay on track. This section describes any major issues that might affect the company's marketing strategy and implementation.

Observational research Gathering primary data by observing relevant people, actions, and situations.

Occasion segmentation Dividing the market into segments according to occasions when buyers get the idea to buy, actually make their purchase, or use the purchased item.

Online advertising Advertising that appears while consumers are browsing the web, including display ads, search-related ads, online classifieds, and other forms.

Online focus groups Gathering a small group of people online with a trained moderator to chat about a product, service, or organization and to gain qualitative insights about consumer attitudes and behaviour.

Online marketing Efforts to market products and services and build customer relationships over the Internet.

Online marketing research Collecting primary data online through Internet surveys, online focus groups, web-based experiments, or tracking consumers' online behaviour.

Online social networks Online social communities—blogs, social networking websites, or even virtual worlds—where people socialize or exchange information and opinions.

Operating expense percentage The portion of net sales going to operating expenses—calculated by dividing total expenses by net sales.

Operating ratios The ratios of selected operating statement items to net sales.

Opinion leader Person within a reference group who, because of special skills, knowledge, personality, or other characteristics, exerts social influence on others.

Optional-product pricing The pricing of optional or accessory products along with a main product.

Outside sales force (or field sales force) Salespeople who travel to call on customers in the field.

Packaging The activities of designing and producing the container or wrapper for a product.

Partner relationship management Working closely with partners in other company departments and outside the company to jointly bring greater value to customers.

Percentage-of-sales method Setting the promotion budget at a certain percentage of current or forecasted sales, or as a percentage of the unit sales price.

Perception The process by which people select, organize, and interpret information to form a meaningful picture of the world.

Personality The unique psychological characteristics that distinguish a person or group.

Personal selling Personal presentation by the firm's sales force for the purpose of making sales and building customer relationships.

Pleasing products Products that give high immediate satisfaction but may hurt consumers in the long run.

Political environment Laws, government agencies, and pressure groups that influence and limit various organizations and individuals in a given society.

Portfolio analysis The process by which management evaluates the products and businesses that make up the company.

Positioning and value proposition A position built on a meaningful value proposition, supported by appropriate strategy and implementation, can help the company build competitive advantage. A positioning statement provides a compass for the company, directing it to the place it wishes to occupy in the mind of its target market.

Positioning Arranging for a market offering or product to occupy a clear, distinctive, and desirable place relative to competing products in the minds of target consumers.

Positioning statement A statement that summarizes company or brand positioning—it takes this form: To (target segment and need) our (brand) is (concept) that (point of difference).

Preapproach The step in the selling process in which the salesperson learns as much as possible about a prospective customer before making a sales call.

Presentation The step in the selling process in which the salesperson tells the "value story" to the buyer, showing how the company's offer solves the customer's problems.

Price The amount of money charged for a product or a service, or the sum of the values that customers exchange for the benefits of having or using the product or service.

Price elasticity A measure of the sensitivity of demand to changes in price.

Primary data Information collected for the specific purpose at hand.

Private brand (store brand, private label) Brand names applied by the marketer to products manufactured for them under contract.

Product Anything that can be offered to a market for attention, acquisition, use, or consumption that might satisfy a want or need.

Product bundle pricing Combining several products and offering the bundle at a reduced price.

Product concept A detailed version of the new-product idea stated in meaningful consumer terms.

Product concept The idea that consumers will favour products that offer the most quality, performance, and features and that the organization should therefore devote its energy to making continuous product improvements.

Product development Developing the product concept into a physical product to ensure that the product idea can be turned into a workable market offering. Also a strategy for company growth by offering modified or new products to current market segments.

Production concept The idea that consumers will favour products that are available and highly affordable and that the organization should therefore focus on improving production and distribution efficiency.

Product life cycle The course of a product's sales and profits over its lifetime. It involves five stages: product development, introduction, growth, maturity, and decline.

Product line A group of products that are closely related because they function in a similar manner, are sold to the same customer groups, are marketed through the same types of outlets, or fall within given price ranges.

Product line pricing Setting the price steps between various products in a product line based on cost differences between the products, customer evaluations of different features, and competitors' prices.

Product/market expansion grid A portfolio-planning tool for identifying company growth opportunities through market penetration, market development, product development, or diversification.

Product mix (or product portfolio) The set of all product lines and items that a company markets.

Product position The way the product is defined by consumers on important attributes—the place the product occupies in consumers' minds relative to competing products.

Product quality The characteristics of a product or a service that bear on its ability to satisfy stated or implied customer needs.

Product review The product review summarizes the main features for all the company's products, organized by product line, type of customer, market, or order of product introduction.

Product sales force structure A sales force organization under which salespeople specialize in selling only a portion of the company's products or lines.

Profit-and-loss statement (or income statement or operating statement) A statement that shows actual revenues less expenses and net profit for an organization, product, or brand during a specific planning period, typically a year.

Pro forma (or projected) profit-and-loss statement (or income statement or operating statement) A statement that shows projected revenues less budgeted expenses and estimates the projected net profit for an organization, a product, or a brand during a specific planning period, typically a year.

Promotional pricing Temporarily pricing products below the list price and sometimes even below cost to increase short-run sales.

Promotion mix (or marketing communications mix) The specific blend of promotion tools that the company uses to persuasively communicate customer value and build customer relationships.

Prospecting The step in the selling process in which the salesperson or company identifies qualified potential customers.

Psychographic segmentation Dividing a market into different segments based on social class, lifestyle, or personality characteristics.

Psychological pricing Pricing that considers the psychology of prices and not simply the economics; the price is used to say something about the product.

Public Any group that has an actual or potential interest in or impact on an organization's ability to achieve its objectives.

Public relations (PR) Building good relations with the company's various publics by obtaining favourable publicity, building up a good corporate image, and handling or heading off unfavourable rumours, stories, and events.

Pull strategy A promotion strategy that calls for spending a lot on advertising and consumer promotion to induce final consumers to buy the product, creating a demand vacuum that "pulls" the product through the channel.

Push strategy A promotion strategy that calls for using the sales force and trade promotion to push the product through channels. The producer promotes the product to channel members who in turn promote it to final consumers.

Rack jobber A wholesaler who buys merchandise and re-sells it on "racks" inside a retail store, in partnership with the retailer.

Reference prices Prices that buyers carry in their minds and refer to when they look at a given product.

Relevant costs Costs that will occur in the future and that will vary across the alternatives being considered.

Retailer A business that primarily sells products and services to consumers.

Retailing The business of selling goods or services to consumers for their personal use.

Return on advertising investment The net return on advertising investment divided by the costs of the advertising investment.

Return on investment (ROI) A measure of managerial effectiveness and efficiency—net profit before taxes divided by total investment.

Return on investment (ROI) pricing (or target-return pricing) A cost-based pricing method that determines price based on a specified rate of return on investment.

Return on marketing investment (or marketing ROI) The net return from a marketing investment divided by the costs of the marketing investment.

Sales force management Analyzing, planning, implementing, and controlling sales force activities.

Salesperson An individual representing a company to customers by performing one or more of the following activities: prospecting, communicating, selling, servicing, information gathering, and relationship building.

Sales promotion Short-term incentives to encourage the purchase or sale of a product or a service.

Sales quota A standard that states the amount a salesperson should sell and how sales should be divided among the company's products.

Salutary products Products that have low appeal but may benefit consumers in the long run.

Sample A segment of the population selected for marketing research to represent the population as a whole.

Secondary data Information that already exists somewhere, having been collected for another purpose.

Segmentation Dividing a market into distinct groups with distinct needs, characteristics, or behaviours that might require separate marketing strategies or mixes.

Segmented pricing Selling a product or service at two or more prices, where the difference in prices is not based on differences in costs.

Selective distribution A distribution strategy in which the marketer selects a set of retailers that specialize in their product category.

Selling concept The idea that consumers will not buy enough of the firm's products unless it undertakes a large-scale selling and promotion effort.

Selling process The steps that salespeople follow when selling, which include prospecting and qualifying, preapproach, approach, presentation and demonstration, handling objections, closing, and follow-up.

Sense-of-mission marketing A principle of sustainable marketing that holds that a company should define its mission in broad social terms rather than narrow product terms.

Service An activity, benefit, or satisfaction offered for sale that is essentially intangible and does not result in the ownership of anything.

Service inseparability A major characteristic of services—they are produced and consumed at the same time and cannot be separated from their providers.

Service intangibility A major characteristic of services—they cannot be seen, tasted, felt, heard, or smelled before they are bought.

Service perishability A major characteristic of services—they cannot be stored for later sale or use.

Service-profit chain The chain that links service firm profits with employee and customer satisfaction.

Service variability A major characteristic of services—their quality may vary greatly, depending on who provides them and when, where, and how.

Share of customer The portion of the customer's purchasing that a company gets in its product categories.

Shopper marketing Using point-of-sale promotions and advertising to extend brand equity to "the last mile" and encourage favourable in-store purchase decisions.

Shopping product Less frequently purchased consumer products and services that shoppers compare carefully on suitability, quality, price, and style.

Social class Relatively permanent and ordered divisions in a society whose members share similar values, interests, and behaviours.

Societal marketing A principle of sustainable marketing that holds that a company should make marketing decisions by considering consumers' wants, the company's requirements, consumers' long-run interests, and society's long-run interests.

Societal marketing concept The idea that a company's marketing decisions should consider consumers' wants, the company's requirements, consumers' long-run interests, and society's long-run interests.

Spam Unsolicited, unwanted commercial email messages.

Specialty product A consumer product with unique characteristics or brand identification for which a significant group of buyers is willing to make a special purchase effort.

Straight rebuy A business buying situation in which the buyer routinely reorders something without any modifications.

Strategic planning The process of developing and maintaining a strategic fit between the organization's goals and capabilities and its changing marketing opportunities.

Style A basic and distinctive mode of expression.

Subculture A group of people with shared value systems based on common life experiences and situations.

Supplier development Systematic development of networks of supplier-partners to ensure an appropriate and dependable supply of products and materials for use in making products or reselling them to others.

Survey research Gathering primary data by asking people questions about their knowledge, attitudes, preferences, and buying behaviour.

Sustainable marketing A philosophy of socially and environmentally responsible marketing that meets the present needs of consumers and businesses while also preserving or enhancing the ability of future generations to meet their needs.

Sustainable packaging Packaging that meets the requirements of the product while minimizing the environmental, economic, and social impacts of the product and its package.

SWOT analysis An overall evaluation of the company's strengths (S), weaknesses (W), opportunities (O), and threats (T).

Systems selling (or solutions selling) Buying a packaged solution to a problem from a single seller, thus avoiding all the separate decisions involved in a complex buying situation.

Target costing Pricing that starts with an ideal selling price, and then targets costs that will ensure that the price is met.

Targeting The process of evaluating each market segment's attractiveness and selecting one or more segments to enter.

Target market A set of buyers sharing common needs or characteristics that the company decides to serve.

Team selling Using teams of people from sales, marketing, engineering, finance, technical support, and even upper management to service large, complex accounts.

Technological environment Forces that create new technologies, creating new product and market opportunities.

Technology Adoption Life Cycle A marketing theory that proposes that when marketing a technology product, marketers must cross a chasm, or significant gap, between members of the early adopters segment and members of the early majority segment, before a new product will become successful.

Territorial sales force structure A sales force organization that assigns each salesperson to an exclusive geographic territory in which that salesperson sells the company's full line.

Test marketing The stage of new-product development in which the product and marketing program are tested in realistic market settings.

Third-party logistics (3PL) provider An independent logistics provider that performs any or all of the functions required to get its client's product to market.

Total costs The sum of the fixed and variable costs for any given level of production.

Total market demand The total volume that would be bought by a defined consumer group in a defined geographic area in a defined time period in a defined marketing environment under a defined level and mix of industry marketing effort.

Touchpoints Advertising, marketing communications, personal experience with the brand, word of mouth, social media, company and brand websites, store displays, and anything else that brings a consumer into contact with a brand.

Trade promotions Sales promotion tools used to persuade resellers to carry a brand, give it shelf space, promote it in advertising, and push it to consumers.

Undifferentiated (mass) marketing A market-coverage strategy in which a firm decides to ignore market segment differences and go after the whole market with one offer.

Unit contribution The amount that each unit contributes to covering fixed costs—the difference between price and variable costs.

Unsought product A consumer product that the consumer either does not know about or knows about but does not normally think of buying.

Value-added pricing Attaching value-added features and services to differentiate a company's offers and charging higher prices.

Value analysis Carefully analyzing a product's or service's components to determine whether they can be redesigned and made more effectively and efficiently to provide greater value.

Value-based pricing Offering just the right combination of quality and good service at a fair price.

Value chain The series of internal departments that carry out value-creating activities to design, produce, market, deliver, and support a firm's products.

Value delivery network The network made up of the company, suppliers, distributors, and, ultimately, customers who partner with each other to improve the performance of the entire system.

Value proposition The full positioning of a brand—the full mix of benefits upon which it is positioned.

Variable costs Costs that vary directly with the level of production.

Vertical marketing system (VMS) A distribution channel structure in which producers, wholesalers, and retailers act as a unified system. One channel member owns the others, has contracts with them, or has so much power that they all co-operate.

Viral marketing The Internet version of word-of-mouth marketing: a website, video, email message, or other marketing event that is so infectious that customers will seek it out or pass it along to friends.

Wants The form human needs take as shaped by culture and individual personality.

Wholesalers Companies whose primary business is wholesaling.

Wholesaling All activities involved in selling goods and services to those buying for resale or business use.

Word-of-mouth influence The impact of the personal words and recommendations of trusted friends, associates, and other consumers on buying behaviour.

Workload method An approach to determining sales force size based on the workload required and the time available for selling.

Indexes

Companies and Organizations Index

Subject Index

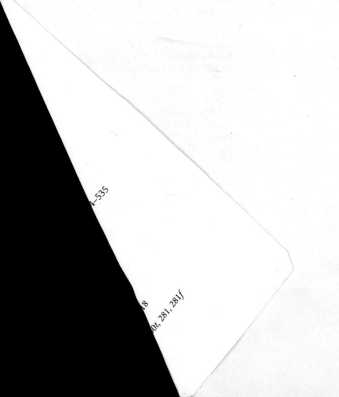